# THE
# BOOK OF
# RESOLUTIONS
## OF THE UNITED METHODIST CHURCH
# 2008

D0874823

# THE
# BOOK OF
# RESOLUTIONS
## OF THE UNITED METHODIST CHURCH
# 2008

The United Methodist Publishing House
Nashville, Tennessee

THE BOOK OF RESOLUTIONS OF THE UNITED METHODIST CHURCH 2008

Copyright © 2008 The United Methodist Publishing House.

All rights reserved.

Permission is hereby granted to any general agency or annual conference of The United Methodist Church or to any local United Methodist church to reproduce, in whole or in part, up to five (5) resolutions from *The Book of Resolutions* on any one topic in any single publication or electronic product for the purpose of study, worship, or advocacy, provided:

- Each use shall contain the words "used by permission" and shall contain the © symbol, the date, and "The United Methodist Publishing House," as follows: Copyright © 2008, The United Methodist Publishing House, used by permission.

- Resolutions may be offered on the Web or in any electronic format for up to ninety (90) days.

- This grant of permission shall not apply to any work that is offered for a fee or with any cost to the user, other than a fee for the costs of mailing or duplication.

Uses that do not comply with these provisions may still be permitted after application to The United Methodist Publishing House at *permissions@abingdonpress.com* or by mail to Permissions Office, The United Methodist Publishing House, 201 8th Avenue South, Nashville, Tennessee 37203 or faxed to 615-749-6128.

Scripture quotations, unless otherwise noted, are from the New Revised Standard Version of the Bible, copyright © 1989 by the Division of Christian Education of the National Council of the Churches of Christ in the USA. Used by permission.

Scripture quotations noted RSV are from the Revised Standard Version of the Bible, copyright 1946, 1952, 1971 by the Division of Christian Education of the National Council of the Churches of Christ in the United States of America. Used by permission. All rights reserved.

Scripture quotations marked (NIV) are taken from the HOLY BIBLE, NEW INTERNATIONAL VERSION®. Copyright © 1973, 1978, 1984 by International Bible Society. All rights reserved throughout the world. Used by permission of International Bible Society.

Scripture quotations marked (GNT) are from the Good News Translation in Today's English Version–Second Edition © 1992 by American Bible Society. Used by Permission.

The Social Principles placed throughout this book are from *The Book of Discipline of The United Methodist Church, 2008*. Copyright © 2008 by The United Methodist Publishing House. Used by permission.

This book is printed on elemental, chlorine-free, acid-free paper.

ISBN 978-0-687-64821-4

2-PACK *Discipline and Resolutions* ISBN 978-0-687-64795-8
CD-ROM Edition (with *Book of Discipline*) ISBN 978-0-687-64749-1

08 09 10 11 12 13 14 15 16 17 —10 9 8 7 6 5 4 3 2 1

MANUFACTURED IN THE UNITED STATES OF AMERICA

# PREFACE

*The Book of Resolutions* has been published after each General Conference since 1968. This edition includes all resolutions that are currently valid. Resolutions that have been rescinded or superseded have been removed from this 2008 edition.

When approved by the General Conference, resolutions state the policy of The United Methodist Church on many current social issues and concerns. Only the General Conference speaks for The United Methodist Church (*Book of Discipline*, ¶ 509).

The 2000 General Conference approved a rule stating: "Resolutions shall be considered official expressions of The United Methodist Church for eight years following their adoption, after which time they shall be deemed to have expired unless readopted. Those that have expired shall not be printed in subsequent editions of the *Book of Resolutions*" (*Book of Discipline*, ¶ 510.2a). This edition has been prepared in accordance with that rule.

This 2008 edition presents the resolutions in seven sections: (I) The Natural World, (II) The Nurturing Community, (II) The Social Community, (IV) The Economic Community, (V) The Political Community, (VI) The World Community, and (X) Other Resolutions. The first six section titles match the sections of the Social Principles, United Methodism's foundational statement on social issues found in *The Book of Discipline of The United Methodist Church, 2008*, ¶¶160-166, pages 97-131. These same paragraphs appear before each section of resolutions in this volume so that users may easily connect the principles to the resolutions.

To assist readers in study and use of the Social Principles and their related resolutions, this edition repeats from previous editions:
—User's Guide
—Index
—Date of General Conference adoption and date of amendment and readoption

**and new features in this edition:**
**—Relocation of the Social Principles to make comparisons with the resolutions easier**
**—Resolution numbering system matching the first digit with the Roman numeral of the Social Principles' six section numbers (I = 1, II = 2, III = 3)**
**—Revised and updated section titles**
**—Resolution numbers from the preceding two volumes to make research easier**
**—Running heads with the resolution numbers on each page**
**—Thumb indexing of the Social Principles**
**—Alphabetical list of resolution titles**

Errata can be found at Cokesbury.com, word search for *Errata.*

The 2008 *Book of Resolutions* is published by The United Methodist Publishing House—Neil M. Alexander publisher and book editor of The United Methodist Church. Marvin W. Cropsey, managing editor of quadrennial resources, The United Methodist Publishing House, served as the principal editor. The late Carolyn D. Minus, former General Board of Church and Society staff member, wrote the User's Guide.

# CONTENTS

## ¶ 160
## I. THE NATURAL WORLD

### Energy

### Environment

CONTENTS

# ¶ 161
# II. THE NURTURING COMMUNITY

CONTENTS

## Pornography

## Spirituality

## Suicide

## ¶ 162
## III. THE SOCIAL COMMUNITY

## Accessibility/Equal Access

## Aging

## Alcohol and Other Drugs

## Black Americans

## Children

CONTENTS

### Church and Community Development

### Cultural Issues

### Ecumenical and Interreligious Issues

CONTENTS

**Organization Memberships:**

## Education

## Genetics

## Health Care

## Hispanic Americans

## HIV and AIDS

## Housing and Homelessness

## Immigration

## Mental Health

CONTENTS

## Population

## Racism

## Rural Issues

## Urban Issues

## Violence

## Women

## Young People

## ¶ 163
## IV. THE ECONOMIC COMMUNITY

## Appalachia

## Boycotts

## Consumption

## Education

## Gambling

## Global Economic Justice

## Investments

## Native Americans

## Poverty

## Stewardship Issues in the Church

### United States Economic Issues

### Workers' Rights

### ¶ 164
### V. THE POLITICAL COMMUNITY

### Basic Freedoms

### Church and State

CONTENTS

## Criminal Justice

## Education

## Military Service

## Political Responsibility

## United States Legislative Issues

CONTENTS

¶ 165
VI. THE WORLD COMMUNITY

Education

Global Mission and Ministry

Justice and Law

National Power and Responsibility

## OTHER RESOLUTIONS

### Mission and Ministry:

### Request for Study:

### United Methodist Guidelines:

### Worship and Liturgy:

# USER'S GUIDE

## What's the purpose of the *Book of Resolutions?*

*The Book of Resolutions, 2008,* published by The United Methodist Publishing House, collects in one volume all current and official social policies and other resolutions adopted by the General Conference of The United Methodist Church. These resolutions are:

• *Official policy statements* for guiding all the work and ministry of The United Methodist Church on approximately 200 subjects;
• *Educational resources* for The United Methodist Church on many of the important issues affecting the lives of people and all God's creation;
• *Guides and models* for helping United Methodist members and groups relate a lively biblical faith to action in daily life;
• *Resource materials* for persons preparing public statements about United Methodist concerns on current social issues.

*The Book of Resolutions, 2008* is primarily a reference tool for church members and leaders. It is not a book that you will sit down to read from cover to cover.

You might not get acquainted with these resolutions until you are in the midst of some controversy in your congregation, or something happens regarding a particular subject in your community (or state, or nation). You may find that your denomination's policies give you more "food for thought." Maybe you will agree with the denomination's position. On the other hand, you may disagree. Either is all right. At the least, you know your church cares and wants you to be a knowledgeable and caring Christian about the issues of the day.

Furthermore, you may look to some of the statements in this book for spiritual guidance as you make an important decision in your life about work, home, family life, or use of money and other resources.

## Can you answer some of my questions?

### Why do we have all these social policies and resolutions?

The resolutions say, "We care!" Delegates to the General Conference of The United Methodist Church believe that we each need and deserve the guidance of the whole denomination as we face daily hopes, struggles, joy, or pain. The resolutions and Social Principles express our Church community's beliefs and give us evidence that the Church means for God's love to reach into situations faced each day, not just on Sunday mornings. Not all of us are intimately involved with each issue, but someone, somewhere, is.

### Isn't *The Book of Discipline* enough?

*The Book of Discipline* establishes a framework for each part of United Methodism. The General Conference decided in 1968 that for reasons of length, these resolutions should be published in a volume separate from the *Discipline*. While *The Book of Resolutions* is not legally binding, it is an official guide from our denomination to be used responsibly for reference, encouragement, study, and support.

### Why do the Social Principles appear in both the *Discipline* and in *The Book of Resolutions*?

The United Methodist Church puts the Social Principles in the *Discipline* (¶¶ 160–165) as one of our denominational foundation statements suggesting how faith is translated into action. Its broad principles (guides, not rules) are declarations to help us be in dialogue with one another about how faith motivates us to "get off the fence" and act.

The United Methodist Church puts the Social Principles in *The Book of Resolutions* to help us relate the broad strokes of the Social Principles to more specific exploration and applications in resolutions.

### Where do these policies and resolutions come from? How do they get adopted by General Conference?

They are sent in as petitions to General Conference every four years by general agencies, annual conferences, local churches, individual members, and groups. Once submitted as petitions, most of them are worked on by delegates in a legislative committee. The legislative committees accept, reject, or amend the petitions, then report their recommendations to the General Conference plenary; all delegates then vote on their recommendations.

**Can I trust the statistics and data in these resolutions?**

General source references are usually given when statistics are used in a resolution. Because such data may change during the years the resolution is valid, sometimes the resolution will provide more general descriptions of social conditions that make it urgent for the church to speak on a particular topic. Resolutions will take on more meaning when you secure local statistics and data on relevant topics.

**Why do church social policies and US government policies or positions seem so far apart on some of these issues?**

The United Methodist Church membership extends beyond the US boundaries; it is global. So, in many cases we are speaking to, from, or with more than one national government. Further, the Christian church must never be a mirror image of any government, whether Democrat or Republican, totalitarian or democratic. We know that Christians are obligated to be responsible and participating citizens under any governmental system, but that response and participation is to be interpreted in light of our faith.

As the Social Principles state, "Our allegiance to God takes precedence over our allegiance to any state" (¶ 164). And our church's public witness is first and foremost to be judged by God by whether it supports justice, love, and mercy, particularly for the poor and powerless.

**Why can't the church just let us make up our own minds on these matters after it presents us neutral information on both sides of an issue?**

Most importantly, The United Methodist Church believes God's love for the world is an active and engaged love, a love seeking justice and liberty. We cannot just be observers. So we care enough about people's lives to risk interpreting God's love, to take a stand, to call each of us into a response, no matter how controversial or complex. The church helps us think and act out of a faith perspective, not just respond to all the other "mind-makers-up" that exist in our society.

No information is truly neutral. This is true even of the most "hard scientific" data secured from the most advanced technology. These resolutions do strive for objectivity, not neutrality. There are usually more than "two sides" in important social controversies. Dialogue between different sides is critical in taking a stand. Faithfulness requires favoring what best demonstrates God's love and being willing to change when new perspectives or data emerge.

### Is this something new in United Methodism?

Taking an active stance in society is nothing new for followers of John Wesley. He set the example for us to combine personal and social piety. Ever since predecessor churches to United Methodism flourished in the United States, we have been known as a denomination involved with people's lives, with political and social struggles, having local to international mission implications. Such involvement is an expression of the personal change we experience in our baptism and conversion.

### Is there a difference between a social policy and a resolution?

The terms are used almost interchangeably in The United Methodist Church. Most social issue resolutions refer to public policy matters, such as local, state, and federal government programs and legislation. Other statements focus on conditions affecting the church and the church's programs or funding.

### How do people use this *Book of Resolutions?*

• An ordained minister went to console neighbor parents after their son committed suicide. At home later that evening, the pastor and his own family struggled in their grief to apply their faith to this troubling situation. What did the church say about suicide? How should a Christian act? The pastor found the 1980 *Book of Resolutions* absolutely silent on this topic. During the six years after that first personal encounter with ministry after a suicide, the pastor wrote letters and articles and talked with seminary faculty and national church staff. As a result, the 1988 General Conference adopted its first resolution on suicide. Instead of merely wishing for guidance from our church on this most difficult subject, this pastor gave constructive leadership in the church, and we now can find helpful perspectives in *The 2008 Book of Resolutions.*

• A bishop and an annual conference board of church and society wanted to share a United Methodist position against the death penalty with their governor, who had to consider clemency for a death row inmate. They visited the governor and delivered a letter stating their own views of this particular situation and describing why The United Methodist Church opposes the death penalty. They used the resolution on capital punishment in *The Book of Resolutions* as the official policy of The United Methodist Church to support their plea for clemency.

• An adult church school group studied the foreign policy discussion topics called "Great Decisions," issued annually by the Foreign Policy Association. They compared its resources with positions in the relevant United Methodist policies from *The Book of Resolutions* for several evenings of lively study.

• Another adult class meeting on Sunday morning always studied faith and contemporary issues. For nearly six months, the members used *The Book of Resolutions* to guide their study and discussion. Different members made presentations on some aspect of the resolutions; then they used the study questions provided on page 38 to stimulate some challenging discussion. Occasionally, they had guest speakers or used an audiovisual resource from their conference media center to amplify the subject.

• A nurse who is an active church member found the resolutions on "Health Care for All in the United States" and "Ministries in Mental Illness" to be helpful as she reflected on the strains in her job. She found it more possible to connect her faith to her discussions with coworkers about some of the major issues facing her profession in a big city hospital.

• A local church's outreach work area asked its administrative council to approve a congregational statement to the county zoning board favoring the construction of several low-income housing units. As part of their homework, the work area members reviewed the "Housing in the USA" resolution in *The Book of Resolutions.* That resolution then served as a basis for their initiative; they even quoted from it when they testified at the zoning board.

## How do I use *The Book of Resolutions?*

Read the preface. ─────────────► It provides an orientation to the whole book.

Skim through the ─────────────► Note: Resolutions are
table of contents.                          listed under the section
                                                      of the Social Principles
                                                      to which they most
                                                      closely relate.

Check index for ─────────────► Key words will help you
for specific references                    locate resolutions

Example:     If you want to know whether our denomination has spoken about AIDS or HIV, you look for those entries in the index. These subjects are referred to in a number of resolutions.

Example:     What is there on "racism"? The index includes a number of references. You may also choose to look under "African Americans," "Native Americans," or "White Privilege."

Find the text of the
Social Principles.

• Note that the Social Principles include broad, fundamental statements grouped in six topical sections. Immediately following this study guide you will find "Our Social Creed" and a new "Companion Litany" designed for worship use. Following that, come the Social Principles Preface and the Preamble, then ¶ 160, the first of the Social Principles. The remaining Social Principles can easily be found by using the new thumb index on the outer edge of the pages. The Resolutions are placed after the Social Principles to which they relate.

• Review the "How can I understand the Social Principles?" section in this User's Guide. Use the diagrams in this section to help interpret and look for meaning in the Social Principles.

# How can I understand the Social Principles?

*The Book of Resolutions* organizes almost all resolutions into the six areas of concern that form the major sections of the Social Principles. You may find it helpful to consider these six areas of concern as you explore specific resolutions.

One way of understanding the Social Principles is to consider the six sections as areas of concern: (1) the natural world, (2) the nurturing community, (3) the social community, (4) the economic community, (5) the political community, and (6) the world community.

The Natural World, the starting point for the areas of concern, provides the essential resources of life for all humankind.

Then add to the natural world the people of the world—of the World Community. All of us live in community, oftentimes becoming part of several communities. Together we make up the world community.

All of us also become a part of the Nurturing Community. Through the people with whom we interact most often—family, friends, local church, and others—we shape our lives and the way we relate to other communities.

Three other communities impact both the nurturing community and the world community.

The Social Community (or cultural community) provides the arena where we live out our responsibilities and rights in our treatment of others.

The Economic Community, in which each of us functions, establishes production, distribution and employment systems; it creates both wealth and poverty.

The Political Community determines whether our rights are guaranteed and our basic freedoms are upheld. Directions and goals of our social and economic communities are debated and decided in this arena.

Decisions in all these communities have an impact on the natural world and vice versa.

## Our Social Creed

"Our Social Creed" (Section VII of the Social Principles) is a summary of the foregoing sections of the Social Principles in the form of a creed. While it is recommended by the general church for separate use in worship services, "Our Social Creed" is an integral part of the Social Principles. The Companion Litany was approved by General Conference 2008 and is also intended for use in worship.

Another way of considering the six sections of the Social Principles (the six areas of concern) is to look at: (1) the role of each section, (2) the predominant faith statement in each section, (3) our responsibility defined in each section, and (4) the issues discussed in each section. The chart on the next two pages summarizes the Social Principles in this way.

# The Social Principles

| CATEGORY | I The Natural World | II The Nurturing Community | III The Social Community | IV The Economic Community | V The Political Community | VI The World Community |
|---|---|---|---|---|---|---|
| ROLE | Provides for sustenance of all creation to be used with integrity | Provides the potential to nurture human beings into the fullness of their humanity. | Provides for means for determining the rights and responsibilities of the members toward one another | Provides directions for influencing economic policies. | Provides for the ordering of society. | Provides the setting for the interaction of nations. |
| FAITH STATEMENT | All creation is God's. | All persons are important and loved by God. | All persons are equally valuable in the sight of God. | All economic systems are under God's judgment. | All political systems are under God's judgment. | All of God's world is one world. |

| | | | | | | |
|---|---|---|---|---|---|---|
| **OUR RESPONSI-BILITY** | To value and conserve all natural resources. | To innovate, sponsor, and evaluate new forms of community. | To work toward societies in which social groups and individual values are recognized, maintained and strengthened. | To ensure that sound policies are developed that provide for full employment, adequate income, and so forth. | To take active responsibility for our government. | To work to develop the moral and spiritual capacity to achieve a stable world of love. |
| **ISSUES** | Water, air, soil, plants, energy utilization, animal life, space. | Family, marriage, human sexuality, abortion, death. | Rights of minorities, children, youth and young adults, the aging, women, men, immigrants, people with disabilities; alcohol/drugs, rural life. | Property, collective bargaining, work/leisure, consumption, poverty, foreign workers, gambling. | Basic liberties, political responsibility, freedom of information, civil obedience and civil disobedience, crime and rehabilitation, military service. | Nations and cultures, national power and responsibility, war and peace, justice and law. |

## How can I better understand the resolutions?

Each resolution shows:

- the rationale or reasons for the resolution;
- the Social Principles paragraph to which that resolution relates (found at the conclusion of any resolution);
- the biblical references and/or theological concerns identified in this resolution;
- the major actions called for in that resolution for churches; individuals; church agencies; local, state, or national governments;
- the date the resolution was passed or amended and readopted by General Conference.
- the resolution number from the preceding two volumes.

## The Natural World

| Resolution | Social Principles Paragraph | Biblical References Theological Concerns | Actions called for | Hymns to use |
|---|---|---|---|---|
| A Dioxin-Free Future | ¶ 160A | Jesus' abundant life embraced physical well-being as well as emotional and spiritual health. Wesley and his followers have a long record of health/welfare ministries. | • Urge local churches, all church agencies and institutions to learn of suffering due to background levels of dioxin<br><br>• Urge general United Methodist agencies to work with companies and governments to support a gradual phase out of the production of dioxin<br><br>• Ask all United Methodists to take action to stop harm being done by the nonessential incineration of medical waste and encourage healthcare workers to adopt policies that will reduce or eliminate use of PVC plastic | "Open my eyes, that I may see" (*Hymnal*, 454)<br><br>"O God who shaped creation" (*Hymnal*, 443) |

## The Natural World

| Resolution | Social Principles Paragraph | Biblical References Theological Concerns | Actions called for | Hymns to use |
|---|---|---|---|---|
| Nuclear Safety in the United States | ¶ 160F | The God-given charge to humans to "guard and keep the earth" (Genesis 2:15).<br><br>To ensure that God's creation is protected for present and future generations. | • Urge general United Methodist agencies to assist annual conferences in all aspects of information and action strategies on this issue.<br><br>• Advocate for public policy, particularly regarding nuclear power, reviewing safety of operating plants, researching designs for plant safety, phasing out nuclear weapons production, establishing uniform safety standards for civilian and military nuclear operations, reevaluating US nuclear waste policy, and conserving energy and enhancing alternative energy sources. | "A charge to keep I have" (*Hymnal*, 413)<br><br>"Creating God, your fingers trace" (*Hymnal*, 109) |

# The Social Community

| Resolution | Social Principles Paragraph | Biblical References Theological Concerns | Actions called for | Hymns to use |
|---|---|---|---|---|
| Rural Communities in Crisis | ¶ 162P | God's gift of the land is a common gift to all humanity, requiring just patterns of land use (Leviticus 25).<br><br>Jesus commands us to love neighbor as self.<br><br>The gospel challenges an ethic based on "bigness is better." | Issues over 72 comprehensive calls for change by the church at all levels, by local communities, and by state and federal governments. For example:<br><br>• Churches to develop intentionally ministry to meet major needs in today's rural USA; to become public policy advocates; to model and support team and cooperative ministries; to emphasize ecology as part of Christian stewardship.<br><br>• Federal legislation and programs to enable farm families to receive just return for their labor and investments; to develop just water and energy policies to recognize and protect rights of farm workers.<br><br>• State and governments, private lending agencies, local governments, and community groups to be involved, together and separately overall, to develop a vision for agricultural life where programs and relations are just, participatory, and sustainable. | "Great is thy faithfulness" (*Hymnal*, 140)<br><br>"Faith, while trees are still in blossom" (*Hymnal*, 508) |

## What do I do next?

Consider these questions for study and response to any of the resolutions:

• How familiar am I with the situation(s) described in this resolution?

• What are my reactions to this call for action by our church?

• How might reactions be different if we lived in another part of this country? lived in another country? were of a different economic class? attended a different church? if members of my family were present (or not present)?

• How could our local congregation creatively respond to the calls for action in the resolution?

• Are there groups in my area or state at work on this issue where I could join in action or learn more?

• What have I communicated to our congressional members or state legislators about our church's position on an issue of great importance?

• Who could we contact for more information or resources? Write to or call: Communications, General Board of Church and Society, 100 Maryland Avenue, N.E., Washington, DC 20002; (202) 488-5600 (www.umc-gbcs.org).

# SOCIAL CREED

## ¶ 166. VII. OUR SOCIAL CREED

We believe in God, Creator of the world; and in Jesus Christ, the Redeemer of creation. We believe in the Holy Spirit, through whom we acknowledge God's gifts, and we repent of our sin in misusing these gifts to idolatrous ends.

We affirm the natural world as God's handiwork and dedicate ourselves to its preservation, enhancement, and faithful use by humankind.

We joyfully receive for ourselves and others the blessings of community, sexuality, marriage, and the family.

We commit ourselves to the rights of men, women, children, youth, young adults, the aging, and people with disabilities; to improvement of the quality of life; and to the rights and dignity of all persons.

We believe in the right and duty of persons to work for the glory of God and the good of themselves and others and in the protection of their welfare in so doing; in the rights to property as a trust from God, collective bargaining, and responsible consumption; and in the elimination of economic and social distress.

We dedicate ourselves to peace throughout the world, to the rule of justice and law among nations, and to individual freedom for all people of the world.

We believe in the present and final triumph of God's Word in human affairs and gladly accept our commission to manifest the life of the gospel in the world. Amen.

(It is recommended that this statement of Social Principles be continually available to United Methodist Christians and that it be emphasized regularly in every congregation. It is further recommended that "Our Social Creed" be frequently used in Sunday worship.)

## A COMPANION LITANY TO OUR SOCIAL CREED

God in the Spirit revealed in Jesus Christ,
calls us by grace
> *to be renewed in the image of our Creator,*
> *that we may be one*
> *in divine love for the world.*

Today is the day
God cares for the integrity of creation,
> wills the healing and wholeness of all life,
> weeps at the plunder of earth's goodness.
*And so shall we.*

Today is the day
God embraces all hues of humanity,
> delights in diversity and difference,
> favors solidarity transforming strangers into friends.
*And so shall we.*

Today is the day
God cries with the masses of starving people,
> despises growing disparity between rich and poor,
> demands justice for workers in the marketplace.
*And so shall we.*

Today is the day
God deplores violence in our homes and streets,
> rebukes the world's warring madness,
> humbles the powerful and lifts up the lowly.
*And so shall we.*

Today is the day
God calls for nations and peoples to live in peace,
> celebrates where justice and mercy embrace,
> exults when the wolf grazes with the lamb.
*And so shall we.*

## SOCIAL CREED

*Today is the day*
*God brings good news to the poor,*
    *proclaims release to the captives,*
    *gives sight to the blind, and*
    *sets the oppressed free.*
*And so shall we.*

# SOCIAL PRINCIPLES

## PREFACE

The United Methodist Church has a long history of concern for social justice. Its members have often taken forthright positions on controversial issues involving Christian principles. Early Methodists expressed their opposition to the slave trade, to smuggling, and to the cruel treatment of prisoners.

A social creed was adopted by The Methodist Episcopal Church (North) in 1908. Within the next decade similar statements were adopted by The Methodist Episcopal Church, South, and by The Methodist Protestant Church. The Evangelical United Brethren Church adopted a statement of social principles in 1946 at the time of the uniting of the United Brethren and The Evangelical Church. In 1972, four years after the uniting in 1968 of The Methodist Church and The Evangelical United Brethren Church, the General Conference of The United Methodist Church adopted a new statement of Social Principles, which was revised in 1976 (and by each successive General Conference).

The Social Principles, while not to be considered law, are a prayerful and thoughtful effort on the part of the General Conference to speak to the human issues in the contemporary world from a sound biblical and theological foundation as historically demonstrated in United Methodist traditions. They are a call to faithfulness and are intended to be instructive and persuasive in the best of the prophetic spirit. The Social Principles are a call to all members of The United Methodist Church to a prayerful, studied dialogue of faith and practice. (*See* ¶ 509.)

## PREAMBLE

We, the people called United Methodists, affirm our faith in God our Creator and Father, in Jesus Christ our Savior, and in the Holy Spirit, our Guide and Guard.

We acknowledge our complete dependence upon God in birth, in life, in death, and in life eternal. Secure in God's love, we affirm the goodness of life and confess our many sins against God's will for us as we find it in Jesus Christ. We have not always been faithful stewards of all that has been committed to us by God the Creator. We have been reluctant followers of Jesus Christ in his mission to bring all persons into a community of love. Though called by the Holy Spirit to become new creatures in Christ, we have resisted the further call to become the people of God in our dealings with each other and the earth on which we live.

We pledge to continue to be in respectful conversation with those with whom we differ, to explore the sources of our differences, to honor the sacred worth of all persons as we continue to seek the mind of Christ and to do the will of God in all things.

Grateful for God's forgiving love, in which we live and by which we are judged, and affirming our belief in the inestimable worth of each individual, we renew our commitment to become faithful witnesses to the gospel, not alone to the ends of earth, but also to the depths of our common life and work.

# ¶ 160. I. THE NATURAL WORLD

All creation is the Lord's, and we are responsible for the ways in which we use and abuse it. Water, air, soil, minerals, energy resources, plants, animal life, and space are to be valued and conserved because they are God's creation and not solely because they are useful to human beings. God has granted us stewardship of creation. We should meet these stewardship duties through acts of loving care and respect. Economic, political, social, and technological developments have increased our human numbers, lengthened and enriched our lives. However, these developments have led to regional defoliation, dramatic extinction of species, massive human suffering, overpopulation, misuse and over-consumption of natural and nonrenewable resources, particularly by industrialized societies. This continued course of action jeopardizes the natural heritage that God has entrusted to all generations. Therefore, let us recognize the responsibility of the church and its members to place a high priority on changes in economic, political, social, and technological lifestyle to support a more ecologically equitable and sustainable world leading to a higher quality of life for all of God's creation.

*A) Water, Air, Soil, Minerals, Plants*—We support and encourage social policies that serve to reduce and control the creation of industrial byproducts and waste; facilitate the safe processing and disposal of toxic and nuclear waste and move toward the elimination of both; encourage reduction of municipal waste; provide for appropriate recycling and disposal of municipal waste; and assist the cleanup of polluted air, water, and soil. We call for the preservation of old-growth forests and other irreplaceable natural treasures, as well as preservation of endangered plant species. We support measures designed to maintain and restore natural ecosystems. We support policies that develop alternatives to chemicals used for growing, processing, and preserving food, and we strongly urge adequate research into their effects upon God's creation prior to utilization. We urge development of international agreements concerning equitable utilization of the world's resources for human benefit so long as the integrity of the earth is maintained. We are deeply concerned about the privatization of water resources, the bottling of water to be sold as a commodity for profit, and the resources that go into packaging bottled water. We urge all municipalities and other governmental organizations to develop processes for determining sustainability of water resources and to determine the environmental, economic, and social consequences of privatization of water resources prior to the licensing and approval thereof.

*B) Energy Resources Utilization*—Affirming the inherent value of nonhuman creation, we support and encourage social policies that are directed toward rational and restrained transformation of parts of the nonhuman world into energy for human usage and that de-emphasize or eliminate energy-producing technologies that endanger the health, the safety, and even the existence of the present and future human and nonhuman creation. Further, we urge wholehearted support of the conservation of energy and responsible development of all energy resources, with special concern for the development of renewable energy sources, that the goodness of the earth may be affirmed.

*C) Animal Life*—We support regulations that protect the life and health of animals, including those ensuring the humane treatment of pets and other domestic animals, animals used in research, and the painless slaughtering of meat animals, fish, and fowl. We encourage the preservation of all animal species including those threatened with extinction.

*D) Global Climate Stewardship*—We acknowledge the global impact of humanity's disregard for God's creation. Rampant industrialization and the corresponding increase in the use of fossil fuels have led to a buildup of pollutants in the earth's atmosphere. These "greenhouse gas" emissions threaten to alter dramatically the earth's climate for generations to come with severe environmental, economic, and social implications. The adverse impacts of global climate change disproportionately affect individuals and nations least responsible for the emissions. We therefore support efforts of all governments to require mandatory reductions in greenhouse gas emissions and call on individuals, congregations, businesses, industries, and communities to reduce their emissions.

E) *Space*—The universe, known and unknown, is the creation of God and is due the respect we are called to give the earth. We therefore reject any nation's efforts to weaponize space and urge that all nations pursue the peaceful and collaborative development of space technologies and of outer space itself.

F) *Science and Technology*—We recognize science as a legitimate interpretation of God's natural world. We affirm the validity of the claims of science in describing the natural world and in determining what is scientific. We preclude science from making authoritative claims about theological issues and theology from making authoritative claims about scientific issues. We find that science's descriptions of cosmological, geological, and biological evolution are not in conflict with theology. We recognize medical, technical, and scientific technologies as legitimate uses of God's natural world when such use enhances human life and enables all of God's children to develop their God-given creative potential without violating our ethical convictions about the relationship of humanity to the natural world. We reexamine our ethical convictions as our understanding of the natural world increases. We find that as science expands human understanding of the natural world, our understanding of the mysteries of God's creation and word are enhanced.

In acknowledging the important roles of science and technology, however, we also believe that theological understandings of human experience are crucial to a full understanding of the place of humanity in the universe. Science and theology are complementary rather than mutually incompatible. We therefore encourage dialogue between the scientific and theological communities and seek the kind of participation that will enable humanity to sustain life on earth and, by God's grace, increase the quality of our common lives together.

G) *Food Safety*—We support policies that protect the food supply and that ensure the public's right to know the content of the foods they are eating. We call for rigorous inspections and controls on the biological safety of all foodstuffs intended for human consumption. We urge independent testing for chemical residues in food, and the removal from the market of foods contaminated with potentially hazardous levels of pesticides, herbicides, or fungicides; drug residues from animal antibiotics, steroids, or hormones; contaminants due to pollution that are carried by air, soil, or water from incinerator plants or other industrial operations. We call for clear labeling of all processed or altered foods, with pre-market safety testing required. We oppose weakening the standards for organic foods. We call for policies that encourage and support a gradual transition to sustainable and organic agriculture.

# THE NATURAL WORLD
# THE RESOLUTIONS

## ENERGY

### 1001. Energy Policy Statement

Humankind enjoys a unique place in God's universe. On the one hand, we are simply one of God's many finite creatures, made from the "dust of the earth," bounded in time and space, fallible in judgment, limited in control, dependent upon our Creator, and interdependent with all other creatures. On the other hand, we are created in the very image of God, with the divine Spirit breathed into us, and entrusted with "dominion" over God's creation (Genesis 1:26, 28; 2:7; Psalm 8:6). We are simultaneously caretakers with all creation and, because of the divine summons, caretakers with God of the world in which we live. This hybrid human condition produces both the opportunity and the twin dangers for humans on this planet.

The first danger is *arrogance:* that we may overestimate the extent of human control over our environment and the soundness of human judgments concerning it; that we may underestimate the limits of the planet where we live; and that we may misunderstand "dominion" to mean exploitation instead of stewardship.

The second danger is *irresponsibility:* that we may fail to be the responsible stewards of the earth. As stewards entrusted with dominion, then, we will demonstrate our faith in God by shaping the new human society that will emerge in the twenty-first century. We cannot, therefore, neglect the task of seeking to embody in the world the values that we hold in covenant with God. Nor can we forget the forgiving grace in Jesus Christ, which alone makes us bold enough, or the hope in Christ, which alone keeps us from despair.

## The Values Involved in Energy Policy

The decisions that humans are now making will either enhance or degrade the quality of life on the planet. We have entered an era of greater energy interdependence. As the world confronts global issues such as climate change, energy inequity, and pollution, energy-related problems will require international solutions based upon the values of justice and sustainability.

The Scripture that provides the motive for our action in the present energy crisis also lays the foundation for the values that we seek to realize. These values underlying the policies we advocate are justice and sustainability.

1. *Justice.* Ever since the first covenant between God and Israel, and especially since the eighth-century prophets, the people of God have understood that they bear a special concern for justice.

> "Let justice roll down like waters,
> and righteousness like an everflowing stream" (Amos 5:24)

is a cry echoed in hundreds of contexts throughout the Old and New Testaments. Biblical righteousness includes a special concern for the least and the last: the poor, the captive, the oppressed (Luke 4:18; Isaiah 61:1-2). Energy policies that Christians can support, then, will seek to actualize the multifaceted biblical vision of justice. They will be policies that close rather than widen the gap dividing wealth and poverty, rich nations and poor. They will be measures that liberate rather than oppress. They will be programs that distribute fairly the benefits, burdens, and hazards of energy production and consumption, taking into consideration those not yet born as well as the living. They will thus be strategies that give priority to meeting basic human needs such as air, water, food, clothing, and shelter.

2. *Sustainability.* Only recently have we humans come to recognize that creation entails limits to the resources entrusted to us as stewards of the earth. In particular, we have come up against limits to the non-renewable fuels available for our consumption and limits to our environment's capacity to absorb poisonous wastes. These double limits mean that humans can betray their stewardship either by using up resources faster than they can be replaced or by releasing wastes in excess of the planet's capacity to absorb them. We now know that humans have the capacity to destroy human life and perhaps even life

itself on this planet, and to do so in a very short period of time. Energy policy decisions, therefore, must be measured by sustainability as a criterion in addition to justice. In terms of energy policy, sustainability means energy use that will not: (a) deplete the earth's resources in such a way that our descendants will not be able to continue human society at the level that is adequate for a good quality of life, and (b) pollute the environment to such an extent that human life cannot be sustained in the future. These guidelines for sustainability must include considerations of quality of life as well as mere biological continuance.

Technological advances have created an increasingly sophisticated and industrialized world community. As we pursue an energy policy that is just and sustainable it is not a realistic option to ask all global citizens to return to an era where wood and candles provided the only sources of heat and light. Also, we should be aware of the tragic effects that steadily increasing energy costs will have, especially upon the aged and those living in poverty. Furthermore, some cleaner energy options available to wealthier nations are not available to peoples in all parts of the world; hence, we should endeavor to develop just and equitable energy policies.

We must creatively explore all sustainable energy options available to us. There are environmental and social problems connected with certain energy options. We believe that the economic, environmental, and social implications of each energy source should be fully assessed.

Today, the leading source of global energy consumption is fossil fuels including oil, coal and natural gas. From extraction to end-use, the life cycle of energy produced from fossil fuels has led to severe strain on both the local and global environment.

Underground mining of coal, in addition to operational accidents, causes disabling illness or death from black lung. Strip-mining and mountaintop removal despoil lands and ruin them for further use if restoration measures are not practiced. The burning of coal causes large-scale pollution and seriously alters the environment by increasing the carbon dioxide content of the atmosphere, contributing to global warming.

In addition to fueling regional instability, the use of oil resources poses significant environmental dangers. Tankers and offshore wells have created spills that have devastated seacoast areas often with long-lasting or permanent ecological damage. The emissions produced from the use of oil as fuel are a leading source of air pollution, particularly in centers of dense population.

Hydroelectric dams, particularly those in areas with considerable seismic activity, pose dangers to nearby communities and the environment. Furthermore, the building of hydroelectric dams and reservoirs destroys communities, wildlife habitats and natural scenic beauty.

There are considerable concerns with regard to the nuclear energy option. The destructive potential of a catastrophic accident involves a great risk of irreversible damage to the environment and all living species. Nuclear waste remains active and dangerous for thousands of years. Additionally, the development of nuclear energy possibly has masked ambitions for nuclear armament.

Today, cleaner alternatives to traditional energy sources are available and increasingly cost-competitive. Harnessing solar and wind power can produce energy with far fewer net emissions. Facing increased global demand for energy resources and ever-increasing strain on the global environment, we must chart a new course rooted in our shared principles of justice and sustainability. To this end:

1. We support strenuous efforts to conserve energy and increase energy efficiency. A transition to energy efficiency and renewable energy sources will combat global warming, protect human health, create new jobs, and ensure a secure, affordable energy future. Economists have concluded that a greater increase in end-use energy can be gained through conservation and energy efficiency than through any single new source of fuel. Furthermore, conservation is nonpolluting and job producing. We include under conservation: insulation, co-generation, recycling, public transportation, more efficient motors in appliances and automobiles, as well as the elimination of waste, and a more simplified lifestyle. The technology for such steps is already known and commercially available; it requires only dissemination of information and stronger public support, including larger tax incentives than are presently available.

2. All United Methodists, including churches, annual conferences, general boards and agencies are to be models for energy conservation by doing such things as: installing dampers in furnaces, insulating adequately all church properties, heating and lighting only rooms that are in use, using air circulation, purchasing energy efficient appliances, and exploring alternative energy sources such as solar energy. Local churches, camps, and agencies are urged to become involved in programs such as the Energy Stewardship Congregation and Interfaith Power and Light programs, thereby witnessing our shared values of justice and sustainability.

3. All United Methodist Church programs and mission projects must model our sustainable and just energy values. We particularly

urge the United Methodist Committee on Relief (UMCOR) and the General Board of Global Ministries (GBGM) to support and fund renewable and energy efficient mission projects; and we urge the Church Architecture Office of the General Board of Global Ministries to make energy conservation and the use of renewables a prime design feature in new building design and renovations.

4. We support increased government funding for research and development of renewable energy sources, especially solar energy, and government incentives to speed the application of the resulting technologies to our energy needs, wherever appropriate. The greatest national and international effort should be made in the areas of conservation and renewable energy sources.

5. We encourage international lending institutions and aid agencies to promote sustainable and just energy policies.

6. We oppose any energy policy that will result in continuing exploitation of indigenous peoples' lands. The despoiling of indigenous peoples' lands and the increased health and social-economic problems that have resulted because of oil exploration, hydroelectric projects, and the mining of coal and the milling of uranium must cease.

7. We support national energy programs that will not increase the financial burden on the poor, the elderly, and those with fixed incomes. If a rapid rise in the price of fuel is necessary to smooth out distortions in the energy economy, as many economists believe, then means should be found to cushion the impact of such price increases on the poor. Furthermore, energy policies must guarantee universal service to all consumers, protecting low-income and rural residents.

8. We support full cooperation of all nations in efforts to ensure equitable distribution of necessary energy supplies, the control of global warming, and rapid development and deployment of appropriate technologies based on renewable energy resources such as solar, wind, and water energy generation.

9. We strongly encourage The United Methodist Church at all levels to engage in a serious study of these energy issues in the context of Christian faith, especially the values of justice and sustainability.

ADOPTED 1980
AMENDED AND READOPTED 2000
AMENDED AND READOPTED 2008
RESOLUTION #5, 2004 *BOOK OF RESOLUTIONS*
RESOLUTION #6, 2000 *BOOK OF RESOLUTIONS*

*See* Social Principles, ¶ 160B.

## 1002. US Energy Policy and United Methodist Responsibility

Resolved:

1. Energy policy in the US must be based on sound scientific and ethical principles of respect for and justice within the World Community, focusing not on expanding supply through large scale projects but on managing the demand and developing renewable, alternative sources of energy. Specifically, the US must:

- move beyond its dependence on high carbon fossil fuels that produce emissions leading to climate change,
- ratify the Kyoto Protocol under the UN Framework Convention on Climate Change,
- concentrate on reducing carbon dioxide emissions within the US and not rely on mechanisms such as emission trading with other countries to meet our targets for emission reductions under international agreements,
- reduce our reliance on nuclear power, a technology for which there are still unresolved problems such as the safe disposal or safe storage of high level waste of nuclear reactors,
- manage demand through a high priority on conservation and energy efficiency,
- increase significantly research and development into such renewable energy sources as solar, wind, biomass, etc.,
- support development and utilization of appropriate technologies for small-scale, decentralized energy systems,
- support expansion of the infrastructure needed for public transportation and carpooling, and
- provide necessary support for individuals, families, and communities adversely affected by a transition away from fossil fuels, nuclear power, and large-scale hydro in order to allow for alternative economic development, retraining, relocation, etc.

2. Members of local United Methodist churches are urged to show leadership as stewards of God's creation and take concrete actions to:

- educate our congregants on energy production and usage in relation to global warming,
- conduct an energy audit of our homes, church facilities, and camp structures to identify sources of energy waste and the potential financial savings of energy-related improvements,
- make energy improvements to our homes, church facilities, and camp structures,

- replace light bulbs with compact fluorescent bulbs,
- expand our use of public transportation, carpooling, and tele-conferencing to reduce fossil fuel consumption,
- choose a cleaner vehicle that is the least polluting and most efficient,
- keep our vehicle's engine tuned and tires properly inflated,
- study the consequences of our consumer choices and take action to lessen our impact on the environment, and use our votes by telling our elected officials that we need laws that support the most important solutions to climate change: cleaner cars and cleaner power plants.

ADOPTED 2004
RESOLUTION #6, 2004 *BOOK OF RESOLUTIONS*

*See* Social Principles, ¶ 160B.

## 1003. Nuclear Safety in the United States

*Theology*

God has given humans a special charge to "guard and keep" the earth (Genesis 2:15). Nuclear technology presents a special challenge to our call to be stewards of God's creation (Psalm 8:6-8) because of the risks involved in the production, handling, and disposal of long-lived nuclear byproducts (such as plutonium) in the energy and weapons-production cycles. Until society discontinues the use of nuclear power to produce energy and weapons, we have a special responsibility to ensure that God's creation be protected for present and future generations by insisting that the entire production cycle be as safe as possible.

The problem of nuclear safety is of worldwide concern. It is the responsibility of the church to use its influence internationally to prevent the devastation that could result from nuclear disasters.

### *United Methodist Policy*

Through its Energy Policy Statement, The United Methodist Church affirmed the need to explore all sustainable energy options while highlighting the environmental risks posed by certain options including nuclear power. "The hazards in storing radioactive wastes for thousands of years and the destructive potential of a catastrophic accident involve a great risk of irreversible damage to the environment or to the human genetic pool."[1] Furthermore, the Church has reiterated its opposition to "the production and testing of weapons designed to destroy or harm God's creation, such as . . . nuclear weapons. We urge the abolishment of chemical, biological, and nuclear weapons and urge the cleanup of sites contaminated by chemical, biological, and nuclear weapons waste."

## Background

### Nuclear Power

Although there has been a pause in construction of new nuclear capacity in the United States—no nuclear plants have been ordered since 1978 and none has come online since the Tennessee Valley Authority's Watts Bar 1 reactor ordered in 1970 and licensed to operate in 1996—the waste generated by current nuclear operations continues to pile up and policy-makers are debating the merits of encouraging construction of new nuclear reactors. In the United States there are currently 103 licensed reactors operating at 65 plants in 31 states. Worldwide, nearly 433 reactors generate roughly 17 percent of global electricity.

The accident at Chernobyl on April 28, 1986—and its legacy of radiation, contamination, and cancer—demonstrated the dangers involved in the production of nuclear energy. This accident was much larger than the one at Three Mile Island in 1979. However, the Nuclear Regulatory Commission's Reactor Safety Study points out that accidents even larger than Chernobyl are possible for US reactors. Despite the difference between the design of the Chernobyl plants and the designs of most US plants, there are, according to the Reactor Safety Study, many accident scenarios possible in US plants that could lead to substantial releases of radiation. In March 2002, at the Davis-Besse nuclear plant near Toledo, Ohio, authorities discovered that leaking boric acid had corroded a six-inch hole in the reactor vessel head leaving only a quarter-inch-thick stainless steel liner to prevent a potentially catastrophic release of reactor cooling water. This most recent example of safety-related shortcomings at nuclear plants further

1. Joshua Gordon, as cited by Christopher Flavin, Worldwatch Paper 75: "Reassessing Nuclear Power: The Fallout from Chernobyl"; March 1987.

increases concerns raised after the September 11, 2001 terrorist attacks that the Nuclear Regulatory Commission's oversight is insufficient and additional security and safety measures are needed.

## Department of Energy Reactors

The Department of Energy (DOE) operates more than 200 nuclear facilities. Among its main responsibilities are the production and testing of this country's nuclear weapons program. The DOE facilities are generally more antiquated than civilian plants and are not subject to review by outside agencies. Five of these facilities are the main nuclear weapons production reactors. Four are located on the Savannah River in South Carolina; the fifth is the "N-Reactor" at Hanford, Washington (a complex where poor disposal of wastes in the past has created a radioactive landfill known as "one of our largest contaminated areas"). The containment systems in these plants have been criticized as being inadequate and not capable of meeting minimum civilian standards. In 1986, the DOE agreed to submit its five weapons reactors to state and federal waste disposal rules and shut down the Hanford "N-Reactor" for safety improvements. The cleanup of the Hanford site alone could cost over $100 billion. Yet most DOE plants continue to be exempt from the far more rigorous examination of commercial reactors by the Nuclear Regulatory Commission.

## Emergency Planning and State Rights

After the Three Mile Island accident, rules were instituted to improve public safety in case of a nuclear accident. The new rules required the participation, in emergency planning exercise, of local and state officials. In 1986, the Nuclear Regulatory Commission, in response to two state governors' challenge to the viability of utility-produced emergency plans, requested that it be allowed to approve utility emergency evacuation plans in the event that state and local officials refuse to participate in the emergency-planning process. This rule change would ease the licensing of future nuclear reactors and seriously diminish public participation and review of safety measures, as well as increase the dangers of a serious accident.

## Nuclear Wastes

One of the most controversial and costly components of the nuclear fission process is the creation of radioactive byproducts. The Nuclear

Regulatory Commission divides wastes into two different categories according to the level and duration of radioactivity: high-level and low-level wastes. Each reactor produces an annual average of 20 tons of highly radioactive spent nuclear fuel and 50-200 cubic meters of low-level radioactive waste. Since the 1950s, the Department of Energy has been searching for a viable way to dispose of the wastes created by commercial nuclear reactors (irradiated fuels) and high-level wastes from weapons production. These wastes are highly radioactive and will remain radioactive. Presently, these wastes are stored within nuclear facility sites, creating what one member of Congress called hundreds of "de facto nuclear waste dumps." Over the past six decades, these by-products have been accumulating at storage sites throughout the country, including an estimated 45,000 tons of spent nuclear fuel at civilian nuclear power plants with another 2,000 tons generated annually.

The Nuclear Waste Policy Act of 1982 (NWPA) set a schedule for the location, construction, and operation of two high-level waste geologic repositories, one in the east, and one in the west. Amendments to NWPA in 1987 restricted the repository site studies to one location: Yucca Mountain. This site is located in Nevada, a state which itself has no nuclear reactors, and on land considered sacred to the Western Shoshone and Paiute. To a large extent, political considerations have taken precedence over safety and scientific considerations, and there has been improper and inadequate consultation and cooperation with state governments and Native American tribes. In 2002, Yucca Mountain was designated as the nuclear fuel repository over the objections of Nevada's elected officials, tribal representatives, and environmental advocates. Proponents of the site highlighted the area's geological stability despite the occurrence of an earthquake registering 4.3 on the Richter scale the month of the Congressional vote.

Construction of the Yucca Mountain repository will not be completed for years and shipments of the radioactive waste—raising deep safety concerns for the millions of residents living along shipment routes—will take decades. While billed as creating a "central repository" for waste, spent nuclear fuel must remain for years on site before it is "cool" enough to transport, so this process would merely create a new, larger storage site in addition to the 100-plus on-site storage facilities that would continue to store nuclear waste.

## Recommendations

The United Methodist Church expresses its deep concern over the use of a technology with severe environmental and health impacts without appropriate and extensive safety measures in the production, handling, and disposal processes. We also reiterate our opposition to the use of nuclear technology for the production of weapons.

*We recommend:*

1. *Reviewing the safety of operating plants.* Each of the 107 operating commercial plants in the US should be reviewed by the Nuclear Regulatory Commission and the Office of Technology Assessment of the US Congress to identify design deficiencies and weaknesses that could contribute to or cause an accident.

2. *Instituting improvement programs.* Improvement programs should be instituted in areas of demonstrated weak performance such as management, personnel performance, equipment reliability, and contractor accountability.

3. *Researching new designs for plant safety.* New designs for existing and future nuclear plants should be researched and developed so as to eliminate the potential of a core meltdown accident.

4. *Phasing out nuclear weapons production.* We urge the closing down of the five weapons-producing reactors and the Rocky Flats Plutonium Processing Plant, a thorough cleanup of any remaining nuclear wastes at these sites, and no more nuclear arms testing.

5. *Establishing uniform safety standards for civilian and military nuclear operations.* We support having all nuclear operations in the US subject to uniform basic safety provision. All Department of Energy nuclear operations should be licensed and reviewed by an independent agency such as the Nuclear Regulatory Commission or the Environmental Protection Agency. Department of Energy contractors should be held accountable to the same standards as civilian facility contractors and operators.

6. *Protecting neighboring populations.* We urge that due attention be given to the protection of populations living near nuclear power plants or along routes used to transport nuclear materials by ensuring the communities' participation in emergency evacuation plans. We support maintaining evacuation planning zones for all areas within ten miles from a nuclear facility, and engaging the full participation of

state and local officials in the planning process. We believe that the safety of all potentially exposed populations should be the guide in safety improvements to nuclear power plants, not narrow cost-benefit analysis.

7. *Instituting full liability and compensation.* We hold that those corporations and governments responsible for nuclear accidents should be liable for cleanup and restitution to all victims of an accident.

8. *Reevaluating the US nuclear waste policy:*

    a. We urge a moratorium on DOE's proposed nuclear waste repository program;

    b. We urge Congress to establish an independent commission to review DOE's nuclear waste repository and Monitored Retrievable Storage Programs and to provide increased funding for the development of waste management technologies that will allow prolonged storage at the reactor site;

    c. We urge that full public participation and consultation in any future nuclear waste repository siting and transportation routing be guaranteed through provision of grants to affected localities, states, and Native American tribes; and

    d. We urge a moratorium of the building of nuclear power facilities until an adequate national plan is developed and implemented for the permanent disposal of nuclear waste products.

9. *Decommissioning.* We urge that the full cost of decommissioning (the dismantling and disposing of obsolete or closed power plants) be paid by the entities responsible for the construction and operation of nuclear facilities, not ratepayers or taxpayers.

10. *Conserving energy and finding alternative energy sources.* The greatest national effort should be made in the areas of conservation and renewable energy sources. We support increased government funding for research and development of technologies that would decrease dependence upon nuclear energy as an electricity source and urge the development of incentives, including tax and appliance standards, to speed the adoption of these technologies.

11. *Cooperating with annual conferences.* We urge the general church agencies of The United Methodist Church to assist central and annual conferences in their efforts to learn more about nuclear safety. Specifically, we urge general agencies of The United Methodist Church to assist annual conferences who have identified nuclear safety problems related to nuclear facilities, waste sites, and transportation routes within the bounds of those annual conferences.

We particularly urge the General Board of Church and Society to identify qualified nuclear safety experts who could assist annual conferences to understand and respond to nuclear waste and nuclear safety concerns in their areas.

ADOPTED 1988
AMENDED AND READOPTED 1992
AMENDED AND READOPTED 2004
RESOLUTION #15, 2004 *BOOK OF RESOLUTIONS*
RESOLUTION #15, 2000 *BOOK OF RESOLUTIONS*

See Social Principles, ¶ 160F.


## ENVIRONMENT


### 1021. Cease Mountaintop Removal Coal Mining

As stewards of God's creation, we are called to care for all of the earth, including the land itself. In Leviticus, God reminds us ". . . the land is mine; with me you are but aliens and tenants. Throughout the land that you hold, you shall provide for the redemption of the land" (Leviticus 25:23). Understanding land as a gift and a sacred trust, we are compelled to action to protect and defend God's sacred creation from abuse and destruction.

Today, communities in central Appalachia are facing the devastating consequences of mountaintop removal coal mining. This practice, which is extremely profitable to the coal companies, in large part because fewer miners are required, literally blasts the tops off of mountains to extract the coal. Where majestic mountains once stood in areas of Kentucky, Tennessee, Virginia, and West Virginia, decimated landscapes remain—along with a legacy of health and environmental concerns for nearby residents.

The blast rock and dust created by the removal of mountaintops has caused human death and severe damage to homes and wells in the nearby communities. The millions and millions of tons of earth and rock removed from the tops of mountains are dumped into the valleys next to these mountains, totally destroying the springs and headwaters of streams in these valleys, along with all plant and animal life in them. More than 500,000 acres of land have been destroyed and 1000 miles of biologically crucial streams have been buried under the debris.[1] Environmental replenishment efforts at former mountaintop removal mining sites do not replicate the sites' God-created biodiversity.

Mountaintop removal mining, by destroying home places, is also destroying ancestral ground, sacred ground where generations after generations have lived, gone to church, married, made and birthed babies, taken family meals, slept in peace, died and been buried.

Believing that the sanctity and sacredness of human life and the natural environment should not be destroyed in the name of corporate profit, we call for the end of this economically, environmentally, and socially destructive practice. We ask that companies halt mountaintop removal coal mining and be held accountable for the devastation in nearby communities that has resulted from this practice. We call on elected leaders and administrators to reject permit applications for further mountaintop removal operations and enforce fully laws designed to protect both the land and waters from destruction. We call on United Methodists to stand in solidarity with the residents of these communities and advocate on their behalf to their elected representatives.

In Deuteronomy, God says, "For the LORD your God is bringing you into a good land, a land with flowing streams, with springs and underground waters welling up in valleys and hills" (Deuteronomy 8:7). We believe that acting together just such a land can be restored to the communities of central Appalachia.

1. Ohio Valley Environmental Coalition

ADOPTED 2000<br>
REVISED AND READOPTED 2008<br>
RESOLUTION #2, 2004 <i>BOOK OF RESOLUTIONS</i><br>
RESOLUTION #3, 2000 <i>BOOK OF RESOLUTIONS</i>

*See* Social Principles, ¶ 160A.

## 1022. A Dioxin-Free Future

*Theological Foundation:*

Psalm 24:1 reads, "The earth is the LORD's and the fullness of it, the world and they who dwell in it."

According to the Social Principles, "All creation is the Lord's and we are responsible for the ways in which we use and abuse it" (Social Principles ¶ 160).

*Background:*

For nearly three decades, the scientific and health communities, including government agencies such as the US Environmental Protection Agency (EPA) and the World Health Organization (WHO) have been assessing the human health risks of dioxin—a class of chlorine-based persistent organic pollutants. The catalyst for this assessment was a finding through animal testing in the 1970s that dioxin was the most potent cancer-causing chemical ever studied.

Since the first EPA study, issued in 1985, major advances have been made in the scientific and health communities' analytical abilities to detect—and determine the impact of—trace amounts of dioxin. A major milestone in exposing the health risks associated with dioxin was the EPA's 1994 report entitled *The Scientific Reassessment of Dioxin.* This report affirmed health warnings made twenty years ago—that the "background" levels of *dioxin* pose a serious threat to the health of the general US population.

Since 1994, the EPA report has been reviewed and revised based on comments from scientific peer review panels. An updated document was issued in 2003 titled Exposure and Human Health Reassessment of 2, 3, 7, 8, Tetrachlorodibenazo-p-dioxin (TCDD) and Related Compounds. Like the October, 2001 draft reviewed and released by panels, the conclusion remained the same: dioxin should be classified as a known human carcinogen—a view shared by the international community as expressed by WHO and within the United States through the US Department of Health and Human Services and the National Institute of Health's National Toxicology Program. In October 2004, the EPA asked the National Research Council (NRC) of the National Academies to review the 2003 draft. After receiving comments from the NRC in 2005, the EPA completed its reassessment and characterized TCDD as "carcinogenic to humans." In July 2006 the NRC issued a report on the 2005 completed report entitled Health Risks from Dioxin and Related Compounds (Evaluation of the EPA Reassessment). In that report the NRC Committee unanimously agreed on a classification for TCDD of at least "likely to be carcinogenic to humans." The committee agrees with the EPA in classifying other dioxins and DLCs as "likely to be carcinogenic to humans."

The EPA report stated that there is reason to believe that dioxins at extremely low levels cause a wide range of other serious health effects, including reproductive impairment, learning disabilities, developmental injuries, and the increased risk of diabetes and endometriosis. Furthermore, even low levels of dioxin impair the ability of the immune system to right infectious disease. The EPA report says that there is no level of dioxin below which the immune system is not affected.

Breast cancer is the second leading cause of cancer death in US women. Breast cancer is the most frequently diagnosed cancer in US women. It accounts for nearly one out of three cancers diagnosed in US women. The EPA concluded that the levels of dioxins already lodged in human bodies are already close to levels known to cause serious health problems. According to the EPA, the average person is exposed to dioxin levels 50 to 100 times greater than the maximum allowable amounts designated by the federal government in 1985.

Some persons have what the EPA calls "special" exposures, including certain occupational groups, people living near dioxin emitters, and people who consume higher than average levels of meat, fish, and dairy products. Human exposure to dioxins begins early in life, since dioxin crosses the placenta. Nursing infants take in four to twelve percent of their lifetime dose of dioxin within the first year of their lives, a period during which they are most susceptible to the effects of such toxins.

Ending toxic pollution, maintaining a clean environment, and using efficient, nonpolluting technologies are essential to a sound economy and a sustainable lifestyle. With a single program—dioxin phaseout—much of the world's most severe toxic pollution could be stopped.

The three largest sources of dioxin are incineration of chorine containing wastes, bleaching of pulp and paper with chlorine and the life-cycle of polyvinyl chloride (PVC). Of continued concern is the use of PVC products by the health care industry, especially the single use or short term use applications (i.e. "disposables"). These account for most of the organically bound chlorine in medical waste.

The American Public Health Association (APHA) has issued warnings, recognizing that "virtually all chlorinated organic compounds that have been studied exhibit at least one of a wide range of serious toxic effects such as endocrine dysfunction, developmental impairment, birth defects, reproductive dysfunction and infertility, immuno-suppression and cancer, often at very low doses."

Remembering that "First Do No Harm" is a binding principle in medical ethics, the health care industry should pursue alternatives to PVC products. Appropriate alternative products composed of nonchlorinated material are currently available for many, though not all, health care uses of chlorinated plastics. Highly effective programs for the reduction of hospital waste have been initiated in the US and programs for the substitution of other materials for PVC are in place in some hospitals in Europe.

Acknowledging the ongoing risks associated with dioxin, The United Methodist Church:

- Calls on cancer research organizations to move to a prevention-based approach to cancer research and funding, including more studies on the relationship between cancer and chlorine-based toxins in the environment.
- Supports a phaseout of the production of dioxin.
- Supports worker production programs for people working in industries that make toxic chemicals or result in toxic byproduct and related chemicals, who may lose their jobs with a phaseout of these chemicals. Such programs could include a "Workers' Superfund" program.
- Challenges all United Methodist-related health care institutions, United Methodist health care professionals and workers, and United Methodist individuals and congregations to begin immediately to take action to change health care policies and practices in order to stop the harm being caused by nonessential incineration of medical waste and by generating a waste stream that is more toxic than necessary.
- Urges all health care facilities to explore ways to reduce or eliminate their use of PVC plastics.
- Calls upon all health care professionals and workers to encourage health care institutions with which they are associated to adopt policies that will lead to the reduction and elimination of the use of PVC plastics.
- Suggests that health care facilities hire or assign professional staff to evaluate the potential for persistent toxic pollution associated with the life-cycle of products the facility purchases.
- Strongly urges medical suppliers to develop, produce, and bring to market appropriate, cost-competitive products that can replace those that contain PVC or other chlorinated plastics. Any substitution for a chlorinated plastic product must provide a less toxic alternative with concern for the full public health implications of the replacement, including infections considerations.

- Encourages government oversight agencies and private accrediting bodies to incorporate requirements for education about the reduction of toxic pollution in their certification standards.
- Encourages study and evaluation of alternative products and practices that will lead to the reduction and elimination of the use of PVC products; also encourages programs to provide technical assistance and training to health care facilities that seek help in the reduction of their reliance on chlorinated plastics.
- Directs the General Board of Church and Society to cooperate with the General Board of Global Ministries to work with companies, governments, and medical institutions to implement the above recommendations.

ADOPTED 1996
AMENDED AND READOPTED 2004
AMENDED AND READOPTED 2008
RESOLUTION #3, 2004 *BOOK OF RESOLUTIONS*
RESOLUTION #4, 2000 *BOOK OF RESOLUTIONS*

*See* Social Principles, ¶ 160.

## 1023. Environmental Justice for a Sustainable Future

Humankind is destroying the global ecological balance that provides the life-support systems for the planet. Signs of the crisis are evident all around us. The global ecological imbalance produces environmental destruction.

Polluted air pervades the atmosphere. Garbage abounds, with little space for disposal. Polluting gases destroy the ozone layer and cause global warming. Deforestation leads to soil erosion, a lack of carbon storage, inadequate water quantity and poor quality, and the loss of species, resulting in a reduction in biological diversity. The misuse of pesticides and fertilizers contributes to the poisoning of our soils and creates products harmful to all life.

Present social, political, and economic development structures fail to provide the basic necessities of food, clothing, and shelter for all our brothers and sisters around the world with more than 1.2 billion people currently living in absolute poverty. And the world population is projected to grow by another 3 billion people in the next fifty years.

This growth, combined with higher standards of living, will pose severe strains on land, water, energy, and other natural resources.

## Historical and Theological Concerns

Through the ages, a theological base for the domination of creation was found in Genesis 1:28: "Be fruitful and multiply, and fill the earth and subdue it; and have dominion over . . . every living thing that moves upon the earth." Misinterpretation of "subdue" and "domin-ion" has been used to justify much of the nature-destroying aspects of modern civilization.

The scale of human activity has grown so large that it now threatens the planet itself. Global environmental problems have become so vast that they are hard to comprehend. Between 1955 and 2000, the human population has more than doubled to 6.1 billion. During the same time, the consumption of fossil fuels has quadrupled with North Americans using fossil fuels at a per capita rate ten times greater than citizens of developing nations. The vast majority of scientific evidence suggests that the carbon dioxide from fossil fuels has already caused a measurable warming of the globe. Destruction of habitat, especially tropical rain forests, is causing the loss of species at an ever-increasing rate. Valuable topsoil is being depleted. There is a recurring hole in the ozone layer. More ultraviolet radiation now reaches the earth, which may cause more cancers, poorer crop growth, and damage to the immune systems of humans and other animals.

Confronted with the massive crisis of the deterioration of God's creation and faced with the question of the ultimate survival of life, we ask God's forgiveness for our participation in this destruction of God's creation. We have misused God's good creation. We have confused God's call for us to be faithful stewards of creation with a license to use all of creation as we see it. The first humans had to leave the garden of Eden when they decided they had permission to use all of creation despite warnings to the contrary. We have denied that God's covenant is with all living creatures (Genesis 9:9). We have even denied that all of the human family should enjoy the covenant. We forget that the good news that we are called to proclaim includes the promise that Jesus Christ came to redeem all creation (Colossians 1:15-20).

We believe that at the center of the vision of shalom is the integration of environmental, economic, and social justice.

We are called to eliminate overconsumption as a lifestyle, thus using lower levels of finite natural resources.

We are called to seek a new lifestyle rooted in justice and peace.

We are called to establish new priorities in a world where 40,000 children die of hunger each day.

Therefore, we are called to a global sense of community and solidarity leading to a new world system of international relationships and economic/environmental order. In this way, the misery of 1.2 billion poor now living in absolute poverty can be alleviated and the living ecosystem be saved.

*Principles for a Sustainable Future*

The Social Principles of The United Methodist Church remind us that "all creation is the Lord's, and we are responsible for the ways in which we use and abuse it" (¶ 160). Development must be centered in the concept of sustainability as defined by the World Commission of Environment and Development: "to meet the needs of the present without compromising the ability of future generations to meet their own needs." The Christian understanding of sustainability encompasses this concept. Fundamental to our call as faithful witnesses is the meeting of human needs within the capacity of ecosystems. This ensures the security of creation and a just relationship between all people. Sustainable development, therefore, looks toward a healthy future in three vital areas: the social community, the economy, and the environment.

*Conclusion*

The United Methodist Church will strive for a global sense of community to help achieve social, economic, and ecological justice for all of creation.

We will focus on the conversion to sustainable practices in the following areas:

*Atmosphere*

- Support measures calling for the reduction of carbon dioxide, methane, nitrogen oxides, and sulfur dioxide, which contribute to acid rain and global climate change.
- Enforce agreements banning the use of chlorofluorocarbons (CFCs) to stop the depletion of the ozone layer.

- Support ratification and enforcement of international frameworks, such as Kyoto Protocol, that seek to reduce global greenhouse gas emissions.
- Support the cleanup of environmental problems through economic incentive, appropriate enforcement measures, and sanctions against those causing pollution.

### Earth

- Support integrated and sustainable natural resource management.
- Commit to the "Greening of the World" through the limiting of all emissions of pollutants that damage forests and reforestation.
- Work for ecologically sound agricultural practices that produce healthy food and a clean environment.
- Protect biodiversity among both animals and plants.

### Water

- Maintain that water is a basic human right not a commodity to be traded for profit.
- Support integrated, sustainable management to reduce or eliminate factors contributing to limited water quantity and poorer quality.

### Energy

- Support improved energy conservation and greater reliance on new and renewable sources of energy.
- Support the development of eco-efficient mass transportation.
- Support a call for a sustainable national energy policy.

*Actions/Recommendations*

We call upon the agencies and local congregations of The United Methodist Church to take the following actions:

### Council of Bishops

- Communicate to the church the urgency of responding to the ecological crisis.

- Model for the church a "ministry of presence" by going to places where humans and ecosystems are endangered by environmental destruction.

### Connectional Table

- Initiate basic research on the changing attitudes on environmental issues among United Methodist members.
- Request each United Methodist agency to include an evaluation of their corporate action taken toward sustainable environmental practices as a part of their 2004-2008 Quadrennial Report.

### General Board of Church and Society (GBCS)

- Develop programs that help annual conferences and local churches become more involved in sustainable practices in public policy and personal aspects of the ecological crisis. These programs would emphasize conversion to a sustainable society.

### General Board of Discipleship (GBOD)

- Develop curriculum and programs (for all ages), in consultation with GBCS, that emphasize ecological responsibility as a key element of discipleship.

### General Board of Global Ministries (GBGM)

- Join with the GBCS in working with mission partners to prepare for and participate in the implementation of Agenda 21 and the ongoing global dialogue on sustainability through the United Nation's Commission on Sustainable Development.
- Conduct a survey, with the assistance of all mission partners, to identify environmental concerns and develop projects geared to the solution of common concerns.
- Initiate an audit of all sponsored projects and meetings as to their environmental effect on the global ecological balance.
- Establish an eco-mission intern group to work on ecology issues.
- Include global environmental issues in the training of all GBGM missionaries.

- Facilitate dialogue between religious groups, other non-government organizations, and government agencies on the formation and methods of popular participation.

*General Board of Higher Education and Ministry (GBHEM)*

- Include a greater awareness in clergy education and training of the global ecological crises.

*United Methodist Communications (UMCom)*

- Produce programs that stress Christian responsibility for the future of creation and include models of The United Methodist Church's involvement in environmental justice.

*General Council on Finance and Administration (GCFA)*

- Assist the church in its effort to be ecologically responsible in its own use of resources by collecting statistics on local churches' and general agencies' use of energy, water, paper, and recycling to monitor the progress of the church in these aspects of stewardship.

*General Board of Pension and Health Benefits (GBPHB)*

- Develop investment guidelines, in consultation with agencies, to evaluate its securities on adherence to high standards of environmental accountability as evidenced by the adoption of an environmental code of conduct and a practice of transparency in public environmental reporting.

*Local Congregations*

- Develop programs to incorporate the concerns of ecological justice into their work in evangelism, social concerns, mission activities, stewardship, trustees, and worship.

ADOPTED 1992
AMENDED AND READOPTED 2004
RESOLUTION #7, 2004 *BOOK OF RESOLUTIONS*
RESOLUTION #7, 2000 *BOOK OF RESOLUTIONS*

*See* Social Principles, ¶ 160.

## 1024. Environmental Law: The Precautionary Principle

As God's people we are called to stewardship of the earth and all that dwells therein (Genesis 1:29-31; 2:4-15). Further, God commands, "You shall not pollute the land in which you live . . . you shall not defile the land in which you life, in which I also dwell" (Numbers 35:33-34).

Presently, the human race is experiencing warning signs that our bodies and the natural environment have limits to their abilities to absorb and overcome the harm from some of our actions, technologies, and substances. These warning signs include the extinction of plant and animal species, the depletion of stratospheric ozone, global climate instability and increased rates of some learning disabilities, reproductive disorders, cancers, respiratory diseases including asthma, and other environmentally related illnesses.

In addition to the immediate impact of pollution, the earth is experiencing environmental problems such as global climate instability, the loss of biodiversity, and the destruction of marine fisheries, which may threaten food supplies and lead to disastrous human health consequences.

Controversy continues in the promotion of world trade regarding the appropriate level of caution and protection of the environment. Where the preponderance of evidence would indicate that an activity will be harmful to the earth's environment, producers of pollutants have insisted that there be "scientific certainty" on each point in question before caution is exercised. In recent years, "think tanks" and research groups funded by corporations and industry allies have been established to create the appearance of scientific uncertainty—challenging the consensus of the peer-reviewed scientific findings on critical issues such as global warming. By creating uncertainty while insisting on certainty, these interests have caused substantial harm to the earth and its creatures.

Current environmental regulations are aimed primarily at controlling pollution rather than taking the preventative approach of limiting the use, production or release of toxic materials in the first place. Under the current system, enterprises, projects, technologies and substances are in effect "innocent until proved guilty", and the vast majority of chemicals in production have not been adequately tested for their effects on humans and ecosystems.

Producers of pollutants have repeatedly used their influence to delay preventative action, arguing that the immediate expense of redesign to achieve pollution prevention is unwarranted in the face of any uncertainty about eventual harmful health effects.

The Precautionary Principle is considered to be an emerging general principle of international environmental law. The United States signed and ratified the Rio Declaration on Environment and Development which states: "In order to protect the environment, the precautionary approach shall be widely applied by states according to their capabilities. Where there are threats of serious or irreversible damage, lack of full scientific certainty shall not be used as a reason for postponing cost-effective measures to prevent environmental degradation." (Rio Declaration on Environment and Development, June 14, 1992, 31 ILM 874)

Likewise the International Joint Commission in 1994 stated that "the burden of proof concerning the safety of chemicals should lie with the proponent for the manufacture, import or use of at least substances new to commerce in Canada and the United States, rather than with society as a whole to provide absolute proof of adverse impacts . . . The onus should be on the producers and users of any suspected toxic substance to prove that it is, in fact, both 'safe' and necessary, even if it is already in commerce." (International Joint Commission, Seventh Biennial Report Under the Great Lakes Water Quality Agreement of 1978 to the Governments of the United States and Canada, 1994)

Furthermore, the *Wingspread Statement* of January 1998, formulated by prominent members of the environmental community, states: "When an activity raises threats of harm to human health or the environment, precautionary measures should be taken even if some cause and effect relationships are not fully established. In this context the proponent of an activity rather than the public should bear the burden of proof. The process of applying the Precautionary Principle must be open, informed, and democratic and must involve potentially affected parties. The process must include a comprehensive, systematic examination of the full range of alternatives, including no action." More recently, the European Commission adopted a communication on the Precautionary Principle explaining its intended application to environmental, health, food safety, and consumer protection concerns.

We urge all United Methodists in their daily lives and official capacities to hold society to this higher standard of care for God's creation; that where the preponderance of evidence indicates the probability of harm from some action, even in the absence of full scientific certainty, that an alternative path must be found.

In this context we advocate for significant increases in efforts toward pollution prevention, for identifying goals for reducing exposure to toxic chemicals, for incentives to replace known toxic chemicals with the least toxic alternatives, and we support the practice of organic farming methods in order to reduce the use of toxic chemicals in agriculture.

We encourage government at all levels to promote and abide by the Precautionary Principle in order to protect human health and the environment.

We urge the United States to honor the Precautionary Principle during the negotiations of international agreements and to work toward the establishment of the Precautionary Principle as a guiding principle of international law.

ADOPTED 2000<br>
REVISED AND READOPTED 2008<br>
RESOLUTION #8, 2004 <i>BOOK OF RESOLUTIONS</i><br>
RESOLUTION #8, 2000 <i>BOOK OF RESOLUTIONS</i>

See Social Principles, ¶ 160A, B, F, and G.

## 1025. Environmental Racism

*Theological Background*

In Isaiah we are given divine insight into our relations with one another "If you do away with the yoke of oppression, with the pointing finger and malicious talk and if you spend yourselves in behalf of the hungry and satisfy the needs of the oppressed then your light will rise in the darkness and your night will become like the noonday" Isaiah 58:9. We are further called both in Leviticus and by our Lord Jesus Christ to love our neighbors as ourselves. When we turn from this divine will, we as a broken people promote systems that are unjust and inequitable. One manifestation of these injustices is the persistent problem of racism.

*Background:*

The United Methodist Church is committed to understanding and eliminating racism. One generally ignored aspect of this issue in industrial nations is environmental racism. For example, in the United

States, people of color are disproportionately affected by toxic contamination due to the production, storage, treatment, and disposal process of hazardous materials and wastes. African American, Hispanic North American, Asian American, Native American, and citizens of developing nations are usually the least able, politically and economically, to oppose the sitings of these facilities.

As a result, their communities have become the dumping grounds for waste with devastating economic and health consequences.

The pervasive problem of environmental racism within the United States first came to light in the early 1980's. The birth of the environmental justice movement can be traced to the historic protest in 1983 in Warren County, North Carolina where over 500 people were arrested for blocking the shipment of toxic waste (PCBs) to a landfill in a predominantly African American county. That same year, a General Accounting Office (GAO, now Government Accountability Office) study concluded "blacks make up the majority of the population in three out of four communities where landfills are located."

In 1987, the United Church of Christ Commission for Racial Justice issued the landmark report *Toxic Wastes and Race*. This report, expanding on the GAO findings, established that race—rather than poverty, land value, or home ownership—is the most reliable predictor of proximity to hazardous waste sites in the United States. And in 1992, the National Law Journal study, *Unequal Protection*, uncovered racial disparities in the enforcement of environmental protection laws. The report highlighted a "racial divide in the way the US government cleans up toxic waste sites and punishes polluters." According to the report, "white communities see faster action, better results and stiffer penalties than communities where blacks, Hispanics and other minorities live. This unequal protection often occurs whether the community is wealthy or poor."

These and other reports provided strong empirical evidence of environmental racism.

*Among the findings:*

1. "The current and future health status of African American, Hispanic, and Native American children in particular continues to fare poorly compared to the rest of the population. Due to the fact that children are so vulnerable to harm, without a political voice and not large players within the world economy, they have historically been

swept under the rug and almost forgotten about when it comes to true public health protection.

2. "National Disparities: More than nine million people (9,222,000) are estimated to live in circular host neighborhoods within 3 kilometers of the nation's 413 commercial hazardous waste facilities. More than 5.1 million people of color, including 2.5 million Hispanics or Latinos, 1.8 million African Americans, 616,000 Asians/Pacific Islanders and 62,000 Native Americans live in neighborhoods with one or more commercial hazardous waste facilities.

"Host neighborhoods of commercial hazardous waste facilities are 56 percent people of color whereas non host areas are 30 percent people of color. Percentages of African Americans, Hispanics/Latinos and Asians/Pacific Islanders in host neighborhoods are 1.7, 2.3 and 1.8 times greater (20 percent vs. 12 percent, 27 percent vs. 12 percent, and 6.7 percent vs. 3.6 percent), respectively. Poverty rates in the host neighborhoods are 1.5 times greater than non host areas (18 percent vs. 12 percent)."

3. "EPA: Regional Disparities: Racial disparities for people of color as a whole exist in nine out of 10 US EPA regions (all except Region 3). Disparities in people of color percentages between host neighborhoods and non host Areas are greatest in: Region 1, the Northeast (36 percent vs. 15 percent)• Region 4, the southeast (54 percent vs. 30 percent)• Region 5, the Midwest (53 percent vs. 19 percent)• Region 6, the South (63 percent vs. 42 percent)• and Region 9, the southwest (80 percent vs. 49 percent). For Hispanics, African Americans and Asians/Pacific Islanders, statistically significant disparities exist in the majority or vast majority of EPA regions. The pattern of people of color being especially concentrated in areas where facilities are clustered is also geographically widespread throughout the country."

4. "African Americans are three times more likely to die from asthma. African American women have the highest asthma mortality rate of all groups, more than 2.5 times higher than Caucasian women. Ethnic differences in asthma prevalence, morbidity and mortality are highly correlated with poverty, urban air quality, indoor allergens, and lack of patient education and inadequate medical care."

5. "Lead poisoning continues to be the number one environmental health threat to children in the United States, especially poor children, children of color and children living in inner cities. Black children are

five times more likely than white children to have lead poisoning. One in seven black children living in older housing has elevated blood lead levels. About 22 percent of African American children and 13 percent of Mexican American children living in pre 1946 housing are lead poisoned, compared with 6 percent of white children living in comparable types of housing. Recent studies suggest that a young person's lead burden is linked to lower IQ, lower high school graduation rates and increased delinquency. Lead poisoning causes about 2 to 3 points of IQ lost for each 10 ug/dl lead level."

6. Toxic Wastes and Race describe the extent of environmental racism and the consequences of people of color and indigenous communities disproportionately affected by polluted environments. Collectively, the two coal plants on the Navajo reservation release over 365 million pounds of cancer and lung disease causing pollutants every year. The groundwater is also contaminated as the pollutants leach into the water banks.

The 2007 "Toxic Waste at Twenty" 1987-2007 Report of the United Church of Christ Justice and witness Ministries Conclusions–most recent report:

"Twenty years after the release of Toxic Wastes and Race, significant racial and socioeconomic disparities persist in the distribution of the nation's commercial hazardous waste facilities. Although the current assessment uses newer methods that better match where people and hazardous waste facilities are located, the conclusions are very much the same as they were in 1987. In fact, people of color are found to be more concentrated around hazardous waste facilities than previously shown.

"Race matters. People of color and persons of low socioeconomic status are still disproportionately impacted and are particularly concentrated in neighborhoods and communities with the greatest number of facilities. Race continues to be an independent predictor of where hazardous wastes are located, and it is a stronger predictor than income, education and other socioeconomic indicators. Indeed, a watershed moment has occurred in the last decade. People of color now comprise a majority in neighborhoods with commercial hazardous waste facilities, and much larger (more than two-thirds) majorities can be found in neighborhoods with clustered facilities. People of color in 2007 are more concentrated in areas with commercial hazardous sites than in 1987. African Americans, Hispanics/

Latinos and Asian Americans/Pacific Islanders alike are dispropor-tionately burdened by hazardous wastes in the US.

"Unequal protection places communities of color at special risk. Not only are people of color differentially impacted by toxic wastes and contamination, they can expect different responses from the govern-ment when it comes to remediation—as clearly seen in the two case studies in Post-Katrina New Orleans and in Dickson County, Tennessee. Thus, it does not appear that existing environmental, health, and civil rights laws and local land use controls have been ade-quately applied or adapted to reducing health risks or mitigating var-ious adverse impacts to families living in or near toxic "hot spots."

"The current environmental protection apparatus is "broken" and needs to be "fixed." The current environmental protection system fails to provide equal protection to people of color and low-income com-munities. Various levels of government have been slow to respond to environmental health threats from toxic waste in communities of color."

Despite the clear evidence and growing awareness, our society's attitude toward the production and disposal of hazardous products is one of "out of sight, out of mind." But "out of sight, out of mind" is most often where the poor and powerless live and work. These com-munities have thus become toxic "sacrifice zones."

The continued pattern of environmental racism represents a serious challenge to the conscience of all Christians. We therefore ask our local churches, conferences, and general agencies to join with other reli-gious bodies and groups in actions to end this form of racism:

1. We request the Council of Bishops to address environmental racism in any formal communication to the denomination concerning racism or the environment.

2. We urge annual conferences, districts, local churches, and general agencies to become more involved with community groups working to end environmental racism.

3. We urge all general program agencies and the General Commission on Religion and Race to:

   a. disseminate the "stories" of people and communities affected by environmental racism; and

   b. find expertise, build leadership, and develop networks that can help empower people within communities in crisis,

4. We call upon the General Board of Church and Society to:
   a. advocate comprehensive legislation that remedies these injustices and adequately protects all citizens and the environment; and
   b. develop educational resource programs that help annual conferences, districts, and local churches respond to these concerns; and
   c. urge industry to develop industry-wide standards for environmental accounting and auditing procedures similar to those requires for financial accounting.

[Editor's note: Quotations in this resolution are from *Toxic Wastes and Race at Twenty: 1987-2007*. It can be found at http://www.ejnet.org/ej/twart.pdf.]

ADOPTED 1992
AMENDED AND READOPTED 2004
AMENDED AND READOPTED 2008
RESOLUTION #9, 2004 *BOOK OF RESOLUTIONS*
RESOLUTION #9, 2000 *BOOK OF RESOLUTIONS*

*See* Social Principles, ¶ 160, *Book of Discipline*; Resolution 1023, "Environmental Justice for a Sustainable Future"; and Resolution 3371, "A Charter for Racial Justice Policies in an Interdependent Global Community."

## 1026. Environmental Stewardship

*I. A Theology of Stewardship and the Environment*

All creation is under the authority of God and all creation is interdependent. Our covenant with God requires us to be stewards, protectors, and defenders of all creation. The use of natural resources is a universal concern and responsibility of all as reflected in Psalm 24:1: "The earth is the Lord's and the fullness thereof."

In the Bible, a steward is one given responsibility for what belongs to another. The Greek word we translate as steward is *oikonomos*, one who cares for the household or acts as its trustee. The word *oikos*, meaning household, is used to describe the world as God's household. Christians, then, are to be stewards of the whole household (creation) of God. *Oikonomia*, "stewardship," is also the root of our word "economics."

*Oikos*, moreover, is the root of our modern word, "ecology." Thus in a broad sense, stewardship, economics, and ecology are, and should be, related.

The Old Testament relates these concepts in the vision of *shalom*. Often translated "peace," the broader meaning of *shalom* is wholeness. In the Old Testament, *shalom* is used to characterize the wholeness of a faithful life lived in relationship to God. *Shalom* is best understood when we experience wholeness and harmony as human beings with God, with others, and with creation itself. The task of the steward is to seek *shalom*.

*Stewards of God's Creation.* The concept of stewardship is first introduced in the creation story. In Genesis 1:26, the Bible affirms that every person is created in God's image. But this gift brings with it a unique responsibility. Being created in God's image brings with it the responsibility to care for God's creation. God chose to give human beings a divine image not so we would exploit creation to our own ends, but so we would be recognized as stewards of God. To have dominion over the earth is a trusteeship, a sign that God cares for creation and has entrusted it to our stewardship. Our stewardship of all the world's resources is always accountable to God who loves the whole of creation and who desires that it exist in *shalom*. The intention of creation was that all should experience *shalom*, to know the goodness of creation. In the Old Testament, "fullness of life" means having enough, sufficient, to experience the goodness of creation. By contrast, our age has come to define "fullness of life" as more than enough. The desire of many for excess begins to deny enough for others, and *shalom* is broken. That all should participate in creation's goodness is a fundamental of stewardship.

Another theme of *shalom* is that in creation we are all related. Humans are not self-sufficient. We need God, others, nature. The story of the garden (Genesis 2) attempts to picture the complete and harmonious interrelatedness of all creation. There is *shalom* only when we recognize that interrelatedness and care for the whole. When we violate the rules of the garden, we are dismissed. In ecological terms, when we violate the principles of ecology, we suffer environmental damage.

As the story of the garden shows, God's intention of *shalom* was not carried out. Sin intervened, and the *shalom* was broken. But God offered a way to restore *shalom*—redemption. And as God's stewards we have a role in that redemption. Stewardship, then, is to become involved wherever wholeness is lacking and to work in harmony with God's saving activity to reconcile, to reunite, to heal, to make whole.

Stewardship has to do with how we bring all of the resources at our disposal into efficient use in our participation in the saving activity of God. Environmental stewardship is one part of our work as God's stewards. As stewards of the natural environment we are called to preserve and restore the air, water, and land on which life depends. Moreover, we are called to see that all life has a sufficient share of the resources of nature. With new hope rooted in Christ and with more obedient living as stewards of the earth, we can participate in God's healing of creation.

## II. United Methodist Historical Concerns

Since the beginnings of the Methodist movement, there has been a concern with what we today call "environmental concerns." Wesley's emphasis on "cleanliness" came as he observed a land of open sewers, impure water, unplanned cities, and smoke-filled air. In the mines and mills, squalor and filth were everywhere, as was disease. The substantial decline in the death rate in England from 1700 to 1801 can be traced to improvements in environment, sanitation, and a wider knowledge of concepts of basic health such as those advocated by Wesley.

## III. Principles for Christian Stewardship of the Environment

### A. Responsible and Equitable Use of Natural Resources.

We support measures which will lead to a more careful and efficient use of the resources of the natural world. We urge United Methodists to analyze their consumption patterns and to seek to live a simple and less resource-dependent life.

We encourage programs which will recycle solid materials of all sorts—paper, glass, wood, building materials, metals, plastics, etc.

We urge United Methodists to participate actively in community recycling programs and urge the establishment of such programs in communities without these programs.

We believe that natural resources, outside the control of different nations, from the genes that form life to the air and outer space, are the common heritage of all humanity, and therefore must be developed and preserved for the benefit of all, not just for the few, both today and for generations to come.

We support the concept of common heritage where people have the right to enough of the resources of the universe to provide for their health and well-being; and we believe that God's creation is intended to be used for the good of all as a precious gift, not for warfare or economic oppression of others.

## B. *Right to Live in a Community Free of Toxic and Hazardous Substances.*

We advocate that governments:

1. aggressively assess the extent of possible toxic and hazardous waste disposal problems within their jurisdictions;

2. require that the entity or entities responsible for the problem pay for hazardous waste cleanup and for any health damages caused by the improper or inadequate disposal of such substances; and

3. severely penalize those convicted of illegal disposal of hazardous and toxic materials.

We encourage measures to minimize the use of toxic and hazardous substances.

We oppose the practice of exporting materials banned in one nation for use in another nation.

We advocate that all parties with information on the health effects of a potentially toxic or hazardous substance make these data available to users of the substance.

We support measures to strengthen the public's right-to-know about chemical substances in their communities. Communities have a right to know whether their water, air, soil, or food is clean and free of toxic pollution.

We support applying the "Precautionary Principle," shifting the burden of proof to polluters to show that their air and water emissions are safe, rather than making citizens prove that emissions pose a health threat.

We support the right of those groups that would be affected by a nuclear, toxic, or hazardous material waste repository or incinerator to be involved actively in all decisions to locate such repositories or incinerators in their neighborhoods or jurisdictions.

We urge a halt to nuclear and toxic waste disposal at sea and stringent controls on toxic waste disposal in the soil.

## C. Right to Clean Air.

We believe clean air is a basic right and necessity for all life. We must clean up and prevent air pollution, which threatens the health of our families and the survival of all life on the planet.

To ensure that we protect future generations and our natural environment from the harmful effects of air pollution and leave a legacy of clean air:

We advocate the adoption and strict enforcement of adequate standards (health-based air quality standards to protect vulnerable populations such as children, the elderly, and people with asthma) to control outdoor air pollutants such as vehicle and industrial smokestack emissions.

We urge all United Methodists to car pool, use mass transit, drive fuel efficient cars, and find other ways of reducing vehicle and industrial emissions.

We must give special attention to the long-term effects of air pollution, such as the depletion of the ozone layer, global warming, and acid rain; we support international and bilateral efforts to eliminate the cause of these problems.

We advocate that all large polluters, specifically power plants, refineries and chemical manufacturers, irrespective of age or fuel use, meet standards based on the least polluting process in each industrial sector.

We advocate the adoption and strict enforcement of adequate standards to control indoor air pollutants, such as chemical fumes from gas stoves and furnaces, pesticides, cleaning materials, formaldehyde, candles, paint, photocopy machines, radon and carpets, as well as particulates such as dust, mold, and asbestos fibers.

We advocate prohibiting smoking and providing adequate fresh air ventilation in all indoor facilities.

## D. Minimization of Chemical Use.

We recommend the concept of integrated pest management (IPM), natural control systems, and crop rotation.

We urge that greater restrictions be placed on the export of restricted agricultural chemicals and that development and aid agencies encourage the use of agricultural techniques which rely less heavily on agricultural chemical use.

We recommend that industry, consumer groups, and governmental agencies aggressively investigate and study the long-range effects of chemicals used for the processing and preservation of food products, since many of these chemicals are harmful to animals and humans.

*E. Responsible Land Use.*

We encourage economic and farming practices which conserve and promote the improvement of topsoil.

We urge that governments provide farmers with incentives for more careful management of this precious resource.

We urge that the careful maintenance of the productivity of farm land be the central goal of all management of agricultural lands.

We urge governments to preserve the most productive soils for agricultural purposes.

We advocate for the preservation of forests (including reforestation), wetlands and wild areas for ecological balance, wildlife production, water quality, air quality, and the human spirit.

*F. Preservation of the Diversity of Life.*

We believe that the wondrous diversity of nature is a key part of God's plan for creation. Therefore, we oppose measures which would eliminate diversity in plant and animal varieties, eliminate species, or destroy habitats critical to the survival of endangered species or varieties.

We support national and international efforts to protect endangered species and imperiled habitats.

*G. Right to Abundant and Clean Water.*

The water on this planet is a sacred gift from God. To ensure that water remains pure and available to all:

We urge that steps be taken by all people to ensure more careful management and preservation of ground water sources.

We support the right of native peoples to the first use of waters on their lands.

We urge that industrial, municipal, agricultural and individual consumers of water develop and use water-conserving technology and practices.

We believe that water is a gift from God that needs to be kept clean. We advocate measures that will address polluted runoff that is threatening to public health; protection of waters for future generations; wetlands preservation to clean water and sustain wildlife; the public's right to know that their water is safe for drinking, swimming, and fishing; and effective enforcement against illegal pollution.

## H. Responsible and Ethical Use of Technology.

We urge that the ethical and environmental effects of new technologies be fully examined before these technologies are used on a widespread basis. We acknowledge the constantly imperfect state of our knowledge of the effects of new technology and urge the development of those technologies most in accord with God's plan of wholeness for all creation.

## I. Minimization of the Military's Impact on the Environment.

We oppose the production and testing of weapons designed to destroy or harm God's creation, such as all chemical, biological, and nuclear weapons.

We urge the abolishment of chemical, biological, and nuclear weapons and urge the cleanup of sites contaminated by chemical, biological, and nuclear weapons waste.

## IV. Involvement

We urge all United Methodists, their local churches, boards and agencies to examine their roles as stewards of God's earth and to study, discuss, and work to implement this resolution.

All general agencies shall develop appropriate resources to implement this resolution.

ADOPTED 1984
REVISED AND READOPTED 2000
READOPTED 2008
RESOLUTION #10, 2004 *BOOK OF RESOLUTIONS*
RESOLUTION #10, 2000 *BOOK OF RESOLUTIONS*

*See* Social Principles, ¶ 160A.

## 1027. God's Creation and the Church

As disciples of Christ, we are called to be good stewards of God's creation. Accordingly, we call upon The United Methodist Church to adopt fresh ways to respond to the perils that now threaten the integrity of God's creation and the future of God's children.

Specifically, The United Methodist Church:

- designates one Sunday each year, preferably the Sunday closest to Earth Day, as a Festival of God's Creation, celebrating God's gracious work in creating the earth and all living things, incorporating it into the church's liturgical calendar, and developing appropriate ways for congregations to celebrate it;
- endorses The Clergy Letter Project and its reconciliatory programs between religion and science, and urges United Methodist clergy participation;
- endorses the work of the National Religious Partnership for the Environment, and the World Council of Churches Climate Change Program and urges conferences and congregations to support their activities and programs;
- supports the annual observance of the United Nations' World Environment Day and encourages conferences and churches to participate in programs such as Environmental Sabbath;
- recommends that annual conferences establish annual awards to honor prophetic defenders of God's creation from within their own constituencies;
- affirms the importance of nurturing, community-building approaches such as the Global Action Plan's Household Eco-Team Program designed to foster resource efficient lifestyle practices;
- encourages a simplified and environmentally sound lifestyle throughout the church and requests that Church agencies, conferences, and congregations be stewards of God's creation by reducing levels of consumption and participating in programs that reuse and recycle goods; and
- encourages United Methodist institutions to perform energy audits, improve energy efficiency, and pursue use of alternative clean energy sources such as wind and solar power where available.

ADOPTED 1996
AMENDED AND READOPTED 2004
AMENDED AND READOPTED 2008
RESOLUTION #11, 2004 *BOOK OF RESOLUTIONS*
RESOLUTION #11, 2000 *BOOK OF RESOLUTIONS*

*See* Social Principles, ¶ 160*B, E.*

## 1028. Law of the Sea

We recognize that "All creation is the Lord's, and we are responsible for the ways in which we use and abuse it" (¶ 160).

We are called to repent of our devastation of the physical and non-human world, because this world is God's creation and is therefore to be valued and conserved.

Nowhere is this need greater than in relation to the sea. In 1970 the United Nations agreed that those areas of the seabed beyond national boundaries were the "common heritage" of humankind. This means that the resources belong to everyone.

The best hope for global cooperation is through the United Nations, where representatives of the nations of the world developed the Law of the Sea.

The Law of the Sea conference worked to produce a fair and just law for the ocean, in which all nations will benefit. No one nation will have all of its interests satisfied, but mechanisms will be set up to maintain order and peace, and both developed and developing countries will have worked on the regulations.

The Law of the Sea Treaty is concerned with protecting this "common heritage" of humanity. It would:

- guarantee unimpeded access to over 100 straits, facilitating commercial transportation;
- prevent conflicts over fishing waters;
- enforce environmental regulations forbidding countries to dump harmful wastes that spoil the ocean waters;
- share equitably the ocean resources, oil, fish, minerals, and prohibit unjust exploitation of these resources by the powerful;
- regulate access to the waters of coastal countries to permit research of the marine environment;
- limit the continuing extension of national sovereignty over international waters and settle legal disputes arising therefrom;
- prevent the division of the world into competing camps depending on powerful navies; and
- create an international agency to manage cooperatively the international seabed resources.

We also affirm our support for the evolution of effective "commons" law, such as the treaties for the Antarctic, climate, biodiversity, and outer space, which support our obligations of stewardship, justice, and peace.

Further, we urge all United Methodists to become informed about the Law of the Sea and to call upon their governments to commit themselves to just and equitable implementation of the Law of the Sea and to the ratification of the treaty.

ADOPTED 1980
AMENDED AND READOPTED 1996
READOPTED 2004 AND 2008
RESOLUTION #12, 2004 *BOOK OF RESOLUTIONS*
RESOLUTION #12, 2000 *BOOK OF RESOLUTIONS*

*See* Social Principles, ¶ 160A.


## 1029. Protection of Water

In the Bible water, in both its physical and spiritual dimensions, is a gift. God covenants with Gods people and extends invitations to them to experience fullness of life. A measure of this abundant life is Gods offer of water as a free gift without cost or price (Isaiah 55:1). Both water as an element and water of life as a healing agent (Revelation 22:17) are a gift of God to everyone who thirsts. Further, the Bible offers examples of God and humans intervening in people's water crises, and providing water (Genesis 21:19; Genesis 24:15-21; Numbers 20:9-11). Water is an integral part of God's radical expression of God's love to all humanity. Water cannot be monopolized or privatized. It is to be shared like air, light, and earth. It is God's elemental provision for survival for all God's children together on this planet.

The problem is:

- Water use is increasing everywhere. The world's six billion inhabitants appropriate 54 percent of all accessible water.
- Globally, 69 percent of all water used on a yearly basis is used by agriculture; industry accounts for 23 percent, and domestic households account for 8 percent.
- Excess withdrawals, withdrawal at a rate greater than can be charged naturally is occurring in parts of the Arabian Peninsula, China, India, Mexico, the former Soviet Union, and the United States.

- One toilet flush uses as much water as an average person in a developing country uses in a whole day, to drink, cook, wash, and clean.
- Many of the 840 million people in the world who go hungry live in water scarce regions.
- 2.3 billion people suffer from diseases linked to dirty water.
- Around the world there is a cumulative pollution of aquifers and water sources by agriculture, industry, and mining waste.
- "If water usage continues in its present form the results will be devastating to the earth and its inhabitants. Each generation must ensure that the abundance and quality of water is not diminished as a result of its activities . . . water must be protected at any cost" (Maude Barlow: *Blue Gold: The Global Water Crisis and the Commodification of the World's Water Supply*).

*Therefore be it resolved* the people called United Methodists

- shall affirm and educate that water is a basic human right to be shared and enjoyed by all God's people;
- shall encourage and develop strategies for guiding principles protecting our water supply;
- shall support the United Nations World Summit on Sustainable Developments commitment to reduce by half the number of people without sustainable access to safe drinking water by 2015;
- shall affirm and teach methods to support the International Year of Freshwaters commitment to protect and respect our water resources as individuals, communities, countries, a global family of concerned citizens;
- shall encourage and commit to good water management by all entities, corporations and communities;
- shall push companies that pollute to provide funds and services to clean waters that they pollute; and
- shall urge that all countries take responsibility for the way they use water.

Other resolutions:

*Book of Resolutions,* 1996, page 90, "Reduction of Water Usage"

*Book of Resolutions,* 1996, page 78, "Environmental Stewardship": Water

Resolution #1026, "Environmental Stewardship": Right to Abundant and Clean Water

Resolution #1023, "Environmental Justice for a Sustainable Future": Water

ADOPTED 2004
READOPTED 2008
RESOLUTION #13, 2004 *BOOK OF RESOLUTIONS*

*See* Social Principles, ¶ 160A.


## 1030. Recycling and the Use of Recycled Products

In Genesis 1:26-28, 2:7 and Psalm 8:6, God created all people in God's image, and gave them responsibility for creation. The Social Principles of The United Methodist Church state: "all creation is the Lord's and we are responsible for the ways in which we use and abuse it" and that as Christians we are called to "place a higher priority on changes in economic, political, social, and technological lifestyle to support a more ecologically equitable and sustainable world leading to a higher quality of life for all of God's creation" (Social Principles ¶ 160). As members of God's human community, we are called to be stewards of the land.

Unfortunately, humankind too often has neglected this sacred duty and chosen instead to misuse God's gifts of creation through overconsumption and wasteful practices. Today, earth's precious resources are threatened by our actions with millions of acres of forests disappearing each year along with thousands of animal and plant species. Given the projected increase in population and economic development, we must take immediate and decisive action to reverse these patterns.

In addition to reducing consumption and reusing materials in lieu of purchasing new ones, recycling is an important and easy step toward a more sustainable future.

Since 1972 the General Conference has requested boards and agencies to use recycled paper and since 1996, the General Conference has called for a phase-out of the production of dioxin, a carcinogenic byproduct of the bleaching of pulp and paper with chlorine. The use of recycled and chlorine-free paper products saves trees, reduces air pollution and greenhouse gas emissions, lowers water pollution, and reduces the amount of dioxin released into the environment.

*Therefore,* The United Methodist Church recommends that:

- United Methodist general boards, agencies and publishers use recycled and "processed chlorine free" paper;
- United Methodist publishers continue to report to subsequent General Conferences on progress made toward achieving this goal;
- United Methodist agencies and congregations educate the public and promote awareness of the benefits of recycling on the environment; and
- United Methodist agencies and congregations participate in all available recycling programs and advocate for their expansion.

ADOPTED 2000
REVISED AND READOPTED 2008
RESOLUTION #14, 2004 *BOOK OF RESOLUTIONS*
RESOLUTION #13, 2000 *BOOK OF RESOLUTIONS*

*See* Social Principles, ¶ 160.

## 1031. Resolution on Global Warming

WHEREAS, global warming is an issue of concern, interest, and action among many United Methodists; and

WHEREAS, global warming is "an average increase in the temperature of the atmosphere near the Earth's surface and in the troposphere <http://www.epa.gov/climatechange/glossary.html>, which can contribute to changes in global climate patterns."[1] Global warming can occur from a variety of causes, both natural and human-induced; and in common usage, "global warming" usually refers to the warming which is thought to occur from increased emissions of human-produced greenhouse gases;[2] and

WHEREAS, a greenhouse gas is "any of the atmospheric gases which contribute to the greenhouse effect."[3] Carbon dioxide, water vapor, and methane are three such examples. The greenhouse effect is "the overall warming of the earth's lower atmosphere <http://www.weather.com/glossary/a.html> primarily due to carbon dioxide <http://www.weather.com/glossary/c.html> and water

1. US Environmental Protection Agency, *Climate Change: Basic Information*, December 2006. <http://www.epa.gov/climatechange/basicinfo.html>
2. Ibid.
3. The Free Dictionary by Farlex, Definition of global warming as found in the *American Heritage Dictionary of the English Language* (Fourth Edition), 2003. <http://www.thefreedictionary.com/greenhouse+gas>

vapor <http://www.weather.com/glossary/w.html>, which permit the sun's rays to heat the earth, but then restrict some heat-energy from escaping back into space."[4] "The greenhouse effect is unquestionably real and helps to regulate the temperature of our planet," making life on Earth possible.[5] Without a natural greenhouse effect, the average temperature of the Earth would be about zero degrees F (-18°C) instead of its present 57°F (14°C).[6] However, too much greenhouse effect can produce conditions on Earth unfavorable to various species of life, including some human populations. Human activity has increased the concentration of greenhouse gases in the atmosphere—mostly carbon dioxide <http://www.ncdc.noaa.gov/img/climate/globalwarming/sio-mlgr.gif> from fossil fuel (coal, oil, gas) combustion;[7] and

WHEREAS, the largest international body critically examining issues related to greenhouse gases and global warming is the Inter-governmental Panel on Climate Change (IPCC). In their 2007 preliminary report, the IPCC reported, with a certainty of 90 percent, that this increase in human-produced greenhouse gases has increased the greenhouse effect, thereby contributing to Earth's recent warming.[8] Prior to the Industrial Revolution, levels of carbon dioxide, the most significant greenhouse gas, were about 280 parts per million by volume (ppmv), and current levels are about 370 ppmv.[9] The concentration of $CO_2$ in our atmosphere today has not been exceeded in the last 420,000 years <http://www.ncdc.noaa.gov/oa/climate/carbdiox.html>, and likely not in the last 20 million years.[10] According to the IPCC Special Report on Emission Scenarios (SRES), by the end of the 21st century, we could expect to see carbon dioxide concentrations of anywhere from 490 to 1260 ppmv (75-350 percent above the pre-industrial concentration);[11] and

---

4. The Weather Channel, Weather Glossary, 2007. <http://www.weather.com/glossary/g.html>
5. National Oceanic and Atmospheric Administration, *Global Warming: Frequently Asked Questions*, February 2006. <http://www.ncdc.noaa.gov/oa/climate/globalwarming.html#Q1>
6. Ibid.
7. Ibid.
8. Intergovernmental Panel on Climate Change, Climate Change 2007: *The Physical Science Basis: Summary for Policymakers*, 2007. http://www.ipcc.ch/SPM2feb07.pdf
9. National Oceanic and Atmospheric Administration, *Global Warming: Frequently Asked Questions*, February 2006. <http://www.ncdc.noaa.gov/oa/climate/globalwarming.html#Q1>
10. Ibid.
11. Ibid.

WHEREAS, such an increase in future carbon dioxide concentration is very likely to cause significant warming of the Earth's climate, resulting in a variety of changes.[12] Scientists have observed some changes already occurring, including: sea level rise, shrinking glaciers, changes in the range and distribution of plants and animals, trees blooming earlier, lengthening of growing seasons, ice on rivers and lakes freezing later and breaking up earlier, and thawing of permafrost.[13] Some of these changes, and other changes not mentioned, may have significant detrimental impacts upon human populations in the future; and unfortunately, many of the impacts may occur in nations with the least ability to adapt, given the economic and social challenges within those nations.

Now therefore, be it resolved, that as a global church community, we call on our members to reduce human-related outputs of greenhouse gases;

Be it further resolved, that members should make an effort to learn about human production and release of greenhouse gases and evaluate their own lifestyles to identify areas where reductions in production and release of greenhouse gases can be made. There are many informative resources for learning how one can reduce his/her greenhouse-gas impact;

Be it further resolved, that members should also work to make their own congregations more aware of the issue of global warming and create policies and practices which reduce greenhouse gas emissions from congregational infrastructure (church buildings, parsonages, vehicles, etc.);

Be it further resolved, that members call on the nations of the world to require reductions in greenhouse emissions using the most efficient and cost-effective mechanisms;

Finally, be it resolved, that members should also attempt to educate others outside their church communities on the need to take action on this issue.

12. Intergovernmental Panel on Climate Change, Climate Change 2007: The Physical Science Basis: Summary for Policymakers, 2007. http://www.ipcc.ch/SPM2feb07.pdf
13. US Environmental Protection Agency, Climate Change: Basic Information, December 2006. <http://www.epa.gov/climatechange/basicinfo.html>

**ADOPTED 2008**

See Social Principles, ¶ 160D.

# ¶ 161. II. THE NURTURING COMMUNITY

The community provides the potential for nurturing human beings into the fullness of their humanity. We believe we have a responsibility to innovate, sponsor, and evaluate new forms of community that will encourage development of the fullest potential in individuals. Primary for us is the gospel understanding that all persons are important—because they are human beings created by God and loved through and by Jesus Christ and not because they have merited significance. We therefore support social climates in which human communities are maintained and strengthened for the sake of all persons and their growth. We also encourage all individuals to be sensitive to others by using appropriate language when referring to all persons. Language of a derogatory nature (with regard to race, nationality, ethnic background, gender, sexuality, and physical differences) does not reflect value for one another and contradicts the gospel of Jesus Christ.

*A) The Family*—We believe the family to be the basic human community through which persons are nurtured and sustained in mutual love, responsibility, respect, and fidelity. We affirm the importance of loving parents for all children. We also understand the family as encompassing a wider range of options than that of the two-generational unit of parents and children (the nuclear family). We affirm shared responsibility for parenting where there are two parents and encourage social, economic, and religious efforts to maintain and strengthen relationships within families in order that every member may be assisted toward complete personhood.

*B) Marriage*—We affirm the sanctity of the marriage covenant that is expressed in love, mutual support, personal commitment, and shared fidelity between a man and a woman. We believe that God's blessing rests upon such marriage, whether or not there are children of the union. We reject social norms that assume different standards for women than for men in marriage. We support laws in civil society that define marriage as the union of one man and one woman.

C) *Divorce*—God's plan is for lifelong, faithful marriage. The church must be on the forefront of premarital, marital, and postmarital counseling in order to create and preserve strong marriages. However, when a married couple is estranged beyond reconciliation, even after thoughtful consideration and counsel, divorce is a regrettable alternative in the midst of brokenness. We grieve over the devastating emotional, spiritual, and economic consequences of divorce for all involved, understanding that women and especially children are disproportionately impacted by such burdens. As the church we are concerned about high divorce rates. It is recommended that methods of mediation be used to minimize the adversarial nature and fault-finding that are often part of our current judicial processes.

Although divorce publicly declares that a marriage no longer exists, other covenantal relationships resulting from the marriage remain, such as the nurture and support of children and extended family ties. We urge respectful negotiations in deciding the custody of minor children and support the consideration of either or both parents for this responsibility in that custody not be reduced to financial support, control, or manipulation and retaliation. The welfare of each child is the most important consideration.

Divorce does not preclude a new marriage. We encourage an intentional commitment of the Church and society to minister compassionately to those in the process of divorce, as well as members of divorced and remarried families, in a community of faith where God's grace is shared by all.

D) *Single Persons*—We affirm the integrity of single persons, and we reject all social practices that discriminate or social attitudes that are prejudicial against persons because they are single. This also includes single parents, and we recognize the extra responsibilities involved.

E) *Women and Men*—We affirm with Scripture the common humanity of male and female, both having equal worth in the eyes of God. We reject the erroneous notion that one gender is superior to another, that one gender must strive against another, and that members of one gender may receive love, power, and esteem only at the expense of another. We especially reject the idea that God made individuals as incomplete fragments, made whole only in union with another. We call upon women and men alike to share power and control, to learn to give freely and to receive freely, to be complete and to respect the wholeness of others. We seek for every individual opportunities and freedom to love and be loved, to seek and receive justice, and to practice ethical self-determination. We understand our gender diversity to be a gift from God, intended to add to the rich variety of human experience and perspective; and we guard against attitudes and traditions that would use this good gift to leave members of one sex more vulnerable in relationships than members of another.

*F) Human Sexuality*—We affirm that sexuality is God's good gift to all persons. We call everyone to responsible stewardship of this sacred gift.

Although all persons are sexual beings whether or not they are married, sexual relations are affirmed only with the covenant of monogamous, heterosexual marriage.

We deplore all forms of the commercialization, abuse, and exploitation of sex. We call for strict global enforcement of laws prohibiting the sexual exploitation of children and for adequate protection, guidance, and counseling for abused children. All persons, regardless of age, gender, marital status, or sexual orientation, are entitled to have their human and civil rights ensured and to be protected against violence. The Church should support the family in providing age appropriate education regarding sexuality to children, youth, and adults.

We affirm that all persons are individuals of sacred worth, created in the image of God. All persons need the ministry of the church in their struggles for human fulfillment, as well as the spiritual and emotional care of a fellowship that enables reconciling relationships with God, with others, and with self. The United Methodist Church does not condone the practice of homosexuality and considers this practice incompatible with Christian teaching. We affirm that God's grace is available to all. We will seek to live together in Christian community, welcoming, forgiving, and loving one another, as Christ has loved and accepted us. We implore families and churches not to reject or condemn lesbian and gay members and friends. We commit ourselves to be in ministry for and with all persons.[1]

*G) Family Violence and Abuse*—We recognize that family violence and abuse in all its forms—verbal, psychological, physical, sexual—is detrimental to the covenant of the human community. We encourage the Church to provide a safe environment, counsel, and support for

1. See Judicial Council Decision 702.

the victim. While we deplore the actions of the abuser, we affirm that person to be in need of God's redeeming love.

*H) Sexual Abuse*—Violent, disrespectful, or abusive sexual expressions do not confirm sexuality as God's good gift. We reject all sexual expressions that damage the humanity God has given us as birthright, and we affirm only that sexual expression that enhances that same humanity. We believe that sexual relations where one or both partners are exploitative, abusive, or promiscuous are beyond the parameters of acceptable Christian behavior and are ultimately destructive to individuals, families, and the social order. We deplore all forms of the commercialization and exploitation of sex, with their consequent cheapening and degradation of human personality. To lose freedom and be sold by someone else for sexual purposes is a form of slavery, and we denounce such business and support the abused and their right to freedom.

We call for strict global enforcement of laws prohibiting the sexual exploitation or use of children by adults and encourage efforts to hold perpetrators legally and financially responsible. We call for the establishment of adequate protective services, guidance, and counseling opportunities for children thus abused.

*I) Sexual Harassment*—We believe human sexuality is God's good gift. One abuse of this good gift is sexual harassment. We define sexual harassment as any unwanted sexual comment, advance, or demand, either verbal or physical, that is reasonably perceived by the recipient as demeaning, intimidating, or coercive. Sexual harassment must be understood as an exploitation of a power relationship rather than as an exclusively sexual issue. Sexual harassment includes, but is not limited to, the creation of a hostile or abusive working environment resulting from discrimination on the basis of gender.

Contrary to the nurturing community, sexual harassment creates improper, coercive, and abusive conditions wherever it occurs in society. Sexual harassment undermines the social goal of equal opportunity and the climate of mutual respect between men and women. Unwanted sexual attention is wrong and discriminatory. Sexual harassment interferes with the moral mission of the Church.

*J) Abortion*—The beginning of life and the ending of life are the God-given boundaries of human existence. While individuals have always had some degree of control over when they would die, they now have the awesome power to determine when and even whether new individuals will be born. Our belief in the sanctity of unborn human life makes us reluctant to approve abortion.

But we are equally bound to respect the sacredness of the life and well-being of the mother and the unborn child.

We recognize tragic conflicts of life with life that may justify abortion, and in such cases we support the legal option of abortion under proper medical procedures. We support parental, guardian, or other responsible adult notification and consent before abortions can be performed on girls who have not yet reached the age of legal adulthood. We cannot affirm abortion as an acceptable means of birth control, and we unconditionally reject it as a means of gender selection.

We oppose the use of late-term abortion known as dilation and extraction (partial-birth abortion) and call for the end of this practice except when the physical life of the mother is in danger and no other medical procedure is available, or in the case of severe fetal anomalies incompatible with life. Before providing their services, abortion providers should be required to offer women the option of anesthesia.

We call all Christians to a searching and prayerful inquiry into the sorts of conditions that may cause them to consider abortion.

The Church shall offer ministries to reduce unintended pregnancies. We commit our Church to continue to provide nurturing ministries to those who terminate a pregnancy, to those in the midst of a crisis pregnancy, and to those who give birth.

We particularly encourage the Church, the government, and social service agencies to support and facilitate the option of adoption. (*See* ¶ 161L.) We affirm and encourage the Church to assist the ministry of crisis pregnancy centers and pregnancy resource centers that compassionately help women find feasible alternatives to abortion.

Governmental laws and regulations do not provide all the guidance required by the informed Christian conscience. Therefore, a decision concerning abortion should be made only after thoughtful and prayerful consideration by the parties involved, with medical, family, pastoral, and other appropriate counsel.

*K) Ministry to those who have experienced an abortion*—We urge local pastors to become informed about the symptoms and behaviors associated with post-abortion stress. We further encourage local churches to make available contact information for counseling agencies that offer programs to address post-abortion stress for all seeking help.

*L) Adoption*—Children are a gift from God to be welcomed and received. We recognize that some circumstances of birth make the rearing of a child difficult. We affirm and support the birth parent(s) whose choice it is to allow the child to be adopted. We recognize the agony, strength, and courage of the birth parent(s) who choose(s) in hope, love, and prayer to offer the child for adoption. In addition, we also recognize the anxiety, strength, and courage of those who choose in hope, love, and prayer to be able to care for a child. We affirm and support the adoptive parent(s)' desire to rear an adopted child as they would a biological child. When circumstances warrant adoption, we support the use of proper legal procedures. When appropriate and possible, we encourage open adoption so that a child may know all information and people related to them, both medically and relationally. We support and encourage greater awareness and education to promote adoption of a wide variety of children through foster care, international adoption, and domestic adoption. We commend the birth parent(s), the receiving parent(s), and the child to the care of the Church, that grief might be shared, joy might be celebrated, and the child might be nurtured in a community of Christian love.

*M) Faithful Care for Dying Persons*—While we applaud medical science for efforts to prevent disease and illness and for advances in treatment that extend the meaningful life of human beings, we recognize that every mortal life will ultimately end in death. Death is never a sign that God has abandoned us, no matter what the circumstances of the death might be. As Christians we must always be prepared to surrender the gift of mortal life and claim the gift of eternal life through the death and resurrection of Jesus Christ. Care for dying persons is part of our stewardship of the divine gift of life when cure is no longer possible. We encourage the use of medical technologies to provide palliative care at the end of life when life-sustaining treatments no longer support the goals of life, and when they have reached their limits. There is no moral or religious obligation to use these when they impose undue burdens or only extend the process of dying. Dying persons and their families are free to discontinue treatments when they cease to be of benefit to the patient.

We recognize the agonizing personal and moral decisions faced by the dying, their physicians, their families, their friends, and their faith community. We urge that decisions faced by the dying be made with thoughtful and prayerful consideration by the parties involved, with medical, pastoral, and other appropriate counsel. We further urge that all persons discuss with their families, their physicians, and their pastoral counselors, their wishes for care at the end of life and provide advance directives for such care when they are not able to make these decisions for themselves. Even when one accepts the inevitability of death, the church and society must continue to provide faithful care, including pain relief, companionship, support, and spiritual nurture for the dying person in the hard work of preparing for death. We encourage and support the concept of hospice care whenever possible at the end of life. Faithful care does not end at death but continues during bereavement as we care for grieving families. We reject euthanasia and any pressure upon the dying to end their lives. God has continued love and purpose for all persons, regardless of health. We affirm laws and policies that protect the rights and dignity of the dying.

¶ 161

*N) Suicide*—We believe that suicide is not the way a human life should end. Often suicide is the result of untreated depression, or untreated pain and suffering. The church has an obligation to see that all persons have access to needed pastoral and medical care and therapy in those circumstances that lead to loss of self-worth, suicidal despair, and/or the desire to seek physician-assisted suicide. We encourage the church to provide education to address the biblical, theological, social, and ethical issues related to death and dying, including suicide. United Methodist theological seminary courses should also focus on issues of death and dying, including suicide.

A Christian perspective on suicide begins with an affirmation of faith that nothing, including suicide, separates us from the love of God (Romans 8:38-39). Therefore, we deplore the condemnation of people who complete suicide, and we consider unjust the stigma that so often falls on surviving family and friends.

We encourage pastors and faith communities to address this issue through preaching and teaching. We urge pastors and faith communities to provide pastoral care to those at risk, survivors, and their families, and to those families who have lost loved ones to suicide, seeking always to remove the oppressive stigma around suicide. The Church opposes assisted suicide and euthanasia.

# THE NURTURING COMMUNITY
# THE RESOLUTIONS

## CHRISTIAN EDUCATION

### 2001. Christian Education

WHEREAS, every elder, at ordination covenants to "preach the word of God, lead in worship, read and teach the Scriptures and engage the people in study and witness and to ensure faithful transmission of the Christian faith" (2004 *Discipline* ¶ 340.1); and every deacon at ordination covenants to "create opportunities for others to enter into discipleship" (2004 *Discipline*, ¶ 329.1); and

WHEREAS, the early Methodist movement was guided by the educational genius of John Wesley, who crafted an ecology of faith formation and leadership development for making disciples; and

WHEREAS, question number fourteen of the Historic Examination for Admission into Full Connection is "Will you diligently instruct the children in every place?" (¶ 336), but yet, two-thirds of our baptized children leave the church because they are not rooted in the traditions of The United Methodist Church, as acknowledged by the Council of Bishops' Episcopal Initiative on Children and Poverty; and

Whereas, the document "Our Shared Dream: The Beloved Community" emphasizes the bishops' vision of building Beloved Community, including a deep commitment to children, and their seven "Vision Pathways" includes reaching and transforming "the lives of new generations of children" and "teaching the Wesleyan model of reaching and forming disciples of Jesus Christ," and the "Provocative Propositions" of the general agencies and commissions includes preparing leadership for the church; and the bishops' Call to Action lists four ways to move forward on the vision, including to "Reach and Care for the Children" and to "Live the United Methodist Way";

*Therefore, be it resolved,* that the 2008 General Conference affirm the imperative to engage in the work of Christian education and direct United Methodist seminaries and colleges, the General Board of Higher Education and Ministry, the General Board of Discipleship, The United Methodist Publishing House, annual conferences, and local churches to assess and expand how they advance the work of Christian education in the church. This includes promoting the professional and para-professional certification in Christian education, youth ministry, spiritual formation, camping and retreat ministry, and older-adult ministry, and, where appropriate, monitoring all approved seminary M.Div. programs to ensure that future leaders are being trained in the ministries of Christian education.

ADOPTED 2008

*See* Social Principles, ¶¶ 161 and 162.

## 2002. Faith Communities on Campus

WHEREAS, just as parish churches are the center of spiritual life for their communities, so too are campus ministries a center of spiritual life for their campuses. Students often find their place and spirituality within these ministries, substituting time spent in fellowship with peers for time spent in a formal worship setting. Oftentimes, these fellowships serve as an introduction to the church and as settings for affirmation of faith; and

WHEREAS, many people find their faith, change their faith, and challenge their faith during their formative young adult years, it is important to have a presence and the technology to answer questions and attract seekers. We believe The United Methodist Church is a strong spiritual home with a table open to any who want to participate. Through campus ministries, students are given the chance to find their "home" in our church; and

WHEREAS, as representatives from campuses across the country, we embrace common challenges found today and envision ways to work with annual conferences to strengthen our ministries; and

WHEREAS, the common challenges of campus ministries include:
- a rapid turnover of population;
- an inability to be self-sustaining through the traditional parish methods of tithing and lay leadership;

- a disconnection in the transfer between high school and college fellowships;
- ministers who face unique challenges outside that of parish churches; and

WHEREAS, we see a higher percentage of young adults attending college, demanding a proportional increase in campus ministry support; and

WHEREAS, many universities are the size of small cities, the same size as other population centers where we maintain a United Methodist presence;

*Therefore, be it resolved,* that we see a growing importance for campus ministries within the church. The 2008 General Conference affirms the work of our campus ministries. With the support of annual conferences across the nation, we envision a growing body of young adults with an increased presence and place in The United Methodist Church; and

*Be it further resolved,* that we ask annual conferences to:
- acknowledge the unique challenges campus ministries face;
- support their campus ministry programs and campus ministers; and
- help high school graduates and young adults connect with campus ministries.

**ADOPTED 2008**

*See* Social Principles, ¶¶ 161 and 162.


## 2003. Support Campus Ministers

WHEREAS, campus ministry is essential to the mission, growth, and future of The United Methodist Church;

WHEREAS, campus ministries are dependent on the commitment and passion of campus ministers;

WHEREAS, campus ministry often can be isolating for campus ministers and unrecognized by the church;

*Therefore, be it resolved,* that the 2008 General Conference affirms the campus ministers of United Methodist and ecumenical campus ministries, who have committed themselves to the work of the church in college environments and calls the entire church to join in acknowledging this important contribution. The 2008 General Conference also remains committed to working with campus ministers to further campus ministry.

ADOPTED 2008

*See* Social Principles, ¶¶ 161 and 162.

## 2004. Revitalizing The United Methodist Church and Theological Education

The United Methodist Church has a long, rich tradition in American higher education. American Methodism has been committed to education since its inception. At the Christmas Conference of 1784, the first action was the election of a bishop and the establishment of Cokesbury College in Abingdon, Maryland. This action was symbolically and substantively important because the conference unquestionably spoke and acted on two high priority items. One was leadership (electing the bishop), and the other was program (establishing Cokesbury College).

Soon thereafter, newly elected Bishop Francis Asbury wrote to all Methodists, reminding them of their obligation to erect a school in the vicinity of every church, "to give the key of knowledge in a general way to your children, and those of the poor in the vicinity of your small towns and villages."[1] Bishop Asbury set the church-wide vision "to give the key of knowledge" as a program priority, and securing local church resources "to erect a school in the vicinity of every church." Thus, "millions of working-class Methodists gave their nickels, dimes, and crumpled dollar bills . . . to the apportionments and special appeals that built our hospitals, orphanages and colleges. Motivated by their commitment to Christ, ordinary people made extraordinary sacrifices to accomplish visionary goals."[2]

The United Methodist education pipeline became an integral part of the connectional system. The pipeline is leadership development, and it must start in the local church, continue in the schools, colleges, universities, theological schools and campus ministry units, and then produce leaders for the church and world. Local churches, together with

1. Elliott, T. Michael, et al., eds. *To Give the Key of Knowledge: United Methodists and Education, 1784-1976*, (Nashville: National Commission on United Methodist Higher Education, 1976), 13.
2. Snyder, Dean, "Too few stars in our crown," *UMConnection*, February 20, 2002.

scholarship support, sent their youth to our colleges and universities. World-class graduates, equipped with general and professional education, were gushing out of the United Methodist education pipeline and became leaders in the church and the world. In the early 1960s, however, The United Methodist Church's program priorities shifted away from education, and today, the historic partnership between church and campus has been weakened therefore contributing to the erosion and rusting of the pipeline.

*The pipeline has eroded and rusted as there are fewer young people in the church and the leadership pool is dwindling. We struggle to get the best and brightest for clergy as research shows there are declining numbers of clergy with MDIVs; there is a small percentage of students entering college who plan to attend seminary; and there are fewer young people who see ordination as elder as a significant vocation.*

It is very alarming to review the membership composition of The United Methodist Church in the United States, for these data further explain how the pipeline is rusted. Membership below the age of 18 consists of only 4.6% (or 383,000), while membership above the age of 40 consists of 80.1%. The average age of church members is 57 years old. Only 9.9% of clergy members are below the age of 39. Of 8,292,809 members of The United Methodist Church, Asian Americans comprise only 0.8%, African Americans 5.1%, Hispanic Americans 0.6%, Native Americans 0.2%, Pacific Islanders 0.1%, and white Americans 93.2%. Among the clergy members, Asian Americans comprise 2.2%, African Americans 5.6%, Hispanic Americans 1.2%, Native Americans 0.4%, Pacific Islanders 0.3%, and white Americans 90.4%. Female clergy members comprise only 18.5% of 44,539 clergy members, while 63% of the members of the church are females.

In facing this reality, we must ask, "What is the future of The United Methodist Church?" In order to resolve this most urgent issue, The United Methodist Church must have a clear vision, dynamic leadership, purposeful and focused programs, and faithful stewardship, such as the early Methodists had at the 1784 Christmas Conference.

The General Board of Higher Education and Ministry (GBHEM) proposes that the 2004 General Conference adopt the following strategic vision and goals as a denominational priority:

*Vision*

A new generation of Christian leaders will commit boldly to Jesus Christ and be characterized by intellectual excellence, moral and spiritual courage, and holiness of heart and life.

*Goal 1*

The United Methodist Church, throughout its connection, will identify, recruit, educate, and prepare young people for Christian vocations with a special focus on first generation United Methodists.

*Goal 2*

The United Methodist Church, throughout its connection, will collaborate with United Methodist-related schools, colleges, universities, theological schools, and campus ministry units to build a new education pipeline that will generate dynamic leaders for the church and world.

*Goal 3*

The United Methodist Church, throughout its connection, will embrace its tradition of excellent, educated leadership by sharing success stories from its ministries in higher education, theological education, and campus ministry in ways that create a desire to be a part of its vibrant ministries.

We urge the 2004 General Conference to approve this resolution for the purpose of revitalizing The United Methodist Church and to mandate that the General Board of Higher Education and Ministry be fully responsible for implementing the resolution.

ADOPTED 2004
RESOLUTION #99, 2004 *BOOK OF RESOLUTIONS*

*See* Social Principles, ¶ 162.

# FAMILY

## 2021. Adoption in a Global Context

Every child is a child of God and deserves to grow up in a safe, healthy, and loving family environment. For a variety of reasons, including unwanted pregnancy, family violence, addictions, or poverty, children are placed for adoption with hopes for a better future.

Those seeking to adopt a child are faced with many challenges and concerns about the high costs of adoption, international laws and restrictions, interracial or intercultural differences, the availability of licensed agencies, and the long waiting times for processing adoptions.

International adoptions have increased dramatically in recent years. In some cases, this has created a lucrative multi-million dollar a year market in the business of "baby selling." High costs of international adoption call into question issues of stewardship while making it cost-prohibitive for families with moderate or low incomes. An international adoption may give a child a new opportunity to live a more abundant life with greater opportunities. However, removing children from their native land can have dire consequences, either because of unresolved prejudices held by the adoptive parents or because the children are unable to adjust emotionally or socially to their new homes. Neither is intercountry adoption a solution to the problems of high birth rates or poverty in the countries of origin. Countries where babies are being considered for adoption are concerned whether they may suffer a "brain drain" since typically only healthy babies, without disabilities or birth defects, are chosen by adoptive parents.

While some may pursue the adoption of children from other countries, many thousands of children in the foster care system wait in vain for families to adopt them. Adoption advocates point out that children who are under care in the foster care system are viewed as "less desirable" by potential adoptive parents, because these children may come from difficult or painful families of origin or may have been harmed by years in successive and less-than-ideal placements. A form of "ageism" prevails in the adoption process, both in the selection of parents and the placement of children.

Cross-racial adoption also presents many challenges. There are divisions over the "correctness" of interracial or cross-cultural adoption. Too often interracial adoption is based on economic class differences, or ability to provide for the child's needs. A family becomes a biracial or multicultural family when they adopt a child of a different race or culture than their own and, therefore, should be sensitive to the societal impact of racism or xenophobia upon the child. Adoptive parents should not neglect the history and heritage of the child's family of origin (if known) and should affirm racial ancestry and culture. Studies have shown that children from ethnic backgrounds different from their parents grow up with a stronger sense of identity and self-esteem if their birth ethnicity has been positively communicated within the family. Great sensitivity also needs to be expressed with regard to the intricacies of the social welfare system and the impact that adoption may have on Native Americans and other ethnic minorities.

Complex social problems which severely impact children, including racism, poverty, alcoholism, and family violence, need other approaches in addition to foster care and adoption.

In a time when many parents are seeking to adopt children, and when many children are needing a loving, caring family, The United Methodist Church affirms adoption as a means to create and strengthen families. Given the multiple challenges posed by adoption, we call upon all United Methodists, local churches, annual conferences, and general agencies to:

- encourage adoptive parents to respect and affirm the cultural and racial background of the adopted child;
- make adoption more affordable by supporting increased financial assistance to middle- and low-income families considering adoption;
- support regulations and policies that enable more qualified foster care families and qualified extended family members to more easily adopt children in their care;
- promote conditions which would make adoption unnecessary by supporting programs which will improve the living conditions of children in their families, their communities and their countries of origin; and provide access to counseling services for adoptive parents;
- in cases where information and contact is desirable for the well-being of the child, work through recognized organizations to make contact between adoptive and birth families; and
- encourage those entering into the adoption process to work only with licensed adoption agencies.

ADOPTED 2000
READOPTED 2008
RESOLUTION #20, 2004 *BOOK OF RESOLUTIONS*
RESOLUTION #19, 2000 *BOOK OF RESOLUTIONS*

*See* Social Principles, ¶ 161L.

## 2022. Support for Adoption

The Social Principles of The United Methodist Church, in the section on "The Nurturing Community," ¶ 161A) "The Family," state: "We believe the family to be the basic human community through which persons are nurtured and sustained in mutual love, responsibility, respect, and fidelity." They further acknowledge that the family encompasses a wide range of options. One of those options is the family that includes adopted children.

Clinical and social service agencies that relate professionally to adoption issues look for and encourage the same attitudes and behaviors that should apply for birth children. These attitudes and behaviors include: parental love; parental responsibility; encouragement of identity development of the child; physical, emotional, and economic security of the child; educational growth of the child; and socialization of the child.

Studies done by a variety of clinical and educational agencies and institutions concur that the six factors mentioned above, expressed in various forms, are vital for a sense of stability and dependability experienced by children in a family system.

Some of the most recent studies of families and children have been done by the Search Institute of Minneapolis, Minnesota, which has identified forty developmental assets that help children grow in a healthy, caring, and responsible environment.

External assets include: support (e.g., the family provides a high level of love and support; the child experiences caring neighbors); empowerment (e.g., children are valued by being placed at the center of family life; the parent(s) serve(s) others in the community); boundaries and expectations (e.g., the parent(s) and other adults model positive, responsible behavior; the parent or parents have realistic expectations for children's growth and development); and constructive use of time (e.g., the parent(s) expose(s) children to a variety of creative activities; the parent(s) provide(s) positive, supervised time at home).

Internal assets include: commitment to learning (e.g., family members are motivated to do well in school, work, and community; the parent(s) enjoy(s) learning and demonstrate(s) this through personal learning activities); positive values (e.g., the family values caring, helping behaviors; the family values honesty); social competencies (e.g., parental planning and decision-making behaviors are modeled and observed; peaceful conflict resolution is modeled and observed); and positive identity (e.g., the family models high self-esteem; the family has a positive view of the future).

It has been observed that as the above-mentioned assets are experienced, children and families demonstrate stability and growth regardless of whether children are of birth origin or adopted. *Therefore,* The United Methodist Church supports and encourages adoption by all persons who demonstrate these attitudes, behaviors, and assets.

ADOPTED 2004
RESOLUTION #21, 2004 *BOOK OF RESOLUTIONS*

*See* Social Principles, ¶ 161L.

## 2023. Support for Clergy Families

Over the last many years, clergy and their families have continued to express serious concerns for the stresses they bear in their congregations and districts. This phrase, "life in the fishbowl," describes how pastor and staff therapist Frank J. Stalfa sees the lives of clergy and their spouses and family members in our local congregations. The image is painfully accurate about the situation filled with unrealistic expectations, virtually nonexistent boundaries for privacy and personal time, disrupted lives, crisis in careers and educational programs, unending demands of congregational needs, and pressure for spouses and "PKs" (preacher's kids) to be perfect, "model" Christians.

PK syndrome is documented in research on children and youth in clergy families, and it names the pressure on clergy children to set a high standard for other children to follow (the perfect student, the model son/daughter, the high-achieving youth)—potentially limiting their individuality and development.

In a 1992 survey by *Leadership*, on the causes for marriage problems in clergy families, these were the most frequently named: insufficient time together (81%); use of money (71%); income level (70%); communication difficulties (64%); congregational differences (63%); differences over leisure activities (57%) followed by difficulties raising children, pastor's anger toward spouse, differences over ministry career and spouse's career. A significant and troubling 80% of clergy reported that they believed their pastoral ministry negatively affected their families.

In a study of spouses of district superintendents, *Giving Voice: A Survey and Study of District Superintendents' Spouses in The United*

*Methodist Church,*[1] the detailed list of concerns and problems included the following: gossip and criticism, lack of family time, raising children alone, constant stress, unrealistic work loads, emotional and energy drains, sense of isolation in times of conflict, and the struggle to find spiritual nurture in that setting. This survey and study found these key issues:

- Family lifestyle;
- Careers of spouses;
- Self-care or lack of it;
- Sense of isolation, anger, and frustration.

It is important to note that while the majority of clergy spouses are female, a growing number of these spouses are male. Noteworthy is the difference in how these men are treated: rather than being called the clergy spouse, they are the "men married to ministers," and the expectations placed on female clergy spouses are not placed on these male clergy spouses. Their development of a separate personal and professional identity may not be the struggle it is for many female spouses who fight to keep a career or family time or educational opportunities. This survey suggests that expectations of clergy spouses may be not only traditional but gender-related.

With the changing nature of our clergypersons in the Church, roles of their spouses and families have changed, blurred, shifted. Dual career clergy families can see career-ending moves and increased pressure on spouses to leave careers and educational programs. Anger, frustration, hostility, and isolation are all mentioned by clergy spouses in surveys of their feelings about this developing crisis in congregational relationships.

The increasing concerns heard from these "model" or "invisible" or "fishbowl" families are similar across the denomination in US and global congregations. And it is unthinkable to believe that congregations intentionally wish this stress and pain. Certainly, many parishioners would find it unacceptable that their expectations and demands (spoken and unspoken) would cause such stress on their clergy family.

### Christian Community for All Our Families

As United Methodists we envision churches and congregations in which all of God's children are welcome at the Table, all are nurtured

---

1. *Giving Voice: A Survey and Study of District Superintendents' Spouses in The United Methodist Church,* by Sylvia B. Corson, published by the General Board of Higher Education and Ministry, Nashville, 1999.

and respected for their own gifts and talents, and all are transformed to be Christ to others in the world. We are a Church of Open Hearts, Open Minds, and Open Doors, regardless of gender, regardless of family status.

Our Church places high value on our families, yet the needs and crises of our clergy family, "the invisible family," may go unnoticed, unidentified, unaddressed. Clergy families are like every other family with strengths and stresses similar to our own. They need privacy and boundaries that protect personal life just as our families do.

*What Can Be Done?*

The roles of clergy spouse and family are unique and frequently taken for granted. These roles are, nonetheless, critical to the success of the clergy's ministry. Sustaining the emotional, spiritual, physical, and economic health of our clergy families is a ministry to be recommended to every congregation and district.

We can support our clergy families by doing the following:

- First, examining our own attitudes, perceptions, and expectations and identifying where we are unrealistic;
- Asking ourselves the questions that will identify any sexism or racism in our expectations and assumptions: *If this clergy spouse/family member were another gender or another race, would I have the same expectations? Would I make the same assumptions?*
- Remembering they are human and have their own personal and professional lives;
- Providing safe and honest sharing for clergy families when stress mounts;
- Encouraging clergy families to seek help, even taking the initiative to provide resources and support;
- Regularly clarifying and keeping our expectations realistic, recognizing that pedestals are for statues;
- Reserving family time and protecting family life boundaries;
- Avoiding stereotypic demands of a clergy spouse as an extension of the clergy or as another professional at the service of the congregation.

We can share the effective and renewing models working in Episcopal areas and conferences around the Church, including but not limited to these:

- The Arkansas Episcopal Area's Partners in Ministry Surveys and Renewal Retreats.
- Iowa Conference's *"What Do I Do If . . . ?" Basic Information Handbook for Clergy Spouses,* similar to those used in Northern Illinois, Memphis, and Southern Indiana conferences.
- Clergy Transitions Programs in several conferences.
- Florida Conference's program of nurture, healing, and preventative care to clergy and their families, *Shade and Fresh Water.* (The three-part approach includes a therapeutic presence for families in crisis or need, including professional counseling and safe space; a preventative program for clergy families in transition in appointments; and a sustaining program encouraging healthy modeling of well-balanced lives.)
- Varied programs, guidance, and initiatives of organizations like The Center for Ministry, the Center for Pastoral Effectiveness and Spiritual Direction, and websites like "Desperate Preacher's Site."
- Ongoing collaboration between the General Commission on the Status and Role of Women, the General Board of Higher Education and Ministry, and the General Commission on Religion and Race.

*Therefore, be it resolved that,* the General Conference of The United Methodist Church calls on each of the following to address this growing crisis among our clergy families:

1. The General Commission on the Status and Role of Women will work collaboratively with the General Board of Higher Education and Ministry and other general boards and agencies to convene a denominational forum focusing on clergy spouse and families issues as experienced globally, the programs and resources available to clergy families, cabinets and bishops, conferences, and local congregations. The commission will report the feedback from the forum to the 2008 General Conference with recommendations for further study or action.

2. Bishops, cabinets, and boards of ordained ministry will promote specific conference resources, training and orientation models, and counseling assistance programs to all clergy and families.

3. The General Board of Higher Education and Ministry will enhance the training for staff-parish relations committees to provide useful strategies and resources.

4. Staff-parish relations committees will use strategies and training resources for their members in these specific concerns of clergy and families.

5. The General Commission on the Status and Role of Women and the General Board of Higher Education and Ministry will convene a summit of staff and members of related general agencies including the Board of Pension and Health Benefits, the Commission on Religion and Race, the Board of Church and Society, and the General Board of Global Ministries, to research issues affecting clergy spouses and families in the global United Methodist Church, to identify and promote existing relevant resources, plan the development of needed additional resources to address these concerns, and make any legislative recommendations to the 2008 General Conference.

6. District superintendents and their spouses may be called on to provide modeling and leadership for their clergy families in successful strategies. Superintendents will prioritize this issue as they work with local congregations in transitions and ongoing appointments.

7. Annual conference commissions on the status and role of women will survey spouses and families of clergy to assist annual conferences, bishops and cabinets, and general agencies in gathering data and developing resources and strategies in response to the challenges of life in the clergy family.

8. The research findings of GCSRW, GBHEM, and other general boards and agencies, will be published in a summary document and made available for use by United Methodist annual and central conferences, and other denominations and religious bodies.

ADOPTED 2004
RESOLUTION #22, 2004 *BOOK OF RESOLUTIONS*

*See* Social Principles, ¶ 161A.

## 2024. Caring for Clergy Spouses, Children, and Youth During Divorce

WHEREAS, clergy families may experience severe tensions that sometimes lead to marital separation and/or divorce; and

WHEREAS, clergy and their spouses in such situations may need mediation and counseling and may not seek it voluntarily; and

WHEREAS, children of clergy families that are going through divorce often find that their normal pattern of spiritual formation and their congregational lives are interrupted during those times of painful transitions; and

WHEREAS, clergy spouses are often vulnerable in such situations, being unaware of provisions in *The Book of Discipline* of *The United Methodist Church* and the General Board of Pension and Health Benefits of The United Methodist Church; and

WHEREAS, spouses may need assistance in obtaining guidance, support and temporary housing; and

WHEREAS, members of the Board of Ordained Ministries and the cabinet encounter situations in which assistance is needed,

*Therefore, be it resolved,* that each annual conference be encouraged to make available through the Board of Ordained Ministries a trained team of children and youth advocates. The role of advocates will be to represent the concerns of children and youth throughout the divorce review process to include providing parents with resource information on those persons or agencies that provide mediation and counseling for children and youth who are experiencing the divorce of their parents; and

*Be it further resolved,* that each annual conference be encouraged to study and make available to families of clergy an explanation of the requirements for clergy and the rights of spouses during a marital separation or divorce, in accordance with the *Book of Discipline* and the General Board of Pension and Health Benefits.

ADOPTED 2000
AMENDED AND READOPTED 2004
RESOLUTION #23, 2004 *BOOK OF RESOLUTIONS*
RESOLUTION #20, 2000 *BOOK OF RESOLUTIONS*

*See* Social Principles, ¶ 161C.

## 2025. May as Christian Home Month

WHEREAS, we believe that families in our world, at this hour, stand at a critical juncture, in the midst of destructive pressures that are daily taking their toll; and that The United Methodist Church has the opportunity, potential, and responsibility to respond to the urgent needs of families,

*Therefore, be it resolved*, that General Conference declare the month of May Christian Home Month, with emphasis upon family worship in the home, worship and program planning in the congregation, and prayer on behalf of families. We call upon the Office of Family Ministries of the General Board of Discipleship to produce resources for the support of Christian Home Month for use in the congregation and in the home.

ADOPTED 1992
AMENDED AND READOPTED 2004
RESOLUTION #24, 2004 *BOOK OF RESOLUTIONS*
RESOLUTION #21, 2000 *BOOK OF RESOLUTIONS*

*See* Social Principles, ¶ 161*A*.

## 2026. Responsible Parenthood

We affirm the principle of responsible parenthood. The family, in its varying forms, constitutes the primary focus of love, acceptance, and nurture, bringing fulfillment to parents and child. Healthful and whole personhood develops as one is loved, responds to love, and in that relationship comes to wholeness as a child of God.

Each couple has the right and the duty prayerfully and responsibly to control conception according to their circumstances. They are, in our view, free to use those means of birth control considered medically safe. As developing technologies have moved conception and reproduction more and more out of the category of a chance happening and more closely to the realm of responsible choice, the decision whether or not to give birth to children must include acceptance of the responsibility to provide for their mental, physical, and spiritual growth, as well as consideration of the possible effect on quality of life for family and society.

To support the sacred dimensions of personhood, all possible efforts should be made by parents and the community to ensure that each child enters the world with a healthy body and is born into an environment conducive to the realization of his or her full potential.

When an unacceptable pregnancy occurs, we believe that a profound regard for unborn human life must be weighed alongside an equally profound regard for fully developed personhood, particularly when the physical, mental, and emotional health of the pregnant woman and her family show reason to be seriously threatened by the new life just forming. We reject the simplistic answers to the problem of abortion that, on the one hand, regard all abortions as murders, or, on the other hand, regard abortions as medical procedures without moral significance.

When an unacceptable pregnancy occurs, a family—and most of all, the pregnant woman—is confronted with the need to make a difficult decision. When a pregnancy occurs that appears to cause the parent or parents hardship, we in the church should bring all our resources of compassion and support to their aid, including prayer and encouragement. We believe that continuance of a pregnancy that endangers the life or health of the mother, or poses other serious problems concerning the life, health, or mental capability of the child to be, is not a moral necessity. In such cases, we believe the path of mature Christian judgment may indicate the advisability of abortion. We support the legal right to abortion as established by the 1973 Supreme Court decision. We encourage women in counsel with husbands, doctors, and pastors to make their own responsible decisions concerning the personal and moral questions surrounding the issue of abortion (*see* ¶ 161J).

We therefore encourage our churches and common society to:

1. provide to all education on human sexuality and family life in its varying forms, including means of marriage enrichment, rights of children, responsible and joyful expression of sexuality, and changing attitudes toward male and female roles in the home and the marketplace;

2. provide counseling opportunities for married couples and those approaching marriage on the principles of responsible parenthood;

3. build understanding of the problems posed to society by the rapidly growing population of the world, and of the need to place personal decisions concerning childbearing in a context of the well-being of the community;

4. provide to each pregnant woman accessibility to comprehensive health care and nutrition adequate to ensure healthy children;

5. make information and materials available so all can exercise responsible choice in the area of conception controls. We support the free flow of information about reputable, efficient, and safe nonprescription contraceptive techniques through educational programs and through periodicals, radio, television, and other advertising media.

We support adequate public funding and increased participation in family planning services by public and private agencies, including church-related institutions, with the goal of making such services accessible to all, regardless of economic status or geographic location;

6. make provision in law and in practice for voluntary sterilization as an appropriate means, for some, for conception control and family planning;

7. safeguard the legal option of abortion under standards of sound medical practice;

8. make abortions available to women without regard to economic standards of sound medical practice, and make abortions available to women without regard to economic status;

9. monitor carefully the growing genetic and biomedical research, and be prepared to offer sound ethical counsel to those facing birth-planning decisions affected by such research;

10. assist the states to make provisions in law and in practice for treating as adults minors who have, or think they have, venereal diseases, or female minors who are, or think they are, pregnant, thereby eliminating the legal necessity for notifying parents or guardians prior to care and treatment. Parental support is crucially important and most desirable on such occasions, but needed treatment ought not be contingent on such support. This statement shall not be used to assert or imply that The United Methodist Church opposes any requirements, with or without exceptions, of parental notification for abortion procedures performed on girls who have not yet reached the age of legal adulthood;

11. understand the family as encompassing a wider range of options than that of the two-generational unit of parents and children (the nuclear family); and promote the development of all socially responsible and life-enhancing expressions of the extended family, including families with adopted children, single parents, those with no children, and those who choose to be single;

12. view parenthood in the widest possible framework, recognizing that many children of the world today desperately need functioning parental figures, and also understanding that adults can realize the choice and fulfillment of parenthood through adoption or foster care;

13. encourage men and women to actively demonstrate their responsibility by creating a family context of nurture and growth in which the children will have the opportunity to share in the mutual love and concern of their parents; and

14. be aware of the fears of many in poor and minority groups and in developing nations about imposed birth-planning, oppose any coercive use of such policies and services, and strive to see that family-planning programs respect the dignity of each individual person as well as the cultural diversities of groups.

ADOPTED 1976
AMENDED AND READOPTED 1996
READOPTED 2004
REVISED AND READOPTED 2008
RESOLUTION #25, 2004 *BOOK OF RESOLUTIONS*
RESOLUTION #22, 2000 *BOOK OF RESOLUTIONS*

*See* Social Principles, ¶ 161A, F, G, J.

## 2027. Gender-Selective Abortion

Gender-selective abortion—choosing abortion solely or primarily because of not preferring the unborn child's sex—is often practiced in several places in the world. Due to cultural biases, female fetuses are generally targeted for abortion in such cases much more often than males.

In the November 9, 2001, cover story of the Indian magazine, *Frontline*, Nobel Laureate Amartya Sen wrote that "sex-selective abortion" is "particularly prevalent in East Asia, in China and South Korea in particular, but also in Singapore and Taiwan, and it is beginning to emerge as a statistically significant phenomenon in India and South Asia as well."[1]

A 1998 study published by the Alan Guttmacher Institute, which was founded as a division of the Planned Parenthood Federation of America, also lists Thailand among the nations in which "sex selection is believed to play a role in abortion."[2]

Jyotsna Patro, an Indian delegate to the Asian Church Women's Conference and former president of the Church of North India Women's Fellowship, has recently reported that "[t]he callousness in

1. Amartya Sen, "Many Faces of Gender Inequality," *Frontline*, 9 November 2001; available from <http://www.flonnet.com/fl1822/18220040.htm>; Internet; accessed 20 August 2007.
2. Akinrinola Bankole, Susheela Singh and Taylor Haas, "Reasons Why Women Have Induced Abortions: Evidence from 27 Countries," *International Family Planning Perspectives* 24, no. 3 [September 1998]; available from: <http://www.guttmacher.org/pubs/journals/2411798.html>; accessed 20 August 2007.

allowing female feticide is worsening," with "[p]arents hav[ing] no qualms about aborting female fetuses."[3]

The widespread practice of sex-selective abortion is believed to be a main cause of the extremely skewed sex ratios at birth in India, where it was recently estimated that only 882 girls are born for every 1,000 boys, and China, where 832 girls are born for every 1,000 boys.[4]

While precise estimates vary, there are now tens of millions of "missing women" in the world thanks to sex-selective abortions. In India alone, about 10 million female fetuses are estimated to have been selectively aborted in the last two decades.[5] The Voice of America news service recently reported that "by the year 2020," China is expected to "have 30 million more men than women, making it difficult for many men to find wives."[6] Chinese population expert Chu Junhong has reported that "[p]renatal sex selection was probably the primary cause, if not the sole cause, for the continuous rise of the sex ratio at birth" in China since the implementation of that country's one-child policy. These growing gender imbalances are believed to exacerbate such problems as prostitution and human trafficking.[7] Furthermore, according to Dr. Therese Hesketh, a researcher at the University College London Institute of Child Health and co-author of

3. Anto Akkara, "Indian Christian Women Warn of Female Extinction from Feticide," Ecumenical News International, 26 July 2007; available from <http://www.eni.ch/featured/article.php?id=1077>; Internet; accessed 20 August 2007.

4. Raekha Prasad and Randeep Ramesh, "India's Missing Girls," Guardian [London], 28 February 2007; available from: <http://www.guardian.co.uk/india/story/0,,2022983,00.html>; Internet; accessed 20 August 2007. Cf. "China Riots Rooted in Child Policy, Financial Woes," Turkish Daily News, 2 June 2007.

5. Prasad and Ramesh; Cf. Neil Samson Katz and Marisa Sherry, "India: The Missing Girls," Background Facts and Links, PBS FRONTLINE/World "Rough Cut," 26 April 2007; available from: http://www.pbs.org/frontlineworld/rough/2007/04/the_missing_girlinks.html <http://www.pbs.org/frontlineworld/rough/2007/04/the_missing_gir.html>; Internet; accessed 20 August 2007.

6. Daniel Schearf, "China Acknowledges Family-planning Policy Affects Sex-Ratio Imbalance," Voice of America news, available from: <http://www.voanews.com/english/archive/2007-01/2007-01-23-voa18.cfm>; Internet; accessed 20 August 2007. Cf. Katharine Mieszkowski, "Millions of Lonely Would-Be Grooms in China," Salon.com, 12 January 2007; available from <http://www.salon.com/mwt/broadsheet/2007/01/12/china/index.html>; Internet; accessed 20 August 2007.

7. Eric Baculinao, "China Grapples with Legacy of its 'Missing Girls': Disturbing Demographic Imbalance Spurs Drive to Change Age-Old Practices," NBC News, 14 Sept 2004; available from <http://www.msnbc.msn.com/id/5953508>; Internet; accessed 17 August 2007. Cf. Prasad and Ramesh; Isabelle Attane, "The Boys Are Wanted, The Girls Aborted: Asia's Missing Women," trans. Krystyna Horko, Guardian Weekly [London], 11 August 2006, Le Monde Diplomatique section, p. 6.

a recent study on societal gender imbalances, this emergence of large numbers of young men unable to find wives "could lead to increased levels of antisocial behavior and violence."[8]

At the March 2007 meeting of the United Nation's Commission on the Status of Women, in New York, a resolution supported by South Korea, the United States, and others would have condemned sex-selective abortion and infanticide and encouraged steps to eliminate them. However, the resolution was ultimately not adopted.[9]

The United Methodist Social Principles affirm "[o]ur belief in the sanctity of unborn human life" and "unconditionally reject" abortion being used "as a means of gender selection" (¶ 161J). While the members of our denomination are not of one mind over the precise conditions in which abortion can be supported, we cannot support abortion for such trivial reasons as not preferring the gender of the fetus.

The widespread practice of sex-selective abortion horribly treats females as inferior before they are even born. This is absolutely contrary to The United Methodist Church's long history of championing the biblical principle of gender equality.

*Therefore, be it resolved*, that the General Conference of The United Methodist Church strongly condemns sex-selective abortion as a particularly lamentable and violent expression of sexism. We call on religious, government, and community leaders to proactively pursue humane means for stopping the practice of sex-selective abortion. The General Board of Church and Society is encouraged to seek out and take advantage of opportunities to make this concern of our church known to national leaders of the United States and of other nations.

8. "GENDER RESEARCH: Too Many Men Could Destabilize Society," *Biotech Week*, 20 September 2006, expanded reporting, p. 564. Cf. Baculinao; Prasad and Ramesh.
9. Andrea Mrozek, "A Recipe for Social Disaster," *Calgary Herald* [Alberta], 28 March 2007, p. A16.

**ADOPTED 2008**

*See* Social Principles, ¶ 161J.


## 2028. Putting Children and Their Families First

"We believe the family to be the basic human community through which persons are nurtured and sustained in mutual love, responsibility, respect and fidelity." Children are "acknowledged to be full human beings in their own right, but beings to whom adults and society in general have special obligations. All children have the right to quality education. Moreover, children have the rights to food, shelter, clothing, health care, and emotional well-being as do adults, and these rights we affirm as theirs regardless of actions or inactions of their parents or guardians. In particular, children must be protected from economic, physical, emotional, and sexual exploitation and abuse." (From Social Principles of The United Methodist Church in *The Book of Discipline*.)

## The Problem

Growing up whole and healthy is increasingly difficult for children. They face weakening support systems throughout society, from home to school to church, at the very time they are struggling with unprecedented stresses. They are forced to grow up too quickly, to make significant life choices at a younger and younger age.

The percentage of children in poverty is the most widely used indicator of child well-being. Growth in the ranks of poor children in the United States over the past few decades has not been due to an increase in the number of welfare-dependent families; rather, it is because the ranks of the working poor have been growing. For example, between 1976 and 2000, the number of children living in economically poor families who were totally dependent on welfare fell from 2.8 million to 1.1 million. At the same time, the number of children living in economically poor families who had income from jobs, but no financial public assistance, increased from 4.4 million to 6.9 million. A major reason for these discrepancies was a significant change in the way the US government provides public assistance to low- and no-income families. Despite the enormous wealth in the United States, the child poverty rate is among the highest in the developed world. (from "KIDS COUNT DATA BOOK 2002")

Globally, children are increasingly at risk from the effects of poverty. UNICEF reported, in its 2002 Annual Report, that "a child born today has a one-in-four chance of being born into poverty—a life of poor health, missed education and increased violence, insecurity and discrimination." Poverty inflicts irreparable damage on young bodies and minds. Nearly 11 million children under the age of five die each year from common illnesses and malnutrition associated with poverty. Poverty undermines the health, abilities and potential of millions more children.

*Public Policy Implications*

In light of the critical nature of the problems described above, The United Methodist Church should press for public polices that:

1. guarantee basic income for all families regardless of structure;

2. provide basic support services for families in economic crisis, including food and nutrition programs, crisis respite care, and home care services;

3. mandate full and complete access to health and medical care, including health maintenance, prenatal and well-baby services, and mental health services for all family members, including a highly under-served group: young children and teens;

4. assure safe and affordable housing for families without regard to number and ages of children; and

5. safeguard protective services for children at risk of abuse.

Too often we engage in public policy debate, make new laws and cut budgets and programs without putting the highest priority on how any change or policy will affect children and their families.

We call upon United Methodists to ask the following questions of any pending legislation, any budget cut, any new policy:

1. Are children's needs and well-being considered first and foremost in evaluating health and welfare, or any other national, state, or local policy?

2. Will this program or policy make fewer children poor or increase the likelihood of children growing up healthy, educated, and pre-pared to work and contribute to the future productivity of the economy?

3. Will this program or policy make families more self-sufficient, enabling parents to work by providing them with jobs and the tools of work (education and training, child care, health care, child support enforcement, before and after-school care)?

4. Will this program or policy support families in providing care, nurture, safety, and stability to children?

5. Will this program or policy help the many who have little rather than the few who have much?

6. Will this program or policy help families stay together and care for children?

7. Does this program or policy refrain from punishing children for the actions or inactions of their parents or guardians?

8. Will this program or policy actually save money in the long run,

rather than gain a shortsighted savings that leaves the next generation to pay the price?

9. Is this program or policy as fair to children as to adults, to women as to men, and to poor as to affluent families?

10. Will this program or policy provide young people with opportunities for a meaningful future, while celebrating the contributions they make in the present?

11. Will this program develop in children a sense of responsibility for themselves and their communities?

Legislators and other public leaders should be held accountable to citizens and voters for their answers to these questions and for the results of their actions.

### Church Program and Policy Implications

Churches must strengthen and expand their ministry and advocacy efforts on behalf of children and their families. A coordinated ministry that serves families with children in the congregations and in the larger community, that works hand-in-hand with human service providers and ecumenical colleagues, and that addresses the public policy concerns listed above is needed in every church and community.

The church has traditionally emphasized the integrity of the institutions of marriage and family and the responsibilities of parenthood. While these emphases should be maintained, a holistic ministry with families must, of necessity, be based on the broadest possible definition of family so that the great variety of structures and configurations will be included. Grandparents often function as parents, and many families are headed by single parents or "blended" through divorce and remarriage. Adoption, fostering, and extended family structures are among those that need the church's ministry.

Churches need to understand that all the problems described here happen to individuals and families inside the congregation as well as in the community. It is critically important that each congregation deal openly with the needs of its members and its community and begin developing appropriate ministry responses for children and their families. Support groups, hotlines, shelters, parenting classes, treatment programs. home care services, nutrition and feeding programs, and after-school tutoring and mentoring programs are especially needed in many communities; they are programs that churches are often well-suited to sponsor or support.

A network of child-serving institution and agencies, from community centers to residences for at-risk children and youth, exists across the church. Many are local expressions of national or international mission, and others are related to annual conferences. These agencies meet critical needs and urgently require the financial, volunteer, and prayer support of congregations.

The Council of Bishops, in its 2001 document on the Initiative on Children and Poverty, said that: "In a world constituted by division and competition, in which the gap between the rich and the poor widens like a yawning chasm and human life is reduced to a marketable commodity, while the impoverished majority of the earth becomes invisible to the prosperous few, it is the church that is called to be the visible and tangible presence of a community built upon grace."

*We Call upon The United Methodist Church to:*

1. generate a plan in every local church for assessing ministry with children (in the congregation and in the community) and implementing a vision for ministry with children and their families that takes seriously the facts and perspectives presented above. This plan is to be overseen by the official decision-making body of every local church. The manual Putting Children and Their Families First: A Planning Handbook for Congregations* can guide the process.

2. use the Bishops' Initiative on Children and Poverty manual Community with Children and the Poor: A Guide for Congregational Study* in every local church.

3. celebrate the Children's Sabbath in every local church each October. Utilize the resource manual* developed annually by the Children's Defense Fund.

4. increase awareness of the needs of children and their families by challenging the church's leaders (including bishops, general agency staff, director of connectional ministries, superintendents as well as local church clergy and lay leaders) to spend the equivalent of one full day each year as a volunteer at a local outreach ministry that serves children, such as a community center, child care center, tutoring or parenting program, or shelter for homeless families.

5. continue and strengthen a task force formed of persons from general church agencies who work on issues of child and family advocacy,

*Order from Service Center (1-800-305-9857).

in order to coordinate work. The task force will be convened annually by the Office of Children's Ministries of the General Board of Discipleship.

ADOPTED 2004
RESOLUTION #26, 2004 *BOOK OF RESOLUTIONS*

*See* Social Principles, ¶ 161A.

## 2029. Nurturing Marriage and Family

WHEREAS, according to the Social Principles of The United Methodist Church, "We believe the family to be the basic human community through which persons are nurtured and sustained in mutual love, responsibility, respect, and fidelity"; and

WHEREAS, we recognize that support from a faith community can help every family, no matter what its configuration, to more effectively provide safety, nurture growth, and sustain healthy relationships; and

WHEREAS, many families throughout our world today suffer because of poverty, inadequate health care, violence in the home, violence in their communities, lack of knowledge for developing healthy relationships, and inadequate resources for times of transition or crisis; and

WHEREAS, we recognize that healthy marriages have a positive impact on all members of a family; and

WHEREAS, we believe that United Methodist general agencies, annual conferences, and congregations can join together to strengthen and support marriages and families;

*Therefore, be it resolved,* that the 2004 General Conference of The United Methodist Church support efforts to nurture families and marriages.

1. We call upon pastors to take seriously the importance of premarital counseling for those seeking marriage.

2. We call upon congregations to offer classes and programs related to parenting, relationships, faith formation in the family, communication skills, conflict management, marriage preparation, marriage enrichment, and coping with crisis.

3. We call upon pastors and congregations to offer support and resources for families in all their various configurations.

4. We call upon annual conferences to assist congregations through the development, identification, and promotion of programs and resources for family ministries.

5. We call upon the General Board of Higher Education and Ministry to offer resources for clergy in marriage preparation and marriage enrichment and in developing healthy relationships within their own families.

6. We call upon seminaries to train clergy in marriage preparation, marriage counseling, and marriage enrichment.

7. We call upon the General Board of Church and Society to study state and federal legislation (both proposed and already in effect) related to strengthening marriages and families and to make recommendations to Boards of Church and Society in annual conferences regarding the possible impact of such legislation.

8. We call upon The United Methodist Publishing House to continue publication of materials in support of marriage, parenting, and family life.

9. We call upon the General Board of Discipleship to continue to develop, identify, and promote resources and materials for marriage and family ministries, including but not limited to the yearly development of resources for Christian Home Month.

**ADOPTED 2004**
**RESOLUTION #27, 2004** *BOOK OF RESOLUTIONS*

*See* Social Principles, ¶ 161A.

## HUMAN SEXUALITY

### 2041. Church to Be in Ministry to Persons of All Sexual Orientations

We affirm our belief in the inestimable worth of each individual because we are human beings created by God and loved through and by Jesus Christ, and we affirm all persons as equally valuable in the sight of God (Preamble to Social Principles). Baptism is God's gift of unmerited grace through the Holy Spirit and marks the entrance of persons into the church and its ministries of love, justice, and service (¶ 305, 2008 *Book of Discipline*), and we affirm that through baptism

God has made us members of one body of Christ so that all who follow Jesus have spiritual gifts to share for the common good (1 Corinthians 12:4-27). In addressing the nurturing function of Christian fellowship, our United Methodist Social Principles assert that human sexuality is a complex gift of which we have limited understanding (¶ 161F). We also believe that homosexual persons no less than heterosexual persons are individuals of sacred worth and that all persons need the ministry and guidance of the church in their struggles for human fulfillment, as well as the spiritual and emotional care of a fellowship that enables reconciling relationships with God, with others, and with self (¶ 161F). An individual confronting his or her own minority sexual orientation and/or that of a close family member, friend, or associate often experiences isolation, confusion, and fear when he or she needs information, guidance, and support ("Teens at Risk," 2000 *Book of Resolutions*); and we recognize that teens dealing with questions about sexual orientation are at a greater risk for suicide ("Teen Sexual Identity and Suicide Risk," 2004 and 2008 *Book of Resolutions*). The teachings and actions of Jesus demonstrated radical inclusion of those rejected by mainstream society, we are called to renew our commitment to become faithful witnesses to the gospel, not alone to the ends of the earth, but also the depths of our common life and work (Preamble to the Social Principles).

*Therefore, be it resolved,* that The United Methodist Church dedicate itself to a ministry of Christ-like hospitality and compassion to persons of all sexual orientations, and to a vision of unity through openness to the spiritual gifts of all those who have been baptized into the Body of Jesus Christ. Such ministry and openness may include: welcoming sexual minorities, their friends, and families into our churches and demonstrating our faith in a loving God; a willingness to listen and open our hearts to their stories and struggles in our churches, districts, annual conferences, and General Conference; encouraging study and dialogue around issues of sexuality; and praying for all those who are in pain and discord over our Christian response to this controversial issue.

ADOPTED 2000
AMENDED AND READOPTED 2008
RESOLUTION #33, 2004 *BOOK OF RESOLUTIONS*
RESOLUTION #28, 2000 *BOOK OF RESOLUTIONS*

*See* Social Principles, ¶ 161F.

## 2042. Report of the Task Force on Homosexuality and the Unity of the Church

WHEREAS, The United Methodist Church has struggled for many years over the issue of homosexuality, and

WHEREAS, the General Commission on Christian Unity and Interreligious Concerns (GCCUIC) remains committed to pursuing unity within the church as a gift and calling of God, and

WHEREAS, the 2000 General Conference directed the GCCUIC to lead the church in dialogue on issues related to homosexuality and the unity of the church (Resolution Number 29, *Book of Resolutions 2000*, page 134), and

WHEREAS, the 2000 General Conference directed the GCCUIC to report on this work within The United Methodist Church; and

WHEREAS, the GCCUIC has been privileged to listen to the hopes, fears, concerns, and suggestions of hundreds of persons across The United Methodist Church, and

WHEREAS, the GCCUIC has worked to create open, grace-filled spaces for persons with contending viewpoints to learn to know each other authentically, to explore divergent understandings through prayerful and civil dialogue, and whenever possible, to experience healing and reconciliation, and has developed models that promote this kind of grace-filled and civil dialogue, and

WHEREAS, the GCCUIC has employed these models to engage the Council of Bishops, the General Council on Ministries, representatives of the five national racial/ethnic caucuses of The United Methodist Church, as well as youth and young adults in productive conversations; and has developed resources for dialogue in local churches, districts, and annual conferences, and

WHEREAS, the GCCUIC was directed by the 2000 General Conference to forgo any advocacy on this issue at the 2004 General Conference related to the position or language of *The Book of Discipline*,

*Therefore, be it resolved*, that the 2004 General Conference of The United Methodist Church receives the report of the Task Force on Homosexuality and the Unity of the Church of the GCCUIC and commends the report to the whole Church, and

*Be it further resolved*, that the 2004 General Conference encourages further dialogue throughout The United Methodist Church designed with worship at the center to lead to greater understanding, love, and care for each other, and with the hope that our struggles with these concerns will take a more civil character to the benefit of us all.

ADOPTED 2004
RESOLUTION #35, 2004 *BOOK OF RESOLUTIONS*

*See* Social Principles, ¶ 161F.

## 2043. Opposition to Homophobia and Heterosexism

WHEREAS, homophobia[1] is the discrimination of people perceived to be nonheterosexual, regardless of the victim's actual sexual orientation or sexual identity; and

WHEREAS, heterosexism[2] is a self-justifying system of homophobia that:

1) perpetuates stereotypical categories of what is essentially "masculine" and what is essentially "feminine";

2) provides a privileged status for people who identify as culturally defined heterosexuals; and

3) discriminates against persons who, regardless of their sexual orientation or sexual identity, do not appear to fit within the particular category defined as appropriate for their gender; and

WHEREAS, actions rooted in homophobia and heterosexism, including violence, threats, ridicule, humiliation, discrimination, isolation, and rejection, are damaging to persons of all sexual orientations and identities; and

WHEREAS, homophobia and heterosexism are manifestations of sexism in general in that they foster stereotypes based on arbitrary distinctions of gender categories; and

WHEREAS, The United Methodist Church is committed to the eradication of sexism (#3444, 2008 *Book of Resolutions*);

1. Homophobia, A commonly used definition from the *American Heritage Dictionary* (1992): "Fear or contempt for lesbians and gay men."
2. Heterosexism, A commonly used definition from the *American Heritage Dictionary* (1992): "Discrimination or prejudice against lesbians or gay men by heterosexual people."

*Therefore, be it resolved,* that The United Methodist Church strengthen its advocacy of the eradication of sexism by opposing all forms of violence or discrimination based on gender, gender identity, sexual practice, or sexual orientation; and

*Be it further resolved,* that the General Board of Church and Society provide resources and materials aimed at educating members of the local churches about the reality, issues, and effects of homophobia and heterosexism and the need for Christian witness against these facets of marginalization.

**ADOPTED 2008**

*See* Social Principles, ¶ 161G and *I*.

## 2044. Sexual Misconduct Within Ministerial Relationships

The abuse of power occurs when we use power to gratify our own needs rather than to carry out God's sacred trust. It happens when we refuse to own the responsibility of guardianship that comes with the privilege of power . . . until we understand that power is the responsibility to give, instead of the opportunity to take, we will continue to abuse it."[1]

"There is little doubt that sexual misconduct in church and society is significant and troubling for our communities and congregations worldwide. This unwanted behavior damages the moral environment where people worship, minister, work, and learn. In 1996, the General Conference made a commitment to focus on sexual misconduct within the church and took action to address this brokenness and pain within The United Methodist Church." (*The Book of Resolutions, 1996*, p. 128; *2000*, p. 135; *2004*, p. 150)

### Sacred Trust, Power, and responsibility

*The Book of Discipline,* ¶ 161F, declares all human beings have equal worth in the eyes of God. As the promise of Galatians 3:26-29 states, "all are one in Christ"; therefore, we as United Methodists support equity among all persons without regard to ethnicity, situation, or gender. In our congregations and settings for ministry, we seek to

1. Ann Smith, *Alive Now*, Sept./Oct. 1996.

create an environment of hospitality for all persons, male or female, which is free from misconduct of a sexual nature and encourages respect, equality, and kinship in Christ.

Those in positions of authority in the church, both clergy and lay, have been given much responsibility, vested with a sacred trust to maintain an environment that is safe for people to live and grow in God's love. Misconduct of a sexual nature inhibits the full and joyful participation of all in the community of God. Sexual misconduct in church and ministry settings impedes the mission of Jesus Christ. Ministerial leaders have the responsibility not only to avoid actions and words which hurt others, but also to protect the vulnerable against actions or words which cause harm.

As our children, youth, and adults come to worship, study, camps, retreats, and schools of mission, they bring a heightened awareness of the issues of sexual abuse, sexual harassment, incest, rape, and sexual assault. Ministerial leaders have the responsibility not only to avoid actions and words that hurt others, but also to protect the vulnerable against actions or words that cause harm. In the safety and sanctity of the church's settings, we as church leaders, both clergy and lay, paid and volunteer, must be held to the highest standard of conduct as we lead, provide guidance and support, and work with children, youth, and adults in ministry settings. Sexual misconduct in any form is a violation of the membership and ordination vows we take as laity and clergy in The United Methodist Church. Sexual abuse, sexual misconduct, and sexual harassment are chargeable offenses both for clergy and laity per *The Book of Discipline*, ¶ 2702.

## Definitions

Sexual misconduct is a betrayal of sacred trust. It is a continuum of unwanted sexual or gender-directed behaviors by either a lay or clergy person within a ministerial relationship (paid or unpaid). It can include child abuse, adult sexual abuse, harassment, rape or sexual assault, sexualized verbal comments or visuals, unwelcome touching and advances, use of sexualized materials including pornography, stalking, sexual abuse of youth or those without capacity to consent, or misuse of the pastoral or ministerial position using sexualized conduct to take advantage of the vulnerability of another. In includes criminal behaviors in some nations, states, and communities.

Sexual harassment is a form of sexual misconduct and is defined in ¶ 161*I* in the Social Principles. To clarify further, it is unwanted sexual or gender-directed behavior within a pastoral, employment, ministerial (including volunteers), mentor, or colleague relationship that is so severe or pervasive that it alters the conditions of employment or volunteer work or unreasonably interferes with the employee or volunteer's performance by creating a hostile environment that can include unwanted sexual jokes, repeated advances, touching, displays, or comments that insult, degrade, or sexually exploit women, men, elders, children, or youth.

Sexual abuse is a form of sexual misconduct and occurs when a person within a ministerial role of leadership (lay or clergy, pastor, educator, counselor, youth leader, or other position of leadership) engages in sexual contact or sexualized behavior with a congregant, client, employee, student, staff member, coworker, or volunteer (1996 *Book of Resolutions*, p. 130). It can include coerced or forced sexual contact (including those unable to give informed consent), sexual interaction or contact with children or youth, and sexual exhibitionism or display of sexual visuals or pornography.

Sexualized behavior is behavior that communicates sexual interest and/or content. Examples include, but are not limited to displaying sexually suggestive visual materials; use of pornography in church programs on or with church property, making sexual comments or innuendo about one's own or another person's body; touching another person's body; touching another person's body/hair/clothing; touching or rubbing oneself in the presence of another person; kissing; and sexual intercourse. Sexualized behavior can be a form of sexual misconduct when this behavior is unwanted by the recipient or witness, is a violation of society's or the Church's law, breaks the sacred trust in the ministerial role, or violates the vows taken at membership or ordination.

The continuum of behaviors called sexual misconduct within the ministerial relationship represents an *exploitation of power* and not merely "inappropriate sexual or gender-directed conduct." Sexual misconduct in any form is unacceptable in church and ministry settings whether it is clergy-to-lay, lay-to-clergy, clergy-to-clergy, lay-to-lay, staff-to-staff, staff-to-volunteer, volunteer-to-volunteer, or volunteer-to-staff. Anyone who works or volunteers under the authority or auspices of the Church must be held to the highest standards of behavior, free of sexual misconduct in any form.

*Those in Ministerial Roles*

Both laity and clergy fill ministerial roles in our Church. In addition to clergy or professional staff, any United Methodist may fill a ministerial role by participating in ministries including, but not limited to:

- leading and participating in lay speaking ministries;
- counseling or leading events for children, youth, and adults;
- teaching and leading in church schools for children, youth, and adults;
- counseling victims of violence, domestic violence, or sexual abuse;
- counseling couples about marriage, divorce, or separation;
- leading in worship as speaker from the pulpit, liturgist, communion server, or usher;
- volunteering to chaperone trips, work camps, or special events;
- working in Walks to Emmaus and Chrysalis retreats;
- mentoring;
- supervising church staff members; and
- working with computers, Web sites, and the internet in church property/programs.

*Progress and Troubling Trends*

The General Conference not only has mandated adoption of policies in our churches, conferences, agencies, and schools, it called for training, advocacy practices, and surveys of progress as a denomination conducted by the General Commission on the Status and Role of Women.

Now twenty years after General Conference first committed to the elimination of sexual misconduct in the Church (1988), good work has been done:

- Thirty-five annual conferences now assign oversight of sexual misconduct issues to a "team";
- Many conferences require sexual misconduct awareness training for all clergy, lay leadership, and appointees;
- The General Commission on the Status and Role of Women has provided support and counsel to victims and church officials in hundreds of cases.

Work remains to be done. Recent findings show the experiences of leadership of the Church on many levels—local church, seminary, annual and general conferences in particular:

- Awareness of the denomination's policy on sexual misconduct is high, but awareness of the resources for victims and congregations is much lower;
- Harassment is still a significant problem: well over three-fourths of the clergy (men and women) and half of the lay-women had experienced sexual harassment in the Church (about one third of laymen);
- Holding offenders accountable, removing errant pastors, lay staff, or volunteers as needed, and requiring counseling, training, and supervision before resumption of ministerial roles are remedial steps our episcopal and superintending leaders should use;
- Follow-up on situations of misconduct so that appropriate and effective remediation is achieved so that the behavior stops, does not reoccur, and relationships and ministry are returned to wholeness as much as possible;
- Placing justice for victims above protection of offenders, including pastors, is an equally pressing need;
- With this global *internet age* and the growing use of computers by clergy and laity has come more frequent reports of the use of pornography and sexualized materials by laity and clergy within church programs or with church computers or property.

Progress in four areas is not adequate: prevention, education, intervention, and healing. Additional work is now needed:

1. resources for various constituencies addressing prevention, education, intervention, and healing after lay or clergy sexual misconduct (including the United Methodist Web site on sexual etthics—www.umsexualethics.org);

2. updated training (initial, follow-up, and advanced) for the various constituencies within the church, *including education on the prevention of the use of pornography, its destructive impact on users, and its potential for abuse in or with church programs or property;*

3. implementation of models for intervention and healing in order to provide a consistent and thorough response when complaints are initiated;

4. development of a model for ongoing assessment of policies, practices, and responses of conferences;

5. appropriate handling of the presence and involvement of legally convicted sexual offenders in local congregational activities and ministry;

6. opportunities for annual conferences to share their resources and experience.[2]

*Therefore be it resolved,* that The United Methodist Church renews its stand in opposition to the sin of sexual misconduct within the Church worldwide. It further recommits all United Methodists to the eradication of sexual misconduct in all ministerial relationships, and calls for:

1. the General Commission on the Status and Role of Women to continue to convene and coordinate a cooperative interagency group to address the areas of prevention, education, intervention, and healing including a representative of the Council of Bishops, the General Boards of Discipleship, Higher Education and Ministry, Global Ministries, Church and Society, the General Council on Finance and Administration, the Division on Ministries with Young People, and representatives of annual conference Response/Crisis Teams and Safe Sanctuary Teams (each agency member responsible for his or her own expenses and a share of the expenses of the annual conference representatives);

2. the General Commission on the Status and Role of Women be provided resources sufficient to develop/distribute resources for leaders of lay events and programs within the church in order to help train and equip them to raise this important issue with laity (including lay speakers, lay leaders, Christian educators, persons in mission, leaders in Schools of Christian Mission, Walks to Emmaus, Chrysalis, and leaders of events with young people;

3. the General Commission on the Status and Role of Women, through the interagency group, to ensure that resources for laity and clergy in ministerial roles are identified and promoted for use in conferences, districts or clusters, and local congregations;

4. the Council of Bishops to reaffirm its commitment to preventing and eradicating sexual harassment, abuse, and misconduct in the church through education, training, and sharing of resources. Each episcopal area will implement policies, procedures, and ongoing plans to coordinate persons involved in prevention and intervention, including but not limited to: district superintendents, boards of ordained

2. For more information, see the United Methodist Web site on Sexual Ethics, www.umsexualethics.org.

ministry, boards of laity, advocates, intervention and healing teams, trained mediators, and staff-parish relations committees;

5. United Methodist-related schools of theology to provide training on the prevention and eradication of sexual harassment, abuse, and misconduct within the ministerial relationship;

6. annual conference boards of ordained ministry to provide education (entry level, follow-up, advanced) for all appointed clergy, local pastors, and commissioned members. Annual conferences are also encouraged to provide similar education and training for those employed in ministerial leadership;

7. episcopal areas to require that all clergy, local pastors, assigned laity, and commissioned members appointed in each annual conference have regular, up-to-date sexual ethics training to be in good standing for appointment;

8. the General Board of Church and Society to continue to advocate for just laws that address or counter sexual harassment and abuse in our larger societies.

ADOPTED 1996<br>
REVISED AND READOPTED 2000<br>
REVISED AND READOPTED 2004<br>
REVISED AND READOPTED 2008<br>
RESOLUTION #36, 2004 *BOOK OF RESOLUTIONS*<br>
RESOLUTION #30, 2000 *BOOK OF RESOLUTIONS*

*See* Social Principles, ¶ 161*I*.

## 2045. Eradication of Sexual Harassment in The United Methodist Church and Society

Since the mid 1970s when the term "sexual harassment" was first recognized, the world has seen an evolution in awareness, laws and litigation, policies, advocacy, and international collaboration to eradicate sexual harassment in the workplace. In our own communities we have moved from debating whether or not sexual harassment is even a problem to witnessing women and men join together across national boundaries to address it in global settings, churches and ministries, and multinational workplaces.

Since the 1990s, sexual harassment is a recognized form of sexual violence and misconduct in our societies and in The United Methodist Church. The Church declared sexual harassment a sin against individuals and communities, and a chargeable offense against our clergy or laity. Critical to our understanding of the impact of harassment is the recognition that it is certainly an abuse of power over another, not only inappropriate sexual or gender-directed conduct.

## Definitions

Beginning with the continuum of behaviors that includes sexual harassment: Sexual misconduct is a betrayal of sacred trust. It is a continuum of unwanted sexual or gender-directed behaviors by either a lay or clergy person within a ministerial relationship (paid or unpaid). It can include child abuse, adult sexual abuse, harassment, rape or sexual assault, sexualized verbal comments or visuals, unwelcome touching and advances, use of sexualized materials including pornography, stalking, sexual abuse of youth or those without capacity to consent, or misuse of the pastoral or ministerial position using sexualized conduct to take advantage of the vulnerability of another. It includes criminal behaviors in some nations, states, or communities.

Sexual harassment is a form of sexual misconduct. The Social Principles define it as "any unwanted sexual comment, advance or demand, either verbal or physical, that is reasonably perceived by the recipient as demeaning, intimidating, or coercive. Sexual harassment must be understood as an exploitation and abuse of a power relationship rather than as an exclusively sexual issue. Sexual harassment includes, but is not limited to, the creation of a hostile or abusive working environment resulting from discrimination on the basis of gender" (¶ 161I).

To clarify further, it is unwanted sexual or gender-directed behavior within a pastoral, employment, ministerial (including volunteers), mentor, or colleague relationship that is so severe or pervasive that it alters the conditions of employment or volunteer work or unreasonable interferes with the employee or volunteer's performance. It can create a hostile, offensive environment that can include unwanted sexual jokes, repeated advances, touching, displays, or comments that insult, degrade, or sexually exploit women, men, elders, children, or youth.

Generally, anyone can be a target and anyone can harass—women, men, youth, interns, volunteers, all racial/ethnic groups, any level of employee, clergy, or laity. In the learning place, it affects any student of either gender, any grade, any teacher or professional, or any volunteer.

Businesses, governments, congregations, and organizations lose significant human and financial resources when harassment is permitted to devastate workers, customers, or members. It damages self-esteem, productivity, and ability to minister or earn wages. It can result in illness, absenteeism, poor performance, loss of promotions and opportunities. For students it can result in failure, absenteeism, isolation from peers, loss of self-esteem and learning potential, withdrawal from teams and groups, and illness. Families of the harassed and others in work, worship, and learning places are also victims of the hostile, intimidating environment harassment creates.

## Harassment in the Church

In the church, harassment can occur between a staff person, pastor, committee or council chairperson, church school teacher or helper, student, camper, counselor, youth worker, volunteer, or chaperone, paid or unpaid. It can happen on the bus to camp, in a youth group or Bible study, on a church computer or in choir rehearsal. The devastating effects on persons when it happens in a faith community jeopardize spiritual life, theological meaning, and relationships. For some, the loss of a sense of safety and sanctuary can permanent.

In 1990, the General Council on Ministries released the study mandated by General Conference in 1988 examining sexual harassment in The UMC. Then, half of the clergy, 20 percent of laity, nearly half of students, and 37 percent of church staff had had an experience of harassment in a church setting. Nearly 20 years ago we had much work go do to eradicate this form of sexual misconduct and violence.

For quadrennial later, good work has been done toward the elimination of sexual harassment in the Church. Thirty-five annual conferences now assign oversight of harassment issues to a "team," and many conferences require sexual misconduct awareness training for all clergy. Since the General Conference mandated sexual harassment policies in 1996, more and more churches of every size continue to report policies in place (in 2007: 34 percent of smallest and 86 percent of largest membership congregations have policies—up from 9 percent and 36 percent, respectively, in 1995). The General Commission on the Status and Role of Women has provided support and counsel to victims and church officials in hundreds of cases.

But the most recent surveys of our progress in eradicating sexual harassment (2005 and 2007[1]) are very troubling: sexual harassment remains a significant problem for women and men, lay and clergy in our church settings, programs, and with church property (including computers and the Internet):

1. Awareness of the denomination's policy on sexual harassment is relatively high (higher among clergy than laity), but awareness of the resources for victims and congregations is much lower.

2. While every local congregation is required to have a policy and procedure on sexual misconduct, including sexual harassment, in 2007 only 34 percent of small and 86 percent of largest membership churches report that they do.

3. Ninety percent of pastors have attended at least one sexual ethics training, but only one of four pastors has attended supplementary training.

4. More than three-fourths of the clergywomen and half of the laywomen had experienced sexual harassment in the Church (only a third of laymen had); the most commonly reported settings were church meetings and offices, and workplaces and social gatherings at seminary.

5. Perpetrators are most often men and increasingly laypersons in the local church. Clergy commit over a third of reported offenses. A significant change since the 1990 study was significant increases in the number of laity harassing laity, and laity harassing clergy.

6. Local churches were most likely to trivialize reports/complaints while seminaries and UM offices were more likely to result in action against offenders.

7. Personal friends and relatives were most helpful to victims, while district superintendents, personnel officers, and seminary administrators were among the least helpful.

8. The most lasting negative effects were inability to work with the offender, emotional impacts, and worsened feelings about self and the church.

9. Smaller membership churches need resources and training specifically developed for their unique settings and dynamics.

In The United Methodist Church, constant vigilance is needed to keep effective, updated policies and procedures in all places in the church. Regular training of our lay and clergy leaders is a a critical

1. "Sexual Harassment in The United Methodist Church 2005," and the "Quadrennial Local Church Survey 2007," by the General Commission on the Status and Role of Women," Chicago, Illinois, Gail Murphy-Geiss, Principal Investigator.

ongoing ministry of our church, with focus on the troubling use of "cyber-sex" (sexualized material in telecommunications) in church programs, with church property, or on church premises.

In 2006, a significant national symposium addressing sexual misconduct in The United Methodist Church, "Do No Harm," was held. At that critical event, participants asked episcopal leaders to focus on clergy training, lay leadership training, and early intervention with problem clergy. Advocacy and intervention teams have been working in many conferences but not all, and every episcopal area needs to maintain working, effective channels and procedures. We need and are grateful for strong episcopal leadership across the Church who maintain our achievements and forcefully address existing barriers to a harassment-free denomination.

### A Vision of God's Hospitable Community

Sexual harassment destroys community. This alienating, sinful behavior causes brokenness in relationships—the opposite of God's intention for us. From the first biblical stories of human community in the garden to the letters of Paul to the first Christian communities, we learn that all of us, both female and male, are created in the image of God, and thus have been made equal in Christ. We are called to be stewards of God's community of hospitality where there is not only an absence of harassment, but also the presence of welcome, respect, and equality.

*Therefore,* the General Conference calls for intensified efforts worldwide to eradicate sexual harassment in the denomination and its institutions including these strategies:

1. Episcopal leaders implement plans to address and eradicate sexual harassment in each episcopal area including regular, updated training of clergy, early intervention with problem clergy, and regular training of lay man and women, especially in smaller membership churches;

2. The General Commission on the Status and Role of Women, in collaboration with appropriate agencies (including the General Board of Discipleship's Safe Sanctuaries ministry), continue to develop and distribute resources to reduce the risk of abuse in local churches and increase United Methodists' understanding and action on sexual harassment in church and society;

3. The General Board of Higher Education and Ministry, in collaboration with appropriate agencies, develop and distribute resources on sexual harassment specific to those in ordained ministry and to lay

leaders, students, faculty, and administrators of United Methodist-related educational institutions;

4. Annual conferences throughout the connection will encourage their local and national governments to collect accurate data on the incidence and nature of sexual harassment in their workplaces, and encourage their national governments to adopt laws, policies, and procedures for eradicating sexual harassment;

5. The General Commission on the Status and Role of Women continue to monitor and assess the church's progress in eradicating sexual harassment and will report to the 2012 General Conference on the specific areas to be strengthened within the life of the Church including policy development, prevention, education, and training;

6. The General Board of Church and Society and the General Board of Global Ministries advocate for laws that prohibit sexual harassment in US workplaces, and continue to provide resources to the denomination on international initiatives to eradicate harassment and other forms of violence against women;

7. The General Commission on Christian Unity and Interreligious Concerns work cooperatively with the World Council of Churches "Decade to Overcome Violence" (2001-2010); and

8. The General Commission on the Status and Role of Women continue to conduct assessments of The United Methodist Church's progress to eradicate this behavior from the Church worldwide.

For more information and resources, see Resolution "Sexual Misconduct Within Ministerial Relationships" (#2044) and the original text of this resolution in *The Book of Resolutions, 2004*, p. 155.

ADOPTED 1992
REVISED AND ADOPTED 2000 AND 2008
RESOLUTION #37, 2004 *BOOK OF RESOLUTIONS*
RESOLUTION #31, 2000 *BOOK OF RESOLUTIONS*

*See* Social Principles, ¶ 161I.

## 2046. Rights of All Persons

A portion of the world's population is gay, lesbian, bisexual, and transgender (GLBT). Around the world, political and religious institutions have targeted GLBT persons for discrimination in housing, employment, health care, and access to redress for such discrimination. Some falsely portray the basic human rights laws that protect GLBT persons from hate crimes as unfair "legal preference."

It is particularly disturbing when religious values are used to justify persecution of select groups. Christians proclaim that all people are God's children deserving the protection of their human and civil rights. Our Social Principles gives us clear direction in this matter:

We insist that all persons, regardless of age, gender, marital status, or sexual orientation, are entitled to have their human and civil rights ensured (¶ 161F).

The rights and privileges a society bestows upon or withholds from those who comprise it indicate the relative esteem in which that society holds particular persons and groups of persons. We affirm all persons as equally valuable in the sight of God. We therefore work toward societies in which each person's value is recognized, maintained, and strengthened (¶ 162).

*Therefore,* all United Methodists are called upon:

1. to refrain from signing petitions and to vote against measures that advocate the denial of basic human and civil rights to anyone;

2. to educate congregation and community alike about the position of the United Methodist *Discipline* on civil rights and its broad applications; and

3. to stand against any political or physical acts that deny human and civil rights and the sacred worth of all persons.

4. to advocate for initiatives which would prohibit job and housing discrimination based on sexual orientation and gender identity throughout the world; and

5. to advocate for initiatives which provide for extra penalties for crimes which are expressly committed for the purpose of harming someone based solely on their race, color, national origin, religion, sexual orientation, gender identity, gender, or disability.

*Therefore, be it resolved,* that the General Board of Church and Society develop education tools designed to provide for open and healthy dialogue and understanding of sexuality in the world with the specific goal of protecting the human and civil rights of gay, lesbian, bisexual and transgender persons.

We do this as part of our Christian witness and ministry. Never let it be said that United Methodists were silent during this attack on the rights of all.

ADOPTED 1996
AMENDED AND READOPTED 2004
RESOLUTION #50, 2004 *BOOK OF RESOLUTIONS*
RESOLUTION #42, 2000 *BOOK OF RESOLUTIONS*

*See* Social Principles, ¶ 161F and ¶ 162A and J.

## INTOLERANCE/TOLERANCE

### 2061. Being the Church Amid Disagreement

To the people called United Methodists, with the hope that through prayer and holy conferencing, we will engage each other in love and grace as we deal with issues upon which we disagree:

As a church facing a new millennium we continue to disagree, sometimes bitterly. Important biblical, theological, and scientific questions remain in dispute among persons of good will. Called as United Methodists to be vigilant on issues of inclusiveness, we reflect on the process of disagreement. When we engage in deeply felt struggles for the truth, emotions run high. Our human nature moves us to yearn for "victory"—for winning the debate, making judgment in hopes it will settle the controversy that causes us discomfort and pain as a community. In prolonged disagreement, we may find ourselves stepping on the feelings of others in our urgency to find the true, winning position. We remind ourselves as a community of faith to remember who we are, how we are perceived by both civil and religious communities when we disagree, and what we have called ourselves to be as a church.

*Our Calling*

In "Called to Inclusiveness" (¶ 139, 2008 *Book of Discipline*), we hold ourselves accountable to this call: "We recognize that God made all creation and saw that it was good. As a diverse people of God who bring special gifts and evidences of God's grace to the unity of the church and to society, we are called to be faithful to the example of Jesus' ministry to all persons."

We can heed this call to value all of God's creation as good, and all of God's children as capable of bringing special gifts to our church and to society: gifts of engaged listening, careful feedback during disagreement, and suspension of judgment and retribution. The diverse people of God do not always agree. But if we heed this call to value all of God's creation, we show our world how to disagree in remarkable and loving ways.

*How Shall We Disagree?*

How we disagree, more so than which position prevails, has a powerful impact on many audiences: young people and children, local congregations, community and national leaders, and those targeted by our disagreements. As caring Christians, we carry responsibility for this impact whether or not we are aware of it.

### Power of a Discerning question

In the midst of engaged debate, our ability to listen to one another can weaken. True listening, hearing feelings as well as ideas, can be enhanced when we focus on discerning one another's positions on matters of importance. Questions that might help us do this are:

1. How can we show hospitality to one another while we disagree?

2. What hopes and interests do we have in common?

3. Can we temporarily suspend decision-making in order, through prayer, silence, and study, to discern and deepen our understanding of all positions on the issue?

4. Until we can agree on a resolution, can we agree to suspend motions, decisions, policy development that will assert one position over the other?

5. What are the positive and negative effects of our disagreement on our congregations, our members, our clergy and laity, and on the communities where we serve?

6. What action as a community of faith should we take in light of these effects?

7. What would we like the nature of our church or community to be when this issue that divides us is finally resolved?

### Ministry of Mindfulness

Local congregations, study groups, cabinets, clusters and districts, annual, central and General Conferences can be holy and hopeful places of discord. Regardless of our positions on controversial issues, we can practice a ministry of mindfulness of the impact of our discord. These strategies may be helpful in these settings:

1. Begin by sharing and studying relevant Scripture, our primary authority, and the additional aspects of the Wesleyan quadrilateral—tradition, reason, and experience.

2. Share where we agree.

3. Remember to honor our relationships to each other as children of God.

4. Practice the art of "feedback," true feedback in which positions are heard and repeated back.

5. Emphasize the "spiritual discipline of true listening"—attending and listening for the feelings of the others as well as their ideas.

6. Use facilitators or mediators to maintain safe spaces for difficult feelings and ideas to be shared.

7. Be mindful not to attack the messenger when discussing the message.

8. Use principles of mediation, focusing on interests (what we would like to happen, how we would envision things to be) rather than the positions we take to get there.

9. Practice "holy conferencing" —infusing debate and dialogue with prayer, silence, and more prayer. Pray for each other, for our church, for future possibilities, for hope and reconciliation, and for guidance of the Holy Spirit as we move through discord.

10. Pray for and practice the discipline of patience. Forging new understandings and agreements will take intentional effort.

ADOPTED 2000
AMENDED AND READOPTED 2008
RESOLUTION #32, 2004 *BOOK OF RESOLUTIONS*
RESOLUTION #27, 2000 *BOOK OF RESOLUTIONS*

*See* Social Principles, ¶ 161.


# PORNOGRAPHY


## 2081. Pornography and Sexual Violence

Throughout the Bible, themes exist that highlight the imperfect nature of humanity and the hope for redemption through our relationship as God's children held in God's loving arms. The Old Testament laws of purity invite an understanding of the body created in God's image and accountable to God through right relationship. Christ shared with us a vision of the world that confirms our vulnerability and affirms sacred personhood. Jesus Christ provides a path to a loving and protective relationship with God and with others; treating our neighbors and families with love thereby fostering healthy physical and emotional relationships. John Wesley described the path to right relationship with God toward achieving invitation into God's kingdom as a journey toward Christian perfection. We struggle mightily throughout life to move toward that vision of Christian perfection in an imperfect world.

In the midst of our imperfect world we grieve at actions of sexual exploitation and pornography. Our Social Principles declare that, "We deplore all forms of commercialization, abuse, and exploitation of sex. We call for strict global enforcement of laws prohibiting sexual exploitation of children and for adequate protection, guidance, and counseling for abused children. All persons, regardless of age, gender, marital status, or sexual orientation, are entitled to have their human and civil rights ensured and to be protected against violence. The Church should support the family in providing age-appropriate education regarding sexuality to children, youth, and adults."

The issue of pornography has undergone a dramatic change over the past two decades, one that shifts the definition, increases the complexity, and requires a new level of discussion. The use of violent, aggressive themes accompanying sexually explicit material has continued to increase. Television, the Internet, and emerging wireless technologies have made sexually aggressive media widely available, particularly to children and youth. Pornography is frequently relied upon as a source of information about sexuality. The church is called to lead society in articulating an ethic that affirms God's good gift of human sexuality and that protects the vulnerable from sexual violence and coercion.

Common understandings of pornography no longer serve us well. Some of us may believe pornography is a social evil because it is sexual, while others may defend pornography as a universal right to freedom of expression because it is sexual. Yet the truth is that pornography is not about sexuality; it is about violence, degradation, exploitation, and coercion.

While there is not widespread agreement on definitions, the following are suggested as the basis for dialogue:

Pornography is sexually explicit material that portrays violence, abuse, coercion, domination, humiliation, or degradation for the purpose of arousal. In addition, any sexually explicit material that depicts children is pornographic.

The impact of pornography on behavior is difficult to measure. While there is little evidence that consuming pornography causes an individual to commit a specific act of sexual aggression, several studies suggest that such consumption is addictive and may predispose an individual to sexual offenses, and that it supports and encourages sexual offenders to continue and escalate their violent and abusive behavior. Few dispute the fact that a society that supports multibillion dollar industries promoting sexual violence as entertainment and portraying the abuse and torture of women and children in a sexual context is a society in trouble.

"Pornography, by its very nature, is an equal opportunity toxin. It damages the viewer, the performer, and the spouses and the children of the viewers and the performers. It is a distortion of power and fosters an unhealthy understanding about sex and relationships. It is more toxic the more you consume, the "harder" the variety you consume and the younger and more vulnerable the consumer. The damage is both in the area of beliefs and behaviors. The belief damage may include Pornography Distortion, Permission-Giving Beliefs and the attitudes about what constitutes a healthy sexual and emotional relationship. The behavioral damage includes psychologically unhealthy behaviors, socially inappropriate behaviors and illegal behaviors."[1]

Pornography is inextricably linked to the oppression of women. Its appeal will continue as long as sexual arousal is stimulated by images of power and domination of one person over another, most often male over female. Pornography is also fundamentally linked to racism; women of color are invariably portrayed in the most violent and degrading ways. The destructive power of pornography lies in its ability to ensure that attitudes toward sexuality will continue to be influenced by images that negate human dignity, equality, and mutuality. Pornography contributes to alienation in human relationships and distorts the sexual integrity of both women and men.

The expansion of pornography onto the Internet in recent years has made access easier for providers and consumers of pornography, and especially for adults who sexually abuse children. There is mounting evidence that pedophiles routinely use the Internet to lure children into their hands. A staggering number of chat rooms promote rape, incest, sex with children, child prostitution, and other criminal and violent behaviors.

1. Layden, Dr. Mary Anne, Co-Director, Sexual Trauma and Psychopathology Program,Center for Cognitive Therapy University of Pennsylvania, Testimony, The Science Behind Pornography Addiction, US Senate Committee on Commerce, Science and Transportation Web site, (expert witness testimony), http://commerce.senate.gov/hearings/witnesslist.cfm?id=1343 (18 May 2005).

Pornographic materials are being transmitted in cyberspace on a global scale, permitting access by both adults and children. Disclaimers warning of graphic materials on these sites have not prevented children from viewing them. Most sites offer free "previews" of graphic, obscene, and violent images and are linked to other sites. According to the United States Commission on Pornography, 12- to 17-year-old adolescents are among the largest consumers of pornography.

Those portrayed in Internet pornographic images are typically women, especially women of color. Female bodies are treated as objects and commodities, and female body parts are dismembered and magnified for pornographic effect and cyber-sexual consumption. The global nature of the Internet and its lack of regulation enables such materials that may be legal in one country to be accessed in a country where they may be illegal. National boundaries are easily crossed, and there is no international code of conduct to monitor pornographic material.

Care should be taken that children and youth are protected from pornographic materials. The supervision and love of Christian parents and other caring adults, supported by the extended church family, are the primary source of sex education. A comprehensive approach to sex education offers an additional basis for countering pornography. Children, youth, and adults need opportunities to discuss sexuality and learn from quality sex education materials in families, churches and schools. An alternative message to pornography, contained in carefully prepared age-appropriate sex education materials that are both factual and explicit and portray caring, mutually consenting relationships between married adults, is needed. Materials should be measured by the intentions expressed and the goals served, not by the degree of explicitness of sexual imagery. If we fail to provide such materials, accompanied by parental and adult supervision, we risk reliance of children and youth on pornography as the primary source of information about sexuality.

We support laws that protect women and children and incarcerate those who are purveyors in the "industry" that instigates and expands child and adult pornography activities.

Addiction to adult pornography affects marital relationships, familial relationships, and may lead to criminal behavior. The addict must be treated with the best practices toward complete and total recovery and rehabilitation to ensure the best chance at future healthy relationships. Where rehabilitation and recovery fail we stand ready to support the spouses and families of addicts with love and care.

Addiction to child pornography is a deviant and criminal behavior that must be addressed through rehabilitation and legal means. We deplore the use of the criminal justice system to address addiction; however, when the pornography addict resorts to criminal behavior that harms or hurts another person, especially children, or should rehabilitation not succeed, we support legal means by which the addict is held accountable and monitored by the legal system so as to protect the addict and the victims from future harm.

The United Methodist Church is already on record naming sexual violence and abuse as sins and pledging to work for their eradication ("Domestic Violence and Sexual Abuse," 2000 *Book of Resolutions*; "Violence Against Women and Children," 2008 *Book of Resolutions*) and stating that "children must be protected from economic, physical and sexual exploitation and abuse" (Social Principles, ¶ 162C).

Understanding pornography to portray violence, abuse and humiliation in a sexual setting, and understanding any sexually explicit depiction of children to be pornographic, we affirm that The United Methodist Church is opposed to pornography. We further affirm our commitment to quality sex education. To address pornography at its root causes we encourage United Methodists to join in:

1. action toward developing effective societal and governmental policies that eradicate child pornography, adult exploitation and enslavement;

2. education to encourage healthy relationships and behaviors;

3. compassion and encouragement for rehabilitation and recovery of addicts, their families, and victims;

4. sensible laws that focus on a restorative justice model; and encourage incarcerated persons to pursue rehabilitation and recovery.

We call upon The United Methodist Church, its general agencies, annual conferences and local churches, to:

1. educate congregations about the issue of pornography, especially Internet pornography, and enact strict oversight of church-owned computers;

2. seek strategies to reduce the proliferation of pornography;

3. work to break the link between sex and violence;

4. monitor and limit access by children and youth to pornography and sexually explicit material;

5. participate in efforts to ban child pornography and protect child victims;

6. promote the use of United Methodist and other quality sex education materials that help children and youth gain an understanding of and respect for mutually affirming sexuality;

7. provide educational sessions for parents on minimizing the risk to children from Internet usage. Encourage parents to establish rules for teenagers and children; encourage parents to utilize screening technology;

8. call for social responsibility in all media, including the Internet and in all public libraries, and work with local, national, and international groups that advocate for global media monitoring of images of women, men and children; and

9. participate in ecumenical and/or community efforts that study and address the issue of pornography.

ADOPTED 1988
REVISED AND ADOPTED 2000
REVISED AND READOPTED 2008
RESOLUTION #42, 2004 *BOOK OF RESOLUTIONS*
RESOLUTION #36, 2000 *BOOK OF RESOLUTIONS*

*See* Social Principles, ¶ 161G.


## 2082. Prevention of the Use of Pornography in the Church

"We recognize that sexuality is God's good gift to all persons. . . . We reject all sexual expressions that damage or destroy the humanity God has given us as birthright" (Social Principles, ¶ 161G).

For nearly two decades, the global people called United Methodist have strengthened our understanding and practice of sexual ethics. We have adopted policies and procedures to guide behavior and address brokenness. We have trained, educated, and surveyed lay and clergy leaders of our denomination, conferences, and our congregations. We have spent significant resources in addressing the brokenness from sexual misconduct, from healing individuals and congregations to holding the Church accountable through legal proceedings.

As a resource to the Church, the General Commission on the Status and Role of Women takes very seriously its role to alert our leaders, conferences, and congregations of developments in our societies that call us to intensified concern and action. One such concern today is the expansion of the use of pornography, and its appearance in church programs, through the use of church computers and technology, or on church property.

*Definition of Pornography*

While definitions may vary, the 2004 *Book of Resolutions* offers the following:

"Pornography is sexually explicit material that portrays violence, abuse, coercion, domination, humiliation, or degradation for the purpose of arousal. Any sexually explicit material that depicts children is pornographic." (2004 *Book of Resolutions*, "Pornography and Sexual Violence," p. 166.)

The global expansion of wireless internet and telecommunications provides limitless availability to pornography. Schools, businesses, and governments are struggling with the use of pornography by employees or students with the organization's equipment.

The research group Top Ten REVIEWS in 2007 published these troubling indicators:

- every second, 28,258 users are viewing pornography;
- every day there are 266 new pornographic sites on the internet;
- sale of pornography generates more revenue than all sports in the US;
- revenue from pornography in the US reached a record $2.84 billion in 2006.

The use of pornography continues to increase as it becomes more accessible (via the internet, for example), and allows more immediate, realistic, and anonymous sexual contact and gratification (through chat rooms, real-time videos). Research shows it is not an "innocent activity." It is harmful and is generally addictive. Persons who are addicted to pornography are physiologically altered, as is their perspective, relationships with parishioners and family, and their perceptions of girls and women. Persons who are addicted to pornography must be held accountable for the impact of their behavior, yet they also need prayer, care, and therapy. Those laity and clergy in ministerial roles within our churches, conferences, and agencies are just as susceptible to pornography addiction as anyone else.

In the *Harmfulness of Pornography*, Robert Brannon shares the following, now confirmed in social science research:

- a majority of people in the US believe that some "pornography" (such as eroticized rape scenes) influences some men toward real-life sexual aggression;
- young male viewers of pornography become more likely to believe "all women want to be raped"; and
- women are portrayed as stereotypical bodies and sex objects.

## Pornography in the Church

A disturbing trend in the Church is the use of pornography by clergy and lay employees and volunteers, even using computers and other equipment owned by or housed within churches and church-related organizations. We are aware of reports of adults sharing pornographic materials with children and youth during church activities, camps, or programs. But beyond being saddened, shocked, and dismayed by these reports, how do we raise awareness among congregational, conference, agency, school or cabinet leaders, and what do we do to identify, stop, prevent, and then heal from recurrence in our communities of faith?

The United Methodist Church declares that the use of pornography in church programs, on church premises or with church property by persons in ministerial roles (lay and clergy) is a form of sexual misconduct, a chargeable offense for laity and clergy in The United Methodist Church.

The General Conference recommends and urges the following actions:

1. that cabinets and boards of ordained ministry include these issues and ministry concerns in sexual ethics training for candidates, appointed pastors, local pastors, and retired pastors;
2. that laity in positions of leadership in conferences, congregations, agencies, and schools should receive updated training on issues of sexual ethics, including current trends and ways to help persons addicted to pornography;
3. that bishops, cabinets, and chancellors should lead in updating the sexual ethics policies and procedures of conferences and congregations to include use of pornography as a form of sexual misconduct;
4. that seminaries and boards of ordained ministries should provide training to help clergy and lay professionals-in-training avoid addictive or harmful behaviors and to minister effectively with persons addicted to pornography;
5. that congregational, annual conference, and agency leaders should receive training on the issues of pornography, especially internet pornography, and should enact strict oversight

of church-owned computers and technology, including periodic technology audits; and

6. that seminaries should include issues of sexual misconduct, including pornography, in ethics and ministries courses and training for all students.

Resources: The Social Principles, ¶ 161G and H; United Methodist Web site on sexual ethics, www.umsexualethics.org; Resolution on "Pornography and Sexual Violence," 2004 *Book of Resolutions*, and Resolutions on "Pornography" and "Sexual Misconduct Within Ministerial Relationships" proposed for the 2008 *Book of Resolutions*.

ADOPTED 2008

*See* Social Principles, ¶ 161F.

## SPIRITUALITY

### 2101. Support Chrysalis at All Levels of the Church

WHEREAS, this is a ministry given to us from the Upper Room; and

WHEREAS, this brings a spiritual awareness of Jesus Christ to our youth in a unique, loving, patient, and kind way; and

WHEREAS, we rejoice in the truth which is revealed in this effort to involve our youth in a very important ministry in the Chrysalis movement; and

WHEREAS, youth may return to their local churches and be present and future leaders of the church,

*Therefore, be it resolved,* that:

1. The General Conference urge all Annual Conferences to increase their efforts and resources in the Chrysalis movement so that the youth of our churches know and are in touch with Christ; and

2. The General Conference encourages churches to enlist and involve their youth, girls and boys, in the life and work of Chrysalis so that they may return and be leaders within their own congregations.

*Furthermore,* General Conference encourages the General Board of Discipleship and Upper Room ministries to continue their emphasis on Chrysalis.

ADOPTED 2000
AMENDED AND READOPTED 2008
RESOLUTION #38, 2004 *BOOK OF RESOLUTIONS*
RESOLUTION #33, 2000 *BOOK OF RESOLUTIONS*

*See* Social Principles, ¶ 161A.

## 2102. Support the Walk to Emmaus at All Levels of the Church

WHEREAS, the Walk to Emmaus is given to us from the Upper Room; and

WHEREAS, this ministry brings a spiritual awareness of Jesus Christ to all adults in a unique, loving, patient, and kind way; and

WHEREAS, we rejoice in the truth which is revealed in this effort; and

WHEREAS, this ministry involves our members in a very important ministry; and

WHEREAS, this ministry enables members to return to their local churches and be present and future leaders of the church,

*Therefore, be it resolved, that General Conference:*

1. urges all annual conferences to increase their efforts and resources in the Walk to Emmaus so that the adults of our churches know and are in touch with Christ;

2. encourages churches to enlist and involve their adult members, men and women, in the life and work of the Walk to Emmaus so that they may return and be leaders within their own congregations; and

3. encourages the General Board of Discipleship and Upper Room ministries to continue their emphasis on Walk to Emmaus.

ADOPTED 2000
READOPTED 2008
RESOLUTION #39, 2004 *BOOK OF RESOLUTIONS*
RESOLUTION #34, 2000 *BOOK OF RESOLUTIONS*

*See* Social Principles, ¶ 161.

## 2103. Affirmation for the Historic Doctrines of the Christian Faith

WHEREAS, The United Methodist Church has long been guided by the teaching of the Scripture, the United Methodist Articles of Religion, the historical creeds of the Church, and the theological heritage of the Wesleyan tradition; and

WHEREAS, the Constitution of The United Methodist Church, in its Restrictive Rules (*see* ¶¶ 17-22), protects both the Articles of Religion and the Confession of Faith as doctrinal standards that shall not be revoked, altered, or changed (*Book of Discipline*, p. 58); and

WHEREAS, the clergy covenant agreed to by all clergy entering the denomination includes the following question: "In covenant with other elders, will you be loyal to The United Methodist Church, accepting its order, liturgy, doctrine, and discipline, defending it against all doctrines contrary to God's Holy Word, and accepting the authority of those who are appointed to supervise your ministry? (*The United Methodist Book of Worship*, p. 676, c.f.p. 666, also c.f. *Book of Discipline*, ¶ 304.1.i.); and

WHEREAS, we affirm that abiding by our rules and upholding the doctrines of Christianity, is critical to the peace and unity both within The United Methodist Church globally;

*Therefore, be it resolved,* that the 2004 General Conference affirms its commitment to the basic doctrines of the Christian faith as taught in the Scripture, and in the United Methodist Articles of Religion, and in the sermons of John Wesley.

ADOPTED 2004
RESOLUTION #40, 2004 *BOOK OF RESOLUTIONS*

*See* Social Principles, ¶161.

Please note:

Following approval by the General Conference, this resolution was referred to the Judicial Council, which ruled that the resolution is null and void. See Judicial Council Memorandum # 1002.

### 2104. Recover Doctrinal Heritage and Encourage Biblical and Theological Dialogue

WHEREAS, the sharing of theological differences should be a common reality within our church; and

WHEREAS, biblical and theological dialogue needs to be part of the fabric of our life together in all aspects of the church's life; and

WHEREAS, the church needs ways to strengthen our ability for dialogue and doctrinal discernment; and

WHEREAS, the issues of faith and order could be developed, struggled with, and result in new perspectives being shared; and

WHEREAS, using discernment in various levels of the church would truly be a celebration if resources were shared as a gift with one another; and

WHEREAS, all bodies of the church should be encouraged to engage in biblical and theological dialogue.

*Therefore, be it resolved,* that we affirm the disciplinary role of the bishops and the General Commission on Christian Unity and Interreligious Concerns in fostering biblical and theological dialogue at all levels of the church and do not support the establishment of a separate Commission on Faith and Order.

*Be it further resolved,* that we affirm the Church in its desire to recover and develop our distinctive doctrinal heritage, catholic, and reformed and thereby support enabling doctrinal reinvigoration for the sake of authentic renewal, faithful evangelism, and ecumenical dialogue and social witness.

*Be it further resolved,* that we encourage the Church at all levels to offer models and training for leaders (i.e. local church pastors, district superintendents, directors of connectional ministries, laity, etc.) on how to facilitate biblical and theological dialogue. In addition, we urge every general agency to incorporate within its training of church leaders, models of biblical and theological discourse using diverse training modules that reflect upon the diversity of The United Methodist Church.

*Be it further resolved,* that the 2004 General Conference and all entities of the Church be urged to model biblical and theological dialogue for The United Methodist Church.

**ADOPTED 2004**
**RESOLUTION #40, 2004** *BOOK OF RESOLUTIONS*

*See* Social Principles, ¶ 161.


## 2105. Lay Responsibility for Growth of the Church

WHEREAS, The United Methodist Church has steadily lost membership for many years in its country of origin; and,

WHEREAS, in the most recent year's totals, The United Methodist Church lost 70,000 members, thus exceeding the previous year's losses of 60,000 members; and,

WHEREAS, the historic strength of The United Methodist Church lay in well-equipped laity who were passionate in their beliefs; and,

WHEREAS, the clergy of The United Methodist Church continue to equip the laity for the task of winning commitments for Christ through witness, service, and transforming ministry; and,

WHEREAS, too many of our laity no longer claim that core responsibility of every Christian to find those who are lost and lead them into a church home,

*Therefore, be it now resolved,* that we, the laity, working with the clergy, accept primary responsibility for the growth and vitality of The United Methodist Church.

**ADOPTED 2008**

*See* Social Principles, ¶ 161.

## 2106. Spiritual Unity in Human Diversity

WHEREAS, The United Methodist Church is experiencing conflicting expressions of faith and biblical theology; and

WHEREAS, The United Methodist Church incorporates confessional traditions (i.e., the Articles of Religion and the Confession of Faith from *The Book of Discipline, 1992)* and inclusive tradition ("The Catholic Spirit" sermon by John Wesley); and

WHEREAS, *The Book of Discipline, 1992* (Part II: "Doctrinal Standards and Our Theological Task") "preserves the inherent tension between doctrinal standards and theological exploration . . . [and] involves dialogue, debate, and some conflict" ("Biblical Wisdom and Current Theological Ferment," Council of Bishops, October 31-November 4, 1994); and

WHEREAS, maintaining an inclusive spirit about doctrinal, theological, and language issues serves the greater purpose of helping people to affirm faith in Jesus Christ and to appropriate the historic confessions of the Church; and

WHEREAS, confessing faith in scriptural truth honors rich diversity in the biblical witness and informs a deeper understanding of diversity among people of faith; and

WHEREAS, "indeed, the body does not consist of one member but of many. . . . [and] God arranged the members in the body, each one of them, as he chose. . . . The eye cannot say to the hand, 'I have no need of you,' nor again the head to the feet, 'I have no need of you.' On the contrary, the members of the body that seem to be weaker are indispensable, and those members of the body that we think less honorable we clothe with greater honor, and our less respectable members are treated with greater respect; whereas, our more respectable members do not need this. But God has so arranged the body, giving the greater honor to the inferior member, that there may be no dissension within the body, but the members may have the same care for one another" (1 Corinthians 12:14-25);

*Therefore, be it resolved,* that The United Methodist Church reject any spirit that seeks to divide the body of Christ (and especially The United Methodist Church) and that cuts off the confessing and inclusive heritages by which United Methodists know themselves to be people of God; and

*Be it further resolved,* that we affirm our biblical faith in Jesus Christ and the spiritual gift of unity in human diversity.

ADOPTED 1996<br>
READOPTED 2004<br>
RESOLUTION #79, 2004 *BOOK OF RESOLUTIONS*<br>
RESOLUTION #70, 2000 *BOOK OF RESOLUTIONS*

*See* Social Principles, ¶ 162.

## SUICIDE

### 2121. Suicide: A Challenge to Ministry

The apostle Paul, rooted in his experience of the resurrected Christ, affirms the power of divine love to overcome the divisive realities of human life, including suicide:

> For I am convinced that neither death, nor life, nor angels, nor rulers, nor things present, nor things to come, nor powers nor height, nor depth, nor anything else in all creation will be able to separate us from the love of God in Christ Jesus our Lord.       (Romans 8:38-39)

Paul's words are indeed sources of hope and renewal for persons who contemplate suicide, as well as for those who grieve the death of friends and family members who have committed suicide. These words affirm that in those human moments when all seems lost, all may yet be found through full faith.

A Christian perspective on suicide thus begins with an affirmation of faith: Suicide does not separate us from the love of God.

Unfortunately, the church throughout much of its history has taught just the opposite, that suicide is an unforgivable sin. As a result, Christians, acting out of a sincere concern to prevent suicide, often have contradicted Christ's call to compassion.

For example, victims have been denounced and presumed to be in hell, and families have been stigmatized with guilt and inflicted with economic and social penalties.

The purpose of this statement is to challenge and guide our caring ministries to reduce the number of suicides and to share God's grace so that the lives of those touched by suicide may be enriched, dignified and enabled for ministry to others.

### Demography of Suicide

Suicide is the eleventh leading cause of death claiming 30,000 lives each year or one every 18 minutes. More than 4,000 0f those who commit suicide annually are under age 25. Because suicide occurs at all ages, it is the fifth leading cause of lost potential life, according to the US Centers for Disease Control and Prevention (CDC). Furthermore, it is estimated that between 500 and 1,500 people seek care in emergency rooms each day for suicide attempts. Research indicates that in any given year 20 percent of all high school students seriously consider suicide.

Suicide rates vary by age, gender and ethnicity but affects all peoples, regardless of education or socioeconomic status. The highest rate of suicide generally occurs among white males in later life. Among some Native American and Alaskan Native groups, however, rates among youth are several times higher that the US population as a whole. About 80 percent of those who commit suicide are male, but females are much more likely to attempt suicide.

"It is generally agreed that not all deaths that are reported as suicides are reported as such. Deaths may be misclassified as homicides or accidents where individuals have intended suicide by putting themselves in harm's way and lack of evidence does not allow for classifying the death as suicide. Other suicides may be misclassified as accidental or undetermined deaths in deference to community or family." (National Strategy for Suicide Prevention, 2001; p.32)

### Risk and Protective Factors of Suicide

Specific groups in society appear more vulnerable to suicide than others, especially if they experience certain precipants (events in their lives such as disease, loss of family, friends, job, severe trama, or other stress factors) and have easy access to a method for ending their lives, that is, if they are in an enabling environment. Studies show that 90% of those who die by suicide suffer from a diagnosable mental illness, substance abuse, or both. These factors—vulnerability, precipitating events, enabling environment—must be recognized and addressed if there is to be any reduction to the suicide rate.

Youth experience alienation and rejection by society, family, and the church when dealing with sexual-identity issues, including homosexuality. For many youth, the only perceived way out is suicide.

Social interconnections, social support and life skills are shown to provide protection from suicide. These methods can be learned, and youth training, such as that taught annually by the Arkansas Youth Suicide Prevention Commission, is a major force for suicide intervention and prevention.

### Societal Attitudes

The prevailing attitudes of society, both secular and religious, have been to condemn the victim and ignore the victim's family and friends

> There are always two parties to a death; the person who dies and the survivors who are bereaved . . . the sting of death is less sharp for the person who dies than it is for the bereaved survivor. This, as I see it, is the capital fact about the relation between the living and the dying. There are two parties to the suffering that death inflicts; and in the apportionment of the suffering the survivor takes the brunt.
> —Arnold Toynbee, from Man's Concern with Death

Churches have denied funerals and memorial services to bereaved families. Victims' remains have been banned from cemeteries. Medical examiners have falsified records for families so they can receive economic aid. Federal and state surveys of attitudes toward suicide confirm a broad spectrum of responses ranging from fear, denial and resistance to widespread support for suicide prevention. Social and religious stigma is widespread. One report told of a long-time teacher of church youth who lost her son to suicide. When she returned to her class a few weeks later, she was told that because her son had taken his life, she was no longer to teach. In contrast, several denominations have in recent years adopted informed and more compassionate statements on suicide for their members. Frequently mentioned are the needs to remove social stigmas that discourage youth and others from seeking the help they need and for providing mental health opportunities for those who suffer from depression and suicidal ideation. The understanding support of family and friends as a major factor in providing such effective support is now more widely appreciated.

## The Church's Response

Recognizing that the church's historical response to suicide includes punitive measures intended to prevent suicide and that there is no clear biblical stance on suicide, the General Conference of The United Methodist Church strongly urges the employment of major initiatives to prevent suicide, following the guidelines of the National Strategy for Suicide Prevention issued by the US Department of Health and Human Services. Additionally, the General Conference recommends to the boards, agencies, institutions, and local churches of The United Methodist Church that the ministry of suicide prevention should receive urgent attention. Survivors of loss through suicide and suicide attempts should also receive priority concern in the overall ministry of the Church. Harsh and punitive measures (such as denial of funeral or memorial services, or ministerial visits) imposed upon families of suicide victims should be denounced and abandoned. The church should participate in and urge others to participate in a full, community-based effort to address the needs of people at risk and their families. Each annual conference and local church should respond to issues of ministry related to suicide prevention and family-support services.

It must be emphasized that suicide increases in an environment or society that does not demonstrate a caring attitude toward all persons. The church has a special role in changing societal attitudes and harmful social environment of individuals and families. To promote this effort, the church should do the following:

1. the General Board of Discipleship shall continue to develop curriculum for biblical and theological study of suicide and related mental and environmental health problems and promote the programs recommended by the American Association of Pastoral Counseling and the use of scientific research of the Centers for Disease Control and Prevention, the National Institutes of Health, and other credible institutions in the private sector, such as organizations within the National Council of Suicide Prevention;

2. the General Board of Higher Education and Ministry shall develop materials for United Methodist-related seminaries to train church professionals to recognize treatable mental illness associated with suicide (e.g., depression) and to realize when and how to refer persons for treatment; it shall ensure that all pastoral counseling programs include such training and strategies for ministry survivors of suicide loss and suicide attempts ; and seek attention to suicide in courses in Bible, Christian Ethics, Preaching and Religious Education as well as Pastoral Care;

3. the General Board of Church and Society shall continue to support public policies that: (a) promote access to mental-health services for all persons regardless of age, (b) remove the stigma associated with mental illness, and (c) encourage "help-seeking" behavior;

4. embrace all persons affected by suicide, including young children, in loving community through support groups and responsive social institutions, call upon society through the media to reinforce (following published guidelines for reporting suicide and related matters) the importance of human life and to advocate that public policies include all persons' welfare, and work against policies that devalue human life and perpetuate cultural risk factors (i.e., nuclear armaments, war, racial and ethnic prejudice);

5. affirm that we can destroy our physical bodies but not our being in God, and affirm that a person stands in relationship to others, but in our efforts to be more compassionate and care giving, avoid glamorizing the deaths of those who take their lives, especially young people. The loss of every person is a loss in community;

6. support the United Methodist childcare institutions that provide treatment for emotionally disturbed children, youth, and their families and retirement communities that are home for those where suicide rates are highest; and

7. strengthen the youth ministries of the local church, helping the young people experience the saving grace of Jesus Christ and participate in the caring fellowship of the church.

### Conclusion

"The church is called to proclaim the gospel of grace and, in its own life, to embody that gospel. It embodies that gospel when it is particularly solicitous of those within its number who are most troubled, and when it reaches beyond its own membership to such people who stand alone" (Dr. Philip Wogaman, professor of Christian Social Ethics, Wesley Theological Seminary).

ADOPTED 1988
AMENDED AND READOPTED 1996
AMENDED AND READOPTED 2004
RESOLUTION #157, 2004 *BOOK OF RESOLUTIONS*
RESOLUTION #145, 2000 *BOOK OF RESOLUTIONS*

*See* Social Principles, ¶ 161N.

## 2122. Teen Sexual Identity and Suicide Risk

In the year 2003 at least 700,000 high school students will attempt suicide—one in every 13 high school students in the United States. According to the US Centers for Disease Control and Prevention, suicide rates among adults have steadied or even declined over the past few decades but teenage suicide rates have tripled.

A 1989 US Department of Health and Human Services study found that teens dealing with issues of sexual identity are two to three times more likely to attempt suicide than are other youth.

The United Methodist Church, in Social Principles ¶ 162H, states: Certain basic human rights and civil liberties are due all persons. We are committed to supporting those rights and liberties for homosexual persons.

The General Conference will establish and fund a task group which will:

- Publish, in laypeople's terms, a summary of current research on homosexual youth at risk for suicide;
- Work with organizations currently doing research on these issues;
- Provide a directory of agencies working on issues of teen suicide among youth dealing with issues of sexual identity;
- Publish a resource for congregations and families which provides accurate information, recommendations for programs, and pastoral guidance.
- Make recommendations for legislative actions within The United Methodist Church;
- Make recommendations for programs for youth through congregations, districts, conferences, mission agencies, United

Methodist Women, United Methodist Men and other organizational bodies of The United Methodist Church.

* Report to the 2008 General Conference on its findings and work.

ADOPTED 2004
READOPTED 2008
RESOLUTION #158, 2004 *BOOK OF RESOLUTIONS*

*See* Social Principles, ¶¶ 161F and N.

# ¶ 162. III. THE SOCIAL COMMUNITY

The rights and privileges a society bestows upon or withholds from those who constitute it indicate the relative esteem in which that society holds particular persons and groups of persons. We affirm all persons as equally valuable in the sight of God. We therefore work toward societies in which each person's value is recognized, maintained, and strengthened. We support the basic rights of all persons to equal access to housing, education, communication, employment, medical care, legal redress for grievances, and physical protection. We deplore acts of hate or violence against groups or persons based on race, ethnicity, gender, sexual orientation, religious affiliation, or economic status. Our respect for the inherent dignity of all persons leads us to call for the recognition, protection, and implementation of the principles of *The Universal Declaration of Human Rights* so that communities and individuals may claim and enjoy their universal, indivisible, and inalienable rights.

*A) Rights of Racial and Ethnic Persons*—Racism is the combination of the power to dominate by one race over other races and a value system that assumes that the dominant race is innately superior to the others. Racism includes both personal and institutional racism. Personal racism is manifested through the individual expressions, attitudes, and/or behaviors that accept the assumptions of a racist value system and that maintain the benefits of this system. Institutional racism is the established social pattern that supports implicitly or explicitly the racist value system. Racism plagues and cripples our growth in Christ, inasmuch as it is antithetical to the gospel itself. White people are unfairly granted privileges and benefits that are denied to persons of color. Racism breeds racial discrimination. We define racial discrimination as the disparate treatment and lack of full access to resources and opportunities in the church and in society based on race or ethnicity. Therefore, we recognize racism as

*169*

sin and affirm the ultimate and temporal worth of all persons. We rejoice in the gifts that particular ethnic histories and cultures bring to our total life. We commend and encourage the self-awareness of all racial and ethnic groups and oppressed people that leads them to demand their just and equal rights as members of society. We assert the obligation of society and groups within the society to implement compensatory programs that redress long-standing, systemic social deprivation of racial and ethnic people. We further assert the right of members of racial and ethnic groups to equal opportunities in employment and promotion; to education and training of the highest quality; to nondiscrimination in voting, in access to public accommodations, and in housing purchase or rental; credit, financial loans, venture capital, and insurance policies; and to positions of leadership and power in all elements of our life together. We support affirmative action as one method of addressing the inequalities and discriminatory practices within our Church and society.

B) *Rights of Religious Minorities*—Religious persecution has been common in the history of civilization. We urge policies and practices that ensure the right of every religious group to exercise its faith free from legal, political, or economic restrictions. We condemn all overt and covert forms of religious intolerance, being especially sensitive to their expression in media stereotyping. We assert the right of all religions and their adherents to freedom from legal, economic, and social discrimination.

C) *Rights of Children*—Once considered the property of their parents, children are now acknowledged to be full human beings in their own right, but beings to whom adults and society in general have special obligations. Thus, we support the development of school systems and innovative methods of education designed to assist every child toward complete fulfillment as an individual person of worth. All children have the right to quality education, including full sex education appropriate to their stage of development that utilizes the best educational techniques and insights. Christian parents and guardians and the Church have the responsibility to ensure that children receive sex education consistent with Christian morality, including faithfulness in marriage and abstinence in singleness. Moreover, children have the rights to food, shelter, clothing, health care, and emotional well-being as do adults, and these rights we affirm as theirs regardless of actions or inactions of their parents or guardians. In particular, children must be protected from economic, physical, emotional, and sexual exploitation and abuse.

*D) Rights of Young People*—Our society is characterized by a large population of young people who frequently find full participation in society difficult. Therefore, we urge development of policies that encourage inclusion of young people in decision-making processes and that eliminate discrimination and exploitation. Creative and appropriate employment opportunities should be legally and socially available for young people.

*E) Rights of the Aging*—In a society that places primary emphasis upon youth, those growing old in years are frequently isolated from the mainstream of social existence. We support social policies that integrate the aging into the life of the total community, including sufficient incomes, increased and nondiscriminatory employment opportunities, educational and service opportunities, and adequate medical care and housing within existing communities. We urge social policies and programs, with emphasis on the unique concerns of older women and ethnic persons, that ensure to the aging the respect and dignity that is their right as senior members of the human community. Further, we urge increased consideration for adequate pension systems by employers, with provisions for the surviving spouse.

¶ 162

*F) Rights of Women*—We affirm women and men to be equal in every aspect of their common life. We therefore urge that every effort be made to eliminate sex-role stereotypes in activity and portrayal of family life and in all aspects of voluntary and compensatory participation in the Church and society. We affirm the right of women to equal treatment in employment, responsibility, promotion, and compensation. We affirm the importance of women in decision-making positions at all levels of Church and society and urge such bodies to guarantee their presence through policies of employment and recruitment. We support affirmative action as one method of addressing the inequalities and discriminatory practices within our Church and society. We urge employers of persons in dual career families, both in the Church and society, to apply proper consideration of both parties when relocation is considered. We affirm the right of women to live free from violence and abuse and urge governments to enact policies that protect women against all forms of violence and discrimination in any sector of society.

*G) Rights of Men*—Because we affirm women and men to be equal in every aspect of their common life, we also affirm the rights of men. We affirm equal opportunities in employment, responsibility, and promotion. Men should not be ignored or lose opportunities or influence because they are men.

We recognize that men's role in raising children is in equal importance to women's and call for equal rights as women in opportunities for parental leave. When parents divorce, men often have less contact with their children. We call for equal access to child-custody, but emphasize that the best interest of the child always is the most important.

*H) Rights of Immigrants*—We recognize, embrace, and affirm all persons, regardless of country of origin, as members of the family of God. We affirm the right of all persons to equal opportunities for employment, access to housing, health care, education, and freedom from social discrimination. We urge the Church and society to recognize the gifts, contributions, and struggles of those who are immigrants and to advocate for justice for all.

*I) Rights of Persons with Disabilities*—We recognize and affirm the full humanity and personhood of all individuals with mental, physical, developmental, neurological, and psychological conditions or disabilities as full members of the family of God. We also affirm their rightful place in both the church and society. We affirm the responsibility of the Church and society to be in ministry with children, youth, and adults with mental, physical, developmental, and/or psychological and neurological conditions or disabilities whose particular needs in the areas of mobility, communication, intellectual comprehension, or personal relationships might make more challenging their participation or that of their families in the life of the Church and the community. We urge the Church and society to recognize and receive the gifts of persons with disabilities to enable them to be full participants in the community of faith. We call the Church and society to be sensitive to, and advocate for, programs of rehabilitation, services, employment, education, appropriate housing, and transportation. We call on the Church and society to protect the civil rights of persons with disabilities.

*J) Equal Rights Regardless of Sexual Orientation*—Certain basic human rights and civil liberties are due all persons. We are committed to supporting those rights and liberties for all persons, regardless of sexual orientation. We see a clear issue of simple justice in protecting the rightful claims where people have shared material resources, pensions, guardian relationships, mutual powers of attorney, and other such lawful claims typically attendant to contractual relationships that involve shared contributions, responsibilities, and liabilities, and equal protection before the law. Moreover, we support efforts to stop violence and other forms of coercion against all persons, regardless of sexual orientation.

¶ 162

*K) Population*—Since the growing worldwide population is increasingly straining the world's supply of food, minerals, and water and sharpening international tensions, the reduction of the rate of consumption of resources by the affluent and the reduction of current world population growth rates have become imperative. People have the duty to consider the impact on the total world community of their decisions regarding childbearing and should have access to information and appropriate means to limit their fertility, including voluntary sterilization. We affirm that programs to achieve a stabilized population should be placed in a context of total economic and social development, including an equitable use and control of resources; improvement in the status of women in all cultures; a human level of economic security, health care, and literacy for all. We oppose any policy of forced abortion or forced sterilization.

*L) Alcohol and Other Drugs*—We affirm our long-standing support of abstinence from alcohol as a faithful witness to God's liberating and redeeming love for persons. We support abstinence from the use of any illegal drugs. Since the use of illegal drugs, as well as illegal and problematic use of alcohol, is a major factor in crime, disease, death, and family dysfunction, we support educational programs, as well as other prevention strategies, encouraging abstinence from illegal drug use and, with regard to those who choose to consume alcoholic beverages, judicious use with deliberate and intentional restraint, with Scripture as a guide.

Millions of living human beings are testimony to the beneficial consequences of therapeutic drug use, and millions of others are testimony to the detrimental consequences of drug misuse. We encourage wise policies relating to the availability of potentially beneficial or potentially damaging prescription and over-the-counter drugs; we urge that complete information about their use and misuse be readily available to both doctor and patient. We support the strict administration of laws regulating the sale and distribution of alcohol and controlled substances. We support regulations that protect society from users of drugs of any kind, including alcohol, where it can be shown that a clear and present social danger exists. Drug-dependent persons and their family members, including those who are assessed or diagnosed as dependent on alcohol, are individuals of infinite human worth deserving of treatment, rehabilitation, and ongoing life-changing recovery. Misuse or abuse may also require intervention, in order to prevent progression into dependence. Because of the frequent inter-

¶ 162

relationship between alcohol abuse and mental illness, we call upon legislators and health care providers to make available appropriate mental illness treatment and rehabilitation for drug-dependent persons. We commit ourselves to assisting those who have become dependent, and their families, in finding freedom through Jesus Christ and in finding good opportunities for treatment, for ongoing counseling, and for reintegration into society.

M) *Tobacco*—We affirm our historic tradition of high standards of personal discipline and social responsibility. In light of the overwhelming evidence that tobacco smoking and the use of smokeless tobacco are hazardous to the health of persons of all ages, we recommend total abstinence from the use of tobacco. We urge that our educational and communication resources be utilized to support and encourage such abstinence. Further, we recognize the harmful effects of passive smoke and support the restriction of smoking in public areas and workplaces.

N) *Medical Experimentation*—Physical and mental health has been greatly enhanced through discoveries by medical science. It is imperative, however, that governments and the medical profession carefully enforce the requirements of the prevailing medical research standard, maintaining rigid controls in testing new technologies and drugs utilizing human beings. The standard requires that those engaged in research shall use human beings as research subjects only after obtaining full, rational, and uncoerced consent.

O) *Genetic Technology*—The responsibility of humankind to God's creation challenges us to deal carefully with the possibilities of genetic research and technology. We welcome the use of genetic technology for meeting fundamental human needs for health, a safe environment, and an adequate food supply. We oppose the cloning of humans and the genetic manipulation of the gender of an unborn child.

Because of the effects of genetic technologies on all life, we call for effective guidelines and public accountability to safeguard against any action that might lead to abuse of these technologies, including political or military ends. We recognize that cautious, well-intended use of genetic technologies may sometimes lead to unanticipated harmful consequences.

Human gene therapies that produce changes that cannot be passed to offspring (somatic therapy) should be limited to the alleviation of suffering caused by disease. Genetic therapies for eugenic choices or that produce waste embryos are deplored. Genetic data of individuals and their families should be kept secret and held in strict confidence unless confidentiality is waived by the individual or by his or her family, or unless the collection and use of genetic identification data is supported by an appropriate court order. Because its long-term effects are uncertain, we oppose genetic therapy that results in changes that can be passed to offspring (germ-line therapy).

*P) Rural Life*—We support the right of persons and families to live and prosper as farmers, farm workers, merchants, professionals, and others outside of the cities and metropolitan centers. We believe our culture is impoverished and our people deprived of a meaningful way of life when rural and small-town living becomes difficult or impossible. We recognize that the improvement of this way of life may sometimes necessitate the use of some lands for nonagricultural purposes. We oppose the indiscriminate diversion of agricultural land for nonagricultural uses when nonagricultural land is available. Further, we encourage the preservation of appropriate lands for agriculture and open space uses through thoughtful land use programs. We support governmental and private programs designed to benefit the resident farmer rather than the factory farm and programs that encourage industry to locate in nonurban areas.

We further recognize that increased mobility and technology have brought a mixture of people, religions, and philosophies to rural communities that were once homogeneous. While often this is seen as a threat to or loss of community life, we understand it as an opportunity to uphold the biblical call to community for all persons. Therefore, we encourage rural communities and individuals to maintain a strong connection to the earth and to be open to: offering mutual belonging, caring, healing, and growth; sharing and celebrating cooperative leadership and diverse gifts; supporting mutual trust; and affirming individuals as unique persons of worth, and thus to practice shalom.

*Q) Sustainable Agriculture*—A prerequisite for meeting the nutritional needs of the world's population is an agricultural system that uses sustainable methods, respects ecosystems, and promotes a livelihood for people that work the land.

We support a sustainable agricultural system that will maintain and support the natural fertility of agricultural soil, promote the diversity of flora and fauna, and adapt to regional conditions and structures— a system where agricultural animals are treated humanely and where their living conditions are as close to natural systems as possible. We aspire to an effective agricultural system where plant, livestock, and

¶ 162

¶ 162

poultry production maintains the natural ecological cycles, conserves energy, and reduces chemical inputs to a minimum.

Sustainable agriculture requires a global evaluation of the impacts of agriculture on food and raw material production, the preservation of animal breeds and plant varieties, and the preservation and development of the cultivated landscape.

World trade of agricultural products needs to be based on fair trade and prices, based on the costs of sustainable production methods, and must consider the real costs of ecological damage. The needed technological and biological developments are those that support sustainability and consider ecological consequences.

R) *Urban–Suburban Life*—Urban–suburban living has become a dominant style of life for more and more persons. For many it furnishes economic, educational, social, and cultural opportunities. For others, it has brought alienation, poverty, and depersonalization. We in the Church have an opportunity and responsibility to help shape the future of urban–suburban life. Massive programs of renewal and social planning are needed to bring a greater degree of humanization into urban–suburban lifestyles. We must judge all programs, including economic and community development, new towns, and urban renewal, by the extent to which they protect and enhance human values, permit personal and political involvement, and make possible neighborhoods open to persons of all races, ages, and income levels. We affirm the efforts of all developers who place human values at the heart of their planning. We must help shape urban–suburban development so that it provides for the human need to identify with and find meaning in smaller social communities. At the same time, such smaller communities must be encouraged to assume responsibilities for the total urban–suburban community instead of isolating themselves from it.

S) *Media Violence and Christian Values*—The unprecedented impact the media (principally television and movies) are having on Christian and human values within our society becomes more apparent each day. We express disdain at current media preoccupation with dehumanizing portrayals, sensationalized through mass media "entertainment" and "news." These practices degrade humankind and violate the teachings of Christ and the Bible.

United Methodists, along with those of other faith groups, must be made aware that the mass media often undermine the truths of Christianity by promoting permissive lifestyles and detailing acts of graphic violence. Instead of encouraging, motivating, and inspiring its audiences to adopt lifestyles based on the sanctity of life, the entertainment industry often advocates the opposite, painting a cynical picture of violence, abuse, greed, profanity, and a constant denigration of the family. The media must be held accountable for the part they play in the decline of values we observe in society today. Many in the media remain aloof to the issue, claiming to reflect rather than to influence society. For the sake of our human family, Christians must work together to halt this erosion of moral and ethical values in the world community.

¶ 162

*T) Information Communication Technology*—Because effective personal communication is key to being a responsible and empowered member of society, and because of the power afforded by information communication technologies to shape society and enable individuals to participate more fully, we believe that access to these technologies is a basic right.

Information communication technologies provide us with information, entertainment, and a voice in society. They can be used to enhance our quality of life and provide us with a means to interact with each other, our government, and people and cultures all over the world. Most information about world events comes to us by the broadcast, cable, print media, and the Internet. Concentrating the control of media to large commercial interests limits our choices and often provides a distorted view of human values. Therefore, we support the regulation of media communication technologies to ensure a variety of independent information sources and provides for the public good.

Personal communication technologies such as the Internet allow persons to communicate with each other and access vast information resources that can have commercial, cultural, political, and personal value. While the Internet can be used to nurture minds and spirits of children and adults, it is in danger of being overrun with commercial interests and is used by some to distribute inappropriate and illegal material. Therefore, the Internet must be managed responsibly in order to maximize its benefits while minimizing its risks, especially for children. Denying access in today's world to basic information communication technologies like the Internet due to their cost or availability, limits people's participation in their government and society. We support the goal of universal access to telephone and Internet services at an affodable price.

*U) Persons Living with HIV and AIDS*—Persons diagnosed as positive for Human Immune Virus (HIV) and with Acquired Immune

Deficiency Syndrome (AIDS) often face rejection from their families and friends and various communities in which they work and interact. In addition, they are often faced with a lack of adequate health care, especially toward the end of life.

All individuals living with HIV and AIDS should be treated with dignity and respect.

We affirm the responsibility of the Church to minister to and with these individuals and their families regardless of how the disease was contracted. We support their rights to employment, appropriate medical care, full participation in public education, and full participation in the Church.

We urge the Church to be actively involved in the prevention of the spread of AIDS by providing educational opportunities to the congregation and the community. The Church should be available to provide counseling to the affected individuals and their families.

*V) Right to Health Care*—Health is a condition of physical, mental, social, and spiritual well-being. John 10:10b says "I came that they may have life, and have it abundantly." Stewardship of health is the responsibility of each person to whom health has been entrusted. Creating the personal, environmental, and social conditions in which health can thrive is a joint responsibility—public and private. We encourage individuals to pursue a healthy lifestyle and affirm the importance of preventive health care, health education, environmental and occupational safety, good nutrition, and secure housing in achieving health. Health care is a basic human right.

Providing the care needed to maintain health, prevent disease, and restore health after injury or illness is a responsibility each person owes others and government owes to all, a responsibility government ignores at its peril. In Ezekiel 34:4a, God points out the failures of the leadership of Israel to care for the weak: "You have not strengthened the weak, you have not healed the sick, you have not bound up the injured." As a result all suffer. Like police and fire protection, health care is best funded through the government's ability to tax each person equitably and directly fund the provider entities. Countries facing a public health crisis such as HIV/AIDS must have access to generic medicines and to patented medicines. We affirm the right of men and women to have access to comprehensive reproductive health/family planning information and services that will serve as a means to prevent unplanned pregnancies, reduce abortions, and prevent the spread of HIV/AIDS. The right to health care includes care for persons with brain diseases, neurological conditions, or physical disabilities, who must be afforded the same access to health care as all other persons in our communities. It is unjust to construct or perpetuate barriers to physical or mental wholeness or full participation in community.

We believe it is a governmental responsibility to provide all citizens with health care.

*W) Organ Transplantation and Donation*—We believe that organ transplantation and organ donation are acts of charity, agape love, and self-sacrifice. We recognize the life-giving benefits of organ and other tissue donation and encourage all people of faith to become organ and tissue donors as a part of their love and ministry to others in need. We urge that it be done in an environment of respect for deceased and living donors and for the benefit of the recipients, and following protocols that carefully prevent abuse to donors and their families.

¶ 162

# THE SOCIAL COMMUNITY
# THE RESOLUTIONS

## ACCESSIBILITY/EQUAL ACCESS

### 3001. Accessibility Grants for Churches

WHEREAS, it is essential that The United Methodist Church as a denomination find a way to assist individual churches in the annual conferences to find grant money to assist them in becoming more accessible by removing architectural barriers; and

WHEREAS, our denomination establishes many programs around specific groups of people, whether they be ethnic groups or age-targeted groups; and

WHEREAS, each of the groups that the church claims an interest in and sets priorities for includes persons with disabilities. There are more than 54 million in the United States alone. The United Nations recently focused on the issue of disability by calling for institutions to become more accessible; and

WHEREAS, several years ago, $500 grants were awarded to churches that were qualified, to help them increase their accessibility;

*Therefore be it resolved*, that it would be appropriate to set aside monies to again provide accessibility grants or loans to churches in each of the annual conferences. The program could be administered from within the General Board of Global Ministries.

ADOPTED 2000
READOPTED 2008
RESOLUTION #44, 2004 *BOOK OF RESOLUTIONS*
RESOLUTION #38, 2000 *BOOK OF RESOLUTIONS*

*See* Social Principles, ¶ 162I.

## 3002. Compliance with the Americans with Disabilities Act for Employers

WHEREAS, the General Board of Global Ministries, on October 16, 1979, called "United Methodists to a new birth of awareness of the need to include, assimilate, receive the gifts, and respond to the needs, of those persons with mental, physical, and/or psychologically hand-icapping conditions, including their families"; and

WHEREAS, the General Conference resolved in 1980 to take major steps in adapting facilities, new and existing, such as "church sanctu-aries, educational buildings, parsonages, camps, colleges, or other church-related agencies or facilities" so that they meet minimum guidelines for "barrier-free construction" (*see* "Barrier-Free Construction for People with Disabilities"); and

WHEREAS, President Bush signed into law the Americans with Disabilities Act (ADA); and

WHEREAS, love without justice is empty and meaningless, and it is unjust to deny anyone employment based solely on human-created obstacles; and

WHEREAS, it is fitting that Christians be a "cloud of witnesses" for the secular world;

*Therefore, be it resolved,* that all United Methodist churches investigate and attempt to comply with Title I of the ADA, which states that employers "may not discriminate against qualified individuals with disabilities" and will "reasonably accommodate the disabilities of qual-ified applicants or employees unless undue hardship would result."

ADOPTED 1992
AMENDED AND READOPTED 1996
READOPTED 2004 AND 2008
RESOLUTION #45, 2004 *BOOK OF RESOLUTIONS*
RESOLUTION #39, 2000 *BOOK OF RESOLUTIONS*

See Social Principles, ¶ 162*I*.


## 3003. United Methodist Implementation of Americans with Disabilities Act

WHEREAS, our human rights as stated by the United States of America Constitution are God given, and we can set priorities unto ourselves apart from the rest of His creation, and

WHEREAS, these priorities are applied to our life and what it means to us, how we live it, who we are and to become, and *anyone* can have an attainable priority to direct their life, and

WHEREAS, by applying the use of our love with all our heart, soul, mind, and strength in our time, money, and attitudes we can perceive our priorities within ourselves and others, and

WHEREAS, God's grace is with us throughout our lives: birth, disease, accident, crime, and aging, yet, not realizing it till it's been revealed, and

WHEREAS, we *all* are instruments of God's grace in other people's lives when we are open to His grace, and

WHEREAS, we are all priests—the whole church is the holy priesthood, those called to be a mediator between God and a needful world representing Jesus Christ—where *all* are to share God's love and salvation with other people, and

WHEREAS, God's love for us is unconditional; God loves us for who we are—not what we are or how we look; Christ died for us while we were yet sinners, and this great love moves us to accept this gift in our hearts of a living relationship with God as a priority for *all* our lives, and

WHEREAS, we are consciously living our lives in relationship with God that can be nurtured through the spiritual discipline of living in God's presence, and these lives are courageous and joyful—not tragic or brave, and

WHEREAS, study brings our minds to Christ like lives, equips us to fulfill the highest calling of *all* of us, and

WHEREAS, Christian study brings *all* to a knowledge of God and knowledge of the world to serve God, and

WHEREAS, sacred moments and practices (through services and discipline) bring us to know, experience, and live in the presence of Christ through the church *(meaning everyone)*, including the serving and receiving of the sacraments, and

WHEREAS, baptism and Holy Communion are upheld by all Christian traditions and have been given to us so we may live on growing as disciples in every part of our life, and

WHEREAS, showing Christ as being real and important for others, we *all* must live authentically as our serving Christ gives our hands to Christ by making a friend, being a friend, and introducing our new friend to the friend of all friends—Jesus Christ, and

WHEREAS, through the Resolution of the "Annual Accessibility Audit" (#43 2004 *Book of Resolutions*, adopted in 1992), Social Principles, ¶ 162I "Rights of Persons with Disabilities," and the section in the *Book of Discipline* on inclusiveness (¶ 139) gives the opportunity for *each person*, and congregation to make a plan for serving Christ, and

WHEREAS, even with God's gift of grace and a new life in Christ, we can still sin in many forms, yet there is still forgiveness, realizing and admitting our sin (physically and spiritually) in our lives as the first step to overcome them, and

WHEREAS, through prayer, repentance, surrendering anew, counseling, and creating a new plan to reevaluate and prioritize to God's direction in *all* our lives, and

WHEREAS, by becoming disciples, we can reply to the call of Christ with *all* our hearts, minds, souls, strengths, hands, and feet as we are able to walk with Jesus and grow into His likeness as our highest priority; to share Christ and to learn to love as Jesus loved, and

WHEREAS, people all around us, including the church, are in need of God's transforming love for living in this world and can be changed whenever we bring Christ's love and truth working within our church, family, work, social environments, and our private times, and

WHEREAS, we are edified by God's grace for growth in our relationships as we live in obedience to His call, the Holy Spirit teaches and empowers us to love as Jesus loved and to mature in the likeness of Christ as children imitate their parents, to be focused upon our call in humble service, and

WHEREAS, the body of Christ is the gathering of *all* disciples who offer their lives to proclaim Christ in the world, and *every member* of the body of Christ has been given special gifts for ministry that need to be sought and exercised to build up the church, to form healthy, living communities, and to show Christ's life of love in concrete ways "that the world may believe," and

WHEREAS, we are called to persevere in grace for the rest of our lives by weekly attendance, commitment to share support, accountability, and guidance, and

WHEREAS, *all* are sent out by Christ's Great Commission, to be Christ's apostles in today's world in the midst of obstacles that can be overcome through Christ and other Christians, and

WHEREAS, there are 56 million disabled citizens at any one time in the United States, and

WHEREAS, disabled persons are real people, with real voices and real choices whose lives have been stolen within ALL cultures within America comprised of young, middle-aged, seniors, veterans, parents, husbands, wives, children from all races and all ethnic backgrounds, and

WHEREAS, people with disabilities constitute a discrete and insular minority, subjected to a history of purposeful unequal treatment and placed in a position of political powerlessness in American society and within the church, and

WHEREAS, prejudice and discrimination against people with disabilities based on unjustified stereotypes continues, with disparate treatment and disenfranchisement, and

WHEREAS, such discrimination and prejudice denies people with disabilities the opportunity to pursue opportunities in society and within the Church on an equal basis, to live in their own homes so as to be close to family, friends, work, school, church, recreation, social stimulation, libraries, theaters, community centers, museums, and medical facilities, and

WHEREAS, accommodation for our disabled people (parishioners and visitors alike) are part of our reaching out through the provisions of *The Book of Discipline* through Church and Society empowers and frees us to advocate for personal assistants, accessibility in public and private areas, housing, transportation, and technology to do so, and

WHEREAS, through Church and Society we have a duty to bring justice and fairness in our civil responsibilities (like voting or serving in civil government) for our people with disabilities for Medicaid, Medicare, vocational rehabilitation, housing, education, job training, in-home services, and transportation—all of which are *everyone's* civil right, and

WHEREAS, this inability to participate fully in American society and within the church robs people with disabilities of the opportunity to claim any degree of independence and costs the United States (including the church) billions of dollars annually in unnecessary expenses from enforced dependency and nonproductivity, and

WHEREAS, the body of Christ, the church, need to be vigilant as consumers, advocates, and legislators to reserve funding and accountability to promote choice for persons with disabilities, and

WHEREAS, the Americans with Disabilities Act (ADA) was signed into law by George Bush in 1990 to, in his words, "in the unjustified segregation and exclusion of persons with disabilities from the mainstream of American life," and

WHEREAS, the United States Supreme Court promoted community living through its OLMSTEAD decision, which urges all 50 states to *plan* for people living in the community over institutional placement, and

WHEREAS, the ADA's primary goal is to promote access to *all* aspects of social interaction including education, employment, commerce, recreation, government, and transportation, and

WHEREAS, the ADA provides the means for full implementation of the Act and legal recourse to redress discrimination on the basis of physical disability, and

WHEREAS, The United Methodist Church has brought closely within itself to help people as taught by our Lord Jesus Christ those who are hungry, thirsty, sick or in prison,

*Therefore, be it resolved,* that the assembled delegates to this General Conference of The United Methodist Church 2004 affirm our support of the full implementation of the provisions of the Americans with Disabilities Act of 1990, and

*Be it further resolved,* the General Conference of The United Methodist Church urge all our congregations to implement and enforce the provisions of the ADA and all disability-related programs within every area that members of The United Methodist Church reside with the same vigor and interest as they would any other law affecting their able-bodied constituency.

ADOPTED 2004
READOPTED 2008
RESOLUTION #46, 2004 *BOOK OF RESOLUTIONS*

*See* Social Principles, ¶ 162*I.*

## 3004. Assisting Personal Mobility

WHEREAS, the International Organization of Mobility Providers estimates that some 22 million persons worldwide lack personal mobility because of land mines, polio, wartime injuries, and a host of other causes, and

WHEREAS, these persons usually live in dire poverty, are marginalized from society, hidden away in back rooms, and are often seen as embarrassments, and

WHEREAS, these persons of God's creation often live lives of misery and discomfort, "scuttling around on the ground like crabs" (the description of a missionary in Congo), eating the dust and mud of streets and trails, looking at people's feet, and

WHEREAS, such persons seldom have an adequate social life, being unable to attend school, go to church, visit relatives, or attend community events, and

WHEREAS, they long to be productive members of society, but must depend on others for mobility, and

WHEREAS, mobility devices are available that can provide for these persons a degree of mobility giving to them the fullness of human dignity, comfort, hope and productivity they deserve, and

WHEREAS, personal mobility should be a human right for all of God's people,

*Therefore, be it resolved,* that the next quadrennium shall be declared a time to focus on the need for providing personal mobility as an act of justice and compassion; and

*Be it further resolved,* that every entity of The United Methodist Church respond generously with time and resources: to analyze the mobility needs in their community and other parts of the world; to collaborate with people in need of enhanced mobility and with organizations involved with them; and to seek appropriate ways to address needs that have been identified.

ADOPTED 2004<br>
READOPTED 2008<br>
RESOLUTION #47, 2004 BOOK OF RESOLUTIONS

*See* Social Principles, ¶ 162I.

## 3005. Strengthening Inclusivity of Individuals with Print Handicaps

WHEREAS, the Social Principles of The United Methodist Church declare that our denomination is to be in ministry with persons with disabilities, including those whose particular needs are in the area of communication (2004 *Book of Discipline,* ¶ 162G); and

WHEREAS, our communities in the United States alone include approximately 10 million persons who are blind and visually impaired, 55,200 of whom are children, whose faith journeys might be initiated, nurtured, steadied, or enriched by specialized resources, print or media, or specially designed curriculum, created with the specific goal of promoting independence, equal access, and inclusivity; and

WHEREAS, individual churches in the United Methodist connection wish to be in ministry to all persons, including those that are blind, visually impaired, and print handicapped, and yet often do not have the expertise or the financial resources to develop inclusive resources/curriculum themselves; and

WHEREAS, without resources and curriculum to meet the spiritual needs of persons who are blind, visually impaired, and print handicapped, many individuals, and possibly their families, will feel neglected by and excluded from the body of Christ; and

WHEREAS, the offerings of The United Methodist Publishing House, Discipleship Resources, and United Methodist Communications in terms of resources in Braille, audio recorded, electronic format suitable for speech readers, and accessible Web-based formats are limited at best, resulting in exclusion from worship, Sunday school classes, Bible studies, small group ministries, evangelism, and stewardship activities;

*Therefore, be it resolved,* that the General Conference of The United Methodist Church calls upon The United Methodist Publishing House, Discipleship Resources, and United Methodist Communications to address this lack of accessible resources and limited curriculum available for people who are blind, visually impaired and print handicapped, with resolve that our denomination, through the ministries of its publication and marketing agencies, might deepen the faith of those experiencing blindness, visual impairment, and print handicaps and enable them and their families to be more fully included in the body of Christ and its ministries.

ADOPTED 2008

*See* Social Principles, ¶ 162*I*.


### 3006. Care for People Who are Hard-of-Hearing

WHEREAS, an inclusive church seeks to be accessible to people who are deaf/hard-of-hearing,

*Therefore, be it resolved,* that the Commission on General Conference, beginning in 2004, budget for the full funding of Professional American Sign Language Interpretation for delegates and nondelegates to General Conference. This is to be coordinated by the General Board of Global Ministries.

ADOPTED 2000
READOPTED 2008
RESOLUTION #105, 2004 *BOOK OF RESOLUTIONS*
RESOLUTION #92, 2000 *BOOK OF RESOLUTIONS*

*See* Social Principles, ¶ 162*I*.

## 3007. Closed Captioning

WHEREAS, United Methodists and other engaged in ministry and mission with The United Methodist Church include those who have reduced or no ability to hear sounds; and

WHEREAS, these persons are thereby denied access to the rich resources of videotaped messages, stories and programs; and

WHEREAS, technology exists to provide such productions with "closed captioning";

*Therefore, be it resolved,* that The United Methodist Church encourages all videos produced by the general church, its agencies, committees, or authorized task forces to include closed captioning.

ADOPTED 2000
READOPTED 2008
RESOLUTION #106, 2004 *BOOK OF RESOLUTIONS*
RESOLUTION #93, 2000 *BOOK OF RESOLUTIONS*

*See* Social Principles, ¶ 162I.


## 3008. Communications Access for People Who Have Hearing and Sight Impairment

Because The United Methodist Church believes that all United Methodists are full members of the church and is committed to ministry by and with people with disabilities; and

Public accommodations such as restaurants, hotels, theaters, doctors' offices, pharmacies, retail stores, museums, libraries, parks, private schools, and daycare centers may not discriminate on the basis of disability, effective January 26, 1992.

Auxiliary aids and services must be provided to individuals with vision or hearing impairments or other individuals with disabilities so that they can have an equal opportunity to benefit, unless an undue burden would result. (from a synopsis prepared by the Civil Rights Division, US Department of Justice)

And because, despite sincere efforts on the part of the church, people with disabilities are still confronted by barriers to communications within the church;

*We call upon the church to:*

1. increase its awareness; and

2. use appropriate technologies to make essential communications accessible to people who are deaf and hearing impaired, including:

    a. considering production of alternative versions of church-produced video, films, or other audiovisuals at meetings for people who are deaf or hearing impaired, and people who are blind or partially sighted; and

    b. considering the use of assistive technologies in telephone communications for persons who are deaf or hearing impaired.

ADOPTED 1992
AMENDED AND READOPTED 1996
READOPTED 2004 AND 2008
RESOLUTION #107, 2004 *BOOK OF RESOLUTIONS*
RESOLUTION #94, 2000 *BOOK OF RESOLUTIONS*

*See* Social Principles, ¶ 162*I*.

## 3009. The Church and Deaf Ministries

### *A Time for Action*

Strategy and Structure for Strengthening the Connection with the Greater Deaf Community for the New Century.

A new era demands a new approach. As the greater deaf community desires to serve the church and become a resource for the whole connection, it is recommended that the General Conference of 2000 adopt the proposed plan for "Strengthening the Connection with the Greater Deaf Community for the New Century."

### *Structure*

1. A Steering Committee shall be established by an assigned staff member of the General Board of Global Ministries.

2. There shall be ten (10) members recruited for the steering committee as follows: two deaf, two deafened, two hard of hearing, one deaf-blind, one deaf institutional ministry professional, and two clergy with experience in ministry with the greater deaf community.

3. It is strongly urged that the committee be inclusive with regard to gender, ethnicity, jurisdictions, and different sign language and hearing abilities.

4. The initial meeting will be called by the staff member of the General Board of Global Ministries during the first year of the quadrennium and the Steering Committee members shall elect their own officers.

## Tasks and Objectives of the Steering Committee

1. The initial meeting of the Steering Committee shall be to establish and organize an overall agenda for the quadrennium. This agenda will include two training events where the Steering Committee and other invited members of the greater deaf community and hearing advocates will be trained in various areas of outreach to include but not be restricted to:

- presentation and advocacy skills for strengthening the connection with the greater deaf community;
- becoming resources for the general church, annual conferences, faith communities, and local churches;
- working with general boards and agencies for strengthening the connection with the greater deaf community;
- creating action plans and legislation for annual conferences and General Conference.

2. The Steering Committee shall also identify general boards and agencies as well as target annual conferences and seminaries for strengthening the connection with the greater deaf community.

3. All trained persons will be expected to serve in teams of two or more to provide resources, leadership, and a presence for the greater deaf community at annual meetings of the targeted general boards and agencies, annual conferences, and seminaries.

4. Targeted general boards and agencies will provide adequate agenda time at their annual meetings for the 2000-2004 quadrennium for these trained teams to educate, inform, and lead them to strengthen their connection with the greater deaf community.

5. Targeted annual conferences will agree to provide adequate time and access to conference staff and cabinet to educate, inform, and lead them to strengthen their connection with the greater deaf community.

6. Targeted seminaries will agree to provide adequate time and access to administration, faculty, and staff to educate, inform, and lead them to strengthen their connection with the greater deaf community.

7. Teams shall report back to the Steering Committee for direction and development as the process of strengthening the connection with the greater deaf community continues through the quadrennium.

## Accountability

The Steering Committee of "Strengthening the Connection with the Greater Deaf Community for the Next Century" will be accountable to an assigned section of the General Board of Global Ministries sharing yearly progress reports and evaluation. The steering committee shall also report to The United Methodist Congress of the Deaf for discussion, sharing information, and plans for implementation.

## Summary

As The United Methodist Church prepares to enter into a new century, one of our most pressing concerns is to strengthen our connection with one another and with our world. Methodism has a long history from its origins with John Wesley of commitment to its connection with the forgotten communities of our world. The United Methodist Church's connection with the greater deaf community is a history of forgotten stories and forgotten people. Never has there been a more important time to act as God's people and strengthen our connection with the greater deaf community for the next century.

ADOPTED 2000<br>
READOPTED 2008<br>
RESOLUTION #111, 2004 <i>BOOK OF RESOLUTIONS</i><br>
RESOLUTION #101, 2000 <i>BOOK OF RESOLUTIONS</i>

See Social Principles, ¶ 162I.

# AGING

## 3021. Abuse of Older Adults

WHEREAS, 1.5 to 2 million older adults are maltreated annually in the US; and

WHEREAS, only one in every eight of these cases is reported; and

WHEREAS, the older adult population will double by the year 2030; and

WHEREAS, elder abuse and neglect take many forms, such as beatings, sexual abuse, improper use of restraints, improper use of medications, verbal abuse, isolation abuse, stealing possessions, misuse or waste of assets, and a failure to provide food/fluids, medication, medical care, shelter and clothing.

*Therefore, be it resolved,* that we call on The United Methodist Church to break the silence and to address this social ill through education and awareness, information, counseling and referral services, support systems, and reports to the proper authorities when abuse is suspected.

*Therefore, be it further resolved,* that the Older Adult Committee and the appropriate general agencies provide resources and materials to address the issue.

ADOPTED 2000
READOPTED 2008
RESOLUTION #155, 2004 *BOOK OF RESOLUTIONS*
RESOLUTION #143, 2000 *BOOK OF RESOLUTIONS*

*See* Social Principles, ¶ 162E.


## 3022. Aging in the United States: The Church's Response


### I. The Situation

Older adult membership in The United Methodist Church is growing rapidly. In the past, the role of older people in congregations was limited, either by choice or circumstance. Congregations often viewed older adults as a liability rather than emphasizing the potential for a renewed or visionary ministry. Many of the myths and stereotypes of aging and older persons are changing.

According to the US Social Security Administration, the number of persons 65 years of age and older has grown from 3.1 million in 1900 (4 percent of the total population) to 38 million in 2007 (13 percent). This number is expected to increase to 72 million in the year 2032 (20 percent of the total population). This increase is due both to the aging of the "baby boomers" (persons born between 1946 and 1964) and increased life expectancy. In 1935 persons reaching age 65 had an average life expectancy of an additional 12.5 years; while in 2007 the life expectancy of persons reaching age 65 is an additional 17.4 years (an increase of 40 percent). The US Census Bureau projects that by 2030, minority populations will represent 25 percent of the older adult population, up from 13 percent in 1990. The older population includes a disproportionate number of women (145 women to 100 men) and persons with a wide range of capacities, from active, healthy, and employed to fragile, frail, and chronically disabled.

As a result of better health care, nutrition, and job safety, many more Americans are living into older adulthood. However, the constantly rising cost of health care in the US puts a considerable strain on the budgets of the older population. Recent studies by the AARP indicate that noninstitutionalized Medicare beneficiaries age 65 and older spend an average of $3,455 per year, or 22 percent of their income, on out-of-pocket health care expenses. While the vast majority of current Medicare beneficiaries have some type of supplemental insurance, those programs are becoming both more expensive and less available. For example, employer-based health insurance plans are becoming either much more expensive for the individual, or even being discontinued altogether for persons beyond 65 who receive Medicare.

Medicare is a health insurance program primarily for persons over the age of 65. Medicaid provides a supplement to Medicare primarily for low-income persons. Older adults who have need for specialized residences, or their families, often have no choice but to opt for a nursing home that is covered by Medicaid. This is more costly and often not the choice of the parties involved.

Although most older persons live in urban places, they also comprise a large proportion of rural populations where facilities and resources for them are extremely limited. Health care availability, transportation, and job opportunities are often lacking in rural areas. This condition is complicated further by a disproportionately low allocation of federal funds to meet the needs of the rural older adults.

Race and ethnicity are important determinants of the residential patterns of older adults. While about one third of all older persons live in central cities, one half of all African Americans and Hispanics over 65 is heavily concentrated in urban areas. The demographic shifts in housing patterns brought about by urban renewal and gentrification (higher-income persons buying property in formerly poor neighborhoods) and the resultant increase in homeowner taxes have a major impact on older adults, especially minorities. Houses that have been paid for are lost because of the tax increases, or low rents rise astronomically.

We need to dispel the common misunderstanding that aging is synonymous with senility and dementia, and that older persons are unable or unmotivated to learn, grow, and achieve. Opportunities for continuing education and growth have long been unmet by a system geared to the needs of the young. Hearing and vision loss and other physical or biological changes may impede or change the way an older adult learns; however, old age can be a time of continual learning.

Like society, faith communities are "graying," but at an even faster rate. It isn't unusual to find many local churches having an older adult membership that represents over 60 percent of their total membership, with some even higher! This is due in part to younger and middle-aged adults choosing not to participate in congregations.

Some problems that beset older persons are the result of the social and physical process of aging. These include changes in work, family, and community roles; the reduction of energy; and the increase in chronic illness and impairments. These conditions can lead to increased dependence on others for life's necessities. Other problems faced by older adults are the result of subtle and overt discrimination by social and political institutions. Being old today is not easy, in either the church or society. If the situation of older persons is to be improved, the church must act.

## II. A Theological Response

Aging is a process involving the whole life span from birth to death. The response of the church begins with a theological understanding of aging concerned with the whole life process rather than with only its final stages. The meaning of life, rather than death, is the central point from which to theologize about aging. In The United Methodist Church, there are many legitimate theological understandings of the meaning of life in its progression from birth to death. The position presented here is one attempt to express this meaning.

1. All of creation is God's work (Genesis 1). Human beings are only a small part of the totality of life forms. The aging process is universal in all life forms. Birth, aging, and death are all part of divine providence and are to be regarded and taught as positive values.

2. As Christians, the mystery of God's involvement in the person of Jesus Christ provides us with a unique source of divine help (grace) in our passage through life's successive stages. This is especially significant in the later stages, when spiritual maturation and well-being can be experienced even in times of physical decline. The power of the cross is a special revelation of how suffering can be reconciling and redemptive. Faith in the Resurrection provides us with an assurance of the abiding presence of the Risen Lord (Matthew 28:20) and the Holy Spirit (John 14:16-19; 2 Corinthians 3:17-18; Romans 8:9-11), and

the permanence of our relationship with God beyond the mystery of death. In this spiritual presence we also find the source of the potential of all persons for self-transcendence. God's act in Christ was for life abundant (John 10:10) in all stages of life. Christ also gives us our traditional Wesleyan vision of the goal of ultimate perfection (Matthew 5:48). The grace of God in Christ is therefore important throughout life, including its last stages.

3. In response to this saving grace, we believe in the inevitable need to walk in the ways of obedience that God has enabled (Ephesians 2:8-10). These ways are defined by love for God and neighbor (Mark 12:28-31; Romans 13:8-9). It is therefore the privilege of Christians to serve all persons in love, including older persons with their special needs. Furthermore, since God's grace is not conditioned by any human standards of worthiness or usefulness (2 Corinthians 5:19), all persons are valuable to God (Matthew 6:25-30). In the larger pattern of human needs and rights, those of older adults must be consciously and intentionally included.

4. Older persons are not simply to be served but are also to serve; they are of special importance in the total mission of the church. Since the Christian vocation has no retirement age, the special contributions of older adults need conscious recognition and employment. The experience of all older persons, and the wisdom of many, is a special resourcefor the whole church.

5. The church as the body of Christ in the world today (1 Corinthians 12:27) is God's method for realizing the reconciliation accomplished by Christ (Colossians 1:16-20). As such, it intentionally sponsors institutional forums that help reconcile persons of all ages to one another and to God. This especially includes those institutions designed to meet the needs of older adults and to keep them fully incorporated into the body of Christ. The church also is charged with an abiding concern for justice for all. It should work tirelessly for the freedom of all persons to meet their own fullest potential and to liberate those who are captive to discrimination, neglect, exploitation, abuse, or poverty.

### III. Calls to Action

#### A. By society at all levels

United Methodists are called to advocate for the elimination of age discrimination in personal attitudes and institutional structures. We should pursue this advocacy vigorously and in cooperation with appropriate private and public groups, including all levels of government. Our efforts should be based on the following:

1. Religious institutions make a unique and significant contribution to human life. Living involves ethical issues and value decisions. Therefore, a religious presence is important to the quality of total community life.

2. Governments should play a critical role in ensuring that all benefits are available to all older adults to improve their quality of life. Christians should support governmental policies that promote sharing with those who are less fortunate. This does not absolve either the institutional church or individual Christians from responsibility for persons in need.

3. A standard of basic survival support systems should be accepted and established in our society and made available to all persons. These systems should include: health care, transportation, housing, and income maintenance at a minimum. Christians need to identify and promote those facilities and services that ensure opportunities for prolonged well-being. These services need to be provided within the financial means of older adults, with appropriate public subsidy when necessary. They include the following:

    a. universal comprehensive health insurance program;

    b. national legislation correcting the disparity in Medicare's failure to cover full prescription drug needs;

    c. health-resources systems special to the needs of older adults that are comprehensive, accessible, and feasible within available resources (these include long-term care, hospice care, home health care, and health maintenance organizations);

    d. health-education systems that emphasize proper nutrition, proper drug use, preventive health care, and immunization as well as information about the availability of health resources within the community;

    e. training for medical and social service personnel concerning the special cultural, physical, psychosocial, and spiritual aspects and needs of older adults;

    f. adequate housing that is both affordable and secure, with protections that massive tax and rental increases will not create displacement, and transportation systems that meet the special needs of older adults;

  g. national legislation correcting the disparity in Medicare's failure to cover either assisted living residences or dementia-specific housing, or home nursing care;
  h. a basic governmental income-maintenance system adequate to sustain an adequate standard of living affording personal dignity;
  i. basic pension systems benefit levels adequate to meet economic needs at least equal to the defined poverty level, supplementation by benefits from public funds;
  j. continuing educational and counseling opportunities for older adults in pre-retirement planning, in work-related training, in interpersonal retirement relationships, and in personal enrichment;
  k. formal and informal community associations such as public and private centers that foster social, recreational, artistic, intellectual, and spiritual activities to help persons overcome loneliness and social isolation;
  l. continuing employment opportunities for those who desire them in flexible, appropriate work settings related to varying lifestyles; and
  m. opportunities for volunteer work and paid employment that best utilize the skills and experiences of older adults.

4. Finally, our society is called upon to respond to a basic human right of older adults: the right to faithful care in dying and to have personal wishes respected concerning the number and type of life-sustaining measures that should be used to prolong life. Living wills, requesting no heroic measures be used, and other such efforts to die with faithful care should be supported.

## B. By the church at all levels

*1. All levels of the church are called to:*
  a. practice nondiscrimination in the church on the basis of age in hiring, deployment, and promotion of older workers, including the appointment of clergy;
  b. include ministries by, with and for older adults as an essential and intentional component of the church and its mission;
  c. promote flexible retirement and eliminate mandatory retirement based solely on age;
  d. develop theological statements on death and dying recognizing the basic human right to faithful care of the dying;

e. address the questions raised by the declining quality of life; stimulate research to connect the improvement of the quality of life with longevity of life, raised by increased longevity;

f. develop ethical guidelines for dealing with difficult medical decisions that involve the use of limited resources for health and life insurance;

g. authorize appropriate research, including a demographic study of members of The United Methodist Church, to provide greatly needed information on the psycho-social and spiritual aspects of aging; and

h. establish a properly funded pension system with an adequate minimum standard for all clergy and church-employed lay persons and their spouses, including the divorced spouse.

2. *Each local church is called to:*

a. become aware of the needs and interests of older people in the congregation and in the community, including the places in which they reside, and to express Christian love through person-to-person understanding and caring;

b. intentionally sponsor ministries in institutions designed to meet the needs of older adults, such as nursing homes, assisted living residences, and dementia-specific housing as well as the homes of older adults living alone, as we keep these older persons fully incorporated in the body of Christ;

c. affirm the cultural and historical contributions and gifts of ethnic older adults;

d. acknowledge that ministry by, with, and for older adults is needed in congregations of all sizes;

e. support, equip, and train lay volunteers with a dedication for this important ministry;

f. develop a barrier-free environment in which older adults can function in spite of impairments;

g. develop an intentional ministry with older adults that:
   • ensures life maintenance for each person related to adequate food, health service, mobility, personal security, income, and other personal services;
   • offers opportunities for life enrichment including intellectual stimulation, social involvement, spiritual cultivation, and artistic pursuits;

- encourages life reconstruction when necessary, including motivation and guidance in making new friends, serving new roles in the community that help people cope with loss, and providing support systems for older adults experiencing losses; and
- affirms life transcendence, including celebration of the meaning and purpose of life through worship, Bible study, personal reflection, and small-group life;
- recognizes that older persons represent a creative resource bank available to the church and to involve them in service to the community as persons of insight and wisdom (this could include not only ministry to one another, but also to the larger mission of the church for redemption of the world, including reaching the unchurched);
- relates to secular retirement communities within its boundaries;
- fosters intergenerational experiences in the congregation and community including educating all age groups about how to grow old with dignity and satisfaction;
- ensures that the frail are not separated from the life of the congregation but retain access to the sacraments and are given assistance as needed by the caring community;
- provides support and information for adults caring for aging parents;
- cooperates with other churches and community agencies for more comprehensive and effective ministries with older persons;
- accepts responsibility for an advocacy role in behalf of older adults; and
- develops older-adult ministries responsible to the church council. A staff position or older adult council may be needed to facilitate this ministry with older adults.

3. *Each annual conference is called to:*
   · a. provide leadership and support for an intentional ministry to older persons in its local churches, with special attention to the needs of women and minorities;

b. develop a program of job counseling and retirement planning for clergy and lay employees;

c. share creative models of ministry and a data bank of resources with the local churches and other agencies;

d. define the relationship between the annual conference and United Methodist-related residential and nonresidential facilities for older adults, so that the relationships can be clearly understood and mutually supportive;

e. recruit persons for professional leadership in working with older adults;

f. serve as both a partner and critic to local church and public programs with older adults, promoting ecumenical linkages where possible;

g. support financially, if needed, retired clergy and lay church workers and their spouses who reside in United Methodist long-term care settings;

h. promote Golden Cross Sunday and other special offerings for ministries by, for, and with older adults; and

i. recognize that older persons within the conference, both lay and clergy, represent a significant and experienced resource that should be utilized in both the organization and mission of the conference.

4. *General boards and agencies are called to:*

a. examine the pension policies of the general church and their impact related to the needs of those who are single (retired, divorced, or surviving dependents of pensioners);

b. create specific guidance materials for ministry by, for, and with older adults;

c. prepare intergenerational and age-specific materials for church school and for other special studies in the local church;

d. promote advocacy in behalf of all older adults, but especially those who do not have access to needed services because of isolation, low income, or disability (this might include advocacy for health care, income maintenance, and other social legislation);

e. assist institutions for older adultsto maintain quality care and to develop resource centers for ministry with and by older adults;

f. create a variety of nonresidential ministries for older adults;

g. coordinate general church training in ministry with older adults;
h. provide for formal coordination on aging issues;
i. advocate the special concerns and needs of older women and minorities; and
j. utilize older persons as a creative resource bank in the design and implementation of these objectives.

5. *Retirement and long-term care facilities related to the church are called to:*
   a. develop a covenant relationship with the church to reinforce a sense of joint mission in services with older adults;
   b. encourage the provision of charitable support and provide a channel for the assistance of the whole church; and
   c. encourage both residential and nonresidential institutional settings that emphasize the spiritual, personal, physical, and social needs of older adults.

6. *Finally, seminaries and colleges are called to:*
   a. provide seminarians with instruction on aging and experiences with older persons in the curriculum;
   b. prepare persons for careers in the field of aging;
   c. develop special professorships to teach gerontology, and to provide continuing education for those who work with older adults;
   d. engage in basic and applied research related to aging, and communicate the findings;
   e. develop a system for sharing research results with the church;
   f. enable older adultsto enroll in courses and degree programs and to participate generally in the life of educational institutions; and
   g. develop and offer lay courses in locations accessible to older persons.

## IV. Summary

Concern for older persons in the church is theologically grounded in the doctrine of Creation, in the meaning of God's work in Christ, in the response to grace that leads us into service, in the continuing value of older persons in the larger mission, and in the nature of the church as an agent of redemption and defender of justice for all.

Older adults deserve respect, dignity, and equal opportunity. The United Methodist Church is called to be an advocate for older adults, for their sense of personal identity and dignity, for utilization of experience, wisdom, and skills, for health maintenance, adequate income, educational opportunities, and vocational and avocational experiences in cooperation with the public and private sectors of society.

The aging process is part of God's plan for life, with the good news of Christ's redemption giving hope and purpose. United Methodists are called to live this message through words and deeds in the church and in society.

ADOPTED 1988
REVISED AND ADOPTED 2000
REVISED AND ADOPTED 2008
RESOLUTION #156, 2004 *BOOK OF RESOLUTIONS*
RESOLUTION #144, 2000 *BOOK OF RESOLUTIONS*

*See* Social Principles, ¶ 162E.

## 3023. Older Adult Recognition Day

WHEREAS, special observances in The United Methodist Church are intended to illustrate the nature and calling of the church and are celebrated annually; and

WHEREAS, special observances are placed on the calendar to make clear the calling of the church as the people of God; and

WHEREAS, both the population in the United States and throughout the world is increasingly aging and growing older as more people are living longer; and

WHEREAS, the average age of the membership in The United Methodist Church is comprised of persons 60 years of age and older; and

WHEREAS, older adults make significant and important contributions in the life of The United Methodist Church and to the spreading of the gospel throughout the world; and

WHEREAS, the scripture commands us to "honor your father and your mother,"

*Therefore, be it resolved,* that The United Methodist Church observe an annual Older Adult Recognition Day; and

*Be it further resolved,* that an Older Adult Recognition Day may be observed annually, preferably during the month of May. The day is to recognize and celebrate the gifts, talents, and contributions older adults make within and beyond the local church. The day should also provide congregations with the opportunity to learn more about the issues and concerns related to aging and older adulthood. The Committee on Older Adult Ministries will have responsibility for the supervision and promotion of the observance of this special day.

ADOPTED 2008

See Social Principles, ¶ 162E.


## 3024. Mission and Aging of the Global Population

Throughout the world, many older persons look to religion for meaning in life, for opportunities to serve, and for a way to address human suffering. The achievement of long life among increasing numbers of global citizens holds possibilities for an invigorated ministry by, for, and with older persons. In taking action, older people challenge discriminatory perceptions of the aged and reveal abundant talents and capacities.

From the earliest days reported in our Scripture, the stories of our faith have looked at aging realistically but positively. Ecclesiastes 12 catalogues the physical miseries of old age with the warning to "remember your creator in the days of your youth, before the days of trouble come" (12:1, NRSV). Nevertheless, the patriarchal stories, depicting individuals who lived hundreds of years, expressed the belief that life itself was good and, therefore, extended life was very good. Age was presumed to bring wisdom, and the elders of Israel were looked to for guidance (Exodus 12:21, etc.), as were, later, the elders of the church (Acts 20:17). Age brings its own pleasures, including grandchildren (Proverbs 17:6), and is marked by the beauty of gray hair (Proverbs 20:29). A life well lived, that is righteous in the sight of God, gives purpose to our aging; Psalm 92 vividly pictures the righteous elderly, "who flourish like the palm tree . . . in old age they still produce fruit; they are always green and full of sap" (92:12, 14, NRSV). Those who survive to old age are, therefore, to be honored, especially one's father and mother (Deuteronomy 5:16; Mark 10:19). It can be assumed that when Paul spoke of giving "honor to whom honor is due" (Romans 13:7), he meant to include respect for older persons. A sign of the coming of the Lord is that not only young but also old shall be merry (Jeremiah 31:13). Zechariah's vision of a truly restored Jerusalem was one in which not only would once again the streets be full of boys and girls playing, but of old men and old women sitting, "each with staff in hand because of their great age" (Zechariah 8:4-5, NRSV).

Through the centuries, the church has held varying attitudes toward older persons, but the prevailing tradition accords dignity to persons in old age. This tradition underpins our United Methodist Social Principles statement on rights of the aging, in which social policies and programs are called for "that ensure to the aging the respect and dignity that is their right as senior members of the human community" (¶ 162E).

In 2002, the United Nations' World Assembly on Ageing stated clearly the demographic facts that confront this century: "The world is experiencing an unprecedented demographic transformation. By 2050, the number of persons aged 60 years and over will increase from 600 million to almost 2 billion; the proportion of persons aged 60 years and over is expected to double from 10 percent to 21 percent. The increase will be greatest and most rapid in developing countries where the older population is expected to quadruple during the next fifty years. This demographic transformation challenges all societies to promote increased opportunities, in particular, for older persons to realize their potential to participate fully in all aspects of life."

Advances in public health and education, as well as control of infectious diseases, have contributed to these changes. Nevertheless, the extreme conditions of poverty, war and hunger, and the HIV/AIDS pandemic prevent realization of the biblical hope for a blessed old age. In situations of armed conflict, combatants increasingly target older persons. All too frequently, families and other caregivers abuse older persons in domestic and institutional settings. Income support and access to health care in old age apply only to a small minority in many countries. Age and gender discrimination often blocks access to the participation and involvement throughout the world. In these challenging situations, a greater proportion of older persons now take their own lives.

Many older persons live in vulnerable situations. They live in rural areas, working the land, and are predominantly female. Older persons are heavily concentrated in agriculture, with manufacturing jobs ranking a distant second. Women outlive men in virtually all countries.

Most women past age sixty-five are widows, a trend likely to continue. They suffer low incomes and chronic illnesses. Less than 10 percent of older women in many poor societies read or write. Across the globe, traditional social support based on family structures continues to erode, leaving many elders in isolation with no one to care for them in their last years.

In some developing countries, older persons attract love and respect precisely because of their experience and their place as wise leaders and survivors within the community. Contrast this love and respect with some attitudes in the United States and other Western nations that deprecates old age because it is less "productive," or because physical energy and commercial images of beauty replace spiritual energy and the beauty of the inner soul. For this reason, the United States and other developed societies can learn much from other societies.

Responding to these challenges, the United Nations, in its 2002 International Plan of Action on Ageing, recommends action in three directions: assuring older persons right to social and economic development; advancing health and well being into old age; and ensuring enabling and supportive environments.

In the United States, the great majority of older persons have access to public social insurance through Social Security and Medicare. Those in The United Methodist Church celebrate the inclusion of older persons in decision-making structures throughout the church. Appreciation for these advances does not blind us to misguided efforts to depict older persons as benefiting, at the expense of the young, to the low quality of care in many nursing homes and to outright abuse in families, institutions, and organizations that employ older persons. We must remain vigilant to keep government programs publicly available to all, free of privatized substitutes that sharply limit many older persons' access to income support and health care.

The United Methodist Church calls upon

   A.  Local churches to:

        1.  involve older adults intergenerationally and in ways that empower and encourage them to use resources for skills, knowledge, experience, and spiritual insight; and

        2.  use resources from general agencies of The United Methodist Church that suggest actions and models for

learning from other cultures and countries in their understanding of and appreciation of older persons.

B. Annual conferences to:

1. involve older adults in the full range of programs of the conference, including Volunteer in Mission (VIM) projects; health ministries in which able older adults care for the frail elderly; public advocacy; and use of resources and action suggestions from the Committee of Older Adult Ministries of The United Methodist Church;

2. ask itinerating missionaries to speak to constructive ways churches in the United States can: (a) learn from the customs, values, and practices of churches in other countries and cultures; and (b) support older persons in other countries and cultures through Advance Specials, VIM projects, and mission support; and

3. study the United Nations International Plan of Action on Ageing adopted in 2002 as a basis for action initiatives and guide to programming.

C. All general program agencies of The United Methodist Church to:

1. develop resources and programs that support and undergird the faith development of older adults and encourage their full participation in ministry;

2. identify specific actions in their ongoing programs and ministries by which families on a global basis can be assisted in caring for their frail elderly;

3. include older persons in training for care-giving in relation to mission and ministry globally; and

4. provide analysis and advocacy training to equip older adults to defend and expand public policies and programs that serve all elders.

D. The General Board of Church and Society and the General Board of Global Ministries to:

1. advocate support for older persons' needs and capacities in governmental and nongovernmental organizations, including the United Nations, the US government, and ecumenical and other nongovernmental international organizations; and

2. study and share with the whole Church pertinent issues related to the well-being of older persons, such as allocation of governmental resources for support and care, end-of-life issues, and avoidance of age discrimination in employment and community life.

E. The General Board of Global Ministries to include in mission education:

1. positive images of older persons in all countries and cultures, along with images realistically depicting the difficulties many of these persons have under conditions of poverty and isolation;

2. information about the "double bind" in which many poor societies find themselves by virtue of the demands of a growing young population and the demands of a growing older population; and

3. resources for annual conferences and local churches that provide models for appropriate mission and ministry on the local level, and specific action and program suggestions.

F. All general agencies and all episcopal leadership to:

1. include older persons as full participants in programs and ministries from planning through decision making and evaluation;

2. seek opportunities by which The United Methodist Church can affirm its aging members, and offer ways that older members can collaborate with younger persons in evangelism and renewal of the whole church, to the end that persons of all ages are called to the discipleship of Jesus Christ; and

3. lift the prophetic voice of Christian faith to proclaim a vision of human community in which older persons are accorded respect and dignity as those made in the image of God and part of the human family.

ADOPTED 2004
READOPTED 2008
RESOLUTION #313, 2004 *BOOK OF RESOLUTIONS*
RESOLUTION #297, 2000 *BOOK OF RESOLUTIONS*

*See* Social Principles, ¶¶ 162 and 165.

## ALCOHOL AND OTHER DRUGS

### 3041. Alcoholic Beverage Advertising at the Olympics

WHEREAS, the Bible tells us that our bodies are "temples of the living God" (1 Corinthians 6:13-20) and since we are created in God's own image, we should strive to perfect our bodies in God's image;

WHEREAS, the founders United Methodism provide historical under-girdings for our strong witness on abstinence from alcohol; Susanna Wesley in a letter to John Wesley influenced and urged piety with these words: *"Take this rule: whatever weakens your reason, impairs the tenderness of your conscience, obscures your sense of God, or takes off the relish of spiritual things; in short, whatever increases the strength and authority of your body over your mind, that thing is sin to you, however innocent it may be in itself"; and*

WHEREAS, John Wesley in his sermon on the use of money urges, *'Neither may we gain by hurting our neighbor in his body. Therefore we may not sell anything which tends to impair health. Such is, eminently, all that liquid fire commonly call 'drams' or spirituous liquor"; and*

WHEREAS, sports events display athletic ability, and the Olympics are an exhibition of the highest achievement in athletic ability; and

WHEREAS, the consumption of alcoholic beverages inhibits athletic ability rather than increases it; and

WHEREAS, the consumption of alcoholic beverages contributes to many problems in society such as automobile accidents, assaults on women and children, suicide, and drowning, to mention a few; and

WHEREAS, advertising of alcoholic beverages will associate them in the mind of the public with the highest achievement in athletic ability, which is a false message;

*Therefore, be it resolved,* that The United Methodist Church strongly protests beer or any alcoholic beverage being advertised at or near all Olympics games or any other sporting event,

*And be it further resolved,* that we consider it scandalous for any alcoholic beverage to be listed as a sponsor of the Olympics event, or any other national or international sports organization,

*And be it further resolved,* that the secretary of the General Conference is instructed to send a copy of this resolution to the Olympic Organizing Committees.

ADOPTED 2000
AMENDED AND READOPTED 2004
RESOLUTION #82, 2004 *BOOK OF RESOLUTIONS*
RESOLUTION #72, 2000 *BOOK OF RESOLUTIONS*

*See* Social Principles, ¶ 162L.

## 3042. Alcohol and Other Drugs

As God's children and participants in the gift of abundant life, we recognize the need to respond to those who know brokenness from the widespread abuse of alcohol and other drugs in our world. The experience of God's saving grace offers wholeness to each individual. In light of the reality of alcohol and other drug abuse, the church has a responsibility to recognize brokenness and to be an instrument of education, healing, and restoration. First, we must be committed to confronting the denial within ourselves that keeps individuals and nations from overcoming their struggle with alcohol and other drug abuse. Second, the alcohol and other drug problem must be understood as a social, economic, spiritual, and health problem. Third, the church has a fundamental role in reorienting the public debate on alcohol and other drugs by shifting the focus from punishment to prevention and treatment. This is rooted in the Christian belief in the ongoing possibilities for transformation in the life of each individual and in our world.

The alcohol and other drug crisis has reached global proportions. More alcohol and other drugs are produced and consumed than ever before. In consuming countries, with their attendant problems of poverty, racism, domestic violence, hopelessness, and material despair, alcohol and other drug abuse is a part of a continuing cycle of economic and spiritual turmoil.

Abuse of legal drugs (alcohol, tobacco, and pharmaceuticals) remains a leading cause of disease and death around the world. While recreational use of illegal drugs in the United States has declined, the use of drugs remains socially acceptable as levels of addiction and abuse continue to rise.

Growing numbers of cities, small towns, and rural areas around the world are caught in a web of escalating alcohol and other drug-related violence. As the findings of the regional hearings in the United States stressed: "Drug addiction crosses all ethnic, cultural, and economic backgrounds." Social systems are dangerously strained under the heavy weight of alcohol and other drug-related health and social problems. Meanwhile, the supply of drugs from developing countries continues to grow in response to high demand from the developed countries.

The United States policy response to the drug crisis has focused almost exclusively on law enforcement and military solutions. This policy, in some cases, has led to the erosion of precious civil liberties and human rights, especially for poor and minority communities.

International strategies should reflect the need for balanced, equitable economic growth and stable democratic governments in drug-producing developing countries. Most importantly, any alternative strategy must be rooted in local communities. The most creative and effective approaches to the present crisis begin at the local level.

The United Methodist Church has long opposed abuse of alcohol and other drugs. In 1916, the General Conference authorized the formation of a Board of Temperance, Prohibition, and Public Morals "to make more effectual the efforts of the church to create public sentiment and crystallize the same into successful opposition to the organized traffic in intoxicating liquors."

During the 1988-92 quadrennium, The United Methodist Church launched a comprehensive Bishops' Initiative on Drugs and Drug Violence, which, through regional hearings across the United States, deepened the denomination's awareness of alcohol and other drug problems. The report of these hearings concluded: "Therefore, The United Methodist Church must play a key role in confronting drug and alcohol addiction. . . ." Today, The United Methodist Church remains committed to curbing drug traffic and the abuse of alcohol and other drugs.

In response to the alcohol and other drug crisis, The United Methodist Church commits itself to a holistic approach, which emphasizes prevention, intervention, treatment, community organization, public advocacy, and abstinence. Out of love for God and our neighbors, the church must have a positive role by offering a renewed spiritual perspective on this crisis. We commend local congregations, annual conferences, and general agencies and seminaries to take action in the areas of alcohol, tobacco, and other drugs.

## I. Alcohol

Alcohol is a drug, which presents special problems because of its widespread social acceptance. We affirm our long-standing conviction and recommendation that abstinence from alcoholic beverages is a faithful witness to God's liberating and redeeming love.

This witness is especially relevant because excessive, harmful, and dangerous drinking patterns are uncritically accepted and practiced. Society glamorizes drinking, and youthful immaturity can be exploited for personal gain. The costs associated with alcohol use/abuse are more than the costs associated with all illegal drugs combined. Worldwide, millions of individuals and their families suffer as a result of alcoholism. The medical consequences of alcohol abuse include fetal alcohol syndrome—which is a preventable cause of mental retardation, cardiac defects, and pre- and postnatal growth retardation. Chronic alcohol consumption can have a damaging effect on every body organ, including brain, liver, heart, stomach, intestines, and mouth. Alcohol is a factor in many other social problems such as crime, poverty, and family disorder. The societal costs of alcohol abuse include lost productivity, increased health-care costs, loss of lives in vehicular accidents, and criminal activity.

Thus, The United Methodist Church bases its recommendation of abstinence on critical appraisal of the personal and societal costs in the use of alcohol. The church recognizes the freedom of the Christian to make responsible decisions and calls upon each member to consider seriously and prayerfully the witness of abstinence as part of his or her Christian commitment. Persons who practice abstinence should avoid attitudes of self-righteousness that express moral superiority and condemnatory attitudes toward those who do not choose to abstain. Because Christian love in human relationships is primary, abstinence is an instrument of love and sacrifice and always subject to the requirements of love.

Our love for our neighbor obligates us to seek healing, justice, and the alleviation of the social conditions that create and perpetuate alcohol abuse.

*Therefore:*

1. We urge individuals and local congregations to demonstrate active concern for alcohol abusers and their families. We encourage churches to support the care, treatment, and rehabilitation of problem drinkers.

2. We urge churches to include the problems of alcohol and the value of abstinence as a part of Christian education.

3. We encourage individuals and local congregations to develop prevention education for family, church, and community. We encourage sound empirical research on the social effects of alcohol.

4. We oppose the sale and consumption of alcoholic beverages within the confines of United Methodist Church facilities and recommend that it be prohibited.

5. We ask individuals and local congregations to study and discuss the problem of driving while intoxicated and impaired by alcohol or other drugs, and we support legislation to reduce such activity.

6. We direct the General Board of Discipleship and The United Methodist Publishing House to incorporate educational material on alcohol and other drug problems, including the material on prevention, intervention, treatment, and the value of abstinence throughout its graded literature.

7. We expect United Methodist-related hospitals to treat the alcoholic person with the attention and consideration all patients deserve. We urge the worldwide health-care delivery system to follow this example.

8. We urge all legislative bodies and health-care systems and processes to focus on and implement measures to help meet the special needs of those disproportionately affected by alcohol use.

9. We favor laws to eliminate all advertising and promoting of alcoholic beverages. We urge the General Board of Church and Society and local churches to increase efforts to remove all advertising of alcoholic beverages from the media. We urge special attention to curbing promotions of alcoholic beverages on college campuses as well as racial minority communities.

10. We urge the US Federal Trade Commission and agencies of other governments to continue developing better health hazard warning statements concerning the use of alcohol.

11. We urge the United States government to improve interagency coordination of drug and alcohol abuse efforts so that there are uniform policies and regulations, and we urge the cooperation of all governments in these areas.

## II. Tobacco

The use of tobacco is another form of drug abuse, even though it is legal. Overwhelming evidence links cigarette-smoking with lung cancer, cardiovascular diseases, emphysema, and chronic bronchitis. In addition, cigarette-smoking can negatively affect a developing fetus, and secondary smoke is a known carcinogen. The United Methodist Church discourages all persons, particularly children, youths and young adults, from using any form of tobacco.

We commend the suspension of cigarette advertising on radio and television. We are concerned about other advertisements that associate smoking with physical and social maturity, attractiveness, and success, especially those targeted at youth, racial minorities, and women. We support the rules of the US Federal Trade Commission and agencies of other governments requiring health warning statements in cigarette packaging. We are also concerned that the tobacco industry is marketing tobacco in developing countries. *Therefore:*

1. We recommend that tobacco use be banned in all church facilities.
2. We recommend a tobacco-free environment in all public areas.
3. We recommend the prohibition of all commercial advertising of tobacco products.
4. We support expanded research to discover the specific mechanisms of addiction to nicotine. We urge the development of educational methods that effectively discourage the use of tobacco and methods to assist those who wish to stop using tobacco.
5. We urge the Department of Agriculture and other government agencies to plan for and assist the orderly economic transition of the tobacco industry—tobacco growers, processors, and distributors—into industries more compatible with the general welfare of the people.
6. We support comprehensive tobacco control policies and legislation that includes provisions to: a) support The Framework Convention on Tobacco Control (FCTC), the Global Tobacco Treaty and its provisions; b) reduce the rate of youth smoking by increasing the price of cigarettes; c) protect tobacco farmers by helping them shift from tobacco to other crops;d) give the US Food and Drug Administration full authority to regulate nicotine as a drug in the United States; and e) fund anti-tobacco research and advertising, as well as education and prevention campaigns.

### III. Drugs

Pharmacologically, a drug is any substance that by its chemical nature alters the structure or function of any living organism. This broad definition encompasses a wide range of substances, many of which are psychoactive and have the potential for abuse. These include marijuana, narcotics, sedatives and stimulants, psychedelics, and hallucinogens. Additionally, commonly used products such as glue, paint thinners, and gasoline have the potential to be abused as inhalants. The United Methodist Church grieves the widespread misuse of drugs and other commonly used products that alter mood, perception, consciousness, and behavior of persons among all ages, classes, and segments of our society.

## A. Marijuana

Like alcohol and tobacco, marijuana is frequently a precursor to the use of other drugs. The active ingredient is THC, which affects the user by temporarily producing feelings of euphoria or relaxation. An altered sense of body image and bouts of exaggerated laughter are commonly reported. However, studies reveal that marijuana impairs short-term memory, altering sense of time and reducing the ability to perform tasks requiring concentration, swift reactions, and coordination. Some countries permit the use of marijuana in medicines. Recently, some states in the United States have passed legislation permitting the medical use of marijuana. The medical use of any drug should not be seen as encouraging recreational use of the drug. We urge all persons to abstain from all use of marijuana, unless it has been legally prescribed in a form appropriate for treating a particular medical condition.[1]

## B. Sedatives and Stimulants

Sedatives, which include barbiturates and tranquilizers, are prescribed appropriately for treatment of anxiety. These legally prescribed drugs need to be taken only under appropriate medical supervision. The use of this class of drugs can result in dependence.

Severe physical dependence on barbiturates can develop at doses higher than therapeutic doses, and withdrawal is severe and dangerous. The combination of alcohol and barbiturates is potentially lethal.

Stimulants range from amphetamines such as methamphetamine ("crystal meth") to mild stimulants such as caffeine and nicotine. Prescribed for obesity, sleep disorders, hyperactivity, fatigue, and depression, stimulants produce a temporary sense of vitality, alertness, and energy.

Unlike other stimulants, cocaine has limited medical uses. When the powder form is inhaled, cocaine is a highly addictive central nervous system stimulant that heightens the body's natural response to pleasure and creates a euphoric high, and has the potential to be extremely lethal. "Crack," a crystallized form of cocaine, is readily available because of its lesser cost. Addiction often comes from one use of the substance.

1. Performance Resource Press, Inc., Troy, Michigan.

## C. Psychedelics or Hallucinogens

Psychedelics or hallucinogens, which include LSD, psilocybin, mescaline, PCP, and DMT, produce changes in perception and altered states of consciousness. Not only is there limited medical use, the use of these drugs may result in permanent psychiatric problems.

## D. Narcotics

Narcotics are prescribed for the relief of pain, but the risk of physical and psychological dependencies is well documented. Derived from the opium plant, natural narcotics include heroin, morphine, codeine, and percodan, while synthetic narcotics include oxycodone, methadone, and meperidine.

*Therefore,* as The United Methodist Church:

1. We oppose the use of all drugs, except in cases of appropriate medical supervision.

2. We encourage the church to develop honest, objective, and factual drug education for children, youths, and adults as part of a comprehensive prevention education program.

3. We urge the church to coordinate its efforts with ecumenical, interfaith, and community groups in prevention, rehabilitation, and policy statements.

4. We encourage the annual conferences to recognize the unique impact of drugs and its related violence upon urban and rural areas and provide appropriate ministries and resources.

5. We strongly encourage annual conferences to develop leadership training opportunities and resources for local church pastors and laity to help them with counseling individuals and families who have alcohol and other drug-related problems; counseling those bereaved by alcohol and other drug-related deaths and violence; and teaching stress management to church workers in communities with high alcohol and other drug activity.

6. We support comprehensive tobacco control policies and legislation that includes provisions to: a) reduce the rate of youth smoking by increasing the price of cigarettes; b) protect tobacco farmers by helping them shift from tobacco to other crops; c) give the US Food and Drug Administration full authority to regulate nicotine as a drug in the United States; d) fund anti-tobacco research and advertising, as well as education and prevention campaigns.

7. We urge redevelopment of more effective methods of treatment of drug abuse and addiction.

8. We support government policies that restrict access to over-the-counter drugs such as ephedrine derivatives that can be converted to illegal and addictive drugs; for example, "crystal meth."

9. We support government policies concerning drugs that are compatible with our Christian beliefs about the potential transformation of all individuals.

10. We urge all United Methodist churches to work for a minimum legal drinking age of twenty-one years in their respective states/nations.

11. We support strong, humane law-enforcement efforts against the illegal sale of all drugs, and we urge that those arrested for possession and use of illegally procured drugs be subject to education and rehabilitation.

12. We note with deep concern that law enforcement against possession and use of illegally procured drugs has resulted in a dramatic increase in jail and prison populations, often consisting disproportionally of poor minority young persons, often due to huge sentencing disparities between possession of "crack" cocaine (the cheaper form, used more by poor minorities, where possession of only 5 grams is subject to a five-year mandatory minimum sentence) and possession of powder cocaine (the more expensive and purer form where possession of 500 grams or more is necessary to invoke a five-year mandatory minimum sentence), even though the two forms are pharmacologically identical, and therefore call for fairness in sentencing through reform of sentencing guidelines governing the possession and use of powder and crack cocaine.

ADOPTED 1996
AMENDED AND ADOPTED 2000
AMENDED AND READOPTED 2004
AMENDED AND READOPTED 2008
RESOLUTION #83, 2004 *BOOK OF RESOLUTIONS*
RESOLUTION #73, 2000 *BOOK OF RESOLUTIONS*

*See* Social Principles, ¶ 162L.

## 3043. Keep Children and Youth Free from Alcohol and Other Drugs

Our Christian faith calls us to teach and lead children and youth through Jesus' example. By his example, we are called to give children special attention enabling them to be free from harm (Matthew 19:13-15, NRSV). Alarming statistics make it clear that the United States and many other countries have not given the proper attention to the use of alcohol and other drugs by children and youth and that as a society, we tolerate access to alcohol and other drugs by underage young people. For example, it is illegal in most US states to sell or give alcoholic beverages to those under 21, and illicit use and sale of controlled substances is a crime at any age, yet more than a third of children begin using alcohol before they are teens and one in ten young teens is a regular user of marijuana and other drugs. Research shows that alcohol and other drugs bring harm to growing bodies and minds. Young people with inner stamina, self-esteem, and a strong and vital faith can more readily say, "no" to alcohol and other drugs. To address this critical problem, many schools have instituted programs on alcohol and other drugs. However, the Justice Department reports that many school programs aimed to help young people have not deterred their use of alcohol and other drugs. Inattention to this critical issue and the failure of many school programs demonstrates the importance of a comprehensive action plan among faith communities to address this crisis.

*Therefore, be it resolved,* that The United Methodist Church supports efforts to keep children and youth alcohol free, drug free, and safe from access to illicit drug use. By following a comprehensive approach to this issue young people can understand the importance of avoiding use of alcohol and other illicit drugs to ensure that they live full and healthy lives.

### An Action Plan for the Church to Combat the Use of Alcohol and Other Illicit Drugs Among Children and Youth

1. We call upon individual families to pray for their children and to teach their children by precept and example the preference of avoiding beverage alcohol and illicit drugs and resisting peer pressures as a commitment to a healthy life and faith..

2. We call upon all people to pray and give moral and financial support to community, church and other efforts to discourage children and teens from the use of alcohol and other drugs.

3. We call upon our local congregations to include in their Christian education programs and their worship services; resources, studies, and seminars that emphasize to children and youth the detrimental effects of alcohol and other drugs.

4. We call upon local congregations to observe an annual Drug and Alcohol Awareness Sunday, and to prioritize this issue within the life of the congregation as a way to challenge young people and their elders to say "no" as an aspect of their commitment to grow in their Christian faith.

5. We further call upon local congregations to create a substance abuse ministry incorporating education, resources, and support for prevention and recovery which emphasizes our commitment to healing and love that is free of judgment, particularly as it relates to children and youth.

6. We call upon our fellow citizens and countries to support legislation that will help to curtail availability of alcoholic beverages to youth and to support public programs that help to instill values in young people that will help them to have drug-and-alcohol-free lives.

7. We call upon other religious bodies to join us in adopting resolutions and supporting efforts to curtail alcohol and drug abuse in our communities, states, and nation.

8. We direct the General Board of Church and Society and the General Board of Discipleship to develop and promote resource materials to implement this concern within the connection.

ADOPTED 2000
REVISED AND READOPTED 2008
RESOLUTION #84, 2004 *BOOK OF RESOLUTIONS*
RESOLUTION #74, 2000 *BOOK OF RESOLUTIONS*

*See* Social Principles, ¶ 162L.

### 3044. Drinking on Campus

Our Christian faith calls us to care for each other. Jesus said, "Love your neighbor as yourself" (Matthew 19:19). Jesus also said, "Let the children come to me, and do not hinder them; for to such belongs the kingdom of heaven" (Matthew 19:14). Jesus' example clearly directs us to care for each other and to give young people special attention enabling them to be free from harm.

The National Institute of Alcohol Abuse and Alcoholism defines binge drinking as a pattern of drinking that brings a person's blood alcohol concentration (BAC) to 0.08 grams percent or above. This typically happens when men consume more than 4 drinks and women consume more than 3 drinks in about 2 hours.[1] Binge drinking is an alarming and growing problem in the United States that can lead to many alarming health-related injuries and illnesses.

According to national surveys:

- Approximately 92 percent of US adults who drink excessively, report binge drinking in the past 30 days.[2]
- The rate of binge drinking among men is 3 times the rate of women.[3]
- Binge drinkers are 14 times more likely to report alcohol-impaired driving than non-binge drinkers.
- About 90 percent of the alcohol consumed by youth under the age of 21 (who are too young to drink legally) in the United States is in the form of binge drinks.[4]
- About 75 percent of the alcohol consumed by adults in the United States is in the form of binge drinks.[5]
- The proportion of current drinkers that binge is highest in the 18 to 20 year old groups (52.1 percent).[6]

The alarming increase in binge drinkers 18-20 years old indicates that many college students in the United States continue to engage in binge drinking and drinking to get drunk, with a disturbing percentage of students reporting alcohol-related incidents, such as missing classes, personal injuries, sexual assault, or other forms of violence and vandalism.

The CDC reports that binge drinking is associated with many health problems, including but not limited to:

- unintentional injuries (e.g. car crash, falls, burns, drowning).
- intentional injuries (e.g. firearm injuries, sexual assault, domestic violence).
- alcohol poisoning
- sexually transmitted diseases

1. National Institute of Alcohol Abuse and Alcoholism. *NIAAA council approves definition of binge drinking* (PDF–1.6Mb). NIAAA Newsletter 2004; No. 3:3. Accessed March 6, 2006.

2. Town M, Naimi TS, Mokdad AH, Brewer RD. *Health care access among US adults who drink alcohol excessively: missed opportunities for prevention.* Prev Chronic Dis [serial online] 2006 Apr.

3. Centers for Disease Control and Prevention. *Behavioral Risk Factor Surveillance System, Trends Data, Alcohol Use: Binge Drinking.* Accessed November 29, 2005.

4. Office of Juvenile Justice and Delinquency Prevention. *Drinking in America: Myths, Realities, and Prevention Policy* (PDF–103K). Pacific Institute for Research and Evaluation in support of the OJJDP Enforcing the Underage Drinking Laws Program. US Department of Justice. November 2001.

5. Ibid.

6. Serdula MK, Brewer RD, Gillespi C, Denny CH, Mokdad A. *Trends in alcohol use and binge drinking, 1985–1999: Results of a multi-state survey.* Am J Prev Med 2004;26(4):294–298.

- unintended pregnancy
- liver disease
- neurological damage.[7]

United Methodist colleges and universities provide an environment suitable for pursuing a higher education in a Christian atmosphere. Within this environment, United Methodist colleges and universities establish policies to address alcohol use and abuse on their campuses.

To continue to provide clear direction in addressing this issue at United Methodist colleges and universities, The United Methodist Church:

1. urges United Methodist-related colleges and universities to use the United Methodist Social Principle on Alcohol and Drugs (162L), its companion resolution on "Alcohol and Other Drugs" (#3042, 2008 *Book of Resolutions*), and the latest research and proven strategies on alcohol prevention to guide the alcohol and drug policies of their institutions;
2. encourages and upholds abstinence from drinking alcohol as a viable and faith-based option;
3. provides counseling, programming, and social events that foster an amenable environment for an abstinence-only campus; and
4. strongly urges the removal of alcohol-promoting advertisements from campuses and campus sports events.

To undergird and assist United Methodist colleges and universities in meeting these goals:

1. The Special Program on Substance Abuse and Related Violence (SPSARV), the General Board of Church and Society, and the General Board of Higher Education and Ministry will partner with United Methodist higher education institutions in providing training and resources to address the issue of reducing college drinking;

2. The General Board of Church and Society will continue to actively advocate and engage the Church in advocating for legislation and regulations that discourage the use of alcohol by youth and young adults and the use of alcohol advertising to market to youth and young adults.

7. US Department of Health and Human Services, Centers for Disease Control website (CDC), Binge Drinking Statistics, /www.cdc.gov/alcohol/quickstats/binge_drinking, 2007.

ADOPTED 2004
REVISED AND READOPTED 2008
RESOLUTION #85, 2004 *BOOK OF RESOLUTIONS*
RESOLUTION #75, 2000 *BOOK OF RESOLUTIONS*

*See* Social Principles, ¶ 162L.

## 3045. A Call to Action on Alcohol

The Scriptures provide many dimensions to understanding the issue of alcohol. For example, Proverbs 23:20-21 and 29-32 (NRSV) illustrates the cautious attitude of Scripture with respect to alcohol: "Do not be among winebibbers, or among gluttonous eaters of meat; for the drunkard and the glutton will come to poverty, and drowsiness will clothe them in rags . . . Who has woe? Who has sorrow? Who has strife? Who has complaining? Who has wounds without cause? Who has redness of eyes? Those who linger late over wine, those who keep trying mixed wines. Do not look at wine when it is red, when it sparkles in the cup and goes down smoothly. At the last it bites like a serpent, and stings like an adder." On the other hand, Jesus affirmed the use of alcohol at the wedding in Cana (John 2:1-10, NRSV): "When the wine gave out, the mother of Jesus said to him, 'They have no wine.' . . . Jesus said to them, 'Fill the jars with water.' And they filled them up to the brim. . . . The steward tasted the water that had become wine . . . and said to him, . . .you have kept the good wine until now."

The United Methodist Church is challenged to apply the ethical guidelines of Scripture to a contemporary culture in which alcoholic beverages play a prominent role, for which we pay a heavy price in both human and economic terms. Further, there is substantial evidence that patterns of casual alcohol use, problematic use, dependence and addiction are prevalent within our fellowship, and may be as prevalent among members of The United Methodist Church as they are in society at large.

John Wesley, the founder of the Methodist Movement, was vividly aware of the effects of drunkenness on individuals and families, including members of his own extended family, but was charitable to those individuals affected by alcohol in his culture. Christian discipleship, stewardship, and justice demand that we attend to the human and economic damage caused by high-risk consumption, recognizing the needs of our addicted brothers and sisters, whether they are within our fellowship or outside of it; and fostering understanding and good will among people who are not addicted or in recovery and choose abstinence or scripture-led judicious use of alcohol. Our Social Principle, ¶ 162L, and several of the resolutions within the *Book of Resolutions* further explain our position on a variety of matters as it relates to alcohol.

The Social Principles place emphasis on abstinence as "a faithful witness" and allow for persons to exercise reasonable discernment regarding "judicious use with deliberate and intentional restraint, with Scripture as a guide," while at the same time encouraging us to "assist those who have become dependent, and their families." Often, there is a divide in understanding on a continuum with abstinence at one end and dependence on the other end, between prohibition and judicious use. Sole concentration on prohibition or abstinence may invite judgmental attitudes, driving troubled people even deeper into despair and secretive behavior, discriminating against people who need healing, inviting hypocrisy while closing off opportunities to witness to God's love and grace. Conversely, judicious use awakens concern and fear among advocates for abstinence that the Church is encouraging and even inviting abuse or addiction to alcohol, especially among young people. The void between these two approaches often prevents meaningful dialogue and education and creates divisions among faithful Christians, thereby cutting off any real hope of transformative change within the Church.

The Social Principles encourage us to assist dependent people "in finding freedom through Jesus Christ and in finding good opportunities for treatment, for ongoing counseling, and for reintegration into society." Resources dedicated to prevention, treatment and rehabilitation exist that can lend considerable support to creating and fostering understanding, education, and dialogue on effective prevention and recovery methods and toward being a faithful witness as it relates to abstinence and prevention. However, we acknowledge that there are no substantive resources for individuals and local churches that explicate and interpret our position for "judicious use with deliberate and intentional restraint, with Scripture as a guide" and foster dialogue between the two approaches to alcohol—abstinence and judicious use.

The legacy of the Temperance Movement of an earlier century has been transformed by new social forces and scientific findings into a vigorous public health movement, with emphasis on alcohol policies and education that place individual responsibility in the context of social norms and practices.

More than three decades of research have shown that alcohol abuse, dependence and addiction have widespread effects on persons, families, communities, and institutions, and have documented not only the extent of the physical and social consequences but also the economic effects on health care, medical services, workforce productivity, crime and violence, child welfare, corrections, public safety, social services, education, and mental health.

Recent research has shown that underage drinkers account for almost 20 percent of all alcohol consumed and adults who drink excessively are responsible for more than 30 percent of the alcohol consumed in the US, and industry profits are derived from those consumers.

Marketing research has shown that youth are 60 times more likely to see alcoholic beverage commercials than "responsibility ads" created by the industry, and that for every drinking and driving prevention ad, alcohol companies aired 172 product promotion ads.

We acknowledge that a global health policy on alcohol lags far behind those of some countries and that there are also many countries in which alcohol policy is not fully developed, is inadequate, and is underfunded. Levels of low-risk, acceptable consumption and guidelines for responsible use have been issued by the US Department of Agriculture and the US Department of Health and Human Services that can be used as guidelines for enacting a global policy on alcohol. These policies call for limiting consumption to one standard drink per day for women and two standard drinks per day for men, but abstinence for (a) persons under the age of 21, (b) persons who are in recovery from alcohol dependence or alcoholism, (c) persons whose parents or other family members have experienced alcohol-related problems, (d) women who are trying to conceive or are pregnant, (e) persons who plan to drive or engage in activities that require attention or skill, and persons using prescription or over-the-counter medications; (f) persons who may put self or others at risk in other ways as a result of consumption.

We acknowledge that "moderation" and "judicious use" are problematic and can be ambiguous concepts, given the psychoactive properties of ethyl alcohol, which challenges our judgment and awareness, so that slogans such as "know when to say when" or "just say no" make little sense to a person who is in the grip of addiction. Furthermore, the alcohol industry has shown in many ways that it is far more interested in profits than in the health, safety and welfare of the people, more interested in expanding its customer base to insure its economic viability, blaming its customers for alcohol-related problems, and refusing steadfastly to define what it means by "responsible drinking," to the point that even their "responsibility" messages serve their own self-interests, attempting thereby to absolve themselves of corporate responsibility.

Those who profit from the production, distribution, promotion, and sale of alcoholic beverages have been allowed to assume a privileged position in the formation of public policy and legislation at local, state, regional, and national levels, a degree of power and influence which has succeeded in dissuading the public, including the faith community, from taking appropriate action as citizens.

Funding for prevention and for treatment of addicted people continues to be woefully inadequate, considering the magnitude of the problem, leaving millions without needed services, and the social costs of alcohol-related problems continue to rob economies of resources needed to deal with poverty and disease, while the alcohol industry opposes every effort to offset these costs by increases in alcohol excise taxes.

Prevention research strongly recommends a comprehensive community-wide approach, which acknowledges that individual behavior is powerfully shaped by one's environment, the rules and regulations of social institutions, community norms, mass media messages, and accessibility of alcohol. A community, state, and nation that allows a product with high potential for misuse and abuse to be produced, promoted, distributed and valued for routine consumption is ethically obligated to care about those who succumb to the risks and adverse consequences, especially when those risks and consequences are incompletely understood by the consumer.

The call for faith community leadership on this issue, leadership that transcends special economic interests and considers the public interest, leadership that pursues action rather than continued pronouncements; able and willing to challenge industry practices, when others have a defeatist attitude and consider the industry invincible in matters of social policy is a critical need.

*Therefore, be it resolved*, that the members of The United Methodist Church take a firm stand to reduce alcohol-related problems, not only as a personal matter, but as a concern for congregation, community, regions, states, and nations, and communicate that stand actively and effectively, rather than passively, through action to change the social norms; and

*Be it further resolved*, that the gap between abstinence and addiction be closed, using the entire Bible as our ethical guide, and that The United Methodist Church promote an ethic that is consistent with personal, spiritual and societal concern for health, safety and well-being; that such ethic be one that (a) accepts abstinence in all situations;

(b) accepts judicious consumption, with deliberate and intentional restraint, in low-risk situations; (c) actively discourages consumption for those under the age of 21; (d) actively discourages consumption in high-risk situations; and (d) actively discourages heavy consumption in all situations; and

*Be it further resolved*, that guidelines for moderate consumption, as issued by the US Department of Agriculture (US Dietary Guidelines) and the US Department of Health and Human Services, as stated above, be encouraged in educational efforts, and used as a tool to persuade the World Health Organization to adopt a global alcohol policy that is effective and active throughout he world; and

*Be it further resolved*, that The United Methodist Church pursue a course of action that reflects the ethical imperative, that prevention of alcohol-related problems and treatment and rehabilitation of those who become addicted should be available and accessible to all those in need, as well as their families, neighbors, fellow church members, employers, and others whose lives are directly affected; and

*Be it further resolved*, that the members of The United Methodist Church take action to reduce the domination of industry agenda on state and local levels and encourage our legislators to place the health and safety concerns ahead of profitability; and

*Be it further resolved*, that The United Methodist Church support public policy proposals that would increase the rates of fees and excise taxes paid by the industry to the various states for the privilege of selling beer, wine and spirits, with proceeds earmarked for the development of prevention, treatment and other measures to reduce alcohol-related problems; and

*Be it further resolved*, that the General Board of Church and Society provide resources and materials to foster action, education, understanding, and dialogue regarding abstinence, judicious use, and addiction; to provide guidance to annual conferences; to work toward wholeness, compassion, reconciliation and healing, community, alternatives to incarceration and restorative justice; to give help and hope to those who feel helpless and hopeless; and to advise congregations on ways in which members can advocate for pro-health alcohol policies at local, state, regional, and national levels.

**ADOPTED 2004**
**REVISED AND READOPTED 2008**
**RESOLUTION #86, 2004** *BOOK OF RESOLUTIONS*

*See* Social Principles, ¶ 162L.

## BLACK AMERICANS

### 3061. African American Family Life

Our Social Principles state that "we believe the family to be the basic human community through which persons are nurtured and sustained in mutual love, responsibility, respect, and fidelity" (¶ 161*A*).

Families of all types in the United States are vulnerable to social and economic change.

African American families today face problems of epidemic proportions from violence within the geographical community, new and virulent health problems, a high rate of cardiovascular illness, and economic stress.

We call upon the General Board of Discipleship to identify or create resources and materials to assist local churches in developing a program of mentoring, counseling, and referral that includes strategies to strengthen African American family life and to produce a listing of these resources to be distributed to and promoted in each annual conference.

ADOPTED 1992
AMENDED AND READOPTED 2000 AND 2004
RESOLUTION #57, 2004 *BOOK OF RESOLUTIONS*
RESOLUTION #51, 2000 *BOOK OF RESOLUTIONS*

*See* Social Principles, ¶ 162*A*.

### 3062. A History of Blacks

An examination and assessment of the Methodist legacy in America reveals that Black persons and their contributions continue to receive inadequate credits, and there are more written resources available about Blacks in the history of Methodism.

Literature about Black persons in the Methodist history and/or literature written from the perspective of the Black ethos is perceived as resources primarily for Black persons, while an important element in the interrelationship of the different groups within the church family is to respect thoroughly and understand the uniqueness and contributions of Black persons in the evolving history of Methodism and the USA.

We call upon the General Commission on Archives and History and The United Methodist Publishing House, in joint consultation with the General Commission on Religion and Race, to determine the most effective means to identify additional Black literary and historical records that have not been acknowledged and/or published; promote the use of these and other such resources among whites and other racial and ethnic minorities; and encourage training sessions led by Blacks using these resources that acknowledge the contributions of Black persons to the legacy and heritage of Methodism in the United States of America and the world and that a listing of these resources be distributed to each conference.

ADOPTED 1992
AMENDED AND READOPTED 2004
RESOLUTION #58, 2004 *BOOK OF RESOLUTIONS*
RESOLUTION #52, 2000 *BOOK OF RESOLUTIONS*

*See* Social Principles, ¶ 162A.

### 3063. African American Methodist Heritage Center (AAMHC)

*Preamble*

The history, heritage, and hopes of United Methodists of African American descent are inextricably intertwined with the history, heritage, and hopes of John Wesley's Methodism since its beginnings in North America. Yet, the whole church has been slow to celebrate that linkage, perhaps due to a lack of knowledge and understanding of that story of trials and triumphs.

It is not widely known that:

- in 1760 the first person of African heritage to be converted to Methodism was Peter Denis;
- in 1765 when Robert Strawbridge preached in Baltimore one of the speakers was a man of African heritage, Caleb Hyland who later became a member of Sharp Street Methodist Church, one of Methodism's oldest African American churches;
- the first Methodist class meeting in New York included a Black woman named Betty, a servant of Barbara Heck;

- John Wesley himself chided a group at Fells Point in Baltimore for failing to include a group of Black persons as full participants; and
- Black Harry Hosier was a great preacher and colleague of Francis Asbury and, along with Richard Allen, was among the attendees at the Christmas Conference of 1784, when the Methodist Church in North America was organized.

The full and rich history of African Americans in Methodism is still to unfold.

African American United Methodists are seeking to recover and preserve the stories and the artifacts of the celebrations and the calamities, the accomplishments and the adversities, the connection and the separation, and the whole gamut of experiences encountered over the nearly three hundred years of the church's journey in America. The hope and the dream is to establish a first-class African American Methodist Heritage Center.

The African American poet, Langston Hughes raised the question in his poem "Harlem," ". . . What happens to a dream deferred? Does it dry up like a raisin in the sun? . . . or does it just explode?" The question is very relevant to the initiative to establish the African American Methodist Heritage Center should there not be adequate support from the total denomination to implement the dream and maintain the Center.

But, we know that God "makes a way out of no way," and reality out of dreams. An African American Methodist Heritage Center that is affirmed, supported, and sustained by ALL of United Methodism, will be a living testimony to how those who were victimized and those who caused their victimization have been able with God's help to make of trials and tribulations, everlasting triumph! The Center will tell the story of the rocky road Methodism has traveled, but it will also be an expression of how a people who believed and trusted when there was no reason to believe and trust sustained themselves and made visible, the "Amazing Grace" of God.

As people with a memory and as people of hope, the General Conference of The United Methodist Church affirms the need to remember the past and to live through the present into a future that is richer and stronger because of our journey together. Therefore:

WHEREAS, Black Methodists for Church Renewal (BMCR), and other interested United Methodists, had the vision that there be an African American Methodist Heritage Center to recover, preserve, and share the rich history and invaluable contributions of African Americans in The United Methodist Church and its predecessor denominations; and

WHEREAS, the initiative was taken to create a Board of Directors that established the African American Methodist Heritage Center, which was properly organized and incorporated as a nonprofit organization under the laws of the state of Maryland and approved as a 501(c) 3 tax-exempt organization by the Internal Revenue Service; and

WHEREAS, the 2004 General Conference of The United Methodist Church approved a resolution, "African American Methodist Heritage Center" [#71, *Book of Resolutions, 2004*], that affirmed the concept of the Heritage Center and authorized the Board of Directors to pursue funding through the United Methodist Development Fund; and

WHEREAS, the General Commission on Archives and History has agreed to partner with the Board of Directors in the development of the African American Methodist Heritage Center by officially accepting the center to be housed in the Archives Building where the collection will be protected by proper scientifically controlled systems for preservation, catalogued, maintained by staff to enable the research into the story of African Americans in Methodism; and

WHEREAS, the Board of Directors continues to plan to develop additional programming and Exhibit/Display space in one or more of the historically African American institutions related to The United Methodist Church; and

WHEREAS, the fund-raising efforts to date have not yielded adequate resources for the housing, staffing, equipping, and maintenance of the collection; and

WHEREAS, The United Methodist Church, in its entirety, desires accelerated realization of the African American Methodist Heritage Center;

*Therefore, be it resolved,* that permission is continued for fund raising by the African American Methodist Heritage Center and for the development of an endowment through the United Methodist Church Foundation; and

*Be it further resolved,* that the General Conference recognize that the General Board of Discipleship, the General Board of Higher Education and Ministry, the General Commission on Christian Unity and Interreligious Concerns, and the General Commission on Religion and

Race have been cooperative in the undergirding of this project and encourage all of the general agencies to determine ways and means whereby they can undergird this task; and

*Be it further resolved,* that all United Methodists work, study, and pray for the recovery, preservation, and sharing of the unique story of African Americans in Methodism, recognizing that to do so is embracing and remembering the WHOLE story of Methodism.

ADOPTED 2008

*See* Social Principles, ¶ 162A.

### 3064. Resourcing Black Churches in Urban Communities

WHEREAS, the struggle for social, economic, and political survival of Black people in the United States is manifested in their historical migration to urban centers; and

WHEREAS, the problems that have evolved through the decade now face this population of people, isolated from access to the material resources needed to unleash its power and creativity in a manner that will build rather than destroy communities; and

WHEREAS, the Black United Methodist churches in urban communities have historically been centers of spiritual nurture and social and political action that have cared for the youth and offered viable alternatives to the negative aspects of decaying urban centers; and

WHEREAS, there is a demonstrated need in all urban communities in this country for strong, vital Black congregations to reach into the hurts and pains of the community and provide the spiritual revival that is needed in order to reclaim individuals and communities and manifest the healing power of God to combat drugs, violence, and a growing sense of hopelessness; and

WHEREAS, the gospel mandates that we "seek the welfare of the city where I have sent you into exile, and pray to the LORD on its behalf, for in its welfare you will find your welfare" (Jeremiah 29:7); and

WHEREAS, Black United Methodist congregations in urban communities are called, as are all churches, to minister to the needs of persons in the communities where the church is located; and

WHEREAS, the conditions in urban communities for Black persons continue to worsen, and the need for grounding in a faith and reliance on the power of God for the strength and vision to reclaim and rebuild strong, proud, faith-centered communities grows daily while the resources and persons in Black urban congregations decrease;

*Therefore, be it resolved,* that the General Conference direct the General Board of Discipleship to develop programs and strategies that will enable the development of Black leadership, and specific programs and strategies that will foster financial self-sufficiency, such as launching a stewardship education program.

*Be it further resolved,* that the General Board of Global Ministries work with existing Black churches in urban communities to develop and maintain vital congregations providing practical ministries that address the spiritual, social, and economic decline in these communities.

*Be it further resolved,* that the General Board of Global Ministries coordinate its work in strengthening Black urban congregations with the General Board of Discipleship, the annual conferences and urban ministry units of annual conferences, the Strengthening the Black Church for the Twenty-First Century initiative.

ADOPTED 1992
AMENDED AND READOPTED 2004
READOPTED 2008
RESOLUTION #59, 2004 *BOOK OF RESOLUTIONS*
RESOLUTION #53, 2000 *BOOK OF RESOLUTIONS*

*See* Social Principles, ¶ 162A.

## 3065. Black Leadership

*Be it resolved,* that The United Methodist Church in all of its annual conferences will actively seek to identify Black clergy and laity for leadership positions at the local, district, annual conference, jurisdictional, and general church levels. Such active identification may be accomplished through:

- the conducting of district leadership training seminars, to which at least three members of each predominantly Black church have been invited;
- the establishment of a "mentor system" in which an effective Black leader would become a mentor to a potential Black leader and would encourage and assist that person in the full development of his or her leadership skills;

- the frequent fellowshipping of racial and ethnic congregations, leading to an understanding and knowledge of racial differences; and
- bishops and district superintendents actively choosing Black United Methodists to fill appointive positions in the district, annual conference, jurisdictional, and general church levels.

*Be it further resolved,* that each conference shall include a report of its progress in its annual conference journal.

ADOPTED 1992
AMENDED AND READOPTED 2004 AND 2008
RESOLUTION #60, 2004 *BOOK OF RESOLUTIONS*
RESOLUTION #54, 2000 *BOOK OF RESOLUTIONS*

*See* Social Principles, ¶ 162A.

### 3066. Observance of Martin Luther King Jr. Day

The prophetic witness of Dr. Martin Luther King, Jr. for justice and peace embodies the spirit of the Social Creed, the Social Principles of The United Methodist Church and the inclusiveness of our denomination. His words continue to inspire and guide our commitment to the whole Gospel:

"We cannot be truly Christian people so long as we flaunt the central teachings of Jesus: brotherly love and the Golden Rule." —Martin Luther King, Jr.

"Was not Jesus an extremist for love—'Love your enemies, bless them that curse you, pray for them that despitefully use you.' Was not Amos an extremist for justice—'Let justice roll down like waters and righteousness like a mighty stream.' Was not Paul an extremist for the gospel of Jesus Christ—'I bear in my body the marks of the Lord Jesus.' Was not Martin Luther an extremist—'Here I stand; I can do none other so help me God.' Was not John Bunyan an extremist—'I will stay in jail to the end of my days before I make a butchery of my conscience.' Was not Abraham Lincoln an extremist—'This nation cannot survive half slave and half free.' Was not Thomas Jefferson an extremist—'We hold these truths to be self-evident, that all men are created equal.' So the question is not whether we will be extremist but what kind of extremist will we be. Will we be extremists for hate or will we be extremists for love? Will we be extremists for the preservation of injustice—or will we be extremists for the cause of justice?

In that dramatic scene on Calvary's hill, three men were crucified. We must not forget that all three were crucified for the same crime—the crime of extremism. Two were extremists for immorality, and thusly fell below their environment. The other, Jesus Christ, was an extremist for love, truth and goodness, and thereby rose above his environment. —Martin Luther King, Jr.

The observance of Martin Luther King Jr. Day enriches and strengthens our social witness today.

*Therefore, be it resolved,* that each annual conference observe Martin Luther King Jr. Day with appropriate services of commemoration in recognition of Dr. King; and on that day we strongly recommend that we close the bishops' office, all conference offices, all district offices, all local church offices, and, where feasible, business offices of church-related institutions; and that we support local activities surrounding the celebration of Dr. King's life and ministry; that we encourage local school districts not to hold classes on Martin Luther King Jr. Day; and that if local school districts hold classes, we encourage them to use Martin Luther King Jr. Day to celebrate Dr. King's work and address the need for the continuing struggle for justice.

ADOPTED 1992
AMENDED AND READOPTED 2004 AND 2008
RESOLUTION #61, 2004 *BOOK OF RESOLUTIONS*
RESOLUTION #55, 2000 *BOOK OF RESOLUTIONS*

*See* Social Principles, ¶ 162A.

## 3067. Support Reparations for African Americans

WHEREAS, the General Conference acknowledges and profoundly regrets the massive human suffering and the tragic plight of millions of men, women, and children caused by slavery and the transatlantic slave trade; and

WHEREAS, at the conclusion of the Civil War, the plan for the economic redistribution of land and resources on behalf of the former slaves of the Confederacy was never enacted; and

WHEREAS, the failure to distribute land prevented newly freed Blacks from achieving true autonomy and made their civil and political rights all but meaningless; and

WHEREAS, conditions comparable to "economic depression" continue for millions of African Americans in communities where unemployment often exceeds 50 percent; and

WHEREAS, justice requires that African American descendants of the transatlantic slave trade be assured of having access to effective and appropriate protection and remedies, including the right to seek just and adequate reparation or satisfaction for the legacy of damages, consequent structures of racism and racial discrimination suffered as a result of the slave trade; and

WHEREAS, Isaiah 61:1-3 provides a model for reparations: "He has sent me to bind up the brokenhearted, to proclaim freedom for the captives, . . . to proclaim the year of the Lord's favor,... and provide for those who grieve in Zion—to bestow on them a crown of beauty instead of ashes, the oil of gladness instead of mourning, and a garment of praise instead of a spirit of despair."; and,

WHEREAS, January 5, 1993, Congressman John Conyers Jr. (D-Mich.) introduced H.R. 40 to the House of Representatives, calling for the establishment of the Commission to Study Reparation Proposals for African Americans, "acknowledging the fundamental injustice, cruelty, brutality and inhumanity of slavery in the United States from 1619 to the present day," for the purpose of submitting a report to Congress for further action and consideration with respect to slavery's effects on African American lives, economics, and politics;

*Therefore, be it resolved:*

1. that we support the discussion and study of reparation for African Americans;

2. that we petition the President, the Vice President, and the United States House of Representatives to support the passage and signing of H.R. 40;

3. that a written copy of this petition be delivered to the President and Vice President of the United States, the United States Senate Majority Leader, the House Speaker, and House Member John Conyers Jr.

4. that the General Commission on Religion and Race and the General Board of Church and Society develop a strategy for interpretation and support of passage of H.R. 40;

5. That the appropriate general boards and agencies of The United Methodist Church develop and make available to its members data on the history of slavery and the role of theology in validating and supporting both the institution and the abolition of the slave trade; and

6. That we call upon The United Methodist Church to acknowledge the memory of the victims of past tragedies and affirm that, wherever and whenever these tragedies occur, they must be condemned and their recurrence prevented

ADOPTED 1996
AMENDED AND ADOPTED 2004
RESOLUTION #62, 2004 *BOOK OF RESOLUTIONS*
RESOLUTION #56, 2000 *BOOK OF RESOLUTIONS*

*See* Social Principles, ¶ 162A.

# CHILDREN

## 3081. Child Care and the Church

### *Our Call*

As people of faith, we are called to teach children through scripture, our tradition as Methodists, the Social Principles, the ritual of baptism, and our concern for families. In responding to the call set before us, we will provide environments for children to be nurtured in the faith and to grow as children of God.

Scripture tells us to teach children the words of God (Deuteronomy 4:10; 6:7) and not to prevent them from discovering Jesus (Matthew 19:14; Mark 10:14; Luke 18:16). We can also help children to grow as Jesus grew, "strong, filled with wisdom; and the favor of God" (Luke 2:40*b*).

John Wesley set the example for us as Methodists as he began health clinics and schools for the children to learn to read and encouraged the pastors to meet with the children regularly. His call to meet the needs of people where they were stands as a marker for us today. Using our buildings that otherwise might sit empty six days a week to meet the physical, mental, and emotional needs of children and their families clearly meets Mr. Wesley's expectations.

Our Social Principles (¶ 162C) state, "Once considered the property of their parents, children are now acknowledged to be full human beings in their own right, but beings to whom adults and society in general have special obligations. . . ." This Social Principle calls us to take responsibility for meeting the needs of children, including education and protection. Additionally, it calls us to meet the needs of not just our children but all children.

Our service of infant baptism in The United Methodist Church recognizes the sacredness of each person from birth and our responsibility to nurture each child in the faith. In proclaiming that sacredness and recognizing each child as a child of God, we in the church carry a commitment to help enable people to live life in the fullness that Jesus proclaimed.

We promise "We will surround these persons with a community of love and forgiveness, that they may grow in their service to others . . ." (*The United Methodist Hymnal*, page 40). In recognition of this promise and in response to the sacredness of all children as set forth in scripture, through the teachings of John Wesley, and in our Social Prinicples, our vision for child care must include a vision of services available to all families on an equitable basis. Through the particular ministry of child care, we extend the nurturing ministry of the church and proclaim justice to children, families, and communities.

The church has important responsibilities in initiating, encouraging, and participating in the highest quality of child care for children and families, not only in the local community but also nationwide.

*Therefore*, we recommend the following:

*1. See child care as planned ministry.*

Each congregation of The United Methodist Church that houses or supports any child-care program must intentionally assess its understanding of discipleship as it relates to weekday ministry. Child care is a valid expression of the Christian faith. However, programs in local churches too often exist without much thought to intentional ministry. Concerns often focus on budgeting and facility use instead of the ministry of the programs. When this happens, misunderstandings arise between the child-care program and the congregation, and missed opportunities occur for witnessing and mirroring the Christian faith. Each child-care program may encompass one or all of the following expressions of ministry: nurture, outreach, and/or witness. A particular congregation may choose any avenue of ministry, but it is important that each congregation be intentional, involving thought and prayer. What are the congregation's gifts for ministry with children? What is the mission of child care? How is intentional ministry a part of the daily operation of the program?

Congregations must determine how the child-care program embraces the church's mission.

a. Nurture includes Christian education, stewardship, and worship. In a program that focuses on nurture, spiritual development through Christian education is central. An intentional part of the curriculum should be the selection of stories (biblical and secular) and methods, and the integration of "God talk" and Christian values into daily conversations and interactions. When celebrations follow the church year, and when themes are based on Christian concepts, our faith traditions are an intentional part of the curriculum.

Also included is stewardship. In our child-care programs, we reflect our commitment to being God's stewards in the ways we use and allocate our physical resources. We also reflect an understanding of the precarious balance of the world in an ecological sense. When children are cared for, they learn to care for others and for their world.

b. Outreach includes the areas of advocacy, safety, health, welfare, and equity, and how well they are addressed in our communities. Embracing outreach as a part of a weekday ministry program follows our traditional roots of caring for the needs of the community. As a congregation responds to the needs of people in the community through weekday ministry, the community and the congregation discover many blessings. Such a program addresses safety issues, social justice issues, equity issues, and health issues. Specialty child care that addresses community issues might include care for infants, ill children, children of families at risk, children with special needs, children who are survivors of abuse, children with language barriers, migrant or refugee children, school-age children, and young adolescents. Each congregation should determine the unmet needs of their surrounding community. When possible, congregations should work collaboratively with other community agencies and groups to assure that needs are being met without duplication of efforts and in support of each other. When unable to meet the needs of a community, congregations must be outspoken advocates for needs of children in their community.

c. Witness includes the areas of evangelism, membership care, and spiritual formation. In embracing witness as our particular expression of ministry, we proclaim God active in our lives. As Jesus told us to proclaim the good news, so we must through our child-care ministries. Through these ministries, we can minister to the spiritual needs of children and their families. A witness to our faith speaks clearly through the actions of weekday ministry boards, through the caring love of the staff, through the use of developmentally appropriate practices, through gentle and caring words, through the curriculum, through the environment of the facilities, and through the attitude of the congregation.

Every congregation of The United Methodist Church needs to define its ministry through child care and include a statement of this ministry through weekday programs as part of employee handbooks, parent handbooks, community statements, and church reports.

2. *Uphold the quality of child care in the Church.*

Any time a child enters a child-care program housed in a church, expectations are raised regarding quality of the program, behavior of the child-care staff and church staff, and adherence to the Christian doctrines of love and justice. Whether a congregation sees itself as actually sponsoring the program or as merely a landlord, since the program is in the church, families have different expectations than if they are taking their child to a commercial child-care facility. A church cannot divorce itself, either morally or legally, from what takes place in its building through child-care programs.

a. Program Reviews: For this reason, annual review of the child-care program should take place. Concern should be given to the curriculum, the involvement of the congregation with the program, pastoral availability to families and staff involved in child care, safe and clean buildings and equipment, and the highest quality in staff and staff support. The process for the program review must be jointly determined by the child-care staff, church personnel, and informed, interested laity. A plan must be in place.

b. Licensing: The purpose of licensing standards is to protect children. Safety, health, space, and staff requirements provide a foundation for establishing and maintaining good programs for children. The regulations of basic health and safety conditions in a building/program that serves children are the appropriate responsibility of the state and do not interfere with the free exercise of religion. United Methodists have been meeting such standards for years in other areas of the life of the church, such as camping. A congregation is responsible to provide the best care for children when they gather in a church building. Regarding licensing procedures, congregations should seek to at least meet, if not surpass, the standards set in their community. Even if a program is license-exempt by the state, an effort should be made to meet licensing requirements for safety and for integrity. Congregations should also seek to be actively informed about such licensing procedures and requirements and should work to reform such regulations when they do not mandate standards that serve the best interests of children.

c. Self-Study: Through a self-study process, every child-care facility can look for ways to evaluate the care provided. Churches should follow some process of self-study for their child-care programs on a regular basis. Such studies involve both the child-care providers and the congregation and allow them to continuously assess the effectiveness of the ministry they are providing. These self-studies are available through some annual conferences, the National Association for the Education of Young Children, and the United Methodist Association of Preschools—Florida.

d. Personnel: As congregations seek to support child-care programs, salary, benefits, and support of the staff of these programs should be of concern and subject to review and discussion to insure the best for the children and families involved. Congregations must assure that children are served through the best caregivers. Congregations have a responsibility to advocate for higher pay and benefits for child-care workers. These professional caregivers should maintain excellence and integrity in the important job they do, and they should be appropriately compensated for it. With increased concern around issues of child abuse, congregations need to assure that all child-care providers have been adequately screened for child abuse and neglect in accordance with laws of local jurisdiction, especially in the area of sexual misconduct. Appropriate screening protects the children, the child-care providers, and the congregation. It is important to meet any government regulations and the Safe Sanctuaries policies of your local church regarding the screening of child-care workers as appropriate. The personnel issue also includes a concern for the education and training of child-care workers.

A yearly plan for continuing education should be part of the congregation's support for child-care providers. Many child-care providers have extensive training and education in the field. They are good sources for training of those who work with children in other areas of the church, including child-care workers for Sunday services, Sunday school teachers, and vacation Bible school teachers. For those who are hired without proper training and education, the congregations should sponsor and encourage attendance at continuing education events.

3. *Be advocates for quality child care.*

Going beyond the congregation, United Methodists should be diligent advocates for child care nationwide. The following suggestions are for individuals and groups within congregations who seek to better the place of children in American society:

a. Become informed about child-care conditions existing today and the issues involved in the design of an adequate public policy for child care. Address the issues through eliciting a response of commitment from the policy makers.

b. Use the appropriate councils and agencies of the church to monitor public policy at federal, state, and local levels of government.

c. Become involved not only in church conferences and meetings but in the larger arena of child care through such organizations as the Children's Defense Fund and the National Association for the Education of Young Children.

d. Call upon staff at the General Board of Church and Society in Washington, DC, and within each annual conference. They are charged with particular responsibility for the church's involvement in public policy processes in order to monitor, serve as an advocate for, raise issues concerning, and bring the voice of the church to bear on child-care policy development.

e. Call upon the staff of the General Board of Discipleship and the United Methodist Publishing House to express arising needs as they relate to program support, needed curriculum, and policies regarding church and child-care center relationships.

f. Call upon the General Board of Global Ministries to assist churches in responding to child-care needs in their communities with appropriate programs and resources.

g. Call upon the General Board of Discipleship in consultation with the General Council on Finance and Administration to make available to local congregations resources that address legal aspects and procedures to follow in establishing child-care facilities and/or programs.

ADOPTED 2000
REVISED AND READOPTED 2008
RESOLUTION #63, 2004 *BOOK OF RESOLUTIONS*
RESOLUTION #57, 2000 *BOOK OF RESOLUTIONS*

*See* Social Principles, ¶ 162C.

## 3082. Church Support of Caregivers of Children

WHEREAS, children are the most precious resource of our societies, but also the most vulnerable. Children need loving adult support to flourish. In turn, the adult caregivers of children need parenting support systems as well. Our churches, schools, societal groups, and governments help provide the support system children and their caregivers need; and

WHEREAS, children are being raised in a variety of household structures headed by various caregivers; and

WHEREAS, children of these various families are in many of our churches and schools. To flourish, they need a family support system that embraces their household's structure;and

WHEREAS, some church programs assume a traditional mother/father two parent family. Consider the name of programs in a local church, such as *"Mothers* of Preschool Children," *"Mother's* Day Out";

*Now, therefore, be it resolved,* that we call upon each local United Methodist Church to:

1. make a conscious effort in its ministry action, as well as in its words, to nurture children by supporting their family unit and its caregivers, regardless of that family structure;
2. examine the structure of existing ministries to determine if they can be more effective and inclusive by changing titles, timing of events, group expectations, or other norms;
3. determine if new ministries are needed to help nontraditional caregiver groups, and create them as appropriate; and

4. prayerfully consider opportunities to minister and love children and their caregivers without limit.

ADOPTED 2008

See Social Principles, ¶ 162C.


## 3083. Eradicating Abusive Child Labor

In the Gospels, the disciples' attitude toward God was measured by their attitude toward children and their ability to "become as a little child." The protection of childhood and the nurture of children are, therefore, among our most sacred human responsibilities. Reflecting this, the Social Principles of The United Methodist Church uphold the rights of children to growth and development, adequate nutrition, health services, housing, education, recreation, protection against all forms of racial discrimination, cruelty, neglect, and exploitation.

However, throughout the world, childhood itself is under assault by new as well as historic forces. Today's child, in too many parts of the world, must not only cope with warfare, famine, and pestilence at an early age, but is too often denied childhood itself by being forced into labor under abusive and destructive conditions. Many millions of children around the world labor in work that is coerced, forced, bonded, enslaved or otherwise unfair in wages, injurious to health and safety, and/or obstructive of educational or moral development.[1]

WHEREAS, the majority of child labor is found in informal sectors of the world's poorest economies, a growing element in global competition is the employment of children in developing-country export industries harvesting crops such as coffee, tea, cocoa, vegetables, seafood, and fruit; mining and shaping raw goods, such as gemstones, leather, gold, silver, and diamonds; and making products such as garments, leather goods, brassware and glassware, jewelry, and hand-knotted carpets for sale on the international market. As many as 300,000 South Asian children between the ages of 4 and 14 are kidnapped, trafficked, or sold into bondage in the hand-knotted carpet industry.

1. A. Bequele and W.E. Myers, First Things First in Child Labor: Eliminating Work Detrimental to Children, ILO and UNICEF, 1995; pages 1-27.

In the United States, as many as 400,000 children work in agriculture as paid or unpaid labor, often under dangerous conditions without adequate protection, and at significant risk to their education. "Children working in agriculture in the US represent only 8 percent of the population of working minors, yet account for 40 percent of work-related fatalities among minors. An estimated 100,000 children suffer agriculture-related injuries annually in the United States."

The United Nations and the International Labor Organization (ILO) have established universal principles to protect children from such abuse, including the UN International Covenant on the Rights of the Child and the ILO Convention No. 138 for Minimum Age for Admission to Work. These international conventions have been ratified by many countries, but not including the United States. The United States has ratified ILO Convention No. 182 concerning the Prohibition and Immediate Action for the Elimination of the Worst Forms of Child Labour.

*We therefore call on The United Methodist Church:*

1. to support public policies that include the ratification and enforcement of international labor conventions regarding child labor, affirmed by The United Methodist Church in the resolution on the "Rights of Workers" (adopted 1988), and the United Nations Convention on the Rights of the Child, affirmed by The United Methodist Church in the resolution on ; "Ratification of Human Rights Covenants and Conventions" ("Globalization and Its Impact on Human Dignity and Human Rights," adopted in 2004);

2. to work to eradicate the evils of child labor through encouraging the appropriate agencies and units to join the Child Labor Coalition, a broad-based coalition of medical, welfare, religious, consumer, labor, and human-rights organizations in the United States;

3. to join the Education Campaign of the Global March Against Child Labour, a movement to mobilize worldwide efforts to protect and promote the rights of all children, especially the right to receive a free meaningful education and to be free from economic exploitation and from performing any work that is likely to be harmful to the child's physical, mental, spiritual, moral, or social development;

4. to support consumer initiatives such as the RUGMARK campaign, which was established by a coalition of nongovernmental organizations, businesses, government entities, and multilateral groups such as UNICEF to label and market oriental carpets made without exploited child labor;

5. to support legislative and administrative measures to enforce bans against the international trafficking in goods made by child labor;

6. to support unilateral and multilateral aid and development policies that attack the root causes of child labor, such as lack of basic education; gender, religion, and caste prejudice; and unbalanced development schemes that disadvantage certain populations; and

7. to work toward the reform of United States labor laws to provide better protection of farm workers' rights and to bring child labor restrictions into conformity with international standards.

ADOPTED 1996
REVISED AND ADOPTED 2000
REVISED AND READOPTED 2008
RESOLUTION #64, 2004 *BOOK OF RESOLUTIONS*
RESOLUTION #58, 2000 *BOOK OF RESOLUTIONS*

*See* Social Principles, ¶ 162C.

## 3084. Reducing the Risk of Child Sexual Abuse in the Church

Jesus said, "Whoever welcomes [a] child . . . welcomes me" (Matthew 18:5). Children are our present and our future, our hope, our teachers, our inspiration. They are full participants in the life of the church and in the realm of God.

Jesus also said, "If any of you put a stumbling block before one of these little ones . . . it would be better for you if a great millstone were fastened around your neck and you were drowned in the depth of the sea" (Matthew 18:6). Our Christian faith calls us to offer both hospitality and protection to the little ones, the children. The Social Principles of The United Methodist Church state that "children must be protected from economic, physical, emotional and sexual exploitation and abuse" (¶ 162C).

Tragically, churches have not always been safe places for children. Child sexual abuse, exploitation, and ritual abuse occur in churches, both large and small, urban and rural. The problem cuts across all economic, cultural, and racial lines. It is real, and it appears to be increasing. Most annual conferences can cite specific incidents of child sexual abuse and exploitation within churches. Virtually every congregation has among its members adult survivors of early sexual trauma.

Such incidents are devastating to all who are involved: the child, the family, the local church, and its leaders. Increasingly, churches are torn apart by the legal, emotional, and monetary consequences of litigation following allegations of abuse.

1. "Ritual abuse" refers to abusive acts committed as part of ceremonies or rites; ritual abusers are often related to cults, or pretend to be.

2. God calls us to make our churches safe places, protecting children and other vulnerable persons from sexual and ritual abuse. God calls us to create communities of faith where children and adults grow safe and strong. In response to this churchwide challenge, the following steps should be taken to reduce the risk of child sexual abuse:

*A. Local churches should:*

1. develop and implement an ongoing education plan for the congregation and its leaders on the reality of child abuse, risk factors leading to child abuse, and strategies for prevention;

2. adopt screening procedures (use of application forms, interviews, reference checks, background clearance, and so forth) for workers (paid and unpaid) directly or indirectly involved in the care of children and youth;

3. develop and implement safety procedures for church activities such as having two or more nonrelated adults present in classroom or activity; leaving doors open and installing half-doors or windows in doors or halls; providing hall monitors; instituting sign-in and sign-out procedures for children ages ten or younger; and so forth;

4. advise children and young persons of an agency or a person outside as well as within the local church whom they can contact for advice and help if they have suffered abuse;

5. carry liability insurance that includes sexual abuse coverage;

6. assist the development of awareness and self-protection skills for children and youth through special curriculum and activities; and

7. be familiar with annual conference and other church policies regarding clergy sexual misconduct.

*B. Annual conferences should:*

1. develop safety and risk-reducing policies and procedures for conference-sponsored events such as camps, retreats, youth gatherings, childcare at conference events, mission trips, and so forth; and

2. develop guidelines and training processes for use by church leaders who carry responsibility for prevention of child abuse in local

churches. Both sets of policies shall be developed by a task force appointed by the cabinet in cooperation with appropriate conference agencies. These policies shall be approved by the annual conference and assigned to a conference agency for implementation. It is suggested that the policies be circulated in conference publications and shared with lay professionals and clergy at district or conference seminars.

C. *The General Board of Discipleship and the General Board of Global Ministries should:*

1. cooperatively develop and/or identify and promote the following resources;

2. sample policies, procedures, forms, and so forth for reducing the risk of sexual abuse and exploitation of children and youth in local churches, both in relation to their own sponsored programs and to any outreach ministries or other programs for children or youth that use church space;

3. child abuse prevention curriculum for use in local churches;

4. training opportunities and other educational resources on child sexual abuse and exploitation and on ritual abuse; and

5. resources on healing for those who have experienced childhood sexual trauma.

ADOPTED 1996
READOPTED 2004 AND 2008
RESOLUTION #65, 2004 *BOOK OF RESOLUTIONS*
RESOLUTION #59, 2000 *BOOK OF RESOLUTIONS*

*See* Social Principles, ¶ 162C.

## 3085. Child Soldiers

"Jesus loves the little children. All the children of the world. Red and yellow, black and white, they are precious in his sight. Jesus loves the little children of the world."

"Let the little children come to me, and do not stop them; for it is to such as these that the kingdom of God belongs" (Luke 18:16 NRSV).

Children represent the future of human civilization and the future of every society. To permit them to be used as pawns of warfare, whether as targets or perpetrators, is to cast a shadow on the future.

As armed conflict proliferates around the world, increasing number of children are exposed to the brutalities of war. In numerous countries, boys and girls are recruited as child soldiers by armed forces and groups, either forcibly or voluntarily. Reports by the United Nations and nongovernmental organizations such as Amnesty International and the Coalition to Stop the Use of Child Soldiers reveal:

- The majority of the world's child soldiers are involved in a variety of armed political groups. These include government-backed paramilitary groups, militias, and self-defense units operating with government support in many conflict zones. Others include armed groups opposed to central government rule, groups composed of ethnic, religious, and other minorities; and clan-based or factional groups fighting governments and each other to defend territory and resources.
- Most child soldiers are aged between 14 and 18. Children as young as 8 years of age are being forcibly recruited, coerced and induced to become combatants. The children most likely to become soldiers are from impoverished and marginalized backgrounds of separated from their families.
- Hundreds of thousands of under-18-year-olds are estimated to have become a part of armed forces in at least 60 countries. While thousands were recruited, others were forcibly conscripted in military roundups to replenish numbers in unpopular armies. Still others were enlisted in countries where the lack of a functioning birth registration system made it impossible to verify the age of recruits and ensure protection of under-18-year-olds from active military service. Forced abductions, sometimes of large numbers of children, continue to occur in some countries.
- Sometimes, children become soldiers in order to survive. A military unit can be something of a refuge, serving as a kind of surrogate family. Children may join if they believe that this is the only way to guarantee regular meals, clothing, or medical attention. Parents may encourage their daughters to become soldiers if their marriage prospects are poor.

Much has been achieved to stop the use of child soldiers since the General Conference adopted a resolution on the matter in 2000. Substantial progress has been made in establishing an international legal and policy framework for protecting children from involvement in armed conflict. The Optional Protocol to the UN Convention on the Rights of the Child on the involvement of children came into force in 2002. It sets 18 as the minimum age for direct participation in hostilities, for compulsory recruitment by governments, and for all recruitment into armed groups. The International Criminal Court defines all recruitment of children under the age of 15, by governments and armed groups, and their active participation in hostilities as a war crime in both international and noninternational armed conflict. Central Conferences in Africa, such as the Liberia Conference, have initiated programs to rehabilitate and integrate ex-combatant children for productive and peaceful life in their families and communities.

The use of children as soldiers is abhorrent and unacceptable. The General Conference of The United Methodist Church urges the General Board of Church and Society and the General Board of Global Ministries to:

- work with international organizations, faith groups, and other nongovernmental organizations ban the use of child soldiers;
- urge governments to sign the Optional Protocol to the UN Convention on the Rights of the Child on the involvement of children in armed conflict; and
- promote and advocate for government funding of demobilization, disarmament and reintegration programs specifically aimed at child soldiers, taking particular account of the needs of former girl soldiers provide financial assistance to Central Conferences for programs to rehabilitate and reintegrate former child soldiers into their families and communities.

ADOPTED 2000
REVISED AND READOPTED 2008
RESOLUTION #66, 2004 *BOOK OF RESOLUTIONS*
RESOLUTION #60, 2000 *BOOK OF RESOLUTIONS*

*See* Social Principles, ¶¶ 162C and 164I.

## 3086. Children's Sabbath

WHEREAS, "The program calendar of the denomination shall include only the Special Sundays approved by General Conference, Special Sundays approved by ecumenical agencies to which The United Methodist Church is officially related, and the days and seasons of the Christian Year" (2008 *Book of Discipline*, ¶ 262); and

WHEREAS, the General Board of Global Ministries, Women's Division and the General Board of Church and Society have officially endorsed the Children's Sabbath of the ecumenically endorsed Children's Defense Fund; and

WHEREAS, the National Council of the Churches of Christ in the USA, an ecumenical agency of which The United Methodist Church is a member, also endorses the National Observance of the Children's Defense Fund Children's Sabbath;

*Therefore, be it resolved,* that the second weekend of October be identified as the Children's Sabbath on the program calendar of The United Methodist Church throughout the next quadrennium,

*Be it further resolved,* that this weekend is not to be classified as a churchwide special Sunday with offerings, or a special Sunday without churchwide offerings. The inclusion of said weekend is the inclusion of a special date approved by an ecumenical agency to which The United Methodist Church is officially related, with said observance requiring no financial support on the part of The United Methodist Church.

**ADOPTED 1996**
**REVISED AND READOPTED 2000**
**REVISED AND READOPTED 2008**
**RESOLUTION #67, 2004** *BOOK OF RESOLUTIONS*
**RESOLUTION #61, 2000** *BOOK OF RESOLUTIONS*

*See* Social Principles, ¶ 162C.

## 3087. Prohibit Corporal Punishment in Schools and Child-Care Facilities

WHEREAS, schools and child-care facilities are the only institutions in America in which striking another person for the purpose of causing physical pain is legal,

WHEREAS, corporal punishment is humiliating and degrading to children and sometimes causes physical injury,

WHEREAS, it is difficult to imagine Jesus of Nazareth condoning any action that is intended to hurt children physically or psychologically,

WHEREAS, corporal punishment sends a message that hitting smaller and weaker people is acceptable,

WHEREAS, corporal punishment is used most often on poor children, minorities, children with disabilities, and boys,

WHEREAS, there are effective alternatives to corporal punishment that teach children to be self-disciplined rather than to submit out of fear,

WHEREAS, schools and child-care centers should inspire children to enjoy learning and school and child-care personnel should be able to encourage positive behavior without hitting children,

*Therefore, be it resolved,* that The United Methodist Church calls upon all states to enact laws prohibiting corporal punishment in schools and day and residential child-care facilities.

ADOPTED 2004
RESOLUTION #69, 2004 *BOOK OF RESOLUTIONS*

*See* Social Principles, ¶ 162C.


## 3088. Discipline Children Without Corporal Punishment

WHEREAS, corporal punishment models aggressive behavior as a solution to conflict,

WHEREAS, some research has associated corporal punishment with increased aggression in children and adults, increased substance abuse, increased risk of crime and violence, low self-esteem, and chronic depression,

WHEREAS it is difficult to imagine Jesus of Nazareth condoning any action that is intended to hurt children physically or psychologically,

WHEREAS, time-outs and deprivation of privileges are as effective as corporal punishment in stopping undesirable behavior,

WHEREAS, the effectiveness of corporal punishment decreases with subsequent use and therefore leads caretakers to hit children more severely,

WHEREAS, children must eventually develop their own conscience and self-discipline, which are fostered by a home environment of love, respect, and trust,

*Therefore, be it resolved,* that The United Methodist Church encourages its members to adopt discipline methods that do not include corporal punishment of their children.

*And be it further resolved,* that The United Methodist Church encourages congregations to offer opportunities for dialogue and education on effective discipline of children.

ADOPTED 2004
RESOLUTION #70, 2004 *BOOK OF RESOLUTIONS*

*See* Social Principles, ¶ 162C.

### 3089. The Girl Child

WHEREAS, The United Methodist Church affirms the rights of children and of women and recognizes that "children are now acknowledged to be full human beings in their own right, but beings to whom adults and society in general have special obligations." Moreover that, "children have the rights to food, shelter, clothing, health care, and emotional well-being, as do adults." And "In particular, children must be protected from economic, physical, emotional, and sexual exploitation and abuse." And that women are affirmed as equal to men "in every aspect of their common life" (Social Principles ¶ 162C and F); and

WHEREAS, there are challenges faced by all children, but there are also challenges that are unique to girls; and

WHEREAS, although girlhood should be a time of growth and learning as the girls of today develop into the women of tomorrow, for millions of girls it is a time of perilous dangers; and

WHEREAS, girls are not valued as boys are, from the time of birth, in many societies. Girls everywhere may often have limited opportunities in education, training, and employment. In addition many face dangerous practices, such as female genital mutilation/cutting (FGM/C)[1] and child marriage that often lead to psychological trauma, infection by sexually transmitted diseases, and frequent pregnancies, jeopardizing their health and economic well-being. Furthermore, many girls are forced into hazardous and exploitative work situations, while bearing most if not all the burden of housework at home; and

WHEREAS, according to Reports from the United Nations Children's Fund (UNICEF) and the International Labour Organization (ILO):

1. decades after commitments and reaffirmations of those commitments have been made to ensure a quality education for every child—some 117 million children, among them 62 million girls—are still denied this right[2];

2. the International Labour Organization estimates that 352 million or 23 percent of all children between 5 and 17 years of age were economically active in the year 2000. About half of these children are

1. WHO, UNICEF and UNFPA (1997), Female Genital Mutilation: A Joint Statement, World Health Organization, Geneva, pp.1-2.
2. UNICEF Statistics, Basic Education, updated January 2006, http://www.childinfo.org/areas/education.

estimated to do work that is likely to harm their health, safety, or moral development[3];

3. given its hidden nature, it is impossible to have reliable figures on how many children are globally exploited as domestic workers. According to the ILO, though, more girl-children under 16 are in domestic service than in any other category of child labour. Common risks children face in domestic service are: long and tiring working days, use of toxic chemicals, carrying heavy loads, handling danger-ous items, such as knives, axes and hot pans, insufficient or inade-quate food and accommodation, and humiliating or degrading treatment, including physical and verbal violence, and sexual abuse[4];

4. it is estimated that more than 130 million girls and women alive today have undergone FGM/C, primarily in Africa and, to a lesser extent, in some countries in the Middle East[5];

5. pregnancy-related deaths are known to be a leading cause of mor-tality for both married and unmarried girls between the ages of 15 and 19, particularly among the youngest of this cohort[6];

6. young people are at the center of the HIV/AIDS epidemic. About half of all new HIV infections worldwide are in young people aged 15-24. Adolescent girls and young women are especially vulnerable to HIV and account for 60 percent of all HIV-positive young people. Of the 10 million young people living with HIV/AIDS, 6.2 million are young women and 3.9 million are young men[7, 8]; and

WHEREAS, "The achievement of goals for children, particularly for girls, will be advanced if women fully enjoy all human rights and fun-damental freedoms, including the right to development, are empow-ered to participate fully and equally in all spheres of society and are protected and free from all forms of violence, abuse and discrimination.

3. UNICEF Statistics, Child Labour, updated May 2006, http://www.childinfo.org/areas/childlabour.
4. International Labour Organization (ILO) Domestic Labour: Global Facts and Figures in Brief, http://www.ilo.org/ipec/areas/Childdomesticlabour/lang—en/index.htm
5. UNICEF Statistics, Female Genital Mutilation/Cutting, updated February 2006, http://www.childinfo.org/areas/fgmc/
6. UNICEF Statistics, Child Marriage, updated March 2006, http://www.childinfo.org/areas/childmarriage.
7. UNICEF Statistics, HIV/AIDS, updated 2006, http://www.childinfo.org/areas/hivaids/young.php. General Assembly Resolution A/RES/S-27/2 – A World Fit for Children, adopted 10 May 2002, III. Plan of Action, A. Creating a World Fit for Children, paragraph #23.
8. General Assembly Resolution A/RES/S-27/2 – A World Fit for Children, adopted 10 May 2002, III. Plan of Action, A. Creating a World Fit for Children, paragraph #23.

We are determined to eliminate all forms of discrimination against the girl child throughout her life cycle and to provide special attention to her needs in order to promote and protect all her human rights, including the right to be free from coercion . . . " ("A World Fit for Children" United Nations)[9]; and

WHEREAS, we have a special concern toward underserved populations, including indigenous children and children in isolated communities, The United Methodist Church has a history of supporting work with children, including girl children, through the advocacy work of the Women's Division, the General Board of Global Ministries and the General Board of Church and Society;

*Therefore, be it resolved,* that The United Methodist Church, in accordance with the recommendations of the Report of the Expert Group meeting organized by the United Nations Division for the Advancement of Women in collaboration with UNICEF, calls on local churches, conferences, general agencies, and church-related organizations, where appropriate, to:

1) give priority and active support to the empowerment of girls in all aspects of life and include girls in the design of programs and projects to ensure that their specific needs are reflected and addressed;

2) ensure girls' access to youth centers and other youth-specific initiatives, including age and sex-specific spaces and activities;

3) use the home visits that are part of health and child health initiatives to identify girls at risk of child marriage, out-of-school girls, girls living apart from their parents, and girls in other social conditions that are often associated with lack of immunization and elevated risk of sexual coercion and labor exploitation;

4) combine social and health promotion activities within maternal and child health initiatives to prioritize reaching the youngest, first time child-brides and child mothers;

5) develop financial literacy and microfinance (including savings and credit) programs for girls that are targeted specifically to age, sex, marital status, life cycle and context needs;

6) develop strategies and action plans to build girls' stakes in their societies and to recognize and acknowledge their rights and citizenship at an earlier age, ideally close to puberty when specific risks often undermine the rights of adolescent girls;

9. The Expert Group Meeting was organized by the Division for the Advancement of Women in collaboration with UNICEF. Their Report, "Elimination of all Forms of Discrimination and Violence against the Girl Child," was presented September 25-28. 2000, Innocenti Research Center, Florence, Italy.

7) develop strategies and action plans to encourage and foster a healthy family envirnonment and provide parental education when needed; and

8) support public education programs and spaces for girls to, for example, carry out national level consultations, essay contests, and national media events that include the voices of girls and boys in questioning gender inequalities.

ADOPTED 2008

See Social Principles, ¶ 162C.

## CHURCH AND COMMUNITY DEVELOPMENT

### 3101. National Cooperative Ministry Leadership

WHEREAS, the effectiveness of cooperative projects, ministries, and parishes for the purposes of congregational nurturing, outreach to communities of the poor and marginalized, and witnessing to Christian commitments in rural, urban and suburban communities has long been recognized; and

WHEREAS, The United Methodist Church is experiencing a decline in the number of ordained clergy persons and will need to find ways to enlist and train persons for new models of ministry, among such models being those that will seek to work in cooperative projects, ministries, and parishes;

*Therefore, be it resolved* that the General Board of Global Ministries, the General Board of Discipleship, the General Board of Higher Education and Ministry, and the General Commission on Christian Unity and Interreligious Concerns be called upon to work together to provide leadership for the continued development of the delivery of cooperative forms of ministry to The United Methodist Church and ecumenically;

*Be it further resolved,* that the annual conferences, districts, and local churches of The United Methodist Church be called on to implement processes that will eventuate in understandings of how to initiate needed cooperative projects, ministries, and parishes and to facilitate their movement toward local and global mission and ministry.

ADOPTED 2004
REVISED AND READOPTED 2008
RESOLUTION #51, 2004 *BOOK OF RESOLUTIONS*

See Social Principles, ¶ 162P.

## 3102. Plan of Support for Cooperative Ministry

WHEREAS, cooperative ministry is an intentional style of team ministry that enables groups of congregations and their pastors and laity in a defined geographic area, as United Methodists and ecumenically, to work together in ministries of nurture, outreach, and witness; and

WHEREAS, cooperative forms of ministry are proven to enhance lay leadership development, to provide greater support and peer accountability among clergy, and to further connectional awareness and increased resourcing from the connectional church; and

*Therefore, be it resolved,* that the cooperative ministry movement be supported by:

1. all boards and agencies of The United Methodist Church collaborating and working together around issues concerning cooperative ministries, i.e., training, resources, financial assistance, technical assistance, etc.;

2. bishops and cabinets fulfilling the requirements that are in *The Book of Discipline of The United Methodist Church,* concerning cooperative ministries, i.e., training, consultation, deployment of personnel, etc.;

3. bishops and cabinets giving priority to cooperative ministries in the appointment making process;

4. seminaries including training and field experiences for students to learn skills for working in team settings such as cooperative projects, ministries, and parishes;

5. courses of study for local pastors including training and field experience to learn skills for working in team settings that include cooperative projects, ministries, and parishes;

6. cabinets encouraging United Methodist congregations to work together in cooperative ecumenical parishes;

7. cabinets and conference administrative leaders giving special attention to cooperative projects, ministries, and parishes as effective strategies for developing and maintaining ministry in a wide variety of congregations and communities, i.e., rural, urban, declining, stable, growing, racial/ethnic and multicultural, large and small membership churches, etc.;

8. cabinets and other annual conference leaders giving attention to encouraging cooperative projects, ministries, and parishes, as means by which to reach out and start new congregations in areas such as

apartment complexes, mobile home parks, recreational areas, prisons, retirement homes, unincorporated sections of communities, etc.

ADOPTED 2004
REVISED AND READOPTED 2008
RESOLUTION #52, 2004 *BOOK OF RESOLUTIONS*

See Social Principles, ¶ 162P.

### 3103. Cooperative Parish Ministry

WHEREAS, numerous changes have taken place within the Cooperative Parish Ministry movement of The United Methodist Church, including general church oversight and new and creative processes and patterns; and,

WHEREAS, historically responsibility for Cooperative Parish Ministry was lodged, first, with the Office of Town and Country Ministry and, later, also with the Office of Urban Ministry in the General Board of Global Ministries; and

WHEREAS, in the past several years Cooperative Parish Ministry has included, for administrative and support purposes, the General Board of Discipleship, the General Board of Higher Education and Ministry, and the General Commission on Christian Unity and Interreligious Concerns, as well as the General Board of Global Ministries; and,

WHEREAS, some annual conferences are exploring the effectiveness of clusters in which all pastors agree to meet regularly for purposes of holding each other accountable for ministry, outreach, and for leading their churches to develop both individual and collaborative cooperative ministry action plans; and,

WHEREAS, at this time staff of the General Boards of Global Ministry, Higher Education and Ministry, Discipleship, and the General Commission on Christian Unity and Interreligious Concerns are creating a new administrative pattern to carry forward work done by the National Cooperative Ministry Leadership Team, which planned and carried to completion six national cooperative ministry consultations;

*Therefore, be it resolved,* that appreciation be expressed for the good work done by the National Cooperative Ministry Leadership Team across the quadrennia; and,

*Further be it resolved,* that the general boards and agencies, the annual conferences, districts, and charge conferences of The United

Methodist Church be called on to implement processes which will eventuate in understandings of how to initiate cooperative projects, ministries, and parishes and to facilitate their movement toward local and global mission and ministry; and

*Further be it resolved,* that the above boards and agencies be expected to continue providing encouragement and financial support to expand the effective use of cooperative patterns and processes within the Church; and,

*Further be it resolved,* that the above boards and agencies be called upon to bring together a group composed of persons from across the church who are knowledgeable and experienced in cooperative parish ministry to plan and carry forward a national cooperative parish consultation no later than two years following the General Conference of 2008 in order to facilitate broader use of existing cooperative forms and the incorporation of new patterns and processes that continue to emerge throughout the Church.

**ADOPTED 2008**

*See* Social Principles, ¶ 162.

### 3104. Affirmation and Celebration of Professional Lay Ministry

WHEREAS, "Christian ministry is the expression of the mind and mission of Christ," and "All Christians are called through their baptism to this ministry" (¶ 125); the forms of this ministry are as diverse as the gifts and talents with which God has graced each life; and "The ministry of all Christians is complementary. No ministry is subservient to another. All United Methodists are summoned and sent by Christ to live and work together in mutual interdependence and to be guided by the Spirit" (¶ 129); and

WHEREAS, "Within The United Methodist Church, there are those called to servant leadership, lay and ordained," and "Such callings are evidenced by special gifts, evidence of God's grace, and promise of usefulness," and "God's call to servant leadership is inward as it comes to the individual and outward through the discernment and validation of the Church" (¶ 136); and

WHEREAS, the General Board of Higher Education and Ministry, Division of Ordained Ministry, in cooperation with other agencies of the church has developed standards and requirements to certify and renew biennially persons in professional ministry careers (¶¶ 1110.11 and 634.2.*t*); and

WHEREAS, the General Board of Higher Education and Ministry, Division of Ordained Ministry and the General Board of Discipleship continue to encourage and resource conference boards of ordained ministry, boards of discipleship, and other appropriate bodies for the ongoing recognition and support of persons in professional careers (¶¶ 634.2*t* and 1102); and

WHEREAS, the General Board of Higher Education and Ministry, Division of Ordained Ministry works with seminaries, graduate schools, universities, and colleges by providing guidance, standards, and technical support for the academic preparation for professional ministry careers; and

WHEREAS, the Discipleship Ministries Unit of the General Board of Discipleship produces training events and resources for continuing leader formation in the church (lay leadership, youth ministry, Christian education, and so forth);

*Therefore, be it resolved,* that in order to recognize, authenticate, and celebrate those serving in professional lay ministry on behalf of The United Methodist Church, the 2004 General Conference affirm the following recommendations:

1. The focus for continuing development of persons in professional ministry will be shared by GBHEM and GBOD in cooperation with colleges, universities, seminaries, and annual conferences as partners in the educational and development process.

2. A more cooperative approach among the appropriate general agencies, professional associations, conference boards and leadership, and United Methodist colleges, universities, and seminaries will be developed to provide a variety of educational avenues and resources for lay persons serving in the church who seek to enhance their learning and increase their knowledge and skills to become more effective workers in their area of service on behalf of the church. Such avenues may include continuing education, certification, professional development, degree programs, conference programs, regional programs, and so forth. (For example: A college will partner with an annual conference to develop and implement a certificate program or course of study program to prepare and credential persons for youth ministry, Christian education, and so forth.)

3. General agencies; colleges, universities, and seminaries; and conferences will cooperate to broaden and make more accessible the

delivery systems for the education and development of church workers, for example college/university/seminary settings, extension sites, lay academies, other conference settings, regional settings, distance learning, e-learning, conferencing, and so forth.

4. An intentional cooperative approach will be shared by GBHEM and GBOD in consultation with conference leadership to develop and expand resources, methods, and rituals for acknowledgment and authentication by the church for those serving in professional/specialized lay ministry. These acts of recognition and celebration may take place where appropriate, including:

- recognition ceremonies at annual conference sessions;
- recognition celebrations where study is completed (either by residence or distance learning)—colleges, universities, seminaries, conference lay academies, and so forth;
- acknowledgment of professional certification in annual conference journals (¶ 632.2*t*);
- district or local church celebrations.

ADOPTED 2004
RESOLUTION #350, 2004 *BOOK OF RESOLUTIONS*

*See* Social Principles, ¶ 162*P* and *R*.


### 3105. Facilitation of Cooperative Ministry Throughout the Church

WHEREAS, cooperative forms of ministry have proven to enhance the ministries of laity, certified lay ministers, and to provide greater support and peer accountability among clergy, and to further connectional awareness and increased resourcing from the connectional church; and,

WHEREAS, cooperative ministry is an intentional style of team ministry that enables groups of congregations and their pastors and laity in a defined geographic area, as United Methodists and ecumenically, to work together in ministries of nurture, outreach, and witness; and,

WHEREAS, during its session at St. Louis in 2003 the Cooperative Ministry Common Table, under leadership of the General Council on Ministries and involving the National Leadership Team on Cooperative Ministry, explicitly affirmed the need for support of cooperative ministries by bishops and cabinets, annual conferences, districts, charge conferences, and their churches, general boards and agencies, and seminaries in order to call disciples to Jesus Christ and shape communities that reflect the reign of God;

*Therefore, be it resolved,* that cooperative ministry be supported by:

1. all boards and agencies of The United Methodist Church by collaborating around issues concerning cooperative ministry, i.e., training, resourcing, and financial and technical assistance, etc.;

2. bishops and cabinets fulfilling the requirements of *The Book of Discipline of The United Methodist Church* regarding cooperative ministries, i.e., training, consultation, deployment of personnel, etc.

3. bishops and cabinets giving priority to cooperative ministries in the appointment making process, including ecumenically cooperative ministries;

4. seminaries including training and field experiences for students to learn skills of working in team settings;

5. courses of study for local pastors, including training and field experience;

6. cabinets, conference staff, and other conference leaders of congregational development, parish and community development, etc., to give special attention to cooperative work in rural, urban, declining, growing, stable, racial/ethnic, multicultural, and large and small membership charges and churches;

7. cabinets and other annual conference leaders encouraging cooperative projects, ministries and parishes as means of reaching out and starting new congregations in apartment complexes, mobile home parks, recreational areas, prisons, retirement homes, unincorporated sections of communities, etc.

**ADOPTED 2008**

*See* Social Principles, ¶ 162.

## 3106. Church and Community Workers

WHEREAS, current social and economic needs across the USA call upon the church for attention and action in accordance with Christ's teachings; and

WHEREAS, financial undergirding of human service programs by the public sector on all levels has failed to meet the needs of people; and

WHEREAS, developing contacts and linkages between local church/cooperative ministries and community groups is key to the understanding of and response to human hurt and need, and is a primary strength of the church and community ministry program; and

WHEREAS, for many decades church and community workers have worked effectively in mission outreach with The United Methodist Church in town and rural, urban, and specialized settings; and

WHEREAS, church and community workers are the only cadre of missionaries serving within the bounds of the USA who are employed and assigned by the General Board of Global Ministries;

*Therefore, be it resolved,* that the General Board of Global Ministries continue to recruit, enlist, train, adequately fund, and deploy church and community workers, and

*Be it further resolved,* that the funding partnership continue between the local area, annual conference, and the General Board of Global Ministries in order to place church and community workers in economically depressed areas where they are desperately needed.

ADOPTED 1992
REVISED AND READOPTED 2000
REVISED AND READOPTED 2008
RESOLUTION #53, 2004 *BOOK OF RESOLUTIONS*
RESOLUTION #45, 2000 *BOOK OF RESOLUTIONS*

*See* Social Principles, ¶ 162R.

## 3107. Church and Community Workers
## Support Mission Initiatives

WHEREAS, several bodies are unified in the development of four "mission initiatives" presented to General Conference 2008 in order to build a collaborative movement in Leadership Development, Building New Congregations and Revitalizing Existing Ones, Ministry with the Poor, and Combating the Preventable Diseases of Poverty; and

WHEREAS, Church and Community Workers are among those leaders involved in a comprehensive approach to the nurture, outreach, and witness of both rural and urban churches; and

WHEREAS, developing contacts and linkages between local church/cooperative ministries and community groups is key to the understanding of and response to human hurt and need, and is a primary strength of the Church and Community Ministry program; and

WHEREAS, for decades Church and Community Workers have worked effectively in mission outreach with The United Methodist Church in town and rural, urban and specialized settings; and

WHEREAS, the goals of the Church and Community Ministry program are closely aligned with the focus of the proposed "mission initiatives" on leadership development, ministry with the poor and combating poverty; and

WHEREAS, Church and Community Workers are an effective cadre of missionaries serving within the bounds of the USA who are employed and assigned by the General Board of Global Ministries;

*Therefore, be it resolved,* that the General Board of Global Ministries, in its support of the "mission initiatives," continue to recruit, enlist, train, adequately fund, and deploy Church and Community Workers; and

*Be it further resolved,* that the funding partnership continue between the local area, annual conference, and the General Board of Global Ministries in order to place Church and Community Workers in economically depressed areas where they are desperately needed.

**ADOPTED 2008**

*See* Social Principles, ¶ 162R.

### 3108. Communities of Shalom

WHEREAS, the Communities of Shalom initiative was created by the General Conference of The United Methodist Church as a response to the Los Angeles riots and subsequent crisis in 1992; and

WHEREAS, through the power of God, Communities of Shalom empowered spiritual renewal, asset-based community development, systemic change, and healthy communities so that God's shalom was experienced among all people in their neighborhoods; and

WHEREAS, God, through the prophet Jeremiah, said: "Seek the shalom of the community where I have sent you . . . for in its shalom you will find your shalom" (29:7);

*Therefore . . .*

*We celebrate:*

That since 1992 the Shalom Initiative has trained more than 5,000 individuals in over 600 sites; and today operates in 250 communities in the United States and two countries in Africa; and

*We give thanks:*

To God, by whose Spirit the Communities of Shalom initiative has mobilized thousands of people, leveraged more than 100 million dollars, developed housing and jobs, improved multicultural relationships, built networks to better serve the health and educational needs within communities, and strengthened congregations;

To the people of Los Angeles in whose tragedy and turmoil the Communities of Shalom ministry was forged;

To all Shalom Sites and their annual conference leadership for their commitment to make God's Shalom tangibly evident in their communities, and for their efforts that will continue with the shepherding of the National Partner;

To all the communities in which the Shalom Initiative lives and works, for their willingness to collaborate, their openness to the Spirit of God, and their desire to be models of peace, wholeness, health, prosperity, and harmony to their neighbors.

To the General Board of Global Ministries who has shepherded the Communities of Shalom initiative since its inception, provided invaluable training and resources to annual conferences and individual sites, and who will continue to work with the initiative in its transition to a National Partner;

To all the men and women who have served on the National Shalom Committee to offer counsel, oversight, prayers, encouragement, creative leadership and loving labor;

*We applaud and affirm:*

The innovative approach to collaborative and sustainable ministry that is modeled by the inclusion of a National Partner under whose leadership the Shalom Initiative will deepen and broaden its impact on congregations and communities in the name of God.

*We therefore challenge:*

The United Methodist Church to empower new Shalom sites and continue its support of the Communities of Shalom initiative through prayer, through advocacy within and among annual conferences and the general boards and agencies, and through financial gifts to the Communities of Shalom Advance (No. 742566).

**ADOPTED 2004**
**REVISED AND READOPTED 2008**
**RESOLUTION #126, 2004** *BOOK OF RESOLUTIONS*
**RESOLUTION #115, 2000** *BOOK OF RESOLUTIONS*

*See* Social Principles, ¶ 162R

### 3109. Mission Personnel in the United States

WHEREAS, mission personnel in the United States, which includes church and community workers, US-2s, mission interns, summer interns, community developers, rural chaplains, lay missioners, and others, have faithfully and effectively enabled The United Methodist Church to facilitate mission and ministry across the United States in settings often neglected and overlooked by others; and

WHEREAS, the mission of the Church is to make disciples of Jesus Christ for the transformation of the world; and

WHEREAS, for many people in the United States, life is becoming increasingly difficult, with the basic necessities of food, shelter, health care, job and educational opportunities, childcare, and transportation required for daily survival often being beyond reach; and

WHEREAS, God continues to hear the cries of the oppressed, impoverished, and neglected people; and

WHEREAS, God continues to call persons to offer themselves for service with the poor to provide both compassionate care and personal empowerment; and

WHEREAS, The United Methodist Church, with its unique Wesleyan traditions of identity and advocacy with the poor and its historical focus on social issues and human development, is challenged by God to be radically attentive and responsive to marginalized and dispossessed people and to bear responsibility for keeping their plight before the total church and world community; and

WHEREAS, mission personnel in the United States provide leadership vital to initiate and maintain cooperative ministries, including communities of shalom and missionary programs, and other efforts that focus attention on the needs of women, children, youth, racial and ethnic populations, the aging, and people with disabilities in both rural and urban areas;

*Therefore, be it resolved,* that The United Methodist Church reaffirm its commitment to impoverished people and oppressed communities in the United States by creating and maintaining among its highest levels of priority the recruitment, training, and placement of mission personnel in the United States who can offer Christ and enable people, churches, and communities to move beyond their present circumstances to participate in healthy, whole communities;

*Be it further resolved,* that new and innovative means of providing financial support for mission personnel in the United States be developed as The United Methodist Church at all levels confronts the challenge to deal with limited available resources.

ADOPTED 1996<br>
AMENDED AND READOPTED 2004<br>
AMENDED AND READOPTED 2008<br>
RESOLUTION #127, 2004 *BOOK OF RESOLUTIONS*<br>
RESOLUTION #116, 2000 *BOOK OF RESOLUTIONS*

*See* Social Principles, ¶ 162.


## 3110.  Use of Church Facilities by Community Groups

Encouragement shall be given for the use of local church facilities by community groups and agencies that serve social and service needs of the total community that are in keeping with the mission of The United Methodist Church.

ADOPTED 1970<br>
AMENDED AND READOPTED 2000<br>
READOPTED 2008<br>
RESOLUTION #54, 2004 *BOOK OF RESOLUTIONS*<br>
RESOLUTION #48, 2000 *BOOK OF RESOLUTIONS*

*See* Social Principles, ¶ 162.


## 3111.  Volunteers in Mission

WHEREAS, the United Methodist Volunteers in Mission (UMVIM) movement is one of the most dynamic mission outreach programs of the denomination today; every conference has a UMVIM Coordinator in place. Some jurisdictions have paid full-time UMVIM coordinator who, because of the time commitment, able to assist their respective conferences more effectively than those coordinators in a part-time or volunteer position; and

WHEREAS, although United Methodist Volunteers in Mission is a major mission outreach now, with thousands of United Methodists participating annually, the potential is much greater; and

WHEREAS, the church needs to invest in ways which will enhance the program, involve even more United Methodists, and bring Christ's love to people and churches in need around the world. Full-time jurisdictional coordinators will be a great help in the expansion of this effective, hands-on mission and service outreach of The United Methodist Church,

*Therefore,* we recommend that every jurisdiction include in its budget a line item to cover the salary, professional expenses, and office expenses for a jurisdictional United Methodist Volunteers in Mission coordinator. In addition, we request the General Board of Global Ministries to enter into discussion with the central conferences relative to discovering the possibility of Volunteers in Mission programs in those conferences.

ADOPTED 2000
READOPTED 2008
RESOLUTION #55, 2004 *BOOK OF RESOLUTIONS*
RESOLUTION #49, 2000 *BOOK OF RESOLUTIONS*

*See* Social Principles, ¶ 162.


## CULTURAL ISSUES


### 3121. Affirming the Use of Diverse Languages in the United States and Opposing a Constitutional Amendment Making English the Official Language

The United States is a land whose inhabitants are enriched by diverse traditions, languages, and cultures. While English is the most commonly used or "primary" language of the country, there have always been other languages present throughout the history of the nation. Native American languages and Spanish were already spoken when the first English colonists arrived. Throughout that same history, there have been various efforts to prescribe the use of English and to proscribe the use of other languages. These efforts sometimes resulted in legislation that had the effect of legalizing discrimination against various language minority groups, as was the case for German, Swedish, French, Greek, and Italian immigrants who came to this country in great numbers during the nineteenth century. However, such legislative attempts were eventually overcome by the constitutional principles of equal rights for all. The acknowledgment of English as the primary language of the United States does not deny the right and contribution of other languages or the inherent right of people to retain and speak their mother tongues.

One particular area of concern is the attempt to remove bilingual education. Education has played a very important role in the development of this nation. To have access to it and to receive a sound education are considered inalienable rights of all children. Bilingual education has been and is a critical tool to ensure these rights for non-English-speaking children living now in the United States of America. It has been an instrument of education for children to make the transition from their native tongues to English (without abandoning their native tongues) while at the same time staying at the level correspondent to their age. Bilingual education does work. There are thousands of living examples of bilingual education successes. They are students who learned English in bilingual classrooms and who continue to achieve to the highest of academic and professional standards.

In recent years, there have been renewed efforts in different parts of the country to make English the official language of the nation. Notwith-standing their unsuccessful attempts to pass a constitutional amendment, we are now seeing concerted efforts to bring the same policy to state and local levels. We are concerned that the movement to declare constitutionally English as the official language of the nation is not based upon any real need but, in fact, may be motivated by an effort to deny the pluralistic foundation of the country and to deny the dignity and wholeness of persons from different racial and ethnic groups who rightly considered their languages an integral part of their cultures. We fear the real purpose of some may be not so much to make English the *official* language of the US as to make English the *exclusive* language of the nation.

The English-only "movement" includes efforts to pass a constitutional amendment making English the official language of the United States, opposition to federal legislation for bilingual education, voting-rights bills, and the FCC licensing applications for Spanish-language broadcasts.

The English-only movement is another manifestation of the systemic racism that has infected this country for generations. The English-only movement blames the deterioration of the American fabric on immigration and the use of languages other than English. It contends that the nation's unity rests upon the use of an official language.

It defines multiculturalism and multilingualism as "anti-unity." Consequently, the movement, if successful, could further discriminate against and segregate the racial and ethnic population of the United States. Essential information such as: 1) numbers for the 911 emergency, hospital emergency rooms, police, firefighters, 2) medical and legal forms, language services, bilingual education, and interpreters in the judicial system might be denied.

As Christians, we believe that we are children of God, created in God's image, and members of the family of God.

We believe that diversity is a gift of the creative genius of God and that languages are an expression of the wisdom of God.

We believe that competence in the English language is important to participate fully in the life of the United States, but we also acknowledge the fact that we live in a global context, the global family of God, where people and nations experience interdependency at all levels and where the acquisition of a second language represents a better understanding of other people's cultures, hopes, and dreams.

We believe that our nation needs to take advantage of the rich contributions that the ethnic/language groups bring to this country by preserving those languages and encouraging North Americans to learn other languages.

We believe that it is the will of God that each human being is affirmed as a whole person and that it is in the acceptance and interchange of our uniqueness that we find a witness of God's *shalom*.

We oppose the attempt to rob a person of his or her language as dehumanizing and as a denial of that person's wholeness.

We oppose the English-only movement as a manifestation of the sin of racism.

*Therefore, be it resolved,* that the General Conference shall:

1. express in writing to the President of the United States its support for practices and policies that permit provision of information in languages appropriate to the residents of communities and its opposition to the movement that seeks to make English the only language of the United States, which movement is discriminatory and racist;

2. forward this resolution to members of Congress, governors, and the legislatures of the fifty states and territories;

3. commend this resolution to all United States annual conferences for promotion and interpretation within the annual conferences; and

4. ask the General Board of Church and Society to make this resolution an urgent item in their agenda for lobbying, constituency education, and advocacy.

ADOPTED 1988
AMENDED AND ADOPTED 2000
AMENDED AND READOPTED 2008
RESOLUTION #72, 2004 *BOOK OF RESOLUTIONS*
RESOLUTION #64, 2000 *BOOK OF RESOLUTIONS*

*See* Social Principles, ¶ 162.

## 3122. Biracial/Multiracial Inclusive Language

WHEREAS, in 1967 the US Supreme Court ruled in Loving vs. Virginia that interracial marriages could not be banned, and a rise in interracial marriages has since occurred producing what can be identified as biracial children and a generation following, multiracial children; and

WHEREAS, the US Census Bureau has identified a significant biracial/multiracial population by reporting in 2001 that biracial/multiracial population is 2.4 percent of the total US population, 6,826,228; specifically, stating that the percentage of children being raised by one parent of a different race is 2.3 percent white, 6.3 percent black, 54 percent Native American, 18 percent Asian, and 13 percent other; and

WHEREAS, it has been reported that out of 35 percent of the current population (those born between 1982 and 2002) one in five have one immigrant parent, and when polled, 82 percent stated that they would date or marry outside their race[1]; and

WHEREAS, we are told that in Christ there is no Jew or Greek, there is no longer slave or free, there is no longer male and female (Galatians 3:28), we as a church should not be exclusive toward race, but actively inclusive; and

WHEREAS, in spite of our faith, many of our own forms within our church are exclusive requiring the growing population of biracial/multiracial people to choose between one parent or another, by requiring churchgoers to identify themselves by selecting only one of the six classical racial options: Asian, Black, Euro-American, Hispanic, Native American, and Pacific Islander;

1. Howe, Neil and William Strauss. *Millennials Rising*. New York : Vintage Books, 2000. pp. 14-15, 218.

*Therefore, be it resolved,* that The United Methodist Church expand its inclusive language in all aspects of the church to include biracial/multiracial persons by offering racial identification options that are not limiting but embracing of persons with more than one racial or ethnic background.

ADOPTED 2004
RESOLUTION #73, 2004 *BOOK OF RESOLUTIONS*

*See* Social Principles, ¶ 162A.


### 3123. Replace Term "Ethnic Minority" with "Ethnic Person"

*Be it resolved,* that given the global nature of The United Methodist Church, that General Conference 2004 take action to remove the term *ethnic minority* from all future United Methodist *Disciplines* as a nomenclature for ethnic people or groups. Given the racial history of the United States of America, the term *minority*, for many people, is not only a means for describing the number of persons of a particular ethnic group but is often heard and experienced by ethnic persons to mean less than and not equal to in worth to the whole. Therefore, the term *minority* diminishes our capacity as United Methodists to see ourselves as part of the body of Christ where all persons are considered to be gifted, whole and equal but yet different.

*Be it further resolved,* that the term *racial/ethnic persons* replace the term *ethnic minority* where it is not feasible to name a particular ethnic group.

ADOPTED 2004
RESOLUTION #74, 2004 *BOOK OF RESOLUTIONS*

*See* Social Principles, ¶ 162A.


### 3124. Support for Five Ethnic National Plans

WHEREAS, ¶ 138 of *The Book of Discipline, 2000* states "As a diverse people of God who bring special gifts and evidences of God's grace to the unity of the Church and to society, we are called to be faithful to the example of Jesus' ministry to all persons"; and

WHEREAS, ¶ 162*A* of The Social Principles affirms the ministry to all persons and states "We rejoice in the gifts that particular ethnic histories and cultures bring to our total life"; and

WHEREAS, five ethnic national plans (Asian Language Ministry, Hispanic, Korean, Native American, and Strengthening the Black Church) have affirmed and have made significant contributions to the growth and strengthening of major ethnic ministries; and

WHEREAS, continuing needs for the five ethnic national plans (Asian Language Ministry, Hispanic, Korean, Native American, and Strengthening the Black Church) are clearly demonstrated by their successes in making disciples of Christ; and

WHEREAS, funding for these ethnic national plans are essential and critical in order to continue ministry to ethnic people;

*Therefore, be it resolved that,* this General Conference of The United Methodist Church expresses its support for continuing existence and funding of the ethnic national plans.

ADOPTED 2004
READOPTED 2008
RESOLUTION #80, 2004 *BOOK OF RESOLUTIONS*

*See* Social Principles, ¶ 162*A*.

### 3125. Support for Multicultural and Ethnic-Specific Ministries

"The World is my parish" said John Wesley, the founder of Methodism. These words have been the motto of United Methodists throughout many generations. Today, when we seem to be living in the midst of an explosion of diversity, once again these words come alive and become more relevant. Even when racial/ethnic/cultural diversity has been a reality in the United States from its very beginnings, this diversity has reached a momentum in our common history both in church and in society. Mobility, advanced technology, war, political instability, and socioeconomic realities have brought the diversity of the world into our very own neighborhoods and churches, creating a challenge to old principles of church growth such as the homogenous theory.

In response to this reality, many churches have begun by developing multicultural ministries. However, the concern has been raised that the current trend for multicultural ministries has been placed in opposition to the continued development and strengthening of the racial/ethnic local church. Frequently the choice of a multicultural ministry has been done at the expense of what has been called ethnic specific ministries, e.g. Asian, Black, Hispanic, Pacific Islander, and Native American ministries. In other instances, multicultural ministries are being used to dismiss the uniqueness of the different groups; and/or simply as a superficial face make-up (a few different faces in the congregation) that does not impact the life, leadership style, and decision-making of the congregation. In these cases, multiculturalism can be a disguised form of racism.

WHEREAS, the General Commission on Religion and Race is mandated by the Church to ensure the equal participation of all believers as members of the same body that is the body of Christ; and

WHEREAS, the question of multicultural congregations or ethnic specific congregations is not an either/or proposition for inclusiveness but rather two distinct paths needed to achieve the inclusive spirit revealed to us at Pentecost, when people understood each other, not through a common language, but through the power of the Spirit who affirmed and embraced everyone (each one spoke in his/her own tongue), making of many, One; and

WHEREAS, a truly multicultural congregation is more than "token" participation of racial/ethnic persons, but is one that incorporates into the worship style, leadership, and entire ministry cultural elements of the different racial/ethnic groups present in the congregation thus ensuring that everyone has a place at the table where power is shared (resources and decision-making) and where conflict is managed collaboratively, and where everyone brings gifts to the mutually "owned table," and where the entire congregation is shaped by all and not by one dominant group; and

WHEREAS, ethnic specific ministries have historically been a source of strength, encouragement, and empowerment for people of color, and have enabled people to move outside of their local congregations to participate in the larger church and have contributed greatly to the inclusiveness of the church; and

WHEREAS, it is important that the church is sensitive to the context of all people and reaches people where they are, including culture and language; and

WHEREAS, one of the principles of inclusiveness is self-determination, and people of color in their continued quest for empowerment in the midst of a racist church and society should have the power to determine if their cultural and spiritual needs are best met in an ethnic specific congregation or in a multicultural one; and

WHEREAS, on many occasions an "ethnic specific" congregation can be the beginning of becoming a multicultural church; and

WHEREAS, multicultural ministries should be look upon as one of the models of the inclusive and multicultural church, and that there are many ways in which the church can be multicultural and inclusive without being together in the same worship service always, such as community work, mission, children and youth, church governance, etc.

*Be it resolved that:*

The United Methodist Church's commitment to inclusiveness affirms the continued development and strengthening of the racial/ethnic congregations as well as the development and strengthening of congregations that respect, understand, and embrace diversity becoming truly multicultural congregations as defined above;

The Council of Bishops give direction to their annual conferences on this issue so that local churches are provided with resources and guidance in their efforts to respond to their diverse communities;

The General Board of Global Ministries and the General Board of Discipleship continue providing leadership and resources in the development of racial/ethnic congregations and multicultural congregations where everyone has a place at the table and power is shared;

The General Commission on Religion and Race continues collaborating with the General Board of Global Ministries, the General Board of Higher Education and Ministry, the General Board of Church and Society, and the General Board of Discipleship in the development of resources that undergird the creation and the strengthening of multicultural and ethnic specific ministries;

The United Methodist seminaries incorporate into their curriculums the subjects needed to prepare students who will be able to minister in different and diverse settings.

ADOPTED 2004
RESOLUTION #76, 2004 *BOOK OF RESOLUTIONS*

*See* Social Principles, ¶ 162A.

## 3126. The Church's Response to Ethnic and Religious Conflict

*Would that you knew the things that make for peace.*
—Jesus of Nazareth (Luke 19:42)

The tragic conflicts in such places as Bosnia, India, Indonesia, the Middle East, Nigeria, Rwanda, Northern Ireland, and Sri Lanka, as well as interethnic conflict in the United States, reveal the deep potential for hatred, fear, and religious belief to stir up violence in humankind. These conflicts pose a great challenge to the Christian church as the mediator of Jesus' gospel of love and reconciliation in the world, as well as to the wider religious community. The church's pain is only made greater by the fact that so many of these violent conflicts pit one religious group against another.

*When his disciples James and John saw it, they said, "Lord, do you want us to command fire to come down from heaven and consume them [a Samaritan village]?" But he turned and rebuked them. (Luke 9:54-55)*

We confess that as Christians we too have responded to religious and ethnic differences out of fear, ignorance and even hatred. We have too quickly resorted to violence as a means of resolving conflicts.

The rising tide of violence in the world threatens to engulf communities, nations, and world civilizations. It is time for the church to become proactive in resolving conflict nonviolently and developing alternatives to violence. Specifically:

- we call upon the General Board of Global Ministries to continue discussions with Christian Peacemakers, Witness for Peace, International Solidarity Movement, and other nonviolent movements that provide a Christian presence in situations of international, interreligious, and interethnic conflict, to explore the possibility of including United Methodists on the teams that are sent to areas of conflict;
- we call upon the General Board of Global Ministries to incorporate the principles of nonviolent conflict resolution and interethnic and interreligious dialogue in the Shalom Zone Program;
- we call upon the General Board of Church and Society, together with the General Commission on Religion and Race and the General Commission on Christian Unity and Interreligious Concerns to hold a series of interreligious dialogues to develop new approaches to mutual understanding,

respect, and cooperation, and to develop, for use in local church and community settings, guidelines on how to set up local dialogues and how to develop and implement alternatives to violence;

- we call upon our seminaries and United Methodist-related colleges and universities to offer courses on alternatives to violence and to sponsor local community initiatives to diffuse ethnic and religious conflict. We also call on our seminaries to encourage the study of the theological roots of violence and of Jesus' teachings on nonresistance and resisting evil; and

- we call upon the US government, working with the United Nations, to give leadership **by** redirecting funds from its foreign military exercise training programs to the UN High Commission for Human Rights and other international human rights organizations for the tasks of peacemaking, peacekeeping, reconstruction, and rehabilitation. This means reallocating funds from building weapons to building communities, from teaching to kill to teaching to protect life. Modest beginnings in such an effort can be seen in community policing initiatives in many of our cities, in the peacekeeping force in Bosnia, and in the nonviolent transition to democracy in South Africa;

- we call upon the General Board of Discipleship, together with the General Board of Global Ministries, to address our growing multi-faith contexts in developing church school curriculum by utilizing resources from ecumenical and interfaith organizations;

- we call upon local churches to be engaged in "Creating Interfaith Community"—a Women's Division-initiated mission study—throughout the coming quadrennium;

- we call upon annual conferences to organize high school and adult trips through United Methodist Seminars (a program offered by Women's Division and the General Board of Church and Society) or United Methodist Volunteers in Mission to study Ethnic and Religious Conflicts and alternatives to violence.

ADOPTED 1996
AMENDED AND READOPTED 2004
READOPTED 2008
RESOLUTION #81, 2004 *BOOK OF RESOLUTIONS*
RESOLUTION #71, 2000 *BOOK OF RESOLUTIONS*

*See* Social Principles, ¶ 162*A* and *B*.

## 3127. Holocaust Memorial Day (Yom HaShoah)

In recent years, Jewish communities have honored the custom of remembering the Holocaust (Shoah) on 27 Nisan of the the Jewish calendar This observance has become a powerful means of educating people about this heinous crime against humanity and sensitizing them to present and potential violence rooted in racial hatred.

WHEREAS, "In the twentieth century there is particular shame in the failure of most of the church to challenge the policies of governments that were responsible for the unspeakable atrocities of the Holocaust" ("Building New Bridges in Hope," *Book of Resolutions*); and

WHEREAS, the same document observes, "[t]he Christian Church has a profound obligation to correct historical and theological teachings that have led to false and pejorative perceptions of Judaism and contributed to persecution and hatred of Jews";

*Therefore, be it resolved,* that the General Conference calls The United Methodist Church to contrition and repentance of its complicity in "the long history of persecution of the Jewish people" and asks the General Commission on Christian Unity and Interreligious Concerns to give special programmatic emphasis to Holocaust awareness and to prepare resources for use in local churches, annual conferences, and their Conference Commissions on Christian Unity and Interreligious Concerns or equivalent structures to enable them to become more aware of the Holocaust and its impact, and

*Be it further resolved,* as a sign of our contrition and our solidarity with the Jewish community, the General Conference urges the observance of *Yom HaShoah,* Holocaust Memorial Day, each spring in United Methodist local churches and urges the General Commission on Christian Unity and Interreligious Concerns, in cooperation with other agencies of The United Methodist Church, in a time of increasing anti-Semitism, to work within the structure of our own Church to find ways to support the work against anti-Semitism in the world today and to prepare resources for local churches to use in observing *Yom HaShoah.*

We continue to pray for God's grace to speak in Jesus' name against bigotry, hatred, genocide, or other crimes against humanity whenever and wherever they are perpetrated.

ADOPTED 2000
REVISED AND READOPTED 2008
RESOLUTION #75, 2004 BOOK OF RESOLUTIONS
RESOLUTION #66, 2000 *BOOK OF RESOLUTIONS*

See Social Principles, ¶ 162.

### 3128. Prejudice Against Muslims and Arabs in the USA

Today in the United States of America there are approximately 3 million persons who are adherents of Islam. Arab Americans, both Christian and Muslim, constitute a growing number of persons in the American population. These persons are suffering the effects of a particularly virulent prejudice too often aided and abetted by statements and images in the media and by rhetoric from some of the highest political leadership. The suffering of this community has increased dramatically since the tragic events of September 11, 2001. As part of the fabric of racism in the USA, in which both subtle and violent acts continue against ethnic groups and persons, such acts are also being perpetrated against the Arab and Muslim communities in the USA. These expressions of racism manifested in violent acts have also increased since September 11, 2001.

Arab American organization offices, mosques, and Islamic centers have been bombed and torched. Leaders of these communities have been murdered and questionable uses of law have been utilized to stifle the rights of association and freedom of expression. Arab persons and/or persons looking like Arabs are being detained in airports and other places without justification. They are continually subjected to harassment and discrimination. Though discriminatory acts against Arabs and Muslims do not stand in isolation from similar acts perpetrated against other racial and ethnic persons in the USA, their existence and effects upon Arabs and Muslims have been little acknowledged in US society, with concomitant deleterious effect on US perceptions, internationally, as they touch upon relations with predominantly Arab and Muslim nations and organizations.

*Therefore,* The United Methodist Church, in the knowledge that Jesus calls us to the blessings of peacemaking and reminds us that the highest law is to love God and neighbor, calls its members and its leaders:

1. To oppose demagoguery, manipulation, and image making that seeks to label Arabs and Muslims in a negative way;

2. To counter stereotypical and bigoted statements made against Muslims and Islam, Arabs and Arabic culture;

3. To increase knowledge of neighbor by study and personal contact that yield a greater appreciation of the Muslim and Arabic contributions to society;

4. To act decisively to include Arabs and Muslims in interfaith and community organizations;

5. To pray for the perfection of community among us and to participate fully in the process of bringing it into being; and

6. To publicly denounce through statements from the Council of Bishops and the General Board of Church and Society current practices that discriminate against this community.

In order to aid United Methodists to respond to this call, all boards, agencies, and institutions of The United Methodist Church are requested to provide resources and program and, where appropriate, to act in advocacy.

ADOPTED 1988
AMENDED AND READOPTED 2000
AMENDED AND READOPTED 2004
READOPTED 2008
RESOLUTION #78, 2004 *BOOK OF RESOLUTIONS*
RESOLUTION #69, 2000 *BOOK OF RESOLUTIONS*

*See* Social Principles, ¶ 162B.


## ECUMENICAL AND INTERRELIGIOUS ISSUES


### 3141. Support of Joint Declaration on the Doctrine of Justification

WHEREAS, in 1999 a Joint Declaration on the Doctrine of Justification was confirmed and signed by the Lutheran World Federation and the Roman Catholic Church, and

WHEREAS, the document is the product of many years of dialogue around this substantive and historically divisive issue, and

WHEREAS, the Joint Declaration "has this intention, namely, to show that on the basis of their dialogue . . . [They] are now able to articulate a common understanding of our justification by God's grace through Jesus Christ. It does not cover all that either church teaches about justification; it does encompass a consensus on basic truths of the doctrine of justification and shows that the remaining differences in its explication are no longer the occasion for doctrinal condemnations" (JDDJ, pg. 5), and

WHEREAS, the Resolution of the Officers of the World Methodist Council at their meeting in Abuja, Nigeria, September 15-19, 2003 supports and affirms this declaration expressing "our deep hope that in the near future we shall also be able to enter into a closer relationship with Lutherans . . . and with the Roman Catholic Church in accordance with this declaration of our common understanding of the doctrine of justification" (WMC, pg. 5).

*Therefore, be it resolved*, that The United Methodist Church expresses its gratitude and appreciation for the Joint Declaration between the Lutheran World Federation and the Roman Catholic Church and the response of the Officers of the World Methodist Council, as well as its encouragement to the Council in its efforts to seek continued dialogue on this, and other matters.

ADOPTED 2004
RESOLUTION #16, 2004 *BOOK OF RESOLUTIONS*

*See* Social Principles, ¶ 162.

### 3142. Called to Be Neighbors and Witnesses: Guidelines for Interreligious Relationships

Nations of the world are growing increasingly interdependent politically and economically. The various world religious communities are also encountering each other in new ways. Religions of Asia and Africa are showing new life and power within their homelands and are spreading to other continents, creating new multireligious societies, especially in western nations. New sects, cults, and ideologies are emerging and ancient traditions are receiving renewed attention. To an unprecedented degree, the wonders of the information age bring the world's rich religious diversity into our homes and communities.

The emergence of religiously diverse societies and the new dynamics in old religious communities have prompted many faith communities to reconsider how they relate to one another and to prevailing secular ideologies. This represents a great opportunity for learning and an enhanced understanding of our common concerns. Yet, there is also danger that religious tensions will lead to oppression of religious minorities and curtailment of religious freedom with real potential for armed conflict. At a time when worldwide problems of human suffering due to poverty, wars, and political oppression are so vast and pervasive that no one faith group can solve them, tensions between religious groups often prevent the level of cooperation needed to respond more adequately. As ancient religions demonstrate new life and power to speak to the deepest human concerns, Christians are pressed toward a deeper understanding of other faith traditions and a reexamination of their our claims to a global mission to all people.

What are the implications of this religiously diverse situation for Christian theology and ministry? What does it mean to be a faithful follower of and witness to Jesus Christ? What does it mean to affirm the Lordship of Jesus Christ in a religiously pluralistic world? Can we, of different faith traditions, live together as neighbors, or will diverse religious loyalties result in mutual antagonism and destruction? What are the resources United Methodist Christians bring for building constructive relationships between persons of different religions?

The United Methodist Church provides this statement as guidance to its members and congregations in facing these questions in their and our relations with persons who hold other faith perspectives.

### Called to Be Neighbors

For some Christians, it may seem strange even to refer to "persons who hold other faith perspectives." Some are accustomed to calling them "non-Christians" or "nonbelievers." These attitudes may have developed out of confidence in the ultimate truth of our own faith perspective or from limited experience of and insensitivity to other traditions, to the truth they may contain, and to the profound meaning and purpose they give to the lives of people. How, then, are we to relate to those who seem different from us religiously?

Scripture gives us many images of neighborliness which extends across conventional boundaries. In the Old Testament (Genesis 12), we find God challenging Abram and Sarai to go live among strangers. In the New Testament, Jesus breaks convention by speaking with the Samaritan woman at the well (John 4:6-30) and shows how she can be reached through dialogue. Speaking with a lawyer (Luke 10:25), Jesus reminds him that his neighbor, the one to whom he should show love and compassion, and from whom he may receive grace, may be a stranger. Today, our Lord's call to neighborliness (Luke 10:27) includes the "strangers" of other faith traditions who live in our towns and cities. It is not just that historical events have forced us together. Christianity itself impels us to love our neighbors and to seek to live in contact and mutually beneficial relationships, in community, with them.

What does it mean to be a neighbor? It means to meet other persons, to know them, to relate to them, to respect them, and to learn about their ways which may be quite different from our own. It means to create a sense of community in our neighborhoods, towns and cities and to make them places in which the unique customs of each group can be expressed and their values protected. It means to create social structures in which there is justice for all and that everyone can participate in shaping their life together "in community." Each race or group of people is not only allowed to be who they are, but their way of life is also valued and given full expression.

Christians distinguish several meanings of "community." One definition expresses their relationships as members of one another in the body of Christ, the church, a people called together by Christ, a "communion of saints" who work toward the reign of God. A broader definition points to the relationship that is shared with others in the wider human community, where Christians are concerned for peace, justice, and reconciliation for all people. Other faiths also have their understanding of "community." The vision of a "worldwide community of communities" commends itself to many Christians as a way of being together with persons of different religious convictions in a pluralistic world.

Ultimately, this is to shift the question from, "To which church do we belong?" to "Have we participated in promoting the work of the Holy Spirit?" That suggests that we United Methodist Christians, not just individually, but corporately, are called to be neighbors with other faith communities (such as Buddhist, Jewish, Muslim, Hindu, and Native American), and to work with them to create a human community, a set of relationships between people at once interdependent and free, in which there is love, mutual respect, and justice.

### Called to Be Witnesses

Within this religiously diverse community, Christians, trusting in Jesus Christ for their salvation, are called to witness to him as Lord to all people (Acts 1:8). We witness to our Lord through words which tell of his grace, through deeds of service and social change that demonstrate his love, and through our life together in the Christian community, exhibiting God's power to heal, reconcile, and unite.

When Jesus issued his famous missionary mandate, "Go therefore and make disciples of all nations" (Matthew 28:20), the Greek word is *poreuthentes.* This literally means "to depart, to leave, to cross boundaries." Thus, a witness to Jesus Christ is one who can bridge boundaries, be they geographic, sociological, racial, or cultural. The gospels tell story after story of Jesus crossing boundaries and reaching to out-siders, drawing them into his circle. As disciples of Jesus, our outreach draws upon the gospel call to be even more than neighbors. We are to proclaim and witness to the God who has bound humanity together in care for one another, regardless of the differences between us.

As relationships with persons of other faith communities deepen, Christians discover how often our witness has been unneighborly, how much we have talked and how little we have listened, and how our insensitive and unappreciative approaches have alienated sincere truth seekers and persons who already have strong faith commit-ments. We become aware that we frequently communicate attitudes of superiority regarding our own faith, thereby perpetuating walls and hostilities between us as human beings. These can only restrict Christian witness.

As United Methodist Christians reflect anew on our faith and seek guidance in our witness to and encounter with our new neighbors, we rediscover that God who has acted in Jesus Christ for the salvation of the whole world, is also Creator of all humankind, the "one God and Father of all, who is Lord of all, works through all, and is in all" (Eph. 4:6 TEV). Here Christians confront a profound mystery—the aware-ness of God who is related to all creation and at work in the whole of it, and the experience of God who has acted redemptively for the whole creation in Jesus Christ. Christians witness to God in Jesus Christ in the confidence that here all people can find salvation and in the trust that because of what we know of God in Jesus, God deals gra-ciously and lovingly with all people everywhere.

### Dialogue: A Way to Be Neighbors

"Dialogue" is the word that has come to signify an approach to per-sons of other faith communities that takes seriously both the call to witness and the command to love and be neighbors. To be engaged in dialogue is to see witnessing and neighborliness as interrelated activ-ities. Rather than a one-sided address, dialogue combines witnessing with listening. It is the intentional engagement with persons who hold other faith perspectives for purposes of mutual understanding, coop-eration, and transformation.

"Dialogue" may be as informal as a conversation in the marketplace or as formal as the leader of one religious group explaining to others its belief or worship life. Dialogue is more than an individual or academic enterprise. It also involves groups or communities of people holding different convictions who reach out to one another. This community orientation gives a practical bent to interreligious dialogue.

In dialogue, one individual or group may seek relationship with another in order to expose misunderstandings and stereotypes and to break down barriers that separate and create hostility and conflict. Ethnic or religious communities may approach each other in dialogue in order to resolve particular problems or to foster cooperation in dealing with a local, national, or even global situation of human suffering. At its deepest level, dialogue is both learning about and sharing our faith through its stories and images. Each partner learns from the rich store of wisdom of the other, and each expresses his or her own deepest conviction in the faith that it has truth worth sharing with the other.

Through dialogue with persons of other faith communities, new insights are received regarding God's activity in the world today, the divine purpose for humankind as a whole, and the place of the Christian community within these purposes. It is also a common experience for Christians to feel the need to express their own faith with greater clarity. We trust in the Holy Spirit to make known new and different insights through such encounters.

Even though Jews, Christians and Muslims share the same covenant, in many of our cities and towns we continue to live as strangers to each other. A positive foundation from which to connect with persons in other faith communities is recognition of some of the gifts they bring to the human community. For instance, through Judaism, Christians can connect to the covenantal faithfulness of God; Islam illustrates the joy of life lived in obedience to God's will; the spiritualities of indigenous peoples encourage a deep reverence for God's natural creation; Buddhism offers contemplative ways to connect to the divine; and Hinduism in its varieties brings the gift of tolerance. Engaging in dialogue with positive expectation offers the possibility of sharing mutually beneficial spiritual gifts as well as overcoming past hostilities.

Dialogue frequently has been misunderstood. Some see it as limited to the commonalities that exist between different religious traditions. It is important to discern and explore those commonalities and to utilize them to strengthen relationships. But there is more! Dialogue offers to both partners the opportunity of enriching their own faith through the wisdom of the other. In the process it helps overcome the deep mistrust, hatred, hostility, and conflict that characterize so many intercultural and interreligious relations. Each religious community asserts that its faith offers a way to resolve conflict in positive ways and has resources for building community among diverse peoples. Dialogue seeks to provide an environment which allows space for differences, builds on the positive affirmations of each faith, and brings them into relationship with each other.

### Dialogue: A Way to Witness

The only precondition for dialogue—sometimes a challenging one—is a true willingness to enter a relationship of mutual acceptance, openness, and respect. Effective dialogue requires that both partners have deep convictions about life, faith, and salvation. True dialogue requires that Christians not suspend their fundamental convictions concerning the truth of the gospel, but enter into dialogue with personal commitment to Jesus Christ and with the desire to witness to that faith. Effective dialogue also requires that Christians be truly open to persons of other faith communities, to their convictions about life, truth, and salvation and to their witness, as others also are called to witness to their faith and teachings about the meaning of life. Engagement in dialogue is a form of Christian ministry.

Is not this urge to witness an obstacle to interreligious dialogue? It often has been, but it need not be. Where there is listening as well as speaking, openness and respect as well as concern to influence, there is dialogue and witness. Indeed, dialogue at its most profound level is an exchange of witness. Participants share with each other their perceptions of the meaning of life, of ultimate reality, salvation and hope, and the resources of their faith for enabling community. In genuine "dialogue," we "witness and are witnessed to." The most effective dialogue takes place when both sides really do care that the other hear, understand, and receive the other's wisdom. Part of our witness is our openness to hearing the witness of the other.

Dialogue at these depths holds great promise. Long-cherished convictions may be modified by the encounter with others. Misunderstanding may be clarified, potential hostilities reconciled, and new insights regarding one's own faith may emerge in contrast to that of another. The depths of another's faith may be so disclosed that its power and attractiveness are experienced. Dialogue is a demanding process, requiring thorough understanding of one's own faith and clear articulation of it to the other person. It asks that we "translate" our perspectives to one another with integrity, that we have the patience and attentiveness to discern what meaning words and images have for the other persons as well as ourselves.

Dialogue is not a betrayal of witness. Dialogue and witness are wrongly placed in opposition to each other. They need each other. Dialogue creates relationships of mutual understanding, openness, and respect. Witness presses dialogue to the deepest convictions about life, death, and hope.

Many persons of other faiths are suspicious that dialogue is a new and more subtle tool for conversion. In some ways this is inevitable since Christians do want others to learn of and receive the truth and grace we know in Jesus Christ. The difference between dialogue and other forms of witness is that it is a context for learning from the other the truth and wisdom of the other faith as well as sharing with the other the truth and wisdom of our own. We leave to the Holy Spirit the outcome of our mutual openness.

Because of our theological understanding of John Wesley's insistence on prevenient grace, we know that our task of witness is set in the context of a world in which God is very much active and where people have already experienced the love of God in good measure through the activity of the Holy Spirit. Because we understand prevenient grace that "goes before," we know that the activity of the Holy Spirit is at work in the church and in the world, in the lives of all persons, including those of other religious traditions. A large part of our task, and foundational to interreligious dialogue and cooperation, is to learn to discern the Spirit's work.

Our concern is to be obedient to our own call to witness and to follow the imperative to be loving and neighborly to persons of other faith communities. In dialogue, these deeply held truths encounter each other in witness and love, so that greater wisdom and greater understanding of truth may emerge which benefit all parties in the dialogue. As we exhibit courtesy, reverence, and respect and become neighbors, fears of each other are allayed, and the Holy Spirit works within these relationships.

*Neighbors and Witnesses: Into the New Millennium*

The command to love one's neighbors and the call to witness to Jesus Christ to all people are inseparably linked. The profound challenge which this represents for United Methodist Christians can be seen most sharply in the new religious movements which have arisen in recent years. These movements have become a source of concern for many Christians. Some groups seem to utilize methods that are manipulative and coercive.

However, many people have found new vision, meaning, and hope in some of these new faith perspectives. These new religious movements are very diverse and they should not be lumped together indiscriminately, condemned, and dismissed. Neither should they automatically be embraced as valid expressions of human dignity and freedom. Careful study and contact will enable Christians to distinguish those which are manipulative and coercive and which are to be challenged for reasons of faith.

As we take seriously this calling to be witnesses and neighbors to people of all faith communities, old and new, we become aware of the biblical caution not to bear false witness (Matthew19:18) and the admonition to live at peace with all people (Hebrews 12:14). How are we to avoid bearing false witness unless we know our neighbors and understand their faith commitments? How can one truly love a neighbor and hold back what to Christians is the greatest of all gifts—God becoming present to people in Jesus Christ? How can we live peacefully together, unless we are willing to be neighborly? How can we say we love our neighbor if we are unwilling to be attentive to the message and the gifts which God has given him or her? Love of neighbor and witness to Christ are the two primary attitudes United Methodist Christians must affirm in their relationship with persons of other faith traditions. When we affirm our love for the neighbor, we discover that God has given us another gift—people in other faith communities. We join hands with them to fight against the evil powers and principalities of this earth.

God is calling United Methodists into a new millennium full of its own challenges and opportunities. We seek to learn how the Holy Spirit works among all peoples of the world, especially among those in other religious traditions. We desire to read the holy texts that others believe to be inspired by God and to open ourselves to the power and spiritual insights held in the stories, images, and rituals of other traditions. And we pray for guidance as we yearn to proclaim the Savior whom we know among people who believe in other saviors and lords. May all our mission and witness to the peoples of this world be inspired by the Holy Spirit and centered in the love taught us by Jesus Christ.

3142.               *BOOK OF RESOLUTIONS*

## *Guidelines for Interreligious Relationships*

The following guidelines will assist United Methodists to be faithful to their call to witness and the call to be neighbors with persons of other faith communities.

1. Identify the various faith communities in your area and begin to familiarize your congregation with them. This may involve planned experiences which bring faith communities into contact with one another or the formation of study groups which provide an introduction to other faith traditions.

2. Initiate dialogues with other faith communities, remaining sensitive to areas of historic tension yet open to the possibilities for deepened understanding and new insight. Each partner must forthrightly face the issues that cause separation as well as those that foster relationship.

3. Work in practical ways with persons of other faith communities to resolve economic, social, cultural and political problems in the community. Soup kitchens, food pantries, Habitat for Humanity projects and other such efforts can be an effective focus for shared concerns for the common good.

4. Together with persons of other faith traditions, plan community celebrations with an interreligious perspective. Prepare carefully. Sensitivity to the integrity of each tradition is essential. Care should be taken not to relativize all religious symbols and practices nor minimize religious differences.

5. Develop new models of community building which strengthen relationships and allow people to dwell together in harmony while honoring the integrity of their differences.

### *Intent*

The intent in developing interreligious relationships is not to amalgamate all faiths into one religion. We Christians have no interest in such syncretism. To engage in interreligious dialogue is neither to endorse nor to deny the faith of other people. In dialogue we mutually seek insight into the wisdom of other traditions and we hope to overcome our fears and misapprehensions. Far from requiring a lessening of commitment to Christ, effective dialogue is only possible when one's own faith is strong, and may ultimately serve to deepen or extend it.

We Christians are seeking to be neighbors with persons whose religious commitments are different from our own and to engage each other about the deepest convictions of our lives. In our assurance of and trust in God's grace in Jesus Christ, we open ourselves to dialogue and engagement with persons of other faith communities and to other Christians whose understandings, cultures, and practices may be different from our own.

This interreligious engagement challenges United Methodist Christians to think in new ways about our lives in the broader human community, about our mission, evangelism, service, and our life together within the Christian church. We seek to promote peace and harmony with persons of other religious traditions in our various towns, cities, and neighborhoods. Yet we do not hide our differences, nor avoid conflicts, but seek to make them constructive. In each place, we share our lives with each other, we witness and are witnessed to, we invite others into the Christian community and we are invited into theirs. Our prayer is that the lives of all in each place will be enriched by the differences of others, that a new sense of community may emerge, and that others may receive the gift of God in Christ, while we receive the gifts which have been given them.

ADOPTED 1980
REVISED AND ADOPTED 2000
REVISED AND READOPTED 2008
RESOLUTION #89, 2004 *BOOK OF RESOLUTIONS*
RESOLUTION #79, 2000 *BOOK OF RESOLUTIONS*

*See* Social Principles, ¶ 162B.

### 3143. Guidelines for Cooperation in Mission

WHEREAS, the World Methodist Council has recommended the following be adopted by its member churches:

People of the Wesleyan heritage look upon the whole world as their parish. They feel committed to preach the gospel of Jesus Christ to all people.

Many of the churches in that Methodist tradition are responding anew to the call for mission in the whole world. There are changing patterns of migration and increasing movements of peoples, both geographically and spiritually. As a result new Methodist missions are started in areas where there are already communities and churches of the Wesleyan tradition working. In places, this has created confusion and unhealthy competition and has been an offense to the gospel. Sometimes, both clergy and laity seek to move from one church to another.

It is natural to those who are in the tradition of John Wesley to seek out and respond to new opportunities and to respond to requests for help. We want to stretch out our hand to all whose heart is as our heart and to work closely together. Our instinct is to share as fully as possible with all who share with us in the same mission. We are therefore committed to support each other in our work and to do nothing that would undermine each other.

In this fluid situation the World Methodist Council finds it necessary for the sake of its common mission to ask its member churches to agree on some principles and guidelines on this matter.

Three basic principles should apply especially to all such Methodist work being done by different member churches in the same area.

• Respect
• Courtesy
• Communication and consultation

Two consequences follow:

1. When any member churches of the WMC are intending to support and endorse new work in an area of the world, before agreeing officially:

• Other member churches should be notified.
• Advice should be sought in order to minimize, or prevent, any duplication of resources.

We are aware that the needs of people of particular languages or cultures may make new mission work necessary. But the principles of respect, courtesy, and communication should ensure that all our traditions can delight in new manifestations of the work of God's Spirit. The Holy Spirit often works beyond our own boundaries and limitations. At the same time, whenever possible, we would encourage those involved in "new" Methodist movements to link with an existing church. We believe it is possible to order our relationships in a cooperative way and to help new fellowships to seek the most appropriate church to join.

2. The same principle should apply where member churches presently find themselves working alongside each other in various countries:

- Different Methodist traditions should be encouraged to join together, or at least to work in a spirit of consultation and cooperation.
- Different Methodist traditions should communicate fully with each other, and thereby share resources and experience for the furtherance of God's Kingdom.

No member churches should be working in competition with each other, because this implies the breakdown of respect, courtesy, and communication. Good practice would be to develop regular meetings and clear protocols governing the relationship of churches together in particular areas.

The World Methodist Council, through its officers, offers its good services to provide a platform and the channels necessary for information and consultation between its member churches on these matters.

*Therefore, be it resolved,* that The United Methodist Church adopts these guidelines in its commitment to the pursuit of Christ's call to Christian unity and in a spirit of solidarity with other member churches of the World Methodist Council.

ADOPTED 2004
RESOLUTION #94, 2004 *BOOK OF RESOLUTIONS*

*See* Social Principles, ¶162.

### 3144. Encounter with Christ in Latin America and the Caribbean

WHEREAS, the missional initiative Encounter with Christ in Latin America and the Caribbean of the General Board of Global Ministries has achieved the initial goal of $1 million on behalf of our United Methodist partnership in mission with the Methodist churches of Latin America and the Caribbean; and

WHEREAS, the stated goal of $25 million to constitute the Encounter permanent fund in order to provide earned income for comprehensive mission partnership provides one means of securing resources to undergird a holistic strategy on Latin America and the Caribbean; and

WHEREAS, the initial success in securing funding for Encounter, and the experience in mission education in sharing the need and opportunities for partnership in witnessing to Christ through the Methodist churches of the region might be utilized in the development of a special program for the region; and

WHEREAS, the Encounter with Christ initiative seeks to strengthen the unity and shared mission outreach of Methodist churches bound together through the Council of Evangelical Churches of Latin America and the Caribbean (CIEMAL) and the Methodist Church of the Caribbean and the Americas (MCCA); and

WHEREAS, the VIII General Assembly of CIEMAL, meeting in Piracicaba, Brazil, in May, 2003, affirmed the importance of Encounter for the churches of the region, and unanimously agreed to make a special contribution to Encounter and include support for Encounter in the yearly CIEMAL budget;

*Therefore, be it resolved,* that General Conference celebrate the achievement of reaching the initial goal of $1 million for this missional initiative that was endorsed as a priority for United Methodists by previous General Conference action, express gratitude to a host of supporters, and call upon annual conferences, local churches, and individuals to renew and increase their commitment in order to reach the $25 million goal.

ADOPTED 2004
READOPTED 2008
RESOLUTION #96, 2004 *BOOK OF RESOLUTIONS*

*See* Social Principles, ¶ 162.

## 3145. Resolution of Intent: With a View to Unity

In 1750, John Wesley wrote the sermon "Catholic Spirit," in which he presented his views on mutual tolerance among those seeking to unite in love:

". . . And 'tis certain, so long as 'we know' but 'in part', that all men [sic] will not see all things alike. It is an unavoidable consequence of the present weakness and shortness of human understanding that several men will be of several minds, in religion as well as in common life. So it has been from the beginning of the world, and so it will be 'till the restitution of all things.'

"Nay farther: although every man necessarily believes that every particular opinion which he holds is true (for to believe any opinion is not true is the same thing as not to hold it) yet can no man be assured that all his own opinions taken together are true. Nay, every thinking man is assured they are not, seeing *humanum est errare et necire*—to be ignorant of many things, and to mistake in some—is the necessary condition of humanity. This therefore, he is sensible, is his own case. He knows in the general that he himself is not mistaken; although in what particulars he mistakes he does not, perhaps cannot, know.

"I say, perhaps he cannot know. For who can tell how far invincible ignorance may extend? Or (what comes to the same thing) invincible prejudice; which is often so fixed in tender minds that it is afterwards impossible to tear up what has taken so deep a root. And who can say, unless he knew every circumstance attending it, how far any mistake is culpable? Seeing all guilt must suppose some concurrence of the will—of which he only can judge who searcheth the heart.

"Every wise man therefore will allow others the same liberty of thinking which he desires they should allow him; and will no more insist on their embracing his opinions than he would have them to insist on his embracing theirs. He bears with those who differ from him, and only asks him with whom he desires to unite in love that single question. 'Is thine heart, as my heart is with thy heart?' " (*The Works of John Wesley*, Volume 2, Sermons II, "Catholic Spirit," 83-85).

Unfortunately, in Wesley's 1784 abridgement of the Thirty-Nine Articles of the Church of England, and not in keeping with the tone of "Catholic Spirit," a number of strong statements against the Roman Catholic Church were included.

In 1970 the General Conference adopted a resolution of intent. It was offered to the conference by Albert Outler on behalf of the Theological Study Commission on Doctrine and Doctrinal Standards. Engaged in the debate, among others, were Harold A. Bosley, Robert E. Cushman, and Georgia Harkness. The resolution was adopted as presented (*Journal of the 1970 General Conference, The United Methodist Church*, 255). However, the resolution was not included in, or was mistakenly deleted from, *The Book of Resolutions of The United Methodist Church*, 1970.

At the General Conference of 1992, a new resolution, "Ecumenical Interpretations of Doctrinal Standards," offered by the General Commission on Christian Unity and Interreligious Concerns, was received, adopted, and subsequently printed in *The Book of Resolutions of The United Methodist Church*, 1992 (245-46). Although grounded in the Study Commisssion's resolution of intent, this document is not as comprehensive in its scope as was the original, with specific reference to our current understanding of the composition of our Doctrinal Standards.

The original resolution of intent is resubmitted as a substitute for "Ecumenical Interpretations of Doctrinal Standards":

WHEREAS, it is common knowledge that the context of the original Thirty-Nine Articles (1563—and specifically Articles XIV, XIX, XXI, XXII, XXIV, XXV, XXVIII, XXX) was bitterly polemical, it is of prime importance in an ecumenical age that they should be reconsidered and reassessed. They were aimed, deliberately, at the Roman Catholic Church in a time of reckless strife, and were a mix of the theological and nontheological convictions of embattled schismatics fighting, as they believed, for national survival and evangelical truth. John Wesley's hasty abridgement (1784) of the original Thirty-Nine Articles (down to twenty-four) retained seven out of the ten of these anti-Roman references (XIV, XV, XVI, XVIII, XIX, XX, XXI) in his enumeration. This reflects his conviction as to their applicability to the Roman Catholic Church as he perceived it at the time. This much must be recognized and acknowledged as belonging to our inheritance from our Anglican-Wesleyan past.

It is, however, one of the virtues of historical insight that it enables persons, in a later age, to recognize the circumstances of earlier events and documents without being slavishly bound to their historical evaluation, especially in a subsequent epoch when relationships have been radically altered. Such a transvaluation will enable us freely to relegate the polemics in these articles (and the anathemas of Trent, as well) to our memories "Of old, unhappy, far-off tales/And battles long ago" and to rejoice in the positive contemporary relationships that are being developed between The United Methodist Church and the Roman Catholic Church, at levels both official and unofficial.

*Therefore, be it resolved,* that we declare it our official intent henceforth to interpret all our Articles, Confession, and other "standards of doctrine" in consonance with our best ecumenical insights and judgment, as these develop in the light of the Resolution of the 1968 General Conference on "The Methodist Church and the Cause of Christian Unity" (*Book of Resolutions 1968*, 65-72). This implies, at the very least, our heartiest offer of goodwill and Christian community to all our Roman Catholic brothers and sisters, in the avowed hope of the day when all bitter memories (ours and theirs) will have been redeemed by the gift of the fullness of Christian unity, from the God and [Creator] Father of our common Lord, Jesus Christ (*Journal of the 1970 General Conference, The United Methodist Church*, 255).

ADOPTED 2000
READOPTED 2008
RESOLUTION #97, 2004 *BOOK OF RESOLUTIONS*
RESOLUTION #86, 2000 *BOOK OF RESOLUTIONS*

See Social Principles, ¶ 162.

## 3146. Resolution on the National Council of Churches

WHEREAS, The United Methodist Church is a longtime member communion of the National Council of the Churches of Christ in the USA (NCCCUSA); and

WHEREAS, the NCCCUSA was founded for the important purpose of advancing unity in the body of Christ in the United States; and

WHEREAS, Christian unity is an important scriptural mandate (John 13:34-35; 17:20-24; 1 Corinthians 12:4-31; Ephesians 4:11-16); and

WHEREAS, the NCCCUSA still defines itself in its constitution as "a community of Christian communions, which, in response to the gospel as revealed in Scriptures, confess Jesus Christ, the incarnate Word of God, as Savior and Lord"; and

WHEREAS, few members of NCCCUSA-affiliated churches are very familiar with the council, and even fewer would connect the NCCCUSA to the ministry of their local congregation; and

WHEREAS, The United Methodist Church, as a significant contributor to the work of the NCCCUSA will seek assurances, through the General Commission on Christian Unity and Interreligious Concerns (GCCUIC) and the Council of Bishops, that the NCCCUSA remain faithful and accountable to the purpose defined in its Constitution;

*Therefore, be it resolved,* that the 2008 General Conference offer its prayers for God's will for the NCCCUSA to be realized.

ADOPTED 2008

*See* Social Principles, ¶ 162.

## 3147. Building New Bridges in Hope

"God whom Christians have come to know in Jesus Christ, has created all human beings in the divine image and . . . God desires that all people live in love and righteousness. . . .

"While we are committed to the promotion of mutual respect and understanding among people of all living faiths, we as Christians recognize a special relationship between Christians and Jews because of our shared roots in biblical revelation."[1]

1. "The Churches and the Jewish People, Towards a New Understanding," adopted at Sigtuna, Sweden, by the Consultation on the Church and the Jewish People, sponsored by the World Council of Churches, 1988.

## A Quest for New Understanding

What is the relationship that God intends between Christianity and Judaism, between Christians and Jews? In The United Methodist Church, a search for understanding and appropriate response to this important theological and relational question has been under way for some time. A significant step in the development of United Methodist understanding of and intention for Christian-Jewish relations was taken in 1972, when the General Conference adopted a position statement under the title Bridge in Hope. This denominational statement urged church members and congregations to undertake "serious new conversations" with Jews in order to promote "growth in mutual understanding."[2] As it has been studied and used, *Bridge in Hope* has served as a strong foundation for United Methodist-Jewish dialogue in many settings.

Since 1972, other Christian denominations, as well as ecumenical bodies in which The United Methodist Church participates, such as the World Council of Churches, have also made statements on Christian-Jewish relations. Those voices have contributed to our further knowledge, reflection, and understanding. At the same time, we have learned much from the many relationships and dialogues that have flourished between Jews and Christians locally, nationally, and internationally.

Especially crucial for Christians in our quest for understanding has been the struggle to recognize the horror of the Holocaust as the catastrophic culmination of a long history of anti-Jewish attitudes and actions in which Christians, and sometimes the church itself, have been deeply implicated. Dialogues with Jewish partners have been central for Christians in our process of learning of the scope of the Holocaust atrocities, acknowledgment of complicity, and responsibility, repentance, and commitment to work against anti-Semitism in all its forms in the future.

We are aware, however, that the Christian-Jewish bridge of understanding has only begun to be constructed. The United Methodist Church is committed to continuing clarification and expansion of our knowledge of Judaism and to strengthening our relationships with Jewish people. We seek mutual exploration of the common ground

2. *Bridge in Hope, Jewish-Christian Dialogue,* adopted by the General Conference of The United Methodist Church, 1972.

underlying Christianity and Judaism as well as that which makes each faith unique. This statement is an expression of the principles of that commitment.

### Foundation for United Methodist Understandings of Christian-Jewish Relations

As expressed in its Constitution, The United Methodist Church has long been strongly committed to the unity of the church: "As part of the church universal, The United Methodist Church believes that the Lord of the church is calling Christians everywhere to strive toward unity. . . ."[3] For many years, The United Methodist Church has devoted itself at all levels of church life to building partnerships with other Christian denominations in striving to reveal the reality of the one Body, the whole church of Jesus Christ. "We see the Holy Spirit at work in making the unity among us more visible."[4]

By its *Book of Discipline,* The United Methodist Church is also dedicated to "serious interfaith encounters and explorations between Christians and adherents of other living faiths in the world." We believe that "Scripture calls us to be both neighbors and witnesses to all peoples. . . . In these encounters, our aim is not to reduce doctrinal differences to some lowest common denominator of religious agreement, but to raise all such relationships to the highest possible level of human fellowship and understanding."[5] In an interdependent world of increasing awareness of the vitality and challenges of religious pluralism, we are called to "labor together with the help of God toward the salvation, health, and peace of all people."[6]

As with all theological questions, United Methodists approach the issues of interfaith relationships, including Christian-Jewish dialogue, by seeking understanding of God's will in Scripture in the context of tradition, reason, and experience. In that spirit and with that intention, we affirm the following principles for continued study, discussion, and action within The United Methodist Church, with other Christians, and especially with Jews.

---

3. *The Book of Discipline of The United Methodist Church, 1992,* Constitution, Division One, Article 5; page 22.
4. *The Book of Discipline of The United Methodist Church, 1992,* Doctrinal Standards, Our Theological Task; page 84.
5. Ibid.
6. Ibid.

*United Methodist Guiding Principles for Christian-Jewish Relations*

In order to increase our understanding of and with peoples of other living faith traditions, of ourselves as followers of Jesus Christ, and of God and God's truth, The United Methodist Church encourages dialogue and experiences with those of other faiths. For important and unique reasons, including a treasury of shared Scripture and an ancient heritage that belong to us in common but which also contain our dividedness, we look particularly for such opportunities with Jews. United Methodist participation in Christian-Jewish dialogue and relationships is based on the following understandings:

*1. There is one living God, in whom both Jews and Christians believe.*

While the Jewish and Christian traditions understand and express their faith in the same God in significantly different ways, we believe with Paul that God, who was in Christ reconciling the world to God's own self (2 Corinthians 5:18-19), is none other than the God of Israel, maker of heaven and earth. Above all else, Christians and Jews are bonded in our joyful and faithful response to the one God, living our faith as each understands God's call.

*2. Jesus was a devout Jew, as were many of his first followers.*

We know that understanding our Christian faith begins by recognizing and appreciating this seminal fact. Neither the ministry of Jesus and his apostles nor the worship and thought of the early church can be understood apart from the Jewish tradition, culture, and worship of the first century. Further, we believe that God's revelation in Jesus Christ is unintelligible apart from the story of what God did in the life of the people of Israel.

Because Christianity is firmly rooted in biblical Judaism, we understand that knowledge of these roots is essential to our faith. As expressed in a statement from the Consultation on the Church and Jewish People of the World Council of Churches: "We give thanks to God for the spiritual treasure we share with the Jewish people: faith in the living God of Abraham, Isaac, and Jacob; knowledge of the name of God and of the commandments; the prophetic proclamation of judgment and grace; the Hebrew Scriptures; and the hope of the coming Kingdom. In all these, we find common roots in biblical revelation and see spiritual ties that bind us to the Jewish people."[7]

7. "The Churches and the Jewish People. . . . "

*3. Judaism and Christianity are living and dynamic religious movements that have continued to evolve since the time of Jesus, often in interaction with each other and with God's continual self-disclosure in the world.*

Christians often have little understanding of the history of Judaism as it has developed since the lifetime of Jesus. As a World Council of Churches publication points out: "Bible-reading and worshiping Christians often believe that they `know Judaism' since they have the Old Testament, the records of Jesus' debates with Jewish teachers and the early Christian reflections on the Judaism of their times. . . . This attitude is often reinforced by lack of knowledge about the history of Jewish life and thought through the 1,900 years since the parting of the ways of Judaism and Christianity."[8]

As Christians, it is important for us to recognize that Judaism went on to develop vital new traditions of its own after the time of Jesus, including the Rabbinic Judaism that is still vibrant today in shaping Jewish religious life. This evolving tradition has given the Jewish people profound spiritual resources for creative life through the centuries. We increase our understanding when we learn about the rich variety of contemporary Jewish faith practice, theological interpretation, and worship, and discover directly through dialogue how Jews understand their own history, tradition, and faithful living.

*4. Christians and Jews are bound to God though biblical covenants that are eternally valid.*

As Christians, we stand firm in our belief that Jesus was sent by God as the Christ to redeem all people, and that in Christ the biblical covenant has been made radically new. While church tradition has taught that Judaism has been superseded by Christianity as the "new Israel," we do not believe that earlier covenantal relationships have been invalidated or that God has abandoned Jewish partners in covenant.

We believe that just as God is steadfastly faithful to the biblical covenant in Jesus Christ, likewise God is steadfastly faithful to the biblical covenant with the Jewish people. The covenant God established with the Jewish people through Abraham, Moses, and others continues because it is an eternal covenant. Paul proclaims that the gift and call of God to the Jews is irrevocable (Romans 11:29). Thus, we believe that the Jewish people continue in covenantal relationship with God.

8. "Ecumenical Considerations on Jewish-Christian Dialogue, 1993," World Council of Churches, paragraph 1.6.

Both Jews and Christians are bound to God in covenant, with no covenantal relationship invalidated by any other. Though Christians and Jews have different understandings of the covenant of faith, we are mysteriously bound to one another through our covenantal relationships with the one God and Creator of us all.

5. *As Christians, we are clearly called to witness to the gospel of Jesus Christ in every age and place. At the same time, we believe that God has continued, and continues today, to work through Judaism and the Jewish people.*

Essential to the Christian faith is the call to proclaim the good news of Jesus Christ to all people. Through the announcement of the gospel in word and work comes the opportunity for others to glimpse the glory of God, which we have found through Jesus Christ. Yet we also understand that the issues of the evangelization of persons of other faiths, and of Jews in particular, are often sensitive and difficult. These issues call for continuing serious and respectful reflection and dialogue among Christians and with Jews.

While we as Christians respond faithfully to the call to proclaim the gospel in all places, we can never presume to know the full extent of God's work in the world, and we recognize the reality of God's activity outside the Christian church. It is central to our faith that salvation is accomplished not by human beings, but by God. We know that judgment as to the ultimate salvation of persons from any faith community, including Christianity and Judaism, belongs to God alone.

It is our belief that Jews and Christians are coworkers and companion pilgrims who have made the God of Israel known throughout the world. Through common service and action, we jointly proclaim the God we know. Together through study and prayer, we can learn how the God we believe to be the same God speaks and calls us continually into closer relationship with one another, as well as with God.

6. *As Christians, we are called into dialogue with our Jewish neighbors.*

Christians and Jews hold a great deal of Scripture, history, and culture in common. And yet, we also share 2,000 painful years of anti-Semitism and the persecution of Jews by Christians. These two apparently discordant facts move Christians to seek common experiences with Jews, and especially to invite them into dialogue to explore the meaning of our kinship and our differences. Our intention is to learn about the faith of one another and to build bridges of understanding.

While for Christians, dialogue will always include testimony to God's saving acts in Jesus Christ, it will include in equal measure listening to and respecting the understanding of Jews as they strive to live in obedience and faithfulness to God and as they understand the conditions of their faith.

Productive interfaith dialogue requires focused, sustained conversation based on willingness to recognize and probe genuine differences while also seeking that which is held in common. We are called to openness so that we may learn how God is speaking through our dialogue partners. As stated in the World Council of Churches' "Guidelines on Dialogue": "One of the functions of dialogue is to allow participants to describe and witness to their faith on their own terms. . . . Participants seek to hear each other in order to better understand each other's faith, hopes, insights, and concerns."[9] Fruitful and respectful dialogue is centered in a mutual spirit of humility, trust, openness to new understanding, and commitment to reconciliation and the healing of the painful wounds of our history.

7. *As followers of Jesus Christ, we deeply repent of the complicity of the church and the participation of many Christians in the long history of persecution of the Jewish people.*

The Christian church has a profound obligation to correct historical and theological teachings that have led to false and pejorative perceptions of Judaism and contributed to persecution and hatred of Jews. It is our responsibility as Christians to oppose anti-Semitism whenever and wherever it occurs.

We recognize with profound sorrow that repeatedly and often in the last 2,000 years, the worship, preaching, and teaching of the Christian church has allowed and sometimes even incited and directed persecution against Jews.

The church today carries grave responsibility to counter the evil done by Christians to Jews in the Crusades, the Inquisition, and the pogroms of Eastern Europe and elsewhere, carried out in the name of Jesus Christ. In the twentieth century there is the particular shame in the failure of most of the church to challenge the policies of governments that were responsible for the unspeakable atrocities of the Holocaust.

Historically and today, both the selective use and the misuse of Scripture have fostered negative attitudes toward and actions against Jews. Use of New Testament passages that blame "the Jews" for the

9. "Guidelines on Dialogue," adopted at London Colney, England, by the Consultation on the Church and the Jewish People of the Unit on Dialogue and People of Living Faiths and Ideologies, World Council of Churches, 1981, paragraph 3.4.

crucifixion of Jesus have throughout history been the basis of many acts of discrimination against Jews, frequently involving physical violence. There is no doubt that traditional and often officially sanctioned and promulgated Christian teachings, including the uncritical use of anti-Jewish New Testament writings, have caused untold misery and form the basis of modern anti-Semitism.

Misinterpretations and misunderstanding of historical and contemporary Judaism continue, including the mistaken belief that Judaism is a religion solely of law and judgment while Christianity is a religion of love and grace. The characterizations of God in the Hebrew Bible (called the Old Testament by Christians) are rich and diverse; strong images of a caring, compassionate, and loving deity are dominant for Jews as well as for Christians. Further, there are parallels between New Testament Christian understandings of the "spirit of the law" and contemporaneous theological developments in first-century Jewish theology.

The church has an obligation to correct erroneous and harmful past teachings and to ensure that the use of Scripture, as well as the preparation, selection, and use of liturgical and educational resources, does not perpetuate misleading interpretations and misunderstanding of Judaism.

It is also essential for Christians to oppose forcefully anti-Jewish acts and rhetoric that persist in the present time in many places. We must be zealous in challenging overt and subtle anti-Semitic stereotypes and bigoted attitudes that ultimately made the Holocaust possible, and which stubbornly and insidiously continue today. These lingering patterns are a call to Christians for ever-new educational efforts and continued vigilance, so that we, remembering and honoring the cries of the tortured and the dead, can claim with Jews around the world to be faithful to the post-Holocaust cry of "Never Again."

*8. As Christians, we share a call with Jews to work for justice, compassion, and peace in the world in anticipation of the fulfillment of God's reign.*

Together, Jews and Christians honor the commandment to love God with all our heart, soul, and might. It is our task to join in common opposition to those forces—nation, race, power, money—that clamor for ultimate allegiance. Together, we honor the commandment to love neighbor as self. It is our task to work in common for those things that are part of God's work of reconciliation. Together, we affirm the sacredness of all persons and the obligation of stewardship for all God has created.

Jews still await the messianic reign of God foretold by the prophets. Christians proclaim the good news that in Jesus Christ, "the kingdom of God is at hand"; yet we, as Christians, also wait in hope for the consummation of God's redemptive work. Together, Jews and Christians long for and anticipate the fulfillment of God's reign. Together, we are "partners in waiting." In our waiting, we are called to witness and to work for God's reign together.

9. *As United Methodist Christians, we are deeply affected by the anguish and suffering that continue for many people who live in the Middle East region that includes modern Israel.*

We commit ourselves through prayer and advocacy to bring about justice and peace for those of every faith.

Within The United Methodist Church, we struggle with our understanding of the complexity and the painfulness of the controversies in which Christians, Jews, and Muslims are involved in the Middle East. The issues include disputed political questions of sovereignty and control, and concerns over human rights and justice. We recognize the theological significance of the Holy Land as central to the worship, historical traditions, hope, and identity of the Jewish people. We are mindful of this land's historic and contemporary importance for Christians and Muslims. We are committed to the security, safety, and well-being of Jews and Palestinians in the Middle East, to respect for the legitimacy of the state of Israel, to justice and sovereignty for the Palestinian people, and to peace for all who live in the region.

As we join with others of many religious communities in wrestling with these issues and searching for solutions, we seek to work together with other Christians, Jews, and Muslims to honor the religious significance of this land and to bring about healthy, sustainable life, justice, and peace for all.

### New Bridges to Christian-Jewish Understanding

The above statements of principle and affirmation offer a foundation for theological reflection within The United Methodist Church and with other Christians on our understanding of our relationships with the Jewish people. They are meant to be the basis of study, discussion, and action as we strive for greater discernment within the church.

Further, we hope that the statements of guiding principle will be important as bases of cooperative efforts, and especially for dialogue between United Methodists (sometimes in the company of other Christians) and Jewish communities, as we mutually explore the meaning of our kinship and our differences.

Using the foregoing foundation and principles, The United Methodist Church encourages dialogue with Jews at all levels of the church, including and especially local congregations. It is also hoped that there will be many other concrete expressions of Jewish-Christian relationships, such as participating in special occasions of interfaith observance, and joint acts of common service and programs of social transformation. These offer great opportunity to Christians and Jews to build relationships and together work for justice and peace (*shalom*) in our communities and in the world, serving humanity as God intends.

We dare to believe that such conversations and acts will build new bridges in hope between Christians and Jews, and that they will be among the signs and first fruits of our sibling relationship under our parent God. Together, we await and strive for the fulfillment of God's reign.

ADOPTED 1996
READOPTED 2004
RESOLUTION #88, 2004 *BOOK OF RESOLUTIONS*
RESOLUTION #78, 2000 *BOOK OF RESOLUTIONS*

*See* Social Principles, ¶ 162B

## 3148. STRENGTHENING BRIDGES

In 1996 The United Methodist Church took a giant step forward in relations with the Jewish community by enacting Resolution 88, *Building New Bridges in Hope*, using as its foundation the 1972 resolution, *Bridge in Hope*. The General Conference of 2000 enacted Resolution 75, furthering United Methodist-Jewish relations in calling all United Methodist churches around the world to observe *Yom HaShoah*, the day of remembrance of those who died in the Holocaust of World War II.

*Building New Bridges in Hope* left to another time and further conversation the question of " . . . evangelization of persons of other faiths, and of Jews in particular" by saying, "These issues call for continuing, serious and respectful reflection and dialogue among

Christians, and with Jews." The United Methodist Church holds that the time for action on this issue is now, and because of the long history of Christian hostility toward Jews, the initiative clearly lies with the Church.

That our lack of clarity on this point is a break in the bridge between United Methodism and the Jewish community is certain. In the 1997 joint commentary on *Building New Bridges in Hope*, Jewish scholar Leon Klenicki said,

> The question considered by this principle is very crucial in the relationship of Christians and Jews. It reminds us of the word 'evangelism' which brings great uneasiness to Jewish hearts. Through the centuries, evangelism has been a way by which Christians tried to convert and persecute Jews in the Western world. As Jews, we need to understand the exact meaning of evangelism.

We cannot know fully the way in which God's Spirit will work, nor can we know in whom the Spirit will be made manifest. We have always proclaimed that God spoke through the prophets of Israel and Judah and that Jesus spoke and acted in the tradition of those prophets. "God's grace is active everywhere, at all times, carrying out this purpose as revealed in the Bible. It is expressed in God's covenant with Abraham and Sarah, in the Exodus of Israel from Egypt, and in the ministry of the prophets." (*Book of Discipline* ¶ 121)

> In a significant way, the path toward Jewish-Christian reconciliation has been paved by the Catholic Church, and we United Methodists can be grateful for that work. (See *Nostra Aetate*, Sect. 4). In his reflection on this landmark declaration from Vatican II, Walter Cardinal Kasper, President of the Pontifical Commission for Religious Relations with the Jews, announced that, " . . . Because we have all this in common and because as Christians we know that God's covenant with Israel by God's faithfulness is not broken (Rom. 11:29 c.f. 3:4), mission as understood as conversion from idolatry to the living and true God (1 Thes. 1:9) does not apply and cannot be applied to the Jews." Therefore, he concluded, "there is no organized Catholic missionary activity toward Jews."

With our Catholic sisters and brothers we believe that God has not abandoned God's covenant with the Jews. We are indebted to our Jewish forebearer through whom the Scriptures of the Old Testament have come to us and through whom the one true God has been revealed in the world. Therefore, we reject any and all forms of evangelism which are coercive in their nature, violent in their means, or anti-Semitic in their intent.

As United Methodist Christians our mission is to make disciples of Jesus Christ. This mission invites us to bear witness to Christ's light. In this context, The United Methodist Church neither makes the Jews a unique focus of our witness-bearing, nor excludes Jews from our longing that all persons may of their own volition believe in Jesus Christ our Savior and Lord. We affirm our responsibility to offer the gospel of Jesus Christ to all in witness that is winsome and respectful of the culture and religious convictions of others. Even as we offer our own faith, we remain open to learn from and be enriched by those who have faith experiences different from our own.

ADOPTED 2008

*See* Social Principles, ¶ 162.

## 3149. Receive Guidelines for Ministering to Mormons Who Seek to Become United Methodists

WHEREAS, United Methodists seek to act in ways that are faithful, compassionate, and just in relationship to other faith traditions, extending hospitality toward all and charity toward those whose faith and practice differ from ours; and

WHEREAS, as an expression of such hospitality and charity, United Methodists need to offer the pathways into membership for persons of other faith traditions with graciousness, consistency, and clarity; and

WHEREAS, the Church of Jesus Christ of Latter-Day Saints presents itself as a faith tradition outside the parameters of historic, apostolic Christianity;

*Therefore,* we continue to recommend that United Methodist churches should receive persons from the Church of Jesus Christ of Latter-Day Saints by offering the sacrament of Christian baptism following a period of catechesis (a time of intensive exploration and instruction in the Christian faith); and

*Further,* we continue to affirm *Sacramental Faithfulness: Guidelines for Receiving People from the Church of Jesus Christ of Latter-Day Saints (Mormons)* as a study resource and guideline for pastors and congregations who seek to offer pathways to receive former Mormons who seek to become United Methodist; and

*Further,* we authorize the General Board of Discipleship to provide ongoing resources in accordance with *Sacramental Faithfulness: Guidelines for Receiving People from the Church of Jesus Christ of Latter-Day Saints (Mormons)* to the Church to guide pastors and congregations who receive such persons who seek to become United Methodists in ways that are faithful to our United Methodist heritage.

ADOPTED 2000
REVISED AND READOPTED 2008
RESOLUTION #16, 2000 *BOOK OF RESOLUTIONS*

*See* Social Principles, ¶ 162.


## 3150. Continuation of Commission on Pan-Methodist Cooperation and Union

WHEREAS, the Constitution of The United Methodist Church states that the dividedness in the church of Jesus Christ "is a hindrance to its mission in the world" and has committed us to ecumenical involvement; and

WHEREAS, the Constitution of The United Methodist Church calls for our church to "seek, and work, for unity at all levels of church life" (¶ 6); and

WHEREAS, The United Methodist Church has a historical relationship and shared tradition with the African Methodist Episcopal Church, The African Methodist Episcopal Zion Church, and the Christian Methodist Episcopal Church; and

WHEREAS, the Third Consultation of Methodist Bishops in 1983 approved a request calling for the creation of a Commission on Pan-Methodist Cooperation as a successor to the Pan-Methodist Bicentennial Committee and the Missional Thrust Convocation; and

WHEREAS, the General Conference of 1984 authorized involvement in a Commission on Pan-Methodist Cooperation "to define, determine, plan, and, in cooperation with established agencies of the several denominations, execute activities to foster meaningful cooperation" (¶ 2403.2); and

WHEREAS, the Commission on Pan-Methodist Cooperation was duly convened and inaugurated on May 27, 1985; and

WHEREAS, the Sixth Consultation of Methodist Bishops in April 1995 approved a resolution to the respective General Conferences calling for the creation of a Commission on Union whose purpose was to build on the work of the earlier Study Commission established in 1994; and

WHEREAS, the Commission on Union was duly convened and inaugurated on December 2, 1997; and

WHEREAS, representatives from the African Methodist Episcopal, African Methodist Episcopal Zion, Christian Methodist Episcopal, and The United Methodist churches labored in the Commission on Pan-Methodist Cooperation on models of cooperation while the representatives of the four denominations labored in the Commission on Union on various models of union; and

WHEREAS, the 2000 and 2004 General Conferences of the four denominations took action to consolidate the Commission on Pan-Methodist Cooperation and the Commission on Union into the Commission on Pan-Methodist Cooperation and Union, which was convened and inaugurated on November 29, 2000; and

WHEREAS, we affirm the consolidation of the two former Commissions to form the Commission on Pan-Methodist Cooperation and Union to better oversee the continuing cooperative work toward union; and

WHEREAS, the first and most difficult lesson that the Commission on Pan-Methodist Cooperation and Union has learned during the past quadrennium is that, as with any worthwhile efforts that are of God, progress is slow and only comes with constant discernment of the will of the Holy Spirit; and

WHEREAS, the work of the Commission on Pan-Methodist Cooperation and Union has produced encouraging opportunities for cooperation in program ministries as noted in the Commission's report to the General Conferences; and

WHEREAS, the Commission on Pan-Methodist Cooperation and Union continues to struggle with the difficult issues of reconciliation, cooperation, and union, in the midst of repentance and forgiveness; and

WHEREAS, we celebrate the changes enacted by the [United Methodist] General Conference of 2000 to include Pan-Methodist representatives as full members of all United Methodist general agencies; and

WHEREAS, events and activities planned and held across the Pan-Methodist connection can work for the unit we seek,

*Therefore, be it resolved,* that the 2004 General Conference of The United Methodist Church continue the work of the Commission on

Pan-Methodist Cooperation and Union and authorize the provision of its membership and budget; and

*Be it further resolved*, that the 2004 General Conference further endorse and promote the implementation of the Pan-Methodist Initiative on Children in Poverty; and

*Be it further resolved*, that the Commission on Pan-Methodist Cooperation and Union be composed of nine (9) persons from each Pan-Methodist denomination: three bishops, three clergy, and three lay persons, one of whom should be a young adult (either clergy or lay), with sensitivity given to continuity of participation.

Models of union shall continue to be instituted and tested by the Commission on Pan-Methodist Cooperation and Union throughout the next quadrennium.

Progress reports shall continue to be made regularly to each body of bishops and to each of the General Conferences no later than 2010.

The quadrennial budget of the Commission on Pan-Methodist Cooperation and Union shall be $140,000 to be allocated proportionately to each Pan-Methodist denomination based on membership.

*Be it further resolved*, that a Pan-Methodist approach be given to any major event planned by a general agency of The United Methodist Church, by the agency's notifying early in the planning stage: (1) the corresponding agency or responsible staff in the other Pan-Methodist denominations, and (2) the members of the United Methodist delegation on the Commission on Pan-Methodist Cooperation and Union; and

*Be it further resolved*, that the General Council on Ministries or its successor agency as defined by *The Book of Discipline* establish a Pan-Methodist approach to its coordinating responsibilities.

ADOPTED 2004
RESOLUTION #95, 2004 *BOOK OF RESOLUTIONS*

*See* Social Principles, ¶ 162A.


### 3151. Continue Membership in the World Methodist Council

WHEREAS, the Constitution of The United Methodist Church states that the dividedness in the church of Jesus Christ "is a hindrance to its mission in the world" and has committed us to ecumenical involvement; and,

WHEREAS, The United Methodist Church and its predecessor churches have been members of the World Methodist Council since its first session in 1881 (under the name of the Ecumenical Methodist Conference); and,

WHEREAS, the World Methodist Council is an appropriate forum for Wesleyans; and

WHEREAS, the United Methodist delegates have offered distinguished leadership to the WMC, and successive General Conferences have supported the continuing membership in the WMC since its founding in 1950;

*Therefore, be it resolved*, that General Conference of 2004 reaffirm its membership in and support of the World Methodist Council, in accordance with the 2004 *Book of Discipline* (¶ 2403.1); and,

*Be it further resolved*, that the General Conference encourage The United Methodist Church to support "Achieving the Vision," the current endowment initiative of the World Methodist Council to ensure the future mission and ministry of the Council.

ADOPTED 2004
RESOLUTION #93, 2004 *BOOK OF RESOLUTIONS*
RESOLUTION #83, 2000 *BOOK OF RESOLUTIONS*

*See* Social Principles, ¶ 162.


## 3152. Continue Membership in the National Council of Churches

WHEREAS, the Constitution of The United Methodist Church states that the dividedness in the church of Jesus Christ "is a hindrance to its mission in the world" and has committed us to ecumenical involvement; and,

WHEREAS, The United Methodist Church and its predecessor churches have been charter members of the National Council of the Churches of Christ in the USA; and,

WHEREAS, The NCCCUSA is a "community through which the churches are seeking to make visible their unity given in Christ"; and,

WHEREAS, the NCCCUSA is "an instrument of the churches' ecumenical witness to live responsibly in mutual accountability and service"; and,

WHEREAS, the NCCCUSA provides a unique opportunity for denominational representatives to share divergent traditions in matters of faith and practice; and,

WHEREAS, the NCCCUSA provides a channel for denominational cooperation in Christian education, mission and justice issues, communications, interfaith matters, evangelism, and relationships with local ecumenical expressions; and,

WHEREAS, United Methodist delegates from each of the jurisdictions have offered distinguished leadership to the NCCCUSA, and successive General Conferences have supported the continuing membership in the NCCCUSA since its founding in 1950; and,

WHEREAS, we rejoiced in the celebration of the fiftieth anniversary of the founding of the NCCCUSA in 2000,

*Therefore, be it resolved,* that the 2004 General Conference of The United Methodist Church reaffirm its membership in and support of the National Council of the Churches of Christ in the USA, in accordance with the 2004 *Book of Discipline,* ¶ 2404.2.a.

ADOPTED 1992
AMENDED AND ADOPTED 2000, 2004
RESOLUTION #91, 2004 *BOOK OF RESOLUTIONS*
RESOLUTION #81, 2000 *BOOK OF RESOLUTIONS*

*See* Social Principles, ¶ 162.

### 3153. Continue Membership in Churches Uniting in Christ

WHEREAS, the Constitution of The United Methodist Church states that the dividedness in the church of Jesus Christ "is a hindrance to its mission in the world" and has committed us to ecumenical involvement; and,

WHEREAS, the predecessor churches of The United Methodist Church were founding members of Churches Uniting in Christ (formerly Consultation on Church Union), and The United Methodist Church has been an active supporter of COCU/CUIC for more than 30 years; and,

WHEREAS, the 1988 General Conference of The United Methodist Church affirmed the COCU Consensus as an authentic expression of the apostolic faith and a sufficient theological foundation for covenanting; and,

WHEREAS, the 1996 General Conference adopted *Churches in Covenant Communion: Churches of Christ Uniting* as the definitive agreement for joining with other churches in covenant communion; and,

WHEREAS, the 1999 plenary of the Consultation on Church Union approved a *Call to Christian Commitment and Action to Combat Racism* and recommends a process using the materials and implementing action within the member communions; and,

WHEREAS, the 2000 General Conference of The United Methodist Church:

- affirmed the progress of the Consultation on Church Union in its journey toward greater visible unity among the member churches under the name of Churches Uniting in Christ; and
- affirmed the following *Marks of Unity* as goals on the journey to be lived out when in accord with *The Book of Discipline*:

1. Mutual recognition of each other as authentic expressions of the one church of Jesus Christ,

2. Mutual recognition of members in one baptism,

3. Mutual recognition that each affirms the apostolic faith of Scripture and tradition which is expressed in the Apostles' and Nicene Creeds and that each seeks to give witness to the apostolic faith in its life and mission,

4. Provision for celebration of the Eucharist together with intentional regularity,

5. Engagement together in Christ's mission on a regular and intentional basis, especially a shared mission to combat racism,

6. Intentional commitment to promote unity with wholeness and to oppose all marginalization

and exclusion in church and society based on such things as race, age, gender, forms of disability, sexual orientation, and class,

7. Appropriate structures of accountability and appropriate means for consultation and decision making,

8. An ongoing process of theological dialogue; and

WHEREAS, the 2000 General Conference of The United Methodist Church directed: (1) the Council of Bishops and the General Commission on Christian Unity and Interreligious Concerns (GCCUIC) to lead The United Methodist Church in its membership in the Consultation on Church Union and to continue dialogue with covenanting partners, clarifying questions and developing a covenanting process; and (2) the Council of Bishops and the GCCUIC to promote the *Call to Christian Commitment and Action to Combat*

*Racism* throughout The United Methodist Church and to advocate for its study and implementation; and

WHEREAS, on January 19, 2002, "A Service of Dissolution" was conducted to mark the dissolution of the Consultation on Church Union; and

WHEREAS, on January 20, 2002, the covenanting partners witnessed the inauguration of a new relationship as Churches Uniting In Christ (CUIC) growing in faith together, worshiping God together, combating racism together, proclaiming the Gospel together, pursuing wholeness together, and being church together;

*Therefore, be it resolved,* that the 2004 General Conference of The United Methodist

Church reaffirm its membership in and support of Churches Uniting in Christ in accordance with *The Book of Discipline* 2000, and

*Be it further resolved,* that the 2004 General Conference direct the Council of Bishops and the General Commission on Christian Unity and Interreligious Concerns to lead The United Methodist Church in its membership in Churches Uniting in Christ and in being a good neighbor.

ADOPTED 2004
RESOLUTION #90, 2004 *BOOK OF RESOLUTIONS*

*See* Social Principles, ¶ 162.


### 3154. Continue Membership in the World Council of Churches

WHEREAS, the Constitution of The United Methodist Church states that the dividedness in the church of Jesus Christ "is a hindrance to its mission in the world" and has committed us to ecumenical involvement; and,

WHEREAS, The United Methodist Church and its predecessor churches were founding members of the World Council of Churches (WCC); and,

WHEREAS, United Methodist delegates in leadership positions among the over 330 member churches continue to make significant contributions to this world wide body, and the General Conference and the Council of Bishops have continued to offer strong commitment for the WCC; and,

WHEREAS, we rejoice in the continuing leadership of Kathryn Bannister (Kansas West Annual Conference) as a president of the WCC; and,

WHEREAS, the United Methodist delegates from each of the jurisdictions and central conferences have offered distinguished leadership in the WCC, and successive General Conferences have supported the continuing membership in the WCC since its founding in 1948;

*Therefore, be it resolved,* that the 2004 General Conference of The United Methodist Church reaffirm its membership in and support of the World Council of Churches, in accordance with the 2004 *Book of Discipline* (¶ 2404.3).

ADOPTED 2004
RESOLUTION #92, 2004 *BOOK OF RESOLUTIONS*
RESOLUTION #82, 2000 *BOOK OF RESOLUTIONS*

See Social Principles, ¶ 162.


### 3155. Gideons International Membership Eligibility

WHEREAS, Gideons International provides an important ministry in the distribution of Scripture; and

WHEREAS, many United Methodist congregations and individuals support Gideons International through memberships and financial donations; and

WHEREAS, the membership of Gideons International is limited to Protestant business and professional men; and

WHEREAS, their membership criteria stand in opposition to the *Discipline* of The United Methodist Church (see Social Principles); and

WHEREAS, the membership criteria of Gideons International detract from the strength of their ministry;

*Therefore, be it resolved,* that the General Conference of The United Methodist Church and its member congregations strongly encourage Gideons International to open their membership to all Christians, regardless of gender, socioeconomic class, or denominational background.

ADOPTED 2004
RESOLUTION #348, 2004 *BOOK OF RESOLUTIONS*

## EDUCATION

### 3161. Education: The Gift of Hope

WHEREAS, John Wesley was a "unique and remarkable educator (who) gave to the whole Methodist movement . . . a permanent passion for education"[1], and

WHEREAS, Wesley believed that persons develop their full God-given potential when they educate their mind as well as nurture their spirit; and

WHEREAS, the historic United Methodist concern for education is witnessed through commitment to educational opportunity for all persons regardless of gender, sexual orientation, ethnic origin, or economic or social background; and

WHEREAS, this commitment continues as United Methodist individuals, congregations, colleges, campus ministries, and other groups become involved in local education in their communities; and

WHEREAS, these efforts make a significant contribution to furthering access, advancing and enhancing student learning, and advocating for the continued improvement of educational opportunity; and

WHEREAS, educators, families, and communities are concerned about substance abuse and violence in our schools and communities, along with other social problems which undermine the safety of children and the quality of their lives in school and in society at large; and

WHEREAS, United Methodists have a moral concern to take initiatives to support and create alliances involving educators, community leaders, and students to address the challenges of contemporary education and to work to resolve the threats to quality education; and

WHEREAS, the 1996 General Conference of The United Methodist Church received *Education: The Gift of Hope,* a study of the historic and current United Methodist concern for education, and urged every local church to use the study to understand our historic educational concern and to become enlivened in educational partnerships in the local community; and

WHEREAS, the General Board of Higher Education and Ministry has revised *Education: The Gift of Hope,* to address concerns about drugs and violence in our schools and to further remind United Methodists of the Wesleyan challenge to become involved in local efforts in education;

1. *The Story of Methodism,* Halford E. Luccock, Paul Hutchinson, Robert W. Goodloe (Abingdon Press, 1926; page 361).

*Therefore, be it resolved,* that every local United Methodist congregation is encouraged to study *Education: The Gift of Hope* to learn of our heritage and concern; and

*Be it further resolved,* that each local congregation develop a strategy for being in partnership with local educators, community leaders, and students in providing a positive, safe, helpful, and hopeful environment in which students can live and learn and grow.

ADOPTED 1996
AMENDED AND READOPTED 2000
AMENDED AND READOPTED 2008
RESOLUTION #98, 2004 *BOOK OF RESOLUTIONS*
RESOLUTION #87, 2000 *BOOK OF RESOLUTIONS*

*See* Social Principles, ¶ 162C and *D*.

## 3162. The Right of All to Quality Education

The Social Principles acknowledge that children are full human beings in their own right (Social Principles, ¶ 162C). Children have a right to education, and parents and governments have an obligation to provide them with the access to an adequate education. "Thus, we support the development of school systems and innovative methods of education designed to assist every child toward complete fulfillment as an individual person of worth. All children have the right to quality education" (¶ 162C).

The United Methodist Church is committed to the "achievement of a world community that is a fellowship of persons who honestly love one another. We pledge ourselves to seek the meaning of the gospel in all issues that divide people and threaten the growth of world community" (¶ 165).

In our tradition, education is not just about learning to read and write, or about mathematics and geography, or about history and science. Education is about acquiring the necessary skills and knowledge we need for the survival of a democratic society. Education is the vehicle through which the community secures its continued existence and development through the transmission of its accumulated knowledge and ideological aims to other generations.

This is also true for the Israelites as for any of the peoples of the ancient world. Walter A. Elwell points out that in the Hebrew Scripture we find "repeatedly that the success of the community and the continuity of its culture were conditioned by the knowledge of and obedience to God's revealed law (Joshua 1:6-8). Thus, to ensure their prosperity, growth, and longevity as the people of Yahweh, Israel's mandate was one of education—diligently teaching their children to love God, and to know and obey his statutes and ordinances (Deuteronomy 6:1-9). Likewise, the New Testament record links the success of the church of Jesus Christ, as a worshiping community of 'salt and light' reaching out to a dark world, to the teaching of sound doctrine"[1] (see also John 13:34-35; Romans 12:1-2; Ephesians 4:14; Titus 2:1).

Clearly, the above example highlights the importance of teaching children about the faith, however; it also illustrates the importance of educating children in general. The above illustrates the need to instill in our children values that could benefit the entire human family. Thus, we can echo the international community in asserting that education is a human right. We can also affirm that education is a social and spiritual benefit from which no one should be barred or impeded.

Unfortunately, the right to education remains one of the most widely and systematically violated of all human rights. Today, 115 million children are not enrolled in school; the majority of them girls. Forty percent (40%) of children in Africa receive no education. Another 150 million children start primary school but drop out before they have completed four years of education, the vast majority before they have acquired basic literacy skills. Unless urgent action is taken, they will join the ranks of nearly 1 billion illiterate adults in the world.

The benefits of an education are enormous. A good education helps people gain access to better paying jobs, thus, helping reduce the number of people who live in poverty. By the same token, a good education is essential for a sustained economic growth. Education provides people with skills and empowers them to take advantage of new opportunities. Completing just five years of education can increase agricultural efficiency significantly. In addition, studies have shown that educating girls not only raises their future wages, but dramatically reduces infant and maternal mortality rates.

People across the world are increasingly demanding that the right to education for all children be upheld. Governments, local communities

---

1. Elwell, Walter A. "Entry for 'Education in Bible Times'" *Evangelical Dictionary of Theology*.<http://www.biblestudytools.net/Dictionaries/BakerEvangelicalDictionary/bed.cgi?number=1218. 1997

and community-based organizations in poor countries are striving, often in spite of the most appalling adversity, to educate their children. In April 2003, two million people took part in the Global Campaign for Education's week of action and called for an end to the global crisis in education.

In 2000 many communities around the world responded to The United Nations' call to "Education for All." In addition, the United Nations' "Millennium Development Goals" document includes a goal to achieve universal primary education by 2015. Rich countries have repeatedly promised that poor countries with credible national education plans would not be allowed to fail due to a lack of resources, but this promise has not yet been translated into action. The World Bank estimates that $10 billion to $15 billion will be needed each year to achieve this goal. If current trends continue, 88 countries will not deliver primary education for all their children by 2015. Rich countries and the World Bank must increase and improve aid for basic education.

Therefore, the General Conference of The United Methodist Church calls on the United States, the European Union, Japan and other rich nations as well as the International Monetary Fund and the World Bank to deliver on their promises to the world's children by providing substantial and sustained increases in aid for basic education in poor countries. The International Monetary Fund must not press governments to cut education spending as a means to "balance" their budgets, or to stimulate the economy.

In addition, we urge United Methodists in countries around the world to advocate their governments to provide such support for their children's education.

ADOPTED 2004
RESOLUTION #100, 2004 *BOOK OF RESOLUTIONS*

*See* Social Principles, ¶ 162C and *D*.

## 3163. Equity in Access to High School Education

Our Social Principles affirm that the rights of children include "the right to quality education" (¶ 162C). This right expresses a basic American belief that all children should have the opportunity to realize their full potential. Today, such education must include not only "reading, writing and arithmetic" but also a wide range of knowledge, understanding, and skills that will equip each student for either college or gainful employment and for the exercise of citizenship responsibilities necessary for the survival of a democratic society. For such reasons, our Social Principles support "the development of school systems and innovative methods of education designed to assist every child toward complete fulfillment as an individual person of worth" (¶ 162C).

Unfortunately, most schools in the United States are far from achieving this goal. Schools often report that 90-95 percent of seniors (12th graders) graduate from high school. But these figures overlook the fact that nationally 30 percent of all 9th graders fail to finish high school with a diploma. Even those who later earn a GED are much more likely than diploma holders "to be unemployed or eventually need some form of government assistance." As the US economy shifts increasingly to service and information industries, "failing to earn a diploma has become devastating to an individual's opportunity for economic and social advancement. One telling fact is that approximately two-thirds of all state prison inmates have not completed high school by any measure."

Failure to finish high school with a diploma, with the devastating consequences this has for an individual's future prospects, is a bitter reality that disproportionally impacts minority youth—especially minority males. Nationally, 78 percent of white females entering the 9th grade graduate with a diploma four years later, while 72 percent of white males do so. Graduation rates are substantially lower for minority students of all backgrounds: among Hispanics, only 60 percent of all females entering the 9th grade graduate four years later, while just 50 percent of males do so; among African Americans the figures are 59 percent for females and only 44 percent for males, with similar figures for American Indian youth. These high attrition rates have been attributed to both "drop out" and "push out"—to students dropping out of school because they find no help or encouragement to overcome a challenge, and to low achieving students being pushed out into alternative programs such as GED to improve a school's test scores.

The above sobering figures clearly indicate that, despite some "success stories," schools in the US are largely failing to equip nearly one-third of all students, and a much higher percentage of minority youth, with the knowledge, understanding, and skills needed for entering college or gainful employment and for the exercise of citizenship responsibilities necessary for the survival of a democratic society. These failings are indicative of a crisis that is marginalizing millions of American youth, especially minority youth, consigning them to second-class citizenship, contributing to an erosion of American democracy, and leaving many members of faith communities less equipped to bear witness to issues of justice and peace.

In view of this crisis and the urgent need to hold our educational system accountable to providing equity in access to a high school education for students from all social backgrounds, we:

1. call upon local, state, and federal educational agencies to annually and publicly report graduation rates by sex, race and ethnicity;

2. call upon local, state and federal educational agencies to annually and publicly report the retention rate for students entering $9^{th}$, $10^{th}$, $11^{th}$, and $12^{th}$ grades by sex, race, and ethnicity;

3. call upon local, state, and federal educational agencies to make increasing the percentage of entering $9^{th}$ grade students who graduate on time with a high school diploma a major focus of educational reform;

4. call upon local, state, and federal educational agencies to make such changes as needed in accountability systems to provide incentives for schools to keep their most challenged students in school — such as smaller class size, support for teachers' professional development, and opportunities for students to recover from failure;

5. call for equitable distribution of financial and other educational resources to all school districts so that no school district will be at a disadvantage in striving to provide quality education for all children within its boundaries;

6. recommend that in each annual conference concerned United Methodists ask their state and federal legislators to support legislation that will help implement concerns 1-5 above;

7. request that the General Board of Church and Society develop and promote an educational program to help equip United Methodists to advocate on the above issues.

ADOPTED 2008

*See* Social Principles, ¶ 162C and *D.*

## GENETICS

### 3181. New Developments in Genetic Science

#### I. Foreword

The ethical implications of new developments in genetic science continue to make themselves known as new aspects of the technology are introduced in medicine, agriculture, and forensic science.

The 1988 General Conference approved a statement affirming the positive prospects and warning of the potential dangers of genetic technologies and  authorized the establishment of a Genetic Science task force to:

1. review and assess scientific developments in genetics and their implications for all life;

2. take initiatives with industrial, governmental, and educational institutions involved in genetic engineering to discuss further projections and possible impact;

3. convey to industry and government the sense of urgency to protect the environment as well as animal and human life;

4. support a moratorium on animal patenting until the task force has explored the ethical issues involved;

5. cooperate with other churches, faith groups, and ecumenical bodies sharing similar concerns;

6. explore the effects of the concentration of genetic engineering research tasks and applications in a few crops; and

7. recommend to the 1992 General Conference such further responses and actions as may be deemed appropriate.

The task force included scientists, educators, health professionals, ethicists, theologians, a social worker, a lawyer, and a farmer. They held hearings in Houston and College Station, Texas; Boston, Massachusetts; Washington, DC; San Leandro, California; Ames, Iowa; Durham, North Carolina; and Oak Ridge, Tennessee.

Testimony was received from geneticists, physicians, theologians, ethicists, social workers, attorneys, officers of biotechnology companies, journalists, insurance executives, governmental regulatory agency representatives, educators, and persons with genetic disorders and the family members of such persons. The hearing process formed the original basis of the recommendations contained in this resolution.

A more complete discussion of issues is in the complete report of the task force to the 1992 General Conference. Subsequent General Conferences appointed other bioethics task forces that advised on amendments to this document.

## II. Our Theological Grounding

The United Methodist doctrinal/theological statement affirms that "new issues continually arise that summon us to fresh theological inquiry. Daily we are presented with an array of concerns that challenge our proclamation of God's reign over all of human existence" (1988 *Book of Discipline*, ¶ 69).

One of the concerns that merits critique in light of theological understandings is genetic science. The urgent task of interpreting the faith in light of the biotechnology revolution and evaluating the rapidly emerging genetic science and technology has only begun. The issues demand continuing dialogue at all levels of the church as persons from diverse perspectives seek to discern and live out God's vision for creation.

The following affirmations provide the theological/doctrinal foundation of the task force's work and recommendations. These historic affirmations represent criteria by which developments and potential developments in biotechnology are evaluated by the community of faith, the church. The task force urges the whole church to join in the urgent task of theological inquiry in what has been called the genetic age.

### A. All creation belongs to God the creator

Creation has its origin, existence, value, and destiny in God. Creation belongs to God, whose power and grace brings the cosmos out of nothingness, order out of chaos, and life out of death. Creation is a realm of divine activity as God continually seeks to bring healing, wholeness, and peace. All creation is accountable to God; therefore, all existence is contingent, finite, and limited. The Creator has declared Creation "good," and its goodness inheres in its fulfillment of God's purpose. The goodness of our genetic diversity is grounded in our creation by God.

### B. Human beings are stewards of creation

While human beings share with other species the limitations of finite creatures who owe their existence to God, their special creation "in the image of God" gives them the freedom and authority to exercise stewardship responsibly. This includes the knowledge of human life and behavior as it is being expanded by genetic science. The biblical imperative is that human beings are to nurture, cultivate, and serve God's creation so that it might be sustained. Humans are to participate in, manage, nurture, justly distribute, employ, develop, and enhance creation's resources in accordance with their finite discernment of God's purposes. Their divinely conferred dominion over nature does not sanction exploitation and waste; neither does responsible stewardship imply refusal to act creatively with intelligence, skill, and foresight.

The image of God, in which humanity is created, confers both power and responsibility to use power as God does: neither by coercion nor tyranny, but by love. Failure to accept limits by rejecting or ignoring accountability to God and interdependency with the whole of creation is the essence of sin. Therefore, the question is not, Can we perform all prodigious work of research and technology? But, should we? The notion that the ability to do something is permission to do it ignores the fundamental biblical understanding of human beings as stewards accountable to the Creator and as contingent, interdependent creatures. Although the pursuit of knowledge is a divine gift, it must be used appropriately with the principle of accountability to God and to the human community and the sustainability of all creation.

## C. Technology in service to humanity and God

God has given human beings the capacity for research and technological invention, but the worship of science is idolatry. Genetic techniques have enormous potential for sustaining creation and, for some, improving the quality of human life when they are applied to environmental, agricultural, and medical problems. When wisely used, they often provide positive—though limited and imperfect—solutions to such perplexing social problems as insufficient food supply, spread of disease, ecological deterioration, overpopulation, and human disease. When used recklessly, for greedy profit, or for calculated improvement of the human race (eugenics), genetic technology becomes corrupted by sin. Moreover, we recognize that even the careful use of genetic technologies for good ends may lead to unintended consequences. We confess that even our intended consequences may not be in the best interest of all.

## D. From creation to redemption and salvation

Redemption and salvation become realities by divine grace as we respond in faith to God's action in Jesus Christ to defeat the powers of sin that enslave the human spirit and thwart the realization of God's purposes for creation. Jesus Christ is the incarnation of God's eternal Word and wisdom. His redemptive life, ministry, death, resurrection, and sending of the Spirit reveal God's vision for humanity. Having distorted God's good intention for us in creation, we now are called to be conformed to God's true image in Jesus Christ.

Through the affirmation of the goodness of creation and the saving work of Christ, God has claimed all persons as beloved sons and daughters with inherent worth and dignity. Therefore, we understand that our worth as children of God is irrespective of genetic qualities, personal attributes, or achievements. Barriers and prejudices based on biological characteristics fracture the human family and distort God's goal for humanity. The community of Christ bears witness to the truth that all persons have unity by virtue of having been redeemed by Christ. Such unity respects and embraces genetic diversity, which accounts for many differences among people. Love and justice, which the Scriptures uplift and which Jesus Christ supremely expresses, require that the worth and dignity of the defenseless be preserved and protected. As the community of Christ, the church seeks to embody love and justice and to give of itself on behalf of the powerless and voiceless.

## E. God's reign is for all creation

The coming of God's reign is the guiding hope for all creation. Hebrew Scripture and the life, teaching, death, and resurrection of Jesus Christ affirm that God's reign is characterized by liberation from all forms of oppression, justice in all relationships, peace and good will among all peoples, and the healing of all creation. It is both the vision of God's new heaven and new earth and the recognition of our limits that must inform and shape our role as stewards of earth and life in the age of genetics. It is in the context of God's sovereignty over all existence, our hope for the coming of God's reign, our awareness of our own finitude, and our responsibility as stewards that we consider these issues and the following recommendations.

### III. Issues in the Development of Genetic Research and Technology

#### A. Why the Church is addressing these issues

God's sovereignty over all creation, our status as stewards of creation's resources, and the church's nature as a nurturing and prophetic community living toward God's reign over all existence propel us to consider the theological/ethical implications of genetic science. As genetic science probes the very structure of biological life and develops means to alter the nature of life itself, the potential for relief of suffering and the healing of creation is enormous. But the potential for added physical and emotional suffering and social and economic injustice also exists. Developments in genetic science compel our reevaluation of accepted theological/ethical issues, including determinism versus free will, the nature of sin, just distribution of resources, the status of human beings in relation to other forms of life, and the meaning of personhood.

#### B. Genetic science affects every area of our lives

The food we eat, the health care we receive, how crimes are prosecuted, our biological traits, and the environment in which we live are all affected by research and developments in genetic science. As stewards of and participants in life and its resources, we seek to understand, to evaluate, and to utilize responsibly the emerging genetic technologies in accordance with our finite understanding of God's purposes for creation. The divine purpose includes justice, health, and peace for all persons, and the integrity and ecological balance of creation. The uses of genetic science have the potential for promoting as well as thwarting these aspects of the divine purpose.

Genetic issues are much more pressing than is generally recognized. Every community contains individuals and families who daily face genetic concerns in the workplace or as result of their own genetic makeup. The rapid growth of genetic science has increased our awareness of these concerns, has created new concerns, and has accelerated the theological, ethical, and pastoral challenges that genetics poses to persons of faith.

#### C. Scientific change now leads societal change

The rise in importance of science and technology has been one of the most significant developments in the last 400 years. Beginning with the industrial revolution, we have witnessed a succession of revolutions: the technological, the atomic, and the biological. Each of these revolutions has presented society with a host of religious challenges and threats that have taken enormous and ongoing efforts to resolve constructively. The very nature of work, perceptions of the world, international relations, and family life has changed in part because of these revolutions.

A major dimension of the biological revolution is genetic science. Less than fifty years ago, the actual genetic substance of living cells, DNA, was firmly identified. Now, altering DNA in plants and animals, even humans, in order to correct disorders or to introduce characteristics that are more desirable is being done. Genetic developments in medicine and agriculture promise to alter the very nature of society, the natural environment, and even human nature. Christians must evaluate these developments in light of our basic understanding of God as creator and of humans as stewards of creation, including technology.

## D. Genetic science challenges society

Biotechnology based on genetic research is already upon us. Thousands of people and millions of dollars are devoted to genetic science. Gene therapy has already been introduced as an experimental medical treatment. Extensive research has been conducted in plant and animal genetics, with significant implications for the food supply, farm policy, agricultural economics, and ecological balance.

In spite of the rapid growth in genetic research, many people tend to see genetics merely as an extension of the changes in medical, agricultural, and other technologies. In fact, genetic science crosses new frontiers as it explores the essence of life. The implications of genetic research and development are so far-reaching that society must consider the effect of these developments on persons, animal and plant life, the environment, agriculture, the food supply, patent policies, criminal justice, and medicine. Delays in commercializing some of the technologies may afford society and the church additional time to address the implications, but the time available for serious reflection on the consequences of these technologies prior to their implementation is brief.

## IV. Questions about Biotechnology

New developments in technology always challenge society's imagination and understanding. Technology is often viewed either with awe or with fear. The popular view of the geneticist alternates between a saint who cures all disease and a mad scientist who creates monsters or perverts life. These extreme images must be avoided as society raises questions about the technologies themselves and questions how they should be properly developed and controlled. Although genetic technologies are similar to other technologies, genetic science and technology force us to examine, as never before, the meaning of life, our understanding of ourselves as humans, and our proper role in God's creation. Just as Jesus was tempted by the devil to turn stones into bread, we, too, can be tempted to believe that these new technologies can solve problems that they were not intended to solve.

Several basic questions can provide a framework within which to evaluate the effect of genetics (or any other new technology) on any segment of society. The questions revolve around issues of appropriateness, availability, efficacy, and accessibility.

## V. The Patenting of Life Forms

The patenting of life forms is a crucial issue in the debate over access to genetic technologies. Some claim that patenting of life will give complete control to the owner and so limit access. Others insist that the scientists and funding agencies or institutions must have some return on their investment. A compromise that many societies have worked out in order to provide economic returns for those who have developed a technology while providing access, eventually, to the entire society is the patent or exclusive control of a technological invention for a period of years. But should exclusive ownership rights apply to the gene pool? In 1984, the General Conference of The United Methodist Church declared genes to be a part of the common heritage of all peoples. The position taken by the church in 1984 is consistent with our understanding of the sanctity of God's creation and God's ownership of life. Therefore, exclusive ownership rights of gene, organisms, and cells as a means of making genetic technologies accessible raises serious theological concerns and profound ethical concerns. While patents on organisms, cells, and genes themselves are opposed, process patents—wherein the method for engineering a new organism is patented—provide a means of economic return on investment while avoiding exclusive ownership of the organism and can be supported.

## VI. Affirmations/Recommendations/Conclusions

### A. General

1. We affirm that knowledge of genetics is a resource over which we are to exercise stewardship responsibly in accordance with God's reign over creation. We believe the use of genetic knowledge in ways that destabilize and fragment creation violates God's vision of justice, peace, and wholeness.

2. We caution that the prevalent principle in research that what *can* be done *should* be done is insufficient rationale for genetic science. This principle should be subject to legal and ethical oversight in research design and should not be the prevalent principle guiding the development of new technologies. Applications of research to technologies need moral and ethical guidance.

3. We urge adequate public funding of genetic research so that projects not likely to be funded by private grants will receive adequate support and so that there will be greater accountability to the public by those involved in setting the direction of genetic research.

4. We urge that genes, cells, and all living organisms be held as common resources and not be exclusively controlled, or patented. We support improvements in the procedures for granting patents on processes and techniques as a way to reward new developments in this area, although we recognize that even process patents should be limited when they are in effect discoveries of how God makes the processes of living organisms.

### B. Medical recommendations

1. Testing and Treatment
   a. We support the right of all persons to health care and health-care resources regardless of their genetic or medical conditions.
   b. We support equal access to medical resources, including genetic testing and genetic counseling by appropriately educated and trained health-care professionals. We affirm that responsible stewardship of God's gift of human life implies access of all persons to genetic counseling throughout their reproductive life.
   c. We support human somatic gene therapies (recombinant DNA therapies that produce genetic changes in an individual

that cannot be passed to offspring) that prevent or minimize disease and its effects. But we believe these therapies should be limited to the alleviation of suffering caused by disease. We urge that guidelines and government regulations be developed for the use of all somatic gene therapies. We oppose human germ-line therapies (those that result in changes that can be passed to offspring) because of the possibility of unintended consequences and of abuse. With current technology it is not possible to know if artificially introduced genes will have unexpected or delayed long-term effects not identifiable until the genes have been dispersed in the population.

We oppose both somatic and germ-line therapies when they are used for eugenic purposes or enhancements, that is, to provide only cosmetic change or to provide athletic or social advantage.

Furthermore, we urge that government regulations and professional organization guidelines be developed and effectively implemented for all gene therapies. Given the reports of deaths from somatic gene therapies and the development of genetically engineered leukemia in some patients undergoing somatic gene therapy, we urge a careful reexamination of the appropriateness of this therapy.

d. We call on all nations to ban human cloning (the intentional production of genetically identical or essentially identical human beings and human embryos), whether such cloning is funded privately or through government research.

e. We call for a ban on medical and research procedures that intentionally generate "waste embryos" that will knowingly be destroyed when the medical procedure or the research is completed. The exception to this is when ova (eggs) are being collected for use in in vitro fertilization. A woman is at risk for complications each time drugs are given to stimulate ovulation and ova are removed. Obtaining and fertilizing multiple ova may be justified to avoid the necessity of multiple attempts to obtain ova. The first attempt at IVF results in a living child less than 30% of the time thus making multiple attempts necessary.

2. Privacy and confidentiality of genetic information

a. We support the privacy of genetic information. Genetic data of individuals and their families shall be kept secret and held in strict confidence unless confidentiality is waived by the individual or his or her family, or unless the collection and use of genetic identification data are supported by an appropriate court order.

b. We support wide public access to genetic data that do not identify particular individuals, but we oppose using genetic data gathered for purposes other than that to which consent was given.

c. We oppose the discriminatory or manipulative use of genetic information, such as the limitation, termination, or denial of insurance or employment.

## C. Agriculture

1. We support public involvement in initiating, evaluating, regulating, and funding of agricultural genetic research.

a. We believe the public has an important policy and financial role in ensuring the continuation of research that furthers the goal of a safe, nutritious, and affordable food supply.

b. We believe that the public should have input into whether a research effort, or its products, will serve an unmet need in food and fiber production and processing. We urge United Methodists to be active participants in achieving this accountability in all areas of the world.

c. We believe that the benefits of research applications should accrue to the broadest possible public, including farmers and consumers.

2. We support the sustainability of family farms, natural resources, and rural communities and urge that genetic research in agriculture and food products promote these goals.

3. We urge that genetically modified crops and genetically engineered or cloned animal products be labeled so that consumers have a choice in which kind of agricultural products they buy.

## D. Environment

1. As stewards of the planet Earth, we should strive to perpetuate all of God's living creations as long as possible. We should be concerned not only with the well-being of humans, but also with the wholeness of the rest of creation. We should try to maintain ecological balance as God intended. Technologies such as genetic engineering can affect

ecological balance. Genetic technologies must be used carefully to help sustain the planet.

2. We caution that genetically engineered organisms be released into the environment only after careful testing in a controlled setting that simulates each environment in which the organisms are to be used.

3. We urge the development of criteria and methodologies to anticipate and assess possible adverse environmental responses to the release of genetically engineered organisms.

4. We urge that prior to the release of each organism, plans and procedures be developed to destroy genetically engineered organisms that may cause adverse environmental responses.

### E. What the church can do

1. Expand education and dialogue around ethical issues in the development of genetic science and technology.

    a. We request that The United Methodist Church and its appropriate boards and agencies educate laity and clergy on the issues of genetic science, theology, and ethics by conducting workshops and seminars, producing resource materials, and training pastors and laypersons to deal constructively with these issues. Sessions on the ethical implications of genetics technology should be included as part of seminary training, continuing education requirements for clergy, Christian educators' training events, adult and youth Sunday school curriculum, schools of mission and schools of church and society, training for military, prison, hospital chaplains, and campus ministry programs.

    b. We request that clergy be trained to provide pastoral counseling for persons with genetic disorders and their families as well as those facing difficult choices as a result of genetic testing. These choices might include decisions such as those related to reproduction, employment, and living wills. Churches are encouraged to provide support groups for individuals and families affected by genetic disorders.

    c. We call on the church to support persons who must make difficult decisions regarding genetic information related to reproduction. We urge that the church support efforts to improve the quality of genetic testing on embryos and fetuses so that accurate information is provided to couples and their doctors about genetic conditions. We reaffirm the 1988

General Conference (1988 *Book of Discipline,* ¶ 71G) position opposing the termination of pregnancy solely for the purpose of gender selection.

d. We urge theological seminaries to offer courses and continuing education events that equip clergy to address theological and ethical issues raised by scientific research and technology.

e. We urge the church to establish and maintain dialogue with those persons working to develop or promote genetics-based technologies.

The complexity and multifaceted implications of genetic science require continuing interaction among scientists, technologists, theologians, ethicists, industrial and corporate leaders, government officials, and the general public.

The ethical concerns of the church need to be interjected into the laboratory, the factory, and the halls of government in an ongoing manner. Local churches, districts, annual conferences, and appropriate general agencies should participate in dialogues with university, industry, and government bodies.

2. Produce resources to educate on genetics issues. General agencies of the church should develop additional interpretive resources on genetics issues.

3. Continue and increase The United Methodist Church's work in the area of genetics.

a. All general agencies are urged to cooperate with ecumenical groups as they seek to coordinate actions regarding the use of knowledge gained from genetic science. Concern for justice for persons and the integrity of all life should form the basis of our ecumenical witness.

b. Local churches are urged to study the issues raised in this statement and to act on the recommendations. We also urge United Methodists to study the recent (2007) reports on genetics developed by the World Council of Churches—"Transforming Life: Genetics, Agriculture, and Human Life"—and the National Council of Churches—"Fearfully and Wonderfully Made."

ADOPTED 1992<br>
AMENDED AND READOPTED 2000<br>
AMENDED AND READOPTED 2008<br>
RESOLUTION #102, 2004 <i>BOOK OF RESOLUTIONS</i><br>
RESOLUTION #90, 2000 <i>BOOK OF RESOLUTIONS</i>

*See* Social Principles, ¶ 162O.

## 3182. Human Cloning

Cloning has sparked enormous and sustained concern in the general public, including the church. For the purposes of this document, human cloning means the intentional production of genetically identical or essentially identical human beings and human embryos. Cloning touches on many crucial questions about human nature, raises hopes and expectations, and brings to the fore uncertainties and fears. While we do not see obvious benefits of human cloning and while we recognize potential dangers of cloning, we also acknowledge the excitement that this new research generates for advances in medicine, agriculture, and other scientific endeavors.

As United Methodists, our reflections on these issues emerge from our faith. We remember that creation has its origin, value, and destiny in God, that human beings are stewards of creation, that technology has brought forth both great benefit and great harm to creation. As people of faith, we believe that our identity as human beings is more than our genetic inheritance, our social environment, or the sum of the two. We are created by God and have been redeemed by Jesus Christ. We recognize that our present human knowledge on this issue is incomplete and finite. We do not know all of the consequences of cloning (psychological, social, or genetic). It is important that the limits of human knowledge be considered as policy is made.

*Therefore*, we submit the following policy positions:

1. We call for a ban on all human cloning, including the cloning of human embryos. This would include all projects, privately or governmentally funded, that are intended to advance human cloning. Transcending our concerns with embryo wastage are a number of other unresolved and barely explored concerns with substantial social and theological ramifications: use or abuse of people, exploitation of women, tearing of the fabric of the family, the compromising of human distinctiveness, the lessening of genetic diversity, the direction of research and development being controlled by corporate profit and/or personal gain, and the invasion of privacy. These unresolved concerns generate significant distrust and fear in the general public.

2. We call for a ban on therapeutic, medical, research, and commercial procedures which generate unused embryos for the purpose of cloning. The methods of concurrent research protocols in cloning necessitate the production of excess or "unused embryos," which are ultimately destroyed.

3. We commit to the widespread discussion of issues related to cloning in public forums, including United Methodist schools, seminaries, hospitals, and churches. Given the profound theological and moral implications, the imperfection of human knowledge, and the tremendous risks and social benefits, we urge that there be a moratorium on cloning-related research until these issues can be discussed fully by both the general public including significant participation from communities of faith, as well as by experts in agricultural and biological science, public policy, ethics, theology, law, and medicine, including genetics and genetic counseling. The psychological and social effects of cloning on individuals, families, parental relationships, and the larger society should be fully discussed. Those presently affected by in vitro fertilization, surrogacy, artificial insemination, and other reproduction technologies should be consulted to provide insight into some related psychological and social issues.

4. We call on all nations to ban human cloning and to identify appropriate government agencies to enforce the ban. Appropriate social and governmental bodies must monitor and guide research and developments in the field. Concern for profit and commercial advantage should be balanced by consideration for individual rights, the interest of wide constituencies, and the common good of future generations.

ADOPTED 2000
REVISED AND READOPTED 2008
RESOLUTION #103, 2004 *BOOK OF RESOLUTIONS*
RESOLUTION #91, 2000 *BOOK OF RESOLUTIONS*

*See* Social Principles, ¶ 1620.

## 3183. Stem Cell Research

WHEREAS, God calls each of us to full personhood and wishes for us well-being; and

WHEREAS, God desires health and healing for every human being; and

WHEREAS, some believe this century will be the "Century of Biology"; and

WHEREAS, medical science will continue to discover new forms of healing for humankind; and

WHEREAS, stem cell research, including somatic nuclear cell transfer, offers great potential for healing;

*Therefore, be it resolved,* that the 2008 General Conference join with other faith communities to support and dialogue with the medical and scientific communities concerning the ethical standards for its use; and

*Be it further resolved,* that the General Board of Church and Society identify and publish on their Web site educational resources. We encourage each pastor to use the resources to become informed concerning the debate regarding the use of embryonic stem cells for medical research and to offer these resources for study in her or his local church.

ADOPTED 2008

*See* Social Principles, ¶ 162O.


### 3184. Guidelines for Developing Genetically Modified Organisms

"In the beginning when God created the heavens and the earth, the earth was a formless void and darkness covered the face of the deep, while a wind from God swept over the face of the waters. . . . And God said, "Let the waters bring forth swarms of living creatures, and let birds fly above the earth across the dome of the sky. . . . So God created the great sea monsters and every living creature that moves, of every kind, with which the waters swarm, and every winged bird of every kind. And God saw that it was good" (Genesis 1:1-2, 20-21).

All of creation is a good gift of God, brought into glorious being out of nothingness and shaped out of chaos. All life, including human life, is created. It is finite, contingent, and limited and is sustained through God's loving care and attention, calling forth of new creation, moment-to-moment, in uncountable abundance in God's world. The tapestry of God's creation is woven with the beauty of extravagant diversity. From bacteria to begonias to our own lives, the diverse interconnected fabric of life calls forth our awe and wonder.

Human communities, in our incredibly diverse web of relationships, carry with them complex and widely differing traditions, (his/her) stories, and relationships with the rest of creation. In addition to nurturing the spirit, God's creatures provide nourishment and sustenance for each other in abundant and diverse ways. In human culture, hunting and gathering, plowing and planting, breeding and feeding, have grown in ways that reflect God's penchant for difference. The climates, soils and lands of different geographical regions differ dramatically in their ecologies. Farming, hunting, and other patterns for sustaining human life vary widely within countries and across the world. These differences also are a reflection God's gloriously expressed diversity.

Reflecting on this diversity and the continuing presence of God's grace in our lives, United Methodists must address the threats to bio- and agricultural diversity posed by current activities in genetic engineering of plants and animals. These technologies are emerging within the context of a history of the overuse of land, the homogenization of agriculture, and the brutal exploitation of nonhuman animal life in search of ever higher profits.

We have exploited God's soils, landscapes, plants, and animal life merely for their commercial value, forgetting our proper roles as limited, graced stewards of God's creation. Our relationship with creation is one of "entrustment." And we have not fulfilled that trust.

Humans, and particularly North American agricultural practices have lost or obliterated strains of corn and apples, reduced the varieties of cattle and sheep to a virtual handful, bred chickens that do not ever get to walk, and turkeys so large they cannot even stand, much less fly. Multinational agribusiness has sought to expand profits and control of agricultural practices by exporting such exploitative practices to peoples in the developing world. These practices have also threatened the diversity of the human community. The voices of farmers in such developing contexts urge North American Christians to seek repentance and wisdom as we embark on the next wave of bio-engineering: genetic modification.

Given this context, we urge extreme caution. The General Conference of The United Methodist Church in 2000 stated, "At this point in human history, the human race is experiencing warning signs that our bodies and the natural environment have limits to their abilities to absorb and overcome the harm from some of our actions, technologies, and substances." (*See* "Environmental Law: The Precautionary Principle.") Medical and scientific research is only beginning to identify the long-term synergistic effects of what we have done to our ecosystems and what we are doing to our food.

Genetic modifications of plants, animals, and microbes must not speed the destruction of God's creation. With genomic technology, we are involved in the manipulation of life at a basic level. There may be possibilities for significant benefits for humanity. There are also, perhaps even greater, possibilities for unforeseen catastrophe. As finite recipients of God's grace and God's call to stewardship, we can only proceed with repentance for past transgression and a willingness to cultivate the crucial virtue of patience. We must proceed on the basis of faithful precaution, seeking God's help in discerning temptations to do apparent "goods" from faithful loving action as Jesus did in his sojourn in the desert (Luke 4:1-44).

Among the specific concerns that warrant our study and action are:
- The distribution of genetically engineered grains to starving, impoverished, and war-ravaged peoples where the grain cannot be used later for crops to be sold in developed world markets. Many African countries that might receive genetically modified grain from the US would not be able to later export that grain to Europe or Japan where genetically modified grain imports are restricted. They also may not be able to export the grain if the strains have been patented.
- The refusal by food donor nations to mill genetically modified grains before distribution so the grains' seeds would not contaminate genetically engineered, organism-free ecosystems is an additional problem.
- the failure of grain exporters to disclosure of the genetically modified nature of the grain being distributed
- Engineering plants and animals to produce pharmaceuticals
  - Including the moral aspects of these procedures particularly on animals
  - Including the dangers of such animals and plants ending up in the food supply
- Release of genetically engineered (GE) seeds and growing GE crops without adequate safety and ecological impact testing
  - Including the role of profit-oriented corporate interests in the process
  - Including the lack of scientific evidence supporting a declaration of "substantial equivalence between GE and non-GE foods"
  - Including the dearth of knowledge of the long-term health effects of genetically modified organisms.

- Including genetic contamination of nongenetically modified species and varieties and the impact on organic farmers
- Including issues of legal liability and intellectual property
- Including the problem of contaminating exports to preclude organic farming standards
- The effects of genetically modified traits in the overall food system of a region
  - Increasing trend toward monoculture of crops
  - Increasing elimination of farm animal diversity
- The engineering of genetically modified organisms to allow greater use of specific pesticides
  - Including the need to use more rather than less pesticides as advertised
- The adverse economic impacts on farmers of using genetically modified crops
- The engineering of toxins into food crops as insecticides and the concomitant expansion of insect resistance to those toxins.
  - Including the adverse impact on organic farmers whose only pesticide has been naturally occurring insect toxins
  - Including the impact of pesticide-resistant insects on the spread of disease
- The lack of labeling of fields containing GE crops
  - Including the impact on surrounding farmers seeking to use non-GE crops
- The lack of regulation and universal labeling of genetically modified foods
  - Including clear labeling to distinguish true organic foods and organically grown products that involved genetically modified organisms
- The production and marketing of agricultural products that have been engineered to produce no seed or sterile seed so that farmers cannot plant seed from the crops they have raised
- Multinational financial and trade institutions' promotion of GE as a solution to global problems of hunger
  - Including interpretation of World Trade rules to prevent local governments from determining their own rules regarding genetically modified organisms
  - Including the imposition of the use of GE crops as a condition of receiving international assistance

- The loss of genetic diversity, including the consequences of the loss of native seed and animal varieties, is a concern.
  - Including the impact of "industrial agriculture" on the impetus to create monocultures
- The genetic engineering of plants and animals and the patenting of genes, plants, and animals raise major theological and ethical concerns.
  - the moral and ethical questions surrounding the proscription of "use" of any for of life to a single party or entity in the face of creation as a gift
  - Including the moral and ethical issues surrounding the proscription of access to knowledge that might help diagnose or treat diseases

*Three Ethical Guidelines*

It is possible to change the technology-driven direction of agriculture and rural development to one that is respectful and appreciative of creation as a gift of God that reflects our responsibilities as stewards and establishes right relationships of sustainability with creation. But we need guidelines. A sustainable agriculture must have three attributes:

1. It must be just. A just society and a just agriculture provide the means whereby people can share in the inheritance of the earth so that all life can fully be maintained in freedom and community. The purpose of a just agriculture should be the maintenance and renewal of the necessary resources for food, clothing, and shelter, for now and for the future, recognizing the needs for space and sustenance of all of God's creatures.

2. It must be participatory. For an agriculture to be just, everyone has the right to be consulted and the needs of all species to thrive be considered. Participation in human society and in the ongoing process of creation is the necessary condition for justice. Ethical human participation requires recognition of everyone's right to be consulted and understood, regardless of that person's economic, political, or social status. Participation is not possible without power. In such decision-making, everyone has the right to be consulted about such issues as expenditures for armaments, nuclear power, and forms of employment, social services, and so forth. However, the power of participation in decision making should be weighted to local participation due

to local community relationships and local risks rather than to economic or political centers of power.

3. It must be appropriate. Appropriate agriculture is appropriate to the region, context, and conditions of the area. It is one where the idea of permanent carrying capacity is maintained, where success (agriculture, energy production, forestry, water use, industrial activity) is measured by whether or not it sustains the soil and the ecosystems necessary to assure continuing supplies of healthful food. Rather than by the criteria of yields per acre or profits, appropriate agriculture ensures that waste products can be absorbed back into the ecosystem without damage.

Sustainable agriculture—just, participatory, and appropriate—would meet basic human needs for food and fiber, regenerate and protect ecosystems, be economically viable, enhance the quality of life for farm families, be supportive of rural communities, be socially just, and be compatible with spiritual teachings that recognize the earth as a common heritage and responsibility. For Christians, the idea of sustainability flows directly from the biblical call to human beings to be stewards of God's creation.

*Be it resolved that:*

The General Board of Church and Society continue to monitor developments in this area, but especially advocate for the following:

1. The right of nations to set their own standards related to genetically modified organisms and their importation.

2. Labeling of genetically modified organisms.

3. Testing of genetically modified organisms to assure their safety to human health and the environment.

That other agencies of the church work to educate about the concerns raised in this resolution.

ADOPTED 2004
RESOLUTION #104, 2004 *BOOK OF RESOLUTIONS*

*See* Social Principles, ¶ 162O.

## 3185. Repentance for Support of Eugenics

Eugenics, the belief that certain "genetic" traits are good and others bad, is associated in the public mind mostly with the extreme eugenics policies of Adolf Hitler, which ultimately led to the Holocaust. The study of eugenics did not begin with Hitler or his German scientists, but rather was first promoted by Sir Francis Galton, in England. Galton, a cousin of Charles Darwin, expanded on Darwin's theories and applied them to the human population. In an article entitled "Hereditary Character and Talent" (published in two parts in *MacMillan's Magazine*, vol. 11, November 1864 and April 1865, pp. 157-166, 318-327), Galton expressed his frustration that no one was breeding a better human:

"If a twentieth part of the cost and pains were spent in measures for the improvement of the human race that is spent on the improvement of the breed of horses and cattle, what a galaxy of genius might we not create! We might introduce prophets and high priests of civilization into the world, as surely as we can propagate idiots by mating cretins. Men and women of the present day are, to those we might hope to bring into existence, what the pariah dogs of the streets of an Eastern town are to our own highly-bred varieties."

Galton in the same article described Africans and Native Americans in derogatory terms making it clear which racial group he thought was superior. Francis Galton, the founder of the Eugenics Society, spoke hopefully about persuading people with desirable genes to marry and have large families. Galton's successor at the helm of the Eugenics Society was Major Leonard Darwin (1850-1943), a son of Charles Darwin. Leonard Darwin, who ran the Eugenics Society until 1928, made the transition from positive to negative eugenics and promoted plans for lowering the birthrate of the unfit.

Built into the idea of natural selection is a competition between the strong and the weak, between the fit and the unfit. The eugenicists believed that this mechanism was thwarted in the human race by charity, by people and churches who fed the poor and the weak so that they survived, thrived, and reproduced.

Ironically, as the Eugenics Movement came to the United States, the churches, especially the Methodists, the Presbyterians, and the Episcopalians, embraced it.

Methodist churches around the country promoted the American Eugenics Society "Fitter Family Contests" wherein the fittest families were invariably fair skinned and well off. Methodist bishops endorsed one of the first books circulated to the US churches promoting eugenics.[1] Unlike the battles over evolution and creationism, both conservative

---

1. George Henry Naply, The Transmission of Life, Philadelphia: J. Fergus, 1871 endorsed by Bishop Levi Scott and Bishop T. A. Morris, both of the Methodist Episcopal Church.

and progressive church leaders endorsed eugenics. The liberal Rev. Harry F. Ward, professor of Christian ethics and a founder of the Methodist Federation for Social Service, writing in *Eugenics*, the magazine of the American Eugenic Society, said that Christianity and eugenics were compatible because both pursued the "challenge of removing the causes that produce the weak."[2]

Conservative Rev. Clarence True Wilson, the General Secretary of the Methodist Episcopal Board of Temperance, Prohibition and Public Morals, and the man chosen to debate Clarence Darrow after William Jennings Bryan's death, believed that only the white Aryan race was the descendant of the lost tribes of Israel.[3] Methodists were active on the planning committees of the Race Betterment Conferences held in 1914, and 1915.[4] In the 1910s, Methodist churches hosted forums in their churches to discuss eugenics. In the 1920s, many Methodist preachers submitted their eugenics sermons to contests hosted by the American Eugenics Society. By 1927, when the American Eugenics Society formed its Committee on the Cooperation with Clergymen, Bishop Francis McConnell, president of the Methodist Federation for Social Service, served on the committee. In 1936, he would chair the roundtable discussion on Religion and Eugenics at the American Eugenics Society Meeting.[5] The laity of the church also took up the cause of eugenics. In 1929, the *Methodist Review* published the sermon "Eugenics: A Lay Sermon" by George Huntington Donaldson. In the sermon, Donaldson argues, "the strongest and the best are selected for the task of propagating the likeness of God and carrying on his work of improving the race."[6]

Both the Methodist Episcopal Church and the Methodist Episcopal Church, South promoted eugenics.[7] Most of the time, church advocates

2. Harry F. Ward, "Is Christian Morality Harmful, Over Charitable to the Unfit?" Eugenics I (December 1928):20.

3. Robert Dean McNeil, Valiant for Truth, Oregonians Concerned About Addiction Problems, Portland, (1992), pp.19,141 Prohibition was Wilson's main concern as the head of the Methodist Episcopal Board of Temperance, Prohibition, and Public Morals, but eugenics, anti-immigrant programs, anti-Catholic sentiments were a key part of his message. He believed that Indians and Negros were especially prone to alcoholism. (See his The Pocket Cyclopedia of Temperance, p.252.)

4. Methodist Episcopal Bishop John Hamilton of the San Francisco Area served on the planning committee for the 1915 Conference. See Proceedings of the Second National Conference on Race Betterment, August 4-8, 1915.

5. American Eugenics Society, program for "Round Table Conferences and Annual Meeting," New York, 1936.

6. George Huntington Donaldson, "Eugenics: A Lay Sermon" Methodist Review, 112 (1929), p. 60.

7. See C. L. Dorris, "The Impending Disaster," Methodist Review, 75 (1926):720-724.

of eugenics supported positive eugenics—essentially careful selection of mates. Nevertheless, sterilization became an acceptable kind of eugenics along with marriage laws limiting marriage between whites and nonwhites. Some annual conferences supported such laws and a few opposed them.

Indiana passed the first forced sterilization law in 1907; eventually 33 states passed similar laws. Most used Harry Laughlin's model law that provided for the sterilization of "feeble minded, insane, criminalistic, epileptic, diseased, blind, deaf, deformed, and dependent" including "orphans, ne'er do wells, tramps, homeless, and paupers."[8] Virginia passed in 1924 a sterilization law based on the Laughlin model and on the same day passed a law making marriage between a white person and a nonwhite person a felony.[9]

Thirty-three US States eventually passed laws authorizing sterilization of criminals, the mentally ill, the "feeble minded." Sterilization of the allegedly mentally ill continued into the 1970s in several states, by which time about 60,000 Americans had been involuntarily sterilized. In 1933, Hitler's Nazi government used Laughlin's Model Law as the basis for their sterilization law that led to the sterilization of some 350,000 people.

State-sponsored eugenics reached an abhorrent extreme in the Nazi extermination programs of the 1930s and 1940s. Initially directed at people with similar health or social problems as were targeted by the US sterilization laws, these were eventually expanded to cover entire populations—Jews, Gypsies, Poles—judged by the Nazi regime to represent "worthless lives" (*lebensunwerte Leben*). While certain overt state policies such as the use of gas chambers have not been used recently, "ethnic cleansing" has emerged in several countries— including Bosnia, Rwanda, Cambodia, and Sudan and shows that eugenic horrors have not disappeared.

8. www.eugenicsarchive.org <http://www.eugenicsarchive.org>, Essay 8-Sterilization Laws.

9. On March 20, 1924, the Virginia Legislature passed two closely related eugenics laws: SB 219, entitled "The Racial Integrity Act[1]" and SB 281, "An ACT to provide for the sexual sterilization of inmates of State institutions in certain cases", henceforth referred to as "The Sterilization Act". The Racial Integrity Act required that a racial description of every person be recorded at birth, and felonized marriage between "white persons" and nonwhite persons. The law was the most famous ban on miscegenation in the US, and was overturned by the US Supreme Court in 1967, in Loving v. Virginia. Virginia repealed the sterilization in 1979. In 2001, the House of Delegates voted to express regret for the state's selecting breeding policies that had forced sterilizations on some 8,000 people. The Senate soon followed suit.

While Germany now has a strong sensitivity to the issues of eugenics, in the US apology for past eugenic excesses has been slow in coming. California did not repeal its law until 1979 and, in 1985, around 20 states still had laws on their books that permitted the involuntary sterilization of "mentally retarded" persons. Family planning programs around the world have included forced sterilization as a tool even recently. In 2002, Peru's Minister of Health issued an apology for the forced sterilization of indigenous women during the recent presidency of Alberto Fujimori. The state governments of Virginia, California, Oregon, and North Carolina have apologized for their support of eugenics including sterilization. United Methodist General Conferences have called for an end to forced sterilization, but have not yet apologized on behalf of Methodist predecessors who advocated for eugenic polices.

## The New Eugenics

The new eugenics is not so much the negative eugenics of state coercion or the oldest positive eugenics of better baby contests, but rather the eugenics made possible by the emerging biotechnology sciences, such as Preimplantation Genetic Diagnosis. Parents, not the state are the new eugenicists. They, as never before, are confronted with choices about which children they should have based on an incomplete science pointing to the genetic links of many conditions.

Preimplantation Genetic Diagnosis (PGD) is only one of many emerging genetic and reproductive technologies in need of broad public discussion and regulation, but we view PGD as a gateway technology. PGD, if permitted to continue unregulated, could pave the way to new eugenics, where children are literally selected and eventually designed according to a parent's desires and fears.

Recent rapid developments in PGD indicate that we are stumbling down a slippery slope toward this future, rendering a policy response an urgent matter. Finally, unfettered developments of PGD applications in the US attest to the general failure of the US policy regarding genetic and reproductive technologies. This policy failure must be corrected if we are to prevent a new eugenics in the US and abroad.

Germany, Austria, Ireland, Switzerland, and Southwest Australia have banned PGD outright. Other nations, including the United Kingdom, France, the Netherlands, Belgium, Italy, and Greece have limited the use of PGD. Even in the US, until recently, PGD was used exclusively for medical purposes.

Today, two thirds of the fertility clinics in the world offering PGD are in the US. Some clinics are blatantly performing PGD for selection.[10] Many other clinics have used PGD to avoid late-onset diseases like Alzheimer's and recently breast cancer. A growing number of couples are using PGD to select an embryo that would grow into a child intended to be a tissue match for its sibling. None of these applications was subject to formal regulatory review or public deliberation prior to their use. In the case of sex selection, the practice specifically violates the voluntary guidelines of the American Society of Reproductive Medicine.[11]

The US lack of regulation has resulted in advocates of expanded PGD in other countries to push for more permissiveness abroad. Some of the advocates, including Robert Edwards, who in 1977 performed the first successful IVF procedure in humans, explicitly promote the new eugenic approach. Edwards has predicted that "Soon it will be a sin for parents to have a child which carries the heavy burden of genetic disease. We are entering a world where we have to consider the quality of our children."[12]

Today, thirty years after the birth of Louise Brown from Edward's IVF technique, more than one million children have been born from the process of IVF. The parallel development of genetic testing has resulted into the merger of genetic testing and assisted reproduction into preimplantation genetic diagnosis (PGD). Parents can now choose which of their embryos to implant in the mother's womb based on the outcome of more than 1000 genetic tests that potentially could be performed on the embryos. These tests at present only indicate probabilities for most conditions. We lack an adequate understanding of how the 98 percent of the human genome that is not made up of genes affects the genes that we can measure. The church needs to help its members sort through the implications of this new information that will never be complete.

The overt racism of the eugenic campaigns of the last century is no longer acceptable in today's civic square or pulpits, but the impetus

10. Aron Zitner, "A girl or a boy, you pick," Los Angeles Times, July 23, 2002, A1.
11. American Society of Reproductive Medicine,1999, "Sex selection and preimplantation genetic diagnosis," Fertility and Sterility 72(4):595-598.
12. Edwards speaking at European Society of Human Reproduction and Embryology as reported in Metro (UK), July 5, 1999.

toward eugenics remains. Controlling the reproduction of the social body and individual bodies, controlling the quality and quantity of the next generation in order to form a more perfect union—these impulses remain part of culture. The church needs to remind its members that as Christians were are called to stand apart from culture and rejoice that our identity comes from being 'adopted' by Christ and where we are all welcomed as children of God regardless of our genetic makeup. Matthew in the opening of his Gospel (Matthew 1:1-16) reminds us that in Jesus' earthly family were not just Jews, but also four Gentile women. As Christians, we are not called because of our genetic identity; we are not called to reengineer our bodies or those of our children, or destroy those different from us, but rather to follow Christ.

### Repentance for Support of Eugenics

The United Methodist General Conference formally apologizes for Methodist leaders and Methodist bodies who in the past supported eugenics as sound science and sound theology. We lament the ways eugenics was used to justify the sterilization of persons deemed less worthy. We lament that Methodist support of eugenics policies was used to keep persons of different races from marrying and forming legally recognized families. We are especially grieved that the politics of eugenics led to the extermination of millions of people by the Nazi government and continues today as "ethnic cleansing" around the world.

**ADOPTED 2008**

*See* Social Principles, ¶ 1620.

## HEALTH CARE

### 3201. Health Care for All in the United States

*Theological and Historical Statement*

From our earliest days United Methodists have believed that providing health care to others is an important duty of Christians. John Wesley found ways to offer medical services at no cost to the poor in

London. The first Methodist Social Creed (adopted in 1908) urged working conditions to safeguard the health of workers and community.

The provision of health care for all without regard to status or ability to pay is portrayed in the parable of the Good Samaritan (Luke 10:24-35) as the duty of every neighbor and thus of every person. In a conversation that began with the question of how one might obtain eternal life, Jesus asserted that one must love God and one's neighbor. In response to the next question as to who one's neighbor is, Jesus portrayed a Samaritan, an outsider, who coming upon a wounded traveler, provided him with health care. Jesus portrayed the duty to provide health care as (1) one that is owed regardless of the merit or ethnicity of the person in need; (2) one that is owed to the limit of one's economic capacity – the Samaritan told the innkeeper, "Take care of him; and when I come back, I will repay you whatever more you spend", and (3) a duty that one neglects at the peril of one's eternal life. In a democracy, our duty to our neighbor merges with the duties that the Hebrew scriptures assign to government: the prophet Ezekiel denounced the leaders of ancient Israel whose failure of responsible government included failure to provide health care: "you have not strengthened the weak, you have not healed the sick, you have not bound up the injured, you have not brought back the strayed, you have not sought the lost, but with force and harshness you have ruled them" (Ezekiel 34:4, NRSV). The United Methodist Church therefore affirms in our Social Principles (¶ 162V) health care as a basic human right and affirms the duty of government to assure health care for all.

In the United States today, however, fulfillment of this duty is thwarted by simultaneous crises of access, quality, and cost. The result of these crises is injustice to the most vulnerable, increased risk to health care consumers, and waste of scarce public and private resources.

### Access Barriers Are an Injustice to the Most Vulnerable

In today's United States, health care access is disproportionately afforded to the affluent, the employees of government and large corporations, the very poor, and many receiving adequate pensions plus Medicare. Forty-seven million Americans are uninsured, largely the self-employed, recently unemployed, middle income, and working poor. Lack of health care access affects minorities disparately, and the results of the devastating expense of a long-term or terminal illness, inadequate care in general, and the extraordinary cost of insurance all contribute to keeping many minorities in the poverty cycle, dependent on welfare and other forms of assistance, and imprisoned in struggling and dangerous communities. Disparities in access lead to disparities in treatment. The poor, the aging, women, children, people with disabilities, and persons of color are most at risk. The infant mortality rate in the United States is the worst among the "developed" countries. African-American women die from cervical cancer at three times the rate of Caucasian women. African-Americans have a significantly lower life span than Caucasians and Hispanics have the least access to the health care system of any group. Native Americans, besides suffering greatly from alcoholism, have a substantially higher diabetes and tuberculosis rate than average US rates. Recent immigrants who experience health problems find the health care system poorly equipped to meet their needs. We believe it is unconscionable and abhorrent that any human being should ever be denied access to adequate health care due to economic, racial, or class barriers.[1]

Such barriers, however, are endemic to our current system of employer-sponsored health coverage. This system is eroding, covering a smaller percentage of Americans each year, and rendering American employers less competitive in a world market. When a covered employee has a health crisis affecting his or her ability to work, a whole family's coverage is jeopardized. Other difficulties with private insurance are that in a health care crisis, even those with insurance may have expenses that exceed the lifetime maximum under their policy. In some cases, the insurance policy may be cancelled just when it is needed most. Businesses are overwhelmed with the cost of health insurance. Persons with chronic diseases face special challenges of inadequate resources both in availability of health-care professionals and economic support. United Methodist Conferences increasingly find health care costs consuming dollars intended for ministry.[2]

Forcing Americans to rely on a safety-net program like Medicaid is unjust because if a health catastrophe should strike, those who have no coverage must deplete all assets in order to qualify for Medicaid, including selling of a home or surrendering a lifetime of savings. Even if this family is not among those who must declare bankruptcy in order to survive, these circumstances contribute to poverty, constant worry, and despair among many. While Medicaid provides some care

1. United States Bureau of the Census, Centers for Disease Control and Prevention, and US Department of Health and Human Services—Office of Minority Health.
2. *United Methodist Reporter*, 1990, 2004.

to the poor, it does not encourage primary nor comprehensive care and disqualifies applicants with borderline incomes. Persons with episodic incomes are denied Medicaid during the period they have incomes, and therefore also receive episodic care. In addition, Medicaid systems remain under constant attack as one of the first places to cut the federal and state budgets, belying the claims of many civil leaders that health care is their priority.

## Quality Issues Put All Patients At Risk

In the United States, the provision of health care has been transformed from a ministry to a commodity measured in patient encounters, tests performed, medications dispensed, and beds filled. In the process, quality of care suffers as the primary concern is often cost, not care. The physician-patient relationship is thereby compromised. Insurance companies in their efforts to reduce costs seek to control physicians' practice of medicine, thereby interfering with the physician-patient relationship. As a result, medical decisions are often made with primary consideration for the costs to the corporation, not for the optimum health of the patient. In the current climate physicians who prescribe treatments or tests not preapproved by the insurance corporation face severe financial penalties or other disincentives to optimum patient care. Physician time is consumed with excessive paperwork, malpractice suits, and inadequate government programs.[3]

The American claim-based system produces enormous administrative burdens as well as denial of needed care. When claims are not denied by policy, they are often denied by the sheer burden of bureaucracy that must be overcome to obtain approvals. It has been estimated that today's physician spends about one-third of his or her time satisfying these insurance company regulations and seeking approvals for treatment, time the physician could be spending with patients. Competition for premium dollars and concern for high profits have taken priority over necessary care at actual cost. It is evident that private insurance companies are prone to deny claims while continuing to receive premiums, favoring higher profit over the "health and wholeness" of the weakened, the worried, and the sick. These same companies want to limit a patient's right to sue in civil court when the

---

3. The Directives of the American Medical Association House of Delegates address these issues at each meeting.

company breaches its own contract to provide benefits, regardless of the suffering or death a benefit denial may cause. In these types of cases a benefit denial is tantamount to medical malpractice.

Care Management has often been taken over by funding agencies rather than physicians. Managed care companies, HMOs, PPOs, and the like, interfere with the physician's ability to develop comprehensive treatment plans for his or her patients. They require that a decision be made by the corporation about treatment cost and efficacy. Medical decisions are in effect made by persons much less qualified than the patient's physician or the specialist a physician may recommend. In fact, persons with little or no medical training often make those decisions. Many insurance companies hire nurses to review the physicians' diagnoses and treatment plans. While it is unusual for nurses to oversee doctors, it is also evident that these nurses have had no contact with the patient under review.

Hospitals are required to provide uncompensated care. As a result, patients who are unable to pay for small primary care bills are able to incur large hospital bills when their untreated illness has become life-threatening. It has been estimated that the cost of uncompensated care included in each individual policy is $341, and in each family policy is $942.[4] Hospitals can no longer stay financially sound under existing policies.

Hospital staffing, due to cost concerns, imposes burdens on patient care that compromises quality, issues reflected in unhappy staff and increased numbers of union complaints and strikes in recent years. Error rates due to overwork and other factors are a crisis; the Institute of Medicine estimates that 100,000 persons die in American hospitals each year as a result of medical errors.

### *Spiraling Costs Waste Scarce Resources*

Per capita health care costs in the United States are more than twice the median level for the 30 industrialized nations in the Organization for Economic Cooperation and Development. The Centers for Medicare and Medicaid Services have estimated that by 2010, health care expenditures in the United States will reach $2.6 trillion.[5]

4. Impact of Health Care for the Uninsured on Health Insurance Premiums, for Private Employer Coverage, 2005, National Average. Families USA, "Paying a Premium: The Added Cost of Care for the Uninsured, 2005."
5. "Building a Better Health Care System: Specifications for Reform." National Coalition on Health Care. 2004, p. 8.

While some of the escalating costs of health care can be attributed to advances in technology and the aging of the population, a very significant part is due to the nature of America's health insurance market, in which:

- Today's physician spends one third or more of his or her time satisfying insurance requirements and seeking approvals for service.
- Multiple insurance companies, programs, coverage, claims processes, ceate confusion, duplication, and unnecessary administrative costs. It has been estimated that the cost of administration of Medicare is 4 percent to 5 percent of its budget, while the typical private company's budget for administration and profit is about 25 percent. Health care provision is managed by a massive bureaucratic complex: more than fifty state and state-level Medicaid systems, the Department of Veterans Affairs, the Railroad Employees insurance program, Indian Health Service, federal and state employee systems, health care for retired military personnel, Medicare and countless programs of the various private insurance companies: HMOs, PPOs, Medicare Supplemental Plans, etc. These entities rarely communicate in similar terms: neither to patients, to physicians, or to hospitals, thereby complicating efforts of providers and patients to properly file and receive payments on legitimate claims.
- Premium increases are driven by requirements to show a profit rather than rises in actual costs of treatment. High premiums to support the high profit margins of private health insurance companies force people to choose between health insurance and sustenance, housing, or other needs of a family, making even basic health insurance too expansive for an average individual or family. High co-payments and uncovered costs lead to significant impoverishment.
- Costs are shifted to the consumer through increasing deductibles and co-payments for care.
- Ever smaller insurance pools are promoted, with increasing portions of risk borne by the patient. The culmination of this trend is promotion of personal policies, with high deductibles and extraordinarily high premiums of thousands of dollars per month, that an average family, much less the working poor, simply cannot afford.

- Annual or lifetime limits are often imposed on policies, whether individual, group, or institutional, as a means of limiting the risk of private insurance companies. These harsh policies simply pass the risk back to individuals at the very time they can least cope with it, leaving the lingering worry that with a catastrophic illness or injury such limits may be reached, abruptly stopping all insurance benefits and leaving the policy beneficiary completely uninsured.
- More than half of all personal bankruptcies are now the result of illness. Even individuals with ostensibly good insurance, let alone those who are uninsured, find themselves in situations where they must sell and/or spend all assets, including homes, financial holdings, lifetime savings accounts, etc., in order to qualify for Medicaid and restore any medical coverage at all.

Increased costs of health care inevitably impact state and federal resources available for Medicaid, often leading to reduction in the number of providers willing to participate, and ultimately to decreased access to health care for the poor and the physically or mentally challenged.

More and more Annual Conferences and even congregations are feeling the burden of providing health care to their clergy and their lay staff. Small churches, even multiple point parishes, have difficulty paying for increasing health premiums for clergy. Funds going to this purpose are in effect diverted from other important ministries.

### The Vision of Health Care for All

The United Methodist Church is committed to health care for all in the United States and therefore advocates for a comprehensive health care delivery system that includes access for all, quality care, and effective management of costs.

1. *Access for All.* In a just society, all people are entitled to basic maintenance and health-care services. We reject as contrary to our understanding of the gospel, the notion of differing standards of health care for various segments of the population. The American Health Care system must serve and be sensitive to the diversity of all people in the United States and its territories. Regional planning processes should coordinate the services rendered by all health-care institutions, including those funded by governments, to create a more

effective system of health services in every area. Priorities should be established for the provision of health services, such as preventive care, mental-health services, home care, and health education. Corrective measures should be taken where there is maldistribution or unavailability of hospital beds, intermediate care and nursing home care, home-delivered care, neighborhood health centers, community mental-health centers, and emergency care networks.

2. *Quality Care.* Health care should be comprehensive, including preventive, therapeutic, and rehabilitative services. The American health care system should provide comprehensive and portable benefits to everyone; including preventive services, health promotion, primary and acute care, mental-health care, and extended care. It should promote effective and safe innovation and research for women and men in medical techniques, the delivery of health services, and health practices. It should assess the health impacts of environmental and occupational safety, environmental pollution, sanitation, physical fitness, and standard-of-living issues such as housing and nutrition. Professional health-care personnel should be recruited and appropriately educated to meet the health-care needs of all persons. Especially urgent is the need for physicians trained in geriatric medicine. Special priorities should be established to secure among the professional group at least proportional representation of women and minorities who are now seriously under-represented. We encourage development of community support systems that permit alternatives to institutional care for such groups as the aging, the terminally ill and mentally ill, and other persons with special needs. We encourage medical education for laypersons that will enable them to effectively evaluate medical care they need and are receiving. Religious and other appropriate forms of counseling should be available to all patients and families when they are called upon to make difficult medical choices, so that responsible decisions, within the context of the Christian faith, may be made concerning organ transplants, use of extreme measures to prolong life, abortion, sterilization, genetic counseling, institutionalization, and death with dignity. We support the medical community in its effort to uphold ethical standards and to promote quality assurance.

3. *Effective Administration of Care and Management and Financing of Costs.* The American health care system must incorporate an equitable and efficient financing system drawn from the broadest possible resource base. It must reduce the current rapid cost inflation through cost-containment measures. It must provide services based on equity,

efficiency, and quality, with payments to providers that are equitable, cost-efficient, and easy to administer and understand. The system must be sensitive to the needs of persons working in the various components of the health care system and gives special attention to providing not only for affirmative action in the recruitment, training, and employment of workers, but also for just compensation for all workers at all levels and for retraining and placement of those displaced by changes in the health care system.

## Advocacy Steps

Globally, the church has a continuing duty to provide, in many parts of the world, the ministry of health care that government is unable to provide. In the United States, however, government has the capability to provide health care for all; doing so will extend health care to many who presently have no access, and doing so without the wastefulness of the current system will represent far better stewardship of resources than at present. The United Methodist Church supports a three-tiered approach to health care advocacy:

1. *Single Payer.* We call for swift passage of legislation which will entitle all persons within the borders of the United States to the provision of health care services, the cost of such services to be equally shared by American taxpayers, and the government to distribute the funds to providers in a coordinated and comprehensive manner. This concept, known as "single-payer," would extend health care to all persons in the United States. Choice of private doctor and other health care providers would be maintained. Public funds would make payment, and these funds would be generated by individual premiums and payroll tax. Studies have shown that this method can be achieved with no increase over what is already being spent on health care from all sources. It therefore not only accomplishes the objective, but it best exercises our stewardship of public resources.[6]

2. *Incremental Steps toward Single Payer.* We recognize that much of the cost savings of "single payer" flow from the virtually total elimination of the health insurance industry. We cannot wait to overcome the current barriers to a single payer plan, and therefore support all initiatives that move segments of our population closer to a single

6. Lewin Group, "Analysis of the Costs and Impact of Universal Health Care Models for the State of Maryland: The Single-Payer and Multi-Payer models." Report to Maryland Citizens Health Initiative Educational Fund. May 2, 2000.

payer system. Particular incremental steps that we support include the State Child Health Improvement Program (SCHIP), which should be extended to achieve health care for all children. We do not support legislation that requires individuals to choose to purchase health insurance from multiple insurance companies, because such bills radically waste resources through duplication of service, burdensome administration, marketing costs, and profits. They inherently promote "adverse selection" in which the sickest people sign up for the plans with the best benefits. Such plans drive up the costs, while healthy young workers sign up for plans with the poorest benefits, therefore removing them from the risk pool.

3. *Recognizing that the nation is deeply divided nationally* on the philosophical bases for addressing America's health care delivery problems, we support state-level initiatives in which individual states, at their own initiative become laboratories for trying out varying approaches to providing health care for all. We support in particular efforts at the federal level to support state-based efforts through necessary waivers of federal regulations.

Bringing America's health care crisis under control will call upon the efforts of every sector of society and demand both personal and social responsibility. We therefore call upon all United Methodist persons and entities to do their part:

- Individuals. We call upon United Methodist individuals and families to pursue a healthy lifestyle, preventing many health problems before they start and strengthening physical capacity to combat problems which do arise.
- Health Care Institutions. We call upon United Methodist affiliated health care institutions to adopt, reaffirm, and strengthen policies supporting care delivery that is Christlike, compassionate, and wholistic rather than fee-driven and compartmentalized. We call upon such institutions as a requirement of their affiliation, to develop United Methodist standards of care that distinguish them from profit-driven, secular institutions.
- Seminaries. We call upon United Methodist seminaries to develop curricula linking sound biblical theology with clergy self-care and advocacy for universal health care.
- General Agencies. We call upon all agencies, commissions, and annual conferences of The United Methodist Church in

the United States to adopt principles and support policies that are consistent with this resolution.

We charge the General Board of Church and Society with primary responsibility for advocating health care for all in the United States Congress and for communicating this policy to United Methodists in the USA.

ADOPTED 2008
RESOLUTION #108, 2004 *BOOK OF RESOLUTIONS*
RESOLUTION #95, 2000 *BOOK OF RESOLUTIONS*

*See* Social Principles, ¶ 162V.

## 3202. Health and Wholeness

*Theological and Historical Statement*

Health is the ultimate design of God for humanity. Though life often thwarts that design, the health we have is a good gift of God. When God created humankind, God declared it to be very good (Genesis 1:31). Among Jesus' statements on the purpose of his presence is the statement that he came that we might have abundant life (John 10:10). Every account of Jesus' ministry documents how Jesus saw restoration to health as a sign of the Kingdom of Heaven becoming present amongst us. When John the elder wrote to Gaius (3 John 1:2), he wished for him physical health no less than spiritual. The biblical narrative is filled with stories of God's healing presence in the world. This includes spiritual, psychological, emotional, social, as well as physical healing.

For John and Charles Wesley, health was integral to salvation. In the Wesleyan understanding of salvation, Christ's self-giving on the cross not only freed us from the guilt of sin, but restored us to the divine image in which we were created, which includes health. John Wesley not only preached spiritual health, but worked to restore physical health among the impoverished people who heard his call. He wrote *Primitive Physick*,[1] a primer on health and medicine for those too poor to pay for a doctor. He encouraged his Methodists to support the health-care needs of the poor. Charles Wesley's hymns reflect early Methodism's awareness of spiritual health as a component of salvation.

1. Wesley, John, *Primitive Physick: Or, An Easy and Natural Method of Curing Most Diseases.* (London: J. Palmar, 1751).

## Achieving Health

Health has, for too long been defined only as the absence of disease or infirmity. The World Health Organization took a more wholistic view when it termed health as "a state of complete physical, mental and social well-being."[2] We who are people of faith add spiritual well being to that list, and find our best definition in the biblical concept of "shalom." Shalom conveys or expresses a comprehensive view of human well being including "a long life of happiness ending in natural death (Gen 15:15)."[3] From the perspective of Shalom, health includes biological well being but necessarily includes health of spirit as well. From the perspective of Shalom, health is social harmony as well as personal well being, and necessarily presumes the elimination of violence. Thus the health that God wants for humanity both presumes and seeks the existence of justice as well as mercy, the absence of violence as well as the absence of disease, the presence of social harmony as well as the presence of physical harmony.

As disciples of the One who came that we might have life and have it abundantly, our first and highest priority regarding health must be the promotion of the circumstances in which health thrives. A leading health expert encourages the study of health not from the perspective of what goes wrong, but of what goes right when health is present. These "leading causes of life" include coherence, connection, agency (action), blessing, and hope.[4] Our lives are healthy when we are linked to a source of meaning, when we live in a web of relationships that sustain and nurture us, when we know we have the capacity to respond to the call God has placed on our lives, when we contribute to the affirmation of another at a deep level, and when we lean into a future that is assured, in this life and forever.

No one portion of the six billion members of God's global family has a monopoly on the expertise of achieving health. Achieving health, therefore, assumes mutual respect among the peoples of this Earth and the sharing of lessons learned in each society among the others.

Physical and emotional health is the health of the bodies in which we live, and we are therefore urged to be careful how we live (Ephesians 5:5).

2. World Health Organization. *Constitution of the World Health Organization*, Geneva, 1946.
3. Richardson, Alan, *A Theological Word Book of the Bible*, New York: MacMillan,1950, p. 165.
4. Gunderson, Gary and Larry Pray, *The Leading Causes of Life*, The Center of Excellence in Faith and Health, Methodist LeBonheur Healthcare, Memphis, TN, 2006.

As spiritual beings, our physical health affects our spiritual health and vice versa. St. Paul has termed our bodies as "temples of the living God (1 Corinthians 3:16; 6:16, 19-20), echoing Jesus himself (John 2:21). We therefore are stewards, custodians, managers of God's property: ourselves, our bodies, minds and spirits. Paul urges us to present to God our bodies as a living sacrifice and this is our spiritual worship (Romans 12:1, 2), and to do everything for the glory of God (1 Corinthians 10:31). When we honor our bodies and those of others, we are honoring God and God's good creation.

The biblical mandate has specific implications for personal care. We must honor our bodies through exercise. We must honor our bodies through proper nutrition, and reducing consumption of food products that we discover add toxins to our bodies, excess weight to our frames, and yet fail to provide nourishment. We must recognize that honoring our bodies is a lifelong process.

The second priority must be the correction of those circumstances in which health is hindered or thwarted. The interconnectedness of life is such that those things that diminish our health are most often things beyond the control of physicians, clinics, or insurers. The Ottawa Charter for Health Promotion identified the basic prerequisites for health as peace, shelter, education, food, income, a stable ecosystem, sustainable resources, social justice, and equity.[5] One estimate of factors influencing health gives medical health delivery only 10 percent of the impact; family genetics account for 20 percent of the variability in health, environment 20 percent, and lifestyle 50 percent.[6] John Wesley recognized the great influence of lifestyle on health and its impact on the ability to perform excellent ministry in his caution against works of supererogation,[7] "voluntary works—besides, over and above God's commandments to do more, for His sake, than bounden duty is required" highlight that faith-influenced lifestyle factors are a factor in health.[8] Thus the achievement of health requires attention to:

5. Ottawa Charter for Health Promotion, cited in Dennis Raphael, *"Toward the Future: Policy and Community Actions to Promote Population Health,* in Richard Hofrichter, Editor, *Health and Social Justice: Politics, Ideology, and Inequity in the Distribution of Disease.* San Francisco: Jossey-Bass, 2003.

6. Daughters of Charity National Hospital System, 1994.

7. *Supererogation* is the technical term for the class of actions that go "beyond the call of duty, obligation, or need." *Merriam-Webster Dictionary* (2007 online version). 2004 *Book of Discipline* ¶ 103, Section 3, Our Doctrinal Standards and General Rules, Article XI, p.62.

8. Wesley, John, Article XI, *United Methodist Book of Discipline*, Doctrinal Standards and General Rules, 2004.

- Environmental Factors. Environmental factors include clean air, pure water, effective sanitary systems for the disposal of wastes, nutritious foods, adequate housing, accessible, people-oriented transportation, work for all who want to work, and hazard-free workplaces are essential to health. Environmental factors include not only the natural environment, but the spiritual environment, the social environment, and the political environment, including issues of war and peace, wealth and poverty, oppression and justice, environmental profiling and environmental racism. The best medical system cannot preserve or maintain health when the environment is disease-producing.
- Public Health Factors. Disease prevention, public health programs, and health education including sex education, appropriate to every age level and social setting are needed globally. Services should be provided in a compassionate and skillful manner on the basis of need, without discrimination as to economic status, mental or physical disability, race, color, religion, gender, age, national origin, language, or multiple diagnoses.
- Social Lifestyle Factors. Lifestyle factors detrimental to good health include inadequate education, poverty, unemployment, lack of access to food, stress-producing conditions which include such critical issues as domestic violence and other crimes and social pressures reinforced by marketing and advertising strategies that encourage the abuse of guns, tobacco, alcohol, and other drugs. Other societal pressures that affect health are overachievement, overwork, compulsion for material gain, and lack of balance between family/work responsibilities and personal renewal.[9]
- Spiritual Lifestyle Factors. A relationship with God, learning opportunities throughout life, personal renewal, recreation, green space and natural beauty add essential positive spiritual focus to life which influences health through fulfillment and positives attitudes of hopefulness and possibility.[10]

9. *Supererogation* is the technical term for the class of actions that go "beyond the call of duty, obligation, or need." *Merriam-Webster Dictionary* (2007 online version). 2004 *Book of Discipline* ¶ 103, Section 3, Our Doctrinal Standards and General Rules, Article XI, p.62.

10. *CAM at the NIH Newsletter*, National Center for Complementary and Alternative Medicine, National Institutes of Health (US), Vol. XII, No.1, 2005. Various research and ongoing research; see www.nccam.nih.gov/health.

- Personal Lifestyle Factors. Those factors, which may be choices, habits or addictions destructive to good health include overeating or eating nonnutritious foods, substance abuse, including alcohol, tobacco, barbiturates, sedatives, and so forth. Failure to exercise or to rest and relax adequately is also injurious to health.
- Cultural Factors. Harmful traditional practices such as child marriage can result in serious health problems such as obstetric fistula[11] and the spread of HIV & AIDS. Other practices such as female circumcision can result in pain and the spread of infection.[12] Having multiple partners, a practice in many countries, has significantly increased the spread of AIDS and other diseases.[13]

The biblical view of health integrates the physical and the spiritual, and therefore both are needed in the achievement and restoration of health. In Western Protestant interpretation of health and healing, however, the union of the body and spirit is often dismissed. Cultures that respect and revere that union are often disregarded or looked upon in a condescending manner. Jesus did not make these distinctions, and the early church struggled with it. An illustrative narrative is that of the healing of the woman who suffered from a hemorrhage (Matthew 9:20-22).

She believed that touching his garment would make her well. He told her that her faith had made her whole, which includes physical wellness. We must, if we are to achieve good health, unite the body and spirit in our thinking and actions.

11. C. Murray and A. Lopez, *Health Dimensions of Sex and Reproduction*. Geneva: World Health Organization, 1998. Obstetric fistula is a rupturing of the vagina and rectum causing persistent leakage of feces and urine. It is a health risk commonly associated with child marriage because of the mother's physical immaturity at the time of childbirth. (Source: International Center for Research on Women) A majority of women who develop fistulas are abandoned by their husbands and ostracized by their communities because of their inability to have children and their foul smell. It is estimated that 5 perecent of all pregnant women worldwide will experience obstructed labor. In the United States and other affluent countries, emergency obstetric care is readily available. In many developing countries where there are few hospitals, few doctors, and poor transportation systems, and where women are not highly valued, obstructed labor often results in death of the mother. (Source: The Fistula Foundation)

12. Hosken, Fran P., *The Hosken Report: Genital and Sexual Mutilation of Females*, 4th rev. ed. (Lexington (Mass.): *Women's International Network News*, 1994.

13. *Multiple Partners and AIDS – UNAIDS, Practical Guidelines for Intensifying HIV Prevention: Towards Universal Access*, March 2007-03-19.

## Restoring Health

The experience of ill health is universal to humankind. When environmental factors have contributed to ill health of body or mind, the restorative powers given to the body and spirit by God, even with the best medical care, will be severely challenged if the environmental factors themselves are not changed.

God challenges our global church, as God has challenged God's servants through the ages, to help create networks of care around the world for those who are sick or wounded. Global networks of care should emphasize:

1. health care as a human right[14];
2. transforming systems that restore health care to its identity as a ministry rather than as a commodity, and reforming those economic, financial and legal incentives to treat health care as a commodity to be advertised, marketed, sold, bought and consumed;
3. citizen leadership from the lowest levels to the highest in each society so that all can have active involvement in the formulation of health-care activities that meet local needs and priorities;
4. public financing mechanisms suited to each society that assures the greatest possible access of each person to basic health services;
5. advocacy care that engages the broader community in what the Ottawa Charter for Health Promotion terms the Five Pillars of Action: building healthy public policy, creating supportive environments that promote health, strengthening community action, developing personal skills, and reorienting health services[15];
6. health promotion and community health education that enables each person to increase control over his or her health and to improve it[16] and then to be a neighbor to another, in the fashion of the Good Samaritan, who took the steps that he could, simply because he was there (Luke 10:29-37);

14. UM Social Principle ¶ 162V, *Book of Discipline*, Nashville: United Methodist Publishing House.

15. Ottawa Charter for Health Promotion, cited in Dennis Raphael, *Toward the Future: Policy and Community Actions to Promote Population Health*, in Richard Hofrichter, Editor, *Health and Social Justice: Politics, Ideology, and Inequity in the Distribution of Disease*. San Francisco: Jossey-Bass, 2003.

16. World Health Organization, 1986.

7. primary care workers who are drawn from the community and are trained to assist with the most common illnesses, as well as educate about the impact that can be achieved by improving environmental factors, such as health and sanitation;

8. basic health services that are accessible and affordable in each geographic and cultural setting;

9. medical care when the degree of illness has gone beyond what can be assisted by primary health workers;

10. hospital care, compassionate and skilled, that provides a safe environment for surgery and healing from illness under professional care; and

11. complete and total transparency to persons (or their designees) under the care of a medical practitioner, of their medical condition, so they can be an active director in their own care.

## The Call to United Methodists

*Therefore,* we call upon United Methodists around the world to accept responsibility for modeling health in all its dimensions. Specifically, we call upon our members to:

- continue the redemptive ministry of Christ, including teaching, preaching, and healing. Christ's healing was not peripheral but central in his ministry. As the church, therefore, we understand ourselves to be called by the Lord to the holistic ministry of healing: spiritual, mental emotional, and physical;

- examine the value systems at work in our societies as they impact the health of people and promote the value of shalom in every sphere;

- work for programs and policies that eliminate inequities around the world that keep people from achieving quality health;

- work for policies that enable people to breathe clean air, drink clean water, eat wholesome food, and have access to adequate education and freedom that enable mind and spirit to develop;

- make health concerns a priority in the church, being careful not to neglect the special issues of gender or age, treatment or prevention;

- collaborate as the body of Christ through establishment of networks for information sharing and action suggestions; and
- work toward healthy societies of whole persons.
  a) Part of our task is to enable people to care for themselves and to take responsibility for their own health.
  b) Another part of our task is to ensure that people who are ill, whether from illness of spirit, mind, or body, are not turned aside or ignored but are given care that allows them to live a full life.
  c) A related obligation is to help society welcome the sick and the well as full members, entitled to all the participation of which they are capable.
  d) People, who are well, but different from the majority, are not to be treated as sick in order to control them. Being old developmentally disabled, mentally or physically disabled is not the same as being sick. Persons in these circumstances are not to be diminished in social relationships by being presumed to be ill.
  e) We see this task as demanding concern for spiritual, political, ethical, economic, social, and medical decisions that maintain the highest concern for the condition of society, the environment, and the total life of each person.

In addition, we call upon specific entities within our United Methodist connection to take steps toward health and wholeness as follows:

## Congregations

United Methodist congregations are encouraged to:
- organize a *Health and Wholeness Team* as a key structure in the congregation. Among the team's responsibilities would be to seek each member to develop their spiritual gifts in order that the body of Christ be healthy and effective in the world. The apostle Paul commented that "many are sickly and die among you" (1 Corinthians 11:27-29, NRSV). We suggest that this may have resulted not simply from failing to discern the body of Christ present in the communion bread, but from failing to discern the body of Christ as the congregation. When church members are not allowed to use their spiritual gift,

they stagnate or die spiritually and the spiritual affects the physical health of the individual. The spread of health and wholeness should be discerned clearly as a guiding factor in why it is that we make disciples;

- accept responsibility for educating and motivating members to follow a healthy lifestyle reflecting our affirmation of life as God's gift;
- become actively involved at all levels in the development of support systems for health care in the community; and
- become advocates for a healthful environment; accessible, affordable health care; continued public support for health care of persons unable to provide for themselves; continued support for health-related research; and provision of church facilities to enable health-related ministries.

*Annual Conferences*

We encourage annual conferences to:
- continue their support and provision of direct-health services where needed through hospitals and homes, clinics, and health centers;
- work toward a comprehensive health system which would provide equal access to quality health care for all clergy and lay employees, including retirees;
- undertake specific actions to promote clergy health, physical, mental, emotional and spiritual; and
- support the establishment of Health and Wholeness teams in every congregation.

*Seminaries*

We call on our United Methodist theological schools to:
- become involved in a search for Christian understanding of health, healing, and wholeness and the dimensions of spiritual healing in our congregations. Include coursework that will train clergy not only in pastoral care, but also in intentional caring of the congregation that promotes the physical and spiritual health of each church member; and
- work toward a comprehensive health system that would provide equal access to quality health care for all clergy and lay employees of seminaries, including retirees.

*Educational and Health Care Institutions*

We call on our United Methodist colleges, universities, hospitals, and seminaries to gain an added awareness of health issues and the need for recruitment and education of persons for health-related ministries who would approach such ministries out of a Christian understanding and commitment.

*General Agencies*

We call on:

- the General Board of Discipleship to develop educational and worship resources supporting a theological understanding of health and stewardship of our bodies;
- the General Board of Church and Society and General Board of Global Ministries to support public policies and programs that will ensure comprehensive health-care services of high quality to all persons on the principle of equal access; and
- the General Board of Pension and Health Benefits to undergird the social teachings of the Church by enacting policies and programs for United Methodist employees that ensure comprehensive health-care services of high quality to all persons on the principle of equal access.

ADOPTED 1984
AMENDED AND READOPTED 2000
AMENDED AND READOPTED 2008
RESOLUTION #109, 2004 *BOOK OF RESOLUTIONS*
RESOLUTION #96, 2000 *BOOK OF RESOLUTIONS*

*See* Social Principles, ¶¶ 162V and 165C.


### 3203. Observance of Health Care Justice Sabbaths

Health Care Justice Sabbaths have been observed by the United Methodist and other congregations since their inauguration in 1994 by the Interreligious Health Care Access Campaign.

Health Care Justice Sabbath observances permit persons of faith to demonstrate their faithfulness to the goal of health care for all in keeping with the healing ministry of Jesus Christ and in recognition of the restoration of health as a sign of the presence of God's kingdom. Rather than specifying a particular date for this observance, the campaign encouraged communions and congregations to select a Sabbath date that reflected their individual commitment to issues of health and wholeness. In support of this interfaith effort and in faithful witness to the beliefs articulated in the United Methodist Social Principles on Heath Care. The United Methodist Church calls congregations to designate one Sunday during the calendar year for the observance of a Health Care Justice Sabbath.

The Health Care Justice Sabbath is a day of rejoicing and reflection. It is a time for thanksgiving for the health and well-being enjoyed by many in our world community and thanksgiving for the diverse caregivers who minister to our needs. It is a time to reflect on those who are sick, who struggle with chronic illnesses, who lack access to the health-care services they need, and who are denied those basic elements essential to achieving health. It is a time to reflect on acts of health care mercy and acts of health care justice and how each supports the other. It is a time to focus on our belief that health care is a right and a responsibility, public and private. It is a time to challenge our communities of faith to seek their role in making "Health Care for All" a reality.

To assist congregations in their observance of a Health Care Justice Sabbath, resources will be made available by the General Board of Church and Society.

ADOPTED 1996
AMENDED AND READOPTED 2004
RESOLUTION #110, 2004 *BOOK OF RESOLUTIONS*
RESOLUTION #100, 2000 *BOOK OF RESOLUTIONS*

*See* Social Principles, ¶ 162V.


## 3204. Support for the Religious Coalition for Reproductive Choice

WHEREAS, The United Methodist Church was a founding member of the Religious Coalition for Reproductive Choice in 1973; and

WHEREAS, the General Board of Church and Society and the Women's Division of the General Board of Global Ministries are currently members of the Religious Coalition, along with national organizations from 14 denominations, including the Episcopal Church, Presbyterian Church (USA), United Church of Christ, Unitarian Universalism, Reform and Conservative Judaism; and

WHEREAS, these Coalition member organizations hold a wide variety of views regarding policies relating to specific issues of reproductive choice such as when life and personhood begins but, nevertheless, share common religious values, have official pro-choice policies, and are committed to working together to ensure reproductive choice for all persons through the moral power of religious communities; and

WHEREAS, the Religious Coalition supports the right of all persons to have access to a wide range of reproductive health services including sexuality education, family planning services, contraception, abortion services, affordable and quality health and child care; and

WHEREAS, the Religious Coalition's All Options Clergy Counseling program trains clergy of many faiths to assist women in discerning the course of action that they believe is best in a case of unintended pregnancy; and

WHEREAS, internationally, the Religious Coalition is an accredited nongovernmental organization with the United Nations Department of Public Information which supports international family planning services in such areas as South Africa where the Coalition works with churches on HIV/AIDS education and prevention; and

WHEREAS, the Coalition's efforts help counter attempts to enact restrictive legislation that would impose specific religious views about abortion and reproductive health on persons of all faiths; and

WHEREAS, factions within The United Methodist Church whose stated goal is to have the General Conference go on record in opposition to all abortions regardless of the reason are working towards the goal of severing all United Methodist ties with the Religious Coalition for Reproductive Choice;

*Therefore, be it resolved,* that the United Methodist 2008 General Conference go on record in support of the work of the Religious Coalition for Reproductive Choice, and

*Be it further resolved,* that the 2008 General Conference affirm the continued membership of the General Board of Church and Society and the Women's Division of the General Board of Global Ministries in the Religious Coalition for Reproductive Choice.

ADOPTED 2004
READOPTED 2008
RESOLUTION #114, 2004 *BOOK OF RESOLUTIONS*

*See* Social Principles, ¶ 162V.

## 3205. Faithful Care for Persons Suffering and Dying

Christians affirm that human beings are creatures of God. As such, we are not the authors of our own existence, but receive our lives as gifts from God, who has made us as embodied spirits, capable of transcendence but also vulnerable to illness, accident, and death. God has endowed human beings with capacities for freedom, knowledge, and love, so that we might freely enter into the communion with God and each other for which we were made. The Creator's gift of liberty has been abused and distorted by sin. In Jesus Christ and the Holy Spirit we meet God as Savior, Redeemer, and present Advocate, who has acted in love to free us and all creation from captivity to the power of sin and death. To know God in these ways enables us to receive God's sovereignty over life and death not just as a limit or a neutral fact. It is a source of comfort and peace, as we wait for the final victory over death which is the hallmark of the finished work of redemption.

Therefore, Christians gather as forgiven sinners, redeemed by Christ and empowered by the Holy Spirit to discern and to choose the path of faithfulness to God and one another, as a community seeking to know and to do the truth. It is within the framework of these affirmations, and within the context of these relationships, that we grapple with the questions of faithful care for the sick and the dying.

Through the examples and command of Jesus Christ, the church receives the task of ministering to the sick, relieving what suffering can be relieved and undertaking to share and to lighten that which cannot be eliminated. This mandate calls upon us to address all the needs of the sick. These needs include relief from pain and other distressing symptoms of severe illness, but they also embrace the need for comfort and encouragement and companionship. These needs are expressed particularly by the very ill and the dying who confront fear and grief and loneliness. They are in critical need for emotional and spiritual care and support. The duty to care for the sick also calls upon us to work to reform the structures and institutions by which health care is delivered when they fail to provide the comprehensive physical, social, emotional, and spiritual care needed by those facing grave illness and death.

Care for the dying is an aspect of our stewardship of the divine gift of life. As human interventions, medical technologies are only justified by the help that they can give. Their use requires responsible judgment about when life-sustaining treatments truly support the goals of life, and when they have reached their limits. There is no moral or religious obligation to use them when the burdens they impose outweigh the benefits they offer, or when the use of medical technology only extends the process of dying. Therefore, families should have the liberty to discontinue treatments when they cease to be of benefit to the dying person. However, the withholding or withdrawing of life sustaining interventions should not be confused with abandoning the dying or ceasing to provide care. Even when staving off death seems futile or unreasonably burdensome to continue, we must continue to offer comfort care-effective pain relief, companionship and support for the patient in the hard and sacred work of preparing for death.

Historically, the Christian tradition has drawn a distinction between the cessation of treatment and the use of active measures by the patient or caregiver which aim to bring about death. If death is deliberately sought as the means to relieve suffering, that must be understood as direct and intentional taking of life, whether as suicide or homicide. This United Methodist tradition opposes the taking of life as an offense against God's sole dominion over life, and an abandonment of hope and humility before God. The absence of affordable, available comfort care can increase the pressure on families to consider unacceptable means to end the suffering of the dying.

## Health Insurance in the United States

(While this section explores this topic in the United States context, we encourage further understanding and knowledge of practices and traditions around the globe.)

In the United States today, many millions of people have either no health insurance or grossly inadequate coverage which gives them no reliable access to medical treatment. Even for those who do have basic access, good quality comfort care—including effective pain relief, social and emotional support and spiritual counsel—is often not available from a medical system geared toward cure and rehabilitation rather than care for the dying. Such circumstances leave people with a distorted choice between enduring unrelieved suffering and isolation, and choosing death. This choice undermines rather than enhancing our humanity. When cost control measures and for-profit health care institutions bring economic pressures directly to bear on treatment decisions such as the cessation of care, the United States system of health care financing and administration has distorted and corrupted the practice of medicine. We as a society must assure patients situations where their desire not to be a financial burden does not tempt them to choose death rather than receiving the care and support that could enable them to live out their remaining time in comfort and peace.

*Pastoral Care*

The church's unique role for persons facing suffering and death is to advocate for and provide care in all of its dimensions to the very sick in the form of pastoral care. Such pastoral care is the calling of the whole community of faith, not only pastors and chaplains. Because Christian faith is relevant to every aspect of life, no one can cope successfully with life's pain and suffering and ultimate death without the help of God through other people. In Pastoral care God's help and presence are revealed. Persons offering and receiving pastoral care include the patient, the community of faith, family, friends, neighbors, other patients, and health-care teams.

Those offering pastoral care empathize with suffering patients and share in the wounds of their lives. They listen as patients express their feelings of guilt, fear, doubt, loneliness, hurt, and anger. They can provide resources for reconciliation and wholeness and assist persons in reactivating broken or idle relationships with God and with others. They can provide comfort by pointing to sources of strength, hope, and wholeness, especially reading Scriptures and prayer.

This same pastoral care must be provided to the family and friends of those who are suffering and dying. They too, must have an opportunity to share their feelings of guilt, hurt, anger, fear, and grief. Grieving persons need to be reminded that their feelings are normal human responses that need not cause embarrassment or guilt. Families have long-established patterns of relationships and attention to the entire family unit must be incorporated into pastoral care. Religious, cultural, and personal differences among family and friends must be considered with special sensitivity.

Health care workers also need pastoral care. Doctors and, especially, support staff have intimate contact with dying persons in ways experienced by few others. They live in the tension of giving compassionate care to patients while maintaining professional detachment. Pastoral care for health-care workers means helping them take loving care of themselves as well as their patients.

Pastors and chaplains are called especially to sustain the spiritual growth of patients, families, and health-care personnel. They bear witness to God's grace with words of comfort and salvation. They provide nurture by reading the Scriptures with patients and loved ones; by Holy Communion; by the laying on of hands; and by prayers of repentance, reconciliation, and intercession. They provide comfort and grace with rituals of prayer or anointing with oil after miscarriage, or after a death in a hospital, nursing home, or hospice. They develop rituals in connection with a diagnosis of terminal illness, of welcome to a hospice or nursing home, or of return to a local congregation by persons who have been absent for treatment or who have been in the care of a loved one.

In all these ways, pastoral-care givers and the community of faith are open to God's presence in the midst of pain and suffering, in order to engender hope, and to enable the people of God to live and die in faith and in holiness. They assist persons in coming to peace with themselves and others as they accept the realization that death is not always an enemy. They affirm that there is only one possible ending to the Christian story. Regardless of the tragedies and triumphs, the youthfulness or the age, the valleys of doubt and despair, the suffering and loss, and the soaring as things turn out all right—we come to the only one certain end: "I am the resurrection and the life. Those who believe in me, though they die, will live, and every one who lives and believes in me shall never die" (John 11:25-26, NRSV).

In addition to offering comfort and hope, pastoral-care givers are trained to help patients understand their illness and can assist families in understanding and coming to grips with information provided by medical personnel. Pastoral-care givers are especially needed when illness is terminal and neither patients nor family members are able to discuss this reality freely.

The complexity of treatment options and requests by physicians for patient and family involvement in life-prolonging decisions require good communication. Pastoral-care givers can bring insights rooted in Christian convictions and Christian hope into the decision-making process. If advance directives for treatment, often called "living wills," or "durable powers of attorney" are contemplated or are being interpreted, the pastoral-care givers can offer support and guidance to those involved in decision-making. They can facilitate discussion of treatment options, including home and hospice care.

Decisions concerning faithful care for the suffering and the dying are always made in a social context that includes laws, policies, and practices of legislative bodies, public agencies and institutions, and the social consensus that supports them. The social context of dying affects individual decisions concerning treatment and care and even the acceptance of death. Therefore, pastoral-care givers must be attentive to the social situations and policies that affect the care of the suffering and dying and must interpret these to patients and family members in the context of Christian affirmations of faithful care.

### United Methodist Response

To insure faithful care for the suffering and dying it is recommended that United Methodists:

1. Acknowledge dying as part of human existence, without romanticizing it. In dying, as in living, mercy and justice must shape our corporate response to human need and vulnerability.

2. Accept relief of suffering as a goal for care of dying persons rather than focusing primarily on prolonging life. Pain control and comfort-giving measures are essentials in our care of those who are suffering.

3. Educate and equip Christians to consider treatments for the suffering and the dying in the context of Christian affirmations of God's providence and hope. This should be done especially through preaching and adult Christian education programs addressing these issues.

4. Train pastors and pastoral-care givers in the issues of bioethics as well as in the techniques of compassionate companionship with those who are suffering and dying.

5. Acknowledge, in our Christian witness and pastoral care, the diverse social, economic, political, cultural, religious and ethnic contexts around the world where United Methodists care for the dying.

ADOPTED 2004
READOPTED 2008
RESOLUTION #115, 2004 *BOOK OF RESOLUTIONS*

*See* Social Principles, ¶¶ 161M and 162V.

## 3206. Protecting Children from Mercury-Containing Drugs

Theological Foundation: Mark 10:13-16 says, "People were bringing little children to him in order that he might touch them; and the disciples spoke sternly to them. But when Jesus saw this, he was indignant and said to them, 'Let the little children come to me; do not stop them; for it is to such as these that the kingdom of God belongs. Truly I tell you, whoever does not receive the kingdom of God as a little child will never enter it.' And he took them up in his arms, laid his hands on them, and blessed them."

Policy Base: The United Methodist Social Principles, ¶ 162J ("Alcohol and Other Drugs"), ¶ 162T ("Right to Health Care")

WHEREAS, as demonstrated in the Social Principles, The United Methodist Church affirms[1]:

". . . wise policies relating to the availability of potentially beneficial or potentially damaging prescription and over-the-counter drugs; we urge that complete information about their use and misuse be readily available to both doctor and patient"; and

WHEREAS, Thimerosal (synonyms include: Thiomseral, Merthiolate, Thimerasol) is a severely toxic, antiquated, organic mercury compound[2] (approximately 50 percent mercury by weight) that has been added to some vaccines and pharmaceutical products since the 1930s[3]; and

---

1. *The Book of Discipline of The United Methodist Church, 2004* , ¶ 162J, p. 108.

2. Pfab R, Muckter H, Roider G, Zilker T. Clinical course of severe poisoning with thiomersal. J Toxicol Clin Toxicol. 1996;34(4):453-60.

Axton JH. Six cases of poisoning after a parenteral organic mercurial compound (Merthiolate). Postgrad Med J. 1972 Jul;48(561):417-21.

Mercury poisoning in child treated with aqueous merthiolate. Md State Med J. 1983 Jul;32(7):523.

Fagan DG, Pritchard JS, Clarkson TW, Greenwood MR. Organ mercury levels in infants with omphaloceles treated with organic mercurial antiseptic. Arch Dis Child. 1977 Dec;52(12):962-4.

Rohyans J, Walson PD, Wood GA, MacDonald WA. Mercury toxicity following merthiolate ear irrigations. J Pediatr. 1984 Feb;104(2):311-3.

Nascimento LO, Lorenzi Filho G, Rocha Ados S. Lethal mercury poisoning due to ingestion of merthiolate. Rev Hosp Clin Fac Med Sao Paulo. 1990 Sep-Oct;45(5):216-8.

James SJ, Slikker W 3rd, Melnyk S, New E, Pogribna M, Jernigan S. Thimerosal neurotoxicity is associated with glutathione depletion: protection with glutathione precursors. Neurotoxicology. 2005 Jan;26(1):1-8.

Hornig M, Chian D, Lipkin WI. Neurotoxic effects of postnatal thimerosal are mouse strain dependent. Mol Psychiatry. 2004 Sep;9(9):833-45.

Ohno H, Doi R, Kashima Y, Murae S, Kizaki T, Hitomi Y, Nakano N, Harada M. Wide use of merthiolate may cause mercury poisoning in Mexico. Bull Environ Contam Toxicol 2004;73:777-80.

3. Ball LK, Ball R, Pratt RD. An assessment of thimerosal use in childhood vaccines. Pediatrics. 2001 May;107(5):1147-54.

WHEREAS, numerous peer-reviewed scientific/medical studies published over many decades, at least since the 1930s, have recommended removing or restricting the use of Thimerosol in medicinal products and have demonstrated its significant toxicity[4]; and

4. Ellis FA. The sensitizing factor in merthiolate. J Allergy 1947;18:212-13.

Ellis published in 1947, " . . . it may be dangerous to inject a serum containing merthiolate into a patient sensitive to merthiolate."

Nelson EA, Gottshall RY. Enhanced toxicity for mice of pertussis vaccines when preserved with Merthiolate. Appl Microbiol. 1967 May;15(3):590-3.

Nelson and Gottshall published in 1967, "Pertussis vaccines preserved with 0.01% Merthiolate are more toxic for mice than unpreserved vaccines prepared from the same parent concentrate and containing the same number of organisms . . . An increase in mortality was observed when Merthiolate was injected separately, before or after an unpreserved suspension of pertussis vaccine."

Fagan DG, Pritchard JS, Clarkson TW, Greenwood MR. Organ mercury levels in infants with omphaloceles treated with organic mercurial antiseptic. Arch Dis Child. 1977 Dec;52(12):962-4.

Fagan et al. published in 1977, "Organic mercurial antiseptics should be heavily restricted or withdrawn from hospital use, as the fact that mercury readily penetrates intact membranes and is highly toxic seems to have been forgotten. Equally effective and far less toxic broad-spectrum antifungal and antibacterial...antiseptics are currently available."

Heyworth MF, Truelove SC. Problems associated with the use of merthiolate as a preservative in anti-lymphocytic globulin. Toxicology. 1979 Mar-Apr;12(3):325-33.

Heyworth and Truelove published in 1979, "For many years, merthiolate has been known to have anti-microbial activity. When it was first introduced as an anti-microbial preservative, little information about the fundamental biological effects of organic mercury compounds was available. We would like to suggest that merthiolate should now be regarded as an inappropriate preservative for anti-lymphocytic globulin preparations and other materials which are indented for administration to human subjects."

Forstrom L, Hannuksela M, Kousa M, Lehmuskallio E. Merthiolate hypersensitivity and vaccination. Contact Dermatitis. 1980 Jun;6(4):241-5.

Forstrom et al. published in 1980, " . . . reactions can be expected in such a high percentage of merthiolate-sensitive persons that merthiolate in vaccines should be replaced by another antibacterial agent."

Kravchenko AT, Dzagurov SG, Chervonskaia GP. Evaluation of the toxic action of prophylactic and therapeutic preparations on cell cultures. III. The detection of toxic properties in medical biological preparations by the degree of cell damage in the L132 continuous cell line. Zh Mikrobiol Epidemiol Immunobiol. 1983 Mar;(3):87-92.

Kravchenko et al. published in 1983, "Thus thimerosal, commonly used as preservative, has been found not only to render its primary toxic effect, but also capable of changing the properties of cells. This fact suggests that the use of thimerosal for the preservation of medical biological preparations, especially those intended for children, is inadmissible."

Cox NH, Forsyth A. Thiomersal allergy and vaccination reactions. Contact Dermatitis. 1988 Apr;18(4):229-33.

Cox and Forsyth published in 1988, "However, individual cases of severe reactions to thiomersal demonstrate a need for vaccines with an alternative preservative."

Seal D, Ficker L, Wright P, Andrews V. The case against thiomersal. Lancet. 1991 Aug 3;338(8762):315-6.

Seal et al. published in 1991, "Thimerosal is a weak antibacterial agent that is rapidly broken down to products, including ethylmercury residues, which are neurotoxic. Its role as a preservative in vaccines has been questioned, and the pharmaceutical industry itself considers its use as historical."

WHEREAS, the Food and Drug Administration (FDA) recommended, in 1982, that Thimerosal be banned from topical over-the-counter products, and the American Academy of Pediatrics (AAP) and United States Public Health Service called for its removal from all vaccines in July of 1999, as did the Institute of Medicine of the United States National Academy of Sciences in 2001[5]; and

WHEREAS, Thimerosol (mercury) still remains in some vaccines (including childhood vaccines and the flu shot) and many other pharmaceutical products in the US, and the mercury content of vaccines manufactured for use in developing nations has not been reduced,[6] and in both cases, remains well in excess of Federal Safety Guidelines; and

WHEREAS, the Environmental Protection Agency of the State of California officially declared that Thimerosol is a developmental toxin, meaning that it can cause birth defects, low birth weight, biological dysfunctions, or psychological or behavior deficits that become manifest as the child grows, and that maternal exposure during pregnancy can disrupt the development or even cause the death of the fetus[8] (The State of California has banned administration of Thimerosol-containing vaccines to children and pregnant women[8]); and

Van't Veen AJ. Vaccines without thiomersal: why so necessary, why so long coming? Drugs. 2001;61(5):565-72.

Van't Veen published in 2001, "The very low thiomersal concentrations in pharmacological and biological products are relatively non-toxic, but probably not in utero and during the first 6 months of life. The developing brain of the fetus is most susceptible to thiomersal and, therefore, women of childbearing age, in particular, should not receive thiomersal-containing products."

Schumm WR, Reppert EJ, Jurich AP, Bollman SR, Webb FJ, Castelo CS, Stever JC, Sanders D, Bonjour GN, Crow JR, Fink CJ, Lash JF, Brown BF, Hall CA, Owens BL, Krehbiel M, Deng LY, Kaufman M. Self-reported changes in subjective health and anthrax vaccination as reported by over 900 Persian Gulf War era veterans. Psychol Rep. 2002 Apr;90(2):639-53.

Schumm et al. published in 2002, "We also recommend that safer alternatives to thimerosal (a mercury sodium salt, 50% mercury) be used to preserve all vaccines."

5. Subcommittee on Human Rights and Wellness, Government Reform Committee. Mercury in Medicine Report. Washington, DC: Congressional Record, May 21, 2003:E1011-30.

6. http://www.rollingstone.com/politics/story/7395411/deadly_immunity/ "Even more alarming, the government continues to ship vaccines preserved with thimerosal to developing countries—some of which are now experiencing a sudden explosion in autism rates."

7. California Environmental Protection Agency – Office of Environmental Health Hazard Assessment. Response to the petition of Bayer Corporation for clarification of the Proposition 65 listing of "Mercury and Mercury Compounds" as chemicals known to cause reproductive toxicity. February 2004.

8. California Legislation – Bill AB2943. CHAPTER 837. An act to add Article 9 (commencing with Section 124172) to Chapter 3 of Part 2 of Division 106 of the Health and Safety Code, relating to vaccinations. Approved by Governor September 28, 2004. Filed with Secretary of State September 28, 2004. This bill, with certain exemptions, would prohibit, on and after July 1, 2006, a person who is knowingly pregnant or who is under 3 years of age from being vaccinated with a mercury-containing vaccine or injected with a mercury-containing product that

WHEREAS, the public is given limited opportunity of informed consent in regard to these known risks of mercury exposure incurred through mandated injections and from many other pharmaceutical products, both prescription and over-the-counter, including topical antiseptic solutions and antiseptic ointments for treating cuts, nasal sprays, eye solutions, vaginal spermicides, diaper rash treatments, and perhaps most importantly, as a preservative in vaccines and other injectable biological products, including immune globulin preparations; and

WHEREAS, while vaccines are promoted for the prevention of diseases, it is also important to guard against any unintentional harm through their administration. It is a violation of human life to inject poison into any being, especially a pregnant woman or a newborn baby; and

WHEREAS, there are some presently marketed vaccines and pharmaceutical products that use safe, effective, and economical methods to eliminate the need for Thimerosal (mercury) preservatives, thereby increasing the safety of vaccines[9];

*Therefore, be it resolved,* that The United Methodist Church support all efforts to protect the public, especially children, from mercury-containing drugs by calling on the World Health Organization, international and national health officials/agencies, including the US Secretary of Health and Human Services, the US Food and Drug Administration and the US Centers for Disease Control and Prevention to:

- immediately prioritize mercury-free stocks of vaccines and other pharmaceutical products for pregnant women, newborn infants and children;
- provide "the opportunity of informed consent" and promote product education to individuals about mercury exposure through their pharmaceutical products or vaccines, detailing the known risks of toxicity and Federal Safety Guidelines for exposure to mercury; and

contains more than a specified amount of mercury. The bill would require notice to be given to the Legislature and interested parties regarding any exemptions and requests for exemptions.

9. www.fda.gov/CBER/vaccine/thimerosal.htm "While the use of mercury-containing preservatives has declined in recent years with the development of new products formulated with alternative or no preservatives, thimerosal has been used in some immune globulin preparations, anti-venins, skin test antigens, and ophthalmic and nasal products, in addition to certain vaccines."

- ban the presence of any mercury compound in pharmaceutical products or vaccines, prescribed or over-the-counter.

*And be it further resolved,* that, until mercury is banned from medicine, the medical missions, hospitals, clinics and ministries of The United Methodist Church strongly encourage use of mercury-free vaccines over mercury-containing ones. Acknowledging the difficulties in some contexts, we strongly urge that other organizations who are responsible for immunization efforts to prevent disease such as the Global Alliance for Vaccines and Immunizations, United Nations Children's Fund (UNICEF), Rotary International, the Bill and Melinda Gates Foundation, as well as any other organization from which vaccines are purchased, join The United Methodist Church in the educating the public about and advocating for mercury-free drugs and vaccines.

**ADOPTED 2008**

*See* Social Principles, ¶ 162C and V.

## 3207. Quality in United Methodist Health Care

I was a stranger and you invited me in; I needed clothes and you clothed me; I was sick and you cared for me (Matthew 25: 35-36).

"There was scarcely any form of social advance and improvement in which he (Wesley) was not interested—establishing societies and institutions, workshops, credit unions, children's homes and schools, homes for the aged, nurses training, and hospitals. He believed that a satisfying spiritual experience could not survive apart from enthusiasm for service to mankind." (Parkinson, *History of the Board of Hospitals and Homes*)

Instead, whoever wants to become great among you must be your servant, and whoever wants to be first must be your slave . . . just as the Son of Man did not come to be served but to serve (Matthew 20:26-28).

"The servant-leader is servant first. It begins with the natural feeling that one wants to serve. Then conscious choice brings one to aspire to lead. The best test is: do those served grow as persons? Do they, while being served, become healthier, wiser, freer, more autonomous, more likely themselves to become servants? And, what is the effect on the least privileged in society? Will they benefit or, at least, not be further deprived?" (Greenleaf, *The Servant Leader*)

WHEREAS, Christ demonstrated a concern for healing of body, mind, and soul throughout his ministry; and

WHEREAS, John Wesley repeatedly demonstrated his concern for health and social ministry; and

WHEREAS, The United Methodist Church has a nearly 250-year history of service in hospitals and ministries to older adults, children, youth, and families. Today there are over 400 such United Methodist-related health and welfare organizations; and

WHEREAS, there is a growing recognition in scientific and medical literature of the role of faith in wellness and healing; and

WHEREAS, numerous studies have documented that not-for-profit health care organizations provide higher-quality care; and

WHEREAS, there is a growing recognition in management literature of the application of Christian principles in management and leadership; and

WHEREAS, the United Methodist Association of Health and Welfare Ministries has a long tradition of promoting quality service, Christian leadership, and connection with annual conferences and local churches;

*Therefore,* The United Methodist Church calls upon:

A. health-care providers and government agencies to:

    1) devote needed resources to the promotion of quality health care;

    2) engage in programs of continuous quality improvement; and

    3) recognize the role of faith in health and wellness.

B. United Methodist–related health and welfare institutions to:

    1) maintain membership and participation in the United Methodist Association of Health and Welfare Ministries (¶ 633.4.b (31)*);

    2) participate in EAGLE accreditation (¶ 633.4.b (29)*);

    3) suggest that annual conferences address participation in these programs when updating covenant relationship statements (¶ 633.4.b (27)*); and

    4) recruit and select paid and volunteer leadership which recognizes and values the church connection and the role of faith in health and wholeness.

C. Annual conference and local churches to:

    1) encourage or require membership in the United Methodist Association of Health and Welfare Ministries when updating covenant relationship statements (¶ 633.4.b (27)*);

* All citations are from *The Book of Discipline of The United Methodist Church, 2008.*

2) encourage or require participation in EAGLE accreditation when updating covenant relationship statements (¶ 633.4.b (29)*); and

3) encourage awareness and use of United Methodist–related Health and Welfare Ministries (¶ 633.4.b (31)*).

* All citations are from *The Book of Discipline of The United Methodist Church, 2008.*

**ADOPTED 2008**

*See* Social Principles, ¶ 162V.

### 3208. United Methodist Response to Hospital Mergers

WHEREAS, a crisis in health care is occurring in communities across the United States because of the ever-increasing number of hospital mergers, and

WHEREAS, such mergers often put the availability of AIDS prevention information, fertility services, artificial insemination, tubal ligations, vasectomies, condom distribution, contraceptive medication and devices, "morning after" pills, and abortion services at risk; and

WHEREAS, such mergers can result in the denial of certain types of end-of-life health care; and

WHEREAS, the effect of these mergers is most severe in poorer communities that have limited health care options to begin with; and

WHEREAS, these mergers are usually completed, often with the assistance of public money, before the public is even aware they are happening or what the consequences will be;

*Therefore, be it resolved,* that the General Board of Church and Society and the Women's Division work to alert their constituencies concerning this crisis in reproductive and end-of-life health care, and

*Be it further resolved,* that the General Board of Church and Society and the Women's Division expand their health and wholeness public policy advocacy to include this critical issue of reproductive and end-of-life health care; and

*Be it further resolved,* that the General Board of Church and Society and the Women's Division work in cooperation with appropriate community groups to make resource materials available to local churches; such materials to include briefing papers, articles, action alerts, sample sermons, and information on gaining legal intervention when necessary to deal with the crisis of increasingly limited reproductive and end-of-life health care in their communities.

ADOPTED 2000<br>
READOPTED 2008<br>
RESOLUTION #112, 2004 *BOOK OF RESOLUTIONS*<br>
RESOLUTION #102, 2000 *BOOK OF RESOLUTIONS*

*See* Social Principles, ¶ 162V.

# HISPANIC AMERICANS

## 3221. Rio Grande Conference

WHEREAS, the Hispanic population continues to grow in the Southwest, especially in the states of Texas and New Mexico; and

WHEREAS, the Hispanic people continues to struggle as a marginalized people in a process of cultural, political, economic, social and educational transition; and

WHEREAS, the Hispanic people are in need of spiritual support in this transitional process to facilitate the development of its spiritual life so it will be a means to a complete and total transformation; and

WHEREAS, the Rio Grande Conference, the only Hispanic annual conference of The United Methodist Church, historically and traditionally exists to minister with and to the Hispanic people of Texas and New Mexico; and

WHEREAS, the Rio Grande Conference has provided leadership and resources as part of its connectional responsibilities to all levels of The United Methodist Church,

*Therefore,* General Conference is committed to a real spirit of accompaniment with the Rio Grande Conference as an extension of its mission and ministry with the Hispanic people, and this commitment is expressed in the following ways:

1. acknowledging the historic tradition of the Rio Grande Annual Conference as the only Hispanic conference of The United Methodist Church ministering to the Hispanic people;

2. affirming the ministry of the Rio Grande Conference as collaborators with The United Methodist Church in mission with and to the Hispanic people;

3. supporting the ministry of the Rio Grande Conference in its commitment to the Hispanic people in Texas and New Mexico with resources from general agencies of The United Methodist Church for a continued development of the leadership and resources appropriate to minister to Hispanics in those states.

ADOPTED 2000
READOPTED 2008
RESOLUTION #28, 2004 *BOOK OF RESOLUTIONS*
RESOLUTION #23, 2000 *BOOK OF RESOLUTIONS*

*See* Social Principles, ¶¶ 161 and 162.

### 3222. Annual Conference Strategic, Comprehensive Plans for Hispanic/Latino-Latina Ministries

WHEREAS, God calls us to proclaim God's mighty acts (1 Peter 2:9) and to be good stewards of God's manifold grace, serving one another with whatever gift each has received (1 Peter 4:10), and to organize ourselves for the work of ministry (Ephesians 4:7-13); and

WHEREAS, our United Methodist heritage integrates missional action with organizational support; and

WHEREAS, *The Book of Discipline, 2004* declares that "the mission of the Church is to make disciples of Jesus Christ by proclaiming the good news of God's grace and thus seeking the fulfillment of God's reign and realm in the world" (¶ 121), and that "each annual conference is responsible to focus and guide the mission and ministry of The United Methodist Church within its boundaries by envisioning the ministries necessary to live out the mission of the church in and through the annual conference; providing encouragement, coordination, and support for the ministries of nurture, outreach, and witness in districts and congregations for the transformation of the world; . . . developing and strengthening ethnic ministries, including ethnic local churches and concerns. . . . " (¶ 607); and

WHEREAS, according to the 2006 United States census analysis, nearly 67 million people of Hispanic origin (who may be of any race) would be added to the nation's population between 2000 and 2050. Their numbers are projected to grow from 35.6 million to 102.6 million, an increase of 188 percent. Their share of the nation's population would nearly double, from 12.6 percent to 24.4 percent. The US is the third largest Latino country in the world and Hispanics remain the largest minority group, with 44.3 million on July 1, 2006—14.8 percent of the total population. With a 3.4 percent increase between July 1, 2005, and July 1, 2006, Hispanics are the fastest-growing minority group; and

WHEREAS, these figures represent an undercount and do not reflect information about undocumented persons; and

WHEREAS, according to the General Board of Global Ministries Office of Research's analysis of the census data, every annual conference of The United Methodist Church in the United States has within its boundaries a growing Hispanic/Latino-Latina population; and

WHEREAS, for three quadrennia the General Conference has approved the National Plan for Hispanic/Latino-Latina Ministry as a mission initiative of the whole church, and it is a comprehensive plan of evangelization with Hispanic/Latino-Latina communities by the whole church; and

WHEREAS, in direct relationship to the implementation of the National Plan for Hispanic/Latino-Latina Ministry, 700 faith communities have been established in 52 conferences, 1,000 lay missioners have been equipped and deployed; 200 pastor mentors; 100 new Hispanic/Latino-Latina congregations have been started in 35 conferences; 100 existing Hispanic/Latino-Latina churches in 35 conferences have been strengthened; and 1,000 outreach ministries have been established in 52 conferences; 30 annual conferences have been developing a comprehensive plan; more than 50 Portuguese-speaking leaders have been trained; 5 new Portuguese-speaking leaders had been trained; 50 new consultants already trained; more than 600 non Hispanic/Latino leaders trained through the convocations; and

WHEREAS, according to the Office of the National Plan for Hispanic/Latino-Latina Ministry's estimates, the Hispanic/Latino-Latina membership in The United Methodist Church has increased by 40 percent from 2004 to 2008; and

WHEREAS, according to the Office of the National Plan for Hispanic/Latino-Latina Ministry's estimates, Hispanic/Latino-Latina persons represent less than 1 percent of the total membership of The United Methodist Church and Hispanic/Latino-Latina congregations represent approximately 1 percent of all United Methodist chartered churches; and

WHEREAS, these figures represent an undercount due to difficulties in reporting the number of Hispanic/Latino-Latina members in multicultural churches and non-Hispanic/Latino-Latina congregations, and the number of Hispanic/Latino-Latina congregations sharing facilities with other ethnic and cultural churches; and due to difficulties in the lack of reports from some Hispanic/Latino Latina congregations; and

WHEREAS, in spite of the National Plan for Hispanic/Latino-Latina Ministry and other missional efforts, advances and success in reaching the people group called Hispanic/Latino-Latina and the increased presence of Hispanic/Latino-Latina persons in the United Methodist connectional system, the people group in the United States called Hispanic/Latino-Latina represents a huge mission field,

*Therefore, be it resolved,* that by December 31, 2011, every annual conference in the United States shall develop a strategic, comprehensive plan for Hispanic/Latino-Latina ministries within its boundaries, and this plan will include, but not be limited to, socioeconomic, cultural, and religious analysis of the Hispanic/Latino-Latina communities that will be served; and strategies to strengthen existing Hispanic/Latino-Latina ministries and congregations, to start new ministries and congregations, to identify, equip, and deploy clergy and laity leaders, and to identify and deploy material and financial resources; and

*Be it further resolved,* that the Council of Bishops, the National Plan for Hispanic/Latino-Latina Ministry, the General Board of Discipleship and the General Board of Global Ministries ensure that the conference comprehensive plans are in place by the indicated date and provide support and consultation in the development of the plans.

ADOPTED 2004
REVISED AND READOPTED 2008
RESOLUTION #29, 2004 *BOOK OF RESOLUTIONS*

*See* Social Principles, ¶¶ 161 and 162.


# HIV AND AIDS


## 3241. A Covenant to Care: Recognizing and Responding to the Many Faces of AIDS in the USA

United Methodists have been in ministry since the beginning of the of the HIV/AIDS pandemic. They have followed the way of healing, ministry, hospitality, and service shown by Jesus Christ. According to the Gospel of Luke (4:16-21), Jesus identified himself and his task with that of the servant Lord, the one who was sent to bring good tidings to the afflicted, hope to the brokenhearted, liberty to the captives, and comfort to all who mourn, giving them the oil of gladness and the mantle of praise instead of a faint spirit (Isaiah 61:1-3). God's Word calls us to a ministry of healing, a ministry that understands healing not only in physiological terms but also as wholeness of spiritual, mental, physical, and social being.

## The Context of Caring Ministry in the United States

In recent years, AIDS in the United States has received less media attention, but that does not mean the disease has gone away. Though medical drugs can prolong the life of people who have been infected, there is no cure for AIDS. Not only must our commitment to ministry continue, but it must also expand, particularly in the area of prevention education.

HIV/AIDS affects and infects a broad cross-section of people in the United States and Puerto Rico: all ages, all races, both sexes, all sexual orientations. The cumulative number of AIDS cases reported to Centers for Disease Control (CDC) through December 2001 is 816,149. Adult and adolescent AIDS cases total 807,074 with 666,026 males and 141,048 females.[1]

In the early 1980s, most people with AIDS were gay white men. Overall incidences of new cases of AIDS increased rapidly through the 1980s, peaked in the early 1990s, and then declined. However, new cases of AIDS among African Americans increased. By 1996, more cases of AIDS were reported among African Americans than any other racial/ethnic population. The number of people diagnosed with AIDS has also increased among Hispanics, Asians/Pacific Islanders, and Native Americans/Alaska Natives.[2] In 2001, the rate of adult/adolescent AIDS cases per 100,000 population was 76.3 among African Americans, 28.0 among Hispanics, 11.7 among Native Americans/Alaska Natives, 7.9 among whites, and 4.8 among Asians/Pacific Islanders.[3] Though

1. Centers for Disease Control and Prevention (CDC). *HIV/Aids Surveillance Report 2001,* 13, no. 2:1-44. http://www.cdc.gov/hiv/stats/hasr1302.htm (31 January 2003).

2. " HIV and Aids-United States, 1981-2000," Morbity and Mortality Weekly Report, 50, no. 21 (June 01, 2001): 430-4. http://www.cdc.gov/mmwr/preview/mmwrhtml/mm5021a2.htm (31 January 2003).

3. National Institute of Allergy and Infectious Diseases (NIAID), Fact Sheet: HIV Statistics (December 2002). http://www.niaid.nih.gov/factsheets/aidsstat.htm (31 January 2003).

national surveillance data does not record the hearing status of people with HIV/AIDS, the Department of Health and Human Services believes that deaf and hard of hearing people have been disproportionately infected with HIV.[4]

As of December 2001, according to CDC estimates, 850,000 to 950,000 people in the United States were infected with HIV. One-quarter of these were unaware of their status! Approximately 40,000 new HIV infections occur each year: about 70 percent men and 30 percent women. Of these newly infected people, half are younger than 25. Almost half of the men are African American, 30 percent are white, 20 percent are Hispanic. Among newly infected women, approximately 64 percent are African American, 18 percent are white, and 18 percent are Hispanic. A small percentage of men and women are part of other racial/ethnic groups.[5] No longer is HIV a disease of white gay men or of the east and west coast; it has not been for more than a decade. In 2001, 39 percent of persons with AIDS were living in the South, 29 percent in the Northeast, 19 percent in the West, 10 percent in the Midwest, and 3 percent in the US territories.[6]

United Methodist churches, districts, and conferences can help to stop the spread of HIV/AIDS by providing sound, comprehensive, age-appropriate preventive education, including information that abstinence from sex and injection drug use is the safest way to prevent HIV/AIDS. In addition, the church can provide grounding in Christian values, something that cannot be done in public schools or in governmental publications on HIV/AIDS.

Youth and Young Adults: AIDS is increasingly affecting and infecting our next generation of leaders, particularly among racial and ethnic minorities. In the United States, HIV is the fifth leading cause of death for people between the ages of 25 and 44. Among African American men in this age group, HIV has been the leading cause of death since 1991. In 1999, among African American women, 25 to 44 years old, HIV was the third leading cause of death. Many of these young adults were infected in their teens and early twenties. At least

4. Department of Health and Human Services (HRSA) "Programs: The Deaf and Hard of Hearing and HIV/AIDS." http://hab.hrsa.gov/programs/factsheets/deaffact.htm (4 March 2003).
    5. National Institute of Allergy and Infectious Diseases (NIAID), Fact Sheet: HIV Statistics (December 2002). http://www.niaid.nih.gov/factsheets/aidsstat.htm (31 January 2003).
    6. Centers for Disease Control and Prevention, "US HIV and AIDS Cases Reported Through December 2001 Year-End Report," Surveillance Report, 13, No. 2. http://www.cdc.gov/hiv/stats/hasr1302/commentary.htm (31 January 2003).

half of all new HIV infections are estimated to be among people under 25 with the majority of infections occurring through sexual contact.[7]

Racial and Ethnic Minorities: African Americans, Hispanics and Native Americans have been disproportionately infected with HIV/AIDS. Representing only an estimated 12 percent of the total US population, African Americans make up almost 38 percent of all AIDS cases reported in the country. Almost 63 percent of all women reported with AIDS were African American.[8]

It is critical to prevent patterns of risky behaviors that may lead to HIV infection before they start. Clear communications between parents and their children about sex, drugs, and AIDS is an important step. Church, school, and community-based prevention education is another step. Youth and young adults must be actively involved in this process, including peer education.

The large and growing Hispanic population in the United States is also heavily affected by HIV/AIDS. In 2000, Hispanics represented 13 percent of the US population (including residents of Puerto Rico) but accounted for 19 percent of the total number of new cases of AIDS reported that year.[9]

Women: AIDS among women has been mostly "an invisible epidemic" even though women have been affected and infected since the beginning. AIDS has increased most dramatically among women of color. African American and Hispanic women together represent less than 25 percent of all women in the United States, yet account for more than 75 percent of reported cases of AIDS. In 2000, African American and Hispanic women represented an even greater proportion (80 percent) of cases of AIDS reported in women.[10] Of newly infected women in 2001, approximately 64 percent were African American and 18 percent were Hispanic.[11] In 2000, 38 percent of women reported with AIDS were infected through sexual contact with HIV-positive men while injection drug use accounted for 25 percent of cases. In

7. Centers for Disease Control and Prevention, "Young People at Risk: HIV/AIDS Among America's Youth" http://www.cdc.gov/hiv/pubs/facts/youth.htm (31 January 2003).

8. Centers for Disease Control and Prevention, "HIV/AIDS among African Americans." http://www.cdc.gov/hiv/pubs/facts/afam.htm (31 January 2003).

9. Centers for Disease Control and Prevention, "HIV/AIDS among Hispanics in the United States." http://www.cdc.gov/hiv/pubs/facts/hispanics.htm (31 January 2003).

10. Centers for Disease Control and Prevention, "HIV/AIDS among US Women," 2002. www.cdc.gov/hiv/pubs/facts/women.httm) (31 January 2003).

11. Centers for Disease Control and Prevention, "HIV Prevention Strategic Plan Through 2005." January 2001. http://www.cdc.gov/nchstp/od/hiv_plan/default.htm (31 January 2003).

addition to the direct risks associated with drug injections (sharing needles), drug use is also fueling the heterosexual spread of the epidemic. A significant proportion of women infected sexually were infected by injection drug-using men. Reducing the toll of the epidemic among women will require efforts to combat substance abuse and reduce HIV risk behaviors.[12]

People who are Deaf, Late-Deafened, and Hard of Hearing: In the United States, as many as 40,000 deaf and hard-of-hearing individuals are believed to be living with HIV disease.[13] Health experts suspect that HIV prevalence in the deaf community may be higher than in the hearing community, but comprehensive data is lacking. An indicator is that one in seven deaf people has a history of substance abuse, compared with one in ten hearing people.[14] Research has also shown that deaf high school students have much less knowledge about HIV transmission than their hearing counterparts. Because 75 percent of the culturally deaf community uses American Sign Language (ASL) as their primary means of communication, ASL is the most effective means of communication of HIV/AIDS information for this group; but the message must be clear. At a United Methodist HIV/AIDS event in 2002, a speaker noted that deaf people have died and others have delayed medical treatment because they believed themselves healthy when they saw the sign for "HIV" and "positive" conveyed to them in ASL. They thought HIV positive meant "good result" and did not realize that they were being told they were infected.[15] It also should be noted that over 98 percent of those with hearing loss, including many elderly people, do not know sign language. In prevention education contexts, assistive listening systems and devices, such as "pocket talkers," should be used to aid those who are hard of hearing.

Older Adults: The number of those 50 and older infected with HIV is increasing at twice the rate of those under 50, according to experts on aging at Baylor College of Medicine in Houston who are targeting

12. Centers for Disease Control and Prevention, "HIV/AIDS among Hispanics in the United States," 2002. http://www.cdc.gov/hiv/pubs/facts/hispanics.htm (31 January 2003).

13. Office of HIV/AIDS Policy. Conference proceedings: National Meeting on the Deaf and Hard of Hearing. Washington, DC: US Department of Health and Human Services; 2000.

14. Peinkoffer JR. HIV education for the deaf, a vulnerable minority. Public Health Rep. 1994;109:390-6.

15. Melissa Lauber, "Silence on HIV/AIDS Spells Death, Church Leaders Warn," December 10, 2002. http://gbgm-umc.org/health/aids/dcconference.cfm (5 March 2003).

older Americans for safer sex education.[16] The myth that older people are sexually inactive has produced dreaded consequences. The most prevalent behavior risks for older adults are multiple sexual partners and having a partner with risk behavior. Since they are not worried about pregnancy, older couples are less likely to use condoms and, therefore, increase their risk of infection. Most older people mistakenly believe that if they are heterosexual and don't inject drugs, they cannot get AIDS. Reaching this group of people with HIV prevention messages means exploring avenues such as church, widows' support groups at senior centers, and Golden Age Clubs at community centers and churches.

Drug-Associated HIV Transmission: Since the epidemic began, injection drug use (IDU) has accounted for more than one-third (36 percent) of AIDS cases in the US Racial and ethnic minorities in the US are most heavily affected by IDU-associated AIDS. In 2000, IDU-associated AIDS accounted for 26 percent of all cases among African Americans and 31 percent among Hispanic adults and adolescents, compared with 19 percent of all cases among white adults/adolescents. Noninjection drugs such as cocaine also contribute to the spread of the epidemic when users trade sex for drugs or money, or when they engage in risky sexual behavior that they might not engage in when sober.

HIV prevention and treatment, substance abuse prevention, and sexually transmitted disease treatment and prevention services must be better integrated to take advantage of the multiple opportunities for intervention—first, to help uninfected people stay that way; second, to help infected people stay healthy; and third, to help infected individuals initiate and sustain behaviors that will keep themselves safe and prevent transmission to others.[17]

## The Challenge for Ministry

Across the United States, in churches large and small, pastors and laity have asked, "What can my church do?" Churches can build on

16. Centers for Disease Control and Prevention, *CDC HIV/STD/TB Prevention News Update* (November 11, 2002) citing Carolyn Poirot, "Risk of AIDS Rising for Older Adults" *Star-Telegram* (November 6, 2002) http://lists.cdcnpin.org/pipermail/prevention-news/2002-November/000353.html (31 January 2003).

17. Centers for Disease Control and Prevention, "Drug-Associated HIV Transmission Continues in the United States," 2002. http://www.cdc.gov/hiv/pubs/facts/idu.htm (31 January 2003).

areas which are already doing well; they can covenant to care. Churches and other United Methodist organizations need to continue or begin compassionate ministry with persons living with HIV/AIDS and their loved ones. In terms of prevention education, United Methodists have an opportunity to teach not only the facts about HIV transmission and how to prevent infection but to relate these facts to Christian values. Congregations can do HIV/AIDS prevention education in broader contexts, such as human sexuality and holistic health, as well as addressing societal problems, such as racism, sexism, addiction, and poverty. We call on United Methodists to respond:

1. Churches should be places of openness and caring for persons with AIDS and their loved ones. We ask congregations to work to overcome attitudinal and behavioral barriers in church and community that create stigma and discrimination of persons with AIDS and their loved ones. Congregations can offer Christian hospitality and become arks of refuge to all. We must remember that:

- the face that AIDS wears is always the face of a person created and loved by God;
- the face that AIDS wears is always the face of a person who is someone's mother or father, husband or wife, son or daughter, brother or sister, loved one or best friend;
- the face that AIDS wears is always the face of a person who is the most important person in someone else's life.

2. Each congregation and annual conference, through their Church and Society committees, should mobilize persons for legislative advocacy at the local, state and national levels to support for HIV/AIDS initiatives in the United States. These advocacy efforts will be strengthened through partnerships with organizations/coalitions who are currently involved in this issue.

3. Educational efforts about AIDS should use reliable medical and scientific information about the disease, transmission, and prevention. Spiritual resources must also be included to enable people to address issues related to discipleship, ministry, human sexuality, heath and wholeness, and death and dying. Education helps to prepare congregations to respond appropriately when they learn that a member has been infected by the HIV virus or diagnosed with AIDS. It can lead to the development of sound policies, educational materials and procedures related to the church school, nurseries, and other issues of institutional participation. Prevention education can save lives.

4. Each congregation should discern the appropriate response for its context. Ministries should be developed, whenever possible, in consultation and collaboration with local departments of public health and with other United Methodist, ecumenical, interfaith, and community-based groups concerned about the HIV/AIDS pandemic. Congregations can organize to provide spiritual, emotional, physical and/or financial support to those in their community who are caring at home or elsewhere for a person who has AIDS. Projects might include observing events such as World AIDS Day (December 1) and the Black Church Week of Prayer for the Healing of AIDS (first week in March), sponsoring support groups for people with AIDS and their loved ones, developing strong general church programs for children and youth that also include AIDS education, pastoral counseling, recruiting volunteers, and offering meeting space for community-based organizations, including groups trying to overcome substance abuse and sexual addiction.

5. The United Methodist Church has a congregational HIV/AIDS ministry called the Covenant to Care Program, whose basic principle is "If you have HIV/AIDS or are the loved one of a person who has HIV/AIDS, you are welcome here." We commend those who have been in ministry through this program and recommend "Covenant to Care" to all United Methodist organizations. More information is available on the General Board of Global Ministries' Web site at http://gbgm-umc.org/health/aids/.[18]

18. For more information about the Covenant to Care program or the church and HIV/AIDS Ministries, contact: Health and Welfare Ministries, General Board of Global Ministries, Room 330, 475 Riverside Drive, New York, NY 10115; Voice Phone: 212-870-3871; FAX: 212-870-3624; TDD: 212-870-3709; E-Mail: aidsmin@gbgm-umc.org.

ADOPTED 2004
READOPTED 2008
RESOLUTION #152, 2004 *BOOK OF RESOLUTIONS*
RESOLUTION #141, 2000 *BOOK OF RESOLUTIONS*

*See* Social Principles, ¶ 162U.

## 3242. World AIDS Day Observance

Each year, World AIDS Day is observed on December 1. It is a time for special programs on HIV/AIDS education and religious worship services that focus on intercessory and healing prayer, hope in God, and love and compassion in the midst of the HIV/AIDS pandemic.

We recommend that United Methodists be encouraged to observe World AIDS Day on or around December 1. We further recommend that voluntary offerings be given to "Global HIV/AIDS Program Development" (UMCOR Advance #982345-7).

Materials for World AIDS Day are available each year from UNAIDS (*http://www.unaids.org*), the General Board of Church and Society(*http://www.umc-gbcs.org*), and the General Board of Global Ministries (*http://gbgm-umc.org/health/*) of The United Methodist Church.

ADOPTED 1996
AMENDED AND READOPTED 2004
READOPTED 2008
RESOLUTION #153, 2004 *BOOK OF RESOLUTIONS*
RESOLUTION #142, 2000 *BOOK OF RESOLUTIONS*

*See* Social Principles, ¶ 162U.

## 3243. The Church and the Global HIV/AIDS Pandemic

In response to the global HIV/AIDS pandemic, The United Methodist Church will work cooperatively with colleague churches in every region. The Bible is replete with calls to nations, religious leaders, and faithful people to address the needs of those who are suffering, ill, and in distress. Jesus Christ reached out and healed those who came to him, including people who were despised and rejected because of their illnesses and afflictions. His identification with suffering people was made clear when he said that "whatsoever you do to the least of these, you also do to me" (Matthew 25:40, paraphrased). His commandment to "do to others as you would have them do to you" (Matthew 7:12) is a basis for the church for full involvement and compassionate response.

### The Global Impact of HIV/AIDS

The global statistics are grim. At the end of 2006, 39.5 million adults and children were living with HIV/AIDS in the world; of these 37.2 million were adults and 2.3 million were children.

At this time, there is no cure for HIV/AIDS. It is mainly spread through intimate sexual contact with an infected person, by needle-sharing among injecting drug users, and, less commonly, through transfusions of infected blood or blood clotting factors. HIV can also be contracted if unsterilized needles tainted with infected blood are used by health care workers, tattooists, and acupuncturists. Other routes of transmission are through transplantation of organs from infected individuals, donated semen, and skin piercing instruments used in cosmetic, traditional, and ceremonial practices. AIDS is not caused by witchcraft, mosquito bites, or nonsexual contact such as shaking hands or hugs.

The HIV/AIDS pandemic compounds the strain on institutions and resources, while at the same time undermining social systems that enable people to cope with adversity. In seriously affected nations, HIV/AIDS compromises education and health systems, shrinks economic output and undermines sociopolitical stability. With life expectancy falling and the labor force becoming decimated, many countries are facing low economic growth rates. In parts of southern Africa, a food shortage has added to the woes. Agricultural productivity is declining as more and more women and young people are infected and become unable to work in the fields. The ramifications of HIV/AIDS are particularly grave for societies where the extended family is the system of social security for the care of elderly people, those who are ill, and orphans.

### *Women and Children*

Women and children have been affected in increasing numbers. Deaths from AIDS have left 13 million orphans in Africa; the number is expected to rise to 25 million by 2010. These children are being looked after by extended families, older siblings in child-headed households, and orphan trusts. Older relatives, especially women, have to bear an enormous burden of taking care of the orphans. In countries that are also affected by war and civil strife, children and young people are more vulnerable to becoming infected with HIV because they are at the higher risk of sexual abuse, forced military recruitment and prostitution.

This burden is increased when women are also faced with stigma and discrimination and the hardships of civil strife, war, and famine. Women often have less status and less access to education, health care, and economic security than men, which in turn affect their ability to protect themselves from infection. Many cannot say "no" or negotiate the use of condoms because they fear they will be divorced or that their husband or other male partner will respond by battering them. Pregnant women who are HIV positive may be subjected to forced sterilizations or abortions. The use of rape and sexual violence as instruments of war adds a further serious dimension. As of 2006 according to UNAIDS, 17.7 million of the 39.5 million persons infected with AIDS are women.

Health budgets and resources are being adversely affected in countries that have to care for increasing numbers of citizens afflicted with HIV/AIDS. For example, it costs $300 to treat a person for a year using the cheapest form of generic antiretroviral drugs, but very few can afford this medicine in sub-Saharan Africa. Antiretroviral drugs and other medicines must be made available at an affordable cost, especially in sub-Saharan Africa. Until effective preventive strategies are implemented, helpful medicines are made universally available, and an effective vaccine is introduced, the future is bleak for deterring the spread of HIV/AIDS.

The suffering borne by individuals, families, and communities and the strain placed on health-care facilities and national economies, call for intensified cooperative efforts by every sector of society, including the church, to slow and prevent the spread of HIV, provide appropriate care of those already ill and speed the development of an effective and affordable vaccine. Those caring for AIDS patients need support too. Communities, health-care workers, and home-care programs must be equipped to meet the challenge.

## Drugs and AIDS

Of the 40 million persons living with HIV, two to three million are injecting drug users. Many more have used, and continue to use, alcohol and other drugs.

The international drug trade knows no boundaries or frontiers and has no specific national identity. It is now worth an estimated $400 billion per year and is organized and managed like a multinational corporation. Drugs of all kinds are now produced in all regions of the world. Despite its illegality, drug production and distribution has become a major source of revenue for many countries. The most lucrative markets remain in the United States and Western Europe, but consumption is spreading fast in Eastern Europe, Southeast Asia, and throughout Africa.

In the United States, an estimated one-third of HIV/AIDS cases are related to injecting drug use. Substance abuse is directly tied to the increase in HIV/AIDS among women. Women are primarily infected with HIV through injecting drugs (48 percent) or heterosexual transmission from an infected partner, who is often himself a drug user (54 percent).

Research has shown over and over again that drug use, injected or otherwise, can affect decision-making, especially about engaging in unsafe sex, which in turn promotes the spread of AIDS. A research study conducted by The National Center on Addiction and Substance Abuse revealed that of the 15- to 24-year-olds surveyed:

- 50 percent say "people their age" mix alcohol or drugs and sex "a lot";
- percent believe that their peers often don't use condoms when alcohol and drugs are in the picture;
- percent want more information about how alcohol or drugs might affect their decisions about having sex.

### The Role of United Methodists

The global AIDS pandemic provides a nearly unparalleled opportunity for witness to the gospel through service, advocacy, and other healing ministries. United Methodist public health specialists, health workers, social workers, teachers, missionaries, clergy, and laity live and work in areas where the AIDS pandemic is spreading. United Methodist congregations, schools, health facilities, women's, men's, and youth groups can play a major role by providing awareness, support, education, and care to those affected by HIV/AIDS.

### Recommendations:

In response to the HIV/AIDS crisis in the world, The United Methodist Church commits itself to a holistic approach of awareness, education, prevention, treatment, community organizing and public advocacy. Out of our love and concern for our brothers, sisters and children in our local and global communities, the following actions are strongly recommended.

### A. Local congregations worldwide to:

1. be places of openness where persons whose lives have been touched by HIV/AIDS can name their pain and reach out for com-

passion, understanding, and acceptance in the presence of persons who bear Christ's name;

2. provide care and support to individuals and families whose lives have been touched by HIV/AIDS;

3. be centers of education and provide group support and encouragement to help men, women, and youth refrain from activities and behaviors associated with transmission of HIV infection;

4. advocate for increased levels of funding for HIV/AIDS. In the United States, persons should contact their US Congresspersons and urge adequate funding for the Global Fund for AIDS, Tuberculosis, and Malaria as well as the United States' bilateral initiatives on AIDS. Additionally, funding for the United Nations Population Fund (UNFPA) must be guaranteed from the United States each year. UNFPA works diligently to provide resources for reproductive health of women and girls as well as HIV/AIDS prevention;

5. observe World AIDS Day on or around December 1 each year. Materials for World AIDS Day are available from the Web sites of UNAIDS (http://www.unaids.org), the General Board of Global Ministries (http:/gbgm-umc.org/health/), and the General Board of Church and Society (http://www.umc-gbcs.org);

6. include problems of alcohol, drug abuse and unsafe sex and the value of abstinence as part of Christian education;

7. provide support, comfort, and care to those afflicted with alcohol-related problems, drug addiction and HIV/AIDS within their given mandate;

8. make available creative programs and activities for school children, youth, and young adults that keep them away from alcohol and drug abuse; and

9. promote and make available peer education models based on empowerment and self-determination.

*B. General program agencies to:*

1. assist related health institutions to obtain supplies and equipment to screen donated blood and provide voluntary HIV testing;

2. support efforts by churches, projects, and mission personnel within regions to promote disease prevention and to respond to the needs of family care providers and extended families;

3. facilitate partnership relationships between institutions and personnel from region to region, as appropriate, to share models and

effective approaches regarding prevention, education, care, and support for individuals and families with HIV/AIDS;

4. assist health workers to obtain regional specific, timely updates on the diagnosis, treatment, and prevention of HIV/AIDS;

5. facilitate the sharing of pastoral-care resources and materials dedicated to the care of persons and families whose lives have been touched by HIV;

6. respond to requests from the regions to develop training seminars and workshops for church-related personnel in cooperation with ecumenical efforts, private voluntary organizations, and programs already existing in the regions;

7. advocate national, regional, and international cooperation in the development, availability, and transport of appropriate/relevant equipment and supplies for infection control, disease prevention, and treatment;

8. support programs that focus on the enhancement of women through economic justice and education as well as programs that provide comprehensive reproductive health services, family planning, and HIV/AIDS prevention information;

9. work cooperatively with the Office of the Special Program on Substance Abuse and Related Violence (SPSARV) of the General Board of Global Ministries on issues related to drugs and AIDS; and

10. urge the federal government to improve interagency cooperation and coordination to fight the double scourge of drugs and AIDS. (General Board of Church and Society and General Board of Global Ministries).

C. *Annual conferences to:*

1. explore HIV prevention and care needs within their areas and to develop conference-wide plans for appropriate, effective responses;

2. promote pastoral responses to persons with HIV/AIDS that affirm the presence of God's love, grace, and healing mercies;

3. encourage every local church to reach out through proclamation and education to help prevent the spread of HIV infection and to utilize and strengthen the efforts and leadership potential of men's, women's, and youth groups.

D. *Episcopal leaders to:*

1. issue pastoral letters calling for compassionate ministries and the development of educational programs that recognize the HIV/AIDS

epidemic as a public health threat of major global and regional significance; and

2. provide a level of leadership equal to the suffering and desperation that individuals, families, and communities are experiencing.

### God's Unconditional Love and Christ's Healing Ministry

The unconditional love of God, witnessed to and manifested through Christ's healing ministry, provides an ever-present sign and call to the church and all persons of faith to join efforts to prevent the spread of HIV, provide care and treatment to those who are already infected and ill, uphold the preciousness of God's creation through proclamation and affirmation, and be harbingers of hope, mercy, goodness, forgiveness, and reconciliation within the world.

The United Methodist Church unequivocally condemns stigmatization and discrimination of persons with HIV/AIDS and violence perpetrated against persons who are or presumed to be infected with HIV. The United Methodist Church advocates the full involvement of the church at all levels to be in ministry with, and to respond fully to the needs of, persons, families, and communities whose lives have been affected by HIV/AIDS. In keeping with our faith in the risen Christ, we confess our belief that God has received those who have died, that the wounds of living loved ones will be healed, and that Christ, through the Holy Spirit, is present among us as we strive to exemplify what it means to be bearers of Christ's name in the midst of the global HIV/AIDS pandemic.

ADOPTED 2004
REVISED AND READOPTED 2008
RESOLUTION #298, 2004 *BOOK OF RESOLUTIONS*
RESOLUTION #278, 2000 *BOOK OF RESOLUTIONS*

*See* Social Principles, ¶¶ 165B and 162U.

## 3244. United Methodist Global AIDS Fund Distribution

WHEREAS, for twenty years the General Conference of The United Methodist Church has spoken with prophetic compassion to the global issue of HIV/AIDS. Our resolutions, however, have not been matched by a resolve to commit significant financial and denominational resources in the struggle for education, prevention, treatment and care in the worldwide struggle against HIV/AIDS; and

WHEREAS, the United Nations has now declared the pandemic a "global emergency," saying human life is threatened everywhere and world security is at risk as the planet faces the worst health crisis in 700 years; and

WHEREAS, with 42 million people infected, more than 20 million already deceased, and 16,000 new infections daily, the leaders of all the nations in the world unanimously asked faith-based organizations to join them in the battle to save human life; and

WHEREAS, to date the response of Christians, including United Methodists, has been minimal, particularly in comparison to our resources and other commitments;

*Therefore, be it resolved,* that the 2004 General Conference commits itself to establishing the United Methodist Global AIDS Fund (UMGAF). During the 2009-2012 quadrennium, United Methodists will raise $3 million through apportionments and match this with an additional $5 million through Advance gifts;

*Be it further resolved,* that of the total money raised in each annual conference for UMGAF, 25 percent shall be retained by the annual conference that raised it, to be used in programs combating HIV/AIDS in their region and in other global connectional projects. Each annual conference shall designate an appropriate agency for the promotion and distribution of these funds.

*Be it further resolved,* that of the total money raised in each annual conference for the United Methodist Global AIDS Fund, 75 percent shall be remitted by the conference treasurer to the treasurer of the General Council on Finance and Administration for distribution to a new Global AIDS Initiatives Committee (with no more than ten total representatives from the General Board of Global Ministries, Council of Bishops, General Board of Church and Society, Youth and Young Adults Ministries, and three persons not serving with any of these agencies).

*Be it further resolved,* that this Global AIDS Initiatives Committee will be responsible for the promotion, use, supervision and distribution of these funds. The United Methodist Global AIDS Fund will:

1. assist local congregations and conferences in identifying and creating global partnerships for mutual HIV/AIDS ministry;

2. provide support for projects sponsored by local congregations or organizations related to The United Methodist Church, partner autonomous Methodist churches and the ecumenical church;

3. encourage partnerships between congregations and conferences in the United States and Methodist congregations and ecumenical organizations globally that are engaged in the struggle against HIV/AIDS;

4. advocate for social justice, particularly related to increasing governmental and nongovernmental funding and issues regarding the role of pharmaceutical companies;

5. develop appropriate promotional materials and funding guidelines; and

6. Engage the leadership of a person with appropriate skills for a special global AIDS assignment (#4091c).

ADOPTED 2004
READOPTED 2008
RESOLUTION #154, 2004 *BOOK OF RESOLUTIONS*

*See* Social Principles, ¶ 162U.

## HOUSING AND HOMELESSNESS

### 3261. Homelessness in the United States

The biblical mandate to care for the poor is clear as put forth in Isaiah 58:6-7 where God says "Is not this the fast that I choose . . . to share your bread with the hungry, and bring the homeless poor into your house; [and] when you see the naked, to cover them?" The homeless are most assuredly the people of God—the people of God who call the church to both repentance and action. They are the hungry we are asked to feed, the strangers we are to welcome, and the naked that we are to clothe. They are the sick and imprisoned we are commanded to visit (Matthew 25:31-36). Theologian Walter Brueggemann says, "The Bible itself is primarily concerned with the issue of being displaced and yearning for a place." What we must seek for all people is safe, sanitary, and affordable housing. The church is called to not only seek to provide shelter but we must do more than house the homeless, we must build community. Home as a promise to the homeless must be the ongoing commitment of the church.

In the most materially rich nation in the world, the homeless are all around us. They are the lonely who pass their time talking to themselves in every big city and small town in the nation. They are rural families without the economic means to travel long distances to shelters and other public services. The homeless are people who have been displaced and discarded. Their numbers alone make them a nation of strangers, highly mobile and rootless, surrounded by wealth, glamour, and excess of all of that which they so desperately lack. Even in a strong economy, no less than 2.3 million adults and children, nearly one percent of the population is likely to experience a spell of homelessness at least once during a year; the numbers grow larger as the economy recedes.

Homelessness is a crisis that strikes at the soul of the nation and at the heart of the church. A study by the US Conference of Mayors revealed a sharp rise of homelessness in major cities in 2006. Officials estimate that, on average, single men comprise 51 percent of the homeless population, families with children 30 percent, single women 17 percent, and unaccompanied youth 2 percent. The homeless population is estimated to be 42 percent African-American, 39 percent white, 13 percent Hispanic, 4 percent Native-American, and 2 percent Asian. An average of 16 percent of homeless people is considered mentally ill; 26 percent are substance abusers. Thirteen percent are employed; 9 percent are veterans.

Homelessness has many faces and many causes, but its root is in the failure of the nation to commit itself through public policies and programs to eradicate poverty. Homelessness and poverty cannot be separated. A comprehensive, all-out attack on poverty must be waged. In order to wage this attach the following factors must be addressed:

- Lack of community support for de-institutionalized people with chronic mental illness
- Discontinuance or reduction of public benefits to significant numbers of elderly and disabled people
- A minimum-wage structure that locks the working poor into poverty
- Loss of family farms
- Closure of plants and businesses
- An economy increasingly built on low-paying temporary and seasonal jobs with few or no benefits
- The increasing number of single-parent households with associated low incomes
- The lack of housing for people with AIDS
- Displacement of inner-city residents by urban renewal.

In addition to the above, the shortage of affordable housing also contributes greatly to this plight of homelessness. In its 2002 report, the Millennial Housing Commission, a bipartisan commission created by Congress, found that housing affordability is the single greatest challenge facing the nation.

Homelessness is both a rural and an urban problem. The rural homeless tend to be young, white, and female. Rural shelters are scarce, so homeless people often double up with friends and relatives. The Housing Assistance Council has found that rural homeless people are migrant workers, displaced renters, bankrupt farmers, and laid-off workers. Native Americans and other residents on Indian reservations are increasingly found among the rural homeless. Extremely high unemployment, coupled with the increased numbers of Native American people returning to live on reservations, has placed undue burdens on an already overtaxed and inadequate social service system. Rural homeless people often migrate to cities, thus contributing to urban homelessness.

The United Methodist Church must continue to affirm the right of all persons to live without deprivation in safe, sanitary, and affordable housing. The United Methodist Church must clearly assert that inequitable public policies, unfair and discriminatory private-sector practices have deprived many of that right. The church must teach its constituents that homelessness is a violation of human dignity and an affront to the biblical mandate to do justice. We must use all our power to eliminate the causes of homelessness and to work along with others to eradicate it. The Bible calls us to commit ourselves to welcoming the stranger into our midst and to seeing all people as belonging to the family of God. The church must recognize in deed as well as word that homeless people are our neighbors, seek to learn who are the homeless in our communities and speak out on their behalf in our congregations and in the larger community.

The following actions are recommended to general agencies, annual conferences, and local churches:

1. General Agency Recommendations:
    a. Provide to clergy and laity educational, training resources and opportunities that address the root causes of homelessness and provide models for addressing the problem.
    b. Urge seminaries to include courses in their curriculum that help prepare clergy for effective leadership around systemic

contradictions in our society that create poverty and homelessness.
c. Encourage annual conferences to include courses in their
plans for continuing education for clergy at least once a quadrennium.
d. Continue to support and work with national, regional, and
local housing advocacy groups to implement this resolution.
e. Join with other communions to promote affordable housing
for low-income persons through the National Low-Income
Housing Coalition, the National Coalition for the Homeless,
the National Alliance to End Homelessness, and other appropriate networks.
f. Document and affirm the work of local churches and service
providers who provide needed ministries of compassion to
homeless persons through church-based soup kitchens, transitional housing programs, shelters, food pantries, clothes
closets, and rent and utility assistance programs. Promote
their efforts throughout the local church by soliciting financial
contributions and volunteer support, and by encouraging
members to contribute specialized skills and technical assistance.
g. Identify effective existing models and provide new models for
local congregations and clergy who wish to undertake Bible
study and theological reflection around the root causes of
homelessness.
2. Annual Conference Recommendations:
a. Participate in "End Homelessness in Ten Years" grassroots
efforts led by the National Alliance to End Homelessness
b. Inform clergy and laity of the avenues available to churches to
become involved in housing development by exposing them
to different models used to address the lack of affordable
housing.
c. Adopt a resolution on homelessness encouraging actions at
the congregational level to address the homeless crisis in local
communities.
d. Encourage local churches to conduct a survey on homelessness in their areas to determine what services are currently
being provided and to discover gaps in services toward which
the church should direct its efforts.

 e. Support cooperative parishes as a major strategy for responding to the problem of homelessness.

3. Local Church Recommendations:

 a. Involve clergy and laity in local church volunteers networks, direct-service programs, ecumenical coalitions for the homeless, directories of local service providers, speaking opportunities for groups such as Habitat for Humanity, and workshops led by local homeless advocates and the homeless themselves.

 b. Promote local church-based community organizing efforts to empower neighborhoods and influence government at every level.

4. All Levels of the Church: Call upon Congress to pass comprehensive national housing legislation, as outlined in the General Conference resolution on housing.

ADOPTED 2004
REVISED AND READOPTED 2008
RESOLUTION #116, 2004 *BOOK OF RESOLUTIONS*
RESOLUTION #105, 2000 *BOOK OF RESOLUTIONS*

*See* Social Principles, ¶ 162 and 162A.

## 3262. Housing in the USA

The Scriptures look ahead to that ideal day when all persons will enjoy pleasant, peaceful, and secure shelter under their own vines and fig trees and "no one shall make them afraid" (Micah 4:4 NRSV).

In many portions of the Gospel, we find Jesus seeking out homes for retreat and renewal, for fellowship and hospitality. Similarly, all persons are entitled to dwelling places that provide for safety, privacy and recreation.

The Social Principles statement of The United Methodist Church declares: "We hold governments responsible for . . . guarantee of the rights to adequate . . . shelter" (¶ 164A). We reaffirm this right as well as the assertion of the 1972 General Conference that "housing for low income persons should be given top priority" (1972 *Book of Resolutions*).

The need for adequate housing at affordable costs is critical today.

Love for neighbor demands that Christians care about how adequately their neighbors are sheltered. Christians should identify with those who suffer daily from a shortage of available, decent, safe, and sanitary housing. There are many levels and forms of deprivation. Nearly every American town and city has its "homeless," those who exist literally without any form of shelter, living under bridges, in cars and abandoned buses, carrying their entire possessions with them in a few shopping bags.

Millions of families huddle together in densely overcrowded apartments, rural shacks, ancient house trailers, converted warehouses, and condemned or abandoned buildings. Many of our fellow citizens live in housing that lack such necessities as running water or plumbing, and others have no permanent housing (the homeless) because the remainder of us fail to recognize their plight or simply do not care enough.

Since December of 1986, families with children have become the fastest growing homeless group. While The United Methodist Church affirms the pervasive powers of families as "creators of persons, proclaimers of faith perspectives and shapers of both present and future society," it must continue its condemnation of policies that ignore the causal relationship between shortages of low-income housing and the lack of initiative or political will to ensure that safe and affordable housing is available to all citizens.

The deinstitutionalization of persons diagnosed as mentally ill or recovering, or who could live full lives with minimal supervision, is a concept of worth. However, a lack of regional and community planning has allowed many people to be released from a variety of institutions with no place to go, no affordable housing on the budgets allotted to persons through federal or state funds, and no supervised environment for those who need it. Few services exist to maintain supervised, semi-independent, safe, affordable housing. The National Institute of Mental Health estimates that one third of the homeless have mental health problems. Some are persons who were deinstitutionalized with no support; others became ill because of the environment of homelessness.

"Am I my brother's keeper?" (Genesis 4:9, NRSV) becomes a challenging alternative when concerned United Methodists begin to address the phenomenon of increased homeless families in our country. We must grapple with ways to meet the needs of the homeless. We must be more open to using church buildings that are outmoded and excess land in urban and rural areas. We must examine needs and services in our communities and develop a better understanding of our role in local, state, and federal policy development. We commend United Methodists who are engaged in the effort to change such intolerable housing conditions. We commend every such individual, local church, interfaith group, nonprofit, for-profit, and government effort. We endorse with gratitude and appreciation the thousands of dollars and untold hours of voluntary service that United Methodists dedicate to this battle to improve human shelter in our country. We urge local churches, districts, and annual conferences to strengthen every housing ministry taking place within their communities by providing additional financial, technical, counseling, and spiritual resources.

Many specific activities deserve greater United Methodist support.

## A. At the local level

Local churches, individually or in cooperation with other churches, can identify specific housing needs existing in their communities. Often, bringing to public consciousness the plight of people in need of shelter is the first step toward alleviating such need. Sometimes the use of existing church buildings can graphically demonstrate both the need and a solution that then can be developed more fully through the use of other facilities and financial resources.

Formation of nonprofit and limited-divided housing corporations or housing cooperatives is a viable approach in many situations. There are excellent opportunities for establishing housing construction, management, and advocacy programs. However, expert consultative and technical services generally are needed from the earliest conception. We urge the use of the services provided by the General Board of Global Ministries. We urge landowners, apartment and housing managers, and policy boards to allow federally subsidized tenants to inhabit their dwellings. This is a serious problem at this time, because US government policy recommends selling up to 30 percent of public housing units for private development. The net result is displacement of the poor. Availability of housing for them is limited because of discrimination and a reluctance on the part of the government to maintain federally subsidized housing monies for privately owned housing.

## B. At the regional level

The atmosphere of conflict infects the relationship between cities, towns, suburban areas, counties, and states throughout our nation.

Too often, competition for use of land cloaks subtle racism. Economic profit, likewise, often is used to justify a lack of concern for the impact of taxation measures. Uncoordinated planning and development results in jobs being located beyond the reach of those most in need of work. The "trickle-down theory" of housing occupancy masks a self-ish motivation and results in the maintenance and expansion of existing ghettos, causes the formation of new ghettos, and enforces negative attitudes that support class and racial segregation. We urge United Methodists to challenge all such practices and to engage in every activity to eliminate such vestiges of discrimination from our nation.

Every urbanized area in our country is required to have some form of a regional planning agency. Most rural areas have some similar agency, such as an area development district. Generally these political structures have considerable influence upon housing patterns, planning, production, and usage. Most can have citizens' advisory groups that develop strategy proposals and monitor private and governmental housing activities. We urge United Methodists to become knowledgeable of and involved in such planning agencies.

## C. At the national level

Since the enactment of the National Housing Act of 1949, the United States has set a goal that every citizen be housed in "decent, safe and sanitary housing." Yet the reality is that we are farther from that goal today than ever before. In part, this is due to growth of population and the ever-increasing gap between those who are economically well-off and those who are not. But in large measure, the disparity is due to an unwillingness of our elected representatives to use general tax revenues to achieve the goals more fully. Generally, legislators feel they represent the views of their electorate and receive very little support for using tax dollars to build more housing for low- and moderate-income families. The moral commitment first stated in 1949 and restated in every subsequent Housing Act by Congress (1959, 1968, 1974, 1978) has gone greatly unheeded. If "decent, safe and sanitary housing" is to be a citizen's right, a much greater moral outcry must be raised.

Therefore, we call upon United Methodists to undertake a concerted effort to impress upon their elected representatives a profound concern over the continuing housing deficiencies existing in our cities, towns, and rural areas. Much more effort needs to be made to influence the legislative processes that affect housing, including improving existing laws, developing more imaginative approaches where possible, and providing adequate funding for housing designated to meet the needs of the ill-sheltered.

### (1) Subsidized Rental Housing (Section 8) and Public housing

Under the Section 8 Housing Assistance Payments Program, renters normally pay a percentage of their income for rent, and the federal government makes up the difference between that and the HUD-(Department of Housing and Urban Development) established Fair Market Rent. We support this program for subsidizing rents as one way of opening up more housing units to low-income families and yet expecting such families, when possible, to provide their fair share of costs. However, the reality is that there are just not enough units of housing available at a cost that can be afforded by the poor, even with payment assistance. There is a great need for developing more housing units. The Temporary Aid to Needy Families (TANF) is the primary source of income for many people who now find themselves homeless. The amount of money that many families with children receive is lower than the average cost of housing in many states. This situation will exacerbate when TANF recipients are terminated due to the term limits now imposed by federal and state governments.

We are greatly concerned over the rapidly increasing trend toward converting rental housing to condominiums for sale. Too often in practice this means pushing people out of housing they can afford to rent but can't afford to buy. We therefore recommend that the rate of condominium conversion of rental units be slowed, or that percentages of the units be set aside with affordable rental rates. Further, we urge local housing authorities to offset this trend by encouraging increased housing stock of subsidized rental units.

We support use of a wide variety of subsidized housing approaches in order to meet a greater demand to house needy people. However, the development of a "voucher" program with no ceiling on the actual rent that can be charged and no local community guarantee of housing set aside for the poor will not alleviate the present situation.

Public housing continues to be a vital necessity in both urban and rural areas. Every incorporated city, town, and county can and should provide public, well-constructed, and well-managed rental housing for those who cannot obtain it on the open market. Nearly 50 percent of all housing is now occupied by the elderly. Since the church has traditionally expressed concern and provided care of the aging, it is especially crucial that this program is continued, expanded, and adequately funded.

We must at all times critically examine the setting at the local, state, and federal levels, because governmental policies affect the funding, improvement, and provision of housing resources for any given community. The Federal Administration between 1981 and 1988 tried to eliminate or reduce the main federal programs used by states and local governments to help the poor and the homeless. The Community Development Block Grant Program, General Revenue Sharing, and the Temporary Emergency Food Assistance Program (TEFAP) have all been affected. The Community Development Block Grant Program budget has been cut almost yearly. General Revenue Sharing was eliminated. The Administration has targeted for elimination the Temporary Emergency Food Assistance Program. Congress has repeatedly come to the rescue of these programs and in 1986 passed a law allowing the homeless to receive Aid to Families with Dependent Children (Now Temporary Aid to Needy Families), social security, and Medicaid.

### (2) Fair housing

Fair housing in our nation has regressed dramatically. Because housing remains segregated in most places in the United States, schools tend to be segregated and jobs tend to be located at inconvenient distances from ethnic neighborhoods.

We therefore call upon the US Congress to provide the Department of Housing and Urban development with "cease and desist" enforcement powers, and we encourage HUD to apply these powers evenly and with relentless determination to ensure equal access to affordable housing in all markets. We support state and local legislation that would strengthen fair housing enforcement across the country. We also support HUD funding for states with laws that are substantially equivalent to federal law. We also call for the expansion of coverage in the Fair Housing Act to provide protection for people with disabilities.

Equal access to housing not available represents an unrealizable right. Therefore, to fulfill equal opportunity objectives we urge that more housing be built and offered at prices most persons can afford to pay.

## A. Redlining

We deplore the practice of "redlining" as it occurs in many urban areas. This generally means that financial institutions, insurance companies, and mortgage brokers collectively make it difficult for homeowners to secure adequate financing and insurance at reasonable rates in a certain neighborhood of a given urban community. We ask that all necessary steps be taken, through negotiation and legislation, to eliminate this immoral practice, and that churches take the lead in encouraging financial support arrangements that rejuvenate instead of destroy our neighborhoods. Vigilant monitoring by the religious community can forestall such unhealthy practices.

We support existing laws such as the Home Mortgage Disclosure Act, which provides information to the public on where banks and savings and loans make their loans, and the enlarged Community Reinvestment Act, which mandates that banks and savings and loans have the responsibility to serve the credit needs of moderate and lower-income communities.

We urge compliance of the institutions in which the church deposits funds with the Home Mortgage Act; and we support such additional regulations and laws that will ensure reinvestment in currently redlined communities, in a way that will not result in unjust displacement of elderly, poor, ethnic, and other persons.

## B. Housing for older adults and people with disabilities

The Section 202 federal program is a bright spot in an otherwise dismal picture of housing for older adults and people with disabilities of any age. Restricted to sponsorship by nonprofit groups (the majority of which are related to religious groups), the 202 continues to offer a direct ministry opportunity. Since it is a loan guarantee program with lower-than-market interest rates, it needs to be funded at much more realistic levels than in the past. There is also a need for expanding the congregate housing services project for semi-independent older adults or people with disabilities. The steady increase in age of our population is evidence for the need to expand the 202 program until the need for this type of rental housing for the elderly has been met. This program provides support services for persons using 202 housing and is cost effective because it allows people who might have to be institutionalized to live in much lower-cost housing.

### (3) Housing for Native Americans

Housing policy, as in other aspects of national policy and practices toward Native American tribes, is grossly inadequate. We call for a substantial increase in programs at the federal level and for the implementation of state and local housing programs in every possible way, so that the shocking condition of substandard reservation housing can be quickly improved. Special efforts through programs of United Methodist general agencies, in partnership with ethnic conferences and funds for ethnic ministry, should be supportive of actions to improve housing for Native Americans.

### (4) Financing of Housing

Traditionally, the vast majority of housing in our country has been financed through the private money-lending industry. There is little likelihood that this would need to change if the traditional principles against usury are followed. But more attention needs to be given to developing ways mortgage money can be made available to low-income persons for home ownership, and to provide rental housing for low-income people. Federal and state programs aid the moderate- and upper-income segments of our population quite well, but similarly helpful programs for the lower-income sector of the population do not exist. The 1980s saw the greatest benefit go not to the neediest families, but to those who are sufficiently well off to purchase homes.

The higher the family income, the more these tax immunities breaks help. Three fourths of these tax immunities breaks go to homeowners in the top 15 percent of the income bracket. Poor or lower-middle class homeowners get only 3 percent of the tax immunities breaks. Government-subsidized mortgage programs need to be developed that can also aid the lower-middle class and poor individuals and families.

In contrast to the rapid growth in federal aid to move well-to-do homeowners through the Internal Revenue Code, Congress has continued to cut the federal budget in areas that greatly affect poor working families.

New methods of private financing need to be developed so that traditional money sources are not withdrawn from the housing industry in favor of other, more profitable forms of investment.

*Recommendations*

A number of federal programs as well as some state programs exist today to make possible the meaningful participation of church groups in providing adequate housing in a wholesome environment. We encourage United Methodist churches to join in such programs that require minimal capital investment but substantial commitment of time and energy. Churches should be aware that these programs are available in both urban and rural areas. More church groups ought to:

1. Be concerned about the conditions of housing in their communities;

2. Use the tools available (e.g., General Board of Global Ministries Housing Consultant Services) to provide better housing;

3. Dedicate a special day or Sunday as a Day of Prayer and Action for Shelter, as has been developed by Habitat for Humanity (contact the General Board of Global Ministries for special resources); and

4. Develop a sense of mission and assume responsibility as stewards to meet these needs without expectation of monetary reward.

5. Encourage the establishment and full funding of a Community and State Fair Housing Trust Fund.

In implementing any housing ministry, church people must maintain great sensitivity to community needs and work to achieve community participation and control. Tenants' need for adequate, reasonably priced and energy-efficient housing should be recognized. Care must always be exercised to ensure our Christian involvement as "enablers" rather than "controllers." Our goal must always be to enable those we help to be in control of their own lives, futures, and destinies. Whatever the form of community organization, housing production, management, or ownership of a housing project, every effort should be made at each developmental step to ensure that those who are being aided are afforded the opportunity, and indeed, are required, to take every action necessary to direct the undertaking. Wherever possible, we must train rather than service, transfer power rather than decide, empower rather than control. In this as in all other aspects of housing ministries, United Methodists should seek the best technical guidance and ensure the greatest professional competence for such a ministry. Let us equip ourselves and provide the widest possible range of supportive assistance to individuals, congregations, districts, conferences, and all forms of cooperative groups sharing similar goals and policies so that our fellow citizens may achieve, as their right, "decent, safe and sanitary housing" as soon as possible.

**ADOPTED 1988**
**AMENDED AND READOPTED 2000**
**AMENDED AND READOPTED 2008**
**RESOLUTION #117, 2004** *BOOK OF RESOLUTIONS*
**RESOLUTION #106, 2000** *BOOK OF RESOLUTIONS*

*See* Social Principles, ¶ 162 and 162A.

# IMMIGRATION

## 3281. Welcoming the Migrant to the US

### The Historical Context

From the dawn of creation human beings have migrated across the earth. The history of the United States is a migration narrative of families and individuals seeking safety, economic betterment, and freedom of religious and cultural expression. The reasons for those who immigrated willingly are numerous and varied depending on the context, but what all immigrants share is the promise of what they believe lies in another land other than their own. Migrants today continue to travel to North America because of the effects of globalization, dislocation, economic scarcity, persecution, and other reasons.

The arrival of migrants to the United States from so many parts of the world has also meant that there is a diversity of cultures and worldviews. The diversity of cultures, worldviews, and languages has placed an enormous strain upon migrants. To effectively deal with this trauma and ease the process of acculturation, migrants should be encouraged to preserve strong cultural and familial ties to their culture of origin.

The arrival of new cultures has also felt threatening to US citizens, and this has too often resulted in conflict and even violence. Throughout the history of the United States, the most recently arrived group of migrants has often been a target of racism, marginalization, and violence. We regret any and all violence committed against migrants in the past and we resolve, as followers of Jesus, to work to eliminate racism and violence directed towards newly arriving migrants to the United States.

## The Biblical and Theological Context

Reflecting upon the Scriptures, we are reminded that United Methodists are a global church. In the United States, we may be descendants of economic immigrants or forced migrants, or we may have recently arrived in the US. We may have formal documents proving US citizenship, or we may be undocumented. Regardless of legal status or nationality, we are all connected through Christ to one another. Paul reminds us that when "one member suffers, all members suffer" as well (1 Corinthians 12:26). The solidarity we share through Christ eliminates the boundaries and barriers which exclude and isolate. Therefore, the sojourners we are called to love are our brothers and sisters, our mothers and fathers, our sons and daughters; indeed, they are us.

Throughout Scripture the people of God are called to love sojourners in our midst, treating them "as the citizen among you" and loving them as we do ourselves (Leviticus 19:33-34). Love for the sojourner is birthed out of the shared experience the Israelites had as a people in sojourn searching for the Promised Land. The attitudes and actions required of God's people were to emanate from the reflection of their liberation from slavery by God's hand. As the people of God were liberated from oppression, they too were charged to be instruments of redemption in the lives of the most vulnerable in their midst—the sojourner (Exodus 22:21; 23:9; Leviticus 19:34; Deuteronomy 10:19; 16:12; 24:18, 22).

In the New Testament, Jesus' life begins as a refugee to Africa when he and his family flee to Egypt to escape Herod's infanticide (Matthew 2:13-18). Jesus fully identifies with the sojourner to the point that to welcome the sojourner is to welcome Jesus himself (Matthew 25:35). Jesus teaches us to show special concern for the poor and oppressed who come to our land seeking survival and peace.

In Scripture, Jesus continually manifests compassion for the vulnerable and the poor. Jesus incarnated hospitality as he welcomed people and ministered to their greatest need. Jesus' presence on earth initiated the Kingdom reality of a new social order based on love, grace, justice, inclusion, mercy, and egalitarianism, which was meant to replace the old order, characterized by nepotism, racism, classism, sexism, and exclusion. The broken immigration system in the United States and the xenophobic responses to migrants reflect the former social order. The calling of the people of God is to advocate for the creation of a new immigration system that reflects Jesus' beloved community.

The fear and anguish so many migrants in the United States live under are due to federal raids, indefinite detention, and deportations which tear apart families and create an atmosphere of panic. Millions of immigrants are denied legal entry to the US due to quotas and race and class barriers, even as employers seek their labor. US policies, as well as economic and political conditions in their home countries, often force migrants to leave their homes. With the legal avenues closed, immigrants who come in order to support their families must live in the shadows and in intense exploitation and fear. In the face of these unjust laws and the systematic deportation of migrants instituted by the Department of Homeland Security, God's people must stand in solidarity with the migrants in our midst.

In Scripture, sojourners are also identified as heralds or messengers bringing good news. This is seen in many stories of the Bible:

- Abraham welcomed three visitors and then was promised a child even though Sarah was past the age of bearing children (Genesis 18:1-11);
- Rahab hid the spies from Israel, and her family was ultimately spared (Joshua 2:1-16);
- the widow at Zarephath gave Elijah her last meal and received food and ultimately healing for her dying son (1 Kings 17:7-24); and
- Zaccheus, upon welcoming Jesus into his home, promised to share half his possessions with the poor and repay those he stole from four times the amount owed. As Jesus entered Zaccheus's home he proclaimed that salvation had come to his house (Luke 19:1-10).

All of these stories give evidence to the words of the writer of Hebrews who advises the listeners to "not neglect to show hospitality to strangers for by doing that some have entertained angels without knowing it" (13:2). God's people are called to welcome the sojourner not only because of God's commands to do so, but because God's people need to hear the good news of the gospel incarnated in their stories and in their lives. Welcoming the sojourner is so vital to the expression of Christian faith that to engage in this form of hospitality is to participate in our own salvation.

There is theologically and historically an implied nature of mutuality in migration. Both the migrant and the native are meant to benefit from migration. Welcoming the migrant is not only an act of mission; it is an opportunity to receive God's grace. The globalization of international economies and the continuing movement of migrants have created an increasingly diversified US population and should be reflected in United Methodist congregations and national church leadership.

Therefore, The United Methodist Church understands that at the center of Christian faithfulness to Scripture is the call we have been given to love and welcome the sojourner. We call upon all United Methodist churches to welcome newly arriving migrants in their communities, to love them as we do ourselves, to treat them as one of our native-born, to see in them the presence of the incarnated Jesus, and to show hospitality to the migrants in our midst, believing that through their presence we are receiving the good news of the gospel of Jesus Christ.

### The Current Context

Immigration to the United States has changed in the last 20 years largely because the world has changed. Globalization has lessened the geographical distance between the poor and affluent, but it has also greatly exacerbated the chasm between those with access to resources and those denied that same access. Vast inequities between the global North and South are a continuing source of conflict and a draw of resources and people from the South to the North. Globalization has localized issues which used to be hidden or detached by geographical boundaries, but has not created forms of accountability or mediated the necessity of cross-cultural reconciliation between those victimized by international economic policies and those who benefit from them. Global media enable the poor of the global South to see the lifestyles of the affluent in the global North, while rarely seeing the intense poverty that also exists there. This creates both tensions and a draw to attain that same lifestyle.

Although unregulated trade and investment have economically benefited some, many more have been sentenced to a lifetime of poverty and marginalization. In poorer countries natural resources have been removed by transnational corporations which have no stake in the continuing welfare of the local people, the enhancement of

415

their cultural traditions, or their ecological environment. The lack of these resources often leads to a drastic reduction in jobs, wages, and labor protections. Public social benefits are eliminated and the nation sinks deeper into debt as it turns to such institutions as the World Bank and International Monetary Fund.[1] As the affluent North continues to expand its wealth, this expansion occurs at the expense of the impoverished South. Every region in the world is affected in some way by the global economic divide. Yet, while money and products easily flow across borders, the movement of people who have been forced to migrate because of intolerable economic conditions is increasingly restricted.

When those whose livelihoods have been eradicated in favor of corporate globalization attempt to sojourn to North America to work and provide for their families, they receive a mixed message that is confusing and ultimately oppressive. Immigrants have moved into areas of the United States where there are economic opportunities that US citizens have largely ignored. Employers often prefer undocumented workers in order to increase profit margins. Until all jobs provide a livable wage employers will be able to pit US citizens against undocumented workers in a downward spiral that undermines the labor rights for all.

Because the US immigration system has not kept up with the changing pace of migration and the US economy, the population of undocumented migrants has grown dramatically. Yet, the growing population of undocumented migrants has not yet been harmful to most US workers because they are not competing for the same jobs. While the United States labor force is growing older and more educated, the need for unskilled workers remains strong. The Migration Policy Institute reports that the economic necessities for repairing the immigration system are clear, as they predict by 2030 immigrant workers will comprise between one-third and one-half of the US labor force.[2] Testifying before the Senate Committee on Aging in 2003, then-Chairman of the Federal Reserve Board, Alan Greenspan, called for increased numbers of migrants to sustain an aging labor force and a continued economic vacuum among low-skilled workers.

1. Moe-Lobeda, Cynthia D. *Healing a Broken World: Globalization and God.* Minneapolis, MN: Fortress Press, p.28.
2. B. Lindsay Lowell, Julia Gelatt & Jeanne Batalove, *Immigrants and Labor Force Trends: The Future, Past, and Present.* Washington, DC: Migration Policy Institute, July 2006, p. 1.\

Although the economic necessity of migrant workers is clear, any immigration or economic system which calls for a perpetual class of second-class workers cannot be supported by people of faith. Undocumented migrants are exploited for their labor and economic contribution to the United States. They are denied their rights to collectively bargain for livable wages and safe working conditions, and they are shut out of access to the social services of which they support through their difficult labor. Any reform of the immigration system must also allow for the full protections of all workers which includes the opportunity to gain legal status for all migrants.

Even though migrants have proven a tremendous benefit to the United States' economy, migrants have been systematically excluded from receiving any benefits. Excluding access to health care promotes an increase in the demand on emergency rooms to provide that daily care or it forces migrants fearful of seeking medical care to live in continued pain and suffering. The United States benefits from migrant labor, but migrants have been forced to live in the shadows, unable to fully contribute or receive appropriate care.

*Immigration: A Human Rights Issue*

Since 9/11 the debate surrounding immigration has unfortunately been framed as an issue of national security. All of this emphasis on border security has not stemmed the flow of undocumented migration, even though the United States has poured millions of dollars into militarizing the border.

The use of local law enforcement as immigration agents should be stopped as well. When local law enforcement officials engage in immigration enforcement, migrants are often unwilling to report crimes and are forced to live in situations where they are exploited, abused, and victimized.

All nations have the right to secure their borders, but the primary concern for Christians should be the welfare of immigrants. Between 1995 and 2004 more than 2,640 migrants have died crossing the border between the United States and Mexico, and since 2004 more than one migrant has died per day.[3]

3. Wayne Cornelius, *Evaluating Enhanced US Border Enforcement.* Migration Policy Institute, May 2004.

Raids of workplaces, homes, and other social places have often violated the civil liberties of migrants. Migrants should be given due process and access to adequate legal representation. Due to these raids and the ensuing indefinite detentions and deportations that follow them, families have been ripped apart and the migrant community has been forced to live in a constant state of fear.

To refuse to welcome migrants to this country—and to stand by in silence while families are separated, individual freedoms are ignored, and the migrant community in the United States is demonized by members of Congress and the media—is complicity to sin.

### A Call to Action

The United Methodist Church affirms the worth, dignity, and inherent value and rights of all persons regardless of their nationality or legal status. United Methodist churches throughout the United States are urged to build bridges with migrants in their local communities, to learn from them, celebrate their presence in the United States and recognize and appreciate the contributions in all areas of life that migrants bring. We call upon all United Methodist churches to engage in the following:

- advocate for legislation that will uphold the civil and human rights of all migrants in the United States and will provide an opportunity to attain legal status for all undocumented migrants currently in the United States, as well as for those arriving in the future;
- begin English as a Second Language classes as part of a ministry to migrant communities and advocate for federal and state support of expanded ESL classes;
- denounce and oppose the rise of xenophobic, racist, and violent reactions against migrants in the United States, and support all efforts to build relationships among people, instead of building walls among diverse ethnicities and cultures;
- oppose the building of a wall between the United States and Mexico, which the communities of both sides of the border are in opposition to;
- call the United States government to immediately cease all arrests, detainment, and deportations of undocumented immigrants, including children, solely based upon their immi-

gration status until a fair and comprehensive immigration reform is passed;

- provide wherever possible pastoral care and crisis intervention to refugees and newly arrived migrants, identifying and responding compassionately to their spiritual, material, and legal needs;
- work with civic and legal organizations to support migrant communities affected by harsh immigration laws and overreaching national security measures;
- support those churches that prayerfully choose to offer sanctuary to undocumented migrants facing deportation;
- continue the work of the Immigration Task Force composed of staff from the general boards and agencies, representatives of the Council of Bishops, and members of caucuses and national plans that was created by the resolution, "Opposition to the Illegal Immigration Reform and Immigration Resolution Act" (2004 *Book of Resolutions*, #118).

Further, The United Methodist Church is urged to advocate for the comprehensive reform of the US immigration system. Any legislation to reform the US immigration system must affirm the worth, dignity, and inherent value and rights of migrants, and must also include:

- an opportunity for legal status for all undocumented migrants. Any pathway created for undocumented migrants should have minimal obstacles, and those requirements should not be designed to preclude migrants from eligibility for legalization;
- clearing the backlogs and reunifying families separated by migration or detainment;
- an increase in the number of visas for short-term workers to come into the United States to work in a safe, legal, and orderly way. Opportunities for legalization should be available for those who wish to remain permanently;
- the protections of all workers who come to stay for a certain period of time as well as for those who stay permanently. The right to bargain for higher wages, to protest against poor working conditions, and to preserve their human rights should be maintained by all workers, documented and undocumented alike;

- elimination of privately-operated detention centers, which are not regulated by the federal or state governments[4] ;
- elimination of indefinite detention, incarceration of children, and the expanding prison population, which also benefits privately owned detention centers and prisons;
- preservation of due process and access to courts and to adequate legal representation for all migrants regardless of legal status.

4. In the 2004 *Book of Resolutions*, "Prison Industrial Complex," it states that "Many states where private prisons are now operating have no laws regulating their operations (including health, safety, security, legal access for prisoners, and disciplinary policies). Many private prisons are under no obligation to ensure access to information about prisoners held in them or how they are classified, and often regard this as proprietary information."

**ADOPTED 2008**

*See* Social Principles, ¶¶ 162H and 163F.

## 3282. Sons and Daughters of Our Fathers

(To amend the Immigration and Nationality Act to give a visa to an alien who was fathered by a US citizen after 1950 in Korea, Vietnam, Laos, Kampuchea, or Thailand.)

### Biblical/Scriptural Foundation

*Do not be afraid, for I am with you; I will bring your children from the east and gather you from the west. I will say to the north, "Give them up!" and to the south, "Do not hold them back." Bring my sons from afar and my daughters from the ends of the earth—everyone who is called by my name, whom I created for my glory, whom I formed and made (Isaiah 43:5-7 NIV).*

WHEREAS, in 1992 when the military bases pulled out from the Philippines, they returned to the US taking almost everything. Very little was left behind except for most of the Amerasian children, fathered by American servicemen and tactical support civilians. These children, called Amerasians, are still receiving a deaf ear and blind eye from Washington; and

WHEREAS, it is estimated that there are 50,000 Amerasians in the Philippines as a whole who are the children of both our servicemen and civilian contractors. Amerasians in Vietnam, Laos, Cambodia, and Thailand are granted immediate US citizenship, but those born in the

Philippines and Japan live as outcasts and are given no special consideration from the United States government.

WHEREAS, Amerasians, regardless of the specific country where they were born, are Asian Americans. They could only become Amerasians by having one parent as an American at the time of their birth. In today's modern society, if an American woman gives birth to an Amerasian child, that child is automatically seen and accepted as a US citizen and has rights to immigrate to the US; and

WHEREAS, when an Amerasian child is born of an American father, the situation changes drastically. Acceptance as a US citizen is questioned, criticized, and microscopically examined.

WHEREAS, Public Law 97-359 was passed to set right the unfortunate situation of Amerasians, who due to their illegitimate birth or blended race makeup, have little or no possibility of evading their plight. However, the Filipino and Japanese Amerasians were excluded from eligibility because the Congress ruled that the Philippines and Japan were not considered war zones; and

WHEREAS, though the Philippines and Japan were not considered war zones, the extent and nature of the US military involvement in both countries were no different to US military involvement in other Asian countries during the Korean and Vietnam Wars. The Philippines and Japan played vital roles during those times of war as supply and stationing bases that brought tens of thousands of US military personnel to these countries; and

WHEREAS, since they were as vital as the other Asian countries, why does the United States government not give Amerasians in these two countries equal rights to other Asian countries that are benefiting from PL 97-359? Filipino and Japanese Amerasians are no different than the Amerasians in Laos, Korea, Kampuchea, Thailand, or Vietnam. They were all fathered by American servicemen and contractors who the US government stationed in the Philippines and Japan to win the war against North Korea and Vietnam; and

WHEREAS, the Fourteenth Amendment mentions two types of citizenship—citizenship by birth and citizenship by law (naturalized citizens)—all persons born in the United States are citizens by birth. Current US statutes define certain individuals born overseas as citizens by birth; and

WHEREAS, the United States Congress has the power to define citizenship to children born outside the United States. Congress can set different citizenship requirements for children born to American mothers versus American fathers;

*Therefore, be it resolved,* that the General Conference of The United Methodist Church petition our US Senators and Representatives to amend Public Law 97-359 to extend and grant US citizenship to Filipino and Japanese Amerasians and give them the right to immigrate to the United States of America to join their parents and to give them the chance to have a better life free from oppression.

**ADOPTED 2008**

*See* Social Principles, ¶ 162H.

## 3283. US Immigration and Family Unity

WHEREAS, family unity is a significant issue of faith.

In Scripture it is the family that is created by God to provide the economic and practical necessities, the religious instruction, the emotional stability and care, and the primary means of socialization for the individual. Policies, which devalue families, ultimately devalue individuals and entire societies. The US immigration system must continue to preserve and maintain families; and

WHEREAS, the unity of family as a basis for immigration should qualify on that merit alone.

Family members should qualify to immigrate to the US if they fall within any of the family immigration categories currently designated by Congress. They should not have to compete with other immigrants who are coming to the US for employment;

WHEREAS, family unity is vital to our society and the foundation for effective integration.

Family members motivate each other to learn English, purchase homes, pursue job opportunities, start their own businesses, participate in spiritually fulfilling activities, send their children to college, and contribute to their communities; and

WHEREAS, US citizens should not be barred from being united with their family members;

*Let it be resolved,* that the General Conference is in support of just and fair immigration policies that benefit and allow the family to preserve and maintain its unity.

**ADOPTED 2008**

*See* Social Principles, ¶ 162H.

## MENTAL HEALTH

### 3301. Abusive Treatment Methods for Persons with Mental Disabilities

A large part of the ministry of our Lord focused on persons with mental disabilities. Such persons are children of God and, therefore, our brothers and sisters within God's family. The full and equal rights of persons with mental disabilities are enshrined in the Social Principles of The United Methodist Church.

Yet the use of abusive treatment methods as "therapy" for persons with mental disabilities still occurs. Such abusive treatment methods are used both on adults and children, and programs that rely on such abusive treatment methods are often funded by tax revenues. A number of organizations that advocate for persons with mental disabilities have already taken a stand against abusive treatment methods.

The United Methodist Church joins in affirming the right of persons with disabilities to freedom from abusive treatment methods. We oppose the use of any form of punishment for children or adults with mental disabilities in any case where such punishment would be considered illegal, abusive, or unconscionable if applied to a child or adult who is not disabled. In particular, we condemn as unacceptable the following practices:

1. treatment methods that result in physical injury or tissue damage to the person;

2. verbal abuse or insult, humiliation, or degradation;

3. prolonged isolation from others;

4. denial of food, warmth, hygiene, contact with other human beings, or other necessities of life;

5. the use of electric shock or noxious substances as a form of punishment;

6. the use of any punishment on a child with a mental disability that would be considered child abuse if used on a child with no disabilities;

7. neglect;

8. the misuse of physical or chemical restraint; and

9. the threat of any of the above treatments.

Any therapy used in the treatment of persons with mental disabilities must be potentially beneficial to the person. As an alternative to abusive treatment methods, we support the use of positive approaches in the treatment of persons with mental disabilities. Positive approaches affirm the humanity of these persons and recognize that the needs and desires of such persons are not significantly different from those of other persons. Our obligation to persons with mental disabilities is to support and assist them in their efforts to live lives as rich and rewarding as possible.

We call upon all public and private agencies and service providers involved in treating persons with mental disabilities to adopt and uphold the standards set forth in this resolution.

We call upon United Methodist Church-related institutions and agencies, including hospitals, homes, schools, and universities, to adopt and uphold the standards set forth in this resolution and to support research on positive treatment methods.

We call upon governments at all levels to end immediately the expenditure of public revenues on any agency or program that fails to adopt and uphold the standards set forth in this resolution.

The United Methodist Church declares itself to be open to persons with mental disabilities and their families, and the church commits itself to support such persons and families and to accommodate their needs within our community. We further pledge our support to help persons with mental disabilities and their families find appropriate services, programs, and supports, and to protect them from abusive treatment methods.

ADOPTED 1996
READOPTED 2004
READOPTED 2008
RESOLUTION #120, 2004 *BOOK OF RESOLUTIONS*
RESOLUTION #108, 2000 *BOOK OF RESOLUTIONS*

*See* Social Principles, ¶ 162*I.*


### 3302. Caring Communities: The United Methodist Mental Illness Network

The mission to bring all persons into a community of love is central to the teachings of Christ. We gather as congregations in witness to that mission, welcoming and nurturing those who assemble with us.

Yet we confess that in our humanity we have sometimes failed to minister in love to persons and families with mental illness. We have allowed barriers of ignorance, fear, and pride to separate us from those who most need our love and the nurturing support of community.

To support United Methodist congregations in their goal to reach out to persons and families with mental illness, the General Board of Church and Society established the United Methodist Mental Illness Network of "Caring Communities," congregations and communities in covenant relationship with persons and families with mental illness.

United Methodist congregations are called to join the Caring Communities Program:
- to educate their members about mental illness;
- to enter into a covenant relationship of understanding and love with persons and families with mental illness, in order to nurture them; and
- to reach out to the larger community.

ADOPTED 1996
AMENDED AND READOPTED 2004
RESOLUTION #121, 2004 *BOOK OF RESOLUTIONS*
RESOLUTION #109, 2000 *BOOK OF RESOLUTIONS*

*See* Social Principles, ¶ 162*I* and *V*.

### 3303. Mental Illness, Mental Health Courts, and the Christian Community

We believe all persons with a mental illness diagnosis should have access to the same basic freedoms and human rights as other persons living in a free society. We understand that there is a fine line of distinction between criminal violation of the law and behavior that is criminalized because law enforcement agencies have had no other recourse for handling persons whose behavior and actions have been the result of mental illness symptoms which affect thinking, perceptions, and behavior. We oppose the use of jails and prisons for the incarceration of persons who have serious, persistent mental illnesses for whom treatment in a secure hospital setting is far more appropriate. Moreover, many incarcerated persons with mental illness need psychiatric medications. Citing economic reasons as the cause for failure to provide medications to a person who needs them is unacceptable as is imposing medication compliance as a condition of release or access to treatment and other services. We believe that all states should understand and embrace an ethical understanding of the compassionate intent of the law in the establishment of mental health courts when mental illness is a factor in law enforcement. We believe all persons confined for the purpose of mental illness treatment in an accredited psychiatric facility, either public or private, shall have all their human rights respected, including their [legal] right to have input into their treatment plan, medications, and access to religious support as State laws allow. We also hold all treatment facilities, public and private, responsible for the protection of these rights.

We further believe all mental health treatment facilities; public and private, including outpatient treatment programs, should take seriously the religious and nonreligious spiritual needs of persons with a mental illness who find help and hope for their life through their faith in God or in a power higher than themselves.

We acknowledge that persons with a mental illness diagnosis who exhibit difficult or disruptive behaviors often do so because they have experienced traumatic events such as abuse or domestic violence, have lived a life of physical or emotional poverty, or have been deprived of social experiences and have limited social skills and etiquette. We believe that some persons with a mental illness who exhibit acting-out or difficult behaviors do so because they have often been lonely, misunderstood, powerless, or are without joy in their lives.

We believe mental illness courts, properly established, regulated and administered could be maintained in every jurisdiction to handle cases involving persons with serious mental illnesses; insure compassionate and ethical treatment, and avoid whenever possible criminalizing the behaviors that result from symptoms which affect thinking, perceptions, and behavior.

We believe The Church and local congregations have a responsibility for the role they play in advocating for the lives of adults as well as children and teens who have mental illnesses; whose experiences have included pastoral care and other spiritual opportunities they have had prior to diagnosis and may be denied now because of stigma and their difficult behaviors. We believe these responsibilities include educational opportunities and the right to literacy. We believe in the perpetuation of Christian and spiritual values in our society relating to the development of pastoral leadership skills to understand mental illness and be able to mediate with persons in their congregations and their communities concerning the issues and needs of persons who have a mental illness. We further believe congregations and private foundation boards on which Christians sit and have authority or influence have a significant role to play in advocating for the support of ministries that address these issues.

ADOPTED 2004
RESOLUTION #125, 2004 *BOOK OF RESOLUTIONS*

*See* Social Principles, ¶ 162V.

### 3304. The Church and People with Mental, Physical, and/or Psychological Disabilities

We call United Methodists to a new birth of awareness of the need to accept, include, receive the gifts of, and respond to the concerns of those persons with mental, physical, and/or psychological disabilities, including their families.

*Because* the experience of disabilities is included in all racial, social, sexual, and age groupings, and this experience is common to every family and at some time in every life;

*And because* a large part of the ministry of our Lord focused on persons with conditions such as mental, physical, psychological, and/or neurological disabilities;

*And because* the body of Christ is not complete without people of all areas of life;

*And because* we cannot afford to deny ourselves fellowship with these persons and must intentionally develop more healthy attitudes and behavioral responses to people with disabilities;

*And because* there exist inadequacies in the church and in society with regard to concerns for the rights of people with disabilities, utilization of talents, and their full participation within the life of the church and society;

*And because* of more suffering and exclusion from the fellowship of the church of persons with mental, physical, and/or psychological conditions;

*And believing* that the church is most faithful to the teachings and example of Jesus when it expresses love in concrete ways in a mutual ministry with those who are outcasts, neglected, avoided, or persecuted by society;

*And believing* in the legacy of John Wesley, Phillip Otterbein, and Jacob Albright, who held that vital piety flows into compassionate ministry;

*And knowing* that prevailing societal norms unduly glorify the conditions of youthful beauty, mental alertness, and material affluence to the exclusion and avoidance of those whose disabilities put them outside these norms,

*Therefore, we pledge ourselves to:*

### Accessibility:

1. Renew and increase our commitments as a church to the development of a barrier-free society, especially in the many facilities of the church and parsonages. To indicate the seriousness of our intent, we must set time limits to ensure the greatest physical accessibility in the shortest feasible periods and extend our policy of not providing funding through or approval by United Methodist agencies unless minimum guidelines are met, which include but are not limited to:

   a. providing adequate access to sanctuary pews, altars, chancel areas and pulpit, classrooms, and restrooms;
   b. providing curb cuts, ramps with at least a 1:12 inclination or platform lifts; and
   c. providing facilities with equipment and supplies to meet the needs of persons with seen and unseen disabilities, including persons with vision and/or hearing impairments.

2. All meetings of The United Methodist Church, beyond the local church, be accessible to people with disabilities. As general church agencies, jurisdictions, annual conferences, and districts nominate people with disabilities to their boards and committees, it is necessary for these boards and committees to accommodate these persons.

3. All United Methodist churches are asked to conduct an audit of their facilities to discover what barriers impede the full participation of people with disabilities. Steps should then be taken to remove those barriers. The accessibility audit for churches is a recommended resource available from the General Board of Global Ministries.

### Awareness:

1. Sensitize and train local church pastors to the needs and opportunities for those who have a disability and their families to better minister to and with them.

2. Lead the local churches in attitudinal change studies, to the end that the people called United Methodists are sensitized to the gifts, needs, and interests of people with disabilities, including their families.

3. Take advantage of the great opportunities for our church to work cooperatively with other denominations who also are addressing these issues and extend an active invitation to work jointly where possible.

4. Suggest one Sunday each year as Access Sunday to sensitize people to our accessibility concerns.

*Adequate Resources:*

1. Provide resources through the church at all levels, including curricula, for persons with various disabilities, such as those who are blind, deaf, para- or quadriplegic, mentally retarded, psychologically or neurologically disabled, and so forth, so that each individual has full opportunity for growth and self-realization with the community of faith and the society at large.

2. Strongly recommend that all curriculum material be so designed that it can be adapted to meet the needs of people with disabilities; that curriculum material portray people with disabilities in leadership roles within church and society; that curriculum material reflect the Guidelines for the Elimination of Handicappist Language as produced by the General Council on Ministries.

*Affirmative Action:*

1. Include in all our efforts of affirmative action the concerns and interests of people with disabilities, particularly in the active recruitment and encouragement of these persons for leadership roles, both clergy and lay, within the church and its agencies, in hiring practices, job security, housing, and transportation.

2. Urge the General Board of Higher Education and Ministry to monitor annual conference boards of ordained ministry so that people with disabilities are given equal treatment in the steps to ordained ministry.

3. Strongly urge that our schools of higher education and theological training provide specialized courses for faculty and students in the awareness and appreciation of gifts, needs, and interests of people with disabilities. This must include the emphasis of accessibility and equal employment in these institutions, as well as those in the larger

society. Accreditation by the University Senate should be withdrawn where persons who are disabled are excluded, either from attendance, services, or employment.

4. Strongly urge local churches to conduct needs-assessment surveys. Such a survey would suggest to a local church what particular actions must be taken to fully include people with disabilities within the life of the church.

### Advocacy Within the Church:

Implement within each annual conference methods of recruiting, sensitizing, and training persons as advocates to work with and on behalf of people with disabilities on a one-to-one basis and to enable them to achieve their human and civil rights as well as to assume their rightful place in the life of the church and community. Each annual conference should also develop the larger concern of advocacy for people with disabilities to enable them to achieve appropriate housing, employment, transportation, education, and leisure-time development.

### Advocacy Within the Society:

While there is much to be done within the church to make real the gospel of inclusiveness with regard to people with disabilities, there is a world society that also must be made aware of the concerns and needs of these persons. We admonish the church and its people to stand alongside people with disabilities and to speak out on their rights in society. These rights include access to jobs, public transportation and other reliable forms of transportation, adequate housing, and education. We are people under orders to minister to and with all God's children. We are all a people in pilgrimage! We have too often overlooked those of God's children who experience life in different ways from ourselves. We pledge ourselves to an inclusive, compassionate, and creative response to the needs and gifts of people with mental, physical, and/or psychological disabilities.

### Barrier-Free Construction for People with Disabilities:

Be it resolved, that church monies from agencies of The United Methodist Church beyond the local church be granted, loaned, or otherwise provided only for the construction of church sanctuaries, educational buildings, parsonages, camps, colleges, or other church-related agencies or facilities that meet minimum guidelines in their plans for barrier-free construction;

That local churches utilizing their own funds or funds secured through lending agencies and institutions beyond The United Methodist Church be urged to make adequate provision in their plans to ensure that all new church buildings shall be of barrier-free construction;

That local churches be urged to adapt existing facilities through such programs as widening doorways, installing ramps and elevators, eliminating stairs where possible, providing handrails, adequate parking facilities, and rest rooms so that people with disabilities may take their appropriate place in the fellowship of the church; and

That the appropriate national agencies provide technical information for local churches to assist in providing barrier-free facilities.

ADOPTED 1984
AMENDED AND READOPTED 1996, 2004
READOPTED 2008
RESOLUTION #122, 2004 *BOOK OF RESOLUTIONS*
RESOLUTION #110, 2000 *BOOK OF RESOLUTIONS*

*See* Social Principles, ¶ 162I.

## 3305. Ministries in Mental Illness

*Mental illness* is a group of brain disorders that cause disturbances of thinking, feeling, and acting. Treatment should recognize the importance of a nonstressful environment, good nutrition, and an accepting community. Treatment should also recognize the importance of medical, psychiatric, emotional and spiritual care, psychotherapy or professional pastoral psychotherapy in regaining and maintaining health. Churches in every community are called to participate actively in expanding care for the mentally ill and their families and communities.

John Wesley's ministry was grounded in the redemptive ministry of Christ with its focus on healing that involved spiritual, mental, emotional, and physical aspects. His concern for the health of those to whom he ministered led him to create medical services at no cost to those who were poor and in deep need, refusing no one for any reason. He saw health as going beyond a simple biological well-being to wellness of the whole person. His witness of love to those in need of healing is our model for ministry to those who are suffering from mental illness.

All aspects of health—physical, mental, and spiritual—were of equal concern to Jesus Christ, whose healing touch reached out to mend broken bodies, minds, and spirits with one common purpose: the restoration of well-being and renewed communion with God and neighbor. But those whose illness brought social stigma and isolation, such as the man of Gadara, whose troubled spirit caused fearsome and self-destructive behavior, were embraced and healed with special compassion (Mark 5:1-34). When the man of Gadara said his name was "Legion; for we are many" (verse 9), his comment was suggestive of the countless individuals, in our time as well as his, whose mental dysfunction—whether genetically, environmentally, chemically, socially, or psychologically induced—causes fear, rejection, or shame, and to which we tend to respond with the same few measures no more adequate for our time than for his: stigmatization, isolation, incarceration, and restraint.

We confess that our Christian concepts of sin and forgiveness, at the root of our understanding of the human condition and of divine grace, are sometimes inappropriately applied in ways that heighten paranoia or clinical depression. Great care must be exercised in ministering to those whose brain disorders result in exaggerated self-negation, for while all persons stand in need of forgiveness and reconciliation, God's love cannot be communicated through the medium of forgiveness for uncommitted or delusional sins.

We reaffirm our confidence that God's unqualified love for all persons beckons us to reach out with fully accepting love to all, but particularly to those with disabling inability to relate to themselves or others due to mental illness.

Research published since 1987 has underscored the physical and genetic basis for the more serious mental illnesses, such as schizophrenia, manic-depression, and other affective disorders.

Public discussion and education about mental illness are needed so that persons who suffer from brain disorders, and their families, can be free to ask for help. This includes freedom from the stigma attached to mental illness that derives from a false understanding that it is primarily an adjustment problem caused by psychologically dysfunctional families. Communities need to develop more adequate programs to meet the needs of their mentally ill members. This includes the need to implement state and local programs that monitor and prevent abuses of mentally ill persons, as well as those programs that are intended to replace long-term hospitalization with community-based services.

The process followed in recent years of deinstitutionalizing mental patients has corrected a long-standing problem of "warehousing" mentally ill persons. However, without adequate community-based mental-health programs to care for the dehospitalized, the streets, for too many, have become a substitute for a hospital ward. Consequently, often the responsibility, including the costs of mental-health care, have simply been transferred to individuals and families or to shelters for the homeless that are already overloaded and ill-equipped to provide more than the most basic care. Furthermore, the pressure to deinstitutionalize patients rapidly has caused some mental-health systems to rely unduly upon short-term chemical therapy to control patients rather than upon more complex programs that require longer-term hospitalization or other forms of treatments where research provides successful outcomes achieved. Such stopgap treatment leads to repeated short-term hospitalizations, with little or no long-term improvement in a person's ability to function.

The church, as the body of Christ, is called to the ministry of reconciliation, of healing, and of salvation, which means to be made whole. We call upon the church to affirm ministries related to mental illness that embrace the role of community, family, and the healing professions in healing the physical, social, environmental, and spiritual impediments to wholeness for those afflicted with brain disorders and for their families.

1. We call upon all local churches, districts, and annual conferences to support the following community and congressional programs:
   a. adequate public funding to enable mental-health systems to provide appropriate therapy;
   b. expanded counseling and crisis intervention services;
   c. workshops and public awareness campaigns to combat stigmas;
   d. housing and employment for deinstitutionalized persons;
   e. improved training for judges, police, and other community officials in dealing with mentally ill persons;
   f. community and congregational involvement with patients in psychiatric hospitals and other mental-health-care facilities;

g. community, pastoral, and congregational support for individuals and families caring for mentally ill family members;

h. more effective interaction among different systems involved in the care of mentally ill persons, including courts, police, employment, housing, welfare, religious, and family systems;

i. education of their members in a responsible and comprehensive manner about the nature of the problems of mental illness facing society today, and the public-policy advocacy needed to change policies and keep funding levels high;

j. active participation in helping their communities meet both preventive and therapeutic needs related to mental illness; and

k. the work of the National Alliance for the Mentally Ill (NAMI), Washington, D.C., a self-help organization of mentally ill persons, their families, and friends, providing mutual support, education, and advocacy for those persons with severe mental illness and urging the churches to connect with NAMI's religious outreach network. We also commend to the churches Pathways to Promise: Interfaith Ministries and Prolonged Mental Illnesses, St. Louis, Missouri, as a necessary link in our ministry on this critical issue.

2. We call upon seminaries to provide:

a. technical training, including experience in mental-health units, as a regular part of the preparation for the ministry, in order to help congregations become more knowledgeable about and involved in mental-health needs of their communities.

3. We call upon the general agencies to:

a. advocate systemic reform of the health-care system to provide more adequately for persons and families confronting the catastrophic expense and pain of caring for mentally ill family members;

b. support universal access to health care, insisting that public and private funding mechanisms be developed to ensure the availability of services to all in need, including adequate coverage for mental-health services in all health programs;

c. advocate community mental-health systems, including public clinics, hospitals, and other tax-supported facilities, being especially sensitive to the mental-health needs of culturally or racially diverse groups in the population;

d. support adequate research by public and private institutions into the causes of mental illness, including, as high priority,

further development of therapeutic applications of newly discovered information on the genetic causation for several types
of severe brain disorders;

e. support adequate public funding to enable mental-health-care
systems to provide appropriate therapy; and

f. build a United Methodist Church mental illness network at
the General Board of Church and Society to coordinate men-
tal-illness ministries in The United Methodist Church.

ADOPTED 1992
AMENDED AND READOPTED IN 2004
RESOLUTION #123, 2004 *BOOK OF RESOLUTIONS*
RESOLUTION #111, 2000 *BOOK OF RESOLUTIONS*

*See* Social Principles, ¶ 162V.

## 3306. Healing of Post-Abortion Stress

WHEREAS, we recognize that there is a legal right to an abortion, we
also recognize that some regret that event later in life,

WHEREAS, the church should be about offering healing ministries for
all types of brokenness,

*Therefore, be it resolved* that the 2004 General Conference of The
United Methodist Church urge pastors to become informed about the
symptoms and behaviors associated with post-abortion stress; and

*Be it further resolved* that the 2004 General Conference of The United
Methodist Church encourage local churches to make available contact
information for counseling agencies that offer programs to address
post-abortion stress for all seeking help.

ADOPTED 2004
RESOLUTION #124, 2004 *BOOK OF RESOLUTIONS*

*See* Social Principles, ¶ 162V.

## NATIVE AMERICANS

## 3321. Comity Agreements Affecting Development
of Native American Ministries

WHEREAS, certain annual conferences of The United Methodist
Church have used the alleged Comity Agreement as the basis for their

functional relationship among Native Americans, limiting their capability to develop Native American ministries in certain geographical areas; and

WHEREAS, the effects of practicing the concept of a Comity Agreement by The United Methodist Church have resulted in the failure of the Church to follow through with the biblical mandate of propagating the gospel to all nations and, further, have caused the failure of the church to create the climate for leadership development of Native Americans; and

WHEREAS, such a Comity Agreement would be discriminatory in that it would violate the right of Native Americans to associate with the denomination of their choice;

*Therefore, be it resolved,* that The United Methodist Church states, as a matter of policy, that it is not a party to any interdenominational agreement that limits the ability of any annual conference in any jurisdiction to develop and resource programs of ministry of any kind among Native Americans, including the organization of local churches where necessary.

ADOPTED 1980
READOPTED 2000
READOPTED 2008
RESOLUTION #129, 2004 *BOOK OF RESOLUTIONS*
RESOLUTION #118, 2000 *BOOK OF RESOLUTIONS*

*See* Social Principles, ¶ 162A.

## 3322. Confession to Native Americans

WHEREAS, the gospel calls us to celebrate and protect the worth and dignity of all peoples; and

WHEREAS, the Christian churches, including The United Methodist Church and its predecessors, have participated in the destruction of Native American people, culture, and religious practices; and

WHEREAS, the churches of this country have not sufficiently confessed their complicity in this evil; and

WHEREAS, the churches have been blessed by having members who are Native Americans as well as by engaging in dialogue with Native Americans who practice their traditional religions; and

WHEREAS, confession of our guilt is a first step toward the wholeness that the churches seek through the ecumenical movement;

*Therefore, be it resolved,* that the United Methodist General Conference confesses that The United Methodist Church (and its predecessor bodies) has sinned and continues to sin against its Native American brothers and sisters and offers this formal apology for its participation, intended and unintended, in the violent colonization of their land; and

*Be it further resolved,* that The United Methodist Church pledges its support and assistance in upholding the American Indian Religious Freedom Acts (P.L. 95-134, 1978) and within that legal precedent affirms the following:

1. the rights of the native peoples to practice and participate in traditional ceremonies and rituals with the same protection offered all religions under the Constitution of the United States of America;

2. access to and protection of sacred sites and public lands for ceremonial purposes; and

3. the use of religious symbols (feathers, tobacco, sweet grass, bones, and so forth) for use in traditional ceremonies and rituals.

*Be it further resolved,* that the General Conference recommends that local churches develop similar statements of confession as a way of fostering a deep sense of community with Native Americans and encourages the members of our Church to stand in solidarity on these important religious issues and to provide mediation when appropriate for ongoing negotiations with state and federal agencies regarding these matters.

ADOPTED 1992
READOPTED 2004 AND 2008
RESOLUTION #132, 2004 *BOOK OF RESOLUTIONS*
RESOLUTION #120, 2000 *BOOK OF RESOLUTIONS*

*See* Social Principles, ¶ 162A.

## 3323. Healing Relationships with Indigenous Persons

WHEREAS, historically United Methodism and its predecessor bodies have desired to reach indigenous persons around the world with the good news of the gospel, yet at the same time that Good News has sometimes been perceived as bad news, as Christian efforts have not only introduced Jesus Christ, but in many cases resulted in indignities, cultural genocide, and atrocities against the tribal peoples, and

WHEREAS, God has been present with all peoples since creation, and through prevenient grace has been a living and moving Spirit among the world's diverse cultures, and WHEREAS, in many parts of the world, to become a Christian may mean one is expected to abandon one's culture and traditional religion, resulting in tension and division within families and tribes, and the loss of the unique identity associated with family and clan, including in some places: the requirement to stop speaking one's own language, to change one's clothing and hair, to discontinue participation in prayer ceremonies of the tribe and any number of cultural activities such as music and dance, and

WHEREAS, God so loved the world that he sent his son Jesus, and many missionaries have befriended and suffered with indigenous peoples in tragic circumstances and thereby have been a true witness of the love of God, we celebrate and confess the faithful and painful journey of our church's relationship with indigenous peoples, seeking to learn the lessons from our past and to avoid the pitfalls that would hinder the sharing and receiving of the gospel of Christ among indigenous persons, and

WHEREAS, the General Commission on Christian Unity and Interreligious Concerns has participated in conversations with persons who practice their indigenous religion and have yet to hear the gospel as good news;

*Therefore, be it resolved,* that United Methodist churches throughout the world seek ways to build bridges of respect and understanding, that our churches listen and become educated about the history of the relationship between indigenous persons and Christian colonizers in their own geographic location, and that through prayer and relationship building, develop means for reconciliation and celebrate the gifts that indigenous people bring to the body of Jesus in the world, and

*Be it also resolved* that the General Commission on Christian Unity and Interreligious Concerns facilitate and make available to annual conferences and local churches resources to suggest models and guidelines for building relationships with indigenous persons, and

*Be it also resolved* that the General Conference hold an Act of Repentance Service at the 2012 gathering of the Conference, and that that service will launch study, dialogue, and acts of repentance in all annual conferences over the following quadrennium, and

*Be it also resolved* that the General Commission on Christian Unity and Interreligious Concerns be charged with the necessary study and preparation of resources for the process of listening, repentance, and reconciliation to occur.

ADOPTED 2000
REVISED AND READOPTED 2008
RESOLUTION #133, 2004 *BOOK OF RESOLUTIONS*
RESOLUTION #121, 2000 *BOOK OF RESOLUTIONS*

*See* Social Principles, ¶ 162*A*.

## 3324. Native American Representation in The United Methodist Church

WHEREAS, the population of Native Americans has grown dramatically during the past two decades; and

WHEREAS, this trend of population growth is accompanied by a substantial positive interest in Native American culture and history in regard to The United Methodist Church participation among traditionally noninterested individuals; and

WHEREAS, leadership of The United Methodist Church has recently demonstrated a sincere desire to "include" Native Americans in the decision-making activity of the church; and

WHEREAS, there is a significant need to recruit Native Americans into "role model" positions within the church as a means to enhance church membership, ministry numbers, and an overall understanding of contemporary Native American life as related to racial communication; and

WHEREAS, current attitudes among Native Americans reflect a critical desire to present and communicate accurate Native American perspectives to, and for, decision-making bodies of The United Methodist Church; and

WHEREAS, there is currently a minute number of Native Americans serving on the national United Methodist Church policy-making boards, management committees, education boards, finance committees, information areas, and such; and

WHEREAS, current trends suggest a decrease in church membership and attendance among Native American citizenry;

*Therefore, be it resolved,* that General Conference strongly support the following tasks as related to accurate Native American representation and participation on local, regional, and national policy-making, managerial, and implementation/evaluation boards/committees of The United Methodist Church:

1. Establish a policy of defining Native American identity as "any individual who can provide verification of membership in a tribe of the United States";

2. Develop a policy that will ensure that Native Americans will be identified, selected, and placed on pertinent boards and/or committees as previously stated; and

3. Urge national, regional, and annual conference activities to select Native American representation from Native American individuals who have a background of relevant Native American history, cultural sensitivity, and contemporary affairs.

*Be it further resolved*, that The United Methodist Church supports the integration of a policy on Native American definition within *The Book of Discipline*, specific to the current and future regard of Native American representation on such national, regional, and local efforts.

ADOPTED 1992
READOPTED 2004
RESOLUTION #144, 2004 *BOOK OF RESOLUTIONS*
RESOLUTION #132, 2000 *BOOK OF RESOLUTIONS*

*See* Social Principles, ¶ 162A.

## 3325. Native American Ministries Sunday

WHEREAS, the Native American population continues to shift in larger numbers from the rural areas to the urban population centers; and

WHEREAS, the human conditions of numerous Native Americans in the rural and urban environments reflect a legacy of poverty and socioeconomic denial; and

WHEREAS, there is a serious shortage of Native American pastors and trained professionals to respond to the human conditions in the Native American communities; and

WHEREAS, there is a National United Methodist Native American Center, which has been created to recruit, train, and deploy Native American leadership; and

WHEREAS, the financial support that is required to sustain the center is beyond the capability of the Native American communities; and

WHEREAS, the 1988 General Conference approved Native American Awareness Sunday (now known as N.A.M. Sunday) as a means for providing opportunities for the denomination to support Native American ministries;

*Therefore, be it resolved,* that all annual conferences promote the observance of the Native American Ministries Sunday and encourage local churches to support the Sunday with programming and offerings.

*Be it further resolved,* that the agencies that develop and provide resources for this special day report to the General Commission on Religion and Race their plans, strategies, and timelines for addressing the goals and objectives related to Native American Ministries Sunday.

ADOPTED 1992
READOPTED 2004 AND 2008
RESOLUTION #137, 2004 *BOOK OF RESOLUTIONS*
RESOLUTION #125, 2000 *BOOK OF RESOLUTIONS*

*See* Social Principles, ¶ 162A.

## 3326. Native American Young Adults in Mission

WHEREAS, by treaty obligation many Native American tribes are recognized as "nations" within the territorial boundaries of the United States; and

WHEREAS, the General Board of Global Ministries of The United Methodist Church sponsor the Mission Intern Program, and the Mission Personnel Program Area of the Board assigns young adults overseas , and within the boundaries of the United States to develop leadership skills; and

WHEREAS, opportunities for mission and evangelism exist within Native American nations and tribes within the territorial boundaries of the United States;

*Therefore, be it resolved,* that the Mission Personnel Program Area be directed to assign Native American young adults in "Native American Nations and Tribes" within the boundaries of the United States and in overseas assignments.

ADOPTED 1992
AMENDED AND READOPTED 2004
READOPTED 2008
RESOLUTION #145, 2004 *BOOK OF RESOLUTIONS*
RESOLUTION #133, 2000 *BOOK OF RESOLUTIONS*

*See* Social Principles, ¶ 162A.

## 3327. Respecting the Native American Legacy and Tradition

The United Methodist Church has denounced the continued use of Native American names as nicknames for sport teams as racist and dehumanizing. Respecting the Native American legacy and tradition has been a critical issue for the General Commission on Religion and Race and the General Commission on Christian Unity and Interreligious Concerns.

United Methodists have not been the sole voice on this issue. Many other communions, religious groups, and secular organizations have addressed this concern in the form of statements, articles, protests, and resolutions. However, in spite of these efforts, Native American names and symbols are still being used by sport teams.

WHEREAS, The United Methodist Church is committed to the elimination of racism within the church and within society, and

WHEREAS, The United Methodist Church is equally committed to participate actively in the continued struggle of building the true community of God where reconciliation comes together with justice and peace, and

WHEREAS, The United Methodist Church rejects the use of Native American names and symbols for sport teams, and considers the practice a blatant expression of racism:

*Therefore, be it resolved,* that the General Conference calls upon all the general agencies, annual conferences, and United Methodist Church-related organizations and institutions, upon selecting locations for their meetings and events in cities that sponsor sport teams using Native American names and symbols, to hold meetings and events in cities that do not sponsor sport teams using Native American names and symbols, and make public the position of The United Methodist Church regarding sport teams using Native American names and symbols.

ADOPTED 2004
RESOLUTION #131, 2004 *BOOK OF RESOLUTIONS*

*See* Social Principles, ¶162A.


## 3328. Native American History and Contemporary Culture as Related to Effective Church Participation

WHEREAS, current literature and research suggest a substantial "communication gap" between Native Americans and non-Indian

United Methodist Church entities, specifically as it relates to non-Indian entities comprehending the concept of Native American life, culture, language, spirit, values, and such; and

WHEREAS, this vague communication has been a consistent problem over history, with minimal effort from non-Indian entities to change their attitudes toward Native Americans until recent trends; and

WHEREAS, such attitude of society reflects a growing trend toward developing and implementing a system accommodating, to a high degree, cultural diversity; generally speaking, society is beginning to demonstrate comprehension of the term *multicultural* education as related to the year 2000 and is making efforts to become even more informed; services that once perpetuated Eurocentric society only are now examining the values of the ever-growing ethnic populations and attempting to integrate these values into their service activities (education, government, health, business, and such); and

WHEREAS, there are substantial numbers of ethnic professionals capable of providing effective instruction in cultural diversity as related to The United Methodist Church's current and future thrusts; and

WHEREAS, there still is a critical need for The United Methodist Church to become concretely familiar with its Native American membership in order to ensure their religious, denominational, spiritual, and emotional well-being; and

WHEREAS, there is an expressed concern from The United Methodist Church's Native American membership that racism and prejudice are significant contributors to the absence of Native American representation in the church's hierarchy; and

WHEREAS, the formal means of eliminating this condition is through the formal instruction in Native American history, culture, and contemporary affairs of non-Indian entities of The United Methodist Church;

*Therefore, be it resolved,* that General Conference advocate the development and implementation of a training policy whereby Native American history, culture, and contemporary affairs will be an integral part of ministry and administrative training for all aspects of The United Methodist Church;

*Be it further resolved,* that General Conference designate the Native American International Caucus, to provide for the research, development, and training components of the requested curriculum;

*Be it further resolved,* that General Conference support a policy that the concept of "Indian preference" be utilized in the selection of instructors and speakers for the proposed training components. The Native American International Caucus will provide a list of qualified Native American leaders

ADOPTED 1992
READOPTED 2004
REVISED AND READOPTED 2008
RESOLUTION #142, 2004 *BOOK OF RESOLUTIONS*
RESOLUTION #130, 2000 *BOOK OF RESOLUTIONS*

*See* Social Principles, ¶ 162A.

## 3329. Native American Religious Freedom Act

WHEREAS, tribal people have gone into the high places, lakes, and isolated sanctuaries to pray, receive guidance from God, and train younger people in the ceremonies that constitute the spiritual life of Native American communities; and

WHEREAS, when tribes were forcibly removed from their homelands and forced to live on restricted reservations, many of the ceremonies were prohibited; and

WHEREAS, most Indians do not see any conflict between their old beliefs and the new religion of the Christian church; and

WHEREAS, during this century the expanding national population and the introduction of corporate farming and more extensive mining and timber industry activities reduced the isolation of rural America, making it difficult for small parties of Native Americans to go into the mountains or to remote lakes and buttes to conduct ceremonies without interference from non-Indians; and

WHEREAS, federal agencies began to restrict Indian access to sacred sites by establishing increasingly narrow rules and regulations for managing public lands; and

WHEREAS, in 1978, in an effort to clarify the status of traditional Native American religious practices and practitioners, Congress passed a Joint Resolution entitled "The American Indian Religious Freedom Act," which declared that it was the policy of Congress to protect and preserve the inherent right of Native Americans to believe, express, and practice their traditional religions; and

WHEREAS, today a major crisis exists in that there is no real protection for the practice of traditional Indian religions within the framework of American constitutional or statutory law, and courts usually automatically dismiss Indian petitions without evidentiary hearings; and

WHEREAS, while Congress has passed many laws that are designed to protect certain kinds of lands and resources for environmental and historic preservation, none of these laws is designed to protect the practice of Indian religion on sacred sites; and

WHEREAS, the only existing law directly addressing this issue, the American Indian Religious Freedom Act, is simply a policy that provides limited legal relief to aggrieved American Indian religious practitioners,

*Therefore, be it resolved,* that the General Board of Global Ministries and the General Board of Church and Society make available to the church information on the American Indian Religious Freedom Act; and

*Be it further resolved,* that the General Board of Church and Society support legislation that will provide for a legal cause of action when sacred sites may be affected by governmental action; proposed legislation should also provide for more extensive notice to and consultation with tribes and affected parties; and

*Be it further resolved,* that the General Board of Church and Society may enter and support court cases relating to the American Indian Religious Freedom Act; and

*Be it further resolved,* that the General Board of Church and Society communicate with the Senate Committee on Indian Affairs, declaring that the position of The United Methodist Church, expressed through the 1992 General Conference, is to strengthen the American Indian Religious Freedom Act of 1978 and preserve the God-given and constitutional rights of religious freedom for Native Americans.

ADOPTED 1992
AMENDED AND READOPTED 2004
RESOLUTION #143, 2004 *BOOK OF RESOLUTIONS*
RESOLUTION #131, 2000 *BOOK OF RESOLUTIONS*

*See* Social Principles, ¶ 162A.

### 3330. Concerning Demeaning Names to Native Americans

In our society today, there is a growing debate and discussion about the appropriateness of using Native American names as nicknames for professional sports teams and university mascots. As the publication *Words That Hurt, Words That Heal,* produced by The United Methodist Church, highlights, the use of names and language is a powerful instrument for good and destructive purposes. It is demeaning to Native Americans and other members of our society to depict Native Americans as violent and aggressive people by calling a sports team the "Braves" or the "Warriors." The implication is that all Native Americans are aggressive and violent people. This use of nicknames is not conducive to the development of a society committed to the common good of its citizenry.

In "The United Methodist Church and America's Native People" (*The Book of Resolutions, 1992;* page 178; *The Book of Resolutions, 2004,* page 375), The United Methodist Church has issued a call for repentance for the church's role in the dehumanization and colonization of our Native American sisters and brothers. In light of this stand and the fact that we strongly believe the continued use of Native American names as nicknames is demeaning and racist, we urge all United Methodist-related universities, colleges, and schools to set an example by replacing any nicknames that demean and offend our Native American sisters and brothers; and we support efforts throughout our society to replace such nicknames, mascots, and symbols.

ADOPTED 1996
READOPTED 2004
RESOLUTION #130, 2004 *BOOK OF RESOLUTIONS*
RESOLUTION #119, 2000 *BOOK OF RESOLUTIONS*

*See* Social Principles, ¶ 162A.

### 3331. Regarding Native American Culture and Traditions as Sacred

For hundreds of years Native Americans, Native Alaskans, and Native Hawaiians, compelled by the gospel have chosen to become disciples of Jesus Christ. In doing so, we have affirmed with the voices of the saints that all that is necessary for salvation, relationship with God and our brothers and sisters, is contained in the gospel of Jesus Christ. We bear witness to the mercy of God through our faith, continuing in discipleship and ministry.

Government and religious institutions intentionally destroyed many of our traditional cultures and belief systems. To assimilate our peoples into mainstream cultures, as children many of our ancestors were forcibly removed to boarding schools, often operated by religious institutions, including historical Methodism. Historically, Native peoples have been targets by those seeking land and other natural resources. Genocide became a tool of greed and a response to fear. While attempting to erase Native people from existence, traditional cultures also fell victim to acts of genocide.

As Native Christians, we affirm for the church and ourselves that many elements of our traditions and cultures are consistent with the gospel of Jesus Christ, and the teachings of the church. We affirm that the Holy Spirit is faithful in guiding us in holy living within our cultures and the broader culture. We recognize that just as in the broader culture, not all expressions of traditional cultures are appropriate for all believers; God is faithful in leading us to acceptable worship and continued growth in grace, as tribal people. We further affirm that our identity as Native, or tribal persons is pleasing to our Creator, and vital to the body of Christ. We affirm for each other that our languages, cultures, identities, and many traditions are pleasing to God and have the potential to refresh the church and offer hope to the world. To be less is to be other than what God is asking us to be in our time.

We further believe that many of our Native traditions affirm the presence of God, our need for right relationship with our Creator and the world around us, and a call for holy living. Both through corporate and personal conviction our people individually and tribally are led by the Spirit of God to a greater awareness of God. Traditional beliefs, consistent with the gospel and the historic witness of the church should not be understood as contrary to our beliefs as Native Christians. Furthermore, the testimony of historic and contemporary Native Christians should be counted in the historic witness of the church.

WHEREAS, we believe that God's creating presence speaks to us through our languages and cultures and that such testimony is vital to the ongoing work of the church among our people and;

WHEREAS, many Native traditions were erroneously feared, rather than understood as vehicles for the grace of God, and;

WHEREAS, such fears have resulted in persecution of traditional Native peoples and Native Christians, and;

WHEREAS, many traditions have been misinterpreted as sin, rather than varying cultural expressions leading to a deeper understanding of our creator;

*Therefore, be it resolved,* that the General Conference of The United Methodist Church affirms the sacredness of Native people, their languages, their cultures, and their gifts to the church and the world.

*Be it further resolved,* that we believe in the faithful leadership of the Holy Spirit in assisting us as individuals and communities in the preservation of those cultures and the continuation of their faith; that just as there are many parts of the body of Christ, there are many Native traditions, languages, customs, and expressions of faith; that in the best of Native traditions, the church, and the spirit of ecumenism, we allow for the work of the Spirit of God among our communities and tribes without prejudice.

*Therefore, be it further resolved,* that being justified by faith, we will honor as sacred those practices that: call us back to the sacredness of Native people; affirm as beautiful their identity among the world's peoples; lead us into right relationship with our Creator, creation, and those around us; and call us into holy living. We call upon the world, the church, The United Methodist Church, and the people of The United Methodist Church to receive the gifts of Native people as people of God.

ADOPTED 2004
RESOLUTION #147, 2004 *BOOK OF RESOLUTIONS*

*See* Social Principles, ¶ 162A.

## 3332. The Protection of Native American Sacred Sites

In 1978 and 1992 Congress passed legislation entitled "The American Indian Religious Freedom Act" and "The Religious Freedom Restoration Act," which declared that it was the policy of Congress to protect and preserve the inherent right of American Indians to believe, express, and practice their traditional religions. Native American love for and identity with the land resonates with the theology of land in Scripture. The loss of sacred land leads to a loss of identity and even freedom for the people of Israel (Genesis 15:13), and that loss of freedom can prevent full religious expression, as the psalmist asks, "How could we sing the LORD's song in a foreign land?" (Psalm 137:4). Native American religious understandings of the sacredness of land resound and even precede the Christian theology of land by thousands of years. Today a crisis exists in that there is no real protection for the practice of traditional Indian religions within the framework of American constitutional or statutory law, and courts usually automatically dismiss Indian petitions without evidentiary hearings. While Congress has passed many laws that are designed to protect certain kinds of lands and resources for environmental and historic preservation, none of these laws are designed to protect the traditional sacred sites of Native American tribes for the purpose of Native American traditional religious practice.

The only existing law directly addressing this issue, the American Indian Religious Freedom Act, is simply a policy that provides limited legal relief to aggrieved American Indian religious practitioners. The 1992 General Conference of The United Methodist Church went on record as supporting the rights of all Native Americans, Christian and traditional alike,

*Therefore,* the General Board of Church and Society shall continue to support legislation that will provide for a legal cause of action when sacred sites may be affected by governmental action and proposed legislation should also provide for more extensive notice to and consultation with tribes and affected parties. On behalf of the whole United Methodist Church, the General Board of Church and Society may enter and support court cases relating to the American Indian Religious Freedom Act.

The General Board of Church and Society shall communicate with the Senate Select Committee on Indian Affairs, declaring that the position of The United Methodist Church, expressed through the 2008 General Conference, is to strengthen the American Indian Religious Freedom Act of 1978 and preserve the God-given and constitutional rights of religious freedom for American Indians, including the preserving of traditional Native American sacred sites of worship.

ADOPTED 2000<br>
AMENDED AND READOPTED 2008<br>
RESOLUTION #148, 2004 *BOOK OF RESOLUTIONS*<br>
RESOLUTION #137, 2000 *BOOK OF RESOLUTIONS*

*See* Social Principles, ¶ 164A.

## 3333. Native American Tribal Sovereignty

Indigenous people were once sole occupants of this continent. Scholars vary greatly in their estimates of how many people were living in the Americas when Columbus arrived in 1492; however, estimates range from 40 million to 90 million for all of the Americas.[1] American Indian tribal populations were decimated after the arrival of the Europeans. This decimation was rationalized according to (a) the European belief in their "discovery" of the new world, (b) the arrogance of "manifest destiny," (c) the cavalier destruction of the Native concept of tribal communal land, and (d) lack of immunity to diseases carried by Europeans to the Americas. According to the 2000 census, the American Indian population stands at 2.48 million people.

Prior to European contact, the indigenous nations of this continent were sovereign, autonomous, and self-regulating.

During the American Revolution, American Indian tribes and confederations of tribes were recognized as sovereign indigenous nations in nation-to-nation relationships with the major European powers. Later, these relationships were maintained with the newly formed US government, which formulated 371 treaties with Indian nations between 1778 and 1871.

Treaties are regarded as binding, sacred, and enduring texts by American Indians and Alaska Natives, comparable to the US Constitution and US Bill of Rights. Therefore, it is disturbing that the U.S government ignored its trust responsibilities through the violation of treaties and other promises.

Tribal sovereignty is an inherent international right of Native nations, and it encompasses various matters, such as jurisdiction over Indians *and* non-Indians on tribal lands, education and language, child welfare and religious freedom. Land is both the physical and spiritual foundation of tribal identity, as stated by Kidwell, Noley and Tinker (2001) in their book, *A Native American Theology:* "Land is today the basis upon which tribal sovereignty rests, the rights of Indian people to live upon, use and to govern in a political sense the members of the tribe who live on the land and those whose tribal membership gives them an association with it" (p. 15). Early US Supreme Court decisions support and affirm tribal sovereignty, most notably the Marshall trilogy of cases in the 19th century, and Winter v. S. (1908).

1. MSN Encarta Web site 2007.

However, recent Court decisions have ignored previous precedent and contradicted earlier rulings undermining tribal sovereignty.

A survey conducted by an independent research firm demonstrated that 75 percent of the American public supports tribal governance over Native lands, and 74 percent believe that federal and state officials should make tribal self-governance a priority.

A United Methodist resolution[2] outlined support for the rights of Native people relative to self-determination and sovereignty, which includes the right of Native people to:

- be self-determining, and make their own decisions;
- plan for a future in this nation, and to expect a fulfillment of commitments that have been made previously by the government, as well as equitable treatment of those who were not afforded legal protection for their culture and lands; and
- exercise their sovereignty consistent with treaty provisions, executive orders, and acts of Congress.

The National Congress of American Indians (NCAI) has appealed to religious institutions and their congregations to urge the US government to exercise moral responsibility in upholding treaty obligations and trust responsibilities with Native peoples. NCAI has implemented the Tribal Sovereignty Protection Initiative as a proactive effort to counter recent threats to tribal sovereignty from the federal government, especially within the US Supreme Court that has disregarded the historic agreements with American Indian tribes.

*Therefore, be it resolved,* that The United Methodist Church reaffirms its support for tribal sovereignty and commends the following guiding principles for the total Church:

Guiding Principles:

1. We believe in redemption, transformation, and reconciliation; people can change and that is representative of the incarnational witness in the world.
2. We believe in John Wesley's directive to connect social and personal holiness; that advocacy and action, speaking out in the public square, truth-telling in love are intrinsic to who we are as United Methodists.
3. We believe that the intentions and politicization of Christianity distorted the gospel/good news for the purpose of colonization and must be decolonized.
4. We affirm that American Indian sovereignty:

2. Resolution #4081, 2008 *Book of Resolutions.*

- is a historical fact, is significant, and cannot be disregarded in favor of political expediency
- is a right; American Indians have a right to self-govern
- preserves culture, land, religious expression, and sacred spaces
- ensures survival; allows for the survival of American Indian people

5. We need to demythologize and move from fiction to fact in our understanding of American Indians and Indian country.
6. We affirm the sacredness of humankind:
   - affirming all persons as equally valuable in God's sight
   - resources of the world are sacred and we deplore practices of exploitation
7. We reject stereotypes and frames that depict American Indians as less than sacred or in harmful or distorted ways.
8. We observe that there are belief systems of Native American Indians and nonnatives and that they do not always have commonality (i.e. "fair play"/justice, land claims, treaties vs. constitutional rights, citizen's rights)

In response to the Tribal Sovereignty Protection Initiative, The United Methodist Church:

1. calls upon the United States government to exercise moral responsibility in upholding and honoring all treaty obligations and trust responsibilities to Native peoples;
2. directs the General Board of Church and Society to present this resolution to members of the United States Congress, the President of the United States, the US Secretary of the Interior, the US Assistant Secretary of the Interior-Bureau of Indian Affairs, and the National Congress of American Indians; and
3. urges all clergy and laity to educate themselves and their congregations about historical and contemporary aspects of tribal sovereignty, including action steps that concerned individuals and congregations can take to support American Indians and Alaska and Hawaiian Natives.

ADOPTED 2004
REVISED AND READOPTED 2008
RESOLUTION #149, 2004 *BOOK OF RESOLUTIONS*

*See* Social Principles, ¶ 162*A* and Resolution #4081.

### 3334. Return to the Earth

WHEREAS, in 1990 the national Native American Graves and Repatriation Act mandated the return of human remains and ritual objects to Native American tribes and nations, it further specified that proper respect be shown toward human skeletal remains, and proper interment be provided when ancestors are identified. Presently, over 100,000 human remains still exist in various repositories; and

WHEREAS, the "Return to the Earth" project of the Mennonite Central Committee has developed a study guide, maintains a Web site, established a model cemetery (series of regional cemeteries) to receive culturally unidentifiable Native American remains, plans for construction of small cedar boxes and sewing of linen burial cloths; and

WHEREAS, the Bible tells significant stories through Abraham, Sarah, and Joseph of the importance of burial site and interment of bones (Genesis 23). Native American traditions and Christian faiths have similar views; and

WHEREAS, a program of this nature would provide an opportunity for The United Methodist Church to engage in its commitment for Restorative Justice;

*Therefore, be it resolved,* that The United Methodist Church pledge its support to the "Return to the Earth" project in the following ways:

1. use the study guide "Return to the Earth Project" as an educational resource;
2. engage in dialogue with Native Americans in their local area;
3. advocate when appropriate;
4. assist with construction of small cedar burial boxes and sewing of burial cloth; and
5. monetary contributions to the project.

**ADOPTED 2008**

*See* Social Principles, ¶ 162A.

### 3335. Treaty Obligations with Native Americans

WHEREAS, the United States government has failed to honor its obligations in treaties adopted by Congress with Native American tribes; and

WHEREAS, treaty agreements are solemn promises and must be honored; and

WHEREAS, The United Methodist Church has long been a champion of Native American rights;

*Therefore, be it resolved,* that The United Methodist Church calls on the President and the Congress of the United States to honor its obligations to and its treaties with Native American people throughout the United States.

**ADOPTED 2008**

*See* Social Principles, ¶ 162A.


## 3336. Increased Support for Programs Impacting Native American Higher Education

WHEREAS, the National United Methodist Native American Center, Inc., supports and endorses the goal of optimum educational achievement for all United Methodist Church members; and

WHEREAS, the concept of illiteracy is unacceptable in a time when society projects a formal demeanor of progress and opportunity for all members; and

WHEREAS, past support for The United Methodist Church for the participation of Native Americans in higher education has been minimal, productive, and appreciated; and

WHEREAS, a trend of decreasing Native American participation in higher education is beginning to appear at the national and regional levels; and

WHEREAS, the consistently rising costs of higher education contribute considerably to the decrease of Native American participation in higher education; and

WHEREAS, recent statistics suggest an upward trend of academic success for Native Americans currently participating in higher education; and

WHEREAS, the National United Methodist Native American Center, Inc., supports the philosophy that every person has a right to an education and it is society's responsibility to enable every person to obtain this right; and

WHEREAS, the foundation to Native American growth and progress in society lies within the domain of formal education;

*Therefore, be it resolved,* that the General Conference endorse and support the funding, development, implementation, and assessment of a higher education recruitment/retention forum, sponsored by The United Methodist Church for Native Americans throughout the denomination's regions, to be organized and managed by the National United Methodist Native American Center, Inc., in cooperation with local churches reflecting a significant population of Native Americans.

*Be it further resolved,* that the General Conference encourage The United Methodist Church to utilize the information and materials generated as a result of the forum for sensitizing and familiarizing non-Indian membership about Native Americans in their respective communities.

ADOPTED 1992
READOPTED 2004 AND 2008
RESOLUTION #136, 2004 *BOOK OF RESOLUTIONS*
RESOLUTION #124, 2000 *BOOK OF RESOLUTIONS*

*See* Social Principles, ¶ 162A.

## 3337. Health Care for Native Americans

Native Americans are the most socioeconomically deprived minority group in the United States. The poverty level for children on reservations is more than twice the national average and unemployment rates are three times that of other Americans.[1] Health statistics are consistent with this: in January 2006, Native Americans had 7 times the rate of tuberculosis, 6 times the rate of alcoholism, nearly 3 times the rate of diabetes, and a 62 percent higher rate of suicide than the American population as a whole.[2]

Matthew 25:36b says, "I was sick and you took care of me." The United States government is bound by treaty to provide health care for all Native Americans. In exchange for millions of acres of land, the United States government obligated itself to provide medical and health care services to members of the Tribes with whom they wrote treaties.

1. Patricia Wilson, Reuters, September 4, 1997, http://www.sisis.nativeweb.org/clarke/sep04us.html
2. Catherine Komb, "Congress, President, Still Ignoring Obligation to Indian Health Care," *The New Standard,* July 14, 2006; Peninsula Peace and Justice Center, www.peaceandjustice.org

The United States government now provides medical services through Indian Health Services, United States Public Health Service, Department of Health and Human Services to 1.5 million American Indians/Native Americans who belong to more that 557 federally recognized Tribes in 35 states.[3]

Since the establishment of the Indian Health Service, infant mortality in the population it serves has been reduced by more than 80 percent through the "provision of safe drinking water, nearly universal immunization of Indian children, and emphasis on comprehensive, community-oriented programs focused on maternal and child care."[4]

Despite these successes, the federal government's legislative and executive branches frequently threaten to reduce funding for the Indian Health Services Program. Any funding cuts could severely curtail or cancel health care for a large number of eligible Native Americans.

Only a small number of Native Americans can afford to buy private health insurance, and even so, such insurance has the grave defect of the absence of a large enough risk pool to spread the risk of costly serious illness.

Our Christian faith calls on all to support the poor—"For the needy shall not always be forgotten, nor the hope of the poor perish forever" (Psalm 8:18).

*Therefore* for all Native Americans, The United Methodist Church supports access to adequate medical services to ensure a balance of physical, mental, and spiritual well-being for the "Journey Toward Wholeness" and asks that the United States Congress increase rather than decrease federal funds to operate Indian health facilities.

The General Board of Church and Society will submit this resolution, on behalf of the General Conference, to all United States senators and legislators who have Indian Health Services within their respective state.

3. http://www.ihs.gov/PublicInfo/PublicAffairs/Welcome_info/IHSintro.asp
4. E. R. Rhoads, et al, *Mortality of American Indian and Alaska Native Infants, Annual Review of Public Health*, 1992;13:269-85.

**ADOPTED 1988**
**AMENDED AND READOPTED 2000**
**AMENDED AND READOPTED 2008**
**RESOLUTION #134, 2004 *BOOK OF RESOLUTIONS***
**RESOLUTION #122, 2000 *BOOK OF RESOLUTIONS***

*See* Social Principles, ¶ 162A.

## 3338. Pastoral Care and the AIDS Epidemic in Native American Communities

WHEREAS, the AIDS disease is of epidemic proportions; and

WHEREAS, pastoral care training does not take into consideration the unique cultural and spiritual healing methods of the Native American community; and

WHEREAS, a national consultation on pastoral care and AIDS for Native Americans would provide sound cultural insights for The United Methodist Church in the area of pastoral care for Native American pastors; and

WHEREAS, a program of this nature would provide nurture for Native American pastors and their continuing education,

*Therefore, be it resolved,* that the General Board of Higher Education and Ministry and the National United Methodist Native American Center continue to develop culturally relevant curriculum materials regarding pastoral care and AIDS in the Native American community; and

*Be it further resolved,* that General Conference encourage the National United Methodist Native American Center and the General Board of Higher Education and Ministry to hold, as soon as possible, a National Consultation on Pastoral Care and AIDS in the Native American community using this curriculum, consistent with the availability of independent funding.

ADOPTED 1992
READOPTED 2004
RESOLUTION #139, 2004 *BOOK OF RESOLUTIONS*
RESOLUTION #127, 2000 *BOOK OF RESOLUTIONS*

*See* Social Principles, ¶ 162*A* and *U.*

# ORGAN AND TISSUE DONATION

## 3351. Organ and Tissue Donation

Consistent with the Great Commandment to love God with all our heart, soul, and mind, and our neighbors as ourselves (Matthew 22:37-39), selfless consideration for the health and welfare of all persons is at the heart of the Christian ethic.

Organ and tissue donation is a life-giving act, since transplantation of organs and tissues is scientifically proven to save the lives of persons with terminal diseases and improve the quality of life for the blind, the deaf, and persons with life-threatening illnesses.

Organ donation may be perceived as a positive outcome of a seemingly senseless death and is thereby comforting to the family of the deceased and is conducted with respect, and with the highest consideration for maintaining the dignity of the deceased and his or her family.

Moral leaders the world over recognize organ and tissue donation as an expression of humanitarian ideals in giving life to another.

Thousands of persons who could benefit from organ and tissue donation continue to suffer and die due to lack of consent for donation, due primarily to poor awareness and lack of an official direction from the church.

The United Methodist Church recognizes the life-giving benefits of organ and tissue donation and therefore:

1. encourages all United Methodist members and others to become organ and tissue donors by signing and carrying cards, driver's licenses, or other forms of identification, attesting to their commitment of such organs upon their death to those in need, as a part of their ministry to others in the name of Christ, who gave his life that we might have life in its fullness; and

2. encourages its congregations to join in the yearly ecumenical and interfaith celebration of National Donor Sabbath in the interest of urging United Methodist members and others to consider becoming future organ and tissue donors. Usually held two weekends before Thanksgiving, this national event is an expression of our Christian gratitude for the gift of life. Congregations may choose a variety of ways to educate persons about organ and tissue donation. Examples of ways churches currently participate include developing special liturgies, bulletin inserts, sermons on the subject, and church school discussions. Additional examples may be found on the Internet at http://www.organdonor.gov/natldonorsabbath.htm and on the Web sites of United Methodist and other faith groups and general agencies. Waiting lists for organ and tissue transplants are long and the need is great. National Donor Sabbath provides yet another way United Methodists can help save lives.

ADOPTED 1984
AMENDED AND READOPTED 2000
AMENDED AND READOPTED 2008
RESOLUTION #151, 2004 BOOK OF RESOLUTIONS
RESOLUTION #139, 2000 BOOK OF RESOLUTIONS

See Social Principles, ¶ 162W.

# POPULATION

## 3361. World's Population and the Church's Response

The creation of the world out of chaos into order is the initial biblical witness. In this witness is the affirmation of the freedom and responsibility of humankind. We affirm God to be the Creator, the one who grants us freedom, and the one to whom we are responsible.

God's ongoing creative and re-creative concern for the universe was expressed through Jesus Christ, who has called us to find the meaning of our lives in dual love of God and neighbor. In this context, we live responsibly before God, writing history by the actions of our lives. The imperative for the individual Christian and the Christian community is to seek patterns of life, shape the structures of society, and foster those values that will dignify human life for all.

We are living in an age of possibility in which we are called under God to serve the future with hope and confidence. Christians have no alternative to involvement in seeking solutions for the great and complex set of problems facing the world today. These issues are closely interrelated: hunger, poverty, disease, lack of potable water, denial of human rights, economic and environmental exploitation, overconsumption, technologies that are inadequate or inappropriate, rapid depletion of resources, and continuing growth of population. None can be addressed in isolation.

Nor can hunger, poverty, disease, injustice, and violence in the world be simplistically blamed on population growth. The rapidly swelling numbers of people, however, makes addressing these issues more challenging. The world's population is estimated to reach 9.2 billion by 2050, with the least developed countries having the highest fertility and population growth. The populations of those nations are expected to triple in the next 50 years, from 600 million to 1.8 billion. With each passing day we are discovering more and more connections between population and with sustainable development. As the population grows, it has an obvious impact on land use, water consumption, and air quality. Communities are called to be responsible stewards of all these resources. How can we protect God's gift of the natural environment and at the same time provide a place of sustainability for humans?

The high rates of malaria and HIV/AIDS diminish life for many of God's children. According to UNAIDS, it is predicted that by 2010 more than 80 million persons will have contracted the AIDS virus. And today malaria is found throughout the tropical and sub-tropical regions of the world and causes more than 300 million acute illnesses and at least one million deaths annually. (World Health Organization, 2001-2010 UN Decade to Roll Back Malaria)

Gender inequality in parts of the world exacerbates these complex issues. We know that in many nations, women are considered property and lack basic human rights such as protection under the law and access to education, housing, and jobs. Women comprise 70 percent of the world's poor and many are captives (knowingly or unknowingly) within patriarchal structures, policies, and practices.

We also recognize the growing numbers of elderly in the world's population. Many of them are among the world's most poor. According to the United Nations Population Fund, there are almost 400 million people over the age of 60 in the developing world, and the majority are women. While just 8 percent of persons in developing countries today are older than 60, the proportion will jump to 20 percent in the next 50 years. As communities engage in sustainable development, it will be important for the needs of the aging to be considered, such as economic sustenance, health care, housing, and nutrition. We must also insure the elimination of violence against older persons and provide support and care for the many elderly who are caring for their children and grandchildren, including those affected by the HIV/AIDS pandemic.

As people of faith, we are called to educate ourselves about the interconnectedness of life's critical concerns and live as responsible stewards. The church can address these complex population-related issues on several fronts. We call on all United Methodists to:

1. access educational opportunities that focus on the issue of population and its inter-relatedness to other critical issues such as poverty, disease, hunger, environment, injustice, and violence, and to promote these opportunities in the local church;

2. urge that the United Methodist medical and mission facilities and programs provide a full range of reproductive health and family planning information;

3. take the lead in upgrading the status of women in societies and include women in all development planning and processes. One such action would be advocating for the United States to ratify the United Nations Convention for the Elimination of Discrimination Against Women (CEDAW) and to adopt the Equal Rights Amendment;

4. implement programs within The United Methodist Church that provide and/or enhance educational opportunities for girls and women, making it possible for them to achieve levels of self-sufficiency and well-being;

5. call upon governments to give high priority to addressing the malaria crisis and HIV/AIDS pandemic and urge adequate funding to eradicate and prevent these diseases;

6. call on the US Congress and legislative bodies of the developed nations to recognize the crucial nature of population growth and to give maximum feasible funding to programs of population, environment, health, agriculture, and other technological-assistance programs for developing nations. International assistance programs should be based on mutual cooperation, should recognize the diversities of culture, should encourage self-development and not dependency, and should not require "effective population programs" as a prerequisite for other developmental assistance;

7. call on governments and private organizations to place a high priority on research aimed at developing a range of safe, inexpensive contraceptives that can be used in a variety of societies and medical situations. Promote greater understanding of attitudes, motivations, and social and economic factors affecting childbearing; and

8. call on governments to implement systems of social insurance and support for older  persons to ensure adequate economic sustenance and housing, and quality health care and nutrition.

ADOPTED 2004
RESOLUTION #159, 2004 *BOOK OF RESOLUTIONS*

*See* Social Principles, ¶ 162K.

# RACISM

## 3371. A Charter for Racial Justice Policies
## in an Interdependent Global Community

*Racism* is the belief that one race is innately superior to all other races. In the United States, this belief has justified the conquest, enslavement, and evangelizing of non-Europeans. During the early history of this country, Europeans assumed that their civilization and religion were innately superior to those of both the original inhabitants of the United States and the Africans who were forcibly brought to these shores to be slaves. The myth of European superiority persisted and persists. Other people who came and who are still coming to the United States, by choice or by force, encountered and encounter racism. Some of these people are the Chinese who built the railroads as indentured workers; the Mexicans whose lands were annexed; the Puerto Ricans, the Cubans, the Hawaiians, and the Eskimos who were colonized; and the Filipinos, the Jamaicans, and the Haitians who lived on starvation wages as farm workers.

In principle, the United States has outlawed racial discrimination; but in practice, little has changed. Social, economic, and political institutions still discriminate, although some institutions have amended their behavior by eliminating obvious discriminatory practices and choosing their language carefully. The institutional church, despite sporadic attempts to the contrary, also still discriminates.

The damage of years of exploitation has not been erased. A system designed to meet the needs of one segment of the population cannot be the means to the development of a just society for all. The racist system in the United States today perpetuates the power and control of those of European ancestry. It is often called "white racism." The fruits of racism are prejudice, bigotry, discrimination, and dehumanization. Consistently, African Americans, Hispanics, Asians, Native Americans, and Pacific Islanders have been humiliated by being given inferior jobs, housing, education, medical services, transportation, and public accommodation. With hopes deferred and rights still denied, the deprived and oppressed fall prey to a colonial mentality that acquiesces to the inequities, occasionally with religious rationalization.

Racist presuppositions have been implicit in US attitudes and policies toward Asia, Africa, the Middle East, and Latin America. While proclaiming democracy, freedom, and independence, the US has been an ally and an accomplice to perpetuating inequality of the races and colonialism throughout the world. The history of The United Methodist Church and the history of the United States are intertwined. The "mission enterprise" of the churches in the United States and "Westernization" went hand in hand, sustaining a belief in their superiority.

We are conscious that "we have sinned as our ancestors did; we have been wicked and evil" (Psalm 106:6 GNT). We call for a renewed commitment to the elimination of institutional racism. We affirm the

1976 General Conference Statement on The United Methodist Church and Race, which states unequivocally: "By biblical and theological precept, by the law of the church, by General Conference pronouncement, and by Episcopal expression, the matter is clear. With respect to race, the aim of The United Methodist Church is nothing less than an inclusive church in an inclusive society. The United Methodist Church, therefore, calls upon all its people to perform those faithful deeds of love and justice in both the church and community that will bring this aim into reality."

*Because we believe:*

1. that God is the Creator of all people and all are God's children in one family;

2. that racism is a rejection of the teachings of Jesus Christ;

3. that racism denies the redemption and reconciliation of Jesus Christ;

4. that racism robs all human beings of their wholeness and is used as a justification for social, economic, and political exploitation;

5. that we must declare before God and before one another that we have sinned against our sisters and brothers of other races in thought, in word, and in deed;

6. that in our common humanity in creation all women and men are made in God's image and all persons are equally valuable in the sight of God;

7. that our strength lies in our racial and cultural diversity and that we must work toward a world in which each person's value is respected and nurtured; and

8. that our struggle for justice must be based on new attitudes, new understandings, and new relationships and must be reflected in the laws, policies, structures, and practices of both church and state.

We commit ourselves as individuals and as a community to follow Jesus Christ in word and in deed and to struggle for the rights and the self-determination of every person and group of persons. Therefore, as United Methodists in every place across the land, we will unite our efforts within The United Methodist Church:

1. to eliminate all forms of institutional racism in the total ministry of the church, giving special attention to those institutions that we support, beginning with their employment policies, purchasing practices, and availability of services and facilities;

2. to create opportunities in local churches to deal honestly with the existing racist attitudes and social distance between members, deepening

the Christian commitment to be the church where all racial groups and economic classes come together;

3. to increase efforts to recruit people of all races into the membership of The United Methodist Church and provide leadership-development opportunities without discrimination;

4. to create workshops and seminars in local churches to study, understand, and appreciate the historical and cultural contributions of each race to the church and community;

5. to increase local churches' awareness of the continuing needs for equal education, housing, employment, and medical care for all members of the community and to create opportunities to work for these things across racial lines;

6. to work for the development and implementation of national and international policies to protect the civil, political, economic, social, and cultural rights of all people such as through support for the ratification of United Nations covenants on human rights;

7. to support and participate in the worldwide struggle for liberation in church and community; and

8. to support nomination and election processes that include all racial groups employing a quota system until the time that our voluntary performance makes such practice unnecessary.

ADOPTED 1980
READOPTED 2000 AND 2008
RESOLUTION #161, 2004 *BOOK OF RESOLUTIONS*
RESOLUTION #148, 2000 *BOOK OF RESOLUTIONS*

*See* Social Principles, ¶ 162A.

## 3372. Act of Repentance for Racism

*There is no longer Jew or Greek, there is no longer slave or free, there is no longer male or female; for all of you are one in Christ Jesus.*

(Galatians 3:28)

WHEREAS, the Constitution of The United Methodist Church in Article IV mandates racial inclusiveness; and

WHEREAS, The United Methodist Church and its predecessor organizations in years past have participated, as institutions, in acts which have perpetuated the sin of racism, which continues to be a barrier to Christian unity; and

WHEREAS, at this time, The United Methodist Church is involved in conversations of the Commission on Pan-Methodist Cooperation and Union, which has helped bring to the forefront of consciousness the particular acts of racism which led to the formation of the African Methodist Episcopal, African Methodist Episcopal Zion, and the Christian Methodist Episcopal denominations, and also the formation of the Central Jurisdiction within The United Methodist Church; and

WHEREAS, there is a need among United Methodists for education concerning the church's past history, especially in the areas of African-American race relations; and

WHEREAS, the Commission on Pan-Methodist Cooperation and Union affirms United Methodist efforts toward repentance for past and present sins of racism; and

WHEREAS, the Council of Bishops has joined the General Commission on Christian Unity and Interreligious Concerns in preparation for a liturgical act of repentance for racism; and

WHEREAS, confession and repentance for racism is but a first step toward the changing of hearts leading to healing and wholeness;

*Therefore, be it resolved,* General Conference adopts *Steps Toward Wholeness: Learning and Repentance,* a study guide which addresses the church's role in racism, concluding with a call for repentance; and requests all local congregations in the United States to engage in study sessions using *Steps Toward Wholeness.* All annual conferences are also requested to engage in a liturgical act of repentance.

ADOPTED 2000
AMENDED AND READOPTED 2008
RESOLUTION #162, 2004 *BOOK OF RESOLUTIONS*
RESOLUTION #149, 2000 *BOOK OF RESOLUTIONS*

*See* Social Principles, ¶ 162A.

### 3373. Affirmative Action

The United Methodist Church has long been committed to the principle of social inclusiveness. That is, in keeping with the spirit of the gospel, we affirm that all persons—whatever their racial or ethnic identity, whatever their gender or national origin, whatever their physical state or condition—are full-fledged members of the human community with every one of the rights and privileges that such membership entails. The implementation of "affirmative action" reflects a shared understanding that diversity is a positive outcome of social inclusion that yields benefits for the entire community.

In light of that commitment, the church has, in years past, adopted a strong stand supportive of the concept of "affirmative action." Recently, this concept has been subjected to intense opposition. While some of the particular policies adopted under that rubric may be in need of revision—given developments that have occurred over the course of time—we would, at this moment, reconfirm our support for the basic concept. Inclusionary efforts that lead to diversity yield enriched environments for our daily living and learning.

The Declaration of the United Nations World Conference against Racism, Racial Discrimination, Xenophobia and Related Intolerance (Durban, South Africa, 31 August to 8 September 2001) contains the following affirmations:

- recognition of the need for special measures or positive actions for the victims of racism, racial discrimination, xenophobia and related intolerance in order to promote their full integration into society;
- recognition that such measures should aim at correcting the conditions that impair the enjoyment of rights;
- recognition of the need to encourage equal participation of all racial and cultural, linguistic and religious groups in all sectors of society; and,
- recognition of the need for measures to achieve appropriate representation in educational institutions, housing, political parties, legislative bodies, employment, especially in the judiciary, police, army and other civil services.

The concept of affirmative action emerged in response to the civil rights movements of the 1960s as one of a set of public policies designed to overcome a tragic history of racist and sexist practices throughout this nation and to create a more equitable social system in keeping with the spirit of the gospel and in keeping with the proclaimed democratic ideals of the American people.

Affirmative action is not intended to enable class privilege for the wealthy, such as using family legacies or donor contributions to gain personal advantages. The specific intent of affirmative action, given its origins, was to bring the prestige and power of government to bear on economic and educational institutions, requiring them to put into effect carefully conceived plans to admit qualified persons who traditionally had been excluded from participating in them—women, ethnic and racial minorities, and, at a later time, persons with disabilities.

Over the past three decades, programs of affirmative action have had a significant effect in the employment patterns of corporations and public agencies and in the character of the professional staff and student bodies of educational institutions, private and public. Proportionately, more women, racial and ethnic minorities, and people with disabilities have found their talents and training recognized than before such programs were instituted.

At the same time, however, many women, racial and ethnic minorities, and persons with disabilities, though fully competent, have confronted obstacles in these settings, stifling their advancement in education and in employment. Unemployment of racial and ethnic minorities remains appreciably higher than the national average. Women workers continue to earn less than male workers in the same or similar positions, and they continue to confront limitations in promotion to a more prestigious and responsible level of jobs. Persons with disabilities are bypassed regardless of their motivations.

Despite these persistent inequities, the concept of affirmative action is currently under severe attack. In some locations, it has been abolished as a public policy on several (somewhat different and not altogether compatible) grounds:

- that it promotes the hiring (in business) or admission (to institutions of higher education) of unqualified persons;
- that it discriminates unduly against white males;
- that it has a negative impact on the self-esteem of affirmative action candidates; and
- that its goals have been at this time fully realized and therefore it is no longer necessary.

In light of the evidence, however, (except in those cases where policies of affirmative action have been badly or improperly administered) all of these alleged grounds seem specious. The implementation of affirmative action has resulted in concrete gains for people of color and women in higher education and the corporate world. However persuasive they seem on the surface, they tend to slough off or to ignore the persistence of significant and widespread inequalities of opportunity affecting women, ethnic and racial minorities, and persons with disabilities throughout our social system.

From the perspective represented by The United Methodist Church, the most fundamental premise underlying the concept of affirmative action is both moral and spiritual. Concern for the disadvantaged and the oppressed is a major feature of the message of the Hebraic prophets and of Jesus. According to biblical teaching, we are mandated, in the face of inhumane discrimination—whether that discrimination is intended or unintended—to do what we can to redress legitimate grievances and to create a society in which the lives of each and all will flourish.

For this fundamental reason, we reconfirm our commitment to the concept of affirmative action. The use of numerical goals and timetables is a legitimate and necessary tool of effective affirmative action programs. This concept retains its pertinence as a means of attaining a more inclusive society in our educational systems, in our businesses and industries, and in religious and other institutions. No persons— whatever their gender, their ethnic or racial heritage, their physical condition—should be deprived of pursuing their educational or employment aspirations to the full extent of their talents and abilities.

Fairness is the rule for affirmative action guaranteeing more opportunities for all to compete for jobs. Indeed, the purpose of affirmative action has always been to create an environment where merit can prevail.

Rather than curtail or abolish programs in affirmative action, we should instead move toward the reallocation of the resources of our society to ensure the fullest opportunities in the fulfillment of life.

At the same time, given the tenacity of many forms of racism, sexism, and ableism—both blatant and subtle—the concept of affirmative action retains its relevance as part of an overall effort to create a more just and equitable social system.

*Therefore, be it resolved,* that the 2008 General Conference of The United Methodist Church calls upon all its members to:

1. affirm our Judeo-Christian heritage of justice and inclusiveness as a foundation for the concept of affirmative action;

2. constitute a model for others in society by practicing and strengthening our own affirmative action policies, whatever our station in life;

3. declare our support of efforts throughout the society to sustain and, where needed, strengthen affirmative action legislation and programs;

4. collaborate with movements and initiatives seeking to ensure effective participation of ethnic and racial minorities, women, and persons with disabilities in all sectors of our society; and

5. interpret the genuine meaning of affirmative action, dispelling the myths and responding to the specious appeals that would undercut and vilify affirmative action policies and programs.

*Be it further resolved,* that the 2008 General Conference reaffirm its mandate to implement affirmative action programs in all general church boards and agencies, annual conferences, church-related institutions, districts, and local churches.

*Be it further resolved,* that the General Commissions on Religion and Race and the Status and Role of Women continue to monitor The United Methodist Church and related institutions and to provide assistance in helping them move toward greater conformity with the principle of inclusiveness.

ADOPTED 1996
AMENDED AND READOPTED 2004 AND 2008
RESOLUTION #163, 2004 *BOOK OF RESOLUTIONS*
RESOLUTION #150, 2000 *BOOK OF RESOLUTIONS*

*See* Social Principles, ¶ 162A.

## 3374. Annual Conferences', Districts', and Local Congregations' Responsibilities for Eradication of Racism

WHEREAS, conferences, districts, and local congregations within the United States are becoming more diverse; and

WHEREAS, it is predicted that within the United States, the population of persons of European descent will be less than 50 percent before 2050; and

WHEREAS, racism has been a systemic and personal problem within the US and The United Methodist Church (UMC) and its predecessor denominations since its inception; and

WHEREAS, The UMC is committed to the eradication of racism; and

WHEREAS, it takes significant change, learning, time, and healing to eradicate racism; and

WHEREAS, it takes significant attitudinal and systemic change to learn and to incorporate the gifts and contributions of the different racial-ethnic persons within the church's ministry, structures, and mission; and

WHEREAS, since 1980 the Charter for Racial Justice Policies has served as an articulation of United Methodist understanding of the biblical imperative for the eradication of racism and a guide for action

(#161 2004 *Book of Resolutions*—"A Charter for Racial Justice Policies in an Interdependent Global Community");

*Therefore, be it resolved,* that every annual conference, district, and local congregation within the US have a strategy and program which educates and supports systemic and personal changes to end racism and work multiculturally, and

*Be it further resolved,* that an educational program which will include understanding systemic racism, a strategy for its eradication, appreciation and valuation of diversity, and guidelines for working with different groups in communities toward becoming an inclusive church be offered at least yearly within the annual conference, and

*Be it further resolved,* that all clergy and lay leadership be encouraged to participate in such programs and that all newly ordained clergy be required to participate in these programs, and

*Be it further resolved,* that between 2008 and 2012 the Women's Division of the General Board of Global Ministries and the General Commission on Religion and Race make available to annual conferences, districts, and local congregations resources such as the Charter for Racial Justice Policies and the Reflection and Action Planning Resource to assist them in their efforts, and

*Be it further resolved,* that the General Commission on Religion and Race include as part of its review process the adherence of annual conferences, districts, and local congregations in equipping and supporting leadership to eradicate racism and work multiculturally, and that as annual conferences, districts, and local congregations develop and implement programs, results will be forwarded by the Conference Commission on Religion and Race (or other conference structures dealing with those responsibilities) to the General Commission on Religion and Race.

ADOPTED 2000
REVISED AND READOPTED 2008
RESOLUTION #164, 2004 *BOOK OF RESOLUTIONS*
RESOLUTION #151, 2000 *BOOK OF RESOLUTIONS*

*See* Social Principles, ¶ 162A.


### 3375. Affirmation of the Commission on Religion and Race

WHEREAS, United Methodists reject racism as sin and a violation of our human dignity as children of God, and

WHEREAS, racism is still alive in both church and society, and

WHEREAS, The United Methodist Church has been committed to the elimination of racism since 1968 when it established the GCORR, and

WHEREAS, it is still crucial that the task of eliminating racism within the church is given to an independent agency with the sole purpose of seeking racial justice and racial inclusiveness,

*Therefore, be it resolved* that the 2004 General Conference affirms the existence of the Commission of Religion and Race as an independent monitoring agency for the elimination of racism, and that the GCORR continues with its explicit mandate of helping the church to be free of racism and become racially inclusive.

ADOPTED 2004
RESOLUTION #165, 2004 *BOOK OF RESOLUTIONS*

*See* Social Principles, ¶ 162A.


## 3376. Affirmation of the Joint Task Force on Racism

WHEREAS, the annual conferences ratified a constitutional amendment adopted by the 2000 General Conference, pledging to work toward the elimination of racism within the society, the Church, its policies, and organizations; and

WHEREAS, "The United Methodist Church acknowledges that all persons are of sacred worth. All persons without regard to race, color, national origin, status, or economic condition, shall be eligible to attend its worship services, participate in its programs, receive the sacraments, upon baptism be admitted as baptized members, and upon taking vows declaring the Christian faith, become professing members in any local church in the connection" (The Constitution, Division One, ¶ 4, Article IV); and

WHEREAS, "Racial Justice—The United Methodist Church proclaims the value of each person as a unique child of God and commits itself to the healing and wholeness of all persons. The United Methodist Church recognizes that the sin of racism has been destructive to its unity throughout its history. Racism continues to cause painful division and marginalization. The United Methodist Church shall confront and seek to eliminate racism, whether in organizations or in individuals, in every facet of its life and in society at large. The United Methodist Church shall work collaboratively with others to address concerns that threaten the cause of racial justice at all times and in all places" (The Constitution, Division One, ¶ 5, Article V); and

WHEREAS, racism is an evil that knows no borders, affects people of all socioeconomic backgrounds, spares no one person as its victim, creates resentment and rage among those affected and erases the circle of humanity replacing it with dividing lines between the races. While the potential for racism lies in all of us, through the power of Jesus Christ the potential to eliminate it is well within our reach; and

WHEREAS, Christians must work together to help eliminate the lines of division and establish that all of God's children are members of the human race, regardless of racial and ethnic origin or the color of one's skin; and

WHEREAS, The United Methodist Church must acknowledge that steps have been made toward the goal of eliminating racism, celebrate and salute the groups that have made proactive efforts to alleviate tension caused by racism; and

WHEREAS, in love, the Church must hold accountable the groups in our midst that have not made efforts to alleviate racism and to bring together the children of God to live and be treated as Jesus intended; and

WHEREAS, Christians have a duty to spread the good news of Jesus Christ who loved each of us, died for us and was resurrected to prove his ultimate victory over death to win our souls. This duty requires much of the household of faith, one of which is to show and live in love with one another and to eliminate the destructive and life-taking sin of racism;

*Therefore, be it resolved,* that the 2004 General Conference affirm the work of the Joint Task Force on Racism to eliminate racism in church organizations and practices by recommending that:

1. All agencies or their equivalent within districts, annual conferences, and the general church, assign a person with the specific responsibility to work on the elimination of racism;

2. All elected district leadership groups, annual conferences, and general agencies establish a covenant that reflects how its members will live out its life in the performance of assigned responsibilities with the goal of eliminating racism. Each member and staff will be asked to embrace the covenant; and

3. All local churches, districts, annual conferences, and general agencies find ways to celebrate diversity through Jesus' prophetic, redemptive, and incarnational presence throughout the Church.

ADOPTED 2004
RESOLUTION #166, 2004 *BOOK OF RESOLUTIONS*

*See* Social Principles, ¶ 162.


## 3377. Membership in Clubs or Organizations that Practice Exclusivity

WHEREAS, membership held in any club or organization that practices exclusivity based on gender, race, or socioeconomic condition is clearly in violation of the stance of the United Methodist Social Principles;

*Therefore, it is recommended,* that United Methodists who hold memberships in clubs or organizations that practice exclusivity based on gender, race, or socioeconomic condition prayerfully consider whether they should work for change within these groups or resign their membership. If one decides to resign, we urge that the decision and reasons be made public. This reflects the intent and purpose of the Social Principles of The United Methodist Church.

ADOPTED 1992
READOPTED 2004 AND 2008
RESOLUTION #167, 2004 *BOOK OF RESOLUTIONS*
RESOLUTION #155, 2000 *BOOK OF RESOLUTIONS*

*See* Social Principles, ¶ 162A.


## 3378. Racial Profiling in the USA

According to a study prepared by the Institute on Race and Poverty of the University of Minnesota Law School, and entitled "Components of Racial Profiling Legislation," racial profiling is one of the most pressing civil rights of our time. Racial profiling negatively affects all persons of color of all generations and income levels. It undermines the legitimacy of the criminal justice system and hinders effective policing in the communities that need it the most.

"A Resource Guide on Racial Profiling Data Collection Systems," published by the US Department of Justice defines racial profiling as "any police-initiated action that relies on the race, ethnicity or national origin rather than behavior of an individual or information that leads the police to a particular individual who has been identified as being, of having been, engaged in criminal activity."[1]

Racial profiling is present at traffic stops by police officers when the use of race or ethnicity is the decisive factor that makes the officer stop, question, search, or arrest someone.

Racial profiling has been monitored in a number of jurisdictions, and in nearly all of these jurisdictions, it was found to be a significant problem. For example, a 1996 study in Maryland found that while African Americans accounted for only 16.9 percent of the drivers on I-95, they constituted 72.9 percent of the drivers stopped and searched by the Maryland police.[2]

Racial profiling affects law-abiding citizens as well as offenders. Innocent persons of color are stopped, questioned, and searched for reasons that would not lead to stops of white drivers. People of color report stops based on minor equipment violations such as items hanging from rearview mirrors and even stops followed by inquiries such as, "whose car is this you're driving?" or "what are you doing in this neighborhood?"

Racial profiling not only subordinates the civil rights of entire communities to the goals of criminal justice, but it is an ineffective crime prevention tool that ultimately victimizes the very people that it is supposed to protect—the noncriminal public.

A 1999 Gallup poll found nationally 42 percent of African Americans believe that they have been stopped by police because of their race, 77 percent of African Americans believe racial profiling is widespread, and 87 percent disapprove of the practice. Similar answers have been received among persons from other races and ethnic background. The same poll showed that although only 6 percent of whites believed they had been stopped by police because of their race or ethnic background, 56 percent of whites believe racial profiling was widespread, and 80 percent disapproved of racial profiling.[3]

1. Deborah Ramrez, Jack McDevitt, and Amy Farrel. "A Resource on Racial Profiling Data Collection Systems: Promising Practices and Lessons Learned," 3 (2000).
2. David A. Harris. "Driving While Black." Racial Profiling on Our Nation's Highways, and American Civil Liberties Union Special Report 21-22 (1999).
3. The Gallup Poll, September 21-November 16, 1999.

The widespread perception among people of color that they are unfairly targeted by the police because of their race or ethnic background has led to a lack of trust in the police. This mistrust harms both the police and communities of color, by impeding effective police work precisely within the communities of color that are the ones who need it the most. It is well known that people of color are more likely than whites to be victims of crime. However, mistrust of police hinders the cooperation that is needed between the communities and the police officers.

WHEREAS, racial profiling is an abhorrent manifestation of racism, and it is a painful and tragic reality in our lives, we call The United Methodist Church to:

- denounce through an official communication of the Council of Bishop, to the President of the United States of America, Congress, and the Attorney General, racial profiling as an unjust and evil reality that needs to be corrected; and
- enable the church body: annual conferences, districts and local churches, and under the leadership of the General Board of Church and Society and the General Commission on Religion and Race, to be proactive in educating the constituency about this issue and in establishing networks of cooperation with the criminal justice and the law enforcement systems.

ADOPTED 2004
RESOLUTION #169, 2004 *BOOK OF RESOLUTIONS*

*See* Social Principles, 162A.


### 3379. White Privilege in the United States

European Americans enjoy a broad range of privileges denied to persons of color in our society, privileges that often permit them to dominate others who do not enjoy such privileges. While there are many issues that reflect the racism in US society, there are some cases where racism is the issue, such as affirmative action, housing, job discrimination, hate crimes, and criminal justice. In addition, there are many broader social issues where racism is one factor in the equation, albeit often the major one.

Poverty is a serious problem in the US, but a far greater percentage of Black and Hispanic persons are poorer than white persons.

Police brutality is much more prevalent in ethnic minority communities, partly because police in minority communities are usually a nonresident, mostly white occupying force.

Schools in white communities receive a far higher proportion of education dollars than those in minority communities, leading to larger class size, fewer resources, and inferior facilities.

While welfare affects the entire society, it hits minorities hardest. Although both Democrats and Republicans support tax credits for families to enable middle-class mothers to stay home with their children, welfare "reform" forces poor, single mothers to take low-paying jobs and leave their children to inadequate or nonexistent day care. Because more and better job opportunities are open to white persons, they are leaving the welfare rolls faster than minority persons, making minority persons a disproportionate segment of the welfare population.

Criminal "justice" is meted out more aggressively in racial minority communities than white communities. Nearly half of inmates in the US are African American; one out of every fourteen Black men is now in prison or jail; one out of every four is likely to be imprisoned at some point during his lifetime.

If only one of these areas impacted ethnic minorities disproportionately, an explanation might be found in some sociological factor other than race. But where race is a common thread running through virtually every inequality in our society, we are left with only one conclusion: White, European Americans enjoy a wide range of privileges that are denied to persons of color in our society. These privileges enable white persons to escape the injustices and inconveniences which are the daily experience of racial ethnic persons. Those who are White assume that they can purchase a home wherever they choose if they have the money; that they can expect courteous service in stores and restaurants; that if they are pulled over by a police car it will be for a valid reason unrelated to their skin color. Persons of color cannot make these assumptions.

We suggest that the church focus not only on the plight of people living in urban or rural ghettos, but also on white privilege and its impact on white persons. For example, churches in white or predominantly white communities need to ask why there are no persons of color in their community, why the prison population in their state is disproportionately Black and Hispanic persons, why there are so few Black and Hispanic persons in high-paying jobs and prestigious universities, why schools in white communities receive more than their fair share of education dollars, and why white persons receive preferential treatment from white police officers.

We ask the General Conference to recognize white privilege as an underlying cause of injustice in our society including our church and to commit the church to its elimination in church and society.

The rights and privileges a society bestows upon or withholds from those who comprise it indicate the relative esteem in which that society holds particular person and groups of persons.

We direct the General Board of Discipleship (GBOD), in consultation with the General Commission on Religion and Race (GCORR), to prepare a study guide on white privilege and its consequences in church and society.

We ask the Board of Church and Society in every annual conference to sponsor workshops on white privilege.

We direct the GCORR and the GBOD to jointly review and develop UM curriculum materials, with particular attention to those for children and youth, for the purpose of affirming children of all racial and ethnic groups, and to communicate in our curriculum materials that in our society, privileges that are taken for granted by white persons are often denied to others because of their racial and ethnic identity.

We ask each local church with a predominantly white membership: 1) to reflect on its own willingness to welcome persons without regard to race and to assess the relative accessibility in housing, employment, education and recreation in its community to white persons and to persons of color; and 2) to welcome persons of color into membership and full participation in the church and community and to advocate for their access to the benefits which white persons take for granted.

We challenge individual white persons to confess their participation in the sin of racism and repent for past and current racist practices. And we challenge individual ethnic persons to appropriate acts of forgiveness.

Finally, we call all persons, whatever their racial or ethnic heritage, to work together to restore the broken body of Christ.

ADOPTED 2000
AMENDED AND READOPTED 2008
RESOLUTION #170, 2004 *BOOK OF RESOLUTIONS*
RESOLUTION #166, 2000 *BOOK OF RESOLUTIONS*

*See* Social Principles, ¶ 162A.

## RURAL ISSUES

### 3391. Call to the Churches for the Renewal of Rural Ministries

For 70 years the religious community has joined together through Agricultural Missions, Inc. as one way of supporting and accompanying rural communities around the world in their efforts to end poverty and injustice. For many years now rural communities in the United States and across the world have faced daunting new challenges in the wake of increasing globalization of food systems and promotion of policies that favor corporations over family farms.

Using global and regional trade agreements, corporations are controlling decisions that profoundly affect the lives of rural people. Trade regulations and treaties, both current and under negotiation, such as the Free Trade Area of the Americas (FTAA), have conferred on corporations the right to supersede national farm policies in any nation, to demand access to local markets, and to purchase and own local water distribution systems and other essential services.

The market-based model of economic development fostered by the World Trade Organization, the World Bank and the International Monetary Fund and imposed through international trade agreements, such as the North American Free Trade Agreement (NAFTA), has resulted in and/or hastened the:

1. displacement of people from the land and the decline in the culture of the family farm;

2. belief among rural residents, particularly the youth, that there is no future in agriculture, leading to the impoverishment and eventual death of many rural communities;

3. increasing rates of farmer suicides and farm worker exploitation, as well as violence in the family and the community, substance abuse and related problems; and

4. violation of the integrity of God's creation as typified by the pollution of the air, land, and water and disruption of the ecology and climate on a global scale.

It is essential that the churches stand with those who work the land in their struggles and witness to their work. As churches, we need to provide material and moral support and raise our voices, lest by our silence the structures of power assume our consent to the injustices being committed against rural peoples and communities. We bear witness that alternatives that are just and sustainable are being developed, despite enormous odds, by the shared efforts of rural communities in many countries and regions. The Church needs to renew and expand relationships with these communities and struggles and make common cause with them.

The Church possesses the lenses of the gospel and has the responsibility to bring moral and ethical scrutiny to social and economic policy. The Church must play a critical and essential role in evaluating economic policies for consistency with the Scripture and the Christian principles of justice.

Therefore, we call The United Methodist Church to respond as worshiping congregations and as institutions responsible for providing moral guidance and prophetic vision to society at large and to impoverished people, in particular:

1. At the congregational level, pastors must be better equipped to address the despair affecting rural people, by working closely with local organizers and grassroots organizations.

2. At the institutional level, The United Methodist Church should:

    a. work with universities in the United States in rural areas and reclaim land-grant colleges, including historically black and Indian tribal colleges, to promote the interests of small-scale farmers instead of agribusinesses;

    b. consider setting up an ecumenical fund to assist small farmers threatened with bankruptcy to keep their farms and assist them in engaging in sustainable farming practices;

    c. promote a culture and economy of sufficiency, conservation, and thrift for corporate and individual lifestyles as best models of stewardship of God's creation;

    d. advocate a process of public audits to call to accountability agribusinesses, banks and other financial institutions (including the international financial institutions), and transnational corporations and call on them to remedy the negative impact of their policies and activities on rural communities;

    e. strengthen its partnership with farm and rural community-based organizations and networks to educate and engage members on critical policy issues, including agricultural subsidies, food and trade policies, economic justice, and the integrity of creation;

    f. accompany farm workers in their struggles to secure healthy living conditions, decent wages, and the right to organize, and to support rural grassroots organizations that work with them in these endeavors; and

g. develop concrete programs to demonstrate its solidarity with and accompaniment of small-scale, minority, and indigenous producers to secure their rights to their land and the fullness of life promised by Jesus Christ.

ADOPTED 2004
READOPTED 2008
RESOLUTION #174, 2004 *BOOK OF RESOLUTIONS*

*See* Social Principles, ¶ 162P.

## 3392. Rural Communities in Crisis

The United Methodist Church has long witnessed to rural peoples and their concerns. Each General Conference since 1940 has suggested responses for improving rural church and community life and the economic and environmental well-being of rural peoples. The 1988 General Conference accepted a study on US Agriculture and Rural Communities in Crisis, yet the crisis continues. Today we reaffirm that historical study and call The United Methodist Church to continue its commitment to rural church ministry and advocacy for agricultural and rural community concerns.

### *Theological Statement: Land, People, and Justice*

God is the owner of the land (Leviticus 25); thus it is a gift in covenant that involves the stewardship of keeping and tending the land for present and future generations. As God's creation, land must be regenerated that it may sustain life and be a place of joy. It is a common gift to all of life, requiring just patterns of its use.

Social, economic and ecological justice with regard to the use of land is central to biblical law. The land itself is to receive a rest every seven years (Leviticus 25:4). Voluntary charity or occasional care of the land is not enough. Israel's failure to follow the laws related to the land was counted a cause of their exile to Babylon (2 Chronicles 36:21). Care of the land and the rights of the poor and needy are at the center of the Law. Adequate food is considered an inherent right, such that the poor could eat grapes in a neighbor's vineyard or pluck grain when passing by a field (Deuteronomy 23:24-25). Land owners are urged not to be too efficient in their harvest (Leviticus 19:9-10), so that it is possible for the needy to glean the fields.

Indeed, the concept of equal access to community resources according to one's need formed the basis of the covenant the community was expected to embody. Caring for one's neighbor, especially a poor neighbor, is a religious obligation. Jesus both inherits and fulfills this tradition when he says the commandment to love one's neighbor as oneself is second only to the commandment to love God (Matthew 22:38-40).

The prophets viewed patterns of economic exploitation, social class consciousness, judicial corruption, political oppression, failing to care for the land, and exclusiveness as in opposition to God's desire for full life and wholeness for all (Amos 2-8; Isaiah 5:1-13; 58:3-7; Jeremiah 2:7-8; Hosea 4:1-3). Some would suggest that both the contemporary world and Israel under the monarchy came to worship "bigness" more than God.

Today, rural parts of our world suffer from many of the same maladies as ancient Israel. Land holdings are increasingly concentrated in the hands of fewer owners. People pursue material wealth as the solution to other spiritual and economic problems. Creation itself groans under a burden of eroding topsoil, toxic waste and polluted waters. Neither the land nor most of the people who work the land can celebrate the wholeness God intended.

### The US Farm Crisis

Agriculture is a major component in the US economy. Through the production of goods and services, agriculture has added about $90 billion annually to the national economy from 1995 to 2000. About 18 percent of all civilian jobs are in agriculture and related input and marketing industries. In addition, the agricultural sector regularly has a positive balance of trade. Women and ethnic minorities, including African Americans, Hispanics, Native Americans, and Asians, have contributed immensely to the country's food production.

The benefits of the agricultural economy are widely skewed. Agriculture is recognized as an inherently volatile industry, especially for family farmers.

### The Crisis Affecting Agriculture Is:

1. The Loss of Family Farmers—Amid chronically difficult rural economics, the patterns of land ownership and control are ever less

diverse. The U.S Department of Agriculture National Commission on Small Farms reported in 1998 that there are 300,000 fewer farmers than in 1979, and farmers are receiving 13 percent less income for every consumer dollar spent. The loss of ethnic-owned and small-scale farms are even greater. Today there are 2.1 million farmers and ranchers. About 94 percent of US farms are small, but they receive only 41 percent of all farm receipts. Most disappearing farms are family-sized units. A family farm is not defined by acreage but as an agricultural production unit and business in which the management, economic risk, and most of the labor (except in peak seasons) are provided by the family and from which the family receives a significant part, though not necessarily the majority, of its income. Family farms vary by region and commodity.

2. Increased Concentration and Corporate Agriculture—US government policy choices have perpetuated the greater concentration of assets and wealth into fewer larger farms and agribusiness firms. Federal farm programs and tax policies have historically benefited large farms the most. Large farms that depend on hired farm workers receive exemptions from federal labor laws allowing them the advantage of low-wage costs. (See 2008 Resolution #4134, "Rights of Farm Workers in the US") The ownership and control over agricultural assets is increasingly concentrated in fewer and fewer hands. Factory farms have become the dominant method of raising meat in the United States. Four firms now control over 80 percent of the beef market. Farmers have little to no control over the prices set for their products. Many family farmers are caught in a web of contracts with large, vertically-integrated agribusiness conglomerates that dictate almost everything farmers do: erecting farm buildings, choosing feed, installing lighting. Emerging agricultural technologies use ever greater levels of capital to enable fewer people to produce food. As a result, income and opportunities have shifted from farms to the companies that produce and sell products to farmers. The dominant trend is a few, large, vertically-integrated firms controlling the majority of food and fiber products in an increasingly global processing and distribution system.

3. Farm Income—Net farm income and net farm operator household income are two measures of the relative ability of farmers to finance and sustain their farming operations and provide for their families. By either measure, it is apparent that the combination of plummeting commodity prices, high input expenses and production

risks continue to threaten the economic sustainability of family farmers. Without government farm programs and disaster assistance as a partial replacement for adequate commodity prices, even more producers would be forced off their farms.

4. Ecological Damage—Factory farms, especially those that produce livestock such as hogs, are poisoning their communities. These farms have taken root mainly where zoning laws were weak or nonexistent or in states that prohibited lawsuits against agricultural operations. The inevitable byproduct of huge concentrations of animals is huge concentrations of manure that is stored in open lagoons. The water is eventually sprayed on farmland, although there is usually far more manure than local fields can absorb. In such quantities, manure becomes a toxic substance. Spills and groundwater contamination are always a risk as is airborne contamination of water from ammonia, which rises from the lagoons and falls into low-lying rivers and estuaries. More than five billion tons of topsoil is lost every year and the intensive use of pesticides results in more than 14 million Americans drinking water that routinely contains pesticides.

5. Pervasive Discrimination—African American and other racial ethnic farmers are even less likely than white farmers to benefit from any changes in the rural/farm economy. Surveys of Native American farmers suggest that their situation may be nearly as bleak. Farming is the leading occupation among Native Americans living on reservation lands. Asian and Hispanic Americans have historically been excluded from significant farm ownership. African Americans, Hispanics and Native Americans have not received fair and equitable service from the US Department of Agriculture. The USDA has long tolerated discrimination in the distribution of program benefits and has misused its power to influence land ownership and farm profitability. Farm program regulations shut out racial ethnic farmers from the benefits that have helped larger white producers survive the changes in agriculture. The USDA remains insensitive to the needs of racial ethnic farmers and neglects its responsibility to reach out and serve all who need their services. (*See* 2008 Resolution #4133, "Rights of African American Farmers.")

6. Trade—Trade agreements have brought few benefits to family farmers. Current trade negotiations fail to address the causes of and needs for the many types of practices that characterize agricultural trade: domestic food safety, security for all countries, agricultural commodity/supply demand imbalances that results in adequate

returns to producers, and the concentrated market power that exists among a limited number of agricultural market participants.

7. Biotechnology/Genetically Modified Organisms (GMOs)—The rapid introduction of commercial genetically engineered animals, seeds and crops with inadequate research, testing and regulation may cause unintended ecological, health, social, economic and cultural consequences. GMOs affect the entire food chain and pose an indirect threat to the future well-being of farmers and nations hoping to ensure food security. The majority of genetically engineered crops currently on the market are produced and marketed by large private companies seeking primarily to generate a return on shareholders' investments. Private control of genetically engineered agriculture, coupled with emerging global trade policies that protect the interests of patent rights holders, makes food systems more vulnerable to shifting global economic trends and threatens the sovereignty and very existence of local food systems. Nonsegregated and unlabeled genetically engineered crops put farmers at risk of losing highly profitable markets, fail to protect the consumers from agricultural products whose safety is not yet proven, and deny consumers' the right to choose. Genetically engineered seeds and crops are promoted as a solution to world hunger and malnutrition. Moral, consumer and producer concerns, informed by independent scientific knowledge, need to be addressed.

### Rural Community in Crisis

The rural United States today is a contrast between beauty and desecration, isolation and industrialization, wealth and poverty, power and oppression, freedom and exploitation, abundance and hunger, individualism and dependence. US Census data and other sources count the overall rural poverty rate at 14.6 percent, while 33 percent of African Americans, 27 percent of Hispanics, and 30 percent of Native Americans in rural areas are poor. More children in rural areas live in poverty than children in urban areas. Of the 50 counties in the US with the lowest per capita income, only one is in a metropolitan area; of the other 49, many are very rural with income based on agriculture. For six years in a row (1996 to 2001), the people living in the great plains of the United States have had the lowest income regionally. Only 6.3 percent of rural Americans live on farms. Farming accounts for only 7.6 percent of rural employment, which is dominated by low wage industries. Rural incomes remain lower than the urban median.

Among poor families, those in rural areas are more likely to be working poor.

Nearly 30 percent of nonmetropolitan households—more than 6.2 million—have at least one major housing problem, most often the burden of cost (paying more than 30 percent of income for housing). A 2000 survey found eighth-graders in rural schools were 32 percent more likely than those in metropolitan areas to have used marijuana, 52 percent more likely to have used cocaine, 29 percent more likely to have used alcohol, and twice as likely to have smoked cigarettes. Rural residents tend to have poorer health care access, lower health insurance coverage, and little or no managed care availability. Rural communities have little or no public transportation.

## Call for Change: What Needs to Be Done?

A. Local churches and annual conferences are called to:

1. Develop specific ministries to meet major needs that exist today in rural United States, including:
   a. taking responsibility for assisting with mending the brokenness of community life in rural society;
   b. strengthening their ministry and mission with rural churches and communities;
   c. lifting up the responsible stewardship of natural resources; and
   d. building bridges of understanding and partnership between rural, suburban and urban congregations and communities.

2. Place personnel strategically in order to respond to rural needs; insist that pastoral appointments be made with the needs of entire communities in mind, and not just the needs of the congregation.

3. Become public policy advocates, speaking out as a church, creating awareness and understanding, and bringing about positive change.

4. Be in partnership with seminaries to develop programs, including "teaching" parishes and internships, to equip ministers to serve in rural areas.

5. Develop programs to invest conference foundation funds in rural economic development needs.

6. Discover ways to enable the racial ethnic ownership of farmland.

*B. The general church is called to:*

1. Use its seminaries to prepare clergy to be more effective pastors in rural areas, using the "missionary training" model, knowing that many ministers not accustomed to rural life enter into areas where there is a new "language," a new lifestyle, a new culture.

2. Cooperate ecumenically and with other groups beyond the church to develop responses to the problems of rural areas.

3. Better learn the skills of personnel placement so that appointed ministers in rural areas will tenure long enough to build trusting, understanding relationships necessary for pastoring the community. Place more mission (and similar) personnel in rural ministries.

4. The General Board of Church and Society and the General Board of Global Ministries work with family farm organizations to address the crisis facing family farmers and rural communities and monitor agricultural genetically engineering developments and educate United Methodists of its impact on the food chain.

5. Recognize Rural Life Sunday as a special day in the church year, combining in the one day the emphases of Rural Life Sunday, Soil Stewardship Day, Earth Day, World Environment Day, and Rogation Sunday.

*C. Federal legislators and administrators, as they develop farm and rural policies, are called to:*

1. Develop national agricultural policies that enable farmers to significantly increase net farm income, improve the quality of rural life and increase the number of family farmers so that farmers may continue to provide a reliable supply of food and fiber and serve as stewards of the nation's resources. These new policies would:

   a. reverse the loss of family farms;
   b. ensure a fair price at the marketplace;
   c. provide credit to family farmers at affordable interest rates;
   d. develop a marketing and government support system that will guarantee the cost of production to farm families;
   e. initiate participatory democratic processes with farmers to determine if mandatory production goals, which would discourage overproduction of some commodities, are needed to move toward a balance between supply and demand;
   f. reform government payments to benefit family farmers, rather than large corporate and wealthy farming interests;

    g. create programs that would enable new families to enter farming as a vocation;

    h. create incentives for family farmers to shift from current production-oriented modes to a sustainable and regenerative agriculture;

    i. ensure the participation of family farmers regardless of race and sex; and

    j. implement the recommendations of the reports National Commission on Small Farms and the Civil Rights at the United States Department of Agriculture.

2. Discourage concentration in ownership and control of land and money and move toward land reforms that broaden ownership of land by stronger anti-trust laws and enforcement, a ban on corporate meatpacker ownership of livestock, and create safeguards and amend laws for growers involved in contract agriculture to give them the bargaining power they need to demand fair contracts.

3. Require soil and water conservation practices as well as increased funding for farm operations that participate in federal programs; include farmers in the planning of such requirements and the enforcement of national organic standards.

4. Reform federal tax laws to remove unfair competition and discourage tax shelter-motivated capital in agriculture.

5. Maintain an emphasis on direct loan activity, resist attempts to reduce the level of direct loans in favor of guarantees, and increase the Limited Resources Loan program for qualified farmers.

6. Provide for commodity reserves, isolated from the market, to be established at a level adequate to protect consumers from supply disruption and meet domestic agricultural disaster and global humanitarian food aid requirements.

7. Ensure that most federally-supported programs of research and education in agriculture focus on small and medium-sized family farm operations, with special attention paid to racial ethnic farmers, and that county committees, which administer these programs, be inclusive of women and racial ethnic farmers.

8. Fund major new research initiatives and programs through the federal land grant institutions, including black land grant colleges, to ensure the development of long-term, sustainable, and regenerative agriculture.

9. Develop farm policies that will encourage farm-owned and controlled businesses and cooperatives for processing, distributing, and marketing farm products.

10. Develop policies that will respect the guaranteed land and water rights of all racial ethnic peoples.

11. Develop and support programs in cooperation with community-based organizations and cooperatives to improve the quality of life in depressed rural areas, with attention given to health care, transportation, education, employment, value-added agriculture, law enforcement, housing, job training, and environmental protection.

12. Develop national and regional water and energy policies that assure that those who benefit from energy and water projects pay a substantial portion of those costs.

13. Recognize and protect the right of farm workers to organize into unions of their own choosing, to be covered by minimum wage laws, and to receive adequate benefits, including social security, health care, and unemployment.

14. Develop a fair trade policy that stabilizes domestic markets, ensures consumer access to an adequate, safe and affordable food supply, discourages dumping[1], allows all countries to develop farm programs that provide fair prices, reduces agricultural subsidies by rich countries, and respects each country's needs and traditions for food security, policies on the importation of genetically modified food, conservation of natural resources, and fair distribution of economic opportunity.

15. Prohibit the importation of produce containing residues of pesticides or other chemicals that are banned for US producers, and revise permitted residue levels when the pesticide is banned.

16. Seek out international cooperation in developing an international food policy.

17. Address GMOs/genetically engineered agriculture by prohibiting patents and exclusive rights to products and processes by companies and individuals that are in the public domain; ensuring that protecting the reward system for innovations does not impede the distribution of the necessities of life; not requiring a country to import genetically engineered seeds and crops; and requiring truthful and accurate labeling so that dietary needs and nutritional considerations can be attended to and, if warranted, epidemiological studies can be done.

1. Dumping: The intentional export of goods priced below the cost of production leading to a disruption of global markets. However the power of participation in decision making should be weighted to local participation due to local community relationships and local risks rather than to economic or political centers of power.

## Three Ethical Guidelines

Food is not merely another market commodity. Food is essential to life and is sacred culturally to all people. We can change the direction of US agriculture and rural development, but we need guidelines. A preferred agriculture must have three attributes:

1. It must be just. A just society and a just agriculture provide the means whereby people can share in the inheritance of the earth so that all life can fully be maintained in freedom and community. The purpose of a just agriculture should be for the maintenance and renewal of the necessary resources for food, clothing, and shelter, for now and for the future.

2. It must be participatory. For agriculture to be just, everyone has the right to be consulted. Participation in society and in the ongoing process of creation is the necessary condition for justice. Participation requires recognition of everyone's right to be consulted and understood, regardless of that person's economic, political, or social status.

Participation is not possible without power. In such decision-making, everyone has the right to be consulted about such issues as expenditures for armaments, nuclear power, forms of employment, social services, and so forth.

3. It must be sustainable. A sustainable agriculture is one where the idea of permanent carrying capacity is maintained, where yields (agriculture, energy production, forestry, water use, industrial activity) are measured by whether or not they are sustainable rather than by the criteria of yields per acre or profits. In a sustainable agriculture, waste products can be absorbed back into the ecosystem without damage.

A just, participatory, and sustainable agriculture would meet basic human needs for food and fiber, regenerate and protect ecosystems, be economically viable, enhance the quality of life for farm families, be supportive of rural communities, be socially just, and be compatible with spiritual teachings that recognize the earth as a common heritage and responsibility. For Christians, the idea of sustainability flows directly from the biblical call to human beings to be stewards of God's creation.

ADOPTED 2004
READOPTED 2008
RESOLUTION #177, 2004 *BOOK OF RESOLUTIONS*

*See* Social Principles, ¶ 162P.

## 3393. Support and Protection of Rural People

WHEREAS, rural people, rural communities and rural congregations are of great value in God's creation and have many gifts and strengths to share with the world community; and

WHEREAS, farming, ranching, other agricultural endeavors, trucking, migrant work, timbering, recreation, fishing and river work, rural factories, and small businesses of numerous kinds, as elements of rural life, undergird the economy of the world; and

WHEREAS, rural people contribute to the abundance of our world economy, but often do not receive benefits commensurate with their efforts; and

WHEREAS, developments in communication technology and improved transportation systems have done much to eliminate problems of isolation and distance in some parts of the world, while further isolating people from each other in other parts of the world; and

WHEREAS, the health and well-being of God's creation rests upon the vitality of our worldwide rural people who are caretakers of the land, water, and air; and

WHEREAS, The United Methodist Church, recognizing the sacredness of creation care, has a long history of ministry within rural places throughout the world;

*Therefore be it resolved,* that The United Methodist Church, as it is in ministry in rural places, affirms that:

1. rural residents around the world deserve the option of living and prospering in the communities where they live, and the goals and policies of the governments that relate to rural places should provide this option;

2. rural people around the world deserve a sense of purpose and authentic hope, equitable and continuing spiritual care; satisfying economic opportunity to meet basic needs for food, clothing, and shelter; nurture and protection for children and youth; security for the elderly and those who abilities are challenged; equitable access to affordable health care and education; and opportunities for recreation and spiritual renewal;

3. as stewards of creation, rural people around the world have a right to determine how land, water, air, and other resources within their communities, especially in areas of limited population, are to be used, with particular attention given to land use and control being exercised by all who live within an area and/or own land

within a given area while respecting the legal rights of owners of real property.

ADOPTED 2004
READOPTED 2008
RESOLUTION #179, 2004 *BOOK OF RESOLUTIONS*

*See* Social Principles, ¶ 162P.

## 3394. Support for All Who Minister in Rural Settings

WHEREAS, rural churches and communities provide unique settings for ministry; and

WHEREAS, this uniqueness calls for specially gifted people, both laity and clergy, who desire to serve in rural communities;

*Therefore, be it resolved,* that The United Methodist Church is called upon to affirm the value and worth of all those who minister in rural settings, to celebrate their gifts and grace, and to recognize their witness within The United Methodist Church.

*Resolved,* that The United Methodist Church is called upon to give particular recognition to licensed local pastors, laypersons assigned, lay missioners, and church and community workers.

*Further be it resolved,* that The United Methodist Church is called upon to support these persons in ways that promote more effective ministry.

*Further be it resolved,* that annual conferences and districts are called upon to explore with these individuals their unique gifts as they relate to service in rural areas, to identify those with gifts particularly suited to rural ministry, and to encourage such uniquely gifted persons to pursue ministry in rural settings.

*Finally be it resolved,* that annual conferences are called upon to establish support structures that provide for:
- enhancement of pastoral family life,
- resources for maintaining pastoral well-being,
- structures and technology that encourage connectedness and accountability to the larger church, and
- creative ways to address geographic dynamics.

ADOPTED 2004
READOPTED 2008
RESOLUTION #172, 2004 *BOOK OF RESOLUTIONS*

*See* Social Principles, ¶ 162P.

### 3395. Affirmation of Rural Chaplains

WHEREAS, the General Conference since 1996 has affirmed the ministries of rural chaplains and the Rural Chaplains Association, and called on The United Methodist Church to pursue rural chaplaincy as a significant means of enabling renewal in towns/villages and rural churches and communities throughout the world; and,

WHEREAS, the Rural Chaplains Association now has 214 members (women, men, laity and clergy, United Methodist and ecumenical), including several persons from the international community; and,

WHEREAS, rural chaplains are lay and clergy persons who have sensed the call to live in, work with, and advocate for town and rural persons, families, congregations, and communities; and,

WHEREAS, special emphasis is placed on responses to hate and violence, and advocacy for justice issues among all people, regardless of ethnicity, gender, age, or economic status; and,

WHEREAS, rural chaplains meet annually for support, encouragement, resourcing, and enrichment by means of workshops/consultations which explore biblical understandings and focus on person-related chaplaincy-type skills as well as understanding issues of food production and multinational economics that impact family farmers, farm workers, migrants, and rural businesses and communities; and,

WHEREAS, rural chaplains work with other prophetic persons/ groups on the local level who are committed to long-term involvement aimed at developing local and outside resources to enhance the lives of rural congregations and communities; and,

WHEREAS, the Rural Chaplains Association greatly empowers the development of lay leadership, serves as one way of recognizing the gifts and graces of rural peoples, and unleashes new possibilities for God's Spirit to move across the countryside; and,

WHEREAS, rural chaplains will be an asset in the implementation of the National Comprehensive Plan for Town and Country Ministry approved by General Conference of 2000; and,

WHEREAS, the Rural Chaplains Association continues to establish and develop international/global linkages, especially with Russia, and Guatemala, by exposing participants to the cultural, economic, political, ecological and religious life of their people;

*Therefore, be it resolved,* that rural chaplains are recognized as having a special relationship to the General Board of Global Ministries as those called to serve others in town and rural settings; and,

*Be it further resolved,* The United Methodist Church commend and reaffirm its commitment to rural chaplains as the Rural Chaplains Association increases its work nationally, internationally, and ecumenically with lay and clergy persons, many of whom carry out their ministries under trying conditions and in difficult places; and,

*Be it further resolved,* that the General Board of Global Ministries be encouraged to continue a relationship with the Rural Chaplains Association in the future.

ADOPTED 2004
REVISED AND ADOPTED 2008
RESOLUTION #173, 2004 *BOOK OF RESOLUTIONS*

*See* Social Principles, ¶ 162P.


## 3396. Ministries of Rural Chaplains

WHEREAS, the General Conference since 1996 has affirmed the ministries of rural chaplains and the Rural Chaplains Association, and called on The United Methodist Church to pursue rural chaplaincy as a significant means of enabling renewal in town/villages, and rural churches and communities throughout the world; and

WHEREAS, the Rural Chaplains Association now has more than 100 active members (women, men, laity, and clergy, United Methodist and ecumenical), including several persons from the international community; especially Russia, and

WHEREAS, the rural chaplains are lay and clergy persons who have sensed the call to live in, work with, and advocate for town and rural persons, families, congregations, and communities; and

WHEREAS, special emphasis is placed on responses to hate and violence, and advocacy for justice issues among all people, regardless of ethnicity, gender, age, or economic status; and

WHEREAS, rural chaplains meet annually for support, encouragement, resourcing, and enrichment by means of workshops/focus events that explore biblical understandings and focus on person-related chaplaincy-type skills as well as understanding issues of food production and multinational economics that impact family farmers

and farm workers, the growth of ethnic/migrant and other new populations, emerging challenges of forestry, fisheries, and other industries
such as small manufacturing enterprises and prisons, changing patterns of land use and control, and struggles over environmental issues,
global warming, water quality, and hazardous waste disposal; and

WHEREAS, each quadrennium the annual meeting and focus event
is held in an international setting in order to continue developing
international/global linkages by exposing participants to the cultural,
economic, political, ecological, and religious lives of people; and

WHEREAS, rural chaplains work with other prophetic persons/groups
on the local level who are committed to long-term involvement aimed
at developing local and outside resources that enhance the lives of
rural congregations and communities; and

WHEREAS, the Rural Chaplains Association greatly empowers the
development of lay leadership, serves as a vital means of recognizing
the gifts and graces of rural peoples, and unleashes new possibilities
for God's Spirit to move across the countryside; and,

WHEREAS, rural chaplains will be an asset in the implementation of
the National Comprehensive Plan for Town and Country Ministries
approved by General Conference of 2000;

*Therefore, be it resolved,* that rural chaplaincy continue to be recognized as a special type of ministry for town and rural settings; and

*Be it further resolved,* that The United Methodist Church commend
and reaffirm its commitment to rural chaplains as the Rural Chaplains
Association continues its work nationally, internationally, and ecumenically with lay and clergy, many of whom carry out their ministries under trying conditions and in difficult places; and

Be it further resolved, in particular that the General Board of Global
Ministries be encouraged to continue relationship with the Rural
Chaplains Association in the future.

**ADOPTED 2008**

*See* Social Principles, ¶ 162P.

## 3397. Accessible and Affordable Leadership Training

WHEREAS, the 2000 General Conference adopted the "National
Comprehensive Plan for Town and Country Ministry of The United
Methodist Church: Born Again in Every Place"; and

WHEREAS, among the goals summarized in the National Comprehensive Plan for Town and Country Ministry was "To Recognize, train and utilize lay leadership in town and country ministries"; and

WHEREAS, also among the goals summarized in the National Comprehensive Plan for Town and Country Ministry was "To Provide effective pastoral leadership for all town and country churches"; and

WHEREAS, the foundational study that lead to the development of the National Comprehensive Plan for Town and Country Ministry found that "The laity made two overwhelming appeals to the connectional system: 1) 'provide us with training and resources appropriate to town and country situations,' and 2) 'listen to us about matters affecting church life and potential in our communities'"; and

WHEREAS, "one of the most critical issues facing the church is the quality of pastoral leadership"; and

WHEREAS, town and country churches are best served by pastors who are sensitive and understand the nature of town and country ministries and are adequately supervised; and

WHEREAS, the distances to educational facilities and training make it difficult for many clergy and laity to take advantage of and receive adequate training;

*Therefore, be it resolved,* that the General Board of Discipleship and conference agencies responsible for lay training and leadership develop distance learning, internet options, and other methods to recognize, train, and utilize lay leadership in ways that are accessible, affordable, and context appropriate to town and country settings, and

*Be it further resolved,* that United Methodist agencies, seminaries, Course of Study schools, licensing schools and other avenues of preparing pastoral leadership further develop accessible, affordable, and context appropriate methods that will prepare those appointed or assigned to understand the culture of town and country communities in order to serve more effectively in those settings.

ADOPTED 2004
RESOLUTION #178, 2004 *BOOK OF RESOLUTIONS*

*See* Social Principles, ¶ 162P.

## URBAN ISSUES

### 3411. Holy Boldness: Pathways to Transformation 2009–2012

## A United Methodist Urban Ministry Plan for Making Disciples of Jesus Christ for the Transformation of the World

WHEREAS, change is inevitable but transformation is optional, The United Methodist Church has the opportunity to transform and energize urban churches and communities with holy boldness; and

WHEREAS, the Holy Boldness: Pathways to Transformation Plan has been developed to continue and strengthen the National Urban Ministry Plan adopted at the 1996 General Conference and reaffirmed in 2004; and

WHEREAS, the primary goal of the Plan calls for The United Methodist Church to provide a vision for the future: identify areas of focus and collaboration; organize and mobilize resources; and equip leaders to carry out the Plan; and

WHEREAS, according to the "State of the World Population 2007" report, "in 2008, half of the world's population will be in urban areas," and "without proper planning, cities across the globe will face the threat of overwhelming poverty, limited opportunities for youth, and religious extremism"; and

WHEREAS, ultimately, the Pathways to Transformation Plan will be effective if annual conferences, districts, and, especially, local churches and faith-based community organizations and agencies develop strategies and carry out the agreed-upon goals and objectives; and

WHEREAS, it is also critical for the whole church (congregations in and outside urban areas, annual conferences, and general church agencies) to work in collaboration to support those working locally to transform urban congregations and the communities to meet the need of growing urban areas; and

WHEREAS, the priorities, goals, and objectives identified for this Plan were determined through a national survey of laity, pastors, faith-based community organization staff, annual conference staff, seminary presidents and deans, and bishops; and

WHEREAS, the primary goals are to accomplish the following:

1. transform existing urban congregations through training, coaching, and mentoring;
2. establish new urban churches and faith communities;
3. identify and develop urban pastors and laity;
4. assist annual conferences and districts in urban strategic planning;
5. challenge and assist urban congregations to transform the communities in which they reside; and

WHEREAS, the priorities that will inform and guide these goals are:
- urban theology and leadership development;
- urban evangelism and congregational development;
- living in community with the poor;
- strengthening and developing multicultural relationships and congregations;
- eradicating racism and other forms of oppression;
- creating and developing urban/suburban collaboration and partnerships;
- community economic development;
- wholeness, healing, and health; and

WHEREAS, these goals and priorities further support the four areas of collaboration developed by the Connectional Table: 1) leadership development, 2) starting new congregations, 3) partnering with the poor, and 4) global health. This Plan is particularly synergistic with the third proposal, "partner with the poor to seek justice and address the causes of human suffering that result from poverty," which has been assigned to Global Ministries to take the lead on; and

WHEREAS, urban transformation will require a collaborative effort by local churches working in cooperation with other denominations, community organizations, businesses, and governmental institutions; collaboration will need to occur beyond the city limits by collaborating with exurban churches that share similar challenges, and churches in suburban areas that have committed persons, resources, and relational roots in urban neighborhoods, all of which strengthen ministry; and

WHEREAS, collaboration will also need to occur at the national level with the National Urban Strategy Council and general agency teams (Global Ministries, Church and Society, Discipleship, Higher Education and Ministry, Religion and Race, and Communications) working together to identify common strategies that they can mutually accomplish; the national strategies linking with local strategies and needs; national collaboration involving the ethnic ministry plans already adopted by our Church with a particular sensitivity to those who are poor; and finally, national collaboration involving other ecumenical and inter-faith bodies and national urban resources;

*Therefore, be it resolved* that we call upon the general agencies, the National Urban Security Council, jurisdictional networks, annual conferences, districts, and, especially, local churches to take authority and responsibility in being holy and bold to accomplish the goals and objectives of the Plan; and

*Be it further resolved* that the General Board of Global Ministries Office of Urban Ministries will be responsible for the coordination and implementation of the Plan. Objectives and action steps have been developed and will be implemented as funding is made available; and

*Be it further resolved* in order to facilitate this coordination and implementation, the Office of Urban Ministries will have copies of the plan available for any who wish to partner in this effort, and that with God's help, we can reclaim our cities for United Methodism and, in the process, meet Christ on the streets walking with his people.

ADOPTED 2008
RESOLUTION #180, 2004 *BOOK OF RESOLUTIONS*
RESOLUTION #171, 2000 *BOOK OF RESOLUTIONS*

*See* Social Principles, ¶ 162R.


## 3412. Special Emphasis for Ministries Within Major Urban Centers

WHEREAS, the Christian church—and the Methodist movement—began in city communities; and

WHEREAS, a majority of the world's population now lives in cities for the first time in history; and

WHEREAS, the fastest-growing populations in the United States are among the Asian, Hispanic, and African American people; and

WHEREAS, The United Methodist Church has a deep commitment to build ministry among the poor and the marginalized; and

WHEREAS, there are high concentrations of human needs, and incidences of human injustice within the communities of our cities;

*Therefore be it resolved*, that The United Methodist Church continue a special emphasis on ministry within our major urban centers by:

1. incorporating intentional, multiracial ministry;

2. implementing outreach and inclusion within the local church congregational life;

3. evangelizing the poor and oppressed;

4. providing strong pastoral and lay leadership;

5. increasing the financial and human resources available for ministry in our cities;

6. uniting our Methodist families—the African Methodist Episcopal Church, the African Methodist Episcopal Zion Church, the Christian Methodist Episcopal Church, and The United Methodist Church—to make one powerful Methodist voice and presence in our cities; and

7. leading the way for ecumenical and interfaith initiatives to revitalize the communities.

*Be it further resolved*, that each general agency and each jurisdictional conference take appropriate steps to implement this ongoing initiative.

ADOPTED 2004
READOPTED 2008
RESOLUTION #181, 2004 *BOOK OF RESOLUTIONS*

*See* Social Principles, ¶ 162R.

## VIOLENCE

### 3421. Grieving and Repenting from Acts of Hate and Violence

*Confessing the Sins of Hate and Violence*

Violence permeates our society, perpetrated by those who hurt others because of the color of their skin, their sexual orientation, their religious identity, or no reason at all. Violence exists as persons and groups from around the world have lashed out in anger and fear, persecuting those whom they see as different. These acts of hate include such actions as "ethnic cleansing," deportations, genocide, torture, tyrannical rule, religious intolerance and persecution, church burnings, rape, murder, war, and civil unrest that scar the lives of millions.

One deplorable form of violence is hate crimes. Hate crimes result from the intentional selection of victims or property as the object of violence because of the actual or perceived race, color, religion, national origin, class, ethnicity, gender, gender identity, disability, or sexual orientation of the individual victim or owners of the property.

The United Methodist Church must be proactive in resisting hate and teaching all members how to live in our diverse social world without passively accepting the rise of hate and bigotry. When church members do nothing about hate language or horrifying atrocities, we participate in the social support of hate.

It is not just hate groups who perpetrate such crimes. According to a study by the American Psychological Association, "most hate crimes are carried out by otherwise law-abiding young people who see little wrong with their actions. Alcohol and drugs sometimes help fuel these crimes, but the main determinant appears to be personal prejudice . . . such prejudice is most likely rooted in an environment that disdains someone who is 'different' or sees that difference as threatening."

In recent years the homeless have been a group that has often been targeted for violence. The National Coalition for the Homeless reports that between 1999 and 2005 there were 169 attacks against homeless people in the US alone that resulted in their deaths.

Immigrants are another group against which violent acts have been increasing. The demeaning of immigrants by media organizations and political leaders has lent itself to attitudes that view immigrants as less than human. In addition, refugees and internally displaced persons attempting to return to their homes are particularly vulnerable to acts of violence. The chaos that so often results from armed conflict prevents protection of refugees by law enforcement. Women and children become especially vulnerable as they seek asylum and flee from fighting. And in returning to their homes, they often face violence as a form of retribution or social and political marginalization. Thus, there is no way of knowing how many immigrants are being terrorized in communities throughout the world.

Racism and crimes against persons based on their actual or perceived race, color, religion, national origin, class, ethnicity, gender, gender identity, disability, or sexual orientation is not limited to the United States alone. Unfortunately, racism and the violence that emanates from racist attitudes are global. According to Amnesty International, an estimated 300 million indigenous peoples face widespread discrimination and cultural marginalization. Ethnic groups such as the Kurds in Turkey, the Roma in Eastern Europe, the Karen in Myanmar, and the Uighurs and Tibetans in China all face discrimination and violence.

The United Methodist Church upholds the International Covenant on Civil and Political Rights (ICCPR), which was adopted by the General Assembly of the United Nations in December of 1966 and ratified by the United States in 1992. The ICCPR states that, "Each State Party to the present Covenant undertakes to respect and to ensure to all individuals within its territory and subject to its jurisdiction the rights recognized in the present Covenant, without distinction of any kind, such as race, color, sex, language, religion, political or other opinion, national or social origin, property, birth or other status."

Assaults against people perceived to be gay or lesbian are increasing at alarming rates and are characterized by viciousness. According to the 2004 US Federal Bureau of Investigation statistics, hate crimes based on sexual orientation constituted the third highest category reported and made up 15.5 percent of all reported hate crimes in the United States. Human Rights organizations such as Human Rights Watch and Amnesty International regularly report discrimination and violence against people throughout the world based solely on their sexual orientation or gender identity.

*Conviction and Sorrow about the Sins of Hate and Violence*

Although The United Methodist Church is in conflict over the place of gay and lesbian people in The United Methodist Church, we grieve over the violence committed against the gay and lesbian community. We also grieve over the violence committed against transgender persons. We urge United Methodist congregations, youth and campus ministries, and church agencies to promote opportunities where we may be a witness, helping to heal wounds of violence in our communities and congregations, witnessing through work groups, Bible studies, community missional outreach, prayer, and involvement in ecumenical and interfaith groups and coalitions.

The United Methodist Church grieves as God grieved when Cain killed Abel and Abel's blood cried out to the Lord from the ground (Genesis 4:10). We grieve as God grieved over the oppression and enslavement of the Israelites. God saw their misery, heard their cries, and was concerned for their suffering (Exodus 3:7). We grieve as Jesus grieved over Jerusalem which killed and stoned the prophets sent by God to proclaim the word of God to the people of God (Matthew 23:34-37). Yet, in each of these passages God does not meet violence with violence. Instead, God offers the option of repentance to those who perpetuate violence and hate.

## Repentance from Sins of Hate and Violence

Therefore, we as United Methodists and individuals within the global community seek to reconcile the violence found within our own hearts. We seek forgiveness for the injustices we ourselves have committed against each other, our friends and family, and the global community. Whether it is our actions or our thoughts, our words or our deeds, our voice or our silence, where we have done wrong, we seek forgiveness. We pray for mercy as we seek to walk humbly with God, and in peace with our families and friends, with our communities, and with ourselves.

We as United Methodists express our grief for the broken covenants of the church, both in The United Methodist Church and the church universal. We define a broken covenant as being actions that we may have committed in the name of faith that have locked persons out of relationships with Jesus Christ and the church, whether it be because of differences, prejudices, or through ignorance. We seek forgiveness for acts of hate and violence committed in the name of faith.

## Redemption from Sins of Hate and Violence

Yet, our grief is only the first step towards what God desires for creation. "For godly grief produces a repentance that leads to salvation and brings no regret" (2 Corinthians 7:10a). Repentance entails a turning away from sin, from actions and attitudes of hate and violence and a turning to acceptance, compassion, hospitality, and love. Jesus requires all of his followers to deny ourselves, take up our cross and follow him (Matthew 16:24).

Therefore, repentance must lead to redemptive action and social change. Violence, hate, and civil rights violations go against the long heritage of United Methodist commitment to justice for all persons. Today, it is increasingly apparent that such commitment must be translated into action in new ways for Jesus has called us to rise up and minister to a broken world that it may heal and that we may one day live in a world free from violence where "Death will be no more; mourning and crying and pain will be no more, for the first things have passed away" (Revelation 21:4).

*Therefore, we resolve,* that The United Methodist Church, with assistance from the appropriate boards, agencies, and local churches continue to educate:
- children and youth on the sins of hate and bigotry;
- seminary students and clergy on the trends of hate in the world and how the church can faithfully prevent and respond to acts of hate; and
- all persons in The United Methodist Church about the sins of hatred and bigotry that have been committed in our United Methodist Church against our members and against those with whom we seek to minister.

*We also resolve,* that the members of The United Methodist Church:
- be active participants in civic or religious organizations that promote unity and diversity and work to eradicate acts of hate;
- take strong nonviolent action in opposition to hate groups;
- develop support group(s) for persons active in antiracism strategies and for persons ministering to victims of hate crimes.
- evangelize those individuals who would choose to be a part of hate groups or who commit acts of hate and violence individually and show them the compassion and saving grace of Jesus Christ;
- promote diversity dialogue and programs in all churches, annual conferences, central conferences, general agencies, campus ministry units, and any other place where The United Methodist Church has a witness;
- support a restorative-justice response to hate crimes, which aims at dialogue, accountability, and healing between victims and offenders rather than adding more punishment of offenders if their crime was motivated by hate; and
- speak up when you are a victim of hate crimes. If you are subject to an act of bigotry or racial violence, tell someone. Tell your family, your friends, neighbors, the church; seek support for yourself. Report the incident to police. Insist that the crime be reported as a "hate crime."

*We resolve,* that all United Methodist congregations, under the leadership of the General Board of Church and Society, will advocate for:

- law-enforcement personnel to maintain records on hate
  crimes and to bring to justice the perpetrators of such violence
  and intimidation;
- hearings on hate crimes, particularly in those states where statistics reveal an increase in the activity of the Ku Klux Klan
  and other hate groups;
- hate crimes prevention legislation that includes gay, lesbian,
  bisexual and transgender persons.

ADOPTED 2008

*See* Social Principles, ¶ 162A and J.

### 3422. Resisting Hate, Fear, and Scapegoating; and Transforming the Context of Hate in the United States

Whoever does not love does not know God, for God is love. . . .
Those who say, "I love God, and hate their brothers or sisters, are liars;
for those who do not love a brother or sister whom they have seen,
cannot love God whom they have not seen."

(1 John 4: 8, 20 NRSV)

WHEREAS, in the post 9/11 world, reports of hate crimes or acts such
as the following have become part of the daily lives of people both in
the United States and around the world:

- a Muslim Arab-American woman receives a threat from a
  coworker "You and your kids will pay . . . death";
- a Catholic high school student is punched and kicked on a bus
  by a group of youth for looking "Chinese";
- a teenage boy is beaten with a baseball bat because of his perceived sexuality;
- anti-Semitic graffiti is spray painted on a store selling kosher
  meat products;
- four men attack and kill one of twelve undocumented immigrants;
- a cross is burned on the lawn of a house for sale after being
  viewed by an African American family.

These acts encourage social movements that promote bigotry based
on race, religion, gender, sexual orientation and national origin (white
supremacists/nativists) to appeal to racial and other fears.

If we look only at these acts as the acts of individuals or groups of individuals we will fail to recognize the wide context of fear and hate that gives rise to these individual acts. That context has both historical roots and grounding in current economic and political realities. Demographic change and economic uncertainties contribute to a sense of insecurity and anxiety about the future leading to old animosities and prejudices being revived and new ones.

The United Methodist Church reaffirms its historical commitment opposing acts of hate, hate speech, and violence in both church and society. The church commits itself to redouble its efforts to speak out against hate crimes and work to transform the context of fear and hate that gives permission to these acts, naming and challenging the culture that perpetuates it.

*Be it resolved,* that The United Methodist Church, with assistance from the appropriate boards, agencies, and local churches, implement the following recommendations:

*Faith and Biblical Resources:*

- provide biblically based resources for young people and adults that address the historic and systemic roots of hate that lead to hate speech and hate crimes;
- create resources to help United Methodists analyze the language of hate among groups that use religious language to justify hatred and bigotry;
- work with ecumenical and interfaith groups to create worship resources, and develop community activities to unite religious groups on behalf of justice for all;

*Educational Resources:*

- develop educational materials to build understanding of the systemic, institutionalized culture of racism, sexism, homophobia, and other forms of marginalization;
- develop materials to explore and challenge expressions of hate, including: personal attitudes, scapegoating, individual violence, media distortions to public policy, and collective violence, including state violence;
- educate United Methodists about trends of hate in the US and the world and how the church can prevent and respond to acts of hate;

*Action/Organizing/Advocacy:*

- encourage United Methodists to report hate incidents to the police, and to organize support for victims of hate crimes;
- ecourage United Methodists to end complicity with hate by speaking out when jokes, disparagements, and stereotypes are based on identity or status;

*Annual Conferences—Responding to Hate Crimes:*

- annual conferences develop data bases of information of local and state hate groups and explore the connections between anti-immigrant/refugee groups and white supremacist organizations in order to develop strategies for response for use by local churches;
- organize letter writing campaigns and denominational and ecumenical delegations to meet with state government officials to advocate for the passage, funding, and implementation of strong and comprehensive state hate crimes laws that extend civil rights protections to all individuals and groups;
- encourage law-enforcement personnel to maintain records on hate crimes and to bring to justice the perpetrators of such violence and intimidation;

*Annual Conferences—Transforming the Culture of Hate:*

- strongly encourage local churches, annual conferences, general agencies, campus ministry units, and any other place where The United Methodist Church has a witness, to create opportunities to hear from excluded groups about the reality and impact of hate and to partner with them to act for justice;
- be active participants in civic or religious organizations that promote unity and diversity and work to eradicate acts of hate, as well as working with diverse grassroots and national organizations;
- engage in efforts to enable communities to unearth the truth about past hate violence, to bring perpetrators (including state actors) to trial, and to heal wounds and seek reconciliation based on justice and more equitable power relationships. This effort is based on the South African Truth and Reconciliation

Commission and other efforts now linked through the Center for Transitional Justice;

- work through local organizations and local schools to ensure their policies and training programs adequately address various forms of discrimination and sexual harassment based on gender and perceived sexual identity;
- use United Nations and other resources for adults and children in efforts to build a global culture of peace;
- create an annual conference taskforce to develop strategies to address actions of the media that use or condone hate speech, stereotypes, or racial profiling.

The United Methodist Church calls on annual conferences to report on their work on the culture of hate and hate crimes at their annual conference meeting; to include hate crimes in their conference report to the General Commission on Religion and Race; and to work with the General Board of Church and Society and the General Board of Global Ministries, including the Women's Division on this concern.

**ADOPTED 2008**

*See* Social Principles, ¶ 162*A*, *H*, and *J*.

## 3423. Violence Against Women and Children

The deafening and disabling silence that has surrounded the abuse of women and children is being broken. We now know that overwhelming numbers of women and children in our churches and communities are being battered, raped, emotionally and psychologically abused, and physically and sexually assaulted. The abuse occurs in communities of every racial composition and every economic status, in rural areas as well as cities, in families adhering to every religion and to no religion. Silence will no longer shield us from our complicity in the violence nor from our failure to overcome it.

The Social Principles of The United Methodist Church affirm the family as "the basic human community through which persons are nurtured and sustained in mutual love, responsibility, respect, and fidelity." Clearly violence and abuse cannot be tolerated within such an understanding. The Social Principles are explicit: "We recognize that family violence and abuse in all its forms—verbal, psychological, physical, sexual—is detrimental to the covenant of the human community. We encourage the Church to provide a safe environment, counsel and support for the victim. While we deplore the actions of the abuser, we affirm that person to be in need of God's redeeming love."

We acknowledge the ways in which misinterpretation and misuse of Christian Scriptures and traditions have contributed to violence against women and children, and to the guilt, self-blame, and suffering which victims experience, and to the rationalizations used by those who abuse. A reexamination of those misused passages can help us reclaim traditions in ways that support victims and challenge abuse in the family.

Stories of violence against women and children are so common that we scarcely notice them, even in the Bible. Yet, they are there. Women, only a few of them even named, are abused, rejected, and raped by brothers, husbands, and strangers. Daughters are traded and sacrificed. A concubine wife is sliced into pieces by the master who traded her body for his own safety. Yet even this last, most violent story, in Judges 19, cannot be used to justify abuse for it ends with this command: "Consider it, take counsel and speak" (vs. 30). It is the silence, the unwillingness to acknowledge the horror, which leaves victims isolated, protects perpetrators, and thwarts healing. We are commanded to break the silence, to give credence to the stories, to be agents of wholeness and justice.

Jesus' concern for the victim is seen in the story of the Good Samaritan (Luke 10:25-37). By concluding this parable with the words, "Go and do likewise," Jesus indicates that we are to receive all people who have been violated or abused, who are weak or vulnerable, with particular compassion and caring. Jesus made it clear that meeting a legalistic obligation is not enough; we must go beyond the letter of the law in reaching out to comfort and assist those who have been harmed.

The church must reexamine the theological messages it communicates in light of the experiences of victims of domestic violence and sexual abuse. We must treat with extreme care the important, but often-misused, concepts of suffering, forgiveness, and the nature of marriage and the family.

Situations of violence and abuse exist in families in virtually every congregation; tragically, no church or community is exempt. As part of a research project conducted by the Ministries with Women, Children and Families program of the General Board of Global

Ministries, pastors who had asserted their conviction that there were no families experiencing violence or abuse in their congregations were asked to mention the issues from the pulpit, using words like battering, rape, incest and child abuse. All those who reported related that members subsequently came to them with current stories of abuse in their families. Clearly, church families are not immune, and many are waiting for a signal that these concerns are appropriate ones with which to share and struggle in the community of faith.

The church is challenged to listen to the stories of victims and survivors and to seek information and guidance that will lead to wiser and more effective ways to minister with persons who experience domestic violence and sexual abuse. The church must be a refuge for people who are hurting, and it is an entirely appropriate place for these issues to be addressed. Many congregations are finding ways to demonstrate that the church is a place where people can feel confident in turning to first, not last, for comfort and healing.

People of faith should take the lead in calling for a just response by the community in the face of domestic violence and sexual abuse. Justice-making involves several steps: righteous anger; compassion for the victim; advocacy for the victim; holding the offender legally and spiritually accountable for his or her sin against the victim and the community; treatment for the offender; and prevention of further abuse by addressing the societal roots and not merely the symptoms of violence and abuse.

## Policy Statements and Actions

The United Methodist Church affirms the sacredness of all persons and their right to safety, nurture and care. It names domestic violence and sexual abuse as sins and pledges to work for their eradication. The church commits itself to listen to the stories of battered spouses, rape victims, abused children, adult survivors of child sexual abuse, and all others who are violated and victimized. The church further commits itself to provide leadership in responding with justice and compassion to the presence of domestic violence and sexual abuse among its membership and within the community at large.

*The following actions are commended to local congregations:*

1. Create a church climate of openness, acceptance, and safety that encourages victims to speak of their pain and seek relief and healing.

2. Encourage all clergy and lay leaders to work collaboratively with community agencies on prevention strategies and to provide for the physical, emotional, and spiritual needs of victims, offenders, and other family members.

3. Adopt policy and procedures for keeping children and vulnerable adults safe from abuse in church facilities and programs.

4. Assess currently available prevention and response resources in the community and, where indicated as appropriate, initiate new programs and services. Wherever possible, undertake new programs ecumenically or as part of a community coalition.

5. Set up peer support groups for battered spouses, for adults who were sexually abused as children, and for rape victims. A trained resource person or professional counselor should be consulted for assistance in setting up peer support groups.

6. Encourage church members to volunteer their services to existing shelters, crisis centers, and other community services. Insist upon training for volunteers.

7. Reexamine, and change if necessary, scriptural and theological messages, cultures, and traditions that validate violence or abuse or support a view of women as subordinate to men or children as property of adults. Pay particular attention to church teachings on repentance and forgiveness.

8. Maintain a library of printed and video resources on domestic violence, sexual assault, child abuse and the role of the church. Develop a utilization plan.

9. Participate in Domestic Violence Awareness Month each October and Child Abuse Prevention Month each April in the United States, or similar emphases in other countries.

10. Urge clergy to preach on domestic violence and sexual abuse topics; urge congregants to host or cooperate in community education events and to highlight opportunities for involvement in prevention and service activities.

*The following actions are commended to annual conferences, general agencies, and seminaries:*

1. Provide, for clergy and laity, education and training that address domestic violence, sexual assault and child sexual abuse. Seminaries are urged to include courses in their curriculum, and annual conferences are urged to offer courses in their continuing education programs for clergy.

2. Support policies, programs, and services that protect victims, hold offenders accountable, and provide support for family members.

3. Provide training in abuse prevention, detection, and intervention to church school teachers, youth leaders and pastors, and encourage them to use abuse prevention curriculum. Include specific guidelines and training for abuse reporting procedures.

4. Develop and implement clear policies to deal with sexual abuse by clergy and others who provide leadership in the church.

5. Encourage governments to ratify the United Nations Conventions on "The Elimination of All Forms of Discrimination Against Women" and on "The Rights of the Child" as minimum global standards to protect women and children.

ADOPTED 2004
READOPTED 2008
RESOLUTION #186, 2004 *BOOK OF RESOLUTIONS*
RESOLUTION #177, 2000 *BOOK OF RESOLUTIONS*

*See* Social Principles, ¶ 162C and F.

## 3424. Violent Video Games

The United Methodist Church advocates at state and federal levels for the elimination of violent games that specifically target children and youth, specifically those games that glorify death, show killing, and depict all acts of violence.

General Conference requests the General Board of Church and Society, the General Board of Global Ministries, and the General Board of Discipleship to develop resources, curriculum, and advocacy strategies that will seek to provide creative avenues to address conflict and violence in our society.

The denomination will use legislative and nonlegislative means at federal and state levels to reduce violence in our society, especially among the young, and to teach our young people conflict resolution strategies as an alternative to violence.

ADOPTED 2000
REVISED AND READOPTED 2008
RESOLUTION #187, 2004 *BOOK OF RESOLUTIONS*
RESOLUTION #178, 2000 *BOOK OF RESOLUTIONS*

*See* Social Principles, ¶ 162S.

## 3425. Prohibition of Bullying

*Be it resolved,* and it is hereby resolved, that The United Methodist Church at all levels will:

- categorically oppose the practices of adult, youth, and child bullying, mobbing (also known as scapegoating);
- diligently work to increase societal awareness of these destructive behaviors; and
- intentionally validate, enlighten, support, and empower persons being injured by such behaviors in workplaces, in schools and in all environments.

ADOPTED 2004
RESOLUTION #188, 2004 *BOOK OF RESOLUTIONS*

*See* Social Principles, ¶ 162.

## 3426. Gun Violence

Violence and, more particularly, violence to children and youth is a primary concern for United Methodists. We recognize and deplore violence which kills and injures children and youth. In the name of Christ, who came "and proclaimed peace to you who were far off and peace to those who were near" (Ephesians 2:17) and challenged all his disciples to be peacemakers (Matthew 5:9), we call upon the church to affirm its faith through vigorous efforts to curb and eliminate gun violence.

Gun violence is killing children throughout the world, including the United States. In the United States alone, there are an estimated 223 million firearms. Approximately one out of every three households owns a handgun. The risk of handgun violence to children and youth is more prevalent in the United States today than in any previous generation. Communities and schools in the United States are so exposed to large numbers of privately owned guns that no mere attempts at providing slightly better security can match the awful threat of guns finding their way through our well-intentioned safety systems.

Many children go to school amidst passionately violent segments of current youth culture. No appeals to individual autonomy are sufficient to justify our church's ignorance of this threat. The need to prevent the incidence of firearm-related injury and death is an issue of increasing concern and a priority public health issue. The United Methodist Church is among those religious communions calling for social policies and personal lifestyles that bring an end to senseless gun violence.

Gun violence in US schools has emerged as a growing and disturbing trend. The United Methodist Church supports ministries that address the issue of violence and crime prevention for children/youth in urban areas through the Communities of Shalom. Violence is no longer confined to the streets of urban areas but has occurred at an increasing rate in US suburban communities. Over the past several years, high-profile cases of school shootings involving suburban youth killing and injuring teachers and peers alike have once again brought the issue of guns and youth to the forefront of national attention.

Amnesty International reports that hundreds of thousands of people throughout the world are killed every year because of the unregulated small arms trade. The small arms trade, which includes such arms as assault weapons and shoulder-fired missiles, is legal but out of control. Amnesty International reports that as many as 639 million small arms and light weapons are in circulation around the world. The small arms trade incites local conflicts, which so often leads to unnecessary human rights abuses. The proliferation of small arms has led to the forced recruitment of children into war and local ethnic conflicts escalating into destabilizing regional warfare. We urge all nations where there is a presence of The United Methodist Church to participate in the process of developing a legally-binding Arms Trade Treaty through the United Nations to regulate the transfer of all small arms and light weapons so as to curb gun violence throughout the world.

These acts of senseless violence should not be an acceptable occurrence in any community: suburban, urban, or rural. The church must continue to address these issues of violence and develop programs to enrich the lives of all children/youth.

In light of the increase of gun violence affecting the lives of children and youth, we call upon The United Methodist Church to:

1. convene workshops of clergy and mental health care professionals from communities (urban, rural, and suburban) in which gun violence has had a significant impact in order to discuss ways by which The United Methodist Church should respond to this growing tragedy, and to determine what role the church should take in facilitating dialogue to address the issue of gun violence in our schools and among our children;

2. educate the United Methodist community (parents, children, and youth) on gun safety, violence prevention, adult responsibility around gun violence prevention, and the public health impact of gun violence;

3. identify community-based, state, and national organizations working on the issue of gun violence and seek their assistance to design education and prevention workshops around the issue of gun violence and its effect on children and youth;

4. develop advocacy groups within local congregations to advocate for the eventual reduction of the availability of guns in society with a particular emphasis upon handguns, handgun ammunition, assault weapons, automatic weapons, automatic weapon conversion kits, and guns that cannot be detected by traditionally used metal detection devices. These groups can be linked to community-based, state, and national organizations working on gun and violence issues;

5. support federal legislation in the US Congress to regulate the importation, manufacturing, sale, and possession of guns and ammunition by the general public. Such legislation should include provisions for the registration and licensing of gun purchasers and owners, appropriate background investigation and waiting periods prior to gun purchase, and regulation of subsequent sale;

6. call upon all governments of the world in which there is a United Methodist presence to establish national bans on ownership by the general public of handguns, assault weapons, automatic weapon conversion kits, and weapons that cannot be detected by traditionally used metal-detection devices;

7. call upon the print, broadcasting, and electronic media, as well as the entertainment industry, to refrain from promoting gun usage to children;

8. discourage the graphic depiction and glorification of violence by the entertainment industry, which greatly influences our society, and recommend that these issues be addressed through education and consciousness raising;

9. call upon the federal and state governments to provide significant assistance to victims of gun violence and their families;

10. recommend that annual conferences make visible public witness to the sin of gun violence and to the hope of community healing; and

11. reflecting the traditional role of The United Methodist Church has been one of safety and sanctuary, every United Methodist Church is officially declared a weapon-free zone.

ADOPTED 2000
REVISED AND READOPTED 2008
RESOLUTION #251, 2004 *BOOK OF RESOLUTIONS*
RESOLUTION #235, 2000 *BOOK OF RESOLUTIONS*

See Social Principles, ¶ 162.

## WOMEN

### 3441. Affirmation for the Women's Division

WHEREAS, the Women's Division of the General Board of Global Ministries is charged by the Discipline to "be an advocate for the oppressed and dispossessed with special attention to the needs of women and children; (to) work to build a supportive community among women; and (to) engage in activities that foster growth in the Christian faith, mission education, and Christian social involvement" (paragraph 1317); and

WHEREAS, the Women's Division continues its educational ministries, its outreach in the name of Christ, its work for justice, peace, human community, and its compassionate service with women, children and youth; and

WHEREAS, for over 135 years, the Women's Division has never wavered from its total commitment to the Gospel of Jesus Christ and serving women, youth and children with mission education, opportunities for spiritual growth, opportunities for Christian social involvement and financial support for mission at home and around the world; and

WHEREAS, the Women's Division continues to stand in solidarity with women, youth and children by addressing issues such as violence, rape, incest, terrorism, exploitation and all levels of discrimination and work with other Christian groups to address and eliminate poverty and hunger as the Gospel of Jesus Christ requires; and

WHEREAS, the Women's Division continues to be at the heart of the denomination's missionary movement by working with Bible women, missionaries and deaconesses and to function as an integral structure and administrative entity with the General Board of Global Ministries;

*Therefore, be it resolved,* that the General Conference affirms the powerful witness of the Women's Division in our church and our world; 135 years of faithful service to Christ and the church, its current commitment to mission and its dedication to work within the General board of Global Ministries;

*Be it further resolved,* that the General Conference affirm the powerful witness of the Women's Division in our church and our world;

*Be it further resolved,* that the General Conference upholds the current structure of the Women's Division and the organization of United Methodist Women.

ADOPTED 2004
READOPTED 2008
RESOLUTION #19, 2004 *BOOK OF RESOLUTIONS*

*See* Social Principles, ¶ 161.


## 3442. Celebration of Full Clergy Rights for Women

WHEREAS, God has given women gifts and graces for ministry to witness faithfully to Jesus Christ; and

WHEREAS, The Church of the United Brethren in Christ gave full clergy rights to women in 1889; and

WHEREAS, in 1947 The Church of the United Brethren in Christ merged with The Evangelical Church to become The Evangelical United Brethren Church and ceased giving full clergy rights to women; and

WHEREAS, in 1956 the General Conference of The Methodist Church granted full clergy rights for women and 2006 will be the 50th anniversary of that event; and

WHEREAS, some women from The Central Jurisdiction of The Methodist Church were dissuaded from seeking full clergy rights; and

WHEREAS, in 1968 The Evangelical United Brethren Church and The Methodist Church, having abolished The Central Jurisdiction, merged to form The United Methodist Church; and

WHEREAS, there are now more than 10,000 clergywomen in The United Methodist Church; and

WHEREAS, the predecessor denominations of The United Methodist Church have a tradition of granting full clergy rights for women reaching back 117 years with 50 continuous years of full clergy rights for women;

*Be it resolved,* that in 2006 every annual conference of The United Methodist Church celebrate full clergy rights for women including a liturgical act during the conference session; and

*Be it further resolved,* that all conferences celebrate the anniversary by honoring the names of the conference's clergywomen, past and present; and

*Finally, be it resolved,* that in 2006 every local congregation observe the celebration of full clergy rights for women.

ADOPTED 2004<br>
RESOLUTION #359, 2004 *BOOK OF RESOLUTIONS*

## 3443. Every Barrier Down: Toward Full Embrace of All Women in Church and Society

*As many of you as were baptized into Christ have clothed yourselves with Christ. There is no longer Jew or Greek, there is no longer slave or free, there is no longer male and female; for all of you are one in Christ Jesus*

(Galatians 3:27-28 NRSV).

As the Church of Jesus Christ enters its third millennium, women continue to heed the call to transform the Church and the world in the name of the One who names us and claims us all for witness, mission and earth-shaking transformation.

As much as he was a product of his era—one admittedly marked by gender, class, religious, and community exclusion—Jesus Christ brought to us a ministry of transformational invitation. The Living Christ invited—and still invites—to a common table of grace, justice, and power, people who had never before been invited to the religious power tables, including women, cultural and religious minorities, social outcasts, and disreputable community sinners.[1] And women, in claiming their voice in the new faith movement ignited by the Messiah, became leaders in expanding that movement and in pushing further for inclusion of Gentiles in what was then viewed as Jesus' renewal of Judaism.

Women, in fact, advocated for and sought to protect the inclusive equality of discipleship called forth by Jesus. In this way, they challenged the Jesus movement to remain true to the new vision of human

---

1. *An End to This Strife: The Politics of Gender in African American Church* by Demetrius K. Williams, Augsburg Fortress Press, 2004.

relationship that Jesus initiated by extending its table fellowship, sharing the message of the coming Reign of God and inviting Gentiles (non-Jews) to share in that Reign.1 Jesus treated women with dignity and respect, challenged the conventional sexism of his day, and forever redefined the role of women in the church and society.

As with many expressions of the Christian faith, it took The United Methodist Church and its forebears a while to capture Christ's vision. In 1770, the first Methodist woman was appointed a class leader in the United States; in 1817, women were allowed to hold prayer meetings but denied a license to preach; in 1884 Anna Howard Shaw's ordination by the Methodist Protestant Church was ruled out of order; and full voting rights for women in the Methodist tradition were not universally recognized until 1956.

Since that time, however, God's call to women as preachers, teachers, administrators, mission workers, treasurers, lay leaders, trustees, peace-with-justice advocates, voting rights' workers, Christian educators, and evangelists has blown a fresh breath across the globe and throughout the Church on the wings of the Holy Spirit, despite the rise and fall of our denominational enthusiasm for addressing sexism, gender bias, prejudice, and bad theology. God has done great things with us and, sometimes, in spite of us. Among the victories celebrated throughout our denomination's history:

- one in four United Methodist pastors in local churches today are women, compared with less than one in 100 in 1972;
- of the 63 active United Methodist bishops around the world, 16 are women; in 2004 an unprecedented six women were elected in the same week as United Methodist episcopal leaders. The first woman bishop (the late Marjorie Swank Matthews) was elected in 1980;
- The United Methodist Church gave to the world the first African American (Leontine T.C. Kelly, 1984) and first Latina (Minerva Carcano, 2004) bishops in mainline Christendom;
- women comprise half of all students enrolled in United Methodist seminaries and seeking ordination;
- the Women's Division of the General Board of Global Ministries is the largest and most prolific mission working entity on behalf of women, children, and youth in our denomination, with ministries of education, discipleship, economic and social development, health care, advocacy, and empowerment in over 120 nations around the world.

In many ways The United Methodist Church has been a standard-bearer among Judeo-Christian faith communions in terms of full inclusion of women in the life, ministry, and witness of the institutional church and its regional and local expressions. However, if we ask, "Is The United Methodist Church a credible and reliable witness to Christ's exemplary embrace of all women as valued, respected partners in the total institutional life and global witness and impact of the Church?"—the honest answer is not yet. We still fall short when it comes to living out the challenge of Galatians 3:27-28, which declares men and women are truly one in Christ. There are still areas of leadership, of professional ministry, of decision-making, and of areas of discipleship for which the Church will not trust, value, revere, or allot resources to women to the same degree as their brothers in the faith. Some recent examples include:

- a number of United Methodist congregations in 2007 still flatly refuse to accept a woman as senior pastor and are especially opposed to receiving a woman in a cross-racial clergy appointment. In 2006, a racial-ethnic clergywoman assigned to an Anglo church was allegedly menaced by members to dissuade her acceptance of the appointment. In another instance, laity threatened to leave the congregation unless the woman pastor wore a dress instead of slacks to prove she was "a real lady";
- in a 2007 survey of local United Methodist congregations, 18 percent said they do not have women serving as ushers (an increase over 2004), and local church chairpersons of the Church Council, Finance, and Trustees are still overwhelmingly men and not women;
- United Methodist membership in the US is declining among young women (and men) and people of color, particularly among those in low-income communities. According to a Wesley Theological Seminary survey, women under 35 comprise less than 2 percent of elders in our denomination;
- a number of lay and clergy respondents to a survey on sexual harassment in the church mandated by the 2004 General Conference dismissed any ministries related to empowering women and addressing sexism as "political crap," which "has nothing to do with spreading the good news of Jesus Christ";
- a woman district superintendent reportedly was called a "bitch" when she disagreed with a male colleague during a meeting of the conference cabinet;

- several prominent Church leaders—including bishops—have joined with secular society in decrying "the tyranny of diversity" and retreating from the work of undoing racism and sexism. such things as: "We need to stop worrying about politics and focus on the gospel . . ." (that is, as long as the gospel is interpreted in a way that continues to privilege North Americans, white people, and males); and "We'll accept a woman or person of color as long as she's qualified" (Could this infer that white men are automatically assumed to be qualified and that women and people of color get their jobs because of some other criteria, not because of their gifts and talents?);
- the Women's Division of the General Board of Global Ministries is under attack for having too much money and too much power in the hands of a women-controlled board of directors. Proposals by opponents include reducing the number of Women's Division directors who can also serve on the General Board of Global Ministries in the interest of "gender balance";
- complaints of alleged sexual abuse of women by lay and clergy leaders in church settings are on the rise, according to the General Commission on the Status and Role of Women;
- women comprise 57 percent of total members of our denomination, yet account for less than 20 percent of ordained ministers, and only 22 percent of the top-paying offices in US annual conferences (treasurers, chancellors, and directors of connectional ministry);
- of 30 active bishops who oversee the work of the church in Europe, Africa, and the Philippines, only one is a woman.

According to United Methodist theologian and ethicist Rosetta Ross, the defining characteristic of an authentic Christian community is that we love one another as God loves us. Such love is not a passive, merely personal emotion, but requires that we constantly strive to be in right relationship with one another, that we pursue justice and well-being for all, and that we be courageous in undoing that in the community that stymies the building of God's beloved—and loving community.[2]

In fact, Dr. Ross asserts that agapé love in the Christian understanding is love that "affirms the dignity and value of life," and depends on the "interrelatedness of all relationships—intimate or cor-

2. "Blazing Trails and Transcending Boundaries Through Love: Women of Color and 'Religious Work'" by Rosetta E. Ross, Associate Professor of Philosophy and Religious Studies, Spelman College, Atlanta Georgia, 2006.

porate, public or private," as expressed through the actions, practices, and behaviors of individuals and the corporate Christian community.

"Whatever we love with the social love of agapé—our understanding of a particular movement; persons living in war zones or without clean drinking water; communities of which we are a part; the cause of justice; or the natural beauty of creation—is evident in our expressions of faithful attentiveness to it," concludes Dr. Ross, who is also a South Carolina United Methodist clergywomen.

The United Methodist Church, as a community conceived as a corporate expression of Christ's love for us all, has declared its belief in the full equality of women and its desire to embrace women, and has historically decried institutional sexism in all forms in every corner of the world. Yet, we are still on the journey to faithful living; to "walking our talk"; to emulating Jesus' model of turning convention on its ear in favor of doing God's new thing when it comes to engaging women as universally respected, full participants in every aspect of our corporate and congregational lives. We are still living into what it means to extend agape love to all the daughters and sons of God, beyond the historic patriarchy and misogyny that has marred full participation of women in church and society.

Our reliability as an agency of God's love assumes that we are paying attention to one another and we are seeking to empower, to unshackle, to raise up those who are still oppressed, repressed, derided, treated as "less than." This agape love seeks to make the world better through persistently affirming all life, and we are willing to call all people and systems—including our own denomination—to account for how we either empower or repress the children of God. Agapé love fears no risk of ridicule or of interrupting business as usual. In fact, God's love requires that we act, even if it means taking positions that are uncomfortable, unpopular, inconvenient, or even frightening. Further, it requires courage. To quote Dr. Ross, "We are behaving courageously when we have the resolve to take the actions and create the context needed for overcoming challenges we face in seeking to be faithful to what we love and are committed to."

Until we fully affirm the dignity and value, the contributions, the theological perspectives, the concerns, the hopes, the recommendations, and even the discourse of and among women, The United Methodist Church will not be adequately equipped to make of all disciples, to carry a word of hope and peace and love to a broken world, and to demonstrate our authenticity as the incarnation of the life-transforming and barrier-breaking body of Christ.

We therefore ask the General Conference to recommit The United Methodist Church to fulfilling the following recommendation as we continue our journey toward dismantling sexism in the church and inviting all women from every station to share in God's welcome table, by challenging the denomination to:

1. *Listen anew to women, with new emphasis on women of color.* The experiences of racial-ethnic women in the United States and women from The United Methodist Church in Africa and the Philippines mirror the parables and other Gospel stories of triumph over obstacles, being strangers in a strange land, reinterpreting familiar stories for new disciples, and bringing our talk about love and justice in line with our walk, especially as the Church also exists in a society that is still racist and sexist. We ask the general agencies to create evangelistic tools, programs, educational materials, networks, and opportunities to empower women in the church and society, including specific resources for and leadership opportunities offered to women under 35, racial-ethnic women in the United States, women from nations beyond the United States, women in recovery from addiction, divorced women, professional women, farm women, and skeptical-about-the-church women. We further urge church growth teams to include women from these groups in order to help the Church focus more on being a vibrant movement in people's lives instead of just a religious institution. In our leadership development at all levels, the Church must put energy, resources, skill and prayerful action into engaging new women in lay and clergy leadership.

2. *Champion economic parity and justice, beginning in our own communities.* Our largely Western-focused denomination must witness in our giving and our living to the power of agape by working actively for the well-being of all people. This is particularly critical in our work with women around the world who, with their children, are more likely that any other demographic group to live in poverty; to lack access to adequate health care, housing, and education; and to lack political power sufficient to transform systems. The United Methodist Church must lead the way by valuing the comparable work and worth of women in our churches, agencies, and related entities, and by championing such things as affordable child care and health care, pay equity, financial aid, and educational support for single women in Africa and the Philippines. Each agency and annual conference should report to the 2012 General Conference on how they have engaged

women, including women of color, women from Africa and the Philippines, and women under 35.

3. *Evangelize and identify, recruit and develop leaders among women.* In recent years, some church pundits have claimed that Christian churches have become "too feminized," and therefore irrelevant and unappealing to men. However, these same observers fail to consider that even with decades of male-only leadership among churches, and even in the face of narrow and misogynist misreading of the Bible to exclude and blame them for human sin, many women have continued to stay actively and joyfully involved in the life of the institutional Church. We challenge general agencies and annual conferences to include in church growth and new discipleship strategies efforts to reach women of color, young women, poor women, career women, teen girls, older women, immigrant women, women survivors of violence, women in prison, women leaving prison, women seeking, women rearing children on limited incomes, etc.

4. *Adopt a posture of "no tolerance" to sexual violence, harassment, and abuse in church and society.* According to some estimates by denominational advocates and legal experts, The United Methodist Church has paid more than $50 million from 2000 to 2004 in legal fees, counseling, mediation, and reparations related to sexual misconduct and abuse in church settings committed by lay and clergy. While sexual misconduct can impact anyone and be perpetrated by anyone, most cases involve men as offenders and women and children as victims. If women cannot trust the Church to believe them, protect them from abuse, and offer them clear justice when abuse happens, it again calls into question the authenticity of the Church's witness. It could suggest to them that the Church—and, by extension, God—does not care about, want, or value the participation of women. We call on the Council of Bishops to collaborate with the General Commission on the Status and Role of Women to continue to develop and enforce effective policies, laws, and practices and consistent application of those policies and practices to reduce risk of misconduct and offer swift and just recompense and remediation for victims when abuse happens.

5. *Engage women in theological exploration and shaping and teaching church doctrine.* There is no one women's perspective or women's theology or women's view of Christianity. What is common among many women in The United Methodist Church, however, is that their participation in theological discourse is typically treated as "in addition to" the "classical" biblical and theological teachings. Feminist/womanist/mujerista perspectives are often considered subversive and treated as suspect. Discussions of gender-inclusive language, reading the Hebrew and

Greek text through women's eyes, and liberation theology—especially as discussed by women—are regarded by many as a threat to the Christian faith, instead of new and perhaps even more authentic perspectives on it. Further, laywomen and clergywomen in local parishes often do not see themselves as theologians, with as much right to explore Scripture, to embrace the gospel anew, and to offer their learnings to the wider Church. We urge the denomination to affirm the importance of women's perspectives in theological discussions in the denomination, and we applaud the General Board of Higher Education and Ministry for its Women of Color Scholarship Program that empowers and engages women of color in theological education and discourse. Further, we ask that the board monitor United Methodist seminaries for inclusion of women's theological perspectives as expressed in the number of tenured faculty, etc. Also, we invite the General Commission on the Status and Role of Women to create curricula for local churches with teaching tools on inclusive language, sexism, creating a girl-friendly church, and myths about women and church leadership. And we ask active members of the Council of Bishops to study with pastors and lay leaders in their respective annual conferences on the history of women as preachers and teachers in the church, using "Women Called to Ministry," a six-part curriculum developed by the General Commission on the Status and Role of Women and the General Board of Higher Education and Ministry, and available at www.gcsrw.org.

6. *Create a "report card" on overcoming sexism for each agency and annual conference.* The General Commission on the Status and Role of Women shall create sufficient monitoring tools, focus-group interviews, desk audits and surveys, along with baseline standards in order to evaluate the progress of each annual conference and each general agency in terms of full participation of women, dismantling institutional sexism, and addressing sexual misconduct. The Commission will report its findings to the 2012 General Conference, along with recommendations for further improvements.

Recommended resources: www.gcsrw.org, www.umsexualethics.org; *The Journey Is Our Home: A History of the General Commission on the Status and Role of Women,* by Carolyn Henninger Oehler, 2005; 2008 Resolutions #2044, "Sexual Misconduct Within Ministerial Relationships," and #2045, "Eradication of Sexual Harassment in Church and Society."

**ADOPTED 2008**
**RESOLUTION #190, 2004** *BOOK OF RESOLUTIONS*
**RESOLUTION #180, 2000** *BOOK OF RESOLUTIONS*

*See* Social Principles #163.

## 3444. Eradication of Sexism in the Church

WHEREAS, sexism continues to be a pervasive and systematic force within our church and our society; and

WHEREAS, sexism deprives the church and society of the opportunity to use the skills and talents that women have; and

WHEREAS, a General Commission on the Status and Role of Women 2003 survey of local churches in the United States found that only 57% have policies against sexual harassment; inclusive language studies are rare in local congregations; and urban congregations more frequently have inclusive language studies, harassment policies, and diverse use of female lay persons (as Board of Trustees members and ushers, for example); and

WHEREAS, this survey also found that bishops who are female appointed more district superintendents who were female, and their conferences had more local congregations with sexual harassment policies in place than conferences with Bishops who were male; and

WHEREAS, the Church remains committed to the eradication of sexual harassment against children, employees, volunteers, clergy and their families, and congregants. Yet sexual misconduct remains a serious problem in our conferences, and an alarming number of local congregations do not have policies, procedures, or training in place for laity and clergy in stopping and preventing sexual harassment and misconduct; and

WHEREAS, the Church continues to lose clergywomen (particularly clergywomen of color) from local church ministry into more welcoming forms of ministry. A persistent, subtle, and often unchallenged sexism denies women in The United Methodist Church the opportunity to participate fully and equally in all areas of the Church;

*Therefore, be it resolved,* that the General Conference affirm the work and the necessity for the continuance of the General Commission on the Status and Role of Women and of the annual conference related commissions and counterparts; and

*Be it further resolved,* that each annual conference commission or counterpart be given the financial backing to pursue projects that are aimed at educating the members of the local churches about the issues of sexism and at sponsoring the leadership events that enable the annual conference commission members to be better advocates for all who seek equity and inclusiveness; and

*Be it further resolved,* that each annual conference, United Methodist seminary, and all United Methodist-related institutions are called to have policies on sexual harassment and equal opportunity; and

*Be it further resolved,* that each annual conference and local congregation is called have policy, procedures, and training opportunities in place for lay and clergy in stopping and preventing sexual harassment and misconduct; and that progress to full compliance will be reported through the Episcopal Office to the General Commission on the Status and Role of Women at the Commission's request. The Commission will be responsible to report to General Conference 2008; and

*Be it further resolved,* that the General Conference support the General Commission on the Status and Role of Women as the advocacy and monitoring agency of women's issues for increasing opportunities for females in leadership, promoting equality in filling decision-making posts, and fostering inclusiveness in all facets of The United Methodist Church.

ADOPTED 1996
AMENDED AND READOPTED 2004
RESOLUTION #48, 2004 *BOOK OF RESOLUTIONS*
RESOLUTION #40, 2000 *BOOK OF RESOLUTIONS*

*See* Social Principles, ¶ 162F.

## 3445. The Status of Women

### I.

Christianity was born in a world of male preference and dominance. Practices, traditions, and attitudes in almost all societies viewed women as inferior to men, as having few talents and contributions to make to the general well-being of society aside from their biological roles. This was true of the Judaic society of which Jesus was a part.

But the life of Jesus, the Redeemer of human life, stood as a witness against such cultural patterns and prejudices. Consistently, he related to women as persons of intelligence and capabilities. He charged women as well as men to use their talents significantly in the cause of God's kingdom. His acts of healing and ministry were extended without distinction to women and men.

The central theme of Jesus' teaching is love for God and neighbor. Jesus embodied this message in his life, and, in the early church, women held prominent positions of leadership. Christian love as exemplified in the New Testament requires that we relate to others as persons of worth. To regard another as an inferior is to break the covenant of love; denying equality demeans, perpetuates injustice, and falls short of the example of Jesus and the early church.

## II.

The movement to improve the status of women is one of the most profoundly hopeful of our times. The United Methodist Church, recognizing that equality between women and men is a matter of social justice, in various ways has sought to support that movement.

Although change is taking place, in most societies women are still not accorded equal rights and responsibilities.

There is increasing awareness that we cannot solve world problems associated with globalization and unequal distribution of resources population growth, poverty, and war so long as the talents and potential of half the world's people are disregarded and even repressed. There are strong interrelationships between all these problems and the status of women.

The International movement for the equality of women formally began in 1975, with the proclamation of International Women's Year by the United Nations General Assembly. The United Nations Decade for Women (1976-1985) which followed was a worldwide effort to examine the status and rights of women at all levels. For Christians, it was a time for repentance and for new dedication to Christ's ideal of equality.

In 1995, the Fourth World Conference on Women succeeded in bringing about a new and international commitment to the goals of equality, development and peace for all women, and moved the global movement for the advancement of women into the twenty-first century. The Beijing Declaration and the Platform for Action constitute a powerful agenda for women's empowerment and gender equality.

The Beijing Platform for Action defined a set of strategic objectives and spelled out actions to be taken by governments and civil society in the following twelve critical areas of concern: poverty, economy, power and decision-making, education, media, health, armed conflict, environment, violence, human rights, the girl child and the institutional mechanisms for the advancement of women.

*Economics:* As part of the Beijing Platform for Action, statisticians were called upon to develop a more comprehensive knowledge of all forms of work and employment. Often the productive labor of women is ignored in economic statistics, reinforcing the impression that work done by women is peripheral, of secondary importance, even dispensable. For that reason, few studies have actually evaluated the importance of contributions by women. As one example, when women grow food to feed their families, they are "just" tending kitchen gardens, but when men grow cash crops such as tobacco and coffee, they are engaged in agricultural and commercial enterprises. In more industrialized societies, the enormous amount of volunteer work done by women is not counted as adding to the nation's wealth.

Although the gender gap in rates of economic activity is narrowing, the nature of women's and men's participation in the labor force continues to be very different. Women have always engaged in the less formal types of work, working as unpaid workers in a family business, in the informal sector or in various types of household economic activities. They also continue to receive less pay than men. In manufacturing, for example, in 27 of the 39 countries with data available, women's wages were 20 to 50 per cent less than those of men.

*Power and Decision-making.* In 1945, only 31 countries allowed women to vote; today women have the right in more than 125 nations. Only eight countries exclude women entirely from political processes open to men. Still, many areas of legal discrimination remain. In some nations, women are still considered the chattels of their husbands, with few rights in family law, landholding, inheritance, and guardianship of children.

In the United States, some of the more glaring inequities are being corrected step by step. However, women are still under represented in all branches of the government. The 75 women sworn into the 108th Congress in January 2003, account for only 13.8% of the 540 members.

*Education.* The perception of women as inferior and dependent is perpetuated through many institutions in society—the media, school textbooks and curricula, political structures, and, often, religious organizations. Education is one of the principal ways of opening doors to wider participation in society. Thus, it is distressing that, while the percentage of literate women is at an all-time high, the absolute number of illiterate women is greater than at any time in the past. The fact that two thirds of the world's 876 million illiterates are female is evidence of continuing disparity in importance given to the education of boys and girls.

*Violence Against Women.* Traditional perceptions of female qualities also are a factor in the widespread domestic violence against women, now coming to be recognized as a tragically widespread occurrence. Nearly one third of women in the world report being physically or sexually abused by a husband or boyfriend at some point in their lives (according to World Health Organization).

*Human Rights in Fertility Decisions.* Throughout the centuries, women have been little consulted or involved in the decisions regarding fertility-related laws or practices. For women, particularly, the ability to make choices concerning fertility is a liberating force, helping to safeguard their health and that of their children, to plan for the future, to assume wider roles and responsibilities in society.

The United Nations has declared that education and access to means for determining the number and spacing of children is a human right, yet this is an ideal far from realization.

Coercion is still common, sometimes aimed at increasing births, sometimes at limiting them. Evidence now clearly shows that many poor, particularly ethnic, women have been sterilized without their understanding of what was being done to them and without their informed consent. In many places, safe and legal abortion is denied, in some cases even to save the life of the pregnant woman. In other cases, women are threatened that welfare payments or aid programs will be cut if the pregnancy continues. Such inconsistency reflects lack of value-centered decision making, as well as insensitivity to the personhood of the woman involved.

While societal needs should be considered more and more in fertility matters, this should never be at the price of demeaning the individual or applying restrictive measures only to the poor. Women should be fully informed and fully involved in the decision making.

*HIV/AIDS and Women.* According to 2004 Joint United Nations Program on HIV/AIDS report, women now account for almost half of the 38 million adults currently living with HIV/AIDS and of the 20 million adults who have died from the disease since the epidemic began. In 1999, 52 per cent of the 2.1 million adults who died from AIDS worldwide were women. The majority of these deaths occurred in sub-Saharan Africa. where women account for 57 per cent of those infected with HIV/AIDS. Women's risk of becoming infected with

HIV during unprotected sexual intercourse is also known to be two to four times higher than that of men.

The Beijing Platform for Action recognizes that social and cultural factors often increase women's vulnerability to HIV and may determine the course that the infection takes in their lives. Women too often do not have the power to insist on safe and responsible sex practices and have little access to public health information and services, both of which have been found to be effective in preventing the disease and/or slowing its progress.

*Women and Armed Conflict.* Although the threat of global conflict has been reduced, wars of aggression, colonial or other forms of alien domination and foreign occupation, civil wars, and terrorism continue to plague the world. Grave violations of the human rights of women occur, particularly in times of armed conflict, and include murder, torture, systematic rape, forced pregnancy and forced abortion, in particular under policies of ethnic cleansing. Women and girls are among those most affected by the violence and economic instability associated with armed conflict Yet, when it comes to negotiating peace and facilitating the reconstruction of societies after war, women are grossly under represented. For example, no Bosnian women were present at the Dayton Peace negotiations in 1995. With Security Council Resolution 1325 on Women, peace and security (2000), the United Nations has affirmed that women's protection in armed conflict and the integration of women's voices and experiences in the process of building peace are a primary concern of the international community.

## III.

Across the nations of the world, new movements are growing that address the serious handicaps and harsh realities of the lives of many women. In the context of this increasing momentum for a more just society, we call on local congregations and the agencies of the church:

1. to exert leadership in working, wherever possible, for legal recognition of equal rights for women. In the United States, this means a strengthened determination to secure passage for the Equal Rights Amendment,[1] in line with the United Methodist Conference affirmations of 1972 and 1976. We need to recognize that this measure has become

---

1. Proposed 27th Amendment: Section 1. Equality of rights under the law shall not be denied or abridged by the United States or by any State on account of sex. Section 2. The Congress shall have the power to enforce, by appropriate legislation, the provisions of this article. Section 3. This amendment shall take effect two years after the date of ratification.

a symbol of the drive for equality. It has meaning far beyond the borders of one nation in the search for equal rights in other societies;

2. to urge governments to ratify the Convention on the Elimination of Discrimination Against Women, which was adopted by the United Nations in December 1979;

3. to encourage support of studies by scientific and governmental bodies of the economic contributions made by women outside the formal economic sector, and to include this information in the gross national product of nations or compilations of national wealth;

4. to urge governments to ratify the Statute of the International Criminal Court, adopted in June 1998, which specifically addresses gender-based crimes and crimes against humanity such as rape, sexual slavery, enforced prostitution, forced pregnancy and enforced sterilization;

5. to support the need to enact specific legislation and develop policies to strengthen women's executive and professional abilities, in particular to allow them to manage their own businesses. To this end, governments should develop policies and projects that use local, national and international networks to facilitate information, technology, credit and training for women entrepreneurs, as well as programs that aim to enhance women's education;

6. to examine governmental policies and practices, including development assistance, as to their impact on women's lives; to work to ensure that policies upgrade the status of women and that women are included in decision-making regarding development goals and programs. The key roles of women as workers and consumers and as transmitters of culture must be given adequate weight in national development activities;

7. to examine the impact of transnational corporations on women's lives, and to work to eradicate exploitative practices where identified. One such area is the promotion and selling of inappropriate products and technologies;

8. to encourage steps that promote legal literacy by publicizing and disseminating information on laws relating to the equal rights of men and women;

9. to encourage private charitable organizations, including churches, to initiate and support more programs of leadership education for women and other educational programs that upgrade the status of women; In many parts of the world, illiteracy remains high among adult women because of the lack of access to education in childhood. Strategies to combat female illiteracy must focus on ensuring girls' equal access to, and completion of, basic education. In addition, there

is a need to reach out to adult women through massive literacy campaigns using all modern means available;

10. to monitor printed and audio/visual media and other means of communication on their portrayals of the roles and nature of women and men, and to seek ways to eradicate narrow stereotypes that limit the possibilities of useful contributions by both sexes. The church should encourage study of the impact of Western—particularly US—television, radio, and other media on cultural patterns and national development around the world, and it should draw public attention to cases where such influence is destructive to other cultures;

11. to support programs providing knowledge of the access to resources in the area of family planning and contraception, including that which is Christian based, to encourage abstinence outside of marriage as a method of birth control, and to involve women in the preparation and distribution of these resources. Attention should particularly be given to ensuring access to safe, legal, and noncoercive contraception; well-informed choice regarding abortion and its alternatives (adoptions and so forth); informed consent for sterilization procedures; and safe women's health-care facilities. We also oppose profit-making referral agencies, which charge fees for providing information freely available elsewhere; and

12. to examine the impact of judicial decisions at all levels upon the daily lives of women in such areas as child custody, employment, civil rights, racial and sexual discrimination, credit practices, estate settlements, reproduction and education, and socioeconomic status.

ADOPTED 1992
AMENDED AND READOPTED 1996
AMENDED AND READOPTED 2004
READOPTED 2008
RESOLUTION #191, 2004 *BOOK OF RESOLUTIONS*
RESOLUTION #181, 2000 *BOOK OF RESOLUTIONS*

*See* Social Principles, ¶ 162F.

## YOUNG PEOPLE

### 3461. Local Church Support for Young People

WHEREAS, The United Methodist Church supports young people and is called to minister to them; and

WHEREAS,  the young people in The United Methodist Church are in need of growth and revival churchwide; and

WHEREAS,  in order for young people to grow in the worldwide church, they must first grow in the local church,

*Therefore, be it resolved,* that the Global Young People's Convocation and Legislative Assembly and General Conference call upon each local church to do all in its power to support and strengthen young people's ministries at its local level, so that they may be strengthened worldwide.

**ADOPTED 2008**

*See* Social Principles, ¶ 162D.

# ¶ 163. IV. THE ECONOMIC COMMUNITY

We claim all economic systems to be under the judgment of God no less than other facets of the created order. Therefore, we recognize the responsibility of governments to develop and implement sound fiscal and monetary policies that provide for the economic life of individuals and corporate entities and that ensure full employment and adequate incomes with a minimum of inflation. We believe private and public economic enterprises are responsible for the social costs of doing business, such as employment and environmental pollution, and that they should be held accountable for these costs. We support measures that would reduce the concentration of wealth in the hands of a few. We further support efforts to revise tax structures and to eliminate governmental support programs that now benefit the wealthy at the expense of other persons.

*A) Property*—We believe private ownership of property is a trusteeship under God, both in those societies where it is encouraged and where it is discouraged, but is limited by the overriding needs of society. We believe that Christian faith denies to any person or group of persons exclusive and arbitrary control of any other part of the created universe. Socially and culturally conditioned ownership of property is, therefore, to be considered a responsibility to God. We believe, therefore, governments have the responsibility, in the pursuit of justice and order under law, to provide procedures that protect the rights of the whole society as well as those of private ownership.

*B) Collective Bargaining*—We support the right of all public and private employees and employers to organize for collective bargaining into unions and other groups of their own choosing. Further, we support the right of both parties to protection in so doing and their responsibility to bargain in good faith within the framework of the public interest. In order that the rights of all members of the society may be maintained and promoted, we support innovative bargaining procedures that include representatives of the public interest in negotiation and settlement of labor-management contracts, including some that may lead to forms of judicial resolution of issues. We reject the use of violence by either party during collective bargaining or any labor/management disagreement. We likewise reject the permanent replacement of a worker who engages in a lawful strike.

*C) Work and Leisure*—Every person has the right to a job at a living wage. Where the private sector cannot or does not provide jobs for all who seek and need them, it is the responsibility of government to provide for the creation of such jobs. We support social measures that ensure the physical and mental safety of workers, that provide for the equitable division of products and services, and that encourage an increasing freedom in the way individuals may use their leisure time. We recognize the opportunity leisure provides for creative contributions to society and encourage methods that allow workers additional blocks of discretionary time. We support educational, cultural, and recreational outlets that enhance the use of such time. We believe that persons come before profits. We deplore the selfish spirit that often pervades our economic life. We support policies that encourage the sharing of ideas in the workplace, cooperative and collective work arrangements. We support rights of workers to refuse to work in situations that endanger health and/or life without jeopardy to their jobs. We support policies that would reverse the increasing concentration of business and industry into monopolies.

*D) Consumption*—Consumers should exercise their economic power to encourage the manufacture of goods that are necessary and beneficial to humanity while avoiding the desecration of the environment in either production or consumption, and to avoid purchasing products made in conditions where workers are being exploited because of their age, gender, or economic status.

And while the limited options available to consumers make this extremely difficult to accomplish, buying "Fair Trade Certified" products is one sure way consumers can use their purchasing power to make a contribution to the common good. The International Standards of Fair Trade are based on ensuring livable wages for small farmers and their families, working with democratically run farming cooperatives, buying direct so that the benefits and profits from trade actually reach the farmers and their communities, providing vitally important advance credit, and encouraging ecologically sustainable farming practices. Consumers should not only seek out companies whose product lines reflect a strong commitment to these standards, but should also encourage expanded corporate participation in the Fair Trade market.

Consumers should evaluate their consumption of goods and services in the light of the need for enhanced quality of life rather than unlimited production of material goods. We call upon consumers, including local congregations and Church-related institutions, to organize to achieve these goals and to express dissatisfaction with harmful economic, social, or ecological practices through such appropriate methods as boycott, letter writing, corporate resolution, and advertisement.

*E) Poverty*—In spite of general affluence in the industrialized nations, the majority of persons in the world live in poverty. In order to provide basic needs such as food, clothing, shelter, education, health care, and other necessities, ways must be found to share more equitably the resources of the world. Increasing technology, when accompanied by exploitative economic practices, impoverishes many persons and makes poverty self-perpetuating. Poverty due to natural catastrophes and environmental changes is growing and needs attention and support. Conflicts and war impoverish the population on all sides, and an important way to support the poor will be to work for peaceful solutions.

As a church, we are called to support the poor and challenge the rich. To begin to alleviate poverty, we support such policies as: adequate income maintenance, quality education, decent housing, job training, meaningful employment opportunities, adequate medical and hospital care, humanization and radical revisions of welfare programs, work for peace in conflict areas, and efforts to protect creation's integrity. Since low wages are often a cause of poverty, employers should pay their employees a wage that does not require them to depend upon government subsidies such as food stamps or welfare for their livelihood.

Because we recognize that the long-term reduction of poverty must move beyond services to and employment for the poor, which can be taken away, we emphasize measures that build and maintain the wealth of poor people, including asset-building strategies such as individual development savings accounts, micro-enterprise development programs, programs enabling home ownership, and financial management training and counseling. We call upon churches to develop these and other ministries that promote asset-building among

¶ 163

the poor. We are especially mindful of the Global South, where investment and micro-enterprise are especially needed. We urge support for policies that will encourage equitable economic growth in the Global South and around the world, proving a just opportunity for all.

Poverty most often has systemic causes, and therefore we do not hold poor people morally responsible for their economic state.

F) Foreign Workers—For centuries people have moved across borders in search of work. In our global world this is still a relevant and increasing form of immigration. Improved wages, better working conditions, and jobs available are reasons for immigration due to work opportunities. Workers from other countries are in many societies an important resource to fill the society's need of workers. But foreign workers too often meet exploitation, absence of protecting laws, and unreasonable wages and working conditions.

We call upon governments and all employers to ensure for foreign workers the same economic, educational, and social benefits enjoyed by other citizens.

Foreign workers also need a religious fellowship, and we call for the churches to include these in their care and fellowships and to support them in their efforts for better conditions.

G) Gambling—Gambling is a menace to society, deadly to the best interests of moral, social, economic, and spiritual life, destructive of good government and good stewardship. As an act of faith and concern, Christians should abstain from gambling and should strive to minister to those victimized by the practice. Where gambling has become addictive, the Church will encourage such individuals to receive therapeutic assistance so that the individual's energies may be redirected into positive and constructive ends. The Church acknowledges the dichotomy that can occur when opposing gambling while supporting American Indian tribal sovereignty and self-determination. Therefore, the Church's role is to create sacred space to allow for dialogue and education that will promote a holistic understanding of the American Indians' historic quest for survival. The Church's prophetic call is to promote standards of justice and advocacy that would make it unnecessary and undesirable to resort to commercial gambling—including public lotteries, casinos, raffles, Internet gambling, gambling with an emerging wireless technology and other games of chance—as a recreation, as an escape, or as a means of producing public revenue or funds for support of charities or government.

*H) Family Farms*—The value of family farms has long been affirmed as a significant foundation for free and democratic societies. In recent years, the survival of independent farmers worldwide has been threatened by various factors, including the increasing concentration of all phases of agriculture into the hands of a limited number of transnational corporations. The concentration of the food supply for the many into the hands of the few raises global questions of justice that cry out for vigilance and action. We call upon the agribusiness sector to conduct itself with respect for human rights primarily in the responsible stewardship of daily bread for the world, and secondarily in responsible corporate citizenship that respects the rights of all farmers, small and large, to receive a fair return for honest labor. We advocate for the rights of people to possess property and to earn a living by tilling the soil.

We call upon governments to revise support programs that disproportionately benefit wealthier agricultural producers, so that more support can be given to programs that benefit medium and smaller sized farming operations, including programs that build rural processing, storage, distribution, and other community food security measures.

We call upon our churches to do all in their power to speak prophetically to the matters of food supply and the people who grow the food for the world and to develop ministries that build food security in local communities.

*I) Corporate Responsibility*—Corporations are responsible not only to their stockholders, but also to other stakeholders: their workers, suppliers, vendors, customers, the communities in which they do business, and for the earth, which supports them. We support the public's right to know what impacts corporations have in these various arenas, so that people can make informed choices about which corporations to support.

We applaud corporations that voluntarily comply with standards that promote human well-being and protect the environment.

*J) Trade and Investment*—We affirm the importance of international trade and investment in an interdependent world. Trade and investment should be based on rules that support the dignity of the human person, a clean environment and our common humanity. Trade agreements must include mechanisms to enforce labor rights and human rights as well as environmental standards. Broad-based citizen advocacy and participation in trade negotiations must be ensured through democratic mechanisms of consultation and participation.

¶ 163

# IV. THE ECONOMIC COMMUNITY
# THE RESOLUTIONS

## APPALACHIA

### 4001. Appalachia: A Call to Action

The General Conference of 1972 directed its boards, agencies and conferences to coordinate denominational and ecumenical ministries within the Appalachian region through the United Methodist Appalachian Ministry Network (UMAMN), and the Commission on Religion in Appalachia (CORA). The region encompasses 23 United States Annual Conferences that span more than 400 counties in 13 states.

The United Methodist Church is called upon to reaffirm its commitments to integrated strategies for mission and ministry in the region and to work denominationally and ecumenically to be present with and supportive of the people and churches of Appalachia by directing its boards, commissions, annual conferences and local churches to examine ways that they might address the systemic issues that contribute to the ongoing plight and exploitation of the people and land of Appalachia.

This can be accomplished by studying the history, culture, social and economic realities of the region called Appalachia: developing opportunities for involvement in mission and ministry in Appalachian communities, enhancing spiritual renewal, addressing social recovery, developing leadership opportunities, working toward economic transformation through advocacy and economic development, securing environmental integrity, promoting political involvement and responsibility, and ministering with compassion.

In recent years, bishops in the Appalachian region of The United Methodist Church have joined with other religious leaders and Roman Catholic bishops of Appalachia in producing pastoral letters calling attention to the continued exploitation of the people and of the land.

ADOPTED 2004
READOPTED 2008
RESOLUTION #193, 2004 *BOOK OF RESOLUTIONS*

*See* Social Principles, ¶ 163.

## BOYCOTTS

### 4011. Guidelines for Initiating or Joining an Economic Boycott

As Christians we are called to stand with those on the economic margins of society. The Hebrew prophets decried economic exploitation and warned against economic systems based on greed and indifference to the plight of the worker (Jeremiah 22:13-17). When Christ began his public ministry, he proclaimed that he was anointed to bring good news to the poor and to free the oppressed (Luke 4:18). Following the warnings of the prophets and the teachings of Christ, The United Methodist Church remains committed to a ministry of economic justice.

Today's economy is too often biased toward profits rather than the common good. As participants in this economy, consumers have power to perpetuate or challenge this bias. As Christian consumers, we are called, through individual and collective actions, to ensure that our participation in the economic system is valuing people and perpetuating justice, rather than simply maximizing profits. One effective mechanism to challenge injustice and to reclaim this often-overlooked power is an economic boycott.

### Preamble

An economic boycott is understood to be a combined effort to abstain from the purchase or use of products or services provided by a specific company, government, or other agency. The purpose of a boycott is to persuade that body to cease from certain practices judged to be unjust, and/or to perform certain practices deemed to be just.

Acknowledging the boycott as a legitimate Christian response to an identified social or economic injustice, we recommend the following criteria as a process for guiding the church and its agencies in decisions regarding boycott. This process includes the following steps:

- Preparation
- Decision making
- Monitoring
- Suspension/termination

The process and steps outlined in this resolution are intended as a guide for discernment and action for those exploring the option of an economic boycott, not an exhaustive or mandated checklist required prior to action. The decision-making body, however, should document and distribute widely relevant information including the theological and factual underpinnings of its decision.

### Clarifying Who May Call

Any local church, district, annual conference, or general church board or agency can initiate or join a boycott if it has completed or has ascertained that another part of The United Methodist Church, or an ecumenical agency that the church is a member of, has completed the initiation process described below. The initiating body is responsible for monitoring and suspending and/or terminating such a boycott.

Any of the above may request the General Conference to join it in the boycott in the name of The United Methodist Church. Only the General Conference shall be empowered to initiate a boycott in the name of The United Methodist Church.

### Preparation

I. Identify in writing the biblical and theological imperatives that address the issues involved in this particular conflict.

II. Document the social-justice issues in the dispute with input from each of the major parties in the dispute, United Methodist and/or ecumenical leadership in the impacted region, and objective third parties.

Among the questions to explore in the discernment and fact-finding phase are:

1. How do the social justice issues affect various segments of society and the communities in the area?
2. What sources of political, economic, or social power does each party in the dispute or alleged injustice have?
3. How will a boycott affect a potential resolution of the situation?

    4. Are the leaders in the dispute or grievance supported by the persons for whom they speak, and are they committed to nonviolent action?

    5. What denominational reviews have been made on this issue?

    6. What groups, agencies, or governmental bodies have been seeking resolution in the conflict?

III. Evaluate the conflict described by the gathered information in relation to the theological, ethical, and social principles of Christian tradition and The United Methodist Church.

    1. Is intervention needed, and what magnitude of response is appropriate to the scope of the injustice?

    2. Is the desired end clearly specified?

IV. Generate a list of potential public and private means of intervention in the situation, and evaluate the probable results of each. Track attempts at mediation, dialogue, and negotiations and explore the likely positive and negative consequences of a boycott.

    1. What methods of mediation, dialogue, and negotiations have been attempted and evaluated?

    2. Have these means of intervention been publicized and shared with connectional leadership in the region of the conflict and other constituencies?

    3. Is the injustice of sufficient scope to warrant the mobilization of a boycott?

    4. Is a boycott a more constructive and effective means of achieving justice than more coercive means?

    5. What are likely to be the positive and negative consequences of a boycott?

    6. What will the effects likely be in the local community?

    7. Are the issues adequately clarified so as to provide support for a boycott?

    8. How can negative stereotyping of contending parties be avoided?

V. Develop a written document detailing the theological foundation for the action, the intended objectives of the boycott, and the relationship of this action to other strategies being used to achieve the goal.

    1. How will these objectives be shared with the disputing parties?

    2. Is it clear as to how the objectives of the potential boycott relate to other strategies being used by this or other church bodies?

    3. Are these objectives in harmony with the theological, ethical, and social principles? (See criteria I and III.)

VI. Develop a plan and identify resources for carrying out a potential boycott, including mechanisms for:

    1. communicating to church constituencies the objectives of the boycott; the issues as seen by the various parties; and the biblical, theological, and ethical imperatives for involvement;

    2. informing disputing parties of an intention to call or participate in a boycott;

    3. coordinating efforts with other United Methodist bodies, interfaith coalitions, and groups dealing with the issues;

    4. monitoring the progress of the boycott (see VIII);

    5. suspending/terminating the boycott when objectives are met (see IX, X, XI);

    6. developing ministries of reconciliation between aggrieved parties, during and following the boycott action.

    7. deciding what resources and plans have been made to ensure that the potential boycott will be carried out effectively and responsibly; and

    8. providing the presiding bishop(s), council director(s), superintendent(s), pastors, and membership in the region with the opportunity to participate in the development of this plan.

## Decision Making

VII. On the basis of the information obtained in I and II above, decide whether a boycott action is merited and determine the most effective time to initiate or join the boycott.

    1. Why is this the best time for this decision-making body to enter the boycott?

    2. Is the boycott likely to achieve the stated objectives and assist in resolution of the dispute?

## Monitoring

VIII. If a boycott is called, a monitoring group should be established by the decision-making body with the goal of evaluating progress toward the stated objective; reporting to the appropriate local, regional, and/or national bodies; and coordinating activities with other ecumenical, interfaith, and coalition partners.
   1. regular evaluation and reporting of progress toward the stated objective;
   2. regular written reporting of such progress to the local area affected and to the constituencies of the decision-making bodies through appropriate denominational channels;
   3. reporting substantial changes in the conditions under which the boycott is being carried out;
   4. a process for issuing public statements; and
   5. coordination with designated coalitions and interfaith groups.

## Suspension/Termination

IX. In those cases where circumstances have changed, making it unclear whether the objectives of the boycott are being met, in consultation with the designated coalition and/or participating groups that are coordinating the boycott action, the decision-making body, or its designate, may call for suspension of the boycott while monitoring and evaluation continues.

X. When the clearly stated written objectives of the boycott have been met, in consultation with the designated coalition and/or participating groups that are coordinating boycott action, the decision-making body or its designate shall terminate boycott participation.

XI. Notification of suspension/termination shall be made in writing to all parties in the dispute and should be widely publicized to all constituencies of the decision-making body.

XII. Following this notification, monitoring of compliance with objectives and ministries of reconciliation shall be continued by the decision-making body for a responsible period of time.

ADOPTED 1988
REVISED AND READOPTED 2000 AND 2008
RESOLUTION #195, 2004 *BOOK OF RESOLUTIONS*
RESOLUTION #187, 2000 *BOOK OF RESOLUTIONS*

*See* Social Principles, ¶ 163B.

## CONSUMPTION

### 4021. Tobacco Marketing by Altria/Philip Morris and RJR Nabisco

As people of faith in the living God, we are reminded that Jesus spoke out for justice for the poor, the disenfranchised and the powerless and called us to love one another. The Bible reminds us that our bodies are "temples of the living God" (1 Corinthians 6:13-20) and since we are created in God's own image, we are then called by God to perfect our bodies in God's image. Moreover, we are called by God to ensure that all of God's creation has access to the knowledge of God's love and God's concern for our well-being and welfare. Through our historic Wesleyan heritage and by John Wesley's words, we are reminded as United Methodists that "the world is our parish," and we are called to minister in and throughout the whole world.

The United Methodist Church and its predecessor denominations have a long history of witness against the use and marketing of tobacco products. There is overwhelming evidence linking cigarette smoking with lung cancer, cardiovascular diseases, emphysema, chronic bronchitis, and related illnesses.

We are outraged by the use of marketing techniques aimed at children by leading cigarette manufacturers. Specific companies using marketing strategies aimed at children are Altria/Philip Morris, which sells Marlboro cigarettes, and RJR Nabisco, which sells Camel cigarettes.

*Therefore*, as people of faith who believe our bodies are temples of the living God (1 Corinthians 6:13-20), we:

1. direct the General Board of Church and Society to maintain and publish a current list of consumer products produced by Altria/Philip Morris and RJR Nabisco so that United Methodists are made aware of their indirect support of the tobacco industry;

2. commend the General Board of Pensions and Health Benefits for its long-standing exclusion of tobacco manufacturers from its investment portfolio and ask it to challenge public media in its portfolio not to carry advertisements and promotion of tobacco products;

3. ask all United Methodist agencies and related institutions to take into account the church's Social Principles and tobacco concerns and, specifically, to consider the role of Altria/Philip Morris and RJR Nabisco in tobacco marketing as a factor in any decision concerning purchasing food products manufactured by them;

4. request the United Methodist general agencies to communicate, interpret, and advocate for this concern with their affiliated institutions;

5. ask all local churches and annual conferences to educate their membership about the tobacco industry's marketing tactics aimed at children. It is equally important we understand the connection between our purchasing food products and our indirect support of the tobacco industry;

6. request the General Board of Church and Society to explore productive measures aimed at stopping tobacco companies from marketing cigarettes and other tobacco products to children and, if necessary, organize a boycott; and

7. direct the General Board of Church and Society to communicate this resolution to the tobacco companies, serve as a continuing advocate of the United Methodist position within The United Methodist Church and with the companies, and monitor the implementation of this resolution for report at the next General Conference.

ADOPTED 1996
AMENDED AND READOPTED 2004
RESOLUTION #198, 2004 *BOOK OF RESOLUTIONS*
RESOLUTION #189, 2000 *BOOK OF RESOLUTIONS*

*See* Social Principles, ¶ 163D.

## 4022. United Methodist Church Use of Fair Trade Coffee and Other Fair Trade Products

WHEREAS, coffee is one of the world's most heavily traded commodities; it originates from either large plantations that are traditionally run and owned by wealthy landowners or small operations that are primarily owned by impoverished farmers. These small farmers frequently live in isolated communities relying on middlemen to buy their coffee invariably at the lowest price possible. The way the system is set up, the farmers' inability to get a just return for their labor is essentially guaranteed and they are condemned to a life of extreme poverty; and,

WHEREAS, tea and cocoa are also major commodities grown on large plantations that often exploit farm laborers and impoverish small farmers; and,

WHEREAS, biblical justice brings all into the economic community, with a share in productive power as seen in the provision of land to every family unit (Numbers 26; Leviticus 25); and,

WHEREAS, our Social Principles state that "we support measures that would reduce the concentration of wealth in the hands of the few," that "we advocate for the rights of people to possess property and to earn a living by tilling the soil"; and that "we call upon our churches to do all in their power to speak prophetically to the matters of food supply and the people who grow the food for the world" (¶ 163); and,

WHEREAS, the United Methodist Committee on Relief (UMCOR) partnered in April 2002 with Equal Exchange to launch a denomination-wide coffee program and through the partnership, any United Methodist church or individual buying coffee through Equal Exchange's Interfaith Program can now order coffee through UMCOR (at the Equal Exchange Web site), and who, for every case of coffee ordered, receives approximately 5 percent of purchase price from Equal Exchange to be used in UMCOR's small farmer economic development programs; and,

WHEREAS, the annual conferences of New England, East Ohio, and Nebraska have resolutions and programs to foster purchase of fair trade coffee by their member churches to support impoverished family farmers in the developing world provide for their families; and

WHEREAS, many of our agencies and congregations, their administrations and their committee organizations serve coffee at meetings, programs, and fund-raising events; and,

WHEREAS, purchasing domestic coffee brands at the least expensive price makes us unintentional participants in an exploitative system that has trapped thousands of developing world farmers, their families and children in an inescapable cycle of poverty; and,

WHEREAS, economic justice can be fostered by consumers exercising their economic power to avoid purchasing products in conditions where workers are being exploited; and,

WHEREAS, the International Standards of Fair Trade focus on ensuring that small farmers are compensated with a fair and true living wage, working with democratically run farming cooperatives that are owned and governed by and for the farmers themselves, buying directly from the co-ops so that the benefits and profits from the trade actually reach the farmers and their communities, providing vital advance credit to farmers and encouraging sustainable farming practices; and,

WHEREAS, fair trade tea, cocoa, olive oil, and other produce are now more widely available from small farmer cooperatives around the world; and,

WHEREAS, the purchase of fair trade olive oil and other olive products from Palestinian farmers provides crucial income to small farmers; and,

WHEREAS, the General Board of Global Ministries has long partnered with and supported the Palestinian and Israeli women's cooperative, Sindyanna; and,

WHEREAS, the General Conference of The United Methodist Church seeks to address the underlying systemic justice issues throughout the world and to provide opportunities for supporting systems based on the values of justice, cooperation, sustainability, and the common good, we therefore create a partnership with a key US Fair Trade organization, Equal Exchange, and join over 5,000 places of worship and faith-based organizations who support small coffee, tea, and cocoa farmers in developing nations;

*Therefore, be it resolved,* that in seeking an authentic Christian response to the plight of developing world small individual coffee farmers, their families, and their communities, the General Conference of The United Methodist Church urges all agencies of the church, local congregations and their affiliated organizations that use coffee, tea, cocoa, and/or olive oil to purchase coffee, tea, cocoa, olive oil, and other fair trade products for corporate and personal use through the fair trade partner, Equal Exchange, or through another fair trade organization.

ADOPTED 2004
REVISED AND READOPTED 2008
RESOLUTION #199, 2004 *BOOK OF RESOLUTIONS*

*See* Social Principles, ¶ 163D.

# EDUCATION

## 4031. The Methodist Global Education Fund for Leadership Development

*Reaffirmation and Reauthorization of the World Service Special Gift—*
*#05-06-04*

WHEREAS, the 2004 General Conference of The United Methodist Church approved the Global Education Fund and authorized the General Board of Higher Education and Ministry to raise $4 million under the World Service Special Gift (#05-06-04) during the 2005-2008 quadrennium for the purpose of developing a new generation of Christian leaders who will inspire and transform the people of the world, and lead The United Methodist Church to become a truly global church through the world wide cooperative network of Methodist schools, colleges, universities, and theological schools; and

WHEREAS, the General Board of Higher Education and Ministry has been working on developing a case statement, creating a Methodist leadership development model, developing marketing and fund-raising strategies, and conducting educational and technological infrastructure assessment in Africa, Asia, Europe, Latin America, and the United States; and

WHEREAS, at a request of the General Board of Higher Education and Ministry, the General Council of Finance and Administration, and the Connectional Table of The United Methodist Church, approved the name change from the "Global Education Fund" to the "Methodist Global Education Fund for Leadership Development" in September, 2006; and

WHEREAS, leadership development is recognized as one of The United Methodist Church's most prominent and galvanizing issues and needs, and the Methodist Global Education Fund for Leadership Development is a dynamic mechanism for leveraging the connectional resources of The United Methodist Church to address its leadership crisis and to support the Church's global mission; and

WHEREAS, the General Board of Higher Education and Ministry serves as the lead program board for leadership development; and

WHEREAS, reaffirming the Methodist Global Education Fund for Leadership Development and reauthorizing the raising of $4 million under the World Service Special Gift by the 2008 General Conference are absolutely necessary to undertake this initiative;

*Therefore, be it resolved,* that the 2008 General Conference of The United Methodist Church reaffirms the Methodist Global Education Fund for Leadership Development and reauthorizes the General Board of Higher Education and Ministry to raise $4 million under the World Service Special Gift during the 2009-2012 quadrennium; and

*Be it further resolved,* that said fund will be raised and managed under the leadership of the General Board of Higher Education and Ministry; and

*Be it finally resolved,* that this resolution be recorded in the *Book of Resolutions* of the 2008 General Conference.

**ADOPTED 2008**

*See* Social Principles, ¶ 163.

### 4032. In Support of Hispanic/Latino Undocumented Students

WHEREAS, the Office of Loans and Scholarships, a unit of The General Board of Higher Education and Ministry, about 60 scholarship programs that provided $4.8 million in awards to about 3,540 students in 2006; and

WHEREAS, this office provided another $1.2 million in loans to 500 students; and

WHEREAS, applicants must be active, full members of a United Methodist Church; and

WHEREAS, these programs require enrollment in colleges or universities accredited by professional accrediting agencies in the USA; and

WHEREAS, the requirement of US citizenship or permanent resident status excludes a significant portion of our members from access to these loans and scholarships; and

WHEREAS, The United Methodist Church is maturing rapidly as a global denomination with over 30 percent of this membership outside the USA, and with increasing US membership from among various immigrant groups such as Hispanics and Latinos;

*Therefore, be it resolved*, that the 2008 General Conference instructs the General Board of Higher Education and Ministry to compete a review as soon as possible of all policies and legal restrictions governing its student loans and scholarships and eliminate any requirements for US citizenship or legal resident status for applicants.

ADOPTED 2008

*See* Social Principles, ¶¶ 162C, D, and 163.

### 4033. The Black College Fund

WHEREAS, since 1866 when Rust College was established to address the educational needs of freed slaves, and over the next 142 years, the mission to empower African Americans through education continued with the founding of Bennett College for Women, Bethune-Cookman University, Claflin University, Clark Atlanta University, Dillard University, Huston Tillotson University, Meharry Medical College, Paine College, Philander Smith College, and Wiley College, The Methodist Church's commitment to higher education has been unequivocal; and

WHEREAS, since the founding of these colleges, they have added value to our society, educating some of the world's great teachers, scientists, bishops, doctors, ministers, politicians, and professionals in other walks of life, and some of the world's best and brightest students are today enrolled in these schools and are receiving a quality education through the work of dedicated and committed faculties and staffs; and

WHEREAS, since 1972, the Black College Fund has been an apportioned item and continues to provide necessary funds for daily operation, capital improvements, and academic program enhancement at these schools, and this funding is a critical investment in the dreams of young people and all those who thirst for knowledge; and

WHEREAS, these institutions are and have been since their founding, open to people of all ethnicities, races, creeds and nationalities, and all are treated with dignity and respect, and therefore the mission and ministry of these schools is still vital and important; and

WHEREAS, many annual conferences are going the extra mile to pay their 100 percent apportionments and this commitment and faithfulness to this important cause continues to make a difference;

*Now, therefore, be it resolved,* that the General Conference reaffirms its commitment to the ministry of the eleven church-related historically black colleges and universities;

*Be it further resolved,* that the General Conference reaffirms its commitment to the Black College Fund and expresses its intention to continue the Black College Fund as an apportioned item for the 2009-2012 quadrennium.

**ADOPTED 2008**

*See* Social Principles, ¶ 163.

## GAMBLING

### 4041. Gambling

The Social Principles state that, "Gambling is a menace to society, deadly to the best interests of moral, social, economic, and spiritual life, and destructive of good government. As an act of faith and concern, Christians should abstain from gambling and should strive to minister to those victimized by the practice. Where gambling has become addictive, the church will encourage such individuals to receive therapeutic assistance so that the individual's energies may be redirected into positive and constructive ends. The church should promote standards and personal lifestyles that would make unnecessary and undesirable the resort to commercial gambling—including public lotteries—as a recreation, as an escape, or as a means of producing public revenue or funds for support of charities or government" (¶ 163G).

When asked which commandment is first of all, Jesus answered, "Hear, O Israel: the Lord our God, the Lord is one; you shall love the Lord your God with all your heart, and with all your soul, and with all your mind, and with all your strength" (Mark 12:29-30 NRSV). Gambling feeds on human greed and invites persons to place their trust in possessions rather than in God. It represents a form of idolatry that contradicts the first commandment. Jesus said: "You shall love your neighbor as yourself" (Mark 12:31b NRSV). In relating with compassion and love to our sisters and brothers, we are called to resist those practices and systems that exploit them and leave them impoverished and demeaned. The apostle Paul wrote in 1 Timothy 6:9-10a: "People who want to get rich fall into temptation and a trap and into many foolish and harmful desires that plunge men into ruin and destruction. For the love of money is a root of all kinds of evil."

Gambling, as a means of acquiring material gain by chance and at the neighbor's expense, is a menace to personal character and social morality. Gambling fosters greed and stimulates the fatalistic faith in chance. Organized and commercial gambling is a threat to business, breeds crime and poverty, and is destructive to the interests of good government. It encourages the belief that work is unimportant, that money can solve all our problems, and that greed is the norm for achievement. It serves as a "regressive tax" on those with lower income. In summary, gambling is bad economics; gambling is bad public policy; and gambling does not improve the quality of life.

We oppose the growing legalization and promotion of gambling.

Dependence on gambling revenue has led many governments to exploit the weakness of their own citizens, neglect the development of more equitable forms of taxation, and thereby further erode citizen confidence in government.

We oppose the legalization of pari-mutuel betting, for it has been the opening wedge in the legalization of other forms of gambling that has fostered the growth of illegal bookmaking. We deplore the establishment of lotteries and their use as a means of raising public revenues. The constant promotion and the wide advertising of lotteries have encouraged large numbers of persons to gamble for the first time.

We express our concern for the increasing development of the casino enterprises, which have taken captive entire communities and corrupted many levels of government with its fiscal and political power.

Public apathy and a lack of awareness that petty gambling feeds organized crime have opened the door to the spread of numerous forms of legal and illegal gambling.

We especially express our deep concern at the rapid growth of two forms of gambling:

Internet Gambling: Because computer usage is available in the privacy of one's home and even in churches, the potential for access to gambling websites and addiction to Internet gambling is great. Internet gambling is an international problem and it is virtually unregulated which has led to corruption, money laundering, and funding of terrorist organizations. Individuals and local churches should seek to educate themselves on the easy access to Internet gambling Web sites. The social cost of addiction to Internet gambling is great and leads to bankruptcy, suicide, and family discord. Young adults and senior citizens are among the most vulnerable populations at risk to gambling addiction. Parents and caregivers should take steps to ensure that children and the elderly with access to computers not be exposed to Internet gambling Web sites. Local churches and annual conferences should provide educational resources for parents and caregivers on the dangers of Internet gambling and enact strict oversight of church-owned computers.

US Tribal Gambling: We grieve over the expansion of gambling onto tribal reservations and lands. Gambling expansion on tribal lands has fostered racism and hate crimes, has caused discord between and among tribal members, and has led to divisions in churches and families. While we support tribal self-determination and self-governance, resorting to gambling as a form of economic development is regrettable. We acknowledge and recognize the dichotomy created when the Church's positions oppose gambling and at the same time support tribal self-determination. We urge annual conferences and local churches, which reside near tribal casinos or are facing expansion of tribal gambling ventures, to build partnerships with churches on reservations and Indian lands to foster mutual trust and understanding of tribal history and of the United Methodist position on gambling without resorting to diminishing tribal sovereignty.

The church has a key role in fostering responsible government and in developing health and moral maturity that free persons from dependence on damaging social customs. We urge national, tribal, state, and local governments to read, analyze, and implement the recommendations of the National Gambling Impact Study report released by the United States in 1999. We encourage tribal governments to wean themselves from gambling as a form of economic development; and we encourage and fully support tribal efforts to diversify economically away from gambling.

We support the strong enforcement of antigambling laws and the repeal of all laws that give gambling an acceptable and even advantageous place in our society.

It is expected that United Methodist churches abstain from the use of raffles, lotteries, bingo, door prizes, other drawing schemes, and games of chance for the purpose of gambling or fundraising. United Methodists should refrain from all forms of gambling practices and work to influence community organizations and be supportive of American Indian tribes in developing forms of funding that do not depend upon gambling. Furthermore, it is incumbent upon local churches to reach out with love to individuals who are addicted, compulsive, or problem gamblers and support efforts at recovery and rehabilitation. We oppose coalitions, groups, organizations, and campaigns that claim opposition to gambling, yet at the same time undermine or oppose tribal sovereignty, which fosters a climate of hate and racism. An alarming trend is the attempt to use local churches in order to increase support for this destructive agenda. We believe that these groups operate contrary to Christian teachings. Therefore we strongly discourage United Methodist members and local churches from participating in such efforts.

The General Board of Church and Society will provide materials to local churches and annual conferences for study and action to combat gambling and to aid persons addicted to gambling. The General Board of Church and Society, annual conferences, and local churches shall work with coalitions and grassroots organizations (such as the National Coalition Against Legalized Gambling) that are compatible with the position of The United Methodist Church (Social Principles ¶ 163).

ADOPTED 1980
AMENDED AND READOPTED 1996
AMENDED AND READOPTED 2004
AMENDED AND READOPTED 2008
RESOLUTION #203, 2004 BOOK OF RESOLUTIONS
RESOLUTION #193, 2000 BOOK OF RESOLUTIONS

See Social Principles, ¶ 163G.

## GLOBAL ECONOMIC JUSTICE

### 4051. The United Methodist Church, Justice, and World Hunger

*Is not this the fast that I choose: to loose the bonds of injustice, to undo the thongs of the yoke, to let the oppressed go free, and to break every yoke? Is it not to share your bread with the hungry, and bring the homeless poor into your house; when you see the naked, to cover them, and not to hide yourself from your own kin? Then your light shall break forth like the dawn, and your healing shall spring up quickly; your vindicator shall go before you, the glory of the LORD shall be your rear guard* (Isaiah 58:6-8, NRSV).

### I. Introduction

In 1996, the World Food Summit held in Rome, Italy, reaffirmed "the right of everyone to have access to safe and nutritious food, consistent with the right to adequate food and the fundamental right of everyone to be free from hunger." It declared that urgent action must be taken to create food security. "Food security exists when all people, at all times, have physical and economic access to sufficient, safe and nutritious food to meet their dietary needs and food preferences for an active and healthy life."[1]

Although globally enough food is produced to feed everyone, 840 million people are undernourished, 799 million of them in the developing world. Children and elderly are particularly at risk. Each year, six million children die as a result of hunger. Although hunger is also a problem in cities, seventy-five percent of the world's hungry people live in rural areas.[2]

The reasons for this continuing tragedy are complex and interrelated. Some causes of world hunger are:
- drought and other weather-related problems;
- poverty and greed;
- inequitable distribution of wealth and unjust economic systems;

1. "Rome Declaration on Food Security," World Food Summit 13-17 November, 1996, http://www.fao.org/docrep/003/w3613e/w3613e00.htm 8 May, 2003.
2. *Agriculture in the Global Economy* (Washington, D.C.: Bread for the World Institute, 2003), pp. 2-5; Bread for the World Hunger Basics: International Facts on Hunger and Poverty, http://www.bread.org/hungerbasics/international.html; *The State of Food Insecurity in the World 2002* (Rome: Food and Agriculture Organization of the United Nations, 2002), 8 May http://www.fao.org/docrep/005/y7352e/y7352e00.htm 8 May, 2003.

- insufficient food production in developing nations;
- use of arable land for nonfood and cash crops such as tobacco;
- increasing emphasis on export-oriented agriculture;
- overfishing of the oceans;
- population growth;
- internal displacement of people;
- wasteful consumerism in richer countries;
- militarism, war, and civil unrest;
- HIV/AIDS pandemic;
- corruption in governments;
- lending policies of the World Bank (IBRD) and the International Monetary Fund (IMF);
- production of unnecessary goods and services that waste resources;
- environmental degradation;
- use of farm subsidies in richer nations that export to poor countries causing them to reject their own products;
- lack of participation in decision-making processes and access to land by women;
- poor regulations on multinational corporations; and
- dwindling water resources.

(Refer to 2000 *Book of Resolutions*, "Global Economic Justice," #195, section III, for more detailed information.)

It is especially important to note that the causes of hunger are intricately related to the problems of poverty and greed. Hunger cannot be dissociated from people and systems that keep people in poverty.

## II. Theological Bases for Action

The Bible reveals that, from the earliest times, God's faithful community has been concerned about hunger and poverty. Helping those in need was not simply a matter of charity, but of responsibility, righteousness, and justice (Isaiah 58:6-8; Jeremiah 22:3; Matthew 25:31-46). For example, the Israelites were commanded to leave the corners of their fields and the gleanings of harvests for the poor and aliens (Leviticus 19:9-10). Jesus taught that whatever people do to "the least of these," they also do him (Matthew 25:31-46). That Jesus was born to a poor, unmarried woman who was living in a small nation, occupied and oppressed by a mighty foreign empire, concretely reveals God's full identification with poor, powerless, and oppressed people.

As Christians, a key question that we must ask ourselves is: What does God require and enable us individually and corporately to do? We know that God loves and cares for all creation. Jesus stressed that the two greatest commandments were to love God and to love our neighbors as ourselves (Matthew 22:34-40). He also challenged the rich young ruler who said he was keeping all of the commandments to sell all of his possessions and give his money to the poor (Matthew 19:16-26).

In the incarnation, life, death, and resurrection of Jesus Christ, the promise and the first fruits of redemption were brought to sinful and selfish humanity. Jesus' own concern for human need in his ministry is a model for the church's concern. His opposition to those who would ignore the needs of the neighbor makes clear that we grossly misunderstand and fail to grasp God's grace if we imagine that God overlooks, condones, or easily tolerates our indifference to the plight of our neighbors, our greed and selfishness, or our systems of injustice and oppression.

We believe that God's Holy Spirit continues to move today, refashioning lives, tearing down unjust structures, restoring community, and engendering faith, hope, and love. The work of the Holy Spirit impels us to take action, even when perfect solutions are not apparent. We engage in the struggle for bread and justice for all in the confidence that God goes before us and guides us. That struggle includes examination of our personal and congregational lives in the light of God's love and concern for all and Jesus' question, "Who is your neighbor?"

As United Methodists, we also look to our ongoing tradition of social concern. Methodism's founder, John Wesley, preached and wrote about the importance of simpler lifestyles. He emphasized ethical stewardship of time, money, and resources as important means to enable ministry with those suffering from hunger and poverty. Wesley preached the gospel to people who were poor, visited them, and lived with them. He donated most of the money that he earned—not just a tithe (ten percent of his income)—to the church and charitable ends.

Wesley's teachings about ministry and frugal lifestyle stand in stark contrast to today's reality. According to the United Nations Development Program (UNDP), 20 percent of the world's people in the highest-income countries account for 86 percent of total private consumption expenditures, whereas the poorest 20 percent account for only 1.3 percent (1998). For example:

- The richest fifth consumes 45 percent of all meat and fish—the poorest fifth, 5 percent.
- The richest fifth consumes 58 percent of total energy—the poorest fifth, less than 4 percent.
- The richest fifth consumes 84 percent of all paper—the poorest fifth, 1.1 percent.[3]

In faithfulness to our understanding of God's good intentions for all peoples, we, as members of The United Methodist Church, set for ourselves, our congregations, institutions, and agencies no lesser goals than repentance for the existence of human hunger and increased commitment to end world hunger and poverty.

### III. A Call for United Methodists

Change is not easy. Movement toward the abolishment of hunger and poverty requires commitment and stamina. All nations, particularly the developed nations, must examine and modify those values, attitudes, and institutions that are the basic causes of poverty and underdevelopment, the primary sources of world and economic hunger. United Methodists must act corporately and individually.

1. We call for The United Methodist Church to engage in an educational effort that would provide information about the scale of world and domestic hunger and its causes, and to engage in study and effort to integrate the church's missional programs into a coherent policy with respect to a just, sustainable, and participatory development.

2. We call for The United Methodist Church to develop effective public policy strategies and educate the constituency on hunger issues, through its appropriate agencies, that would enable church members to participate in efforts to:

   a. decrease mother/child mortality;
   b. promote environmental justice and sustainable practices for using and restoring natural resources;
   c. provide safe drinking water and sustainable water-management systems;
   d. support community organizing to effect change in systems that keep people poor and powerless;

3. United Nations Development Programme, "Overview," *Human Development Report 1998: Comsumption for Human Development* http://hdr.undp.org/reports/global/1998/en/ 8 May, 2003.

e. organize and work to retain programs such as Women, Infants, and Children (WIC), food stamps, and food co-ops;

f. develop and implement policies that enable family farms to compete in the global market, provide just wages and working conditions for farm workers, and provide incentives that enable and promote sutainable agriculture and equitable access to land by all;

g. become advocates for reduction of military spending and reallocation of resources to programs that provide human services, convert military facilities to provide for civilian needs, and protect and restore the environment;

h. become advocates of trade policies that alleviate economic disparities between rich and poor countries while protecting labor and human rights; environmental, health, and safety standards; and respecting the need for agricultural and food security;

i. protect craftspeople and artisans from exploitative trade practices; and

j. support community-based economic development that provides jobs; recycles money within communities; provides low-cost, high-quality services to meet basic human needs; and combats unemployment and underemployment.

3. We specifically call upon each local church, cooperative parish, district, and conference to:

a. increase sharing resources through support of church and community agencies dedicated to eliminating hunger and poverty at home and abroad;

b. become involved in Fair Trade activism through efforts such as purchasing fair trade products from fair trade companies such as SERVV International, asking grocery and specialty stores to carry fair trade coffee and other fair trade items, and participating in UMCOR's Coffee Project. (More ideas are on Global Exchange's Web site at: http://www.globalex change.org)); and

c. promote World Food Day, which is observed on October 16 (*see* http://www.worldfooddayusa.org) and National Hunger Awareness Day observed on June 5 (*see* http://www.hunger day.org).

4. We call on United Methodists to strive for "Christian perfection" and to recover the Wesleyan tradition of simpler lifestyles and

generosity in personal service and financial giving. Therefore, individuals are encouraged to:

    a. study and discuss John Wesley's sermons (and related scripture passages) that address "acts of mercy" and Christian stewardship, including "The More Excellent Way," "The Use of Money," "On the Danger of Riches," "On the Danger of Increasing Riches," "On Dress," and "On Visiting the Sick;"[4]

    b. simplify their lifestyles, moving away from consumerism and toward caring;

    c. compost, recycle, conserve energy, practice or support organic gardening, and participate in other environment-friendly practices;

    d. commit themselves to give more of their time and money to programs that address hunger and poverty, including United Methodist Advance projects and UMCOR's World Hunger/Poverty Advance (#982920); and

    e. participate in projects such as "The Souper Bowl of Caring" and Bread for the World's annual "Offering of Letters."

5. We urge the General Board of Church and Society and the General Board of Global Ministries to:

    a. work with the Food and Agriculture Organization, the International Fund for Agricultural Development, and grassroots small farmer and peasant organizations for the right of everyone to have access to safe and nutritious food acceptable within their culture. This would require many countries to implement genuine agrarian reforms that allow for the fair distribution of incomes, new management models which place human needs before profits, and access for the poor to land, natural resources, capital, and markets. Many developed countries would have to reform their agricultural subsidies programs.

    b. work with other churches and agencies in the United States and internationally:

        1) for the achievement of the United Nations Millennium Development Goals (MDGs) which set targets for 2015 in the areas of basic education, infant and maternal mortality, clean water supplies and poverty reduction throughout the developing nations;

---

4. These sermons are available in books and online at: http://gbgm-umc.org/umhistory/wesley/sermons/.

and, because progress is currently not fast enough to meet those targets by 2015,

2) to urge governments to support any proposals for an International Finance Facility (IFF). The concept is that, in addition to regular aid flows, donor governments in rich countries should guarantee additional flows of funds from the private sector to the developing world. These would allow investments by developing economies to enable them to converge more closely onto the MDGs. This private sector finance would be a liability of the rich country governments and therefore not increase the debt burden of the poorer nations. It would eventually be repaid out of rich country aid budgets but mostly after 2015. The IFF is therefore a means of bringing forward potential investment money to enable much earlier progress towards the MDGs.

ADOPTED 2004
READOPTED 2008
RESOLUTION #205, 2004 *BOOK OF RESOLUTIONS*

*See* Social Principles, ¶ 164A.

## 4052. Economic Justice for a New Millennium

### I. *Wesleyan Tradition and The United Methodist Church Witness for Economic Justice*

The United Methodist Church and its predecessor bodies have a long history of public witness on matters of economic justice. John Wesley set the example in his famous sermon on "The Use of Money," his public stand against slavery, and his witness among England's working class. The 1908 "Social Creed" committed The Methodist Episcopal Church to work for the protection and rights of people disadvantaged by society. The Evangelical United Brethren Church made a comparable commitment to personal, social, and international justice in its Discipline statement, "Moral Standards of The Evangelical United Brethren Church" (Section IX). As United Methodists at the dawn of a new millennium, "We claim all economic systems to be under the judgment of God no less than other facets of the created order" (Social Principles, ¶ 163, 2004 *Discipline*).

## II. Biblical/Theological Background

In Luke 4:18-19, Jesus began his public ministry with these words from Isaiah:

*The Spirit of the Lord is upon me, because the Lord has anointed me to preach good news to the poor. God has sent me to proclaim release to the captives and recovery of sight to the blind, to let the oppressed go free, to proclaim the year of the Lord's favor* (New Revised Standard Version, adapted)

Christ teaches that faith requires action for social and spiritual well-being and especially care for the poor and the oppressed. The early church understood that all were to share all that they had and especially care for the widows and orphans (Acts 2:44-45; 2 Corinthians 8:13-15). Israel's early law codes required persons to meet human needs and guarantee basic economic and legal rights: food (Leviticus 19:9-10; Deuteronomy 23:21-22; 24:19-22), clothing (Exodus 26-27), just business dealings (Deuteronomy 25:13-16), and access to just juridical process (Exodus 23:6-8). Special concern is expressed for the marginalized in society: the poor (Exodus 23:6; Deuteronomy 15:7-11), the disabled (Mark 2:1-12), the stranger (Exodus 22:21-24; 23:9), the sojourner (Deuteronomy 10:19), the widow and the orphan (Deuteronomy 24:19-22).

The covenant community was called to observe sabbatical years in which the land was not worked and its produce was available to the poor (Exodus 23:10-11), and slaves were set free (Exodus 21:2). In the fiftieth year the Jubilee is to be celebrated (Leviticus 25:8-55) as the year of God's release, when prisoners are set free, debts are canceled, and land is returned to families. But throughout the ages people elected to break covenant with God and instead worship the idols of greed, privilege, materialism, and oppressive power. Likewise, our age worships economic privileges that benefit the rich and powerful. Still, the prophets warn us that an economic system based on greed, economic exploitation, and indifference to the needs of the poor is contrary to God's will and leads to ruin for the society (Amos 8:4-6; Jeremiah 22:13-17).

## III. Structures of Injustice

Today, the world economy continues to change dramatically. The results of rapid consolidation of wealth and power by fewer individuals, corporations, and banks, the shift in government priorities from social to military expenditures, and the growing interconnections between national economies have led to increases in poverty, hunger, and despair in the human family. Technology, which has the potential to benefit all humanity, is being developed, produced, and marketed to serve rich nations. Materialism and selfishness are undermining the values of community and mutual sharing. Within this context, The United Methodist Church, in following its traditional commitment to justice, must analyze economic systems and work for ministries rooted in justice.

## A. Concentration of Wealth and Power

"We support measures that would reduce the concentration of wealth in the hands of a few" (Social Principles, ¶ 163, 2008 *Discipline*).

As transnational corporations and banks have extended their ownership and control of agriculture, industry, land, finances, and communications, two consequences have emerged:

1. The separation between the rich and the poor has become greater. The United Nations 2005 Human Development Report found that the 2.5 billion people living on less than $2.00 per day (40 percent of the world's population) account for 5 percent of global income. The richest 10 percent, almost of all of whom live in the high-income countries, account for 54 percent of global income. The United Nations 2006 Human Development Report found "The world's 500 richest people have an income of more than $100 billion dollars not taking into account asset wealth." That total exceeds the combined incomes of the poorest 416 million persons. The 50 Least Developed Countries (the world's poorest countries), as established by the United Nations Conference on Trade and Development (UNCTAD), in 2006 collectively had a Gross Domestic Product (GDP) of $ 236.3 billion while the net worth of the five wealthiest persons in 2006 was $248.5 billion.

2. Many corporations have become increasingly anonymous and unaccountable to their employees, to the communities in which they operate, and to governments.

## B. Production and Work

Every person has the right to a job at a living wage. Where the private sector cannot or does not provide jobs for all who seek and need them, it is the moral responsibility of government to encourage the creation of such jobs (Social Principles ¶ 163C, 2008 *Discipline*).

Around the world, working people share many of the same concerns: unjust hours and wages; unsafe workplaces; sexual harassment; and discrimination because of race, age, disability, and sexual orientation. Some workers encounter harassment, violence, or job loss for even raising issues of concern with their employer; aging workers are quickly "let go" from their jobs for having reached a company-imposed `senior' status and are suddenly replaced with `more energetic,' younger persons; young workers accept lower wages more readily; and many workers are employed full-time but are unable to live above poverty conditions. Women are profoundly vulnerable to poverty because women's labor, whether in the home or community, has traditionally gone unrecognized, undervalued, unpaid, or underpaid. Overall, women have yet to attain pay equity for their time, dexterity, or expertise in the workplace.

Many transnational corporations have transferred their manufacturing base from industrial countries to developing countries, seeking cheap labor and less stringent environmental practices, consumer protection, and occupational safety and health codes. They have taken advantage of favorable tax treatment for overseas investment, employer or government suppression of labor organizing, and the employment of the most vulnerable persons for the lowest of wages. Women, especially young women, indigenous persons, and even children toil for long hours under harsh and unsafe conditions.

## C. Development, Debt, and Structural Adjustment

"We affirm the right and duty of the people of developing nations to determine their own destiny. We urge the major political powers to use their power to maximize the political, social, and economic self-determination of developing nations rather than to further their own special interests . . . We urge Christians in every society to encourage the governments under which they live and the economic entities within their societies to aid and work for the development of more just economic orders" (Social Principles, ¶ 165B, 2008 *Discipline*).

The global economic system and external debts continue to force developing countries to allocate major resources to produce goods with heavy emphasis on production for export rather than for domestic use. Many of these countries are locked into exporting primary commodities at widely fluctuating prices. Few manage to export manufactured goods and most face uncertain markets due to rapid changes in the terms of trade.

Encouraged by Western banks, many developing countries found that by the early 1980s (when interest rates rose and raw material prices collapsed), they could no longer meet the service payments on their debts. The creditor banks and governments turned to the World Bank and International Monetary Fund (IMF), which makes loans contingent on strict austerity or `structural adjustment' programs. The Bank and IMF remedies have placed the burden of debt repayment squarely on the shoulders of poor and working people by devaluing currencies, freezing wages, curbing government price subsidies (on rice, cooking oil, beans, and other essential items), and cutting subsidized credits in rural areas. In addition, the corruption by some government officials has made it impossible to provide an adequate food supply, health care, education, and other services. Compelled to commit their natural and human resources to compete in world markets, the irony is that developing nations may have no other options, but to sacrifice their domestic economy, social welfare programs, and possibly the life and spirit of the people.

## D. Military Spending

"Human values must outweigh military claims as governments determine their priorities; . . . the militarization of society must be challenged; . . . the manufacture, sale, and deployment of armaments must be reduced and controlled" (Social Principles ¶ 165C, 2008 *Discipline*).

Many governments, in shifting major resources to the military, have hurt the most vulnerable people in their societies: women, children, and youth. Some economies, such as that of the United States, increasingly depend on the military for jobs, exports, and economic growth. Among developing countries, some produce weapons to pay their foreign debt, while others import military equipment to control their own populations. And in so doing, the basic needs of the average residents go unmet or are severely diminished.

## IV. The Effects of the Global Economic System

According to the 2006/2007 Globalization mission study book, *Globalization and Its Impact on People's Lives*, that was used at School of Mission, injustices are imposed upon the people of the world by economies characterized by a concentration of wealth and power, an export-based development, heavy indebtedness, and reliance on a militarized national security system. The belief that competition results in greater economic growth underlies much of the emerging global economic order. In the production and consumption of goods, corporations are to compete with corporations, individuals with one another, and societies with other societies. These conditions produce a culture that has little use for those who lack the means to consume. The following evidence shows the effects of the global economy:

1. Worldwide, poverty and hunger have increased, especially among women and children. Human rights have become untenable. Homelessness remains rampant in major cities, while many rural communities are in rapid decline as family farms go bankrupt in record numbers. In developing countries, shantytowns surround major cities as people leave rural areas in search of jobs. These resulting poor populations, with a disproportionate share being of a different ethnic racial heritage of a nation's elites, are also faced with discriminatory obstacles to overcome.

2. As transnational corporations shift centers of production, unemployment and underemployment is increasing in some parts of the world, while education and job training have not kept pace with the global economy.

According to the 2006 International Labor Organization (ILO) World Employment Report, in 2005 noted that out of the 2.8 billion workers in the world, nearly 1.4 billion still did not earn enough to lift themselves and their families above the USA $2-a-day poverty line. In a 2006 ILO report on the International Program on the Elimination of Child Labor (IPEC) some 211 million children aged 5-14 can be found at work,

3. The increasing ability of large corporations to shift their resources around the globe has contributed to an erosion of worker rights everywhere. Sweatshops and child labor have increased. Many corporations have shifted to the use of temporary and part-time workers in order to avoid paying benefits, such as insurance, health care, and pensions. As wages and benefits decline, the number of full-time employees living in poverty increases.

4. Beyond business owners, employers, and contractors, the international stock markets and corporate traders are not accountable for the wages and workplace conditions of workers. Usually, workers are excluded from profit-sharing schemes. Women and some racial and ethnic groups are denied promotions to high-level positions.

5. The unrestrained business and development pursuits have negative social, economic, and ecological ramifications: shifts in agricultural

production have led to indigenous seed crops being replaced by chemically dependent cash crops or genetically engineered seeds; destruction of fragile environments and exploitation of nonrenewable natural resources have occurred; and the forced dislocation of people and indigenous cultures has devalued human dignity and life.

6. Churches and social-service agencies have struggled to meet the spiritual and psychological needs caused by economic injustice. But they are not able to keep up with the problems. In communities under economic stress, there is a rising incidence of crime, family break-down, child and spouse abuse, suicide, substance abuse, gambling, and other worrisome behavior.

7. Millions of low wage workers affected by the global economy are migrants. A migrant worker refers to a person "who is to be engaged, is engaged or has been engaged in a remunerated activity in a State [country] of which he or she is not a national." In 2005, 191 million migrants (3 percent of the world population) lived outside their country and nearly half of them were female. In 1990, the United Nations adopted the International Convention on the Protection of the Rights of all Migrant Workers and Members of their Families which states in its preamble, "Convinced that the rights of migrant workers and members of their families have not been suffi-ciently recognized everywhere and therefore require appropriate international protection . . . "And, further gives consideration to the fact that " . . . workers who are nondocumented or in an irregular sit-uation are frequently employed under less favourable conditions of work than other workers and that certain employers find this an inducement to seek such labour in order to reap the benefits of unfair competition." Migrants are among the most vulnerable in any soci-ety and women and children more often than not become the objects of abuse and brutality.

## V. Call to Action

The United Methodist Church, as a covenant community commit-ted to God's justice, must work toward a just global economy. Our Social Principles remind us that "in spite of general affluence in the industrialized nations, most of the persons in the world live in poverty. To provide basic needs such as food, clothing, shelter, education, health care, and other necessities, ways must be found to share more equitably the resources of the world" (Social Principles, ¶ 163E, 2008

*Discipline*). Faced with securing economic justice for a new millennium, the General Conference calls upon:

1. each local congregation and every central and annual conference to use this resolution and related resources as a foundation to initiate a study curriculum and social actions on global economic justice issues;

2. the whole church to work with people in local communities to identify specific economic issues that affect families, communities, and individuals, especially the impacts upon the lives of women.These issues include jobs with livable wages and benefits, debt, plant closings and relocation, public education, homelessness, affordable housing, and meeting sanitation, clean water, and energy needs. These issues should be addressed through the strategies of prayer, study, service, advocacy, community organizing, and economic development;

3. the General Board of Church and Society and the General Board of Global Ministries to engage in ongoing searches for and study of alternative and sustainable systems of economic order, shall work with local congregations, central and annual conferences to initiate and support legislative efforts at the local, state, national, and international levels that will address "Structures of Injustice" (Section III). Attention should be given to marginalized and indigenous people; the accountability or reform of transnational corporations and banks; personal and corporate investment responsibility; land reform, and the dependency of national economies on the military;

4. the general program agencies of the church and the General Board of Pension and Health Benefits to work with the Interfaith Center on Corporate Responsibility and support its *Principles for Global Corporate Responsibility*; and

5. all bodies of the church to be more intentional in using their investment portfolios to strengthen developing national economies and global economic justice. We also encourage central and annual conferences, local churches and individuals in wealthy nations to live a simpler, more modest lifestyle.

In order to be God's real community, we must realize that people are not here to serve an economic system, but economic systems must serve all people so all live in God's abundance.

ADOPTED 1988
REVISED AND READOPTED 2000 AND 2008
RESOLUTION #206, 2004 *BOOK OF RESOLUTIONS*
RESOLUTION #197, 2000 *BOOK OF RESOLUTIONS*

*See* Social Principles, ¶ 163D and E.

## 4053. Global Debt Crisis: A Call for Jubilee

### I. Introduction

Since the inception of the global Jubilee Campaign in 2000, we can celebrate important strides. The debt of twenty nations to the International Monetary Fund and the World Bank has been wiped out, with the proceeds going to fight poverty in these nations. Despite this important step, the global debt crisis continues to cripple poor countries. Countries in Africa, Asia, the Pacific, Latin America, and the Caribbean owe over $2 trillion to rich nations and international financial institutions. The poorest countries in the world are still among the most heavily indebted, owing around $380 billion. For many countries left behind by world leaders, the burden of repaying the debt continues to prevent them from providing adequate health care, education, and food for their people. This debt burden—often incurred illegitimately by dictators—inhibits the social and economic change that is needed to lift people out of poverty. Throughout the world there is a call for Jubilee, a call for debt cancellation in a Sabbath Year.

### II. Biblical Foundation

Scriptures mandate periodically overcoming structural injustice and poverty and for restoring right relationships by forgiving debt and reforming land holding. In the earliest Sabbath traditions, consumption and exploitation of the land were limited by the Sabbath and the Sabbath year. People and animals were to rest every seventh day (Exodus 23:10-12). In the Sabbath year, there was to be release from debts and slavery and during the jubilee year—every 50th year—a restoration of all family lands (Leviticus 25). Fulfilling these commandments proclaims "the year of the Lord's favor" (Isaiah 61:1-2) and anticipates "new heavens and a new earth" (Isaiah 65:17-25). Jesus emphasized this jubilee vision of proclaiming good news to the poor, release of the captives, sight to the blind, and liberation of the oppressed (Luke 4:16-19). He taught his disciples to pray for the forgiveness of debts (as we forgive our debtors) (Matthew 6:12). Pentecost results in the voluntary sharing of possessions, so that "there was not a needy person among them" (Acts 4:34; Deuteronomy 15:4).

The Sabbath tradition of the jubilee vision is as relevant today as it was thousands of years ago. Debt bondage by the poorest countries to rich nations and financial institutions is today's new slavery. The accelerating concentration of wealth for a few in the richest countries and the devastating decline in living standards in the poorest countries call for correction along the lines of the ancient Sabbath and jubilee cycles. The social, political, and ecological costs of the debt crisis are intolerable and must be challenged and stopped. Only when we have implemented the Sabbath-jubilee mandate can we "turn to God" and "rejoice in hope."

### III. Causes of the Debt Crisis

The causes of the debt crisis are complex. Colonialism has tied the developing world's economies to the export of agricultural, mineral, and other raw materials while creating a dependence on imported goods. This export-oriented and import-dependent economic arrangement sunk poor and debtor countries even more into debt. For decades, prices for agricultural, mineral, and most raw materials have steadily declined in relation to the cost of manufactured goods. Poor countries that still depend on these exports find themselves increasingly disadvantaged in the global marketplace and often deeper in debt. Declining commodity prices between 1986 and 1990 alone cost Africa $50 billion in export earnings, more than double the funds received in foreign assistance from all nations.

In the 1970s, the oil-producing nations deposited billions of dollars in Western commercial banks. In turn, many banks aggressively marketed their loans to developing countries who were short of cash, facing high oil costs, and eager to borrow. Banks' normal loan-review procedures were often abandoned in the rush to lend large amounts of money quickly. Some of the loans went to productive uses, such as water purification and sewage systems, education and health programs, and subsidies for basic food staples. However, a large percentage of the money has supported militarization and, sometimes, repressive regimes and corrupt leadership.

By the mid 1970s, developing countries, encouraged by the West to grow cash crops, suddenly found that they were not getting the prices they used to for the raw materials they sold. The reason: too many countries—advised by the West—were producing the same crops, so prices fell. Soon after, US interest rates began to rise dramatically and oil prices rose again. This led to a global recession that depressed demand and commodity prices of products from developing countries. Receiving less for their exports and forced to pay more on loans and imports, indebted countries had to borrow more money just to pay off the interest.

In 1982, Mexico, Brazil, and other middle-income countries announced that they were about to default on billions of dollars in loans. Banks suddenly stopped new lending to developing countries. By late 1980s, the crisis had eased for most middle-income countries, as a result of some debt restructuring by commercial banks, intervention by international financial institutions, and export growth. However, the poorest countries continue to struggle under heavy unpayable debt burden and are essentially bankrupt.

Today, debt campaigners across the globe are increasingly focused on the origins of much of the debt of countries in Africa, Asia, and Latin America. Campaigners in these regions are questioning whether much of the debt is really owed. A growing number of governments are undertaking official audits to assess the legitimacy of debts. Debts are odious if they result from loans contracted without the knowledge or consent of the population or if government officials used the money for personal purposes or to oppress their people. In cases where borrowed money was used in ways contrary to the peoples' interest, with the knowledge of the creditors, the creditors may be said to have committed a hostile act against the people. Creditors cannot legitimately expect repayment of such debts. Examples of odious debt are money from loans stolen by the ruling elite of the then Indonesia dictator Suharto; debts contracted by the apartheid regime of South Africa; and debts accrued during the dictatorial rule of Mobbutu Sese Seko in the Democratic Republic of Congo, Ferdinand Marcos in the Philippines, and the military junta in Argentina.

## IV. Consequences of the Global Crisis—Everyone Loses

The World Bank and International Monetary Fund (IMF)—the two main international financial institutions—lend money and reschedule the debt of poor countries. However, these loans to highly indebted poor countries come with conditions known as Structural Adjustment Programs (SAPs). SAPs consist of measures designed to help a country repay its debts by earning more hard currency (i.e., increasing exports and decreasing imports). While a few countries appear to have been helped by SAPs, poverty and inequality have increased in most countries due to the externally imposed programs. This is because, in order to obtain more foreign currency, governments implementing SAPs usually must:

- reduce government spending, resulting in cuts in health care, education, and social services—many people are forced to go without;
- devalue the national currency, which increases the cost of imported goods and increases taxes, especially regressive sales taxes;
- reduce or eliminate transportation and food subsidies—because of this, prices of essentials soar out of the financial reach of many citizens;
- reduce jobs and wages for workers in government industries and services;
- encourage privatization of public industries which benefits the country's business elite and foreign investors; and
- shift agricultural and industrial production from food staples and basic goods for domestic use to commodities for export, which results in a transfer of land holdings from small subsistence farmers to large-scale agribusiness leaving many farmers with no land to grow their own food and few are employed on these new cash crop farms.

Children and women bear the full costs of debt repayment. In addition, by concentrating on exports in order to repay their debts, poor countries strip forests and overexploit land and nonrenewable resources, further aggravating serious environmental problems. Reports on the impact of debt repayment show that many indebted governments spend two to four times as much money "servicing"—that is, making timely interest and principal payments—their international debt as they spend on health care (such as basic medicines and clean water) and education combined. These IMF and World Bank policies, by taking away indebted country's sovereignty, undermine accountability by debtor governments, which in turn erodes local democratic institutions. In short, IMF and World Bank policies do more harm than good. The debt burden carried by impoverished nations hurts everyone—including citizens of rich nations such as the United States. The environmental damage magnified by indebtedness, such as destruction of forests, has global repercussions. Growing poverty—worsened by the debt—is linked to the spread of disease.

Indebted countries are forced to use scarce dollars for debt payments instead of importing goods and services. This directly affects jobs and incomes in the rich countries. Indebtedness creates the climate that fosters the production and trafficking of illicit drugs. Debt also causes an increase of economic migration. It should trouble the conscience of citizens of rich nations that people living in misery have to spend their money for debt servicing that they need for their own survival.

## V. Principles to Guide Debt-Crisis Solutions

As Christians, our love of God and neighbor must be reflected by our actions within the global family. Thus, we affirm the following policies and principles as necessary to ensure a just resolution to the debt crisis:

- We need to examine patterns of greed that may cause us as individuals and nations to become debtors and lenders. Debt cancellation and relief should be fashioned in a way that benefits the poor and helps move debtor nations to sustainable human development.
- The poor should not bear the burden of repayment and structural adjustment. Living standards of those least responsible and most vulnerable should not be sacrificed in order to meet external obligations. Developing countries have the right to choose their own development paths without military or economic interference from outside. They should not be forced to surrender their right to political or economic self-determination in exchange for relief.
- The debt burden should be shared equitably among credit institutions and the debtor governments, corporations, banks, and elites that incurred the debt. Factors adding to and perpetuating the debt problem but beyond the control of debtor countries—such as previous US budget deficits, high interest rates, unfair commodity prices, and trade barriers—should be alleviated.
- Long-term solutions should promote a more just international economic system in order to prevent such crises from recurring. New structures and mechanisms, involving participation and dialogue between creditors and debtors, including civil society groups such as community and faith-based organizations are critically needed.

- There is a need for a new just process of arbitration for international debt cancellation, such as the introduction of an international insolvency law, which ensures that losses and gains are equally shared.
- New mechanisms involving civil society must produce ethical, mutually responsible and transparent solutions, which not only satisfy requirements for economic efficiency, but also for the protection of basic human needs and rights as well as protecting of the environment.
- Where funds are released through debt cancellation or other relief measures, civil society organizations must be enabled to take part in determining how monies are reallocated for social priorities.

*VI. Recommended Actions for The United Methodist Church*

The United Methodist Church, as a covenant community committed to Christian discipleship and advocacy with the poor, must work toward "measures that would reduce the concentration of wealth in the hands of a few" (¶ 163, 2008 *Discipline*). Thus, the General Conference of The United Methodist Church:

1. celebrates the worldwide movement to cancel the crushing debt of the world's poorest countries and the participation of the General Board of Church and Society and the General Board of Global Ministries in the campaign;

2. recognizes even with the progress made to cancel the debt of impoverished countries, much more remains to be done: 9 out of 10 people in the developing world saw no benefit from the 2005 debt deal at the G8 Summit in Gleneagles, Scotland; and debts are accumulating faster than they are being cancelled;

3. calls for the United States, governments of other leading industrial nations, private commercial lending institutions, and international financial institutions such as the World Bank and IMF to:

   a. cancel the debts of the poorest countries to enable them to meet human development goals, beginning with the Millennium Development goals;

   b. audit their lending portfolios, including loans made to middle-income countries, in order to assess the legitimacy of these loans;

    c. support measures to promote accountability of debtor countries when debts are relieved; these measures must be determined and monitored by local community organizations, including churches, and other communities of faith, and representative organizations of civil society, to ensure that debt cancellation leads to a more just distribution of wealth;

    d. use their powers to ensure that funds illegitimately transferred to secret foreign bank accounts are returned to debtor nations; and

    e. engage, in consultation with civil society, in a process of global economic reform toward the development of responsible financing standards for a more just distribution of wealth and prevention of new cycles of debt.

4. urges the General Board of Church and Society and the General Board of Global Ministries to

    a. work with annual and central conferences to become advocates for debt cancellation and relief, for new structures and mechanisms involving participation and dialogue between creditors and debtors, that is open and transparent and includes civil society;

    b. develop and distribute appropriate curriculum and study materials to annual conferences and local congregations; and

    c. organize and assist speaking tours on the human impact of the global debt crisis.

5. urges United Methodist theological seminaries to include Christian responsibility for economic justice, including the global debt crisis, as a necessary part of education for ministry; and

6. urges the General Board of Church and Society and the General Board of Global Ministries to continue public policy work for major reforms of the International Monetary Fund, the World Bank, the World Trade Organization, and other international financial institutions to promote equitable development through poverty alleviation, protection of the environment, openness, democracy, and human rights.

ADOPTED 1988
REVISED AND ADOPTED 2000
REVISED AND READOOPTED 2008
RESOLUTION #207, 2004 *BOOK OF RESOLUTIONS*
RESOLUTION #198, 2000 *BOOK OF RESOLUTIONS*

*See* Social Principles, ¶ 163D and E.

## 4054. Pathways to Economic Justice

Growing economic inequality in the world is a challenge to the conscience of all followers of Christ. Fed by markets that value profits over people and a culture that sanctions and encourages personal greed, the increasing disparity between those who live on the economic margins and those who amass vast riches threatens to further tear the social fabric of our global community.

In a world where over one billion people live on less than a dollar a day and the richest five individuals have wealth surpassing the combined economies of the poorest 37 nations,[1] the church must stand in this gap and proclaim a new economic order grounded in justice.

The church is set in a world of growing inequality. Even in the United States where there are 268 billionaires, a large percentage of all children live below the poverty line. The richest 1 percent of Americans had as much income in 1999 as the bottom 38 percent combined. In many poor countries in Africa and Asia, the poverty is deeper and the gap between rich and poor exceeds the gap that existed in life between Dives and Lazarus. In such a situation, the church must decide whether its mission to preach good news to the poor is good news only for their spiritual life or whether it is good news to the whole person.

From the beginnings of Methodism, we have always been a movement that sees the whole person, body and soul. Wesley's class meetings emphasized both acts of piety and acts of mercy. He organized and used the class meetings to support groups like sewing collectives, that helped those who didn't have much money, bring their resources together to start small businesses that would be a witness to God's abundance in the midst of poverty. The church has many opportunities to continue that witness if we make the commitment that Wesley made: every congregation not only gives to mission, but has an opportunity to use its assets for the building of a more just economy.

Drawing on the teachings of Jesus and the prophets, the writings and example of our founder John Wesley, and on an analysis of current economic conditions, we can discern pathways leading to a more just and equitable sharing of the riches which God has given us as a human family. These pathways are personal, local, and global.

1. World Bank/Forbes 2007

*Personal Pathways to Economic Justice May Include*

- Support locally based businesses.
- Model sustainable living by recycline waste products and avoiding the use of disposable products.
- Buy organic, locally produced foods and/or fairly traded goods.
- Invest personal savings in stocks and mutual funds which are socially screened.
- Buy "sweat-free" clothing and other articles rather than those manufactured by child labor, sweatshop, or slave labor.
- Engage in Bible study on economic justice.
- Take part in study groups on economic issues, using materials available from general agencies and community-based organizations.

*Local Paths to Economic Justice May Include*

- Support local initiatives to ensure availability of moderate and low income housing.
- Support policies of Affirmative Action and Equal Opportunity employment.
- Open your church to house the homeless and feed the hungry.
- Commit as a congregation a tithe (10 percent) of its budget to promote economic justice and care for those living on the economic margins.
- Support full rights for farm workers, especially the right to organize and bargain collectively.

*National and Global Paths to Economic Justice May Include*

- Support efforts by annual conferences and Conference United Methodist Women organizations to take up at least one specific action project for economic justice in the next quadrennium.
- Make every annual conference staff racially and ethnically diverse at all levels.
- Support the right of governments to limit the international flow of capital.

- Deny Most Favored Nation Trade Status to nations which permit sweatshop, child, or slave labor, do not permit workers to organize, and do not guarantee workers a living wage by accepted international standards.
- Strengthen campaign finance reform laws that prevent corporations and special interest groups from dominating elections and the legislative process.
- Support public sector job creation to build highways, schools, and housing when the private sector is unable to provide jobs for all who need them.
- Support policies that encourage the use of renewable resources and limit the destruction of nonrenewable resources, leading to a sustainable environment.
- End the fiction that the corporation is a "person," a doctrine never envisioned by the founding fathers.
- Support Jubilee USA and Jubilee Debt Campaign through living out their spirit and principles in the life of the community.

The church has too often neglected the full call of the gospel and left economics in the hands of government and business. The kingdom of God is a form of economy that calls forth from each of us a commitment to the abundance of God in our midst. It is a call to renounce the politics of greed and acquisitiveness which dominate the institutions of government and business and reclaim their true calling in the service of people. Economy is how we order our lives, our politics, our world. It is time that we manifest gospel values in the economic order. It is after all, our calling.

ADOPTED 2000
REVISED AND READOPTED 2008
RESOLUTION #208, 2004 *BOOK OF RESOLUTIONS*
RESOLUTION #199, 2000 *BOOK OF RESOLUTIONS*

*See* Social Principles, ¶ 163*D* and *E*.

## 4055. Bread for the World Covenant Church

In developing countries, 1.3 billion people (equaling the entire population of China) live in absolute poverty, with individual purchasing power equivalent to less than one US dollar a day and 70 percent of childhood deaths are associated with malnutrition and preventable diseases. Approximately 35,000 children worldwide die each day from hunger-related causes, and another 841 million other people will suffer from malnutrition (Bread for the World Institute).There is significantly more hunger-related pain, suffering and death in the world than that caused by all the wars in the world. Approximately 18 million people die each year from hunger, malnutrition and resulting diseases. In the US, approximately 31 million people go to bed hungry a part of each month.

The prophets promised a messiah who would establish justice and the knowledge of God, and Jesus later announced himself as the fulfillment of those promises: "The Spirit of the Lord is upon me, because he has anointed me to preach the good news to the poor. He has sent me to proclaim release to the captives. . .to set at liberty those who are oppressed . . ." (Luke 4:18-21). Jesus asked that we see that the hungry are fed (Matt. 25:35), and Jesus also said "in as much as you have done it unto the least of these, you have done it unto me" (Matt. 25:40). Jesus fed hungry people, befriended outcasts and called for radical sharing. He embodied forgiveness and mercy. Those of us who have been embraced by this "good news" are drawn to be concerned about people in need and we are compelled to work to make our society's laws fair and helpful toward poor and hungry people.

The Social Principles of The United Methodist Church state that, "In order to provide basic needs such as food, clothing, shelter, education, health care, and other necessities, ways must be found to share more equitably the resources of the world. Increasing technology, when accompanied by exploitative economic practices, impoverishes many persons and makes poverty self-perpetuating" (¶ 163E).

Our General Conference resolution, "Call for a Rebirth of Compassion" (Resolution #196, 2000 *Book of Resolutions*), reinforces this sentiment when it states that "we call upon United Methodists throughout the land not only to feed the hungry and house the homeless, but also to work for policies that will end hunger and homelessness."

Bread for the World (BFW), established in 1974, is a nonprofit, nonpartisan Christian citizens' movement which performs a unique and critical role within the faith community by working to eradicate hunger from the face of the earth by using their network of thousands of local Covenant Churches across America to lobby elected officials to change policies to provide opportunities to establish a sustainable livelihood for all people. BFW's main campaign is an annual nationwide "Offering of Letters," which not only provides church members with the opportunity to write members of Congress concerning hunger-related issues, but also enables congregations to incorporate into their worship experience, their passionate concerns for those that are starving and suffering from malnutrition.

Covenant Church membership includes training, Bible study and worship aids (resources/materials) on the Christian response to world hunger. The BFW Covenant Church network (www.bread.org) is an essential component of the hunger program of The United Methodist Church, and its efforts complement UMCOR's (http://gbgm-umc.org/umcor) and the General Board of Church and Society's ministry (http://umc-gbcs.org) in alleviating the root causes of hunger/poverty. Direct feeding (soup kitchens) provides relief one day at a time (and may always be needed) but does little to eradicate causes of hunger. Holistic spirituality and development (putting love in action) prepares persons for sustainable livelihoods, but only if government policies are changed to permit this. The Bread for the World Covenant Church program provides opportunities to change government policies. Bread for the World works, but more grassroots initiative is needed. Otherwise, at the current rate of change, between 1.5 and 2 billion people will die during the next 75 years due to hunger/malnutrition.

BFW's Covenant Church program focuses on an annual nationwide "Offering of Letters" and helps prepare United Methodists to effectively change public policy through new legislation each year.

The United Methodist Church, along with more than 45 denominations and church agencies, generously supports BFW, and in fact, The United Methodist Church has a 25-year history of collaboration with BFW's fight against the root causes of both global and domestic hunger. The United Methodist Advance Special Number is: 982325-3. BFW has said that, "[It] owes much to Methodism's historic commitment to social justice and active concern for the poor and downtrodden. John Wesley's conviction that `the world is my parish' is at the heart of BFW's work,"

*Therefore, be it resolved,* that The United Methodist Church significantly enhance its efforts to END HUNGER by increasing participation in the Bread for the World (BFW) Covenant Church program. We further urge that The United Methodist Church achieve a minimum of a 5 percent increase in the number of churches participating in the BFW Covenant Church program each year.

ADOPTED 2000
AMENDED AND READOPTED 2004
READOPTED 2008
RESOLUTION #210, 2004 *BOOK OF RESOLUTIONS*
RESOLUTION #201, 2000 *BOOK OF RESOLUTIONS*

*See* Social Principles, ¶ 163D and E.

## 4056. Greed

God's vision of abundant living is a world where we live out of a theology of "enough," a theology based in the knowledge that we are grounded in Christ, that our sense of personal value and esteem grows from our Christ-centered life. (*Book of Resolutions, 2000,* #188)

Scripture calls us to be compassionate and just stewards of our wealth and warns us of the sin of greed and its devastating effects. The Law ensured that the basic needs and rights of the poor were protected from the greedy (Exodus 23:6-11; Leviticus 25:35-55). The prophets warned that an economic system based on greed is contrary to God's will and leads to ruin of the society (Amos 8:4-7; Jeremiah 22:13-17). Echoing the Law and the prophets, Jesus condemned the rich for the hypocrisy of greed and the barriers greed creates to salvation (Luke 6:24; 16:1-15; Matthew 18:16-22). He taught that in the Reign of God everyone would have enough (Matthew 13:31-32; 20:1-16). The early church rejected greed by sharing their wealth among their members (Acts 2:44-45). When their salvation was jeopardized by greed, Paul warned them that "the love of money is the root of all kinds of evil" (1 Timothy 6:6-10).

In our Wesleyan tradition, greed is an impediment to holiness. John Wesley taught and practiced that excessive wealth, absent of effective stewardship and radical charity, prevents a believer from growing in grace and cultivates sinful actions and attitudes. Wesley said that greed is "destructive of that faith which is of the operation of God; of that hope which is full of immortality; of love of God and of our neighbor, and of every good word and work. ("The Danger of Riches" I.11) Wesley also believed that stewardship that centers on care for the poor is a means of Grace. "O let your heart be whole with God. Sit as loose to all things here below as if you was a poor beggar. Be a good steward of the manifold gifts of God." ("On Riches" II.12)

Furthermore, John Wesley encouraged government leaders to develop public policies that provided for the well-being of the poor and the just distribution of wealth through taxation. For example, he praised the mayor of Cork for public policies which curbed the negative effects of greed on the poor. In his tract, "Thoughts on the Present Scarcity of Provisions" he described the widespread suffering of the poor due to changes in the English economy. Among his solutions was a call for the wealthy to pay taxes on their carriages and for the government to regulate the amount the poor could be charged for land rent.

Therefore, we support measures that would reduce the concentration of wealth in the hands of the few. We encourage personal lifestyles that embody good stewardship of wealth on behalf of the poor. We further support efforts to revise tax structures and to eliminate governmental support programs that now benefit the wealthy at the expense of other persons. (Social Principles, ¶ 163; see also 2008 *Book of Resolutions*, #4052, "Economic Justice for a New Millennium") Gandhi predicted: "There is enough in the world for everyone's need; there is not enough for everyone's greed."

*Call to Action:*

At the General Church Level:

That the General Board of Global Ministries and General Board of Church and Society study and support measures in the US Congress that would reject new trade agreements that allow continuing subsidies to the richest nations and multinational corporations of the world and restrict the possibilities of advancement of the poorest nations and individuals including family farmers everywhere.

That The United Methodist Church oppose tax reduction measures that would increase the concentration of wealth in the hands of the few and support progressive income taxes.

That The United Methodist Church advocate for revisions of tax structures to reduce the regressive taxes paid by the poor worldwide and redouble our efforts toward debt cancellation for the poorest nations.

That the General Board of Global Ministries and the General Board of Church and Society research public policy solutions to practices in global financial markets which create currency speculation that destroys the ability of countries to protect their currency from devastating ruin

At the Local Church Level:

That local congregations organize "simple-living" seminars in our churches and UMW units.

That local congregations examine their investments and endowment funds to determine how they can be better utilized for the poor.

That local congregations expand their stewardship programs to include education about the effects of materialism on discipleship.

That local congregations advocate for fairness in local taxes that ensure the well-being of the poor.

*Be it resolved,* that the people called United Methodists search the scriptures concerning greed and pray for forgiveness.

ADOPTED 2004
READOPTED 2008
RESOLUTION #211, 2004 *BOOK OF RESOLUTIONS*

*See* Social Principles, ¶ 163A, D, and E.

## 4057. Protecting Health Care, Labor, and Environment in Trade Negotiations

Under the World Trade Organization (WTO) and its General Agreement on Trade in Services (GATS) first negotiated in 1994, the concept of free trade has moved beyond the lowering of trade barriers at a country's borders, focusing now on what are called "internal barriers to trade." But what appear to trade interests to be barriers to trade are often laws and regulations passed by national, regional, and local legislatures to protect health care, labor, and the environment. Past WTO decisions have compromised Ontario's ability to discourage the sale of alcoholic beverages, Guatemala's ability to promote breast feeding in preference to use of infant formula, and Europe's ability to support public health by restricting the sale of hormone-treated beef. In the future, GATS rules under discussion could prevent member countries, including the United States, from considering a full range of solutions to problems in their health-care systems or from protecting standards for working conditions. Countries could be challenged under GATS for subsidizing hospitals that disproportionately serve the poor or that seek to extend current "monopolies" such as the US Medicare program to include additional services, such as prescription drugs. Proposed GATS rules could allow foreign corporations and governments to challenge laws requiring reasonable staffing ratios, use of safe needles, and professional licensing as "more burdensome than necessary." The United Methodist Church supports economic development around the globe, but we insist that economic development be sustainable, safeguard human beings and the environment, support the health of workers and communities, and provide a safety net for the most vulnerable among us.

We call upon governments around the world to take steps to protect the right of legislatures at all levels—national, regional and local—to safeguard the health care, environment, and labor of their citizens. In countries like the United States where "fast track" legislation permits Congress to only give a yes or no to new trade legislation, Congressional leaders must involve themselves more in the trade negotiations or be prepared to vote no to the entire trade package when it is presented.

We call upon the General Board of Church and Society to represent these concerns before the US Congress, the United Nations, and the WTO, and to assist United Methodists in all nations to seek attention of their own governments to health care, labor, and environmental issues when trade issues are negotiated.

ADOPTED 2004
READOPTED 2008
RESOLUTION #212, 2004 *BOOK OF RESOLUTIONS*

*See* Social Principles, ¶ 163*I* and *J*.

## 4058. Privatization

"The earth is the Lord's and everything in it" (1 Corinthians 10:26). The Lord's people have been given enough—an abundance of all of the things we need for life.

"We believe [that] governments have the responsibility, in the pursuit of justice and order under law, to provide procedures that protect the rights of the whole society as well as those of private ownership" (Social Principles, ¶ 163*A*).

One of our values as Christians is to provide an economy that serves God's vision of abundance to all. (Ecclesiastes 3:22 "So I saw that there is nothing better than that all should enjoy their work for that is their lot," Luke 10:7 and 1 Timothy 5:18 "the laborer deserves to be paid," Matthew 20:8 "Call the laborers and give them their pay.")

Jesus singled out the poor and the sick and imprisoned for special care and the special responsibility of the faithful. Under many privatization schemes, responsibility by the public has been abandoned to private enterprise. Our responsibility to the sick and poor and imprisoned has been left to the devices of private profit. Privatized prisons, nursing homes, hospitals, welfare programs and other social services have sometimes been less dedicated to service and rehabilitation than to cutting service and increasing profits (2008 *Book of Resolutions*, #4052, "Economic Justice for a New Millennium").

(Social Principles ¶ 162) "We support the basic rights of all persons to human services with oversight by the public. "

(2008 Resolution #3201,"Health Care for All in the United States") "private health insurance in all its forms, continues to increase its premium cost while limiting care and /or increasing deductibles and co-payments for care." Just 20 years ago, only about 18 percent of HMOs (Health Maintenance Organizations) were for-profit. By 1995, the market share was 70 percent. HMOs charge up to 25 percent out of every premium dollar for CEO salaries, profits and bureaucracy; Medicare has administrative costs of only 1.2 percent.

(2008 Resolution #1026) "We are called to see that all life has a sufficient share of the resources of nature."

## Introduction

Corporate interests are rushing to privatize many of the resources of the earth—water, energy, education, natural plants, human and animal genes, cultures and public services such as social security, health care and public safety. Everything from prescription drugs to prisons to welfare programs is considered fair game for corporate profit-making. Wall Street, according to the Economic Policy Institute, is fighting hard for a privatized Social Security system because it would reap an estimated $240 billion in fees for managing these funds during the first 12 years of such a system.

## Private Control

Supporters of privatization accuse government of inefficiency and claim that, if allowed to make a profit, these same corporations could control resources more effectively and efficiently, saving public money and delivering services better. The expectation of privatization is that government would continue to collect taxes from the citizens and then provide that tax money to the corporate CEO's who would manage salaries, resources, and functions better. Those who favor privatization argue that they would earn a profit, benefit the economy, and be less encumbered by inefficient bureaucracy and public controls.

The World Bank is actively subsidizing the privatization of public resources worldwide. The World Trade Organization has been quietly renegotiating and expanding the General Agreement on Trade in Services (GATS). The range of services on the negotiating table is vast, covering such vital areas as water and energy, banking, communications and retail services. Eighty additional countries have been targeted by the European Union for this invasion by foreign corporations. If governments refuse to cooperate, they may be faced with world trade disputes claiming "barriers to free trade."

### Public Control

Opponents of privatization point to corporate abuses and criminality in the management of pensions, energy and communications systems.

Those who favor continued public control and regulation of these common resources and services argue that, when private forces take control, there is less accountability to the citizens. They claim that ever-growing profits are the primary interest of the corporations doing the privatizing. They also note that worker salaries and working conditions are usually forfeited in the name of efficiency and in order to increase private profits. Loss of well-paid public sector jobs is a burden to society in many ways, including reduced tax revenues and increasing the need for social welfare programs.

People worldwide are challenging the privatization of commonly held resources such as native seeds and plants under intellectual property rules established under international financial institutions such as the World Trade Organization. Many are calling for public control of resources such as the drugs necessary for stamping out the most devastating diseases of our world and the water that is essential to life on earth.

### Discernment

There may be instances where privatization is appropriate. However, the role of Christians requires us to honor the earth's resources and to protect our God-given common heritage. The public must be vigilant to regulate and control any privatization of public resources.

### New Laws to Protect Our Common Property

We have rules that protect our private property and our individual property. We also need strong, ethical governments and new laws to protect our common property—the common resources that belong to all of us and the common services that constitute the basis of universal human rights. Responsive governments must be strengthened and supported to provide protection for all, particularly in the most exploited and vulnerable nations and particularly in support of the elements that are necessary to the abundant life provided by God.

There are efforts by the international financial institutions to impose new rules that increase the private invasion of common property. The sovereignty of underdeveloped countries would be undermined by Rule 11 of NAFTA and other free trade agreements such as the proposed Free Trade Area of the Americas. These trade rules strengthen the ability of private interests to force local communities to allow their free trade operations and privatization of common resources without effective regulation. Under Rule 11, if the governments move to regulate the activities of the corporations on behalf of their own workers or their own environment, they face multimillion dollar penalties in private trade courts unattended and unregulated by the public. These rules, called "takings," are increasing the poverty and devastation of communities worldwide.

## The Need for Effective Governments

Effective and democratic governments worldwide must be strengthened in order to function on behalf of the interest of their citizens. Our common resources do not belong to government or market, but responsible and effective government is essential for protecting those public properties. Privatization of common property rights should be viewed as a "form of taking" from the people. For decades a body of international rules has been developing led by corporations that would challenge the rights of governments to protect their workers and their natural resources from corporate exploitation.

## Call to Action

The United Methodist Church and its predecessors have always had a history of public witness on matters of economic justice. Faced with protecting and securing the common resources and services needed by all humanity, the General Conference calls upon:

1. the General Board of Global Ministries to develop an educational program on the issues posed by privatization worldwide and join in challenging privatization where it endangers public interest;

2. the boards and agencies of The United Methodist Church to create and disseminate materials explaining proposed trade agreements

and oppose them when they violate United Methodist ideals supporting a just economy;

3. the General Board of Global Ministries and the General Board of Church and Society to invigorate efforts to acquire national publicly-provided health care for everyone in the United States and that the issue of worldwide health care be put on the agenda for increased support;

4. members of The United Methodist Church to urge our governments to challenge and change the International Monetary Fund (IMF), World Bank and World Trade Organization rules supporting massive privatization;

5. the United Methodist Church to question the IMF investment of billions of public dollars into support for the efforts of private corporations to take over public services and public resources in poor countries;

6. the General Board of Global Ministries and the General Board of Church and Society study ways of supporting world trade rules that would protect our commons resources from the growing trend toward "takings" by private entrepreneurs;

7. the General Board of Global Ministries and the General Board of Church and Society to lead an effort to discern effects to society of privatization of  services in the United States and globally and join in opposing detrimental privatization;

8. the General Board of Church and Society to provide studies and actions on the importance of responsible government and ways to enact good governance; and

9. United Methodists to study and act in support of our local governments by insisting that the Federal budget provide for adequate tax money for running public services and regulating private service initiatives for the benefit of all.

ADOPTED 2004
READOPTED 2008
RESOLUTION #361, 2004 *BOOK OF RESOLUTIONS*

*See* Social Principles, ¶ 163*I*

## 4059. Global Economy and the Environment

The United Methodist Church has been rightly concerned about the environment and its sustainability, given the rapid depletion of natural resources and the contamination of the air, water, and land. However, we have been slow to recognize the impact of the emerging global economy and its impact upon the environment.

When the economic institutions were contained within the boundaries of countries, governments had the power to regulate. Particularly, in the area of the environment, communities could exercise control so that pollution and waste could be regulated and conservation encouraged. Of course, this adds costs to doing business. However, if everyone is under the same constraints, no one is at a disadvantage.

As countries rush to open up markets in the name of free trade, it is obvious that those countries that have strict environmental regulations are going to be at a competitive disadvantage in attracting and keeping business. Business will seek countries in which to operate that have lower environmental standards and, therefore, lower operating costs. Pressures will increase on countries with higher standards to lower them, and developing countries will be hesitant to enact environmental legislation.

*The United Methodist Church therefore recommends:*

1. that every country, including the United States, require that there be roughly equivalent environmental standards between itself and any other country with which it enters into a free-trade agreement, so that there is not a competitive disadvantage for the country with the stricter standards. Mechanisms should also be included in the agreement that will allow for further new standards of environmental regulations in the future;

2. that the General Board of Church and Society develop a statement outlining the relationship of the world economy to the environment and communicate this to appropriate governmental agencies and the church;

3. that the General Board of Church and Society develop study materials for local congregations; and

4. that local congregations study the implications of the global economy on the environment. Study materials might include: *For the Common Good: Redirecting the Economy Toward Community, The Environment, and a Sustainable Future,* by Herman E. Daly and John B. Cobb; *Sustaining the Common Good, A Christian Perspective on the Global Economy;* or materials to be developed by the General Board of Church and Society.

ADOPTED 1996
READOPTED 2004
READOPTED 2008
RESOLUTION #308, 2004 *BOOK OF RESOLUTIONS*
RESOLUTION #288, 2000 *BOOK OF RESOLUTIONS*

*See* Social Principles, ¶ 165B and D.

## 4060. Global Living Wage

Our Holy Scriptures speak repeatedly of the God who reminds us that it is unjust to construct or perpetuate barriers to physical wholeness or full participation in community.

Jesus' commandment to love our neighbor—a love that extends to all persons in all places—is incompatible with exploitation or underpayment of workers.

The Social Principles instruct us on the rights of all people including children to have food, shelter, clothing, health care, and emotional well-being and, that in particular, children must be protected from economic, physical, emotional, and sexual exploitation.

One hundred years ago, The Methodist Episcopal Church, in adopting the first social creed, responded to the call for worker justice by proclaiming support for "a living wage in every industry" (1908 Social Creed).

*Therefore*, in the global community of the twenty-first century, the church has no choice but to be concerned about and involved in contemporary issues of globalization including the impact of changing global economic structures, particularly in the world's poorer countries, if we are to be faithful to our biblical roots and theological traditions. A living wage in a safe and healthy workplace with reasonable hours of work is a universal right not restricted by national borders.

We call upon all members of the global United Methodist Church to work in partnership with persons, communities, and governments everywhere around the world to bring about the creation of conditions that encompass fundamental workers' rights, fair wages, a safe and healthy workplace, reasonable hours of work, decent living standards, support for community infrastructure, and commitment to community economic development.

ADOPTED 2008

*See* Social Principles, ¶ 163B, C, and E.

## INVESTMENTS

## 4071. Investment Ethics

The United Methodist Church believes that social justice and social usefulness must be given consideration together with financial security and financial yield in the ivestment of funds by individuals, churches, agencies, and institutions in the United Methodist family. When we take account of both fiduciary obligations (including financial returns) and denominational values (including social returns), we are investing in a socially responsible manner.

The Church's investment philosophy is based on the biblical concept that all resources are God-given and can be used to promote the reign of God on earth.

### Economic Witness in the Wesleyan Tradition

Churches in the Wesleyan tradition have a long history of witness for justice in the economic order. John Wesley and early Methodists, for example, were firmly opposed to the slave trade, to smuggling, and to what we today call conspicuous consumption. Beginning in 1908, social creeds adopted by our predecessor churches stressed social justice in the economic world, with special attention to child labor and inhumanely long working hours.

Throughout the 20th and into the 21st century, the Church has promoted decent working conditions and the right to organize and bargain collectively, and it has opposed discrimination in the workplace on the basis of race, ethnic background, gender, age, or disability. Historically our tradition has opposed church investments in companies manufacturing liquor or tobacco products or promoting gambling.

Since the 1960s, our denomination and its predecessors have built a solid record based on our belief that every financial investment has ethical dimensions with consequences that are both fiscal and social. United Methodist agencies and conferences fought against the manufacture of napalm and were involved in the social-justice issues raised by religious shareholders. In the mid-1970s, the General Council on Finance and Administration (GCFA) issued official social responsibility guidelines for general Church investments.

Historically, apartheid in South Africa was the major issue for many church-related investors, but United Methodist agencies, affiliated institutions, conferences, congregations, and individual members have brought the Church's Christian witness to business on numerous issues, including employment discrimination, environmental preservation, militarism, nuclear weapons production, reevaluation of infant formula use and addressing the HIV/AIDS pandemic. The Church also continues to advocate on such issues as:

- international fair labor practice;
- domestic and global human rights;
- lending practices or policies for lesser developed communities and nations;
- violence to persons;
- firearms sales and gun policies;
- best corporate governance practices;
- environmental reporting;
- risks of global warming and climate change;
- genetically modified organisms; and
- food safety.

### *Socially Responsible Investing Strategies*

The Church's witness through investments takes four forms, each of which may be employed with the others. They are:

1. Portfolio Screening

Because some companies and enterprises, such as those manufacturing alcoholic beverages and tobacco-related products and manufacturing, selling, or distributing pornography and gambling opportunities, violate basic church teaching, they are excluded from investment. In addition, many church investors refuse to invest in major military contractors or companies with nuclear weapons contracts. Historically, many investors refused to invest in companies doing business in South Africa during the apartheid era. In some cases, they divested of such companies, making public their action as a moral statement.

2. Social Impact Investing

The members of The United Methodist Church expect all Church-related investments to make a positive contribution toward the goals outlined in the Social Principles and *The Book of Resolutions.* Investment strategy, therefore, is based on careful consideration of not only financial returns, but also of social returns across a wide range of issues and concerns. Some investments, however, are undertaken to achieve very specific social outcomes, such as the construction of affordable housing, the renewal of a particular neighborhood or the expansion of business ownership among those traditionally excluded from such ownership.

3. Shareholder Advocacy

Companies may meet the broad investing guidelines of the Church but still fall short of the standards expressed in the Social Principles and *The Book of Resolutions*. Responsible Christian investing includes seeking to change company policies and practices to match more closely articulated Church values. As shareholders of corporations, Church investors may engage corporate management in a variety of ways—from gentle persuasion to public pressure, from dialogue to voting proxies, from filing shareholder resolutions to building coalitions. In many cases, such advocacy has resulted in important policy changes at the corporate level.

4. Strategic Partnerships

Working in collaboration with others strengthens the socially responsible witness and allows the synergy of strategies more forcefully to engage corporations on issues of governance, and environmental and social importance. Strategic partners may include United Methodist boards, agencies, foundations, and universities; other faith-based investors; domestic and global nongovernmental organizations; and other socially responsible investors.

*Investment Policy*

The policy goals of the General Conference of The United Methodist Church, its general agencies, and the entities under its control shall be:

1. to invest in corporations, companies, institutions, or funds making a positive contribution to the realization of the goals outlined in the Social Principles and *The Book of Resolutions*, especially those pursuing such specific targeted goals as:
   - recycling and the use of recycled products;
   - working within legally imposed discharge limits for toxic chemicals, noise and water temperature;
   - the refusal to sell chemicals that would be banned in the company's country of origin;
   - the use of power supplies from renewable resources that do not have undue adverse environmental, socioeconomic, and human rights upon indigenous peoples;
   - the reduction of greenhouse gas emissions in order to minimize impact on climate change;
   - the provision of low-income housing, affordable housing, and community development projects in urban and rural areas;

- the hiring and promoting of women and racial and ethnic persons;
- programs, benefits, and wages that assure quality of life for employees and their families;
- policies and practices that preclude predatory or harmful lending practices; and
- maintaining a commitment to sustainability so that current business practices do not detract from future viable business operations.

2. to exclude from investment companies that:
- manufacture alcoholic beverages or tobacco-products;
- manage or own gambling enterprises;
- produce, distribute, or sell pornographic material;
- make components for nuclear explosive devices;
- manufacture chemical or biological warfare materials;
- make components for anti-personnel weapons;
- have as their primary business the production, distribution, or sale of handguns and assault-type weapons or ammunition for such weapons; or
- manufacture, or purchase through subcontracting, a significant number of products made with sweatshop, forced, or child labor.

3. to persuade corporations to integrate responsible business practices on environmental, social, and governance issues into their operations and to be transparent in documenting these endeavors in public reports by using any combination of the following shareholder advocacy activities:
- letters directed to company management;
- dialogue or discussions with company management;
- voting proxies;
- soliciting votes from other investors for a particular reason,
- sponsoring resolutions for consideration at stockholder meetings;
- speaking at stockholder meetings;
- legal action;
- press releases;
- working in coalitions with other concerned stockholders; and
- petitioning the US Securities and Exchange Commission or Congress for changes in the proxy rules.

4. to seek opportunities to invest in companies, banks, funds, or ventures owned by women and by racial and ethnic persons or have positive records in hiring and promoting women and racial and ethnic persons or that invest or have operations in:

- Native American communities;
- Africa; and
- developing countries, provided that those countries respect human and labor rights and have a record of trying to raise national living standards while working to maintain ecological integrity.

5. to encourage companies to adopt, implement, and then monitor for compliance a supplier code of conduct that is consistent with the International Labor Organization's core labor standards and designed to prevent the manufacture, or purchase through subcontracting, of products made with sweatshop, forced, or child labor.

6. to encourage companies to honor and promote human rights and the dignity of human life;

7. to seek opportunities to commend corporations publicly for transparency, disclosure, socially responsible behavior, and efforts to raise industry standards on environmental, social, and governance issues that are of major concerns to The United Methodist Church.

8. to consider using investment-portfolio managers and funds that specialize in corporate social responsibility screening or are owned by women and persons of color.

The GCFAis responsible for preparing and distributing the socially responsible investment guidelines that are to be used by all general agencies receiving general Church funds. The council shall review and update these guidelines periodically, inviting the input of the agencies and other interested sectors of the Church. GCFA encourages investing agencies to be actively involved in the overview of socially responsible investing described in this policy.

Each general agency receiving general Church funds shall provide GCFA with  a copy of their investment policy. The policy shall be made available upon request to any interested member of the Church.

These investing guidelines are strongly recommended to all organizations affiliated with The United Methodist Church, including annual conferences and local churches and the foundations related to them. It is strongly recommended that a copy of the investment guidelines of any United Methodist-related organization be available upon request.

Where financial considerations preclude immediate divestment of securities held in violation of the above policies, the affected boards, agencies, and institutions of The United Methodist Church shall develop a plan for complying with the guidelines no later than the 2012 General Conference.

All United Methodist investors and users of financial services, whether institutional or individual, are strongly encouraged to use these guidelines.

ADOPTED 1992
AMENDED AND ADOPTED 2000
AMENDED AND READOPTED 2004
AMENDED AND READOPTED 2008
RESOLUTION #213, 2004 *BOOK OF RESOLUTIONS*
RESOLUTION #202, 2000 *BOOK OF RESOLUTIONS*

*See* Social Principles, ¶ 163D.

## 4072. Divestment and Sudan

Let justice roll down like waters, and righteousness like an ever-flowing stream (Amos 5:24).

Resolution 6043, "Guidelines for the Imposition of Sanctions," reminds us that "sanctions, in whatever form, lay conditions upon love and on the extension of humanitarian aid and succor; they fall short of the gospel imperative for unconditional love. Yet sanctions as political and economic tools of pressure and leverage can play a critical role in the mitigation and deterioration of conflicts. It is in this sense that sanctions are sometimes seen as a more tolerable alternative to war" (2008 *Book of Resolutions*).

The humanitarian crisis in Darfur is well documented. The United Methodist Church has called repeatedly for action to end this crisis, and has worked hard to alleviate suffering on the ground. Additional steps are needed to bring economic pressure on the government of Sudan to end the genocide.

The Sudanese government is susceptible to well-placed economic pressure because of its dependence upon direct foreign investment. For example, in 2002 when the Canadian company Talisman led other oil companies in withdrawing from Sudan, the Khartoum regime entered into negotiations that finally ended the country's 21-year civil war. According to the Sudan Divestment Task Force, a project of the

Genocide Intervention Network, "divestment is still likely to dispro-portionately affect the government of Sudan since Khartoum allocates little government revenue towards social spending." Most develop-ment and relief programs are financed largely by international humanitarian concerns. Therefore, a targeted divestment from com-panies doing business with the Sudanese government is unlikely to harm those in need.

US government policy has eased most investment restrictions related to South Sudan, while maintaining a ban on oil investment in the entire country. Such targeted divestment promotes strict criteria for oil companies throughout Sudan, but otherwise relaxes standards for most other kinds of investment necessary in South Sudan. Companies that provide agricultural, consumer, and educational products and services also engage in commerce that benefits the peo-ple of Sudan directly. Investment in these corporations provide posi-tive alternatives to those whose products and services are primarily consumed by the government and military forces.

The United Methodist Church should not own or profit from com-panies whose products or services are used by corrupt governments or regimes to murder, suppress, or displace its citizens and neighbors. Therefore, we ask every United Methodist member and United Methodist general board and agency, administrative agency and insti-tution, including hospitals, homes and educational institutions, annual conferences, foundations, and local churches, to prayerfully consider divestment of the personal and pension assets under their control from any company doing business with the government of Sudan, and request that other investment managers such as mutual fund companies, pension plans and bank trustees do the same.

**ADOPTED 2008**

*See* Social Principles, ¶ 163*I* and *J*.

## NATIVE AMERICANS

### 4081. Economic Development for Native American People

Christians are called to celebrate and protect the worth and dignity of every human being and to struggle against oppression and exploitation. We are called to "proclaim release to the captives . . . to set at liberty those who are oppressed" (Luke 4:18, RSV).

Economic realities, such as "one world economies" and "mega-mergers," can have a negative impact on both the rich and poor of this world. Native American spirituality speaks to and challenges inequities with its understanding of how to care for the whole family of God. Native American United Methodists believe their cultural understanding of stewardship is God-given and has been distorted from its intended purpose; God's creation has been used with greed rather than care. Native Americans in The United Methodist Church believe that the Church must take a proactive stand for reform of church and society that will introduce a radically different model of economic relationships into the new century—a God-centered model. The United Methodist Church believes that models of economic development should not have a negative impact on Native American people.

For more than five hundred years, Native Americans have lived and survived in the context of first, colonialism and second, capitalism and have been impacted by the economics of greed. Many have been forced to live in poverty; however, a small segment of the Native American population is surviving through tribal economic development based on gambling. Unfortunately, tribal gambling casinos have had negative social consequences beyond and even within tribes.

The need for economic development and growth is critically acute in most Native American communities across the United States. Economic conditions are appalling, with some reservations facing exceptionally high rates (some as high as 80-90 percent) of unemployment, well above the national average.

In fact, many reservations have very high poverty rates in the United States and rank very low in health and education indicators. There is little or no tax base on many reservations. Equity for investment is practically nonexistent or equity comes from questionable sources and at an exorbitant rate. As a result some tribes have resorted to gambling endeavors in an effort to improve their economies. However. the vast majority of tribes remain in desperate need of meaningful, diversified economic development.

Economic development encompasses everything from job creation to reform in tax codes, from the creation of banking institutions to the expansion of tribal autonomy, development of basic physical infrastructure (roads and sewers); telecommunications to bridge the digital divide; fiscal literacy development for Native American people. Collectively, these basic essentials are requirements for effective economic development.

Tribal sovereignty is historical, legal, and sacred to American Indian people. We affirm autonomous decision-making by Native American tribes. After all, the primary goal of economic development is to create self-sufficiency in Native American tribes. Ultimately, sovereignty ensures and enables tribes to deliberate and map out a strategy that will hopefully lead to self-sufficiency.

The US Department of the Interior has grossly mismanaged tribal lands and has lost track of billions of dollars in mining, logging, and other royalties that should have gone to benefit Native American tribes. Fiscal accountability and ethical management of trust funds is an absolute necessity in the quest for tribal economic self-sufficiency.

*Therefore, be it resolved*, that The United Methodist Church:

1. supports the efforts of sovereign Native American nations to create means and methods of economic development that do not depend on gambling and do not disrupt or destroy sacred sites;

2. urges the US government to affirm tribal sovereignty and work with Native American tribes in a genuine partnership to support economic development and trust reform;

3. directs the General Board of Church and Society and the General Board of Discipleship in collaboration with Native Americans to develop educational tools for local churches and individuals as a study on contemporary Native American issues; especially tribal sovereignty as it relates to effective economic development. The studies should also include the Church's role in influencing contemporary mission and ministry with Native people and create strategies and actions which can allow active participation of local churches in assisting Native Americans to find a God-centered alternative to gambling as a form of economic development;

4. authorizes the General Board of Church and Society to work with the National Congress of American Indians and other Native American organizations in advocating for federal economic development programs and initiatives;

5. encourages the General Board of Church and Society to facilitate participation of United Methodist Native Americans in the work of the United Nations Permanent Forum on Indigenous Issues and other advocacy events which influence economic development for Native Americans;

6. urges the General Board of Global Ministries to support funding of economic development projects of Native American tribes;

7. urges the General Board of Pension and Health Benefits to invest funds in Native American financial institutions and community.

ADOPTED 2004
REVISED AND READOPTED 2008
RESOLUTION #215, 2004 *BOOK OF RESOLUTIONS*

*See* Social Principles, ¶ 163.


# POVERTY

## 4091. Principles of Welfare Reform

As people of faith and religious commitment, we are called to stand with and seek justice for people who are poor. Central to our religious traditions, sacred texts, and teachings is a divine mandate to side with and protect the poor. Thus the scripture says: However, there should be no poor among you, for in the land the LORD your God is giving you to possess as your inheritance, he will richly bless you, if only you fully obey the LORD your God and are careful to follow all these commands I am giving you today. If there is a poor man among your brothers in any of the towns of the land that the LORD your God is giving you, do not be hardhearted or tightfisted toward your poor brother. Rather be openhanded and freely lend him whatever he needs. If one refuses to help the needy, the scripture continues:

"He may then appeal to the LORD against you, and you will be found guilty of sin . . . Give generously to him [the poor] and do so without a grudging heart; then because of this the LORD your God will bless you in all your work and in everything you put your hand to. There will always be poor people in the land. Therefore I command you to be openhanded toward your brothers and toward the poor and needy in your land" (Deuteronomy 4-5 and 7-11, NIV).

We share a conviction, therefore, that welfare reforms must not focus on eliminating programs but on eliminating poverty and the damage it inflicts on children (who are two thirds of all welfare recipients), on their parents, and on the rest of society.

We recognize the benefit to the entire community of helping people move from welfare into the job market when possible and appropriate. We fear, however, that reform will fail if it ignores labor-market issues such as unemployment and an inadequate minimum wage, and important family issues such as the affordable housing affordable childcare, pay equity, access to health care, and the economic value of care-giving in the home. Successful welfare reform must address these concerns as well as other issues, such as pay equity, affordable housing, and the access to health care.

We believe that people are more important than the sum of their economic activities. Successful welfare reform demands more than economic incentives and disincentives; it depends on overcoming both biased assumptions about race, gender, and class that feed hostile social stereotypes about people living in poverty and suspicions that people with perspectives other than our own are either indifferent or insincere. Successful welfare reform will depend ultimately upon finding not only a common ground of policies but a common spirit about the need to pursue them for all.

The following principles neither exhaust our concerns nor resolve all issues raised, but these principles will serve as our guide in assessing proposed legislation. We hope they may also serve as a rallying point for a common effort with others throughout the nation.

The General Conference of The United Methodist Church adopts "Principles of Welfare Reform," and directs them to be sent to the President of the United States, the speaker of the United States House of Representatives, and the United States Senate majority leader. In addition, annual conferences are asked to send this statement to appropriate state officials.

## A Statement of Shared Principles of Welfare Reform

The goal of Welfare Reform must be to lift people out of poverty, thus requiring systemic changes.

On February 8, 2006, the President of the United States signed legislation authorizing the Work Opportunity and Personal Responsibility Act, commonly known as Temporary Assistance for Needy Families (TANF) Act. Originally signed into law in 1966, the new provisions will shape the nature of America's welfare policies through 2010. Addressing the needs of the most vulnerable of our citizens, particularly women and children, should be the aim of any welfare program. The TANF reauthorization heightens the work mandate as a condition to receive benefits, without ensuring adequate family supports such as child care or reducing medical and/or mental health barriers to employment.

As states now consider the challenge of meeting Federal requirements, we must continue to advocate for policies that:

1. insure that poverty reduction is a central goal. All welfare policies must work together to enable recipients and their families to leave poverty and achieve self-sufficiency. For example, cash benefits combined with wages and supportive services must be sufficient to allow each family to meet its basic needs.

2. provide sufficient federal and state funding. Funding for welfare should at a minimum be indexed to the rate of inflation. Continuation of state maintenance of effort should be required.

3. acknowledge the dignity of work, eliminate barriers to employment and provide training and education necessary for unskilled workers to get and hold jobs. Participation in post-secondary education should count as work. Supportive services provided should include childcare, transportation, and ancillary services to make participation possible and reasonable.

4. continue and encourage public/private partnerships to train workers and help them find jobs. If public jobs are created, they should lead to family-sustaining wages, comply with workplace protection laws, and not displace current workers. States should provide means by which employment programs can be evaluated at the local level for effectiveness and fairness and allow welfare recipients to retain a substantial portion of wage earnings and assets before losing cash, housing, health, child care, food assistance or other benefits. In no case should former welfare recipients receive less in combined benefits and income as a result of working than they received while they were on welfare.

5. be available to all people in need. Immigrants should have access to the same benefits that are available to citizens. Those who receive benefits should receive them according to their needs and for as long as the need exists.

6. do not impose time limits on people who are complying with the rules of the program. It is the state's responsibility to assure access to counseling, legal assistance, and information on eligibility for child support, job training and placement, medical care, affordable housing, food programs, and education.

7. acknowledge the responsibility of both parents and government to provide for the well-being of children. Welfare should insure that

children benefit from the active and healthy participation of parents—whether custodial or not—in their lives. The barriers to participation by married parents in federal programs should be removed. There should be no family caps and no full-family sanctions. Children should benefit from successful state efforts to collect child support assistance from noncustodial parents through increasing the amount of collected child support that children receive.

8. address the needs of individuals with special situations. People who have been victims of domestic violence or stalking must be protected and have their privacy maintained. Some with disabling conditions may need extended periods of time to become employable; and it must be recognized that some people cannot or should not work under any circumstances.

9. uphold and affirm every person's value, whether employed or not. In compassion, we recognize that a small proportion of people on welfare may never be in a position to work outside the home. Exemptions should be offered for people with serious physical or mental illness, disabling conditions, or responsibilities as caregivers who work at home. States should have the option to use federal funds to help families to cope with multiple barriers to employment.

## Call to Action

Therefore, we call on annual conference boards of church and society or their equivalents to urge their state and county governments to create programs that assist current and former welfare recipients in making the transition from dependence to economic health, including: training, public sector job creation, child care, and resources for parenting.

We urge local churches to familiarize themselves with the issues regarding welfare reform. As states develop changes to TANF regulations, we urge local churches to work with community organizations, local advocates, and state officials to protect the right of all people to dignity and well-being, to improve education and training opportunities, and to ensure a safety net for the most vulnerable among us.

ADOPTED 1996
AMENDED AND READOPTED 2004 AND 2008
RESOLUTION #160, 2004 *BOOK OF RESOLUTIONS*
RESOLUTION #147, 2000 *BOOK OF RESOLUTIONS*

*See* Social Principles, ¶ 163E.

## 4092. Statement of Concern on Poverty

We commonly believe:

1. that God loves all persons and God wants all human beings to live and experience an abundant life;

2. that all persons should act as responsible stewards of God's creation and equally share the fruits of these resources among each other.

However, we also understand that inequality exists in our time between nations and among people. In our society today, there are poor people living in miserable conditions while a small segment of the population is living in affluence and controlling the majority of resources.

We also recognize that certain social structures and policies contribute to the worsening of poverty especially in developing and poor countries:

1. governments in poor countries not prioritizing education in their budget allocation, thus limiting the access of poor people to quality education and thus depriving poor people of chances to get high-paying jobs;

2. failure of the governments of developing nations to provide enough decent jobs;

3. lack of welfare and support programs for the unemployed and underemployed;

4. failure of the government of these poor countries to uphold the rights of workers to decent wages and instead, through legislation, protect the interest of big businessmen and corporations;

5. rampant graft and corruption in government bureaucracies and offices;

6. unequal trade relations between poor and wealthy nations and the debt crisis that diverts the country's resources to debt servicing;

7. dysfunctional families that have neglected the welfare of children.

Given this situation, as people of The United Methodist Church, called by God to become world-changing disciples and to be stewards and keepers of our brothers and sisters who have been marginalized, we recommend to the local churches/agencies of The United Methodist Church that

1. local churches create groups that will study and understand the root causes of and extent of poverty in their communities;

2. the church agencies find ways on how to alleviate poverty in consultation with the community;

3. the general church urge the governments of wealthy nations to forgive the debts of poor nations and work out ways to ease the burden of debt servicing;

4. the local churches and agencies educate their constituencies on preventing corruption in the government and demanding investigation and prosecution of violators;

5. local churches advocate for just wages for workers and urge the government to provide decent jobs for the workers;

6. the local churches review and evaluate trade treaties or agreements promoting unequal/unfair trade relations and urge the government to repeal such laws or agreements;

7. the local churches and agencies urge the government to prioritize education in their national budget allocations; and

8. the local churches launch programs that promote caring and support for the poorest of the poor.

**ADOPTED 2008**

*See* Social Principles, ¶ 162E.

### 4093. Society of St. Andrew

*Be it resolved,* that The United Methodist Church commend the Society of St. Andrew, a national Christian hunger-relief ministry, as a partner organization with The United Methodist Church in the alleviation of hunger in the United States.

*Furthermore,* we commend this partnership between local churches and the Society of St. Andrew through volunteer service and gifts through the Advance Special.

**ADOPTED 2008**

*See* Social Principles, ¶ 162E.

## STEWARDSHIP ISSUES IN THE CHURCH

### 4101. Living Wage Model

Throughout Scripture, God commands us to treat workers with respect, dignity, and fairness. Exploitation or underpayment of workers is incompatible with Christ's commandment to love our neighbor

—a love that extends to all persons in all places, including the workplace. The Old Testament and New Testament include explicit warnings to those who would withhold fair pay to workers. "Woe to him . . . who makes neighbors work for nothing and does not give them their wages" (Jeremiah 22:13). "Listen! The wages of the laborers who mowed your fields, which you kept back by fraud, cry out, and the cries of the harvesters have reached the ears of the Lord of hosts" (James 5:4).

A century ago, the Methodist Episcopal Church, in adopting the first social creed, responded to this call for worker justice by proclaiming support for "a living wage in every industry" (1908 Social Creed). Today, The United Methodist Church reaffirms its historic support for the living wage movement and calls upon businesses and governments to adopt policies to ensure employees are paid sufficient wages to afford shelter, food, clothing, health care and other basic expenses, according to local costs of living.

In calling for a living wage in every industry, The United Methodist Church recognizes its own responsibility to model fair and faithful compensation. To this end, The United Methodist Church adopts the living wage as a model for justice in the world and in the household of faith, holding all levels of the church accountable—local United Methodist congregations, annual conferences, and their agencies, the general church and its agencies—to adjust compensation for all employees, including support staff, to effect the following:

- reflect the local cost of living;
- provide for adequate health coverage for employees and their dependents;
- provide mechanisms for training, promotion, and advancement for all United Methodist employees at all levels; and
- ensure that fair and consistently applied personnel policies pertain to all employees of The United Methodist Church and its agencies.

ADOPTED 2000
REVISED AND READOPTED 2008
RESOLUTION #217, 2004 *BOOK OF RESOLUTIONS*
RESOLUTION #210, 2000 *BOOK OF RESOLUTIONS*

*See* Social Principles, ¶ 163*B* and C.

## 4102. Provide Financial Incentives for Clergy in Churches with Small Membership

WHEREAS, churches with small memberships require clergy with specialized training and skills; and

WHEREAS, such training is available at various times/places involving personal costs; and

WHEREAS, clergy with such training are often influenced by financial concerns to move to churches that provide higher salaries,

*Therefore, be it resolved,* that annual conferences be creative and intentional in providing clergy in churches with small memberships salary increments for each continuous year of service in churches with small membership; and/or in town and country settings; and

*Be it further resolved,* that annual conferences be creative and intentional in providing financial support to clergy who desire specialized training for ministry in churches with small memberships, and/or town and country settings.

ADOPTED 2000
READOPTED 2008
RESOLUTION #221, 2004 *BOOK OF RESOLUTIONS*
RESOLUTION #210, 2000 *BOOK OF RESOLUTIONS*

*See* Social Principles, ¶ 163D and E.

## 4103. Stewardship Education for Small Membership Churches

WHEREAS, there is a general absence of financial development and stewardship education in small membership and rural churches; and

WHEREAS, there is a need to guide small membership and rural churches to change the concept of stewardship from "meeting the budget" to "sharing the resources God has given to us"; and

WHEREAS, tithing has a long history in The United Methodist Church which resulted in the 1996 Resolution, "A Tithing Church"; and

WHEREAS, stewardship responsibilities are outlined in the 2008 *Book of Discipline*, ¶¶ 258.4, 630.5, and 1115,

*Therefore, be it resolved,* that the General Board of Discipleship and the General Board of Global Ministries be called on to network with the United Methodist Rural Fellowship on the issue of financial development and stewardship education; and

*Be it further resolved,* that we encourage a new resource packet on stewardship be developed for today's small membership and rural churches; and

*Be it further resolved,* that we encourage resources be developed for training pastors and lay leadership regarding personal tithing, speaking about stewardship and finances, and negotiating pastoral compensation.

ADOPTED 2000
REVISED AND READOPTED 2008
RESOLUTION #224, 2004 *BOOK OF RESOLUTIONS*
RESOLUTION #213, 2000 *BOOK OF RESOLUTIONS*

*See* Social Principles, ¶ 163D.

## UNITED STATES ECONOMIC ISSUES

### 4111. Enabling Financial Support for Domestic Programs

In Genesis 4:3-9, Cain displays the selfishness that exploits and destroys and God calls him into accountability for his treatment of his brother. Acts 2:44-45 provides us with an early glimpse of the transformation in community that is the gift of the Holy Spirit, especially in our responsibility to each other. It is apparent that God calls us to be responsible for how we live and share the resources of community with others.

The United Methodist Church has declared war to be "incompatible with the teachings of Jesus Christ"; and

Dr. Martin Luther King Jr. wrote that "racism and its perennial ally," economic exploitation, "provide the key to understanding most of the international complications of this generation."

While unemployment is increasing among minority groups, tens of thousands of African American, Hispanic, and Native American male and female young adults have never been employed and are, therefore, not counted in current unemployment statistics; and

Many public school districts (especially those that serve the masses of urban Black, Hispanic, and poor people) find themselves facing severe financial shortfalls, staff cuts, the elimination of vital programs, and school closings.

Those same communities are experiencing social trauma due to plant closings and the relocation of industry to countries where the wages are from fifty cents to one dollar an hour. All of these are examples that we have not heard God's answer to Cain, that we are our sisters' and brothers' keepers and have not sought to usher in the community that is blessed by the Spirit.

We petition the President and Congress of the United States to reduce the US military presence by recognizing principles of sovereignty in every region of the world.

We petition the President and Congress of the United States to reapportion dollars, saved by reduced military spending and base closings, for domestic programs that will enable the financial support for an increase in quality educational offerings in the public school systems of the country, adequate health care, affordable housing, the creation of sufficient employment opportunities, and a new comprehensive employment training act, that will appropriate federal dollars into elements of the private sector that are currently in compliance with affirmative action guidelines for the purpose of encouraging their participation in the retraining of US workers and for redevelopment of plants within the continental United States.

ADOPTED 1992
AMENDED AND READOPTED 2004
RESOLUTION #227, 2004 *BOOK OF RESOLUTIONS*
RESOLUTION #216, 2000 *BOOK OF RESOLUTIONS*

*See* Social Principles, ¶ 164.

## 4112. Establish Annual Conference State Taxation Task Force

WHEREAS, the Bible enjoins all Christians to establish a just society, called "the Kingdom of God" by our Lord Jesus; the Hebrew prophets condemn in no uncertain terms depriving the poor of fair treatment and Jesus described his mission as liberating the oppressed and preaching good news to the poor and further identified with "the least of these"; and

WHEREAS, tax laws are necessary to raise revenues to meet the minimum health, safety, educational, and welfare needs of the community, the Judeo-Christian standards of justice require that the taxes imposed be fair to poor and low-income citizens and raise adequate revenues for the society's common good; and

WHEREAS, Susan Pace Hamill, United Methodist layperson and professor of law at the University of Alabama School of Law in Tuscaloosa, has convincingly documented in her thesis "An Argument for Tax Reform Based on Judeo-Christian Ethics" http://www.law.ua.edu/pdf/hamill-taxreform.pdf that the State of Alabama tax code, by oppressively burdening poor and low-income Alabamians and failing to raise adequate revenues for basic services, does not meet the Judeo-Christian standards of justice; and

WHEREAS, the North Alabama Conference and the Alabama-West Florida Conference both organized to work to reform their state's regressive tax code;

*Be it hereby resolved that*, State Taxation Task Forces are established in each annual conference at their next session to examine the tax codes of their states, following the guidelines in Professor Hamill's book *The Least of These (Fair Taxes and the Moral Duty of Christians)*;

*and that* the task forces in each Conference prepare a strategy for action to promote and establish a just tax code in every state;

*and that* strategies seek to enlist the cooperation and support of all local churches through tax education and advocacy;

*and that* their results are communicated annually to the General Board of Church and Society in Washington D.C.;

*and that* the General Board of Church and Society report on the effectiveness of these strategies and recommend continued action to the General Conference of 2008.

ADOPTED 2004
RESOLUTION #228, 2004 *BOOK OF RESOLUTIONS*

*See* Social Principles, ¶ 163 *D* and *E*.

## 4113. Guidelines for Social Security Reform in the United States

The Old and New Testaments share prophetic-messianic traditions in which God stands with the oppressed against a dehumanizing and destructive social order. The emphasis on the protection of those in deepest need was a theme of the events of Exodus. And Jesus, drawing on intimate knowledge of the Hebrew Scriptures, inaugurated his ministry with a quotation from Isaiah:

"The spirit of the Lord . . . has anointed me to preach good news to the poor . . . to set at liberty those who are oppressed" (Luke 4:18-19, RSV; cf. Isaiah 61:1-2).

The early Christian church in Jerusalem, following this tradition, established a community in which all things were held in common. Special attention was given to those who were living on the economic margins of society, including widows, the elderly, children, and the disabled. Israel and the early church exemplified the role of the community of faith as they addressed concern for the welfare of the poor and establishment of a just social order.

It is the birthright of every child of God to live a life with dignity and access to the basic necessities of life. It is our responsibility as individuals, as churches and as expressed collectively through our government, to ensure that all God's children are cared for through all stages of life.

In modern society, the establishment of retirement security programs has greatly reduced the number of individuals living in poverty in their older years. Retirement security is often described as a three-legged stool composed of workplace retirement plans, private savings and government sponsored income security programs, such as Social Security. In recent decades workplace retirement plans, particularly traditional pension plans, and private savings have weakened thus increasing the importance of programs such as Social Security. At the same time, however, Social Security is experiencing long-term financing challenges which have given rise to proposals that would fundamentally alter and weaken the program.

The United Methodist Church celebrates the success of the Social Security program and advocates changes that would preserve and strengthen the program for this and future generations.

## History

The Social Security system in the United States, with its disability, survivors and retirement benefits, has historically functioned as a basic insurance program to provide income and medical expenses for those persons who are retired or disabled or are the survivors of deceased workers. Since its enactment in 1935, The Social Security has been a cornerstone of the social policy of the United States and remains the most successful antipoverty program in US history.

*Principles of Reform*

Because of the important role of Social Security, people of faith have a special interest in ensuring that it is operated fairly and securely and that its benefit structure and financing are regularly reviewed to ensure that it is flexible enough to adjust to the changing needs of society. We affirm the following principles when discussing potential changes to the Social Security program:

- Compassion: The program must embody our collective responsibility to care for one another.
- Economic Security: Security for the elderly, survivors and persons with disabilities should not be left to fragile family support systems, charity or stock market cycles.
- Equity, Fairness and Progressivity: The program must continue to provide universal coverage based on compulsory employee and employer contributions with costs and benefits distributed progressively in proportion to each person's ability to pay and level of need.
- Savings and Pensions: In addition to preserving Social Security, we advocate government actions which expand access and availability of employer pension plans as well as a higher level of personal savings.
- Stewardship of Public Trust: Social Security has demonstrated the positive role that the government can play in advancing the common good. Future generations deserve nothing less.

In addition to these broad principles for reform, The United Methodist Church recognizes that Social Security is an issue of particular and critical importance to women. Since its inception, Social Security has often been the only income source keeping women from living in poverty. Today, while women's lives have changed, women are still overrepresented in the lowest wage jobs and earn only 77 percent of what men earn. Women leave the labor force for an average of 15 percent of their working careers, primarily to fulfill responsibilities as caregivers to their children, spouses, or elderly family members. In addition, women live an average of seven years longer than their male counterparts. In recent years, advisory commissions have issued proposals that have caused turmoil in the debate over the future of Social Security in the United States. Especially pernicious were the proposals to divert portions of workers' current payments from the Social Security system into individually held private accounts.

The United Methodist Church affirms Social Security's central role in family income protection. We believe that all proposals to address the future solvency of the Social Security Trust Fund must be viewed through the eyes of beneficiaries—particularly the most vulnerable recipients—and with the goal of addressing remaining inadequacies in the current system affecting women  If we strengthen the Social Security system so that it works well for women, we will have a system that works well for all persons in the United States.

To truly strengthen the Social Security system, we believe any reform effort must:

- continue to help those with lower lifetime earnings, who are disproportionately women;
- maintain full cost-of-living adjustments;
- protect and strengthen benefits for wives, widows, and divorced women;
- preserve disability and survivor benefits;
- protect the most disadvantaged workers from across-the-board benefits cuts;
- ensure that women's guaranteed benefits are not reduced by individual account plans  that are subject to the uncertainties of the stock market;
- address the care-giving and labor force experiences of women; and
- further reduce the number of elderly living in poverty.

*Action*

The United Methodist Church supports the above principles and guidelines for reform and directs The General Board of Church and Society to distribute these principles to policymakers and to advocate on their behalf.  Furthermore, The United Methodist Church shall continue to educate its constituents about the importance of preserving a strong social insurance program for future generations with particular attention paid to the needs of women and vulnerable populations.

ADOPTED 1984
REVISED AND READOPTED 2000
REVISED AND READOPTED 2008
RESOLUTION #230, 2004 *BOOK OF RESOLUTIONS*
RESOLUTION #219, 2000 *BOOK OF RESOLUTIONS*

*See* Social Principles, ¶ 163D and E.

## 4114. Support of Employment Retirement Income Security Act (ERISA)

WHEREAS, as United Methodists, we have a long history of public witness on matters of economic justice. As we view questionable business practices in our world, we must speak out for ethical behavior and call our Congress to action; and

WHEREAS, hundreds of thousands of people have lost their jobs and life savings to illegal, corrupt, or questionable business practices that manipulate short term stock prices and tend to benefit the very few individuals in upper management positions, and we see that the brunt of this mismanagement is borne by employees who have been downsized, forced into early retirement, or forced to work longer hours; and

WHEREAS, loyal employees have seen their retirement savings eroded in an atmosphere of growing bankruptcy and a more skewed distribution of wealth and income throughout the nation, we realize we must call for action to protect the futures of these peoples; and

WHEREAS, procedures of corporations such as Enron, Tyco, WorldCom, and others enabled financial officers aware of financial difficulties within their structures to divest themselves of stock during freeze-out periods, creating steep drops in stock prices. When employees were finally able to sell stock, stock prices had plummeted because of the "dumping" of stock by managers, thus leaving employees with great losses in the value of their Employment Retirement Income Security Act (ERISA) managed plan.

*Therefore,* we United Methodists as employees, investors, and consumers in the Kansas East Conference adopt and petition the General Conference to petition Congress to enact legislation that would protect ERISA managed plan participants through limitation of company-owned stock, through eliminating freeze-out periods restricting sale of company stock, and by increasing investment options available to ERISA managed plan participants;

*Further,* we petition Congress to tighten the requirements for converting traditional pension plans to cash balance plans, especially for long-term employees.

ADOPTED 2004
RESOLUTION #231, 2004 *BOOK OF RESOLUTIONS*

*See* Social Principles, ¶¶ 162E and 163E and I.

## 4115. Negative Implication of US Deficit Spending

All expenditures by governments are funded either by current taxation or by borrowing from future revenues. Experience has shown that when governments borrow from the future by making expenditures for which no current source of income exists, frequently the effect is inflation. Inflation erodes the purchasing value of funds held by common people of the country, sometimes dramatically. While inflation affects all persons, it especially affects those persons, primarily retired, whose incomes, such as pensions, annuities, and interest from savings, are fixed.

We note with consternation the willingness of the US Congress to essentially fund foreign conflicts by printing currency not backed by income at the same time it is legislating tax reductions. In effect, without so stating, the government is confiscating the financial security of the vulnerable poor and elderly in order to fund the military costs of foreign conflicts.

We call upon all United Methodists to contact their legislators to remind them of the negative implications of deficit spending. We especially call upon United Methodists in the United States to request that their senators and representatives assure an adequate tax base for all expenditures for military conflicts. We call upon the General Board of Church and Society to provide all appropriate resources in support of this resolution.

ADOPTED 2004
RESOLUTION #232, 2004 *BOOK OF RESOLUTIONS*

*See* Social Principles, ¶ 163.

# WORKERS' RIGHTS

## 4131. Concern for Workers Task Force

WHEREAS, Scripture and Wesleyan tradition call us to do justice and demonstrate mercy for workers as an expression of our witness for Jesus Christ;

WHEREAS, transitions in the global economy and local communities have created systems and practices of unfairness and persecution of workers; and

WHEREAS, The United Methodist Church continues to need guidance and support in developing ministries of justice for workers,

*Therefore, be it resolved,* that the 2008 General Conference authorize the continuation of the Concern for Workers Task Force. The General Conference shall direct the General Board of Global Ministries and the General Board of Church and Society to appoint a task force composed of clergy and laity. All appointees will be persons who are informed about the issues and are presently engaged in ministry to working people, the unemployed, and the underemployed. The task force will be gender, racial, and class inclusive.

*Be it further resolved,* that the task force shall fulfill the following goals:

A. *Educate the church about the integration of justice for workers with the Christian faith by:*

1. providing resources and opportunities for United Methodists who are employers and directors of church-related institutions to become aware of workers' concerns and to integrate our social teachings on workers' rights into their vocations. The task force may organize a forum for United Methodist employers and directors for this purpose;

2. providing resources and opportunities for United Methodists who are leaders of labor unions and workers' rights organizations to integrate our social teachings on workers' rights into their vocations. The task force may, for example, organize a forum for such persons;.

3. providing resources and training for United Methodist clergy and seminarians to engage in ministry to and advocacy with workers who are engaged in labor struggles; and

4. providing congregations and lay members with resources and opportunities to develop their awareness of workers' concerns and our social teachings.

B. *Empower the church to advocate for workers' rights in local and international struggles by:*

1. guiding the development of the United Methodist Concern for Workers Network, through the General Boards of Church and Society and Global Ministries. The purpose of the network will be:

    a. to help United Methodists connect with local struggles for workplace peace and justice;

    b. to provide information about national and international campaigns and legislation that are endorsed by the General Boards of Church and Society and Global Ministries;

    c. to promote the observance of Labor Sunday; and

    d. to receive and share information from members of the network;

2. exploring collaborations with labor unions, Pan Methodist denominations, ecumenical organizations and other workers' rights organizations.

3. assisting the General Boards in the implementation of General Conference resolutions related to the rights of workers.

ADOPTED 2000
AMENDED AND READOPTED 2004
AMENDED AND READOPTED 2008
RESOLUTION #233, 2004 *BOOK OF RESOLUTIONS*
RESOLUTION #220, 2000 *BOOK OF RESOLUTIONS*

*See* Social Principles, ¶ 163B and C.

## 4132. Environmental Health and Safety in Workplace and Community

God's covenant with humanity affirms that God is involved in the healing of individuals (Proverbs 3:7-8) and includes the mandate to protect the community from dangers that threaten the health and safety of the people. At the beginning of Methodism, John Wesley provided medicine and medical treatment at no cost to the poor in London and Bristol. In addition to pioneering free dispensaries in England, Wesley emphasized prevention of illness. In his book *Primitive Physick*, he dealt with nutrition and hygiene, as well as treatment of the sick. The first Social Creed, adopted by the 1908 General Conference of The Methodist Episcopal Church, declared that workers must be protected "from dangerous machinery, occupational disease, injuries, and mortality," and that working conditions must be regulated to safeguard the physical and moral health of the community. Today as well, the church is called to declare that the health of every individual is part of community health, including safe and healthy conditions in places where people work. The church has a responsibility to pronounce clearly the implications of God's law of love for human health. Where human life and health are at stake, economic gain must not take precedence.

## A. Public Health and Safety Hazards

Public health hazards originate from a variety of sources, including organisms (e.g., bacteria, fungi, and viruses), physical conditions (e.g., hazardous machinery, excessive noise, repetitive motion), toxic chemicals, and radiation. Such hazards can produce infectious diseases, disabling injuries, incapacitating illnesses, and death. Toxic substances and related hazards such as ionizing radiation threaten the exposed individual to additional hazards such as cancer and sterility, and they also threaten future generations with birth defects and gene mutations.[1]

## B. Declaration

Public health and safety is dependent on effective prevention and active protection before illness or injury have occurred. To fulfill God's commandment to love our neighbor as ourselves, we should support action to protect each individual's health and to preserve the health of the community. To this end, we declare:

1. Every individual, including those with disabilities, has a right to a safe and healthful environment unendangered by a polluted natural world, a hazardous workplace, an unsanitary community, dangerous household products, unsafe drugs, and contaminated food. This human right must take precedence over property rights. Moreover, the necessary preservation of human life and health must not be sacrificed or diminished for economic gain. It is unconscionable that anyone should profit from conditions that lead to the disease, disability, or death of another.

Furthermore, the essential protection of the physical and moral quality of human life must not be compromised by competing considerations of capital investment and return, or diminished by society's insistence on affluence, luxury, and convenience. Environmental health and safety regulations must not be compromised by private property rights or risk-benefit analysis.

2. Public health hazards must be prevented in order to avoid the serious individual and community consequences of injury, illness, and

---

1. *Estimates of the Fraction of Cancer in the United States Related to Occupational Factors*, prepared by the National Cancer Institute, National Institute of Environmental Health Sciences, National Institute for Occupational Safety and Health, mimeographed report, September 14, 1978; page 24. One substance alone, asbestos, is expected to claim the lives of 1.6 million of the 4 million individuals heavily exposed since World War II, including a substantial number of shipyard workers.

untimely death, including disability, physical pain, mental anguish, lost human potential, family stress, and the diversion of scarce medical resources.

3. Public health hazards to future generations, such as toxic substances and wastes that produce birth defects and gene mutations, must be prevented in order to avoid a legacy of disease, disability, and untimely death. No generation has the right to assume risks that potentially endanger the viability of future life.

4. The public health risks of technological development must be fully researched and openly assessed before new technologies are introduced into the home, the workplace, the community, or the environment. Consumers and workers have the right to know what technologies and substances are used in the workplace, in foods, and other products.

5. The preservation and protection of human life from public and environmental health hazards is a fundamental responsibility of government that must be maintained by active public support and adequate public funds. All levels of government must enforce public and environmental health and safety laws.

6. Preventive health care should be taught in educational institutions to persons in every age group at every level of society. Health professionals in all branches of medicine and public health, and those in related fields, should be encouraged to practice preventive medicine, implementing community preventive health strategies, and assist patients in the adoption of healthy lifestyles. Programs should be implemented that educate and inform consumers and workers about physical, chemical, biological, and radiological hazards of products, services, working conditions, and environmental contaminants.

7. The right to a healthy and safe workplace is a fundamental right. Employers must assume responsibility to eliminate hazards in their workplaces which cause death, injury, and disease and to work together with their employees and employee organizations to achieve this objective.

## C. General Recommendations

We call upon all local churches, annual and central conferences, and general boards and agencies of The United Methodist Church to provide for the safety and health of persons in their meeting places and work places; and to educate and to encourage advocacy for public and environmental health and safety in the community as indicated in the declarations above.

ADOPTED 1988
REVISED AND ADOPTED 2000
READOPTED 2008
RESOLUTION #234, 2004 *BOOK OF RESOLUTIONS*
RESOLUTION #221, 2000 *BOOK OF RESOLUTIONS*

*See* Social Principles, ¶ 163C.


## 4133. Rights of African American Farmers

Since the initial charge from God to till and keep the Garden of Eden (Genesis 2:15), farming has been an integral part of humankind's existence—providing nourishment for our bodies and a connection with the Creation. As agribusiness has grown and population centers shifted toward urban areas, the intimate connection between our food, the hands that harvest it, and God's Creation has been strained.

While The United Methodist Church supports "the right of persons and families to live and prosper as farmers" (Social Principles, ¶ 162N), society has failed to fully value the essential contributions of farmers. This growing disconnect, combined with long-established patterns of racism in the United States, has created a crisis among African American farmers.

Over the past 100 years, the number of African American farmers in the United States has shrunk from over 925,000 to fewer than 18,000 today. The share of farmland owned by African American farmers likewise has shrunk from roughly 14 percent to less than 1 percent.

These losses have been accelerated by a lack of access to capital, technical information, and legal resources needed to train and develop agricultural holdings into stable, income-producing, self-sustaining operations. Although the United States Department of Agriculture (USDA) is charged with assisting all farmers, a 1997 report by the USDA entitled, Civil Rights at the United States Department of Agriculture, confirmed widespread discrimination within the agency. These discriminatory practices denied farmers access to loan approval, loan servicing, and farm management assistance.

Despite a landmark class action settlement reached with USDA in 1999 providing a system of payments for farmers who faced discrimination, the struggle for justice continues. Many African American farmers were shut out of the settlement process and thousands of others heard about the settlement only after the deadline for filing a claim had passed.

In order to ensured justice for all farmers and the preservation of a unique and vital heritage of rural communities, The United Methodist Church:

1. reaffirms its support for a settlement aimed at redressing discriminatory practices by USDA;
2. calls on USDA to establish a process to reevaluate pending claims by African American farmers based on the merits rather than flawed bureaucratic deadlines;
3. calls on USDA to establish and enforce strict guidelines on agency outreach and action to guard against further discrimination;
4. calls on the United States Congress to fully fund the Minority Farm Outreach and Technical Assistance Program;
5. and, recognizing the critical need for community, government, and private sector collaboration to help stem the decline of African American farmland, calls on the General Board of Church and Society and the General Board of Global Ministries to work with community-based organizations such as the Federation of Southern Cooperatives/Land Assistance Fund to care for the needs of African American farmers in the United States.

ADOPTED 2008
RESOLUTION #235, 2004 *BOOK OF RESOLUTIONS*
RESOLUTION #222, 2000 *BOOK OF RESOLUTIONS*

*See* Social Principles, ¶ 163A and H.


## 4134. Rights of Farm Workers in the US

And the cries of the *harvesters* have reached the ears of the Lord of Hosts.

—James 5:4b [emphasis added]

Throughout Scripture we are taught the importance of respecting and rewarding work. The prophets decried economic systems that denied workers fair compensation and dignity and Christ's ministry was centered on those individuals marginalized by society. Today, workers whose hands gather the fruits of God's good earth are among the most marginalized – both economically and socially – in our communities. As the cries of the harvesters continue, we are called as a church to respond.

Farm workers are the men women and children who climb for our apples, oranges and peaches, stoop for our cucumbers and strawberries, and dig for our sweet potatoes. Eighty-five percent of fruits and vegetables in the United States are handpicked by some of the nation's most vital workers, essential to the economic well-being of the United States. While conditions have improved for some farm workers through successful, and long-fought, organizing campaigns, the majority of farm workers continue to struggle with low wages, minimal legal protections, and unhealthy work environments.

The average wage of the more than two million farm workers in the United States is $11,000. In some areas workers earn significantly less, often paid by piece rate earning as little as forty cents per bucket of tomatoes or sweet potatoes collected. Women may receive less pay than men for the same work and face sexual discrimination, harassment, and abuse by crew leaders who control their jobs.

Agriculture is consistently ranked as one of the most dangerous occupations in the United States. Farm workers face pesticide risks and suffer from the highest rate of toxic chemical injuries and skin disorders of any workers in the country. Women who work in the fields have given birth to babies with severe birth defects, attributed by many to pesticide exposure. In recent years, workers across the United States have died in fields nationwide from heat exposure combined with lack of drinking water, shade, or breaks.

Farm workers face numerous obstacles to receiving health care including lack of transportation, lack of paid sick leave and risk of job loss if they miss work; only ten percent of farm workers report having employer-provided health insurance. Most farm workers are immigrants who have come to the United States to seek a better life for their families. Many here today were once farmers in their own countries who have been driven from their land, unable to compete with the price of subsidized crops from the United States. At their workplace and in communities in which they live here, these workers face discrimination and exploitation based on ethnicity, socioeconomic and immigration status. An increasing number of farm workers arrive through the H2-A guest worker program, some from as far away as

Thailand. Isolated in remote labor camps without transportation, these workers are in particular need of outreach, support, and ministry from the community.

Farm workers were excluded from federal laws passed in the 1930's to protect workers, such as the National Labor Relations Act and those mandating overtime pay and minimum wage. Few states require overtime pay for farm workers and minimum wage statutes apply to workers on large farms only. Laws designed to protect farm workers are often not enforced. Furthermore, workers often fear firing or deportation if they speak up about abuses.

Farm workers call on us to stand in solidarity with them to change unjust conditions and scripture calls us to respond. As Christians, we cannot sit silently as our brothers and sisters are exploited and abused. We proclaim our outrage at their living and working conditions. Following the teachings of Christ we must ensure that the men and women who harvest our food are invited to share fully in the fruits of their labor.

*The United Methodist Church:*

- publicly denounces any and all mistreatment of farm workers and repents of any complicity that we hold as consumers and often-silent participants in and beneficiaries of an exploitive food production and distribution system;
- demands that employers treat farm workers and their families with dignity and respect; and that corporate processors, food retailers, and restaurants take responsibility in proportion to the power they possess for the treatment of the farm workers in their supply chains;
- calls on the General Board of Church and Society, the General Board of Global Ministries, annual conferences, and local churches to support state and federal legislation that would strengthen the laws protecting farm workers' rights and provide the funding necessary for adequate enforcement of laws protecting farm workers rights, health, and safety;
- celebrates that farm worker organizing campaigns have resulted in labor agreements producing significant change in farm workers lives, including wage increases, benefits, pesticide protection, and treatment with respect;

- commits itself to work in cooperation with the National Farm Worker Ministry whose primary mission is supporting farm workers organizing for justice and empowerment;
- urges annual conferences, especially where farm workers live and work, to use personal and institutional resources to encourage recognition of farm workers' rights to a voice in the agricultural industry, including representation and good faith bargaining;
- urges local churches to identify and reach out to farm workers in their communities, including those in the H2-A guest worker program;
- urges local churches to hold a yearly service to remember and honor farm workers, including worship, education and a call to action; and
- urges the United Methodist Committee on Relief to consider the needs of farm workers when administering relief efforts.

ADOPTED 2008
RESOLUTION #236, 2004 *BOOK OF RESOLUTIONS*
RESOLUTION #223, 2000 *BOOK OF RESOLUTIONS*

*See* Social Principles, ¶ 163H.

## 4135. Rights of Workers

### I. Biblical/Theological Background

Scripture teaches that human beings, created in the image of God, have an innate dignity (Genesis 1:27). God grants dignity to work by commanding human beings to be stewards of the land and to till and keep the earth (Genesis 1:28, 2:15). Work is one way through which human beings exercise their God-given creativity.

Scripture also teaches that an economic system should be ordered so that employees receive justice at their place of work and that concern for right relationships among people and with all of creation should be the heart of any economic system. Society and its institutions are to be structured so that marginalized persons participate fully in the shaping of society and their own future. Both the Old and the New Testaments show God's desire that wealth and prosperity of society be shared. God's covenant with the Jewish people required them to respect the gifts that God gave them and share them with one another. God condemned the bondage and abusive conditions the Pharaoh imposed upon the Israelites. The Hebrew Prophets decried the growing disparities of wealth and poverty. The Book of Acts describes an early Christian community that shared its goods with one another and throughout both Testaments, God's people are urged to give special concern for widows, orphans, and immigrants. The basic principles are clear: all workers should be treated with respect and dignity, disparities of wealth and poverty should be avoided, workers should earn wages that sustain themselves and their families, and employers have a particular responsibility to treat workers fairly and empower them to organize to improve conditions.

The concern of The United Methodist Church for the dignity of workers and the rights of employees to act collectively is stated in the Social Principles. Both employer and union are called to "bargain in good faith within the frame work of the public interest" (¶ 163B). In response to the increasing globalization of the economic system, the widening disparity between rich and poor, and attempts to deprive workers of their fundamental rights, the church reaffirms its position in support of workers and their right to organize.

## II. Historic Witness of The United Methodist Church

Historically, The United Methodist Church has been concerned about the plight of working men and women. In the United States, we were among the first supporters of the labor movement where both lay and clergy members played leadership roles in supporting garment workers, textile workers, farm workers, and factory workers and advocating passage of the Fair Labor Standards Act and the National Labor Relations Act. From our beginnings and across the globe, we have led the way in seeking improved conditions and stronger unions for workers. Through public policy work, shareholder advocacy, and consumer power, the church and its members have sought to influence political and corporate decisions affecting working conditions around the world.

## III. Supporting Workers in the International Economy

Although the phenomenon of globalization has been occurring for hundreds of years, the pace of globalization has increased dramatically with the widespread mobility of capital and labor. Companies are no longer subject to the rules of one country and search the globe for resources, cheap labor, and access to markets. Although there are social, economic, and educational benefits to globalization, workers face many challenges in the new global economy. The rapid process of unchecked globalization in many countries has produced sweatshops, encouraged the contracting out of skilled workers to richer nations, undermined local food production, exacerbated child labor and forced labor, and drawn young people out of rural areas to urban ones or to other countries. Too few multinational corporations have taken leadership in setting higher standards for wages, benefits, and working conditions, and fewer still have supported international workers' right to organize. Workers, governments and the church have had little ability to challenge the negative aspects of rapid globalization and improve working conditions around the world.

Despite the challenges and complexities of engaging in the international arena, The United Methodist Church is a participant in the global economy and thus must witness for justice in the international labor arena. To this end, The United Methodist Church:

1. supports the conventions of the International Labor Organizations that advance safety in the workplace; freedom from bonded or forced labor; the elimination of discrimination in respect to employment and occupation; effective abolition of child labor; fair compensation; just supervision; and the right of collective action for employees in all nations. The United Methodist Church shall continue to seek ratification and enforcement of these conventions;

2. encourages the General Board of Pensions and Health Benefits to continue to invest in companies that set high standards for treatment of workers throughout the world and to file or join shareholder resolutions that encourage such high standards;

3. urges the General Board of Church and Society and the General Board of Global Ministries to partner with United Methodists around the globe and international advocacy organizations such as International Labor Rights Fund to challenge unjust working conditions;

4. urges the United States government to protect the rights of migrant workers through the ratification of the International Convention on the Rights of Migrant Workers and their Families;

5. encourages United Methodist youth groups and mission trips to meet with sweatshop workers, factory workers, farm workers or trade

unions to learn about working conditions and how they can improve conditions through personal actions and advocacy; and

6. lifts up workers in prayer and reaffirms our belief in workers' rights on the Sunday nearest Labor Day or May Day.

### IV. Supporting Living Wages and the Sharing of Prosperity

Since 1908, the church has advocated for a living wage in every industry (1908 Social Creed) and continues to support the rights of workers to share fully in the prosperity of society. Unfortunately, too many workers earn poverty wages with few benefits, and disparities are growing between high wage earners and low-wage earners. Despite rising productivity and profits in recent years, these gains have not been shared by a majority of workers. Therefore, The United Methodist Church:

1. encourages all employers—and especially United Methodist employers – to share prosperity with workers and seek ways to reduce disparity between top and bottom wage earners;

2. supports efforts in the US Congress to raise the minimum wage to a living wage and index it to inflation, expand health care benefits to workers, expand and protect worker pension programs, set core national standards for workers for paid sick days and paid vacation days, and limit mandatory overtime;

3. calls upon the US Department of Labor to expand its targeted investigations of industries that routinely violate wage and hour laws, partner with workers' centers and congregations that are in ministry with low-wage and immigrant workers, and develop new print and online resources for educating workers about their rights in the workplace;

4. affirms efforts by governments to explore new mechanisms and policies to improve standards for wages, benefits and conditions for workers in low-wage jobs;

5. asks United Methodist seminaries to expose seminary students to worker concerns through teaching, internships and field placement opportunities; and

6. urges the General Board of Church and Society and the General Board of Global Ministries to partner with organizations such as the National Farm Worker Ministry and Interfaith Worker Justice to engage United Methodists in education and advocacy to improve wages, benefits and working conditions for workers in low-wage jobs.

## V. Supporting Workers' Right to Organize and Bargain Collectively

The United Methodist Church through its Social Principles recognizes and supports the right of workers to organize into unions of their own choosing and to bargain collectively regarding hours, wages and conditions of employment (Social Principles ¶163B). Workers around the world are finding it harder and harder to form labor unions to achieve economic and social justice in the workplace. Many employers interfere with employees' efforts to exercise their right to unionize by firing or retaliating against union supporters, threatening to close their facilities, or speciously challenging bargaining units or election results.

Affirming its historic position and in response to new challenges facing workers, The United Methodist Church:

1. calls upon United Methodist institutions and organizations to exemplify the teachings found in the Social Principles and to support the right of their employees to organize for collective bargaining;

2. calls upon United Methodist agencies and congregations to use their purchasing and contracting dollars to support employers who pay living wages and support workers' right to organize;

3. encourages all employers to respect workers' right to organize and recognize the inherent power that employers have over workers in most workplaces. This power over workers' livelihoods means that employers must be especially careful not to bully or threaten employees, if workers are indeed to experience a "freedom of association." In particular, employers are encouraged to clearly communicate to their employees that they are neutral on their employees' choice and will deal fairly with any union they select; abide by their employees' decision when a majority has signed union authorization cards or otherwise indicated their desire to be represented by a union, and refrain from using hearings, elections, and appeals as a means for delaying or avoiding representation for their employees. The United Methodist Church is particularly concerned about the unethical practices of locking workers out of their workplaces and permanently replacing striking workers;

4. expresses additional concern about the erosion of rights guaranteed in the United States since 1935 by the National Labor Relations Act and urges adoption of legislation to reclaim these rights. This legislation should allow workers to choose union representation by signing cards, require mediation and binding arbitration if a first contract

agreement is not reached in a reasonable period of time, and expand penalties for employers violating workers' right to organize;

5. calls on all governments to take strong measures to prevent violent attacks against labor organizers and to engage in prompt and full prosecutions whenever such attacks occur; and

6. calls upon all workers and labor unions to refrain from violence, be truthful about employers, and bargain in good faith. We also call upon United Methodists who are union members and leaders to express their Christian witness by promoting a prophetic witness, democratic process, and financial integrity in their unions.

ADOPTED 2008
RESOLUTION #237, 2004 *BOOK OF RESOLUTIONS*
RESOLUTION #224, 2000 *BOOK OF RESOLUTIONS*

*See* Social Principles, ¶ 163B and C.

## 4136. Smithfield Foods, Inc. and Union Organizing

WHEREAS, Smithfield Foods is the largest pork producer and processor in the world, and the Smithfield plant in Tar Heel, NC, is the largest pork processing facility in the world, employing 5,000 workers and slaughtering more than 32,000 hogs a day; and

WHEREAS, Human Rights Watch has found that Smithfield has violated internationally recognized human rights standards by using intimidation, threats, and violence against workers in Tar Heel, NC, for attempting to improve workplace conditions through the formation of a union; and

WHEREAS, previous union elections at Smithfield's Tar Heel, NC, plant in 1994 and 1997 were marred by widespread violations of the law; and

WHEREAS, numerous court rulings show that Smithfield has a history of intimidating, threatening, and harassing workers who engage in union organizing activities to improve plant conditions; and

WHEREAS, Human Rights Watch also reported evidence that shows that Smithfield Packing discourages workers from reporting workplace injuries; and

WHEREAS, reported injuries rose by 200 percent at the plant from 2003 to 2006 according to data from the Occupational Safety and Health Administration; and

WHEREAS, in a report issued by Research Associates of America, many injured Smithfield workers have reported being denied workers compensation benefits for legitimate workplace injuries and/or being terminated after becoming injured on the job; and

WHEREAS, in 2006 Smithfield was found in violation of federal labor law by the National Labor Relations Board for using a now defunct Company Police force to physically assault contracted sanitation workers, cause the false arrest of a worker, and threaten bodily harm in retaliation for legal activities to protest working conditions; and

WHEREAS, a majority of Smithfield workers signed and delivered a petition to the company in August of 2007 asking for union representation and for an election process "without the threats, abuses and interference that we have seen in the past"; and

WHEREAS, the United Food and Commercial Workers Union engaged in six weeks of good faith negotiations with Smithfield at the behest of workers from late August through mid-October of 2007 in an attempt to agree on a free and fair process for a new union election; and

WHEREAS, throughout negotiations with UFCW, Smithfield interfered in workers' organizing efforts by showing an anti-union video to new employees, prominently posting a flier that described union organizers as cockroaches, and collaborating with a consulting firm to air advertisements portraying union organizers as intimidating bullies; and

WHEREAS, The United Methodist Church recognizes and supports the rights of workers to organize and bargain collectively; and

WHEREAS, in 2000 The United Methodist Church adopted resolution #238, which urges all employers to allow their employees to "freely choose whether to unionize or not" and "urges all employers to clearly communicate to their employees that they are neutral on their employees choice, and will deal fairly with any union they select."

Therefore, be it resolved, that The United Methodist Church supports justice for workers at Smithfield Packing; and

Be it further resolved, that we call on Smithfield to agree to remain completely neutral and not discourage workers from choosing union representation at the Tar Heel, NC, plant and resume negotiations with the United Food and Commercial Workers to formulate a neutrality agreement for another union election at the Tar Heel, NC, plant.

Be it further resolved, that we urge annual conferences, local congregations, and clergy to actively support Smithfield workers in this struggle for justice.

*Be it further resolved,* that we will communicate this call for justice to:

1. The United Methodist Church through its board, agencies, conferences, and local congregations, and

2. Larry Pope, CEO and Joseph Luter, III, Chairman of the Board, Smithfield Foods, Inc, 200 Commerce St, Smithfield, VA 23430.

**ADOPTED 2008**

*See* Social Principles, ¶ 163B.

# ¶ 164. V. THE POLITICAL COMMUNITY

While our allegiance to God takes precedence over our allegiance to any state, we acknowledge the vital function of government as a principal vehicle for the ordering of society. Because we know ourselves to be responsible to God for social and political life, we declare the following relative to governments:

*A) Basic Freedoms and Human Rights*—We hold governments responsible for the protection of the rights of the people to free and fair elections and to the freedoms of speech, religion, assembly, communications media, and petition for redress of grievances without fear of reprisal; to the right to privacy; and to the guarantee of the rights to adequate food, clothing, shelter, education, and health care. The form and the leaders of all governments should be determined by exercise of the right to vote guaranteed to all adult citizens. We also strongly reject domestic surveillance and intimidation of political opponents by governments in power and all other misuses of elective or appointive offices. The use of detention and imprisonment for the harassment and elimination of political opponents or other dissidents violates fundamental human rights. Furthermore, the mistreatment or torture, and other cruel, inhumane, and degrading treatment or punishment of persons by governments for any purpose violates Christian teaching and must be condemned and/or opposed by Christians and churches wherever and whenever it occurs.

The Church regards the institution of slavery, the practice and commissioning of genocide, war crimes, crimes against humanity, and aggression as infamous and atrocious evils. Such evils are destructive of humanity, promote impunity, and therefore must be unconditionally prohibited by all governments and shall never be tolerated by the Church.

*B) Political Responsibility*—The strength of a political system depends upon the full and willing participation of its citizens. The church should continually exert a strong ethical influence upon the state, supporting policies and programs deemed to be just and opposing policies and programs that are unjust.

C) *Church and State Relations*—The United Methodist Church has for many years supported the separation of church and state. In some parts of the world this separation has guaranteed the diversity of religious expressions and the freedom to worship God according to each person's conscience. Separation of church and state means no organic union of the two, but it does permit interaction. The state should not use its authority to promote particular religious beliefs (including atheism), nor should it require prayer or worship in the public schools, but it should leave students free to practice their own religious convictions. We believe that the state should not attempt to control the church, nor should the church seek to dominate the state. The rightful and vital separation of church and state, which has served the cause of religious liberty, should not be misconstrued as the abolition of all religious expression from public life.

D) *Freedom of Information*—Citizens of all countries should have access to all essential information regarding their government and its policies. Illegal and unconscionable activities directed against persons or groups by their own governments must not be justified or kept secret, even under the guise of national security.

E) *Education*—We believe that every person has the right to education. We also believe that the responsibility for education of the young rests with the family, faith communities, and the government. In our society, this function can best be fulfilled through public policies that ensure access for all persons to free public elementary and secondary schools and to post-secondary schools of their choice. Persons in our society should not be precluded by financial barriers from access to church-related and other independent institutions of higher education. We affirm the right of public and independent colleges and universities to exist, and we endorse public policies that ensure access and choice and that do not create unconstitutional entanglements between church and state. We believe that colleges and universities are to ensure that academic freedom is protected for all members of the academic community and a learning environment is fostered that allows for a free exchange of ideas. We affirm the joining of reason and faith; therefore, we urge colleges and universities to guard the expression of religious life on campus.

¶ 164

*F) Civil Obedience and Civil Disobedience*—Governments and laws should be servants of God and of human beings. Citizens have a duty to abide by laws duly adopted by orderly and just process of government. But governments, no less than individuals, are subject to the judgment of God. Therefore, we recognize the right of individuals to dissent when acting under the constraint of conscience and, after having exhausted all legal recourse, to resist or disobey laws that they deem to be unjust or that are discriminately enforced. Even then, respect for law should be shown by refraining from violence and by being willing to accept the costs of disobedience. We do not encourage or condone any form of violent protest as a legitimate exercise of free speech or civil disobedience. We offer our prayers for those in rightful authority who serve the public, and we support their efforts to afford justice and equal opportunity for all people. We assert the duty of churches to support those who suffer because of their stands of conscience represented by nonviolent beliefs or acts. We urge governments to ensure civil rights, as defined by the International Covenant on Civil and Political Rights, to persons in legal jeopardy because of those nonviolent acts.

*G) The Death Penalty*—We believe the death penalty denies the power of Christ to redeem, restore, and transform all human beings. The United Methodist Church is deeply concerned about crime throughout the world and the value of any life taken by a murder or homicide. We believe all human life is sacred and created by God and therefore, we must see all human life as significant and valuable. When governments implement the death penalty (capital punishment), then the life of the convicted person is devalued and all possibility of change in that person's life ends. We believe in the resurrection of Jesus Christ and that the possibility of reconciliation with Christ comes through repentance. This gift of reconciliation is offered to all individuals without exception and gives all life new dignity and sacredness. For this reason, we oppose the death penalty (capital punishment) and urge its elimination from all criminal codes.

¶ 164

*H) Criminal and Restorative Justice*—To protect all persons from encroachment upon their personal and property rights, governments have established mechanisms of law enforcement and courts. A wide array of sentencing options serves to express community outrage, incapacitate dangerous offenders, deter crime, and offer opportunities for rehabilitation. We support governmental measures designed to reduce and eliminate crime that are consistent with respect for the basic freedom of persons.

We reject all misuse of these mechanisms, including their use for the purpose of revenge or for persecuting or intimidating those whose race, appearance, lifestyle, economic condition, or beliefs differ from those in authority. We reject all careless, callous, or discriminatory enforcement of law that withholds justice from persons with disabilities and all those who do not speak the language of the country in which they are in contact with the law enforcement. We further support measures designed to remove the social conditions that lead to crime, and we encourage continued positive interaction between law enforcement officials and members of the community at large.

In the love of Christ, who came to save those who are lost and vulnerable, we urge the creation of a genuinely new system for the care and restoration of victims, offenders, criminal justice officials, and the community as a whole. Restorative justice grows out of biblical authority, which emphasizes a right relationship with God, self, and community. When such relationships are violated or broken through crime, opportunities are created to make things right.

Most criminal justice systems around the world are retributive. These retributive justice systems profess to hold the offender accountable to the state and use punishment as the equalizing tool for accountability. In contrast, restorative justice seeks to hold the offender accountable to the victimized person, and to the disrupted community. Through God's transforming power, restorative justice seeks to repair the damage, right the wrong, and bring healing to all involved, including the victim, the offender, the families, and the community. The Church is transformed when it responds to the claims of discipleship by becoming an agent of healing and systemic change.

*I) Military Service*—We deplore war and urge the peaceful settlement of all disputes among nations. From the beginning, the Christian conscience has struggled with the harsh realities of violence and war, for these evils clearly frustrate God's loving purposes for humankind. We yearn for the day when there will be no more war and people will live together in peace and justice. Some of us believe that war, and other acts of violence, are never acceptable to Christians. We also acknowledge that many Christians believe that, when peaceful alternatives have failed, the force of arms may regretfully be preferable to unchecked aggression, tyranny, and genocide. We honor the witness of pacifists who will not allow us to become complacent about war and violence. We also respect those who support the use of force, but only in extreme situations and only when the need is clear beyond reasonable doubt, and through appropriate international organizations. We urge the establishment of the rule of law in international affairs as a means of elimination of war, violence, and coercion in these affairs.

We reject national policies of enforced military service as incompatible with the gospel. We acknowledge the agonizing tension created by the demand for military service by national governments. We urge all young adults to seek the counsel of the Church as they reach a conscientious decision concerning the nature of their responsibility as citizens. Pastors are called upon to be available for counseling with all young adults who face conscription or who are considering voluntary enlistment in the armed forces, including those who conscientiously refuse to cooperate with a system of conscription.

We support and extend the ministry of the Church to those persons who conscientiously oppose all war, or any particular war, and who therefore refuse to serve in the armed forces or to cooperate with systems of military conscription. We also support and extend the Church's ministry to those persons who conscientiously choose to serve in the armed forces or to accept alternative service. As Christians we are aware that neither the way of military action, nor the way of inaction is always righteous before God.

¶ 163

# V. THE POLITICAL COMMUNITY
# THE RESOLUTIONS

## BASIC FREEDOMS

### 5001. Taking Liberties: On the Stifling of Dissent

The Social Principles affirm, "We hold governments responsible for the protection of the rights of the people" (¶ 164A). Yet governments often use wartime and/or perceived threats to national security to justify restrictions on civil rights, immigrant rights, and the right to express political dissent.

In ancient Egypt, Pharaoh appealed to a mixture of patriotic loyalty and national security fears to justify the repression of immigrants: "Come let us deal shrewdly with them, or they will . . . in the event of war, join our enemies and fight against us and escape from the land" (Exodus 1:10).

The prophet Jeremiah, like many of the other biblical prophets, voiced his dissent to the unjust practices of his government during war. The powers-that-be repeatedly condemned Jeremiah, charging him with "desertion" (Jeremiah 37:13-15). The prophets invariably faced beatings, imprisonment, and death threats for their political dissent in times of national crisis (*See* 1 Kings 22:13-27; Jeremiah 20:10; 26:11; 37:13-18; 38:4; Psalm 120).

The early church often faced beatings, imprisonment, and death for their religious and political dissent. The early church, as a religious minority, was frequently accused of being a political opposition group that must be suppressed: *see* Acts 6:11 on charges brought against Stephen. In Acts 17, early Christians are accused: "They are all acting contrary to the decrees of the emperor"(17:7).

Yet in the midst of repression, Paul affirms the importance of due process respect for civil liberties. He insists that government officials acknowledge their own human rights violations: " 'They have beaten us in public, uncondemned, men who are Roman citizens . . . and now are they going to discharge us in secret? Certainly not! Let them come and take us out themselves.' So they came and apologized to them" (Acts 16:37, 39).

The recent US-led "war on terrorism," the USA PATRIOT Act ("Uniting and Strengthening America by Providing Appropriate Tools Required to Intercept and Obstruct Terrorism") legislation, the creation of military tribunals which lack due process or independent means of appeal, as well as draft legislation known as PATRIOT Act II, or the Domestic Security Enhancement Act, have created a political climate in which an increasing number of governments have adopted executive orders and legislation restricting the rights of immigrants and opposition groups. Such measures include:

- use of "unlawful combatants" to designate political opposition,
- detention without charges or a trial,
- use of secret evidence and secret hearings,
- expanded wiretap and government surveillance,
- denial of access to legal counsel,
- deportation of asylum seekers, refugees and others who face persecution in their home country,
- use of racial and religious profiling,
- threatening to strip someone's citizenship,
- denying rights of peaceable assembly and freedom of speech based on political beliefs,
- use of military tribunals that lack due process and independent judicial review, and
- the combination of restrictive government measures with appeals to unquestioning patriotic loyalty often foster a climate of mounting intolerance and repression against foreigners and any who voice peaceful political dissent.

The international human rights organization, Human Rights Watch, has compiled a report entitled, "Opportunism in the Face of Tragedy: Repression in the name of anti-terrorism." (www.hrw.org) The report analyzes various repressive laws and measures adopted by 17 nations in the name of fighting terrorism. In reality, most of these measures seek to stifle internal political and religious dissent, as well as restrict the rights of refugees, asylum seekers, and foreigners. Those who are targeted are often the most vulnerable and violated in a society.

Legitimate security concerns of any nation are best met by upholding and protecting the full human rights of all, including the rights of political opposition, immigrants, and minority groups. The church has a long history of advocating and protecting the rights of religious and political dissent.

Even in a context of heightened fears and violence, The Social Principles clearly declare, "We also strongly reject domestic surveillance and intimidation of political opponents by governments in power. . . . The use of detention and imprisonment for the harassment and elimination of political opponents or other dissidents violates fundamental human rights" (¶ 164*A*).

We affirm the prophetic tradition of dissent and call on all United Methodists to publicly speak out for the protection of all human rights for all—including the right to dissent through peaceable assembly, freedom of the press, freedom of speech and other nonviolent means.

We call for the following actions:

- local congregations to undertake educational efforts (studying the Social Principles ¶ 164, the Universal Declaration of Human Rights, and the US Bill of Rights) to promote greater understanding of international human rights and civil liberties, especially the rights of immigrants, political opposition groups and religious minorities, and that these educational programs build toward the 60th anniversary of the Universal Declaration of Human Rights on December 10, 2008;

- General Board of Global Ministries and General Board of Church and Society, working with national and international civil liberties and human rights organizations, such as the Center for Constitutional Rights, Amnesty International, Human Rights Watch, and American Civil Liberties Union, to develop resources and advocacy materials for use in local congregations, to: 1) monitor potentially restrictive government measures that effect people's civil liberties; 2) challenge repressive legislation and executive orders already in place (such as ones listed above); and 3) protect the rights of peaceful dissent;

- to call on the US government and all other national governments to submit timely reports on their compliance with the International Covenant on Civil and Political Rights and the UN Convention Against Torture, and that governments especially document steps taken to insure full civil liberties to religious and political minority groups, immigrants, and the right to peaceful dissent; and

- local congregations, working with others in their communities, organize to defend civil liberties by encouraging local authorities to adopt Civil Liberties Safe Zone resolutions, and by forming local Bill of Rights (or Human Rights) defense committees to create a climate of tolerance and respect for different views.

ADOPTED 2004
READOPTED 2008
RESOLUTION #240, 2004 *BOOK OF RESOLUTIONS*

*See* Social Principles, ¶ 164*A* and *F*.

# CHURCH AND STATE

## 5011. Church Is a Weapon-Free Zone

WHEREAS, in keeping with the spirit of Isaiah 2:4: God shall judge between the nations, and shall arbitrate for many peoples; they shall beat their swords into plowshares, and their spears into pruning hooks; nation shall not lift up sword against nation, neither shall they learn war any more;

WHEREAS, reflecting the church's traditional role as a place of safety and sanctuary,

*Therefore,* every United Methodist church is officially declared a weapon-free zone.

ADOPTED 2000
READOPTED 2008
RESOLUTION #241, 2004 *BOOK OF RESOLUTIONS*
RESOLUTION #227, 2000 *BOOK OF RESOLUTIONS*

*See* Social Principles, ¶ 164.

## 5012. Church-Government Relations

In Luke 20:20-26, the teachers of the law and the scribes sent "spies" to watch Jesus closely hoping to entrap him in either a theological or political error. They asked him whether or not it was right to pay taxes to Caesar. Considering that taxes were a means of Roman oppression and the inscription on the coin represented submission to Caesar, this is a dangerous question for Jesus. For the Israelites suffering under Roman imperialism, to answer in the affirmative would imply that Roman colonization is an appropriate form of governance and that God's people should accept whatever form of government, no matter how repressive, they find themselves under. However, we know that Jesus did not uphold the right of government to oppress its people because he was brought before Pilate on charges of treason, which he never refuted (Luke 23:1-2). If Jesus had answered the question negatively he would have been openly calling for revolt against the ability of Rome to tax its people. In Jesus' answer, "Then give to the emperor the things that are the emperor's, and to God what is God's," he refuses to incriminate himself through the questions of those out to trap him. We know that Scripture presents various examples and ways for the people of God to relate with the governing authorities. Jesus does not call his followers to open revolt although there are times when biblical faithfulness will necessitate civil disobedience to the ruling authorities (Acts 4:1-20). Jesus does not call his followers to submit blindly to all governing authorities although there are times when biblical faithfulness necessitates compliance (Romans 13:5-6). While declaring our ultimate allegiance is to God, Scripture recognizes that faithfulness to God requires political engagement by the people of God. The nature of this engagement is determined by the particular situation and biblical faithfulness. The Social Principles of The United Methodist Church assert: "We believe that the state should not attempt to control the church, nor should the church seek to dominate the state. `Separation of church and state' means no organic union of the two, but it does permit interaction. The church should continually exert a strong ethical influence upon the state, supporting policies and programs deemed to be just and opposing policies and programs that are unjust" (¶ 164B).

As we consider the religious protections of the First Amendment of the US Constitution—the free exercise and nonestablishment of religion—we are profoundly grateful for the major statement made by the 1968 General Conference on "Church/Government Relations." In recognizing that debt, we reaffirm the substance of that declaration.

## A Statement Concerning Church-Government Relations and Education

The fundamental purpose of universal public education at the elementary and secondary levels is to provide equal and adequate educational opportunities for all children and young people, and thereby ensure the nation an enlightened citizenry.

We believe in the principle of universal public education, and we reaffirm our support of public educational institutions. At the same time, we recognize and pledge our continued allegiance to the US constitutional principle that citizens have a right to establish and maintain private schools from private resources so long as such schools meet public standards of quality. Such schools have made a genuine contribution to society. We do not support the expansion or the strengthening of private schools with public funds. Furthermore, we oppose the establishment or strengthening of private schools that jeopardize the public school system or thwart valid public policy.

We specifically oppose tuition tax credits, school vouchers, or any other mechanism that directly or indirectly allows government funds to support religious schools at the primary and secondary level. Persons of one particular faith should be free to use their own funds to strengthen the belief system of their particular religious group. They should not, however, expect all taxpayers, including those who adhere to other religious belief systems, to provide funds to teach religious views with which they do not agree.

To fulfill the government's responsibility in education, sometimes government and nonpublic educational institutions need to enter a cooperative relationship. But public funds should be used only in the best interests of the whole society. Extreme caution must be exercised to ensure that religious institutions do not receive any aid directly or indirectly for the maintenance of their religious expression or the expansion of their institutional resources. Such funds must be used for the express purpose of fulfilling a strictly public responsibility, and should be subject to public accountability.

By providing a setting for contact at an early age between children of vastly different backgrounds, public schools have often been an important unifying force in modern pluralistic society. We recognize in particular that persons of all religious backgrounds may have insight into the nature of ultimate reality, which will help to enrich the common life. It is therefore essential that the public schools take seriously the religious integrity of each child entrusted to their care.

Public schools may not properly establish any preferred form of religion for common exercises of worship, religious observance, or study. At the same time, however, education should provide an opportunity for the examination of the various religious traditions of humankind.

We believe that every person has a right to an education, including higher education, commensurate with his or her ability. It is society's responsibility to enable every person to enjoy this right. Public and private institutions should cooperate to provide for these educational opportunities.

Freedom of inquiry poses a risk for established ideas, beliefs, programs, and institutions. We accept that risk in the faith that all truth is of God. Colleges and universities can best perform their vital tasks of adding to knowledge and to the perception of truth in an atmosphere of genuine academic freedom.

We affirm the principle that freedom to inquire, to discuss, and to teach should be regulated by the self-discipline of scholarship and the critical examination of ideas in the context of free public dialogue, rather than by censorship by supervisors, school boards, or any control imposed by churches, governments, or other organizations. In the educational process, individuals have the right to appropriate freely for themselves what they believe is real, important, useful, and satisfying.

Experience has demonstrated that freedom to inquire, to discuss, and to teach is best preserved when colleges and universities are not dependent upon a single base or a few sources of support. When an educational institution relies upon multiple sources of financial support, and where those sources tend to balance one another, the institution is in a position to resist undue pressures toward control exerted from any one source of support. In the case of church-related colleges and universities, we believe that tuitions; scholarships; investment return; bequests; payments for services rendered; loans; government grants; and gifts from individuals, business corporations, foundations, and churches should be sought and accepted in as great a variety as possible. Care must be exercised to ensure that all support from any of these sources is free from conditions that hinder the college or university in the maintenance of freedom of inquiry and expression for its faculty and students.

We are very much aware of the dangers of church-sponsored colleges and universities being overly dependent upon government funding. However, we are also aware that given the independent thought of most college students today, there is little danger of using government funds to indoctrinate students with religious beliefs. Therefore, institutions of higher learning should feel free to receive government funds (except for religious teaching and structures for worship). At the same time, they should be eternally cognizant of the dangers of accompanying government oversight that might threaten the religious atmosphere or special independent character of church-sponsored educational institutions.

No church-sponsored higher education institution should become so dependent upon government grants, research projects, or support programs, that its academic freedom is jeopardized, its responsibility for social criticism (including criticism of governments) inhibited, or its spiritual values denied.

We recognize that the freedom necessary to the existence of a college or university in the classical sense may be threatened by forces other than those involved in the nature and source of the institution's financial support. Institutional freedom may be adversely affected by governmental requirements of loyalty oaths from teachers and students, by public interference with the free flow of information, or by accreditation and certification procedures and requirements aimed at dictating the content of college and university curricula.

With respect to church-related institutions of higher education, we deplore any ecclesiastical attempts to manipulate inquiry or the dissemination of knowledge, to use the academic community for the promotion of any particular point of view, to require ecclesiastical loyalty oaths designed to protect cherished truth claims, or to inhibit the social action activities of members of the academic community. We call upon all members of The United Methodist Church, in whatever capacity they may serve, to be especially sensitive to the need to protect individual and institutional freedom and responsibility in the context of the academic community.

We are persuaded that there may be circumstances or conditions in which the traditional forms of tax immunities granted to colleges and universities may be a necessary requirement for their freedom. Therefore, we urge a continuation of the public policy of granting reasonable and nondiscriminatory tax immunities to all private colleges and universities, including those that are related to churches.

We believe that colleges and universities should consider the benefits, services, and protections that they receive from the community and its governmental agencies and should examine their obligations to the community in the light of this support. We believe it is imperative that all church-related institutions of higher education determine on their own initiative what benefits, services, and opportunities they ought to provide for the community as a whole, as distinct from their usual campus constituencies.

### A Statement Concerning Church-Government Relations and Governmental Chaplaincies

We recognize that military and public institutional chaplaincies represent efforts to provide for the religious needs of people for whom both churches and governments are responsible. We recognize that in such a broad and complex undertaking there are bound to exist real and serious tensions that produce genuine uneasiness on the part of government officials as well as church leaders. Great patience and skill are required to effect necessary accommodations with understanding and without compromising religious liberty.

We believe that there are both ethical and constitutional standards that must be observed by governments in the establishment and operation of public chaplaincies. At a minimum, those standards are as follows:

First, the only obligation that governments have is to ensure the provision of opportunities for military personnel, patients of hospitals, and inmates of correctional institutions to engage in religious worship or have access to religious nurture.

Second, participation in religious activities must be on a purely voluntary basis; there must be neither penalties for nonparticipation nor any rewards for participation.

Third, no preferential treatment should be given any particular church, denomination, or religious group in the establishment and administration of governmental chaplaincies.

Fourth, considerable care should be exercised in the role assignments of chaplains so they are not identified as the enforcers of morals. Precaution should also be taken to avoid chaplains being given duties not clearly related to their primary tasks.

Standards should be maintained to protect the integrity of both churches and governments. The practice of staffing governmental chaplaincies with clergy personnel who have ecclesiastical endorsement should be continued. The practice of terminating the services of such personnel in any instance where it becomes necessary for ecclesiastical endorsement to be withdrawn should also be continued.

Supervision of clergy personnel in the performance of their religious services in governmental chaplaincies should be clearly effected through ecclesiastical channels with the cooperation of the public agencies and institutions involved. In the performance of these administrative functions, churches and agencies of government have an obligation to be fair and responsible and to ensure that due process is observed in all proceedings.

The role of a governmental chaplain should be primarily pastoral but with important priestly, prophetic, and teaching roles. The chaplain has an obligation to perform these ministries in as broad an ecumenical context as possible. A chaplain is responsible for the spiritual welfare and religious life of all the personnel of the military unit or the public institution to which he or she is assigned.

There are many persons, and some groups, whose personal religious practices or whose church's rules make it impossible for them to accept the direct ministry of a particular chaplain. In such instances, the chaplain, to the full extent of his or her powers, has an obligation to make provision for worship by these persons or groups. A chaplain is expected to answer specific questions by members of faith groups other than his or her own. Chaplains must know the basic tenets of their denominations in order to protect such members in the expression and development of their faith. The absence of parochialism on the part of a chaplain is more than an attitude; it necessitates specific, detailed, and accurate knowledge regarding many religions.

The churches should strive to make public chaplaincies integral expressions of their ministry and to face the implications of this for supervision and budget. The chaplain represents the church by affirming the dignity of all persons in military service through the chaplain's function in upholding their freedom of religion and conscience. Every person exists within a broader set of values than those of the military, and within a broader spectrum of responsibilities than those created by military orders. The chaplain is a bearer of the gospel to affirm the freedom of the individual and represents The United Methodist Church at that point of tension. Whether the freedom of the gospel is compromised or limited may be a result of either external pressures or internal submission, or both. Failure to sustain the freedom of the gospel lies within any human system or any individual. It is the task of the church to confront prophetically institutions or chaplains who compromise the gospel. The United Methodist Church provides presence, oversight, and support to chaplains who risk ministry in such a setting.

There are degrees of tension in present arrangements whereby a chaplain is a commissioned officer of the armed forces or an employee of a public institution. As such, he or she is a member of the staff of the military commander or of the director of the public institution involved. Government regulations and manuals describe him or her as the adviser on religion, morals, morale, and welfare. Therefore, we believe it is the chaplain's duty in faithfulness to his or her religious commitments to act in accordance with his or her conscience and to make such viewpoints known in organizational matters affecting the total welfare of the people for whom the chaplain has any responsibility. The chaplain has the obligation and should have the opportunity to express his or her dissent within the structures in which the chaplain works, in instances where he or she feels this is necessary. With respect to such matters, it is the obligation of religious bodies to give the chaplain full support.

Churches must encourage chaplains who serve in the armed forces to resist the exaltation of power and its exercise for its own sake. They must also encourage chaplains who serve in public institutions to maintain sensitivity to human anguish. Churches and chaplains have an obligation to speak out conscientiously against the unforgiving and intransigent spirit in people and nations wherever and whenever it appears.

### A Statement Concerning Church-Government Relations and Tax Exemption

We believe that governments recognize the unique category of religious institutions. To be in this unique category is not a privilege held by these institutions for their own benefit or self-glorification but is an acknowledgment of their special identity designed to protect their independence and to enable them to serve humankind in a way not expected of other types of institutions.

We urge churches to consider at least the following factors in determining their response to the granting of immunity from property taxes:

1. responsibility to make appropriate contributions for essential services provided by government; and

2. the danger that churches become so dependent upon government that they compromise their integrity or fail to exert their critical influence upon public policy.

We support the abolition of all special privileges accorded to members of the clergy in US tax laws and regulations and call upon the churches to deal with the consequent financial implications for their ministers. Conversely, we believe that all forms of discrimination against members of the clergy in US tax legislation and administrative regulations should be discontinued. We believe that the status of an individual under ecclesiastical law or practice ought not to be the basis of governmental action either granting or withholding a special tax benefit.

## A Statement Concerning Church Participation in Providing Social Services

We believe that all the organizations and resources of the private sector, as well as those of governments, should be taken into account in the formulation and execution of social welfare policies.

We recognize that appropriate government bodies have the right to prescribe minimum standards for all public and private social welfare agencies. We believe that no private agency, because of its religious affiliations, ought to be exempted from any of the requirements of such standards.

Governmental provision of material support for church-related agencies inevitably raises important questions of religious establishment. In recognition, however, that some health, education, and welfare agencies have been founded by churches without regard to religious proselytizing, we consider that such agencies may, under certain circumstances, be proper channels for public programs in these fields. When government provides support for programs administered by private agencies, it has the most serious obligation to establish and enforce standards guaranteeing the equitable administration of such programs and the accountability of such agencies to the public authority. In particular, we believe that government resources should not be provided to any church-related agency unless it meets the following minimum criteria:

1. The services to be provided by the church-related agency shall meet a genuine community need.

2. The services of the agency shall be designed and administered in such a way as to avoid serving a sectarian purpose or interest.

3. The services to be provided by the agency shall be available to all persons without regard to race, color, national origin, creed, or political persuasion.

4. The services to be rendered by the agency shall be performed in accordance with accepted professional and administrative standards.

5. Skill, competence, and integrity in the performance of duties shall be the principal considerations in the employment of personnel and shall not be superseded by any requirement of religious affiliation.

6. The right to collective bargaining shall be recognized by the agency.

We recognize that all of the values involved in the sponsorship of a social welfare agency by a church may not be fully expressed if that agency has to rely permanently on access to government resources for its existence. We are also aware that under certain circumstances, sponsorship of a social welfare agency by a church may inhibit the development of comprehensive welfare services in the community. Therefore, the church and the agency should choose which pattern of service to offer: (1) channeling standardized and conventional services supplied or supported by government, or (2) attempting experimental or unconventional ministries and criticizing government programs when they prove inadequate. We believe that these two patterns are difficult, if not impossible, to combine in the same agency, and that the choice between them should be made before dependence upon government resources makes commitment to the first pattern irreversible. In their efforts to meet human needs, churches should never allow their preoccupation with remedial programs under their own direction to divert them or the larger community from a common search for basic solutions. In dealing with the elimination of the conditions of poverty and hunger, churches should have no stake in programs that contribute to promote dependency or embody attitudes and practices that fail to promote self-sufficiency.

We believe that churches have a moral obligation to challenge violations of the civil rights of the poor and marginalized. They should direct their efforts toward helping the poor overcome the powerlessness that makes such violations of civil rights possible. Specifically, churches should protest such policies and practices by welfare personnel as unwarranted invasions of privacy and oppose any requirement of attendance at church activities in order to qualify for social services.

*A Statement Concerning Church Participation in Public Affairs*

We recognize that churches exist within the body politic, along with numerous other forms of human association. Like other social groups, their existence affects, and is affected by, governments. We believe that churches have the right and the duty to speak and act corporately on those matters of public policy that involve basic moral or ethical issues and questions. Any concept of, or action regarding, church-government relations that denies churches this role in the body politic strikes at the very core of religious liberty.

The attempt to influence the formation and execution of public policy at all levels of government is often the most effective means available to churches to keep before humanity the ideal of a society in which power and order are made to serve the ends of justice and freedom for all people. Through such social action churches generate new ideas, challenge certain goals and methods, and help rearrange the emphasis on particular values in ways that facilitate the adoption and implementation of specific policies and programs that promote the goals of a responsible society.

We believe that any action that would deny the church the right to act corporately on public policy matters threatens religious liberty. We therefore oppose inclusion of churches in any lobby disclosure legislation.

This does not mean, in any way, that we wish to hide actions taken by the church on public issues. On the contrary, we are usually proud of such actions. It does recognize, however, that the church is already responding to members who request information with respect to church action on public policy questions. In effect, in accordance with legislation enacted by the 1976 General Conference, The United Methodist Church already has its own lobby disclosure provisions in place.

It is quite another matter, however, for the government to insist that it must know everything about what a church is saying in its private communications with its own members.

When the US Supreme Court acted in the 1971 landmark case of *Lemon* v. *Kartzman* (403 US 602, 612-13), the Court applied a test to determine the constitutionality of legislation on First Amendment grounds as it deals with religion. Among its three criteria were these two: (1) its principal or primary effect must neither advance nor inhibit religion; (2) the statute must not foster an excessive government entanglement with religion.

Lobby disclosure legislation before the US Congress over the last several years has required: (1) extremely burdensome record keeping and reporting of all legislative activity; (2) reporting of contributions of churches giving $3,000 or more annually to a national body if a part of this is used for legislative action; (3) criminal penalties with up to two years in jail for violations; and (4) unwarranted subpoena powers to investigate church records.

Legislation that passed the House in 1978 would have required detailed records of expenditures of twenty-two items. As such, it would have been burdensome and would inhibit religion in that The United Methodist Church would have been severely handicapped in implementing its Social Principles due to being neutralized by minutia.

Furthermore, if the government insists on knowing everything the church is doing on public policy questions over a five-year period (as was required) and imposes a criminal sentence for violations, this could inhibit religion to the extent that the church might be tempted to limit severely its activity to avoid noncompliance.

If the government is going to require that religious groups keep burdensome records and make voluminous reports, and there is some question as to whether the churches are complying, federal authorities would be authorized to step in and check church records and files. Such action would undoubtedly represent an unconstitutional excessive government entanglement with religion.

The United Methodist Church would have great difficulty in complying with the provision that all organizational contributions of $3,000 annually be reported if some of these funds are used for lobbying. Since local churches contribute generously to the World Service Fund, and a small portion of those funds is used for legislative action, this brings our church under coverage of this provision. Such a requirement could mean that reports of contributions of some 30,000 United Methodist churches would have to be made to the government shortly after the close of each year. This could not be done, and we would be in violation, having knowingly omitted material facts required to be disclosed. As a result, church officials would be subject to criminal penalties of up to two years in prison.

For these reasons, we oppose lobby disclosure measures for the churches. In its most stringent form, legislation such as this would inhibit our free exercise of religion. It would be impossible for the church to comply with certain provisions, thus subjecting our church leaders to criminal penalties.

We believe that churches must behave responsibly in the arena of public affairs. Responsible behavior requires adherence to ethically sound substantive and procedural norms.

Churches should seek to enlarge and clarify the ethical grounds of public discourse and to identify and define the foreseeable consequences of available choices of public policy.

In participating in the arena of public affairs, churches are not inherently superior to other participants; hence the stands that they take on particular issues of public policy are not above question or criticism.

Responsible behavior in the arena of public affairs requires churches to accept the fact that in dealing with complex issues of public policy, good intentions and high ideals need to be combined with as much practical and technical knowledge of politics and economics as possible.

Another norm of responsible behavior derives from the fact that no particular public policy that may be endorsed by churches at a given point in time should be regarded as an ultimate expression of Christian ethics in society. Churches should not assume that any particular social pattern, political order, or economic ideology represents a complete embodiment of the Christian ethic.

When churches speak to government, they also bear the responsibility to speak to their own memberships. Cultivation of ethically informed public opinion is particularly crucial in local congregations. It is essential to responsible behavior that procedures be established and maintained to ensure full, frank, and informed discussion by religious groups within the arena of public affairs. In the present period of human history, attention should be given to the dignity of every person, and appeal should be made to the consciences of all persons. Churches must acknowledge and respect the role of the laity as well as the clergy in determining their behavior in the arena of public affairs.

Because of their commitment to unity, and in the interest of an effective strategy, churches should, to the maximum extent feasible, coordinate their own efforts and, where appropriate, cooperate with other organizations when they seek to influence properly the formation and execution of public policy at all levels of government.

Finally, churches should not seek to utilize the processes of public affairs to further their own institutional interests or to obtain special privileges for themselves.

United Methodism is a part of the universal church. In the formulation and expression of the United Methodist voice in public affairs, we must listen to the concerns and insights of church members and churches in all nations. It is imperative that our expressions and actions be informed by participation in the universal church.

With particular reference to The United Methodist Church and public affairs, we express the following convictions: Connectional units of the denomination (such as General Conference, jurisdictional conference, annual conference, local congregation, or general board or agency) should continue to exercise the right to advocate government policies that involve basic moral or ethical issues or questions. In exercising this right, each such connectional unit, or any other official group within The United Methodist Church, should always make explicit for whom or in whose name it speaks or acts in the arena of public affairs. Only the General Conference is competent to speak or act in the name of The United Methodist Church.

ADOPTED 1980
AMENDED AND READOPTED 2000
AMENDED AND READOPTED 2008
RESOLUTION #242, 2004 *BOOK OF RESOLUTIONS*
RESOLUTION #228, 2000 *BOOK OF RESOLUTIONS*

*See* Social Principles, ¶ 164*A* and *E.*

### 5013. Separation of Church and State

We believe in the Christian church, the community of God's people founded on the confession of Christ. Jesus is the head of the body, the universal church, which is united by its common faith in Him. The church participates in the worship of God, the fellowship and training of believers, and the spread of God's love in the world. This ministry of God's love continues in the church as people are called to love and to bring together those who are separated from God and each other (Matthew 16:16-18; John 3:16-17; 2 Corinthians 5:14-20). On the other hand, we believe that government is an institution established by God for the welfare of society. Government, as many other things in creation, is a part of God's common grace to humanity. This is a grace where all members of society benefit, whether they are Christians or not. Wayne Grudem has said, "Human government is also a result of common grace. . . . One of the primary means God uses to restrain evil in the world is human government."

There are several places in Scripture that help us understand this gracious act of God. In the Flood story (Genesis 9:6ff) God reestablishes God's covenant with Noah and sets forth the truth of the sanctity of life. The Bible does not speak much of the role of civil government; however, when it does it gives us a clear idea as to the reason God has for the establishment of governments and its leaders (*see* 1 Samuel 10:17-25). For the biblical tradition the role of the government (as seen through the work of the kings and leaders) was very clear.

The psalmist says regarding kings and rulers: "Endow the king with your justice, O God, / the royal son with your righteousness. / He will judge your people in righteousness, / your afflicted ones with justice. . . . / He will defend the afflicted among the people / and save the children of the needy; / he will crush the oppressor" (Psalm 72:1-2, 4, NIV). Thus the prayer for the king continued by describing the task of the rulers (i.e., governments): "For [they] will deliver the needy who cry out, / the afflicted who have no one to help. / [They] will take pity on the weak and the needy / and save the needy from death. / [They] will rescue them from oppression and violence, / for precious is their blood in [their] sight" (Psalm 72:12-14, NIV). And, thus, adds Isaiah regarding the ruler whom God will bring: "But with righteousness [they] will judge the needy, / with justice [they] will give decisions for the poor of the earth. . . . / Righteousness will be [their] belt / and faithfulness the sash around [their] waist" (Isaiah 11:4-5, NIV; *see also* Isaiah 3:14; 1 Kings 3:8-9; Proverbs 8:14-16; Daniel 4:32).

The fact that God allows for the establishment of governments cannot be interpreted to mean that they are all good, as we can see in Scripture. As a matter of fact many governments act contradicting God's will. The reality is that governments fail as human beings fail to live according to God's will. Nevertheless, God uses governments for God's purposes. In the New Testament we also see the important role that governments play according to Paul. When Paul speaks of those in authority he states: "For he is God's servant to do you good. But if you do wrong, be afraid, for he does not bear the sword for nothing. He is God's servant, an agent of wrath to bring punishment on the wrongdoer. Therefore, it is necessary to submit to the authorities, not only because of possible punishment but also because of conscience. This is also why you pay taxes, for the authorities are God's servants, who give their full time to governing" (Romans 13:4-7, NIV).

The above in no way equates God and government, on the contrary there is no way to reconcile God's purpose for government with a government that acts contrary to God's will. There are many examples where governments pervert this God-given authority. It is in situations such as this where the prophetic voice of the church best honors its responsibility to the state, and its faithfulness to the gospel, by calling the state to accountability. Christians must become the conscience of government, in the best sense of the prophetic tradition. As Martin Luther King, Jr. once stated: "The church must be reminded that it is not the master or the servant of the state, but rather the conscience of the state. It must be the guide and the critic of the state, and never its tool." Over the years The United Methodist Church has come to a clearer understanding of this relationship. Hence, our church has historically supported the separation of church and state and the free exercise of religion because of our direct experience of exclusion and persecution, due to religious intolerance and bigotry. During the early years of the republic The Methodist Church was seen as a group of outsiders and as an inconsequential religious body that was not part of the Protestant establishment, thus resulting in the exclusion of the Methodist preachers from many towns and pulpits in many places around the new nation.

This experience, which the Methodists shared with the Baptists, Moravians, and a few other nonestablishment religious groups of the time, helped the Methodists to affirm the need to support the first constitutional amendment: "Congress shall make no laws respecting an establishment of religion or prohibiting the free exercise thereof" (also known as the establishment clause).

The Social Principles of The United Methodist Church assert: "We believe that the state should not attempt to control the church, nor should the church seek to dominate the state. 'Separation of church and state' means no organic union of the two, but it does permit interaction. The church should continually exert a strong ethical influence upon the state, supporting policies and programs deemed to be just and opposing policies and programs that are unjust" (Social Principles, ¶ 164B). The notion of the separation of the state from the church deals with the relationship of institutions that are independent of each other, although interrelated. Religion and politics are two spheres of activities in the life of Christians that cannot be separated. Citizens who belong to religious groups are also members of the secular society, and this dual association generates tensions. Religious beliefs have moral and social implications, and it is appropriate and necessary for people of faith to express these through their activities as citizens in the political arena. The fact that ethical convictions are rooted in religious faith, does not disqualify them from the political realm.

On the other hand these ethical convictions do not have secular validity merely because they are thought by their exponents to be religiously authoritative. They must be argued for in appropriate social and political terms in harmony with broad social values, including competing values.

The appropriate place of religion in our society has been in a constant flux, its nature and relations have been clarified in ongoing social debates. "It may not be easy," James Madison wrote, "in every possible case, to trace the line of separation between the rights of religion and civil authority with such distinctness as to avoid collisions." Clearly, collisions are what provide opportunities for careful deliberations of religious liberty issues, helping us to fine-tune this important pillar, in an increasingly pluralistic society.

Therefore, we should be prepared to deal with the complexities, ambiguities, and overlapping interests of church and state. We must discern workable principles that are compatible with fundamental constitutional imperatives, as well as our theological imperatives, in order to act morally and in accordance with God's will. As the Book of Acts reminds us: "We must obey God rather than any human authority" (5:29, NRSV).

Thus, The United Methodist Church has supported that "[e]veryone has the right to freedom of thought, conscience and religion; this right includes freedom to change his [or her] religion or belief, and freedom, either alone or in community with others and in public or private, to manifest his [or her] religion or belief in teaching, practice, worship and observance" (The Universal Declaration of Human Rights, Article 18).

In addition, The United Methodist Church also agrees with the Universal Declaration of Human Rights (Article 18), which is not limited in its application to traditional religions or to religions and beliefs with institutional characteristics or practices analogous to those of traditional religions. Given our Church's history, the Church views with concern any tendency to discriminate against any religion or belief for any reasons, including the fact that they might be newly established or represent a religious minority that may be the subject of hostility by a predominant religious community.

The United Methodist Church, in agreement with the International Covenant on Civil and Political Rights, affirms that the freedom to manifest one's religion or beliefs may be subject only to such limitations as are necessary to protect public safety, order, health, or morals or the fundamental rights and freedoms of others (Article 18, Paragraph 3).

Furthermore, The United Methodist Church has understood this to mean that government must be neutral in matters of religion and may not show preference of one religion over others, for religion in general, for religion over nonreligion, or for nonreligion over religion.

*Therefore, be it resolved*, that the General Conference of The United Methodist Church continue to affirm its historical position that government may not engage in, sponsor, supervise, aid, or lend its authority to religious expressions or religious observances.

*Be it further resolved*, that the General Conference urge rejection of any attempt of legislative bodies at the federal and state levels to bridge this important separation between church and state by providing direct financial assistance to houses of worship and religiously affiliated organizations in order for them to evangelize or proselytize. The state should not support any religious group's interest to evangelize or proselytize, the state is not the defender of the faith, whichever that faith might be.

*Be it further resolved*, that the General Conference reaffirms its historical position in opposition to any government legislation or constitutional amendment that would allow the use of public funds to support nonpublic elementary and secondary schools, or in regards to religious observances in public schools.

ADOPTED 2004
RESOLUTION #243, 2004 *BOOK OF RESOLUTIONS*
RESOLUTION #229, 2000 *BOOK OF RESOLUTIONS*

*See* Social Principles, ¶ 164C.

## 5014. On Humility, Politics, and Christian Unity

WHEREAS, in recent years, there has been significant discussion of public policy issues within The United Methodist Church, as well as a significant amount of religious rhetoric in the political arenas of the societies surrounding many of our churches; and

WHEREAS, The United Methodist Church, as well as the broader body of Christ, includes faithful members with a very wide spectrum of political views; and

WHEREAS, this diversity should be celebrated as a strength rather than ignored or suppressed; and

WHEREAS, the unity that United Methodists enjoy in Christ Jesus transcends worldly divisions (Mark 9:38-41; 1 Corinthians 1:10-25; Galatians 3:28; Colossians 3:11); and

WHEREAS, our unity as Christians is found in repentance for our sins, acceptance of Christ's atoning sacrifice, and submission to the will of God as revealed in Scripture, rather than in any secular or partisan political agenda; and

WHEREAS, an important maxim of John Wesley for the Methodist movement was "As to all opinions which do not strike at the root of Christianity, we think and let think" (*Book of Discipline* ¶ 102); and

WHEREAS, many, if not most, disagreements over public policy issues amount to differing prudential judgments about the most effective means for advancing commonly desired ends, such as improving the economy or effectively protecting citizens from terrorism; and

WHEREAS, scriptural teaching does not unambiguously mandate a specific position that all Christians must take on every piece of legislation discussed in modern local, state, and national legislatures; and

WHEREAS, the spirit of love and unity that Christians are called to have with one another (John 13:34-35; 1 Corinthians 13:1-13; Galatians 6:1-10; Ephesians 4:1-16; Colossians 3:12-17) stands in sharp contrast to the harsh divisiveness that characterizes secular politics; and

WHEREAS, there is risk of an unnecessary and unscriptural (Romans 13:13; Galatians 5:20) divisiveness being injected into some United Methodist and other Christian churches because of fights over divisive public policy debates whose underlying principles "do not strike at the root of Christianity";

*Therefore, be it resolved,* that the 2008 General Conference hereby affirms that differing opinions in public policy debates generally "do not strike at the root of Christianity"; and

*Be it further resolved,* that we call on all Christian people in political and ecclesiastical realms to have the humility to be cautious of asserting that God is on their side with regard to specific public policy proposals; and

*Be it further resolved,* that we continue to affirm the importance of conscientious and humble Christian social engagement for the sake of advancing justice and the common good.

**ADOPTED 2008**

*See* Social Principles, ¶ 164C.

## 5015. Guidelines for "Charitable Choice" Programs

WHEREAS, the term "charitable choice" entered the vocabulary of human service delivery in the United States of America (USA) in social welfare reform legislation in 1996, with particular reference to religious provider access to and utilization of public funds; and

WHEREAS, the term has come to be widely used in USA legislation, government regulations, and public discourse on the role of religious organizations as providers of publicly funded programs; and

WHEREAS, the term and its implications have become the source of ongoing debate on appropriate relations between religious organizations and governments, including the issue of church-state separation and religious nondiscrimination in hiring by religious service providers using public funds; and

WHEREAS, many United Methodist congregations, church-related institutions, and programs in the USA, are potentially or actually affected by charitable choice issues; and

WHEREAS, United Methodist agencies, related institutions, and some congregations have long histories of partnership with government in the delivery of human services; and,

WHEREAS, The United Methodist Church, through policy and practice, has developed sound and practical guidelines on the use of public funds by churches and church-related entities;

*Therefore, be it resolved,* that the 2004 General Conference urge congregations, agencies, related institutions, and programs in the USA to:

- adhere to the minimum nondiscrimination criteria to be met by church and church-related recipients of public funds;
- abide by the historical and prudent principle of separate non-profit incorporation for organizations and programs receiving public service funds, including the setting up of separate service corporations by congregations so engaged, in large measure as a means of protecting the Church from liability claims;
- carefully investigate the terms and implications of all public grants and contracts to ensure that the tasks undertaken and expected outcomes are consistent with the United Methodist Social Principles; and
- engage in informed dialogue on the public policy and religious liberty implications of charitable choice.

ADOPTED 2004
READOPTED 2008
RESOLUTION #244, 2004 *BOOK OF RESOLUTIONS*

*See* Social Principles, ¶ 164C.

## CRIMINAL JUSTICE

### 5031. Equal Justice

It must be remembered that the verse "Let every person be subject to the governing authorities" (Romans 13:1, NRSV) is preceded by "Live in harmony with one another; do not be haughty, but associate with the lowly; never be conceited. Repay no one evil for evil, but take thought for what is noble in the sight of all" (Romans 12:16-17, NRSV). The admonition to "live in harmony" is directed to the authorities who govern as well as those who may be subject.

The Social Principles of The United Methodist Church state (¶ 164B and H): "The church should continually exert a strong ethical influence upon the state, supporting policies and programs deemed to be just and opposing policies and programs that are unjust. . . . In the love of Christ, who came to save those who are lost and vulnerable, we urge the creation of a genuinely new system for the care and restoration of victims, offenders, criminal justice officials, and the community as a whole."

Deeply rooted racial and economic injustices in most nations' criminal justice systems form barriers to the realization of this vision. Some of the challenges include:

- media's disproportionate portrayal of poor people and people of color as criminals;
- legislation that results in ever-increasing rates of arrests and longer sentencing of the poor and people of color;
- racial profiling and arrest quota systems; and
- court-appointed legal representation for poor people that is often inferior to that available to those who can afford private representation.

### The Police

In a democratic society, the police fill a position of extraordinary trust and power. Usually the decision of whether a citizen is to be taken into custody rests solely with the police. For these reasons, law enforcement officers must be persons who possess good judgment, sound discretion, proper temperament, and are physically and mentally alert.

Unusual care must be exercised in the selection of those persons to serve as police officers. We recommend psychological testing prior to employment of police officers and periodically thereafter. During the period of training and continually thereafter, police must be instilled with the knowledge that the rights of many will never be secured if the government, through its police powers, is permitted to prefer some of its citizens over others. The practice of citizen preference in the enforcement of our criminal laws must not be tolerated. Our laws must be fairly enforced and impartially administered. No one is immune from the requirements of the law because of power, position, or economic station in life. Further, the power of the police must never be used to harass and provoke the young, the poor, the unpopular, and the members of racial and cultural minorities.

Where there is heavy pressure upon police officers by police departments to regularly make a large number of arrests as a demonstration of their initiative and professional performance, we urge that such practice be discontinued.

In a democratic society, however, a large majority of police work encompasses peacekeeping and social services rather than crime control functions. Police routinely use more than 85 percent of their duty time in giving assistance to citizens and making referrals to other governmental agencies. It is important for police to be recognized and promoted for their effectiveness in such roles as diverting youths from disorderly activities, peacefully intervening in domestic quarrels, anticipating disturbances through the channeling of grievances, and the building of good community relationships.

The United Methodist Church recommends that police departments publicly establish standards of police conduct and policies for promotion. To this end, congregations should encourage the police to conduct public hearings among all classes of citizens, giving adequate weight to peacekeeping, life-protecting, and other service roles, as well as the bringing of criminal offenders to justice. The standards must include strict limits on the police use of guns.

We further recommend that police officers live within the jurisdiction in which they are employed.

We make these recommendations not only in concern about the frequent abuses of people by the police, but also because we are concerned for more effective control of crime. We observe that only about one half the victims of serious crime, and a far smaller proportion of witnesses, report to the police. If offenders are to be apprehended and convicted, police and law-abiding citizens must work closely together. Such cooperation can occur only when the police are fair and humane and when they are publicly known to be sensitive and considerate.

The United Methodist Church urges that communities establish adequate salary scales for police officers and develop high standards for recruiting both men and women, and members of all ethnic groups. Recruitment must be followed by adequate training in social relations and dispute settlement as well as in law and the skills of crime detection investigation and the apprehension of offenders. As police officers continue to meet those improved qualifications, we will recognize law enforcement as a profession with status and respect.

## Criminal Laws and the Courts

Restorative justice practices should be utilized within the community as a first response to any criminal behavior. Justice can only prevail when there is healing of the victim, repentance of the offender, and when forgiveness and reconciliation are shared throughout the community. Victim-offender mediation, family group conferencing, and various other restorative justice techniques are urged to be considered as an alternative to the criminal courts.

Overwhelmingly, criminal convictions are by guilty pleas, a large proportion of those by plea bargaining. Where the law recognizes and permits plea bargaining, and in those instances where the ends of justice dictate that a renegotiated plea be considered, we recommend it should be permitted and approved only after full disclosure in open court of the terms and conditions of such plea-bargaining agreement. Equal justice requires that all trials and the sentencing of those convicted under our criminal laws must be conducted in the public courtroom.

However, that work should be correspondingly eased by changes in the law, such as the moving of most traffic offenses out of criminal court to administrative procedures, and by relieving the court of great numbers of civil cases through the adoption of genuine no-fault motor-vehicle insurance laws. The courts must also organize their work efficiently, employing modern management procedures. Many improvements could be made by the use of administrative volunteers, including retirees who can furnish professional services to the court at minimal costs.

Other changes needed to obtain equal justice in the courts include:

1. the repeal of some criminal laws against certain personal conditions or individual misconduct. Examples are criminal prohibitions of vagrancy, personal gambling, public drunkenness, drug use, and prostitution. Together, these charges alone account for more than half of all arrests in some jurisdictions. They result in little social good, but great evil in class discrimination, alienation, and waste of resources needed for other purposes. Some related laws such as those against drunken driving and those limiting and controlling the operation of gambling establishments need to be tightened;

2. the adoption of systematic new penal codes prescribing penalties proportionate to the predictable damage done by the various kinds of crime, without regard to the race or class of the offender. For example, in the United States, there are discriminatory high penalties for the use of crack cocaine (most often used by blacks) as opposed to powder cocaine (most often used by whites);

3. the training of judges of juvenile and criminal courts in the use of nonincarcerating community sanctions wherever the offense does not involve persistent violence;

4. the adoption of systematic new penal codes prescribing a range of penalties without regard to the race or class of the offender, but utilizing nonincarceration community sanctions wherever consistent with community protection;

5. the provision for court-fixed sentences, rather than mandatory ones, in order to draw upon the skill and the training of qualified judges;

6. a statement by the sentencing judge of the reason or reasons why he or she is selecting from the range permitted by the law the particular sentence being pronounced;

7. the development of appropriate jury selection procedures that would ensure the most inclusive representation, including representatives of the socioeconomic class and ethnic group of the defendants and of the crime victims, as well as balance between male and female jurors;

8. the adoption by all courts of: (a) speedy trial provisions, which the Constitution guarantees; and (b) that degree of personal recognizance and supervision which each defendant's situation warrants, regardless of race and class identity, in place of the present, inherently discriminatory bail bond, pretrial release process that exists in some courts;

9. when fines are assessed, they should be scaled to the magnitude of the crime and the ability of the offender to pay. In suitable cases, fines should be made payable in installments;

10. governmentally regulated programs of compensation for reimbursement of financial loss incurred by innocent victims of crime should be encouraged, with preference being given for programs in which specific offenders provide restitution to their specific victims as an alternative to incarceration; and

11. changes in state self-defense laws to allow for cases in which persistently battered persons, especially women and children, are driven to violence against their batterers, when they believe with good reason, that another attack is forthcoming.

We recommend that local churches consider setting up court monitoring panels to observe court operations and proceedings. Such panels may well adopt a role of friends of the court or of advocacy on behalf of accused persons and/or on behalf of crime victims. They may adopt other appropriate procedures in the interest of restorative justice, including close scrutiny of plea bargaining and/or evidence of unequal imposition of sentences.

We call upon the General Board of Global Ministries, through the Restorative Justice Ministries Program, to give leadership and training to congregations to participate in these actions, and to create and sustain new ministries of justice to help eliminate racism and classism in the criminal justice system. We call upon the General Board of Church and Society to advocate for legislation which will eliminate racism and classism in the criminal justice system by:

- promoting equity in courts by legal representation of equal quality, regardless of financial ability;
- reassessing incarceration guidelines and reducing incarceration of persons guilty of nonviolent crimes;
- creating laws prohibiting discrimination against ex-offenders;
- reinstating voting rights for ex-offenders; and
- eliminating mandatory minimum sentences for drug-related crimes.

**ADOPTED 1980**
**AMENDED AND READOPTED 2000**
**AMENDED AND READOPTED 2008**
**RESOLUTION #248, 2004** *BOOK OF RESOLUTIONS*
**RESOLUTION #233, 2000** *BOOK OF RESOLUTIONS*

*See* Social Principles, ¶ 164H.

## 5032. Grand Jury Abuse

Scripture reveals that hidden judgments often lead to destruction. In the Book of Esther, Haman schemed behind the scenes and manipulated his relationship with the king in his attempt to destroy all of the Jews throughout the kingdom (Esther 3:8-10). In the New Testament, the Pharisees plotted to kill Jesus, even using false witnesses against him (Matthew 26:59-60). Scripture also shows how righteous judgments made in full public view can lead to truth and accountability. The prophet Nathan rebuked David for his sin against Uriah and it led to David's repentance (2 Samuel 12). Jesus publicly exposed the hypocrisy of the Pharisees (Matthew 23:13-36), and still counted among his followers were some of these same religious leaders (Mark 15:42-43; John 3:1-9).

The Social Principles of The United Methodist Church state boldly that "governments, no less than individuals, are subject to the judgment of God" (¶ 164F). Such a social principle causes us, appropriately, to view with concern the government's use of the grand jury to control dissent and to harass those who act under the constraint of conscience.

The grand jury is envisioned in American law as a protector of citizens from unwarranted prosecutions. It is for this reason that its proceedings are secret and it has the power to subpoena witnesses.

Evidence indicates that in recent years, the extraordinary powers of the grand jury often have been used not for the *protection* of citizens, but in subjecting them to harassment and intimidation. Historically, political dissidents, antiwar activists, and leaders of minority groups and religious organizations have been particularly vulnerable to these abuses.

A government prosecutor can control the grand jury, thus distorting the grand jury's power to monitor and moderate the actions of the prosecution. The prosecutor can use the subpoena powers of the grand jury to conduct investigations that are the responsibility of law enforcement agencies. As an example, the United States Congress has never given the Federal Bureau of Investigation subpoena powers, yet agents routinely threaten uncooperative persons with subpoenas from a grand jury. In fact, subpoenas are often served at the request of the Federal Bureau of Investigation.

The use of the powers of the grand jury to harass and pursue political dissidents is a departure from its proper constitutional function, and it is a threat to public order, lawful government, and true domestic security.

Witnesses called before a grand jury may be given little or no warning of their subpoenas, may be forced to travel to court at distances from their homes, may not know whether they are targets of prosecution, may have little understanding of their rights, and cannot have legal counsel in the chambers.

Comprehensive grand jury reform legislation is needed to restore the constitutional guarantees of protection for citizens. The United States Constitution's Fifth Amendment right against self-incrimination and false accusation must be reestablished and reinforced.

The United Methodist Church calls on all United Methodist congregations, under the leadership of the General Board of Church and Society, to advocate for legislation designed to enhance the rights to due process of law, including preserving habeas corpus, freedom of association, effective legal counsel for witnesses excluded from immunity appearing before the Grand Jury, the presumption of innocence, and the privilege against self-incrimination of persons subpoenaed to testify before grand juries.

ADOPTED 1980
AMENDED AND READOPTED 2000
AMENDED AND READOPTED 2008
RESOLUTION #250, 2004 *BOOK OF RESOLUTIONS*
RESOLUTION #234, 2000 *BOOK OF RESOLUTIONS*

*See* Social Principles, ¶ 164F and H.

## 5033. Justice with Young Persons

"Let the little children come to me; do not stop them; for it is to such as these that the kingdom of God belongs" (Mark 10:14, NRSV).

Our Lord particularly identified with children and illustrated the loving care which they need to grow and mature.

The Social Principles of The United Methodist Church calls for special attention to the rights of children and youth. From these perspectives we are concerned that in many states, children are arrested and incarcerated for truancy, incorrigibility, stubborn altercations with parents, and other conduct which would not be criminal if performed by an adult. Such status offenses should not be considered as grounds for involving a young person in processes of criminal or delinquency procedures. Rather, a child in trouble should be helped by caring communities, such as churches, mentoring programs, and boys/girls clubs.

There is considerable evidence that the punitive methods of dealing with children play a major part in developing criminal tendencies. Most adults who repeat violent crimes began their conflict with law and order as children ten to fourteen years old. If treatment by the state or local agencies leads the child to think of him or herself as a tough young criminal, he or she is likely to act out that role.

The United Methodist Church urges that all status offenses be eliminated from the juvenile codes and from the processes for determining juvenile delinquency. We urge further that all offenses by children and youth be handled with extreme reluctance to incarcerate the offender. We especially oppose solitary confinement of children and youths in official detention. Institutions where young persons classified as delinquent often are segregated from the general population often become schools of crime. As an alternative, we encourage greater use of supportive and restorative services for parents and children in their home settings; foster child care; neighborhood group homes, Parents Anonymous, and other alternatives.

There are communities within the states in which children are routinely locked up in jails because of a lack of temporary shelter, care or an unwillingness to use home detention. We urge the prohibition of placing dependent and neglected children in jails or facilities for juvenile delinquents.

For many children, the quality of life continually declines due to poverty, gangs, school violence, emotional, sexual and physical abuse, and other social ills that have yet to be recognized. The United Methodist Church must take a stand against juvenile delinquency and work to prevent it.

The church can witness to children in a restorative and prophetic way. The church must continue to address the social issues that children and adolescents face and become a safe haven where the children can come. By addressing the issues that children face, we help bring God's children back to their Creator.

*Therefore, be it resolved,* that General Conference of The United Methodist Church takes a stand against harsh and punitive measures applied to youth and children for nonviolent status offenses. Such punitive policies serve to criminalize many youth—especially in poor communities and communities of color.

*Be it further resolved,* that The United Methodist Church works to strengthen youth empowerment programs that provide positive avenues for youth participation in their communities.

*Be it further resolved,* that The United Methodist Church, through the appropriate churches, annual conferences, agencies, or coalitions work to prevent juvenile delinquency and treat offenders by:

- updating the *Urban and Rural Life Youth Mentoring Guide*;
- continuing to develop and distribute peer mentoring guides to local churches;
- continuing to develop and distribute up-to-date information on social problems facing children and youth today and strategies on how local churches can help prevent both self-destructive and anti-social behavior as well as to end punitive policies that serve to criminalize children and youth;
- encouraging local churches to create ministry partnerships with local juvenile justice officials and agencies;
- forming alliances with other international, national, state, and local civic and religious groups that work on juvenile justice issues; and
- encouraging conference council on youth ministries or other similar boards to create ministry teams and/or programs for their peers.

ADOPTED 2000
REVISED AND READOPTED 2008
RESOLUTION #254, 2004 *BOOK OF RESOLUTIONS*
RESOLUTION #237, 2000 *BOOK OF RESOLUTIONS*

*See* Social Principles, ¶ 164*H*.

## 5034. Mission Plan for Restorative Justice Ministries

### *I. Biblical/Theological Grounding*

*The words of Micah ring out clearly, setting the tone for justice ministries in the church: "He has told you, O mortal, what is good; and what does the Lord require of you but to do justice, and to love kindness, and to walk humbly with your God?"*

(Micah 6:8)

Justice is the basic principle upon which God's creation has been established. It is an integral and uncompromising part in God's redemptive process, which assures wholeness. Compassion is characterized by sensitivity to God's justice and, therefore, sensitivity to God's people.

The gospel, through the example of Jesus Christ, conveys the message for Christians to be healers, peacemakers, and reconcilers when faced with brokenness, violence, and vengeance. Through love, caring and forgiveness, Jesus Christ is able to transform lives and restore dignity and purpose in those who are willing to abide by his principle.

Jesus was concerned about victims of crime. In the story of the Good Samaritan, Jesus explored the responsibility we have for those who have been victimized: " 'Which of these three, do you think, was neighbor to the man who fell into the hands of the robbers?' He said, 'The one who showed him mercy.' Jesus said to him, 'Go and do likewise'" (Luke 10:36-37).

Jesus was concerned about offenders, those who victimize others. He rejected vengeance and retribution as the model of justice to being used for relating to offenders: "You have heard that it was said, 'An eye for an eye and a tooth for a tooth.' But I say to you, Do not resist an evildoer. But if anyone strikes you on the right cheek, turn the other also; . . . " (Matthew 5:38ff). Jesus also indicated the responsibility Christians have for offenders: "I was sick and you took care of me. I was in prison and you visited me . . . Truly I tell you, just as you did it to one of the least of these . . . you did it to me" (Matthew 25:36, 40).

The apostle Paul believed that this biblical concept of justice which was reflected in the life of Christ was a primary molder of Christian community and responsibility: "All this is from God, who reconciled us to himself through Christ, and has given us the ministry of reconciliation; that is, in Christ God was reconciling the world to himself, not counting their trespasses against them, and entrusting the message of reconciliation to us" (2 Corinthians 5:18-19).

While acknowledging that the biblical concept of justice focuses on the victim, the offender, and the community in the hope of restoring all to a sense of God's wholeness, it is also important to understand that our Methodist heritage is rich with examples of ministries carried out in jails and prisons. John Wesley (and others in his inner circle, including a brother, Charles) had a passion for those in prison. As early as 1778, the Methodist Conference adopted action making it the duty of every Methodist preacher to minister to those who were incarcerated. United Methodists have reaffirmed and expanded the mandate for prison ministry and reform in many different chapters of our denominational history. This is a part of our identity and call.

Criminal justice in our world rarely focuses on the biblical initiatives of restoration, mercy, wholeness, and shalom. Out of a desire to punish rather than restore, governments around the world have made retribution the heart of their criminal justice systems, believing that this will deter crime and violence. The statistics indicate the colossal failure of retributive justice. Therefore, we call on the church to embrace the biblical concept of restorative justice as a hopeful alternative to our present criminal justice codes. Restorative justice focuses on the victim, the offender, and the community in the desire to bring healing and wholeness to all.

## II. Our Current Criminal Justice System: A Retributive Justice System

### A. Victims

When crime is defined as the breaking of a law, the state (rather than the victim) is posited as the primary victim. Criminal justice, as we know it, focuses little or no attention on the needs of the victim. Legal proceedings inadvertently cause crime victims, including loved ones, to experience shock and a sense of helplessness which is further exacerbated by financial loss, spiritual or emotional trauma and, often, a lack of support and direction. Many victims feel frustrated because, in most cases, there seems to be little or no provision for them to be heard or to be notified of court proceedings. Victims, moreover, are seldom given the opportunity to meet with their offenders, face to face, in order to personally resolve their conflicts and to move toward healing, authentic reconciliation, and closure.

### B. Offenders

Our criminal justice systems around the world have become increasingly based on retribution. Although it is often cloaked or justified in the language of accountability, this focus on punishment has resulted in massive increases in the number of incarcerated persons across the globe. In the United States, for example, the prison population doubled between 1990 and 2000, even as the crime rate decreased during this period. Because prisons are often places where dehumanizing conditions reinforce negative behavior, present criminal justice systems actually perpetuate a cycle of violence, crime, and incarceration, especially among those whose race, appearance, lifestyle, economic conditions, or beliefs differ from those in authority.

Incarceration is costly. In the United States, the cost of incarcerating someone for a year ranges between $15,000 and $30,000. Citizens are, therefore, paying billions of dollars for the support of systems that consistently engender a grossly dehumanizing experience characterized by the loss of freedom, the loss of contact with family and friends, the loss of self-determination, the loss of education, the loss of adequate medical care, and the loss of religious freedom and opportunities for spiritual growth.

## C. Community

Criminal justice, as we know it, is retributive justice. It is consumed with blame and pain. It is a system of retribution that pays little or no consideration to the root causes of criminal behavior. It does not aim at solutions that will benefit the whole community by helping the community to repair the breach and often fails to come to terms with the social conditions that breed crime. Retributive justice permanently stigmatizes the offender for past actions, thereby creating such a sense of alienation from the community that social reintegration is virtually impossible. An offender who is held in exile away from the community cannot be held accountable to the community for his or her wrongdoing. An ex-offender who is ostracized and kept in exile after paying his or her debt to society is further violated. He or she is stripped of the opportunity to fully understand the consequences of the crime committed, to make restitution to the victim, to be reconciled with the community, or to heal and become a viable member of the community.

## III. Our Vision of Restorative Justice

The gospel, through the example of Jesus Christ, conveys the message for Christians to be healers, peacemakers, and reconcilers when faced with brokenness, violence, and vengeance. The concept of restorative justice shows us specific ways by which to transform lives and effect healing.

Restorative justice asks: Who has been hurt? What are their needs? Whose obligations are they?

We label the person who has been hurt "the victim." But the victim is essentially a survivor who need not remain a victim for his or her entire life. The victim needs healing and emotional support. Victims (survivors) want people to recognize the trauma they have endured and how this trauma has affected their lives and the lives of their loved ones. Often survivors/victims need counseling, assistance, compensation, information, and services. Victims/survivors need to participate in their own healing. They may need reparations from the offender, or the victim may want to meet the offender and have input during the trial, sentencing, and rehabilitation process.

During the healing process, the victim often asks: Why me? What kind of person could do such a thing? Therefore, they may want to meet their offender to receive answers to such questions. Victims deserve to have these questions answered and to hear that the offender is truly sorry.

Victims suffer real pain; however, encouraging vengeance does not heal pain. The community needs to aid in the recovery of the victim. The community can help the victim by not ostracizing him or her, by learning how to accept him or her as a person and not just a victim.

Offenders are harmed as well. An offender is harmed by being labeled for life as an offender. One or more bad decision or action sometimes measures the total of an offender's life. Offenders are further harmed when they are denied the opportunity to make amends, to have respectful interaction with others, and to develop healthy social skills before, during, or after incarceration. Often young offenders do not have constructive guidance or a good role model in the community. Sometimes they need treatment for a disorder, life skills development, or mentoring with clear and achievable expectations of heightened self-awareness and accountability.

The victim and the community need to identify ways the offender can remedy hurt and harm caused. The offender needs to understand how his or her behavior affected others, and acknowledge that the behavior was indeed harmful. The offender needs to be transformed into a contributing citizen of the community with a system of limits and support.

Crime hurts the community. When crime occurs, the neighborhood is disrupted; people become more isolated, fearful, distrusting, and uninterested in the community. Restorative justice helps to release the community members from their fear of crime; it empowers them with the knowledge that circumstances are not out of their control. The community needs to express pain and anger to the one or ones who caused the harm. However, we need to take one step further by helping in the healing process. We need to understand and address the causes of crime to prevent future occurrences. The victim, community, and offender (when possible) need to help others who face similar struggles.

Restorative justice opens the opportunities for personal and community transformation. This transformation cannot be mapped, planned, or put into a program or structure. Nevertheless, it can be encouraged and nurtured.

United Methodists have the will, the vision, the opportunity and the responsibility to be advocates for systemic change. We are called to minister with all parties affected by crime: the victim, the offender, and the community.

Expectations are high for the faith community to lead the way in practicing restorative justice. We need to own and advocate a vision for restorative justice. We need to be supportive to members of the congregation who are victims, offenders, and their families, and especially to those who work toward restoration in the criminal justice system.

The church must initiate models of restorative justice with service providers, policy makers, and law enforcement. We need to work in partnership with the criminal justice system to make it more open, accessible, humane, effective, rehabilitative, and less costly. We need to see our own capacity in community breakdowns and in the racism and classism present in the enactment and enforcement of criminal law. We must also advocate for social and economic justice to see the restoration and strengthening of our communities.

### IV. A Call to Action

As United Methodists we are called to:
- repent of the sin we have committed that has fostered retributive justice;
- speak prophetically and consistently against dehumanization in the criminal justice system;
- establish restorative justice as the theological ground for ministries in The United Methodist Church and build bridges of collaboration and cooperation to advance the practice of

restorative justice with boards and agencies within The United Methodist Church, with United Methodist and other Methodist communions around the globe, with other faith communities in the United States and worldwide, and with nonprofit organizations and/or governmental organizations; and

- intensify our redemptive ministries with those who work within criminal justice, victims of crime and their families, those who are incarcerated in jails and prisons and their families, and communities traumatized by crime.

1. At the General Church Level:

Restorative Justice Ministries Committee:

Continue and expand the work of The United Methodist Church's Restorative Justice Ministries through the Restorative Justice Ministries Committee, which serves as the global coordinating committee for criminal justice and mercy ministries mandated by the 1996 General Conference of The United Methodist Church. The members should include:

- two bishops named by the Council of Bishops, attending with funds from the Episcopal Fund;
- one elected board member and one staff person (responsible for Restorative Justice Ministries within the named agency) from each of the General Board of Global Ministries, the General Board of Church and Society, the General Board of Discipleship, the General Board of Higher Education and Ministry, the General Council on Ministries and the General Commission on Religion and Race—all to be selected and funded by their respective agencies;
- one member from United Methodist Women and one member from United Methodist Men—each selected and funded by their respective agency; and
- up to seven members-at-large selected by the Council of Bishops in order to ensure that the committee as a whole reflects the varied constituency of the church by gender, age, laity, and clergy; and that the committee have persons who can contribute to Restorative Justice Ministries.

Fulfill these specific functions:

- Provide a biblical/theological basis for a restorative justice approach to criminal justice.
- Be a center for resourcing, teaching, learning, and networking.

- Work collegially with other groups and organizations whether they are inside or outside the denomination, religious or secular, by finding common ground to bring about systemic change in the spirit of mediation (even when there is disagreement about theological rationale).
- Coordinate the training, networking, and advocacy for Restorative Justice Ministries of The United Methodist Church by working with jurisdictions, annual conferences, central conferences, districts, local United Methodist churches and their communities.
- Serve as the primary advocate and interpreter of Restorative Justice Ministries.
- Identify and expand critical models and facilitate the development of Restorative Justice Ministries, on a global basis, at all levels of The United Methodist Church.

2. Specific General Church Agencies:

We reaffirm the 1996, 2000, 2004, and 2008 General Conference mandate which led to a program of Restorative Justice Ministries and recommend that the church continue to support and strengthen its commitment. We recommend the following:

- that the Restorative Justice Ministries Committee continue to give guidance and oversight to the operation of the Restorative Justice Ministries with each board/agency providing the funds to continue the work of Restorative Ministries as outlined below;
- that the General Board of Global Ministries provide resources to annual and central conferences to enable them to develop Restorative Justice Ministries with victims, offenders, prisoners, their families, and communities;
- that the General Board of Global Ministries provide funding to enable the assignment of missionaries, including youth and young adults, to serve in restorative justice ministries with victims, offenders, prisoners, and communities;
- that the General Board of Global Ministries provide funding to support gatherings of United Methodists working in the fields of criminal justice, community corrections, and restorative justice. The events will be focused on the relationship between faith and work;
- that the General Board of Global Ministries provide funding to organize global consultations on restorative justice to be

held in central conferences, bringing together United Methodist leaders from across the globe who are using restorative justice ministry strategies and techniques to transform and resolve social, political, religious, economic, racial, and ethnic conflicts and end violence within their churches and communities;

• that the General Board of Global Ministries work with annual and central conferences and their ecumenical, interfaith, and community partners to develop victim offender reconciliation programs and neighborhood conflict resolution programs based on restorative justice ministries models to serve the church and community;

• that the General Board of Global Ministries, in consultation with annual and central conferences, continue to organize training events in restorative justice ministries;

• that the General Board of Global Ministries continue to work to evaluate and identify model programs of restorative justice ministries and develop the network for these ministries;

• that the General Board of Global Ministries work with the boards and agencies to develop written resources to assist the church in their work in these ministries;

• that the General Board of Global Ministries work with the DISCIPLE Bible Study Ministries in order to increase the involvement of annual conferences and local congregations in ministries with prisoners, ex-offenders and juvenile offenders;

• that the General Board of Global Ministries develop a group of United Methodist trained mediators who can respond to conflicts in the community and who can assist in training other United Methodists to serve as mediators in their communities;

• that the General Board of Global Ministries develop electronic resources and a quarterly newsletter to provide information and updates on new developments in restorative justice ministries around the world to serve The United Methodist Church;

• that the General Board of Church and Society intensify their advocacy for social and economic justice in order to restore and strengthen communities;

• that the General Board of Church and Society continue to advocate for a criminal justice system that is not racist, less costly, more humane, effectively rehabilitative and accessible to family members of victims and offenders;

- that the General Board of Church and Society provide training and resourcing to annual and central conferences and local churches that intend to advocate for a more just system of justice;
- that the General Board of Church and Society intensify its advocacy for the abolition of the death penalty throughout the world;
- that the General Board of Discipleship work to develop print and training resources, including Sunday school resources, for local churches to use as they embrace restorative justice ministries. This directive includes: the development of resources and training for reconciling parents and youth offenders; the development of small group resources that support victim and offender reconciliation; and the provision of material for small groups that wish to explore restorative justice issues within the local church;
- that the General Board of Discipleship work to explore the development of a training and certification process for laity and local church pastors carrying out restorative justice ministries;
- that the General Board of Higher Education and Ministry continue to provide certification for chaplains and explore the development of certification for others interested in professional ministry with restorative justice ministries;
- that the General Board of Higher Education and Ministry work with United Methodist seminaries to promote curriculum and practicum offerings in those seminaries in areas of violence, crime, and criminal justice from a restorative justice perspective;
- that United Methodist Women continue to start units within jails and prisons to promote restorative justice;
- that United Methodist Women continue ministries with families of prisoners;
- that United Methodist Men work jointly with the General Board of Church and Society to resource UMM to become involved in the various aspects of Restorative Justice; and
- that United Methodist Women and United Methodist Men consider working with DISCIPLE Bible Study Ministries,

KAIROS, and other Bible studies/retreats to start units of Christian disciple making with prisoners, ex-offenders and juvenile offenders.

3. At Jurisdictional/Central Conference and Annual Conference Levels:

- support jurisdictional/central conference and annual conference networking as modeled by the Southeastern Jurisdiction's and South Central Jurisdiction's Restorative Justice Network Group, or bring together clusters of contiguous conferences or expedite processes of training and resource sharing;
- encourage conferences to establish inter-agency restorative justice task forces to coordinate Restorative Justice Ministries within their bounds, with special emphasis on partnership with the Restorative Justice Ministries Inter-agency Task Force and the facilitation and resourcing of local church ministries.

4. At the Local Level:

- encourage local congregations to provide adult and youth education programs on restorative justice: theory, practice, issues, models, and use of resources (utilizing curriculum resources, printed and audiovisual, provided through the above-mentioned connectional sources);
- encourage congregations to provide safe space to enable people to share real experiences of victimization, incarceration, or other direct encounters with the criminal justice system and/or restorative justice processes;
- encourage congregations to schedule a "Restorative Justice Ministries Sunday" to generate deeper awareness by the entire congregation regarding the contrasting paradigms of retributive justice and restorative justice—and their different outcomes;
- encourage congregations to organize or form direct service and/or advocacy efforts to support the work of restorative justice; and
- work with local ecumenical and/or interfaith agencies and other community agencies to:
  * convene consultations of representatives of the restorative justice community to define policy/legislative needs and strategies;

* encourage/resource congregations to work on restorative justice through regional judicatories and media;
* encourage/initiate dialogue with correctional/criminal justice system officials;
* identify and nurture criminal justice system leaders (e.g., judges, attorneys, wardens, police, etc.) regarding restorative justice;
* involve local congregations in ministries with juvenile detention centers and domestic violence centers;
* build covenant discipleship groups at the local level for restorative justice advocates, as well as for other persons involved in the criminal justice system;
* provide victim-offender mediation and other restorative justice processes;
* identify and develop coalition partnerships with victim assistance groups, advocacy groups, jail and prison ministry groups, ex-offender assistance groups; and.
* plan and implement strategies for advocacy that encourage legislative support for restorative justice programs.

ADOPTED 2004
REVISED AND READOPTED 2008
RESOLUTION #258, 2004 *BOOK OF RESOLUTIONS*
RESOLUTION #241, 2000 *BOOK OF RESOLUTIONS*

*See* Social Principles, ¶ 164*A* and *F*.

## 5035. In Opposition to Capital Punishment

The United Methodist Church declares its opposition to the retention and use of capital punishment and urges its abolition. In spite of a common assumption to the contrary, "an eye for an eye and a tooth for a tooth," does not give justification for the imposing of the penalty of death. Jesus explicitly repudiated retaliation (Matthew 5:38-39), and the Talmud denies its literal meaning and holds that it refers to financial indemnities.

Christ came among us and suffered death. Christ also rose to new life for the sake of all. His suffering, death, and resurrection brought a new dimension to human life, the possibility of reconciliation with God through repentance. This gift is offered to all without exception, and human life was given new dignity and sacredness through it. The death penalty, however, denies Christ's power to transform and restore all human beings. In the New Testament, when a woman having committed a crime was brought before Jesus, He persisted in questioning her accusers, so that they walked away (John 8:1-11).

The Social Principles of The United Methodist Church condemn "... torture of persons by governments for any purpose," (¶ 164A) and assert that it violates Christian teachings. The church, through its Social Principles, further declares, "we oppose capital punishment and urge its elimination from all criminal codes" (¶ 164A).

During the 1970s and 1980s a rapidly rising rate of violent crime and an even greater increase in the fear of crime generated support in some countries and within the North American society, for the institution of death as the punishment for certain forms of homicide. It continues to be wrongly asserted, that capital punishment uniquely deters criminals and protects law-abiding citizens from violent crime.

Studies conducted over more than sixty years have overwhelmingly failed to support the thesis that capital punishment deters homicide more effectively than does imprisonment. In fact, in the United States "ten of the twelve states without the death penalty have homicide rates below the national average, whereas half of the states with the death penalty have homicide rates above the national average." (Source: New York *Times*, September 22, 2000) The United Methodist Church is deeply concerned with the rate of crime throughout the world, and the value of a life taken by murder or homicide. When another life is taken through capital punishment, the life of the victim is further devalued.

In the 1980s and 1990s, "the homicide rate in states with the death penalty had been 48-101% higher than in states without the death penalty." (Source: New York *Times*, September 22, 2000) Use of the death penalty gradually increased until peaking in the late 1990s; however, the number of executions has steadily declined in recent years. Also steadily waning is public support for the death penalty as more people support other forms of punishment as alternatives to death. A further development since 2000 is that a majority of people also no longer believe that the death penalty acts as a deterrent or is administered fairly. (Source: Death Penalty Information Center Web site) As United Methodist Christians, part of our mission is to reform the criminal justice system and to eliminate social conditions which breed crime and cause disorder.

Sixty-seven percent of law enforcement officials do not think capital punishment decreases the rate of homicide. A poll of police chiefs found that they ranked the death penalty least effective in reducing violent crime.[1]

In 1993, the US Supreme Court ruled that executing an innocent person was not "cruel and unusual" if all the proper and legal procedures were followed. The court thus does not have to reopen a case if new evidence, exonerating the defendant, comes to light after a legally established deadline for new information. Between 1972 and 2007 more than one hundred twenty people have been released from death row as a result of being wrongly convicted. On average, for every eight people executed, one person under a death sentence is found innocent. (Source: Death Penalty Information Center Web site)

The practice of executing child offenders remains a global problem and has been condemned in numerous human rights treaties. We applaud the United States Supreme Court decision on March 1, 2005, which ruled that executing child offenders is unconstitutional. Justice Kennedy, writing for the majority opinion of the Court, stated that the growing international outrage against the executions of juveniles was a "significant" factor in ruling against its practice in the United States. Therefore, it is our hope that further international outrage against the use of the death penalty for all people might bring about its abolition in the United States and throughout the world.

According to the 2007 statistics from Amnesty International, the top five nations known to carry out executions were China (470), Iran (317), Saudi Arabia (143), Pakistan (135), and the United States of America (42). Some of the nations often use the death penalty as a method of political repression to eliminate political opponents.

The death penalty falls unfairly and unequally upon marginalized persons including the poor, the uneducated, ethnic and religious minorities, and persons with mental and emotional illnesses. In the United States, persons who receive the death penalty are usually convicted of killing middle or upper class white persons, and are almost always poor and unable to afford a lawyer. In the US, methods for selecting the few persons sentenced to die from among the large number who are sentenced for comparable offenses are entirely arbitrary. What warrants the death penalty and what sentencing options are

1. Eric Pooley. "Death or Life?" *TIME*, June 16, 1997.

available vary among the few countries that impose capital punishment and even among the states in the United States.

The United States Supreme Court, in *Gregg v. Georgia* (1976), in permitting use of the death penalty, conceded the lack of evidence that it reduced violent crime, but permitted its use for the purpose of sheer retribution.

The United Methodist Church cannot accept retribution or social vengeance as a reason for taking human life. It violates our deepest belief in God as the Creator and the Redeemer of humankind. In this respect, there can be no assertion that human life can be taken humanely by the state. Indeed, in the long run, the use of the death penalty by the state will increase the acceptance of revenge in our society and will give official sanction to a climate of violence.

*Therefore*, we call upon United Methodists individually, at the district and conference level and through the Council of Bishops and the general boards and agencies to:

- work in collaboration with other ecumenical and abolitionist groups for the abolition of the death penalty in those states which currently have capital punishment statutes, and against efforts to reinstate such statutes in those which do not;
- promote the work of United Methodists Against the Death Penalty in mobilizing United Methodists to the work of abolition;
- advocate against the death penalty to state governors, state and federal representatives;
- develop education materials on capital punishment; and
- oppose all executions through prayer and vigils.

ADOPTED 2000
REVISED AND READOPTED 2008
RESOLUTION #255, 2004 *BOOK OF RESOLUTIONS*
RESOLUTION #238, 2000 *BOOK OF RESOLUTIONS*

*See* Social Principles, ¶ 164*A* and G.

## 5036. Seek Moratorium on Capital Punishment

Because Jesus explicitly repudiates retaliation (Matthew 5:39-39), The United Methodist Church values the sanctity of human life, and desires that no human being be executed by capital punishment.

Although The United Methodist Church stands unequivocally in opposition to the death penalty, we realize there are states within the United States that might be open to a moratorium on the death penalty as a gradual step toward abolition. There are numerous reasons for seeking a moratorium that include:

- the possibility of innocence, as seen in the exoneration of 128 people wrongfully placed on death row in the United States since 1976 (Note Death Penalty Information Center),
- the American Bar Association has currently called for a moratorium on the death penalty,
- thorough investigations and competent experienced capital case lawyers that are often not appointed to defend poor defendants in capital cases,
- highly publicized capital cases that seem often to be decided in an emotionally charged atmosphere, and
- DNA evidence was not available when most current death row prisoners were convicted.

The General Conference of The United Methodist Church calls upon US federal and state government officials to enact, within forty days of the closing of the 2008 General Conference, an immediate moratorium on carrying out of the death penalty sentence.

This request should be sent to US federal and state government officials by the secretary of the General Conference, the Council of Bishops, and the general secretary of the General Board of Church and Society immediately upon the close of the 2008 General Conference.

ADOPTED 2000
REVISED AND READOPTED 2008
RESOLUTION #259, 2004 *BOOK OF RESOLUTIONS*
RESOLUTION #242, 2000 *BOOK OF RESOLUTIONS*

*See* Social Principles, ¶ 164A and G.

## 5037. Texas Death Penalty

WHEREAS, The United Methodist Church strongly opposes capital punishment; and

WHEREAS, in the state of Texas:

- over 400 persons have been put to death since the state resumed executions in 1982;

- among the persons executed since 1982 at least six were mentally retarded, at least twenty suffered from mental illness, and thirteen were juveniles when their crimes were committed;
- among those executed eighty-three African Americans were put to death for crimes against white victims, and only one white person was executed for crimes against African Americans;
- eight persons sentenced to die have later been proven innocent and removed from death row;
- capital trials have at times been characterized by "unreliable witnesses, lack of evidence, incorrect experts, official misconduct, and inadequate defense attorneys";
- the Innocence Project of Texas has pointed to the likelihood that one or more innocent persons have been executed; and

WHEREAS, over 250 organizations of all kinds, including religious, civic, political, legal, and humanitarian groups, have officially called either for a moratorium on executions or for the abolition of the death penalty in Texas; and

WHEREAS, at least ten major newspapers in Texas have endorsed either a moratorium on executions or the abolition of capital punishment in the state;

*Therefore, be it resolved,* that the 2008 General Conference of The United Methodist Church, meeting in Fort Worth, Texas:

- express its deepest appreciation to all those organizations and individuals in the state of Texas who have valiantly struggled and continue to struggle for a more humane society in which the death penalty is rare or nonexistent;
- call upon the Texas Legislature either to abolish the death penalty completely or to stop executions in the state until such time as all capital cases can be tried in a completely equitable way;
- call upon the Texas Pardon and Parole Board and the governor to commute the sentences of persons currently on death row to life in prison without parole or to life in prison; and
- instruct the secretary of the General Conference to have copies of this resolution sent immediately to all members of the Texas Legislature, to each member of the Pardon and Parole Board, to the governor of Texas, to the Texas Conference of Churches, and to the Texas Coalition to Abolish the Death Penalty.

**ADOPTED 2008**

*See* Social Principles, ¶ 164G and H.

## 5038. Opposition to USA PATRIOT ACT to Violate Human Rights

WHEREAS, the United States Constitution guarantees rights to everyone living in the United States, including temporary and permanent aliens as well as citizens; and

WHEREAS, these rights are threatened by the October 2001 USA PATRIOT ACT that includes provision for indefinite detention or deportation of noncitizens, even if they have not committed a crime; grants the FBI access to medical, financial, and educational records without a court order; creates a new crime, "domestic terrorism," which is so broadly defined it could apply to acts of civil disobedience; and

WHEREAS, the PATRIOT ACT includes Federal Executive Orders that establish secret military tribunals for terrorism suspects; permit wiretapping of conversations between federal prisoners and their lawyer; lift Justice Department regulations against covert, illegal counter-intelligence operations by the FBI; and limit the disclosure of public documents under the Freedom of Information Act; and

WHEREAS, despite the fact that this law and these executive orders particularly target foreign nationals and people of color, anyone in the USA could be affected even when acting and speaking legally in opposition to government policy; and

WHEREAS, this law has resulted in the detention and arrest of at least 2,000 Muslims, Arabs, and Southeast Asians in the United States without due process of law; and

WHEREAS, at the outbreak of WW II, the United States government interned 120,000 persons of Japanese ancestry, two-thirds of whom were American citizens, in just such a manner without semblance of due process of law; and

WHEREAS, after extensive investigation, a Presidential Commission in 1982 concluded that such internment was the result of "war hysteria, racial prejudice and a failure of political leadership"; and

WHEREAS, a token monetary award and an apology signed by Presidents Bush (first) and Clinton on behalf of the USA was made to those affected as a result of this finding;

*Therefore, be it resolved,* that the 2004 General Conference of The United Methodist Church go on record as opposed to the use of the USA PATRIOT ACT to violate fundamental rights guaranteed by the United States Constitution; and

*Be it further resolved,* that all members of the General Conference be encouraged to ask their elected representatives to work toward the repeal of those portions of the USA PATRIOT ACT that could be used to violate fundamental rights guaranteed by the United States Constitution; and

*Be it further resolved,* that the General Conference Secretary be directed to immediately forward a copy of this resolution to the President of the United States, members of Congress; and

*Be it further resolved,* that the 2004 General Conference incorporate the language of this resolution into *The Book of Resolutions of The United Methodist Church.*

ADOPTED 2004
RESOLUTION #253, 2004 *BOOK OF RESOLUTIONS*

*See* Social Principles, ¶ 164A, B, D, and F.

# EDUCATION

## 5051. Public Education and the Church

### I. Historic Church Support for Public Education

The United Methodist Church has issued statements supportive of public education, and now at a time when public education has become a political battleground, the church is called to remember, first and foremost, the well-being of all God's children. Education is a right of all children and is affirmed by Scripture which calls us to "train them in the right way" (Proverbs 22:6). Furthermore, the Social Principles affirm that education "can best be fulfilled through public policies that ensure access for all persons to free public elementary and secondary schools and to post-secondary schools of their choice" (¶ 164D).

The public school is the primary route for most children into full participation in our economic, political, and community life. As a consequence of inequities in our society, we have a moral responsibility to support, strengthen, and reform public schools. They have been, and continue to be, both an avenue of opportunity and a major cohesive force in our society, a society becoming daily more diverse racially, culturally, and religiously.

Historically, education has been held to contribute to the development of religious faith. To that end, the great figures of the Reformation called for the establishment of schools. Our founder, John Wesley, was dedicated to the education of poor and underprivileged children. The Sunday School Movement of the latter 18th century was an outgrowth of this ministry and largely established a model for access to public education, regardless of social or economic status. Our heritage should lead us to defend the public schools, and to rejoice that they now more nearly reflect the racial, ethnic, and religious diversity of our country than they have ever done before.

## II. The Larger Social Context

We welcome the fact that many public schools now teach about diversity and the role of religion in human life and history; and we applaud the schools' efforts to promote those virtues necessary for good citizenship in a pluralistic democracy. These reforms help to accommodate the constitutional rights of all students and their parents. Just as we encourage schools to ensure that all religions are treated with fairness and respect, so we urge parents and others to refrain from the temptation to use public schools to advance the cause of any one religion or ethnic tradition, whether through curriculum or through efforts to attach religious personnel to the public schools. We believe that parents have the right to select home schooling or private or parochial schools for their children. But with that personal right comes an obligation to support quality public education for all children. The long-range solution is to improve all schools so that families will not be forced to seek other educational alternatives.

At a moment when childhood poverty is shamefully widespread, when many families are under constant stress, and when schools are limited by lack of funds or resources, criticism of the public schools often ignores an essential truth: we cannot improve public schools by concentrating on the schools alone. In this context, we must address with prayerful determination the issues of race and class that threaten both public education and democracy in America.

## III. Public Funding Issues

By almost any standard of judgment, the schools our children attend can be described in contradictory terms. Some are academically excellent; others are a virtual disgrace. Some are oases of safety for their students; others are dangerous to student and teacher alike. Some teachers are exceptionally well qualified; others are assigned to areas in which they have little or no expertise. Some school facilities are a fantasy land of modern technology; others are so dilapidated that they impede learning.

The wide disparities among public schools exist largely because schools reflect the affluence and/or the political power of the communities in which they are found. Within virtually every state, there are school districts that lavish on their students three or four times the amount of money spent on other children in the same state. A new phenomenon in our society is "re-segregating of communities" which further diminishes the effectiveness of public schools. Most tellingly, the schools that offer the least to their students are those serving poor children, among which children of color figure disproportionately, as they do in all the shortfalls of our common life. Indeed, the coexistence of neglect of schools and neglect of other aspects of the life of people who are poor makes it clear that no effort to improve education in the United States can ignore the realities of racial and class discrimination in our society as a whole.

We acknowledge the debate over whether public funds might appropriately be used to remedy the lingering effects of racial injustice in our nation's educational system. We do not purport to resolve our differences over this issue, but we do affirm our conviction that public funds should be used for public purposes. We also caution that government aid to primary and secondary religious schools raises constitutional problems and could undermine the private schools' independence and/or compromise their religious message.

## IV. What the Church Can Do

Local churches and all communities of faith must become better informed about the needs of the public schools in their communities and in the country as a whole. Only through adequate information can we defend public education and the democratic heritage which it supports. Full knowledge of our religious and democratic traditions helps us ensure that those elected to school boards are strongly committed to both public education and religious liberty.

*Therefore*, we call upon local churches, annual conferences, and the general agencies of The United Methodist Church to support public education by:

1. establishing partnerships with local public schools such as providing after-school and vacation enrichment programs, adopt-a-school programs, and literacy and reading emphases;

2. monitoring reform efforts in public schools, including the creation of charter and magnet schools, of schools-within-schools, and of classes sized to best serve all children;

3. honoring teachers for the crucial work they do with young People; and advocating for appropriate salaries commensurate with their vital role in society;

4. encouraging young people of our congregations to enter the teaching profession;

5. encouraging school libraries to provide quality materials, including those of religious perspectives, that will broaden students' understanding of human life all over the world;

6. insisting that all curricula present the best textbooks and teaching at all levels acknowledging that we encourage children to read, to imagine, and to understand the many wonders of God's creation;

7. encouraging teaching about religion as an essential dimension in the development of civilization;

8. encouraging teaching basic character and civic virtues such as honesty, truthfulness, and respect for life and property;

9. providing parenting classes to emphasize the special responsibilities of families to schools and school-aged children;

10. encouraging the use of curricula in all schools that reflect the role of the many racial, ethnic, and religious groups in the history and culture of the United States;

11. rejecting racial- and gender-biased curricula and testing which limit career options of children and youth;

12. advocating for quality, age-appropriate, comprehensive health education in the public schools;

13. advocating for the inclusion of differently-abled students in our classrooms, and ensuring that teachers have the special training needed to meet these children's needs;

14. supporting thoughtful reform and innovation in local schools to improve teaching and learning at all levels;

15. advocating at the state and local level for adequate public school funding and equitable distribution of state funds; and supporting efforts to end unjust educational disparities between rich and poor communities;

16. learning about public school issues, offering candidate forums during school board elections, and educating church members about

local funding ballot issues and about the historical role of churches in creating and supporting public schools;

17. advocating for strengthened teacher training, for enhanced professional development for teachers and administrators, and for policies that assign teachers only to disciplines in which they are fully prepared, to classes whose size encourages individualized assistance, and to schedules that give teachers time to prepare or consult with other teachers, students, and parents;

18. supporting standards-based school reforms and working in districts and states until the country as a whole has reasonable and challenging standards by which to assess students and schools;

19. encouraging the development of smaller schools (including "schools within schools") to provide a caring environment;

20. calling upon the United States Congress to pass and fully fund legislation to repair and modernize school facilities and to create new facilities as needed;

21. advocating for universal, early, and quality preschool education for all children; and

22. advocating for public education as a basic human right; and not relying solely on school fund raising and state alternative revenues, such as gambling, for financial support.

ADOPTED 2000
AMENDED AND READOPTED 2004
READOPTED 2008
RESOLUTION #263, 2004 *BOOK OF RESOLUTIONS*
RESOLUTION #246, 2000 *BOOK OF RESOLUTIONS*

*See* Social Principles, ¶ 164E.

## 5052. Evolution and Intelligent Design

WHEREAS, The United Methodist Church has for many years supported the separation of church and State (¶ 164C, *Book of Discipline, 2004*, p. 119);

*Therefore, be it resolved,* that the General Conference of The United Methodist Church go on record as opposing the introduction of any faith-based theories such as Creationism or Intelligent Design into the science curriculum of our public schools.

ADOPTED 2008

*See* Social Principles, ¶ 164E.

## MILITARY SERVICE

### 5061. Prayer and Support for Members of the Armed Forces and Veterans

Whereas, our Social Principles state that war is incompatible with the teachings and example of Christ (165.C); and

Whereas, the pervasiveness of violence and the threat of violence in social ordering on the local, national, and international levels present conscientious Christians with profound challenges in living out the Church's rejection of war and violence; and

Whereas, reflecting these challenges, our Social Principles state that we support and extend the ministry of the Church to those persons who conscientiously oppose all war, or any particular war, and who therefore refuse to serve in the armed forces or to cooperate with systems of military conscription, and that we also support and extend the Church's ministry to those persons who conscientiously choose to serve in the armed forces or to accept alternative service (164.I); and

Whereas, United Methodist men and women have served in various capacities in the armed forces and need the acceptance and pastoral ministry of the Church, regardless of the Church's view of the wisdom or moral justification of the military operations into which national political leadership sent them; and

Whereas, the hardships and risks faced by members of the armed forces and the separations inherent in military service impact their families and especially their children; and

Whereas, many of those who serve in the military return with physical or emotional injuries, some of which may persist throughout life or first become apparent many years after their return from service; and

Whereas, expenditures for medical and readjustment services and the needs of military families should be recognized as a cost of war and an obligation of society as a whole; and

Whereas, many military veterans return with experiences that could be an asset in the ministries of the Church, for example, insights arising from the direct experience of military life and war, the perspective gained from having faced one's own mortality, and an understanding of disciplined commitment to a team of people who depend on one another;

*Therefore, be it resolved*, that the 2008 General Conference of The United Methodist Church honors, supports, and upholds in our prayers those men and women who serve in our armed services and, in addition, honors and supports those United Methodist clergy who serve as chaplains; and

*Be it further resolved*, that the Church commits itself to extend its pastoral ministry to members of the armed forces and their families during their time of service and after their return; and

*Be it further resolved*, that we call upon national governments to fully provide medical care and other benefits that promote the welfare of military veterans and their reintegration into civilian society; and

*Be it further resolved*, that we call upon our churches to extend a welcome home to persons who return from service in the armed forces, to respect their stories and interpretations of their experiences, and to value and encourage expression of their potential contributions to the ministry of our churches; and

*Be it further resolved*, that we call upon our churches and members to pray for persons serving in the armed forces and their families, to pray for persons whom circumstances have caused us to relate to as enemies, to pray for other persons for whom war has caused suffering, and to pray for peace.

ADOPTED 2008
RESOLUTION #268, 2004 *BOOK OF RESOLUTIONS*
RESOLUTION #251, 2000 *BOOK OF RESOLUTIONS*

*See* Social Principles, ¶ 164I.


## 5062. Military Service Regardless of Sexual Orientation

The United Methodist Church has historically been opposed to discrimination in society including the military. Our anti-discrimination stance is supported primarily through Jesus' teachings about radical love and the acceptance of those persons living on the margins of society. Throughout Jesus' life, this radical love was shared when Jesus healed the sick, conversed with women, ate with the rejected and brought hope to the hopeless. We see visibly the call to embrace others and not make judgment: "Do not judge, so that you may not be judged. For with the judged, and the measure you give will be the measure you get" (Matthew 7:1-2). Although The United Methodist

Church "deplores war and urges the peaceful settlement of all disputes among nations" it "also support[s] and extend[s] the Church's ministry to those persons who conscientiously choose to serve in the armed forces. . . . " A commitment to the civil rights of people and their ability to follow a "call" to ministry, such as military service, should not be denied.

The United States of America, a nation built on equal rights, presently denies the right of professing homosexuals to actively serve their country, forcing men and women who are gay, lesbian, bisexual, or transgender to assume a "don't ask, don't tell" position when enlisting into military service. This situation is discriminatory, unethical, and regrettable; therefore, we affirm the stance that the US military should not exclude persons from service solely on the basis of sexual orientation or gender identity.

**ADOPTED 2008**

*See* Social Principles, ¶¶ 164*I* and 161*F*.

## 5063. Military Conscription, Training, and Service

1. *Conscription.* We affirm our historic opposition to compulsory military training and service. We urge that military conscription laws be repealed; we also warn that elements of compulsion in any national service program will jeopardize seriously the service motive and introduce new forms of coercion into national life. We advocate and will continue to work for the inclusion of the abolition of military conscription in disarmament agreements.

2. *Conscientious objection.* Each person must face conscientiously the dilemmas of conscription, military training, and service and decide his or her own responsible course of action. We affirm the historic statement: "What the Christian citizen may not do is to obey persons rather than God, or overlook the degree of compromise in even our best acts, or gloss over the sinfulness of war. The church must hold within its fellowship persons who sincerely differ at this point of critical decision, call all to repentance, mediate to all God's mercy, minister to all in Christ's name" ("The United Methodist Church and Peace," 1968 General Conference).

Christian teaching supports conscientious objection to all war as an ethically valid position. It also asserts that ethical decisions on political matters must be made in the context of the competing claims of biblical revelation, church doctrine, civil law, and one's own understanding of what God calls him or her to do.

We therefore support all those who conscientiously object to preparation for or participation in any specific war or all wars, to cooperation with military conscription, or to the payment of taxes for military purposes, and we ask that they be granted legal recognition.

Since 1936, The United Methodist Church or one of its predecessors has provided to those of its members who claim to be conscientious objectors the opportunity to register. Certified copies of such registration are supplied for use with the draft authorities. It is the responsibility of the church at all levels to inform its members of the fact that conscientious objection, as well as conscientious participation, is a valid option for Christians and is recognized in many countries as a legal alternative for persons liable to military conscription.

The local church's support of an individual participating in this process does not express agreement or disagreement with the convictions of the applicant member. Rather, the church's task is to record which of its members are opposed to participation in military service on grounds of conscience and to assist them in securing proper counsel. When a member has registered as a conscientious objector and his or her registration has been certified by the proper authorities, that action should be recorded with the annual conference and the General Board of Church and Society.

The United Methodist Church also supports those persons who refuse to register for the draft and deplores discrimination against those persons by any institution.

3. *Amnesty and reconciliation.* We urge understanding of and full amnesty or pardon for persons in all countries whose refusal to participate in war has placed them in legal jeopardy. We urge governments to grant political asylum to persons whose countries fail to recognize their conscientious objection to war.

**ADOPTED 2008**

*See* Social Principles, ¶ 164*I*.

## POLITICAL RESPONSIBILITY

### 5071. Campaign Finance Reform in the United States

Campaign finance reform is a moral matter for the religious community. The temptation to buy unjust favors is an ancient one that is addressed often in Scripture. The prophet Amos thundered against those merchants in Israel who "sell the righteous for silver and the needy for a pair of sandals . . . and push the afflicted out of the way . . ." (Amos 2:6-7, NRSV). Psalm 15 defines upright persons as those who ". . . stand by their oath even to their hurt . . . and do not take a bribe against the innocent."

The pouring of tens of millions of dollars into political campaigns in order to buy special influence with legislators has become a scandal. Citizens forsake participation in the political process because they believe policies are shaped by money from special interests—not by the national interest or the needs of the people.

The issue of campaign financing is far more than a political matter. It goes to the heart of the ethical and moral life of a nation.

Many elected officials continually court monied special interests in order to finance their next election campaign. It is time to free electoral politics from this corrupting pressure—through a system of public campaign financing that would take government away from special interests and return it to the people.

If politicians are to focus on the well-being of the people and the nation, they must be able to depend on public financing rather than pursuing special-interest money.

We commend those politicians of all parties who are working to achieve real campaign financing reform.

We call upon all United Methodists to work within their own countries to build support for measures that would end the flood of special-interest monies to political campaigns and restore integrity to decision making.

In 2002, the bipartisan Campaign Reform Act was enacted in the United States. The long-term goal of campaign finance reform is the public financing of campaigns at the national level. The next short-term steps for reform are strengthening the oversight of the Federal Election Commission, changing the presidential public financing system, and establishing a system that will enable federal candidates and parties to air on television and radio stations a limited amount of free advertising. Similar legislation is ongoing in Germany and other countries. Candidates for public office should focus their campaigns on the issues and on their own qualifications to serve in office. They should refrain from personal attacks and name-calling of opponents, not distort an opponent's views by taking quotes out of context or misrepresenting the opponent's positions or voting record, and set an example of truthfulness and integrity for the public. Similar legislation is ongoing in Germany and other countries.

ADOPTED 1996
AMENDED AND READOPTED 2004
RESOLUTION #269, 2004 *BOOK OF RESOLUTIONS*
RESOLUTION #253, 2000 *BOOK OF RESOLUTIONS*

*See* Social Principles, ¶ 164*A* and *B.*

## 5072. Encouragement to Vote in Elections

WHEREAS, members of The United Methodist Church have a history of being proactive in all levels of governmental activity; and

WHEREAS, the first sentence of ¶ 164 of the Social Principles states, ". . . we acknowledge the vital function of government as the principal vehicle for the ordering of society"; and

WHEREAS, Resolution # 228 in *The Book of Resolutions of The United Methodist Church, 2000* entitled "Church-Government Relations" presents a broad discussion of the relationship that is or should exist between the church and the government; and

WHEREAS, the decision-making power and administrative leadership of the government is vested primarily in elected officials; and

WHEREAS, in many jurisdictions within the United States there may be propositions, amendments and/or resolutions appearing on the election day ballot; and

Whereas, in some jurisdictions within the United States there is provision for initiative and referendum, the consideration of which may appear on the election day ballot;

*Therefore, it is resolved,* to urge churches in our global community to encourage their members to take advantage of the opportunities to vote; and

*Be it further resolved*, those registered voters be encouraged to inform themselves concerning the qualifications of persons running for office and the merit(s) of items requiring decision(s) that are to appear on the election day ballot, and, after thoughtful and prayerful consideration, to vote their choices on the various election days.

ADOPTED 2004
RESOLUTION #270, 2004 *BOOK OF RESOLUTIONS*

*See* Social Principles, ¶ 164*A* and *B*.


## UNITED STATES LEGISLATIVE ISSUES

### 5081. Call for Comprehensive Immigration Reform

*When an alien lives with you in your land, do not mistreat him. The alien living with you must be treated as one of your native-born. Love him as yourself, for you were aliens in Egypt. I am the* LORD *your God.*
                                            —*Leviticus 19:33-34, NIV*

*Background:*

As followers of Christ we are called to love the stranger in our midst because we were once strangers in a foreign land. The stranger in the midst at one time or another has been your own family member.

In 1996 the Illegal Immigration Reform and Immigrant Responsibility Act (IIRAIRA) went into effect. This immigration law severely restricted the opportunities of immigrants in the United States to reunite with their families, to obtain permission to work legally, and to avoid being exploited by unscrupulous employers and employment practices. It restricted the opportunities for the elderly to obtain needed social services and for children to obtain an education at a reasonable cost. The IIRAIRA also strengthened border security with the idea of reducing the numbers of people who enter this country every year without permission in search of opportunities to earn wages with which they can support their families back home. The law has not worked. The current immigration system is broken.

Approximately 850,000 immigrants enter the United States without permission every year. America benefits and prospers as a result of their labor; yet denies many of them basic rights like fair wages, health benefits, the opportunity to be with their families, and social services.

We are living in a time of persecution and oppression due to igno-rance and fear. There is frustration on all sides about the state of our immigration laws. We must work to channel that frustration into advocacy for the passage of a comprehensive immigration reform bill.

Fear, ignorance, and debate over immigration has generated dan-gerous racial dynamics that have led to racial profiling and intoler-ance toward Latino/Hispanic Cultures, an increase in the English-only language movements, and racism. The United Methodist Church has historically stood against racism, cultural prejudice, and other forms of intolerance. On the contrary, we as a church have affirmed and celebrated God's diverse human creation.

As Christians and United Methodists we are called to love the stranger in our midst and to treat that stranger as we would our own family. We must be a church that welcomes the foreigners into our cities, our towns, our neighborhoods, our churches, our homes. We must keep ourselves open to the opportunity and blessing of enter-taining angels unawares. If we are to truly live out our mandate of having open hearts, open minds, open doors, we must work to ensure the just treatment of the foreigners living among us.

*Therefore, be it resolved*, that the 2008 General Conference of The United Methodist Church assert that immigrants are children of God made in God's image, affirm the labor and struggle of the undocu-mented worker, and assert that immigrant children deserve to be edu-cated and provided with basic social services.

*Be it further resolved*, that The United Methodist Church stand against all forms of oppression and prejudices, and will work through its general agencies, especially the General Commission on Religion and Race and the General Board of Church and Society, to resist racism, intolerance, and prejudice in the context of the immigration debate.

*Be it further resolved*, that the General Conference urge all the local congregations to oppose unjust local and state ordinances that seek to deprive undocumented persons of basic social services including the access to adequate housing and protection under the law.

*Be it further resolved*, that the 2008 General Conference join with M.A.R.C.H.A. (Methodists Associated to Represent the Cause of Hispanic/Latino Americans) and urge the United States Congress to pass comprehensive immigration reform that makes family unity, students being able to get an education at an affordable rate, fair and just treatment of laborers, and a reasonable path towards citizenship a priority.

*Be it further resolved,* that the Council of Bishops be asked to be sensitive to the immigration situation as it is important not only to demand this of the United States Government, but that they also improve policies inside the church that reflect this sensitivity on immigration.

*Be it further resolved,* that the 2008 General Conference send a copy of this resolution and a letter to the President of the United States and the United States Congress urging them to work towards the passage of a fair and just comprehensive immigration bill.

*Finally, be it resolved,* that the 2008 General Conference of The United Methodist Church request the Council of Bishops to urgently establish a Plan of Action of Advocacy and Welcoming the Sojourner to enable their annual conferences to immediately respond to the needs and challenges of the Hispanic/Latino immigrant population, and all immigrant populations in the community, by creating opportunities of service and equipping local churches to effectively respond in their ministry.

**ADOPTED 2008**

*See* Social Principles, ¶ 164B.

## 5082. Establish US Department of Peace

WHEREAS, the people of the United States overwhelmingly support peace in the world; and

WHEREAS, the current structure of our government has not been designed to research and advocate new strategies for peace; and

WHEREAS, the Department of Defense consumes an increasingly large portion of our national budget (currently 40 percent of outlays—Friends Committee on National Legislation, March 24, 2003); and

WHEREAS, Congressman Dennis Kucinich (D-OH), Congresswoman Barbara Lee (D-CA) and Congressman John Conyers Jr. (D-MI), and others have advocated for a Department of Peace, and have introduced H.R. 2459 for the establishment of a Department of Peace; and

WHEREAS, the bill defines the mission of the Department of Peace such that it shall: 1) hold peace as an organizing principle, coordinating service to every level of American society; 2) endeavor to promote justice and democratic principles to expand human rights; 3) strengthen nonmilitary means of peacemaking; 4) promote the development of human potential; 5) work to create peace, prevent violence, divert from armed conflict, use field-tested programs, and develop new structures in nonviolent dispute resolution; 6) take a proactive, strategic approach in the development of policies that promote national and international conflict prevention, nonviolent intervention, mediation, peaceful resolution of conflict, and structured mediation of conflict; 7) address matters both domestic and international in scope; and 8) encourage the development of initiatives from local communities, religious groups, and nongovernmental organizations; and

WHEREAS, the Social Principles of The United Methodist Church states that "we deplore war and urge the peaceful settlement of all disputes among nations" (¶ 164I of the *Book of Discipline, 2008*); and

WHEREAS, Jesus taught us that "blessed are the peacemakers," and valued all human life;

*Therefore, be it resolved*, that the 2008 General Conference endorse the establishment of a US Department of Peace.

ADOPTED 2004
REVISED AND READOPTED 2008
RESOLUTION #272, 2004 *BOOK OF RESOLUTIONS*

*See* Social Principles, ¶ 164B and I.

## 5083. Right to Privacy

### *Theological Statement*

The Christian faith stresses the dignity of and respect for human personality and the need to protect its privacy. Our human right to privacy has an importance in this age of electronic communication and information data bases that it did not have in the days when our scriptures were written. The right to privacy, however, and the corollary duty to protect the privacy of others, are not without mention in the Bible.

Jesus tells us to give our alms in secret so that God may bless us (Matthew 6:4). What God commands us to do, we surely must have a right to do. And with that right, comes a duty. We are to protect the secrets of others and not disclose them, for doing so will bring us both shame and ill repute (Proverbs 25:9-10). Vulnerability is closely linked with our need for privacy and we have a positive duty to make the vulnerable less vulnerable; when we see the naked, we are to cover them (Isaiah 58:7), and by extension, when we encounter information which is better kept private, we are to keep it from going farther.

The ability to respect the privacy of others is a virtue: he who is trustworthy in spirit keeps a thing hidden (Proverbs 11:13). Conversely, because gossip leads to the invasion of others' privacy and the revelation of their secrets, gossips are viewed as destructive people, and a careful steward of private information will not let oneself become vulnerable to them (Proverbs 20:19).

At the same time, our scriptures recognize that privacy can be abused. Employing privacy to slander another in secret is an offence against God, who will destroy the violator (Psalm 101:5). Delilah abuses her relationship with Samson to learn the secret of his strength, then violates his privacy, jeopardizing his life by sharing his secret with his enemies (Judges 16:9). The Bible recognizes that privacy can be abused in the service of oppression; the poor are devoured in secret, Habakkuk (3:14) reminds us, for frequently evil is the result of conspiracies undertaken in secret. The prophets of Israel denounced the repression of the poor, widows, orphans, and others of their society, and our Lord's ministry began with the announced purpose to set at liberty the poor and disadvantaged.

Privacy takes on special meaning in the context of our spirituality. The Psalmist identifies privacy with inwardness; "You desire truth in the inward being; therefore teach me wisdom in my secret heart" (Psalm 51:6). Privacy is an attribute of God, who owns secrets (Deuteronomy 29:29), and who creates humanity in secret (Psalm 139:15). We have no privacy, however, from God, from whom no secret is hidden (Ezekiel 28:3, Mark 4:22), and who will reveal all secrets (Luke 8:17). The secrets of our heart are disclosed to God (1 Corinthians 14:25) who judges these secrets by Christ (Romans 2:16). These scriptural roots claim our attention in several areas of modern life.

### Privacy as a Civil Liberty

Because privacy is a human right, it is also a civil liberty. Privacy is meaningless if it does not include privacy from the intrusion of government bodies. Implicit in the right to privacy is the assumption that humans are the owners of their private information, and it is from that position of ownership that the right to choose whether or not to disclose flows. The power to control one's own information is the mark of a free person rather than a slave.

We recall among the many offenses of slavery how slaves were exhibited naked on the auction block so that potential buyers might examine them as a commodity. Invasion of the privacy of an ordinary citizen of society negates this dignity and respect. Further, the Christian faith is supportive of a society that elicits hope and trust, not a society that foments fear and threatens with oppression. The packaging and sale in today's world of information about persons represents a commodification of their humanity and is an offence against their freedom.

We recognize that many of the obligations of government necessitate the collection of personal information by the government. Every instance of such collection must be justified through due process where challenge is possible.

The Social Principles of The United Methodist Church affirm that "illegal and unconscionable activities directed against persons or groups by their own governments must not be justified or kept secret, even under the guise of national security" (¶ 164C). "We strongly reject domestic surveillance and intimidation of political opponents by governments in power and all other misuses of elective or appointive offices" (¶ 164A).

## Law Enforcement

We recognize that privacy can be abused for idolatry and murder (Deuteronomy 27:24), for political intrigue (2 Samuel 15:10), and for treachery (Judges 3:19). The psalmist prays that God will protect us from the secret plots of the wicked (Psalm 64:2) and Psalm 10:9 warns its readers of the wicked who lurk in secret like a lion.

We therefore recognize that law enforcement in particular requires the collection and presentation of data to prove a defendant's guilt. We affirm, however, the principle that all are innocent until proven guilty, and, as innocent persons, enjoy the right to privacy.

## Medical Privacy

The purpose of health care, whether provided by physicians or other professionals, whether provided by solo practitioners or large institutions, is to restore the health of individual human beings.

Persons who seek healing entrust medical practitioners and institutions with their private information, which remains their property.

We therefore support the understanding that patient records and the information in them are the property of the patients to whom the individual pertains, and are not the property of the medical institutions which maintain the records. Institutions are trustees of such information, and must use it for its intended purpose, namely the restoration to health of the affected individuals and, where appropriate, for the health of the public.

We oppose the use of private medical information to promote the products of commercial enterprises. We oppose the provision of private medical information to employers or creditors without the consent of the persons who own the information. We oppose the use of private medical information in legal situations without the person's consent, as this amounts to involuntary self-incrimination.

We oppose the use of private medical information without the owner's permission, to discriminate against the owner of the information in employment, in housing, in the provision of credit.

## Genetic Privacy

We are particularly opposed to the use of genetic information concerning an individual in order to discriminate in the provision of credit, employment, and various forms of insurance.

We support genetic privacy and nondiscrimination legislation that seeks to prohibit discrimination on the basis of genetic information with respect to life insurance, health insurance, employment, and other areas of life in which genetic information can be used for injustice and oppression.

## National Security and Government Privacy

Governments are comprised of human beings and it is understandable that governments will have the same desire for privacy that individual humans will have. In addition, governments have responsibilities for national security that individuals do not have, and have a legitimate right to keep certain information secret, whose transmission could leave a nation vulnerable. In Isaiah 39, the King of Judah unwisely allowed the Babylonians information on both the treasure and the defense of Judah; this information was then used by Babylon to defeat Judah. We oppose, however, the extension of government's legitimate need for security to include information which is of little value to an enemy, but which might be embarrassing to the government, or might subject the government to greater accountability from a concerned public.

Citizens of all countries should have access to all essential information regarding their government and its policies. Openness is a redemptive gift of God, calling for trust and honesty between various segments of the community. Justice is the cornerstone of that trust we have come to expect in our elective and appointive representatives of the community. Communal wholeness is attained through the concerted use of these elements.

In the United States, we support the Freedom of Information Act, and encourage its widespread use. We support sunshine laws which require that the business of government not be conducted in secret. We recognize that agencies charged with public and national security need information in order to discharge their duties. We believe that when government needs private information, all three branches of government must agree that the public need outweighs the private right—the legislative branch to create appropriate laws, the executive branch to identify particular needs, and the judicial branch to approve them. We strongly oppose, however, in the United States the provisions of the USA Patriot Act that permit warrantless intrusion into private communications by telephone, mail, and email, and the secret searching of bank records and other records. Revelations that intelligence agencies, local police, the Internal Revenue Service, and the United States military have, over a number of years, developed a domestic espionage apparatus involving the gathering of information about the lawful political activities of millions of citizens is a continuing cause for concern. It is deplorable that in a society that is democratic in theory and structure there are signs of increasing repression: dragnet arrests; police and the intelligence community's harassment of minority leaders; charges of conspiracy; summary acquittals of police accused of brutality; the rising militancy of rank-and-file police; support for the use of preventive detention; the utilization of wiretaps; censorship of journalism in educational and correctional institutions; heavy punitive action against dissidents; the confinement of those who protested within the military forces; the utilization of grand juries for the purpose of harassment rather than indictment; and the use of church members, clergy, and missionaries for secret intelligence purposes by local police departments, the Federal Bureau of Investigation, and the Central Intelligence Agency.

We call for restoration of legal protections against any kind of wire-tapping without a warrant of a court and restraint in the use of wire-tapping and electronic surveillance. Surveillance creates an air of suspicion throughout the whole society and contributes to the insecurity of law-abiding American citizens.

We affirm the many civil, school, and church authorities who are working toward the elimination of these abuses through their work and example; and we note that many of the most flagrant of these acts of repression no longer occur. Congress, the press, and the American people have begun watching agency activities more closely and with a greater demand for public accountability.

This vigilance must not be relaxed, for if it is, there may be renewed acts of repression and fresh attempts to curtail the rights of citizens whenever redress is sought for economic and social grievances.

We are particularly appalled when the promotion of fear appears to be a means of undermining our civil liberties including the right to privacy. We agree with Benjamin Franklin in his statement that, "They who would give up an essential liberty for temporary security, deserve neither liberty nor security."

## Sexual Privacy

Of all topics related to privacy, the Bible is most clear regarding our right to sexual privacy. In the Biblical narrative, privacy is addressed in the very first pages of Genesis. Immediately upon eating the fruit of the tree of good and evil, Adam and Eve cover their loins (Genesis 3:7), a recognition not only that human beings need privacy, but that it is in the area of sexual relationship that human beings are most vulnerable to each other, and that we legitimately seek a degree of privacy in the area of sex and reproduction that exceeds what we require in other areas.

Subsequent statements of the Hebrew Scriptures emphasize the primacy of sexuality in matters of privacy. When identification is made of those for whom sexual relationships are forbidden, what is forbidden is described in euphemisms of privacy: one must not "uncover the nakedness" of those with whom sexual intercourse is forbidden. (Deuteronomy 22:30; Leviticus 18:6-19; 20:18-19). By extension, one must also not "uncover the nakedness" of those for whom sexual intercourse is protected. We therefore support the privacy rights of men and women regarding reproductive health decisions. The Scriptures also acknowledge our need for privacy in meeting our bodies' needs; the servants of Eglon, king of Moab, do not rush into his chamber after his murder, thinking that he is relieving himself (Judges 3:19).

We therefore maintain the appropriateness of a greater degree of privacy regarding sexuality than in other areas.

We oppose strip searches by law enforcement personnel of the opposite sex. We oppose the employment of prison guards of the opposite sex where prisoners have no privacy for dressing, undressing, or the performance of bodily functions. We support the right of medical patients to have a chaperone of the same sex present when being examined by a practitioner of the opposite sex. It is in the deprivation of the right to sexual privacy that the most degrading forms of dehumanization occur in our society.

*Charge*

We call upon:
- The General Board of Church and Society to represent this perspective to American legislators in Washington and to the global community at the United Nations in New York. We respectfully request the Congress of the United States to:
1. enact comprehensive charter legislation for all of the intelligence agencies that would prohibit them from engaging in surveillance or disruption of lawful political activity. We oppose any charter provision that permits intelligence agencies to recruit and use as agents clergy or missionaries;
2. place statutory limitations upon the demand by governmental bureaus and agencies for personal information about any citizen or family for statistical purposes. When such requests by agencies are for information not required by law, the respondent should be informed that compliance is voluntary. Restrictions should be placed by law on private agencies in gathering, storing, and disseminating personal information; and
3. retain the Freedom of Information Act as it is, in support of the right of all citizens to know the actions of their government.
- The General Board of Discipleship to include in its curricula an understanding of the biblical bases for the right to privacy. they have influence, both personally and as members of church congregations.

- All church members and leaders to continue to be sensitive to this situation in their local community and in the nation by:

1. seeking to understand and undergird responsible institutions and agencies of the community and being supportive of measurements that will improve them and upgrade their personnel; and

2. establishing programs in the community sponsored by local churches to:

  - educate church members and their wider community about the potential for repression in the institutions of society;
  - study and affirm the biblical and constitutional basis for justice under law;
  - work in state and federal legislatures to bring about just and responsible criminal code revisions that do not reinforce repressive elements in our nation's life;
  - oppose forms of legislation that would legalize repression; support legislation that would prohibit intelligence agencies from conducting surveillance or disruption of lawful political activities or otherwise violating constitutional rights;
  - develop an awareness of the rights and protection citizens should expect; and
  - work for institutional change in situations where rights are not respected and protection is not furnished.

ADOPTED 2008
RESOLUTION #276, 2004 *BOOK OF RESOLUTIONS*
RESOLUTION #258, 2000 *BOOK OF RESOLUTIONS*

*See* Social Principles, ¶ 164A.

## 5084. Support Legislation Prohibiting Malicious Harassments

The United Methodist Church encourages and supports the introduction, passage, and funding of legislation that prohibits malicious and intimidating actions that are reasonably related to, associated with, or directed toward a person's race, color, religion, ancestry, national origin, sexual orientation, age, gender, or disability.

ADOPTED 1992
READOPTED 2004 AND 2008
RESOLUTION #277, 2004 *BOOK OF RESOLUTIONS*
RESOLUTION #259, 2000 *BOOK OF RESOLUTIONS*

*See* Social Principles, ¶ 164A.

## 5085. The US Campaign for a Tax Fund

We have long supported those persons who cannot in conscience pay taxes in support of war. We believe they should be granted the same legal recognition as that granted to conscientious objectors to military service. Toward that end, we recognize the work of the National Campaign for a Peace Tax Fund (NCPTF). The NCPTF advocates for legislation by the United States Congress to establish a Peace Tax Fund.

The purpose of Peace Tax Fund legislation is to:
- provide each individual the right not to be coerced into any form of participation in killing other human beings—whether that participation is physical or financial;
- offer conscientious objectors the right to pay their full tax obligation without violating deeply held religious or ethical beliefs; and
- give those who are conscientiously opposed to war because of religious or ethical beliefs the right not to have legal penalties imposed because of those beliefs.

We believe all persons have these rights based in the freedom to exercise their beliefs according to the dictates of conscience. To that end, we support the National Campaign for a Peace Tax Fund and affirm the work it does on behalf of those who conscientiously object to payment of taxes for war.

ADOPTED 1996
READOPTED 2004
RESOLUTION #278, 2004 *BOOK OF RESOLUTIONS*
RESOLUTION #260, 2000 *BOOK OF RESOLUTIONS*

*See* Social Principles, ¶ 164F.


## 5086. Food and Drug Administration (FDA) Regulation of Tobacco

WHEREAS, The United Methodist Church historically has opposed the use of tobacco products and their devices in the Social Principles ¶ 162M:

"We affirm our historic tradition of high standards of personal discipline and social responsibility. In light of the overwhelming evidence that tobacco smoking and the use of smokeless tobacco are hazardous to the health of all ages, we recommend total abstinence from the use of tobacco. We urge that our educational and communication resources be utilized to support and encourage such abstinence. Further, we recognize the harmful effects of passive smoke and support the restriction of smoking in public areas and workplaces."

WHEREAS, the sixth commandment says, "Thou shalt not kill";

WHEREAS, the medical community and surgeon general have known the causal effects of tobacco and disease and death for over fifty years;

WHEREAS, annually more than 450,000 people in the United States die because of the over 240 cancer-causing ingredients in tobacco products and their devices and their products of combustion. This is equivalent to all the American casualties in all the wars of the 20th century occurring every eighteen months and the same number of casualties of Sept. 11, 2001 occurring every three days;

WHEREAS, the Congress of the United States has intentionally maintained for itself the authority to regulate the ingredients in tobacco products, their devices, and their products of combustion;

*Therefore, be it resolved,* that the General Conference of The United Methodist Church strongly urges the members of Congress to provide the authority to the Food and Drug Administration to regulate the ingredients of tobacco products, their devices, and their products of combustion in order to render harmless the greatest menace to human life in our country's history.

ADOPTED 2004
READOPTED 2008
RESOLUTION #281, 2004 *BOOK OF RESOLUTIONS*

*See* Social Principles, ¶¶ 162L and M and 164.

## 5087. US Federal Single-payer Health Insurance Program

WHEREAS more than forty million Americans are without health care insurance and countless others are under-insured, and

WHEREAS there already exists within the present federal government a fractured and disjointed set of national health care insurance plans in the form of Medicare, CHAMPUS, Federal Employees Health Benefit Program, Railroad Employees Health Benefit Plan, Medicaid, and possibly others,

*Therefore, be it resolved,* that The United Methodist Church exert influence through all its structures and means to connectionally advocate and fervently lobby the federal government for the adoption and implementation of a totally nonprofit health insurance system, a single-payer system administered by the federal government, and

*Be it further resolved,* that the General Board of Church and Society be charged with initiating conversations with, and developing strategies for, working with other nonprofit groups, such as AARP, the United Health Care Action Network, the Physicians for a National Health Care Program, and other denominations to lobby members of the federal government to develop a national health insurance plan that embodies the principles spelled out in Resolutions 118 and 120.

*Be it further resolved,* that the General Board of Church and Society communicate annually to its annual conference counterparts what actions it has taken on General Conference resolutions pertaining to health care.

ADOPTED 2004
RESOLUTION #282, 2004 *BOOK OF RESOLUTIONS*

*See* Social Principles, ¶¶ 162*V* and 164*A*.


### 5088. Voting Representation for People in the District of Columbia

The District of Columbia was established on the first Monday in December, 1800, by an Act of Congress as a seat for the national government under authority granted to the Congress by Article 1, Section 8, of the US Constitution, under which the Congress has the power to "exercise exclusive legislation in all cases whatsoever, over such District." At no time since has the federal legislature passed any provision for voting representation for the residents of the District of Columbia. Yet, throughout our nation's history, citizens of the District of Columbia have given their undivided allegiance to the United States: fighting and dying in wars, paying their full measure of taxes, and providing labor and resources to the federal government.

Therefore, because we recognize:

- that governments derive their "just powers from the consent of the governed" in order to secure the people's rights "endowed by their Creator";
- the Social Principles contained in *The United Methodist Book of Discipline* state that the "form and the leaders of all govern-

ments should be determined by exercise of the right to vote guaranteed to all adult citizens";

- the Social Principles also state that "the strength of a political system depends on the full and willing participation of its citizens" (¶ 164B);
- it has been the enduring tradition and history of the Methodist movement, from the time of Wesley to the present day, to support the rights of the individual, to provide relief to the disenfranchised, and to champion the equality of all persons before God and before the law; and
- throughout the biblical narrative God desires the inclusion and full participation of all people into society;

The United Methodist Church agrees that the continuing disenfranchisement of the citizens of the District of Columbia is an egregious moral wrong that must be rectified.

Therefore, the General Conference of The United Methodist Church declares its full support, on moral grounds that citizens of the District of Columbia are entitled to political rights equal to those of other United States citizens, including voting representation in both houses of Congress. We call on the President and the Congress of the United States of America to take action to provide congressional representation to the citizens of Washington, DC.

We call on all United Methodist congregations throughout the United States to support the people of the District of Columbia in this cause by calling upon their elected representatives in Congress to demand democratic rights for the District of Columbia.

ADOPTED 1980
REVISED AND ADOPTED 2000
REVISED AND READOPTED 2008
RESOLUTION #280, 2004 *BOOK OF RESOLUTIONS*
RESOLUTION #262, 2000 *BOOK OF RESOLUTIONS*

*See* Social Principles, ¶ 164B.


## 5089. Puerto Rican Political Prisoners

WHEREAS, The United Methodist Church and The Methodist Church of Puerto Rico have advocated for the liberation of Puerto Rican women and men sentenced to excessive punishment due to alleged crimes related to their struggle for the independence of Puerto Rico;

WHEREAS, these persons have been in prison for a long time;

WHEREAS, the sentencing of these persons intended to punish political activity more than the crimes they are accused of; and

WHEREAS, Puerto Rican political prisoners refused to participate in the US court system because of their belief that the US government was the colonial and enemy power; and

WHEREAS a number of Puerto Rican political prisoners were released from prison, but there are still some in prison; and

WHEREAS, the United Nations' resolutions on decolonization have clearly established that colonialism is a crime, and they recognize a colonized people's right to end colonialism. The United Nations also recognizes that these resolutions and laws apply to Puerto Rico. For many years, the United Nations Decolonization Committee has approved resolutions recognizing the inalienable right of Puerto Rico's people to independence and self-determination. The injustice suffered under Puerto Rico's colonial reality cannot be overlooked; and

WHEREAS, the release of these prisoners is being supported by many civic, religious, and international organizations;

*Therefore, be it resolved,* that The United Methodist Church, The Methodist Church of Puerto Rico, and MARCHA continue to advocate for the liberation of Puerto Rican political prisoners; and

*Be it also resolved,* that letters from the General Conference Secretary of The United Methodist Church, the Council of Bishops of The United Methodist Church, and of the Bishop of The Methodist Church of Puerto Rico be sent to the President of the United States requesting that these persons be released from prison.

ADOPTED 1996
AMENDED AND READOPTED 2000
AMENDEDED AND READOPTED 2008
RESOLUTION #274, 2004 *BOOK OF RESOLUTIONS*
RESOLUTION #257, 2000 *BOOK OF RESOLUTIONS*

*See* Social Principles, ¶ 164*A* and *F.*

## 5090. Justice for Cuban Prisoners

WHEREAS, in Matthew 25, Jesus tells us that those who care for those in need are his true disciples (verses 31-46). By the same token, the Lord reminds us that to do justice, and mercy are the most important aspects of the Law, that anyone who forgets these points has forgotten God's purposes for them. Thus, the author of Hebrews urges us to "[r]emember those in prison as if you were their fellow prisoners, and those who are mistreated as if you yourselves were suffering" (13:3).

WHEREAS, taking the scriptural witness to heart we must respond to the injustice suffered today by five Cuban political prisoners in US federal prisons. Since their arrest in 1998 and incarceration following sentencing, they have received inhumane and cruel treatment.

WHEREAS, they are not allowed to visit with their families, and in many occasions their families have been denied visas to come to the US to see them, or have been allowed to come to the US and returned to their country without seen their loved one, and

The following are their names and their sentences:

1. Gerardo Hernández Nordelo: Two lives in prison plus 15 years.
2. Ramón Labañino Salazar: Life in prison plus 18 years
3. Antonio Guerrero Rodríguez: Life in prison plus 10 years
4. Fernando González Llort: 19 years in prison

*Therefore, be it resolved that,* the 2004 General Conference of The United Methodist Church meeting in Pittsburgh, Pennsylvania, request the US government: the State Department, the federal prison system, to allow the families of these prisoners access to their loved ones; to allow them to see their children and their spouses in prison.

*Therefore, be it further resolved,* that The United Methodist Church support these prisoners' families with their prayers and supplications before God, and that the Church through its leadership may accompany these families to visit their loved ones in prison.

*Finally, be it further resolved,* that, given that there have been concerns about the impartiality of their trials, The United Methodist Church gathered in Pittsburgh, Pennsylvania, considers that it would be appropriate for the Justice Department to address these concerns and to truly do justice to these prisoners.

ADOPTED 2004
RESOLUTION #275, 2004 *BOOK OF RESOLUTIONS*

*See* Social Principles, ¶ 164A.


## 5091. Filipino Veterans Equity Act of 2007

WHEREAS, during World War II, the military forces of the Commonwealth of the Philippines were drafted to serve in the United States Armed Forces in the Far East under the command of General Douglas MacArthur; and

WHEREAS, Filipino soldiers fought with Americans in the bloodiest battles of World War II, including the battle at Corregidor; and

WHEREAS, thousands of Filipino prisoners of war died during the 65-mile Bataan Death March, and those who survived were imprisoned under inhumane and degrading conditions; and

WHEREAS, for serving in the US Armed Forces in the Far East (USAFFE), Filipino veterans were promised military benefits and US citizenship; and

WHEREAS, the US Congress passed the Recession Act of 1946, Section 107 of Title 38 of the United States code, that mandated that the service performed by Filipino veterans would not be recognized as "active service," thus denying Filipino veterans the rights, privileges, and benefits that US veterans receive, including health benefits and pension; and

WHEREAS, both President William Clinton and President George H. Bush issued two Presidential Proclamations recalling the sacrifice, courage, and loyalty of Filipino veterans of World War II; and

WHEREAS, the United States Congress passed two resolutions in 1996 and 2005 that recognized and thanked the Filipino veterans of World War II for their service and contribution toward the successful outcome of the war; and

WHEREAS, on January 4, 2007, Senator Daniel Inouye introduced S. 57, and on January 31, 2007, Congressman Bob Filner introduced H.R. 760, both known by the "Filipino WWII Veterans Equity Act of 2007," that would amend Title 38 of the United States Code to deem certain service in the organized military forces of the government of the Commonwealth of the Philippines and the Philippine Scouts to have been active service for purposes of benefits under programs administered by the Secretary of Veterans Affairs; and

WHEREAS, both bills are reintroductions of bills introduced in every Congress since the 105th Congress that would have granted Filipino veterans of World War II the same rights and benefits as US veterans, but have not been enacted; and

WHEREAS, the Philippine Embassy reports that there are only approximately 18,000 veterans left who would be able to take advantage of the Equity Act, and they are dying due to ill-health and old age at a rate of approximately 8 to 10 a day; and

WHEREAS, many Filipino veterans will not receive the benefits that they deserve and are entitled to if S. 57 and H.R. 760 do not pass; and

WHEREAS, it is written in Micah 6:8: "And what does the LORD require of you but to do justice, and to love kindness, and to walk humbly with your God?"

*Now, therefore, be it resolved,* that the 2008 General Conference of The United Methodist Church urges all our elected officials to support pending federal legislation or their more recent equivalents supporting the Filipino-American war veterans: (1) H.R. 4574/S. 146, the Filipino Veterans Equity Act of 2006; (2) H.R. 901, an act to give priority in the issuance of immigrant visas to the sons and daughters of Filipino World War II veterans who are or were naturalized citizens of the United States, and for other purposes; (3) H. Res. 622/S. Res. 307, a Congressional Resolution to formally recognize and honor the Filipino World War II veterans for their defense of democratic ideals and their important contribution to the outcome of World War II, and (4) to complete the commitment to fund the Philippines Veterans Memorial Medical Center in Quezon City pursuant to Title 38, US Code, Section 1732; and

*Be it further resolved,* that the General Conference of The United Methodist Church declares its unqualified support for the "Filipino WWII Veterans Equity Act of 2007," that would amend Title 38 of the United States Code to deem Filipino veterans of WWII to have been in active service of the US military for purposes of benefits under programs administered by the Secretary of Veterans Affairs; and

*Be it further resolved,* that the General Conference instructs appropriate agencies, like the General Board of Church and Society, to monitor this legislation in the US Congress, and to enjoin all of its agencies to work with the National Association of Filipino American United Methodists (NAFAUM) and the National Alliance for Filipino Veterans Equity (NAFVE) in ensuring its passage; and

*Be it further resolved,* that the General Board of Church and Society, the Philippines Central Conference Board of Church and Society, and the National Association of Filipino-American United Methodists work together to advocate with appropriate bodies and officials in the United States Congress and the Philippine government, urging and encouraging these officials to continue in and consummate their efforts to secure these overdue veterans' benefits; and

*Be it further resolved,* that copies of this resolution be transmitted to the President of the US Senate and the Speaker of the US House of Representatives.

**ADOPTED 2008**

*See* Social Principles, ¶ 164.

# ¶ 165. VI. THE WORLD COMMUNITY

God's world is one world. The unity now being thrust upon us by technological revolution has far outrun our moral and spiritual capacity to achieve a stable world. The enforced unity of humanity, increasingly evident on all levels of life, presents the Church as well as all people with problems that will not wait for answer: injustice, war, exploitation, privilege, population, international ecological crisis, proliferation of arsenals of nuclear weapons, development of transnational business organizations that operate beyond the effective control of any governmental structure, and the increase of tyranny in all its forms. This generation must find viable answers to these and related questions if humanity is to continue on this earth. We commit ourselves as a Church to the achievement of a world community that is a fellowship of persons who honestly love one another. We pledge ourselves to seek the meaning of the gospel in all issues that divide people and threaten the growth of world community.

*A) Nations and Cultures*—As individuals are affirmed by God in their diversity, so are nations and cultures. We recognize that no nation or culture is absolutely just and right in its treatment of its own people, nor is any nation totally without regard for the welfare of its citizens. The Church must regard nations as accountable for unjust treatment of their citizens and others living within their borders. While recognizing valid differences in culture and political philosophy, we stand for justice and peace in every nation.

*B) National Power and Responsibility*—Some nations possess more military and economic power than do others. Upon the powerful rests responsibility to exercise their wealth and influence with restraint. We affirm the right and duty of people of all nations to determine their own destiny. We urge the major political powers to use their nonviolent power to maximize the political, social, and economic self-determination of other nations rather than to further their own special interests. We applaud international efforts to develop a more just international economic order in which the limited resources of the earth will be used to the maximum benefit of all nations and peoples. We urge Christians in every society to encourage the governments under which they live and the economic entities within their societies to aid and work for the development of more just economic orders.

C) *War and Peace*—We believe war is incompatible with the teachings and example of Christ. We therefore reject war as an instrument of national foreign policy. We oppose unilateral first/preemptive strike actions and strategies on the part of any government. As disciples of Christ, we are called to love our enemies, seek justice, and serve as reconcilers of conflict. We insist that the first moral duty of all nations is to work together to resolve by peaceful means every dispute that arises between or among them. We advocate the extension and strengthening of international treaties and institutions that provide a framework within the rule of law for responding to aggression, terrorism, and genocide. We believe that human values must outweigh military claims as governments determine their priorities; that the militarization of society must be challenged and stopped; that the manufacture, sale, and deployment of armaments must be reduced and controlled; and that the production, possession, or use of nuclear weapons be condemned. Consequently, we endorse general and complete disarmament under strict and effective international control.

D) *Justice and Law*—Persons and groups must feel secure in their life and right to live within a society if order is to be achieved and maintained by law. We denounce as immoral an ordering of life that perpetuates injustice and impedes the pursuit of peace. Peoples and nations feel secure in the world community when law, order, and human rights are respected and upheld.

Believing that international justice requires the participation of all peoples and nations, we endorse the United Nations, its related bodies, the International Court of Justice, and the International Criminal Court as the best instruments now in existence to achieve a world of justice and law. We commend the efforts of all people in all countries who pursue world peace through law. We endorse international aid and cooperation on all matters of need and conflict. We urge acceptance for membership in the United Nations of all nations who wish such membership and who accept United Nations responsibility. We urge the United Nations to take a more aggressive role in the devel-

¶ 165

722

opment of international arbitration of disputes and actual conflicts among nations by developing binding third-party arbitration. Bilateral or multilateral efforts outside of the United Nations should work in concert with, and not contrary to, its purposes. We reaffirm our historic concern for the world as our parish and seek for all persons and peoples full and equal membership in a truly world community.

¶ 165

# V. THE WORLD COMMUNITY
# THE RESOLUTIONS

## EDUCATION

### 6001. Africa University

WHEREAS, the Africa University initiative formally began by the inspiring address delivered by Bishop Emilio de Carvalho of Angola at the General Board of Higher Education and Ministry of The United Methodist Church in October, 1984; and

WHEREAS, Bishop de Carvalho was joined by Bishop Arthur Kulah of Liberia, Bishop F. Herbert Skeete, then president of the General Board of Higher Education and Ministry, Bishop Felton E. May, then president of the General Council on Ministries, and other members in discussing the educational needs of Africa and ways the denomination might respond to this challenge; and

WHEREAS, the African central conferences of The United Methodist Church asked the General Board of Higher Education and Ministry and the General Board of Global Ministries to assist them in developing significant post-secondary institutions of learning for the churches of Africa; and

WHEREAS, in St. Louis, Missouri, the 1988 General Conference of The United Methodist Church overwhelmingly approved the establishment of a university on the continent of Africa to be built in Zimbabwe and authorized an apportionment of $10 million over a four-year period and an additional $10 million to be raised through World Service Special Gifts; and

WHEREAS, the official groundbreaking for the university occurred on site in Old Mutare in 1991, and Africa University opened in 1992 with two faculties and forty students representing six nations on the African continent; and

WHEREAS, Africa University's enrollment reached a significant milestone in 2006 with its student population reaching 1,123 representing 22 African nations; and

WHEREAS, the number of faculties has grown from two in 1992 to nine in 2006; and

WHEREAS, in February 2003, Africa University launched its Institute of Peace, Leadership and Governance with an initial enrollment of 15 students, each of whom will earn a masters degree in Peace and Governance (MPG); and

WHEREAS, 2,317 Africa University alumni have been deployed across the African continent in fulfillment of the University's mission to train new leaders for the nations of Africa—new leaders like Walter Manyangawirwa, who was in the first graduating class at Africa University and who is now a leader in the field of study of fungi, viruses, bacteria, and other plant diseases; and

WHEREAS, Africa University is the only private institution of higher learning on the African continent that may fly the international flag of the United Nations; and

WHEREAS, Africa University has been called " . . . one of the great success stories of Christian missions in the world today" by Millard Fuller, founder and president of Habitat for Humanity International; and

WHEREAS, in the year that The United Methodist Church is celebrating the 50th anniversary of the ordination of women, the gender ratio in the student body is 53 percent female and 47 percent male; and

WHEREAS, Bishop Daniel Wandabula of Uganda was elected to the episcopacy on 28 May 2006 during a meeting of the denomination's Africa Central Conference on the Africa University Campus in Zimbabwe; and

WHEREAS, the support and enthusiasm of United Methodists worldwide for Africa University are demonstrated in the apportionments remitted annually, the second-mile givings, and contributions from churches and individuals for the Africa University Endowment Fund; and

WHEREAS, the South Carolina Annual Conference calls upon each local church to pay the full Africa University apportioned line item and give generously to the Africa University Endowment Fund;

*Therefore, be it resolved,* that the General Conference affirms that Africa University is a dynamic and important mission project of The United Methodist Church; affirms the leadership of all those involved in the continuing development and day-to-day operations of the university; and commends the Africa University Board of Directors and advisory Development Committee for their persistence, diligence, and visionary leadership in overcoming the obstacles and barriers to fulfilling the dream; and,

*Be it further resolved,* that the 2008 General Conference make Africa University a priority and allocate an apportionment of $10 million over a four-year period and an additional $10 million to be raised through World Service Special Gifts to continue development, construction, and endowment of Africa University as outlined in the planning process determined by the General Board of Higher Education and Ministry and the Africa University Board of Directors.

ADOPTED 2004
REVISED AND READOPTED 2008
RESOLUTION #304, 2004 *BOOK OF RESOLUTIONS*
RESOLUTION #284, 2000 *BOOK OF RESOLUTIONS*

*See* Social Principles, ¶ 165A.

# GLOBAL MISSION AND MINISTRY

## 6011. Global Ministries and Mission Society

WHEREAS, the Methodist Mission Sending Society commonly known as the Mission Society has been in active missionary work for over 25 years; and

WHEREAS, the Mission Society has provided added opportunities for United Methodists to engage in mission and has conducted itself with Christian grace and cooperation; and

WHEREAS, the General Board of Global Ministries and the Mission Society have worked collaboratively and with other mission sending agencies from time to time; and

WHEREAS, there has for too long been some attitudes of competitiveness around the notions of shared ministry between the official mission work of The United Methodist Church and the Mission Society; and

WHEREAS, we believe cooperation rather than competition is the better way for the church;

*Therefore, be it resolved,* that The United Methodist Church acknowledge and commend the positive contribution to the work of mission through the Mission Society and that furthermore the General Board of Global Ministries develop new conversations and liaisons with the Mission Society for new and ongoing partnerships in areas of mutual concern; and

*Be it further resolved,* that we encourage bishops, cabinets, and annual conferences to acknowledge and support, where appropriate, those individuals and projects associated with the work of the Mission Society.

ADOPTED 2008

*See* Social Principles, ¶ 165.


## 6012. Celebrating Diversity Within the Global Methodist Family

WHEREAS, modern developments in transportation, communications, and technology have brought peoples and nations closer together; and

WHEREAS, globality tends to be understood in The United Methodist Church basically in terms of the United Methodist presence beyond the boundaries of the United States and almost exclusively in relation to those sections of the Church that are structurally within it; and

WHEREAS, there are a number of churches in the Methodist family that out of a sense of calling by the Holy Spirit, a desire to affirm their own identity, and their need for self-determination have elected to become autonomous;

*Therefore, be it resolved,* that The United Methodist Church:

1. celebrate the God-given diversity of race, culture, and people at every level of Church life in our worship and other activities;

2. celebrate the global dimension brought to The United Methodist Church by sisters and brothers from all over the globe and the Native American nations, who are a part of US society and The United Methodist Church;

3. celebrate the affiliated autonomous Methodist churches and the Central Conferences of The United Methodist Church as important expressions of the diversity of cultures and peoples called by God to be the church universal;

4. work for a future where The United Methodist Church and the autonomous Methodist churches throughout the world, expressing

their faith through their unique, God-given culture, will share resources, personnel, and perspectives as equals in their common task of evangelizing all the world;

5. continue and strengthen its ecumenical commitment; and

6. embody this vision as possible in all United Methodist programs.

ADOPTED 2004
READOPTED 2008
RESOLUTION #360, 2004 *BOOK OF RESOLUTIONS*

## JUSTICE AND LAW

### 6021. Church Supports Global Efforts to End Slavery

WHEREAS, the institution of slavery controls the lives of over 27 million persons worldwide, including the United States; and

WHEREAS, slavery is a crime against humanity, and is expressly prohibited by international law and a number of international treaties; and

WHEREAS, the United Nations, the United States Congress, the United States State Department, the Department of Justice, as well as a host of international human rights organizations, have recognized and officially documented the current existence of slavery and bonded labor; and

WHEREAS, the existence of slavery is often closely connected with sex trafficking of women and the trafficking of children; and

WHEREAS, in the Exodus, the people of God are liberated from the bondage of Pharaoh; and

WHEREAS, founder of Methodism, John Wesley, in numerous instances, including a tract entitled "Thoughts on Slavery" and sermon entitled "The Use of Money," condemned slavery as wrong and incompatible with Christ's teachings; and

WHEREAS, The United Methodist Church regards the institution of slavery as an "infamous evil" and recognizing that "All forms of enslavement are totally prohibited and shall no way be tolerated by the church" (*Book of Discipline,* ¶ 164A); and

WHEREAS, the General Board on Global Ministries, through the United Methodist Committee on Relief Sudan Emergency campaign, as well as other United Methodist organizations, has worked to aid people subjected to enslavement and bonder labor;

*Therefore, be it resolved,* that The United Methodist Church officially support efforts to end all contemporary forms of slavery and bonded labor; and

*Be it further resolved,* that The United Methodist Church actively champion anti-slavery efforts by petitioning the United Nations, United States Congress, the State Department, the Department of Justice, and the legislative bodies of all countries in which The United Methodist Church has an organized ecclesiastical structure, to demand the freeing of all subjected to modernday forms of enslavement and bonded labor; and

*Be it further resolved,* that The United Methodist Church petition the United Nations and the United States Congress and State Department to abolish slavery through the use of nonmilitary options such as negotiations and sanctions; and

*Be it further resolved,* that The United Methodist Church officially support stock/mutual fund divestment campaigns that urge people to remove funds from organizations whose actions profit from and contribute to slavery's existence; and

*Be it further resolved,* that The United Methodist Church inform all members of the church, via news publications and other communication channels of the connectional system, that slavery currently exists and that The United Methodist Church officially opposes its existence and urge all United Methodists to join with international human rights organizations in working to end all contemporary forms of slavery and bonded labor; and

*Be it further resolved,* that this document be sent to the Secretary-General of the United Nations, the President of the United States, the United States Congress, and the legislative bodies of countries in which The United Methodist Church has an established ecclesiastical structure.

ADOPTED 2000
REVISED AND READOPTED 2008
RESOLUTION #283, 2004 *BOOK OF RESOLUTIONS*
RESOLUTION #263, 2000 *BOOK OF RESOLUTIONS*

*See* Social Principles, ¶ 165B.

## 6022. Compensation for Comfort Women

"So if anyone is in Christ, there is a new creation: Everything old has passed away; see, everything has become new! All this is from God, who reconciled us to himself through Christ, and has given us the ministry of reconciliation; that is, in Christ God was reconciling the world to himself, not counting their trespasses against them, and entrusting the message of reconciliation to us. So we are ambassadors for Christ" (2 Corinthians 5:17-20).

The United Methodist Church affirms all persons as equally valuable in the sight of God. We therefore work toward societies in which each person's value is recognized, maintained, and strengthened. We support the basic rights of all persons to equal access to legal redress for grievances, and physical protection. We deplore acts of hate and violence against groups or persons based on race, ethnicity, gender, sexual orientation, religious affiliation, or economic status (Social Principles, ¶ 162).

The United Methodist Church also regards nations as accountable for unjust treatment of their citizens and others living within their borders. While recognizing valid differences in culture and political philosophy, we stand for justice and peace in every nation (Social Principles, ¶ 165).

The urgency for the ministry of reconciliation has never been greater. For over fifty years the sexual enslavement of more than 200,000 women from Korea (80 percent), Malaysia, Burma, China, Taiwan, East Timor, Indonesia, and the Pacific Islands by the Japanese military and government, remains one of the greatest unresolved injustices of the Second World War as stated by the judges of the Women's War Crimes Tribunal. They further stated, there are no museums, no graves of the unknown comfort women, no education of future generations, and no judgment days, for the victims of Japan's military sexual slavery. Many of the women who have come forward to fight injustice have died unsung heroes. While the names inscribed in history's pages are often those of the men that commit the crimes, rather than the women that suffer them, this judgment bears the names of the survivors that took the stage to tell their stories, and thereby, for four days at least, put wrong on the scaffold and truth on the throne (The Hague, December 4, 2001). The urgency is the need to find justice before the survivors of Japan's sexual slavery die, never knowing whether the Japanese government agreed to be accountable for their monstrous treatment of women inside and outside their borders. David J. Scheffer, United States Ambassador-at-Large for War Crimes suggested that a conservative estimate (based on each woman being raped five times a day for five years) would amount to 125 million rapes. Thousands of women were raped up to 60 times a day.

The United Nations Commission on Human Rights accepted the Final Judgment of the Women's International War Crimes Tribunal of Japan's Military Sexual Slavery (held in Tokyo in 2000) as an official document of its 58th Session and reminded Japan to do the honorable thing and recognize its state responsibility.

The United Methodist Women have taken action to help pass US Federal legislation calling on the Japanese government to apologize to and to compensate comfort women or the surviving family members of comfort women.

We call on The United Methodist Church to:

- urge United Methodists to become informed about and supportive of the continuing struggle of the survivors of sexual slavery and urge the General Board of Global Ministries to make resources available; and,
- urge United Methodists to be supportive of the remedial measures recommended by the Women's International War Crimes Tribunal and find innovative ways in partnership with Asian women to put pressure on the Japanese government to make a response.

*Therefore, be it resolved*, that the 2004 General Conference calls upon the General Board of Global Ministries to continue to to urge the government of Japan to do the following:

- acknowledge fully its responsibility and liability for the establishment of the comfort system and that this system was in violation of international law;
- issue a full and frank apology, taking legal responsibility and giving guarantees of nonrepetition;
- compensate the victims and survivors and those entitled to recover as a result of the violations declared herein through the government and in amounts adequate to redress the harm and deter its future occurrence;
- establish a mechanism for the thorough investigation into the system of military sexual slavery, for public access and historical preservation of the materials;
- consider, in consultation with the survivors, the establishment of a Truth and Reconciliation Commission that will create a historical record of the gender-based crimes committed during the war, transition, and occupation.

- recognize and honor the victims and survivors through the creation of memorials, a museum, and a library dedicated to their memory and the promise of never again;
- sponsor both formal and informal educational initiatives, including meaningful inclusion in textbooks at all levels and support for scholars and writers, to ensure the education of the population and, particularly, the youth and future generations concerning the violations committed and the harm suffered.

*Be it further resolved,* that the General Board of Global Ministries report its efforts and the response of the government of Japan to the 2008 General Conference.

ADOPTED 2004
REVISED AND READOPTED 2008
RESOLUTION #284, 2004 *BOOK OF RESOLUTIONS*

*See* Social Principles, ¶ 165.

## 6023. Abolition of Sex Trafficking

*Again I looked and saw all the oppression that was taking place under the sun: I saw the tears of the oppressed—and they have no comforter; power was on the side of their oppressors—and they have no comforter.*

Ecclesiastes 4:1 NIV

*But this is a people plundered and looted, all of them trapped in pits or hidden away in prisons. They have become plunder, with no one to rescue them; they have been made loot, with no one to say, "Send them back."*

Isaiah 42:22 NIV

These are hard words of Scripture. Yet, even harder is this Scripture's contemporary reality, daily reflected in the tears of millions of women and children who are trafficked into sexual slavery. Former Secretary of State Colin Powell asserts, "It is appalling that in the twenty-first century hundreds of thousands of women, children, and men made vulnerable by civil conflict, dire economic circumstances, natural disasters or just their own desire for a better life, are trafficked and exploited for the purposes of sex or forced labor. The deprivation of a human being's basic right to freedom is an affront to the ideals of liberty and human dignity cherished by people around the world."[1]

1. US Department of State, Trafficking in Persons Report, June 2003. Trafficking Victims Protection Act of 2000. www.state.gov/g/tip/rls/tiprpt/2003/ http://www.state.gov/g/tip/rls/tiprpt/2003/

This resolution addresses a gaping hole that exists in The United Methodist Church's advocacy concerning sexual violence-sex trafficking. The United Methodist Church has never recoiled in the face of controversial and painful issues such as the myriad ways in which human sexuality is abused. It would be wrong to suggest that this hole exists purposefully. Rather, one can rightly assume that the pervasive existence and deep gravity of the sex trafficking industry has only recently begun to be uncovered. Sex trafficking was briefly raised as a concern for "Responsible Travel" in the 2004 BOR. However, the daunting statistics have not been discussed, nor has the direct and indirect compliance of US citizenry and businesses in this matter been exposed to the members of the Church. In its prophetic role, The United Methodist Church is called to inform its members and the public at large that an estimated 700,000 to 4,000,000 people worldwide are trafficked each year. Furthermore, the most overlooked aspect of these statistics is the fact that 18,000 to 20,000 people are trafficked into the United States each year. [2]

Sexual violence in the twenty-first century, through many and varied manifestations, destructively permeates the whole of society. Not only must the Church denounce these issues, such as sex trafficking, both in and outside its own walls, but also, it must embrace its crucial responsibility to witness to the only One who is truly able to offer lasting hope, refuge, restoration, and redemption. The United Methodist Church is called to model that the church universal is the very first place to which people can turn in their hunger for justice, wholeness, and sanctuary. This calling comprises an essential element of the church's identity as the body of Jesus Christ, and, for The United Methodist Church specifically, the identity of being a community that carries the Wesleyan legacy of seeking justice and proclaiming the healing that can only come from our reconciling, Incarnate God. The church is given by God to be a place in which broken people—both victims and perpetrators of sexual violence—can be welcomed, heard, embraced with the gospel, and even healed.

The United Nations defines trafficking to be "the recruitment, transportation, transfer, harboring, or receipt of persons, by means of the threat or use of force or other forms of coercion, of abduction, of fraud, of deception, of the abuse of power or of a position of vulnerability or

2. According to estimates by the CIA and the US State Department. http://usinfo.state.gov/gi/Archive/2003/Jun/10-239681.html..

of the giving or receiving of payments or benefits to achieve the consent of a person having control over another person, for the purpose of exploitation. Exploitation shall include, at a minimum, the exploitation of the prostitution of others or other forms of sexual exploitation, forced labour or services, slavery or practices similar to slavery, servitude . . .";

The church has a difficult and awesome responsibility, by the power of the Holy Spirit, to seek justice and Christ's healing in the face of structures of oppression; and such structures of oppression are well-embedded in the institution of sex trafficking,

Therefore, The United Methodist Church, through education, financial resources, publication, lobbying, and the use of every relevant gift of God, shall join in the active battle against the modernday enslavement of humans for commercial sexual exploitation, i.e., sex trafficking.

The General Board of Church and Society shall lead The United Methodist Church's efforts toward the abolition of sex trafficking for the 2009-2012 quadrennium. On this issue, the GBCS shall work in cooperation with the Women's Division of the General Board of Global Ministries. The United Methodist Church shall recognize the urgency and gravity of this issue through a substantial monetary investment toward the galvanization of the Church at all levels to live out her gifts and calling in relation to the abolition of modern day slavery. To this end, the General Board of Church and Society shall receive an additional $100,000 from World Service Funds to the GBCS quadrennial budget for 2009-2012 toward the concrete implementation of a specific anti-sex trafficking program. [Note: This funding did not get approved in the final budgeting process.]

ADOPTED 2004
REVISED AND READOPTED 2008
RESOLUTION #285, 2004 *BOOK OF RESOLUTIONS*

*See* Social Principles, ¶ 165.

## 6024. Global Racism and Xenophobia: Impact on Women, Children, and Youth

The General Conference of The United Methodist Church affirms the United Nations principles relating to global racism and xenophobia.[1]

1. Principles can be found on the United Nations Web site in various reports including "Declarations World Conference against Racism, Racial Discrimination, Xenophobia and Related Intolerance, Durban, South Africa, 31 August to 8 September 2001."

The General Conference reaffirms the principles of equality and nondiscrimination in the Universal Declaration of Human Rights and encourages respect for human rights and fundamental freedoms for all without distinction of any kind such as race, color, sex, language, religion, political, or other opinion, national or social origin, property, birth, or other status.

We, the General Conference, affirm that all peoples and individuals constitute one human family, rich in diversity. "So then you are no longer strangers and aliens, but you are citizens with the saints and also members of the household of God" (Ephesians 2:19).

We recognize the fundamental importance of nations in combating racism, racial discrimination, xenophobia, and related intolerance [hereinafter referred to as racism]; and, the need to consider signing, ratifying or acceding to all relevant international human rights instruments, with a view to international adherence.

We recognize that religion, spirituality, and belief can contribute to the promotion of the inherent dignity and worth of the human person and to the eradication of racism.

We recognize that racism reveals itself in a different manner for women and girls and can be among the factors leading to deterioration in their living conditions, poverty, violence, multiple forms of discrimination, and the limitation or denial of their human rights.

We recognize the need to develop a more systematic and consistent approach to evaluating and monitoring racial discrimination against women, children, and youth.

Therefore, we, the General Conference, urge:

- that, in light of these affirmations and principles, each nation in which The United Methodist Church is established to adhere to the principles and programs contained in the opening statements;
- that the United States, all nations and The United Methodist Church incorporate a gender perspective in all programs of action against racism;
- that the United States, all nations, and The United Methodist Church undertake detailed research on racism, especially in respect to its effect on women, children, and youth;
- that the United States, all nations, and The United Methodist Church address the burden of such discrimination on women, children, and youth and promote their participation in the economic and productive development of their communities, especially in respect to:

* the increased proportion of women migrant workers, human rights violations perpetrated against them, and the contribution they make to the economies of their countries or their host countries;
* the large number of children and young people, particularly girls, who are victims of racism;
* the rights of children belonging to an ethnic, religious, linguistic minority or indigenous community and their right individually or in community to enjoy their own culture, their own religion, and their own language;
* child labor and its links to poverty, lack of development, and related socioeconomic conditions that can perpetuate poverty and racial discrimination disproportionately, denying children a productive life and economic growth;
* education at all levels and all ages.
• that the United States, all nations and the appropriate structures of The United Methodist Church involve women, children, and youth in decision-making at all levels related to the eradication of racism;
• that the General Commission on Religion and Race, the General Commission on the Status and Role of Women, in consultation with the Women's Division of the General Board of Global Ministries, create a monitoring instrument for assessing evidences of racism in programs for and with women, children, and youth;
• that all national mission institutions, schools, and institutions of higher education, annual conferences, and general agencies evaluate current and projected programs to determine their impact in reducing racism in programs for women, children, and youth; and
• that a report be prepared and presented to each General Conference by the General Commission on Religion and Race, the General Commission on the Status and Role of Women, in consultation with the Women's Division of the General Board of Global Ministries, related to the status of women, children, and youth impacted by racism.

ADOPTED 2004
READOPTED 2008
RESOLUTION #286, 2004 *BOOK OF RESOLUTIONS*

*See* Social Principles, ¶ 165.

## 6025. Globalization and its Impact on Human Dignity and Human Rights

*What are human beings that you are mindful of them,
   mortals that you care for them?
Yet you have made them a little lower than God [or divine beings, or angels],
   and crowned them with glory and honor.*
                         —Psalm 8:4-5 NRSV

*Human rights are what make us human. They are the principles by which we create the sacred home for human dignity. Human rights are what reason requires and conscience commands.*
        —Kofi Annan, United Nations Secretary-General

### *Our Globalized World*

In an age of globalization, the struggle for human rights has become more complex and challenging. While protections for human rights are increasingly passed by governments and international bodies like the United Nations, grave threats to and gross violations of human rights are also on the rise.

The world's financial capital is ever more integrated, and wealth is ever more centralized in the hands of financial elites and institutions. Realizing social and economic rights, especially eradicating hunger and unemployment, is becoming increasingly difficult. Bringing conflicts to a just and durable resolution is more daunting with the increased capacity of individuals, governments and their military forces, and other groups, including paramilitary, to organize and unleash violence. These groups have access to more sophisticated communications technology and more deadly instruments of war than ever before.

Ending violence and wars, and checking impunity and disregard for international human rights and humanitarian laws, will require more than political will and moral courage. Concrete programs and mechanisms are needed to realize the totality of human rights—civil, political, social, economic, and cultural.

Our Christian tradition shows us an alternative to globalization. It is a "counter-globalization" that empowers God's people to "do justice, and to love kindness, and to walk humbly" (Micah 6:8b) with God. What must be globalized is a culture of peace that institutes peace with justice in ways that are visible and tangible in the lives of peoples and communities. We are challenged to globalize an ethos that respects and protects human life with human rights so that all "may have life, and have it abundantly" (John 10:10b) as God intends.

## Biblical and Theological Grounding

The psalmist exclaims: "What are human beings that you are mindful of them, mortals that you care for them? Yet you have made them a little lower than God" [or divine beings, or angels], and crowned them with glory and honor." (Psalm 8:4-5). Every human being bears the likeness of our just, gracious, and loving God: "God created human beings, in the image of God they were created; male and female were created" (Genesis 1:27, adapted).

Human dignity is the foundation of all human rights. It is inherent and inborn. Human dignity is the image of God in each human being. Human dignity is the sum total of all human rights. We protect human dignity with human rights. Human rights are the building blocks of human dignity. They are indivisible and interdependent. It is God's gift of love for everyone. Human rights, being the expression of the wholeness and fullness of human dignity, are indivisible and interdependent.

Human rights—expressed in affirmations and declarations, treaties and conventions, laws and statutes—are products of struggles to affirm and fulfill the wholeness and fullness of life. As peoples and governments increase the catalogue of rights that are recognized and protected, protections not only increase, but so do our approximation of and striving for human dignity. To be engaged in the human rights struggle is to accept God's gift of love in Jesus Christ who has come to affirm all God's people as they are—as individuals and people in community together.

But human rights do not affect humanity alone. The integrity of God's creation is possible only with the affirmation of both the dignity of all persons and the integrity of the whole ecological order. Human rights cannot be enjoyed in an environment of pillage and decay.

Human dignity is the common bond that affirms the individuality of each human being while celebrating the plurality and variety of communities to which each belongs, including the diverse economic, political, religious, ideological, racial, class, gender, and ethnic identities each represents.

## The United Methodist Church and Human Rights

The United Methodist Church's Social Principles provide foundational understanding of rights and freedoms. These principles affirm both the sovereignty of God over all of creation and the duties and responsibilities of each person for the natural and nurturing world, and the social, economic, political, and world communities. At their spring 1998 meeting, and on the occasion of the 50th anniversary of the Universal Declaration of Human Rights, the Council of Bishops called on "United Methodists across the connection worldwide [to] join in . . . safeguarding the worth and dignity of peoples and the integrity and sacredness of all of God's creation."

"As Christians," the bishops said, "loving our God and loving our neighbor together advance the imperatives of human rights. Human rights enable us to express in concrete ways our love for one another by assuring that each person's value is recognized, maintained, and strengthened."

Human rights are safeguards of peoples and communities against violations of their rights and infringements on their freedoms. To this end, the General Conference called on "all governments to accept their obligation to uphold human rights by refraining from repression, torture, and violence against any person" and "to ratify and implement international conventions, covenants, and protocols addressing human rights in the context of justice and peace" (¶ 164, Social Principles).

### Arenas for Human Rights Work

An emerging feature of the new global context is the rise and increasing participation of peoples' and citizens' organizations in leading the establishment of just, participatory, and sustainable communities. This new context must be celebrated; it is one venue of counter-globalization. The so-called "civil society," especially through nongovernmental organizations, is increasingly present in forums where grassroots advocacy and global governance are at stake. Through the presence of nongovernmental organizations in all levels of governance—local, national, regional, global—globalization is challenged in multiple ways, from the local and the global. Human rights monitors, themselves a threatened group of defenders, have increased in the ranks of civil society. As a new millennium is ushered in, we lift the following arenas for human rights work to all United Methodists worldwide, and to the attention of all general agencies, particularly the General Board of Church and Society and the General Board of Global Ministries of The United Methodist Church.

*A. Children's Rights and Well-Being: Receiving the Reign of God as a Little Child*

"Let the little children come to me, and do not stop them; for it is to such as these that the kingdom of heaven belongs" (Matthew 19:14).

The Social Principles strongly support children and children's rights. It says: "Once considered the property of their parents, children are now acknowledged to be full human beings in their own right, but beings to whom adults and society in general have special obligations. All children have the right to quality education. . . . Moreover, children have the rights to food, shelter, clothing, health care, and emotional well-being as do adults, and these rights we affirm as theirs regardless of actions or inaction of their parents or guardians. In particular, children must be protected from economic, physical, and sexual exploitation and abuse" (¶ 162C).

The *United Nations Convention on the Rights of the Child* expresses this same concern for the child. The convention extends the basic concept of protection to the level of human rights. The Convention affirms that the rights described in the *Universal Declaration of Human Rights* are rights that belong also to children.

Children's rights are human rights. United Methodists worldwide must continue to urge their governments to implement the convention, and for the United States to ratify it.

The proliferation of and easy access to small arms have a devastating effect on our children. Children must never have access to or opportunity to use guns. Both the children killed and those wounded by small arms are victims of a culture of violence which denies human rights, snuffs out precious human life, and debases human dignity.

The United Methodist Church is called to join the international campaign to prevent the proliferation and unlawful use of small arms. The campaign raises our awareness of the need for emergency measures to save the lives of children, in our schools, in inner cities, and in many parts of the world, particularly those countries and communities that are highly militarized and governed by national security laws.

Children in situations of conflict and war test our commitment to the future. There is something wrong in our sense of the moral when children are put in harm's way. No boy or girl must be sent to the front lines of war, battles, and conflict. The field of play must not be replaced with the field of combat. War games are not child games. Playgrounds are for children; battlegrounds are not.

The United Methodist Church must oppose the recruitment and use of child soldiers. We must support the call of the United Nations Commission on Human Rights (Resolution 1999/80) to raise the current minimum age limit set by Article 38 of the *Convention on the Rights of the Child* on the recruitment into the armed forces or participation of any person in armed conflicts from 15 to 18. The General Conference of the International Labor Organization (ILO), through Convention 182 (1999), prohibits forced or compulsory recruitment of children under the age of 18 for use in armed conflict. ILO also recommends (Recommendation 190) that governments prohibit the use, procuring or offering of a child for activities which involve the unlawful carrying or use of firearms or other weapons.

## B. Migrant Workers: Entertaining Angels Unawares

"Let mutual love continue. Do not neglect to show hospitality to strangers, for by doing that some have entertained angels without knowing it" (Hebrews 13:1-2).

A complex of factors—civil conflicts, human rights abuse, extreme poverty, and misguided development schemes—have produced in many countries around the world an unprecedented number of migrant workers and people looking for jobs beyond their national borders.

While globalization heralded the swift movement of capital across national borders, the movement of laborers seeking work in richer countries of the world has been slow and increasingly restricted. Transnational corporations have moved to poor countries where labor is much cheaper and workers' organizing is either weak, suppressed, or altogether banned.

The underlying causes of migration are twofold: first, economic competition which forces industrial economies to hire cheap labor in order to remain competitive in the global market, and second, to resolve structural imbalances in the local labor force on the part of the labor-sending countries.

Migrant workers continue to be discriminated against and abused, especially those who are undocumented in their host countries.

Women migrants are particularly vulnerable to exploitation especially when they work in gender-specific jobs that consign them to various forms of sexual, domestic, and menial work. Studies show that the majority of migrants are uprooted because of the lack of jobs at home, or because jobs pay extremely low wages. While globalization has spawned more capital and spurred greater production, workers' wages have been kept low and below a livable wage even in those countries whose governments have a prescribed minimum wage.

Migrants' rights are human rights. It is tragic when migrants, whose rights have already been violated in their home countries, find their human rights also violated in their foreign host countries. Invoking host country laws rarely works in their favor. United Methodists should urge their governments to ratify and implement the *United Nations International Convention on the Protection of the Rights of All Migrant Workers and Members of Their Families*. This Convention will be an instrument to protect, secure, and ensure the human rights of migrant workers and their families.

## C. Indigenous Peoples: Toward Self-Determination

"But they shall all sit under their own vines and under their own fig trees, and no one shall make them afraid; for the mouth of the Lord of hosts has spoken" (Micah 4:4).

Globalization threatens the human rights of indigenous peoples, including their aspirations for self-determination. Exploration and colonization have led to rapid appropriation of indigenous peoples' lands and natural resources, and the destruction of their sciences, ideas, arts, and cultures.

Indigenous peoples struggle against the industries encroaching on their sacred lands. They are fighting for sovereignty over their ancestral lands in the face of systematic campaigns of extermination. They face population transfers, forced relocation, and assimilation, often because of the aggressive development interests of big business.

Indigenous peoples demand respect of their right to their culture, spirituality, language, tradition, forms of organization, ways of knowing and doing, and their intellectual properties. Indeed, it will be hard for indigenous peoples all over the world to exercise their fundamental human rights as distinct nations, societies, and peoples without the ability to control the knowledge they have inherited from their ancestors.

The 1992 General Conference urged The United Methodist Church to "place itself at the vanguard of the efforts to undo and correct the injustices and the misunderstandings of the last 500 years" of colonialism. It raised the church's awareness of "the shameful stealing of the Native's land and other goods and the cruel destruction of their culture, arts, religion, the environment, and other living things on which their lives depended."

Religious intolerance is one form of human rights violation perpetrated on indigenous peoples around the world. The experience of forced relocation by the Dineh (Navajo) of Black Mesa in Arizona is an example of religious intolerance. The Dineh consider their ancestral lands as sacred. For them, to be uprooted is to be exterminated as a people. Big mining companies have been responsible in the destruction of livelihood, sacred sites, and ancestral homelands of indigenous peoples. Indigenous peoples' rights are human rights. United Methodists are urged to support the ongoing drafting and the eventual adoption of the *United Nations Declaration on the Rights of Indigenous Peoples*. United Methodists must also support the establishment of a Permanent Forum of Indigenous Peoples and the appointment of a Special Rapporteur on Indigenous Populations, both within the aegis of the United Nations. We must also continue support for the work and the mandate of the United Nations Special Rapporteur on Religious Intolerance.

## D. Impunity: The Case for an International Criminal Court

"You shall not render an unjust judgment; you shall not be partial to the poor or defer to the great: with justice you shall judge your neighbor" (Leviticus 19:15).

A culture of peace must be globalized today. The prevailing culture of repression, oppression, and exploitation has no place in this culture of peace. Only the pursuit of a just peace, which includes the search for truth and justice for victims, will bring about forgiveness, reconciliation, and healing in many rural villages, towns, cities, nations, and regions of the world that are scarred by conflict and war.

The establishment of an International Criminal Court (ICC), as provided for in a treaty adopted in Rome in June 1998 by the United Nations Diplomatic Conference of Plenipotentiaries on the Establishment of an International Criminal Court, provides an important step in ending impunity. This court will hear cases against war crimes, genocide, crimes against humanity, and crimes of aggression. Faith-based and religious groups, working together with the Coalition for an International Criminal Court (CICC), identified several moral and ethical imperatives and included these in a draft preamble they offered the Rome Conference to consider. The draft stated: "Desirous that the quest for justice includes retributive justice whose purpose is the prosecution and punishment of offenders while insuring the rights of the accused to fair trials, restorative justice whose purpose is that of reparation, restitution and rehabilitation for the victims, and redemptive justice which must be seen as the enablement of communities to deal with the truths of the past in ways which will allow and enable social reconstruction and reconciliation, and the ending of cycles of violence;

"Recognizing that adjudication of crimes of international concerns that have transcended national boundaries are often beyond the scope of national criminal justice systems, and that crimes whose immediate victims have occurred within national contexts are often beyond the competence or ability of national judicial systems; *Noting the basic principles of justice for victims of crime and the abuse of power approved by the United Nations General Assembly; therefore, establish the International Criminal Court . . .*"

As Pope John Paul II stated, "A positive sign of the growing will of the States to acknowledge their responsibility in the protection of the victims of [crimes against humanity], and their commitment to prevent them, is the recent initiative of the Diplomatic Conference of the United Nations that distinctly adopted the Statute for an International Criminal Court that will assess the guilt and punish those responsible of genocide, crimes against humanity and war crimes."

United Methodists all over the world must urge all governments, especially the United States of America, to sign and ratify the treaty to establish the court. The work of the CICC and the Washington Working Group on the International Criminal Court (which focuses on getting the US to ratify the treaty) must be supported. In their support, United Methodists must preserve and strengthen the unprecedented provisions of the Rome Statute calling for an end to impunity for crimes committed against women and children. Also, the ancestral and sacred sites of indigenous peoples must be included in the Court's definition of protected sites.

## E. Religious Liberty: The Case Against Intolerance

Religious liberty forms part of the pantheon of human rights. The Universal Declaration of Human Rights provides that "Everyone has the right to freedom of thought, conscience and religion: this right includes freedom to change his religion or belief, freedom, either alone or in community with others and in public or private, to manifest his religion or belief in teaching, practice, worship and observance" (Art. 18). Religious liberty, according to The United Methodist Church, includes the belief that "it is the right of a person to be allowed to follow the call of conscience when it becomes impossible to live by both the dictates of the State and the decisions of faith" (Religious Liberty, 1996 *Book of Resolutions*, p. 571).

Religious liberty continues to be denied and violated in many parts of the world. Concerns about religious persecution have been raised by almost every religious group especially in places where one particular religion or belief is in a minority position. Religious intolerance, of both the established as well as "nontraditional" religions, is growing both in new and established democracies. The rise in religious extremism, of all sorts, and from all of the established and nontraditional religions, have been convenient pretexts for the curtailment of the exercise of religious liberty by many governments around the world.

The United Methodist Church must continue to foster further cooperation among spiritual, religious, and ecumenical bodies for the protection of religious freedom and belief. It must enter into healthy dialogues with peoples of differing faiths and ideologies, including Native and indigenous peoples, in the search for shared spiritual, social, and ethical principles that engender peace and justice.

The United Methodist Church is already committed to uphold the minimum standards of the right of belief that are contained in the provisions of the *United Nations Declaration on the Elimination of All Forms of Intolerance and of Discrimination Based on Religion or Belief* adopted by the United Nations General Assembly on November 25, 1981. This declaration enunciates that "freedom of religion and belief should also contribute to the attainment of the goals of world peace, social justice and friendship between peoples and to the elimination of ideologies or practices of colonialism and racial discrimination."

United Methodists must urge their governments and encourage civil society to enter into dialogues about racism and discrimination and resolve to address especially those concerns that have religious bases. The United Methodist Church must also support and participate in the World Conference on Racism and Discrimination in 2001 organized by the United Nations.

## F. Peace and Peace-building: The Case for a Culture of Peace

"[God] shall judge between many peoples, and shall arbitrate between strong nations far away; they shall beat their swords into plowshares, and their spears into pruning hooks; nation shall not lift up sword against nation, neither shall they learn war anymore" (Micah 4:3).

In this era of globalization, the icons of war are more prominent and the arsenal of killing machines is more lethal than ever before. Our images of peace and the implements that make for a just peace most often are stymied by these icons and arsenals.

The resolution of conflicts and the establishment of a just and durable peace proceed from a just and liberating practice of governance on all levels of life—local and global. Just governance thrives not on wars and rumors of wars, but in the advancement of a world order that protects human rights, develops sustainable communities, cultivates a culture of peace, empowers people and their associations, and promotes a just and participatory democracy. It is imperative for human rights to be the foundational principle for a just and durable peace. The United Methodist Church must participate in building communities that prioritize the eradication of poverty and the elimination of hunger; the ending of wars and the resolution of conflicts; and the overcoming of ignorance, curing of diseases, and healing of enmities. The United Nations remains the single most important international institution to achieve these ends. The United Methodist Church must continue to support the United Nations. Our participation in its many activities allows us to participate in making it a responsible and effective global force in peacemaking and human rights.

The United Methodist Church must also support The Hague Agenda for Peace and Justice for the 21st Century. This agenda, produced by a historic conference in The Hague in May of 1999, and encompassing fifty areas of concern with:

1. root causes of war and the culture of peace;

2. international humanitarian and human rights law and institutions;

3. the prevention, resolution, and transformation of violent conflict; and

4. disarmament and human security.

The United Methodist Church must also support the Pillars of Peace for the 21st Century, written as a policy statement in support of the United Nations for the National Council of the Churches of Christ in the USA. The seven pillars state that peace rooted in justice requires:

1. increased political collaboration and accountability among governments within the United Nations system, among regional bodies, governments, local authorities, people's organizations, and global economic structures to seek the common good and equality for all;

2. increased moral, ethical, and legal accountability at all levels from governments, financial institutions, multilateral organizations, transnational corporations, and all other economic actors to seek a just, participatory, and sustainable economic order for the welfare and well-being of all people and all creation;

3. a comprehensive international legal system, capable of change as conditions require, in order to prevent and resolve conflicts, to protect rights, to hold accountable those who disturb peace and violate international law, and to provide fair and effective review and enforcement mechanisms;

4. the participation of vulnerable and marginalized groups, seeking to promote justice and peace, in those mechanisms capable of redressing the causes and consequences of injustice and oppression;

5. the nurturing of a culture of peace in homes, communities, religious institutions, and nations across the world, including the use of nonviolent means of resolving conflict, appropriate systems of common security, and the end of the unrestrained production, sale, and use of weapons worldwide;

6. respect for the inherent dignity of all persons and the recognition, protection, and implementation of the principles of the International Bill of Human Rights so that communities and individuals may claim and enjoy their universal, indivisible, and inalienable rights; and

7. a commitment to the long-term sustainability of the means of life, and profound reorientation of economic systems and individual lifestyles to support ecological justice for human communities in harmony with the whole of creation.

The United Methodist Church must also continue its support for the campaign to ban land mines by urging all governments to ratify and implement the landmine ban treaty which prohibits the use, production, stockpiling and transfer of antipersonnel land mines. This treaty also calls on parties to increase mine clearance and victim assistance efforts around the world.

United Methodists must also urge their governments to ratify the Comprehensive Nuclear Test Ban Treaty. Counterglobalization happens when we ban land mines, abolish nuclear weapons, and prevent wars from happening.

## G. Economic, Social, and Cultural Rights: That the Hungry May Be Filled

"When you give a banquet, invite the poor, the crippled, the lame and the blind" (Luke 14:13).

The Lord our God commanded us "to do justice, and to love kindness, and to walk humbly." Justice, kindness, and humility underscore society's obligations to its people. But even with the indivisibility of civil, political, economic, social, and cultural rights, global hunger and poverty challenge our priorities. It is a challenge that confronts and addresses our concern for lifting the poor and marginalized among us. In this era of globalization, poverty is defined as the inability of a human being to take advantage of global and market opportunities that are supposed to be booming and soaring. This globalization process deifies the market even as it commodifies the earth and its resources, if not even people themselves who become pawns to economic production. One's worth and dignity in this globalization process is measured by one's ability to contribute to the gains of the market.

But gain or loss, in this era of globalization, it is the poor, the marginalized, and the vulnerable who suffer from price increases, reductions in government support for needed social and environmental programs, business disruptions, higher unemployment levels, and increased human rights violations.

The sudden devaluation and large outflow of capital from countries such as recent ones in Mexico, Thailand, Indonesia, and South Korea resulted in severe economic downturns, political instability, widespread social turmoil, job loss, and human suffering. The proposal by Professor James Tobin, Nobel laureate in economics, to levy taxes on cross-border speculative financial and currency exchange transactions deserves our support. The so-called "Tobin Tax" aims to:

1. shrink the volume of the currency market;

2. help to restore national control of currency; and

3. generate sizable revenue that would provide resources urgently needed to wipe out extreme poverty.

The indivisibility of human rights underscores the understanding that freedom is hollow without food, that justice without jobs is like a clanging cymbal, and that liberty is a sham when people do not have land to inhabit and farm. The right to food and the right to employment are fundamental economic human rights. Societies become peaceful when the demands of justice are met. Justice becomes not only a dream but a reality when implements of war give way to implements of peace. Food and jobs, also, are implements of peace. Would that indeed, at the end of the day, no child, no woman, and no one, goes to bed with an empty stomach.

United Methodists must continue to urge their governments to ratify the *International Covenant on Economic, Social, and Cultural Rights* and for these governments to make these rights a reality.

We also urge United Methodists worldwide to call on their governments to implement the Millennium Development Compact. Adopted as part of the UN Millennium Declaration in 2000 at the largest-ever gathering at the United Nations of Heads of State, these government leaders pledged together to eradicate poverty, promote human dignity and equality, and achieve peace, democracy, and environmental sustainability.

The compact declared eight goals (known as the Millennium Development Goals) with specific targets to which governments have pledged to implement by the year 2015. These goals include: 1) eradicating extreme poverty and hunger, 2) achieving universal primary education, 3) promoting gender equality and empowering women, 4) reducing child mortality, 5) improving maternal health, 6) combating HIV/AIDS, malaria, and other diseases, 7) ensuring environmental sustainability, and 8) developing a global partnership for development.

In this era of globalization—where profit and profit making at the expense of the needs and welfare of the poor and the vulnerable, and where unbridled pursuit of wealth and power have trampled upon and denied human rights of peoples—peace rooted in God's justice brings about the true globalization that will heal the wounds and scars of wars and conflict peoples and nations have engaged with each other. Peace rooted in God's justice will help bring about forgiveness and wholeness for all God's people and the whole of creation. God's reign on earth, as it is in heaven, is, in the end, the true globalization we must long and work for.

ADOPTED 2000
AMENDED AND READOPTED 2004
READOPTED 2008
RESOLUTION #309, 2004 *BOOK OF RESOLUTIONS*
RESOLUTION #289, 2000 *BOOK OF RESOLUTIONS*

*See* Social Principles, ¶ 165.

## 6026. International Day of Prayer

As Paul writes of the interrelatedness of the body of Christ to the Corinthians saying that when "one member suffers all suffer together with it" (1 Corinthians 12:26), so we recognize the presence of religious persecution throughout the world. As The United Methodist Church condemns religious intolerance and persecution of all faith groups, we heed Paul's words and acknowledge the interconnectedness we have with members of the body of Christ throughout the world who endure persecution because of their faith.

Since The United Methodist Church opposes injustice, intolerance, and bigotry and believes in the power of prayer, we encourage United Methodist congregations to observe in November an International Day of Prayer for the Persecuted Church. It is through our earnest prayers that we grow in our sense of unity with Christians around the world, as well as with all members of religious groups who endure persecution. We become more aware of the needs of our brothers and sisters who suffer because of their faith, as we defend the religious freedoms of all faith communities.

ADOPTED 2000
REVISED AND READOPTED 2008
RESOLUTION #311, 2004 *BOOK OF RESOLUTIONS*
RESOLUTION #292, 2000 *BOOK OF RESOLUTIONS*

*See* Social Principles, ¶ 165A.

## 6027. United Methodists Sharing the Vulnerability in the Process of Alteration

Paul reminded the divided Corinthians, "If one part (of the body) suffers, every part suffers with it; if one part is honored, every part rejoices with it" (1 Corinthians 12:25). It is in this spirit that the European community, its peoples and its churches, are gathering together to respond to a time of change and transformation—a time of alteration in Europe.

The fall of the Berlin wall (1989) was a symbol of a new political order in Europe. Ever since, Europe has been in a process of alteration which has led to both improvements and new challenges.

The United Methodist Church recognizes with gratitude a trend to democratisation and increased freedom in many countries as well as a development towards a larger community of European nations. We affirm that many people, among them numerous Christians, including United Methodists, are now more vigilant in the journey of Europe towards "An Area of Freedom, Security and Justice" (expression from European Community Law).

After September 11, 2001, people all over the world are more than ever experiencing a profound sense of vulnerability. As a people of faith we are recognizing that a shared vulnerabililty may become more important for mutual understanding and caring than privileged security of some. This shared vulnerability has helped to see the European Process of Alteration in the context of an encompassing global transformation which in particular includes the continents of Africa, Asia and Latin America.

A decade ago we rejoiced as we experienced great political changes in Central and Eastern Europe.

Today it is clear that the magnitude and the content of the problems encountered have been underestimated by governments, the media, the general public as well as the churches. Rising unemployment and the falling value of pensions and wages has plunged millions of people into poverty. United Nations Development Reports for Central and Eastern Europe show that in 1989 about 14 million people in the former communist block lived with less than four dollars a day. By the mid-nineties that number had risen to 147 million people. Only a small minority has participated in economic growth and development. In many places health care, schooling and education standards declined dramatically whilst commerce-based criminality grew rapidly.

Given this situation, the United Methodist Minorities in Europe together with the other denominations emphasises the need for human development through witness for Jesus Christ and through working towards justice for the poor and vulnerable like women, children, gypsies and other ethnic minorities. United Methodists are together in mission to safeguard the local initiatives and the dignity of clergy and lay missionaries, women and men, faithfully responding to the calling of Jesus, our Lord and Saviour. We therefore affirm that church-planting, evangelism and social initiatives in Eastern Europe, Russia, the Baltics and the Balkans require continued support by the larger Methodist family, spiritually and financially. Even if local churches may become financially self-sustaining and strong enough to continue the mission among the vulnerable and the poor on their own it should not be forgotten that the Lord's commandment to mission is addressed to the whole Church.

We are thankful for the "Fund Mission in Europe," a solidarity initiative of the European Methodist Council to collect financial means among Methodist congregations in Western and Northern Europe for newly emerging churches and congregations in the East and in the South. The financial and spiritual support generated by local churches and conferences in the USA during the last ten years was an act of rescuing.

### *The process of European integration—hopes and challenges*

The process of change has been strengthened especially by the European Union which aims to work for peace, stability and welfare. The initiation of an unprecedented enlargement involving 13 new candidate countries is an ambition on a new level and on a new scale. Unfortunately, it has become clear that there is a widening gap between the expectations of tangible results on the one hand and loss of patience resulting from dissatisfaction with the actual process on the other hand.

Particular challenges in this context are:
- transparency in the negotiating process;
- free movement of persons / migration;
- human and social costs of the integration process;
- protection of the rights of minorities;
- preservation of indigenous (regional) cultures and identities;
- future borders of the European Union and the relations to the new neighbours;
- commitment to common (Christian) values.

As United Methodists, we affirm that the European integration process is a sign of hope. We support efforts for the creation and development of independent regional cooperation and communities of nations, such as the European Union and the OSCE including USA and Canada. At the same time, we are also aware of the dangers that continue to threaten the process toward a new Europe such as self-serving nationalism, serious economic problems and social upheavel. Against this background, the current priorities of The United Methodist Church's human rights program are as follows:

- protection of refugees, migrants, asylum seekers and dis-placed people;
- social policy questions in the transformation that nations make into market economics;
- social rights for all, in particular respect and justice for women, children and minorities;
- religious freedom;
- environmental and energy policies for a sustainable way of life.

The Churches are not left untouched by the processes of political, economic and cultural integration. The Conference of European Churches, together with the Roman Catholic Council of European Bishops Conferences, the Leuenberg Church Fellowship and the European Methodist Council, are very actively involved in internal and external processes of integration. In particular, the European Churches developed a "Charta Oecumenica" which is meant to be a helpful tool for dialogue and advocacy for the practical life together of the Orthodox, Protestant, Anglican and Roman Catholic Churches.

We believe and affirm that the Churches in Europe have a message of hope. The new Europe can not be built without them. The United Methodist Church is not nationally bound and is, therefore, particularly called upon to advance the goal of integration in the present European process of alteration on the way to a true Area of Freedom, Security and Justice.

Zurich and Budapest, March 5, 2003

ADOPTED 2004<br>READOPTED 2008<br>RESOLUTION #314, 2004 *BOOK OF RESOLUTIONS*

*See,* Social Principles, ¶ 165.


## 6028. Global Migration and the Quest for Justice

"Ways must be found to share more equitably the resources of the world."

—Social Principles, ¶ 163E, The United Methodist Church

The United Methodist Church has frequently addressed general and specific topics related to migration. The Social Principles affirm:

1. "We commit ourselves as a Church to the achievement of a world community that is a fellowship of persons who honestly love

one another. We pledge ourselves to seek the meaning of the gospel in all issues that divide people and threaten the growth of world community" (¶ 165).

2. "In order to provide basic needs such as food, clothing, shelter, education, health care, and other necessities, ways must be found to share more equitably the resources of the world" (¶ 163E).

3. "We advocate for the rights of all migrants and applaud their efforts toward responsibility self-organization and self-determination"(¶ 163F, 2004 *Book of Resolutions*).

Human migration is as old as human history. Individuals, families, tribes, and nations have been on the move since the days of Abraham and Sarah and before. Throughout the centuries, political and economic factors, including wars; health and environmental challenges; and racism, xenophobia, and religious discrimination have at times uprooted people and at others lured them to new venues across continents and oceans as well as national and ethnic boundaries.

Today, migration is at once a critical international issue and a necessary option for millions of human beings. Some people seek to move; others have no alternatives. Contemporary migration involves the linked realities of abundance and poverty and racial/ethnic/religious identities and exclusion. The current global economic system reflects an expectation that many people will live in poverty, or have their nations torn by conflict, so that others may live in abundance. That many people will resist poverty and war through migration is an ancient and modern fact of human existence. As a consequence, elaborate national and international systems of containment and classification based on national origin have been developed over the past quarter-century with regard to migrants.

Global migration as a factor in the quest for justice is of major concern to The United Methodist Church as a denomination that is global in its vision, mission, and ministries.

## I. Contemporary Migrants

Four categories of contemporary migrants can be delineated:
- Refugees—persons outside of their country of origin who are unable or unwilling to return for fear of persecution based on race, religion, ethnicity, political affiliation or opinion; official "refugees" are so recognized by the United Nations High Commissioner for Refugees, which is charged by the

international community to oversee service to, and protection of, refugees.

- Asylum seekers—a type of refugee, persons who have left their homeland to petition for refuge in the country to which they have fled; asylum seekers must be so recognized by the countries whose protection they seek.

In 2007, recognized refugees and asylum seekers totaled 13.9 million.

- Internally displaced persons—those who are displaced within their own country because of military, economic, and social upheaval, and natural disasters such as famine, earthquake and flood; they are generally not protected by the international community, but must depend for protection and assistance primarily on their country of residence, which may be implicit in the cause of displacement. In 2007, such persons numbered 24.5 million.

- Economic migrants—people who move from one country to another to find work. Most frequently they seek to flee from poverty to economic opportunity, and often permanently relocate so they may feed their families. Some are allowed into more affluent nations as immigrants; some enter without documentation and may be welcomed in times of labor shortages and deported in times of economic downturn or public disapproval. Such migrants are among the most vulnerable in any society; many are women and children who become the objects of abuse and brutality. One subcategory in this classification consists of migrant workers, people who move from place to place, often with the agricultural cycle, to find employment. Some return on a periodic or eventually permanent basis to their homelands; others make domestic and other ties in places of employment and wish to remain. The number of current economic migrants is difficult to calculate. Some estimates run as high as 100 million globally, with large numbers in the affluent regions of North America and Europe.

## II. A Context of Migration

Virtually all groups of today's migrants and refugees are battered by the divide between the rich and the poor, a divide rooted in nineteenth and twentieth century colonialism and directly caused by rapid corporate globalization in agriculture, industry, and commerce.

Currently, slightly more than 10 percent of the world's population consumes 85 percent of the world's wealth while the rest make do with just 15 percent of that wealth. For example, agricultural subsidization in Europe and the United States results in the dumping of commodities in the poor countries of the global South, resulting in the disruption of family farming and unemployment. Trade policies and arms deals further enrich the rich and undercut economies in the global South without providing new contexts for prosperity or hope. These realities, along with armed conflict, environmental spoilage, and natural disasters force people to find new homes within their own countries or across national borders. Every region of the world is affected in some way by the global economic divide.

Yet, while money and products easily flow across borders, the movement of people is increasingly restricted, leading to concentrations of the poor along borders and, often, to the building of literal and figurative walls of exclusion, notably around the rich nations of the northern hemisphere and the affluent enclaves in Asia, Latin America, Africa, the Middle East, and the Pacific. While the legal and physical walls seek to exclude flows of undocumented migrants, in fact, there is growing demand in wealthier nations for cheap labor. Millions of migrants do enter—through formal guest worker programs or through informal business networks that actively seek undocumented workers while maintaining them in an exploitative noncitizen underclass. Many of those who are shut out or who migrate without legal status are at the bottom of racial, ethnic and caste hierarchies. They are often poor women and children. On either side of the divide, families are relegated to intense human suffering, inadequate nutrition and health service, lack of educational opportunities, and the reverberating, debilitating experience of oppression. Ironically, and horribly, with regard to economic migrants, the rich say, "Come in, do our dirty work at low wages, and then go away." Significant percentages of the work force are migrants in affluent countries, with the figure exceeding more than 50 percent in parts of the Middle East. Such "guest workers" enjoy limited civil and human rights.

The global South is particularly concerned with the migration of people from rural to urban areas and with the loss of young generations to other countries, the departures dictated either by economic need or wooing by affluent societies seeking to fill jobs with cheap labor. Such émigrés often do not want to leave; they may feel pressured by promises of education, jobs, and economic security for themselves and their families. They become entrapped in unjust global systems that drain the resources of poor, Southern countries for the benefit of the affluent societies of the global North.

### III. Biblical Perspectives: Justice and Shared Resources

Attitudes toward and treatment of migrants are usually conditioned today, even within the church, by nation-state considerations expressed in the language of "us" and "them"—or "we" the home-folks and "they" the intruder/alien. A beneficent attitude sometimes prevails: "'We'" will allow X number of 'them' to come among 'us' provided they acknowledge our generosity and become like us; so long, of course, as they do not threaten our comfort."

There are more biblically and theologically sound perspectives. In the biblical understanding, it is not about us and them, but about one people of God, called to seek justice and share equitably, at the very core of our spiritual and physical survival.

The prophet Isaiah put the matter in context and posed the daunting question: "You serve your own interest on your fast day, and oppress all your workers. . . . Such fasting as you do today will not make your voice heard on high. . . . Is not this the fast that I choose: to loose the bonds of injustice, to undo the thongs of the yoke, to let the oppressed go free, and to break every yoke? Is it not to share your bread with the hungry, and bring the homeless poor into your house?" (Isaiah 58:3-7). Not only does God's understanding of faithfulness entail the achievement of justice, but for the comfortable, the promise of healing and salvation depends on that action. It was only when the people turned from false religiosity to operative justice that they would receive the promise of spiritual wholeness. "Then, . . . the Lord will guide you continually, and satisfy your needs in parched places, . . . you shall be like a watered garden . . . whose waters never fail" (Isaiah 58:10-11).

The Hebrew Scriptures contains many references to "strangers" and "sojourners" among the people of Israel and to provisions for treatment that reflect a tribal framework that had stipulated rules for hospitality and also limits on the outsiders. However, the Books of the Law, and to an even greater extent in the prophetic literature, concern for the stranger focuses on justice and the sharing of resources that flow from the bounty of God. Ezekiel anticipated a time when foreigners would share with the ancient Jewish nation all the blessings of the land, which was understood to belong to God alone (Leviticus 25:23). In a real sense, the ancient scriptures understand both the people of Israel and sojourners to be aliens since the people of Israel had been sojourners in Egypt. God's providence for Israel extends to others (Psalm 146:9; Malachi 2:5), and everything, and everyone, belongs to God (Psalm 24:1-2)

The breadth of God's love permeates the New Testament; that love incorporates faith community and goes beyond it. This is clearly emphasized in a short passage in 1 Thessalonians (3:12), where Paul prays that God will provide the grace for Christians to "abound in love for one another, and for all (people)."

Christians do not approach the issue of migration from the perspective of tribe or nation, but from within a faith community of love and welcome, a community that teaches and expects hospitality to the poor, the homeless, and the oppressed. The Christian community not only welcomes and embraces migrants but can be led by them toward clearer understandings of justice and hospitality. Furthermore, many migrants in many parts of the world today are themselves members of the Christian community, brothers and sisters of the same baptism, gathered around the same sacramental table. And people beyond the Christian community deserve no less hospitality than Christians extend to themselves.

United Methodists should harbor no doubt about their responsibility to all those who live here on the earth, especially the poor, the homeless, and the mistreated. John Wesley's concern for the poor and outcast was constant and extended far beyond acts of charity. He worked for just systems in which persons could with dignity stand on their own feet. Wesley advocated just relationships within the social order. When some have great abundance while others are homeless and hungry, the biblical task is not merely to help those in need, but to seek justice—to shift resources and opportunity so that all are at the table, all are fed, all experience the abundance of Gods' love both physically and spiritually.

## IV. Critical Issues Relating to Migration Today

United Methodists and all Christians face numerous critical situations, causes, and effects relating to migration today, especially in regard to war and economic systems and policies that perpetuate poverty. As a global, denomination, The United Methodist Church experiences the dilemmas of nations that both "send" and "receive" migrants. Citizens and undocumented immigrants are within the church's membership, as are employers and migrant workers, police and detainees, and affluent and poor families. The United Methodist family is a microcosm of migrant issues, a church that through God's grace seeks to respond to the needs of the most physically vulnerable and also address the spiritual needs of the privileged.

The following are among the critical issues demanding attention:

1. The volume of refugees, asylum seekers, and persons displaced within their own countries is growing, as are the numbers of economic migrants with and without documentation.

2. Wealthy nations, especially those with decreasing populations, are increasingly dependent upon migrants to maintain their current economies. They seek both highly skilled professionals and low-wage workers for jobs in construction, health care, agriculture, meat packing, and domestic service. The "receiving" nations or areas on a world scale include Australia, Canada, Europe, Japan, New Zealand, the United States, and some countries of the Middle East (such as Saudi Arabia, United Arab Emirates, Lebanon). Regional migration, often in the form of contract labor, is common in Brazil, Hong Kong, Lebanon, South Africa, South Korea, and other nations.

3. The critical loss of skilled workers and potential leaders in "sending" countries undermines the future economic and social advancement of those societies. Doctors from poorer nations can often earn more in the US as a nurse than as a physician in their country of origin. The "brain drain," often deliberately encouraged by rich countries for their own benefit, affects teachers, engineers, medical personnel, researchers, and technicians.

4. Old wars and territorial occupations have left a critical migration crisis and new wars add to the problem. This can be illustrated in the Middle East, where many Palestinians remain as refugees more than a half century since they lost their homes in Israel. In recent years, millions of Iraqis have fled their country, adding to the displaced population of the greater Middle East.

5. The passage of stricter enforcement of anti-immigrant legislation and the building of exclusionary walls, often in response to increased migration, intensifies cultural tensions, marked by racial, class, and religious "backlash." Restrictive policies also intensify migrant resistance based on fear of arrest and deportation, substandard wages, physical and mental abuse, and even death for crossing a border.

Migrants fall prey to trafficking for economic or sexual purposes and sometimes become virtual slaves in their new place of residence.

6. The increasing percentage of migrant women, who now make up half of the international migrant population and as much as 70 to 80 percent in some countries. Many of these women are domestic workers, who may raise other peoples' children while being separated from their own. Some women and girls who are migrant are subjected to physical and sexual abuse and fear reprisals if they complain.

7. Migration today divides families across generations. Filipino contract workers in Saudi Arabia may serve in those countries for their entire careers, and then watch their children step into their roles as they retire. Families are also divided by deportation of undocumented parents, while children hold citizenship.

8. Remittances (sending "home" the paycheck) have become major sources of financing for poor countries; revenues that threaten to undercut aid assistance from rich nations. The monies migrants send home is massive, an estimated $230 billion in 2005. Some nations, including the Philippines and El Salvador, depend on remittances to support the financial system. In an effort to escape responsibility for the sharing of resources, some officials in the global North tout remittances as replacements for development aid. This attitude violates the spirit of the Millennium Development Goals and other United Nations accords. Through international instruments, northern nations have set the goal of providing 0.7 percent of their gross national product in development aid to poor nations, as well as to cancel some debt and alter trade policies in ways that benefit poor nations.

## V. Response of the Church

The United Methodist Church commits itself to:

1. provide real help for refugees, asylees, and migrants;

2. engage in strong, coordinated advocacy on migration issues and on behalf of actions that overcome poverty, war and other causes leading to the displacement and marginalization of people; and

3. organize through institutional channels and prepare educational resources for the achievement of these objectives.

Assistance includes:

1. relief to refugees and displaced persons around the world, including the resettlement, when possible, of refugees through congregations

and through economic development programs for both those who permanently resettle and those who may return to homelands, this work to be coordinated by the United Methodist Committee on Relief in collaboration with all other levels and organizations of the church;

2. congregational and annual conference programs that humanely respond to migrants within their borders—defending their human rights, advancing just immigration policies by national governments, and tending to their spiritual, material, and legal needs as required, with the General Boards of Global Ministries and Church and Society, in collaboration with other general agencies, responsible for resource materials to help in equipping conferences and congregations for these ministries;

3. education of church members and communities on the causes and realities of migration, including international treaty commitments, the issues of economic and environmental justice, and the obstacles to a just, peaceable world created by anti-immigrant racism and xenophobia;

4. building bridges between diverse races, ethnicities, religions, and cultures, opposing violence against and abuse of migrants;

5. work with civic and legal organizations to help communities to alleviate social conditions caused by harsh immigration laws and heavy-handed national security measures; and

6. recognizing the right of sanctuary in any United Methodist local church for migrants subject to detention or deportation by government security forces.

Advocacy includes promotion of:

1. just and equitable trade and development policies that support human rights and counteract the root causes of migration such as war and militarization, environmental spoilage, and corporate greed;

2. engagement with other Christian and religious organizations in North-South dialogues, study of international economic policies, and joint action;

3. protection for uprooted women and children from all forms of violence and abuse, including full legal protection of children in situations of armed conflict;

4. unification of families divided by borders and legal status wherever this occurs;

5. denunciation of xenophobic and racist reactions against newcomers;

6. defense of civil liberties regardless of the legal status of persons;

7. abolishment of governmental anti-terrorism policies and practices that criminalize or profile refugees and immigrants as threats to national security; and

8. adoption by all nations of the United Nations International Convention on the Protection of the Rights of All Migrants Workers and their Families, and mobilize to promote compliance with the terms of the convention.

Institutional organization includes:

- continuation of a United Methodist Task Force on Immigration to lead the church in a prophetic response to refugee and migrant issues by interpreting official policy in light of current realities, coordinating vision, analysis, education and action. Said task force will be convened by two bishops designated by the Council of Bishops, organized and staffed by the General Boards of Church and Society and Global Ministries, and composed of representatives from all appropriate general agencies (General Commission on Religion and Race, General Board of Discipleship, General Council on Finance and Administration, and others), as well as persons from jurisdictions, central conferences, annual conferences, partner churches, denominational ethnic/racial caucuses, and ethnic and language ministry plans as situations dictate. General agencies will each bear the cost of their participation in the task force and those agencies may underwrite the costs of nonagency participation as needs require and resources permit.

**ADOPTED 2008**

*See* Social Principles, ¶ 165A and D.

## 6029. End Exploitation by United Nations Personnel

United Nations personnel, including staff persons, aid workers, and peacekeeping forces, are responsible for distributing much-needed humanitarian aid the world over. This humanitarian aid such as food, clothing, medical supplies, shelter, and money has been bartered for sex in what has become known as the "Sex for Food" scandal. This exploitation and abuse of women, children, and youth is a clear violation of the trust put in the United Nations to be a force of peace and goodwill.

It has been reported that these abusive acts have occurred in nations where UN personnel are active.

This problem has been the subject of several US government investigations and studies, including those conducted by the Senate and House Foreign Relations Committee and the Governmental Accountability Office. Bipartisan studies acknowledging the abuse and calling for necessary reform measures include:

- Hope for Africa's Forgotten: A Report on the Fact-Finding Mission to Democratic Republic of the Congo, Rwanda and Kenya, issued in 2005 by Senator Sam Brownback and Senator Richard Durbin;
- The United States Institute for Peace's report titled, American Interest and UN Reform, prepared by Newt Gingrich and George Mitchell (This was a comprehensive task force on UN reform that not only reported the problem, but also the structural reasons within the UN that keep the problem from being adequately addressed.); and
- The UN Independent Inquiry Committee.

Although the UN has passed resolutions calling for a zero tolerance policy, the fact remains that the UN has taken no substantive steps other than rhetoric to enforce their policy or hold offenders accountable. The United Methodist Church partners with the United Nations in many programs, treaties, and mission projects involving women, children, and youth, and thus has a great moral and practical interest in assuring the integrity of United Nations relief programs.

*Therefore,* The United Methodist Church calls on the United Nations and all member nations to implement the currently active zero tolerance policy on this issue in order to bring about an end to the abusive acts against women, children, and youth.

ADOPTED 2008

*See* Social Principles, ¶ 165D.

## 6030. Responsible Travel

The travel and tourism industry has become one of the fastest growing and largest sectors in the global economy. The annual revenues are second only to the weapons industry and, according to the United Nations, earnings from tourism are expected to triple in the next 20 years. The impact of travel and tourism on local economies, disadvantaged communities, women and children, indigenous peoples, and the environment has become a serious concern and requires thoughtful reflection by people of faith on our role as participants in these activities.

We are called by Scripture to be sojourners in ways which promote justice:

Exodus 12:48-49—Sojourners are to abide by one law for both the native and for the stranger.

Exodus 22:21—You shall not wrong a stranger or oppress [him/her], for you were a sojourner in the land of Egypt.

Leviticus 19:34—When a stranger sojourns with you in your land, you shall not do [him/her] wrong. The stranger who sojourns with you shall be as a native among you. You shall love [him/her] as yourself.

1 Peter 1:17—Conduct yourselves with reverent fear throughout the time of your exile (sojourning).

To travel is not to take a vacation from our faith. Just as we are called to express hospitality by welcoming the stranger, we are also called to abide in love and justice with our neighbors when we visit them, whether near or far away. When sojourning in a strange land, travelers should behave with reverence and respect for the people, their culture, and the land upon which they live.

Too often travel and tourism is exploitative as a result of the globalization of local economies in ways that transform self-sufficient communities into consumer-oriented and dependent societies. The impact of the travel industry can be viewed as a new form of colonialism in which local people are displaced and priced out of their own communities. Local people are most commonly employed in low-wage service positions without benefits. They are also faced with rising prices for basic needs such as food, transportation, and housing to meet the demand of tourists, hotels, and resorts. In the wake of this transformation, traditional knowledge and skills are forgotten, and the natural environment is exploited to meet the needs of a tourist economy.

Exploitative travel and tourism also impacts women and children who become victims in sex trade or trafficking, child prostitution, and/or pornography.

The impact of tourism is of particular concern to indigenous peoples. Tourism may exploit sacred sites such as burial grounds, ritual areas, and other places which hold significance in the cultural traditions of the indigenous peoples sometimes without their input or permission.

God's creation, the natural environment, can also be a victim of exploitative tourism when the local resources are viewed as a commodity to be consumed by the tourist industry as resources, entertainment, or merely as a dumping ground for the waste products they produce.

A just alternative to exploitative travel and tourism is "sustainable tourism." Sustainable tourism development in the travel industry should include the following principles:

- support for community and indigenous involvement in the planning, implementation, and monitoring of any tourism policies or development plans; and, wherever possible, ownership or joint venture of destination sites/travel programs;
- creation of tourist/travel programs that combat poverty by ensuring that a larger share of the profits and jobs generated by tourism remain in the local communities through purchases of local crafts, foods, and supplies;
- practice of travel behaviors that are respectful of cultural norms and traditions within the society; and
- development of forms of tourism that are not destructive to the local or global environment.

*Therefore*, The United Methodist Church calls on general agencies, annual conferences, and members of local churches to model sustainable travel and tourism and to reflect on the following when traveling:

- Does the travel respect and protect God's creation? Are there ways to lower and/or offset carbon emissions from the mode of transportation? Is the travel respectful of resources in and the natural habitat of the community being visited?
- Are the products/souvenirs purchased on travel locally produced using sustainable materials (e.g. no threatened species of plants or animals?
- Does the travel respect and strengthen the community being visited? Is the visit respectful of local culture and customs? Are members of the local community fullt involved in and benefiting from the site visits and cultural experiences? Is the tourist revenue being shared by the community? Are the workers in the restaurants, hotels, and tour companies being paid a living wage? Are gratuities adequately provided?
- How will the travel inform conversation and action upon returning home? What local stories and experiences will be communicated with colleagues, friends, and family? What

successes and/or challenges of the local community can be connected to actions at home? What organizations advocate for policies and reforms that would further strengthen the community and empower local residents to address systemic challenges?

ADOPTED 2000
REVISED AND READOPTED 2008
RESOLUTION #287, 2004 *BOOK OF RESOLUTIONS*
RESOLUTION #266, 2000 *BOOK OF RESOLUTIONS*

*See* Social Principles ¶ 165*A, B,* and *D.*

## 6031. Holy Land Tours

For many years, some Palestinian Christians have expressed deep dismay that too many United Methodists and other Christian groups traveling to Israel/Palestine, also called the Holy Land, have missed an extraordinary opportunity for ecumenical fellowship and sharing with other followers of the Prince of Peace. Our Christian sisters and brothers indigenous to the area continue to wonder why they are so often ignored by Christian pilgrims to the region. Why, they ask, do travelers tend to honor the inanimate stones that testify to Jesus' life and ministry while ignoring the "living stones," the indigenous Christians who represent an unbroken line of discipleship to Jesus in the land that he called home?

Travelers to this land have the opportunity to be ambassadors of unity and concern to the rapidly dwindling churches and Christians in a troubled land. They also have an opportunity to share in the vocation of peacemaking and to learn from the spiritual traditions of the churches indigenous to the Middle East. Further, they have a special opportunity to discover firsthand the realities of a region of deep meaning and vital importance to Christians, as well as to Jews and Muslims.

We recognize the tragic history that Christians share with Jews, and the complex relationships between particular nations and the state of Israel. We encourage dialogue between Christians, Jewish, and Muslim religious leaders.

*Therefore,* The United Methodist Church:

1. strongly affirms the resolution of the 1984 General Conference, offering "encouragement of all leaders of and participants in `Holy Land tours' to contact indigenous Christian leaders in the Middle

East, and to hear the concerns of both the Israelis and Palestinians who live there, as well as visit the biblical and historical sites" ("The Arab-Israeli Conflict," *The Book of Resolutions, 1984;* page 280);

2. asks the bishops, clergy, members, agencies, and congregations of The United Methodist Church, as they plan visits to the Holy Land, to devote significant program time to contact with indigenous Christian leaders and to hearing the concerns of Palestinians and Israelis on the current crisis of Palestinian self-determination;

3. urges all United Methodists planning, organizing, and/or participating in a trip to the Holy Land to apply the guidelines outlined in the General Conference resolution "Responsible Travel" to their trip—especially 1) to "ask travel agents/agencies whether local people [i.e., Palestinians] are involved in the development of the 'tour packages'; 2) "Practice 'low impact' travel and tourism, which do minimal damage to local culture," and 3) "Monitor ethical, responsible travel practices of conferences, boards, and agencies of The United Methodist Church" regarding Holy Land trips;

4. recommends that United Methodists planning individual or group tours to Israel/Palestine consult with the United Methodist liaison in Jerusalem to seek opportunities to worship with indigenous Christian congregations, to include at least one overnight stay in Bethlehem, and to visit United Methodist-supported mission sites;

5. supports the purchase of local Palestinian-made fair trade products and crafts in keeping with the guidelines in the General Conference resolution on "Responsible Travel"

6. asks the General Board of Global Ministries and the General Board of Church and Society to prepare specific recommendations regarding preparation, participation in, and follow-up education and advocacy actions for United Methodists traveling in the Middle East and other sensitive regions of the world;

7. recommends that United Methodist-sponsored tours use the denomination's seminar program in predeparture seminars for the travelers;

8. urges that travelers use, as advance study materials, positions adopted by General Conference and by general church agencies relating to the Middle East, as well as resources from the 2007-2008 Mission Study on Israel/Palestine;

9. urges seminaries and United Methodist-related colleges to apply the guidelines in this resolution to any school-sponsored trips, internships, and/or semesters of study in Palestine/Israel;

10. extends sincere appreciation to those United Methodists who have facilitated the implementation of the above recommendations in tours they have sponsored or participated in since the adoption of this resolution;

11. expresses deep concern that many tours sponsored or arranged by United Methodist bishops, pastors, and laity do not schedule opportunity for all participants to enter into partnership with the indigenous Christians for the recommended program time and, therefore, fail to "Walk With the Living Stones" in their strides toward Palestinian self-determination, their rich spiritual heritage, and their faithful contemporary witness;

12. expresses deep concern that evidence continues to accumulate that Christianity is dying in the land of Jesus through economic, social, and political pressures, which have greatly diminished the numbers and percentage of Christians in the Holy Land. United Methodist bishops and other organizers of Holy Land tours have a special responsibility to adhere to these recommendations to strengthen the witness of the remaining Palestinian disciples of the Living Lord;

13. affirms the presence of The United Methodist Church in Jerusalem through our liaison office and through our ongoing partnership with Palestinian and Israeli organization working for reconciliation and to establish equal rights for all under international law;

14. encourages tour leaders to consult with the General Board of Global Ministries and the United Methodist liaison office in Jerusalem in order to facilitate adherence to these recommendations;

15. instructs annual conferences and general agencies to monitor and report to the General Conference regarding the implementation of this resolution;

16. urges close cooperation with the Middle East Council of Churches and other indigenous Christian groups to facilitate informed, alternative travel opportunities to the region; and

17. commends the General Board of Global Ministries for initiating visits to the Bible lands that explore issues of justice and peace among all participants in the region, with special emphasis upon the concerns of our Palestinian Christian colleagues.

ADOPTED 1992
AMENDED AND READOPTED 1996
AMENDED AND READOPTED 2000
AMENDED AND READOPTED 2008
RESOLUTION #292, 2004 *BOOK OF RESOLUTIONS*
RESOLUTION #271, 2000 *BOOK OF RESOLUTIONS*

*See* Social Principles, ¶ 165A, B, and D.

## NATIONAL POWER AND RESPONSIBILITY

### 6041. US Training on Global Human Rights

. . . and they shall beat their swords into plowshares, and their spears into pruning hooks; nation shall not lift up sword against nation, neither shall they learn war any more. (Isaiah 2:4 NRSV)

Let us then pursue what makes for peace and for mutual upbuilding. (Romans 14:19 NRSV)

### *Background*

Each year, more than 100,000 foreign soldiers and police officers from over 150 countries receive training from the US government. This training is undertaken with minimal oversight and little assessment of the effects of such instruction on human rights around the world.[1]

The US Army School of the Americas (SOA) provided such training to soldiers from Latin America from 1946 to 2000. Several graduates from the SOA returned to their home countries and committed human rights abuses, including the murders of priests, women, and children. In 1996, it was discovered that training manuals at the SOA advocated such practices as torture, extortion, kidnapping, and execution. In response to these egregious acts, The United Methodist Church called for the closing of the SOA in 2000. In 2001, under pressure from advocacy groups, the name of the institution was changed to the Western Hemisphere Institute for Security Cooperation (WHINSEC) and the curriculum was reformed to include more human rights and democracy training. However, no US army or government officials have been held accountable for the development and use of training manuals advocating practices in clear violation of domestic and international laws.[2]

WHINSEC-SOA is symbolic of a much larger issue. It is one of many institutions providing foreign military training in the US, most of which provide substantially less human rights instruction than WHINSEC-SOA.

1. Amnesty International USA, *Unmatched Power, Unmet Principles: The Human Rights Dimensions of US Training of Foreign Military and Police Forces*, 2002, p. vii-xi, 1-5.

2. Ibid, p. vii-viii, 5-6, 43-49.

Tens of thousands of students come to the US to study at approximately 275 US military institutions. Tens of thousands more receive training from US forces in their home countries. Time and again, the US has provided training to forces directly responsible for human rights abuses, in countries such as Indonesia, East Timor, Rwanda, and Colombia.[3] Such training has helped to prop up large militaries that are often used to suppress government opposition groups and thwart legitimate democratic activity—all in the name of counterinsurgency or counter-terrorism. US military training of Mujahideen forces in Afghanistan (which included Taliban forces) is but one example of how the troops we train today may become the forces (or train the forces) we face tomorrow. Such cases demonstrate how important it is that any US military training plans consider the political realities and level of existing human rights protections in the host country.[4]

Being a good neighbor does not mean providing bombs and sniper training to economically depressed countries in Latin America. Our neighbors need humanitarian aid, civil society support, and judicial reforms. When we favor military institutions over democratic movements we are not working toward sustainable communities in Latin America or elsewhere. We must consider how to best use limited natural, economic, and human resources to create real security and establish acceptable living conditions for all people.

### Action

Based on our historic advocacy for human rights and against the militarization of societies, we urge all United Methodists in the US to work actively to improve the standards for US training of foreign military and police personnel and to educate and inform others about the human rights implications of such training. In the spirit of peaceful cooperation with our neighbors and mutual betterment of all, we urge the US government to focus such foreign training efforts primarily on peacekeeping, disaster assistance, and domestic policing. We call upon the General Board of Church and Society to continue to monitor this issue, including any proposed legislation to close WHINSEC-SOA.

3. Ibid, p. ix-x, 4-6, 9, 51-62.
4. Ibid, p. 1-2.

United Methodists are encouraged to contact the President, their senators and representatives to support legislation in support of the following objectives:[5]

1. Require significant, standardized training in human rights, ethical decision making, humanitarian law, military justice, and civil-military relations (the military's role in a democratic society) for all US education provided to foreign forces, whether on US soil or elsewhere.
2. Improve and standardize the process for screening all foreign students to ensure that known human rights abusers do not receive training.
3. Improve the accountability and oversight of training programs, including better follow-up tracking of trainees (to the extent practicable) and comprehensive assessment of programs to evaluate the level of benefit to the US government and the public.
4. Establish a congressional task force to assess the type of education appropriate for the US to provide to foreign military and police personnel (including the type and amount of training on human rights, humanitarian law, and democratic principles) and to evaluate the effects of foreign military and police training in the areas of human rights and adherence to democratic principles and the rule of law.
5. Establish an independent commission to identify those responsible for creating and approving the training manuals used at the SOA that advocated tactics in clear violation of US and international law.

Our hope, our belief, our desire is to work for peace in the world. While we recognize the importance of military and police institutions to maintain security, we are concerned that, without adequate standards and oversight, such training can lead to severe human rights abuses. It is imperative that US training of foreign military and police personnel operates with the highest degree of integrity and works to maintain the dignity and rights of civilians.

5. Amnesty International USA, *Unmatched Power, Unmet Principles: The Human Rights Dimensions of US Training of Foreign Military and Police Forces*, 2002, p. x-xi, 63-69, and H.R. 1217, "Latin America Military Training Review Act of 2005" (Introduced in House), 109th Congress.

**ADOPTED 2008**

*See* Social Principles, ¶ 165*B* and *D*.

## 6042. Oppose Food and Medicine Blockades or Embargoes

WHEREAS, as Christians we have a moral obligation to support life and stand against any force or action that causes suffering and death; and

WHEREAS, some groups of nations, governments, and /or factions within a country have stopped the flow and free marketing of food and medicines, seeking political gains; and

WHEREAS, such practices cause pain and suffering, malnutrition, or starvation with all its detrimental consequences to the innocent civilian population, especially the children; and

WHEREAS, the blockade of food and medicines is used many times to force riots in the general population, putting them in greater danger; and

WHEREAS, the media have brought to us the terrible images of children and women suffering, sick, and starving due to the blockade of food and medicines in recent conflicts;

*Therefore, be it resolved,* that as United Methodists, we request the United Nations to declare the practice of impeding the flow or free commerce of food and medicines to be a crime against humanity; and, as such, not to be permitted in or by the Security Council; and

*Be it further resolved,* that as United Methodists, we request the President of the United States and the United States Congress to abstain from using embargoes or blockades of food and medicines, with no exceptions, as an instrument of foreign policy;

And we, as Christians, call upon world leaders to affirm life, to affirm and guarantee the right of all human beings to have access to food and adequate health care, regardless of their political or ideological views.

ADOPTED 1992
AMENDED AND READOPTED 2004
READOPTED 2008
RESOLUTION #293, 2004 *BOOK OF RESOLUTIONS*
RESOLUTION #273, 2000 *BOOK OF RESOLUTIONS*

*See* Social Principles, ¶ 165*B* and *C*.

## 6043. Guidelines for the Imposition of Sanctions

The parable of the good Samaritan invites us to see the fundamental character of God's love as unconditional and overflowing. In the face of death and in death-dealing situations, aid and succor are the hallmarks of Christian response. The neighbor in need and the good neighbor were not known for their friendly relations. They were strangers and historical enemies to one another. In the time of need, however, care was made available—unconditioned by tribe, class, kinship, gender, religion, race, and economic or political status.

Sanctions, in whatever form, lay conditions upon love and on the extension of humanitarian aid and succor; they fall short of the gospel imperative for unconditional love. Yet sanctions as political and economic tools of pressure and leverage can play a critical role in the mitigation and deterioration of conflicts. It is in this sense that sanctions are sometimes seen as a more tolerable alternative to war.

A Church World Service and Witness (CWSW) study defines sanctions as "a menu of possible diplomatic, communications and economic measures used by governments, intergovernmental bodies, and nongovernmental entities to force changes in policies and behavior (usually but not exclusively on the part of a government). Sanctions cover a wide variety of measures from moratoria on diplomatic contacts to trade embargoes. Consumer boycotts and disinvestments programs are related measures."

The CWSW study notes that "sanctions can be limited and targeted, such as sports boycotts or restrictions on air travel, or they can be comprehensive, as in the case of trade embargoes. Sanctions can be unilateral (involving a single government) or multilateral (involving more than one)." The term *sanction* is most frequently associated with economic measures intended to inflict economic damage and thereby force a government or other entity to change its behavior and its policies. The effective use of sanctions lies in the political will of the imposer and is to be measured by the positive response of the sanctioned on the desired outcomes.

At the heart of the conflictive character of sanctions is the debate over when or when not to use and impose them. The caution in the use of sanctions arises out of a fundamental ethical and moral dilemma: the impact of sanctions on the innocent, and in situations of armed conflict, on noncombatants. Imposed in any way, those who impose sanctions must always take care to protect the suffering and the innocents with the basic modicum of international and humanitarian laws, uncompromised. This means the minimum guarantee of the right to the protection of human life and of human rights and civil liberties. The Christian community must insist that any and all sanctions include humanitarian exceptions—food, medicine, medical supplies and equipment, basic school supplies, and agricultural inputs and implements.

The CWSW study on the effectiveness of sanctions as an alternative to war concluded with recommendations that include the establishment of decision-making criteria for the imposition of sanctions based on the following guidelines:

- Sanctions must be a part of a broader strategy of peacemaking and an alternative to warfare.
- Sanctions should be adopted only in circumstances of flagrant and persistent violations of international law.
- Sanctions should have a clearly defined purpose.
- Sanctions have their greatest legitimacy and moral authority when authorized by a competent multilateral authority.
- The good achieved must not be exceeded by anticipated harm.
- There must be a reasonable prospect that their stated purpose of effecting political change will be achieved.
- Sanctions are effective only to the extent that they are consistently and thoroughly applied.

There must also be operational criteria to sanction impositions:

- Sanctions should be directed as precisely as possible to those bodies and leaders most responsible for the violation. Humanitarian assistance should be made available to the general population.
- The progress and effects of sanctions should be continually monitored by an independent and impartial multilateral monitoring body.
- Enforcers should be prepared to address the hurts and needs of victims in the sanctioned country and affected third countries.
- Open communication should be maintained with government leaders and civic groups in the sanctioned country.

*Therefore, be it resolved,* that United Methodists

- request the United Nations and the United States ascribe to and use indicators to assess potential humanitarian impacts prior to imposing sanctions and for monitoring impacts once sanctions are in place;
- request the United Nations and the United States to develop a list of humanitarian exceptions and call upon these bodies

to incorporate those exemptions in any and all sanctions regimes;

- call for systematic monitoring of sanctions by independent observers;
- call for consensus to be required on a regular basis, before the United Nations imposes and/or continues Security Council sanctions;
- ensure in our advocacy efforts that sanctions and embargoes meet the requirements of available international human rights and humanitarian laws, including the provisions of the Statute of the International Criminal Court; and
- commit ourselves and our humanitarian aid efforts as United Methodists to be carried out with awareness of this understanding of sanctions, especially because sanctions, especially trade embargoes have been shown to be of limited effectiveness in achieving their stated political goals while resulting in severe hardship for the general population, especially the most vulnerable.

ADOPTED 2004
READOPTED 2008
RESOLUTION #296, 2004 *BOOK OF RESOLUTIONS*

*See* Social Principles, ¶ 165*A*, *B*, and *D*.


## 6044. Understanding Globality in the United Methodist Tradition

WHEREAS, modern developments in transportation, communications, and technology have brought peoples and nations closer together; and

WHEREAS, globality tends to be understood in The United Methodist Church basically in terms of the United Methodist presence beyond the boundaries of the United States and almost exclusively in relation to those sections of the church that are structurally within it; and

WHEREAS, there are a number of churches in the Methodist family that out of a sense of calling by the Holy Spirit, a desire to affirm their own identity, and their need for self-determination have elected to become autonomous,

*Therefore, be it resolved,* that The United Methodist Church:

1. celebrate the God-given diversity of race, culture, and people at every level of church life in our worship and other activities;

2. celebrate the international dimension of The United Methodist Church consisting of sisters and brothers from different parts of the world including sisters and brothers from indigenous communities;

3. celebrate the autonomous affiliated Methodist churches as important expressions of the diversity of cultures and peoples called by God to be the church universal;

4. work for a future where The United Methodist Church and the autonomous Methodist churches throughout the world, expressing their faith through their unique, God-given culture, will share resources, personnel, and perspectives as equals in their common task of evangelizing all the world;

5. continue and strengthen its ecumenical commitment; and

6. embody this vision as possible in all United Methodist programs.

ADOPTED 1992
AMENDED AND READOPTED 2000
READOPTED 2008
RESOLUTION #299, 2004 *BOOK OF RESOLUTIONS*
RESOLUTION #279, 2000 *BOOK OF RESOLUTIONS*

*See* Social Principles, ¶ 165.


## 6045. United States-China Political Relations

*Our Political Understandings*

In late 1978, the governments of the United States and the People's Republic of China (PRC) reached agreement establishing full diplomatic relations. The United States ended official relations—diplomatic and military—with the authorities on Taiwan. The United States recognized the People's Republic of China as the "sole legal government of China" but reserved the right, over PRC objections, to sell "defensive" weapons to Taiwan. At the time of normalization, the PRC refused to rule out the possibility of reunifying with the island of Taiwan by force but offered to allow Taiwan to maintain the political, economic, and military status quo if Taiwan were to recognize PRC sovereignty.

This normalization agreement ended a thirty-year period in which formal American commitments to the authorities on Taiwan blocked closer relations with the People's Republic of China. It laid the foundations for a framework of cooperation and exchanges that continues to develop. Highlights include:

- government-to-government agreements covering consular relations and embassies, civil aviation, scientific and technical cooperation, educational exchange, trade and credit, fisheries, and a wide range of other fields;
- substantial expansion of tourism and specialized visits;
- educational programs facilitating nearly 10,500 scholars and teachers (10,000 Chinese, 500 Americans) to be resident in the other country;
- numerous governmental and private institutional exchange agreements in education, the fine and performing arts, cinema, publishing, and so forth; and
- sister state-province and city-to-city agreements calling for various kinds of cooperation.

The rapid growth and elaboration of these bilateral relations has been unusual and, to many, unexpected. While the direction is generally positive and the initial results heartening, the relationship is still in its early stages. Because the PRC and US systems are so different, translating worthwhile goals into concrete practice has often been difficult.

Fundamentally, the two countries have yet to determine what kind of long-term relationship they want. Misperceptions and misunderstandings are all too common on both sides, even on basic principles.

### Recommendations on US-China Political Relations

The United Methodist Church:

1. recognizes the necessity for China to continue its economic and social development and urges US cooperation to that end within the context of Chinese independence and selfhood;

2. feels the long-term basis of US-China relations should emphasize people-to-people, educational, social, and economic short-term or expedient military or strategic interests; opposes the sale of US military equipment to the PRC;

3. endorses a peaceful approach to ending the long-standing conflict between the governments in the People's Republic of China and in Taiwan while recognizing that the resolution of the status of Taiwan

is a matter for the People's Republic of China and for Taiwan and in that context supports the continued reduction and early cessation of US arms sales in Taiwan;

4. declares our continuing concern regarding the human rights of all people on both sides of the Taiwan Straits; and

5. recognizes that US-PRC relations have an important influence on the peace and stability of the Asian region, particularly in Southeast Asia; and urges the United States and the People's Republic of China and Taiwan to seek peaceful means to contribute to the peace and stability of the region.

ADOPTED 1984
AMENDED AND READOPTED 2000
AMENDED AND READOPTED 2008
RESOLUTION #301, 2004 *BOOK OF RESOLUTIONS*
RESOLUTION #281, 2000 *BOOK OF RESOLUTIONS*

*See* Social Principles, ¶ 165C and *D*.

## 6046. Ending the Colonial Status of Puerto Rico

We direct the secretary of the General Conference of The United Methodist Church to send a copy of this resolution to the President of the United States and to all members of Congress.

The Christian tradition has stood clearly against colonialism, believing instead in God's promise of human liberation, found again and again in the Bible. God breaks the bars of the yoke of oppression and feeds the people with justice (Ezekiel 34:27-30). Moses led the Hebrew people out of Egypt to the promised land, and the Hebrew prophets call us to a world in which all people are secure in their own land and on their own mountains (Ezekiel 36:8-15; Amos 9:14-15). In the synagogue, our savior proclaimed the acceptable year of the Lord (Luke 4:16-19). Jesus calls us to be peacemakers, and to seek justice and peace with one other (Matthew 5:1-12).

We, in The United Methodist Church, need to be part of the struggle against colonialism, dependence, and discrimination. Puerto Ricans have resisted, for more than one hundred years, being assimilated into the American "melting pot" because they are proud of their culture, their language, and their heritage. They are proud of their national identity. The God of Israel, who saw, heard, and descended to liberate God's people from oppression in Egypt (Exodus 3:16-18;

Isaiah 49:24-26) is calling upon us to acknowledge the colonial status of Puerto Rico and to advocate strongly for a decolonization and self determination process following international law and UN guidelines.

## Puerto Rico's Colonial Experience

The control of the political life of Puerto Rico (a "US territory") has never been in the hands of the Puerto Rican government, nor the Puerto Rican people, but in the hands of the US Congress. To put it more bluntly, Puerto Rico has never ceased to be a colony of the US

At the end of the Spanish-American War in 1898, the island and the people of Puerto Rico were given to the United States government as war booty. This was the direct result of the Treaty of Paris, a peace agreement signed in Paris on December 10, 1898 between the Spanish government and the United States.

Under the 1917 Jones Act, the United States imposed American citizenship over all citizens of Puerto Rico, making them eligible for the draft and forcing Puerto Ricans to serve in US wars. When the US Congress approved the current political definition of the island in Public Law 447 on July 7, 1952, Puerto Rico became the "Commonwealth of Puerto Rico," recently redefined by Congress as a territory not incorporated of the USA. Although this measure was meant to end the colonial status of Puerto Rico, it in fact enabled the US to adopt the Constitution of Puerto Rico, which had to be approved and framed by the Constitution of the US.

In a recent case before the 11th Circuit Court of Appeals (*US vs. Sanchez*, 992F2d 1143, June 4, 1994), the court concluded that Puerto Rico remains a territory of the United States of America. The court sustained that Congress has the power to unilaterally revoke or derogate the Constitution of Puerto Rico and the statutes that regulate the relationship between the US and its territory. And, more recently, the subcommittee on Indian and Insular Affairs of the House of Representatives rejected the inclusion of the current political status of Puerto Rico in a new referendum for considering that the current formula is "clearly colonial," the same formula Congress adopted in 1952.

Even former US President George Bush admitted that the Puerto Rican people have never been consulted as equals on their political status. In pursuit of President Bush's idea, Congressman Don Young

(R-AL) introduced the "United States-Puerto Rico Political Status Act" (H.R. 3024), which was passed by the House of Representatives on March 1998. The supporters of this bill affirmed that: "for the first time since the Treaty of Paris entered into force" Puerto Ricans will freely express their wishes regarding their political status. Therefore, they were acknowledging that Puerto Rico is still a colony today under congressional rule.

In July of 1999, the governor of Puerto Rico, the Honorable Pedro Rosello (a pro-statehood advocate), asked the UN Committee on Decolonization to urge the United States to solve the colonial status of Puerto Rico. He argued that the US has the moral and international obligation of solving the colonial status of Puerto Rico.

### Why Won't the US Let Puerto Rico Go?

The United States maintains control over Puerto Rico for military and economic reasons. During the 1898 Spanish American War, Puerto Rico was acquired as one of the "militarily strategic" areas of the Pacific, Central America, and the Caribbean—along with Panama, Cuba (Guantánamo), and others. Captain Alfred T. Mahan, US Naval Strategic Adviser, argued that acquiring Puerto Rico would guarantee the United States' safety from enemy countries: ". . . [I]t would be very difficult for a transatlantic state to maintain operations in the western Caribbean with a United States fleet based upon Puerto Rico and the adjacent islands." Clearly, military necessity was determined by the ideology of "Manifest Destiny," dressed up in religious symbolism. Today, the US controls and uses thousands of acres of Puerto Rican land for military bases (about 10 percent of Puerto Rico's national territory).

Puerto Rico has also remained under US domination for political and economic reasons. After the invasion of the island, Philip C. Hana, the last US consul in Puerto Rico, stated clearly, "The trade of Puerto Rico is of more value to the United States than is the trade of many of the South and Central American countries." The above strategy offered the US economy the possibility of an ample market for a growing capitalist economy. What Puerto Rico had to offer to the United States politically, militarily, and economically, was of too great value to let it pass. As President Theodore Roosevelt wrote, on March 1898, to his good friend, Senator Henry Cabot Lodge: "Do not make peace until we get Puerto Rico. . . ." One can clearly see that this clashes dramatically with General Miles' promise of liberty and equality, a promise suggested in the first official proclamation presented once he was in control of the island.

Today, the US continues to control the island's political and economic policies, leaving the people vulnerable to policies that adversely affect them. As a result, unemployment is disproportionately higher in Puerto Rico than any state of the union (between 10 to 15 percent higher than any state of the union). Puerto Rico is completely dependent on the US economy. It does not have the right (as other nations around the world) to trade with other nations without the consent of the US.

Puerto Ricans have to abide by laws and rules that are established by a Congress where they have but one representative who cannot vote, so that the island's destiny and future are in the hands of people for whom Puerto Ricans are just a problem.

### A Call to Action

All of the island's political parties, in recent years, have expressed their dissatisfaction with Puerto Rico's political status. However, those Puerto Ricans that struggled for the independence of Puerto Rico have been victims of discrimination, persecution, and imprisonment. The injustices suffered under Puerto Rico's colonial reality cannot be overlooked. The UN has clearly established that colonialism is a crime, and recognizes a colonized people's right to end colonialism. The United Nations' Decolonization Committee has approved resolutions recognizing the inalienable right of the people of Puerto Rico to independence and self-determination.

At their 1998 meeting this committee adopted a resolution requesting that steps be taken by the US in order to solve the case of Puerto Rico in accordance with the General Assembly Resolution 1514 (XV). This resolution requires that for self-determination to take place colonial rule has to cease and political and economic powers be returned to the country under colonial domination.

The United Methodist Church has long stood for an end to colonialism and for the self-determination of all peoples. "We affirm the right and duty of people of all nations to determine their destiny" (Social Principles ¶ 165B). We have categorically opposed interventions by more powerful nations against weaker ones. Such actions violate our Social Principles and are contrary to the United Nations Charter and international laws and treaties. As a result of these historical positions, the General Conference asks that United Methodists advocate before the President of the US and Congress for the people of Puerto Rico to be accorded full opportunity for true self determination in accordance with the General Assembly Resolution 1514 (XV), and in accordance with the United Nations Charter, and international laws and treaties.

**ADOPTED 2000**
**READOPTED 2008**
RESOLUTION #290, 2004 *BOOK OF RESOLUTIONS*
RESOLUTION #270, 2000 *BOOK OF RESOLUTIONS*

*See* Social Principles, ¶ 165A, B, and D.

## 6047. Political Status of Puerto Rico

The United States Congress and other entities of the United States government have long been studying the relationship between the United States and Puerto Rico. This topic is a hot and divisive issue in Puerto Rico with many diverse and strong opposing views. The Church enters into this discussion because of its mandate to be a prophetic voice that intends to assist in finding ways that are in accordance with the values of the Reign of God. There are certain principles that need to be emphasized:

1. We believe that all human beings are God's creatures and therefore of equal value and dignity.

2. We recognize that the church must take into consideration the following historical facts as it develops its theological thinking regarding the political status of Puerto Rico:

   a. Puerto Rico officially came to be subject to the United States of America as result of the Treaty of Paris on December 10, 1898, through which Spain surrendered its colonies to the United States. At that point Puerto Rico began to be governed by United States military authorities.

   b. The Foraker Act approved by the US Congress on 1900 put an end to the US military government of Puerto Rico. The President of the United States appointed a governor of Puerto Rico and the administration of the island came to be under the U. S. Department of the Interior.

    c. In 1917 the Jones Act was approved by the United States granting United States citizenship to all Puerto Ricans.

    d. In 1947 the United States Congress approved a law allowing the people of Puerto Rico to elect their own governor.

    e. The United States authorities have persecuted and acted against the Puerto Rico pro independence movements all along. There was even a period when it was forbidden to raise the Puerto Rico flag or to display the shield of arms that served as an emblem of Puerto Rico or to speak advocating for the independence of Puerto Rico.

    f. The people of Puerto Rico, as permitted by the appropriate United States authorities, approved in 1952 the constitution of the "Commonwealth of Puerto Rico" known in Spanish as "Estado Libre Asociado de Puerto Rico." The relationship is described as a pact. The people of Puerto Rico continue to be subjugated to the authorities of the United States of America.

    g. Several proposals are being discussed in the US Congress (2007) intending to address the problem caused by the political subordination of the people of Puerto Rico to the United States of America (see: H.R. 900, Puerto Rico Democracy Act of 2007, and H.R. 1230, the Puerto Rico Self Determination Act of 2007). Representatives of different political parties in Puerto Rico participated in public hearings in reference to the aforementioned law projects.

The present status of Puerto Rico as a nonincorporated territory of the United States, with a clear subordination to the United States, move us to take the following position from a moral and ethical perspective according to the traditions and teachings of our church:

    1. We firmly believe in self-determination for all peoples. Clearly Puerto Rico is a country with its own idiosyncrasy, cultural expressions, and that treasures its Spanish language which has survived under the remnants of a colonial system.

    2. We believe that Puerto Rico's political problem is not just a problem for Puerto Ricans; but also a problem for the people of the United States of America, and therefore, the United States should act to facilitate a real self-determination process that is in agreement with criteria accepted by the international community. The active participation of different social and political entities in the United States is needed to solve the problem.

*Therefore*, we call upon the churches to be educated about the political situation of Puerto Rico without promoting a particular political partisan perspective. We affirm that truth will set us free. We affirm that God has created us equal and with the same dignity. The subordination of a people by another people is contrary to our church's teachings.

As a church we confess that for too long we have kept ourselves uninvolved in this and other important issues for the sake of avoiding conflicts and divisions. Now we recognize that this is contrary to the prophetic tradition of our faith.

We call upon the authorities of the United States government to foster a true process of self-determination for the people of Puerto Rico in which the United States Congress participates in working out alternatives and definitions that achieve a nonterritorial formula. The United States government should clearly define which are  the vested rights of Puerto Ricans as United States citizens that will not change regardless of the political formula selected to solve the territorial problem.

We also call upon the United States government to free the Puerto Rican political prisoners in United States prisons and to drop pending charges against other persons related to their struggle for the independence of Puerto Rico. It is important for the United States to show that the era of persecution has come to an end and that we are at the beginning of a new journey where there will be space for dialogue with all the groups representing different ideologies.

**ADOPTED 2008**

*See* Social Principles, ¶ 165A, B, and D.


## 6048. US Policy in Vieques

The Exodus story of liberation speaks volumes about the experience of the people of Vieques, Puerto Rico. Exodus Chapter 3 describes very well the experience of this courageous people who have confronted the power of the US military and have come out victorious. "And the LORD said: 'I have surely seen the oppression of My people who are in Egypt, and have heard their cry because of their taskmasters, for I know their sorrows. So I have come down to deliver them out of the hand of the Egyptians, and to bring them up from that land to a good and large land, to a land flowing with milk and honey . . . ' " (3:7-8, NKJV). God has surely seen the oppression experienced by the people of Vieques, and today we can celebrate their journey of no more bombs in Vieques and no more military maneuvers.

## *Historical Background*

Vieques is a small island about eight miles east of the island nation of Puerto Rico. In 1938 the US Navy began using the island-municipality of Vieques for military practices. In 1941, during the height of WWII, the United States initiated a campaign of expropriation of territory (evicting over 3,000 people), which ended in the Navy's control of over two thirds of the island's most arable land. Thousands of families were displaced and those remaining were jeopardized in their basic means of subsistence. The net effect of these policies was the clustering of the entire civilian population into a small strip of land right in the middle of the island. Only 25 percent of the island remained under civilian control.

One of the effects of 60 years of bombing has been the degradation, and in some cases destruction, of Vieques' delicate ecosystems. Hundreds of species of plants and animals have been killed as a result of the direct impact of projectiles during military practices. These bombings and military maneuvers have led to serious contamination of the environment due to toxic residues and other contaminants.

In an article published in 1988, engineer and environmental consultant Rafael Cruz-Pérez identified three ways that the military bombs pollute the environment in Vieques: (1) chemicals in the missiles' explosive payloads, (2) dust and rock particles released into the air from the missile impact and/or detonation, and (3) metallic residues left by missiles after they detonate and the junk and scrap heap they use for target practice. "According to information provided by the Navy, this material has never been removed . . . Under the effects of additional explosions and sea breezes, metals are oxidized or decomposed, turning in accelerated fashion into leachates that pollute the environment," wrote Cruz-Pérez. He also cited a scientific study by the US Navy that found the drinking water sources in Vieques' Isabel Segunda village and Barrio Esperanza are polluted with toxic chemicals, including TNT, tetryl and RDX. Cruz-Pérez wrote that "the study doesn't explain how these substances got to the water sources, located more than fourteen kilometers away from the shooting area."

In the 1970s, the US Environmental Protection Agency sampled Vieques' air and soil. After studying the samples, the EPA determined that the air has unhealthy levels of particulate matter and the ground has iron levels above normal.

The net result of this environmental pollution is high levels of cancer and other serious health problems that Viequenes have been experiencing for years. Studies carried out by the Puerto Rico Department of Health have shown that from 1985 to 1989 the cancer rate in Vieques was 26 percent higher than the rest of Puerto Rico's already high levels of cancer.

Dr. Rafael Rivera-Castaño, a retired professor from the University of Puerto Rico's Medical Sciences Campus, has documented the increase in extremely rare diseases, including scleroderma, lupus, thyroid deficiencies, as well as more common ailments like asthma, which are significantly affecting Vieques' children.

According to Dr. Rivera-Castaño there is no reason for the children of a small island like Vieques to develop asthma. "The winds that blow in from the ocean are rich in iodine, which prevents asthma. The only possible cause for this high incidence of asthma is air pollution," he stated. Vieques does not have factories or any large industry that could cause the high incidence of asthma; the only source of air pollution on the island has been the Navy.

Economic development on the island has also been drastically affected by the Navy's presence. About 9,400 people live on Vieques and the unemployment rate is almost fifty percent by most conservative estimates.

General Electric, the only large company in Vieques, ended its operations in the summer of 2003. One of the few viable industries in Vieques today is commercial fishing. The bombing, however, has left this industry barely profitable.

Agriculture, the largest industry in Vieques before the Navy expropriated the most fertile land, is today almost nonexistent. Now the economic inheritance of the people and the children of Vieques is economic stagnation.

## Conclusion

The United Methodist Church has been a key supporter of the struggle in Vieques. The voice of our Church joined with the voices of many organizations in Puerto Rico and around the world to halt the

Navy's maneuvers on the island. The Navy's military presence finally ended on May 1, 2003, which the 2004 General Conference celebrated. Justice, however, is not complete.

The majority of the people of Vieques rejoiced with the announcement that the bombing, mainly by the US Navy, against their island had ended. Regretfully even when now there is no longer any bombing, bombs continue to explode in the former base that was called Camp Garcia. The removal of thousands of live bombs in the area is being done exploding them on site, in the open air. This produces an additional quantity of contaminants that enter different ecosystems and continue to have an adverse impact on the food chain and on the health of the people of Vieques. The US Navy has reported that the open air bomb explosions on site in Vieques may continue until the year 2010 or even 2012. According to information published by the US Navy, by March 16, 2007 as part of the "cleaning" of Vieques, some 5,754 explosive artifacts were detonated in the open air. It is not acceptable to continue to put at risk the peace, health and security of the people of Vieques.

Now the people of Vieques need the Church to call for restoration for their island, urging environmental cleanup of the damage left behind by the US Navy and restoration of the economy through the creation of new jobs and new industry.

Reconstruction in Vieques is only just beginning. It is important that renewal principally benefit the resident people of the island and not the hotel interests, politicians or other powerful forces. Equally important is that restoring agriculture, fishing, ecotourism, housing, archaeologic-historic investigation and environmental study, will be the backbone of a new model of cooperative, community and sustainable development.

Community participation in all steps of reconstruction (the environmental cleanup, return of the lands, future development) is necessary to ensure a process of genuine healing and reconstruction.

The land cannot be developed if they are not returned—and demilitarized. The use proposed by the Navy for some of the land will determine the level of cleanup. The Navy looks to bypass the Viequenses' demands by "passing" the lands to the US Department of the Interior and Fish and Wildlife Service, so that cleanup is not an essential part of the end of military use process.

*Be it resolved that,* The United Methodist Church:

1. request of the appropriate agencies of the United States government that the cleaning of all the contaminants produced by the US Navy activities or activities allowed by the US Navy be done using methods that will keep to a minimum the release of toxic agents into the environment. The health of the residents of Vieques must be protected. Diverse sources have published information on the availability of equipment and methodology that make possible the removal of explosive artifacts without detonating them in open air spaces;

2. urge the US Congress to appropriate sufficient funds to decontaminate Vieques such that the land is again suitable for agriculture, environmental tourism and other social uses;

3. call upon the United States government to assign funds to enable the people of Vieques to have access to new health programs directed to reduce the high incidence of different types of cancer, to provide treatment to all the persons with toxic chemicals in their bodies, and to treat and reduce the high incidence of respiratory diseases;

4. urge Congress and the government of Puerto Rico to establish mechanisms to promote the reconstruction and sustainable economic development of Vieques;

5. call upon the Environmental Protection Agency and all other government agencies responsible for the cleaning to also expedite the cleaning of the island of Culebra, Puerto Ric, that was also contaminated as a result of military maneuvers;

6. urge that civil and religious leaders in Vieques be involved in every decision regarding the future of the island;

7 develop educational resources through the General Boards of Church and Society, Global Ministries, and Discipleship, to help United Methodists and others understand the issues affecting the people of Vieques;

8. send a copy of this resolution to the US House and Senate Armed Services Committees, the governor of Puerto Rico, and the secretary-general of the United Nations; and

9. send a copy of this resolution to the bishop of the Puerto Rico Methodist Autonomous Affiliated Church.

ADOPTED 2004
REVISED AND READOPTED 2008
RESOLUTION #294, 2004 *BOOK OF RESOLUTIONS*
RESOLUTION #274, 2000 *BOOK OF RESOLUTIONS*

*See* Social Principles, ¶ 165B.

## 6049. Haitian Asylum Seekers

WHEREAS, successive governments in Haiti, whether democratically elected or not, have failed to ensure the proper functioning of political, judicial, police, and civil institutions and normal economic and commercial activity, which has led to escalating violence and deepening poverty; and

WHEREAS, thousands of persons have been displaced in Haiti and thousands more have sought refuge in the Dominican Republic, in other countries of the Caribbean, and in the United States; and

WHEREAS, United States law offers opportunity for asylum for those with a well-founded risk of persecution; and

WHEREAS, the United States viewed Haitian refugees as economic migrants and, therefore, not eligible for asylum, and Haiti alone has been subject to an interdiction policy whereby the US Coast Guard turns back refugee boats on the high seas with no offer of protection such as is offered to both interdicted Chinese and Cubans; and

WHEREAS, until December 2002, all asylum seekers arriving in Florida by sea were allowed to remain with family or friends during their asylum application process with the exception of Haitians, all of whom were detained; and

WHEREAS, Haitian families who are detained have been separated, the women and men have been placed for months in jails, in deplorable conditions, and alongside criminals, and others (including small children) have been held in overcrowded hotels unsuitable for detention, without exercise or fresh air; and

WHEREAS, when a boat filled with refugees reached shore in Miami, they were eligible for parole from detention on bond, the Immigration and Naturalization Service (now the Bureau for Customs and Border Control of the Department of Homeland Security), using the authority granted it since 9/11, obtained a stay on bonds granted to Haitians on grounds of "security risk"; and

WHEREAS, the United States, in denying Haitians a full and fair hearing and deporting them, is putting them at great risk on their return, as exemplified in the case of the 200 Haitians who arrived in Miami, December 2002, were given expedited hearings of 30 minutes (including translation time) for their asylum cases with no opportunity to consult with their attorneys, and faced deportation;

WHEREAS, the US, in subjecting Haitian asylum seekers to interdiction, summary return, expedited removal, prolonged detention and accelerated asylum adjudications, violates US obligations under the Geneva Convention of 1951 and of US asylum law; and

WHEREAS, the US, by its own admission, is detaining Haitian asylum seekers in order to deter a mass exodus from Haiti, and so has a policy contrary to international law and applies it in a discriminatory fashion;

*Therefore,* the United Methodist Committee on Relief, in cooperation with other appropriate structures of The United Methodist Church:

A. calls upon the government of the United States to:

1. end the practice of interdiction of Haitian refugees and make provision instead for a full and fair opportunity for those who have a credible fear to present it;

2. end the practice of detaining Haitian asylum seekers without parole and/or returning them, and instead to provide for their parole in the same way as the (former) Miami INS District provided for parole of asylum seekers of other nationalities;

3. grant Haitian asylum seekers full access to refugee determination proceedings and offer protection to those who qualify;

4. extend Temporary Protected Status (TPS), which would allow Haitians who had arrived in the country prior to the date announced for the start of the TPS period, to remain in the US legally until the political situation in Haiti improves;

5. increase resettlement opportunities for Haitian refugees;

6. monitor conditions of return for rejected refugees;

7. take the leadership in calling for the Organization of American States (OAS), especially the countries of the Caribbean, to develop a policy for Haitian refugees in which the US assumes its share of the responsibility for their protection.

B. calls upon the United Nations High Commissioner for Refugees to:

1. place an international staff person in the Dominican Republic to respond to the asylum seekers already there and to provide an existing presence given a possible increased exodus from Haiti;

2. increase this presence so as to be able to meet the needs of refugees and asylum seekers in the region;

3. work with the United States government to implement a more just policy for Haitian refugees that will conform with US asylum law, as well as international law.

C. calls upon The United Methodist Church through its boards and agencies to:

1. advocate for an end to the discriminatory treatment of Haitian refugees that runs counter to the laws of the United States and of the international community;

2. involve itself in the coalition of national organizations that are in process of formation under the leadership of Church World Service and that will advocate for Haitian refugees;

3. monitor government actions with respect to Haitian asylum seekers and be ready to respond in advocacy to them; and

4. work to establish ministries of hospitality and development for Haitian refugees.

ADOPTED 2004
READOPTED 2008
RESOLUTION #291, 2004 *BOOK OF RESOLUTIONS*

*See* Social Principles, ¶ 165.

## 6050. Atomic Testing on the Marshall Islands: A Legacy

WHEREAS, in the Old Testament the Lord spoke to Moses saying: "Speak to the Israelites: When a man or a woman wrongs another, breaking faith with the LORD that person incurs guilt and shall confess the sin that has been committed. The person shall make full restitution for the wrong, adding one fifth to it, and giving it all to the one who was wronged" (Numbers 5:5-7). And in the New Testament Zacchaeus stood there and said to the Lord, "Look, half of my possessions, Lord, I will give to the poor, and if I have defrauded anyone of anything, I will pay back four times as much." (Luke 19:8, NRSV)

WHEREAS, The Marshall Islands government has indicated that new information on the health of its people exposed to radiation from atomic and nuclear testing by the United States in the Marshalls requires more just compensation and expansion of medical care than the $150 million trust fund provided in the Compact of Free Association; and

WHEREAS, evidence from recently declassified US government reports and studies shows that many more Marshall Islanders were exposed to nuclear fallout from the 67 US atomic and nuclear tests than American negotiators admitted when the compensation package in the compact was negotiated in the early 1980s; and

W HEREAS, many questions are arising about the accuracy of medical research done by US government labs on Marshall Islanders who were exposed to fallout from atomic and nuclear testing; and

W HEREAS, although the US government provided full compensation to American citizens living downwind of the Nevada Test Site, Marshall Islanders have not received more than sixty-one percent of their total awards because the compensation level is inadequate; and

W HEREAS, fully one-third of the 1,074 Marshall Islands recipients of nuclear test awards have died without receiving full compensation; and

W HEREAS, the US government provided full compensation to American citizens living in a significantly larger area compared to the Marshall Islands, despite the fact that the total tonnage of US tests in the Marshall Islands was almost 100 times greater than the yield of tests at the Nevada test site; and

W HEREAS, documents now show that the people of Ailuk and other nearby islands were exposed to dangerous amounts of radiation, yet purposely were not evacuated; and

W HEREAS, the Marshall Islanders are increasingly becoming aware that islanders were not evacuated *despite* information that prevailing wind would blow fallout over a number of inhabited islands and that they were likely being used as "guinea pigs" in radiation studies; and

W HEREAS, US government representatives deceived the people of Bikini Atoll by telling that their island would be used "for the benefit of mankind"; and

W HEREAS, the March 1, 1954 "Bravo" hydrogen bomb test at Bikini Atoll was detonated despite weather reports the previous day that winds were blowing to the east toward the inhabited atolls of Rongelap, Utrik, Ailuk and others; and

W HEREAS, a 1985-1989 health survey in the Marshall Islands revealed cancer rates 2-30 times higher among Marshall Islanders than in the US; and

W HEREAS, a nationwide survey of thyroid problems in the Marshall Islands in the mid-1990s by doctors from Tohoku University in Japan confirmed a high rate of thyroid disorders among Marshall Islanders; and

W HEREAS, the economic provisions of a Compact of Free Association implemented in 1986 will expire in 2001 and are up for renegotiation in 1999; and

WHEREAS, the US government has not yet apologized to the Marshallese people for the death of Marshallese citizens and for the damage done to their homeland, waters and people; and

WHEREAS, the $150 million trust fund provided in a Compact of Free Association with the Marshall Islands is woefully inadequate and not just compensation for the health injuries and deaths caused by US nuclear testing to the population, and the loss of the use of their atolls because of radiation contamination since 1946; and

WHEREAS, US funding for medical surveillance and treatment programs is inadequate to meet the needs of the exposed population in the Marshall Islands,

*Therefore, be it resolved,* that this General Conference of The United Methodist Church call upon The United Methodist Church through the General Board of Church and Society and the General Board of Global Ministries to work closely with the Marshallese people and our ecumenical partners, to bring about an official apology and full redress including all necessary funding from the US government; and

*Be it further resolved,* that copies of this resolution be sent to the US attorney general, the secretary of the department of energy, the secretary of defense, the secretary of state, with copies to the Republic of the Marshall Islands Embassy Office in Washington, DC, and to the people in the Marshall Islands.

ADOPTED 2000
READOPTED 2008
RESOLUTION #288, 2004 *BOOK OF RESOLUTIONS*
RESOLUTION #267, 2000 *BOOK OF RESOLUTIONS*

*See* Social Principles, ¶ 165B.

## 6051. United States Role in Colombia

Therefore thus says the LORD, the God of Israel, concerning the shepherds who shepherd my people: It is you who have scattered my flock, and driven them away, and you have not attended to them. So I will attend to you for your evil doings, says the LORD.

(Jeremiah 23:2 NRSV)

The Social Principles on National Power and Responsibility state, "Some nations possess more military and economic power than do others. Upon the powerful rests responsibility to exercise their wealth and influence with restraint (¶ 165).

For many years the nation of Colombia has suffered from internal conflict, which has been exacerbated by United States involvement through Plan Colombia (a joint US and Colombian military effort to fight drug trafficking and guerilla military operations) and the "war on drugs." Large areas of land have been rendered unusable and crops destroyed by indiscriminate spraying of chemicals intended to destroy coca plants.

The land rights of Afro-Colombians, indigenous peoples, and campesinos have been violated by armed groups who violently force them off their land, as well as by Colombian and American corporations exploring and drilling for oil in rain forests.

Paramilitary death squads regularly collude with the Colombian military, which receives millions of dollars of support each year from the United States. These illegal armed groups spear among the Colombian people. Internal civil war has left nearly three million internally displaced people in Colombia.

The United States-Colombian co-sponsored Plan Colombia has not succeeded in curbing the production and export of drugs from Colombia. Instead, it has intensified sharp political and military divisions in that country.

The present policy of the United States has only exacerbated the basic problems of poverty and decades-long armed conflict in Colombia.

*Therefore,* The United Methodist Church urges the United States government to:

- stop all current and future United States military aid to Colombia;
- support negotiations between the Colombian government and the guerrillas to end the civil war;
- divert funds used for DEA military raids and crop fumigation to provide viable economic alternatives to coca production; and
- support Afro-Colombians', indigenous peoples', and campesinos' rights to self-determination and control over resources in their traditional homelands.

The General Conference expresses its profound concern and support for The Methodist Church in Colombia, which has two local congregations in the center of the conflict. This area has mass graves of persons murdered by the paramilitary forces who were cut into pieces. The Methodist Church works with the Ecumenical Network of Colombia to assist people who have been displaced and provide sanctuary to people who have been persecuted.

ADOPTED 2000
REVISED AND READOPTED 2008
RESOLUTION #300, 2004 *BOOK OF RESOLUTIONS*
RESOLUTION #280, 2000 *BOOK OF RESOLUTIONS*

*See* Social Principles, ¶ 165*B*.

## 6052. United States-Mexico Border

The United States-Mexico border is a 2,000-mile-long area where the socioeconomic dynamics of two interacting cultures have a negative impact on the quality of life of adjoining populations. This adverse situation has been exacerbated by domestic and international policies espoused by the US and Mexican governments.

The border region is characterized by:

- political domination by a minority of rich and powerful families;
- drastic economic disparity between segments of the population;
- constant deterioration of the health conditions, particularly those affecting the poor;
- high incidence of crime, drug trafficking, and human trafficking for the exploitation of children and adults; and
- high rates of unemployment and underemployment, These detrimental conditions also affect the constant influx of thousands of refugees and undocumented persons coming to the United States seeking safe haven or better economic conditions. This situation of pain and suffering affects millions of women, children, and men residing on both sides of the border. The impact of these dynamics reaches well into the interiors of both countries.

Confronted by this human suffering along the United States-Mexico border region, we recognize that the vision of the "new heaven and new earth" (Revelation 21) will be only an illusion as long as "one of the least" (Matthew 25) continues to suffer.

We are particularly concerned about the following conditions:

## 1. *Environmental:*

    a. the constant indiscriminate use of pesticides in the growing and harvesting of agricultural products, a problem on both sides of the border; and the export of banned or restricted pesticides across the border;

    b. water contamination caused by corporations dumping industrial toxic waste and the flushing of poisonous compounds into the Rio Grande, the Colorado, and other rivers; and

    c. growing air pollution on both sides of the border.

## 2. *Health:*

    a. a high rate of birth defects and other health problems among industrial workers, many of whom have neither been given proper equipment nor been informed of the hazards of the toxic materials they have been exposed to;

    b. the high incidence of dysentery, tuberculosis, and hepatitis especially among children in the Colonias (rural unincorporated areas), caused by lack of adequate water treatment facilities and a lack of food and fresh water;

    c. the growing number of unsafe, crowded barracks and shanty towns without sanitation and other basic facilities due to a lack of adequate, affordable housing for workers; and

    d. the lack of access to health, education and welfare services, already overburdened by the volume of need, perpetuating the cycle of poverty and dehumanization.

## 3. *Economic:*

    a. wages kept low by repressing workers' bargaining rights, which keeps the border region below the average of Mexican industrial wage levels, despite the fact that the Maquiladoras are the second largest producers of export income (after oil), and the largest source of income for the Mexican border region;

    b. the lack of long-range economic and industrial development strategies, making both the U.S. and the Mexican economies more dependent on quick economic fixes such as Maquiladoras,

quick cash crops, tourism, and services that can help temporarily and superficially, but ignore the needs of most of the
present and future generations;

c. the trade agreements (such as the North American Free Trade
Agreement), which worsen existing economic dependencies
and foster the exploitation of human and natural resources; and

d. the region's low level of educational attainment, high incidence of illiteracy, the high dropout rate, and the availability
and influx of drugs, which have a greater impact on the low-
income population along the border.

4. *Civil and Human Rights:*

a. heightened anxieties of Americans who perceive immigrants
as unwelcomed foreigners who threaten US social, political,
and economic security;

b. strategies devised by US governmental agencies and groups
to harass, intimidate, and repress legal and foreign entrants
into the US territory; and

c. the poor administration of justice; the cultural insensitivity of
border patrol agents; the high incidence of illegal use of force;
and the constant violation of the civil and human rights of
those detained or deported. These situations create an atmosphere of tension and distrust that adds to the polarization
between Mexicans and US residents and transients.

These detrimental conditions create pain and suffering among millions of women, children, and men residing on both sides of the border. The impact of these dynamics reaches well into the interiors of
both countries. As Christians and United Methodists, we express our
sorrow and indignation about this human suffering and accept the
responsibility to use our resources toward the elimination of the root
causes creating this tragic human problem. We are urged by God
through Christ to love our neighbor and to do what we must to bring
healing in the midst of pain, and to restore to wholeness those whose
lives are shattered by injustice and oppression.

*Therefore,* we recommend and urge the Mexican and US governments to:

• develop national and international policies that bring more
economic parity between the two countries, as an integral part
of any trade agreement;

- develop binational and multilateral agreements that improve the quality of life; safeguard water rights; and prevent the contamination of air, water, and land of both sides of the border;
- develop binding and enforceable mechanisms with respect to: labor and human rights; agriculture, including farm workers; environmental standards; and health and safety standards for both nations and in any agreements to which they are a party;
- develop and support national and international policies, such as the UN Convention on the Protection of the Rights of all Migrant Workers and Members of their Families, that facilitate the migration and immigration of peoples across the border while respecting their rights and aspirations; and
- find alternative and creative ways to reduce the foreign debt of Mexico.

We further recommend that the General Board of Church and Society, with churches in Mexico, the United States, and Canada, seek ways to network on fair trade, labor and human rights, agricultural, and environmental concerns.

ADOPTED 1992
AMENDED AND READOPTED 2004
READOPTED 2008
RESOLUTION #302, 2004 *BOOK OF RESOLUTIONS*
RESOLUTION #282, 2000 *BOOK OF RESOLUTIONS*

*See* Social Principles, ¶ 165.

## NATIONS AND CULTURES

### 6061. Our Muslim Neighbors

Christians are called to initiate and promote better relationships between Christians and Muslims on the basis of informed understanding, critical appreciation, and balanced perspective of one another's basic beliefs.

### *The Historical Context*

United Methodists, seeking to be faithful neighbors and witnesses to other members of the human family, recognize with respect peoples of the religion of Islam.

Christians and Muslims acknowledge common roots, along with Jews, in the faith of Abraham, Sarah, and Hagar. As members of one of the monotheistic world religions, Muslims worship and serve the one God with disciplined devotion. Both Christians and Muslims believe that God is ever-inclined toward humankind in justice and mercy. Based on this common ground, we celebrate where Christians and Muslims are working together to make God's justice a reality for all people. The two faiths sometimes understand differently the particular ways in which God deals with human beings, but they agree that the proper human response to the Almighty is a life of humble obedience, including repentance, faith, and good works. Muslims believe that the Qur'an sets forth the principles for righteous conduct and a harmonious life in society. The following verses from the Qur'an show that these principles are similar to the ones found in the Christian Scriptures:

O believers, be steadfast witnesses for God with justice. Do not let the hatred of a people make you act unjustly. Be just, for justice is next to piety (5:8).

Worship only God; be good to parents and kindred, to orphans and the poor; speak kindly to others (92:83).

Do not mix truth with falsehood, nor knowingly conceal the truth (2:42).

O believers, fulfill your obligations (5:1).

Hold to forgiveness and enjoin good; turn aside from the foolish (7:199).

It may be that God will bring about friendship between you and those whom you hold to be your enemies (60:7).

## The Need for Understanding

United Methodists live together with Muslims in many countries of the world and in a variety of social environments. Indeed, in the United States of America, Muslims comprise one of the most rapidly growing religious communities. In places around the world, Muslims may constitute the majority of the population, and in other places, Christians may be the majority. As believers of the two religions build their lives in the same general area, they are often affected by patterns of religious antagonism inherited from the past history of disputes and misunderstanding between the two.

Also, Muslims and Christians experience varying degrees of political and social discrimination, depending on the particular circumstances of each country. In certain areas of tension believers in the two faiths are caught up in struggles for economic, political, and human rights.

We believe that sustained and ever-renewed initiatives of open discussion and sharing of concerns in interfaith settings contribute to the achievement of social justice.

By this statement, we express solidarity with those of either religion who suffer oppression or discrimination.

By this statement, we make a step toward more hospitable and cooperative relationships and encourage dialogical relations.

## Basic United Methodist Documents

### A. Called to Be Neighbors

A clear biblical basis for discussion in interfaith settings is set forth in Guidelines for Interreligious Relationships:

> In conversation with a lawyer (Luke 10:25), Jesus reminded him that his neighbor, the one to whom he should show love and compassion, included a stranger, a Samaritan. Today, Christ's call to neighborliness (Luke 10:27) includes the "stranger" of other faiths. It is not just that historical events have forced us together. The Christian faith itself impels us to love our neighbors of other faiths and to seek to live in contact and mutually beneficial relationship, in community with them.

### B. The Social Community

In our United Methodist Social Principles, we affirm all persons as equally valuable in the sight of God and determine to work toward societies in which each person's value is recognized, maintained, and strengthened.

Religious persecution has been common in the history of civilization. We urge policies and practices that ensure the right of every religious group to exercise its faith free from legal, political, or economic restrictions. In particular, we condemn anti-Semite, anti-Muslim, and anti-Christian attitudes and practices in both their overt and covert forms, being especially sensitive to their expression in media stereotyping.

### C. Our Theological Task

In our United Methodist Doctrinal Standards, our relationship with adherents of other living faiths of the world is set in the context of our ecumenical commitment. We are encouraged to enter into serious interfaith encounters and explorations between Christians and adherents of other living faiths of the world. Scripture calls us to be both neighbors and witnesses to all people. Such encounters require us to reflect anew on our faith and to seek guidance for our witness among neighbors of other faiths.

When Christians enter into such dialogue, they come to it consciously as they seek to live as one people, under the living God who is the Creator of all humankind, the One "who is above all and through all and in all" (Ephesians 4:6).

This theological understanding compels us to a particular kind of dialogue, one in which we reflect critically upon our Christian tradition, gain accurate appreciation of the traditions of others, and engage with love and generosity of spirit as we seek "to raise all such relationships to the highest possible level of human fellowship and understanding."

### Christian-Muslim Discussions

The long-standing commitment of The United Methodist Church to social justice, to theological inquiry, and to just and open relationships places a particular responsibility on its members to develop discussions between Christians and Muslims. Mutual respect requires the church to recognize and affirm that, although individuals may move from one religion to another, we do not enter into formal interfaith dialogue with the intent to convert the Muslim community to Christianity. Although the movement is still small, there is increasing evidence that groups of Christians and Muslims are coming together to witness to their faith and acknowledge the power of God in their lives, to identify problems that challenge all on the deepest theological and moral level, and to try to understand better the complex factors that determine the crucial decisions being made by governments around the world.

Through such interactions, Christians and Muslims are finding that working for better exchange of information and for ways to cooperate in solving mutual problems and concerns often leads to discovery and growth, adding to the depth and understanding of each tradition.

If we observe the unfolding of events in today's world and assess Islamic movement as only reactionary and threatening, we will hinder the advancement of justice and peace and neither gain from nor contribute to mutual understanding.

If we develop friendships with Muslims as members of the human community from whom and with whom we have much to learn, we will increase our respect for Islam as a way of life that calls its millions of followers to the highest moral ideals and satisfies their deepest spiritual aspirations.

In the aftermath of September 11, 2001, The United Methodist Church has intentionally explored what it means to be in relationship with the Muslim community. The United Methodist Church stands in solidarity with Muslims in the struggles for economic, political and human rights.

## Action Statement

Local congregations and United Methodist agencies are encouraged to develop ongoing relationships with Muslims and their respective organizations. They are urged to initiate conversations, programs, and dialogues leading to the understanding of both Islam and Christianity, and appreciation of their particular gifts, while discovering commonalities and differences; and seeking areas of mutual cooperation. They are also urged to exchange information and discuss ways to cooperate when they address common problems and concerns.

## Recommendations

We request the Council of Bishops to support, participate in, and assist United Methodists in implementing this resolution.

We call upon the General Board of Global Ministries, and particularly its Women's Division, to promote a program of ongoing relationships with Muslim women, seeking areas of mutual concern about how to live ethically, morally, and responsibly in today's world and to join in common struggles for peace and justice.

We urge the General Board of Church and Society to work with Muslims in activities designed to achieve common political, social, economic, and ecological goals.

We urge that the General Board of Global Ministries and the General Board of Church and Society develop advocacy programs on behalf of religious freedom and minority rights, particularly regarding nations that are experiencing crisis in Christian-Muslim conflict in which religious minorities are harassed or persecuted. These advocacy programs should be directed toward, among others, the US Department of State, US Embassies, and the United Nations Human Rights Commission.

We recommend that the General Commission on Christian Unity and Interreligious Concerns, as it initiates and engages in dialogue with representatives of Islam, remain mindful of the evangelism imperatives of the gospel and the gospel mandate to seek justice for those who are oppressed.

We recommend that United Methodist Communications, through its Division of Public Media and News Service, monitor and call attention to discrimination against Muslims in both the religious and secular media.

We urge United Methodist members, local churches, and agencies to take the following specific actions:

1. Study Islam, using resources such as: Brochures, "Basic Facts about Islam," "Guidelines for Interfaith Dialogue," (GCCUIC, 2001) "Called to be Neighbors and Witnesses" (General Conference, 2000); *Guidelines on Dialogue with People of Living Faiths and Ideologies*, World Council of Churches (Geneva: 1990); *God Is One: The Way of Islam*, by R. Marston Speight (New York: Friendship Press, updated/revised 2001); *The Holy Qur'an*, New Revised Edition, trans. 'Abdullah Yusuf' Alli (Brentwood, MD: Amana Corp., 2001); National Council of Churches Interfaith Policy Statement 2000; *Silent No More: Confronting America's False Images of Islam*, by Paul Findley (Amana Publications, Beltsville Maryland, 2001); *A New Religious America*, by Diana Eck (Harper Collins, New York, 2001); *Creating Interfaith Community*, by Marston Speight (GBGM, Service Center, 2003); magazines such as *Minaret* (MultiMedia Vera International, 434 South Vermont, Los Angeles, CA 90020).

2. Initiate dialogue with Muslims, utilizing as our guide the resolution of the 2000 General Conference entitled "Called to Be Neighbors and Witnesses, Guidelines for Interreligious Relationships," and models of dialogue developed by the General Commission on Christian Unity and Interreligious Concerns. The dialogue will address theological and justice issues, related to the particular contexts in which those dialogues occur.

3. Develop awareness of the concerns of particular Muslim populations through implementation of other applicable General Conference Resolutions in the 2000 *Book of Resolutions*, such as "Prejudice Against Muslims and Arabs in the USA."

4. Promote understanding between Christians and Muslims in local communities through:

- arranging visits to local mosques;
- developing and participating in cultural exchanges with Muslims;
- inviting Muslims to social occasions;
- seeking Muslim participation in local interfaith councils and interfaith worship;
- sending messages of greeting and good will to Muslims upon the occasion of their religious festivals;
- encouraging authorities of schools, hospitals, prisons, factories, and places of business and government to respect particular features of Muslim life;
- upholding the dignity of individuals, families, and communities; and
- seeking to remedy situations in which Muslims encounter misunderstanding, prejudice, stereotyping, or even hostility from the neighborhood or population when they desire to express their faith in everyday life.

**ADOPTED 1992**
**AMENDED AND READOPTED 2004**
**RESOLUTION #315, 2004** *BOOK OF RESOLUTIONS*
**RESOLUTION #299, 2000** *BOOK OF RESOLUTIONS*

*See* Social Principles, ¶ 165*A, B,* and *C.*


## 6062. Africa Reconstruction and Development

*We applaud international efforts to develop a more just international economic order in which the limited resources of the earth will be used to the maximum benefit of all nations and peoples. We urge Christians in every society to encourage the governments under which they live and the economic entities within their societies to aid and work for the development of more just economic orders.* (Social Principles, ¶ 165*B*)

The continent of Africa is in crisis. A century of colonial rule, preceded by two centuries of a vicious slave trade and followed by a generation of neocolonialism, has left much of Africa's social, political, and economic life in a shambles. The scale of poverty and suffering is daunting. More than 300 million people survive on under $1 per day.

Life expectancy remains lower than 60 in 41 of the 53 countries. Africa is now the epicenter of the greatest catastrophe in recorded human history—the HIV/AIDS pandemic—with women making up 58 percent of those infected and more than 11 million children orphaned since the pandemic started. Corruption and bribery in many African countries places unbearable burdens on the most vulnerable people and blocks progress towards poverty reduction. More than one-third of all children are malnourished, and more than 40 percent have no access to education and are far more likely to die before the age of five than children in any other region. Famine and starvation continue to devastate women, children and men. In December 2002, the United Nation's World Food Programme issued an "African Hunger Alert" appealing for emergency assistance to care for 38 million Africans threatened by famine. Almost half the continent does not have access to safe water.

Conflicts affect one in five people living in Africa. There are more than 3 million refugees throughout the continent. Arms merchants, worldwide, find ready markets for weapons and their components among African governments and the combatant movements that oppose them. Massive numbers of ruinous land mines and explosive traps are installed by both offenders and defenders but, even after the combatants have moved on, the potential for dismemberment and death remains. Demobilized child soldiers have represented a particular challenge to communities. Young people who have proven their murderous effectiveness must be nurtured into positive social productivity.

In 1995, at the United Nations World Summit for Social Development in Copenhagen, Denmark, Africa was singled out as a region requiring special attention by the international community to address the urgent need to develop the economic, social, and human resources of the continent. In the 2000 review of the implementation of the goals set by the Summit the following observations were reported:

"African countries have made real efforts to implement the commitments made at Copenhagen, but internal and external constraints continue to make progress extremely difficult. The mobilization of resources at the national and international levels to accelerate the economic and social development of Africa...through a holistic approach is needed for the full implementation of the commitments. Equitable access to education and health services, income earning opportunities, land, credit, infrastructure and technology, as well as official development assistance and debt reduction are vital to social development in Africa. . . .

"In a rapidly globalizing economic world, Africa continues to be marginalized. A persistent decline in the international terms of trade for commodities exported from African countries has reduced real national income and savings for finance investment. The external debt burden has drastically reduced resources available for social development. Furthermore, promises made to provide official development assistance to developing countries in general and the least developed countries in particular have not been fulfilled. More concerted efforts and an internationally enabling environment are necessary to integrate Africa as well as the least developed countries into the world economy." (World Summit for Social Development and Beyond: Achieving Social Development for all in a Globalizing World—24th Special Session of the UN General Assembly)

Africa is blessed with people of remarkable energy, spirit, and ingenuity. The continent is rich in natural resources needed by the entire world. The spread of democracy and the growing strength of African civil society offer a real chance to tackle the root causes of poverty and conflict. Social movements and organizations throughout the continent have developed to hold governments accountable and to build societies where public institutions and policies will guarantee cultural, economic, political, and social rights of all citizens. There is a call for alternative development programs based on the fundamental principles of democracy, human rights, gender equality and social justice. African leaders have developed their own initiative for establishing new relationships between Africa and the world—New Partnership for Africa's Development (NEPAD) focuses on the eradication of poverty and support for sustainable development. Key priorities of NEPAD are to attract investment in energy, agriculture, communications and human resources as well as to request increased aid and debt relief to build the infrastructure to attract investment. The African Union (replacing the Organization of African Unity) was established in 2002 and endorsed NEPAD at its first meeting in July 2002. The United Nations General Assembly officially endorsed NEPAD in November 2002. African civil society (including the faith communities), which has not been consulted on NEPAD, is organizing to study and offer their suggestions to the initiative. The debate has been heated across the continent.

The United Methodist Church in Africa is continuing to grow rapidly and is a transforming presence in many countries, influential beyond its numbers, engaging in a holistic Wesleyan ministry of outreach, evangelism, and humanitarian service. The church in Africa is part of civil society and has a strong witness to make in participating in the eradication of poverty; in promoting reconciliation, conflict resolution and justice ministries; in humanitarian assistance and refugee resettlement programs; and in pastoral training in HIV/AIDS. The church in the United States and in Europe has a strong role to play in advocating respect for the rights of African governments and peoples to define their economic policies and priorities and for continuing to support—among other things—debt cancellation, increased humanitarian and development aid, removal of trade barriers which discourage African exports, funding to overcome HIV/AIDS, ratification of the Treaty to Ban Landmines, as well as discouraging the militarization of the continent.

As Christians, our faith is in the God of Jesus Christ, who stands with the most vulnerable and oppressed people in our societies. Their well-being must serve as a guidepost for justice. God, sovereign over all nations, has made of one blood all the peoples of the earth. United Methodists, therefore, remain ever-vigilant, listening more attentively than ever to churches and movements around the world, as they struggle for social, political, economic, and spiritual development.

Therefore, we call upon the United Methodist people, local churches, and agencies to:

1. encourage United Methodist churches to increase their participation in programs of missionary support, pastors' salary supplementation, emergency relief, aid to refugees, reconstruction, and development through the appropriate units of the General Board of Global Ministries, regional councils of churches and the World Council of Churches;

2. encourage United Methodists to participate in Volunteers in Mission programs and other volunteer-based projects; and educate themselves (through orientation, cultural sensitivity, and contingency planning) for working alongside African brothers and sisters to, for example, reconstruct schools, clinics and churches. There is a need to emphasize the importance of preparation for the cross-cultural experience by volunteers and receiving partners. Orientation and training for both are available through the Jurisdictional VIM Coordinators and the Mission Volunteers Program of the General Board of Global Ministries. In addition, the United Methodist Seminar Program on

National and International Affairs in Washington, DC, and New York City provides educational opportunities for United Methodists to learn about significant issues affecting Africa;

3. urge United Methodist churches in Africa to advocate with government leaders in every country as to the need for people and justice to be at the center of any concerted national and international efforts toward the eradication of poverty, sustainable and equitable development, and reconstruction on the continent of Africa. Urge United Methodist churches to become knowledgeable about the Copenhagen Commitments, the continuing United Nations plans of action and commitments to Africa and other bilateral and multilateral initiatives—including the Special Program of Assistance to Africa (SPA) and the UN System-Wide Initiative on Africa; Urge the United Methodist Office for the United Nations in New York to be ready with resources regarding the United Nations and Africa;

4. urge United Methodists to persuade their governments to ratify the United Nations Convention to Combat Desertification in Those Countries Experiencing Serious Drought and/or Desertification;

5. be supportive of civil society in Africa as it seeks to continually review, assess and offer constructive suggestions to government leaders implementing the objectives of the New Partnership for Africa's Development (NEPAD). Urge the General Board of Global Ministries and the General Board of Church and Society to stay abreast of the issues involved, be ready to offer resources and opportunities for United Methodist churches and the ecumenical movement in Africa to gather, study and debate the concerns;

6. urge the General Board of Church and Society to develop a grassroots public policy action network to:

   a. address peacemaking concerns including the end of arms sales and landmines sales to government and nongovernment combatants;

   b. urge the reduction of foreign assistance to countries that rely on African arms sales for their own hard currency;

   c. support efforts to end the international trade in stolen diamonds and other minerals to fund chronic African wars. Support the General Board of Global Ministries' efforts to remove landmines safely and in sufficient numbers to return land to productive agriculture.

7. continue and further develop the General Board of Global Ministries' commitment to health care in Africa through comprehensive,

community-based primary health care, recognizing the role that poverty and poor sanitation play in the spread of communicable diseases across the continent; the collapse of the health-care systems in many countries; and the ineffectiveness of total reliance on institutional medical models. Support the revitalization of mission hospitals as critical adjuncts to community-based care. Support AIDS prevention training through the African Churches, AIDS orphan trusts, prevention of mother to child transmission of HIV and equipped and informed home care for terminally ill family members;

8. monitor all programs of relief and development, with special attention to these criteria:

    a. give priority to women and children, who suffer the most during times of social unrest and war;

    b. involve full consultation with African United Methodists relying upon their experience, wisdom, and resourcefulness;

    c. design programs to alleviate the root causes of poverty, oppression, and social unrest;

    d. seek resources for program support from beyond the church to augment the church's contribution to African social development;

    e. implement methods to demonstrate financial transparency and accountability in all development programs and projects; and

    f. program for sustainability, both in terms of ecological integrity and appropriate technologies that do not require continuing input of resources from other countries, capacity building for local hand-off of sustainable size and scale of projects.

*God bless Africa*
*Guard her children*
*Guide her leaders*
*And give her peace*

**ADOPTED 2004**
**READOPTED 2008**
**RESOLUTION #303, 2004** *BOOK OF RESOLUTIONS*
**RESOLUTION #283, 2000** *BOOK OF RESOLUTIONS*

*See* Social Principles, ¶ 165A.

## 6063. Democratic Republic of Congo: A New Beginning

Violence shall no more be heard in your land, devastation or destruction within your borders; you shall call your walls Salvation, and your gates Praise (Isaiah 60:18).

The people of the Democratic Republic of Congo (DRC) have not seen peace since its independence in 1960. Decades of a corrupt dictatorial government, backed by the US and other Western powers, and war have been their history. A war over the country's vast resources involving nine countries broke out in 1998. It is estimated that 4 million died, largely from disease and hunger, or have disappeared without a trace. The war is one of the bloodiest in modern times.

After more than three years of a transitional government, the Congolese people elected a president, Joseph Kabila, and a National Assembly in 2006. The new administration is the first elected in over 40 years. The DRC has a new constitution and security in parts of the country has improved dramatically. The elections and regional security are milestones in the restoration of stability in the Congo and a new beginning for the country.

We pray for the rebirth of the nation and end to war and conflict.

### Life for the Congolese People

The majority of the people live in poverty, despite the country's vast natural resources. Only 20 percent of the population has access to safe water, 70 percent has little or no access to health care, 16 million have critical food needs, and the country has the highest infant mortality rate in Africa. Almost no social services are provided to the population by the government. The conflict has caused the displacement of millions of people. Children have experienced extreme hardships— lifelong physical and psychological harm—due to the war. Each year, more children die in DRC than in China (a country with 23 times the population) and than in all the Latin American countries combined according to a 2006 UNICEF report. The DRC has approximately $12 billion in foreign debt, most of which was incurred by the corrupt government of President Mobutu Sese Seko, a corrupt dictator.

### Challenges for the New Government

The challenges facing the new government are vast. It must consolidate the peace process, rebuild the government's administrative capacity, and restore its authority at all levels throughout the entire country, unify and consolidate its armed forces, and institute an impartial and credible judiciary system. The government has developed a five-year economic development plan for reconstruction. The success of the plan requires reform of laws on the extraction, production, and use of the country's natural resources. The government and its international partners should set up an independent mechanism to monitor the implementation of contracts and ensure transparent and fair management of mining resources.

The country's development cannot be achieved without the active participation of its citizens. Nongovernmental organizations need to be strengthened and given a real voice in the future of their country.

Congolese need and deserve support to consolidate peace, construct democracy, save lives, and rebuild their country. Celebrating with the Congolese people in the rebirth of their nation, the General Conference:

1. urges our churches to support the peoples and the mission of The United Methodist Church in the DRC through Advance Special giving, covenant relationship between annual conferences, and other mission funding. We also urge United Methodists and all Methodist peoples to join in prayer and solidarity for the people, leaders, and churches of the DRC;

2. urges agencies and members of The United Methodist Church worldwide to work with The United Methodist Church in the DRC and with nongovernmental organizations in rebuilding the country, its churches and seminaries, and the repatriation, resettlement, and provision of shelter for displaced persons, child soldiers, and other war victims;

3. urges the government of the DRC to move forward with reforms: security, economic and mining, judiciary, education, and communications;

4. urges governments and international institutions to provide economic assistance for reconstruction and development and debt cancellation to the government of the DRC;

5. urges multinational corporations, especially mining companies, and neighboring countries to respect the sovereignty and integrity of the DRC; and

6. supports the continued presence of MONUC, the UN peacekeeping force in the DRC.

**ADOPTED 2008**

*See* Social Principles, ¶ 165A, B, and D.

## 6064. Liberia

Great is our Lord, and abundant in power; his understanding is beyond measure. The LORD lifts up the downtrodden; he casts the wicked to the ground. (Psalm 147:5-6)

Violence shall no more be heard in your land, devastation or destruction within your borders; you shall call your walls Salvation, and your gates Praise. (Isaiah 60:18)

In 2005, the people of the Liberia "seized the moment" to elect new political leaders after a 14-year civil war that left the country in ruins. Ellen Johnson Sirleaf, a United Methodist, was elected as the first woman president of an African country. The people of Liberia expect the new government to tackle the national ills of bad governance, corruption, poverty, illiteracy, diseases, unemployment, and mediocrity.

During the 14-year civil war more than 270,000 Liberians were killed and over 500,000 were forced to flee their homes. Entire communities were uprooted. Economic activity declined sharply. Poverty increased sharply. Agricultural production dropped as people fled their farms. Exports nearly ceased. Mining and timber industries shut down. The infrastructure of the country was destroyed. Government finances collapsed. More than 75 percent of Liberians now live below the poverty line of $1 a day. Unemployment is as high as 85 percent.

Since President Sirleaf's inauguration in January 2006, Liberia has begun the long journey to recovery. The new government has resettled tens of thousands of refugees and begun training new security forces, increased government revenues, restored electricity and water to part of the capital, substantially increased primary school enrollment, and has begun to rebuild roads and other critical infrastructure.

The government developed a plan for the reconstruction and development of the country. A key element of the plan is restoring and strengthening basic human rights and further empowering the Liberian people. The reconstruction and development strategy is based on four pillars: 1) expanding peace and security; 2) revitalizing economic activity; 3) strengthening governance and the rule of law; and 4) rebuilding infrastructure and providing basis services. The success of the plan must be based on how well it alleviates poverty and empowers people.

United Methodists are encouraged to partake in the journey of the Liberian people for a new future. We commit ourselves to:

1. support the peoples and mission of the Liberian people through Advance Special giving, covenant relationships between annual conferences, and through other mission funding. We also urge all Methodist and United Methodist peoples to join in prayer and solidarity for the people, leaders, and churches of Liberia;

2. urge governments to provide economic assistance for reconstruction and development and debt cancellation to the government of Liberia;

3. support and strengthen Liberian civil society so that all Liberians will be able to fully participate in public life, where government is at the service of its people, and where human rights and the rule of law is respected;

4. urge the United Nations and nongovernmental organizations to join in the effort to help stabilize and rebuild Liberia;

5. provide humanitarian assistance, including medical services for HIV/AIDS and illnesses, food, and water;

6. provide financial assistance to pastors and their families;

7. rebuild churches, parsonages, and church-related institutions;

8. repatriate, resettle, and provide shelter for displaced persons and war victims;

9. assist the transition of soldiers into the civilian sector through counseling, vocational and general education;

10. engage in reconciliation and healing at the grassroots level between and among various ethnic groups;

11. train pastors to be agents of reconciliation, peace, and healing;

12. set up counseling and education programs to help children, women, and others traumatized by war; and

13. urge multinational corporations investing in Liberia to be good corporate citizens by respecting labor laws, training workers, protecting the environment, and supporting value-added production (i.e., rubber products) to the country's present exports.

The United Methodist Church in Liberia is committed to prioritizing ministries on human rights, peace-building, conflict resolution, and reconciliation. We stand with you on this mission.

**ADOPTED 2008**

*See* Social Principles, ¶ 165*A, B*, and *D*.

## 6065. Sudan: A Call to Compassion and Caring

Is not this the fast I choose: to loose the bonds of injustice, to undo the thongs of the yoke, to let the oppressed go free, and to break every yoke? Is it not to share your bread with the hungry, and bring the homeless poor into your house; when you see the naked, to cover them, and not to hide yourself from your own kin? Then your light shall break forth like the dawn, and your healing shall spring up quickly; your vindicator shall go before you, the glory of the Lord shall be your rear guard. (Isaiah 58: 6-8 NRSV)

Dr. Silvia Regina de Lima Silva, a Brazilian theologian, called for the walls to come down and the pathways to be opened toward a culture of compassion and caring, " . . . the words of Isaiah are directed towards those who have the power because they had the power to untie those who had been subjugated. On the other hand, the prophet also makes a call for solidarity among those who are tied to the same yoke. He invites them to change everyday relations, to seek forms of life in which bread can be eaten and shared, to live together, and to cover each other, and to protect and take care of each person's body. We understand this to be a call to compassion and caring."

"One Million People have died since fighting began in our country in 1983. Three million people are now displaced. Yet there is nothing in your [Western] press about it. Are we not human beings?" These words were spoken in March 1989 by the Reverend Ezekiel Kutjok, General Secretary of the Sudan Council of Churches. In 2002 Church World Service (CWS) in the United States expressed similar sentiments "Despite the enormous suffering and flagrant human rights abuses committed on all sides, the Sudan tragedy receives little attention from Western media. Churches and nongovernmental organizations have been at the forefront of efforts to respond to the suffering of Sudan's peoples and support their creative efforts to build a just and lasting peace." That is the solidarity which Isaiah calls for with the people of Sudan as they painstakingly rebuild their country, changing everyday relations and finding ways of sharing with each other.

That same year Church World Service emphasized that the Sudan was as a country 'Hungry for Peace,' "the Sudan suffers from the world's longest running civil war—35 of the last 46 years. Fueled by religious, ethnic, and political differences between the country's northern and southern populations, more than two million Sudanese, mostly in the South, have died as a result of this conflict. Three hundred

Sudanese die each day from war-related causes. More than 4.5 million people are internally displaced, and over 500,000 have fled to other countries as refugees." In this civil war the colonial past and the growing economic concerns were also crucial to understanding the roots of the conflict. They included, among others, the sequels of serious drought and famine in Northern and Western Sudan in 1984-85 and in the South in 1986-88; conflicts between pastoralists and agriculturalists and vast resources of oil in the South.

The churches have been involved with the Sudan for many years and in 1971 the World Council of Churches (WCC) helped broker a peace accord between North and South which lasted 11 years—the country's only peaceful period since independence from joint Egyptian-British rule in 1956. In 2002 the WCC appointed a special ecumenical envoy, the Rev. Dr. Samuel Kobia (the current General Secretary of the WCC) to accompany the peace negotiations between the government of the Sudan/National Congress Party in Northern Sudan and the Sudan People's Liberation Movement (SPLM) in Southern Sudan. Their Comprehensive Peace Agreement (CPA) was finalized January 2005. The agreement included a permanent ceasefire and autonomy for Southern Sudan for 6 years with a referendum about independence to be held in 2011. An autonomous government was formed in the South and a power sharing government was set up in Khartoum with the South represented by a co-vice-president. It was further agreed that North and South would share equally in the oil revenues. The United Nations was authorized to support the CPA and a peacekeeping operation was sent including 10,000 troops and 600 police. International donors pledged $4.5 billion in aid to recover from the decades of war.

The Republic of Sudan is the largest country in Africa. Situated in the Greater Horn of Africa it is surrounded by Egypt to the north and moving clockwise, the Red Sea, Eritrea, Ethiopia, Kenya, Uganda, Democratic Republic of the Congo, Central African Republic, Chad, and Libya. The Sudan was one of the most ethnically and linguistically diverse countries in the world. "In 1999 it had nearly 600 ethnic groups speaking over 400 languages and dialects. During the 80s and 90s smaller ethnic and linguistic groups disappeared. Migration played a part, as migrants often forget their native tongue when they move to an area dominated by another language. Some linguistic groups were absorbed by accommodation, others by conflict." Arabic is the official language but English and many languages and dialects are spoken in the Sudan. The Sudanese population is approximately 37 million people, 70 percent Sunni Muslim, 25 percent have indigenous beliefs and 5 percent are Christians.

While the Comprehensive Peace Agreement was being negotiated, violent conflict broke out in the Western states. In February 2003 world attention was directed to Darfur (the land of the Fur people). There are several other ethnic groups in Darfur. A rebellion began, initiating a number of military activities leading to a grave humanitarian situation. In April 2003 coordinated attacks against military targets in the regional capital of El Fasher were launched by the Sudan Liberation Movement (SLA) and the Justice and Equality Movement (JEM). The Sudan government responded harshly as it had during the conflict with the South, using counterinsurgency tactics and indiscriminate aerial bombings. Its armed forces coordinated with irregular militia (including janjaweed (men on horseback) known for raping women, pillaging, and looting the population in Darfur) to attack not only the rebel forces but the civilian populations causing thousands to die, vast destruction by burning down whole villages, trees, and fields, and the displacement of hundreds of thousands of people. Rebel groups were also involved in the disastrous consequences of their armed attacks against the government.

Violence in Darfur escalated rapidly leading to more than 200,000 deaths caused by killings, illness and starvation due to the scorched earth policy, 2.1 million internally displaced persons and 236,000 as refugees in Chad. The situation became known as one of the worst humanitarian disasters in the 21st century. The cruelty of the armed attacks on the civilian population was reminiscent of the same in South Sudan and in the neighboring Democratic Republic of the Congo where it is estimated that 4 million people died. Women and children were particularly vulnerable to sexual abuse. The age-old struggle for land suggested that attackers, especially the Janjaweed, were killing and burning down homes to move people away and replace them. A rebellion against the government in Khartoum became an opportunity to revive old rivalries, settle scores, and take over the farm lands for grazing cattle.

Solidarity with the people of Sudan raised an outcry around the world demanding an end to the massacres, the atrocities and bringing the perpetrators to justice for crimes against humanity and as some nongovernmental organizations suggested ethnic cleansing. In the United States, officials and legislators, churches and nongovernmental organizations accused the Sudan of genocide. The United Nations sent a team to investigate but in their report they noted that there were crimes against humanity but not enough evidence that the government of the Sudan had "intent to destroy . . . " The Convention on the Prevention and Punishment of the Crime of Genocide does define genocide as any act "committed with intent to destroy, in whole or in part, a national, ethnical, racial or religious group. . . ." The protest against the Sudan promoted many demonstrations, vigils, visits to Darfur, and eventually a divestment movement that promoted international sanctions that the Security Council discussed but never agreed to.

The Sudan government, the militias, the rebel movement, and neighboring governments as the conflict spilled over their borders were among those with influence or power to end the conflict. Other actors included the United Nations Security Council and the African Union, headquartered in Addis Ababa, which responded with help in containing the chaos by sending in monitors, peacekeepers, and police.

The Security Council was sending peacekeeping forces and police to the South of Sudan. The Council was already responsible for 18 peacekeeping operations on four continents involving 100,000 personnel, directly impacting the lives of hundreds of millions of people. Yet, the African forces needed reinforcement and support and the Council began to discuss how they could raise another peacekeeping mission. Other involved powers were the 5 Permanent Members in the Security Council, the United Kingdom, China, France, Russia, and the United States. Each of which have political and strategic interests, as well as economic stakes, in the Sudan that is rich with resources such as oil, natural gas, uranium, gold, silver, chrome, manganese, and other minerals.

Finally, all those in power or with influence including the worldwide protesters against continued violence and those in the solidarity movement with the Sudanese people were able to agree on common solutions symbolized by the renewed peace talks between the Sudanese government, the rebel groups and militias and the unanimous approval in the Security Council to authorize "hybrid UN-African Union operation in Darfur." In the United Nations Press Release of July 31, 2007, the Security Council approved the creation of a hybrid United Nations-African Union peacekeeping force to quell the violence and instability plaguing the Darfur region of Sudan . . . In what Secretary-General Ban Ki-moon called a "historic and unprecedented resolution," Council members unanimously backed the establishment of a force of nearly 20,000 military personnel and more than 6,000 police officers.

Decades of negligence and marginalization by both the former colonial powers and the Sudanese government were major causes for the rebellion. "Over the course of the 20th century, colonial and independence governments in Khartoum (the Capital of Sudan) devoted few resources to developing the human potential of Darfur. There were limited investments in infrastructure, schooling, and economic activity." In addition, since most residents were either involved with raising livestock or in low-productivity agriculture, recent droughts and the advancing desert exacerbated tensions over access to water and fertile land, crucial causes for the rebellion. Fredrick Nzwili, a freelance journalist from Kenya writing for the Ecumenical Water Network agrees. "From Darfur in western Sudan to Mt. Elgon in Kenya, the absence of water for rural communities is emerging as a major cause of conflict on the African continent. In Darfur, the story is one of pain and desperation for the nearly two million displaced persons. And the organizations that work in the area are convinced that it is battles for water and pasture that sparked it off."

The United Nations Environment Program (UNEP) released a report in June 2007, "indeed historical data in Darfur indicates that rainfall declines of between 16 per cent and over 30 percent have occurred turning millions of hectares of marginal semi-desert land into desert. . . . Overall, deserts in some northern regions of Sudan may have advanced by an average of 100km over the past 40 years. . . . The scale of climate change recorded in Northern Darfur is almost unprecedented, and its impacts are closely linked to the conflicts in the region, as desertification has added significantly to the stress on traditional agricultural and pastoral livelihoods . . . the crisis is being aggravated by degradation of water sources in deserts known as wadis or oases. 'Virtually all such areas inspected by UNEP were found to be moderately to severely degraded, principally due to deforestation, overgrazing and erosion.'"

United Methodists praise God for signs of hope. As in the Social Principles (¶ 165*B*), we can applaud worldwide efforts to develop more just international economic systems in which the limited resources of the earth will be used to the maximum benefit of all nations and peoples. Another sign of hope is the ability of UMCOR to work in southern Darfur, an area which its assessment team determined was underserved by other agencies. UMCOR'S programs in southern Darfur assist hundreds of thousands of people, including providing seeds and tools to farmers, schools and supplies to children, training for teachers, vocational training programs, and establishing water points. Ten water points have been completed, giving some 250,000 Sudanese, access to water. In 2006, UMCOR began working in South Sudan to assist the people returning home after nearly 20 years of war.

As Dr. Lima Silva says, solidarity means finding ways "to seek forms of life in which bread can be eaten and shared to live together, and to cover each other, and to protect and take care of each person's body." For United Methodists this is a call to compassion and caring.

*Therefore:*

1. The United Methodist Church shall affirm and call upon all parties to work through and with the United Nations and the African Union to secure justice for all Sudanese.

2. United Methodists in every country shall encourage their governments and the economic entities within their societies to aid and work for the development of more just economic system in the Sudan.

3. United Methodists shall examine all methods of protest and solidarity before undertaking them. Recent efforts by the divestment movement in the United States, in which many United Methodists participated, is an example of a nonviolent strategy to effect change and has contributed to raising awareness of the plight of the people in Darfur. As United Methodists continue to seek a just and lasting peace in Sudan, we shall ensure that none of their actions cause violence.

4. United Methodists shall commend the General Board of Global Ministries for its development of a mission study on the Sudan for 2009 and shall take advantage of all opportunities to study and develop a better understanding of all the people in the Sudan.

5. United Methodists shall continue to contribute to UMCOR and commend them for their ongoing work in the Sudan, remembering that the 2004 General Conference commended them for their concern and caring for Darfur refugees in Chad.

ADOPTED 2008

*See* Social Principles, ¶ 165A, B, and D.

## 6066. Taiwan Security, Stability, and Self-Determination

Taiwan has, since 1624, been continually ruled by military invaders, under the Dutch (1624-1662), under the exiled Pirate King Coxinga of the Ming Dynasty (1661-1683), under the Ch'ing Dynasty (1683-1895), under the imperial Japan (1895-1945), and under the post WWII Allied Military Occupation Forces ordered by General McArthur and represented by General Chiang Kai-shek (1945 and following);

When the only treaty of the 20th century regarding the status of Taiwan was signed at the San Francisco Peace Treaty of 1951, signers stated that Japan was surrendering its sovereignty over Taiwan and intentionally refused to designate any other nation (Article 23 4b & 2b), clearly excluding the designation of Chiang Kai-shek and the Chinese Communist rule of Mao Tze-tung, to exercise sovereignty over the island of Taiwan; and, in accordance to the United Nations Charter, the inhabitants of the island have the right of self-determination as other nations achieved following their decolonization in the post-WWII era;

After decades of opposing the dictatorship of Chang Kai-shek and the Kuo Ming Tang (KMT), the Taiwanese ushered in an era of democracy without bloodshed in 1986 and established reforms by permitting the organization of political parties, establishing freedom of the press, and conducting a democratic election of legislators and the president of the island nation;

With its new Anti-Secession Law (2005), the People's Republic of China (PRC) has threatened to destroy the hard-earned democracy and human rights of the people of Taiwan with more than 800 short-range ballistic missiles if the Taiwanese exercises self-determination and declares independence;

The PRC also aggressively prohibits the nations of the world from providing humanitarian efforts, vividly illustrated by hindering the assistance of the International Red Cross and the World Health Organization following the 1999 earthquake and during the 2003 threat of SARS;

On February 27, 2006, the democratically elected President Chen Shui-bian, with the support of the majority of the population, scrapped the "National Unification Council" and the "National Unification Guidelines," two obscure and unconstitutional symbols from the time when Taiwan was still ruled by the repressive KMT, and vowed to address the threat of military action by the PRC;

With the leadership of the Taiwanese United Methodists, the advocacy of the National Federation of Asian American United Methodists, and support of annual conference delegates to General Conference, the General Conference adopted resolutions on Taiwanese issues from 1980 onward supporting human rights, self-determination, security, and stability in accordance with the United Methodist Social Principles and other resolutions; the future of the 23 million Taiwanese people hinges upon the courage of the democratic nations including the United States to oppose in no ambiguous terms China's military threat against Taiwan; and

Taiwanese President Chen Shui-bian expressed profound appreciation for the support of The United Methodist Church in the Taiwanese struggle for democracy through resolutions at each General Conference from 1980 to 2004 and for the generous and compassionate support of UMCOR following the disastrous 1999 earthquake;

*Therefore, be it resolved,* that the 2008 General Conference of The United Methodist Church reaffirm its supports of the democratic aspirations and achievements of the people of Taiwan and;

*Be it further resolved,* that The United Methodist Church, under the leadership of the Council of Bishops with the assistance of the General Board of Church and Society and its annual conference networks, inform themselves about the history of the Taiwanese people, study contemporary issues involved in the changing application of the "One China" policy, and prayerfully and wisely promote in their own countries and the United Nations the rights of Taiwanese for stability, security, and self-determination of Taiwan's own status in the family of nations.

**ADOPTED 2008**

See Social Principles, ¶ 165*A* and *B*.

## 6067. Support of Taiwan

The human story is one of migration and struggles for self-determination, but often frustrated by the unsolicited intervention of nations into the affairs of other nations. The United Methodist Church continues to stand unequivocally against such interventions. This, too, is the story of the people of Taiwan whose struggles for self-determination call for our solidarity and action.

Taiwan is an island state of two million people, comprised of indigenous Taiwanese, Chinese and a mix of both. After 400 plus years of colonial rule by the Dutch, the Chinese, and the Japanese, the people of Taiwan today have a stable form of democratic government, a thriving economy, and a vibrant national identity and culture.

*Therefore,* we call upon all United Methodists around the world to stand in solidarity with the Taiwanese people as they assert their human rights and their right to self-determination. Self-determination will allow the Taiwanese people to freely determine their political destiny and achieve their democratic aspirations, without influence from, or domination by, foreign powers.

*Further,* that United Methodists support the Taiwanese people's hope for a just and durable peace, secure and stable borders, and sustainable development and cooperation among nations and peoples of the world.

In light of historic United Methodist understanding of self-determination, and its current understanding of the "One China" policy, we therefore call upon the leadership of the Council of Bishops, with the assistance of the General Board of Global Ministries and the General Board of Church and Society and their Annual Conference networks, including the National Federation of Asian American United Methodists, to inform and educate the church about the history, experience, struggles, and hopes of the Taiwanese people.

**ADOPTED 2008**

See Social Principles, ¶ 165A and B.

### 6068. Restore Freedom and Independence/Autonomy to the Land and People of Tibet

WHEREAS, Isaiah prophesies (Isaiah 2:4, NIV) that in the last days (see also Micah 4:3):
"He will judge between the nations
    and will settle disputes for many peoples.
    They will beat their swords into plowshares
    and their spears into pruning hooks.
    Nation will not take up sword against nation,
    nor will they train for war anymore"; and

WHEREAS, *The Book of Discipline of The United Methodist Church* expounds in Part IV, Social Principles, ¶ 165 (VI. The World Community), that "we commit ourselves as a Church to the achievement of a world community that is a fellowship of persons who honestly love one another. . . . The Church must regard nations as accountable for unjust treatment of their citizens and others living within their borders. . . . We affirm the right and duty of people of all nations to determine their own destiny. We urge the major political powers to use their nonviolent power to maximize the political, social, and economic self-determination of other nations rather than to further their own special interests. . . . We affirm our historic concern for the world as our parish and seek for all persons and peoples full and equal membership in a truly world community";

*Therefore, be it resolved,* that The United Methodist Church support the people of Tibet and their struggle for independence and autonomy; and

*Be it further resolved,* that The United Methodist Church affirms the Dalai Lama's 1987 Five Point Peace Plan; and

*Be it further resolved,* that The United Methodist Church support the United Nations' efforts to protect the human rights of all Tibetans and to preserve the distinct religious, cultural, and linguistic heritage of the Tibetan people; and

*Be it further resolved,* that the general boards and agencies of The United Methodist Church continue to monitor this situation and provide opportunities for United Methodist church members to advocate for justice for the people of Tibet.

ADOPTED 2008

*See* Social Principles, ¶ 165*A, B,* and *D.*

## 6069. End the US Embargo of Cuba

The United Methodist Church is linked in Christ with The Methodist Church of Cuba. We share a common heritage and mission. We are mutually responsible for the proclamation of God's love and the nurturing of neighbor love. We celebrate the continued growth of The Methodist Church of Cuba. We acknowledge the difficulties that our two churches continue to face in their mission partnership due to the US embargo and the lack of diplomatic relationships between the two countries.

For over 44 years, the government of the United States has not maintained diplomatic relations with the Cuban government and has, instead, pursued an economic embargo prohibiting trade with Cuba and controlling very tightly travel to that country. The Democracy Act of 1992 (22 U.S.C. 6001) and the 1996 Helms/Burton Act tightened the embargo and brought about additional suffering to the people of Cuba. In addition to that, the embargo has failed its stated purpose of bringing political change to Cuba after all these years.

The United Methodist Church has long advocated for an improved relationship between Cuba and the US The Methodist Church in 1964 made a historical statement entitled "The Reexamination of Policy Toward Mainline China, Cuba and Other Countries," which said: "The Christian gospel involves reconciliation by encounter and by communication regardless of political considerations. Therefore, we cannot accept the expression of hostility by any country, its policies, or its ideologies as excuses for the failure of Christians to press persistently, realistically, and creatively toward a growing understanding among the peoples of all countries."

There are many groups in the United States desiring the end of the United States embargo against Cuba. Among them, US farmers and other business concerns that went through the recently allowed, but very cumbersome, licensing process imposed by the US government to permit sales of food products to Cuba resulting in sales of over $125,000,000.00 by the end of 2002. This development was a step in the right direction, which we celebrate on the basis of the United Methodist-stated position that embargoes of food and medicines should not be part of any country's policies. Individuals and organizations—religious, academic, business—want to exercise their constitutional right to travel freely to Cuba. In 2001 alone, over 176,000 US citizens traveled to Cuba, and some are facing steep fines for not adhering to the embargo travel restrictions.

The General Assembly of the United Nations has overwhelmingly approved, every year since 1992, a resolution called "The Necessity of Ending the Economic, Commercial, and Financial Embargo Imposed by the United States of America Against Cuba." The latest of these, in December 2002, passed by a vote of 173 to 3, demonstrating the international community's concern for what it calls the "adverse effects of the embargo on the Cuban people and on Cuban nationals living in other countries" (UN resolution 57/11 of December 16, 2002).

WHEREAS, the Council of Churches of Cuba, of which The Methodist Church of Cuba is a member; the Cuban Conference of Roman Catholic Bishops; and several other international religious groups and leaders such as CIEMAL [Council of Evangelical Methodist Churches of Latin America and the Caribbean], the Caribbean Conference of Churches, and Pope John Paul II, as well as US religious bodies such as the United Church of Christ, the Presbyterian Church (USA), and the American Baptist Churches have stated or passed resolutions in favor of lifting the embargo; and

WHEREAS, we acknowledge that the embargo also curtails religious freedom by making very difficult the relationship between churches in the United States and churches in Cuba; and

WHEREAS, we believe that stopping the hostility generated by the US embargo policies would facilitate improvements in democratic reforms and human rights in Cuba; and

WHEREAS, we reaffirm the Bible teachings and mandate to "love one another, because love is from God" (1 John 4:7), and to practice mercy as the good Samaritan did (Luke 10:25-37);

*Therefore, be it resolved,* that The United Methodist Church, from its Christian and humanitarian perspective, inspired by the love of God and the historic Methodist commitment to peace and social justice, and in light of historic changes with the end of the Cold War, hereby petitions the President and Congress of the United States to lift its economic embargo against Cuba and any other regulations, practices or measures enforcing the embargo law and to seek negotiations with the Cuban government for the purpose of resuming normal diplomatic relations.

*Note:* The United States broke diplomatic relations with Cuba on January 3, 1961. A partial trade embargo against Cuba by the US government was declared on October 19, 1960. On July 8, 1963, "the Treasury Department, using its authority under the Trading with the Enemy Act of 1917, issued more restrictive Cuba Assets Control Regulations."

(Cuban Foreign Relations, A Chronology, 1959-1982).

ADOPTED 2004
READOPTED 2008
RESOLUTION #316, 2004 *BOOK OF RESOLUTIONS*

*See* Social Principles, ¶ 165A and D.

## 6070. Call for Free Speech in Cuba

WHEREAS, the Scripture calls us to raise our voice for those who have no voice, judge with justice those who have no voice (Proverbs 31:8-9); and

WHEREAS, the right of free expression is one of the most basic rights recognized in the Universal Declaration of Human Rights; and

WHEREAS, over seventy-five (75) Cuban dissidents, among them independent journalists, economists, and human rights activists, were condemned to sentences up to twenty-eight (28) years in prison, for exercising their freedom of expression, and according to the Cuban government, because they were receiving compensations and expensed reimbursements by the US;

*Therefore, be it resolved,* that the 2008 General Conference of The United Methodist Church supports the right of all people to express themselves freely, regardless of where they live, and

*Be it further resolved,* that The United Methodist Church, through the General Board of Church and Society, calls upon the Cuban government to review their sentences and consider their release from prison, seeking reconciliation and understanding among all people in Cuba.

ADOPTED 2004
REVISED AND READOPTED 2008
RESOLUTION #317, 2004 BOOK OF RESOLUTIONS

See Social Principles, ¶ 165*A* and *D*.

### 6071. Violence Against Children in Latin America and the Caribbean

WHEREAS, millions of children in Latin America and the Caribbean struggle daily to survive in the midst of violence:

- the violence of armed conflict;
- the violence of scarce resources taken from children's health and educational needs to support inordinately large military budgets;
- the violence of poverty linked to the massive external debt burdening every nation of the region;
- the violence of hunger;
- the culture of violence permeating television and other mass media;
- widespread domestic violence;
- ecological violence that is destroying and polluting the natural world and all live creatures;

- the violence of HIV-Aids, with the second highest incidence in the world in many Caribbean nations, destroying children's lives from birth;
- the violence of very high infant mortality.

*Therefore, be it resolved,* that the General Commission on Religion and Race endorses MARCHA's petition to the 2004 General Conference to establish a special program to address, in cooperation with the member churches of CIEMAL, the grave crisis of children struggling to survive in the midst of violence and poverty by communicating this concern to the Council of Bishops and be referred to the General Board of Global Ministries (GBGM) and the General Council on Finance and Administration (GCFA) for the implementation of a program.

ADOPTED 2004
READOPTED 2008
RESOLUTION #324, 2004 *BOOK OF RESOLUTIONS*

*See* Social Principles, ¶¶ 162C, 164A, and 165.

## 6072. Latin America and the Caribbean

I seek out my sheep; and I will rescue them from all places where they have been scattered. I will feed them with good pasture. I myself will be the shepherd of my sheep, says the Lord God. I will seek the lost, and I will bring back the strayed, and I will bind up the crippled, and I will strengthen the weak, and the fat and the strong I will watch over; I will feed them in justice. (Ezekiel 34:12-16)

"As individuals are affirmed by God in their diversity, so are nations and cultures. We recognize that no nation or culture is absolutely just and right in its treatment of its own people, nor is any nation totally without regard for the welfare of its citizens. The Church must regard nations as accountable for unjust treatment of their citizens and others living within their borders. While recognizing valid differences in culture and political philosophy, we stand for justice and peace in every nation" (Social Principles, ¶ 165A).

Latin America and the Caribbean are in a period of great transition. No longer existing as colonial territories solely dependent on others for social, political, and economic support, much of Latin America and the Caribbean are trying to create a new identity while continuing to struggle with recurring problems.

The economic state for many is dire. There is a severe lack of development for those living in rural areas and many are being forced to move into overcrowded urban areas in order to have a chance at survival. The United National Human Development Report in 2005 stated that those living in rural areas are facing increasing poverty with a decreased ability to access needed services. For example, the child death rate in Bolivia is almost two times higher for children in rural areas than for children living in urban areas. Additionally, farmers who chose to stay are at risk of being paid unequal wages at a time when the primary export of Latin America coffee is facing uncertain prices and unpredictable natural disasters. When the survival of so many is based on so few agricultural exports, the very lives of these farmers and their families are in jeopardy.

Environmental conditions within the Caribbean and Latin America are facing three great challenges: deforestation, urbanization, and fumigation. The fertile lands of Latin America are being depleted at an alarming rate of over 5.8 million hectares a year through deforestation by the mining industry.

Trade agreements such as NAFTA (North America Fair Trade Agreement) are also negatively impacting people. Privatization of public resources such as water, education, and health care makes it difficult for poor women and children to gain access to these resources. Low wage laborers also face difficulty as new economic plans have created a "race to the bottom" where laborers are being paid as little as possible for their work.

Human rights organizations report staggering rates of human rights violations taking place throughout Latin America. Colombia has the second highest rate of indigenously displaced people after Sudan, with 2.9 million people displaced by threats and reverse land reform between 1995 and 2005.

Other disturbing trends include violence against Protestant churches working to combat injustice and the rapidly deteriorating treatment of women with over 2,500 acts of femicide in the past five years in Guatemala alone.

Ranked 153rd of the 177 countries in the United Nations Human Development Index and with 80 percent of the population living in poverty, the country of Haiti begs for immediate attention. Poverty, when combined with an unstable government and continued conflict, has been a key factor in Haiti's growing AIDS epidemic. Studies conducted by the US Agency for International Development (USAID) have found that some urban areas of Haiti have HIV rates as high as 10 percent. There is growing concern for the World Bank that "what has happened in Africa in less than two decades could now happen in the Caribbean if action is not taken while the epidemic is in the early stages." In 2005, through the President's Emergency Plan for AIDS Relief (PEPFAR), $76 million was provided to the Caribbean and Central America for HIV/AIDS prevention, education, and treatment.

While Haiti has been the focus of much attention within the Caribbean due to its current political and social instability, the Caribbean as a whole warrants additional attention. The ratio of income disparity between the richest 10 percent and the poorest 10 percent is 46:1 for the Caribbean, while sub-Saharan Africa has a ratio of 24:1 and most industrialized nations are at a ratio of 15:1. Many of the poor, both rural and urban, are unable to attain sufficient housing, health care, education, and employment. This is especially true of youth and young adult populations. One example is in St. Kitts where the percentage of all people living in poverty is 35.5 percent and the percentage of people between the ages of 15 and 24 living in poverty is 65 percent. With a lack of development funds for education to prepare youth for the existing labor market, the education rate is decreasing while poverty continues to rise in the Caribbean.

The result of the "War on Drugs" is still unclear. The United Nations Office on Drugs and Crime reports that while over 60,000 acres of legal crops were planted in 2005 to replace coca crops in Colombia, this constitutes only 9 percent of the coca growers. The USAID has budgeted upwards of $75 million for Alternative Development over the past five years and still cocaine production has seen an increase in cultivation.

More emphasis should be placed on sustainable alternative development plans that come from within the country. One example is Bolivia's "Coca Sí- Cocaine No" campaign that recognizes the cultural/economic/religious importance of the coca plant to the indigenous people. Rather than completely eradicate a plant that also has numerous legal uses, the Bolivian government has begun a policy of "rationalization" where each farmer is allowed to grow enough coca for his family. As a result, there have been better relations with the police and an increased willingness to report illegal actions. The political trends in Latin America are moving more toward democracy through populist movements. These movements are in stark contrast to the elitists who have historically run so many Latin American countries. With the election of the first South American female president in Chile, Michelle Bachelet Jeria, and Bolivia's first indigenous president, Evo Morales, there is a transition underway to give a political voice and position to those who have traditionally faced oppression by these same governments. Additionally, countries such as Brazil, Argentina, Venezuela, and Uruguay are all implementing social programs aimed at combating poverty on a widespread scale.

## The United Methodist Church Response

As The United Methodist Church, we must support efforts in Latin America and the Caribbean toward social justice and spreading a gospel of peace and healing. Efforts to build up local churches within Latin America must also create strong leadership and encourage ecumenical efforts. Organizations such as MARCHA (Methodists Associated Representing the Cause of Hispanic Americans) and CIEMAL (Council of Evangelical Methodist Churches of Latin America and the Caribbean) are important in the movement toward sustainable development. We must also be in partnership with the Caribbean Conference of Churches and the Latin America Council of Churches as they work to provide ecumenical, creative, and holistic approaches in response to social issues facing the region.

*Therefore*, the General Conference of The United Methodist Church calls upon:

- all members of The United Methodist Church to act as a source of support and encouragement to our brothers and sisters working as peacemakers in lands of violence;
- the General Board of Church and Society (GBCS) to stay informed as to developments in the region and to encourage advocacy with the peoples of the region;
- Methodist and United Methodist churches in Latin America and the Caribbean to advocate with government leaders to place people and justice at the center of any concerted efforts toward the eradication of poverty and toward sustainable and equitable development in the region. Special attention should be made to people who are marginalized: indigenous communities, Afro-Latinos, women and children;
- the General Board of Global Ministries (GBGM), the General Board of Discipleship (GBOD), and the General Board of Higher Education and Ministries (GBHEM) to support the

growth of United Methodist churches and seminaries in this region through programs of leadership development and congregational development; and

- the General Board of Church and Society and the General Board of Global ministries to monitor programs of relief and development, with special attention to:
  1. collaboration for implement of reforestation and reduction of pollution programs;
  2. funding specifically allocated to human development and HIV/AIDS programs;
  3. small farmers and landless workers, who are struggling to survive in light of globalization; and
  4. internally displaced people who are losing their land and their livelihood in the midst of violence and insecurity.

**ADOPTED 2008**

*See* Social Principles, ¶ 165*A*, *B*, and *D*.

## 6073. Opposition to Israeli Settlements in Palestinian Land

We join with Palestinian Christians as well as our Jewish and Muslim brothers and sisters in feeling a deep sense of rootedness to the land that has special meaning for our three religious traditions. We celebrate the diversity of religious customs and traditions throughout the Middle East.

Jerusalem is sacred to all the children of Abraham: Jews, Muslims, and Christians. We have a vision of a shared Jerusalem as a city of peace and reconciliation, where indigenous Palestinians and Israelis can live as neighbors and, along with visitors and tourists, have access to holy sites and exercise freedom of religious expression. The peaceful resolution of Jerusalem's status is crucial to the success of the whole process of making a just and lasting peace between Palestinians and Israelis.

We seek for all people in the region an end to military occupation, freedom from violence, and full respect for the human rights of all under international law.

WHEREAS, the prophet Isaiah cautioned against coveting the lands and homes of one's neighbors: "Ah, you who join house to house, who add field to field, until there is room for no one but you, and you are left to live alone in the midst of the land!" (Isaiah 5:8); and

WHEREAS, the continuing confiscation of Palestinian land for construction of settlements and the building of a separation wall violates basic understanding of human rights, subverts the peace process, destroys the hope of both Israelis and Palestinians who are working for and longing for peace, and fosters a sense of desperation that can only lead to further violence; and

WHEREAS, continued and often intensified closures, curfews, dehumanizing check points, home demolitions, uprooted trees, bulldozed fields, and confiscation of Palestinian land and water by the government of Israel have devastated economic infrastructure and development in the West Bank and Gaza, have caused a massive deterioration of the living standards of all Palestinians . . . and an increasing sense of hopelessness and frustration; and

WHEREAS, targeted assassinations, suicide bombings, and attacks against civilians by both Israelis and Palestinians heighten the fear and suffering of all; and

WHEREAS, people in the United States, through their taxes, provide several billion dollars in economic and military assistance to the State of Israel each year, which allows for the building of bypass roads and settlements that are illegal according to the Fourth Geneva Convention;

WHEREAS, the church continues to work with ecumenical and interfaith bodies to advocate for Palestinian self-determination and an end to Israeli occupation; to affirm Israel's right to exist within secure borders; to affirm the right of return for Palestinian refugees under international law; to call for region-wide disarmament; to urge Israelis and Palestinians to stop human rights violations and attacks on civilians, such as targeted assassinations and suicide bombings; and to urge the US government to initiate an arms embargo on the entire Middle East region;

*Therefore, be it resolved,* that The United Methodist Church opposes continued military occupation of the West Bank, Gaza, and East Jerusalem, the confiscation of Palestinian land and water resources, the destruction of Palestinian homes, the continued building of illegal Jewish settlements, and any vision of a "Greater Israel" that includes the occupied territories and the whole of Jerusalem and its surroundings.

*Be it further resolved,* that we urge the US government to end all military aid to the region, and second to redistribute the large amount of aid now given to Israel and Egypt; to support economic development efforts of nongovernmental organizations throughout the region, including religious institutions, human rights groups, labor unions, and professional groups within Palestinian communities.

The United Methodist Church requests that the government of the United States, working in cooperation with the United Nations and other nations, urge the state of Israel to:

1. cease the confiscation of Palestinian lands and water for any reason;

2. cease the building of new, or expansion of existing, settlements and/or bypass roads in the occupied territories including East Jerusalem;

3. lift the closures and curfews on all Palestinian towns by completely withdrawing Israeli military forces to the Green Line (the 1948 ceasefire line between Israel and the West Bank);

4. dismantle that segment of the Wall of Separation constructed since May 2002 that is not being built on the Green Line but on Palestinian land that is separating Palestinian farmers from their fields.

We also urge the Palestinian Authority and all Palestinian religious leaders to continue to publicly condemn violence against Israeli civilians and to use nonviolent acts of disobedience to resist the occupation and the illegal settlements.

We urge all United Methodists in the US to:

1. advocate with the US administration and Congress to implement the above steps;

2. encourage members of each congregation to study the Israeli-Palestinian conflict from all perspectives by inviting speakers to church events, reading books, using audiovisual resources in educational forums, and getting information from Web sites.

3. provide financial support to the Palestinian people through contributions to the General Board of Global Ministries;

4. support, and participate in, the work of international peace and human rights organizations to provide protection for Palestinians and Israelis seeking nonviolently to end the occupation; and

5. reach out to local synagogues, mosques, and Christian faith groups by engaging in interfaith and ecumenical dialogue on how to promote justice and peace in the Holy Land; and

That the General Board of Global Ministries, working together with the General Board of Church & Society and interfaith organizations, develop advocacy packets for use in local congregations to promote a just and lasting peace and human rights for all in the region.

ADOPTED 2004
READOPTED 2008
RESOLUTION #312, 2004 *BOOK OF RESOLUTIONS*

*See* Social Principle, ¶ 165.

## 6074. United Nations Resolutions on the Israel-Palestine Conflict

WHEREAS, negotiations between the State of Israel and the Palestinian National Authority still have not achieved a just and lasting peace for the Palestinian people; and

WHEREAS, the United Nations Security Council and General Assembly have passed numerous resolutions since UN Resolution 181, the Partition Plan, first adopted in November 1947, including Resolutions 242 and 338, that outline a framework for a just and lasting peace; and

WHEREAS, The UMC in the Social Principles recognizes and affirms the role of the United Nations in the just and lasting resolution of conflict, "Believing that international justice requires the participation of all peoples, we endorse the United Nations and its related bodies and the International Court of Justice as the best instruments now in existence to achieve a world of justice and law" (¶ 165D); and

WHEREAS, Security Council Resolution 242, unanimously adopted in 1967, declares "the inadmissibility of the acquisition of territory by war and the need to work for a just and lasting peace in which every State in the area can live in security"; and

WHEREAS, the security of every state depends on it having defined borders and not occupying the territory of its neighbors, and

WHEREAS, the 10th commandment in the Bible states, "You shall not covet your neighbor's house . . . or anything that belongs to your neighbor" (Exodus 20:17); and

WHEREAS, for more than 40 years the government of Israel has continued its military occupation of East Jerusalem, the West Bank, and Gaza and the seizing of more and more Palestinian land for illegal settlements in direct violation of UN resolutions as well as United Methodist General Conference resolutions; and

WHEREAS, the International Court of Justice, on July 9, 2004, issued an advisory opinion that declared that Israel's security barrier or wall built on occupied Palestinian territories violates international law; that it must be dismantled; and that compensation must be provided to Palestinians for loss of land and livelihood; and

WHEREAS, Israel's government has continued to build the wall on Palestinian land in ongoing violation of international law, which greatly increases Palestinian suffering as well as heightens the insecurity of both Palestinians and Israelis; and

WHEREAS, May 2008 marks 60 years since the establishment of the state of Israel as well as the dispossession of 750,000 to 900,000 Palestinians who are still seeking their full human rights; and

WHEREAS, ongoing military occupation and armed resistance heightens violence and insecurity for Palestinians and Israelis alike; and

WHEREAS, The United Methodist Church opposes all violence against civilians and considers "war is incompatible with the teachings and example of Christ" (Social Principles, ¶ 165C); and

WHEREAS, the United States' use of its veto more than 30 times in the UN Security Council to block actions by the international community to criticize and prevent the killing of Palestinian civilians has contributed to a climate of impunity and exacerbated the cycle of violence affecting both Palestinians and Israelis;

*Therefore, be it resolved* that The United Methodist Church calls upon Israel, the Palestinian National Authority, and all States to abide by and uphold UN resolutions, International Court of Justice rulings, and international law as the basis for just and lasting peace in Palestine/Israel; and

*Be it further resolved* that The United Methodist Church calls upon the United States, as a permanent member of the UN Security Council, to accept the authority of Security Council resolutions to refrain from vetoing resolutions, and abide by Security Council Resolutions 242 and 338, as well as all other relevant UN resolutions and International Court of Justice rulings, that provide a framework for bringing this conflict to a just and permanent end.

ADOPTED 2000
REVISED AND READOPTED 2008
RESOLUTION #323, 2004 *BOOK OF RESOLUTIONS*
RESOLUTION #305, 2000 *BOOK OF RESOLUTIONS*

*See* Social Principles, ¶ 165A, B, C, and D.

## 6075. Saying No to Violence in Middle East Conflict

WHEREAS, The United Methodist Church has affirmed its commitment to relationship and dialogue with people of other religious traditions ("Called to Be Neighbors and Witnesses—Guidelines for Interreligious Relationships," 2004 *Book of Resolutions*, page 252ff); and

WHEREAS, The United Methodist Church has affirmed its commitment to relationship and dialogue with Jewish people ("Building New Bridges in Hope," 2004 *Book of Resolutions*, page 243ff); and

WHEREAS, The United Methodist Church has affirmed its commitment to relationship and dialogue with Muslims ("Our Muslim Neighbors," 2004 *Book of Resolutions*, page 797ff); and

WHEREAS, The United Methodist Church has affirmed its support for the boundaries of the State of Israel internationally recognized prior to the 1967 war in the Middle East ("United Nations Resolutions on the Israel-Palestine Conflict," 2004 *Book of Resolutions*, page 811ff); and

WHEREAS, The United Methodist Church has strongly stated its opposition to Israeli settlements in occupied territories ("Opposition to Israeli Settlements in Palestinian Land," 2004 *Book of Resolutions*, page 787ff);

*Therefore, be it resolved,* that The United Methodist Church continues to advocate for a peaceful settlement of the conflict between Israel and the Palestinians through negotiation and diplomacy rather than through methods of violence and coercion.

ADOPTED 2008

*See* Social Principles, ¶ 165*A, B,* and *D.*

## 6076. East Timor: Action Still Needed

Tragedy struck East Timor again in 2006-2007, five years after the island territory achieved its independence following twenty-four years of brutal occupation by Indonesia during which more than a quarter of the original population of less than 700,000 perished from the combined effects of the war.

Renewed violence erupted in April and May of 2006, as rival East Timorese security forces turned on each other. There was also an outbreak of violence in August 2007 in the wake of parliamentary elections. Such violence underscored the divisions that emerged after the territory's long quest for freedom, and the unhealed wounds that remain. While the manifestations of the continuing crisis in East Timor are political and institutional, poverty and associated deprivations, including high unemployment, especially among youth, also contributed to the crisis. These issues must be urgently addressed. The world, which ignored East Timor for so long and contributed so much to its suffering, should be patient and find constructive ways to assist East Timor in the challenges ahead.

The UN Security Council responded to East Timor's plight, as did an international peacekeeping force led by Australia, New Zealand, and Portugal. A renewed United Nations assistance mission was constituted, and should be generously supported by the international community for as long as needed.

It is now accepted that the original United Nations transitional mission in East Timor should have continued with strength. Instead, it was far too short in duration, scaling down drastically after less than three years once East Timor became independent in May 2002. The same mistake should not happen again. The current UN mission should be fully supported, stressing institution-building and social and economic development, consolidating stability and enhancing a culture of democratic governance.

Historical responsibility cannot be overlooked. Throughout Indonesia's 24-year-long occupation of East Timor, the United States staunchly backed Jakarta both with arms shipments and by blunting criticism in Congress and the United Nations. But wanting to save money on peacekeeping, the Bush Administration pushed for the withdrawal of UN troops as soon as East Timor became independent in 2002.

Health is a crucial issue in East Timor. Standards remain low, aggravated by the fact that more than 150,000 people were displaced in 2006. Most of the population remains highly vulnerable to respiratory and gastrointestinal diseases, in addition to malaria, dengue fever, tuberculosis, and leprosy. Despite some improvements, the health situation remains worse than in all other Southeast Asian countries. Life expectancy currently (based on 2004 data) is 49, and under-5 mortality rates are the highest in the region. Only 24 percent of births are attended by skilled medical personnel. Malaria incidence has increased threefold since 1999. Some signs of improvement are due to the fact that the Ministry of Health undoubtedly is the most efficient ministry in East Timor. More health awareness information is available locally; local clinics have been opened, enabling doctors and nurses to reach poor households more successfully. Fully 87 percent of the population now has some access to health care, so a basis is being developed for future improvements in health conditions.

Especially in light of the renewed crisis, it is crucial that the United States maintain and expand its relatively modest financial contributions to East Timor's development, including health.

*Therefore, be it resolved,* that The United Methodist Church, its members, local churches, annual conferences, central conferences, and general agencies:

1. recognize our continuing moral and religious duty to assist East Timor in its reconstruction and development, with special emphasis on child mortality and maternal health;
2. call on the United States government and other governments to support a continuing United Nations presence, including for peace keeping, as warranted by conditions in East Timor;
3. exhort the executive and legislative branches of the United States government and the United Nations to take all steps within their respective powers to reduce the suffering of the people of East Timor and promote the new nation's development, and continue to stress the need for justice for the victims of crimes committed throughout the 24 year Indonesian occupation of East Timor as well as during the events of 2006;
4. urge United Methodists, including the General Board of Global Ministries and the General Board of Church and Society, to continue to make the issue of East Timor a priority for social justice and mission purposes, and to support constituency education, direct relief efforts and related projects in East Timor; and
5. direct that The United Methodist Church, immediately following 2008 General Conference, send copies of this resolution to the secretary-general of the United Nations, the president of the UN General Assembly, the President of the United States, all US senators and congressional representatives, and all appropriate ecumenical colleagues.

**ADOPTED 2008**

*See* Social Principles, ¶ 165A, B, and D.

### 6077. Support for Covenant of the Commonwealth of the Northern Mariana Islands

WHEREAS from 1972 to 1976, the United States government and the people of the Northern Mariana Islands negotiated in phased implementation the "Covenant of the Commonwealth of the Northern Mariana Islands" (CNMI) in Political Union with the United States of America"; and

WHEREAS the Northern Mariana Islands district previously was part of the United Nations Trust Territory of the Pacific Islands; and

WHEREAS under the terms of the covenant, citizens of the self-governing commonwealth do not participate in federal elections but enjoy all the other benefits of US citizenship; and

WHEREAS unlike the other Insular Areas of Puerto Rico, the US Virgin Islands, American Samoa, and the territory of Guam, the CNMI do not have a delegate in the United States Congress; and

WHEREAS the Commonwealth of Northern Mariana Islands has always elected a representative to Washington DC; and

WHEREAS in solidarity with the aspirations of the people of the CNMI, members of the Immanuel United Methodist Church of Saipan publicly declared their support for delegate representation in the United States Congress;

*Therefore be it resolved* that the 2004 General Conference direct the General Board of Church and Society to win congressional representation for CNMI in the United States Congress with committee level membership that includes voice and seat.

ADOPTED 2004
RESOLUTION #325, 2004 *BOOK OF RESOLUTIONS*

*See* Social Principles, ¶ 165.

## 6078. Philippines

Justice is turned back, and righteousness stands at a distance; for truth stumbles in the public square, and righteousness cannot enter. Truth is lacking, and whoever turns from evil is despoiled. The Lord saw it and it displeased him that there was no justice. He saw that there was no one, and was appalled that there was no one to intervene . . . (Isaiah 59:14-16 NRSV ).

Jerusalem, Jerusalem, the city that kills the prophets and stones those who are sent to it! How often have I desired to gather your children together as a hen gathers her brood under her wings, and you were not willing! (Matthew 23:37 NRSV).

*Our Concern: Human Rights Violations Continue*

The United Methodist Church continues to be alarmed by and concerned about the unabated and egregious violations of human rights in the Philippines. Such violations continue to take the form of extra-judicial killings, summary executions, abductions, torture, arbitrary political detentions, and enforced disappearances. Victims of human rights violations, according to a September 2007 report by the Philippine human rights group Karapatan, over 900 extrajudicial killings and 179 disappearances. The Philippines has officially collaborated and is widely perceived as having willingly subordinated itself to the United States–prosecuted war on terror, resulting in the designation of the Philippines as the second front in this war. Even more alarming is the recently adopted Human Security Act, which is the Philippine blueprint for counterinsurgency that many Filipinos regard as dismissive of human rights and their protection.

Chief Justice of the Supreme Court of the Philippines, Hon. Reynato Puno, who is the first ever Filipino United Methodist to hold this high and lofty position, said in a university commencement speech: "One visible result of the scramble to end terrorism is to take legal shortcuts and legal shortcuts always shrink the scope of human rights. . . . These shortcuts have searched the landscape of rights in the Philippines. . . . The escalation of extrajudicial killings in the Philippines has attracted the harsh eye of advocates of human Rights. . . . Their initial findings are not complementing to our Constitutional commitment to protect human rights. . . . If there is any lesson that we can derive from the history of human rights, it is none other than these rights cannot be obliterated by bombs but neither can they be preserved by bullets alone. Terrorism is a military-police problem but its ultimate solution lies beyond the guns of our armed forces. . . . The apathy of those who can make a difference is the reason why violations of human rights continue to prosper. The worst enemy of human rights is not its nonbelievers but the fence sitters who will not lift a finger despite their violations."

## The Human Rights Situation Is Appalling

Many international groups—religious bodies, nongovernmental organizations, foreign governments and intergovernmental organizations like the United Nations—have pressed the Philippine government to do more to stop the many disturbing forms of human rights violations in the Philippines, urging the government to fulfill its constitutional and international law obligations.

Prof. Phillip Alston, the United Nations Special Rapporteur on Extrajudicial, Summary or Arbitrary Executions, issued a press statement after a ten-day visit to the Philippines in 2007 that characterized the Philippine Armed Forces as being "in a state of almost total denial" on the need to resolve the "significant number of killings which have been convincingly attributed to them." He called the human rights situation tragic and in a "climate of virtual impunity." In his preliminary report to the UN Human Rights Council meeting in Geneva on March 22, 2007, Prof. Alston emphasized governmental culpability, especially in the military, in the human rights violations.

The 2006 US State Department Country Report on Human Rights Practices dealing with the Philippines opened with the following statement: "During the year there were a number of arbitrary, unlawful, and extrajudicial killings apparently by elements of the security services and of political killings, including killings of journalists, by a variety of actors. Many of these killings went unsolved and unpunished, contributing to a climate of impunity, despite intensified government efforts during the year to investigate and prosecute these cases. Members of the security services committed acts of physical and psychological abuse on suspects and detainees, and there were instances of torture. Arbitrary or warrantless arrests and detentions were common. Trials were delayed and procedures were prolonged. Prisoners awaiting trial and those already convicted were often held under primitive conditions. Corruption was a problem in all the institutions making up the criminal justice system, including police, prosecutorial, and judicial organs. During a brief 'state of emergency' in February, there was some attempted interference in freedom of the press and in the right of assembly. In addition to the killings mentioned above, leftwing and human rights activists were often subject to harassment by local security forces. Problems such as violence against women and abuse of children, child prostitution, trafficking in persons, child labor, and ineffective enforcement of worker rights were common."

Several other reports from international human rights groups echo the same concerns about extrajudicial killings in the Philippines. These include reports from groups like Amnesty International, Human Rights Watch, Human Rights First, and the Asian Human Rights Commission. Even the Philippine government–appointed independent commission to address "media and activist killings," otherwise known as the Melo Report, has pointed to the need for the Philippine government to take firmer action to resolve the killings.

## The Filipino People Deserve our Solidarity and Action

Of the many reports, we welcome especially "Let the Stones Cry Out: An Ecumenical Report on Human Rights in the Philippines and a Call to Action" released by the ecumenical and nongovernmental community in the Philippines, led by the National Council of Churches in the Philippines, whose production and distribution was led and supported by a couple of general agencies of our church.

"This report articulates the protests and indignations of human rights organizations, Church and faith institutions, civil libertarians, justice and peace advocates, parliamentarians, numerous fact-finding missions, multilateral organizations as well as a number of foreign governments and their agencies all over the world on the spate of extrajudicial killings, enforced disappearances, torture, threats and harassment, and other violations of human rights. Their collective call —'Stop the killings!'—is addressed to the government of President Gloria Macapagal-Arroyo given its inadequate action over the deteriorating human rights situation and despite persistent calls for investigation, prosecution and adjudication of the alleged perpetrators of these politically-motivated crimes."

We share with the ecumenical community in the Philippines the perspective posed and the burden of the question raised in the ecumenical report's preface: "Something is wrong when members of the clergy and lay missionaries are being silenced when they are deeply engaged in missions that address the concerns of their constituencies —and the Philippine society as a whole. Something is wrong when members of the church and faith institutions are killed, go missing or arrested while pursuing their calling to bring about justice closer to the poor, to fight for their rights, and advocate peace in a society that is torn asunder by armed conflicts fueled by structural problems. Of greater alarm is that the gross and systematic attacks on these pilgrims of peace and servants of God are forcing their institutions to an inevitable clash with the State. . . ."

We issue this statement not only to support the ecumenical report from the Philippines and the direction in which its call to action points. We issue this statement because the struggle for human rights in the Philippines is at a point when our solidarity and accompaniment, as we have expressed in many ways and many times in the past, are crucial and needed even more so today.

## We Commit to Action with Resolve and Dispatch

Filipino faith communities and other citizens continue to address the situation in the Philippines. And the Philippine judiciary has taken the cudgels for them—ensuring that the rule of law is going to be biased towards a universal adherence and practice of human rights. In a very laudable effort by the Chief Justice of the Supreme Court of the Philippines, a "National Consultative Summit on Extrajudicial Killings and Enforced Disappearances—Searching for Solutions" was conducted. In his opening remarks, Chief Justice Reynato Puno stated: "The time has come to say less and do more. . . . [I]n the crusade to protect constitutional rights there is no room for neutrality. They who seek to remain in the safety of the sidelines when human rights are under assault shall be condemned by history into irrelevance."

General boards and agencies of The United Methodist Church have addressed the human rights situation in the Philippines in a variety of ways and venues, including providing leadership to the Philippine Working Group (PWG), which helped produce the ecumenical human rights report and supported the itineration of a Philippine ecumenical delegation called "Ecumenical Voice for Human Rights and Peace in the Philippines." This ecumenical voice has since expanded its membership and its voice is ever more heard in the Philippines.

The PWG was also instrumental in the holding of a US House of Representatives briefing and a US Senate hearing on March 14, 2007. United Methodists in California played a crucial role in getting Senator Barbara Boxer (D-CA) and Rep. Tom Lantos (D-CA) to hold these watershed meetings by the US Congress. Our church also helped secure meetings with the US State Department and key congressional offices to raise concerns about the Philippine human rights situation. Our church, through a number of its boards and agencies, also accompanied the ecumenical delegation in submitting the ecumenical report to a variety of United Nations–related offices in Geneva, Switzerland, especially the United Nations Human Rights Council, the Office of the UN High Commissioner for Human Rights, on Indigenous Peoples, and on the promotion and protection of human rights while countering terrorism.

Other annual conferences in the United States, such as California-Nevada, Pacific Northwest, Desert Southwest, California-Pacific, and Northern Illinois, have also addressed these issues, including conducting fact-finding, solidarity, and mission trips to the Philippines.

In all these visits, Philippine church leaders and church workers showed them the appalling human rights situation and in turn the visitors voiced their concern with government and military officials, and expressed their solidarity with church and community leaders.

*We Commit to Work on the Following Actions:*

We will submit this statement to concerned governmental and inter-governmental offices, accompanied by the ecumenical report, "Let the Stones Cry Out."

We call on the Philippine government to immediately stop the killings and all the other forms of human rights violations, to take effective measures to bring to justice members of its security forces and their agents for whom there is credible evidence of human rights violations, to comply with its obligations under international human rights and humanitarian laws, to rescind national security policies that make no distinction between combatants and noncombatants, to hold free and fair elections, and to investigate any allegations of electoral fraud.

We call on the Philippine government to stop the practice of listing peace and human rights advocates in its watch lists of individuals banned from entering or leaving the Philippines, and to expunge such record of names already listed.

We call on other governments, but especially the governments of the United States of America, the European Union, the Association of Southeast Asian Nations, and significant development aid and trading partners like Japan, to look into these human rights violations and pressure the Philippine government to stop them. To this end, we also support moves within the US Congress calling for a review of official development aid and trade and economic arrangements to examine whether these do or do not further exacerbate human rights violations.

We especially call for any military appropriations and official development assistance to the Philippine government to be conditioned to a strict adherence to international laws and standards of human rights and good governance, and thereby support the development and use of benchmarks that will guide and measure the Philippine government's adherence to the same. Since human rights thrive under democratic, just, and peaceful conditions we call for the resumption of peace talks by the government, without preconditions, with all of the Philippine rebel groups, so that through negotiations the civil, political, social, economic, and cultural problems that beset the Philippines may result into just and durable peace.

We call on the United Nations and its agencies, to continue investigating human rights violations in the Philippines, and to offer help to the Philippine government in meeting its international obligations, including empowerment and capacity-building of nongovernmental organizations in their work of monitoring Philippine government compliance and promotion of human rights.

Lastly, we call on our general boards, agencies, annual conferences, and local churches in the US and throughout the global connection, including the National Association of Filipino American United Methodists, to work with Philippine annual conferences, ecumenical bodies, and nongovernmental organizations in joint undertakings to address the peace and human rights situation in the Philippines.

"These are the things that you shall do: Speak the truth to one another, render in your gates judgments that are true and make for peace, do not devise evil in your hearts against one another, and love no false oath; for all these are things I hate, says the LORD" (Zechariah 8:16-17 NRSV).

**ADOPTED 2008**

*See* Social Principles, ¶ 165*A*, *B*, and *D*.

## 6079. Statement Against Extrajudicial Killings in the Philippines

WHEREAS, since 2001, Karapatan, a human rights advocacy group in Southeast Asia, tallied more than 800 people killed extrajudicially. This number is increasing, and killings pose a threat to both Filipinos and other nationalities visiting the Philippines. UMC young people appeal to the government to take action on this human rights violation; and

WHEREAS, Matthew 23:37-39 says, "Jerusalem, Jerusalem, the city that kills the prophets and stones those who are sent to it! See, your house is left to you, desolate. For I tell you, you will not see me again until you say, 'Blessed is the one who comes in the name of the Lord'"; and

WHEREAS, human rights are in danger in the Philippines, and the image of God in every person is being assaulted in many ways, including God's servants—bishops, pastors, deaconesses, and women, men, and youth lay leaders. These prophet servants of God have preached, with costly discipleship, the good news to the poor, deprived, and marginalized peoples of the Philippines; and

WHEREAS, the recent and ongoing summary and extrajudicial killings—outright execution of people outside of the judicial process—in the Philippines is an affront to the rights and dignity of peoples. International human rights law, to which the Philippines subscribes, prohibits these kinds of killings. United Methodist social and biblical teachings found in our Social Principles and *Book of Resolutions* consider the "mistreatment . . . of persons by governments for any purpose violates Christian teaching and must be condemned and/or opposed"; and

WHEREAS, respectable human rights organizations, including ecumenical bodies and our own church, local and international, have reported on the rampancy and brutality of these killings under the government of Philippine President Gloria Macapagal-Arroyo. All such reports point to an unacceptable level of impunity with which such killings have been conducted. These reports point to the involvement of government security forces—police and military—in these killings and human rights violations; and

WHEREAS, the failure of government to protect its people and to fairly investigate these killings and human rights violations unjustly encourages impunity and the unnecessary shedding of even more blood and the sacrifice of even more precious lives. To date, these killings total over 900 from all sectors, including 24 from the religious community which counts former United Methodist pastor Isaias Sta. Rosa of the Davao Episcopal Area; and

WHEREAS, the Connectional Table of The United Methodist Church, in cooperation with several general agencies of the church, in its January 2006 visit to the Philippines has joined the worldwide chorus of calls to "stop the killings." It is a call issued to the Philippine government, whose prime duty is the protection of the rights and welfare of its people, to impartially and thoroughly investigate and end these killings and violations. It is also a call for the United States government to rethink its foreign policy toward the Philippines, given its historical colonial and contemporary relations to the Philippines, including economic, political, cultural, and military relations. The United States and other governments and international agencies like the United Nations, European Union, and African Union may exert their influence so that the killings and violations are stopped,

*Therefore, be it resolved,* that as socially responsible young people of The United Methodist Church we are called to respond to social injustices in our society. As in the many wars and conflicts and human rights violations now committed worldwide, the toll on the lives and psyches of young people is very high and unnecessary. But violations are stoppable, and we must help to stop them in the Philippines, and in other places where they happen. Human rights violations in the Philippines threaten human rights everywhere.

*Therefore, be it further resolved,* that as United Methodist young people, we commit to pray for the Filipinos as they disciple among their people and call them to fidelity to our Lord Jesus Christ's imperatives for love, compassion, justice, and peace. Our solidarity and companionship with fellow United Methodists in the Philippines will add courage and hope to them and their people as they bear witness to God's gift of life and struggle against death-dealing forces.

*Finally, be it resolved,* that using the resources available to us as a global connectional church, we will involve ourselves on this issue, guided by our brothers and sisters in the Methodist family in the Philippines and other ecumenical and interreligious bodies that are already in ministries of peace and restorative justice there. We will pray and work with the United Methodist Youth and the Young Adult Fellowships in the Philippines in their ministries on this concern. Specifically, we suggest that awareness-raising on this issue be intensified across the connection, including, if possible, fact-finding missions to the Philippines that include young people.

**ADOPTED 2008**

*See* Social Principles, ¶ 165*A* and *D*.

## 6080. West Papua

*Justice and Self-determination for West Papua (Irian Jaya)*

West Papua is the western half of the island of New Guinea. The independent nation of Papua New Guinea (PNG) makes up the eastern half. The western half, known at the time as Dutch New Guinea, was a colony of The Netherlands until 1961.

In 1949, when the Dutch East Indies became Indonesia, the Dutch colonial power excluded Dutch New Guinea, as it was then called, and started to prepare it for independence by training Papuans for leadership positions within the government and civil society. The people of the area were predominately Melanesian, unlike the rest of the

East Indies who were mainly Malay. Australia, at the time, supported independence for West Papua. The Papuan people, comprised of more than 200 tribes, are mainly Christian and animist, with a high percentage of the Papuan identifying as either Roman Catholic or Protestant Christians.

In 1961, The Netherlands was preparing Dutch New Guinea for independence, but Indonesia objected strongly and sent its troops into the region. The United States subsequently brokered an agreement between Indonesia and The Netherlands in 1963, called the New York Agreement, which handed Dutch New Guinea over to Indonesia for a period of six years, to be followed by an act of self-determination ("Act of Free Choice").

In 1969, the "Act of Free Choice" was conducted under the auspices of the UN, but in reality under control of Indonesia. One thousand twenty-five Papuans handpicked by the Indonesian government from a population of 800,000 voted, under threat from Indonesian troops, to join Indonesia.

The UN sanctioned the vote and Dutch New Guinea became Irian Jaya, a province of Indonesia.

In November 2001, two senior UN officials, including the head of the UN mission to oversee the handing-over of West Papua to Indonesia, admitted that the Act of Free Choice was a sham—"a whitewash, designed to appease the Americans and the Indonesians."

Church groups estimate that since 1961, at least 100,000 West Papuans have been killed or disappeared under the brutal Indonesian military occupation. Murder, torture, rape, summary detentions, and destruction of entire villages, continues to this day.

In 2001, Chief Theys Eluay, perhaps the most important Papuan leader, was assassinated by the Indonesian military's Special Forces in yet another attempt to destroy the Papuans' struggle for a peaceful solution to years of intimidation, torture, and genocide.

Since 2003, the president of Indonesia has banned all journalists and international observers from going to West Papua.

In the last several years there has been increased militarization of West Papua.

Meanwhile, Freeport McMoRan mining operations, a Lousianna-based company, continues to devastate tribal lands, extracting gold from the largest deposit in the world.

After 40 years it is time for a genuine act of self-determination for West Papua.

*Therefore, be it resolved,* that The United Methodist Church calls on the secretary-general of the United Nations to immediately institute a timeline for a review of the United Nations "Act of Free Choice"; and

*Be it further resolved,* that The United Methodist Church, immediately following 2008 General Conference, send copies of this resolution to the secretary-general of the United Nations, the president of the UN General Assembly, the President of the United States, all US senators and congressional representatives, and all appropriate ecumenical colleagues; and

*Be it further resolved,* that The United Methodist Church urges the General Board of Global Ministries to make the issue of self-determination for West Papua a priority for social justice purposes, and to support constituency education and related projects on West Papua.

**ADOPTED 2008**

*See* Social Principles, ¶ 165*A, B,* and *D.*

## PEACEMAKING

### 6091. A Call for Peacemaking

God's earth is aching for peace. Domestic strife, interpersonal violence and abuse, civil conflict, ethnic and racial clashes, religious schism and interfaith rivalry, terrorist attacks, wars between nations, and threatened use of nuclear, chemical, and biological weapons—all of these prevent us from achieving God's shalom. In response we who are disciples of Jesus Christ are called to be peacemakers for the transformation of the world.

The biblical foundation for peacemaking is the Sermon on the Mount where Jesus taught, "Blessed are the peacemakers" (Matthew 5:9), "Don't react violently against the one who is evil" (Matthew 5:39, *Scholars Version*\*), "Love your enemies and pray for those who persecute you" (Matthew 5:44), and pray to forgive those who trespass against us (Matthew 6:12, 14-15). Paul echoed Jesus' teaching when he instructed Christians in Rome, "Do not be overcome by evil, but overcome evil with good" (Romans 12:14-21). He told the church in Corinth that through Christ we have a "ministry of reconciliation" (2 Corinthians 5:17-18).

\**The Five Gospels: The Search for the Authentic Words of Jesus. New Translation and Commmentary* by *Robert W. Funk, Roy W. Hoover, and the Jesus Seminar* [also known as the Scholars Version]; Robert W. Funk, et al. (New York: Macmillan, 1993).

For The United Methodist Church peacemaking is an essential task for achieving success in other initiatives. Working with the poor to eliminate poverty, caring for children, and conducting global health initiatives can be most successful in stable and just societies free from armed conflict. To have sufficient resources for these tasks requires global peace and disarmament in order to redirect vast amounts of public funds now spent on armed forces and weaponry. Moreover, a strong concern for peace and justice is a necessary feature of vital congregations.

*Therefore,* the 2008 General Conference of The United Methodist Church calls upon:

- United Methodist children, youth, and adults as devoted disciples of Jesus Christ to become peacemakers wherever they are—at home, school, work, in the local community and the wider world—and to show the love, compassion, and concern for justice that Jesus taught and lived;
- local congregations as an expression of Wesleyan social holiness to teach and practice peacemaking, to study underlying causes of conflict among social groups and nations, to seek positive remedies and become instruments of peace;
- annual conferences to undergird congregations through training, encouragement, and active support for peacemaking activities and to be voices for peace, justice, and reconciliation within the conference area and beyond;
- bishops to encompass peacemaking in teaching what it means to live the United Methodist way, engage in conflict resolution where appropriate, and offer a prophetic voice for peace and justice; and
- boards and agencies to incorporate peacemaking into their regular programs and budgets.

**ADOPTED 2008**

*See* Social Principles, ¶ 165C.


## 6092. Justice, Peace, and the Integrity of Creation

A World Council of Churches Convocation on "Justice, Peace and the Integrity of Creation" was held in Seoul, Republic of Korea, in March 1990 "to engage member churches in a conciliar process of mutual commitment to justice, peace and the integrity of creation." A set of ten affirmations was approved by the convocation for a process of covenanting:

1. We affirm that all forms of human power and authority are subject to God and accountable to people. This means the right of people to full participation. In Christ, God decisively revealed the meaning of power as compassionate love that prevails over the forces of death.

2. We affirm God's preferential option for the poor and state that as Christians our duty is to embrace God's action in the struggles of the poor in the liberation of us all.

3. We affirm that people of every race, caste, and ethnic group are of equal value. In the very diversity of their cultures and traditions, they reflect the rich plurality of God's creation.

4. We affirm the creative power given to women to stand for life whenever there is death. In Jesus' community women find acceptance and dignity, and with them he shared the imperative to carry the good news.

5. We affirm that access to truth and education, information, and means of communication are basic human rights. All people have the right to be educated, to tell their own stories, to speak their own convictions and beliefs, to be heard by others, and to have the power to distinguish truth from falsehood.

6. We affirm the full meaning of God's peace. We are called to seek every possible means of establishing justice, achieving peace, and solving conflicts by active nonviolence.

7. We affirm that the world, as God's handiwork, has its own inherent integrity; that land, waters, air, forests, mountains, and all creatures, including humanity, are "good" in God's sight. The integrity of creation has a social aspect, which we recognize as peace with justice, and an ecological aspect, which we recognize in the self-renewing, sustainable character of natural ecosystems.

8. We affirm that the land belongs to God. Human use of land and waters should release the earth to replenish regularly its life-giving power, protecting its integrity and providing spaces for its creatures.

9. We affirm the dignity of children that derives from their particular vulnerability and need for nurturing love; the creative and sacrificial role that the young people are playing in building a new society, recognizing their right to have a prophetic voice in the structures that affect their life and their community; the rights and needs of the younger generation as basic for establishing educational and developmental priorities.

10. We affirm that human rights are God-given and that their promotion and protection are essential for freedom, justice, and peace. To protect and defend human rights, an independent judicial system is necessary.

The Social Principles of The United Methodist Church clearly reflect our commitment to justice, peace, and the integrity of creation. In addition, The United Methodist Church has demonstrated its support for justice, peace, and the integrity of creation through its complementary Peace with Justice Program.

In affirming its participation in the justice, peace, and the integrity of creation process of the World Council of Churches, The United Methodist Church specifically pledges to:

1. encourage local churches and individuals to study the documents of "Justice, Peace, and the Integrity of Creation" in order to develop greater understanding and support for those movements of people who struggle for human dignity, liberation, and for just and participatory forms of government and economic structures;

2. join the worldwide ecumenical movement to articulate its vision for all people living on earth and caring for creation;

3. urge the General Board of Global Ministries and the General Board of Church and Society to give priority to integrated programs supportive of the four covenants affirmed by the convocation in Seoul, Korea, which advocate:

- a just economic order and liberation from the bondage of foreign debt;
- true security of all nations and people;
- the building of a culture that can live in harmony with creation's integrity; and
- the eradication of racism and discrimination on national and international levels for all people;

4. urge all United Methodists to implement the Social Principles and General Conference resolutions that address these issues, especially "Economic Justice," "The United Methodist Church and Peace," "Environmental Stewardship," "Global Racism," and "Ecumenical Decade: Churches in Solidarity with Women"; and

5. urge all United Methodists to join in covenant with Christians around the world to work to fulfill the goals of justice, peace, and the integrity of creation.

ADOPTED 1992
AMENDED AND ADOPTED 2004
READOPTED 2008
RESOLUTION #327, 2004 *BOOK OF RESOLUTIONS*
RESOLUTION #308, 2000 *BOOK OF RESOLUTIONS*

*See* Social Principles, ¶ 165.

## 6093. Peace with Justice Sunday and Special Offering

*Background: From Despair to Hope*

The world today has seen unprecedented worsening of economic conditions all over the world. Economically debilitating conditions have sunk the poor of the world further in the quagmire of exploitation and despair. While we have seen the globalization of financial capital that has made possible the unprecedented creation of wealth, we have not seen the globalization of economic justice that would have spread this wealth equitably and sustainably. While there has been increased movement of capital in the world, unemployment and labor conditions remain appalling.

The world, also, has seen unprecedented worsening of political conditions that have mired many countries in ever escalating political tensions, especially those brought about by conflict and wars, genocide and terrorism, and political repression. The wanton disrespect for basic modicums of international cooperation has led to violations of already agreed principles of international law. Human rights continue to be violated and disregarded. Changes taking place in our global community diminish our hope for potential future reductions in military expenditures. These military expenditures drain resources of money and talent to be used for meeting urgent social needs.

Living together on this planet, we have realized that the many threads that connect both fragile and solid foundations of human life and of God's whole creation are endangered. The cultural conditions under which we undergird our citizenship on planet earth continue to be challenged by acts of intolerance and aggression, by acts of racism and xenophobia, by acts of classism, sexism, ageism, and gender discrimination. God's beautiful universe, and all that was good in creation, is in danger of extinction by the unsafe and unsound environmental practices that all too daily governments and peoples around the world inflict upon it. HIV/AIDS continues to escalate to pandemic proportions.

We must renew our call for a social transformation, for the quest to open the doors of opportunity for all, to distribute resources more equitably, and to provide better care for persons in need.

## Biblical Basis for Response

The United Methodist Church, with its historic commitment to peace and justice, can and should provide leadership to this social transformation. This heritage is expressed in the Social Principles and the Social Creed. It gained eloquent articulation by the United Methodist Council of Bishops in the foundation document In Defense of Creation: The Nuclear Crisis and a Just Peace, which offers a well-grounded biblical analysis for peace with justice. The bishops wrote:

> At the heart of the Old Testament is the testimony to *shalom*, that marvelous Hebrew word that means peace. But the peace that is *shalom* is not negative or one-dimensional. It is much more than the absence of war. *Shalom* is positive peace: harmony, wholeness, health, and well-being in all human relationships. It is the natural state of humanity as birthed by God. It is harmony between humanity and all of God's good creation. All of creation is interrelated. Every creature, every element, every force of nature participates in the whole of creation. If any person is denied *shalom*, all are thereby diminished. . . .

The Old Testament speaks of God's sovereignty in terms of *covenant*, more particularly the "covenant of peace" with Israel, which binds that people to God's *shalom* (Isaiah 54:10; Ezekiel 37:26). In the covenant of *shalom*, there is no contradiction between justice and peace or between peace and security or between love and justice (Jeremiah 29:7). In Isaiah's prophecy, when "the Spirit is poured upon us from on high," we will know that these laws of God are one and indivisible:

> *Then justice will dwell in the wilderness, and the effect of righteousness will be peace, and the result of righteousness, quietness and trust forever. My people will abide in a peaceful habitation, in secure dwellings, and in quiet resting places* (Isaiah 32:16-18).

> *Shalom*, then, is the sum total of moral and spiritual qualities in a community whose life is in harmony with God's good creation. . . .
>
> In Defense of Creation, pp. 24, 25-26

In their analysis, the United Methodist bishops pointed out that when the elders of Israel forsook their moral covenant for warrior-kings, the nation descended into generations of exploitation, repression, and aggression—then into chaos, captivity, and exile in Babylon.

Yet we must look to the great prophets of that bitter period of Exile for the renewed vision of *shalom*. If Exodus is liberation, Exile is renewal. Ezekiel and Isaiah (40-66) reaffirm God's creation and redemption as universal in scope. Narrow nationalism is repudiated. Servanthood is exalted as the hopeful path to *shalom* (page 27).

> And the prophets' images—swords into plowshares, peaceable king-doms, new covenants written on the heart—forecast the coming of One who will be the Prince of Peace."

And so he comes. He comes heralded by angels who sing: "Glory to God in the highest, and on earth peace!" He invokes the most special blessings upon peacemakers. He exalts the humanity of aliens. He commands us to love our enemies; for he knows, even if we do not, that if we hate our enemies, we blind and destroy ourselves. *Shalom*, after all, is the heart of God and the law of creation. It cannot be bro-ken with impunity.

New Testament faith presupposes a radical break between the fol-lies, or much so-called conventional wisdom about power and secu-rity, on the one hand, and the transcendent wisdom of *shalom*, on the other. Ultimately, New Testament faith is a message of hope about God's plan and purpose for human destiny. It is a redemptive vision that refuses to wallow in doom.

Paul's letters announce that Jesus Christ is "our peace." It is Christ who has "broken down the dividing wall of hostility," creating one humanity, overcoming enmity, so making peace (Ephesians 2:14-19). It is Christ who ordains a ministry of reconciliation. Repentance pre-pares us for reconciliation. Then we shall open ourselves to the trans-forming power of God's grace in Christ. Then we shall know what it means to be "in Christ." Then we are to become ambassadors of a new creation, a new Kingdom, a new order of love and justice (2 Corinthians 5:17-20).

The promise of peace envisioned by Israel's prophets of the Exile at the climax of the Old Testament is celebrated once more at the climax of the New Testament. The Revelation of John, in the darkest night of despair, sings of a new earth, radiant with infinite love and compas-sion, in which all nations and peoples come together peaceably before the Lord God and in which hunger and hurt and sorrow are no more (Revelation 7) (pp. 27-30).

This is the foundation of faith that enables us in The United Methodist Church to offer hope to those who despair and to bring forth joy to replace sadness. As Saint Francis of Assisi prayed to act in the spirit of Christ, so we too can sow love where there is hatred; where injury, pardon; where darkness, light. As instruments of peace and justice, we can seek to replace discord with harmony and to repair the brokenness that shatters the wholeness of *shalom*.

## Program Activities

The General Board of Church and Society will carry out the following "Peace with Justice" activities:

1. implement "Policies for a Just Peace" as specified in the Council of Bishops' Foundation Document, The United Methodist Church and Peace, Globalization and Its Impact on Human Dignity and Human Rights, and other resolutions on war, peace, disarmament, and terrorism;

2. implement the process of "Justice, Peace, and the Integrity of Creation" as adopted by the 1990 World Convocation for Justice, Peace, and the Integrity of Creation in Seoul, Republic of Korea;

3. work for social-justice policies and programs that seek the wholeness of *shalom* for all of God's people, and

4. work to eradicate attitudinal and systemic behavior patterns that perpetuate the sin of racism as it is lived out in the areas of peace, justice, and the integrity of creation.

To achieve these objectives, the General Board of Church and Society may:

a. assist annual conferences, districts, and local churches to organize and carry out peace with justice activities, and to promote the Peace with Justice Special Sunday Offering;

b. provide a regular flow of information on public issues to local churches, districts, and annual conferences;

c. strengthen its capacity to act as a public-policy advocate of measures that improve global relations and move toward nuclear disarmament and measures that provide jobs, housing, education, food, health care, income support, and clean water to all;

d. assist annual conferences and/or local churches to assess and respond to the disproportionate effect of injustices on racial

and ethnic persons in the United States, and that of people
around the world; and

e. assist annual conference Peace with Justice coordinators to
carry out their duties.

For the purpose of financing activities (a) to achieve the "Policies for
a Just Peace" contained in the Council of Bishops' Foundation
Document *In Defense of Creation*, and (b) to pursue other justice and
peace objectives contained within the vision of *shalom* in this same
document, revenue shall come from the Peace with Justice offering
and other possible sources in accordance with the 2004 *Book of
Discipline* ¶ 264.5 and World Service Special gifts.

### Assignment

The Peace with Justice Sunday and Special Offering shall be
assigned to the General Board of Church and Society.

ADOPTED 1992
AMENDED AND READOPTED 2004
RESOLUTION #332, 2004 *BOOK OF RESOLUTIONS*
RESOLUTION #313, 2000 *BOOK OF RESOLUTIONS*

*See* Social Principles, ¶ 165C.

## 6094. The United Methodist Church and Peace

Longing for safety is a feeling that all human beings share with one
another. . . . The way to real peace and security is reconciliation. We
will not attain full reconciliation between all peoples before God's
final consummation because the forces of evil and destruction are still
at work in the hearts of human beings and in their relationships. But
we are called to be peacemakers and ministers of reconciliation until
our Lord comes. (*In Search of Security*, Council of Bishops Task Force
on Safety and Security)

"Peace is not simply the absence of war, a nuclear stalemate or combination of uneasy cease-fires. It is that emerging dynamic reality
envisioned by prophets where spears and swords give way to implements of peace (Isaiah 2:1-4); where historic antagonists dwell
together in trust (Isaiah 11:4-11); and where righteousness and justice
prevail. There will be no peace with justice until unselfish and
informed life is structured into political processes and international

arrangements" (Bishops' Call for Peace and the Self-Development of Peoples).

The mission of Jesus Christ and his church is to serve all peoples regardless of their government, ideology, place of residence, or status. Surely the welfare of humanity is more important in God's sight than the power or even the continued existence of any state. Therefore, the church is called to look beyond human boundaries of nation, race, class, sex, political ideology, or economic theory and to proclaim the demands of social righteousness essential to peace.

The following are interrelated areas that must be dealt with concurrently in a quest for lasting peace in a world community.

## I. Disarmament

The arms race goes on. However, the danger of a holocaust remains as long as nations maintain nuclear weapons. Meanwhile, millions starve, and development stagnates. Again and again, regional tensions grow, conflicts erupt, and outside forces intervene to advance or protect their interests without regard to international law or human rights.

True priorities in national budgeting are distorted by present expenditures on weapons. Because of fear of unemployment, desire for profits, and contributions to the national balance of payments, the arms industry engenders great political power. Arms-producing nations seek to create markets, then vie with one another to become champion among the arms merchants of the world. Food, health, social services, jobs, and education are vital to the welfare of nations. Yet their availability is constantly threatened by the overriding priority given by governments to what is called "defense."

We support initiatives in every part of the world that move toward the goal of disarmament. This demands a radical reordering of priorities coupled with an effective system of international peacemaking, peacekeeping, and peace building. The church must constantly keep that goal before peoples and governments. In particular, we support the abolition of nuclear weapons. We affirm the prophetic position of our bishops who said in their statement In Defense of Creation: "We say a clear and unconditional 'NO' to nuclear war and to any use of nuclear weapons. We conclude that nuclear deterrence is a position that cannot receive the church's blessing." Accordingly, we reject the possession of nuclear weapons as a permanent basis for securing and maintaining peace. Possession can no longer be tolerated, even as a temporary expedient. We call upon all nations that possess nuclear weapons to renounce these vile instruments of mass destruction and to move expeditiously to dismantle all nuclear warheads and delivery vehicles. As a first step, we support all movement to ban the "first strike" policy from all North Atlantic Treaty Organization (NATO) doctrine.

We support the Comprehensive Nuclear Test Ban Treaty and the Nuclear Non-Proliferation Treaty. We call upon all nations to become signatories of these important treaties and to abide by their provisions.

At the same time, nations must provide for more secure control of weapons-grade nuclear materials. It is clear deterrence comes from international controls on materials from which bombs are made. We support the concept of nuclear-free zones where governments or peoples in a specific region band together to bar nuclear weapons from the area either by treaty or declaration. The United Methodist Church affirms its commitment to a nuclear-free Pacific. As Christian people committed to stewardship, justice, and peacemaking, we oppose and condemn the use of the Pacific for tests, storage, and transportation of nuclear weapons and weapons-delivery systems and the disposal of radioactive wastes. We further affirm the right of all indigenous people to control their health and well-being.

World public opinion justly condemns the use of chemical or biological weapons. Governments must renounce the use of these particularly inhumane weapons as part of their national policy. We support universal application of the Chemical Weapons Convention and the Biological Weapons Convention.

We support treaty efforts to ban the development, trade, and use of weapons that are inhumane, are excessively injurious, and have indiscriminate effects. Such weapons include landmines, booby traps, weapons with nondetectable fragments, incendiary weapons, dirty bombs, cluster bombs, and blinding laser weapons. We call upon all nations to sign and abide by the Convention on the Prohibition of the Use, Stockpiling, Production, and Transfer of Anti-Personnel Mines and on Their Destruction.

We are also concerned about the use of inhumane weapons by civilian or military police. Hollow-point ("dumdum") or other bullets designed to maim are not acceptable weapons for use by civilian or military forces. We support measures that outlaw use of such weapons at all levels. We affirm peoples' movements directed to abolition of the tools of war. Governments must not impede public debate on this issue of universal concern.

## II. Democracy and Freedom

Millions of people still live under oppressive rule and various forms of exploitation. Millions more live under deplorable conditions of racial, sexual, religious, and class discrimination. In many countries, many persons, including Christians, are suffering repression, imprisonment, and torture as a result of their efforts to speak truth to those in power. Action by governments to encourage liberation and economic justice is essential but must be supported by parallel action on the part of private citizens and institutions, including the churches, if peaceful measures are to succeed. Unless oppression and denial of basic human rights are ended, violence on an increasing scale will continue to erupt in many nations and may spread throughout the world. The human toll in such conflicts is enormous, for they result in new oppression and further dehumanization. We are concerned for areas where oppression and discrimination take place. We, as United Methodist Christians, must build the conditions for peace through development of confidence and trust between peoples and governments. We are unalterably opposed to those who instill hate in one group for another. Governments or political factions must not use religious, class, racial, or other differences as the means to achieve heinous political purposes. This concern extends to all situations where external commercial, industrial, and military interests are related to national oligarchies that resist justice and liberation for the masses of people. It is essential that governments which support or condone these activities alter their policies to permit and enable people to achieve genuine self-determination.

## III. The United Nations

International justice requires the participation and determination of all peoples. We are called to look beyond the "limited and competing boundaries of nation-states to the larger and more inclusive community of humanity" (Bishops' Call for Peace and the Self-Development of Peoples).

There has been unprecedented international cooperation through the United Nations and its specialized agencies as they have worked to solve international problems of health, education, and the welfare of people. The United Nations Children's Fund (UNICEF) is one of the agencies that has been successful in this area.

These achievements are to be commended. However, in other areas, political considerations have diminished the support needed for the United Nations to achieve its goals. Many nations, including the most powerful, participate in some programs only when such action does not interfere with their national advantage.

We believe the United Nations and its agencies must be supported, strengthened, and improved. We recommend that Christians work for the following actions in their respective nations:

- The Universal Declaration of Human Rights is a standard of achievement for all peoples and nations. International covenants and conventions that seek to implement the Declaration must be universally ratified.
- Peace and world order require the development of an effective and enforceable framework of international law that provides protection for human rights and guarantees of justice for all people.
- Greater use should be made of the International Court of Justice. Nations should remove any restrictions they have adopted that impair the court's effective functioning.
- The industrialized world must not dominate development agencies. We support efforts to make controlling bodies of such agencies more representative.
- We support the development and strengthening of international agencies designed to help nations or peoples escape from domination by other nations or transnational enterprises.
- Economic and political considerations greatly affect issues of food, energy, raw materials, and other commodities. We support efforts in the United Nations to achieve new levels of justice in the world economic order and work for the realization of the United Nations Millennium Development Goals. [See Res. #6025, "Globalization and Its Impact on Human Rights and Human Dignity."]
- We support the concept of collective action against threats to peace. Wars fought in the search for justice might well be averted or diminished if the nations of the world would work vigorously and in concert to seek changes in oppressive political and economic systems.

## IV. World Trade and Economic Development

The gap between rich and poor countries continues to widen. Human rights are denied when the surpluses of some arise in part as a result of continued deprivation of others. This growing inequity exists in our own communities and in all our nations. Our past efforts to alleviate these conditions have failed. Too often these efforts have been limited by our own unwillingness to act or have been frustrated by private interests and governments striving to protect the wealthy and the powerful.

In order to eliminate inequities in the control and distribution of the common goods of humanity, we are called to join the search for more just and equitable international economic structures and relationships. We seek a society that will assure all persons and nations the opportunity to achieve their maximum potential.

In working toward that purpose, we believe these steps are needed:

- Economic systems structured to cope with the needs of the world's peoples must be conceived and developed.
- Measures that will free peoples and nations from reliance on financial arrangements that place them in economic bondage must be implemented.
- Policies and practices for the exchange of commodities and raw materials that establish just prices and avoid damaging fluctuations in price must be developed.
- Control of international monetary facilities must be more equitably shared by all the nations, including the needy and less powerful.
- Agreements that affirm the common heritage principle (that resources of the seabed, subsoil, outer space, and those outside national jurisdiction are the heritage of humanity) should be accepted by all nations.
- Multilateral, rather than bilateral, assistance programs should be encouraged for secular as well as religious bodies. They must be designed to respond to the growing desire of the "developing world" to become self-reliant.
- Nations that possess less military and economic power than others must be protected, through international agreements, from loss of control of their own resources and means of production to either transnational enterprises or other governments.

These international policies will not narrow the rich-poor gap within nations unless the powerless poor are enabled to take control of their own political and economic destinies. We support people's organizations designed to enable the discovery of local areas of exploitation and development of methods to alleviate these problems.

Economic and political turmoil within many developing nations has been promoted and used by other powers as an excuse to intervene through subversive activities or military force in furtherance of their own national interests. We condemn this version of imperialism that often parades as international responsibility.

We support the United Nations' efforts to develop international law to govern the sea and to ensure that the world's common resources will be used cooperatively and equitably for the welfare of humankind.

We urge the appropriate boards and agencies of The United Methodist Church to continue and expand efforts to bring about justice in cooperative action between peoples of all countries.

## V. Peace Research, Education, and Action

The 1960 General Conference established the landmark study "The Christian Faith and War in the Nuclear Age." That study said, "The Christian Church and the individual must accept responsibility for the creation of a climate of opinion in which creative changes can occur." It called work for these creative alternatives "our mission field as we live as disciples of the Prince of Peace." In a more recent study by the Task Force on Safety and Security on the Council of Bishops, "In Search of Security," they asserted that "fear causes us to accumulate weapons and to devote all too much of our resources to the goal of deterring our supposed enemy. Paradoxically enough, it is the special temptation of the strong and the rich to overreact in this way. This blocks resources that could be used much more creatively for development and social justice around the world." In order to create such a climate of conciliation and compromise, we call upon The United Methodist Church, including its agencies and institutions of higher education, in the light of its historical teachings and its commitment to peace and self-development of peoples, to:

1. seek the establishment of educational institutions devoted to the study of peace;

2. develop alternatives to vocations that work against peace, and support individuals in their quest;

3. explore and apply ways of resolving domestic and international differences that affirm human fulfillment rather than exploitation and violence;

4. affirm and employ methods that build confidence and trust between peoples and countries, including training in multicultural understanding and appreciation of differences, rejecting all promotion of hatred and mistrust;

5. continue to develop and implement the search for peace through educational experiences, including church school classes, schools of Christian mission, and other settings throughout the church; and

6. encourage local churches and members to take actions that make for peace and to act in concert with other peoples and groups of goodwill toward the achievement of a peaceful world.

ADOPTED 1984
AMENDED AND READOPTED 2000
AMENDED AND READOPTED 2008
RESOLUTION #338, 2004 *BOOK OF RESOLUTIONS*
RESOLUTION #318, 2000 *BOOK OF RESOLUTIONS*

*See* Social Principles, ¶ 165*B* and *C*.

## 6095. "Just 1 Day" Ministry of Peace

WHEREAS since the birth of humankind, war and threats of war between nations, religions and ethnic backgrounds have kept the world from knowing a true and lasting peace; and

WHEREAS unfathomable pain, suffering, and grief have come about from the battles humankind has waged throughout history continuing today with humankind having devoted more wealth to weapons of war than any other cause, resulting in parallel pain and suffering from hunger, disease, loss of habitat, and other sins against humanity as well as our environment and wildlife that have no say in our world; and

WHEREAS the fellowship ministry A Circle of Friends, working with other churches around the globe, has set August 22, 2004, for Just 1 Day, 24 hours, of peace requesting that every nation lay down their arms for a period of reflection.

*Be it resolved* by this General Conference that The United Methodist Church supports the initiative brought forth by the ministry of peace at Peoples United Methodist Church and all of its fellowship churches in A Circle of Friends called Just 1 Day and in doing so:

- request that all UM churches support the spirit of Just 1 Day through prayer and active participation, as they see fit, through discussion within each church;
- call upon the leaders of the United States of America and the world to commit to this step toward a permanent world peace;
- invite all faiths and denominations of the world to set forth a common doctrine together with us of peaceful coexistence, understanding of, and respect for each other's beliefs beginning on August 22, 2004.

*Be it further resolved,* that with this vote of support today, The United Methodist Church takes this initiative as an expression of hope for those who live in a world without hope today.

ADOPTED 2004
RESOLUTION #342, 2004 *BOOK OF RESOLUTIONS*

*See* Social Principles ¶ 165B and C.

## 6096. Political and Social Unrest

We, the people of The United Methodist Church, affirm that terrorist activities and harmful radical religious opinions, especially in developing countries, are the consequences of serious social cleavages (i.e. poverty, oppression due to conflict, discrimination, segregation).

Furthermore, we strongly oppose an exclusive religious ideology of any faith that fails to recognize the humanity of all people.

We, the people of The United Methodist Church, agree that within the global community there exist instances where the natural rights of citizens are not upheld. Infringements on these rights as well as instances of political injustice within nations are cause for political unrest and instability. Such events lead to personal and social unrest, leading to violence and war. Whereas the church's stance is to combat violence and war peaceably, it is the responsibility of the church to take action against such infringements and injustices.

ADOPTED 2008

*See* Social Principles, ¶ 165C and D.

## 6097. Young People's Statement on War and Peace

WHEREAS, we believe that war exacts an especially high toll on young people;

*Therefore, let it be resolved,* that we join the young people in calling for the preservation of youth around the world and support the Young People's Statement on War and Peace.

*Young People's Statement on War and Peace*

We are the young people of The United Methodist Church.

We hear God's clear call to be instruments of peace in all corners of the world.

We are among those sent to the front lines of every war, by every nation and organization that chooses to engage in war.

We are among those who pay the price of military action at the expense of our education, our health care, and our security.

We are among those most affected by the insidiousness of war:

- damage to our bodies
- damage to our psyches
- damage to our communities
- damage to our spirits

and yet,

We are among those with the least representation in decision-making bodies around the world.

We strongly support our brothers and sisters who so bravely stand up for our protection, while strongly rejecting the policies that unnecessarily risk their lives and rob them of their youth.

We strongly affirm The United Methodist Church's stance on war and peace, as stated in The Social Principles, ¶ 165, VI, section C.

We empower all young people around the world to actively work for peace within their churches, their communities, and our world.

We are the young people of The United Methodist Church.

We affirm God's clear call to be instruments of peace in all corners of the world.

**ADOPTED 2008**

*See* Social Principles, ¶ 165C.

## 6098. In Defense of International Law and Cooperation: Cornerstone of Multilateralism

"Those who say, 'I love God,' and hate their brothers and sisters, are liars; for those who do not love a brother or sister whom they have seen, cannot love God whom they have not seen. The commandment we have from him is this: those who love God must love their brothers and sisters also" (1 John 4:20-21).

Justice and Law—Persons and groups must feel secure in their life and right to live within a society if order is to be achieved and maintained by law. We denounce as immoral an ordering of life that perpetuates injustice. Nations, too, must feel secure in the world if world community is to become a fact. We commend the efforts of all people in all countries who pursue world peace through law. We endorse international aid and cooperation on all matters of need and conflict . . . Bilateral or multilateral efforts outside of the United Nations should work in concert with, and not contrary to, its purposes. Social Principles, ¶ 165D.

At the beginning of the 21st century, the world is faced with an unprecedented global environmental crisis and a devastated global economy increasingly unequal and exploitative, the pandemic of HIV/AIDS, the spread of weapons of mass destruction, terrorist actions which recognize no borders and gross violations of human rights and humanitarian law. No country can develop solutions to these grave concerns alone. Unfortunately, the United States maintains global military dominance and the right of a preemptive military attack against any country it regards as a current or even a potential future threat.

The USA:

1. devotes more than $1 billion a day to military spending and has the largest number of military bases around the world. The USA has abrogated the Anti-Ballistic Missile (ABM) Treaty and squanders billions in chasing the illusion of national missile defense. It has refused to ratify the Treaty to Ban Landmines;

2. has the largest nuclear arsenal and has undermined the Nuclear Non-Proliferation Treaty and the Comprehensive Test Ban Treaty while expressing support for testing new nuclear weapons and refusing to rule out a nuclear first strike against non nuclear nations;

3. treated human rights as an obstacle to rather than an essential component of civic security at home and abroad. Suspended US support for the UN's family planning programs and balked at supporting the Convention on the Elimination of All Forms of Discrimination

against Women (CEDAW) and the Convention on the Rights of the Child. Walked out on the World Summit against Racism, Racial Discrimination and Xenophobia.

4. withdrew from global efforts to curb global warming thru the Kyoto Protocol on reducing carbon emissions.

5. rejected UN Security Council resolutions supported by previous administrations that provide a framework for conflict resolution containing strict security guarantees for both Israel and the Palestinians.

Therefore, The United Methodist Church urges United Methodists to take seriously the question, "How does God's love abide in anyone who has the world's goods and sees a brother or sister in need and yet refuses to help?" and agree that for the followers of Christ there is but one answer, " . . . let us love, not in word or speech, but in truth and action" (1 John 3:17 and 18).

While this resolution addresses primarily the United States because : of its position of power in the world, we call on United Methodist churches in all countries of the world to work in their own countries and together to advocate for their countries to work in defense of international law and cooperation, through multilateral efforts to be witnesses of God's love for all humanity by promoting the eradication of poverty, sustainable development, justice, human rights, and peace around the world.

We therefore recommend:

1. that The United Methodist Church, including its agencies and institutions of higher education, find ways to implement the resolutions from *The Book of Resolutions of The United Methodist Church:* that

a) encourage local churches and members to take actions that make for peace and to act in concert with other peoples and groups of goodwill toward the achievement of a peaceful world and

b) remind United Methodists that "The indivisibility of human rights underscores the understanding that freedom is hollow without food, that justice without jobs is like a clanging cymbal, and liberty is a sham when people do not have land to inhabit and farm." [From Resolution #6025, "Globalization and Its Impact on Human Dignity and Human Rights"]

2. that United Methodists urge the governments of their countries:

    a. to commit themselves to the fundamental principle of international justice-that no country is above international law;

    b. to increase its commitment to multilateralism including the UN security system, while urging UN action against threats to peace;

    c. to renew efforts to mobilize a global consensus and global action against all forms of terrorism at home and around the world;

    d. to strengthen multilateral, verifiable arms control regimes that aim to curb weapons of mass destruction and their delivery systems, while at the same time promoting nuclear disarmament and international demilitarization. Extend treaties to ban cluster bombs, carbon filament bombs, depleted uranium and herbicides;

    e. to exercise leadership for protection of the environment through the ratification of the Kyoto Protocol and other international environmental agreements while protecting existing multilateral environmental agreements from challenges by free trade agreements;

    f. to increase the Global Fund to fight AIDS, Tuberculosis and Malaria as well as other efforts to respond to the AIDS Pandemic;

    g. to ratify and enforce the new International Criminal Court which judges individuals and groups of individuals who commit crimes against humanity; and

    h. to expand the international human rights regime by ratifying such key international human rights treaties such as the Covenant on Economic, Social and Cultural Rights; the International Labor Organizations core labor rights conventions; the Convention on the Elimination of All Forms of Discrimination Against Women and the Convention on the Rights of the Child.

3. that the General Board of Global Ministries and the General Board of Church and Society, in consultation with each other, develop resources on the concerns described above, including a theological perspective and strategies for advocacy by United Methodists.

4. that United Methodist Churches, in all countries who belong to the G8, work in their own countries and together to advocate for their countries to work in defense of international law and cooperation, through multilateral efforts to be witnesses of God's love for all humanity by promoting the eradication of poverty, sustainable development, justice, human rights and peace around the world.

ADOPTED 2004
REVISED AND READOPTED 2008
RESOLUTION #340, 2004 *BOOK OF RESOLUTIONS*

*See* Social Principles, ¶ 165.

## 6099.  In Support of the United Nations

*Preamble*

The world needs a new vision, a vision of peace rooted in justice, a vision of a world bound together in intentional community dedicated to the well-being of all people and all creation. The United Nations, however limited, represents the best efforts made so far by governments and peoples of the world toward such a vision.

The Christian faith and community are rooted in theological understanding that is global by its very nature. The foundation for the church's involvement in the quest for world peace and justice can be found in the following biblically based beliefs: (1) the transcending sovereignty and love of God for all creation and the expression of that love in the Incarnation of Jesus Christ, whose mission was to reveal understanding about that divine presence, to proclaim a message of salvation, and to bring justice and peace; (2) the unity of creation and the equality of all races and peoples; (3) the dignity and worth of each person as a child of God; and (4) the church, the body of believers, whose global mission of witness, peacemaking, and reconciliation testifies to God's action in history.

The world is the responsibility of each of our communities where the securing of justice for one individual, one community, one nation contributes to the securing of justice and peace for all. To work for justice and peace for all is to affirm God's promise of the fullness of life: "The earth is the Lord's and the fullness thereof" (Psalm 24:1); "I came that they may have life, and have it abundantly" (John 10:10b).

The United Methodist Church, therefore, reaffirms its support for the United Nations and calls upon all governments to fully support the United Nations in the fulfillment of its charter and in its highest calling to work for peace and justice for all the world's people. Furthermore, The United Methodist Church affirms the following principles as *Pillars of Peace for the 21st Century*:

1. *Political Accountability.* Peace rooted in justice requires increased political collaboration and accountability within the United Nations system, and among regional bodies, governments, local authorities, peoples' organizations, and global economic structures to seek the common good and equality for all.

2. *Economic Accountability.* Peace rooted in justice requires increased moral, ethical, and legal accountability at all levels from governments, financial institutions, multilateral organizations, transnational corporations, and all other economic actors to seek a just, participatory, and sustainable economic order for the welfare and well-being of all people and all creation.

3. *Legal Accountability.* Peace rooted in justice requires a comprehensive international legal system, capable of change as conditions require, in order to prevent and resolve conflicts, to protect rights, to hold accountable those who disturb peace and violate international law, and to provide fair and effective review and enforcement mechanisms.

4. *Liberation and Empowerment.* Peace rooted in justice requires the participation of vulnerable and marginalized groups who are seeking to promote justice and peace in those mechanisms capable of redressing the causes and consequences of injustice and oppression.

5. *Peace and Conflict Resolution.* Peace rooted in justice requires the nurturing of a culture of peace in homes, communities, religious institutions, nations, and across the world; the use of nonviolent means of resolving conflict; appropriate systems of common security; and the end of the unrestrained production, sale and use of weapons worldwide.

6. *Human Dignity and Rights.* Peace rooted in justice requires respect for the inherent dignity of all persons and the recognition, protection, and implementation of the principles of the International Bill of Human Rights so that communities and individuals may claim and enjoy their universal, indivisible, and inalienable rights.

7. *Preservation of the Environment.* Peace rooted in justice requires a commitment to long-term sustainability of the means of life, and profound reorientation of economic systems and individual lifestyles to support ecological justice for human communities in harmony with the whole of creation.

### Policy Base

1. NCCC* Policy Statement: "The United Nations and the World Community," adopted May 4, 1977.

2. NCCC Policy Statement: "The National Council of Churches Views Its Task in Christian Life and Work," adopted May 16, 1951.

*National Council of the Churches of Christ in the USA (Web site: http://ncccusa.orc/)

3. NCCC Policy Statement: "Statement on the International Situation," adopted January 17, 1951.

4. Federal Council of Churches Statement: "Six Pillars of Peace," 1943.

ADOPTED 1992
REVISED AND READOPTED 2000
REVISED AND READOPTED 2008
RESOLUTION #326, 2004 *BOOK OF RESOLUTIONS*
RESOLUTION #307, 2000 *BOOK OF RESOLUTIONS*

*See* Social Principles, ¶ 165*A, B, C,* and *D.*

## 6100. Korea: Peace, Justice, and Reunification

Christians in Korea have spoken about the urgency of the reunification of their nation. Celebrating one hundred years of Korean Methodism in 1985, the Korean Methodist Church, in its Centennial Statement, said:

"Faced as we are with the forty years' tragic division of the Korean peninsula, we express our longing for unification of the nation in any form possible through peaceful means in the earliest possible time. This must be done through establishing a democratic political structure based upon freedom and human rights, and must be fulfilled by working toward the establishment of a just society built for the sake of the people. Therefore, we reject any form whatever of dictatorship. Deploring the long history of our nation in which the reality has been the sacrifice of our country's political life, and now with a definite sense of national self-determination which rejects any domination by the superpowers, we disavow any form of war or the taking of life, and commit the whole strength of the Korean Methodist Church to the peaceful reunification of our country."

For the nation of Korea, divided for more than fifty years, justice, peace, and reconciliation are tragically overdue. In 1945 just before the end of World War II, the United States proposed and the Soviet Union agreed to the division of Korea. The division was to have been temporary to facilitate the surrender of Japanese troops in Korea. More than four decades later the country is still divided into the Republic of Korea (ROK) and the Democratic Peoples Republic of Korea (DPRK). The enmity between the superpowers has been played out in the Korean tragedy of war and death, dictatorship and militarization, separation of one people into two hostile camps and divided families with no contact at all. All members of the body of Christ, but especially Christians in the United States, have a special responsibility to support the Korean people in their attempts to build democracy, reduce tension, create trust on the Korean peninsula, heal the divisions, and reunite their country. The threat to peace remains critical with the world's fifth and sixth largest armies facing each other across the Demilitarized Zone.

In many ways, the Korean people, north and south, have expressed their strong desire for reunification. Since 1984, there have been official contacts and conversations on economic and humanitarian issues between ROK and DPRK. Emergency assistance by the DPRK and the ROK following devastating floods in the south and floods and drought in the north was offered and accepted by each other. The first government-sponsored exchange of visits between divided family members occurred in 1985. Thousands of overseas Koreans were able to visit their family members in the DPRK. Christians from north and south met in 1986 in Glion, Switzerland, as part of an ecumenical process on peace and the reunification of Korea led by the World Council of Churches. In 1987, both sides offered proposals to lower military tensions on the peninsula. In June 2000, an unprecedented historic summit between North and South Korean leaders took place in Pyongyang, DPRK. President Kim Dae Jung and Chairman Kim Jong Il pledged themselves to work toward Korean reunification. Since the summit, both Koreas have had numerous exchanges such as reunions of separated families, ministerial level talks, and other economic, social, cultural, and sports exchanges including reconnection of railways and roads through the Demilitarized Zone.

The relationship between the United States and the DPRK, however, has deteriorated due to the issues related to the DPRK's violation of nuclear proliferation since 2001. It has turned out that both signatories of the 1994 Agreed Framework have violated the mandates of the agreement. It is most desirable that the United States and the DPRK, through direct negotiations, redraft or update the 1994 Agreement encompassing all vital matters of interest to both sides including DPRK's nuclear proliferation issues and US recognition of the sovereignty and security of the DPRK.

In 1991, the Agreement on Cooperation of Non-aggression and Exchange was adopted; and in 1992, a Non-nuclearization of the Peninsula was signed by both sides. In 1994, the United States and

DPRK signed the Agreed Framework in reference to the DPRK nuclear programs and bilateral US-DPRK issues. The agreement stipulated that funds would be provided to the DPRK from the United States, Japan, and the Republic of Korea (South Korea) for the construction of two light-water electric power reactors. In addition, the US agreed to provide 500,000 tons of heavy oil annually to the DPRK. In return, the DPRK agreed to forego any further accumulation of fuel rods which could be used to produce atomic bombs. The Agreed Framework remains an important stabilizing element in the US-DPRK relations. It is one of the key tools of engagement by which DPRK uses incentives rather than threats to build inter-Korean and regional cooperation.

In 1986, as a result of consultations in Korea, north and south, with Christians and government representatives, the National Council of the Churches of Christ in the USA (NCCCUSA) adopted an important policy statement on "Peace and the Reunification of Korea." United Methodist representatives participated fully in the development of this statement, in consultations on peace and reunification, and in an official ecumenical delegation to North and South Korea in the summer of 1987.

In support of the Korean people and in cooperation with partner Christian groups, it is recommended that The United Methodist Church, its members, local churches, annual conferences, and agencies undertake the following actions through intercession, education, public advocacy, and support of programs furthering justice, peace, and reconciliation:

1. Engage in prayer of penitence and petition with the Korean people and with Christians in the north and south, scarred and pained by the division of their nation and yearning for reunion, and support the efforts of the Korean Methodist Church, the National Council of Churches of Korea (ROK), and the Korean Christian Federation (DPRK) to seek peace and reconciliation.

2. Commend the policy statement on "Peace and the Reunification of Korea" of the National Council of the Churches of Christ in the USA (NCCCUSA), November 1986, to annual conferences and local churches for study and action. The policy statement affirms the desire of the Korean people for restoration of national unity and reunion of separated families, traces the history of division and hopeful steps toward change, and outlines Recommendations for Advocacy and Action in the areas of "Healing and Reconciliation," "Peace With

Justice," and "New Directions for US Policy." Recommendations 3, 4, and 5, which follow, are in line with the policy statement.

3. Participate in the ecumenical effort of the World Council of Churches (WCC) and NCCCUSA to facilitate the reunion of separated Korean families, including Korean residents in the US and their family members in the DPRK;

4. Urge all governments that have relations with the ROK or the DPRK, or both, to exercise their influence to further mediation, interchange, peace, and reunification.

5. Urge all governments involved to forthright commitment to the following policy directions in support of Korean efforts for peace and reunification:

   a. The peaceful reunification of Korea should be a formal US policy goal.
   b. A peace treaty should be signed among the nations involved to eliminate the threat of war, establish an enduring peace, and minimize tension in the Korean peninsula. The Peace treaty, replacing the existing armistice treaty, should be based on the conditions of a Non-aggression Pact between the Republic of Korea and the Democratic People's Republic of Korea, with the full participation of the United States and the People's Republic of China, as well as other related countries.
   c. ROK and DPRK contacts should be encouraged;
   d. Bilateral diplomatic and human contacts between the United States and the DPRK should be enhanced.
   e. The US should negotiate to end the war and to seek a comprehensive peace settlement in Korea.

6. Continue to provide humanitarian aid to the DPRK through the World Food Program (WFP). This aid is directed to those persons most at risk, and is monitored carefully. The WFP has developed productive working relationships with its DPRK counterparts and continues to push for more open access to the food distribution process.

7. Increase communication with the DPRK. Since 1986, the General Board of Global Ministries, in cooperation with the NCCCUSA, has been exchanging delegations with the ROK and DPRK for dialogue and support. Political, economic, social, and religious delegations are a high priority with the DPRK leadership. They provide Korean middle management with experience outside their country and a greater perspective regarding the situation between Korea and the rest of the developed world. Delegations from the DPRK can also be matched with exchange delegations to the DPRK which allows US residents

and others to see and understand what the country is like, share ideas, and have personal contact with Korean people.

8. Remove economic sanctions against the DPRK. Sanctions limit the engagement of the DPRK with the global market economy. Removing sanctions will also facilitate foreign investment in improving the DPRK production infrastructure. Because of economic and legal obstacles, development of foreign investment will be a difficult and long-term process, even without sanctions. Removing sanctions is a high priority with the DPRK leadership.

9. Continue to redraft or update policies to comply with the Agreed Framework, of which the most positive element is the US-DPRK relations, by supplying heavy fuel oil and supporting the ROK and Japanese financing for the Korea Peninsula Energy Development Office (KEDO) light-water reactors.

10. Encourage a consistent, bipartisan, and long-range US policy formulation regarding both North and South Korea. Policies that engage the ROK and DPRK governments effectively and promote change and moderation will stand a greater chance of resolving the present crisis and bringing the DPRK into the world community.

11. Urge the United Nations to look into the North Korean refugee situations arising from political and economic needs, as thousands of North Koreans are crossing the border seeking asylum in the neighboring countries. The United Nations should declare them refugees, assist them as they seek asylum and, also, provide humanitarian assistance.

When these approaches can be taken, and most of them depend on US government policy decisions, there are still no guarantees that the crisis can be resolved. But it is quite clear that a US policy of isolation, sanctions and military buildup directed against the DPRK will stimulate North Korea to rely more on its military, even at the expense of the lives of its population, and may lead to another catastrophic war on the Korean peninsula. Continued engagement, steadfast negotiation, and careful cultivation of cooperative relationships with the appropriate DPRK organizations provide the only real opportunity for a positive resolution of the Korean stalemate.

ADOPTED 1988
AMENDED AND ADOPTED 2000
AMENDED AND READOPTED 2004
READOPTED 2008
RESOLUTION #328, 2004 *BOOK OF RESOLUTIONS*
RESOLUTION #309, 2000 *BOOK OF RESOLUTIONS*

*See* Social Principles, ¶ 165B and C.

## 6101. Prayer for Military Personnel and for Peace in Iraq

The prophet Micah reminds us that God calls nations to "beat their swords into plowshares, and their spears into pruning hooks," and that nations will no longer "lift up sword against nation, and neither shall they learn war anymore" (Micah 4:3).

The war in Iraq must end. It is a tragedy that wounds the heart of God. Thousands of lives have been lost, millions of Iraqis have fled their country, and hundreds of billions of dollars wasted in a war the United States initiated and never should have fought.

A bipartisan US commission appointed by President Bush chaired by former Governor Tom Keane and former Representative Lee Hamilton established that:

- No weapons of mass destruction were stored in Iraq;
- There was no attempt on the part of the government of Saddam Hussein to purchase uranium from the nation of Niger;
- There were no ties between Saddam Hussein and the events of September 11, 2001;
- There were no ties between Saddam Hussein and al Qaeda.

As people of Jesus Christ, the Prince of Peace, we pray for peace, stability and freedom in Iraq. We believe the Iraqi people can and should ultimately determine how these will be achieved. It is time for the United States to end the conflict and withdraw US troops, to discontinue waging war, and to seek a peaceful political solution in concert with the international community.

In recognition of the Church's responsibility to work for peace, The General Conference of The United Methodist Church calls upon the US government to:

1. end the cycle of violence in Iraq by developing and implementing a plan for the immediate and safe withdrawal of US and partner coalition troops from the country;

2. work with Iraqis of good will, the United Nations, and nations in the Middle East to bring about a peaceful, long-term resolution to the conflict and rebuild Iraq;

3. commit US funds for the rebuilding of Iraq through a plan that ensures the participation of the Iraqis and gives them hope for their future;

4. provide adequate funding for US military personnel returning from Iraq and their families.

We urge United Methodists throughout the world to pray for an immediate end to the war in Iraq and to speak out for public policies that promote peace, justice, and reconciliation.

ADOPTED 2008
RESOLUTION #337, 2004 *BOOK OF RESOLUTIONS*

*See* Social Principles, ¶ 165B and C.

## WAR AND THE MILITARY

### 6111. War and Peace with Iran, North Korea, and the World

Consistent with the Social Principles, ¶¶ 165 B and C of *The Book of Discipline*, the General Conference of The United Methodist Church has clearly stated in Resolution 6094, "The United Methodist Church and Peace" (adopted 1984, amended and readopted in 2000) the meaning of peace and strategies to achieve it. This resolution calls for abolishing all nuclear weapons and cannot justify seeking a nuclear deterrence as a means of achieving peace. It calls on all governments to renounce the use of chemical or biological weapons. Peacemaking and peacekeeping are of the highest priorities. Resolution 6121, "Rejection of Unilateral First-Strike Actions and Strategies" (adopted 2004) states:

"The United Methodist Church strongly protests all unilateral first-strike actions and strategies on the part of any government or military force and calls on the President and Congress of the United States to cease and desist from such actions without ratification by, and collaboration with, the United Nations."

The Constitution of the United States of America outlines specific responsibilities for Congress and the President in declaring war.

*Therefore, be it resolved*, that the 2008 General Conference of The United Methodist Church calls upon the President, Vice President, Secretary of State, Secretary of Defense, and members of the US Senate and House of Representatives to immediately work with all deliberate speed toward peaceful resolution of issues with Iran, North Korea, countries and peoples of the Middle East, and the rest of the world, and to reject any first-strike actions by the US armed forces anywhere. Any US action must only follow full disclosure during open debate in both houses of Congress with formal, recorded votes before any deliberate military action is taken. The General Conference requests the General Board of Church and Society of The United Methodist Church to pursue these peacemaking strategies, with particular focus on Iran and North Korea.

**ADOPTED 2008**

See Social Principles, ¶ 165C.

### 6112. Support and Services for US Military and Rebuilding Iraq

WHEREAS, The United Methodist Church teaches that: "We believe that war is incompatible with the teachings and example of Christ" (¶ 165C); and

WHEREAS, The United Methodist Church also teaches that: "We honor the witness of pacifists who will not allow us to become complacent about war and violence. We also respect those who support the use of force, but only in extreme situations and only when the need is clear beyond reasonable doubt, and through appropriate international organizations" (¶ 164I); and

WHEREAS, The United Methodist Church has expressed its concern about the war in Iraq by stating: "by attacking Iraq without the approval and participation of the United Nations, the United States has squandered its positive reputation as a responsible member of the global community . . ." (page 850 of the 2004 *Book of Resolutions*);

*Therefore, be it resolved,* that The United Methodist Church affirms its commitment to uphold in prayer all military personnel, their families, and all the people of Iraq, even as we pray and work for a speedy and just resolution of the war in Iraq; and

*Be it further resolved,* that we express our respect and prayers for all who choose to serve in the military and for those who, for reason of conscience, seek to separate from the military, and for those who refuse to serve in the war in Iraq while retaining their place in the military; and

*Be it further resolved,* that we call upon the government of the United States and its partners in the Iraq war to provide full support and services for as long as needed for returning veterans, especially for those wounded in body and spirit by their experiences in the war. Such support should include medical treatment, appropriate counseling, training for employment, and a generous pension for those who are not able to provide a living for themselves and their families; and

*Be it further resolved,* that we call upon the United States and its partners in the war in Iraq, in cooperation with the other willing nations, to provide the resources for rebuilding the infrastructure of Iraq, especially the medical system, so that the citizens of Iraq who were injured or damaged in the war will receive the full support and services needed to resume their lives; and

*Finally, be it resolved,* that the Secretary of the General Conference send a copy of this resolution to the President of the United States, to the Vice President, to the Secretary of State, to the Secretary of Defense, and to the leadership of both houses of Congress.

ADOPTED 2008

See Social Principles, ¶ 165.

## 6113. Okinawa: Removal or Reduction of US Military Bases

*Be it resolved,* that the 2004 General Conference support the strong and unceasing efforts of the Okinawan government and its people to achieve the complete removal or substantial reduction of US military bases and US military personnel on the island of Okinawa and other islands in Okinawa Prefecture of Japan, and the return of those lands for peaceful, constructive purposes; and that a copy of this petition be sent to the President of the United States, the US secretary of state, and the US secretary of defense for consideration and action, and that a copy be sent to the governor of Okinawa and the prime minister of Japan for their information.

ADOPTED 1996
AMENDED AND READOPTED 2004
READOPTED 2008
RESOLUTION #330, 2004 *BOOK OF RESOLUTIONS*
RESOLUTION #311, 2000 *BOOK OF RESOLUTIONS*

See Social Principles, ¶ 165B and C.

## 6114. Reduction of US Military Personnel in Okinawa

In recognition of the great investment that The United Methodist Church has made in the mission of the Church in Okinawa (Japan) since the turn of the century, with the arrival of the first Methodist missionary, this resolution is presented to request the support of United Methodist congregations for one of the urgent issues in mission of the Okinawa District of The United Church of Christ in Japan, the Christian body with which The United Methodist Church has a cooperative mission relationship.

In accordance with the US-Japan Mutual Security Treaty, which grants the US use of facilities and areas in Japan, the United States military forces occupy a substantial amount of the land area of Okinawa Island, in addition to having exclusive use of designated air and sea space for military training. This vast military presence greatly hinders the development of Okinawa and threatens the livelihood of Okinawan citizens.

Even after Allied occupation ended on the Japanese mainland in 1952, Okinawa remained under complete US military administration for twenty years, until 1972, when the islands reverted to Japanese jurisdiction

Private property requisitioned by the US military to construct the vast military bases after the war is still held today, denying some 30,000 families the right to live on and utilize their own land. Military aircraft produce ear-splitting noise on a daily basis. Military drills endanger the lives of citizens and destroy the natural environment.

Since 1972, the date of Okinawa's reversion to Japan, US military personnel have committed thousands of crimes. These crimes, which include robbery, murder, and rape, imperil the fundamental human rights of the Okinawan people.

The September 4, 1995, rape of an elementary school girl by three American military personnel and the June 29, 2001, rape of another young woman are not extraordinary cases. Such structural violence is inherent in the enforced "presence of military bases and armed forces which create environment for such incidents" (Okinawa District's July 8, 2001, Statement in Protest Against Rape Incident). The residents of Okinawa living around the bases become the primary targets of this violence, with women and children being especially vulnerable.

This latest rape is only the spark igniting the Okinawans' anger over this and past crimes perpetuated upon them by the US military. In its July 8, 2001, statement, the Okinawa District of the United Church of Christ in Japan demanded "1) apology, mental and physical care, and compensation to the victim, and 2) removal of military bases from Okinawa in order to establish sovereignty and to protect dignity of Okinawan people."

The Okinawa District considers militarization to be an issue that the church is called on to address in its mission of peacemaking.

In light of the above, this resolution requests the General Conference of The United Methodist Church to join with Okinawan Christians in urging the following four appeals to the governments of the United States and Japan:

1. a thorough investigation of all crimes and acts of violence committed by US military personnel stationed on US military bases in Okinawa, and an apology and compensation to the victims of the crimes;

2. an immediate cessation of all military exercises that destroy the environment and threaten the daily life of Okinawans;

3. an immediate review of the US-Japan Mutual Security Treaty (AMPO) which completely ignores the laws of Japan, imposing great hardship on the people of Okinawa; and

4. establishment of a peace not based on military power, and the removal of all US bases from Okinawa.

*Therefore, be it resolved,* that the 2004 General Conference support the prefectural government of Okinawa and the vast majority of the Okinawan people in their strong, unceasing efforts to achieve the complete removal or substantial reduction of US military bases and US military personnel on the island of Okinawa and other islands in Okinawa Prefecture of Japan, and the return of those lands for peaceful, constructive purposes; and that a copy of this petition be sent to the President of the United States, the US Secretary of State, and the US Secretary of Defense for consideration and action, as well as to the Governor of Okinawa and the Prime Minister of Japan for their information.

**ADOPTED 2004**
**READOPTED 2008**
**RESOLUTION #331, 2004** *BOOK OF RESOLUTIONS*

*See* Social Principles ¶ 165B and C.

## 6115.  Rape in Times of Conflict and War

*Their infants will be dashed to pieces*
*before their eyes;*
*their houses will be plundered,*
*and their wives ravished* (Isaiah 13:16).

*Women are raped in Zion,*
*virgins in the towns of Judah* (Lamentations 5:11).

*For I will gather all the nations against Jerusalem to battle, and the city shall be*
*taken and the houses looted and the women raped; half the city shall go into exile,*
*but the rest of the people shall not be cut off from the city* (Zechariah 14:2).

"We believe war is incompatible with the teachings and example of Christ. We therefore reject war as an instrument of national foreign policy, to be employed only as a last resort in the prevention of such evils as genocide, brutal suppression of human rights, and unprovoked international aggression. We insist that the first moral duty of all nations is to resolve by peaceful means every dispute that rises between or among them; that human values must outweigh military claims as governments determine their priorities; that the militarization of society must be challenged and stopped; that the manufacture, sale, and deployment of armaments must be reduced and controlled; and that the production, possession, or use of nuclear weapons be condemned" (Social Principles, ¶ 165C).

For centuries, women have been raped as an act of violence and a demonstration of power—most especially in times of conflict and wars. Rape has been and is sanctioned by military organizations for the gratification of soldiers as was seen in several Asian countries during World War II. The comfort women from Korea (some 80%) and from China, Taiwan, Malaysia, Burma, Indonesia, East Timor, the Philippines and the Pacific Islands are a most blatant example of this practice. Rape during wartime constitutes many individual and group acts of violence perpetrated by soldiers against girls and women of enemy countries or opposing sides, often under orders. Thus rape, in effect, is used as an extension of warfare. But rape is rarely mentioned in resolutions and statements on war and peace. And the conquest of women as spoils of war continues to be tolerated in times of conflict.

Mass rape is an increasingly sophisticated weapon of war, used in the Bosnia-Herzegovina conflict and in other conflicts—such as Haiti, Georgia (CIS), Rwanda, and in other parts of the world today.

Survivors of conflicts speak of rape on the frontline and third-party rape; these rapes are carried out publicly by soldiers to demoralize family members and opposition forces compelled to witness them.

Many stories refer to village communities being rounded up in camps—perhaps a school or community center—where a space is cleared in the middle. It is in this space that public raping takes place. It is reported as repeated and violent and procedural. It is claimed that many of the victims and witnesses know the rapists.

Destruction and violation of women is one way of attacking male opponents who regard the women as their property—and whose male identity is therefore bound to protection of their property.

The United Methodist Church affirms the sacredness of all persons and their right to safety, nurture, and care. And, together with the international community, it is challenged to respond to the rape of women in military conflicts. The extent and frequency of the violation of women in war must not be allowed to deaden sensitivity to this as gross injustice. There must be greater understanding of the use of rape in this manner (as a weapon of warfare). Documentation and analysis of such planned violation of human rights and its root causes must be developed. Strategizing to confront systems that give rise to it and the needs of those who are its victims must be undertaken.

International instruments such as The Hague Conventions and the Geneva Conventions included prohibitions on rape and sexual violence but these crimes were not codified in their charters. And while, evidence on sexual violence was presented at the International Military Tribunals after World War II, the crime did not get singled out but was included in the accusations of Crimes Against Humanity-Inhumane Treatment. Not until the International Criminal Tribunals for the Former Yugoslavia and for Rwanda did the crimes of sexual violence become recognized and prosecuted. In February 2001, in the Hague, three Bosnian Serbs were convicted of rape and sexual enslavement of Muslim women and girls. This was the first time in history that defendants had been condemned exclusively for sexual violence. In addition the judges asserted that the rape was used as an "instrument of terror" and as a "systematic attack "on the Muslim populations. The judgment declared rape as a crime against humanity.

"... crimes against international law are committed by men, not by abstract entities, and only by punishing individuals who commit such crimes can the provisions of international law be enforced." The Judgment of the Nuremberg Tribunal

In 2002, the International Criminal Court was established in The Hague. Unlike the International Court of Justice (also in the Hague) which handles issues between states, the

International Criminal Court deals with individual responsibility for acts of genocide and egregious violations of human rights, crimes against humanity. No longer will there be the need for setting up International Criminal Tribunals. The Treaty setting up the Court has been ratified by more that 90 Countries and represents an international community which will no longer tolerate genocide, ethnic cleansing, murder, rape and brutalization of civilians trapped in military conflicts.

*We call on The United Methodist Church:*

1. to condemn all forms of rape as incompatible with the church's understanding of the sacredness of life; and to affirm the right of all persons to safety, nurture, and care;

2. to urge United Methodists to work towards the ratification by their country of the Treaty establishing the International Criminal Court;

3. to urge the General Board of Global Ministries to develop an anthology of theological and biblical perspectives of rape in times of war, written by survivors and other women who have observed and reflected on this grave concern;

4. to urge both the General Board of Global Ministries and the General Board of Church and Society to act as resources for churches who wish to pressure for legal and political redress for victims of rape in times of war; and

5. to urge the United Methodist Committee on Relief to continue developing assistance and support for women victims of war and their families, to meet their physical and emotional needs. This may mean supporting, as wartime refugees, women who cannot return to their homes because of fear of rape, violence, and condemnation.

ADOPTED 1996
AMENDED AND READOPTED 2004
READOPTED 2008
RESOLUTION #333, 2004 *BOOK OF RESOLUTIONS*
RESOLUTION #314, 2000 *BOOK OF RESOLUTIONS*

*See* Social Principles, ¶ 165.

## 6116. Nuclear-Free Pacific

In 1986, after nearly two years of prayerful study, the United Methodist bishops adopted a pastoral letter, entitled *In Defense of Creation: The Nuclear Crisis and a Just Peace*. The bishops' statement was deeply rooted in biblical faith. They wrote:

"At the heart of the Old Testament is the testimony to *shalom*, that marvelous Hebrew word that means peace. But peace that is *shalom* is not negative or one-dimensional. It is much more than the absence of war. *Shalom* is positive peace: harmony, wholeness, health, and well-being in all human relationships. It is the natural state of humanity as birthed by God. It is harmony between humanity and all of God's good creation. All creation is interrelated. Every creature, every element, every force of nature participates in the whole of creation. If any person is denied *shalom*, all are thereby diminished. . . . New Testament faith presupposes a radical break between the follies, or much so-called conventional wisdom about power and security, on the one hand, and the transcendent wisdom of *shalom*, on the other. Ultimately, New Testament faith is a message of hope about God's plan and purpose for human destiny. It is a redemptive vision that refuses to wallow in doom."

Based upon this faith, the bishops in their letter stated unequivocally that "we say a clear and unconditioned No to nuclear war and to any use of nuclear weapons. We conclude that nuclear deterrence is a position that cannot receive the church's blessing."

We, The United Methodist Church, in solidarity with the Pacific Conference of Churches, affirm our commitment to a nuclear-free Pacific. As Christian people committed to stewardship, justice, and peacemaking, we oppose and condemn the use of the Pacific for development, testing, storage, and transport of nuclear weapons and weapons-delivery systems and the disposal of radioactive wastes. We further affirm the right of all indigenous people to control their health and well-being.

ADOPTED 2008
RESOLUTION #329, 2004 *BOOK OF RESOLUTIONS*
RESOLUTION #310, 2000 *BOOK OF RESOLUTIONS*

*See* Social Principles, ¶ 165B and C.

## 6117. Saying No to Nuclear Deterrence

In 1986, the United Methodist Council of Bishops, after nearly two years of prayerful and penitent study, adopted a pastoral letter and foundation document entitled *In Defense of Creation: The Nuclear Crisis and a Just Peace.*[1]

The bishops' statement was deeply rooted in biblical faith. They wrote:

> At the heart of the Old Testament is the testimony of shalom, that marvelous Hebrew word that means peace. But the peace that is shalom is not negative or one dimensional. It is much more than the absence of war. Shalom is positive peace: harmony, wholeness, health, and well-being in all human relationships. It is the natural state of humanity as birthed by God. It is harmony between humanity and all of God's good creation. All of creation is interrelated. Every creature, every element, every force of nature participates in the whole of creation. If any person is denied shalom, all are thereby diminished. . . .[2] New Testament faith presupposes a radical break between the follies, or much so-called conventional wisdom about power and security, on the one hand, and the transcendent wisdom of shalom, on the other. Ultimately, New Testament faith is a message of hope about God's plan and purpose for human destiny. It is a redemptive vision that refuses to wallow in doom.[3]

Based upon this faith, the bishops in their pastoral letter stated unequivocally that "we say a clear and unconditional *No* to nuclear war and to any use of nuclear weapons. We conclude that nuclear deterrence is a position that cannot receive the church's blessing."[4]

The implication is clear. If nuclear weapons cannot be legitimately used for either deterrence or war fighting, no nation should possess them. Accordingly, in the foundation document the bishops indicated:

> We support the earliest possible negotiation of phased but rapid reduction of nuclear arsenals, while calling upon all other nuclear-weapon states to agree to parallel arms reductions, to the eventual goal of a mutual and verifiable dismantling of all nuclear armaments.[5]

In 1988, the United Methodist General Conference affirmed and supported the statements of the Council of Bishops contained in *In Defense of Creation.*[6] Four years later, in a resolution entitled "Nuclear

---

1. *In Defense of Creation: The Nuclear Crisis and a Just Peace,* the United Methodist Council of Bishops (Nashville: Graded Press, 1986).
2. Ibid., page 24.
3. Ibid., page 28.
4. Ibid., page 92.
5. Ibid., page 76
6. *The Book of Resolutions of The United Methodist Church, 1988,* page 503.

Disarmament: The Zero Option," the 1992 General Conference stated that "now is the time to exercise the zero option: to eliminate all nuclear weapons throughout the globe,"[7] and the conference offered a series of concrete actions for achieving this goal.

## Our Commitment

We reaffirm the finding that nuclear weapons, whether used or threatened, are grossly evil and morally wrong. As an instrument of mass destruction, nuclear weapons slaughter the innocent and ravage the environment. When used as instruments of deterrence, nuclear weapons hold innocent people hostage for political and military purposes. Therefore, the doctrine of nuclear deterrence is morally corrupt and spiritually bankrupt.

In contrast to the goal of total nuclear disarmament, policy of the United States government has moved in the opposite direction in recent years. A series of policy documents—"Nuclear Posture Review" (January 2002), "National Security Strategy" (September 2002), "National Security Presidential Directive 17" (September 2002), and "National Strategy to Combat Weapons of Mass Destruction" (December 2002)—have called for the development of new nuclear weapons, preparation for renewal of nuclear testing, targeting nonnuclear states with nuclear weapons, and using nuclear weapons in response to biological and chemical weapons. Policy statements have asserted the right to take unilateral, preemptive action, including the use of nuclear weapons, against emerging threats by states and terrorist groups before they are fully formed.

These policies undermine the intent of the Nuclear Non-Proliferation Treaty and increase the risk that nuclear weapons will actually be used. We deplore these dangerous and retrogressive policies.

Therefore, we reaffirm the goal of total abolition of all nuclear weapons throughout Earth and space.

## Recommended Actions

Because we unequivocally reject the use or threatened use of nuclear weapons, we call upon all possessors of nuclear weapons to carry out the following actions as soon as possible:

7. Ibid., page 601.

1. renounce unconditionally the use of nuclear weapons for deterrence and war-fighting purposes;

2. pledge never to use nuclear weapons against any adversary under any circumstance;

3. immediately take all nuclear weapons off alert by separating warheads from delivery vehicles and by other means;

4. embark upon a program to systematically dismantle all nuclear warheads and delivery vehicles as soon as possible with adequate safeguards and verification, carried out under multilateral treaties and through reciprocal national initiatives;

5. ratify and implement the Comprehensive Test Ban Treaty;

6. cease all research, development, testing, production, and deployment of new nuclear weapons and refrain from modernizing the existing nuclear arsenal;

7. halt all efforts to develop and deploy strategic antimissile defense systems because they are illusory, unnecessary, and wasteful;

8. respect the requirements of nuclear weapon-free zones where they exist;

9. enter into a multilateral process to develop, adopt, and carry out a nuclear weapons convention that outlaws and abolishes all nuclear weapons under strict and effective international control; and

10. develop and implement a system for control of all fissile material with international accounting, monitoring, and safeguards.

*We call upon all nations that do not possess nuclear weapons to:*

1. cease all efforts to develop these instruments of mass destruction and their delivery systems;

2. ratify and carry out the provisions of the Comprehensive Test Ban Treaty;

3. adhere to all provisions of the Non-Proliferation Treaty; and

4. respect the requirements of nuclear weapon-free zones and extend this approach to other nations and continents.

*Implementation*

To promote the achievement of goals and objectives specified in this resolution:

1. We ask the Council of Bishops to transmit a copy of the resolution to the heads of state of all nations possessing nuclear weapons.

2. We ask the General Board of Church and Society to publicize the resolution with appropriate governmental officials, legislators, the media, and the general public.

3. We call upon the Council of Bishops and the General Board of Church and Society to provide leadership, guidance, and educational material to United Methodists, congregations, and conferences in order to assist them in understanding and working for the goal and objectives of nuclear abolition.

4. We request that the General Board of Church and Society prepare an annual "report card" to be included with Peace With Justice Sunday materials in relation to: a) countries that possess nuclear weapons and their compliance with the recommended actions in this resolution, and b) countries that do not posses nuclear weapons and their compliance with the recommended actions in this resolution.

### Conclusion

We fervently believe that these recommendations will greatly enhance global security by eliminating the possibility of nuclear war. Furthermore, the resources of human talent, production capacity, and money released can become available to deal with urgent human problems around the globe. Nuclear abolition provides great hope for global peace and prosperity.

ADOPTED 1996
AMENDED AND READOPTED 2000
AMENDED AND READOPTED 2004
RESOLUTION #334, 2004 *BOOK OF RESOLUTIONS*
RESOLUTION #315, 2000 *BOOK OF RESOLUTIONS*

*See* Social Principles, ¶ 164C.

### 6118. Plan to Eliminate Terrorism

Biblical visions of a new heaven and a new earth speak of a time when there will be no more death and suffering (Revelation 21) and of a time when swords shall be turned into plowshares and none shall be afraid (Micah 4:3-5). Toward this end, all biblically based codes of ethics, beginning with the Ten Commandments, prohibit the killing of others.

Horrific terrorist attacks of recent years have caused fear and desperation among many people around the world, contributing to feelings of hopelessness and powerlessness. During the past four decades, many nations have suffered acts of terror perpetrated by diverse political and religious groups. In the past several years, however, this tragic global phenomenon has assumed an even greater prominence, and debates over "fighting terrorism" have taken on broader and more varied meanings.

The September 11, 2001 attacks in the United States perpetrated by the al-Qaeda terrorist network that killed more than 3,000 persons from at least 78 countries were a terrible watershed in the world's experience with international terrorism. The attacks galvanized a strong response from the United Nations and the international community, which joined together to fight terrorism through enhanced law enforcement, diplomatic and intelligence cooperation, and actions to restrict terrorist financing. Despite such cooperation, however, thousands of additional persons have been killed since September 11 by acts of terror in the Middle East, Southeast Asia, South Asia, North Africa, East Africa, and Europe; and the threat of other catastrophic attacks continues to challenge governments and societies around the world.

Global terrorism reminds us of how fragile our global community is and points up the continuing weaknesses in the international system. As God's children, all of us are united in an increasingly interdependent world linked in myriad ways, both good and harmful.

The church has a prophetic message to proclaim in what some have called an age of global terror. The image of God and the sacrifice of Christ bestow a worth and dignity on each human being that cannot be rightfully ignored or violated by any human institution or social movement. For this reason, we condemn all acts of terrorism, with no exception for the target or the source.

There is no significant difference between "state terrorism," as the disproportionate response of a state, and group terrorism, whether in the international arena or on the home front. The killing of innocent persons in horrific bombings, hijackings and other malicious acts of violence cannot be justified by any political or other objective.

Working to prevent further acts of terror clearly is a central responsibility of governments and the international community. Unilateral and preemptive actions and policies of nations including the "doctrine of preemption" and the US invasion of Iraq, are disproportionate, deeply disturbing and counter-productive, as they undermine the international cooperation that is key to preventing further terrorist attacks.

WHEREAS,

We are equally concerned about repressive governments that brand those who oppose them as "terrorists;" this label should not be an excuse to justify government oppression or to support colonial or repressive rule.

*Therefore,* The United Methodist Church:

1. stands against acts of terror of all kinds and condemns them unequivocally;

2. urges all world leaders to repudiate violence and the killing and victimizing of innocent people;

3. pledges to examine critically the causes of terrorism and affirm the primacy of international cooperation to confront terrorism effectively;

4. firmly supports the United Nations as an agency for conflict resolution, as a viable alternative to resorting to war or terrorism, and as an effective body to promote cooperation against terrorism, through the Security Council and its Counter-Terrorism Committee;

5. urges support of United Nations Security Council Resolution 1373 and other UN resolutions that urge greater international cooperation to prevent acts of terror, and commends the cooperation of many nations to take steps to halt financing for terrorist organizations, to prevent movement of terrorists across borders, and to take other steps to help prevent further destruction by terrorists;

6. commends the hard work and dedication of persons across the globe who engage in appropriate law enforcement actions, consistent with internationally recognized human rights standards and due process, to prevent further acts of terror;

7. opposes the use of indiscriminate military force to combat terrorism, especially where the use of such force results in casualties among noncombatant persons who are not themselves perpetrators of acts of terror;

8. calls for tolerance toward and dialogue with Muslims to prevent the "war on terrorism" and actions against al-Qaeda from poisoning relations between Christians and Muslims;

9. urges that concerns about acts of terror not be used to impose discriminatory restrictions on immigration and freedom of movement among countries; such restrictions cause unnecessary harm and suffering to many individuals and families and can prove counter-productive;

10. Oppose governmental policies or actions which, in the name of combating terrorism, violate civil and human rights protected by national and international laws and conventions.

11. condemns the use of extremist tactics by groups around the world that resort to violence because of ideological differences, racism, and anti-Arab and anti-Jewish attitudes; and

12. urges churches and United Methodist Christians to support the activities and program of the "Decade to Overcome Violence" led by the World Council of Churches.

*To further these objectives,* we urge United Methodist Church members and congregations to utilize the study on terrorism produced by the General Board of Church and Society. In an "age of terror" the church needs—more than ever—to respond prophetically and pastorally to this critical issue of our time.

ADOPTED 2004
RESOLUTION #336, 2004 *BOOK OF RESOLUTIONS*

*See* Social Principles, ¶ 165*B* and *D*.

## 6119. The Abolition of Torture

Torture is a crime and the biblical mandate is clear that evil must cease and evil deeds must stop. "Cease to do evil, learn to do good, seek justice, rescue the oppressed, defend the orphan, plead for the widow." (Isaiah 1:17 NRSV) The Social Principles remind United Methodists that the "use of detention and imprisonment for the harassment and elimination of political opponents or other dissidents violates fundamental human rights. Furthermore, the mistreatment or torture of persons by governments for any purpose violates Christian teaching and must be condemned and/or opposed by Christians and churches wherever it occurs." (Social Principles ¶ 164*A*)

The United Nations Convention against Torture and Other Cruel, Inhuman or Degrading Treatment or Punishment came into force June 26, 1987. The Convention is a key tool to fight torture and other forms of ill-treatment and protect the rights of the survivors, the women, children, and men in every country. By 2007, 144 governments had ratified the Convention but in102 of these countries there were cases of torture and ill-treatment by security forces, police, and other state authorities, according to Amnesty International.[1] Torture is defined as

1. Amnesty International Report 2007: FACTS and FIGURES, press release, 5/23/2007 Web site: <http://news.amnesty.org>

"... any act by which severe pain or suffering, whether physical or mental, is intentionally inflicted on a person for such purposes as obtaining from him or a third person information or a confession, punishing him for an act he or a third person has committed or is suspected of having committed, or intimidating or coercing him or a third person, or for any reason based on discrimination of any kind, when such pain or suffering is inflicted by or at the instigation of or with consent or acquiescence of a public official or other person acting in an official capacity. It does not include pain or suffering arising only from, inherent in or incidental to lawful sanctions."[2] (Part I, article 1 of the Convention against Torture ... )

The biblical mandate is clear. It is not enough to cease evil. It is imperative to "learn to do good, seek justice, rescue the oppressed, defend the orphan[, and] plead for the widow" (Isaiah 1:17 NRSV). The International Federation of Action by Christians for the Abolition of Torture (FIACAT) proclaimed, on their 20th anniversary in 2007, "... we are bearers of the values of the Gospel, those which Christ—who experienced torture—taught us, among which figure the absolute condemnation of torture, but also the proclamation of truth, of justice of love and of life ... "[3] Justice "is a key element in the abolition of torture. Torturers must be tried and condemned if guilty. Victims must be rehabilitated and compensated."[4]

In the United States the religious community's struggle against torture is inter-religious. The National Religious Campaign against Torture (NRCAT) has a membership of over 115 religious organizations including Christians (Catholic, evangelical, mainline Protestant, and Orthodox), Unitarians, Jewish, Muslim and Sikh communities. Their demands for swift passage of legislation in the United States Congress: 1) to prohibit " ... without exception, all US-sponsored torture and cruel, inhuman and degrading treatment of detainees" 2) to prohibit the practice by the United States of apprehending suspects and transporting them to countries that use torture as an interrogation

2. Convention against Torture and other Cruel, Inhuman or Degrading Treatment or Punishment, adopted and opened for signature, ratification and accession by General Assembly resolution 39/46 of 10 December 1984, entry into force 26 June, 1987, in accordance with article 27 (1)—Office of the High Commissioner for Human Rights, Web site: <http://www.ohchr.org>

3. International Federation of Action by Christians for the abolition of Torture, FIACAT is twenty years old, statement from Sylvie Bukhari-de Pontual, President of FIACAT—FIACAT. NEWS NO. 67.

4. FIACAT Charter, Section on Impunity, second paragraph, Web site: <http://www.fiacat.org>

technique, and 3) to prohibit the use by the United States of secret prisons for their detainees anywhere in the world.[5]

On June 26, 2007, the United Nations International Day to Remember the Victims of Torture, several religious leaders, representing member organizations of NRCAT, spoke. Dr. Ingrid Mattson, President of the Islamic Society of North America, noted, "Torture is a major transgression of God's limits. The impact of such a transgression is not just on the victim, but on the souls of those engaged in and complicit in the evil act." Rabbi Gerry Serrota, Chair of the Board of Rabbis for Human Rights-North America, joined her, ". . . torture shatters and defiles God's image . . . meaning that torture violates the tortured human being, who was created in the likeness of God, as well as the torturer's human soul, which is inevitably defiled and compromised in dishonoring the image of God in his victim." And, Dr. Charles Gutenson, an evangelical leader and Professor at Asbury Theological Seminary, adds, "Jesus not only commanded, but also modeled a way of life that refused to repay evil with evil. When his enemies came for him, he embodied that call to love our enemies. How then can we who seek to imitate this Jesus ever see torture as a legitimate tool wielded to serve our own purposes?"[6]

In 2001 the World Council of Churches sent a message to FIACAT. In this message

Dr. Konrad Raiser, General Secretary of the World Council of Churches (1993-003), reminded that, "The practice of torture became more widespread during the peak of military dictatorships and authoritarian rule in the 70s and the 80s. With the end of the Cold War and the popular demand for democratization and political reforms in many regions, it was hoped that this practice would disappear. This, however, did not happen and torture is still prevalent in many parts of the world. It is now not only practiced by the security forces of the state, but also by private armed groups that are at war not only with the state but also amongst themselves."[7]

5. National Religious Campaign against Torture (NRCAT) WHAT WE ARE ASKING FOR: paraphrase of the entire Section, Web site: www.nrcat.org <http://www.nrcat.org> Note: Both the Board of Global Ministries and Church and Society of The United Methodist Church belong to NRCAT.

6. NRCAT Press Release – June 26, 2007, Religious Leaders' Message to Congress: Restore Habeas Corpus, Abolish Torture.

7. Message from Dr. Konrad Raiser, General Secretary of the World Council of Churches in support of the International Campaign against the Practice of Torture – sent Monday, 12 February 2001 to the International Federation of Actions by Christians for the Abolition of Torture (FIACAT) Web site: <http://www.wcc-coe.org>

In December 2004, Dr. Samuel Kobia, the General Secretary of the World Council of Churches (2004-) also writes to FIACAT, "Despite the progress on human rights concerns in recent years, the practice of torture continues unabated. In fact, since the September 11th attacks in New York that gave rise to an increase in emergency legislation against terrorism, the practice of torture has increased. In some societies, it has been given a legal cover thus allowing impunity to the perpetrators."[8]

In a June 26, 2007 statement, signed by the UN Special Rapporteur on Torture and the President and Secretary General of the International Rehabilitation Council for Torture Victims (IRCT) and read around the world: " In the wake of a series of horrific attacks against civilian targets in a number of countries across the world in recent years, we have seen the absolute prohibition against torture come under enormous pressure in the context of the ill-labeled "War on Terror": outright torture, directly or by proxy; detainees being transferred to secret prisons by clandestine flights; multiyear deten-tion without trial; and full fledged disappearances. Phenomena asso-ciated with history's most repugnant and brutal regimes, but recently employed, directly or with complicity, by otherwise democratic coun-tries." In their statement, the signatories honored the "dignity of tor-ture survivors worldwide and acknowledged the extraordinary courage it takes to attempt to rebuild a life that has been shattered by this heinous crime. We also remind the world that the rehabilitation of torture survivors is not an act of charity, but an inalienable right. And not least, we stress that rebuilding individual lives and families goes hand in hand with restoring broken societies."[9]

*Therefore:*

1. The United Methodist Church must continue to publicly condemn and oppose torture wherever it occurs through legislative and other means. The Council of Bishops and all agencies of the church must work together to develop resources and find ways to keep the informa-tion about torture, its perpetrators, the victims, their families, and their communities continuously in the consciousness of United Methodists.

8. Message by Dr. Sam Kobia, General Secretary of the WCC to the FIACAT, Paris, 3rd December 2004

9. International Rehabilitation Council for Torture Victims (IRCT) Global Reading on 26 June 2007, a statement signed by Manfred Nowak, the UN Special Rapporteur on Torture, Abdel Hamid Afana, President of IRCT, and Brita Sydhoff, Secretary General of IRCT, Web site: <http://www.irct.org>

2. United Methodists must take time in their churches, women's, youth and men's groups to study, reflect, and pray about how to abolish torture and live out the biblical mandate to "love our neighbors" even in the midst of a "war on terror."[10]

3. United Methodists must seek to ensure the ratification by and compliance of their governments with the provisions of the Convention against Torture and all internationally accepted norms and standards on the prevention of torture; fully support the work of the International Criminal Court (ICC) and honor their international obligations to prosecute alleged perpetrators of torture.

4. United Methodists should encourage initiatives to establish international strategies to abolish all forms of torture.

5. United Methodists must express their solidarity with churches and peoples everywhere in the common struggle to have the provisions of the Covenant on Civil and Political Rights and the Convention against Torture strictly applied in all countries. And, United Methodists should organize or join events such as the 26th of June, the United Nations International Day to Remember the Victims of Torture.

6. United Methodists should seek access to places of detention and interrogation centers in order to ensure that persons held are not mistreated. Treatment of prisoners should not be contrary to the Geneva Convention Relative to Treatment of Prisoners of War (1949) particularly Articles 13, 14, 15, 17, 18.[11]

7. United Methodists should find ways to ensure the inalienable right of survivors of torture to rehabilitation, access to adequate reparations, including medical and psychological rehabilitation, restitution, compensation, satisfaction, and the guarantee of nonrepetition. It is recommended that The United Methodist Church work in partnership with international organizations, such as the Center for Victims of Torture, which have for many years developed the skills to care for victims of torture. Most organizations have Centers around the world sensitive to the language and culture of the victims and their families.

10. Letter to the United Methodist Women on Torture, May 11, 2005, sent by Kyung Za Yim, President , Women's Division, Global Ministries, United Methodist Church, and Jan Love, Deputy General Secretary, Women's Division. Paraphrase from the letter.

11. Geneva Convention relative to the Treatment of Prisoners of War, adopted on 12 August 1949 by the Diplomatic Conference for the Establishment of International Conventions for the Protection of Victims of War, held in Geneva from 21 April to 12 August 1949, entered into force: 21 October 1950, Office of the United Nations High Commissioner for Human Rights: Web site: <http://www.ohchr.org>

8. United Methodists should urge governments to fully fund the United Nations Voluntary Fund for Victims of Torture which was established in1981 for humanitarian, legal and financial aid to persons who have been tortured and to members of their families.[12]

12. Fact Sheet No.4, Methods of Combating Torture, Office of the High Commissioner for Human Rights

**ADOPTED 2008**

*See* Social Principles, ¶ 165C and *D*.

## 6120. Opposition to Torture

Our commitment to human rights is grounded in the conviction that each and every human life is sacred. This theme wends its way throughout our Scriptures, in the creation stories as well as in Jesus' teaching and ministry. Among the most significant of human rights is the right to security of person, which includes the right not to be tortured.

Yet around the world today, there are countless number of persons suffering shocking and morally intolerable treatment at the hands of those acting — all too often — on behalf of their governments. Such torture violates the basic dignity of the human person that all religions, in their highest ideals, hold dear. It degrades everyone involved — policymakers, perpetrators, and victims.

*Therefore,* The United Methodist Church:
1. opposes the use of torture and all forms of cruel, inhuman, or degrading interrogation by all agencies, employees, or agents of all governments anywhere in the world;
2. supports the application of the Geneva Conventions to all enemy soldiers and the humane treatment with due process for all combatants held by both government and nongovernment forces anywhere in the world;
3. supports principles as contained in documents such as the Bill of Rights of the Constitution of the United States that call for judicial review and legislative oversight over executive branch operations relating to counter terrorism and domestic surveillance programs, both classified and publicly acknowledged, and similar documents in other countries; and

4. endorses legislative and judicial remedies for the use of torture and illegal detention by agencies of all government, such as the appointment of special counsels, open hearings, appropriate investigation, and legislation outlawing the use of "extraordinary rendition" and extraterritorial prison facilities.

As in the case of conscientious objectors, The United Methodist Church expresses support for the principled refusal on grounds of conscience by military, intelligence, and other personnel who are asked to participate in coercive and/or covert detention of prisoners.

The United Methodist Church's Board of Church and Society and all other church boards and agencies are authorized to express support for the protection of the right of privacy for all citizens against unwarranted intrusion by their government or private entities.

The United Methodist Church encourages all United Methodists:

1. to be attentive to issues of human rights related to policy and practice of their own governments;
2. to continue to advocate for human rights in the many places around the world where those rights are in jeopardy;
3. to seek ways to assist victims of human rights abuse and to prevent further abuse of others; and to pray for all victims of such abuse and for those who persecute them.

**ADOPTED 2008**

*See* Social Principles, ¶ 165C and D.


### 6121. Rejection of Unilateral First-Strike Actions and Strategies

WHEREAS, the United Methodist Council of Bishops has stated its opposition to the first-strike use of nuclear weapons (2008 Resolution $3237);

WHEREAS, our denomination is on record for opposing war as a usual instrument of foreign policy and insists that the first moral duty of all nations is to resolve by peaceful means every dispute that arises among them (*Discipline* ¶ 165C); and that it may only be waged "when peaceful alternatives have failed" (*Discipline* ¶ 164I).

WHEREAS, our denomination is on record that "We urge the establishment of the rule of law in international affairs," and whereas, policies of unilateral first strike military actions without United Nations approval violate established international law;

WHEREAS, by attacking Iraq without the approval and participation of the United Nations, the United States has squandered its positive reputation as a responsible member of the global community in the effort to make the world safe for democracy, instigating instead, a widespread mood of resentment and an attitude of mistrust toward Americans;

*Therefore,* The United Methodist Church strongly protests all unilateral first-strike actions and strategies on the part of any government or military force and calls on the President and Congress of the United States to cease and desist from such actions without ratification by, and collaboration with, the United Nations.

ADOPTED 2004
READOPTED 2008
RESOLUTION #339, 2004 *BOOK OF RESOLUTIONS*

*See* Social Principles, ¶ 165.

## 6122. Prohibition of Arms Sales to Foreign Countries for Purposes of War

WHEREAS, the United States sells more armaments around the world than any other country ($18.6 billion in sales in 2000, of $36.9 billion worldwide-Frida Berrigan, World Policy Institute, August 21, 2001); and

WHEREAS, these arms are frequently used in conflicts which we do not support and have even been used against our own troops in combat; and

WHEREAS, prohibitions against the resale of such arms have proven to be unenforceable in the world market; and

WHEREAS, President Jimmy Carter has said, "We cannot have it both ways. We can't be both the world's leading champion of peace and the world's leading supplier of arms"; and

WHEREAS, the Social Principles of The United Methodist Church states that " . . . the manufacture, sale, and deployment of armaments must be reduced and controlled; and that the production, possession, or use of nuclear weapons be condemned;" (¶ 165C of *The Book of Discipline, 2000*); and

WHEREAS, Jesus taught us that "blessed are the peacemakers," and valued all human life;

*Now, therefore, be it resolved*, that The United Methodist Church supports the strict prohibition of sales of arms for purposes of war to foreign countries.

ADOPTED 2004
RESOLUTION #341, 2004 *BOOK OF RESOLUTIONS*

*See* Social Principles, ¶ 165*B* and C.

### 6123. Crimes Against Humanity, Genocide, and War Crimes

When the days drew near for him to be taken up, he set his face to go to Jerusalem. And he sent messengers ahead of him. On their way they entered a village of the Samaritans to make ready for him; but they did not receive him, because his face was toward Jerusalem. When his disciples James and John saw it, they said, "Lord, do you want us to command fire to come down from heaven and consume them?" But he turned and rebuked them.

—Luke 9:51-56 NRSV

"We confess that as Christians we too have responded to religious and ethnic differences out of fear, ignorance, and even hatred. We have too quickly resorted to violence as a means of resolving conflicts.

"The rising tide of violence in the world threatens to engulf communities, nations, and world civilizations. It is time for the church to become proactive in resolving conflict nonviolently and developing alternatives to violence."

"The Church's Response to Ethnic and Religious Conflict,"
Resolution #81, *BOR 2004*

Seeking nonviolent conflict resolution and alternatives to violence, the Council of Bishops, in June 2004, offered a discussion guide "In Search of Security" that reminded United Methodists that "Our Christian ethic tells us: 'If you want peace, work for justice.' This is the course we should pursue in search for security. . . . Security in the perspective of faith 'is a state of being that flows from the inclusion of all in the bounty of the earth. Security is meant for all and results from a concern of each one for the other. Security results from a concern for the common good and the promotion of solidarity between nations and peoples. Security stems from a recognition and defense of basic human rights. . . .' "

The Social Principles of The United Methodist Church (¶ 165C, "War and Peace") states that "We believe war is incompatible with the teachings and example of Christ . . . and insist that the first moral duty of all nations is to resolve by peaceful means every dispute that arises between or among them." In the same paragraph The United Methodist Church also states, "We therefore reject war as an instrument of national foreign policy, to be employed only as a last resort in the prevention of such evils as genocide, brutal suppression of human rights, and unprovoked international aggression."

How and who will determine when "the last resort" has been reached and war becomes the only way to stop "such evils as genocide, brutal suppression of human rights, and unprovoked international aggression"? The international community has been wrestling with that concern. The 2005 World Summit at the United Nations agreed upon a number of actions as global challenges including a concept emerging since 2001 the International Responsibility to Protect, which states that it is the "clear and unambiguous acceptance by all governments of the collective international responsibility to protect populations from genocide, war crimes, ethnic cleansing and crimes against humanity. Willingness to take timely and decisive collective action for this purpose, through the Security Council, when peaceful means prove inadequate and national authorities are manifestly failing to do it."

In 2006 the Ninth Assembly of the World Council of Churches (WCC) noted that Responsibility to Protect has "shifted the debate from the viewpoint of the interveners to that of the people in need of assistance, thus defining sovereignty as a duty-bearer status. . . . States can no longer hide behind the pretext of sovereignty to perpetrate human rights violations against their citizens and live in total impunity. . . . [T]he responsibility to protect and serve the welfare of its people is central to a state's sovereignty. When there is failure to carry out that responsibility, whether by neglect, lack of capacity, or direct assaults on the population, the international community has the duty to assist peoples and states, and in extreme situations, to intervene in the internal affairs of the state in the interests and safety of the people."

In the twenty-first century as in the twentieth the atrocities during war and peacetime have been and continue to be directed against civilians. The participants at the Ninth Assembly of the WCC called attention to the "cries arising daily in their home countries and regions due to disasters, violent conflicts and conditions of oppression and suffering." But, the Assembly participants knowing that they were empowered by God remained committed " . . . to bear witness to transformation in personal lives, churches, societies and the world as a whole." In other words, "if you want peace, work for justice." "Do not be overcome by evil, but overcome evil with good" (Romans 12:21).

It becomes imperative that the international community find peaceful means to exercise its responsibility to protect and never as a "last resort" have to go to war or even intervene militarily. But, "ending violence and wars, and checking impunity and disregard for international human rights and humanitarian laws" will require more than political will and moral courage. Concrete programs and mechanisms are needed to realize the totality of human rights—civil, political, social, economic, and cultural." One of those mechanisms is the new International Criminal Court, which has been set up to bring to justice individuals who commit war crimes, crimes against humanity, genocide, and the crime of aggression.

It becomes imperative for United Methodists to clarify the definitions of these international crimes and understand existing means for pursuing the perpetrators and caring for the victims.

War Crimes, according to Article 8, paragraph 2, subparagraph (a) of the Rome Statute of the International Criminal Court, are defined, "For the purpose of this Statute, 'war crimes' means: Grave breaches of the Geneva Convention of 12 August 1949, namely, any of the following acts against persons or property protected under the provisions of the relevant Geneva Convention:

    i) Willful killing;

    ii) Torture or inhuman treatment including biological experiments;

    iii) Willfully causing great suffering, or serious injury to body or health;

    iv) Extensive destruction and appropriation of property, not justified by military necessity and carried out unlawfully and wantonly;

    v) Compelling a prisoner of war or other protected person to serve in the forces of a hostile Power;

    vi) Willfully depriving a prisoner of war or other protected person of the rights of fair and regular trial;

    vii) Unlawful deportation or transfer or unlawful confinement;

    viii) Taking of hostages."

Article 8, paragraph 2, subparagraph b) adds "Other serious violations of the laws and customs applicable in international armed conflict, within the established framework of international law, namely, any of the following acts: i) Intentionally directing attacks against the civilian population as such or against individual civilians not taking direct part in hostilities. . . ."

Crimes Against Humanity are: "namely, murder, extermination, enslavement, deportation, and other inhumane acts committed against civilian populations, before or during war; or persecutions on political, racial or religious grounds in execution of or in connection with any crime within the jurisdiction of the Tribunal, whether or not in violation of the domestic law of the country where perpetrated . . . " This definition was established by the Allies and the USA and was contained in Article 6) of the Charter of the International Military Tribunal (IMT) sitting in Nuremberg in 1945. While no specialized convention was ever developed on crimes against humanity, such a category of crimes has been included in the International Tribunals for both the Former Yugoslavia and for Rwanda as well as in the Rome Statute of the International Criminal Court.

The International Convention on the Prevention and Punishment of the Crime of Genocide defines genocide as any act "committed with intent to destroy, in whole or in part, a national, ethnic, racial or religious group, as such: Killing members of the group; Causing serious bodily or mental harm to members of the group; Deliberately inflicting on the group conditions of life calculated to bring about its physical destruction in whole or in part; Imposing measures intended to prevent births within the group; Forcibly transferring children of the group to another group."

Ethnic Cleansing is a "purposeful policy designed by one ethnic or religious group to remove by violent and terror-inspiring means the civilian population of another ethnic or religious group from certain geographic areas. . . . This purpose appears to be the occupation of territory to the exclusion of the purged group or groups." Many resolutions of the United Nations Security Council declare ethnic cleansing to be a violation of international humanitarian law and demand that perpetrators be brought to justice.

Crimes against humanity, war crimes, and genocide all come under the jurisdiction of the International Criminal Court (ICC) and perpetrators are being brought before the court. In 2005 the United Nations Security Council passed Resolution 1593 referring the crimes against humanity, committed in the tragic conflict in Darfur, to the ICC. In 2007 the court's prosecutor named two Sudanese leaders for atrocities in Darfur.

In 2005 the World Council of Churches affirmed the establishment of the ICC as "the most important step forward in International Law. . . . The Court provides the international community with an instrument to defend human rights and pursue justice for specified crimes that otherwise would be committed with impunity. . . ." United Methodists first expressed their support for the Court in the 2000 General Conference. Twenty-five countries where there is a United Methodist Church have ratified the Rome Statute on which the court is based before it entered into force in July 2002. One hundred and four states have ratified as of January 2007.

*Therefore*, The United Methodist Church must search for ways to be a "witness to transformation in personal lives, churches, societies and the world as a whole" and pursue the elimination of violence, war, crimes against humanity, war crimes, and genocide in each of our societies and throughout the world. United Methodists are urged to continue participating in the World Council of Churches' (WCC) Decade to Overcome Violence: Churches Seeking Reconciliation and Peace 2001-2010 and the Council's worldwide mobilization of churches for peace, which will culminate with an International Ecumenical Peace Convocation in May 2011.

The United Methodist Church must urge United Methodists to pray, to gather in study groups to learn about the degrading effects that war crimes, crimes against humanity, and genocide have on the victims, the perpetrators, and those who silently stand by. United Methodists must initiate actions against impunity associated with violations of international humanitarian law by, among others, campaigning in all nations to ratify the Rome Statute especially in those countries where there are United Methodists such as the USA, Russia and Ukraine, Czech Republic, Republic of Macedonia, Philippines, Cote d'Ivoire, Algeria, Angola, Mozambique, Sudan, and Zimbabwe, which have only signed the statute (Macedonia has neither signed nor ratified).

The United Methodist Church calls on the Council of Bishops, all agencies, commissions, local churches, districts, annual and central conferences to witness to the urgent need to stop the destruction of life and to seek resources, develop resources, and share resources, in as many languages as possible and through the varied means available in The United Methodist Church. Such resources should enable members of The United Methodist Church to:

a) remain informed and work toward the prevention of conflicts, atrocities, violence, and suffering that is borne by millions of people in the world;

b) participate in the World Council of Churches' mobilization of the churches for peace and join other organizations and movements that struggle for peace with justice;

c) assure the presence and participation of the Church in those places where people need protection and humanitarian aid. Mindful, that if external intervention, hopefully nonviolent or using force only in rare circumstances, is involved "churches should nevertheless be engaged in increasing the capacity of the local people to be able to intervene themselves by strengthening structures of the civil society and modern public-private partnerships, in terms of prevention as well as protection. Churches are called to offer their moral authority for mediation between differently powerful actors";

d) remain informed on the work of the International Criminal Court and become supportive of the court's work; and

e) support organizations working for human rights and be watchful and critical of the new Human Rights Council of the United Nations as it develops its new structures and procedures.

ADOPTED 2008

See Social Principles, ¶ 165C and D.

## 6124. Support for the Landmine Treaty

Antipersonnel landmines are weapons that claim life or limb of another innocent victim every 20 minutes. Peacekeepers, humanitarian workers, and missionaries daily risk death and injury from landmines. As of now, 151 countries have signed the 1997 Mine Ban Treaty, an international agreement that bans antipersonnel landmines. In March 1999 the treaty became binding under international law. The United States and 39 other countries have not ratified the treaty. Religious leaders, physicians, veterans, humanitarian activists, environmentalists, and human-rights advocates have called upon the United States to sign and ratify the Mine Ban Treaty.

Antipersonnel landmines are a growing threat to human community and the environment, kill or maim hundreds of people every week, bring untold suffering and casualties to mostly innocent and defenseless civilians and especially children, obstruct economic development and reconstruction, inhibit the repatriation of refugees and internally displaced persons, and have other severe consequences for years after emplacement. The United States is one of only 13 countries that refuse to halt production of antipersonnel landmines.

We firmly believe that the world needs a vision of peace rooted in justice and a world bound together under the umbrella of God's love for all humankind.

It is in this spirit that we celebrate the worth and dignity of all races and peoples and call for the end of development and deployment of landmines. Micah 4:3 ". . . They shall beat their swords into plowshares and their spears into pruning hooks" further reveals God's will for humankind.

The General Conference of The United Methodist Church, calls upon:

1. the President of the United States to sign and the US Senate to ratify the "Convention on the Prohibition of the Use, Stockpiling, Production and Transfer of Anti-Personnel Mines and on Their Destruction," commonly called the Mine Ban Treaty;
2. all countries that have not done so to ratify the Mine Ban Treaty;
3. the General Board of Global Ministries, nongovernmental organizations, and governments to increase resources for humanitarian de-mining, mine awareness programs, and increased resources for landmine victim rehabilitation and assistance; and
4. the General Board of Church and Society to advocate against the deployment of landmines and advocate for de-mining and caring for persons who have been wounded by landmines.

We ask that the secretary of the General Conference send this resolution to the President of the United States Senate and to the Speaker of the US House of Representatives as soon as possible after the adjournment of the 2008 General Conference.

ADOPTED 2000
REVISED AND READOPTED 2008
RESOLUTION #335, 2004 *BOOK OF RESOLUTIONS*
RESOLUTION #316, 2000 *BOOK OF RESOLUTIONS*

*See* Social Principles, ¶ 165B and C.

## 6125. Ban Cluster Bombs

Then justice will dwell in the wilderness, the righteousness abide in the fruitful field. The effect of righteousness will be peace, and the result of righteousness, quietness and trust for ever. My people will abide in a peaceful habitation, in secure dwellings, and in quiet resting places (Isaiah 32:16-18).

Cluster bombs kill and injure as they indiscriminately scatter explosives over a wide area. Many of the bombs fail to work properly leaving huge quantities on the ground. Like landmines, they remain a lethal threat to anyone in the area. These weapons kill and injure people trying to rebuild their lives after a conflict. They stop people from being able to use their land and the threat remains for decades Unexploded submunitions can be very sensitive to movement and must be destroyed where they are found, making them especially challenging for clearing operations.

A cluster bomb, or cluster munition, consists of a container filled with lots of smaller bombs (submunitions). These containers are dropped from aircraft or fired from the ground. Breaking open midair, the container releases the submunitions—saturating an area the size of several football fields. Anyone within that area, be they military or civilian, is likely to be severely injured or killed.

The small size and curious shapes of submunitions make them particularly appealing to children, who make up a large proportion of the casualties. Locations affected by cluster bombs include: Afghanistan, Albania, Bosnia and Herzegovina, Cambodia, Chad, Croatia, Eritrea, Ethiopia, Iraq, Kosovo, Kuwait, Laos, Lebanon, Montenegro, Russia, Saudi Arabia, Serbia, Sierra Leone, Sudan, Syria, Tajikistan, Vietnam, and Western Sahara. Billions of submunitions are now stockpiled and ready to be used by more than 70 countries.

The General Conference of The United Methodist Church:
1. condemns the use of cluster bombs,
2. urges governments to stop the use and production of cluster bombs and negotiate a new international treaty prohibiting them.

**ADOPTED 2008**

*See* Social Principles, ¶ 165C.

# OTHER RESOLUTIONS

### 8001. Commitment in Mission and Ministry

WHEREAS, the mission of The United Methodist Church is to make disciples of Jesus Christ for the transformation of the world; and

WHEREAS, the Council of Bishops has expressed a vision of mission and ministry that articulates the aspirations and ministries prevalent across The United Methodist connection, and the general agencies have responded by identifying four areas of emphasis that live out the vision for the current quadrennium and beyond; and

WHEREAS, the spirit of collaboration and shared ministry through the Council of Bishops, the Connectional Table, the general agencies, and the annual conferences is infusing new energy and recommitment to assure vitality and effectiveness across the connection; and

WHEREAS, the following four areas of emphasis provide crucial avenues for shared labor and witness:

1. Leadership development, with particular focus on leading the United Methodist way of discipleship,
2. Congregational development and new church starts,
3. Ministry with the poor, with particular attention to caring for and protecting children;
4. Global health, by confronting the diseases of poverty and health-care access for all; and

The 2008 General Conference supports these four areas of emphasis for this quadrennium.

ADOPTED 2008

### 8002. A Commitment to Unity in Mission and Ministry

WHEREAS, the mission of The United Methodist Church is to make disciples of Jesus Christ for the transformation of the world;

WHEREAS, the Council of Bishops has expressed a vision of mission and ministry that articulates the aspirations and ministries prevalent across the United Methodist connection and the general agencies have responded by identifying four areas of emphasis that live out the vision for the current quadrennium and beyond;

WHEREAS, the spirit of collaboration and shared ministry through the Council of Bishops, the Connectional Table, the general agencies, and the annual conferences is infusing new energy and recommitment to assure vitality and effectiveness across the connection;

WHEREAS, the following four areas of emphasis provide crucial avenues for shared labor and witness:

1. leadership development with particular focus on leading the United Methodist way of discipleship,
2. congregational development and new church starts,
3. ministry with the poor with particular attention to caring for and protecting children,
4. global health by confronting the diseases of poverty and health care access for all,

*Therefore, be it resolved,* that we, the General Board of Discipleship,

- Commit ourselves to work in a spirit of unity with all across the Connection and with our ecumenical partners to give form to new expressions of shared mission and ministry;
- Commit ourselves to cooperatively foster "A Future with Hope" whereby United Methodist Christians are encouraged and equipped to perform mission and ministry as disciples of Jesus Christ;
- Commit ourselves to intentionally and collaboratively address the four emphases of congregational development, leadership development, ministry with the poor, and global health as we prepare in planning and budgeting for mission and ministry in 2009–2012.

ADOPTED 2008

### 8003. Ethics of Embryonic Stem Cell Research

*Preamble*

The following statement addresses the ethical implications of using human embryos as a source of stem cells for research. It also examines in vitro fertilization procedures, as they are the source of most of the

OTHER RESOLUTIONS

embryos that are presently used for research. This statement does not explore in detail other kinds of stem cell research, but finds no moral objections to research involving stem cells derived from adult cells or umbilical cord blood. The United Methodist Church has made a commitment to consider all issues in light of concerns for the welfare of all people and the just distribution of resources. In light of that, we wish to state at the outset our conviction that Christians are called to use their resources to meet the basic health care needs of all people. We reaffirm our theological grounding on these issues as found in Section II of the 2004 *Book of Resolutions,* Resolution #102—"New Developments in Genetic Science."

### Description of In vitro fertilization

In vitro fertilization (IVF) is a clinical practice in which a woman's ovaries are hyper-stimulated to release several eggs, which are extracted and subsequently fertilized in a laboratory dish. This is for the purpose of creating embryos to be introduced into the uterus in the hope of implantation, gestation, and eventual birth. Current practice usually involves the extraction of up to 15-16 eggs for fertilization. The resulting embryos that are judged most viable are either introduced into the womb in the initial attempt or frozen and stored for possible later use. Some of the embryos are judged to be less viable than others and are discarded. (Those stored embryos that are not later used become the "excess embryos" whose use as a source of embryonic stem cells is currently under discussion.)

### Concerns Regarding the Status of Human Embryos

A human embryo, even at its earliest stages, commands our reverence and makes a serious moral claim on us, although not a claim identical to that of a more developed human life. For this reason we should not create embryos with the intention of destroying them, as in the creation of embryos for research purposes. Neither should we, even for reproductive purposes, produce more embryos than we can expect to introduce into the womb in the hope of implantation.

We recommend the following guidelines to minimize the overproduction of embryos:

- We urge clinicians and couples to make the determination of how many eggs to fertilize and implant on a case-by-case basis.

- Only enough embryos should be produced to achieve one pregnancy at a time.
- We insist that rigorous standards of informed consent regarding the procedures, the physical and emotional risks, and the associated ethical issues be applied to all reproductive technologies. This is especially important regarding the disposition of "excess" embryos and should be the norm of practice around the world.

### Some Judgments Regarding the Use of Existing Embryos for Stem Cell Research

There has been a great deal of scientific interest recently generated by research on human stem cells. These are the cells that give rise to other cells. There are a number of potential sources for stem cells, including adult tissues, fetal remains, umbilical cord blood, and human embryos. The use of adult stem cells and stem cells derived from umbilical cord blood raise few moral questions. The use of human embryos as a source for stem cells has been the subject of intense moral debate.

Given the reality that most, if not all, of these excess embryos will be discarded, we believe that it is morally tolerable to use existing embryos for stem cell research purposes. This position is a matter of weighing the danger of further eroding the respect due to potential life against the possible, therapeutic benefits that are hoped for from such research. The same judgment of moral tolerability would apply to the use of embryos left from future reproductive efforts if a decision has been made not to introduce them into the womb. We articulate this position with an attitude of caution, not license. We reiterate our opposition to the creation of embryos for the sake of research. (See *Book of Resolutions*, 2000, p. 254)

### The Issue of "Therapeutic Cloning"

In consideration of the potential therapeutic benefits that might eventually arise from research on embryonic stem cells, particular concerns are raised by a proposed practice called "therapeutic cloning." This involves taking a donated human egg, extracting its nucleus, and replacing it with a nucleus taken from another body cell. This newly formed cell would then be electrically or chemically stimulated to develop into an embryo. This embryo would contain most of the same genes as the person whose body cell was used to obtain the nucleus. The cloned embryo would then be used as a source of stem cells, which would be a closer genetic match for that donor, although they would contain some genes from the egg cell used for the cloning. This procedure might overcome the problem of immune system rejection of cellular treatments that might be developed for an individual from embryonic stem cells. As of March 2007, no human embryos have been successfully cloned. However, we still believe that human embryos should not be created purely for the sake of research, or created with the advance intention of destroying them, or cloned for harvesting stem cells.

The United Methodist Church supports persons who wish to enhance medical research by donating their early embryos remaining after in vitro fertilization (IVF) procedures have ended, and urges the United States Congress to pass legislation that would authorize federal funding for derivation of and medical research on human embryonic stem cells that were generated for IVF and remain after fertilization procedures have been concluded, provided that:

1. these early embryos are no longer required for procreation by those donating them and would simply be discarded;

2. those donating early embryos have given their prior informed consent to their use in stem cell research;

3. the embryos were not deliberately created for research purposes; and

4. the embryos were not obtained by sale or purchase.

The United States Secretary of Health and Human Services is urged to establish an interdisciplinary oversight body for all research in both the public and private sectors that involves stem cells from human embryos, parthenotes, sperm cells, or egg cells, and cells that produce sperm or eggs.

ADOPTED 2004
REVISED AND READOPTED 2008
RESOLUTION #366, 2004 *BOOK OF RESOLUTIONS*

## 8004. Replace "In Defense of Creation" with new Document and Study Guide

WHEREAS, our Abrahamic tradition calls us to seek those things which lead to shalom in our personal lives, our communities, and our world; and

WHEREAS, Jesus Christ calls us to be peacemakers ("blessed are the peacemakers") Matthew 5:9a; and

WHEREAS, our United Methodist Church has a long tradition towards educating and encouraging church members, citizens and governments to seek those things which lead to a just peace; and

WHEREAS, our country is experiencing a new challenge with the escalation of tensions and the rise in worldwide terrorism; and

WHEREAS, the United Methodist Council of Bishops in 1986 at the height of the nuclear arms race published a landmark foundation document and study guide entitled, "In Defense of Creation: The Nuclear Crisis and a Just Peace," the first draft of this document being adopted at the Council's meeting in Wichita, Kansas November 10-15, 1985;

*Therefore, be it resolved,* that the Kansas East Conference of The United Methodist Church recommend to General Conference that the Council of Bishops of The United Methodist Church will be charged and funded to publish a new document and study guide similar to "In Defense of Creation," to be published during the next quadrennium.

ADOPTED 2004
RESOLUTION #367, 2004 *BOOK OF RESOLUTIONS*


## 8005. United Methodist Men Study Committee

WHEREAS, as United Methodists we recognize the critical nature of men's ministries within The United Methodist Church; and

WHEREAS, men's ministry leads to the spiritual growth of men and effective discipleship; and

WHEREAS, each local church or charge shall have an organized unit of United Methodist Men; and

WHEREAS, the purpose of United Methodist Men is to declare the centrality of Christ in every man's life and lead men to spiritual growth and effective discipleship; and

WHEREAS, any organized group of men in a local United Methodist Church constitutes a ministry of men; and

WHEREAS, George Barna's studies indicate that women are 100 percent more likely to be in discipleship than men, 56 percent more likely to be lay leaders, 54 percent more likely to be in a small ministry group, and 39 percent more likely to have personal devotion time; and

WHEREAS, the General Social Survey, shows that three out of ten respondents who attend church weekly also had a father who attended church weekly. Likewise, 3 out of 10 respondents who never attend church also had a father who never attended church at all; and

WHEREAS, research in the area of implied religion shows that men are finding "religion" in groups outside of church—sports, support groups, left wing and right wing radical movements, new religious movements, and new spirituality movements; and

WHEREAS, there is an urgent need to conduct a study of the needs of males in The United Methodist Church in order to develop effective resources, respond to current needs, challenge long-held assumptions, develop effective strategies for reaching men in the 21$^{st}$ century, and effectively understand male spiritual formation issues;

*Therefore, be it resolved*, that the 2004 General Conference direct the General Commission on United Methodist Men, in cooperation with the Office of Research and Planning, General Council on Ministries (or its equivalent structure for the 2005-2008 quadrennium), to create a study committee for the 2005-2008 quadrennium to undertake a study of men across The United Methodist Church. The study committee will report back to the 2008 General Conference as to its findings.

**ADOPTED 2004**
**RESOLUTION #368, 2004** *BOOK OF RESOLUTIONS*

## 8006. Biblical Language

WHEREAS, The United Methodist Church affirms the use of biblical language and images in worship and in our common life together, and affirms the use of language that reflects the long-standing commitment to the inclusiveness and diversity of United Methodist members and constituencies; and

WHEREAS, the use of metaphors of color, darkness, ability, and age in negative ways has had a harmful effect;

*Therefore, be it resolved* that United Methodist clergy and laity be encouraged to use diverse biblical images and titles for God, including masculine/feminine metaphors; use language for humans that reflects both male and female; use metaphors of color, darkness, ability, and age in positive ways; and

*Be it further resolved* that we affirm the use of biblical language and images in all their forms as appropriate for use in hymns, liturgy, teaching, and in all areas of our common life together; and

*Be it further resolved,* that publications, audiovisual media, online resources, and other communication materials of The United Methodist Church shall reflect the diverse biblical metaphors and the diversity and inclusiveness of humanity.

ADOPTED 1988
REVISED AND ADOPTED 2000
REVISED AND READOPTED 2008
RESOLUTION #344, 2004 *BOOK OF RESOLUTIONS*
RESOLUTION #321, 2000 *BOOK OF RESOLUTIONS*

### 8007. Use of the Name: The United Methodist Church in Periodicals and Advertisements

The 1980 United Methodist General Conference, sympathetic toward Evangelical United Brethren moved Heritage Sunday from the anniversary of John Wesley's Aldersgate experience (the former Aldersgate Sunday) to the anniversary of the United Conference and passed a resolution on the "Proper Use of Name: The United Methodist Church."

We call our members to a more thorough understanding of the joint heritage of our Methodist and Evangelical United Brethren forebears, and we call on our members and agencies to implement with energy and enthusiasm, the 1980 resolution on the "Proper Use of Name: The United Methodist Church."

We call on our church periodical editors, where contributors omit the word "United" from "United Methodist" to correct this usage—both in articles and in letters to the editor. With direct quotations, they should insert "United" in brackets. They should further instruct advertisers that advertisements that refer to "Methodist" without "United" are unacceptable.

We further direct the General Commission on Communication, when it becomes aware of the omission of "United" from "United Methodist" in the church or secular press, to notify the responsible parties that this is unacceptable usage and to report to the Church annually in *The Interpreter* of its compliance with this directive.

ADOPTED 2004
RESOLUTION #352, 2004 *BOOK OF RESOLUTIONS*

## 8008. Meeting Times

WHEREAS, The United Methodist Church recognizes the leadership of young people within the church; and

WHEREAS, young people of The United Methodist Church are called by God to serve in leadership roles at the local, district, and conference levels; and

WHEREAS, a churchwide effort in recruiting and retaining young people's participation is growing; and

WHEREAS, the time constraints of young people through school, career, and family are great, making accessibility to leadership roles difficult;

*Therefore, be it resolved,* that in choosing dates and times for all meetings of United Methodist Church boards and agencies, utmost importance is given to the consideration of times, dates, and places between all conferences that will make young people's participation as great as possible.

*Therefore, be it further resolved,* that in choosing dates and times for district, annual/central, and General Conference meetings that utmost importance is given to the consideration of allowing as many youth and young adult delegates to actively participate as is possible.

**ADOPTED 2008**

## 8009. Church Participation by a Registered Child Sex Offender

The Social Principles of The United Methodist Church declare: "We recognize that family violence and abuse in all its forms—verbal, psychological, physical, sexual—is detrimental to the covenant of the human community. We encourage the Church to provide a safe environment, counsel, and support for the victim. While we deplore the actions of the abuser, we affirm that person to be in need of God's redeeming love."

Increasingly, churches are faced with a dilemma in their attempt to be faithful to both of the last two sentences above. Assuring the safety of children in our care, our facilities and our programs is a sacred duty. We must weigh that duty in the balance with what often seems the conflicting value of participation in the life of the church by a convicted child abuser. Being part of a worshiping community is not the only way for a person to experience God's redeeming love, but it is an important one.

Recent studies suggest a low likelihood that pedophiles can or will change. Without extensive professional treatment, virtually all child sexual offenders will re-offend. Repentance, prayer, and pastoral support, always in combination with lifelong professional treatment, can be crucial in helping to change behavior but, in themselves, offer slim hope of changing the behavior of perpetrators. Welcoming a child sex offender into a congregation must be accompanied by thorough knowledge, careful planning, and long-term monitoring.

A convicted and/or registered sex offender who wishes to be part of a church community should expect to have conditions placed on his or her participation. Indeed, offenders who have been in treatment and are truly committed to living a life free of further abuse will be the first to declare that, in order to accomplish that, they must structure a life that includes on-going treatment, accountability mechanisms, and lack of access to children.

The following steps should be taken in order to be faithful to the Social Principles' commitment both to safety from abuse and to ministry with abusers:

A. *Local churches should:*

- hold discussions in the church council and in adult education settings about the possibility of facing the situation of a convicted sex offender returning to or joining the church. These discussions should be held and general agreements reached about actions to be taken should the church find itself in this circumstance;
- develop a carefully constructed and openly negotiated covenant between the offender and the church community. The covenant should include agreements in the following areas: participation in a professional counseling program for at least the entire time of church membership or participation; adult "covenant partners" to accompany the offender while on church property or attending church activities; areas of church facilities that are "off limits;" restrictions on leadership in or on behalf of church; no role in church that includes contact with children or youth; any additional conditions for presence or participation; and
- assure that the covenant is maintained by having it written and signed by the offender, the pastor(s), and the chairperson

of the church council. While confidentiality of victims should be respected, the covenant should not be secret. Monitoring of the covenant should be taken seriously as a permanent responsibility.

*B. Annual conferences should:*

- develop similar plans and covenant for situations in which a convicted and/or registered sexual offender is involved or seeks involvement in the conference, its activities or facilities;
- include information about this concern and assistance with implementation of this resolution in its training and resourcing of clergy and local church lay leaders;

*C. The General Board of Discipleship and the General Board of Global Ministries should:*

- cooperatively develop and promote a process and specific guidelines to assist congregations in the education and covenant tasks outlined above.

ADOPTED 2004
READOPTED 2008
RESOLUTION #355, 2004 *BOOK OF RESOLUTIONS*

## 8010. Guidelines: The UMC and the Charismatic Movement

*Introductory Statement*

In 1976 General Conference approved *"Guidelines: The United Methodist Church and the Charismatic Renewal."* These Guidelines served the church well. At the 2004 General Conference the GBOD was assigned the responsibility to review and revise the Guidelines, while retaining their general focus and purpose.

*Glossary*

Terminology associated with the charismatic movement is confusing because of varying usage.

*Pentecostal.* This term refers to the movement whose roots began late in the nineteenth century, resulting in the formation of a number of pentecostal denominations in the early years of the twentieth century. Classic pentecostalism affirms what is sometimes spoken of as initial evidence, which includes the concept of requisite "baptism in the Holy Spirit," that every Christian must experience the "baptism in the Holy Spirit" that is accompanied by *glossolalia* or speaking in tongues as an "initial evidence." Pentecostals also emphasize strongly the full recovery of the gifts of the Holy Spirit.

*Charismatic.* The word *charismatic* comes from the Greek word charismata, meaning *"gifts."* The root words in Greek mean grace and joy. By definition, a charismatic should be a joyful, grace-gifted Christian. Charismatic Christians emphasize the need to recover the empowerment and the gifts of the Spirit for ministry today. They affirm the importance of all the "gifts of the Spirit."

*Charismatic Movement.* Throughout this report the term charismatic movement is used to identify the movement that began about 1960 in mainline Christian bodies, both Protestant and Roman Catholic. This movement emphasizes the central importance of the "baptism of the Holy Spirit," but without the elevation of "speaking in tongues" as the initial evidence. A focus is placed on the need to recover the Holy Spirit's empowering and gifts for ministry today. These gifts include prophecy, healing, tongues, and interpretation of tongues, because these gifts are perceived to have been neglected by the Church.

In a biblical sense there is no such person as a "noncharismatic Christian," since the term *charismata* refers to the gracious gifts of God bestowed upon all Christians to equip them for ministry: "To each is given the manifestation of the Spirit for the common good" (1 Corinthians 12:7).

*Pentecostals* and *Charismatics* emerged out of Christianity in the West, where for long periods Christianity neglected the importance of the gifts of the Holy Spirit in the life of the church. However, the activity of the Holy Spirit is not merely restricted to Western Christianity. Indeed, when the gospel reached different parts of the non-Western world, many Christians learned of the Holy Spirit's work in the Bible. In simple faith they believed, and many began exercising the gifts of the Spirit. Although the ministries of such individuals and churches are similar to those of the Pentecostals and the Charismatics in many ways, they do not owe their origins to these Western sources. Rather, they sprang up entirely on their own under the direct leading of the Spirit.

*Neo-charismatics, or Third Wave* (the Pentecostals being the first wave and the Charismatics being the second wave). These are Christians who, unrelated or no longer related to the Pentecostal or Charismatic renewals, have become filled with the Spirit, are energized by the

Spirit, and exercise gifts of the Spirit without recognizing a baptism in the Spirit separate from conversion. Speaking in tongues is considered optional or unnecessary. Signs and wonders, supernatural miracles, and power encounters are emphasized. Third-wavers form independent churches and do not identify themselves as either Pentecostals or Charismatics. (Synan, p. 396)

### Guidelines

We believe the church needs to pray for a sensitivity to be aware of and to respond to manifestations of the Holy Spirit in our world today. We are mindful that the problems of discerning between the true and fraudulent are considerable, but we must not allow the problems to paralyze our awareness of the Spirit's presence; nor should we permit our fear of the unknown and the unfamiliar to close our minds against being surprised by grace. We know the misuse of mystical experience is an ever-present possibility, but that is no reason to deny spiritual experiences.

In facing the issues raised by charismatic experiences, we plead for a spirit of openness and love. We commend to the attention of the church the affirmations of Paul on the importance of love in First Corinthians 13 and of Wesley—"In essentials, unity; in nonessentials, liberty; and, in all things, charity" (love that cares and understands). Without an active, calm, objective, and loving understanding of the religious experience of others, however different from one's own, harmony is impossible.

The criteria by which we understand another's religious experience must include its compatibility with the mind and the spirit of our Lord Jesus Christ, as revealed in the New Testament. If the consequence and quality of a reported encounter with the Holy Spirit leads to self-righteousness, hostility, and exaggerated claims of knowledge and power, then the experience is subject to serious question. However, when the experience clearly results in new dimensions of love, faith, joy, and blessings to others, we must conclude that this is "what the Lord hath done" and offer God our praise. "You shall know them by their fruits" (Matthew 7:20).

### Guidelines for All

1. Be open and accepting of those whose Christian experiences differ from your own.

2. Continually undergird and envelop all discussions, conferences, meetings, and persons in prayer.

3. Be open to new ways in which God by the Spirit may be speaking to the church.

4. Seek the gifts of the Spirit that enrich your life and your ministry, as well as the life of the church.

5. Recognize that although spiritual gifts may be abused in the same way that knowledge or wealth or power may be abused, this does not mean that they should be prohibited.

6. Remember that, like other movements in church history, the charismatic renewal has a valid contribution to make to the ecumenical church.

7. Remember the lessons of church history that when God's people rediscovered old truths the process was often disquieting and that it usually involved upheaval, change, and a degree of suffering and misunderstanding.

8. Always be mindful of the spiritual needs of the whole congregation.

9. In witnessing, teaching or preaching, the wholeness of all aspects of the gospel must be presented.

### For Pastors Who Have Had Charismatic Experiences

1. Combine with your charismatic experience a thorough knowledge of and adherence to United Methodist theology, polity, and tradition. Remember your influence will, in large part, be earned by your loving and disciplined employment of the gifts, by your conduct as a pastor of your entire congregation, and by your participation as a responsible pastor.

2. Seek a deepening and continued friendship with your clergy colleagues regardless of their charismatic experience.

3. Remember your ordination vow to "love, serve, and pray for all the people among whom you work . . . to serve rather than to be served . . . to look after the concerns of Christ above all." (*The United Methodist Book of Worship*, "The Order for the Ordination of Elders," 675)

4. Avoid the temptation to force your personal views and experiences on others. Seek to understand those whose spiritual experiences differ from your own.

5. Seek to grow in your skills as a biblical exegete, a systematic theologian, and a preacher in all the fullness of the gospel.

6. Pray for the gifts of the Spirit essential for your ministry; continually examine your life for the fruits of the Spirit.

7. Let your personal experience demonstrate the power of the Spirit in "works of piety" and "works of mercy" as understood and practiced in the Wesleyan tradition.

### For Pastors Who Have Not Had Charismatic Experiences

1. Continually examine your understanding of the doctrine and experience of the Holy Spirit, so you can communicate this with clarity.

2. Remember the lessons of church history when God's people rediscover old truths—the process is often disquieting, that it usually involves upheaval, change, and a degree of suffering and misunderstanding.

3. Seek firsthand knowledge of what the charismatic renewal means to those who have experienced it. Keep your mind open until this firsthand knowledge is obtained. Then observe and respond as a loving Christian, as a United Methodist minister, and as a sympathetic, conscientious pastor. Keep to scriptural teaching regarding all the gifts of the Holy Spirit.

4. When speaking in tongues occurs, seek to understand what it means to the speaker in his/her private devotional life and what it means when used for intercessory prayer, especially in group worship.

5. Seek to understand the meaning of the other "gifts of the Spirit" in the charismatic experience, such as the utterance of wisdom, knowledge, faith, healing, miracles, and prophecy.

6. United Methodist pastors should be intentional about the benefits to be derived by a mutual sharing of a variety of experiences that have biblical foundation. Accordingly, the pastor should seek to keep all meetings called for prayer and fellowship open to all interested members of the congregation.

### For Laity Who Have Had Charismatic Experiences

1. Remember to combine with your enthusiasm a thorough knowledge of and adherence to the United Methodist form of church government. The charismatic movement is closely related to the holiness movement and to the Wesleyan tradition. Consult with your pastor(s) and if they have not also had your experience, help him or her understand what it means to you. Invite your pastor(s) to attend your worship services and prayer meetings.

2. Pray that the Spirit will help you to maintain fellowship with all United Methodists.

3. Strive for a scholarly knowledge of scriptural content in combination with your spiritual experiences. "Seek to unite knowledge and vital piety" (Wesley). Strive to integrate your experiences with the theological traditions of our church.

4. Avoid undisciplined, undiplomatic enthusiasm in your eagerness to share your experiences with others. Resist the temptation to pose as an authority on spiritual experiences. Failure in this area may cause your fellow Christians to interpret your behavior as spiritual pride.

5. Be intentional about keeping your prayer meetings and other gatherings open to all members of your congregation. When those who do not share your experiences do attend, discuss with them the purpose of the meeting with an interpretation of the significance of the content.

6. Remember that there are many types of Christian experiences that lead to spiritual growth; charismatic experience is one of these.

7. Accept opportunities to become personally involved in the work and mission of your own congregation. Let the results of your experience be seen in the outstanding quality of your church membership and service to others. Be an obvious, enthusiastic supporter of your congregation, its pastor and its lay leadership and of your district, your annual conference, the General Conference, and mission of each. This may well be the most effective witness you can offer to the validity and vitality of your charismatic experience.

8. Remember Paul's injunction that when the gift of tongues is spoken to the body in a group context, there must be interpretation to ensure proper order (1 Corinthians 14:27, 40). If the gift is exercised in a worship setting or group prayer, be careful that it does not hinder worship or cause distraction for others.

9. Keep your charismatic experience in perspective. No doubt it has caused you to feel that you are a better Christian. Remember that this does not mean you are better than other Christians but that you are, perhaps, a better Christian than you were before. Jesus commanded us to love one another (John 13:34).

*For Laity Who Have Not Had Charismatic Experiences*

1. We believe God is constantly seeking to renew the Church, including The United Methodist Church. Pray that God may make

known to you your own place in the process of renewal. The advent of the charismatic movement into our denomination is only one aspect of renewal.

2. If there are members of your congregation who have had charismatic experiences, accept them as brothers and sisters. Jesus commanded us to love one another (John 13:34).

3. Be aware of the tendency to separate ourselves from those who have experiences that differ from our own. Observe personally the charismatics in their prayer meetings, in your congregation, and in the mission of your church. Examine scriptural teaching about this. Pray about it. Discuss your concern with your pastor. The United Methodist Church is theologically diverse.

4. Do not be disturbed if your experience is not the same as others. The work and mission of a healthy congregation calls for many gifts (1 Corinthians 12–14). Each Christian is a unique member of the body of Christ and should seek to discover his or her gifts and role.

5. Should your pastor emphasize charismatic experiences, help her or him to be mindful of the spiritual needs of the entire congregation, to be a pastor and teacher to all. Encourage her or him in preaching to present the wholeness of all aspects of the gospel. Be open to what God would say to you through your pastor about the Holy Spirit.

### For Connectional Administration

1. Refer prayerfully and thoughtfully to the other sections of these Guidelines.

2. Remember your pastoral responsibilities toward ordained persons and congregations within the connection, particularly toward those whose spiritual experience differ from your own.

3. Each administrator should consider whether any teaching or practice regarding the charismatic movement involving an ordained minister of a congregation is for the edification of the church.

4. If there is division involved in a particular situation, make as careful an evaluation as possible, remembering that there are other kinds of issues that may divide our fellowship—a lack of openness to something new or an unwillingness to change, for example. Sometimes tensions and conflicts may result in the edification and growth and maturity of the church and therefore need to be handled wisely and prayerfully by all concerned.

5. Administrators and connectional bodies will be required to deal with expressions of the charismatic movement. We urge all involved to seek firsthand information and experience about the movement, its meaning for those involved in it, and its value to the particular congregation.

6. Care should be taken that persons whose theology and experiences align with those of the Charismatic Renewal are not discriminated against in appointments or as candidates for ordination.

7. Where an ordained person seems to overemphasize or de-emphasize some charismatic doctrines/practices, she or he should be counseled to preach the wholeness of the gospel, to minister to the needs of all of the congregation, and as a pastor to grow in understanding of our polity in the mission of the particular annual conference.

8. Annual conferences may also be faced with a situation where there is a charismatic group within a congregation whose pastor or whose lay leadership or both may be hostile to or ignorant of the charismatic movement. The Annual Conference Board of Ordained Ministry, the bishop, and the district superintendent have a pastoral responsibility to mediate and to guide in reconciliation, using these guidelines.

9. Pray continuously for sensitivity to the will and the leading of the Holy Spirit.

## Historical Perspective:

## The Ministry of the Holy Spirit in Church History

### *The Holy Spirit in the New Testament Period*

The Holy Spirit came upon Mary (Luke 1:35), descended upon Jesus at his baptism (Luke 3:22) and filled Jesus before the temptation in the wilderness (Luke 4:2ff). Jesus claimed that the Spirit was upon him when he stood up to preach (Luke 4:18ff) and that the Spirit empowered him to cast out demons (Matthew 12:28). John the Baptist and Jesus both indicated the importance of the power of the Spirit (Luke 3:15-19; John 7:37-39; Acts 1:5, 8).

The coming of the Holy Spirit ushered in the beginning of the Church (Acts 2) and empowered the disciples to be witnesses (Acts 1:8, Acts 2:4ff). Paul writes about the gifts of the Spirit in his letters

(Romans 12:6-8; 1 Corinthians 12:4-11, 27-31; Ephesians 4:11) and describes his missionary outreach to the Gentiles as "by word and deed, by the power of signs and wonders, by the power of the Spirit of God" (Romans 15:18*ff*, 1 Corinthians 2:4-5; 1 Thessalonians 1:5).

## *The Holy Spirit in John Wesley's Life and Ministry*

John Wesley and his followers were bearers of Scriptural Christianity. Their ministry testifies to the dynamic work of the Spirit in early Methodism.

To begin with, Wesley's Aldersgate experience of the assurance of his salvation on 24 May 1738 was certainly a work of the Spirit. He relates in his journal how as he heard of "the change which God works in the heart through faith in Christ, I felt my heart strangely warmed . . . and an assurance was given that he had taken away my sins." Some months later, he was at prayer with seventy others, including his brother Charles and also George Whitefield, on the night of 1 January 1739. In the early hours of the next morning, the Holy Spirit was poured on them in a most powerful manner. He writes: "About three in the morning . . . the power of God came mightily upon us insomuch that many cried out for exceeding joy and many fell to the ground. As soon as we were recovered a little from that awe and amazement at the presence of His majesty, we broke out with one voice, 'We praise Thee, O God, we acknowledge Thee to be the Lord.'"

"On the basis of Scripture, Wesley taught that the Holy Spirit is present and active in *every major stage of Christian experience*." (Stokes, 46) Careful study of Wesley's writings shows clearly that spiritual gifts, including healing and deliverance of the demonized, were clearly manifested in his ministry and that of his coworkers. There were also reported cases of people falling to the ground under the power of the Holy Spirit due to a variety of reasons, including deliverance from demonization, deep conviction of sin and subsequent release, or simply being overcome by the Spirit. (Davies, *Methodism*, pp.60f; Heitzenrater, *Wesley and the People Called Methodists*, pp.100f, 319.) One study has shown that, 'a careful study of Wesley's *Works* and particularly of the lives of the early Methodist preachers reveals evidence that all the spiritual gifts listed in 1 Corinthians 12:810 were exercised, with the one exception of the interpretation of tongues."(Davies and Peart, *The Charismatic Movement and Methodism*, 2)

Finally, Wesley himself has noted that the spiritual gifts were not generally exercised after the first two or three centuries after Christ. But the reason for this was not that these gifts were not available. Rather, as he noted, "The real cause was 'the love of many,' almost all Christians, was 'waxed cold,' because the Christians were turned Heathens again, and had only a dead form left." (Sermon LXXXIX, "The More Excellent Way," *Works*, Vol. 7, 26-27) And Wesley wrote, "I do not recollect any scripture wherein we are taught that miracles were to be confined within the limits either of the apostolic or the Cyprianic age, or of any period of time, longer or shorter, even till the restitution of all things." ("Principles of a Methodist Farther Explained," *Works*, Vol. 8, 465)

*The Pentecostal and Charismatic Movements and the Wesleyan Framework*

It is impossible to speak of Pentecostalism and the Charismatic Renewal apart from their roots in Methodism. It was, after all, the Wesleyans who first applied the title "pentecostal" to their movement and to a variety of their publications. The Methodists were also first to coin the phrase *baptism of the Holy Spirit* as applied to a second and sanctifying grace (experience) of God. (Cf. John Fletcher of Madeley, Methodism's earliest formal theologian.) The Methodists meant by their "baptism" something different from the Pentecostals, but the view that this is an experience of grace separate from and after salvation was the same. However, the roots of Pentecostalism in Methodist soil go much deeper than titles and phrases. While the phenomenon of speaking in tongues, commonly associated with Pentecostalism, was not an experience sought or promoted by early Methodists, other equally startling manifestations of the Spirit did abound. This was particularly so as Methodism spread across the American frontier. When asked once why the gifts of the Spirit, manifest in the early church, had disappeared, as if the church had no more need for them, Mr. Wesley responded: "It should not be reasoned that the absence of such in the church (eighteenth-century Church of England) reflects the reluctance of God to give, rather the reticence of the church to receive." (Tuttle, 106) Methodism then, at its inception, invited God's people to expect and receive whatever blessing God would give "for the common good" (1 Corinthians 12:7). It is not surprising that many of the first Pentecostal leaders were originally Methodists. Pentecostalism has continued to be what Francis Asbury wanted Methodism to remain, a pliable movement more than a static institution. Whether Methodism claims it or not, Pentecostalism is an off-spring and will perhaps be its greatest legacy. Conservative estimates of the number of classical denominational Pentecostals run 200 million. Combined with the millions of charismatics and neo-pentecostals or third-wavers and those in house churches, that number now stands at 500 million (Synan, 2) to 700 million (Rutz, 44-46), making this the second largest group of Christians in the world, second only to the Roman Catholic church as a whole. This group is estimated to be growing worldwide by 8 percent a year (Rutz, 15).

Charismatics should interpret their gifts and experiences in light of their own traditions. When this does not occur, division and/or exploitation sets in. When United Methodist charismatics adopt a classical pentecostal line, they are no longer United Methodist—at least in the Wesleyan sense. United Methodist Charismatics need to recognize that, properly understood within the context of our own tradition, their charismatic gifts and experiences can be considered as fresh wind of the Spirit.

Wesley's theology of grace is in fact a theology of the Holy Spirit. He believed that Reformation theology was built upon the cardinal doctrine of original sin and that it is God's sovereign will to reverse our "sinful, devilish nature" by the work of the Holy Spirit. He called this activity of God prevenient, justifying, and sanctifying grace. Bound by sin and death, one experiences almost from the moment of conception the gentle wooing of the Holy Spirit—*prevenient grace*. This grace "prevents" one from wandering so far from God that when a person finally understands what it means to be a child of God the Holy Spirit enables us to say Yes to this relationship. For Wesley, this Yes was a heartfelt faith in the merit of Christ alone for salvation. It allows the Holy Spirit to take the righteousness that was in Christ and attribute or impute it to the believer—*justifying grace*. For Wesley this begins a *lifelong movement* from imputed to imparted righteousness in which the Holy Spirit moves the believer from the righteousness of Christ attributed through faith to the righteousness of Christ realized within the individual—*sanctifying grace*.

To understand Wesley's experience of "entire sanctification" is to know how far the pentecostal baptism of the Holy Spirit falls short if there are not continuing works of grace. Grace is continual, though we may not always perceive it. It is essential that we do not confuse being "filled with the Holy Spirit" with Wesley's mature doctrine of sanctification. The Spirit-filled life is, rather, a sustained journey of gifts, experiences, and divine support, beginning with conversion, constantly moving us toward the goal of sanctification.

Many charismatics have come to believe that being filled with the Holy Spirit is an experience that begins with justification and continues as a lifelong process of growth in grace. For the charismatic, Spirit-baptism bestows not one but many gifts and not one but many experiences intended to sustain one day after day. Being baptized in the Spirit (Acts 1:4-5) and being continually filled with the Spirit (Ephesians 5:18) and walking with the Spirit (Galatians 5:25) are important parts of the *journey* toward Christ-likeness, but they are only *parts* of the journey. Thus, United Methodist charismatics, within the context of our own rich tradition, can never interpret gifts and experiences as signs of superior spirituality, making them better than others. Rather, the power of God being sustained within them makes them better than they were and able "to press on toward the goal for the prize of the heavenly call of God in Christ Jesus" (Philippians 3:14).

The Charismatic Renewal has been instrumental in providing many gifts to the Church of Christ Jesus and has made a profound impact upon present-day United Methodism.

Methodists throughout history have always worshipped God in a variety of styles—never more so than today. In addition worship itself—from openly free to highly liturgical—is now more broadly and correctly understood as a personal offering from the body rather than simply the service of worship that one attends. *"God is spirit, and those who worship him, must worship in spirit and truth"* (John 4:24).

Contemporary Christian music—a hallmark of the charismatic renewal—fills many of our churches each Sunday, enriches the spiritual life of individuals and enhances small group meetings.

There are a variety of healing services offered in *The United Methodist Book of Worship*. In addition, the church offers a number of helpful resources for beginning and sustaining healing ministries within the local church.

Spiritual formation is now considered an integral part of planning for annual conferences and important in the continuing education for clergy.

The renewing work of the Holy Spirit within The United Methodist Church has supported the *Lay Witness Movement*, the *Walk to Emmaus*, and the *Academy for Spiritual Formation*. In 1978, Aldersgate *Renewal Ministries* (whose purpose is to "encourage United Methodists to be filled, gifted, empowered and led by the Holy Spirit in ministry to the world) became an affiliate of the General Board of Discipleship. These ministries have been used by God to bring thousands of people around the world into a new or deeper relationship with the Lord.

United Methodist charismatics and noncharismatics alike should be encouraged. In fact, the term *noncharismatic* Christian is a misnomer. All Christians have gifts. *Charismatic,* as earlier defined, refers to those who more explicitly acknowledge and emphasize teaching concerning the power of the Holy Spirit at work within them and the church through such gifts.

## Bibliography

Davies, Rupert E. *Methodism*. London: Epworth, 1976. This is a standard reference work written by a British Methodist scholar.

Davies, William R. and Peart, Ross. *The Charismatic Movement and Methodism*. Westminster, UK: Methodist Home Mission, 1973. This resource written by clergy within the Charismatic tradition of the British Methodist Church.

DeArteaga, William. *Quenching the Spirit: Discover the Real Spirit behind the Charismatic Controversy*. Lake Mary, FL: Creation House 2002. This volume contains a historical overview of spiritual gifts from the early church to the date of publication. It also provides the history of opposition to spiritual gifts. www.creationhouse.com <http://www.creationhouse.com>.

Heitzenrater, Richard P. *Wesley and the People Called Methodists*. Nashville: Abindgdon, 1995. This is a standard reference work written by a United Methodist scholar in the USA. www.cokesbury.com <http://www.cokesbury.com>.

"The Holy Spirit and Revival." The Methodist Church in Malaysia, August 2006. This document was recently approved in Malaysia and represents a more global and biblical perspective on spiritual gifts.

Hyatt, Eddie L. *2000 Years of Charismatic Christianity*. Lake Mary, FL: Charisma House, 2002. This book traces the history of Charismatic Christianity from the early church to the present time with significant attention to Methodism. www.charismahouse.com <http://www.charismahouse.com>.

Jennings, Daniel R. *The Supernatural Occurrences of John Wesley*. Sean Multimedia 2005. This resource gathers information from John Wesley's writings on spiritual gifts and the supernatural. www.seanmultimedia.com <http://www.seanmultimedia.com>.

Moore, Gary L. *Life in the Spirit Seminar.* Franklin, TN: Providence House, 2003. This resource is the manual for local church *Life in the Spirit* seminars. It also can be used for small group bible studies on the Holy Spirit from a Wesleyan perspective. www.aldersgaterenewal.org <http://www.aldersgaterenewal.org>.

Rutz, James *Mega Shift.* Colorado Springs: Empowerment Press, 2005. This resource describes the miraculous work of God around the world through ordinary people and the house-church movement.

Stokes, Mack B. *The Holy Spirit in the Wesleyan Heritage.* Nashville: Abingdon Press, 1985, 1993. This is a standard work by a bishop of The United Methodist Church.

Synan, Vinson. *The Century of the Holy Spirit: 100 Years of Pentecostal and Charismatic Renewal.* Nashville: Thomas Nelson, 2001. This book traces the development of the Pentecostal, Charismatic, and Third Wave movements from 1901 to 2001 including references to Methodism.

Tuttle, Robert G. *Sanctity without Starch.* Anderson, IN: Bristol Books, 1992. A standard work by a United Methodist theologian within the Charismatic tradition.

**ADOPTED 2008**

## 8011. Proper Use of Information Communication Technologies

We affirm that the right to communicate and to access information is a basic human right, essential to human dignity and to a just and democratic society.

Our understanding of communication is grounded in Scripture. God is a communicating God.

Christians believe that the creation of the world is rooted in the spoken Word of God.

God made all persons in the divine image. God created the world and all living things for relationship.

The Bible is the inspired Word of God about communication and a God who created the world and all living things for relationship.

The biblical account of the tower of Babel presents a classic example of the integral relationship between communication and being human.

This theme repeats itself in the story of Pentecost, the birthplace of the church. Being filled with the Holy Spirit and in communion with God and one another, the people of God spoke and heard the divine message of God in their own languages. We acknowledge that every right brings with it responsibilities. The whole community—owners, managers and consumers—is responsible for the functioning of communication in society.

Christians have an obligation to advocate that mass media and communication technologies are operated to serve the public good rather than merely commercial interests.

Most peoples of the world have no access to even the most rudimentary communication technologies—telephones, radio—much less the digital, satellite, and other technologies that are rapidly expanding in the developing world.

These technologies allow their owners to manage information and resources at increasingly remote distances from the local cultures and economies affected. The instantaneous nature of global data transmission means that economic powers often have access to information before others do. The global-technological nature of the economy gives tremendous fiscal power to these same developed world and transnational interests.

This system works to advance the cause of the global market and promote commercial values aimed only at profit, often neglecting the aspects of communication and culture that promote the common good. Media companies, as producers and carriers of information, have a far-reaching effect on value formation.

Issues of justice in local and national development cannot be addressed without a consciousness of the role of communication, nor can any people do so without the tools with which to make their views known.

Information Communication Technologies (ICTs) offer enormous benefits. They enable global contact and, when made available for human uses and to address human needs, can significantly enhance life, development, and global consciousness.

Such uses will not become widespread unless concrete enabling steps are taken. Therefore the church's voice is crucial.

The church continues its mission and ministry amid this enormous revolution in communication.

The church quickly embraced the first communication revolution, the invention of the printing press, and used the printed word to disseminate the written word and to teach literacy to millions who were otherwise considered unfit to learn, empowering them to fully engage in the world.

The education of his neighbors was a matter close to John Wesley's heart, and his efforts gave many the education necessary to read and understand the gospel of Jesus Christ and to interpret the events of their world in the light of the gospel.

The Church carries a responsibility for helping its members achieve media literacy, not only to read and understand the gospel but also to discern from the flood of information an understanding of the events of our world today. Citizens cannot get responsible political information without media literacy. The current media revolution challenges all people to resist becoming mere consumers of messages that are created and controlled by a relatively small number of super-powerful transnational media corporations.

Media technologies have great potential to bind the world together, when not beholden entirely to transnational commercial interests.

Therefore, The United Methodist Church commits to:

A. Change of the Church

- Encourage leaders to preach and teach about the impact of media on the quality of life and values of individuals and society and to suggest ways congregations and individuals can both work with the positive forces and resist the negative.
- Use the available ICTs of local churches and other UMC entities to provide training in communication technologies to persons in their communities, particularly children, youth, and the poor, so that they might become active creators of story and culture rather than simply passive consumers.
- Assist members of United Methodist churches, our clergy, seminarians, and those who serve in the Church to become literate and committed to using ICTs for ministry and advocacy. As part of becoming aware of the power of the media, we particularly suggest the study of the Principles of Christian Communication developed by the World Association of Christian Communication.
- Encourage United Methodist institutions of higher education, particularly communication and theology faculties, to address societal communication issues.
- Reevaluate the church's work at every level of the United Methodist connection, including allocation of resources, decisions about programs, ministries, and missions, in light of the vital need to affirm the dignity of all persons by ensuring them equal opportunity to be heard, to have voice in the

shaping of the church and of the world, and to communicate their story.

B. Change of Society

- Devote serious attention to the economic, political, and cultural forces that constrain the press and other communication media, challenging the use of communication as a force that supports the powerful, victimizes the powerless, and marginalizes minority opinion.
- Use ICTs for acts of love that liberate.
- We will work to preserve the right to communication for oppressed and persecuted communities, to oppose efforts to deny citizens the right of information, and to develop communication technologies that can be used to protect children from exploitation and psychological harm.
- Advocate for uses of media and communication technologies that promote peace, understanding, cooperation and multiculturalism and oppose those uses of media that encourage violence, factionalism, militarism, and ethnic strife.
- Advocate for technologies that allow consumers to exclude unwanted commercial messages.
- Encourage the production and broadcast of independently owned media, particularly those of developing nations, which encompass artistic and entertainment programming as well as news and information.

C. Change of the World

- Develop methods to educate persons about the importance of communication as a basic right for all persons and advocate for public policies that promote fair and equitable access to ICTs through educational, advocacy, and communications ministries.
- Identify and eliminate the hindrances to communication technologies with a view toward assisting those without those technologies to acquire, access, and use them. In this context the Church supports the development of open source software (General Public License systems). Its availability in the public domain helps overcome some of the digital divide between the developed and developing countries.
- Work through annual conferences and the general boards and agencies with regional, national, and international bodies to provide support for such activities as:

1. scholarships and training of persons, especially women, in developing countries in communication policy issues and communication management in order that they may be fully prepared to participate in planning for the communications policy, programs, and infrastructure in their respective nations;

2. participation in communication efforts that offer alternatives to the mass media.

- Integrate sustained work for both domestic and global communications justice into current peace and justice advocacy agendas.
- Work through shareholder groups to persuade companies to respect nations' attempts to protect their cultural sovereignty.

Global communications justice, in the end, is about communication that is just and participatory, equitable and sustainable.

ADOPTED 2004
READOOPTED 2008
RESOLUTION #362, 2004 *BOOK OF RESOLUTIONS*

## 8012. Inclusiveness in All Dimensions of the Church

A door of opportunity has been opened to The United Methodist Church—the opportunity to consolidate endeavors to discern the barriers to racial and cultural inclusiveness. Many annual conferences responded to the action of the 1992 and 1996 General Conferences calling upon annual conferences to develop "programs to emphasize inclusiveness in all dimensions of the church." However, many annual conferences have not yet responded to that call.

In recognition of the need to plan in order to implement intentions to be inclusive, the 2004 General Conference reaffirms the commitment that each annual conference, led by the bishop and cabinet, develop comprehensive programs that place fresh emphasis upon inclusiveness—cultural, racial, lingual, gender—throughout the life and ministry of The United Methodist Church.

These plans should provide that strategies similar to those outlined in the resolution adopted in 1992 continue:

1. that this program include a conference-wide enlistment and recruitment program that seeks clergy and laity who will give them-

selves to cross-racial and cross-cultural appointments, to begin new Sunday schools and congregations among poor people and people of color;

2. that the program include a determined effort to enlist and recruit some of the most competent, experienced pastors for such cross-racial and cross-cultural appointments rather than simply enlisting the newest clergy;

3. that local churches are trained and enabled to reach out to their surrounding communities;

4. that this "inclusive" emphasis include asking and actively encouraging all multistaff congregations to deliberately make their staffs inclusive in terms of gender, race, and ethnicity;

5. that goals and strategies be established in each conference so that cross-racial and cross-cultural appointments become normative for the conference and one of the essential ways in which the conference engages in the mission of Christ;

6. that the program include experiences for the conference lay and clergy leadership that increase their knowledge and understanding of all the people and cultures who reside within the borders of the conference;

7. that this conference program include programs for children and youth, such as multicultural camps, human-relations conferences/seminars, and various kinds of work camps;

8. that the conference program include the enlisting and recruitment of young adults to become "people in mission" who work on a subsistence basis or pay their own way;

9. that this program enable the establishment of new congregations—rural, suburban, and urban—in town and country;

10. that this program will encourage diversity in styles and kinds of ministries, in worship styles, and in language and thought forms in order to enable the gospel and The United Methodist Church to again have impact on working-class people, the poor, people of color, and other target groups of people;

11. that this program make appointments of clergy to ministries of justice and peace, to ministries of prevention and rehabilitation in drug abuse, and to children and young people caught in the spiraling crisis of drugs, violence, racism, and poverty;

12. that each conference program will include assisting local congregations and pastors in sharing-facilities situations to develop an "inclusive" model for the congregation, even though worship services

occur in several languages, and in eliminating the "landlord-tenant" model of relationships;

13. that the program include a provision that we will no longer sell church buildings in the urban areas to churches of other denominations but will instead place clergy and laity in those situations, assisting them in finding the way to create a new people in that place for mission to the people in that community;

14. that the conference program will include a major training and additional skills strategy, using pastors' schools, annual conference sessions, and United Methodist theological schools (where a United Methodist seminary is not within the bounds of the conference or area, the conference should enlist schools of other denominations) to create resources for the inclusive ministry and to empower conference clergy and laity; and

15. that this conference program also include innovative ministries in urban, suburban, and rural areas, so that an unfettered gospel can do the work of the Crucified and Risen One.

*Further,* that as annual conferences continue to revise and perfect their inclusiveness programs, that special attention be given to the following points of concentration:

1. that Comprehensive Plans for Racial Ethnic Ministries be reviewed, revised, and implemented. Further, that the Comprehensive Plans incorporate the recommendations of the national plans adopted by General Conference, the National Plan for Hispanic/Latino-Latina Ministries, the Native American Comprehensive Plan, Strengthening the Black Church for the 21st Century, Advancing United Methodist Ministries Among Korean Americans, the Asian American Language Ministry Plan, and other plans for racial and ethnic ministries that may be approved by General Conference;

2. that bishops and cabinets design specific strategies with timelines to make cross-racial and cross-cultural appointments the norm rather than the exception. That these strategies include preparation of pastors, congregations, and pastor-parish relations committees before an appointment is made, and provisions for support for pastors and congregations in cross-racial and cross-cultural appointments;

3. that annual conference leaders at all levels—local church, district, conference, bishops, and cabinets—seek ways to enhance their skills in the areas of interpersonal communication, cross-cultural communication, and conflict management and resolution. The General Commission on Religion and Race may be consulted for resources;

4. that councils on ministries (or their equivalent) provide opportunities for ongoing dialogue among people of different races, cultures, ethnicities, gender, ages, abilities, disabilities, and theological perspectives at all levels of the conference about what it means to be the inclusive church.

*And further,* that the delegates at the various jurisdictional conferences and their nominating committees be urged to be intentional in their nominations to the various general boards and agencies to ensure that racial/ethnic persons are elected to these boards and agencies in representative numbers; and that the nominating committees of each annual conference include in their nomination and election process an equitable number of racial/ethnic persons on every board and agency.

We call upon the General Commission on Religion and Race to monitor the progress of each annual conference's plans for inclusiveness and the content of jurisdictional and conference nominations reports.

**ADOPTED 1996**
**AMENDED AND READOPTED 2004**
RESOLUTION #77, 2004 *BOOK OF RESOLUTIONS*
RESOLUTION #68, 2000 *BOOK OF RESOLUTIONS*

*See* Social Principles, ¶ 162A and J.

## 8013.  By Water and the Spirit:
## A United Methodist Understanding of Baptism

### *A Report of the Baptism Study Committee*

Contemporary United Methodism is attempting to recover and revitalize its understanding of baptism. To do this, we must look to our heritage as Methodists and Evangelical United Brethren and, indeed, to the foundations of Christian tradition. Throughout our history, baptism has been viewed in diverse and even contradictory ways. An enriched understanding of baptism, restoring the Wesleyan blend of sacramental and evangelical aspects, will enable United Methodists to participate in the sacrament with renewed appreciation for this gift of God's grace.

Within the Methodist tradition, baptism has long been a subject of much concern, even controversy. John Wesley retained the sacramental theology which he received from his Anglican heritage. He taught that in baptism a child was cleansed of the guilt of original sin, initiated into the covenant with God, admitted into the church, made an heir of the divine kingdom, and spiritually born anew. He said that while baptism was neither essential to nor sufficient for salvation, it was the "ordinary means" that God designated for applying the benefits of the work of Christ in human lives.

On the other hand, although he affirmed the regenerating grace of infant baptism, he also insisted upon the necessity of adult conversion for those who have fallen from grace. A person who matures into moral accountability must respond to God's grace in repentance and faith. Without personal decision and commitment to Christ, the baptismal gift is rendered ineffective.

Baptism for Wesley, therefore, was a part of the lifelong process of salvation. He saw spiritual rebirth as a twofold experience in the normal process of Christian development—to be received through baptism in infancy and through commitment to Christ later in life. Salvation included both God's initiating activity of grace and a willing human response.

In its development in the United States, Methodism was unable to maintain this Wesleyan balance of sacramental and evangelical emphases. Access to the sacraments was limited during the late eighteenth and early nineteenth centuries when the Methodist movement was largely under the leadership of laypersons who were not authorized to administer them. On the American frontier where human ability and action were stressed, the revivalistic call for individual decision making, though important, was subject to exaggeration. The sacramental teachings of Wesley tended to be ignored. In this setting, while infant baptism continued not only to be practiced, but also to be vigorously defended, its significance became weakened and ambiguous. Later toward the end of the nineteenth century, the theological views of much of Methodism were influenced by a new set of ideas which had become dominant in American culture. These ideas included optimism about the progressive improvement of humankind and confidence in the social benefits of scientific discovery, technology, and education. Assumptions of original sin gave way before the assertion that human nature was essentially unspoiled. In this intellectual milieu, the old evangelical insistence upon conversion and spiritual rebirth seemed quaint and unnecessary.

Thus the creative Wesleyan synthesis of sacramentalism and evangelicalism was torn asunder and both its elements devalued. As a result, infant baptism was variously interpreted and often reduced to a ceremony of dedication. Adult baptism was sometimes interpreted as a profession of faith and public acknowledgment of God's grace, but was more often viewed simply as an act of joining the church. By the middle of the twentieth century, Methodism in general had ceased to understand baptism as authentically sacramental. Rather than an act of divine grace, it was seen as an expression of human choice.

Baptism was also a subject of concern and controversy in the Evangelical and United Brethren traditions that were brought together in 1946 in The Evangelical United Brethren Church. Their early pietistic revivalism, based upon belief in the availability of divine grace and the freedom of human choice, emphasized bringing people to salvation through Christian experience. In the late nineteenth and early twentieth centuries, both Evangelical and United Brethren theologians stressed the importance of baptism as integral to the proclamation of the gospel, as a rite initiating persons into the covenant community (paralleling circumcision), and as a sign of the new birth, that gracious divine act by which persons are redeemed from sin and reconciled to God. The former Evangelical Church consistently favored the baptism of infants. The United Brethren provided for the baptism of both infants and adults. Following the union of 1946, The Evangelical United Brethren Church adopted a ritual that included services of baptism for infants and adults, and also a newly created service for the dedication of infants that had little precedent in official rituals of either of the former churches.

The 1960-64 revision of *The Methodist Hymnal*, including rituals, gave denominational leaders an opportunity to begin to recover the sacramental nature of baptism in contemporary Methodism. The General Commission on Worship sounded this note quite explicitly in its introduction to the new ritual in 1964:

> In revising the Order for the Administration of Baptism, the Commission on Worship has endeavored to keep in mind that baptism is a sacrament, and to restore it to the Evangelical-Methodist concept set forth in our Articles of Religion. . . . Due recognition was taken of the critical reexamination of the theology of the Sacrament of Baptism which is currently taking place in ecumenical circles, and of its theological content and implications.

The commission provided a brief historical perspective demonstrating that the understanding of baptism as a sacrament had been weakened, if not discarded altogether, over the years. Many in the church regarded baptism, both of infants and adults, as a dedication rather than as a sacrament. The commission pointed out that in a dedication we make a gift of a life to God for God to accept, while in a sacrament God offers the gift of God's unfailing grace for us to accept. The 1964 revision of the ritual of the sacrament of baptism began to restore the rite to its original and historic meaning as a sacrament.

In the 1989 *United Methodist Hymnal*, the Services of the Baptismal Covenant I, II, and IV (taken from the 1984 official ritual of the denomination as printed in *The Book of Services*) continue this effort to reemphasize the historic significance of baptism. These rituals, in accenting the reality of sin and of regeneration, the initiating of divine grace, and the necessity of repentance and faith, are consistent with the Wesleyan combination of sacramentalism and evangelicalism.

United Methodism is not alone in the need to recover the significance of baptism nor in its work to do so. Other Christian communions are also reclaiming the importance of this sacrament for Christian faith and life. To reach the core of the meaning and practice of baptism, all have found themselves led back through the life of the church to the Apostolic Age. An ecumenical convergence has emerged from this effort, as can be seen in the widely acclaimed document *Baptism, Eucharist, and Ministry* (1982).

Established by the General Conference of 1988 and authorized to continue its work by the General Conference of 1992, the Committee to Study Baptism is participating in this process by offering a theological and functional understanding of baptism as embodied in the ritual of The United Methodist Church. In so doing, the broad spectrum of resources of Scripture, Christian tradition, and the Methodist-Evangelical United Brethren experience has been taken into account. The growing ecumenical consensus has assisted us in our thinking.

### We Are Saved by God's Grace

*The Human Condition.* As told in the first chapters of Genesis, in creation God made human beings in the image of God—a relationship of intimacy, dependence, and trust. We are open to the indwelling presence of God and given freedom to work with God to accomplish the divine will and purpose for all of creation and history. To be human as God intended is to have loving fellowship with God and to reflect the divine nature in our lives as fully as possible.

Tragically, as Genesis 3 recounts, we are unfaithful to that relationship. The result is a thorough distortion of the image of God in us and the degrading of the whole of creation. Through prideful overreach or denial of our God-given responsibilities, we exalt our own will, invent our own values, and rebel against God. Our very being is dominated by an inherent inclination toward evil which has traditionally been called original sin. It is a universal human condition and affects all aspects of life. Because of our condition of sin, we are separated from God, alienated from one another, hostile to the natural world, and even at odds with our own best selves. Sin may be expressed as errant priorities, as deliberate wrongdoing, as apathy in the face of need, as cooperation with oppression and injustice. Evil is cosmic as well as personal; it afflicts both individuals and the institutions of our human society. The nature of sin is represented in Baptismal Covenants I, II, and IV in *The United Methodist Hymnal* by the phrases "the spiritual forces of wickedness" and "the evil powers of this world," as well as "your sin." Before God all persons are lost, helpless to save themselves, and in need of divine mercy and forgiveness.

*The Divine Initiative of Grace.* While we have turned from God, God has not abandoned us. Instead, God graciously and continuously seeks to restore us to that loving relationship for which we were created, to make us into the persons that God would have us be. To this end God acts preveniently, that is, before we are aware of it, reaching out to save humankind. The Old Testament records the story of God's acts in the history of the covenant community of Israel to work out the divine will and purpose. In the New Testament story, we learn that God came into this sinful world in the person of Jesus Christ to reveal all that the human mind can comprehend about who God is and who God would have us be. Through Christ's death and resurrection, the power of sin and death was overcome and we are set free to again be God's own people (1 Peter 2:9). Since God is the only initiator and source of grace, all grace is prevenient in that it precedes and enables any movement that we can make toward God. Grace brings us to an awareness of our sinful predicament and of our inability to save ourselves; grace motivates us to repentance and gives us the capacity to respond to divine love. In the words of the baptismal ritual: "All this is God's gift, offered to us without price" (*The United Methodist Hymnal,* page 33).

*The Necessity of Faith for Salvation.* Faith is both a gift of God and a human response to God. It is the ability and willingness to say "yes" to the divine offer of salvation. Faith is our awareness of our utter dependence upon God, the surrender of our selfish wills, the trusting reliance upon divine mercy. The candidate for baptism answers "I do" to the question "Do you confess Jesus Christ as your Savior, put your whole trust in his grace, and promise to serve him as your Lord . . .?" (*The United Methodist Hymnal,* page 34). Our personal response of faith requires conversion in which we turn away from sin and turn instead to God. It entails a decision to commit our lives to the Lordship of Christ, an acceptance of the forgiveness of our sins, the death of our old selves, an entering into a new life of the Spirit-being born again (John 3:3-5, 2 Corinthians 5:17). All persons do not experience this spiritual rebirth in the same way. For some, there is a singular, radical moment of conversion. For others, conversion may be experienced as the dawning and growing realization that one has been constantly loved by God and has a personal reliance upon Christ. John Wesley described his own experience by saying, "I felt my heart strangely warmed. I felt I did trust in Christ, Christ alone for salvation; and an assurance was given me that he had taken away my sins, even mine, and saved me from the law of sin and death."

### The Means by Which God's Grace Comes to Us

Divine grace is made available and effective in human lives through a variety of means or "channels," as Wesley called them. While God is radically free to work in many ways, the church has been given by God the special responsibility and privilege of being the body of Christ which carries forth God's purpose of redeeming the world. Wesley recognized the church itself as a means of grace—a grace-filled and grace-sharing community of faithful people. United Methodism shares with other Protestant communions the understanding that the proclamation of the Word through preaching, teaching, and the life of the church is a primary means of God's grace. The origin and rapid growth of Methodism as a revival movement occurred largely through the medium of the proclaimed Gospel. John Wesley also emphasized the importance of prayer, fasting, Bible study, and meetings of persons for support and sharing.

Because God has created and is creating all that is, physical objects of creation can become the bearers of divine presence, power, and meaning, and thus become sacramental means of God's grace. Sacraments are effective means of God's presence mediated through the created world. God becoming incarnate in Jesus Christ is the supreme instance of this kind of divine action. Wesley viewed the sacraments as crucial means of grace and affirmed the Anglican teaching that "a sacrament is 'an outward sign of inward grace, and a means whereby we receive the same.'" Combining words, actions, and physical elements, sacraments are sign-acts that both express and convey God's grace and love. Baptism and the Lord's Supper are sacraments that were instituted or commanded by Christ in the Gospels.

United Methodists believe that these sign-acts are special means of grace. The ritual action of a sacrament does not merely point to God's presence in the world, but also participates in it and becomes a vehicle for conveying that reality. God's presence in the sacraments is real, but it must be accepted by human faith if it is to transform human lives. The sacraments do not convey grace either magically or irrevocably, but they are powerful channels through which God has chosen to make grace available to us. Wesley identified baptism as the initiatory sacrament by which we enter into the covenant with God and are admitted as members of Christ's church. He understood the Lord's Supper as nourishing and empowering the lives of Christians and strongly advocated frequent participation in it. The Wesleyan tradition has continued to practice and cherish the various means through which divine grace is made present to us.

### Baptism and the Life of Faith

The New Testament records that Jesus was baptized by John (Matthew 3:13-17), and he commanded his disciples to teach and baptize in the name of the Father, Son, and Holy Spirit (Matthew 28:19). Baptism is grounded in the life, death, and resurrection of Jesus Christ; the grace which baptism makes available is that of the atonement of Christ which makes possible our reconciliation with God. Baptism involves dying to sin, newness of life, union with Christ, receiving the Holy Spirit, and incorporation into Christ's church. United Methodists affirm this understanding in their official documents of faith. Article XVII of the Articles of Religion (Methodist) calls baptism "a sign of regeneration or the new birth"; the Confession of Faith (EUB) states that baptism is "a representation of the new birth in Christ Jesus and a mark of Christian discipleship."

*The Baptismal Covenant.* In both the Old and New Testaments, God enters into covenant relationship with God's people. A covenant involves promises and responsibilities of both parties; it is instituted through a special ceremony and expressed by a distinguishing sign. By covenant God constituted a servant community of the people of Israel, promising to be their God and giving them the Law to make clear how they were to live. The circumcision of male infants is the sign of this covenant (Genesis 17:1-14; Exodus 24:1-12). In the death and resurrection of Jesus Christ, God fulfilled the prophecy of a new covenant and called forth the church as a servant community (Jeremiah 31:31-34; 1 Corinthians 11:23-26). The baptism of infants and adults, both male and female, is the sign of this covenant.

Therefore, United Methodists identify our ritual for baptism as "The Services of the Baptismal Covenant" (*The United Methodist Hymnal,* pages 32-54). In baptism the church declares that it is bound in covenant to God; through baptism new persons are initiated into that covenant. The covenant connects God, the community of faith, and the person being baptized; all three are essential to the fulfillment of the baptismal covenant. The faithful grace of God initiates the covenant relationship and enables the community and the person to respond with faith.

*Baptism by Water and the Holy Spirit.* Through the work of the Holy Spirit—the continuing presence of Christ on earth—the church is instituted to be the community of the new covenant. Within this community, baptism is by water and the Spirit (John 3:5; Acts 2:38). In God's work of salvation, the mystery of Christ's death and resurrection is inseparably linked with the gift of the Holy Spirit given on the Day of Pentecost (Acts 2). Likewise, participation in Christ's death and resurrection is inseparably linked with receiving the Spirit (Romans 6:1-11; 8:9-14). The Holy Spirit who is the power of creation (Genesis 1:2) is also the giver of new life. Working in the lives of people before, during, and after their baptisms, the Spirit is the effective agent of salvation. God bestows upon baptized persons the presence of the Holy Spirit, marks them with an identifying seal as God's own, and implants in their hearts the first installment of their inheritance as sons and daughters of God (2 Corinthians 1:21-22). It is through the Spirit that the life of faith is nourished until the final deliverance when they will enter into the fullness of salvation (Ephesians 1:13-14). Since the Apostolic Age, baptism by water and baptism of the Holy Spirit have been connected (Acts 19:17). Christians are baptized with both, sometimes by different sign-actions. Water is administered in the name of the triune God (specified in the ritual as Father, Son, and Holy Spirit) by an authorized person, and the Holy Spirit is invoked with the laying on of hands in the presence of the congregation. Water provides the central symbolism for baptism. The richness of its meaning for the Christian community is suggested in the baptismal liturgy which speaks of the waters of creation and the flood, the liberation of God's people by passage through the sea, the gift of water in the wilderness, and the passage through the Jordan River to the promised land. In baptism we identify ourselves with this people of God and join the community's journey toward God. The use of water in baptism also symbolizes cleansing from sin, death to old life, and rising to begin new life in Christ. In United Methodist tradition, the water of baptism may be administered by sprinkling, pouring, or immersion. However it is administered, water should be utilized with enough generosity to enhance our appreciation of its symbolic meanings.

The baptismal liturgy includes the biblical symbol of the anointing with the Holy Spirit—the laying on of hands with the optional use of oil. This anointing promises to the baptized person the power to live faithfully the kind of life that water baptism signifies. In the early centuries of the church, the laying on of hands usually followed immediately upon administration of the water and completed the ritual of membership. Because the laying on of hands was, in the Western church, an act to be performed only by a bishop, it was later separated from water baptism and came to be called confirmation (*see* pp. 955-57). In confirmation the Holy Spirit marked the baptized person as God's own and strengthened him or her for discipleship. In the worship life of the early church, the water and the anointing led directly to the celebration of the Lord's Supper as part of the service of initiation, regardless of the age of the baptized. The current rituals of the baptismal covenant rejoin these three elements into a unified service. Together these symbols point to, anticipate, and offer participation in the life of the community of faith as it embodies God's presence in the world.

*Baptism as Incorporation into the Body of Christ.* Christ constitutes the church as his Body by the power of the Holy Spirit (1 Corinthians 12:13, 27). The church draws new persons into itself as it seeks to remain faithful to its commission to proclaim and exemplify the gospel. Baptism is the sacrament of initiation and incorporation into the body of Christ. An infant, child, or adult who is baptized becomes a member of the catholic (universal) church, of the denomination, and of the local congregation (*see* pp. 729-31). Therefore, baptism is a rite of the whole church, which ordinarily requires the participation of the gathered, worshiping congregation. In a series of promises within the liturgy of baptism, the community affirms its own faith and pledges to act as spiritual mentor and support for the one who is baptized. Baptism is not merely an individualistic, private, or domestic occasion. When unusual but legitimate circumstances prevent a baptism from taking place in the midst of the gathered community during its regular worship, every effort should be made to assemble representatives of the congregation to participate in the celebration. Later, the baptism should be recognized in the public assembly of worship in order that the congregation may make its appropriate affirmations of commitment and responsibility.

Baptism brings us into union with Christ, with each other, and with the church in every time and place. Through this sign and seal of our common discipleship, our equality in Christ is made manifest (Galatians 3:27-28). We affirm that there is one baptism into Christ, celebrated as our basic bond of unity in the many communions that make up the body of Christ (Ephesians 4:4-6). The power of the Spirit in baptism does not depend upon the mode by which water is administered, the age or psychological disposition of the baptized person, or the character of the minister. It is God's grace that makes the sacrament whole. One baptism calls the various churches to overcome their divisions and visibly manifest their unity. Our oneness in Christ calls for mutual recognition of baptism in these communions as a means of expressing the unity that Christ intends (1 Corinthians 12:12-13).

*Baptism as Forgiveness of Sin.* In baptism God offers and we accept the forgiveness of our sin (Acts 2:38). With the pardoning of sin which has separated us from God, we are justified—freed from the guilt and penalty of sin and restored to right relationship with God. This reconciliation is made possible through the atonement of Christ and made real in our lives by the work of the Holy Spirit. We respond by confessing and repenting of our sin, and affirming our faith that Jesus Christ has accomplished all that is necessary for our salvation. Faith is the necessary condition for justification; in baptism, that faith is professed. God's forgiveness makes possible the renewal of our spiritual lives and our becoming new beings in Christ.

*Baptism as New Life.* Baptism is the sacramental sign of new life through and in Christ by the power of the Holy Spirit. Variously identified as regeneration, new birth, and being born again, this work of grace makes us into new spiritual creatures (2 Corinthians 5:17). We die to our old nature which was dominated by sin and enter into the very life of Christ who transforms us. Baptism is the means of entry into new life in Christ (John 3:5; Titus 3:5), but new birth may not always coincide with the moment of the administration of water or the laying on of hands. Our awareness and acceptance of our redemption by Christ and new life in him may vary throughout our lives. But, in whatever way the reality of the new birth is experienced, it carries out the promises God made to us in our baptism.

*Baptism and Holy Living.* New birth into life in Christ, which is signified by baptism, is the beginning of that process of growth in grace and holiness through which God brings us into closer relationship with Jesus Christ, and shapes our lives increasingly into conformity with the divine will. Sanctification is a gift of the gracious presence of the Holy Spirit, a yielding to the Spirit's power, a deepening of our love for God and neighbor. Holiness of heart and life, in the Wesleyan tradition, always involves both personal and social holiness.

Baptism is the doorway to the sanctified life. The sacrament teaches us to live in the expectation of further gifts of God's grace. It initiates us into a community of faith that prays for holiness; it calls us to life lived in faithfulness to God's gift. Baptized believers and the community of faith are obligated to manifest to the world the new redeemed humanity which lives in loving relationship with God and strives to put an end to all human estrangements. There are no conditions of human life (including age or intellectual ability, race or nationality, gender or sexual identity, class or disability) that exclude persons from the sacrament of baptism. We strive for and look forward to the reign of God on earth, of which baptism is a sign. Baptism is fulfilled only when the believer and the church are wholly conformed to the image of Christ.

*Baptism as God's Gift to Persons of Any Age.* There is one baptism as there is one source of salvation—the gracious love of God. The baptizing of a person, whether as an infant or an adult, is a sign of God's saving grace. That grace—experienced by us as initiating, enabling, and empowering—is the same for all persons. All stand in need of it, and none can be saved without it. The difference between the baptism of adults and that of infants is that the Christian faith is consciously being professed by an adult who is baptized. A baptized infant comes to profess her or his faith later in life, after having been nurtured and taught by parent(s) or other responsible adults and the community of faith. Infant baptism is the prevailing practice in situations where children are born to believing parents and brought up in Christian homes and communities of faith. Adult baptism is the norm when the church is in a missionary situation, reaching out to persons in a culture which is indifferent or hostile to the faith. While the baptism of infants is appropriate for Christian families, the increasingly minority status of the church in contemporary society demands more attention to evangelizing, nurturing, and baptizing adult converts.

Infant baptism has been the historic practice of the overwhelming majority of the church throughout the Christian centuries. While the New Testament contains no explicit mandate, there is ample evidence for the baptism of infants in Scripture (Acts 2:38-41; 16:15, 33) and in early Christian doctrine and practice. Infant baptism rests firmly on the understanding that God prepares the way of faith before we request or even know that we need help (prevenient grace). The sacrament is a powerful expression of the reality that all persons come before God as no more than helpless infants, unable to do anything to save ourselves, dependent upon the grace of our loving God. The faithful covenant community of the church serves as a means of grace for those whose lives are impacted by its ministry. Through the church, God claims infants as well as adults to be participants in the gracious covenant of which baptism is the sign. This understanding of the workings of divine grace also applies to persons who for reasons of disabilities or other limitations are unable to answer for themselves the questions of the baptismal ritual. While we may not be able to comprehend how God works in their lives, our faith teaches us that God's grace is sufficient for their needs and, thus, they are appropriate recipients of baptism.

The church affirms that children being born into the brokenness of the world should receive the cleansing and renewing forgiveness of God no less than adults. The saving grace made available through Christ's atonement is the only hope of salvation for persons of any age. In baptism infants enter into a new life in Christ as children of God and members of the body of Christ. The baptism of an infant incorporates him or her into the community of faith and nurture, including membership in the local church. The baptism of infants is properly understood and valued if the child is loved and nurtured by the faithful worshiping church and by the child's own family. If a parent or sponsor (godparent) cannot or will not nurture the child in the faith, then baptism is to be postponed until Christian nurture is available. A child who dies without being baptized is received into the love and presence of God because the Spirit has worked in that child to bestow saving grace. If a child has been baptized but her or his family or sponsors do not faithfully nurture the child in the faith, the congregation has a particular responsibility for incorporating the child into its life.

Understanding the practice as an authentic expression of how God works in our lives, The United Methodist Church strongly advocates the baptism of infants within the faith community: "Because the redeeming love of God, revealed in Jesus Christ, extends to all persons and because Jesus explicitly included the children in his kingdom, the pastor of each charge shall earnestly exhort all Christian parents or guardians to present their children to the Lord in Baptism at an early age" (1992 *Book of Discipline,* ¶ 221). We affirm that while thanksgiving to God and dedication of parents to the task of Christian child-raising are aspects of infant baptism, the sacrament is primarily a gift of divine grace. Neither parents nor infants are the chief actors; baptism is an act of God in and through the church.

We respect the sincerity of parents who choose not to have their infants baptized, but we acknowledge that these views do not coincide with the Wesleyan understanding of the nature of the sacrament. The United Methodist Church does not accept either the idea that only believer's baptism is valid or the notion that the baptism of infants magically imparts salvation apart from active personal faith. Pastors are instructed by *The Book of Discipline* to explain our teaching clearly on these matters, so that parent(s) or sponsors might be free of misunderstandings.

*The United Methodist Book of Worship* contains "An Order of Thanksgiving for the Birth or Adoption of the Child" (pages 585-87), which may be recommended in situations where baptism is inappropriate, but parents wish to take responsibility publicly for the growth of the child in faith. It should be made clear that this rite is in no way equivalent to or a substitute for baptism. Neither is it an act of infant dedication. If the infant has not been baptized, the sacrament should be administered as soon as possible after the Order of Thanksgiving.

*God's Faithfulness to the Baptismal Covenant.* Since baptism is primarily an act of God in the church, the sacrament is to be received by an individual only once. This position is in accord with the historic teaching of the church universal, originating as early as the second century and having been recently reaffirmed ecumenically in *Baptism, Eucharist, and Ministry.*

The claim that baptism is unrepeatable rests on the steadfast faithfulness of God. God's initiative establishes the covenant of grace into which we are incorporated in baptism. By misusing our God-given freedom, we may live in neglect or defiance of that covenant, but we cannot destroy God's love for us. When we repent and return to God, the covenant does not need to be remade, because God has always remained faithful to it. What is needed is renewal of our commitment and reaffirmation of our side of the covenant.

God's gift of grace in the baptismal covenant does not save us apart from our human response of faith. Baptized persons may have many significant spiritual experiences, which they will desire to celebrate publicly in the worship life of the church. Such experiences may include defining moments of conversion, repentance of sin, gifts of the Spirit, deepening of commitment, changes in Christian vocation, important transitions in the life of discipleship. These occasions call not for repetition of baptism, but for reaffirmations of baptismal vows as a witness to the good news that while we may be unfaithful, God is not. Appropriate services for such events would be "Confirmation or Reaffirmation of Faith" (*see* Baptismal Covenant I in *The United Methodist Hymnal*) or "A Celebration of New Beginnings in Faith" (*The United Methodist Book of Worship,* pages 588-90).

*Nurturing Persons in the Life of Faith.* If persons are to be enabled to live faithfully the human side of the baptismal covenant, Christian nurture is essential. Christian nurture builds on baptism and is itself a means of grace. For infant baptism, an early step is instruction prior to baptism of parent(s) or sponsors in the gospel message, the meaning of the sacrament, and the responsibilities of a Christian home. The pastor has specific responsibility for this step (the 1992 *Book of Discipline,* ¶ 439.1*b*). Adults who are candidates for baptism need careful preparation for receiving this gift of grace and living out its meaning (the 1992 *Book of Discipline,* ¶ 216.1).

After baptism, the faithful church provides the nurture which makes possible a comprehensive and lifelong process of growing in grace. The content of this nurturing will be appropriate to the stages of life and maturity of faith of individuals. Christian nurture includes both cognitive learning and spiritual formation. A crucial goal is the bringing of persons to recognition of their need for salvation and their acceptance of God's gift in Jesus Christ. Those experiencing conversion and commitment to Christ are to profess their faith in a public ritual. They will need to be guided and supported throughout their lives of discipleship. Through its worship life, its Christian education programs, its spiritual growth emphases, its social action and mission, its examples of Christian discipleship, and its offering of the various means of grace, the church strives to shape persons into the image of Christ. Such nurturing enables Christians to live out the transforming potential of the grace of their baptism.

*Profession of Christian Faith and Confirmation.* The Christian life is a dynamic process of change and growth, marked at various points by celebrations in rituals of the saving grace of Christ. The Holy Spirit works in the lives of persons prior to their baptism, is at work in their baptism, and continues to work in their lives after their baptism. When persons recognize and accept this activity of the Holy Spirit, they respond with renewed faith and commitment.

In the early church, baptism, the laying on of hands, and Eucharist were a unified rite of initiation and new birth for Christians of all ages. During the Middle Ages in Western Europe, confirmation was separated from baptism in both time and theology. A misunderstanding developed of confirmation as completing baptism, with emphasis upon human vows and initiation into church membership. John Wesley did not recommend confirmation to his preachers or to the new Methodist Church in America. Since 1964 in the former Methodist Church, the first public profession of faith for those baptized as infants has been called Confirmation. In the former Evangelical United Brethren Church, there was no such rite until union with The Methodist Church in 1968. With the restoration of confirmation—as the laying on of hands—to the current baptismal ritual, it should be emphasized that confirmation is what the Holy Spirit does. Confirmation is a divine action, the work of the Spirit empowering a person "born through water and the Spirit" to "live as a faithful disciple of Jesus Christ."

An adult or youth preparing for baptism should be carefully instructed in its life-transforming significance and responsibilities. Such a person professes in the sacrament of baptism his or her faith in Jesus Christ and commitment to discipleship, is offered the gift of assurance, and is confirmed by the power of the Holy Spirit (*see* Baptismal Covenant I, sections 4, 11, and 12). No separate ritual of confirmation is needed for the believing person.

An infant who is baptized cannot make a personal profession of faith as a part of the sacrament. Therefore, as the young person is nurtured and matures so as to be able to respond to God's grace, conscious faith and intentional commitment are necessary. Such a person must come to claim the faith of the church proclaimed in baptism as her or his own faith. Deliberate preparation for this event focuses on the young person's self-understanding and appropriation of Christian doctrines, spiritual disciplines, and life of discipleship. It is a special time for experiencing divine grace and for consciously embracing one's Christian vocation as a part of the priesthood of all believers. Youth who were not baptized as infants share in the same period of preparation for profession of Christian faith. For them, it is nurture for baptism, for becoming members of the church, and for confirmation.

When persons who were baptized as infants are ready to profess their Christian faith, they participate in the service which United Methodism now calls Confirmation. This occasion is not an entrance into church membership, for this was accomplished through baptism. It is the first public affirmation of the grace of God in one's baptism and the acknowledgment of one's acceptance of that grace by faith. This moment includes all the elements of conversion—repentance of sin, surrender and death of self, trust in the saving grace of God, new life in Christ, and becoming an instrument of God's purpose in the world. The profession of Christian faith, to be celebrated in the midst of the worshiping congregation, should include the voicing of baptismal vows as a witness to faith and the opportunity to give testimony to personal Christian experience. Confirmation follows profession of the Christian faith as part of the same service. Confirmation is a dynamic action of the Holy Spirit that can be repeated. In confirmation the outpouring of the Holy Spirit is invoked to provide the one being confirmed with the power to live in the faith that he or she has professed. The basic meaning of confirmation is strengthening and making firm in Christian faith and life. The ritual action in confirmation is the laying on of hands as the sign of God's continuing gift of the grace of Pentecost. Historically, the person being confirmed was also anointed on the forehead with oil in the shape of a cross as a mark of the Spirit's work. The ritual of the baptismal covenant included in The United Methodist Hymnal makes clear that the first and primary confirming act of the Holy Spirit is in connection with and immediately follows baptism.

When a baptized person has professed her or his Christian faith and has been confirmed, that person enters more fully into the responsibilities and privileges of membership in the church. Just as infants are members of their human families, but are unable to participate in all aspects of family life, so baptized infants are members of the church—the family of faith—but are not yet capable of sharing everything involved in membership. For this reason, statistics of church membership are counts of professed/confirmed members rather than of all baptized members.

*Reaffirmation of One's Profession of Christian Faith.* The life of faith which baptized persons live is like a pilgrimage or journey. On this lifelong journey there are many challenges, changes, and chances. We engage life's experiences on our journey of faith as a part of the redeeming and sanctifying body of Christ. Ongoing Christian nurture teaches, shapes, and strengthens us to live ever more faithfully as we are open to the Spirit's revealing more and more of the way and will of God. As our appreciation of the good news of Jesus Christ deepens and our commitment to Christ's service becomes more profound, we seek occasions to celebrate. Like God's people through the ages, all Christians need to participate in acts of renewal within the covenant community. Such an opportunity is offered in every occasion of baptism when the congregation remembers and affirms the gracious work of God which baptism celebrates. "Baptismal Covenant IV" in *The United Methodist Hymnal* is a powerful ritual of reaffirmation which uses water in ways that remind us of our baptism. The historic "Covenant Renewal Service" and "Love Feast" can also be used for this purpose (*The United Methodist Book of Worship*, pages 288-94 and 581-84). Reaffirmation of faith is a human response to God's grace and therefore may be repeated at many points in our faith journey.

### Baptism in Relation to Other Rites of the Church

The grace of God which claims us in our baptism is made available to us in many other ways and, especially, through other rites of the church.

*Baptism and the Lord's Supper (Holy Communion or the Eucharist).* Through baptism, persons are initiated into the church; by the Lord's Supper, the church is sustained in the life of faith. The services of the baptismal covenant appropriately conclude with Holy Communion, through which the union of the new member with the body of Christ is most fully expressed. Holy Communion is a sacred meal in which the community of faith, in the simple act of eating bread and drinking wine, proclaims and participates in all that God has done, is doing, and will continue to do for us in Christ. In celebrating the Eucharist, we remember the grace given to us in our baptism and partake of the spiritual food necessary for sustaining and fulfilling the promises of salvation. Because the table at which we gather belongs to the Lord, it should be open to all who respond to Christ's love, regardless of age or church membership. The Wesleyan tradition has always recognized that Holy Communion may be an occasion for the reception of converting, justifying, and sanctifying grace. Unbaptized persons who receive communion should be counseled and nurtured toward baptism as soon as possible.

*Baptism and Christian Ministry.* Through baptism, God calls and commissions persons to the general ministry of all Christian believers (*see* 1992 *Book of Discipline,* ¶¶ 101-07). This ministry, in which we participate both individually and corporately, is the activity of discipleship. It is grounded upon the awareness that we have been called into a new relationship not only with God, but also with the world. The task of Christians is to embody the gospel and the church in the world. We exercise our calling as Christians by prayer, by witnessing to the good news of salvation in Christ, by caring for and serving other people, and by working toward reconciliation, justice, and peace, in the world. This is the universal priesthood of all believers.

From within this general ministry of all believers, God calls and the church authorizes some persons for the task of representative ministry (*see* 1992 *Book of Discipline,* ¶¶ 108-110). The vocation of those in representative ministry includes focusing, modeling, supervising, shepherding, enabling, and empowering the general ministry of the church. Their ordination to Word, Sacrament, and Order or consecration to diaconal ministries of service, justice, and love is grounded in the same baptism that commissions the general priesthood of all believers.

*Baptism and Christian Marriage.* In the ritual for marriage, the minister addresses the couple: "I ask you now, in the presence of God and these people, to declare your intention to enter into union with one another through the grace of Jesus Christ, who calls you into union with himself as acknowledged in your baptism" (*The United Methodist Hymnal,* page 865). Marriage is to be understood as a covenant of love and commitment with mutual promises and responsibilities. For the church, the marriage covenant is grounded in the covenant between God and God's people into which Christians enter in their baptism. The love and fidelity which are to characterize Christian marriage will be a witness to the gospel, and the couple are to "go to serve God and your neighbor in all that you do."

When ministers officiate at the marriage of a couple who are not both Christians, the ritual needs to be altered to protect the integrity of all involved.

*Baptism and Christian Funeral.* The Christian gospel is a message of death and resurrection, that of Christ and our own. Baptism signifies our dying and rising with Christ. As death no longer has dominion over Christ, we believe that if we have died with Christ we shall also live with him (Romans 6:8-9). As the liturgy of the "Service of Death and Resurrection" proclaims: "Dying, Christ destroyed our death. Rising, Christ restored our life. Christ will come again in glory. As in baptism *Name* put on Christ, so in Christ may *Name* be clothed with glory" (*The United Methodist Hymnal,* page 870).

If the deceased person was never baptized, the ritual needs to be amended in ways which continue to affirm the truths of the gospel, but are appropriate to the situation.

Committal of the deceased to God and the body to its final resting place recall the act of baptism and derive Christian meaning from God's baptismal covenant with us. We acknowledge the reality of death and the pain of loss, and we give thanks for the life that was lived and shared with us. We worship in the awareness that our gathering includes the whole communion of saints, visible and invisible, and that in Christ the ties of love unite the living and the dead.

## Conclusion

Baptism is a crucial threshold that we cross on our journey in faith. But there are many others, including the final transition from death to life eternal. Through baptism we are incorporated into the ongoing history of Christ's mission, and we are identified and made participants in God's new history in Jesus Christ and the new age that Christ is bringing. We await the final moment of grace, when Christ comes in victory at the end of the age to bring all who are in Christ into the glory of that victory. Baptism has significance in time and gives meaning to the end of time. In it we have a vision of a world recreated and humanity transformed and exalted by God's presence. We are told that in this new heaven and new earth there will be no temple, for even our churches and services of worship will have had their time and ceased to be, in the presence of God, "the first and the last, the beginning and the end" (Revelation 21-22).

Until that day, we are charged by Christ to "go therefore and make disciples of all nations, baptizing them in the name of the Father, the Son, and the Holy Spirit, and teaching them to obey everything that I have commanded you. And remember, I am with you always, to the end of the age" (Matthew 28:19-20).

Baptism is at the heart of the gospel of grace and at the core of the church's mission. When we baptize we say what we understand as Christians about ourselves and our community: that we are loved into being by God, lost because of sin, but redeemed and saved in Jesus Christ to live new lives in anticipation of his coming again in glory. Baptism is an expression of God's love for the world, and the effects of baptism also express God's grace. As baptized people of God, we therefore respond with praise and thanksgiving, praying that God's will be done in our own lives:

*We your people stand before you,*
*Water-washed and Spirit-born.*
*By your grace, our lives we offer.*
*Re-create us; God, transform!*
—Ruth Duck, "Wash, O God, Our Sons and Daughters"
(*The United Methodist Hymnal*, 605); Used with permission.

ADOPTED 1996
READOPTED FOR 2005-2008
AND 2009-2012 QUADRENNIA
RESOLUTION #343, 2004 *BOOK OF RESOLUTIONS*
RESOLUTION #320, 2000 *BOOK OF RESOLUTIONS*

### 8014. This Holy Mystery

WHEREAS, the 2000 General Conference directed the General Board of Discipleship in collaboration with the General Board of Higher Education and Ministry, the General Commission on Christian Unity and Interreligious Concerns, and the Council of Bishops, to develop a comprehensive interpretive document on the theology and practice of Holy Communion in United Methodism and report their findings and recommendations to the 2004 General Conference; and

WHEREAS, The United Methodist Church needs an authoritative contemporary statement of its understanding of Holy Communion, both for strengthening its interpretation and practice of the Lord's Supper in its churches and for clarity in its ecumenical conversations with other denominations; and

WHEREAS, in developing its report the Holy Communion Study Committee took intentional steps to heed our United Methodist heritage and history, remain sensitive to the ecumenical church, and hear the voices of United Methodists in the United States as well as in central conferences in the Philippines, Africa, and Europe;

*Therefore, be it resolved,* that the 2004 General Conference approve *This Holy Mystery: A United Methodist Understanding of Holy Communion,* affixed and, thereby, made part of this petition, as an official interpretive statement of theology and practice in The United Methodist Church; and

*Be it further resolved,* that *This Holy Mystery* be used by the Council of Bishops, Church School Publications of The United Methodist Publishing House, the General Board of Higher Education and Ministry, and the General Board of Discipleship as a guide for teaching and formation of both clergy and laity in relation to Holy Communion; and

*Be it further resolved,* that *This Holy Mystery* be used by the General Commission on Christian Unity and Interreligious Concerns and the Council of Bishops in interpreting United Methodist understandings and practices in ecumenical dialogue; and

*Be it further resolved,* that the 2004 General Conference commend to the Church the principles, background, and practices in *This Holy Mystery* for the interpretation and use of the services of Word and Table in our hymnals and *The United Methodist Book of Worship*; and

*Be it further resolved,* that *This Holy Mystery* be published in *The Book of Resolutions,* and that the General Board of Discipleship offer it in study editions with a leader's guide.

## This Holy Mystery:

### A United Methodist Understanding of Holy Communion

*Part One: There Is More to the Mystery*

The story is told of a little girl whose parents had taken her forward to receive Holy Communion. Disappointed with the small piece of bread she was given to dip in the cup, the child cried loudly, "I want more! I want more!" While embarrassing to her parents and amusing to the pastor and congregation, this little girl's cry accurately expresses the feelings of many contemporary United Methodist people. We want more! We want more than we are receiving from the sacrament of Holy Communion as it is practiced in our churches.

According to the results of a survey conducted by the General Board of Discipleship prior to the 2000 General Conference, there is a strong sense of the importance of Holy Communion in the life of individual Christians and of the church. Unfortunately, there is at least an equally strong sense of the absence of any meaningful understanding of Eucharistic theology and practice. United Methodists recognize that grace and spiritual power are available to them in the sacrament, but too often they do not feel enabled to receive these gifts and apply them in their lives. Many laypeople complain of sloppy practice, questionable theology, and lack of teaching and guidance. Both clergy and laity recognize the crucial need for better education of pastors in sacramental theology and practice. The concern for improved education is coupled with a call for accountability. Bishops, district superintendents, and other annual conference and general church authorities are urged to prepare their pastors better and to hold them accountable for their sacramental theology, practice, and teaching. Many of the people surveyed are plainly resentful of the lack of leadership they believe they are receiving in these areas. These results are troubling and must provoke the church to reexamination and recommitment.

These results are also exciting and challenging! They reveal a deep hunger for the riches of divine grace made available to us through Holy Communion, for real communion with Jesus Christ and with Christian people. They show that United Methodists want our faith to be enlivened and made more relevant to our daily lives. How can our church best respond to the wonderful hunger of its people for "this holy mystery" ("A Service of Word and Table I," BOW; page 39)?

United Methodists share with many other Christians an increased interest in the study and celebration of the sacraments. For the last several decades we have been actively seeking to recover and revitalize appreciation of Holy Baptism and Holy Communion. Our current services of the Baptismal Covenant and Word and Table are the fruit of a long process of development that began in the 1960's and culminated in their adoption by the 1984 General Conference and publication in *The United Methodist Hymnal* approved in 1988. The change in location of these sacramental rituals from the back to the front of the *Hymnal* is an intentional expression of their significance in the life of the community of faith. In 1996, the General Conference approved *By Water and the Spirit: A United Methodist Understanding of Baptism* as an official interpretive and teaching document for the church. *This Holy Mystery: A United Methodist Understanding of Holy Communion* is submitted to the 2004 General Conference with the same purpose. Both of these documents reflect United Methodism's efforts to reclaim its sacramental heritage and to be in accord with ecumenical movements in sacramental theology and practice.

*This Holy Mystery* is characterized by the effort to avoid rigidity on the one hand and indifference on the other. Neither extreme is true to our heritage nor faithful to the Spirit who leads the church forward in the work of making disciples living toward the new creation. The document is made up of two main parts. The expository introduction titled "Part One: There Is More to the Mystery" describes the document's development and provides grounding in historical tradition and sacramental theology. "Part Two: Christ Is Here: Experiencing the Mystery" is organized by principles. Under each principle, "Background" provides an explanation for the principle, while "Practice" provides guidelines for applying the principle. The principles make assertions that are truthful and doctrinally clear. They honor the historic and ecumenical center of the Christian church's theology and practice. The committee has endeavored to explain in the "Background" sections how the principles are rooted in the theology and practice of Christians past and present, particularly United Methodist Christians. In the "Practice" sections we have applied the principles to contemporary sacramental practices of the church in the various contexts of United Methodism.

The church is always universal and particular, catholic and local, united and diverse. United Methodists vary geographically, racially, and culturally. *This Holy Mystery* invites United Methodists to share common understandings while allowing for appropriate, faithful applications. Some United Methodist practices differ from those of other Christian traditions. Being truthful about these differences recognizes our ties and responsibility to the wider church while claiming God's work in leading us to affirm distinctive understandings and practices. Both within our own United Methodist community and in fellowship with other traditions, we reject cavalier or arrogant attitudes. We seek to strengthen the bond of unity by "speaking the truth in love" (Ephesians 4:15) as, with humility and openness, we acknowledge our principles, explain our backgrounds, and affirm our practices.

## Names of the Sacrament

Several terms naming the sacrament are used in past and present Christianity. In *This Holy Mystery* some are used more than others, but all are largely synonymous. *The Lord's Supper* reminds us that Jesus Christ is the host and that we participate at Christ's invitation. This title suggests the eating of a meal, sometimes called the Holy Meal, and makes us think of the meals that Jesus ate with various people both before his death and after his resurrection. The term *the Last Supper* is not appropriately used for the sacrament, but it does encourage us to remember the supper that Jesus ate with his disciples on the night when he was arrested. This emphasis is especially meaningful around Maundy Thursday. The early church appears to have referred to their celebrations as breaking bread (Acts 2:42).

The term *Holy Communion* invites us to focus on the self-giving of the Holy God, which makes the sacrament an occasion of grace, and on the holiness of our communion with God and one another. *Eucharist*, from the Greek word for thanksgiving, reminds us that the sacrament is thanksgiving to God for the gifts of creation and salvation. The term *Mass*, used by the Roman Catholic Church, derives from the Latin word *missio*, literally "sending forth," and indicates that this celebration brings the worship service to a close by sending forth the congregation with God's blessing to live as God's people in the world. *The Divine Liturgy* is a name used mostly by churches in the tradition of Eastern Orthodoxy. All of these names refer to the same practice: the eating and drinking of consecrated bread and wine in the worshiping community.

## Background

As early as the Emmaus experience on the day of Resurrection, recorded in Luke 24:13-35, Christians recognized the presence of Jesus Christ in the breaking of bread. The traditional Jewish practice of taking bread, blessing and thanking God, and breaking and sharing the bread took on new meaning for them. When followers of Christ gathered in Jesus' name, the breaking of bread and sharing of the cup was a means of remembering his life, death, and resurrection and of encountering the living Christ. They experienced afresh the presence of their risen Lord and received sustenance for their lives as disciples. As the church organized itself, this custom of Eucharist became the characteristic ritual of the community and the central act of its worship.

Over the centuries, various understandings and practices of Holy Communion have developed. Roman Catholicism teaches that the substance of bread and wine are changed (although not visibly) into the actual body and blood of Christ (sometimes called transubstantiation). Protestant Reformers in the sixteenth century rejected this teaching but had diverse ideas among themselves. Lutherans maintain that Christ's body and blood are truly is present in and with the elements of bread and wine in the celebration (sometimes erroneously called corporeal presence or consubstantiation). Ulrich Zwingli, a Swiss reformer, taught that the Lord's Supper is a memorial or reminder of Christ's sacrifice, an affirmation of faith, and a sign of Christian fellowship. Although his name may be unfamiliar, Zwingli's views are widely shared today, especially within evangelical churches. Denominations in the Reformed tradition, following John Calvin, maintain that although Christ's body is in heaven, when Holy Communion is received with true faith, the power of the Holy Spirit nourishes those who partake. The Church of England affirmed a somewhat similar view in its Catechism and Articles of Religion. These understandings (stated here very simplistically) suggest the range of ideas that were available to John and Charles Wesley and the early Methodists.

## United Methodist Heritage

### Early Methodism

The Methodist movement in eighteenth-century England was an evangelical movement that included a revival of emphasis on the sacraments. The Wesleys recognized the power of God available in the Lord's Supper and urged their followers to draw on that power by frequent participation. The grace available in and through the sacrament was active in conviction, repentance and conversion, forgiveness, and sanctification. John Wesley described the Lord's Supper as "the grand channel whereby the grace of his Spirit was conveyed to the souls of all the children of God" ("Sermon on the Mount—Discourse Six," III.11). During the years in which Methodism was beginning and growing, Wesley himself communed an average of four to five times a week. His sermon "The Duty of Constant Communion" emphasizes the role of the sacrament in the lives of Christians in ways that are keenly meaningful today. The Wesley brothers wrote and published a collection of 166 *Hymns on the Lord's Supper*, which was used for meditation as well as for singing. The Wesleys understood and taught the multifaceted nature of the Lord's Supper. They wrote about love, grace, sacrifice, forgiveness, the presence of Christ, mystery, healing, nourishment, holiness, and pledge of heaven. They knew that Holy Communion is a powerful means through which divine grace is given to God's people. Our sacramental understandings and practices today are grounded in this heritage.

### Evangelical and United Brethren Roots

The movements that developed into the Church of the United Brethren in Christ and the Evangelical Church began in the late eighteenth century and early nineteenth century in America. From the beginning, relationships between these groups and the Methodists were close and cordial. The beliefs and practices of the three churches were similar. Francis Asbury and Philip William Otterbein were close friends, and Otterbein participated in Asbury's consecration as a Methodist Episcopal bishop. Conversations about possible union began at least as early as 1809 and continued intermittently until the churches finally merged in 1968 to form The United Methodist Church.

Unfortunately, Otterbein and Martin Boehm—founders of the United Brethren—left little written material. The same is true of Evangelical founder Jacob Albright. Therefore, we can make comparatively few references to their theology and practice of Holy Communion. The *Journal* of Christian Newcomer (d. 1830), third United Brethren bishop, records so many occasions of administering and participating in the sacrament that its significance in the life of the church is apparent.

### American Methodism

The early American Methodists, who began arriving in the 1760's, were at first able to receive the sacraments from Anglican churches of which they were considered a part. But the situation soon changed, and Methodists began to reject the English church. As rising tensions between the colonies and England led to the Revolutionary War, most Anglican priests left the country. By the mid 1770's, most Methodists had no access to the sacraments. The missionary preachers sent by John Wesley were laymen, as were the Americans who became preachers. They had no authority to baptize or to offer Holy Communion. Methodists were longing for the sacraments, and it was this need that motivated Wesley to take actions to provide ordained elders for America. In 1784, the Methodist Episcopal Church was created and some preachers were ordained. Still, the number of elders was too small to offer the sacraments regularly to the rapidly increasing number of Methodists. During the decades of the circuit riders, most Methodists were able to receive the Lord's Supper quarterly, at best, when the ordained elder came to their community. The camp meetings of the period were also sacramental occasions where large numbers of people communed. By the late nineteenth century and throughout the twentieth, many Methodist churches were served by ordained elders, but the habit of quarterly Holy Communion remained strong.

American Methodists considered Holy Communion a sacred and solemn event. The tone of the ritual was deeply penitential, calling upon people to repent and having less emphasis on celebration of God's grace. During the nineteenth and twentieth centuries the rich Wesleyan understandings of Eucharist were largely lost, and the sacrament became understood only as a memorial of the death of Christ. In many congregations attendance on Communion Sunday was low. Revitalization of the Lord's Supper in Methodism, and in the Evangelical and United Brethren churches, started in the mid-twentieth century when the churches began to reclaim their sacramental heritage and create new rituals to express it.

As Methodism spread to other parts of the world, ritual and practice established in America were followed. Over the years, however, there have been certain influences from surrounding Christian traditions. These are to some extent reflected in Holy Communion practice in the central conferences (those beyond the geographic area of the United States).

## Grace and the Means of Grace

Today Holy Communion must be viewed within the larger context of United Methodist theology. In accord with biblical and Christian teaching, we believe that we are sinners, constantly in need of divine grace. We believe that God is gracious and loving, always making available the grace we need. Grace is God's love toward us, God's free and undeserved gift. Several words describe how grace works in our lives. Prevenient grace is that which "comes before" anything we can do to help ourselves. Although we are all bound by our sinful nature, grace gives us enough freedom of will to be able to respond to God. In truth, all grace is prevenient—we cannot move toward God unless God has first moved toward us. God seeks us out, pursues us, calls us to come into the loving relationship that we were created to enjoy. Convicting grace makes us conscious of our sinfulness and urges us to repentance. Justifying grace forgives and puts us into right relationship with God. Sanctifying grace enables us to grow in holiness of life. Perfecting grace molds us into the image of Christ. The grace of God is made available to us through the life, death, and resurrection of Jesus Christ and works in our lives through the presence and power of the Holy Spirit.

While divine grace reaches us any time and in any way that God chooses, God has designated certain means or channels through which grace is most surely and immediately available. John Wesley expressed it this way: "By 'means of grace' I understand outward signs, words, or actions, ordained of God, and appointed for this end, to be the ordinary channels whereby he might convey to men [and women], preventing, justifying, or sanctifying grace" ("The Means of Grace," II.1). In the General Rules, Wesley listed these means of grace as, "The public worship of God. The ministry of the Word, either read or expounded. The Supper of the Lord. Family and private prayer. Searching the Scriptures. Fasting or abstinence" (*BOD*, ¶ 103; page 74). Elsewhere Wesley added Christian conferencing, by which he meant edifying conversation and meeting together in groups for nurture and accountability. These means are not to be understood as ways of earning salvation, for that is an unmerited gift. They are, rather, ways to receive, live in, and grow in divine grace. The Wesleyan tradition has continued to emphasize the practice of these means of grace throughout our salvation process.

## The Theology of Sacraments

The Greek word used in the early church for sacrament is *mysterion*, usually translated "mystery." It indicates that through sacraments, God discloses things that are beyond human capacity to know through reason alone. In Latin the word used is *sacramentum*, which means a vow or promise. The sacraments were instituted by Christ and given to the church. Jesus Christ is himself the ultimate manifestation of a sacrament. In the coming of Jesus of Nazareth, God's nature and purpose were revealed and active through a human body. The Christian church is also sacramental. It was instituted to continue the work of Christ in redeeming the world. The church is Christ's body—the visible, material instrument through which Christ continues to be made known and the divine plan is fulfilled. Holy Baptism and Holy Communion have been chosen and designated by God as special means through which divine grace comes to us. Holy Baptism is the sacrament that initiates us into the body of Christ "through water and the Spirit" ("The Baptismal Covenant I," *UMH*; page 37). In baptism we receive our identity and mission as Christians. Holy Communion is the sacrament that sustains and nourishes us in our journey of salvation. In a sacrament, God uses tangible, material things as vehicles or instruments of grace. Wesley defines a sacrament, in accord with his Anglican tradition, as "an outward sign of inward grace, and a means whereby we receive the same" ("Means of Grace," II.1). Sacraments are sign-acts, which include words, actions, and physical elements. They both express and convey the gracious love of God. They make God's love both visible and effective. We might even say that sacraments are God's "show and tell," communicating with us in a way that we, in all our brokenness and limitations, can receive and experience God's grace.

## The Meaning of Holy Communion

In the New Testament, at least six major ideas about Holy Communion are present: thanksgiving, fellowship, remembrance, sacrifice, action of the Holy Spirit, and eschatology. A brief look at each of these will help us better comprehend the meaning of the sacrament.

Holy Communion is Eucharist, an act of thanksgiving. The early Christians "broke bread in their homes and ate together with glad and sincere hearts, praising God and enjoying the favor of all the people" (Acts 2:46-47a, NIV). As we commune, we express joyful thanks for God's mighty acts throughout history—for creation, covenant, redemption, sanctification. The Great Thanksgiving ("A Service of Word and Table I," *UMH*; pages 9-10) is a recitation of this salvation history, culminating in the work of Jesus Christ and the ongoing work of the Holy Spirit. It conveys our gratitude for the goodness of God and God's unconditional love for us.

Holy Communion is the communion of the church—the gathered community of the faithful, both local and universal. While deeply meaningful to the individuals participating, the sacrament is much more than a personal event. The first person pronouns throughout the ritual are consistently plural—*we, us, our.* First Corinthians 10:17 explains that "because there is one bread, we who are many are one body, for we all partake of the one bread." "A Service of Word and Table I" uses this text as an explicit statement of Christian unity in the body of Christ (*UMH*; page 11). The sharing and bonding experienced at the Table exemplify the nature of the church and model the world as God would have it be.

Holy Communion is remembrance, commemoration, and memorial, but this remembrance is much more than simply intellectual recalling. "Do this in remembrance of me" (Luke 22:19; 1 Corinthians 11:24-25) is *anamnesis* (the biblical Greek word). This dynamic action becomes re-presentation of past gracious acts of God in the present, so powerfully as to make them truly present now. Christ is risen and is alive here and now, not just remembered for what was done in the past.

Holy Communion is a type of sacrifice. It is a re-presentation, not a repetition, of the sacrifice of Christ. Hebrews 9:26 makes clear that "he has appeared once for all at the end of the age to remove sin by the sacrifice of himself." Christ's atoning life, death, and resurrection make divine grace available to us. We also present ourselves as sacrifice in union with Christ (Romans 12:1; 1 Peter 2:5) to be used by God in the work of redemption, reconciliation, and justice. In the Great Thanksgiving, the church prays: "We offer ourselves in praise and thanksgiving as a holy and living sacrifice, in union with Christ's offering for us . . ." (*UMH*; page 10).

Holy Communion is a vehicle of God's grace through the action of the Holy Spirit (Acts 1:8), whose work is described in John 14:26: "But the Advocate, the Holy Spirit, whom the Father will send in my name, will teach you everything, and remind you of all that I have said to you." The *epiclesis* (biblical Greek meaning "calling upon") is the part of the Great Thanksgiving that calls the Spirit: "Pour out your Holy Spirit on us gathered here, and on these gifts of bread and wine." The church asks God to "make them be for us the body and blood of Christ, that we may be for the world the body of Christ, redeemed by his blood. By your Spirit make us one with Christ, one with each other, and one in ministry to all the world . . ." (*UMH*; page 10).

Holy Communion is eschatological, meaning that it has to do with the end of history, the outcome of God's purpose for the world— "Christ has died; Christ is risen; Christ will come again" (*UMH*; page 10). We commune not only with the faithful who are physically present but with the saints of the past who join us in the sacrament. To participate is to receive a foretaste of the future, a pledge of heaven "until Christ comes in final victory and we feast at his heavenly banquet" (*UMH*; page 10). Christ himself looked forward to this occasion and promised the disciples, "I will never again drink of this fruit of the vine until that day when I drink it new with you in my Father's kingdom" (Matthew 26:29; Mark 14:25; Luke 22:18). When we eat and drink at the Table, we become partakers of the divine nature in this life and for life eternal (John 6:47-58; Revelation 3:20). We are anticipating the heavenly banquet celebrating God's victory over sin, evil, and death (Matthew 22:1-14; Revelation 19:9; 21:1-7). In the midst of the personal and systemic brokenness in which we live, we yearn for everlasting fellowship with Christ and ultimate fulfillment of the divine plan. Nourished by sacramental grace, we strive to be formed into the image of Christ and to be made instruments for transformation in the world.

## Toward a Richer Sacramental Life

Like the little girl who was disappointed with what she received, United Methodist people are looking and hoping for something more in their Eucharistic experience. As we move toward a richer sacramental life, including weekly celebration of Holy Communion, we ask what spiritual benefits we receive from it. What do divine love and power do in and for us through our participation in the sacrament? The answers to this question involve forgiveness, nourishment, healing, transformation, ministry and mission, and eternal life.

We respond to the invitation to the Table by immediately confessing our personal and corporate sin, trusting that, "If we confess our sins, he who is faithful and just will forgive us our sins and cleanse us from all unrighteousness" (1 John 1:9). Our expression of repentance is answered by the absolution in which forgiveness is proclaimed: "In the name of Jesus Christ, you are forgiven!" (*UMH*; page 8). This assurance is God's gift to sinners, enabling us to continue striving to live faithfully. Wesley wrote, "The grace of God given herein confirms to us the pardon of our sins by enabling us to leave them" ("The Duty of Constant Communion," I.3).

We receive spiritual nourishment through Holy Communion. The Christian life is a journey, one that is challenging and arduous. To continue living faithfully and growing in holiness requires constant sustenance. Wesley wrote, "This is the food of our souls: This gives strength to perform our duty, and leads us on to perfection" ("The Duty of Constant Communion," I.3). God makes such sustenance available through the sacrament of Eucharist. In John 6:35, Jesus tells the crowd: "I am the bread of life. Whoever comes to me will never be hungry, and whoever believes in me will never be thirsty." As we return to the Table again and again, we are strengthened repeatedly. We go out empowered to live as disciples, reconcilers, and witnesses. In the words of the prayer after Communion, "Grant that we may go into the world in the strength of your Spirit, to give ourselves for others . . ." (*UMH*; page 11).

As we encounter Christ in Holy Communion and are repeatedly touched by divine grace, we are progressively shaped into Christ's image. All of this work is not done in a moment, no matter how dramatic an experience we may enjoy. It is, instead, a lifelong process through which God intends to shape us into people motivated by love, empowered and impassioned to do Christ's work in the world. The identity and ministry that God bestows on us in our baptism are fulfilled as we continue to be transformed into disciples who can respond to God's love by loving God and others (Romans 12:1-2).

Through Eucharist, we receive healing and are enabled to aid in the healing of others. *Sozo*, the root of the Greek word used in the New Testament for "healing," is also translated as "salvation" and "wholeness." Much of this healing is spiritual, but it also includes the healing of our thoughts and emotions, of our minds and bodies, of our attitudes and relationships. The grace received at the Table of the Lord can make us whole. As those who are being saved, we seek to bring healing to a broken world. *The United Methodist Book of Worship* describes this well: "Spiritual healing is God's work of offering persons balance, harmony, and wholeness of body, mind, spirit, and relationships through confession, forgiveness, and reconciliation. Through such healing, God works to bring about reconciliation between God and humanity, among individuals and communities, within each person, and between humanity and the rest of creation" (page 613). Holy Communion can be a powerful aspect of the services of healing provided in the *Book of Worship* (pages 615-623).

The grace we receive at the Lord's Table enables us to perform our ministry and mission, to continue his work in the world—the work of redemption, reconciliation, peace, and justice (2 Corinthians 5:17-21). As we commune, we become aware of the worth and the needs of other people and are reminded of our responsibility. We express the compassion of Christ through acts of caring and kindness toward those we encounter in our daily lives. In our baptism, we have vowed to "accept the freedom and power God gives [us] to resist evil, injustice, and oppression in whatever forms they present themselves" (*UMH*; page 34). But, in the words of the prayer of confession, we acknowledge our failures: "We have rebelled against your love, we have not loved our neighbors, and we have not heard the cry of the needy" (*UMH*; page 8). Remembering the revolutionary Jesus, we are impelled to challenge unjust practices and systems that perpetuate political, economic, and social inequity and discrimination (Matthew 23; Luke 4:16-21; 14:7-11).

The loving God who meets us at the Table gives us the gift of eternal life. Jesus' presentation of himself as the spiritual bread of life in John's Eucharistic account (6:25-58) makes clear the connection: "Those who eat my flesh and drink my blood have eternal life, and I will raise them up on the last day" (6:54). This life in union with Christ is life eternal. It is not only the promise of our being with Christ after physical death. It is also our being in dynamic loving relationship with Christ here and now. It is life that never ends because it is grounded in the everlasting love of God who comes to us in the sacraments.

> *O Thou who this mysterious bread*
> *didst in Emmaus break,*
> *return, herewith our souls to feed,*
> *and to thy followers speak.*
>
> Charles Wesley
> *The United Methodist Hymnal*, 613

## Part Two: Christ Is Here: Experiencing the Mystery

### The Presence of Christ

*Principle:*

Jesus Christ, who "is the reflection of God's glory and the exact imprint of God's very being" (Hebrews 1:3), is truly present in Holy Communion. Through Jesus Christ and in the power of the Holy

Spirit, God meets us at the Table. God, who has given the sacraments to the church, acts in and through Holy Communion. Christ is present through the community gathered in Jesus' name (Matthew 18:20), through the Word proclaimed and enacted, and through the elements of bread and wine shared (1 Corinthians 11:23-26). The divine presence is a living reality and can be experienced by participants; it is not a remembrance of the Last Supper and the Crucifixion only.

*Background:*

Christ's presence in the sacrament is a promise to the church and is not dependent upon recognition of this presence by individual members of the congregation. Holy Communion always offers grace. We are reminded of what God has done for us in the past, experience what God is doing now as we partake, and anticipate what God will do in the future work of salvation. "We await the final moment of grace, when Christ comes in victory at the end of the age to bring all who are in Christ into the glory of that victory" (*By Water and the Spirit: A United Methodist Understanding of Baptism*, in *BOR*; page 875), and we join in feasting at the heavenly banquet table (Luke 22:14-18; Revelation 19:9).

The Christian church has struggled through the centuries to understand just how Christ is present in the Eucharist. Arguments and divisions have occurred over the matter. The Wesleyan tradition affirms the reality of Christ's presence, although it does not claim to be able to explain it fully. John and Charles Wesley's 166 *Hymns on the Lord's Supper* are our richest resource for study in order to appreciate the Wesleyan understanding of the presence of Christ in the Eucharist. One of these hymns expresses well both the reality and the mystery: "O the Depth of Love Divine," stanzas 1 and 4 (*The United Methodist Hymnal*, 627):

*O the depth of love divine,*
*the unfathomable grace!*
*Who shall say how bread and wine*
*God into us conveys!*
*How the bread his flesh imparts,*
*how the wine transmits his blood,*
*fills his faithful people's hearts*
*with all the life of God!*

*Sure and real is the grace,*
*the manner be unknown;*
*only meet us in thy ways*
*and perfect us in one.*
*Let us taste the heavenly powers,*
*Lord, we ask for nothing more.*
*Thine to bless, 'tis only ours*
*to wonder and adore.*

Article XVI of The Articles of Religion of The Methodist Church describes the sacraments as "certain signs of grace, and God's good will toward us, by which he doth work invisibly in us, and doth not only quicken, but also strengthen and confirm, our faith in him" (*BOD*; page 63).

Article XVIII describes the Lord's Supper as "a sacrament of our redemption by Christ's death; insomuch that, to such as rightly, worthily, and with faith receive the same, the bread which we break is a partaking of the body of Christ; and likewise the cup of blessing is a partaking of the blood of Christ" (*BOD*; page 64). (*See* section "The Communion Elements" in this paper for related material.)

Article VI of The Confession of Faith of The Evangelical United Brethren Church speaks similarly of the sacraments: "They are means of grace by which God works invisibly in us, quickening, strengthening and confirming our faith in him. . . . Those who rightly, worthily and in faith eat the broken bread and drink the blessed cup partake of the body and blood of Christ in a spiritual manner until he comes" (*BOD*; page 68).

United Methodists, along with other Christian traditions, have tried to provide clear and faithful interpretations of Christ's presence in the Holy Meal. Our tradition asserts the real, personal, living presence of Jesus Christ. For United Methodists, the Lord's Supper is anchored in the life of the historical Jesus of Nazareth, but is not primarily a remembrance or memorial. We do not embrace the medieval doctrine of transubstantiation, though we do believe that the elements are essential tangible means through which God works. We understand the divine presence in temporal and relational terms. In the Holy Meal of the church, the past, present, and future of the living Christ come together by the power of the Holy Spirit so that we may receive and embody Jesus Christ as God's saving gift for the whole world.

*Practice:*

Because Jesus Christ has promised to meet us there (1 Corinthians 11:23-26), Christians approach the Communion Table with desire and expectation, with awe and humility, and with celebration and gratitude.

Pastors need to be trained and formed (in seminary, course of study, licensing school, and continuing education) in the theology, spirituality, history, and tradition of the sacraments and in how to most effectively utilize proclamation, ritual, gestures, postures, and material signs in order to convey their full meaning.

### *Christ Is Calling You*

### Invitation to the Lord's Table

*Principle:*

The invitation to the Table comes from the risen and present Christ. Christ invites to his Table those who love him, repent of sin, and seek to live as Christian disciples. Holy Communion is a gift of God to the church and an act of the community of faith. By responding to this invitation we affirm and deepen our personal relationship with God through Jesus Christ and our commitment to membership and mission in the body of Christ.

*Background:*

The Invitation to Holy Communion in "A Service of Word and Table I" and "A Service of Word and Table II" proclaims, "Christ our Lord invites to his table all who love him, who earnestly repent of their sin and seek to live in peace with one another" (*UMH*; pages 7, 12). The more traditional wording in "A Service of Word and Table IV" invites, "Ye that do truly and earnestly repent of your sins, and are in love and charity with your neighbors, and intend to lead a new life, following the commandments of God, and walking from henceforth in his holy ways: Draw near with faith . . ." (*UMH*; page 26). "A Service of Word and Table V," for use with people who are sick or homebound, says that Christ invites "all who love him and seek to grow into his likeness" (*BOW*; page 51).

*Practice:*

When Holy Communion is celebrated, it is important to always begin with the words of Invitation, including Confession and Pardon.

If these are omitted, all those present may not understand either the openness of the Table of the Lord or the expectation of repentance, forgiveness, healing, and entrance into new life in Christ.

The church community has a responsibility to provide ongoing age-appropriate nurture and education about the sacrament of Holy Communion to all its people. Those who are baptized as infants need continual teaching as they mature in faith. Those who come into membership later in life also need ongoing instruction about the significance of the sacrament in their personal faith journey and in the life of the congregation and larger Christian community. All who seek to live as Christian disciples need formation in sacramental spirituality.

Bishops, elders, deacons, pastors, Sunday school teachers, parents and guardians, seminary professors, and others have responsibility for faithfully teaching understandings and practices of Holy Communion. Teaching about the sacraments should emphasize United Methodist positions and practices but should also encourage knowledge of and respect for those of other Christian traditions.

*Principle:*

All who respond in faith to the invitation are to be welcomed. Holy Baptism normally precedes partaking of Holy Communion. Holy Communion is a meal of the community who are in covenant relationship with God through Jesus Christ. As circumcision was the sign of the covenant between God and the Hebrew people, baptism is the sign of the new covenant (Genesis 17:9-14; Exodus 24:1-12; Jeremiah 31:31; Romans 6:1-11; Hebrews 9:15).

*Background:*

Baptism is the nonrepeatable rite of initiation into the body of Christ, while the Lord's Supper is the regularly-repeated celebration of communion of the body of Christ.

Beginning early in its history, the Christian church divided its worship services into the Liturgy of the Word, in which all participated, and the Liturgy of the Faithful, which was the celebration of Holy Communion. Those who were not yet baptized were dismissed before the celebration of the sacrament (*Didache* 9; Justin Martyr, *First Apology,* 66; *The Apostolic Constitutions,* Book VIII; *The Liturgy of St. Basil*).

John Wesley stressed that baptism is only a step in the salvation process and must be followed by justifying faith and personal commitment to Christ when one reaches an age of accountability. He referred to Holy Communion as "a converting ordinance" (Journal from November 1, 1739, to September 3, 1741; Friday, June 27, 1740). In eighteenth-century England, Wesley was addressing people who, for the most part, although baptized as infants and possessing some degree of faith had not yet experienced spiritual rebirth. Therefore, the conversion Wesley spoke of was transformation of lives and assurance of salvation.

Soon after the merger of The Evangelical Church and the United Brethren in Christ, the Evangelical United Brethren *Discipline* of 1947, reads, "We invite to [the Lord's Supper] all disciples of the Lord Jesus Christ who have confessed him before men and desire to serve him with sincere hearts" (page 447).

*The United Methodist Book of Worship* says, "All who intend to lead a Christian life, together with their children, are invited to receive the bread and cup. We have no tradition of refusing any who present themselves desiring to receive" (page 29). This statement means that in practice there are few, if any, circumstances in which a United Methodist pastor would refuse to serve the elements of Holy Communion to a person who comes forward to receive.

*By Water and the Spirit* affirms: "Because the table at which we gather belongs to the Lord, it should be open to all who respond to Christ's love, regardless of age or church membership. The Wesleyan tradition has always recognized that Holy Communion may be an occasion for the reception of converting, justifying, and sanctifying grace" (*BOR*; pages 873-74).

*Practice:*

Invitation to partake of Holy Communion offers an evangelical opportunity to bring people into a fuller living relationship with the body of Christ. As means of God's unmerited grace, Holy Baptism and Holy Communion are to be seen not as barriers but as pathways. Pastors and congregations must strive for a balance of welcome that is open and gracious and teaching that is clear and faithful to the fullness of discipleship.

Nonbaptized people who respond in faith to the invitation in our liturgy will be welcomed to the Table. They should receive teaching about Holy Baptism as the sacrament of entrance into the community of faith—needed only once by each individual—and Holy Communion as the sacrament of sustenance for the journey of faith and growth in holiness—needed and received frequently. "Unbaptized persons who receive communion should be counseled and nurtured toward baptism as soon as possible" (*By Water and the Spirit*, in *BOR*; page 874).

*Principle:*

No one will be turned away from the Table because of age or "mental, physical, developmental, and/or psychological and neurological" capacity (*BOD*, ¶ 162G) or because of any other condition that might limit his or her understanding or hinder his or her reception of the sacrament.

*Background:*

According to *By Water and the Spirit*,

"The services of the baptismal covenant appropriately conclude with Holy Communion, through which the union of the new member with the body of Christ is most fully expressed. Holy Communion is a sacred meal in which the community of faith, in the simple act of eating bread and drinking wine, proclaims and participates in all that God has done, is doing, and will continue to do for us in Christ. In celebrating the Eucharist, we remember the grace given to us in our baptism and partake of the spiritual food necessary for sustaining and fulfilling the promises of salvation" (*BOR*; page 873).

The concluding rubrics of the services make clear that this applies to people of all ages.

The theological basis for baptism of infants and people of varying abilities applies as well to their participation in Holy Communion:

"Through the church, God claims infants as well as adults to be participants in the gracious covenant of which baptism is the sign. This understanding of the workings of divine grace also applies to persons who for reasons of disabilities or other limitations are unable to answer for themselves the questions of the baptismal ritual. While we may not be able to comprehend how God works in their lives, our faith teaches us that God's grace is sufficient for their needs and, thus, they are appropriate recipients of baptism" (*By Water and the Spirit*, in *BOR*; page 868).

Likewise, the grace given through Holy Communion is offered to the entire church, including those who are unable to respond for themselves. Children are members of the covenant community and participants in the Lord's Supper.

*Practice:*

Young children and people with handicapping or incapacitating conditions may need special consideration as the elements are served. Pastors and congregations should develop plans for providing assistance that maintains the dignity and affirms the worth of those receiving.

Children of all ages are welcome to the Table and are to be taught and led to interpret, appreciate, and participate in Holy Communion. Adults need training to help them explain the sacrament to children.

When worship spaces are constructed or renovated, attention needs to be given to providing physical access to the Communion Table for all.

*Principle:*

The Lord's Supper in a United Methodist congregation is open to members of other United Methodist congregations and to Christians from other traditions.

*Background:*

"A baptized or professing member of any local United Methodist church is a member of the global United Methodist connection and a member of the church universal" (*BOD*; ¶ 215).

The United Methodist Church recognizes that it is only one of the bodies that constitute the community of Christians. Despite our differences, all Christians are welcome at the Table of the Lord.

*Practice:*

As a part of the directions before the invitation, it is customary to announce that all Christians are welcome to participate in the sacrament in United Methodist congregations.

Response to the invitation is always voluntary, and care needs to be taken to ensure that no one feels pressured to participate or conspicuous for not doing so.

When Holy Communion is served as part of a service of Christian marriage or a service of death and resurrection, "It is our tradition to invite all Christians to the Lord's table, and the invitation should be extended to everyone present; but there should be no pressure that would embarrass those who for whatever reason do not choose to receive Holy Communion" (*BOW*; page 152). It is not appropriate for only the couple or family to commune.

## The Issue of "Unworthiness"

*Principle:*

Any person who answers in faith the invitation "Christ our Lord invites to his table all who love him, who earnestly repent of their sin and seek to live in peace with one another" (*UMH*; page 7) is worthy through Christ to partake of Holy Communion. Christians come to the Lord's Table in gratitude for Christ's mercy toward sinners. We do not share in Communion because of our worthiness; no one is truly worthy. We come to the Eucharist out of our hunger to receive God's gracious love, to receive forgiveness and healing.

*Background:*

Some deeply committed United Methodist people who hesitate or even refuse to partake of Holy Communion do so because of their sense that they are unworthy. This problem is largely based upon misinterpretation and false fears. Within the United Methodist tradition, people who participate in the sacrament are assured of the forgiveness of their sins and of pardon through their participation in the Invitation and the Confession and Pardon.

Paul's words of warning in 1 Corinthians 11:27-32 have long been a source of confusion and concern. Some people are fearful of communing "in an unworthy manner" and, sometimes out of genuine Christian humility, believe that their participation would be improper. John Wesley addressed this problem in his sermon "The Duty of Constant Communion": "God offers you one of the greatest mercies on this side of heaven, and commands you to accept it. . . . You are unworthy to receive any mercy from God. But is that a reason for refusing all mercy? . . . Why do you not obey God's command? . . . What! unworthy to obey God?" (II.7-8).

Wesley went on to explain that unworthiness does not apply to the people who are to commune, but to the manner in which the consecrated elements are consumed: "Here is not a word said of being unworthy to eat and drink. Indeed he [Paul] does speak of eating and drinking unworthily; but that is quite a different thing. . . . In this very chapter we are told that by eating and drinking unworthily is meant, taking the holy Sacrament in such a rude and disorderly way, that one was 'hungry, and another drunken' [1 Corinthians 11:21]" (II.9).

First Corinthians 11:29 is a word of judgment against "all who eat and drink without discerning the body." A footnote to this passage in *The New Oxford Annotated Bible* (NRSV) explains that this is a reference to "the community, one's relation to other Christians" (page 242). Paul is speaking against those who fail to recognize the church—the body of Christ—as a community of faith within which Christians relate to each other in love.

*Practice:*

Pastors and other leaders can alleviate most of these concerns about worthiness through patient counseling, faithful teaching, and prayers for healing. These efforts can be focused on study of the cited passage in First Corinthians, with clear explanation of what it meant in its first-century context and what it means today.

### The Basic Pattern of Worship: A Service of Word and Table

*Principle:*

The complete pattern of Christian worship for the Lord's Day is Word and Table—the gospel is proclaimed in both Word and sacrament. Word and Table are not in competition; rather they complement each other so as to constitute a whole service of worship. Their separation diminishes the fullness of life in the Spirit offered to us through faith in Jesus Christ.

*Background:*

In *The United Methodist Book of Worship* (pages 13-14), the Basic Pattern of Worship is traced to its Jewish roots:

The Entrance and the Proclamation and Response—often called the Service of the Word or the Preaching Service—are a Christian adaptation of the ancient synagogue service. The Thanksgiving and

Communion, commonly called the Lord's Supper or Holy Communion, is a Christian adaptation of Jewish worship at family meal tables. . . . Christians held an adapted synagogue service and broke bread when they gathered on the first day of the week. (Acts 20:7)

The practice of the Christian church from its earliest years was weekly celebration of the Lord's Supper on the Lord's Day. The *Didache*, a source from the late first century or early second century says, "On every Lord's Day—his special day—come together and break bread and give thanks . . ." (14). Justin Martyr, writing around A.D. 150, relates, "And on the day called Sunday there is a meeting . . . bread is brought, and wine and water, and the president similarly sends up prayers and thanksgivings . . ." (Chapter 67). Most Christian traditions have continued this pattern.

John Wesley was highly critical of the infrequency of Holy Communion in the Church of England of his day. He exhorted his followers to practice "constant communion" because Christ had so commanded and because the spiritual benefits are so great ("The Duty of Constant Communion"). In his 1784 letter to American Methodists, Wesley counseled, "I also advise the elders to administer the supper of the Lord on every Lord's day" ("Letter to Dr. Coke, Mr. Asbury, and Our Brethren in North America").

For decades the scarcity of ordained pastors made it difficult if not impossible for churches in the Wesleyan tradition to observe the Lord's Supper as a part of regular Sunday worship. The custom of celebrating the sacrament at least quarterly, when an ordained elder was present, ensured the opportunity for regular if infrequent participation. With the introduction of new liturgical texts for the Lord's Supper in 1972, United Methodism has been recovering the fullness of Word and Table as the pattern for weekly worship on the Lord's Day.

The *Journal* of Christian Newcomer, third bishop of the United Brethren in Christ, is filled with references to frequent celebrations of Holy Communion. He rejoiced in the "sacramental festivals" that he led and in which he participated.

Recent theology and practice of worship stress both the proclamation of the gospel enacted through Holy Communion and the sacramental power of Christ's presence through preaching. Partaking of Holy Communion is a response to and continued participation in the Word that has been proclaimed. Those seeking to live as Christian disciples have constant need of the nourishment and sustenance made available through both the Word and the sacrament of Holy Communion.

*Practice:*

Congregations of The United Methodist Church are encouraged to move toward a richer sacramental life, including weekly celebration of the Lord's Supper at the services on the Lord's Day, as advocated by the general orders of Sunday worship in *The United Methodist Hymnal* and *The United Methodist Book of Worship*. The sacrament can also be celebrated appropriately on other occasions in the life of the church from the congregational to the denominational level. However, occasions of worship that might not always include Communion are revivals, services of daily praise and prayer, love feasts, and services on days other than Sunday.

Attention should be given to the special needs of churches whose pastoral leadership is neither ordained nor licensed. Cooperative parishes and ecumenical shared ministries (*BOD*; ¶¶ 206.2 and 207) may offer patterns through which such congregations could receive regular sacramental ministry.

### The Gathered Community

### The Whole Assembly

*Principle:*

The whole assembly actively celebrates Holy Communion. All who are baptized into the body of Christ Jesus become servants and ministers within that body, which is the church. The members are claimed by God as a royal priesthood, God's own people (1 Peter 2:9). The one body, drawn together by the one Spirit, is fully realized when all its many parts eat together in love and offer their lives in service at the Table of the Lord.

*Background:*

Those baptized are called "Christ's royal priesthood" in the United Methodist services of the Baptismal Covenant ("The Baptismal Covenant I," *BOW*; page 92). We are "royal" because we belong to Christ, the sovereign. As priests, each of us can have access to God without any human intermediary. This priesthood means, especially, that we are to be priests to each other as together we seek to live as Christians. The exchange of words of forgiveness between pastor and congregation is an example in the ritual of this role (*UMH*; page 8).

All Christians share in the ministry of the church. Our diverse abilities and callings are gifts from God that together form the unity of the body of Christ and carry out its mission (Romans 12:3-8; 1 Corinthians 12:4-30; Ephesians 4:1-16). There is no more powerful expression of this reality than the participation of the whole gathered community in the celebration of Eucharist.

*Practice:*

All in the congregation are participants in the ministry of offering praise and worship to God and in the servant work of mutual ministry. The terms presiding minister and assisting minister describe the work of those who lead and assist the congregation.

### The Prayer of Great Thanksgiving

*Principle:*

The prayer of Great Thanksgiving is addressed to God, is prayed by the whole people, and is led by the presiding minister. The prayer is shaped by our Trinitarian understanding of the nature of God. It includes an introductory dialogue, thankful remembrance of God's mighty acts of creation and the salvation made possible through Jesus Christ, the institution of the Lord's Supper, invoking of the present work of the Holy Spirit, and concluding praise to the Trinity. The prayer recognizes the fullness of God's triune nature, expresses the offering of ourselves in response, and looks toward the joy of sharing in God's eventual victory over sin and death.

*Background:*

The Trinitarian structure is evident in the Great Thanksgiving in the Word and Table services of *The United Methodist Hymnal* (pages 6-16). Following the introductory exchange between presiding minister and people in the Great Thanksgiving, prayer is addressed to "Father [God] Almighty, creator of heaven and earth." Following the Sanctus ("Holy, holy, holy . . ." ), the work of the second person of the Trinity is proclaimed: ". . . and blessed is your Son [Child] Jesus Christ." The presence and work of the Holy Spirit are invoked in the portion beginning "Pour out your Holy Spirit on us gathered here and on these gifts . . . ," words historically known as the *epiclesis*. Throughout the Great

Thanksgiving the congregation prays actively but silently and speaks its responses aloud at designated points in the service.

In their *Hymns on the Lord's Supper,* John and Charles Wesley make clear that divine presence and power come into the Eucharistic experience through the action of the Holy Spirit. Hymn 72 in that collection is a good example:

*Come, Holy Ghost, Thine influence shed,*
*And realize [make real] the sign;*
*Thy life infuse into the bread,*
*Thy power into the wine.*
*Effectual let the tokens prove,*
*And made, by heavenly art,*
*Fit channels to convey Thy love*
*To every faithful heart.*

Biblical worship was expressed in gestures and bodily movements, including bowing (Micah 6:6), lifting the cup of salvation (Psalm 116:13), lifting hands (Psalm 141:2), clapping (Psalm 47:1), and dancing (Psalm 149:3). The Gospels tell of Jesus' characteristic actions at meals that include taking bread, blessing or giving thanks, breaking the bread, and giving the bread. In Luke, the disciples who walked with Jesus on the way to Emmaus without recognizing him had their eyes opened "when he was at the table with them" and "he took bread, blessed and broke it, and gave it to them" (Luke 24:30).

*Practice:*

The prayer of Great Thanksgiving includes the voices of both the presiding minister and the people. The congregation's responses, which may be spoken or sung, include adoration, acclamation, and affirmation.

The whole assembly might join in parts of the Great Thanksgiving that speak for them: (a) the memorial acclamation, beginning, "And so, in remembrance . . ."; (b) an expression of intention to serve the world, beginning, "Make them be for us . . ."; (c) the concluding doxology, beginning, "Through your Son Jesus Christ. . . ." Congregational responses of "Amen" are the affirmation by the people of what has been prayed.

Presiding at Holy Communion involves bodily action as well as verbal communication. Gestures evoke and lead physical and visual participation by the congregation and aid worshipers in recognizing that the action at the Lord's Table is more than reading a script. For the presiding ministers, such gestures may include making welcoming gestures with arms or hands during the Invitation, raising arms or hands to God in praise or supplication, opening arms and hands to indicate including the entire body of Christ, and holding arms and hands over the elements as blessing.

Different postures are appropriate at different points in the ritual. The presiding minister and those in the whole assembly who are physically able appropriately stand throughout the Great Thanksgiving (*BOW*; page 28). Those unable to stand might participate with other gestures of praise as they desire. Standing communicates an attitude of respect and reverence; kneeling and bowing signify humility and confession; hands raised and open express praise and receptivity. The sign of the cross affirms our baptismal identity and the centrality of the cross to our faith. The ancient biblical use of hands and arms in expressing prayer and thanksgiving to God (arms uplifted, called *orans*; see 1 Timothy 2:8) and other gestures are recommended in *The United Methodist Book of Worship*, pages 36-39 and 46-79.

## The Community Extends Itself

*Principle:*

The Communion elements are consecrated and consumed in the context of the gathered congregation. The Table may be extended, in a timely manner, to include those unable to attend because of age, illness, or similar conditions. Laypeople may distribute the consecrated elements in the congregation and extend them to members who are unavoidably absent (*BOD*; ¶¶ 340.2.a and 1117.9). An elder or deacon should offer appropriate training, preparation, and supervision for this important task (¶ 340.2.a).

*Background:*

In his description of worship practices of the early church, second-century writer Justin Martyr noted that consecrated bread and wine were carried to Christians who were unable to attend the service (*First Apology*; 67).

"Since the earliest Christian times, communion has been brought as an extension of the congregation's worship to sick or homebound persons unable to attend congregational worship" (*BOW*; page 51).

*Practice:*

When Holy Communion is extended to those unable to attend, the liturgy should include the reading of the Scripture Lesson(s), the Invitation, Confession and Pardon, the Peace, the Lord's Prayer, distribution, and post-Communion prayer. Elders, deacons, and laity may use this liturgy. A prayer of Great Thanksgiving should not be repeated, since this service is an extension of the Communion service held earlier (*BOW*; page 51).

If Holy Communion is to be celebrated with people who are homebound on a day when the congregation has not gathered at Table, "A Service of Word and Table V" (*BOW*; pages 51-53), which includes the Great Thanksgiving, should be used by an elder or another who is authorized to preside.

The Lord's Supper is to be made available to people who are in hospitals and hospices; nursing, convalescent, and rehabilitation facilities; correctional and custodial institutions; or other situations that make it impossible for them to gather with the community of faith. If a person is unable to eat or drink, one or both of the elements may be touched to his or her lips.

Both "self-service" Communion, where people help themselves, and "drop-in" Communion, where the elements are available over a period of time, are contrary to the communal nature of the sacrament, which is the celebration of the gathered community of faith.

### The Ritual of the Church

*Principle:*

As stewards of the gifts given by God to the church, pastors have a responsibility to uphold and use the texts for Word and Table of The United Methodist Church found in *The United Methodist Hymnal*; *Mil Voces Para Celebrar: Himnario Metodista*; *Come, Let Us Worship: The Korean-English United Methodist Hymnal*; *The United Methodist Book of Worship*; and other liturgical material approved by central conferences in accordance with the *Book of Discipline*, ¶ 544.13. These liturgies, arising from biblical, historical, and ecumenical sources, are expressions of the Christian faith and the worship of God.

*Background:*

Article XXII of The Articles of Religion of The Methodist Church affirms some diversity of "rites and ceremonies" but rebukes "whosoever, through his private judgment, willingly and purposely doth openly break the rites and ceremonies of the church" (*BOD*; page 65).

The *Book of Discipline* specifies in ¶ 1114.3 that "the ritual of the Church is that contained in *The United Methodist Hymnal* (1989), *The United Methodist Book of Worship* (1992), *Mil Voces Para Celebrar: Himnario Metodista* (1996), and *Come, Let Us Worship: The Korean-English United Methodist Hymnal* (2000)."

In the Order for the Ordination of Elders, candidates promise to "be loyal to The United Methodist Church, accepting its order, liturgy, doctrine, and discipline" (*BOW*; page 676).

The preface to "An Order of Sunday Worship Using the Basic Pattern" in *The United Methodist Book of Worship* (page 16) states,

While the freedom and diversity of United Methodist worship are greater than can be represented by any single order of worship, United Methodists also affirm a heritage of order and the importance of the specific guidance and modeling that an order of worship provides. . . . Acts of worship that reflect racial, ethnic, regional, and local customs and heritages may be used appropriately throughout this order.

The ritual officially approved by The United Methodist Church represents the decisions of the church about the theology and practice of Holy Communion. This ritual expresses the unity of the universal church of Jesus Christ and exemplifies our connection within The United Methodist Church. It had its origin in the early Christian community and has evolved in the practice of the church through the centuries. Our ritual is in accord with those currently used in most Christian bodies.

At its best, United Methodist liturgy combines the order and beauty of established ritual with the vitality and freshness of creative expression. The richness of tradition developed through two thousand years of Christian history can be faithfully adapted for present times and situations.

*Practice:*

Bishops, pastors, and congregations are expected to use the services of Word and Table in the official United Methodist hymnals and books of worship. Knowledgeable use of these resources allows for a balance of flexibility to meet contextual needs and order that reflects our unity and connectional accountability.

"An Order of Sunday Worship Using the Basic Pattern" (*UMH*; pages 3-5) offers flexibility for response to the activity of the Holy Spirit as well as the specifics of events and settings. In attending to the season, day, or occasion, presiders may insert words of their own composition or selections taken from fuller ritual texts as indicated in "A Service of Word and Table II" and "A Service of Word and Table III." (See *UMH*, "A Service of Word and Table II," pages 12-15; "A Service of Word and Table III," pages 15-16; musical settings, pages 17-25.) Pastors using *Mil Voces Para Celebrar* or *Come, Let Us Worship* may apply these directions to the use of the respective rituals in those books. Material from different regions and cultures may also enrich our celebrations.

Pastors and congregations in ecumenical shared-ministry settings will necessarily need to incorporate and use the rituals of the denominations comprising those parishes in ways that are responsible and respectful, both of United Methodist understandings and practices and of those of the other traditions represented.

In accord with our commitments to the pursuit of Christian unity and seeking shared Communion, bishops, pastors, and congregations are encouraged to use the Word and Table ritual from other denominations. Such use is to be compatible with our Basic Pattern of Worship and with United Methodist liturgical and theological commitments.

*Servants at the Table*

Presiding Ministers: Elders and Licensed Local Pastors

*Principle:*

An ordained elder or a person authorized under the provisions of the Book of Discipline presides at all celebrations of Holy Communion.

*Background:*

In accord with the practice of the church throughout Christian history, God calls and the church sets apart certain people for leadership within the body of Christians. We believe that the Holy Spirit gives to such people the grace and gifts they need for leadership in obedience to their call. The meaning and purpose of ordination are described in ¶¶ 301-303 in the *Book of Discipline*.

Elders are ordained to a lifetime ministry of service, word, sacrament, and order (*BOD*; ¶ 332) and charged to "administer the sacraments of baptism and the Lord's Supper and all the other means of grace" (*BOD*; ¶ 340.2.a).

John Wesley drew a sharp distinction between the preaching ministry, which was open to lay men and women, and the priestly ministry of administering the sacraments, which was to be exercised only by those ordained as elders. Recounting the 1744 preachers' conference, Wesley wrote, "None of them dreamed, that the being called to preach gave them any right to administer sacraments. . . . 'You are to do that part of the work which we appoint.' But what work was this? Did we ever appoint you to administer sacraments; to exercise the priestly office? Such a design never entered into our mind; it was the farthest from our thoughts" ("The Ministerial Office"). Wesley insisted that there could be no sacramental ministry without ordination as elder. This conviction ultimately determined his decision to perform "extraordinary" ordinations himself.

"The authority of the ordained minister," according to *Baptism, Eucharist, and Ministry* (World Council of Churches, 1982), "is rooted in Jesus Christ who has received it from the Father (Matt. 28:18), and who confers it by the Holy Spirit through the act of ordination. This act takes place within a community which accords public recognition to a particular person" (page 22). Elders administer the sacraments as authorized representatives of the church.

Under the terms of the *Book of Discipline*, several groups of people are authorized to preside at Eucharist in the charges to which they are appointed. These include associate member deacons, deacons ordained under the provisions of the 1992 *Book of Discipline*, licensed local pastors, and commissioned ministers licensed for pastoral ministry (*BOD*; ¶¶ 315, 316, 339, 340). Some of these provisions have been in effect since 1976 in order to enable the sacraments to be served regularly in many small congregations that do not have elders as their pastors. The church continues to seek the best ways to meet this need and still uphold the historic linkage of ordination and administration of the sacraments.

*Practice:*

Bishops and district superintendents are elders who are assigned and appointed to exercise the ministry of superintending (BOD; ¶¶ 403 and 404) as an expression of the connectional nature of The United Methodist Church. To embody the connectional nature of the church and its sacramental life, a bishop or district superintendent who is present may be invited to preside at Holy Communion.

An elder or a person authorized under the provisions of the *Book of Discipline* presides at all celebrations of Holy Communion. While some portions of the order of worship may be led by others, an elder or authorized pastor leads the congregation in praying the Great Thanksgiving, in which the whole assembly takes an active role. (*See* the Sanctus, the memorial acclamation, and the Amen, all printed in bold type, in *UMH*, pages 9-10.)

Elders who are in extension ministries and retired elders may be asked to preside when they are needed in local churches or on other sacramental occasions. "All conference members who are elders in full connection, including those in extension ministries, shall be available and on call to administer the sacraments of baptism and the Lord's Supper as required by the *Discipline* (¶ 340.2.a) and requested by the district superintendent of the district in which the appointment is held" (*BOD*; ¶ 344.3.a). Those in the Order of Elders are encouraged to make every effort to be available for presiding when Holy Communion is needed or desired.

All elders or deacons who are present may be invited to participate in leadership of the service, stand with the presider at the table, and assist in distributing the elements.

All who lead Holy Communion should be knowledgeable and prepared in Eucharistic theology, spirituality, and practice, including the roles of those assisting. This ministry is under the supervision of district superintendents and pastoral mentors (*BOD*; ¶ 316.4).

*Assisting Ministers: Deacons and Laity*

*Principle:*

Deacons are ordained to the ministry of word and service (*BOD*; ¶ 329) and charged to "give leadership in the Church's life" in, among other ways, "assisting the elders in the administration of the sacraments" and "in the congregation's mission to the world" (¶ 328).

*Background:*

"Within the church community, there are persons whose gifts, evidence of God's grace, and promise of future usefulness are affirmed by the community, and who respond to God's call by offering themselves in leadership as ordained ministers" (*BOD*; ¶ 301.2). Deacons, as well as elders, are ordained to the ministry of leadership in The United Methodist Church.

This ordination of a deacon is to a life of linking the church's worship to Christ's service in the world. In worship it is appropriate for deacons to lead, or recruit and support others to lead, those parts of the liturgy that manifest the connection between our worship and Christian witness in daily life.

*Practice:*

In continuity with historic and ecumenical practice (*Baptism, Eucharist, and Ministry*), the role of deacon in services of Word and Table appropriately includes reading the Gospel lesson; leading the concerns and prayers for the world, the church, and the needy; receiving the elements and preparing the table before the Great Thanksgiving; assisting the elder in serving the Communion elements; setting the table in order; and dismissing the people to serve before the elder offers God's blessing. Further, deacons have a significant role in preparing for the service by organizing, assembling the necessary elements and containers, and making assignments for other participants, including those taking the meal to those unable to attend. Deacons are designated to serve as links between the church and the world. Their ministry appropriately includes taking the consecrated elements from their congregations and serving them in their places of ministry.

Deacons need training and preparation for their diverse roles in Eucharistic ministry.

*Principle:*

All members of Christ's universal church are, through their baptism, called to share in the Eucharistic ministry that is committed to the whole church (*BOD*; ¶ 220). Lay people assist the presider in leading the whole congregation to celebrate the Lord's Supper.

*Background:*

In the section titled "The Ministry of All Christians," *The Book of Discipline* says, "All Christians are called through their baptism to this ministry of servanthood in the world to the glory of God and for human fulfillment" (¶ 125).

In depicting the church as a body of many parts, Paul declares in 1 Corinthians 12:7: "To each is given the manifestation of the Spirit for the common good." This diversity of ministry requires cooperation within the body of Christ, since it is only through such cooperation that the body is complete (1 Corinthians 12:12-31). It is important for liturgical celebrations to embody the active participation of all those gathered, as a demonstration of the full ministry of the body of Christ in the world.

As each layperson fulfills his or her vital ministry in worship, some will be called to exercise various leadership roles. "The United Methodist tradition has recognized that laypersons as well as ordained persons are gifted and called by God to lead the Church. The servant leadership of these persons is essential to the mission and ministry of congregations" (¶ 132). The whole of Part III of the *Book of Discipline* elaborates on this idea.

*Practice:*

Pastors and other leaders facilitate the full and active engagement of the ministry of all laity in celebrations of Holy Communion. As part of this general liturgical ministry of all Christians, laypeople exercise leadership of worship by reading Scripture, leading prayers, preparing the table, providing and preparing the elements, distributing the elements, and helping with other parts of the service.

At the appropriate point in the service, laity representing the whole congregation may bring the elements forward to the Table as a part of the offering. The entire congregation responds in unison as indicated throughout the ritual. Laypeople may take the consecrated elements to members who are unable to attend the congregational celebration.

Laypeople need instruction and training for this leadership, under the supervision of pastors and deacons.

*Setting the Table*

The Holy Communion Table

*Principle:*

The people and leaders gather around the elements for Holy Communion. The place where the elements are set is the Holy Communion table.

*Background:*

In the Old Testament, sacrifice was offered on an altar. In the Gospel narratives of the Last Supper, Jesus "took his place at the table, and the apostles with him" (Luke 22:14). Through time, the church increasingly understood the Eucharist as a repetition of Christ's sacrifice on the cross, and the Table came to be seen as an altar of sacrifice. It was moved against the wall of the sanctuary and priests stood before the altar, with their backs to the congregation, to offer sacrifice to God.

The more radical Protestant reformers abandoned altars, preferring simple tables and reenactment of the Last Supper of Jesus with his disciples. Others, including the Church of England, of which John Wesley was a priest, retained the altar against a wall.

A twentieth-century international liturgical renewal movement, expressed in the changes of the Second Vatican Council of the Roman Catholic Church, made major reforms in worship. These reforms included moving the table into an open space so that the priest could stand behind it, giving the assembly a sense of meeting around it. The United Methodist Church, along with many other mainline churches, adopted revised rituals that call for the presiding minister to stand behind the Lord's Table, facing the people, from the offertory through the breaking of the bread (*BOW*; page 36).

In a church building, the place where the elements are set is sometimes called the altar, but the terms *altar-table* and *Lord's Table* are preferable.

The rail that in some churches is located between the congregation and the chancel area, while not properly called the altar, is a sacred area for kneeling to receive Communion. People may also come to one or more stations where the elements are served and receive them standing, with an option of kneeling at the rail for prayer.

*Practice:*

In our churches, the Communion table is to be placed in such a way that the presider is able to stand behind it, facing the people, and the people can visually if not physically gather around it. The table should be high enough so that the presider does not need to stoop to handle the bread and cup. Adaptations may be necessary to facilitate gracious leadership.

While architectural integrity should be respected, it is important for churches to carefully adapt or renovate their worship spaces more fully to invite the people to participate in the Holy Meal. If "altars" are for all practical purposes immovable, then congregations should make provisions for creating a table suitable to the space so that the presiding minister may face the people and be closer to them.

### The Communion Elements

*Principle:*

In accordance with the words of Christ and Christian tradition, the church uses bread in celebrations of Holy Communion.

*Background:*

Bread is used in both the Old and New Testaments to signify God's sustenance of human beings and the importance of our eating together. When God liberated the Hebrew people from slavery in Egypt, they carried their bread with them. The Jews have celebrated this exodus throughout the centuries as Passover. The provision of manna and the showbread (bread of the Presence) kept in the Tabernacle are examples of God's sustenance from the time of Israel's wandering in the wilderness (Exodus 16; 25:23-30). In the New Testament, Jesus shared meals frequently with his disciples and with others (Matthew 9:9-11 and similar passages). He fed the multitudes (Matthew 14:13-21 and parallels) and used bread to signify his identity and mission (John 6). On the eve of his crucifixion, Jesus ate the Last Supper with his disciples (Matthew 26:26-29 and parallels). After his resurrection, he broke bread with the travelers to Emmaus (Luke 24:13-35) and with his disciples on the seashore (John 21:9-14).

*Practice:*

It is appropriate that the bread eaten in Holy Communion both look and taste like bread. The use of a whole loaf best signifies the unity of the church as the body of Christ and, when it is broken and shared, our fellowship in that body (1 Corinthians 10:16-17).

Historical continuity with the practice of the universal church is important; however, worship planners should be sensitive to local situations. Bread may be made from any grain according to availability. In ecumenical and other settings, wafers may be an appropriate choice.

The loaf should be plain bread (no frostings, nuts, raisins, artificial coloring, or other additions). Leavened or unleavened bread is equally acceptable. In congregations where there are people with gluten allergies, gluten-free bread may be offered. The loaf broken at the table is to be the bread distributed to the people. As appropriate to the dignity of the occasion, care should be taken to avoid excessive crumbling of the bread and to remove large pieces that fall to the floor.

*Principle:*

In accordance with Scripture and Christian tradition, the historic and ecumenical church uses wine in celebrations of Holy Communion.

*Background:*

Throughout the Old Testament story of God's relationship with the Hebrew people, blood was the sign of covenant ratification (Exodus 12:12-28; 24:1-8). At his last meal with the disciples, Jesus spoke of the wine as his blood—the blood of the new covenant (Jeremiah 31:31-34) between God and God's people, made possible through Christ's death and resurrection (Revelation 5:9). Jesus also spoke of the wine as a sign of the heavenly banquet that he will celebrate with the church in the future (1 Corinthians 11:23-26; Matthew 26:26-29).

The juice of the red grape in a common cup represents the church's covenant with Christ, established through his atoning death (Hebrews 9:15-28; 13:20-21), and fulfills Christ's commands at the Last Supper (Matthew 26:27-29; Mark 14:23-24; Luke 22:19-20).

Roman Catholicism, Eastern Orthodoxy, and many Protestant denominations have always used wine in the Eucharist. During the movement against beverage alcohol in the late nineteenth century, the predecessor bodies of The United Methodist Church turned to the use of unfermented grape juice. This continues to be the position of the denomination (*BOR*; page 838). (The term *wine* is used in this document because of its biblical and historical antecedents, although United Methodists customarily serve unfermented grape juice in Holy Communion.)

The use of a common cup dates back to the Last Supper where Jesus takes a single cup of wine, blesses it, and gives it to the disciples. It is a powerful symbol of the unity of the body of Christ gathered at the Lord's Table.

*Practice:*

Variations may be necessary in cultural contexts where the juice of the grape is unavailable or prohibitively expensive.

A single cup or chalice may be used for intinction—dipping the bread into the wine—or for drinking. The use of a common chalice best represents Christian unity, but individual cups are used in many congregations. In these situations, unity can be effectively symbolized if each person's cup is filled from a pouring chalice.

*Principle:*

The consecrated elements are to be treated with reverent respect and appreciation as gifts of God's creation that have, in the words of the Great Thanksgiving, become "for us the body and blood of Christ" (*UMH*; page 10).

*Background:*

We do not worship the consecrated elements nor reserve them for adoration. We respect the elements because God is using them for holy purposes—reconstituting the assembly as the body of Christ, conveying grace, forgiving sin, foreshadowing heaven, and strengthening the faithful for the journey of salvation. Although they have undergone no substantive (physical) change, the elements have been consecrated—set apart for sacred use.

While, in the history of the church, reverence for the consecrated elements has sometimes led to superstition, proper respect for the elements helps Christians grow in authentic sacramental piety.

As Article XVIII of The Articles of Religion of the Methodist Church makes clear, United Methodism rejects any suggestion that the bread and wine used in Communion are transformed or transubstantiated into other substances:

"Transubstantiation, or the change of the substance of bread and wine in the Supper of our Lord, cannot be proved by Holy Writ, but is repugnant to the plain words of Scripture, overthroweth the nature of a sacrament, and hath given occasion to many superstitions. The body of Christ is given, taken, and eaten in the Supper, only after a heavenly and spiritual manner. And the mean whereby the body of Christ is received and eaten in the Supper is faith" (*BOD*; page 64).

(The United Methodist Church notes that the anti-Roman Catholic tone of Article XVIII reflects the "bitterly polemical" relationships of past centuries and "rejoice[s] in the positive contemporary relationships that are being developed . . . at levels both official and unofficial" [BOR; pages 272-273].)

The Book of Worship directs, "What is done with the remaining bread and wine should express our stewardship of God's gifts and our respect for the holy purpose they have served" (page 30).

*Practice:*

The practice of consecrating elements ahead of time for the convenience of the pastor not having to go to small or remote congregations, weekend camps, or other such occasions is inappropriate and contrary to our historic doctrine and understanding of how God's grace is made available in the sacrament (Article XVIII, The Articles of Religion, BOD; page 64). If authorized leadership is not available for celebrating the Lord's Supper, other worship services such as love feasts, agape meals, or baptismal reaffirmations are valid alternatives that avoid the misuse of Communion elements.

The consecrated elements of bread and wine are used for distribution to the sick and others who wish to commune but are unable to attend congregational worship. If any bread and wine remain, they should always be disposed of by (1) the pastor and/or others at the pastor's direction consuming them in a reverent manner following the service; (2) returning them to the earth by pouring (2 Samuel 23:16), burying, scattering, or burning.

*Hygiene and Table Setting*

*Principle:*

Those who prepare the elements and give them to the people are to demonstrate care that the bread and cup are administered so as to minimize contamination.

*Background:*

In administering the elements to the people, both perception and reality of hygiene are important. The people have justifiable health concerns that the signs of the body and blood of Christ given to them at the Holy Meal are handled carefully and with concern for hygiene.

This need for care and hygiene should be considered along with scientific studies that make it clear that those who partake in Holy Communion have no higher incidence of illness than those who do not.

Concern and planning are necessary in situations of serious illness and for accommodating at the Table those whose immune systems are compromised. The counsel of Romans 14 and 15 can guide our practice.

*Practice:*

Those who will prepare and serve the elements should wash their hands. This can be done simply and without creating an additional layer of ceremony in the service.

The piece of bread given should be sizeable enough to be a generous sign and to be able to be dipped in the cup without the fingers of the recipient dipping into the liquid.

*Extending the Table*

## Holy Communion and Evangelism

*Principle:*

The Lord's Supper forms the church into a community of evangelism that reaches out to preach, teach, baptize, and make new disciples of Christ (Matthew 28:19-20).

*Background:*

Immediately after his account of the institution of the Lord's Supper in 1 Corinthians 11-12, Paul moves into an extended discussion of the body of Christ composed of many members whose gifts for ministry are diverse. Paul understood the sacrament of Holy Communion to form and shape the church for its mission of redeeming the world. In 2 Corinthians 5:16-6:10, he describes more fully "the ministry of reconciliation" that is the work of the church as "ambassadors for Christ."

United Methodists have inherited a tradition that emphasizes that spiritual benefits are not received for ourselves alone but also to prepare and propel us for the work of evangelism. In our prayer after Communion, we give thanks for what we have received and ask God to "grant that we may go into the world in the strength of your Spirit, to give ourselves for others" (*UMH*; page 11).

*The Book of Discipline* emphasizes the imperative of evangelism: "The people of God, who are the church made visible in the world, must convince the world of the reality of the gospel or leave it unconvinced. There can be no evasion or delegation of this responsibility; the church is either faithful as a witnessing and serving community, or it loses its vitality and its impact on an unbelieving world" (¶ 128).

*Practice:*

Through the grace received in continual participation in the Lord's Supper, the community of faith reaches beyond itself to proclaim and exemplify the good news of salvation in Jesus Christ.

In Christian education and congregational life, we teach about the significance and meaning of the sacraments so that the faithful appreciate their own spiritual journey and are empowered to be knowledgeable and hospitable guides to those who seek Christ.

As members of the congregation partake of the Lord's Supper, the bonds of love within are strengthened and the worshiping community is empowered to reach out in dynamic and meaningful ways to evangelize and to work for peace and justice.

*Principle:*

As followers of Jesus, who ate with sinners and reached out to the marginalized, the church must intentionally concern itself about those who are absent from Christ's Table—those who feel unworthy, the poor, the unconverted, victims of prejudice, and others who are oppressed or neglected.

*Background:*

One of the themes of the Gospels, most prominent in Luke, is Jesus' ongoing efforts to teach the disciples that God's love and favor are extended to all people, not just those of a certain ethnicity, status, economic or political standing, or gender. The Book of Acts records some of the attempts of the early Christian community to define its limits, and God's continued efforts to broaden its inclusiveness. Peter's vision in Acts 10 is a particularly dramatic example.

Early English Methodists were typically (with some notable exceptions) from the socioeconomic groups that we might today speak of as the working poor. Wesley realized that a community of people who lived according to his General Rules (*BOD*; pages 71-74) were inevitably going to rise in status. He preached fervently against the dangers of money and the spiritual weakness that often accompanies prosperity.

In "The Ministry of All Christians," *The Book of Discipline* asserts: "We are called to be faithful to the example of Jesus' ministry to all persons. Inclusiveness means openness, acceptance, and support that enables all persons to participate in the life of the Church, the community, and the world. Thus, inclusiveness denies every semblance of discrimination" (¶ 138).

*Practice:*

The church is to consciously identify and seek out those who feel unwelcome, even excluded, from its congregations and to invite them to become part of the body of Christ and join in its celebrations of Holy Communion.

## Holy Communion and Ethical Christian Discipleship

*Principle:*

The sacraments are God's gifts to the gathered body of believers to form the church into Christ's body in ministry to the world. Through Holy Communion, the Holy Spirit works to shape our moral and ethical lives. In the ongoing process of conversion, we grow in personal and social holiness and are empowered to work for healing, compassion, reconciliation, justice, and peace.

*Background:*

The Old Testament prophets denounced the injustice and oppression that they saw around them. They proclaimed a God who acts in favor of the poor and powerless and calls God's people so to act. (Isaiah 1:16-17; 58:6-9; Amos 2:6-8; 5:11-15, 21-24; and Micah 6:6-8 are among a multitude of such passages.) When Jesus began his public ministry, he announced his mission: "The Spirit of the Lord is upon me, because he has anointed me to bring good news to the poor. He has sent me to proclaim release to the captives and recovery of sight to the blind, to let the oppressed go free, to proclaim the year of the Lord's favor" (Luke 4:16-21). He associated with those who were stigmatized and despised. Much of his teaching addressed economic and social inequality. Following his example, the early Christian community tried to care for the needs of all people (Acts 4:32-35; James 1:27; 2:14-17).

The United Methodist Church has a heritage from John Wesley in which ethical discipleship was inextricably related to sacramental worship. From concern by the Holy Club for the imprisoned, through care of the sick by the societies, to Wesley's own lifelong giving away of most of his money, the early Wesleyan movement sought to ease the suffering of the needy. Wesley made the linkage explicit when he wrote, "The Gospel of Christ knows no religion but social, no holiness, but social holiness" (Preface to *Hymns and Sacred Poems*). Collection at the Lord's Supper of alms to be given to the poor is a historic practice that many congregations in our tradition continue.

By the early twentieth century, Methodists had begun to realize that holy living meant even more than acts of charity. Beginning with the Social Creed, American Methodists started to point out injustices caused by economic, social, and political structures and to call for the reform of such structures. The Social Principles in *The Book of Discipline* and the General Conference positions recorded in *The Book of Resolutions* show ongoing response to these concerns.

In carrying out our mission to make disciples of Jesus Christ, *The Book of Discipline* stipulates that the church is to "send persons into the world to live lovingly and justly as servants of Christ by healing the sick, feeding the hungry, caring for the stranger, freeing the oppressed, being and becoming a compassionate, caring presence, and working to develop social structures that are consistent with the gospel" (¶ 122).

Those who partake of Holy Communion are sent from the Table to be in ministry as Christ's presence in the world. God's people are sent to work compassionately for healing, reconciliation, justice, and peace. Such work requires prophetic, subversive actions: "renounc[ing] the spiritual forces of wickedness, reject[ing] the evil powers of this world, . . . accept[ing] the freedom and power God gives . . . to resist evil, injustice, and oppression in whatever forms they present themselves" (vows from the services of the Baptismal Covenant, *BOW*; for example page 88), claiming and making real the victory of the risen Christ over all evil, sin, and death. Such faithful living in the power of the Holy Spirit answers the prayer in the Great Thanksgiving "that we may be for the world the body of Christ" and the petition "your kingdom come, your will be done" in the Lord's Prayer (*UMH*; page 10). Celebrations of Holy Communion are, therefore, a foretaste of the realm of God, when God's future breaks into our present world. Here the church enacts the words of Jesus, "Then people will come from east and west, from north and south, and will eat in the kingdom of God" (Luke 13:29).

*Practice:*

Holy Communion is to be conducted in ways that make apparent the inherent link between the Table and holy living, both individual and corporate. Participation in the Eucharist bears fruit in the world in attitudes and actions of personal and social holiness.

Communing with others in our congregations is a sign of community and mutual love between Christians throughout the church universal. The church must offer to the world a model of genuine community grounded in God's deep love for every person. As we eat and drink, we are motivated to act compassionately for those whose physical, emotional, and spiritual needs are unmet.

Receiving the bread and wine as products of divine creation reminds us of our duties of stewardship of the natural environment in a time when destruction and pollution imperil the earth and unjust distribution of the planet's resources destroys the hopes and lives of millions.

As we gratefully receive God's abundant grace, we are challenged to accept fully our responsibility and accountability for renewal of the social order, liberation for the oppressed, and the coming of the realm of God.

### Holy Communion and the Unity of the Church

*Principle:*

Holy Communion expresses our oneness in the body of Christ, anticipates Jesus' invitation to feast at the heavenly banquet, and calls us to strive for the visible unity of the church.

*Background:*

In its Constitution, The United Methodist Church affirms its ecumenical commitment: "As part of the church universal, The United

Methodist Church believes that the Lord of the church is calling Christians everywhere to strive toward unity; and therefore it will seek, and work for, unity at all levels of church life" (*BOD*; ¶ 6).

In "Our Doctrinal Heritage" in the *Book of Discipline* (pages 41-43), the church affirms:

"United Methodists share a common heritage with Christians of every age and nation. This heritage is grounded in the apostolic witness to Jesus Christ as Savior and Lord, which is the source and measure of all valid Christian teaching. . . . With Christians of other communions we confess belief in the triune God—Father, Son, and Holy Spirit. This confession embraces the biblical witness to God's activity in creation, encompasses God's gracious self-involvement in the dramas of history, and anticipates the consummation of God's reign."

In the quest for greater visible unity, United Methodism has undertaken numerous concrete actions that express its commitment and promote ecumenical sharing:

1. Since the 1960's, the church has been involved with partners through Churches Uniting in Christ, formerly called the Consultation on Church Union. Throughout most of that history United Methodists have joined the partner churches in Holy Communion using liturgy approved by those churches for celebration together.

2. United Methodists across the world have entered into ecumenical agreements enhancing the unity of the church through recognition and reconciliation of ministries and sacraments.

3. Ecumenical representatives have been invited and encouraged to participate in United Methodist services of Holy Communion.

4. United Methodists have participated in the Eucharist services of other traditions when invited to do so, as an affirmation and reflection of our commitment to the church universal.

*Baptism, Eucharist, and Ministry* affirms the significance of the sacrament for all Christians:

It is in the eucharist that the community of God's people is fully manifested. Eucharistic celebrations always have to do with the whole Church, and the whole Church is involved in each local eucharistic celebration. In so far as a church claims to be a manifestation of the whole Church, it will take care to order its own life in ways which take seriously the interests and concerns of other churches (page 14).

For churches such as the Orthodox and Roman Catholic, sharing the Eucharist between churches that are not in full agreement with one another is unacceptable because the Eucharist is itself a sign that unity and full agreement have been achieved. For other churches, including The United Methodist Church, the Eucharist can be a means to express the unity in Christ that already exists as a gift from God in spite of our failure to manifest it.

*Practice:*

United Methodists are encouraged to continue participating in ecumenical services that include Holy Communion. Special care is to be given to the use of commonly approved texts or the development of liturgy that reflects the beliefs and practices of the different traditions. If bishops or superintendents are present, it is appropriate for them to be invited to preside.

Church members can practice hospitality by participating in each others' liturgies with attitudes of respect and openness to learning. United Methodists are encouraged to receive Communion in other churches when they are invited to do so.

Churches need to address, within official dialogues, the theological barriers to full Eucharistic sharing. Materials already available from the official dialogues shall be part of the study resources of the denomination.

United Methodists need to study and work to answer questions that are critical to ecumenical conversation and sensitive to ecumenical concerns—the presence of Christ ("real presence"), frequency of celebration, who presides at the Table, use of grape juice, and baptism in relation to Eucharist, among others.

*Principle:*

United Methodists enter into the ecumenical conversation about Eucharist grounded in several historic sources of authority and relate most authentically to other Christian bodies as we remain faithful to these sources.

*Background:*

Most prominent among United Methodism's sources of authority are the Scriptures of the Old and New Testaments; the hymns and writings of John and Charles Wesley (especially the Standard Sermons, the General Rules, and *Explanatory Notes Upon the New Testament*); the Constitution, Articles of Religion, Confession of Faith, and other doctrinal standards; the writings and traditions emerging from the evangelical experience, through the Wesleyan, Evangelical, and United Brethren movements; and current ecumenical developments and statements that have had United Methodist involvement, especially multilateral and bilateral agreements, some of which have been approved by the World Methodist Council and/or the General Conference.

"Our Doctrinal Heritage" points out some distinctive aspects of the United Methodist tradition:

"Although Wesley shared with many other Christians a belief in grace, justification, assurance, and sanctification, he combined them in a powerful manner to create distinctive emphases for living the full Christian life. The Evangelical United Brethren tradition, particularly as expressed by Phillip William Otterbein from a Reformed background, gave similar distinctive emphases.

"Grace pervades our understanding of Christian faith and life. By grace we mean the undeserved, unmerited, and loving action of God in human existence through the ever-present Holy Spirit. While the grace of God is undivided, it precedes salvation as 'prevenient grace,' continues in 'justifying grace,' and is brought to fruition in 'sanctifying grace'" (*BOD*; pages 45-46).

These distinctive emphases of United Methodists provide the basis for "practical divinity," the experiential realization of the gospel of Jesus Christ in the lives of Christian people. These emphases have been preserved not so much through formal doctrinal declarations as through the vital movement of faith and practice as seen in converted lives and within the disciplined life of the Church.

Devising formal definitions of doctrine has been less pressing for United Methodists than summoning people to faith and nurturing them in the knowledge and love of God. The core of Wesleyan doctrine that informed our past rightly belongs to our common heritage as Christians and remains a prime component within our continuing theological task (*BOD*; pages 49-50).

The General Commission on Christian Unity and Interreligious Concerns spearheads the ecumenical work of the denomination by fulfilling its purpose: "To advocate and work toward the full reception of the gift of Christian unity in every aspect of the Church's life and to foster approaches to ministry and mission that more fully reflect the oneness of Christ's church in the human community" (*BOD*; ¶ 1902.1).

In "Resolution of Intent—With a View to Unity," the 2000 General Conference declared it "our official intent henceforth to interpret all our Articles, Confession, and other 'standards of doctrine' in consonance with our best ecumenical insights and judgment" (2004 *BOR*; page 273).

*Practice:*

Within all discussions of Holy Communion, United Methodism must remain firmly anchored in its traditional sources of authority. We recognize and respect authorities that other church traditions hold dear. United Methodists remain open to greater Christian unity through the work of the Holy Spirit in response to Jesus' prayer that "they may all be one" (John 17:21).

Committee Members:

*L. Edward Phillips*, Chairperson
*Daniel T. Benedict, Jr.*
*Michael J. Coyner*
*Jerome King Del Pino*
*Gayle Carlton Felton*
Thelma H. Flores
Barbara Thorington Green
*Karen A. Greenwaldt*
*Susan W. Hassinger*
*Sally Havens*
Dong Hyun (David) Kim
*Jon E. McCoy*
Sophie Pieh
Arturo L. Razon, Jr.
Bruce W. Robbins
Frank E. Trotter, Jr.
Karen Westerfield Tucker
Hans Växby
Josiah U. Young, III

*Notes About This Document*

Scripture quotations, unless otherwise indicated, are from the New Revised Standard Version of the Bible, copyright © 1989 by the Division of Christian Education of the National Council of the Churches of Christ in the USA. All rights reserved. Used by permission.

BOD, *Discipline*, and *Book of Discipline* refer to *The Book of Discipline of The United Methodist Church, 2004*, copyright © 2004 The United Methodist Publishing House.

*UMH* refers to *The United Methodist Hymnal*, copyright © 1989 The United Methodist Publishing House.

*BOW* refers to *The United Methodist Book of Worship*, copyright © 1992 The United Methodist Publishing House.

*BOR* refers to *The Book of Resolutions of The United Methodist Church, 2004*, copyright © 2004 The United Methodist Publishing House.

Quotations from John Wesley are from the Jackson edition of *The Works of John Wesley.*

**ADOPTED 2004**
**RESOLUTION #353, 2004** *BOOK OF RESOLUTIONS*

## 8015. Adoption of Services for the Ordering of Ministry

WHEREAS, The United Methodist Church should reflect in the services of ordination the implementation of the ordering of ministry as reflected in *The Book of Discipline*; and

WHEREAS, the 2000 General Conference referred the work of revision of services for the ordering of ministry to the General Board of Discipleship in consultation with the General Board of Higher Education and Ministry and the Council of Bishops; and

WHEREAS, the provisions of the 1992 *Discipline* regarding the consecration of diaconal ministers and the ordination of those in the probationary relationship formally continue until 2008, whereupon further changes in the ritual for ordering ministry will be required;

*Therefore, be it resolved,* that the 2004 General Conference adopt *Services for the Ordering of Ministry in The United Methodist Church* as the approved texts for use by the bishops and annual conferences during the 2005-2008 quadrennium; and

*Be it further resolved,* that the 2004 General Conference direct the General Board of Discipleship in consultation with the General Board of Higher Education and Ministry and the Council of Bishops to further revise these services as needed to conform to the 2004 legislation and to present them for adoption by the 2008 General Conference.

**ADOPTED 2004**
**RESOLUTION #358, 2004** *BOOK OF RESOLUTIONS*

# ALPHABETICAL LIST OF RESOLUTION TITLES

# INDEX

faith statement of, 32
family, 95, 108–45
intolerance/tolerance, 146–48
issues, 33
pornography, 148–56
role of, 32
spirituality, 156–61
suicide, 161–67

**NWPA.** *See* Nuclear Waste Policy Act (1982)

**Nzwili, Fredrick,** 819

## O

**OAS.** *See* Organization of American States

**Occupational Safety and Health Administration,** 631

**Offenders, in criminal justice system,** 674–76

**Office of Family Ministries, on Christian Home Month,** 118

**Office of Loans and Scholarships, of GBHEM,** 552

**Office of Technology Assessment of US Congress, nuclear plant review by,** 59

**Oil, as energy source,** 51

**Okinawa**
military bases removal/reduction, 881
US military personnel reduction in, 882–83

**Okinawa District of the United Church of Christ in Japan,** 882–83

**Okinawa Prefecture of Japan,** 881, 883

**Older Adult Committee,** 193

**Older Adult Recognition Day,** 203–4

**Older adults**
abuse of, 192–93
Census Bureau on, 193–94
HIV/AIDS of, 387–88
Medicare/Medicaid and, 194
race/ethnicity of, 194
Section 202 housing for, 409
Social Security Administration on, 193
in world population, 360

**OLMSTEAD decision,** 185

**Olympic advertisement, of alcoholic beverages,** 209

**"Opposition to the Illegal Immigration Reform and Immigration Resolution Act,"** 419

**Optional Protocol to the UN Convention on the Rights of the Child,** 249

**Organization for Economic Cooperation and Development,** 350

**Organization of American States (OAS),** 791

**Organ/Tissue donation,** 457–58

**Other Resolutions**
baptism, United Methodist understanding of, 941–60
biblical language, 917–18
commitment to mission/ministry, 911
commitment to unity in mission/ministry, 911–12
embryonic stem cell research, ethics of, 912–15
"In Defense of Creation" replacement, 915–16

**White privilege,** 30, 475–77

**Whitefield, Charles,** 929

**Whitefield, George,** 929

**WIC.** *See* Women, Infants, and Children

**Wilson, Clarence True,** 342

**Wine, for Holy Communion,** 997–98

*Wingspread Statement* **(1998), Precautionary principle and,** 73

**Witnesses**
called to be, 282–83
dialogue to be, 285–86

**WMC.** *See* World Methodist Council

**Women,** 96–97, 515–32. *See also* Comfort Women; Women, in church/society; Women, status of
cervical cancer of, 348
Church/Society embrace of all, 517–24
education of, 528–29
full clergy rights for, 516–17
global debt repayment influence on, 574
global HIV/AIDS pandemic and, 392–93
global racism/xenophobia impact on, 735–37
HIV/AIDS and, 386–87, 529–30
human rights of, 530
Japan's sexual enslavement of, 730–33
migrant, 761
pornography/oppression of, 150
rights of, 171
sexism, eradication of, 525–26
sexual violence of Muslim, 885
Social Security and, 614
status of, 526–32
UMC members, 107

violence against, 507–11, 528, 529, 829
Women's Division affirmation, 515–16

**"Women Called to Ministry" curriculum**
of GCSRW/GBHEM, 524

**Women, in church/society,** 517–24
economic parity/justice of, 522–23
evangelize/recruit/develop leaders among, 523
overcoming sexism of, 524
as pastors/bishops, 518
racial-ethnic, 522
respect, lack of, 519–20
sexual violence/harassment/abuse, "no tolerance" policy of, 523
theological exploration of, 523–24

**Women, Infants, and Children (WIC), UMC support of,** 561

**Women, status of**
armed conflict of, 530
Beijing Declaration and the Platform for Action, 527, 528, 530
economics of, 528
education of, 528–29
Fourth World Conference on Women, 527
human rights in fertility decisions, 529
international movement for equality of, 527–30
International Women's Year for, 526
power/decision making of, 528
theological concerns on, 526–27
violence against, 529

**Women's Division, of GBGM,** 366, 379–80, 515–16, 520, 737

**Women's International War Crimes Tribunal of Japan's Military Sexual Slavery,** 732

**Women's War Crimes Tribunal,** 731